AUSTRALIAN DICTIONARY

OF BIOGRAPHY

General Editor

DOUGLAS PIKE

AUSTRALIAN DICTIONARY OF BIOGRAPHY

VOLUME 2 : 1788-1850

I-Z

Section Editors

A. G. L. SHAW 1788-1825
C. M. H. CLARK 1826-1850

MELBOURNE UNIVERSITY PRESS

First published 1967
Reprinted 1979
Printed in Australia by
Wilke and Company Limited, Clayton, Victoria 3168 for
Melbourne University Press, Carlton, Victoria 3053
U.S.A. and Canada: International Scholarly Book Services, Inc.,
Box 555, Forest Grove, Oregon 97116
United Kingdom, Ireland and Europe: Europa Publications Limited,
18 Bedford Square, London WC1B 3JN

National Library of Australia Cataloguing in Publication data

Australian dictionary of biography. Volume 2. 1788-1850, I-Z.
Bibliography
ISBN 0 522 84194 5

1. Australia – Biography. 2. Australia – History –
1788-1850. I. Shaw, Alan George Lewers, 1916-, joint ed. II.
Clark, Charles Manning Hope, 1915-, joint ed.
920'.094

PREFACE

This volume of the *Australian Dictionary of Biography* is the second of two for the period 1788-1850. Four volumes are planned for the period 1851-1890 and probably six for the period 1891-1939. The chronological division was designed to simplify production, for some six thousand articles are likely to be included. A general index volume will be prepared when the three sections are completed. Meanwhile a provisional list of names proposed for inclusion in the 1851-1890 period has been prepared; free copies of this temporary guide are available from the *Dictionary* office.

The placing of each individual's name in the appropriate section has been generally determined by when he did his most important work (*floruit*). For articles that overlap the chronological division, preference has usually been given to the earlier period, although all the important Federationists will appear in the third section.

The selection of names for inclusion in the first two volumes was the result of much consultation and co-operation. After quotas were estimated, Working Parties in each State prepared provisional lists, which were widely circulated and carefully amended. Many of the names were obviously significant and worthy of inclusion. Others, less notable, were chosen simply as samples of the Australian experience. Some had to be omitted through lack of material, and thereby joined the great anonymous mass whose members richly deserve a more honoured place; however, many thousands of these names are accumulating in a 'Biographical Register' at *Dictionary* headquarters in the Australian National University, and copies of this register are circulated at intervals to Australian libraries.

Most authors were nominated by the Working Parties, and nearly all contributed their entries without payment. The burden of writing has been shared almost equally by university historians and by members of Historical and Genealogical Societies and other specialists. Most of the unsigned entries were prepared by *Dictionary* staff.

The *Dictionary* is an all-Australian, Commonwealth-wide venture based on consultation and co-operation. The Australian National University has borne the cost of the small headquarters staff and much research, while other Australian Universities have supported the project in various ways. Each year its policies have been determined by the National Committee of representatives from the Departments of History in each Australian University. At Canberra the Editorial Board has kept in touch with all these representatives and, through them, with the Working Parties. In turn the editorial work has called for much consultation with the Working Parties, librarians, archivists and other local experts, as well as over-seas correspondents and research assistants in each Australian capital. With such varied support the *Australian Dictionary of Biography* can truly be called a national project.

Canberra
December 1966   D.P.

ACKNOWLEDGMENTS

The *Dictionary* is grateful for financial help from the Bushell Trust and the Directors of the Myer Foundation; and for many privileges extended by the Australian Universities, especially those in Canberra, Sydney and Hobart.

For assistance overseas special thanks are due to Mrs Judy Egerton in London and her correspondents in Edinburgh and Dublin, to the officials of the Public Record Office, Somerset House and the County Records Offices, to Colonel J. T. Hall and Captain A. McG. Robertson for information on the Royal Marines, to Captain W. R. Chaplin of Trinity House, and to the host of clergy, archivists and others who have answered Mrs Egerton's calls for help; to F. W. Torrington, Liaison Officer of the National Library of Australia in London, and to Miss Phyllis Mander-Jones for valuable advice; to Dr W. J. de Kock, editor in chief of the *Dictionary of South African Biography*, and to Dr Birgita Lager, editor of the *Svenskt Biografiskt Lexikon*, for generous co-operation; to the officials of the Parliamentary, Alexander Turnbull and Hocken Libraries in New Zealand; to Professor Samuel C. McCulloch as correspondent in America; to Dr David J. Murray (Southern Rhodesia); to Dr E. H. McCormick (Auckland), C. P. Wright (Ottawa), the President of Magdalen College, Oxford, and to the British and New Zealand High Commissioners, Canberra, for advice on particular articles.

Within Australia the *Dictionary* is greatly indebted to countless librarians and archivists in each State, to the secretaries of many Historical and Genealogical Societies, and to the Registrars-General of Births, Marriages, and Deaths, whose generous co-operation has solved many problems of research. Warm thanks for the free gift of their time and talents are due to the contributors of articles; to M. H. Ellis, Period Editor and member of the Editorial Board until January 1962 and of the National Committee until his resignation in June 1963; to Dr Bernard Smith, consultant on the Fine Arts and to Dr H. L. Oppenheim, on the Theatre; and, for particular advice, to M. Aurousseau, Rev. A. A. Dougan, Professor Frank W. Fetter, Miss M. Jacobs, G. L. Little, Robert Stephens, Mrs Annabel Swainston, Mrs Betty Whittakers, J. K. Wilson, Mrs Bertha MacSmith, Dr John Cumpston, Dr Niel Gunson, Miss Louisa F. Carne and many others; to the Chairmen and members of the National Committee, the Editorial Board and the Working Parties. Grateful acknowledgment is also due to the staff of Melbourne University Press; to the editorial staff: Mrs Ann Mozley until January 1962, Mrs Judith Iltis until October 1963, Gavin Long from April 1963, Miss Kathleen O'Donoghue from September 1963, A. W. Bazley in 1964; to the painstaking research assistance of A. J. and Nancy Gray, Mrs Vivienne Parsons and G. P. Walsh in Sydney, Mrs Anne Rand until 1963, and Mrs Decie Denholm in Hobart, Miss Mary O'Keeffe in Brisbane, Mrs Kathleen Thomson in Melbourne; Mrs Marjorie Findlay in Adelaide and E. Zalums in Perth; to the secretarial staff and to the tireless enthusiasm of Mrs Nan Phillips, personal assistant to the General Editor.

COMMITTEES

AUTHORS

ABBOTT, G. J.:
  Kemp, C.
ALLEN, Susan:
  Lord, D.
ANTILL, J. M.:
  Lennox.
ARNOT, Jean F.:
  McGarvie, J.
AUCHMUTY, J. J.:
  Wentworth, D.
AUSTIN, C. G.:
  Lawless; Russell, H.
AUSTIN, M.:
  MacKellar; Minchin; Townson, J.

BACH, J.:
  Spain.
BAKER, D. W. A.:
  Lang, J.; Mitchell, T.
BARKER, Theo:
  Stewart.
BARNARD, Marjorie:
  Macquarie, E.; Piper.
BARRETT, John:
  Kenny; Nicholas.
BARRETT, W. R.:
  Nixon.
BARRY, John V.:
  Maconochie; Price, J.; Willis, J.
BASSETT, Marnie:
  King, A.
BATE, Weston:
  Were.
BATESON, Charles:
  Reid, D. & T.; Savage, A.
BEALE, Edgar:
  Jackey Jackey; Kennedy.
BERGMAN, George F. J.:
  Johnston, E.; Larra; Levey, B. & S., Rümker.
BILLING, C. G.:
  Massey.
BIRMAN, Wendy:
  Wylie.
BLAKE, L. J.:
  Kentish.
BLUNDEN, T. W.:
  Mason, M.; Wallis.
BOLTON, G. C.:
  Morrill; Stokes; Wollaston.
BORDER, Ross:
  Scott, T. H.
BROWN, P. L.:
  Learmonth; Mercer; Russell, P.; Strachan.
BYRNES, J. V.:
  McGarvie, W.; O'Shaughnessy; Stephens, A.; Thompson, A.

CABLE, K. J.:
  Icely; Johnson; McKenny; Sadleir; Stiles; Walsh.

CALABY, J. H.:
  Latham; MacGillivray; Preiss; Shaw, G.
CAMERON, E. J.:
  Kermode.
CARINGTON SMITH, Julie:
  Schaw.
CASHMAN, R. I.:
  Langlands.
CHATE, Alfred H.:
  Moore, G.; Stone.
CHISHOLM, A. H.:
  Lindesay; Wilson, J.
CLARKE, Donovan:
  Robinson, M.
CLAUGHTON, S. G.:
  Lawry; Walker, W., minister.
CLELAND, J. B.:
  Wright.
COBLEY, John:
  Worgan.
COLES, P. J.:
  Scott, D.; Trigg.
CONWAY, Jill:
  Macarthur, E.; Riley, A. & E.
CORBETT, Arthur:
  Struth.
COWPER, Norman:
  McCrae.
CRAIG, C.:
  Lyttleton; Pugh.
CRANFIELD, Louis R.:
  Logan; Stapylton.
CRANFIELD, R. E.:
  Wittenoom.
CRAWFORD, G. H.:
  Scott, T.
CRISP, Peter:
  Pitcairn.
CROWLEY, F. K.:
  Stirling.
CULLEN, John H.:
  Willson.
CURREY, C .H.:
  Stephen, John; Therry, R.; Wardell.

DALEY, Louise T.:
  Manning, E.; Rous.
DALLY, James:
  Jorgenson.
DALY, R. A.:
  Makinson; Sconce.
DAVIDSON, J. W.:
  Kendall.
DENHOLM, Decie:
  Tregurtha.
DOLLERY, E. M.:
  Nairn.
DOUST, R. H.:
  Leigh.

HERMAN, Morton:
Lewis, M.; Lucas, N.
HEYDON, J. D.:
Macarthur, James.
HINDWOOD, K. A.:
Raper.
HITCHCOX, A. C..:
Shepherdson.
HODDINOTT, W. G.:
Milligan.
HODGMAN, V. W.:
Prout; Simpkinson de Wesselow; Waine-
wright.
HODGSON, David:
Meredith.
HOLDER, R. F.:
Jenkins; Macvitie; Williams, F.
HONNIBALL, J. H. M.:
Mackie; Shenton.
HORNER, J. C.:
Rowcroft; Vidal.
HORNIBROOK, J. H.:
Pamphlett.
HORTON, Allan:
Lithgow; Southwell.
HOTIMSKY, C. M.:
Lazarev.
HOWELL, P. A.:
Montagu, A.; Pedder.
HUME, L. J.:
Lynch; Macdermott.

ILTIS, Judith:
Simpson, S.

JACKSON, P. R. S.:
Jackson, S.
JAMES, G. F.:
Joyce.
JONES, Brian L.:
Stow.
JOY, W.:
Walker, T., merchant.

KEMP, Murray C.:
Kemp, A.
KING, Hazel:
Miles; Rossi; Slade; Wilson, H.
KNIGHT, R. L.:
Lowe, R., politician; Thompson, R.
KUNZ, E. F.:
Wortman(n).

LACK, Clem:
Lawless; Russell, H.
LANGDON, H. C. C.:
Read, G.
LEA-SCARLETT, E. J.:
Snodgrass, K.; Watson.
LENEHAN, Marjorie:
Rouse.
LE ROY, Paul Edwin:
Lyons.

LEVY, Michael C. I.:
Parramore.
LEWIS, Hubert C.:
Lewis, R.
LOANE, M. L.:
Moore, T.
LOCKLEY, G. L.:
Price, C.; Quaife; Ross, R., minister;
Schofield.
LONG, Gavin:
Ranken; Tom.
LOVE, A. R.:
Power.

McAULAY, Ida:
Walker, T., commissary.
McCALLUM, C. A.:
King, J. C.; Simpson, J.; Tuckfield; Water-
field.
McKAY, R. J.:
Moore, W.; Wylde.
MACKERRAS, Catherine:
Nathan; Wallace.
McKINNEY, Judith Wright:
Wyndham.
McLACHLAN, N. D.:
Macquarie, L.
McMAHON, Anne:
Laing, H.
McMARTIN, Arthur:
Nichols; Ramsay; Rose, T., farmer; Short-
land, J. & J. jnr.
MACMILLAN, David S.:
King, J.; McLachlan; Macleay, G. & W.;
Milson; Molle; Morehead; Nicholson;
Paterson; Ross, R., major; Uther.
MACNAB, Ken:
Mundy.
MANDER-JONES, Phyllis:
Lewin.
MANIFOLD, W. G.:
Manifold.
MARCHANT, Leslie R.:
La Pérouse; Péron.
MARSHALL, Herbert:
Wilton.
MATHER, Robert:
Mather.
MAUDE, H. E.:
Nobbs; Raine, T.
MEAD, Isabella J.:
Mountgarrett; Oakden; Strange.
MEDCALF, M.:
Landor; Leake, G.
METCALFE, John:
Riddell.
MONKS, Linda:
Knopwood.
MORGAN, E. J. R.:
Robe.
MORRIS, J. R.:
Lord, T.; McLachlan; Shoobridge; Woods.
MORRISON, A. A.:
Petrie; Wickham.

MORTYN, S. M.:
Macarthur, A.
MOSSENSON, David:
Irwin; Nash, R. W.; Samson.
MOZLEY, Ann:
Jukes.
MULVANEY, D. J.:
Thomas, W.
MURRAY, C. R.:
Murray, R.
MURRAY, H. M.:
Murray, H.

NAIRN, Bede:
Macarthur, H.; Polding.
NEWTON, R. J. M.:
Manning, J.

O'BRIEN, J. L.:
Laing, C.
OLDHAM, Ray:
Reveley.
OPPENHEIM, H. L.:
Knowles; McCrone; Simmons; Wyatt, J.
ORTON, J. Russell:
Orton.
OSBORNE, M. E.:
Thomson, E. D.
OSBORNE, P. J. B.:
Osborne.

PAGE, C. A. S.:
Page.
PARRY, Ann:
Parry.
PARSONS, George:
Laidley; Miller, A.; Wemyss.
PARSONS, Nancy:
Parsons.
PARSONS, Vivienne:
Jamieson; Jamison, T.; Lee; Lowe, R.,
grazier; Mann, D.; Mansfield; Mileham;
Miller, G.; Morisset; Murray, J.; Nepean;
O'Flynn; O'Neil; Platt; Prieur; Raven;
Raymond; Redmond; Rose, T., baker;
Savage, J.; Scott, E. & T. A.; Sidaway;
Siddins; Smith, T.; Suttor; Throsby;
Walker, W., merchant; Waterhouse;
Wild; Wiseman.
PENNY, B. R.:
Jackson, J.; Lonsdale.
PERSSE, Michael:
Wentworth, W.
PERRY, T. M.:
Meehan; Westall.
PHILLIPS, Nan:
Vancouver.
PHILLIPS, P. K.:
McEncroe.
PIDGEON, W. E.:
Pidgeon.
PIKE, A. F.:
Mason, T.; Reid, A.; Roemer; Salting;
Smith, H.; Wilson, J. T.; Young.

PONDER, J. B.:
Smith, P.
PREST, Jean:
Kingston.
PRESTON, Harley:
Kay, W.; Russell, R.; Thomson, J.; Verge.
PRETTY, Graeme L.:
Wakefield.
PRETYMAN, E. R.:
Kelly; Lucas, J.; McCarty; Manton;
Miller, F.

RAND, A.:
Leake, J.; Murdoch, J.; Talbot.
RENDELL, Alan:
Newland; Wyatt, W.
REYNOLDS, J. H.:
Péron.
REYNOLDS, John:
Montagu, J.; Pitt; Sorell, W.; West.
RICHARDSON, G. D.:
Scott, J., marine.
RIENITS, Rex:
Lycett; Parkinson; Watling; White.
RIENITS, Thea:
Lord, E.
ROBINSON, N. M.:
O'Flaherty.
ROBSON, L. L.:
Lakeland; Maum; Mulgrave.
ROE, Margriet:
Lascelles.
ROE, Michael:
Lillie ;Margarot; Mealmaker; Morgan, J.;
Wroe.
ROSS, D. Bruce:
O'Halloran.
ROSS, Hugh D.:
Ross, H.
RUDE, G.:
Loveless; Meagher; Mitchel; O'Brien, W.;
Williams, Z.
RUTLEDGE, Martha:
Rutledge.

SALES, P. M.:
Powlett.
SAYERS, C. E.:
Wills.
SCOTT, Peter:
O'Brien, H.; Tucker.
SHARMAN, R. C.:
Solomon, I.
SHAW, A. G. L.:
King, P. G.
SHEEHAN, M. J.:
Raine, J.
SHINEBERG, D.:
Jones, R., merchant.
SKEMP, J. R.:
Kearney; Lovell.
SMITH, Roy S.:
Lambe.

REFERENCES

The following works of reference have been widely used but have not been listed in the sources at the foot of the articles:

D. Blair, *Cyclopaedia of Australasia* (Melbourne, 1881)

B. Burke, A *Genealogical and Heraldic History of the Colonial Gentry* (London, 1891)

J. A. Ferguson, *Bibliography of Australia*, 1-6 (Sydney, 1941-65)

H. M. Green, A *History of Australian Literature*, 1-2 (Sydney, 1961)

J. H. Heaton, *Australian Dictionary of Dates and Men of the Time* (London, 1879)

F. Johns, *An Australian Biographical Dictionary* (Melbourne, 1934)

P. Mennell, *The Dictionary of Australasian Biography* (London, 1892)

E. M. Miller, *Australian Literature . . . to 1935*, 1-2 (Melbourne, 1940); extended to 1950, by F. T. Macartney (Sydney, 1956)

W. Moore, *The Story of Australian Art*, 1-2 (Sydney, 1934)

P. C. Mowle, A *Genealogical History of Pioneer Families in Australia* (Sydney, 1939)

P. Serle, *Dictionary of Australian Biography*, 1-2 (Sydney, 1949)

Australian Encyclopaedia, 1-2 (Sydney, 1925)

Australian Encyclopaedia, 1-10 (Sydney, 1958)

Dictionary of National Biography, 1-22 (London, 1885-1900), and Supplements

REFERENCES

The following works of reference have been widely used but have not been listed in the notes or the foot of the articles:

ABBREVIATIONS

Ac no	Accession number	JRHSQ	Journal of the Royal Historical Society of Queensland
Adm	Admiralty		
ANU	Australian National University, Canberra	JRWAHS	Journal and Proceedings of the Royal Western Australian Historical Society
ANZAAS	Australian and New Zealand Association for the Advancement of Science		
A'sian	Australasian	LA	Legislative Assembly
Assn	Association	LC	Legislative Council
Aust	Australia, Australian	Lib	Library
		LMS	London Missionary Society
		LSD	Lands and Surveys Department
Battye Lib.	J. Battye Library of West Australian History, Perth		
		Mag	Magazine
bibliog	bibliography	MJA	Medical Journal of Australia
BM	British Museum, London	ML	Mitchell Library, Sydney
		MS	manuscript
		mthly	monthly
cat	catalogue		
CO	Colonial Office		
Col Sec	Colonial Secretary	nd	no date of publication stated
Com	Commission	NL	National Library of Australia, Canberra
comp	compiler		
CSIRO	Commonwealth Scientific and Industrial Research Organization	no	number
		np	no place of publication stated
		NSW	New South Wales
CSO	Colonial Secretary's Office	NSWA	New South Wales State Archives, Sydney
cttee	committee		
Cwlth	Commonwealth		
		OD	Outward Dispatches
ed	editor, edition		
encl	enclosure	p	page, pages
		PD	Parliamentary Debates
		PP	Parliamentary Papers
fl.	floruit (he flourished)	PRGSQ	Proceedings of the Royal Geographical Society of Australasia (Queensland)
Gen	Genealogists		
GO	Governor's Office	PRGSSA	Proceedings of the Royal Geographical Society of Australasia (South Australian Branch)
HC	House of Commons	priv print	privately printed
HL	House of Lords	PRO	Public Record Office, London
HO	Home Office	Procs	Proceedings
HRA	Historical Records of Australia	pt	part, parts
HRNSW	Historical Records of New South Wales	PTHRA	Proceedings of the Tasmanian Historical Research Association
J	Journal	Q	Quarterly
JRAHS	Journal and Proceedings of the Royal Australian Historical Society	QA	Queensland State Archives, Brisbane
		Qld	Queensland
JRGS	Journal and Proceedings of the Royal Geographical Society	Qld GJ	Queensland Geographical Journal

ABBREVIATIONS

[q.v.]*	quod vide (which see); cross reference	Tas	Tasmania
		tr	translated, translation
		Trans	Transactions
res	research		
Roy	Royal	Univ	University
SA	South Australia	VA	Victorian State Archives, Melbourne
SAA	South Australian Archives, Adelaide	V & P	Votes and Proceedings
Sel	Select	VDL	Van Diemen's Land
SLV	State Library of Victoria, Melbourne	VHM	Victorian Historical Magazine
		v, vol	volume
SMH	Sydney Morning Herald	Vic	Victoria
Soc	Society		
SPG	Society for the Propagation of the Gospel in Foreign Parts	WA	Western Australia
Supp	Supplement	WAA	Western Australian State Archives, Perth
TA	Tasmanian State Archives, Hobart	wkly	weekly
		WO	War Office

*The note [q.v.] accompanies the names of individuals, other than governors, lieut-governors and Colonial Office officials, who are the subjects of biographies in one of the two volumes of Period 1, 1788-1850.

I

ICELY, THOMAS (1797-1874), land-owner and stockbreeder, was born in November 1797 at Plympton, Devonshire, England, eldest son of Thomas Icely, a merchant and shipowner (d. 1836). Icely received a sound general and commercial education and in September 1818 was given an order for 600 acres in New South Wales. He reached Sydney in September 1820, disposed profitably of the merchandise he had brought, and returned to England where he added to his capital. This resulted in a 2000-acre grant that Icely, back in the colony in 1822, took up at Saltram, near Bathurst, in 1823. He was given permission to buy another 9600 acres and received a further grant in 1825, although these additions were not taken up immediately. Two years later Icely bought Bungarribee with the help of the Macarthurs [q.v.], from whom he had already bought sheep and cattle. Finally in 1831 Icely established the Coombing Park estate and by 1838 had disposed of Saltram and Bungarribee. Coombing, near the later town of Carcoar (Carcuan, Corcoran), comprised about 26,000 acres by 1839. Icely developed the resources of this and other properties. He built large stores, a cheese factory and a foundry, mined for copper and tried to exploit the gold first discovered on his land in 1842. A. G. Mann, book-keeper at Coombing in 1850, reported: 'We have a Mine on the Estate where Mr Icely has found Gold and very soon intends working it'. Icely became famous as a breeder and importer of cattle, sheep and horses. His race-horses and cavalry re-mounts for India were of high quality, his merino experiments achieved success and he made type history in Australia in his selection of Shorthorn stock. Icely was not a large-scale squatter. Rather, he was a landowner with a belief in orderly and scientific development. It was a sign of his careful planning that he did not suffer from the depression of the early 1840s as much as many of his fellows.

Icely's mercantile career in New South Wales had been briefer. In 1824 he had entered into partnership with Matthew Hindson to carry on business as agents and merchants. He gained Governor Brisbane's commendation for trying to set up a timber trade with England and sailed to England in the *Midas* in 1824 to encourage this trade. He retired from active partnership in 1827 and thenceforward his commercial activities were determined largely by his property interests. He was a shareholder in the Bank of Australia, a member of the committee of inquiry into the Savings Bank in 1843 and a trustee of that institution in 1844. These were incidental to his main concern at Coombing.

Icely was a nominee in the Legislative Council from 1843 to 1856. He was a consistent supporter of the governor but did not take a leading part in proceedings. In the stormy session of 1844 he sat on no committees and did not give personal or written evidence before the select committee on crown lands grievances. But in May, when Governor Gipps thought it best to make known his opinion 'on the subject of the occupation of Crown land, [he] . . . put into the hands of Mr Icely . . . a Paper, and intimated to Mr Icely that he was at liberty to make it public'. In December Gipps recommended Icely for a proposed colonial order of merit, not as a reward for subservience but in recognition of his position as a great landowner and a sensible conservative. Icely was 'one of the first gentlemen in the colony' and Colonel Mundy [q.v.] wrote, after a visit to Coombing in 1846, that 'the great graziers and even the wealthiest landed proprietors of the Old Country may hide their diminished heads when compared with [Icely] in point of territory, stock, and numbers of persons employed'.

Icely's conformity in the council involved him in the one case of notoriety in his career. He voted against the motion for a select committee to investigate Earl Grey's strictures on J. D. Lang's [q.v] immigration scheme. In 1851 Lang publicly accused Icely of sycophancy and more directly of having defrauded Joseph Underwood [q.v.] over the sale of the *Midas* in 1824. Lang, who admitted that the charge was inspired by Icely's attitude, apologized but was given a gaol sentence for criminal libel. While in prison he investigated a story that Icely had hired someone in 1824 to fire a shot into Underwood's house 'to shut his mouth about the *Midas*'. B. C. Rodd, who had fired the shot unwittingly, denied that Icely had had anything to do with the affair. The court proceedings did not harm Lang's electoral popularity but they vindicated Icely's reputation for honest, though perhaps hard, dealing. His fellow-landowner, Edward Hamilton, told Deas Thomson [q.v.] that he 'always considered [Icely] as the best gentleman of the old settlers—*facile princeps*', and he was glad that, as a result of the libel case, his 'estimation of him as a friend, and a

1

good citizen, is in the highest sense not misplaced'. Icely was appointed to the Legislative Council once more in June 1864 and retained his seat until his death.

Icely was a firm member of the Church of England. The first resident clergyman of Carcoar lived for a time on the Coombing property and Icely helped to build the parish church of St Paul. He remained a leader in church affairs in the district and acted as trustee, warden and Church Society representative. The synod movement found in Icely a strong supporter, but his attitude to problems of ecclesiastical government was often independent. His relations with Bishops Broughton [q.v.] and Barker were cordial but the squire-parson nexus was his ideal and this did not accord always with official policy.

In England in 1830 Icely married Charlotte, daughter of Nicholas Phillips Rothery, R.N., of Bittern, Hampshire. His wife's brothers accompanied him to New South Wales. Frederick (1804-1860) became a promoter of mining and iron companies of Sydney and William Montagu (1810-1900) a prosperous grazier and stockbreeder at Cliefden, near Carcoar. Icely had two sons and four daughters by his first wife, who died in 1843. In 1856 he married Louisa Bartlett, who bore him a son and daughter and survived him.

In 1862 Icely left Coombing for Greystones and, in 1869, Elizabeth Farm House, Parramatta. He died on 13 February 1874 and was buried at St Peter's, Cook's River.

HRA (1), 12; S. C. Mundy, Our antipodes, 1-3, (Lond, 1852); M. H. Ellis, The beef Shorthorn in Australia (Syd, 1932); W. A. Steel, 'The history of Carcoar, 1815-1881', JRAHS, 17 (1931); SMH, Feb, Apr 1851; MS cat under T. Icely (ML).   K. J. CABLE

IMLAY, PETER (1787-1881), GEORGE (1795-1847), and ALEXANDER (1801-1847), landowners and speculators, were born in Scotland of an Aberdeenshire family. Alexander, an army surgeon, arrived in Sydney in December 1829 in the *Elizabeth* and was appointed to the colony's medical staff in March. Peter, a naval surgeon, reached Hobart Town in the *Greenock* in February 1830. George arrived in Sydney as surgeon superintendent of convicts in the *Roslyn Castle* in February 1833 and joined Alexander on the staff of the Sydney Infirmary.

In 1832 Alexander toured the south coast and the County of Argyle with Governor Bourke and next year was holding 1280 acres on the Breadalbane plains. In that year Peter also called at Twofold Bay,

where he was impressed by the possibilities of shore-based whaling and stock-raising. He soon made his home at Twofold Bay and in 1835 was joined by George, who, although a pastoralist, continued to hold his navy posting until 1841. Alexander resigned from his army medical post in 1833 after ten years service. He went to Hobart in January 1833 and thereafter was chiefly responsible for the brothers' Van Diemen's Land properties. In 1834 he sought and received support from Bourke and Lieut-Governor Arthur for his plans to build up trade in cattle and salted provisions between Twofold Bay and Van Diemen's Land. Alexander also promised to introduce steam navigation and develop trade in wool from the Minarro (Monaro) district. The brothers acquired several properties in Van Diemen's Land, including one of 2560 acres, the only grant on Forestier's Peninsula. This was the site of one of their whaling stations. Despite government objections to their use of convict labour on and near whale-boats, by 1837 the Imlays were among the six leading producers of whale products. Alexander bored for coal on his New Town property near Hobart in 1841, but this attempt at further diversification of his interests was unsuccessful.

In January 1838 Alexander took 120 cows to Adelaide by sea from Twofold Bay. Four days after his arrival with a servant and an Aboriginal, he made a journey across the Mount Lofty Ranges to the Murray River. His diary of the journey was published in the Adelaide *Register* in June and July 1838. David McLaren [q.v.], manager of the South Australian Co., was so impressed with the importance of the journey that he sent a dispatch about it to his London headquarters.

The Imlay brothers' biggest interests were in the Bega district, where George and Peter controlled the pastoral and whaling activities. Peter also opened up trade with New Zealand where he had acquired land at New Plymouth. Although he and his brothers held 1500 square miles of the colony's best land, their fortunes declined disastrously. By the end of 1844 they had surrendered to their creditors all their land except four runs totalling 37,400 acres round Bega and Cobargo. In November Alexander tried to sell his Forrestier Peninsula property to the government, but Lieut-Governor Eardley-Wilmot was not interested. A year later all the brothers' Van Diemen's Land properties were offered for sale as Alexander was going to join his brothers at Bega. A few months later in July 1846 Peter was shipwrecked when his chartered vessel, the *Breeze*, out of Hobart, was wrecked at Upolu on her way from Tahiti to New Zealand. He had been looking for oil.

In December 1847 George, who had contracted an incurable disease, shot himself on top of the mountain overlooking Bega, now known as Dr George Mountain. He was unmarried. Alexander had married Sophia Atkins in Hobart, and a son was born to them at New Town on 2 September 1843. Alexander died in March 1847. Peter married Jane McGuire in 1841, migrated to New Zealand in 1851 and in 1857 settled at Wanganui, whence he controlled trading interests in the south-west Pacific. He died at Wanganui in 1881, leaving three daughters.

H. P. Wellings, 'The brothers Imlay', JRAHS, 17 (1931); True Colonist, 24 Feb 1835, 11 Aug 1837; Colonial Times, 2 Nov 1841, 30 Mar 1847; Hobart Town Courier, 15 Nov 1845; Correspondence file under Imlay (TA).

H. P. WELLINGS

INGLE, JOHN (1781?-1872), merchant and shipowner, sailed with David Collins's expedition to Port Phillip and went with it to Van Diemen's Land in 1804. On the voyage he was appointed an inspector of public mechanics and artificers. In October 1805 he resigned, became a private settler and was granted land which he located near Bagdad. He acquired allotments in Hobart Town and other land by purchase and grant at Sorell and Green Ponds. Ingle soon became a leading merchant, making several voyages to England and acquiring merchandise through relations in London. Friendship with Edward Lord [q.v.] was a major cause of Ingle's prosperity. He benefited handsomely by outfitting the extravaganza of David Collins's funeral procession, and in 1813 stated in a petition that his livestock, buildings and merchandise were worth more than £23,000.

Ingle left Van Diemen's Land for the last time in January 1818 in his own ship, the Spring, although he often expressed his desire to return to the colony. When he left he sold much of his land to Lord and his still considerable financial affairs in the colony were managed by agents. Ingle's opinions of the agricultural prospects in Van Diemen's Land were highly regarded by the meeting which decided to found the Van Diemen's Land Co. but he appeared to have no direct connexion with the company after its formation. In England, Ingle was able to increase his fortune by investments and trading ventures and was appointed a magistrate. When he died, aged 91, on 21 June 1872

at Orleigh, Devon, his English estate was sworn at under £35,000 and his Tasmanian estate was valued at £2081.

On 1 July 1804 at Hobart he married Rebecca, sister of James Hobbs [q.v.]; after his return to England, he married Sophia Browell Currey. He had at least seven children in Van Diemen's Land by his first wife and at least two by his second.

Ingle was probably the most successful of the early merchants in Van Diemen's Land. Governor Macquarie in 1815 considered him a 'low, Vulgar Man who has Accumulated a Considerable Property by Carrying on Trade at the Derwent', an opinion shared by many of Ingle's contemporaries. He is remembered in the name Ingle Hall given to a warehouse he was reputed to have built on property he owned. Its exact date is not known but it is believed to be the oldest building still standing in Hobart.

HRA (1), 7-9, (3), 1-3; Correspondence file under Ingle (TA).

K. A. GREEN

INNES, ARCHIBALD CLUNES (1800-1857), soldier and pastoralist, was born at Thrumster, Scotland, the son of Major James Innes, a distinguished soldier. He was commissioned an ensign in the 3rd Regiment on 23 September 1813 and served in the Peninsular war. He arrived in Sydney as captain of the guard in the convict ship Eliza in 1822. From January 1824 to May 1825 he served in Van Diemen's Land where he distinguished himself in recapturing escaped convicts. In December 1825 he was appointed aide-de-camp to the lieut-governor of New South Wales and became a magistrate in November 1826. He sought and gained the position of commandant of the penal settlement at Port Macquarie, being appointed in December 1826 in succession to Captain Gilman. About six months later he returned to Sydney as brigade major. In 1828 he resigned his commission and was appointed superintendent of police and magistrate at Parramatta, serving there until his resignation in 1829. In 1829, at one of the most magnificent weddings that the colony had then seen, he married Margaret, daughter of the colonial secretary, Alexander McLeay [q.v.].

In 1830 Innes became police magistrate at Port Macquarie and was granted 2568 acres and contracts to supply the convict population with food. This land he worked with convict labour, transforming the wilderness into the fabled Lake Innes, for many years the greatest pastoral property north of Sydney. On this establishment he built, on a typically grand scale, his home, Lake Innes Cottage. As his wealth grew he spread his interests. In his first few years at Lake Innes he produced the first sugar grown in the district. He acquired sheep and cattle stations all over northern New South Wales, among them Yarrows on the Hastings, Brimbine and Innestown on the Manning, Waterloo, Innes Creek, Kentucky and Beardy Plains. He bought Furracabad and the township on this station, the present Glen Innes, was named after him. In 1844 he planted thirty acres of vines and constructed large wine cellars; this venture soon failed. He was largely responsible for the building of a road from Port Macquarie to the New England district. An example of his panache at the height of his career was the hiring in 1842 of the steamship *Maitland* to take his wool from Port Macquarie to Sydney. At his apogee one of the wealthiest men in the colony, he becomes famous for the hospitality he dispensed to all travellers to his regions; a detailed account of a journey through the area by Governor FitzRoy and the vice-regal entourage is given by Colonel Mundy [q.v.] in *Our Antipodes* (London, 1852). During the depression in the 1840s Innes's wealth was almost completely wiped out and he became bankrupt in 1852. He was then appointed assistant gold commissioner and magistrate at Nundle and later police magistrate at Newcastle, where he died on 29 August 1857.

Of his five children, two sons died in 1842; the surviving son, Gustavus Archibald Clunes Innes, became a Church of England minister and served in New South Wales and Victoria. The two daughters married and resided in the colony; his niece, Annabella Boswell, kept a journal in 1845-48 at Port Macquarie, which was published in Sydney in 1962. George Innes, a younger brother of Major Innes, received one of the first land grants in Bathurst plains in 1823, to which he gave the name Yarras.

Innes was largely responsible for transforming Port Macquarie from a penal settlement to a flourishing town. His activities led to the opening of the area between Port Macquarie and New England. His early success in his pastoral endeavours at Lake Innes, including his pioneering of the sugar industry, pointed to the future prosperity of this part of New South Wales. In a time and place when much existence was drab and bitter the doings and the mode of Archibald Clunes Innes wore a cheering brightness.

Two portraits in oils and one in crayon are in the Mitchell Library, Sydney.

HRA (1), 13-16, 18-21, 24; B. W. Champion, 'Major A. C. Innes, 3rd Regiment of Foot', *JRAHS*, 21 (1935); E. S. Lauchland, 'Lake Innes, Port Macquarie', Newcastle and Hunter District Hist Soc, *Procs*, 2 (1947), pt 2; W. J. Goold, 'Port Macquarie', Newcastle and Hunter District Hist Soc, *Procs*, 4 (1950), pt 11; *Hobart Town Gazette*, 6 Feb, 10 Sept 1824; *Australian*, 22 Feb 1840; *Newcastle Morning Herald*, 24 Jan 1953; *Glen Innes Examiner*, 16 Sept 1953; Innes papers (ML).
E. FLOWERS

IRVING, JOHN (d. 1795), a convict 'bred to surgery', was found guilty of larceny at Lincoln, England, on 6 March 1784 and sentenced to transportation for seven years. While in the hulks on the Thames his surgical training was mentioned to Superintendent Duncan Campbell by one of the visiting surgeons, Dr Erskine. Campbell commended Irving to Under-Secretary Nepean who seems to have directed that he be employed professionally on the transports. He embarked in the *Scarborough*, but was transferred to the *Lady Penrhyn* on 20 March 1787 as surgeon's mate and apparently acted in this capacity until 27 April when Surgeon Altree returned from sick leave.

There is no conclusive evidence that he assisted the surgeons on the voyage, but on landing at Sydney Cove he was employed immediately as an assistant at the hospital. During the next two years the surgeons found him such 'a very useful man' that on 28 February 1790 Governor Phillip emancipated him in recognition of his 'unremitting good Conduct and meritorious Behaviour', and directed him to proceed to Norfolk Island in H.M.S. *Sirius* as assistant to Surgeon Considen [q.v.]. Lieutenant Ralph Clark [q.v.] rejoiced in the knowledge that Irving was on board because he was 'the best Surgeon amongst them'. Tench [q.v.], who reacted against the view that the convict settlement was bound to be a sink of infamy, accepted Irving's emancipation, the first granted at Sydney Cove, as a pleasing proof 'that universal depravity did not prevail'.

On his return to Sydney towards the end of 1791 Irving was posted to Parramatta to assist Surgeon Arndell [q.v.]. He was granted thirty acres of land on 22 February 1792 on the north side of the creek leading to Parramatta, between the grants made to Philip Schaffer [q.v.] and Robert Webb, and by 16 October he had nine acres under maize and two ready for planting. Of his professional work, which became increasingly heavy, a few specific records have been preserved. His deposition on the post-mortem of Simon Burn and his evidence at the trial of John Hill for Burn's murder showed his skill in stating matters simply, clearly and convincingly. Irving died at Parramatta on 3 September 1795 and was buried in St John's cemetery. No stone marks his grave but one of Parramatta's streets bears his name. When Collins said that his death 'was much regretted' and that 'his loss would be severely felt' he expressed the popular estimate of Irving's worth.

A. J. Gray, 'John Irving', JRAHS, 40 (1954-55), and for bibliog.   A. J. GRAY

IRWIN, FREDERICK CHIDLEY (1788-1860), soldier and administrator, was the son of Rev. James Irwin, who was born near Enniskillen, Ireland, and became headmaster of the Royal Grammar School, Raphoe, County Donegal. He was descended from a family which had migrated from Scotland in the reign of James I. Frederick began his military career in 1808, seeing active service in Spain and Portugal in 1809-14 and taking part in several of the major sieges, retreats, and battles of the Peninsular war. In 1817-18 he was stationed first in Canada and later in Ceylon. Late in 1828 with the rank of captain, Irwin was commanded to assume charge of a detachment of the 13th Regiment which comprised another officer and sixty-six other ranks, and was to provide military protection for the colony at Swan River, then in the process of establishment.

Irwin arrived in the colony with his detachment in the Sulphur in June 1829, six days after the Parmelia, which brought the lieut-governor and the first settlers. After more than four years in the colony Captain Irwin was transferred to England, where in December 1836 he married Elizabeth Courthope, whose brother was auditor-general and registrar-general at Swan River. They had four sons and three daughters. In 1837, after promotion to major, he returned to the colony and again became commandant of the military forces, an office that he retained for the remainder of his army career. In 1845 he was promoted lieut-colonel. He retired from the army in 1852, and returned to England with his family two years later. He died at Cheltenham in 1860.

Irwin was a severe and stern officer who identified himself with spiritual welfare and religious observance. He devoted much energy to sponsoring the Church of England in the settlement; a bush church called the 'rush church', being walled with rushes, was built not far from the present Anglican cathedral in Perth. In the early days Irwin often organized and conducted church services in his home on the Upper Swan. While in England in 1834-36 he pressed the case of the Western Australian Aboriginals with the Church of England missionary societies, although he had more success at that time in his endeavours to obtain additional clergymen for the young colony, and four arrived in 1841-43. Irwin's sternness and his fondness for moralizing explained some of his unpopularity as an administrator: he tried to found a temperance society in Perth to combat drunkenness, and he encouraged prayer meetings among his troops.

From the beginning Irwin formed a strong and enduring attachment to the new colony. He received an early allotment of land in Perth. Together with Judge Advocate Mackie [q.v.], to whom he was related by marriage, he built one of the first brick houses in Perth. Later he built another home at Henley Park on the Upper Swan, where he lived after his marriage and return to the colony. During his years in England in the 1830s Irwin actively espoused Western Australia's cause in general affairs as much as in the religious field. At that time the colony's reputation was low, the early hopes and promises had failed to materialize, and the need for migrants and capital was very real. In London Irwin helped to form the Western Australian Association in order to disseminate information, create goodwill, and combat unhappy rumours about the colony. His *The State and Position of Western Australia, Commonly Called the Swan-River Settlement* (London, 1835) is a valuable source book for the early days of the settlement.

As commandant Irwin was automatically a senior member of the Swan River administration and he acted twice as head of the government. On the first occasion, in the temporary absence of Governor Sterling from September 1832 to September 1833, the pressing problem was trouble with the Aboriginals. Irwin sought to foster friendliness with them, but he was obliged to execute one of their most aggressive leaders. Later he freed another chief from imprisonment in an effort to achieve a reconciliation.

Irwin's more important period as head of the Western Australian government lasted from the death of Governor Clarke in February 1847 until the new governor, Captain FitzGerald, arrived in August 1848. These nineteen months were difficult because of the long depression into which the colony had sunk. Despite the personal respect he commanded Irwin's administration was intensely unpopular, partly because of the state of the colony, partly because of his manner, and partly because of the attack to which he was subjected by W. H. Sholl, the editor of the *Inquirer*, who had failed to obtain appointment as colonial surgeon. Despite the criticism he received, and the relief and pleasure with which FitzGerald was greeted, Irwin's period of office achieved some important results. One of his most bitterly disliked measures was the imposition of an export tax on sandalwood. Another example of his vigour was the method he employed to overcome the labour shortage: because the revenue had improved slightly and because he was opposed to convictism which was beginning to attract support in the colony, he chartered a schooner and brought a number of Chinese labourers from Singapore to Perth.

It was in the educational field that the acting governor's policies achieved more enduring results. The Catholic Church had been recently established in the colony under the care of Bishop Brady [q.v]. Although his congregation was quite small, Brady brought a large party of priests and several nuns of the Irish Sisters of Mercy to Perth. When Brady proceeded to found schools which Protestant children attended, Anglican leaders including Irwin became infuriated, for at that time the Church of England could not afford schools of its own. Governor Clarke had refused Brady's application for state aid for his schools, and had also attempted to found National schools, though with little success. When Irwin assumed control he pursued Clarke's policy with greater vigour. He clashed with Brady over a proposed marriage bill, over an allotment for a Catholic cemetery, and over the prelate's title of address on official correspondence. In particular Irwin was determined to challenge the superior position in education which the Catholic Church had achieved. Accordingly in 1847 he created a General Board of Education of which he and several other prominent Anglicans were members. Assisted by government subsidies for teachers' salaries, the board founded schools based upon broad Christian principles in Perth and in the other main centres of population. In this way the board originated the state school system of education in Western Australia.

J. S. Battye (ed), *Cyclopedia of Western Australia*, 1 (Adel, 1912); J. S. Battye, *Western Australia* (Oxford, 1924); CO 323/132.

DAVID MOSSENSON

J

JACKEY JACKEY (d. 1854), Aboriginal guide, was a member of a tribe of the Merton district near Muswellbrook. He was probably little more than a boy when at short notice in April 1848 he was selected to accompany the explorer E. B. C. Kennedy [q.v.] on his expedition in Cape York Peninsula. He soon acquired a reputation for hard work, sagacity and superb bushcraft; as privation and disaster gradually overcame the party he steadily emerged as one of its strongest members. The worse conditions became the more it seemed that he could be relied on. Finally a rear party was left at Weymouth Bay; Jackey and Kennedy pressed on towards Cape York, first with three others, then alone, only to find that they were trapped by the mangroves and swamps of the Escape River within a few miles of the waiting supply ship. There blacks attacked them and Kennedy was killed; still in danger Jackey buried him and then made his own escape. With heroic tenacity he made his way at last to the supply ship, reaching it about a fortnight later on 23 December 1848. Though completely exhausted, he could not rest the first night of his return, but grieved for his dead master.

The deep *rapport* between Kennedy and Jackey was again demonstrated in May 1849 when under Captain T. Beckford Simpson Jackey served as guide on another expedition to trace any other survivors and find Kennedy's body. They were unsuccessful, but Simpson praised Jackey's skill, modesty, respectful manner and touching devotion to Kennedy's memory. Ominously, however, he referred to Jackey's one weakness: his 'fondness for ardent spirits'. On his return Jackey was widely honoured by a brass breast-plate presented by Governor FitzRoy, by a government gratuity, and by drinks stood for him by an admiring public. By 1850 he was back with his tribe 'naked, with the exception of his old blanket round him'; he later drifted about aimlessly until, in the early days of 1854 when thirty miles from Albury on an overlanding journey, he fell drunkenly into the camp fire and was burned to death.

One authentic portrait of him survives, a lithograph made in 1849 by Rodius [q.v.] (copy in Mitchell Library), which shows his youth, his sensitive intelligence, and some degree of his suffering.

W. Carron, *Narrative of an expedition . . . for the exploration of the country lying between Rockingham Bay and Cape York* (Syd, 1849); *Argus*, 4 Feb 1854; Col Sec 52/7614 (NSWA); T. B. Simpson, Log-book (ML).

EDGAR BEALE

JACKSON, JOHN ALEXANDER (1809?-1885), public servant and colonial agent, was the son of John Serocold Jackson, major in the 72nd Regiment, who in July 1825 brought his large family to Sydney because his income from a 'valuable paternal estate in Scotland' had become inadequate for their support. By November 1826 J. S. Jackson sold his commission; with greatly diminished means he gratefully accepted appointment as acting barrack master at 10s. a day, but soon proved totally useless and Governor Darling stopped his pay, although he was not dismissed by the Colonial Office until 1837.

J. A. Jackson was appointed a draughtsman in the Surveyor-General's Department at a salary of £100. He appears to have returned to England, for he arrived from London at Launceston in the *David Owen* in June 1831. More successful in every way than his father, by 1834 he was referred to as an agriculturist on a large scale, possessing two large farms and renting Esk Farm, Rosetta; he frequently complained of the shortage of assigned labour to work his farms. In 1833 he became editor of J. P. Fawkner's [q.v.] *Launceston Advertiser*. Next year he tried to become co-proprietor with Henry Dowling [q.v.], and may have succeeded when Fawkner went to Port Phillip in 1835. Later Jackson claimed to have had ten years association with the Launceston press. On 24 March 1834 at Vron, Norfolk Plains, he married Maria Anne, eldest daughter of W. G Walker, who had come to Van Diemen's Land in 1825 and had taken over the Vron estate in 1829.

Jackson was attracted from this successful private life to a public career by an invitation from Governor Gawler of South Australia. Jackson and his wife reached Adelaide in the *Dawsons* on 2 September 1839, and on 1 October he was appointed colonial treasurer and accountant-general. He had been recommended by the colonial secretary, Robert Gouger [q.v.], and his Tasmanian friends, W. E. Lawrence and G. C. Clark [qq.v.] stood as his sureties. The Treasury was in a most confused state and Gawler had instituted an Audit Board to investigate the colony's financial position. Jackson wanted to introduce a more effective accounting system, but the board decided that the head of each government department was to be responsible for the correctness of his own accounts. Jackson was thus left with inadequate powers of audit and little encouragement to be efficient in his methods.

Captain Grey succeeded Gawler in May 1841 and began an era of retrenchment and firm government control. The first reckoning came early in 1842 when Downing Street discovered that Jackson, while still colonial treasurer, had become a local director of the Bank of Australasia. Suspicion had been aroused by the transfer of the government account, from the South Australian Banking Co., to the Adelaide branch of this bank a few months after it opened in 1841, a decision said to have been influenced by Jackson. He was reprimanded by the Colonial Office for holding two positions, but the government account remained with the Bank of Australasia. Meanwhile on 16 October 1841 Jackson had left the Treasury to become colonial secretary. A more serious reckoning came in March 1843 when Grey appointed a new local Audit Board, which examined the confused government accounts, and Jackson was surcharged for certain minor omissions in his accounts for 1840. At the same time the Colonial Office told Grey that money received by the colonial treasurer in 1839-41 from land sales did not appear in his general accounts. As a result some £9800 had been lying in the South Australian Bank for two years without Grey's knowledge. Jackson was summoned to Government House on 26 May 1843 to explain. He was so incensed by Grey's 'alacrity of suspicion' and disrespectful tone that he resigned as colonial secretary on 10 June. Before he left, his friends in Adelaide presented him with plate worth £50 as testimony to his 'able, upright and honorable conduct as a public functionary'. Since the local Audit Board stressed that it had not aspersed Jackson's character but merely condemned his methods of accounting, Grey was irritated when Jackson revived the matter in correspondence in August and announced his intention of going to England to justify his activities as colonial treasurer and explain his resignation as colonial secretary. Probably he was regretting a hasty decision which could blight his career in the colonial public service, for he later claimed that his years in Adelaide had ruined him. On 21 December 1843 Jackson left Launceston in the *Mona* for London. There he sought to vindicate his character, but prolonged correspondence culminated in a refusal by the Colonial Office in July 1846 to give him employment in the colonial service. However, in November 1847 he was fully exonerated and the surcharges held against him were remitted.

Meanwhile Jackson had returned to Australia, going first to Sydney, where he assisted in compiling a census early in 1846, then to Launceston, where he arrived on 26 June. In January he had sent a circular to his Van Diemen's Land acquaintances asserting that colonial affairs were pushed aside or disregarded in London, and proposing the appointment of an agent there. He offered himself for the position. The proposal was well timed, for the colonists were becoming increasingly impatient with delay or indecision in London in meeting long-standing grievances, and Port Phillip and New South Wales colonists were separately arranging to appoint agents in London.

In Van Diemen's Land affairs had reached a climax in October 1845 when the Patriotic Six resigned. On 25 March 1846 a London Agency Association was formed at a meeting in Launceston with J. W. Gleadow [q.v.] as secretary to consider sending Jackson to London to represent colonial interests. Jackson's offer was accepted, and at another meeting in July he received instructions and a formal appointment for two years at a salary of £400 to be subscribed by interested colonists. With the committee Jackson went to Hobart Town to collect more general support than that given by the landowners in the north of the island, and in August he embarked at Launceston in the *Shamrock* as the accredited agent for the colonists of Van Diemen's Land. He was unavoidably delayed at Sydney until December when he sailed for London in the *Penyard Park*. His friend G. C. Clark, a subscriber to the Agency Association, gave him letters of introduction to London acquaintances, and on his arrival on 3 April 1847 Jackson stayed with Clark's family. At once he set about lobbying at the Colonial Office through sympathetic members of parliament. He published pamphlets on emigration, abolition of transportation, steam communication to Australia, and representative assemblies for the colonies. He reported regularly to the Agency committee, and his letters were published in the Van Diemen's Land press. Petitions were sent to him for shepherding through the imperial parliament, and he sent back parliamentary papers, reports of debates and informal news of colonial interest. His activities were much appreciated: he was reappointed for two more years in 1848 and for a further year in 1850. The Van

Diemen's Land colonists continued to subscribe for his salary and expenses, and in 1847-48 some South Australians subscribed £130 a year for him to act as their agent also. At the same time Jackson was busy on his own account, for in October 1847 he had been admitted to the Middle Temple and three years later was called to the Bar.

The London Agency Association exaggerated his part in the achievements of the mid-century: they attributed to him such welcome reforms as the transfer of the land fund to colonial control, the inclusion of Van Diemen's Land in the 1850 Australian Colonies Government Act, the abolition of transportation, and the successful promotion of free emigration: 'a record of exertions untiring, incessant, multiform and judicious . . . in every colonial movement he has been the chief mover'. The results certainly were gratifying, but Jackson was only one of many lobbyists, and the changes in British colonial policy reflected changes in Britain itself as much as deference to colonists' wishes. In 1851 Jackson's work for the London Agency Association was absorbed into the intercolonial Australasian League. When this body voluntarily went out of existence in June 1853 Jackson's agency work ceased. In that year he was appointed colonial inspector for the English, Scottish and Australian Bank at £1200 a year, to reside in Melbourne. He held this position until 1872 when another former colonial agent in London, Sir George Verdon, succeeded him. Jackson died at Ealing, England, on 25 May 1885, at the age of 76.

HRA (1), 12-14, 16-18, 25, 26; J. West, The history of Tasmania, 1-2 (Launceston, 1852); D. Pike, Paradise of Dissent (Melb, 1957); Hobart Town Courier, 25 Mar 1846; Launceston Advertiser, 2, 13 July, 20 Aug 1846; London Agency Assn and Tasmanian administration papers (ML); CSO 787/150, 230, 232 (SAA); CO 13/66, 201/410, 280/252.

B. R. PENNY

JACKSON, SAMUEL (1807-1876), pastoralist and architect, was born in London, the second son of Henry Jackson and Jane Paynter. He received a better education than did other members of his family. He sailed from London in the brig Lion and arrived in Hobart Town on 7 August 1829. He soon established himself as a builder in Brisbane Street, Launceston. In May 1831 he moved to premises in St John Street near the wharf. In 1829-36 he established quite a busy architectural practice. However, only three of his buildings can be traced with certainty: Hythe near Longford, the Paterson Street Methodist Sunday School, Launceston, and a residence for Henry Reed [q.v.] at the corner of Cameron and Charles Streets, Launceston.

In 1835 he and his brother William joined the Fawkner [q.v.] syndicate which hoped to establish a settlement at Port Phillip. William sailed in the Enterprise and after satisfying himself as to the possibilities of the area returned to Launceston. It was decided to migrate at once. In company with Gellibrand, Swanston and Evans [qq.v.], the brothers chartered the brig Chilli, Captain Nixon, and finally landed with their sheep and plant at Williamstown on 10 July 1836. A homestead, situated between the present Rupertswood and Jackson's Creek, was built and became known as Koorakooracup. This property was absorbed in 1850 by the W. J. T. Clarke [q.v.] special survey.

In 1839 Jackson returned to architecture and in 1840 was listed as having an office and residence in Little Collins Street at the rear of the present Scots Church. A brisk practice was soon established. The following are his recorded works: the first St Francis', 1839; the second St Francis', 1841; the first Scots Church, 1841; St Patrick's Hall, 1847; St Mary of the Angels, 1846; Melbourne Hospital, 1846; St Patrick's Church, 1850; St Paul's, Coburg, 1850; the Tower House, Flinders Street; a residence for Colonel Anderson [q.v.]; and a warehouse in North Geelong. In 1841 he made one of the earliest panoramic sketches of Melbourne from the parapet of the partly finished Scots Church; it now hangs in the Newspaper Room, State Library of Victoria.

In 1845 Jackson moved to St Kilda where he lived in the present Acland Street. A few years later he built a larger residence, Wattle House, and eventually owned 200 acres between Fitzroy and Grey Streets from which he later profited greatly. In July 1847 he bought Sandford station (15,000 acres), near Casterton, from John Henty [q.v.]. In 1852 at St James's, Melbourne, he married Mary Ann Lowther; they had one daughter, Mary Ann. In 1862 Jackson and his family returned to England and resided in a fine Georgian mansion, Yarra House, Baker Street, Enfield, Middlesex. He died there on 7 May 1876, leaving a large estate, and was buried in the Highgate cemetery, London.

Although Jackson had little formal architectural training, his artistic sense combined with the strong Georgian influence of his Tasmanian stay enabled him to produce the simplicity and fine proportions of some of the most delightful buildings of pre-gold-rush Melbourne.

H. F. Gurner, *Chronicle of Port Phillip* . . . *from 1770 to 1840* (Melb, 1876); Garryowen (E. Finn), *The chronicles of early Melbourne,* 1-2 (Melb, 1888); R. V. Billis and A. S. Kenyon, *Pastoral pioneers of Port Phillip* (Melb, 1932); A. Henderson, *Early pioneer families of Victoria and Riverina* (Melb, 1936); M. L. Kiddle, *Men of Yesterday* (Melb, 1961); *Kerr's Melbourne Almanac,* 1840; *Hobart Town Courier,* 15 Aug 1829; *Launceston Advertiser,* 16 May 1831, 20 Apr 1835; *Cornwall Chronicle,* 4 Apr 1835; *Port Phillip Herald,* 9 Apr 1846; *Observer* (Enfield), 20 May 1876; *Advocate,* 13 Nov 1897; I. Batey MS (SLV); S. Jackson to W. P. Weston (Weston papers, Queen Victoria Museum, Launceston); E. S. Jackson, Chronicles of the Jacksons (MS in possession of C. M. S. Sinclair, 24 Ormidale Terrace, Edinb).   P. R. S. JACKSON

JAMIESON, JOHN (1766?-1850), superintendent of stock, was a farmer who came to New South Wales with his wife and child in the *Royal Admiral* as one of the first free settlers. He was reputedly forced by misfortune to seek an engagement under the Crown and immediately on his arrival on 7 October 1792 was appointed superintendent of convicts on Norfolk Island in place of Andrew Hume [q.v.]. In October 1795 he applied for permission to settle on the mainland and next April he left for Port Jackson. There he was given the duty of receiving and issuing grain at Toongabbie under the direction of the commissary, and received his first land grant of 100 acres. When Governor King dismissed Hume for dishonesty in September 1800 he appointed Jamieson, whom he had known at Norfolk Island, as superintendent of government stock in Hume's place. To put temptation out of his way and because Jamieson had 'a large family', King raised his salary to £100. Jamieson was 'a proud, touchy but *honest* Scotchman' according to the governor, and therefore a valuable public servant, even though on occasions he earned a reprimand for his brusqueness; his appointment as a lieutenant in the Parramatta Loyal Association in October 1802 indicates the governor's opinion of him.

After the deposition of Governor Bligh in 1808, Jamieson was one of those examined by order of Major Johnston [q.v.] about the 'most shameful abuses' which Bligh was said to have perpetrated, and he testified to cases where Bligh had converted government stock to his own use. Soon afterwards Johnston alleged that Jamieson was incompetent and dismissed him from his position. Jamieson blamed John Macarthur [q.v.] for his removal from office, for he had refused to take the government herds to 'barren ground' near Broken Bay and so leave the pastures near Parramatta free for Macarthur's use. In April Jamieson signed the petition asking Colonel Paterson [q.v.] to take over the government from Johnston, wrote to Bligh asserting his loyalty and that he had only remained in his position for the public good while he hoped freeholders would rise against the rebels, and complained bitterly to John Palmer [q.v.] of Macarthur's misuse of government stock. Next year Jamieson's 'undisputed character for honesty' induced Lieut-Governor Foveaux [q.v.] to reinstate him 'to an employment which [he] could find no other person better qualified to fill'. In 1810 Governor Macquarie confirmed this appointment, but in May 1813 dismissed Jamieson 'for gross Neglect of Duty and Want of Capacity'; he thought Jamieson 'a very honest Man, but extremely ignorant and obstinate and is too Conceited of his own Knowledge to receive or take Advice from anyone'. Jamieson retired to farm his own land which by 1820 amounted to 1200 acres near Liverpool; by 1828 he had moved and held 600 acres at Coomsby Hill, Parramatta.

In 1820 he had been threatened with legal action by the Orphan Committee for feeding his herds on the Orphan School farm despite repeated notice to desist; thereafter his life remained quiet until he died at Parramatta on 7 October 1850, aged 84. His estate was sworn at £3500. His wife Mary had predeceased him on 30 October 1832; their two surviving sons, John and William Thomas, became landholders at Cookbundoon and Cabramatta.

HRNSW, 2; *HRA* (1), 2-7; MS cat under J. Jamieson (ML).   VIVIENNE PARSONS

JAMISON SIR JOHN (1776-1844), physician, landowner and constitutional reformer, was born at Carrickfergus, Antrim, Ireland, the eldest son of Thomas Jamison [q.v.], who arrived in the colony as surgeon's mate in the First Fleet. After education at the University of St Andrews (M.D., 1808) he joined the navy and served in many parts of the world. In 1809, while physician in the hospital ship *Gorgon* with the Baltic Fleet, he was instrumental in curbing a serious outbreak of scurvy in the Swedish navy. This work, which was carried out in the face of great opposition and ignorance, earned him the approbation of King Charles XIII of Sweden, who honoured him in July 1809 with a knighthood of the Order of Gustavus Vasa. In May 1813 he was appointed a knight bachelor by the Prince Regent.

On the death of his father in 1811 Jamison inherited several grazing properties close to Sydney, including 1000 acres near Penrith, together with some city property. He arrived in Sydney in the *Broxbornebury* in 1814 to look after his interests, until then administered by D'Arcy Wentworth [q.v.]. He soon became associated with the public and official affairs of the colony. He accompanied Governor Macquarie on his visit to the interior in June 1815, and in 1818 explored the Warragamba River. In 1817 he was one of the founders of the Bank of New South Wales, and asked the British government to appoint him a member of any proposed colonial council.

His relationships with Governor Macquarie were at first friendly but in December 1817 because he objected to the governor's emancipist policy, called by him 'the very impolitick levelling measures of this Government', Macquarie in a secret report named him one of twelve intriguing and discontented persons. By 1819, however, Macquarie regarded him as loyal and appointed him a justice of the peace, an office which was extended by Governor Brisbane in 1821. Because of his 'wealth, landed possessions and consequent influence', Brisbane included him in the list of ten nominees submitted for a colonial council in 1824, but withdrew his nomination next year. In 1822 Jamison had made serious allegations of immorality among the convicts in the government establishment at Emu Plains but an inquiry did not substantiate his charges; in consequence, he remained *persona ingrata* with the Colonial Office for some years. In 1826 Governor Darling was instructed that on no account whatever should he be employed in any civil office under the colonial government. Jamison appealed against this decision in 1827 and Darling tried without success to persuade the Colonial Office to modify its censure. In 1831, however, Jamison was restored to the magistracy, and next year Governor Bourke recommended him for a vacancy in the council in place of John Macarthur [q.v.]. This time the British government accepted the nomination, but it was not until 1837 that he took his seat in the Legislative Council. He remained a member until January 1843 when he and Robert Campbell [q.v.] were omitted from the nominations for the new council; according to Governor Gipps, both were 'by years and infirmities unable to continue their services to the Public'.

In spite of his differences with the government Jamison always exhibited great public spirit and was prominent in most movements aimed at the improvement of prevailing conditions or at the redressing of an evil. Throughout his colonial life he devoted his time, wealth and influence to the introduction of the free institutions of England into New South Wales. Although not as forceful and prominent a speaker as his friend W. C. Wentworth [q.v.] Jamison, as the chief representative of the immigrant settler class, presided over many important meetings in the 1830s to agitate for representative government and trial by jury. He thus became the first president of the Australian Patriotic Association, founded in 1835. Bourke described him in 1837 as one of the 'many free Emigrants of great wealth and intelligence . . . who advocate liberal principles'.

By the 1820s Jamison was 'one of the first Landed Proprietors in the Colony'; he acquired more land by grant and purchase and extended his Penrith estate, where about 1825 he built Regentville, a famous country house of the early period, named in honour of George IV, the former Prince Regent. Regentville was a model property with vineyards, an irrigation scheme, and a woollen mill built about 1842; it was here that Henry Parkes obtained his first employment in Australia. Commissioner Bigge [q.v.] referred to Regentville as one of the more prosperous and improved properties in the colony. Described by Darling in 1829 as 'holding perhaps the largest Stake in the Colony', Jamison in the 1830s had grazing runs on the Namoi and Richmond Rivers, about 11,000 acres at Bathurst and over 18,000 acres at Capertee. He also took a keen interest in the turf and was an importer of bloodstock. He was a founder and president of the old Sydney Turf Club in 1825-27 and of its successor, the Australian Racing and Jockey Club formed in 1828. He was patron of the Hawkesbury Racing Club in 1829 and had his own race-course at Penrith.

He was prominent in organizations which aimed at the betterment of agriculture and the protection of the grazing interest, being a founder in 1822 and president for many years of the Agricultural and Horticultural Society of New South Wales, and founder and first president of the Northern Districts Stock-owners' Association in 1837. His annual presidential addresses to the Agricultural Society took the form of detailed accounts and criticisms of the state of the primary industries and manufactures. In 1830 the London Society for the Encouragement of Arts, Manufactures and Commerce awarded him a gold medal 'for his successful method of extirpating the stumps of trees', a process outlined in his address to the Agricultural Society in 1829.

Jamison's other public activities were many; he was one of the founders and a president of Sydney College (later Sydney Grammar School) in 1830, and for his charitable contributions he was made a life member of the Benevolent Society. Like many naval and military officers of the period he was a member of the Masonic craft. In 1817 he was admitted to the Royal Arch Chapter, Mount Floreb No. 227, under the Registry of Ireland, and in 1834 was elected president of the United Masonic Fraternity. He was interested in natural history, taking with him a 'collector of natural History productions' on his exploration of the Warragamba in 1818 and sending specimens to England. In 1811 he was elected a non-resident member of the Wernerian Natural History Society of Edinburgh, and admitted as a corresponding member of the Société d'Histoire Naturelle of Mauritius in 1830. In the 1830s he was a member of the Australian Museum and the Botanical Gardens committee.

Sir John Jamison entertained lavishly both at his town house and at his country estate, and in the season of his affluence never lost an opportunity of extending hospitality to visitors to the colony, for whom he arranged outings, picnics and other diversions. He lived like a genial and prosperous English squire, earning by his unlimited bounty the appropriate title, 'the hospitable Knight of Regentville'.

In February 1844 he married his housekeeper Mary, daughter of John Griffiths, an ex-private in the marines, by whom he had already had two sons and five daughters. The eldest son, Robert Thomas (1829-1878), was a member of the first three parliaments under responsible government. The 'hospitable Knight' died on 29 June 1844, comparatively poor through the failure of the Bank of Australia, in which he was the second largest shareholder. His wife died at Hunter's Hill in 1874, aged 74.

HRA (1), 8-24, (4), 1; R. Therry, *Reminiscences of thirty years' residence in New South Wales and Victoria*, 2nd ed (Lond, 1863); E. Sweetman, *Australian constitutional development* (Melb, 1925); SMH, 2 July 1844; MS cat under J. Jamison (ML).

G. P. WALSH

JAMISON, THOMAS (1745-1811), surgeon, was baptized on 17 February 1745, the son of Thomas Jameson, rector of Egremont, Cumberland, England. He was educated at the University of Dublin (B.A., 1768; M.A., 1772). In 1777 he received a warrant as naval surgeon and in 1786 was appointed surgeon's mate of the *Sirius*, arriving in New South Wales in the First Fleet in January 1788. From March 1788, when Norfolk Island was settled, Jamison acted there. His appointment by Governor Phillip as assistant surgeon to the colony, after the wreck of the *Sirius*, was later confirmed in London; however, there was confusion over the date of his commission, and for some time he received only a superintendent's pay because of his being confused with John Jamieson [q.v.].

He remained at Norfolk Island until James Mileham [q.v.] relieved him in October 1799, and then did duty at Sydney until September 1800 when he was granted twelve months leave. In 1801 Lord Hobart informed Governor King that Jamison was to succeed William Balmain [q.v.] as surgeon-general of New South Wales without reference to the date of his commission. Jamison left England in the *Atlas*, but because of a quarrel with the master, Richard Brooks [q.v.], arising out of the overcrowding of the ship with goods brought out for private trade, Jamison left the ship at Rio de Janeiro and took a passage in the *Hercules*. In June 1802 he arrived at Sydney, where he was immediately appointed acting surgeon-general during Balmain's absence. He proceeded to bring a civil action against Brooks on ten charges, but the court only recognized eight of them, rejecting a charge of assault on the grounds that the aggression had been committed outside the limits of its authority. Jamison's claim of £300 for damages to his property in the *Atlas* was rejected by Governor King on appeal, since action for damages could only be made against the owners of the ship; but he was later refunded the cost of his passage from Rio.

In 1804 Jamison, with Surgeons Harris and Savage [qq.v.], carried out the first successful vaccination of children against smallpox, though Savage later claimed that this was due to his initiative. On 14 October Jamison published in the *Sydney Gazette* the first medical paper to be printed in Australia, 'General Observations on the Smallpox', followed by an offer of vaccination to prevent this 'loathsome, disgusting and too often fatal disease'; but he received many setbacks in his official position, finding a shortage of medicines and equipment and above all a lack of skilled assistants. In 1805 he court-martialled two assistant surgeons, Mileham and Savage, for neglect of duty in refusing to attend women in child-birth, but the War Office ruled that these charges did not come under the Articles of War. These incidents emphasized the problem of medical attendance on the growing civilian population in the colony, and led to the granting of permission to the surgeons to engage in private practice. Jamison's reiterated complaints of the lack of medical supplies were of little avail, and his discontent came to a head under Governor Bligh. In 1806 he sought leave to return to England to bring out his family, but Bligh refused permission until other assistant surgeons could be found. Bligh accused Jamison, along with John Macarthur and D'Arcy Wentworth [qq.v.] of becoming discontented when their trade in spirits was checked. Jamison supported Wentworth when the latter was court-martialled by Bligh, gave evidence for Macarthur when he sued Robert Campbell junior [q.v.] for trespass after that officer had removed the heads and worms of Macarthur's stills and had accompanied Major Johnston [q.v.] when that officer had complained to Bligh about improper gubernatorial interference with the affairs of the New South Wales Corps. This, Johnston said later, was the cause of Bligh dismissing Jamison from the magistracy to which he had been appointed in 1802; but the governor complained to the Colonial Office that Jamison was 'not an upright Man, and inimical to Government, as likewise connected in improper transactions'; he allowed him to continue as principal surgeon only because there was no one to take his place. It was not surprising, therefore, that Jamison was among those who deposed Bligh in January 1808. He was appointed a magistrate and Naval Officer by the rebel government, took part in the committees which examined Bligh's supporters and read his personal papers, and was one of those whom the governor forbade to leave the colony when he proclaimed it as being in a state of rebellion. However, Jamison sailed in the *Admiral Gambier* in June 1809 to be a witness for Johnston in the inquiries which were soon to be held in England.

Jamison was deeply embroiled in trade. He was active in bringing wheat and pork from Norfolk Island settlers who, before the evacuation of the island, owed about £15,000 to Jamison and other Sydney merchants. In partnership with Garnham Blaxcell [q.v.] and Macarthur, he invested heavily in the sandalwood trade and quarrelled bitterly with Blaxcell over the sale of the *Favourite* of which he was part owner. The dispute over Jamison's share in this trade was carried on by his son and Macarthur long after his death. Jamison saw no harm in following the example of his colleagues in indulging in mercantile activities in his spare time, which led him first to disregard some government regulations and ultimately to conflict with authority; for all that he was more com-

petent and conscientious than most of his contemporaries among the officials. He was granted 1000 acres on the Nepean in 1805, where Regentville was later built; he also acquired farms at George's River and South Creek, and held 2300 acres in 1807. After returning to England he signed over his property in New South Wales to his son Sir John Jamison [q.v.], who came to the colony in 1814 to take it up.

Thomas Jamison died in London on 27 January 1811, leaving a widow, Rebecca, who was granted a pension of £40. They had seven daughters and one son. Jamison also made provision for an illegitimate son born in the colony.

HRNSW, 2-7; HRA (1), 1-7; E. Ford, 'Thomas Jamison and the beginning of medical journalism in Australia', *MJA*, 16 Oct 1954; J. MacPherson, 'Thomas Jamison', *Univ Syd Medical J*, 27 (1933); MS cat under T. Jamison (ML).   VIVIENNE PARSONS

JANSSEN (contracted to JANSZ), WILLEM (fl. 1603-1628), mariner, of Amsterdam, was, according to Valentijn, a foundling. He received at least enough education to enable him to write a good hand and to become expert in navigation. He is first distinguishable from his many namesakes when, in December 1603, he sailed from Holland for the East as skipper of the small yacht *Duyfken* in the fleet of van der Hagen. In 1605-06 he took part as her skipper in the first discovery of any part of the Australian coastline when he examined the east coast of the Gulf of Carpentaria from 11°S to 14°S. On his return from that expedition he was desultorily employed as a skipper for several years and served for a time in the squadron commanded by Jan Roossengin. In January 1611 he was appointed an upper-merchant and sailed for home in that grade.

He returned to the East in November 1612 and served in Moluccan waters as an upper-merchant and for a time as governor or *commandeur* of Fort Henricus on Solor. At the end of 1616 he again went home as upper-merchant and in July 1617 took his discharge. In August he re-enlisted in his former grade but with the promise of early employment as a vice-governor or *commandeur* at sea. In January 1618 he set out in the *Mauritius* for Java, and on 31 July called at Cloates Land, which he reported as a new discovery, being ignorant of Mibaise's earlier sighting of it. His landing party saw, near North-West Cape, footprints and smoke signals: the earliest evidence that Eendracht's Land was inhabited. On reaching Jacatra he was called into consultation by the governor-general and in March 1619 was appointed to the Council of the Indies. He took part in the operations in which Coen relieved the fort and destroyed the town of Jacatra, and soon afterwards sailed to Tiku where he captured four ships of the English East India Co., which had aided the Javanese. For his part in this he was decorated with a chain of honour.

In June 1620 he was appointed vice-admiral to Robert Adams of an Anglo-Dutch 'Fleet of Defence' against the Iberian powers. The fleet made an unprofitable cruise and next year the positions of the senior officers were reversed, Janssen becoming admiral. When the English withdrew from these operations he continued them for a time as admiral of the Dutch ships, but eventually retired to Batavia. In October 1623, the government of Banda having fallen into disorder, he was appointed governor there and took up the office in December. He soon restored the place to order and established churches and schools, financing the schools by a lottery. He served there until February 1627, then returned to Batavia and was appointed *commandeur* of a fleet for a voyage to Persia. He returned in June 1628, and soon afterwards, when the Mataram laid siege to Batavia, he lent Coen valuable support in its defence, though by reason of his age he was not permitted to face the enemy at the head of troops. In November 1628 he was sent home as one of the three joint-commanders of a fleet which reached Holland in July 1629. On arrival he was sent to report to the States-General and the stadtholder on the state of the Indies, and thereafter he drops out of sight. It does not appear that he ever married.

Janssen was a good disciplinarian, diligent, unassuming and good-tempered. Although he appears to have lacked outstanding ability, his qualities made him a valuable executive officer. By reason of a trick of his speech, he had from contemporaries the nickname 'Ik zeg, ik zeg' (I say, I say).

F. Valentijn, *Oud en nieuw Oost-Indien*, 1-5 (Amsterdam, 1724-26); P. A. Leupe, *Willem Jansz. van Amsterdam, Admiraal* (Amsterdam, 1872); J. P. Coen, *Bescheiden omtrent zijn bedrijf in Indië*, ed W. P. Coolhaas, 1-2 (The Hague, 1952-53); T. D. Mutch, 'The first discovery of Australia', *JRAHS*, 28 (1942).   J. W. FORSYTH

JEFFCOTT, SIR JOHN WILLIAM (1796-1837), judge, was the eldest son of William Jeffcott, merchant, of Tralee, County Kerry, Ireland, and his wife Harriet Jane, née

Hoare. He was educated by private tutor and at Trinity College, Dublin (B.A., 1821; M.A., 1825). Called to the English Bar at the Inner Temple in February 1826, he applied for a legal post in the colonies and in February 1830 was appointed chief justice of Sierra Leone and the Gambia. He carried out the duties of chief justice for two years and in April 1832 returned to England on leave, which was extended from time to time on medical grounds. In April 1833 he agreed, though in ill health, to return to Sierra Leone for a short period. On 1 May he was knighted, and was about to embark to return to Africa when, in a duel at Exeter on 11 May, he shot and mortally wounded Dr Peter Hennis, a young physician of that town. After the duel Jeffcott sailed for Africa before he could be apprehended. He was seriously ill when he reached the Gambia and, on medical advice, went to a neighbouring French settlement and thence to France, without resuming his judicial duties. The seconds in the duel were tried for murder at Exeter in July 1833 and were acquitted. A warrant had been issued for Jeffcott's arrest on a charge of murder. No one wished, however, to press the charge and it was arranged that if he returned to England and stood his trial for murder, no evidence would be tendered against him. He surrendered at Exeter Assizes in March 1834, was arraigned upon the charge of murder and, no evidence being tendered, was acquitted. He had been removed from his position as chief justice, and from 1834 to 1836 was unemployed.

In May 1836 he was appointed judge of the colony about to be founded in South Australia. On his way to the colony he spent several months as the guest of his kinsman William Kermode [q.v.] at Mona Vale in Van Diemen's Land, and became engaged to Kermode's daughter Anne. Reaching South Australia on 21 April 1837, he held the first criminal sessions in the province on 13 May. Having in the meantime lost all his belongings through the wreck of the ship in which they were being sent to Adelaide, he returned to Van Diemen's Land for some months. He came back to South Australia in October and set up the Supreme Court. He supported Governor Hindmarsh in his quarrels with government officials, but was dismayed at 'dreadful dissensions' in the colony and sought a judicial post elsewhere. Having obtained leave to proceed to Hobart Town to consult with the judges there upon legal difficulties which had arisen in South Australia, he was accidentally drowned on 12 December 1837, while awaiting a ship to take him to Van Diemen's Land, by the upsetting of a whaleboat in the mouth of the River Murray. His body was never found. Jeffcott spent only a few months in South Australia, and could not leave any great mark upon the history of the province. He was an able lawyer, whose promising judicial career was ruined by the fatal duel; and his principal claim to distinction, perhaps, is that of being one of the few British judges ever to stand in the dock charged with murder.

R. M. Hague, *Sir John Jeffcott* (Melb, 1963).

R. M. HAGUE

JEFFCOTT, SIR WILLIAM (1800-1855), judge, was the brother of Sir John Jeffcott [q.v.]. He was educated at Trinity College, Dublin (B.A., 1825) and called to the Irish Bar in 1828. He practised as a barrister in Dublin for many years before he came to Australia. In June 1843, within a few weeks of his arrival in Sydney, he was appointed judge of the Supreme Court at Port Phillip at a salary of £1500, in succession to Mr Justice Willis [q.v.], who had been removed from office by Governor Gipps. As a judge Jeffcott proved successful and popular, and was described as bland in his manners, good-tempered, firm, impartial and methodical. 'He was a vast improvement upon the gentleman he succeeded, and the Court business was no longer a series of gratuitous farces for public amusement. From a bear-garden, it became a decent, well-behaved place'. Willis having appealed to the Privy Council against his removal from office, in December 1844 Jeffcott insisted upon resigning because of conscientious scruples, not shared by anyone else, that his appointment as judge might turn out to have been invalid if Mr Justice Willis's appeal should be upheld. He left Melbourne in February 1845 and returned to Ireland, where he resumed practice as a barrister at Dublin. In 1849 he was appointed Recorder of Singapore and Malacca and was knighted. According to Rajah Brooke of Sarawak, the recordership was a comfortable post, 'snug, little to do, well paid, genteel pension &c.'. On 23 October 1855 Jeffcott was advanced to be judge at Bombay, but he had died on the previous day.

Garryowen (E. Finn), *Chronicles of early Melbourne*, 1 (Melb, 1888), p 83-84; J. L. Forde, *The story of the Bar of Victoria* (Melb, nd), p 80-89.

R. M. HAGUE

JEFFREYS, CHARLES (1782-1826), naval officer and author, was born on 16 October 1782 at Cowes, Isle of Wight, England, the son of Ninian and Mary Jeffreys. He joined the navy at 11 and served as midshipman in various ships before his passing certificate as lieutenant was issued by the Admiralty in August 1803. He was commissioned lieutenant in March 1805. In August 1810 at Lambeth, Surrey, he married Jane Gill of London. In January 1814 he arrived with her at Port Jackson in the brig *Kangaroo*.

Jeffreys's first commission was to transport convicts and other passengers in the *Kangaroo* from Port Jackson to the Derwent. After an unsuccessful attempt in May 1814 he finally sailed for the Derwent in August and arrived at Hobart Town in October. Instructed to return to Port Jackson by way of Port Dalrymple to collect a cargo of wheat Jeffreys travelled overland, but though the *Kangaroo* sailed for Port Dalrymple later in October it did not re-enter Port Jackson until February 1815. Governor Macquarie was dissatisfied with Jeffreys's explanation of the delay, wanted to send the brig back to England as unfit for service and to discharge Jeffreys, whom he thought a timid seaman and ignorant of his duties; however, in April he dispatched Jeffreys to Ceylon with the remainder of the 73rd Regiment. Whilst on this voyage Jeffreys named Molle Island in the Whitsunday Passage after Lieut-Governor Molle [q.v.], and Mount Jeffreys on Molle Island after himself. When sailing around Cape York Peninsula in May he discovered and named Princess Charlotte Bay. After his return to Port Jackson in 1816 he made two trips with convicts and stores to the Derwent, which he carried out satisfactorily, but in April 1817 the governor, still critical of Jeffreys's incompetence, reported that he was sending him in the *Kangaroo* to England. Macquarie instructed him not to touch at any port in either of the colonies, but Jeffreys disobeyed his instructions. He entered Hobart at the end of April under the pretext that he had lost a boat and suffered some damage, but with the real purpose of landing a large quantity of spirits. While the brig was in the Derwent it was learned that several prisoners were missing from Hobart, that two prisoners had been stowed at Port Jackson, and that the escaped Sydney merchant, Garnham Blaxcell [q.v.], who owed a large sum of money to the government, was on board. When Lieut-Governor Sorell ordered two boats to patrol the river on the evening of 6 May Jeffreys boarded one of them, beat and abused the commander, Captain Jones, and took him and other crew members on board the *Kangaroo* as prisoners. The captured men were released next day and Jeffreys sailed for England a week later. Macquarie hoped that Jeffreys would be suitably punished, but legal impediments prevented his trial in England; however, at least he had given the British government the means of successfully prosecuting its claims against Blaxcell.

While in London Jeffreys arranged for publication of his *Geographical and Descriptive Delineations of the Island of Van Diemen's Land* in 1820. Most of the information for his work was obtained from the manuscript of Surveyor Evans [q.v.] who had travelled in the *Kangaroo* between Van Diemen's Land and Port Jackson. The book, now rare, was the first of many guides for immigrants intending to settle in Van Diemen's Land.

In May 1820 Jeffreys and his wife returned to Hobart in the *Saracen*, and later obtained a grant at Pittwater of 800 acres, which he named Frogmore. The first house and all its contents were destroyed by fire soon after being built, but he immediately laid the foundations of another. However, Jeffreys did not prosper as a farmer. He died on 6 May 1826 and was buried at Sorell. His widow remained in the colony, and was allowed an additional grant of 500 acres.

HRA (1), 8, 9, (3), 2; G. T. Lloyd, *Thirty-three years in Tasmania and Victoria* (Lond, 1862); P. L. Brown (ed), *Clyde Company papers*, 1 (Lond, 1941); K. R. von Stieglitz, *Edward Markham's voyage to Van Diemen's Land 1833* (Launceston, 1953); Adm 107 (PRO); CSO 1/170/4092 (TA).   E. FLINN

JENKINS, ROBERT (1777?-1822), merchant, was the son of Robert Jenkins, of Arlingham, Gloucestershire, England. His mother's maiden name was Warren, and he was said to be well educated. He arrived in Sydney in 1809 in the *Atalanta* owned by William Wilson, a London merchant, to act as his agent in the colony, replacing Campbell & Co., who had hitherto acted, but were being opposed by the rebel administration.

Wilson's bankruptcy in London encouraged Jenkins to go quickly into business in Sydney on his own account. In 1811 he received some public recognition through his appointment by the Court of Civil Jurisdiction as auditor of the accounts of Lord, Kable & Underwood [qq.v.], at law over a partnership agreement. By 1813 he had won some standing in the community. He was one of those who framed the forthright New Year address to Governor Macquarie and was a member of the committee appointed to draft a memorial to the British government, mainly on the need to encourage a colonial export trade.

On 22 March 1813 at St John's Church, Parramatta, he married Jemima, the widow of Captain Austin Forrest, formerly of the East India Co., who had died in 1812 at Swilly Farm, near Richmond. Mrs Forrest was the daughter of Robert Pitt and Mary, née Matcham. The widowed Mary Pitt had settled in New South Wales with her young family in 1801 on the recommendation of Lord Nelson, with whom she was connected by marriage.

In 1813, when Simeon Lord resigned, Jenkins was appointed auctioneer, a post he held for three years. He was also one of the two appointees to the Court of Civil Jurisdiction. In January 1816 he was appointed as one of the two magisterial members of the Governor's Court when it was reorganized after the death of E. Bent [q.v.] under the acting judge-advocate, F. Garling [q.v.]. In another sphere of public activities Jenkins became in 1814 collector for the New South Wales Philanthropic Society, in 1817 a member of the provisional committee of the Auxiliary Bible Society, which had plans for the establishment of schools, and in 1819 treasurer of the Benevolent Society. Meanwhile Jenkins was one of the 'principal merchants' of Sydney invited to attend the meeting on 19 November 1816 to plan the foundation of the Bank of New South Wales. He was elected a director on the first board of the bank when it was established next year, but resigned in 1819 and became a member of the committee of the Savings Bank (Campbell's Bank). Having an interest in farming, principally through his wife's estate, Jenkins received a land grant of 1000 acres, known as Berkeley, in the Illawarra in 1817. He was among the first five landowners in the district. In 1819 he was one of the convenors of the important assembly of 'free settlers, merchants, land- and house-holders' which met to draft a memorial to the British government on the familiar themes of trial by jury, the disabilities imposed on the colony's trade by shipping restrictions and British import duties, and the need for a distillery. Approval of the last item, which Macquarie had consistently advocated, interested Jenkins because in 1822 he imported the still for the first legal distillery in Australia. By the time it was in operation, however, Jenkins was dead, as a result of a fall from his horse in May 1822. He was survived by his widow and two sons, Robert Pitt and William Warren.

Energetic, capable and successful in business, Jenkins took an active part in the affairs of the colony. He seems to have co-operated amicably with the emancipists on most public issues and mixed freely on such social occasions as the first Anniversary Day dinner, in 1817, where he gave voice to early sentiments of Australian patriotism in a song written by himself. There are indications, however, of some private reservations about his compatriots.

Although collector for the Philanthropic Society he did not become involved in Samuel Marsden's [q.v.] libel suit against J. T. Campbell [q.v.] over the letter to the *Sydney Gazette*, 4 January 1817, containing imputations about the society's funds. Marsden stated that Jenkins, who had just received his land grant, refused to support him for fear of offending the governor. Circumstances may have dictated prudence on this occasion, but Macquarie was eventually to list him in 1821 as one of the 'factious and dissatisfied' persons in the colony. No reason for the governor's criticism was given, but it may be conjectured that Jenkins's interests had led him to favour the demands of the larger settlers for generous land grants and cheap convict labour.

'Biographical sketch of Robert Jenkins', *Illawarra Mercury*, 23, 27 Nov 1901, reprint in JRAHS, 8 (1922); MS cat under R. Jenkins (ML).

R. F. HOLDER

JOHNSON, RICHARD (1753-1827), Church of England clergyman, was the son of John Johnson, of Welton, Yorkshire, England. He was educated at the grammar school at Kingston-upon-Hull, and engaged in farming and teaching until 1780, when he entered Magdalene College, Cambridge, as a sizar (B.A., 1784). He graduated with a good reputation as a scholar and was ordained by the bishop of London in 1786. On 24 October Johnson received a royal warrant appointing him 'Chaplain to the settlement' of New South Wales. The date of Johnson's commission disposes of the story, which Judge Burton [q.v.] reported on Samuel Marsden's [q.v.] authority, that the appointment of a chaplain was due to 'a pious man of some influence', who at the last moment secured the support of Bishop Porteous of London and Sir Joseph Banks [q.v.]. Johnson owed his nomination to the Eclectic Society, a group of evangelical clergy and laymen interested among other things in missions and in prison reform. With William Wilberforce, Henry Thornton and John Newton among its leaders, the society was a powerful force in English religious life and could influence official policy. On the other hand it cannot be stated that, without the Eclectics, there

would have been no chaplain with the First Fleet.

Johnson was taken to inspect the hulks at Woolwich by Thornton and introduced by Wilberforce to the Societies for the Propagation of the Gospel and for Promoting Christian Knowledge. These societies, the long-established and orthodox missionary department of the Church of England, supplied him with a large number of religious books and tracts. After a long sojourn at London and Lymington Johnson took up his appointment with the First Fleet at Portsmouth. There the character of his sermons led Governor Phillip to request him 'to begin with moral subjects'.

These three factors, the Eclectic Society, the church societies and the governor, represented the various parts of Johnson's ministry. As chaplain to the settlement, 'according to the rules and discipline of war', he had to be the guardian of public morality; Phillip considered this to be Johnson's main, if not his only, duty. As a clergyman under the general jurisdiction of the bishop of London he had to carry on the regular ministrations of the church. As the protégé of the evangelicals, and by his own unswerving convictions, he had the task of promoting the conversion of his charges. Johnson never succeeded in reconciling the three or in carrying out any of them to his own satisfaction. Although his faith did not waver he lacked the buoyancy of spirit to apply it. However, his extensive correspondence with English patrons and friends, filled with accounts of the depravity of the convicts and indifference of the officials, was probably more pessimistic in tone than his practical achievements warranted. Johnson doubted the eventual success of the colony and of his mission to it, and after 1791 tended to cast too much blame on himself.

On the voyage in the *Golden Grove* Johnson held services at sea for two of the ships, and at Cape Town for as many as he could. On 3 February 1788 he conducted the first divine service in Sydney 'under some trees' (or 'a great tree') and preached from the text 'What shall I render unto the Lord for all His benefits toward me' (Psalm 116 : 12). On 17 February he celebrated Holy Communion in the 'markee' of Lieutenant Clark [q.v.], who resolved 'to keep this table as long as I live, for it is the first Table that ever the Lord's Supper was eat of in this country'. Johnson soon became one of the busiest men in the colony. Apart from some help after 1791 from James Bain [q.v.], chaplain to the New South Wales Corps, he carried out all the clerical duties of the colony for six years. He held services, either in the open air or in a store-house, at Sydney and Parramatta, performed the occasional offices of the church—baptisms, marriages, churchings, burials—attended the execution of condemned men and worked hard among the convicts. One of them wrote home, amid the sickness and hunger of 1790, that 'few of the sick would recover if it was not for the kindness of the Rev. Mr Johnson, whose assistance out of his own stores makes him the physician both of soul and body'. In the horror of the Second Fleet he ignored Newton's earlier advice that 'it will be madness in you to risk your health, by going down into the hold of a ship, where the air must be always putrid from the breath of a crowd of passengers in chains'. He supported Phillip's policy of befriending the Aboriginals, took a native girl, Abaroo (Boo-ron), into his family, and once remained as a hostage while Bennelong [q.v.] visited the governor.

In October 1792 he wrote *An Address to the Inhabitants of the Colonies, established in New South Wales and Norfolk Island* (London, 1794). Newton amended a section which had made the sensitive Johnson seem 'personally hurt by wickedness you had met with'.

When Phillip was succeeded by Lieut-Governor Francis Grose [q.v.] Johnson's time of troubles began. Grose represented Johnson as 'one of the people called Methodists, [and] a very troublesome, discontented character'. In 1793 Johnson, tired of being a 'field-preacher' and despairing of getting a church built by the government, irritated Grose by putting one up at his own expense at a cost of £67 12s. 11½d. Disputes also arose over the time allowed for Sunday morning service, the chaplain's ministrations to men under sentence, the enforcement of Phillip's regulation for church attendance and the withdrawal of most of Johnson's convict labour. When Samuel Marsden arrived as second chaplain in 1794 he found Johnson and Grose 'involved in a serious quarrel'. Grose and Johnson had different views of the chaplain's office. The lieut-governor considered Johnson's emphasis on personal salvation detrimental to good order and discipline—hence the unfounded but not surprising charge of Methodism—while Johnson believed that the twin aspects of religion could not be separated. So he came to think of Grose's rule as a time when 'things went on from bad to worse, and from worse to worse still, until (I will not say all vital religion and godliness, but) even almost all common morality, and even decency, was banished from the Colony'.

Johnson found Governor Hunter more sympathetic. In 1797 he was recompensed for his church, and in July 1798 wrote in defence of Hunter's administration against the charges of John Macarthur [q.v.], of whose conduct and that of the trader-officers he disapproved strongly. In October his temporary church was burned down and a new store-shed had to be fitted up hastily for divine service. Johnson had general supervision over the increasing number of schools, and in August 1800 Lieut-Governor King set up a committee, with Johnson as treasurer, to conduct an orphan institution. Johnson used money from former subscriptions that he had collected. A month later he was thanked 'for his attention and assiduity in the concerns of the orphans in the colony'. But in October King had to publish yet another order 'respecting a proper attention being paid to the observance of the Sabbath'. He reported that Johnson 'has met with much obstruction formerly in the execution of his duty. I believe him to [be] a very honest man, and I think has been ill-used in this colony by those in it'.

Johnson had been appointed by Phillip to act as a civil magistrate. He was removed by Grose but reinstated by Hunter and remained in the office until he left the colony. Such an appointment was not unusual, for this was the hey-day of the clerical justice of the peace and Johnson, as a civil official, believed it his duty to take part in the administration of justice. However, his main secular occupation and chief solace was farming. Watkin Tench [q.v.] thought him 'the best farmer in the country' in 1790, and Johnson 'flatter[ed] him]self that there are not many here who understand agriculture better'. At first he doubted the durable quality of the soil, but he gained some early success with citrus fruits, grapes, vegetables, wheat, barley and tobacco. The land allotted to him as a glebe under Phillip's additional instructions, 20 August 1789, he considered of little use, '400 acres . . . for which I wd not give 400 pence', but on his own 350 acres at Canterbury Vale, as earlier on his patch at Brickfield, he worked hard and well. Before he sailed for England Johnson sold his Canterbury farm to William Cox [q.v.] and disposed of his land at Ryde, but he does not seem to have engaged in agriculture and stock-raising solely for gain. It gave him personal satisfaction and contributed to the colony's morale and well-being.

Johnson had first applied for leave for reasons of health in 1798; he sailed from

Sydney with Hunter in the *Buffalo* in October 1800. From the time of his arrival in England in May 1801 he tried to secure some compensation for his long colonial service and some preferment in the church at home. For the former he received a year's salary, though he might have had two had he not thought that Marsden should be given an allowance for his extra work at Sydney; in the latter he secured nothing, and late in 1808 was still 'wholly unprovided for, and . . . under the painful necessity of serving as a Curate', as he had been doing chiefly in Kent, Essex and Norfolk. For some time this had been due to uncertainty about his return to Australia. In March and August 1801 King had asked that Johnson be sent back or replaced. Lord Hobart thought it 'probable that Mr Johnson will not return to New South Wales', but Johnson characteristically did not give even a tentative verbal resignation on the ground of illness until March 1802. In 1805 King was still hopefully including him in the list of civil officers on leave, and as the owner of eight colonial cows and two oxen.

In 1808 Marsden, on a long visit to England, made representations on Johnson's behalf to the missionary and evangelical friends who had lost interest in their former protégé. It may have been as a result of this intercession that Johnson was presented by the Crown in 1810 to the united rectories of St Antholin and St John the Baptist in the City of London. Seven years later he also held the sequestrated perpetual curacy of Ingham in Norfolk. In 1812 he made his last contribution to Australia by giving evidence before the select committee of the House of Commons on transportation. He died on 13 March 1827.

Johnson had married just before sailing for New South Wales; his wife, who survived him until 1831, bore him a daughter whom he called by an Aboriginal name, Milbah (b. 1790), and a son (b. 1792).

HRNSW, 1-4; HRA (1), 1-5; W. Tench, *A narrative of the expedition to Botany Bay* (Lond, 1789); J. Bonwick, *Australia's first preacher* (Lond, 1898); G. Mackaness, *Admiral Arthur Phillip* (Syd, 1937); W. H. Rainey, *The real Richard Johnson* (Melb, 1947); G. Mackaness (ed), *Some letters of Rev. Richard Johnson* (Syd, 1954); C. M. H. Clark, *A history of Australia,* 1 (Melb, 1962); R. Border, *Church and state in Australia 1788-1872* (Lond, 1962); *Gentleman's Mag,* Oct 1786, Dec 1790, Apr 1794, Apr 1827; G. A. Wood, 'The Reverend Richard Johnson, Australia's first clergyman', *JRAHS,* 12 (1926); MS cat under R. Johnson (ML).   K. J. CABLE

JOHNSTON, ESTHER (1771?-1846) née Abrahams, was a milliner aged about 15 and of the Jewish faith when she was sentenced on 30 August 1786 at the Old Bailey, London, to seven years transportation for having tried to steal twenty-four yards of silk lace, value 50s. When sent to Newgate prison she was pregnant, and on 18 March 1787 a daughter was born, Rosanna, who in 1805 married Isaac Nichols [q.v.]. On 3 May 1787 Esther was mustered with the child in the *Prince of Wales,* but later transferred to the *Lady Penrhyn.* On board she met Lieutenant Johnston [q.v.], and after the landing at Sydney Cove became his *de facto* wife. On 4 March 1790 her first son, George Johnston junior, was baptized, and two days later she accompanied Johnston to Norfolk Island. In May 1791 she returned with her son to Sydney and two years later her sentence expired. In the following years she bore Johnston two more sons and four daughters. During his absence in 1800-02 she lived on his grant at Bankstown, and after his return at his residence, Annandale House.

From 1800 instead of Abrahams she called herself 'Julian', after a renowned Judeo-Spanish family, originally Juliano and presumably the name of Rosanna's father. Under this name bills were drawn by the Treasury to her for the sale of grain and meat and in 1809 she received a land grant of 570 acres near Bankstown, which was confirmed in 1813. While Johnston stood trial in London for his part in the rebellion against Governor Bligh, she proved an able administrator of his large estates. A year after his return to the colony, at Concord on 12 November 1814, he married Esther, the bride using the name Julian. The marriage was celebrated by Samuel Marsden [q.v.] and witnessed by Isaac and Rosanna Nichols. When Johnston died on 5 January 1823 he bequeathed to his wife 'Esther Johnston or Julian' the estate of Annandale for her natural life.

In the 1828 census she appeared as a free settler in possession of 2460 acres, but the years were beginning to take their toll. In 1829 her son Robert instigated court procedures to have her declared insane and unable to administer her estates. The jury found her 'insane, but having lucid moments', for she was then probably becoming senile. The jury also found that 'Robert Johnston was not heir at law' and application was made to the Supreme Court to appoint trustees for Esther's estate. She retired to the property of her son David, George's Hall at the George's River, where she died on 26 August 1846. She was buried in the Annandale family vault, and when it was demolished her coffin was transferred to the new Johnston vault at Waverley cemetery.

Destiny had allowed her to climb from the depths of degradation to the heights of social respectability; but she was a modest woman who effaced herself and stood always in the background. It was this attitude which probably won her the respect of the 'exclusives' among whom her husband moved. She was very attractive, with black hair, a long face, almond formed eyes, small lips and a long, but straight nose. Deeply devoted to her husband and her children, she remained 'through evil and through good report the faithful wife and companion'.

HRNSW, 7, p 217; HRA (1), 3, 4; G. F. J. Bergman, 'Esther Johnston', *Aust Jewish Hist Soc J*, 6 (1964-65); *Sydney Gazette*, 19 Mar 1829; SMH, 28 Aug 1848.

GEORGE F. J. BERGMAN

JOHNSTON, GEORGE (1764-1823), soldier and farmer, was born on 19 March 1764 at Annandale, Dumfriesshire, Scotland, the son of Captain George Johnston, aide-de-camp to Lord Percy, later duke of Northumberland. This patron secured for the young Johnston a second lieutenancy in the 45th company of marines on 6 March 1776. After serving at New York and Halifax in 1777-78, he was promoted first lieutenant and spent the next two years recruiting in England. In 1781 he embarked in H.M.S. *Sultan* and saw action against the French in the East Indies, where he was severely wounded. After six months leave in England he sailed in the *Lady Penrhyn* with the marine detachment in the First Fleet, and reputedly was the first man ashore at Port Jackson in January 1788.

When the marines were relieved in 1790 Johnston, now a captain-lieutenant, was chosen by Governor Phillip as the 'most deserving' marine officer to raise a company that would be annexed to the incoming New South Wales Corps. Though his detachment included a number of ex-convicts, in 1803 Johnston made trouble when Governor King appointed a bodyguard of five mounted troopers who had been conditionally emancipated the previous year on the ground that their admission would degrade the corps. The governor insisted that transportation 'did not consign the Offender . . . to Oblivion and disgrace for ever' and, ironically, Johnston found the troops so useful that later he recommended the raising of a troop of cavalry for service in the colony.

He was promoted brevet major in Janu-

ary 1800, and during his service in the colony often held positions of responsibility: as Phillip's adjutant of orders, as Hunter's aide-de-camp, and as commanding officer of the corps during the long absences from Sydney of Lieut-Colonel Paterson [q.v.]. A handsome and popular officer, jealous of the honour of the corps, he quarrelled with both King and Bligh when those governors appeared to intrude in military administration. In 1800 he had been sent to England under arrest for illegal trading in spirits, but he was not brought to trial and returned to Sydney next year. In March 1804 he showed his courage and presence of mind by his part in suppressing the armed rising of Irish convicts when, after a year of sporadic raids on the exposed settlers near by, the convicts from the government farm at Castle Hill planned a full scale attack on the settlements at the Hawkesbury, Parramatta and Sydney. After a forced march from Sydney, Johnston and a detachment of twenty-six soldiers sighted the main band of insurgents, ten times their number, at Vinegar (Rouse) Hill. Anxious to prevent their planned junction with convicts at the Hawkesbury, Johnston rode with a trooper to within pistol shot and demanded to parley with the leaders, who naively allowed themselves to be overpowered, leaving their confused fellows to be cut to pieces.

The critical point in Johnston's colonial career was his decision on 26 January 1808 to assume the lieut-governorship and arrest Bligh. In considering the background of this apparently desperate action one must recall the frontier morality that then prevailed in private and public life in New South Wales and other British overseas territories, and the many precedents for such a mutiny. Quarrels had been endemic, not only between governors and garrison but also among the officers themselves, since Phillip's clashes with Major Ross [q.v.]. Johnston himself had been arrested in 1800 when he ignored Governor Hunter's regulations on the sale of liquor, but the disciplinary aims of the English authorities, no less than those of Hunter, were frustrated by the readiness of the officers to protect a fellow profiteer. The rebellion of 1808, the scurrilous 'pipes', the character assassinating letters sent to England, the duels and the horsewhippings indicate the recklessness and malevolence with which colonial quarrels were pursued. John Macarthur's [q.v.] success in aligning the corps with him against Bligh may reflect his ability as a 'manipulator of men', but it was facilitated by the governor's disregard for the feelings of the men of power. Bligh's verbal abuse, parsimony in granting land, preference for the small farmers, attacks on the liquor traders, and finally his threat to court-martial the six recalcitrant officers from the abortive Macarthur trial, ensured a concerted front against him.

In deposing Bligh, Johnston consistently represented himself as an agent of the popular will. He claimed to have found the townsfolk of Sydney on his arrival from Annandale on 26 January 1808 in a state of tumult and apprehension, with no man's life or property safe against a tyrannical governor and his sinister adviser, George Crossley [q.v.]. He stressed the appeal by the 'principal inhabitants' and the 'entire concurrence' of the officers, but showed an apparent lack of self-confidence by marching the whole corps against the undefended Government House. Bligh's evidence at the court martial in 1811 brings out vividly the major's state of mind. After acceding at first to Bligh's request to have his secretary, Edmund Griffin, remain at Government House, Johnston hesitated, checked on the wishes of the 'inhabitants outside', and then announced his refusal.

The officers were soon disappointed in their quest among Bligh's official and personal papers for evidence of behaviour sufficiently culpable to justify the act of mutiny. Johnston must have longed for the arrival of Colonel Paterson [q.v.] as his colleagues quarrelled and showed their resentment of the power wielded by John Macarthur as colonial secretary. Contrary to expectation, Johnston was by no means liberal in granting favours and land, though shortly before being relieved by Colonel Foveaux [q.v.] on 28 July 1808, he gave his son George a conditional grant of 2000 acres, later withdrawn by Governor Macquarie, at Emu Island on the River Nepean.

Accompanied by some of their supporters Macarthur and Johnston returned to England, where the latter, who had been promoted lieut-colonel in May 1808 before news of the rebellion had reached London, pressed for an investigation which he hoped would vindicate his conduct. In the event, he was himself court-martialled in June 1811, and was unable to make capital of Bligh's exchange of land grants with the outgoing King, or of his improper use of government stock and provisions in running his own farm. Against the patent fact of mutiny was set nothing more substantial than the governor's hot temper, and unproven and irrelevant allegations of cowardice at the time of the arrest. Johnston was found guilty and suffered the mild penalty of being cashiered, though Sir David Baird, a member of the court who was absent through illness on the day that sentence was passed, told Macquarie there was not 'the least palliation that was in my mind worthy of consideration'. However, the Colonial Office seems to have thought differently, for, in response to Johnston's appeals, based on his lengthy past services and strongly backed by Hunter, it provided the cashiered officer with a passage to New South Wales, where he arrived on 30 May 1813, and it directed Macquarie to treat him as he would 'any other ordinary Settler'.

Confirming the accepted picture of Johnston as a misled man his barrister, John Adolphus, wrote after the trial: 'I always considered and indeed understood that the parties who led you into your present most unpleasant and unfortunate situation, would, at least, have taken off your shoulders the expense of the present prosecution, but as you refer in your letter to the smallness of your means, I beg you will consider me as entirely satisfied'. A similar note was struck by Johnston himself when he wrote in June 1820, 'Every person that promised [at the time of the deposition of Bligh to support me with their lives and fortunes] has risen upon my ruin. I alone am the sufferer, having lost my commission, and upwards of 6,000 pounds for conceding to their requests'.

At the time of writing this letter Johnston was in failing health and deeply distressed at the loss of his eldest son George [q.v.], killed while riding in the Cowpastures. But in many ways fortune smiled on him during his thirty-five years in the colony. Esther Julian (Johnston) [q.v.], the beautiful convict girl who had come on the same ship in 1788 and had lived with him ever since, had presented him with a large family, of whom three sons, George, Robert and David, achieved some distinction. Four daughters, Julia, Blanche, Isabella and Maria, sprang from this not unusual colonial union which, probably in response to Governor Macquarie's strictures and warnings, was duly regularized at St John's, Parramatta, on 12 November 1814. By this time Macquarie had become convinced that he had nothing to fear from the erstwhile revolutionary, a colleague from the American war of independence, who was living as an exemplary citizen. The family was frequently entertained by the governor and received from him generous grants of land, valuable appointments and other favours. In turn, Johnston gave Macquarie a thoroughbred stallion, Sultan, and acted as chairman of a committee that presented him with an address in 1821 when he returned from his farewell tour of Van Diemen's Land.

Landed activities had occupied much of

Johnston's attention since May 1793 when he received his initial grant of 100 acres, Annandale Farm at Petersham, from Lieut-Governor Grose [q.v.]. Appropriately, the Johnston papers include a letter from England dated 2 September 1803, conveying to Paterson the commander-in-chief's permission, previously refused, for the officers to engage in farming. The crucial contribution made by the military and civil officers to the provisioning of the isolated settlement is well known. By 1801 Johnston had 602 acres at Annandale and Bankstown, with 160 acres sown in wheat and maize, grazing 7 horses, 27 horned cattle, 136 sheep, 85 goats and 29 hogs. Twice in 1804 the *Gazette* recorded presents to the major, including a fine stallion and some Teeswater ewes and a ram, from his old commander and patron, the duke of Northumberland. A grant of 2000 acres at Cabramatta conveyed King's gratitude for his part in quelling the 1804 insurrection, and in April 1817 he wrote enthusiastically of the pastures included in his pioneering 1500-acre grant from Macquarie near Lake Illawarra. All told he received grants amounting to 4162 acres.

Johnston's success as a farmer and grazier (in the latter capacity, as a supplier of meat rather than as a wool-grower), his love of the land and its botanical and feathered curiosities, which his daughters carefully consigned to the Percys in England, and the respect and affection of his fellows must have compensated for the court martial of 1811. He died on 5 January 1823 just as the War Office was inclining favourably towards his claim for compensation. He was buried in the Greenway-designed family vault at Annandale Farm, where a score of years earlier he had planted the colony's first Norfolk Island pines.

HRNSW, 1-7; HRA (1), 2-8; *Proceedings of a general court-martial . . . for the trial of Lieut.-Col. Geo. Johnston* (Lond, 1811); H. V. Evatt, *Rum rebellion* (Syd, 1947); G. Mackaness, *The life of Vice-Admiral William Bligh*, 2nd ed (Syd, 1951); M. H. Ellis, *John Macarthur* (Syd, 1955); CO 201/62, 63; Johnston papers (Dixson Lib, Syd); Piper papers (ML).   A. T. YARWOOD

JOHNSTON, GEORGE junior (1790-1820), farmer, was baptized on 4 March 1790 at Sydney, the eldest child of George Johnston and Esther Julian, later Johnston [qq.v.]. His early ideas of a military life gave way to farming and the civil service. From Governor King he received his first land grant of 500 acres at Bankstown on 23 April 1804. His father, while lieut-governor, made George a conditional grant of 2000 acres on the Nepean; Governor Macquarie rejected this as 'inadmissible', but restored the 100-acre grant, 'Foveaux's Gift', in December 1813, and added 600 acres at Cabramatta on 10 June 1815 and 650 acres at Bankstown on 31 August 1819. Between 1814 and 1816 George and his father supplied a large part of the government's beef requirements, but in 1817 Johnston complained that Commissary Allan [q.v.] was rejecting his tenders, and he strongly criticized Allan's appointment of his own son as a commissariat clerk. Johnston himself held a similar clerkship from April 1814 to June 1818, but when the commissary-general in London refused to confirm it, Macquarie appointed him to the more lucrative posts of deputy-provost-marshal on 6 March 1819 and superintendent of government flocks and herds on 17 July.

George Johnston took charge of the work of yarding, driving and taming the wild cattle descended from the seven which had strayed in 1788. They had defied all attempts to control them and were a public nuisance, sustaining bushrangers and occupying, at a time of growing pressure on coastal land, a sanctuary of thirty-miles river frontage. It is not known whether he received or used the 'machine for taming immediately the most vicious bull' that had been promised by Lord Percy, his father's patron, in April 1816, but by July 1820 some 230 head and in 1823 another 972 had been incorporated in the same herd by means of a plan initiated by George and carried out after his death by his younger brother and successor, David.

George died from a riding accident at the Macarthurs' [q.v.] Camden home on 19 February 1820, unmarried, childless and intestate and 'universally regretted and lamented'. John Macarthur wrote of his death as having 'inexpressibly disturbed us all, for he was a most deserving young person'. Macquarie told the sorrowing father, 'Your son was an honor to his Name, his Family, and the Country that Gave him Birth, of which he was one of the brightest ornaments'. Judging by surviving letters, he was suprisingly literate in spite of the colony's lack of educational facilities, and on 1 March 1819 wrote to W. C. Wentworth [q.v.] a classic statement of the irritation felt by a man of property, notwithstanding favours received, at the commercial restrictions and the despotic form of government experienced by the penal colony.

HRA (1), 8-10; Johnston papers (Dixson Lib, Syd); MS cat under George and David Johnston (ML).   A. T. YARWOOD

JONES, DAVID (1793-1873), merchant, was born on 8 March 1793, the son of Thomas Jones, a farmer near Llandilo, Wales, and his wife Nancy. His parents hoped that he would enter the church but at 15, showing little interest in farming or the ministry, he left home and was apprenticed to a grocer in Carmarthen. At 18 he was offered and accepted the management of a general store in Eglwyswrw, Pembrokeshire, where in 1813 he married Catherine Hughes, daughter of the local pastor. A year later in childbirth she and the baby died.

Jones then went to London and at once found work with a retailer in Oxford Street. He made several changes of employment before accepting appointment with the firm of R. N. Nicholls, Wood Street, Cheapside, where he soon rose to be a confidential assistant. In London in 1828 he married Jane Hall, the daughter of John Hall Mander of East Smithfield. The Mander family were zealous Independents and much interested in the work of the London Missionary Society, and through them David Jones made many friends among his fellow Independents. Through W. Wemyss [q.v.], a friend of the Manders, he met Charles Appleton, a Hobart Town businessman who had opened a store in Sydney in 1825 and was visiting London. Jones resigned from Nicholls's firm and entered into partnership with Appleton which included the Australian branches under the style of Appleton & Co.

In October 1834 Jones sailed with his family in the *Thomas Harrison* for Hobart, whence with plans for expanding business, he travelled overland to Launceston to gauge the needs of the settlers. He arrived in the *Medway* at Sydney in September 1835. Appleton had left his Sydney business under the control of a partner, Robert Bourne, a former missionary, and when Bourne's partnership expired on 31 December 1835 the firm became Appleton & Jones and the latter embarked on the ambitious plan of establishing in Sydney 'a house on the principles of the respectable wholesale London Firms'. When Appleton arrived a rift developed between him and Jones and the partnership was dissolved by mutual consent in 1838. Both Appleton and Jones published their versions of the quarrel in the press; Appleton was uneasy over what he considered a reckless credit policy pursued by Jones, who claimed in defence that since he had taken over the Sydney business in 1836 the turnover had increased tenfold to £80,000 a year, netting in the colony alone a profit of more than £7000 a year. Jones had certainly instituted a policy of liberal credit, for when the

partnership ended the credit figure was over £30,000. Jones moved his business to premises on the corner of George Street and Barrack Lane, where David Jones Ltd still has a branch. To trade with London he formed a mutually protective association with his business friends and fellow Independents, Robert Bourne, Ambrose Foss, G. A. Lloyd and their consulting accountants, Thompson & Giles, with William Wemyss as their chief agent. Jones and his associates regularly secured the whole cargo space of ships bringing out bounty migrants, guaranteeing such profitable backloading as wool or tallow.

Jones survived the depression of the 1840s, business prospered and with his wife he visited England and Wales in 1849. He retired from active management of the business in 1856, taking in partners and leaving in it a capital of £30,000. A few years later the firm failed; faced with bankruptcy, he bought out his partners, returned to manage its affairs and in a few years had fully discharged all obligations to his creditors. He was seriously ill in 1866 but, under the treatment of his son Philip, he made a remarkable recovery. He finally retired in 1868 and died at his home in Lyons Terrace, Liverpool Street, Sydney, on 29 March 1873. His wife died three weeks later, aged 71.

David Jones had a noble and prepossessing presence and a kind and engaging personality; according to his friend Rev. W. Slatyer, 'he suffered from an unsuspicious and charitable judgment in giving others with whom he dealt credit for the integrity with which he himself was activated'. Apart from his family his main interests were business, religion and civic affairs. He had many investments in banks, steamship, insurance, building and other companies; he was a director of the Mutual Fire Insurance Co. formed in 1840, a foundation director of the Australian Mutual Provident Society in 1848, and a trustee and chairman of the Metropolitan and Counties Permanent Investment and Building Society in 1851. He was a deacon of the Congregational Church in Sydney for some thirty-five years, one of the founders and first council members of Camden College and a committee member of the local auxiliaries of the Bible and Religious Tract Societies. He was a generous benefactor to his own and other churches and was one of the Sydney merchants who each gave 1000 guineas to the Crimean war victims' fund. He was a member of the first Sydney City Council in 1842 and of the New South Wales Legislative Council in 1856-60.

He had four sons and four daughters by

his second marriage. The eldest son David Mander (d.1864) married a cousin, Emily Ann Jones, and he with his brother George took up the 300-square-mile property, Boonara, on the Darling Downs. The second son, Philip Sydney (1836-1918), achieved eminence as a physician and was knighted. The youngest son, Edward Lloyd (1844-1893), married Helen Ann, daughter of Richard Jones [q.v] and succeeded his father in the business. In September 1848 the eldest daughter, Eliza, married Robert, son of Dr Robert Ross [q.v.].

HRA (1), 18, ·22; C. Lloyd Jones, 'The history of David Jones Limited', JRAHS, 41 (1955); SMH, 28 May 1838, 31 Mar 1873; A. Jackson, The days of David Jones (Archives David Jones Ltd, Syd).

G. P. WALSH

JONES, RICHARD (1786-1852), merchant and pastoralist, was born at Chirbury, Shropshire, England, the eldest son of Thomas Bowdler Jones, small landowner and brewer, and his wife Elizabeth Ann, née Philips. He was educated in London and early chose a mercantile career, entering a London business as a clerk. He first arrived in New South Wales on 14 August 1809 in the Mary Ann. By May 1815 he was agent for Forbes & Co. of Bombay, importing spirits. In the same year he set up in Sydney as a general merchant in partnership with Alexander Riley [q.v.]. In 1817 Alexander Riley retired and was replaced by Edward Riley [q.v.]. In 1819 Macquarie referred to the fact that they were the only merchants in New South Wales: he complained to London that the order prohibiting convict ships from carrying merchandise made the colony unduly dependent on the goods imported by Jones & Riley, 'our solitary mercantile firm', and that 'this sordid Rapacious House' had consequently raised their prices by 100 per cent. Indeed, he went so far as to conjecture that the measure was suggested by Jones & Riley or their associates in London, Bell & Wilkinson.

In July 1820 William Walker [q.v.] joined the firm which was thenceforth known as Jones, Riley & Walker. In October 1818 Jones sailed to China on the Magnet, and after a short stay there, where he probably began negotiations with W. S. Davidson [q.v.] for a joint pastoral venture, returned to England. In 1823 he married Mary Louisa Peterson, and in that year announced his retirement from the Sydney firm and his intention of acting as their agent in England. By 1823, however, he was making arrangements to return to Australia. It is evident that he intended to return as a pastoralist on a considerable scale: in 1823-24 he set about collecting a flock of pure-bred Saxon sheep to take with him to New South Wales.

In April 1825 he arrived in Sydney in the Hugh Crawford with his wife, his infant son Richard, his sister Elizabeth, his brother Edward and the first shipment of his Saxon sheep. With Davidson, who had a half share of the 'joint flocks', he imported altogether 488 sheep from Saxony, pioneering the introduction of this strain into the country, and bought on importation another 184 merino ewes at a total cost of £11,542.

Jones had been granted 2000 acres and had bought 4000 more during the governorship of Brisbane, but in 1829 applied for an additional grant of 10,000 acres. In his application for this large grant he argued his case on the grounds of the great expense of the experiment in Saxon sheep (although he omitted to mention Davidson's share in it) as well as his other services to the colony. He received 10,000 acres on the Hunter River where he managed the joint flocks and also ran cattle. Jones succeeded in producing wool of the finest description, and his introduction of the Saxon strain must be rated an important contribution to the Australian wool industry. Jones was now one of the most considerable landowners in the country. As well as another property on the Condamine River he also had the Fleurs estate near Penrith, on which he kept a dairy herd, pigs, poultry and a 6-acre vineyard which in 1844 produced 2000 gallons of wine.

It is evident that Jones's heart was in his rural estates, and during the 1830s he repeatedly said that he wished to get clear of his mercantile interests to devote himself entirely to pastoral pursuits. But, in fact, most of his business and trading connexions were maintained until 1838. In 1825, on his return to Australia, he had re-entered the Sydney firm which, after the suicide of Edward Riley in the same year, became known as Jones & Walker. Although they traded with Van Diemen's Land, New Zealand and Mauritius, the business was best known for its commerce with China, the East Indies and India, and especially as large importers of tea and other eastern produce. J. S. Ferriter, who had married his sister Elizabeth, and S. A. Donaldson entered the business briefly in 1836, but the firm dissolved a year later when Donaldson set up in partnership with Dawes.

Jones was a pioneer in several maritime enterprises. He was among the first to commence deep-sea whaling from New

South Wales. By 1825 he was part-owner of five whalers, the *Pocklington, Harriet, Mercury, Saracen* and *Alfred*. With Riley in 1819 he sent the *Governor Bligh* sealing off the coast of New Zealand. Later he had the *Samuel* and the *Mercury* in the New Zealand seal fishery; in 1825 the *Mercury* was taken by the natives of Whangaroa. In concert with Ranulph Dacre[q.v.] and Henry Elgar he bought the secret information of the discovery of sandalwood on the Isle of Pines (near New Caledonia) and organized the first expedition there, with the *Diana* and the *Orwell*, in 1841.

By the late 1820s Jones had become a magistrate and a leading public figure in Sydney. There was scarcely a committee or society of which he was not a member, ranging from the Australian Religious Tract Society to the Agricultural and Horticultural Society and the Chamber of Commerce. He was a director of the Bank of Australia, president of the Gaslight Co., chairman of the Australian Auction Co., a director of the Marine Assurance Co. and on the committees of steamship companies. He was an original subscriber to the Bank of New South Wales of which he became president in 1828. Whenever a merchant was required to sit on a board or committee or act as an assessor, Jones was sure to be called upon officially for his services. In the nominated Legislative Council of New South Wales from 1829 to 1843 he was a particularly active member, sitting on almost every select committee that was appointed. When the council became semi-elective in 1843 he was again a nominated member but resigned in November of the same year because of his financial failure.

He was severely hit by the depression of 1842-44 and declared insolvent in November 1843. All his ships and estates were sold. Although his mercantile activities were thereafter negligible, he again became a landowner, with large properties in southern Queensland, towards the end of the 1840s. He was elected to the Legislative Council in New South Wales as member for Gloucester, Macquarie and Stanley in 1850, and in the next year, under the new Constitution, the first member for Stanley Boroughs.

Jones was well known for his conservative views, and was a determined opponent of Governor Bourke's liberal reforms. He was particularly active in his opposition to the restoration of civil rights to emancipists and to Bourke's attempt to curb the power of the unpaid magistrates. A fervent supporter of the Church of England, in 1836 he also opposed Bourke's plan for National

Schools on religious grounds, and even the grant of £600 to the Roman Catholic Orphan School. Bourke regarded him as a leader of the unofficial opposition to his régime—the so-called 'Hunter River Cabal' —referring to him sourly as 'an acknowledged opponent' of the government, and pointing out that a petition to the Crown and another to the House of Commons in 1836 protesting against his measures, were 'got up at the House of Mr. Jones'. Indeed, Jones played a large part in the incident which led to Bourke's resignation, the election of an 'opposition' candidate for the position of chairman of the Quarter Sessions. Bourke supported Roger Therry [q.v.], who was regarded by Jones and other exclusives as a critic of the magistrates and a friend of the emancipists, and who was moreover a Roman Catholic. Against the express wishes of the governor, C. D. Riddell [q.v.], a member of the Executive Council, was nominated in opposition to Therry and, after a campaign led by Jones, was elected. In his later opposition to transportation Jones found himself in more liberal company.

Jones died at his home, New Farm, Moreton Bay, on 6 November 1852. Of his eight children, Richard became an Anglican clergyman; Mary Australia in 1844 married William Bligh, son of Sir Maurice O'Connell and the maternal grandson of Governor Bligh; Louisa Alexandrine married Robert Ramsay, son of Sir George Mackenzie, baronet, of Coul, Scotland; Frances Sophia married Rev. Thomas Jones, an Anglican clergyman.

HRA (1), 14-18; A. G. Forster, 'Some early homes and epitaphs', *JRAHS*, 11 (1925); *Moreton Bay Courier*, 13 Nov 1852; *SMH*, 8 Dec 1852; E. Jones, Early reminiscences (ML).

D. SHINEBERG

JONES, RICHARD (1816-1892), journalist, politician and company director, was born on 4 October 1816 at Liverpool, England, the son of John Jones, innkeeper, and his wife Elizabeth, née Bond. Both parents died when he was young, and he was educated at free schools of the Church of England in Liverpool. In 1831 he was apprenticed as a printer on the *Liverpool Chronicle*. Indifferent health induced him to emigrate to New South Wales soon after his apprenticeship ended in 1837. He and his wife Martha arrived at Port Jackson as bounty immigrants in the *Fairlie* in 1838.

Jones soon became a compositor on the *Sydney Monitor*, and in August 1839 joined the staff of the *Australasian Chronicle* where he remained until

December 1842. In this period he began to take an active interest in public affairs and politics. He spoke at several meetings in Sydney against the Masters and Servants Act, was one of a delegation who presented a petition to Governor Gipps for extending the municipal franchise, and at the first municipal elections was urged to stand as a candidate but declined. About this time he met Henry Parkes, and their mutual interests and similar political outlook drew them into a close and enduring friendship.

In December 1842 Jones and Thomas William Tucker, a young reporter on the *Sydney Morning Herald*, formed a partnership to establish a newspaper at Maitland. A year earlier Thomas Strode, a printer from Port Phillip, had set up the *Hunter River Gazette*, the first newspaper in the area north of Sydney; unable to run it profitably, he was forced to cease publication in June 1842. Undaunted by Strode's failure Jones and Tucker went to Maitland and on 7 January 1843 issued the first number of their *Maitland Mercury and Hunter River General Advertiser*. Commenced on the eve of the first elections for the Legislative Council it soon prospered and by 1848 was described by Governor FitzRoy as one of the colony's leading newspapers.

Much of the success of the *Maitland Mercury* sprang from provocative editorials written by Richard Jones. Under his keen guidance it became a powerful organ dedicated to the development of local resources and to the education of public opinion in the district. Jones was actively interested in many local movements, at various times serving as president of the Maitland School of Arts, treasurer of the Hunter River Agricultural Society, secretary of the Anti-Transportation Committee, and of the Committee to Establish a Free Port at Newcastle. In 1846 Jones had become sole proprietor; in 1854 he sold out to Tucker, Cracknell & Falls for £6000. In March 1855 he returned to Sydney, and soon accepted nomination as a candidate for the electorate of New England and Macleay, but was defeated by R. G. Massie. Next year he was one of three successful candidates elected for Durham to the first Legislative Assembly under responsible government. In September 1857 he became treasurer in the second Cowper ministry, but resigned in January 1858. He was elected as the representative of the Hunter electorate in 1859 and on the resignation of the Forster ministry was invited to form a government by Denison; Jones refused, and advised the governor to send for John Robertson. In April 1860 he retired from politics and devoted his time to commerce.

He was elected to the board of directors of the Commercial Banking Co. of Sydney Ltd in 1860, and acted as chairman for some twenty years. During his association with the bank its assets rose from £2,500,000 to £14,000,000. In July 1892 the shareholders presented him with a cheque for £2500 in recognition of his 'invaluable services' for thirty-four years. He also served as chairman of directors of the Alliance Assurance Co., and a director of the Sydney Marine Insurance Co., the London, Liverpool and Globe Insurance Co., and the Australian Gaslight Co. In 1862-66 he served on the committee of the Australian Library, later the Public Library of New South Wales.

As a pioneer of the provincial press in New South Wales Jones proved by his astute management of the *Maitland Mercury* and his vigorous editorials that it could be run profitably and with benefit to its readers. As a journalist he was 'a compact, vigorous, plain writer of temperate tone, displaying considerable power of reasoning', and always conscientious in his efforts 'to cultivate a sound public spirit'. In politics he played a major part in the framing of the Electoral Act.

Jones was married twice, first in Liverpool to Martha Olley, a dressmaker, and after her death to Emma Felton of Sydney in 1860. Nine children were born of his first marriage and seven of the second. He died at his home, Stoneleigh, at Darlinghurst on 25 August 1892, after an illness of four months. He was an active member of the Church of England.

In memoriam: Richard Jones (Syd, 1892); *The Commercial Banking Company of Sydney Limited . . . 1834-1934* (Syd, 1934); G. Hendy-Pooley, 'History of Maitland', JRAHS, 2 (1906-09), pt 12; R. C. Pogonoski, 'History of journalism and printing in the north of NSW', JRAHS, 24 (1938); *Empire*, 3 June 1856; SMH, 23 July, 26 Aug 1892; *Sydney Mail*, 30 July 1892; MS cat under Richard Jones (ML).   ELIZABETH GUILFORD

JORGENSON, JORGEN (1780-1841), adventurer, was born on 7 April 1780 at Copenhagen, Denmark, the second son of Jorgen Jorgensen, royal watchmaker, and his wife Anna Lette, née Bruun. He changed his patronymic to Jorgenson in 1817.

Jorgenson's formal education stopped at 14. At 15 he was apprenticed to Captain Henry Marwood of the English collier *Jane*, and served in her four years between Newcastle and Baltic ports. By his own statement, he then served on various vessels, including a British man-of-war into which he had been press-ganged. In 1801 he was aboard the *Harbinger* at Port Jackson, where he soon joined H.M.S. *Lady Nelson* as John Johnson. As he was not discharged from her until April 1804, he probably sailed with Flinders [q.v.] in 1802, witnessed the disbandment of the first settlement at Port Phillip, and certainly was present at the first settlement on the Derwent in Van Diemen's Land. His own testimony has generated the legend that he was first to harpoon a whale in the Derwent. For months in 1804 he was sealing in New Zealand waters and whaling in the *Alexander*. He left Australian waters in her in February 1805 and by way of New Zealand, Tahiti, Cape Horn and St Helena arrived at Gravesend in June 1806. After some months of London pleasures he returned to Copenhagen.

During the Anglo-Danish war Jorgenson commanded the privateer *Admiral Juul* and took three prizes before striking his flag to H.M.S. *Sappho* in March 1808. Next December after ten restricted months in London he made his first visit to Iceland. In June 1809 he returned and, with an English merchant and abetted by English seamen, arrested the Danish governor, placed himself at the head of government, and proclaimed Iceland independent of Denmark. On this escapade Jorgenson's notoriety largely rests, although his 'protectorship' lasted only nine weeks before it was ended by the arrival of H.M.S. *Talbot*. In August Jorgenson sailed, voluntarily, for England.

For the next eleven years Jorgenson's life was compounded of ill fortune, opportunism and debauchery. Until September 1810 he was incarcerated in the prison-hulk *Bahama* at Chatham, then lived on parole at Reading. After months of gambling and drinking he fled England and his creditors in 1812, but soon after his return next year he was in the Fleet prison, heavily in debt. Released in May 1815 he went to the Continent as an English spy for two years, then spent the next three in and about London, with much gambling and drinking. After May 1820, when he was arrested for petty theft, Jorgenson was in and out of Newgate prison, and once condemned to death, until finally sentenced to transportation for life. He arrived in Van Diemen's Land in April 1826. He received a ticket-of-leave in June 1827 and, after a short-lived convict-clerkship, was assigned to the Van Diemen's Land Co. and sent to explore parts of the north and north-west of the island. In 1828 he was appointed a convict-constable of the field police in the Oatlands district and strenuously employed in pursuit of Aboriginals. He was granted a conditional pardon in June 1830.

In January 1831 he married Norah, an illiterate and hard-drinking convict, born in 1800 in County Cork, the daughter of Patrick Cobbett (Corbett) and his wife Catherine, née Fitzgerald. The next decade saw Jorgenson employed in the infamous Black Line, farming briefly and ingloriously, appointed again to the constabulary, acting as scribe for the illiterate, and selling his wits wherever possible, whether to such a one as G. A. Robinson [q.v.], to the government, or to the fevered press. Mostly he lived by his pen, precariously. During this period he accepted with considerable understanding and compassion the problems of his wife's suicidal disposition. Both he and she were granted free pardons in 1835, but did not enjoy them long. She died in July 1840, Jorgenson on 20 January 1841 in the Colonial Hospital of 'inflamation of the lungs'.

Jorgenson was an average-sized man, given to passionate expression and wild gesticulation. Gifted with extraordinary high spirits and unbalancing verve, he was ambitious, diversely talented and appreciably amoral. A measure of self-discipline came later, with reluctance. He would merit little attention had not the whole formless, headlong rush of his life been marked by such wild spirit. His status is, as it was to Marcus Clarke, that of 'a human comet'.

The two men who knew Jorgenson best were both aware of the variance between his accomplishments and his reckless aspirations. To Willam Hooker, his 'talents were of the *highest order*: but for his character, moral and religious, it was always of the lowest order'. To Thomas Anstey [q.v.] Jorgenson was his own worst enemy. Writing of the Icelandic revolution Jorgenson revealed himself in a rare moment of objective candour: 'I . . . fully determined to seize the first opportunity to strike some blow to be spoken of . . . It was not love of liberty . . . which influenced me on this occasion . . . I have in the course of my life been under the malignant influence of other passions besides play'.

Apart from his writings Jorgenson's explorations in 1826-27 have been considered as the most permanent contributions of his Australian years. But the judgments and conclusions of his journals were questioned as early as 1829 and these doubts are now largely confirmed. As for Jorgenson's published works they were numerous and diverse, and included religious works, travelogues and histories.

There are two known likenesses of Jorgenson. The first, an oil painting by C. W. Eckersberg, probably done in 1808, is in the National Historical Museum, Hil-

leröd, Denmark. The second, a small gro-
tesque-humorous oil painting in the National Museum of Iceland, Reykjavik, is
regarded as a self-portrait or self-caricature.

H. P. Briem, *Sjálfstaedi Islands 1809* (Reykjavik, 1936); R. Davies, *Sea urchin* (Lond,
1940); F. Clune and P. R. Stephensen, *Viking
of Van Diemen's Land* (Syd, 1954), and for
partial list of Jorgenson's publications; W. J.
Hooker papers (Egerton MS, British Museum);
Sir George Arthur papers (ML); S. M. Franks,
Land exploration in Tasmania 1824-1842
(M.A. thesis, Univ Tas, 1959); CSO 1 (TA).

JAMES DALLY

JOYCE, ALFRED (1821-1901), grazier
and farmer, was born on 25 March 1821
in Whitechapel, Middlesex, England, the
youngest of five sons of Thomas Joyce,
ironmonger, and his wife Elizabeth, née
Robertson. Apprenticed as a mechanical
engineer and millwright, he attended
evening classes in mensuration, geometry
and mechanical drawing at the London
Mechanics' Institute. Thomas Joyce had
secured the contracts for supplying and
maintaining oil lanterns for the newly-
established Metropolitan Police, and extended his business to oil-refining and then
to shipping. Two barques, *Indemnity* and
London, were bought in partnership with
their captains, and when the *London* sailed
on her first voyage to Port Phillip on 7
June 1840 the passengers included Thomas
Joyce's fourth son, George, who opened
business as a tailor in Bourke Street, Melbourne. Early in 1841 George Joyce sold
his stock, entered into partnership with
Thomas, Henry and Robert Clowes, fellow-
passengers in the *London*, and acquired a
half share in the Woodside run, near
Mount Macedon.

On 7 September 1843 Alfred Joyce sailed
in the *London* and landed in Melbourne
on 30 December, only to find that land,
stock and commodities had dropped to little
more than paper values. George Joyce
faced bankruptcy, and Alfred would have
returned home had not the *London's*
captain agreed to advance the brothers
£150 on Thomas Joyce's account. This enabled them to obtain possession, at a depression price of £50, of 10,000 acres on
the upper Loddon River, together with
two primitive huts, a sheep yard, fifty
hurdles and a watch-box. The run was
stocked with 1200 sheep, George Joyce's
share of the Woodside partnership, and
renamed Plaistow, after the family's
country home in Essex.

In the development of Plaistow Alfred
Joyce derived full advantage from his
earlier apprenticeship; by harnessing wind
and water power, and the construction of
bridges and weirs, maximum benefits were
ensured from successive good seasons. Soon
after George Joyce's marriage to Helen
McNicol on 22 April 1846 Alfred explored
the upper reaches of the Avon and Avoca
Rivers, the first of many searches for land
for Plaistow's surplus stock. On 1 January
1852 the brothers took possession of Norwood, 37,000 acres, about eighteen miles
west of Plaistow; this was acquired, with
5500 sheep, a 10-roomed brick cottage,
farming implements and utensils, for
£3400. The partnership was formally dissolved in June 1854. George Joyce retained
Plaistow and Alfred Joyce, who on 29
March 1853 had married Caroline, only
daughter of E. G. Bucknall, of Rodborough
Vale, adjoining Plaistow, occupied Norwood.

The goldfields at Maryborough and
Dunolly provided ready markets for Norwood stock and produce; they also hastened the surveys of the water frontages
and outlying portions of the run. In order
to buy essential portions of land and develop his farming activities Joyce was compelled by September 1859 to seek assistance
from the London Chartered Bank.

Although installation of large-scale milling equipment in 1861 had necessitated a
full mortgage of his freehold land, Joyce
began the erection of a two-storey stone
homestead in 1863, and imported Victoria's
earliest steam-plough in 1864. Norwood
was at its peak activity, some seventy
people being employed, exclusive of seasonal labour. Liens were established on his
wool clips from 1863 and by 1869 the proceeds had dropped to a mere third of the
1863 total. Norwood had proved to be
particularly vulnerable in poorer seasons.
Good seasons brought temporary recoveries
in 1872 and 1873, but by then the run
had shrunk to little more than half of its
original area, and a particularly bad season
in 1877, on top of a crushing interest
burden, caught Joyce unprepared. The
Norwood freehold and buildings passed to
the bank in December 1878, Joyce accepting tenancy at £1000 a year.

Milling moved to the towns; wool yields
in the early 1880s were low; farming became more widespread and more competitive. In 1887 Joyce relinquished the home
and the estate that had been his pride for
more than thirty years, and where his only
son and one of his eleven daughters were
buried.

In retirement at Mervyn, Nightingale
Street, Maryborough, he maintained his
active interest in local affairs. For more
than twenty years from 1865 he was in the
Shire Council of Tullaroop, being president

in 1865-67 and 1878-79; he had fought hard for free trade and temperance, and in ·1868 had unsuccessfully contested the Maryborough seat in the Victorian Legislative Assembly. He was a trustee of the Maryborough Congregational Church from 1859 until his death.

He died on 18 January 1901, his wife having predeceased him in 1898. The writing of his 'Reminiscences' had been the supreme interest of his later years, and a Melbourne publisher had provisionally accepted them. At the last minute they were declined, on the ground that other memoirs had recently appeared (presumably *Letters from Victorian Pioneers*) and that the market was too small to justify another volume. They were published in 1942 under the title of *A Homestead History* (Melbourne); a second edition appeared in 1949 and the book was re-issued in 1963.

Joyce was survived by nine daughters. Alfreda married David Coutts, composer and musician, and the youngest, Alexandra, married George Merrick Long (1874-1930), bishop of Bathurst 1911-28 and of Newcastle 1928-30.

G. F. JAMES

JUKES, JOSEPH BEETE (1811-1869), geologist, was born in Birmingham, England, the son of John and Sophia Jukes. Educated at Wolverhampton and King Edward's School, Birmingham, he studied geology under Professor Sedgwick at Cambridge (B.A., 1836). In 1839-40 Jukes was geological surveyor of Newfoundland and his *Excursions in and about Newfoundland during the years 1839 and 1840* (London, 1842), contained the fruits of this pioneering work. In 1842 he accepted the post of naturalist in the expedition in H.M.S. *Fly* under the command of Captain F. P. Blackwood [q.v.].

The *Fly* reached Sydney in October 1842 and in the next three years twice circumnavigated Australia, visited Java in 1845, and conducted an intensive maritime survey from the south-east coast of New Guinea and Torres Strait Islands to the southern tip of the Great Barrier Reef. As chronicler of the survey Jukes gave a well ordered account, in the first volume of his *Narrative of the Surveying Voyage of H.M.S. Fly* . . . (London, 1847), of the expedition's activities and of its ethnological and natural history observations. His geological contribution to this volume was a masterly chapter on the Great Barrier Reef, an early classic of Australian geology, its detailed evidence affording strong support for Darwin's theory of coral reefs.

Jukes's major contribution to Australian geology, abstracts of which he read to the British Association in 1846 and to the Geological Society of London in 1847, was *A Sketch of the Physical Structure of Australia* . . . (London, 1850), which contained the first, though imperfect, geological map of the continent. From his own notes of the coastline and from observations during visits to each colony, together with the isolated observations of other authors, Jukes drew a connected outline of Australian geology. He found it 'the very land of uniformity and monotony' whose mountain chains and rock formations stretched for hundreds of miles without interruption or change of character; yet he formed positive conclusions about the country's mineral wealth and, in a paper presented to the Tasmanian Society in 1846, urged the importance of geological surveys in New South Wales and Van Diemen's Land.

In Sydney, Jukes became acquainted with Strzelecki [q.v.] and made several geological excursions around Sydney and Wollongong with Rev. W. B. Clarke. He lent support in his published writing to Clarke's conclusion on the palaeozoic age of Australian coal, during the protracted public controversy that developed on that subject between Clarke and Professor Frederick McCoy of the University of Melbourne.

On the *Fly's* return to England in 1846 Jukes joined the geological survey of Great Britain and was assigned to North Wales and Staffordshire. Three years later the offer of the newly-created post of geological surveyor to the mineral survey of New South Wales tempted him to return to Australia, but his marriage to Georgina Augusta Meredith of Birmingham, and his own lack of faith, confided to Clarke, in the permanency of colonial appointments, led him to decline. The post went to Samuel Stutchbury. In 1850 Jukes became director of the Irish geological survey and held this position until a fall from a horse resulted in his death in Dublin on 29 July 1869.

Jukes was the author of several manuals of geology together with scientific papers and memoirs. In all his geological work he combined the exact and sound observation of a field geologist with a lively insight into origins and causes. At a time when English interest was turning towards Australian geology, Jukes's work provided the first systematic record of known facts enriched by thoughtful speculations and generalizations which mostly proved correct. At the same time he urged a cautious approach towards the rocks of a new continent and underlined the need to keep an eye on 'the solid geometry of the country'

as a corrective against hasty palaeonto-
logical classification. His book on the physical structure of Australia was supplemented by several scientific papers and by
lectures delivered to the Royal College of
Science.

J. B. Jukes et al, *Lectures on gold* (Lond,

1852); C. A. Browne (ed), *Letters and extracts
from the . . . writings of J. Beete Jukes*
(Lond, 1871); R. Tate, 'Presidential address',
ANZAAS 1893; J. B. Jukes, 'Nomenclature
and classification of rock formations in new
countries', *Tas J of Natural Science*, 2 (1846);
J. B. Jukes, Letters 1842-61, in W. B. Clarke
papers (ML).

ANN MOZLEY

K

KABLE, HENRY (1763-1846), businessman, was convicted of burglary at Thetford, Norfolk, England, on 1 February 1783 and sentenced to death. This was commuted to transportation for fourteen years to America, but he remained in prison until he embarked in the transport *Friendship*, in which he sailed in the First Fleet to New South Wales. On 10 February 1788 he married Susannah Holmes, a convict from the same village, who had already borne him a son. Before the young couple left England certain people, moved by their plight, had subscribed £20 to buy them a parcel of goods which Rev. Richard Johnson [q.v.] was to give them on their arrival in the penal colony. The gift was plundered on the voyage, but Kable won damages of £15 against the ship's captain in the first civil suit heard in New South Wales. This oddity may have brought Kable to the governor's notice, although Kable later claimed to have had influential letters of recommendation, for soon afterwards Governor Phillip appointed him an overseer. Three years later he was made a constable and nightwatchman, and a further three years service saw him elevated to chief constable: but he was dismissed in 1802 for misbehaviour, after being convicted for breaches of the port regulations and illegally buying and importing pigs from a visiting ship.

Kable's business activities were to keep him in comparative affluence for at least the next ten years. His early activities as a trader, probably as a middleman between the trading officers of the New South Wales Corps and the consumer, are suggested by his possession of capital sufficient to take part in the sealing industry on a considerable scale after 1800. He was also one of seventy signatories to a petition to Governor Hunter from creditors who were anxious to prevent debtors from frustrating their demands by legal delays.

Kable's association with the emancipist boatbuilder James Underwood [q.v.] dated from at least as early as July 1800, for in that month he signed a partnership agreement with Underwood and a mariner resident in Sydney, Samuel Rodman Chace, who was to command Kable & Underwood's sloop *Diana* in sealing expeditions to Bass Strait. The agreement envisaged the working-up of sealskins into leather for boots and shoes. The partnership was to last two years, with Chace spending the coming year at Cape Barren or on other sealing grounds. The association with Chace proved transient but Kable and Underwood remained partners until 1809. At first they exported sealskins in ships controlled by Robert Campbell [q.v.] and his Calcutta partners who had an agent in Canton, but the depressed state of the China market persuaded them to join forces with Simeon Lord [q.v.] who had a valuable London connexion, T. W. & J. Plummer and Co., through which they could market their skins and oil. During the next two years Kable acted as 'ships' husband' to Lord, Kable & Underwood (Lord & Co.). The firm was involved in a wide range of speculations, including whaling, sealing, sandalwood and wholesale and retail trading, but Lord withdrew in 1808, Underwood split from Kable in 1809 and the firm dissolved in a welter of law suits not finally settled until 1819.

Like Lord and other early Sydney entrepreneurs, Kable always had a substantial landholding as a kind of 'sheet anchor'. He had been granted farms at Petersham Hill in 1794 and 1795, and in the latter year bought out four near-by grantees within a week of their grants being signed. In 1807 he owned at least four farms of about 170 acres; in 1809 in addition he held five farms at the Hawkesbury and 300 acres at the Cowpastures, with a variety of real estate in Sydney itself including his comfortable house and extensive stores. He also had 40 horned cattle, 9 horses and 40 pigs. His business reputation seems to have been dubious, for he was regarded with distrust by Governor King and with active hostility by Governor Bligh who thought him and his partners fraudulent and had them imprisoned for a month and fined each £100 for sending him a letter 'couched in improper terms'. It is certain that Kable played no part in public life comparable with Lord's multifarious activities. His commercial career in Sydney seems to have ended soon after Lord & Co. broke up, for as early as February 1810 he announced that his son Henry had taken over the entire management of his Sydney affairs.

In 1811 Kable moved to Windsor where he operated a store and brewery, the latter in association with a partner, Richard Woodbury, and his Sydney warehouse was let to Michael Hayes [q.v.]. In 1812 he was sending wheat down the Hawkesbury consigned to Robert Campbell junior [q.v.], perhaps partly his own growth, partly the fruits of barter for his beer. He was never again a prominent businessman, although he signed a petition in distinguished commercial company for the granting of an auctioneer's licence to William Baker of Windsor in 1821. Evidence collected by Commissioner Bigge [q.v.] in 1820 shows that, while he had once owned 700 acres by grant and a further 250 by purchase, he then held only ninety acres and a further thirty acres as a tenant.

Kable's commercial career cannot really be considered separately from James Underwood's, and it was of little significance compared with Simeon Lord's. In combination with these two, Kable did much to pioneer sealing and shipbuilding in New South Wales, but it was Lord who marketed the skins and Underwood who built the ships; yet Kable's achievements were remarkable for a man who could barely sign his name and had no other claim to literacy than his ability to add a column of figures.

Kable, in his own words, 'reared ten children'. At least two of them, Henry junior and James, were mariners, commanding vessels owned wholly or in part by their father. James was murdered by Malay pirates in the Straits of Malacca on a return voyage from China about 1810, but Henry remained prominent in Sydney mercantile circles for some time after his father withdrew to Windsor. There are some signs that the elder Kable may have transferred much of his property to his eldest son to avoid having to pay a judgment of £12,000 awarded to Lord in 1811. The property probably included the schooner *Geordy* which Henry junior owned jointly with William Gaudry who had married Kable's daughter in 1809, and the schooner *Endeavour*, of which Henry junior was sole owner, and which he employed in the Tahitian pork trade in 1812. A third son, John, known as 'Young Kable', was a prominent pugilist of the 1820s. Susannah Kable died on 8 November 1825, aged 63, but Henry, who was described as a farmer at Pitt Town in the 1828 census, survived her for twenty-one years and died on 16 March 1846 at the age of 84.

HRNSW, 3-6; HRA (1), 3-7; MS cat under H. Kable (ML); Supreme Court records (NSWA).   D. R. HAINSWORTH

KANE, HENRY PLOW (1825?-1893), schoolmaster, was the son of Benjamin Kane of the British Ordnance Department. In his early twenties he emigrated to Van Diemen's Land and became tutor to the son of William Barnes [q.v.], a Launceston merchant. When the Launceston Church Grammar School opened in temporary pre-

mises in 1846 he was appointed headmaster. In July he was ordained deacon and licensed as a minister and chaplain at Paterson's Plains and Allenvale, where he officiated until 1850. In October 1854 his scholastic services were honoured by the archbishop of Canterbury who conferred on him a Lambeth master of arts degree. During the Crimean war Kane was active in collecting funds for the British Patriotic Fund and as secretary to the supporting committee of Launceston ladies.

Hoping for government employment Kane applied in 1856 for the position of inspector of schools under the Board of Education. He was prepared to accept a decrease in salary for the honour of the new position, in which he felt he would be of real service to the cause of colonial education by reason of his long experience with boys of all denominations. Unfortunately the post had been filled already. In March 1857 he undertook to officiate temporarily at Evandale and Lymington on the death of Rev. J. Bishton, received a testimonial of his parishioners' regard, and a request from them that he be appointed permanently. Kane was ordained priest at Holy Trinity, Launceston, on 11 May 1857; he felt that his services at the school were of greater value than pastoral work, and therefore declined the Evandale living. In 1854-56 he was assistant secretary to the Launceston branch of the Royal Society, and in 1857-59 was secretary. He resigned as headmaster in January 1860 and was succeeded by Rev. F. W. Quilter.

In 1847 he had married Caroline Jeanette, daughter of Captain William Neilley, a Waterloo veteran of the 63rd Regiment, of Rostella, East Tamar. After his father-in-law's death Kane conducted a private school at Rostella, and educated the sons of many prominent Tasmanians until the 1870s, when he accepted the invitation of the bishop of Melbourne to take charge of several small parishes at Cheltenham, Dingley East, South Brighton and Gipsy Village (Sandringham). He had previously been made a surrogate in 1867.

In 1874, on the death of his only son Henry Neilley, aged 15, Kane took his wife and daughter to England. In 1882 his wife died there, and their daughter was entrusted to the care of relatives. A lonely man, Kane retired from the church and returned to Melbourne, where he married Lily Bradish of Dingley, and entered on a business career for which he was unfitted. A sense of responsibility for the bankruptcy of the company of which he was director undermined his health, and he died on 11 November 1893 at his home, Rhyll, Brighton, Melbourne.

Correspondence file under H. P. Kane (TA); Diocesan registry office, Records (Hob).

BETHIA FOOTT

KAVEL, AUGUST LUDWIG CHRISTIAN (1798-1860), Lutheran pastor, was born at Berlin, the son of poor parents. FRITZSCHE, GOTTHARD DANIEL (1797-1863), Lutheran pastor, was born at Liebenwerda, Saxony, the son of the town musician. From his Liebenwerda school he went to the Dresden Gymnasium and then studied theology at the University of Breslau. After graduating in 1823 he taught for some years in a school for Jewish children, and was ordained in 1835.

In the bitter church struggle arising from the King of Prussia's attempt in 1817 to enforce unity of Lutherans and Calvinists within his realm, Kavel was at first inclined to follow the royal decree, but later found obedience incompatible with his conscience. In 1835 he resigned from his parish at Züllichau in Brandenburg and was sent by the congregation to Hamburg, to seek aid in migrating to America where they might worship with free consciences. In Hamburg Kavel heard of George Fife Angas [q.v.] and went to England. After tedious negotiations with the Prussian government over exit permits, Angas advanced the money to enable Kavel and some two hundred of his flock to pay their passages to South Australia. The dispirited southern Prussians reached Adelaide in 1838, and found a land of promise thriving there. They then sent a call to Fritzsche, who had also renounced the state church and as an itinerant pastor had narrowly escaped arrest several times. In February 1840 Fritzsche went to Hamburg where he was invited to be pastor of a group of Lutherans waiting to emigrate to Australia. After many difficulties with money and ships and long delay in Hamburg, the 250 migrants embarked in July 1841 for South Australia, an ill-fated voyage on which more than a fifth of the party died. Fritzsche was accompanied by his young fiancée, Dorette Nehrlich, whom he married on 11 January 1842.

Kavel and Fritzsche with their fellows were among the forerunners of a stream of German colonists. The early days were not without their difficulties. Whether they came in 1838 in the *Prince George* with Kavel, in 1839 in the *Zebra* with the charitable Captain Dirk Hahn, or in 1842 in the *Skjold* with Fritzsche, the colonists had little money and few possessions. Kavel was a great inspiration to them and negotiated with Angas's agents the lease of land near Adelaide, which became the settlement of Klemzig, named after one of Kavel's German parishes. It soon became obvious that this was not large enough for the settlers to fulfil their obligations to Angas and to provide for themselves adequately. Captain Hahn had arranged for his shipload to rent land in the Adelaide hills, their site being named Hahndorf in his honour. Fritzsche's group later founded a settlement called Lobethal.

Inspired by the geologist Johannes Menge [q.v.], Kavel negotiated with Charles Flaxman, Angas's representative, to take over a much larger area in the Barossa valley. The financial terms were hard, but Kavel kept his congregation together in good heart, and their dogged devotion to agriculture helped to pull both Angas and the province through some dangerous times. In the Barossa district were founded the townships of Bethany and Langmeil (Tanunda), where Kavel settled after the death in child-birth of his English wife; he married his German housekeeper in 1851, and died on 11 February 1860.

Since the Hahndorf settlement was not easy for Kavel to visit regularly, Fritzsche's arrival was a relief and it was arranged that he should serve the southern settlement of Lutherans whilst Kavel served the northern. This division became serious when the question of taking up land in the Barossa valley divided the migrants: some felt that the Hahndorf men ought to leave their homes and share in opening up the Barossa. The bad feeling broke out in fierce controversy, when in 1845 and 1846 Kavel and Fritzsche disagreed on doctrinal questions; the division was all the sadder because Fritzsche's wife died early in 1845. Fritzsche died on 22 October 1863.

Fritzsche was a theologian of some standing with works respected in Lutheran circles far beyond Australia; Kavel tended to millenial doctrines then fashionable in Lutheran thought. From their beginnings the German settlements had minor feuds on questions of orthodoxy; at the Bethany synod in 1846, however, Kavel and Fritzsche quarrelled irreconcilably and severed organizational connexions. The split between Kavel and Fritzsche resulted in two separate synods, which, after gathering in Lutheran bodies elsewhere in Australia, later became the United Evangelical Lutheran Church of Australia and Evangelical Lutheran Synod of Australia. But in spite of their divisions, the German settlements led by Kavel and Fritzsche retained some national distinctions, and their industry and culture contributed richly to South Australia's development.

Kavel was a born leader and succeeded

in settling his congregations with no other means than moral authority. He encouraged early naturalization, and kept his followers together in rural occupations until they prospered. Fritzsche had qualities complementary to Kavel's. He was distinguished above all for his devotion to the cause of education. He encouraged the pioneer settlements to support schools and build churches. At Lobethal he started in 1842 the first Lutheran theological seminary in Australia. Himself an excellent musician, he encouraged music in his congregations.

E. Hodder, George Fife Angas, father and founder of South Australia (Lond, 1891); J. S. Lyng, Non-Britishers in Australia (Melb, 1927); A. Grenfell Price, Founders and pioneers of South Australia (Adel, 1929); A. Lodewyckx, Die Deutschen in Australien (Stuttgart, 1932); T. J. Hebart, Die Vereinigte Evangelisch-Lutheran Kirche in Australien (Adel, 1938), and translation with J. Stolz, History of the Evangelical-Lutheran Church in Australia (Adel, 1938); A. Brauer, Under the Southern Cross: history of Evangelical Lutheran Church of Australia (Adel, 1956).

D. Van Abbe

KAY, JOSEPH HENRY (1815-1875), naval officer and scientist, was born in London, the second son of Joseph Kay, architect, and his wife Sarah Henrietta, née Porden. He was a brother of W. P. Kay [q.v.], but broke with family tradition and entered the navy in 1827 and served in H.M.S. Fly. In 1839, with the rank of lieutenant, he left in the Terror under Commander Crozier on a magnetic observation expedition. Scientists were then taking great interest in the geomagnetic field, and the expedition had been organized to gather information on the peculiarities in the behaviour of the geomagnetic field in the southern hemisphere. The leader of the expedition, Captain James Clark Ross, had instructions to establish a chain of more than thirty magnetic observatories from Ceylon to Cape Horn and to determine if possible the existence of an Antarctic continent.

The Terror and the Erebus arrived in Hobart Town on 16 August 1840 and the members of the expedition were enthusiastically received by Lieut-Governor Franklin who, as an Arctic explorer, had a great interest in science and discovery and was a personal friend of both Ross and Crozier. Kay stayed with the Franklins at Government House. Franklin made all necessary preparations for the establishment of the magnetic observatory in Hobart and the building was speedily erected at Rossbank

in the present Government House grounds. Ross and Kay installed the instruments on 23 September 1840 and, when the expedition left on 12 November for Antarctic waters, Kay remained in Hobart with the title of director of the magnetic observatory in Van Diemen's Land. He was responsible for the routine measurement of inclination, declination and horizontal component of the earth's magnetic field and regularly communicated his observations to the Royal Society. The Admiralty financed the observatory so Kay remained in naval service; he was promoted commander in 1849.

On 6 November 1845 in the schoolhouse at Great Swanport Kay married Maria, fourth daughter of George Meredith [q.v.]; their only child, Rosina Maria, was born in 1860. In 1853 when the Admiralty's support was withdrawn from the observatory, its costs were transferred to the land fund, and Kay was recalled. He went to Victoria where he was promoted captain on the retired list in 1865. He held various posts in the Victorian public service and at the time of his death was clerk to the Executive Council. He died from diabetes on 17 July 1875 at South Yarra, Melbourne, and was buried in St Kilda cemetery.

Kay was one of Australia's first geophysicists and, as well as making fundamental contributions to research, his presence in Hobart gave an impetus to interest in science in general. He was a foundation member of the Royal Society of Tasmania and published several papers in its journal, the subjects including solar radiation, the aneroid barometer, and the geology of western Tasmania. He was elected a fellow of the Royal Society of London on 26 February 1846 for his work on geomagnetism.

K. Fitzpatrick, Sir John Franklin in Tasmania 1837-1843 (Melb, 1949); Correspondence file under J. H. Kay (TA).

Ronald Green

KAY, WILLIAM PORDEN (1809-1870?), architect, surveyor, engineer and public servant, was born in England, the son of Joseph Kay (1775-1847) and grandson of the eminent architect William Porden (1755?-1822). He was trained under his father who had been a pupil of S. P. Cockerell, sometime architect to Greenwich Hospital and vice-president of the Institute of British Architects. William then went to New Brunswick to work for the New Brunswick Land Co. and for the government. As the nephew of Sir John Franklin through his first wife Eleanor Porden, Kay was invited to Van Diemen's Land because the Franklins objected that the two most highly qualified architects in Hobart Town, Blackburn and Thomson [qq.v.], were emancipated convicts.

Kay sailed from London as a cabin passenger in the convict transport *Isabella* and arrived at Hobart on 20 May 1842. Five days later he applied for the position of director of public works, lately vacated by the architecturally inept Alexander Cheyne [q.v.]. Amidst implications of nepotism largely unjustified, Franklin appointed Kay provisionally on 16 June, but in 1843 this was disallowed by the secretary of state, who directed that Major J. C. Victor [q.v.] should have the position. In November Kay was appointed colonial architect, but both Victor and Lieut-Governor Eardley-Wilmot were dissatisfied, and in January 1844 Kay was restored to his position as director of public works. In September the Colonial Office again overruled the appointment and Kay resumed duty as colonial architect and surveyor of buildings under Victor. Early in 1847 the Legislative Council deleted Kay's position from the estimates and the acting administrator, La Trobe, appointed him superintendent of the King's Wharf. However, Lieut-Governor Denison reappointed Kay director of public works and in January 1848 gave him additional duties as director of waterworks. From 1846 to 1859 Kay served on the Bridgewater Bridge Commission, in 1850 he became a commissioner under the Market Act, and from 1855 he was director *ex officio* of the New Norfolk Bridge Co. He was given leave to return to England on half-pay from 1 March 1853 until 29 November 1854, owing to the failure of his eyesight, but otherwise remained in office until 31 December 1858. He was pensioned from 1 January 1859, and on 3 February 1860 he sailed for England in the *Isles of the South*. His death has not been traced, although his Tasmanian pension was still being paid in 1870.

On 3 April 1845 at St John's, New Town, Kay had married Clara Ann Elwall; a daughter, Clara Virginia Porden, was born on 19 December 1849. His wife is said to have returned to Tasmania in the 1870s to her profession as governess.

Kay's lively interest in the fine arts is indicated by his musical soirées and by his position of secretary to the second Hobart Art Exhibition in June 1846. He lived always in New Town, for some time at Barrington Lodge, now belonging to the Salvation Army, the classicist house he built about 1850 to his own designs. Over the period of Kay's employment, a varied range of activity occupied the Department of Public Works. Particularly important were the new systems of roads, and necessarily, bridges, extending further into the interior. In addition, harbour repairs and enlargements, the reconstruction of Hobart and Launceston wharves, new transport systems, coastal lighthouses, water supply extensions, river improvements and swamp reclamation are recorded.

Architecturally, this post-depression period is a sparse one, and the practice of supplying church designs was practically abandoned; the simple round-arched Gala Kirk, Cranbrook (1844-45), may be an exception. Innumerable small official dwellings and offices, and particularly watch-houses were designed and built, sometimes masquerading as tiny Italian villas, ornamental cottages in Tudor or other picturesque styles; a rare surviving example is the diminutive gabled Rokeby watch-house of 1850. Generally, however, the period is noted for considerable extensions, alterations and repairs to earlier buildings, the Italianate additions projected variously between 1849 and 1855 for Government Cottage, Launceston, or the ballroom for old Government House, Hobart (1849-50), being examples. Larger commissions reveal the main styles used by Kay: the symmetrical Tudor St Mary's Hospital (1847-48, now the Department of Lands), a fine example of the Italian villa style; the harbourmaster's house and the former post office (1851, demolished); the round-arched, and monumentally classicist Hobart markets (1851-53, destroyed by fire); and, representing purely utilitarian design, the stone-quoined brick Hobart slaughter houses (1844-59). Of similar style are the additions to the Hobart Criminal Court of 1858-60 (extending Lee Archer's [q.v.] Penitentiary Chapel, 1831-33) but the contemporary extensions along the Macquarie Street frontage of the Supreme Court buildings, based on Kay's conception and, in part, on his drawings, are more decoratively mid-Victorian. Indeed, Kay's work marks the end of the early phase of Colonial architecture and the full arrival of the more grandiose and ornamental Victorian manner. One of his smallest works, the Gothic Revival Eardley-Wilmot memorial of 1850, reveals his ideals as clearly as his undoubted masterpiece and largest work, Government House, Hobart (1853-58), with its elaborately picturesque massing and romantic Elizabethan-Jacobean style.

Correspondence file under W. P. Kay (TA).

HARLEY PRESTON

KEARNEY, WILLIAM (1795-1870), settler, was born in Norfolk Island, the son of a reputed squire of County Mayo, Ireland. He arrived in Hobart Town in 1807 with his mother Catherine and younger brother Thomas, after Norfolk Island had been evacuated by order of Governor King. The family was Protestant. Catherine was given a small block of land in Argyle Street on the Hobart Rivulet and set up a dairy. She supplied Governor Macquarie and his wife on their visit to Van Diemen's Land and from him received another small grant in Hobart. With difficulty, William and Thomas were given some schooling, but their interest lay in stock and farming. Both keen horsemen, they accompanied parties in search of new grazing land. Thomas went with the surveyor, Thomas Scott [q.v.], on his exploration of the east coast, and in 1819 William was given a licence to graze stock on the Salt Pan Plains in the midlands near Tunbridge. In 1821 William and Thomas each received small grants of land on the Coal River near Richmond. In 1824 William married Susan, the youngest daughter of Robert Nash, a flour-miller at Sorell and also a Norfolk Islander.

After the death of Thomas, William took over his brother's land and bought 500 adjoining acres on which in 1829 he built a two-storied stone house that he called Laburnum Park. On the strength of his possessions he applied for further grants of land and got 1000 acres, later increased to 1800 acres, on the St Paul's River in the South Esk valley, where he already had property at Avoca. He then had 15,000 sheep, 300 cattle and 25 horses, and employed six free labourers and six assigned servants. By the mid-1830s he had 13,000 acres of land in the Coal River valley alone, including the estates of Laburnum Park, Colebrook Dale and Rosebank Farm.

Kearney freely indulged his passion for horse-racing and hunting. He had been a foundation member of the Tasmanian Turf Club formed in 1826, and kept a stud of blood horses. His best horses were sometimes matched against those of other sportsmen for as much as £500 a side. He also kept hounds and arranged hunts on his properties. A frequent visitor from Hobart to Laburnum Park was his friend John Woodcock Graves, author of the song 'John Peel'. By his sporting activities, hospitality and generosity Kearney became popularly known as the 'Squire of Richmond'. The slump of 1841 practically ruined him. In 1846 he had to sell most of his properties and was left with the Laburnum Park estate, which was heavily mortgaged. He continued, however, to breed and race horses. He died on 31 May 1870 in Hobart at the residence of Captain Riddle.

William and Susan Kearney had eight sons and one daughter. The two elder sons, Thomas and William, married Anne and Margaret, daughters of Esh Lovell [q.v.].

HRA (3), 3; J. R. Skemp (ed), *Letters to Anne . . . 1846-1872* (Melb, 1956); *Hobart Town Gazette*, 17 June 1826, 22 Nov 1828; *Hobart Town Courier*, 4 Mar, 4, 6 May 1846; *Mercury*, 1 June 1870; CSO 1/307/7413 (TA).
                                              J. R. SKEMP

KELLY, JAMES (1791-1859), sealer, pilot and harbourmaster, was born on 29 November 1791 at Parramatta, according to the inscription on the Kelly family tomb in St David's Park, Hobart. By tradition he was the son of an English army officer, but probably of James Kelly, a Greenwich pensioner, who held the titular post of cook in the transport *Queen*, and Catherine Devereaux, a convict transported for life from Dublin in the same ship. Apparently a quickwitted child, Kelly was largely self-taught and before 13 had already made several voyages out of Sydney. On 27 January 1804 he was apprenticed to Kable & Underwood [qq.v.] to learn 'the Art of a Master Mariner'. He was employed as a sealer until 1807 when he sailed in their ship *King George* to Fiji for sandalwood. In 1809, his apprenticeship completed, he sailed in the *Governor Bligh*, commanded by John Grono and in April 1810 he sailed to India in the *Mary Anne (Marian)*. On his return to New South Wales he became chief officer of Kable & Underwood's *Campbell Macquarie*, under Captain Siddins [q.v.], and sailed on a sealing venture to Macquarie Island. The ship was wrecked on 10 June 1812, but Kelly, one of several picked up by the *Perseverance*, reached New South Wales on 29 October and walked overland from Broken Bay to Port Jackson. On 17 November he married the daughter of a former marine, Elizabeth Griffiths, whose sister Mary later married Sir John Jamison [q.v.]. Probably the first white Australian born to become a master mariner, Kelly commanded the *Brothers*, sealer, and left Sydney on 24 December 1812 for Bass Strait, returning five months later with some 7090 skins. Next September, in command of *Mary and Sally* belonging to William Collins [q.v.], he sailed again for Macquarie Island. He returned in March 1814 and was then employed by Dr T. W. Birch [q.v.] to sail between colonial ports as master of the schooner *Henrietta Packet*. Next year he began to build his famous Rock House on a bank of the Hobart Town Rivulet; his wife and family occupied it in 1817.

According to an account he wrote some time after 1821, Kelly set out on 12 December 1815 in a whale-boat on a voyage in which he circumnavigated Van Diemen's Land and discovered Port Davey and Macquarie Harbour; but in a letter written in April 1816 Birch claimed to have discovered Port Davey on 22 December when sailing the *Henrietta Packet*. From there, said Birch, Kelly 'proceeded along the coast and discovered Macquarie Harbour'. Kelly did not refer to his voyage when giving evidence to Commissioner Bigge [q.v.] in 1820, though he said he had been to that harbour seven times and described it in considerable detail.

After a year of sailing in Tasmanian waters, in November 1817, commanding Birch's *Sophia*, Kelly sailed on a sealing venture to New Zealand and landed near the present Otago. The Maoris gave him a friendly reception, but next day attacked and three of his men were killed. He retaliated by destroying canoes and burning their village, which he said had 600 houses. The exact site of the sacking, of interest to archaeologists, has never been established. In April 1818 with an armed detachment he was searching the east coast of Tasmania for escaped convicts; on 19 June he circumvented an attempt at Port Jackson to cut out the *Sophia*, for which he was praised by Sydney merchants and presented with a suitably inscribed piece of plate. In September he returned to Hobart having caught six whales in the river.

Next May he entered on official duties when Governor Macquarie confirmed his appointment as pilot and harbourmaster at the Derwent. In December 1821 in the *Sophia* he assisted in transporting convicts to the newly established penal station at Macquarie Harbour and in 1825 he helped to set up the secondary penal station on Maria Island. With others in 1826 he inaugurated the Derwent Whaling Club. In 1829, because the increasing number of ships entering the port required more of his time as pilot, he gave up the position of harbourmaster, and two years later resigned as pilot. He was then actively engaged in whaling, had an interest in several ships, was extending farming operations on Bruny Island, owned property and built steps at Battery Point and had become a well-to-do identity. He sent two of his sons to Bath Grammar School in England, contributed towards the cost of building the theatre (Royal) in Campbell

Street, was elected one of the Derwent and Tamar Fire, Marine and Life Assurance Co.'s first directors, and soon after became committeeman of the Anniversary Regatta inaugurated by Sir John Franklin.

In 1834 his ship *Australian* had been wrecked and the *Mary and Elizabeth* attacked by Maoris in New Zealand. In 1831 his wife had died. Then in 1841 his eldest son was killed while whaling, and his third son was drowned in the Derwent next year. Hit by the depression of the 1840s he was compelled to assign his properties to creditors, and later was glad to accept employment from the port authorities once more. Although credited with being the 'father and founder of whaling' in Tasmania he saw others reap the benefits without himself being able to re-enter the industry. He died suddenly in Hobart on 20 April 1859. His funeral was attended by numerous merchants and others interested in the port's shipping. Seven of his ten children predeceased him. His name is remembered by Kelly's Steps in Hobart, Kelly Basin at Macquarie Harbour, Kelly Island off Forestier Peninsula and Kelly Point on Bruny Island.

A portrait thought to be of James Kelly is in the Queen Victoria Museum, Launceston.

HRA (3), 2-6; K. M. Bowden, *Captain James Kelly of Hobart Town* (Melb, 1964); PP (LC Tas), 1881 (75); *Tasmanian Almanack*, 1827, p 129; *Sydney Gazette*, Apr 1810, 31 Oct 1812, 5 June 1813, 16 Apr 1814, 1 June 1816, 18, 20 Apr 1818; *Hobart Town Gazette*, 28 Mar, 11 July 1818, 23 Jan 1822; *Colonial Times*, 11 Mar 1827, 15 Nov 1842; *Hobart Town Courier*, 14, 28 Mar, 17 Oct 1834, 20 Dec 1848, 12 Apr 1858, 23 Apr 1859; GO 33/7/1043 (TA); CSO 1/116/2900, 1/438/9803 (TA); LSD 1/2/494 (TA).　　E. R. PRETYMAN

KELSALL, ROGER (1793?-1861), ·soldier and engineer, was educated at Eton and commissioned as a second lieutenant in the Royal Engineers in July 1809. He was promoted lieutenant in May 1811, second captain in June 1815 and captain in December 1829. From April 1819 to March 1825 he was on temporary half-pay. In 1835 he was appointed to command the branch of the Ordnance Department in Van Diemen's Land. He arrived in December and was appointed clerk of works. A few days later Lieut-Governor Arthur reported to the Colonial Office that 'the appointment of a captain of the Royal Engineers, if he be a highly competent, active and zealous person, is one of the first consequence in a country where everything is new, where everything is to be done and where there are many labourers of the most depraved habits to be controlled and to be compelled to work'. He was not happy, however, to see his colonial architect, John Lee Archer [q.v.] superseded.

Kelsall promptly made a tour of inspection of the buildings and stores throughout the colony, a costly journey as a colonial officer had to accompany him under a Treasury instruction for co-ordinating the ordnance and the commissariat, an arrangement which Arthur considered to complicate rather than simplify their work. Kelsall expressed full satisfaction with the works he saw.

Lieut-Governor Franklin, who arrived in January 1837, soon had reason to complain about another Treasury order that ordnance officers should have an adequate supply of convict labour. Kelsall interpreted this order as meaning that he should be given unlimited numbers and his own choice of convicts whether in private or public service. Franklin called Kelsall before the Executive Council where he refused to furnish copies of his reports to the Board of Ordnance because they were 'confidential'. Franklin then ordered him to show copies of the reports, and after five days Kelsall complied but attached a protest that it was inconsistent with his instructions. At this stage a Treasury order arrived that Ordnance officers had to send to London annual estimates of costs for the next year but these had now to be transmitted through the lieut-governor and have his approval.

Kelsall was promoted major in January 1837. Among works he carried out were the church at Port Arthur (1836); guard house at George Town (1838); barracks at Port Arthur (1840); barracks on Maria Island, and the convict hospital (1842). He was succeeded by Major Victor [q.v.] in November 1842 and in January 1843 sailed for England with his wife and son. In April 1845 he was promoted lieut-colonel and in August sold his commission. By 1853 he was on a grazing property in Victoria. He died on 26 March 1861, aged 67 years, and was buried in the Eastern cemetery, Geelong.

P. L. Brown (ed), Clyde Company papers, 5 (Lond, 1963); GO 1/40/70, 33/7/191, 33/21/177 (TA); CSO 1/828/17584 (TA).

KEMBLE, FRANCIS (1784?-1844), company promoter, was a director of the Australian, Colonial and General Life Assurance and Annuity Co. in London, and was said to have a 'mania for promoting sugar companies' when in 1839 he decided that the flourishing condition of New South Wales warranted the establishment of a sugar refinery. Predicting annual profits of £40,000 he persuaded William Knox Child to finance the venture. Child was deputy-lieutenant of Kent and inspecting director of the London and County Joint-stock Bank, and his eldest son was at Cambridge studying for the church, but he sold his estate at Denton Court, Gravesend, invested £20,000 in steam-engines, boilers and machinery, and migrated with all his family to Sydney.

Kemble recruited skilled workers and arrived in Sydney on 12 July 1840 with his wife and family in the Ann Gale. He promptly petitioned the Legislative Council for an increased duty on imports of refined sugar, and bought sixty acres of land at Canterbury from Robert Campbell junior [q.v.]. Within a year the Australian Sugar Refining Co. had 'a magnificent manufactury', 100 ft long, 60 ft wide, 60 ft high and a chimney stack of 130 ft. The costs had been heavy and the onset of depression encouraged the partners to quarrel instead of starting production. After Kemble threatened to go into business as a merchant at Moreton Bay Child came to terms and in March 1842 they formed the new Australasian Sugar Co., with a capital of £23,000 in £50 shares and an impressive list of shareholders. In September, with Child as commercial director and Kemble works manager, the company commenced operations. Orders flowed in from other colonies and hopes of success ran high, but the promoters continued to bicker. As a devout Evangelical Kemble objected to the factory working on Sunday. Child, who had withdrawn his capital, held the confidence of the shareholders until Kemble, with many appeals to divine grace, publicly charged him with lying and acting dishonourably in money matters. In a libel suit in February 1843 the Supreme Court found for Child and awarded him damages of 40s. The company was again reorganized and twelve years later became the Colonial Sugar Refining Co.

Out of employment Kemble gave evidence to select committees on 'monetary confusion' and on land grievances. Early in 1844 he visited Port Phillip and, although opposed to its separation from New South Wales, he was nominated as a candidate for election to the Melbourne Town Council. He soon withdrew and by May was back in Sydney and elected a member of the Sydney Municipal Council. On 19 June he died suddenly at Undercliff, aged 60.

A. G. Lowndes (ed), *South Pacific enterprise* (Syd, 1956); A. Birch, 'The origins of the Colonial Sugar Refining Co. 1841-55', *Business Archives and History*, 5 (1965); *Australian*, 25 Aug, 10, 19 Sept, 24 Oct 1842; *SMH*, 1 Mar 1843, 15 Apr, 5 June 1844.

KEMP, ANTHONY FENN (1773?-1868), soldier and merchant, was born near Aldgate, London, the son of Anthony Fader Kemp, merchant, and Susannah, nee Fenn. After being educated in Greenwich by Dr Knox, he travelled in the United States for about a year and then in France. In July 1793 he was commissioned ensign in the New South Wales Corps and arrived in Sydney with a detachment of the regiment about two years later. During 1795-97 he served a tour of duty on Norfolk Island. He was promoted lieutenant in March 1797 and captain in November 1801. Towards the end of 1800 he left for London on leave. On his return to Sydney in 1802 he married Elizabeth, the sister of Alexander Riley [q.v.], by whom he had seven sons and eleven daughters, and so qualified in one sense for the soubriquet he longed for, 'the father of Tasmania'.

Like many of his brother officers, Kemp was as much occupied with trade as with his military duties. In November 1799 he he was granted a lease of what is now the north-west corner of King and George Streets, where he built a shop. As paymaster of his company and later treasurer of the Committee of Paymastership of the corps, Kemp was strategically placed to dispose of his wares at high prices. Against his bullying and threats the soldiers had no redress, though it must be remembered that 'truck' was then common and, since there was no currency in the colony, payment in kind was inevitable; however, Joseph Holt [q.v.], perhaps with some exaggeration, reckoned Kemp's profits at 100 per cent.

In September 1802 Kemp was received into the grade of Ancient Masonry at the first lodge known to have assembled in Australia. Two of the three members were officers of *Le Naturaliste*, one of the three ships of Captain Nicholas Baudin's [q.v.] expedition. This was not, however, the most important of Kemp's involvements with the French. When the *Atlas* arrived with a cargo of brandy Governor King refused to let the cargo land, but allowed Baudin to buy 800 gallons to stock his ships. Kemp led an outcry against the governor's action and, on doubtful evidence, accused the French of bringing brandy ashore and selling it at 25s. a gallon. King questioned two of the French officers and was convinced of their innocence. Some of them spoke of challenging Kemp, but Baudin restrained them; under pressure from his fellow officers, Kemp tendered Baudin a written apology but the incident reveals his extremism.

Soon afterwards Kemp was involved in the notorious pamphlet war which so plagued King. In January 1803 a paper containing a scurrilous attack on King was found in the yard of Kemp's barracks. King ordered the arrest of Kemp and two junior officers, Nicholas Bayly [q.v.] and Thomas Hobby. The subsequent court martial of Kemp had barely begun when Major Johnston [q.v], who was temporarily in command of the corps, ordered the arrest of Surgeon Harris [q.v.], the officer acting as judge-advocate, on the ground that Harris had disclosed the votes of members of the court at the earlier trial of Hobby. At first King refused to replace Harris and ordered the court martial to dissolve, but Johnston replied that the officers would continue to sit until they had delivered a verdict. The governor then yielded and appointed Richard Atkins [q.v.] to act as judge-advocate in the case. Kemp was acquitted.

In 1804 King appointed Kemp second-in-command to Colonel Paterson [q.v.] of the proposed new settlement at Port Dalrymple. From August 1806 to April 1807, while Paterson was absent in Sydney, Kemp administered the settlement in his stead. During this period provisions ran low and for a time, early in 1807, hunting and fishing were the only sources of food. Disaffection grew and an insurrection was averted only by arresting the leaders of the dissidents.

In August 1807 Kemp returned to Sydney. He was the senior officer in the Criminal Court which assembled on 25 January 1808 to try John Macarthur [q.v.] for sedition. He and the five other officers of the court supported Macarthur when he declared that Judge-Advocate Atkins was unfit to appear in the case. Next morning, when the officers asked Governor Bligh to restore Macarthur to bail and requested Atkins's replacement, Kemp appeared to be one of the most extreme of the governor's opponents. When Johnston decided to depose Bligh, Kemp and three other officers were sent ahead to summon him to resign his authority and to assure him of his personal safety.

On 28 May Johnston, acting as governor, appointed Kemp, who had certainly been one of the leaders in the attack on Bligh, as acting deputy-judge-advocate. In that capacity he was a member of the illegal Criminal Court which tried the provost-marshal, William Gore [q.v.], for perjury, although four of its members, including

Kemp, were among the defendant's accusers. In December Kemp was posted commandant at Parramatta, and thereupon relinquished his position as acting judge-advocate. In 1810 he returned to England when the corps was sent home. He was one of Johnston's witnesses at his court martial in 1811; more fortunate than his superior in not being tried himself, he was able to sell his commission, but his magistrate's warrant and most of his land grants were cancelled. He became a partner in a commercial and shipping agency, though apparently this did not prosper, for he moved into and out of bankruptcy before receiving permission in 1815 to settle in Van Diemen's Land.

Kemp arrived there in January 1816. A year later Lieut-Governor Davey granted him 700 acres at Green Ponds the first grant to be made in the district. By 1829 Kemp had two adjoining grants, making a total of 2000 acres. Soon afterwards, in consideration of his improvements, a further 1000 acres were leased to him, and he bought another 1100 acres. In the 1830s he bought more, as well as renting large areas in the Lakes district. At Green Ponds Kemp bred first-class sheep and helped to pioneer the Tasmanian wool industry. He also bred horses and raised cattle and, about 1831, introduced a hardy, drought-resistant variety of dwarf American corn (Cobbett's) which was suitable for swine, poultry and horses.

However, Kemp was better known as a merchant than as a grazier. He was a foundation director and later president of the Van Diemen's Land Bank. Soon after his arrival in Hobart Town he had established the firm of Kemp & Gatehouse [q.v.], which was changed to Kemp & Co. about 1823 when Richard Barker was taken into partnership. After this was dissolved in 1829, Kemp continued the shipping, mercantile and importing business from a central Macquarie Street store. In 1839 he sold this property and limited his activities to his premises in Collins and Argyle Streets. In 1844, during the general depression, he sold his last city block, and a fellow merchant, Richard Lewis [q.v.], bought his residence and store.

In April 1816 Governor Macquarie appointed Kemp a justice of the peace, but in 1817-19 he was involved in a series of quarrels, first with Lieut-Governor Davey and then with his successor, Sorell. In June 1818 Macquarie confirmed Kemp's suspension from the magistracy. In 1820 Kemp, critical as always, testified at length to Commissioner Bigge [q.v.] about Sorell's immorality, discriminatory administration and the excessive consumption of spirits, but by the time Sorell was recalled one of Kemp's daughters had married one of

Sorell's sons and Kemp had swung round to a profound appreciation of the lieut-governor's virtues. In January 1824 Kemp was chairman of a 'Committee appointed at a Public Meeting of the Landholders, Merchants and Free Inhabitants of Van Diemen's Land' to draft a petition to the King that Sorell's tenure of office be extended; but this was unavailing.

From 1824 to 1836 Kemp found the authority of Lieut-Governor Arthur as irksome as that of his predecessors. Kemp expressed republican sympathies, and opposed many official measures; through the press, public meetings, petitions and correspondence, he advocated the independence of Van Diemen's Land from New South Wales (granted in 1826), the establishment of an elected Legislative Council, the abolition of press censorship, and the adoption of the English jury system. In 1837 Arthur's successor, Sir John Franklin, who was more sympathetic to the development of free institutions, appointed Kemp to the board to inquire into applications for secondary grants, and in October Franklin reappointed him a justice of the peace.

Kemp died at Sandy Bay on 28 October 1868, in his ninety-fifth year and was buried in St George's Church of England cemetery. His wife had predeceased him in October 1865, aged 79. Of his family, George Anthony became the first warden of the Green Ponds municipality and Edward followed the example of the 'pipes' of King's time by writing a bitter attack on Lieut-Governor Wilmot in satirical verse in A Voice from Tasmania (1846). Of Kemp's nine daughters known to have married, Elizabeth Julia became the wife of William Sorell [q.v.], registrar of the Supreme Court of Tasmania; Sophia, the wife of William Seccombe [q.v.], medical practitioner; Fanny Edith, the wife of Captain Algernon Burdett Jones, visiting magistrate and superintendent of the Queen's Orphan Schools; and Ellen, the wife of James Henry Young, member of the New South Wales parliament.

Kemp may be remembered mainly for his notorious early exploits in New South Wales, but he also played a notable pioneering role in Van Diemen's Land, both as merchant and grazier, where his 'inherent aversion of despotism' was harnessed to some worthwhile causes.

M. C. and T. B. Kemp, 'Captain Anthony Fenn Kemp', JRAHS, 51 (1965), and for bibliog.   MURRAY C. KEMP

KEMP, CHARLES (1813-1864), journalist, politician and businessman, was born on 2 June 1813 in London, the eldest son of Simon Kemp, and his wife Mary Ann, née Cox. He came to Australia with his family in 1825. They settled at Port Stephens where his father was employed by the Australian Agricultural Co., becoming mayor of Newcastle in 1866.

In 1831 Charles Kemp moved to Sydney, where he was first employed in a carpenter's shop but soon became interested in journalism. He contributed to the *Monitor* and in 1838, when the Legislative Council first allowed strangers to witness and report its proceedings, he was engaged by F. M. Stokes, owner of the *Sydney Herald*, as its first parliamentary reporter. In November 1838 Kemp married Stella Christie of Sydney.

In March 1841 Kemp and John Fairfax took over the publication of the *Sydney Herald*, which was then the only daily in New South Wales, and next September they entered into partnership to buy the newspaper with long-term credit from Stokes as vendor. In this partnership the duties were divided, with Fairfax supervising the administrative and technical details while Kemp looked after the literary aspects.

By early 1847 the partners had liquidated their debt to Stokes. Kemp, who had already been actively associated with the formation and operation of the Mutual Fire Insurance Association and the Sydney Fire Insurance Co., now began to increase his business activities by engaging in underwriting, and buying real estate and and shares. In September 1853, 'having amassed a comfortable fortune, and being desirous of retiring' from the *Herald*, he arranged to sell his interest to his partner so that he could turn his full attention to politics and business.

He contested the by-election held in 1854 in the city of Sydney constituency for the seat in the Legislative Council left vacant by W. C. Wentworth's [q.v.] departure for England in 1853, but was soundly beaten by Henry Parkes. This was his third unsuccessful election, for he had previously contested polls at Newcastle and Maneroo. Political fortune continued to frown until at last he won a by-election for Liverpool Plains in April 1860. Even then his career in the Legislative Assembly was short lived, for parliament was dissolved in November. He was appointed next year to the Legislative Council.

Kemp was one of the original directors, and for a time chairman, of the Sydney Railway Co. and of the Hunter River Railway Co. He remained a director of both companies till they were taken over by the government, and was appointed in January 1855 as one of the three railway commissioners provided for in the Railways Act 1854 to supervise the operation of the government railways. He resigned this position in February 1856 owing to his imminent departure for England. Kemp was away from Australia for about two years, during which time he visited Great Britain, France, Spain, Germany and Belgium, with his wife and his adopted daughter, Anne Boyle.

On his return Kemp expanded his business activities, and by 1860 was deputy-chairman of the Commercial Banking Co. of Sydney and chairman in 1863-64, a director of the Australian Steam Navigation Co. and chairman in 1862-64, and a trustee of the New South Wales Savings' Bank. In 1863 he became chairman of the United Fire and Life Insurance Co. of Sydney, which had been established in 1862. He served on the committees of the Victoria and Union Clubs, and for many years as a magistrate of the city of Sydney. He was also one of the commissioners for the Exhibition of 1862 held in Sydney.

Kemp was one of the colony's leading Anglican laymen. He served on many church committees, both parochial and diocesan. He was for some time a churchwarden of Holy Trinity, Miller's Point, and later when he moved his home to Macquarie Street of St James's, King Street, then the principal Anglican church in Sydney. As a lay member of the Sydney Diocesan Committee, he took an active interest in the formation of new sees in New South Wales. He helped to found St Paul's, the Anglican college within the University of Sydney in 1856 and later became a fellow. From 1852, as a trustee of the estate of Thomas Moore [q.v.] who had left a substantial legacy to the Anglican Church for the education of young men for the ministry, Kemp was a party to the foundation in 1855 of Moore Theological College. In 1860-64 he was active in raising funds for building St Andrew's Cathedral, Sydney. After a long illness he died of dropsy on 25 August 1864.

Kemp's prominence derived primarily from his various business directorates during the 1850s and early 1860s. While he purported in these activities to advance public welfare by providing services required in a growing economy, he still expected to earn good rates of profit and did not hesitate on occasion to condone monopolistic or quasi-monopolistic practices. However, his business operations would appear to have been marked by more enthusiasm than acumen. In politics his success was less marked, one observer noting that 'Mr Kemp was rashly deemed averse to liberty'. To Henry Parkes, he was 'the personification of the "Herald" influence', a not inconsiderable influence, as Governor Gipps remarked, 'the Sydney Morning Herald—the self-styled Great Leviathan—the Alpha and Omega of the Sydney Press'. Kemp thus found little favour in the eyes of the 'Liberals and Democrats' who saw in him the 'most oleaginous parody on the great idea of Senator that has ever been perpetrated'.

Kemp rose from obscurity to eminence and influence. The pomposity and religiosity of his personal writings reveal his mind and spirit. Extreme concern with his own social status impelled his business enterprise, and simultaneously offered scope for his detractors; yet his religious convictions impelled a zeal for promoting the Anglican church which he saw not merely as a 'denomination . . . but as a branch of Christ's Holy Catholic Church here on earth'. Shrewdly assessed in his obituary in the Sydney Morning Herald, he 'realized an independence by his own prudence and industry, and, as he would have said, by the blessing of God'.

A portrait of Kemp is in the Mitchell Library, Sydney.

A century of journalism. The Sydney Morning Herald, 1831-1931 (Syd, 1931); G. H. Nadel, Australia's colonial culture (Melb, 1957); C. Kemp, Diary 1847-48 and papers (ML).
G. J. ABBOTT

KENDALL, THOMAS (1778-1832), missionary, was born on 13 December 1778 at North Thoresby, Lincolnshire, England, the son of Edward Kendall, a small farmer, and his wife Susanna, née Sorflitt. He became a teacher but at one period combined this work with farming and at another abandoned it to become a grocer and draper. On 21 November 1803 at Kirmington, Lincolnshire, he married Jane Quickfall (1781-1866).

In 1808 Rev. Samuel Marsden [q.v] persuaded the Church Missionary Society to begin work in New Zealand by appointing a group of men able to teach the Maori 'the arts of civilization', as well as to act as catechists. In 1809 Kendall, whose preoccupation with religion had from youth been intense, though discontinuous, volunteered for service in the proposed mission and was accepted. With his wife and five children, he sailed for New South Wales in 1813. He participated, together with Peter Dillon [q.v.], in a preliminary expedition to New Zealand in 1814. At the end of that year Kendall, whom Governor Macquarie had appointed a justice of the peace in order that he could attempt to exercise some restraint on the actions of Europeans in New Zealand, settled permanently at the Bay of Islands with William Hall, a carpenter, and John King, a shoemaker.

Kendall applied himself to his duties with energy and devotion. In particular, he set out to master the Maori language and produced a Maori-English primer, A Korao no New Zealand; or, the New Zealander's First Book (Sydney, 1815). In 1816 he opened a school for Maori children, but he had formidable difficulties. His two colleagues, who possessed equal status with him, resented his non-participation in manual work, and the three quarrelled violently on this and other matters. Attendance at the school soon began to wane, as he lacked the resources to feed his pupils. Finally, the arrival in 1819 of an ordained clergyman as resident superintendent of the mission was a bitter blow to his self-esteem. He continued his work on the language and deepened his study of custom; but, from an early stage, he had sought solace for his troubles in heavy drinking with visiting mariners and, through his contact with them, he became involved in the trade in muskets. In March 1820 he sailed for England accompanied by two Maori chiefs. Though he was censured by the Church Missionary Society for this unauthorized visit, it enabled him to publish, jointly with Professor Samuel Lee of Cambridge, A Grammar and Vocabulary of the Language of New Zealand (London, 1820) and to secure ordination by the bishop of Norwich.

Kendall arrived back at the Bay of Islands in July 1821. Before long he was living with a Maori woman and again trading in muskets. In 1823 he was dismissed. In 1825 he sailed for Valparaiso, where he acted as chaplain and schoolmaster to the English community. He returned to New South Wales in 1827, obtained a land grant at Ulladulla, and entered the timber trade. In August 1832 he was drowned when a small vessel that he used in his business overturned near the mouth of the Shoalhaven River.

As a missionary Kendall was conspicuous for his fine qualities of intellect and imagination; but his career was ruined by the instability of purpose that had marked his religious and professional life from its beginning. He was a man who was equally responsive to the claims of conscience and of the senses, and it seems fitting that the best known of his descendants, his grandson, Henry Kendall, gained his reputation as a poet.

A painting by James Barry of Kendall and two Maori chiefs, Hongi and Waikato, is in the Alexander Turnbull Library, Wellington, New Zealand.

J. R. Elder (ed), *Marsden's lieutenants* (Dunedin, 1934); R. M. Burdon, *New Zealand notables*, 3 (Christchurch, 1950).

J. W. DAVIDSON

KENNEDY, EDMUND BESLEY COURT (1818-1848), explorer, was born on 5 September 1818 on Guernsey, Channel Islands, the sixth of eight children of Colonel Thomas Kennedy and his wife Mary Ann, daughter of Thomas Smith, sometime lord mayor of London. All his brothers later distinguished themselves in either the Church of England or the public service, and a strong parental influence in both these directions is obvious. Edmund himself was educated at Elizabeth College, Guernsey, and trained as a surveyor. Impelled by what his admiring father admitted to be an 'almost mad ambition to distinguish himself', he embarked for Australia, arriving in Sydney in 1840, and while still only 21 was appointed an assistant surveyor in the Surveyor-General's Department.

He began duty on 7 August 1840 and immediately left under C. J. Tyers [q.v.] for the Portland Bay settlement in western Victoria. In 1841 he began general survey work there and earned some praise, but in 1842 incurred official displeasure through an altercation with a local magistrate, James Blair [q.v.]. It was a parochial affair and, though Kennedy's motive was protest against an injustice, his crusade was juvenile. Moreover it left him open to further adverse reports as a result of a youthful and indiscreet alliance with an immigrant Irish girl, Margaret Murphy, by whom he had a daughter. Blair's main allegations were found by Superintendent La Trobe to be not borne out by the facts. However, Kennedy was recalled to Sydney, where he wrote to the governor a manly defence of his action and expressed deep contrition for his alliance with the girl.

After his return to Sydney on 12 June 1843 his duties were slight; because of the falling off in land sales, most of the surveyors were on half-pay, and Kennedy had practically nothing to do for over two years. He did, however, establish himself as a popular and charming member of society, with a rowdy, boyish sense of fun. His gifts included a pleasant singing voice and considerable skill in sketching in pencil and water-colour.

Inactivity was galling to a man of such thrusting energy, and he found an outlet in November 1845 when he was suddenly appointed second-in-command, under Sir Thomas Mitchell [q.v.], of the expedition to find an overland route to the Gulf of Carpentaria. Under this leader Kennedy was kept somewhat in the background, but after minor initial criticisms Mitchell praised his 'temperate and gentlemanly way, and highly honourable principles', with frequent references to his zeal and activity. Kennedy had the difficult assignment, which he performed to the satisfaction of his exacting leader, of maintaining a base camp for over four months while Mitchell probed the central west of Queensland, discovering in excellent country a river which he named the Victoria. The party returned to Sydney in January 1847.

Mitchell felt convinced that his 'Victoria' River flowed into the gulf, but his theory had to be tested, and Kennedy volunteered to lead an expedition to do so. With a small party of eight men and an Aboriginal boy, and with pack-horses and three spring carts, he left Sydney on 13 March 1847, retraced the tracks of Mitchell to his farthest point on the 'Victoria', and followed it down its course, only to find that instead of flowing north-west to the gulf it flowed south-west to become, as he correctly deduced part of Cooper's Creek. He renamed the 'Victoria' the Barcoo, and discovered and named the Thomson River. He then traced the Warrego River down until its waters gave out, whereupon he crossed south-east to the Culgoa, and thence back to Sydney, arriving on 7 February 1848. The result of his exploration was somewhat negative, but he had successfully overcome many difficulties and was acclaimed for his sagacity, patience, skill and perseverance.

Within a few months he was again in the field, this time on an ambitious plan of landing at Rockingham Bay to traverse Cape York Peninsula along the east coast to its most northerly point, where supplies would be replenished from a ship waiting at Albany Passage; thence he was to traverse the west coast southwards to link with the recent discoveries of Mitchell and Leichhardt [q.v.], and to return overland to Sydney. Leaving Sydney on 28 April 1848, the landing was made on 24 May. He found, however, that he was hemmed in by mangrove swamps and mountains, and two months later the party was still in about the same latitude and only about twenty miles inland. Having ascended the mountains, progress became a little better, but misfortune had beset them: sickness, a growing shortage of stores, extreme fatigue. Yet Kennedy maintained his cheerful manner and good spirits and proved thereby his excellent qualities of leadership. Eventually on 13 November Kennedy decided to leave eight of his thirteen men at Weymouth Bay while he and four others made forced marches to the supply ship for help. Starvation now confronted them all; only two of the men at the Weymouth Bay camp ultimately survived. Meanwhile one of the advance party shot himself accidentally, and Kennedy therefore left the wounded man and two others to look after him—they too all perished—whilst he and the Aboriginal boy, Jackey Jackey [q.v.], pressed on alone. With weakening strength but superb courage and endurance, they reached to within about twenty miles of the supply ship, only to find themselves trapped by the Escape River and its crocodile-infested mangrove swamps and thick scrubs. In the second week of December Aboriginals, who had become increasingly hostile, attacked; Kennedy was speared and soon afterwards died in the arms of the devoted Jackey Jackey, who alone reached the ship and was saved.

Kennedy died unmarried. His nature was unaffected and straightforward; actuated by high ideals and a strong religious sense as he was, his character was revealed in his deeds. T. H. Huxley [q.v.], who admired him and nearly joined his last expedition, later commented: 'a fine, noble fellow poor Kennedy was'.

E. Beale, 'Edmund Besley Court Kennedy', JRAHS, 35 (1949) and for bibliog; Kennedy to Col Sec, 1 Sept 1843 (Dixson Lib, Syd); MS cat under Kennedy (ML).

EDGAR BEALE

KENNY, JOHN (1816-1886), Catholic priest and historian, was born in Fife, Scotland, and educated by Benedictines. He was preparing for the priesthood when he came to Australia with Bishop J. B. Polding [q.v.] in 1835. In August the bishop's party reached Hobart Town where Kenny was left as catechist to organize and teach in a Catholic school for which Lieut-Governor Arthur approved annual payment by the government of £35 rent and £50 salary, though the approval was more readily forthcoming than the salary. In March 1836 Kenny went to Sydney where he was prominent among the religious instructors of Catholic convicts, whom Polding gained permission to have taught between their arrival in Sydney and their dispersion throughout the colony.

Ordained priest in 1843 Kenny became assistant-priest at Queanbeyan. Except for two years in England (1861-63), he spent the rest of his life in Australia mostly in parish work: at Penrith (1844-45),

McDonald River (1845-47), Geelong (1847-48), East Maitland (1848-67) and St Leonard's, North Sydney (1867-78). He was responsible for building the first stone Catholic Church at North Sydney, St Mary's, which was opened in June 1868. He also bequeathed to the church several allotments of land and three houses. Of these houses, the first, in Mount Street, went to the Sisters of St Joseph to be used as a home for aged women, the second was directed to be sold and the proceeds invested on behalf of either certain Irish colleges or St John's College, University of Sydney, and the third, his own, was left for the use of elderly priests.

Kenny won his parishioners' respect rather than their affection, for, although described as having led a 'blameless, exemplary and edifying life', he was dour and strict. As a priest he was faithful and reliable, and well regarded by his fellows. Polding always spoke highly of him, honouring him with the title of dean in 1872, and Archbishop Vaughan made him a member of the committee which reported on the Marist brothers in 1874. Next year Kenny had brief interim charge of the diocese of Armidale, and was said to have later declined an offer of the bishopric.

Dean Kenny is remembered mainly for his A History of the Commencement and Progress of Catholicity in Australia, up to the year 1840 (Sydney, 1886), which was the first extended treatment of the subject to be published. It was a creditable and useful achievement, although rather dull and partisan, and now superseded. Kenny intended to take his history further, but was prevented by severe rheumatism. After a brief illness he died on 16 September 1886 and was buried at Gore Hill cemetery.

J. H. Cullen, The Catholic Church in Tasmania (Launceston, 1949); H. A. Johnston A seed that grew: a hundred years of Catholic life on the North Shore (Syd, 1956); Freeman's J, 4 July 1874, 18 Sept, 2 Oct 1886; SMH, 18 Sept 1886; CSO 1/817/17458 (TA).

JOHN BARRETT

KENT, THOMAS (d. 1832), merchant and speculator, had been a druggist in Tonbridge, Kent, England, when Samuel Enderby [q.v.] who knew his family, recommended him to the former governor, P. G. King, as 'rather too gay for business, but is unimpeachable as an honest, good Man'. King in turn interviewed Kent and in December 1807 supported his application to the Colonial Office for a land grant. He was also recommended by Edward Thornton, a director of the Bank of England. With these strong references Kent was given an order addressed to Governor Bligh for 600 acres and six convict servants.

He arrived in Sydney in the *Speke* on 15 November 1808 with little capital but many ideas. He soon formed a partnership with J. C. Burton, a Bengal merchant, with whom he proposed to take up land and seek government aid in importing coolies and machinery for growing and manufacturing hemp. Bligh, who was then under arrest, thought him a 'stranger in this artful school of iniquity', and 'cautioned him how he acted with the usurpers of my government'. However, Lieut-Governor Paterson [q.v.] gave Burton 500 acres near Toongabbie and Kent 1230 acres near Cobbitty. Nothing came of the proposed venture, the partnership dissolved and Kent talked of returning to England. He changed his mind after Governor Macquarie arrived in January 1810 and made a great flourish by proposing, with Simeon Lord and Alexander Riley [qq.v.], to form a settlement in New Zealand for growing flax. Macquarie recommended their plan to the Colonial Office and offered to make Kent a justice of the peace for New Zealand but, when news of the *Boyd* massacre reached Sydney in March, Kent and Riley withdrew from the project. Kent had had to surrender his grant at Cobbitty, but it was restored by Macquarie and he settled there. He grew wool and grain, dabbled in trade, imported Bengal rum, and in August acted as an assessor in the Governor's Court.

In 1812 Kent moved to Van Diemen's Land with an order from Macquarie for 1230 acres, which he located near Sorell. He bought large numbers of sheep and cattle, built a slaughter house on crown land at Kangaroo Point and contracted to supply the commissariat with meat. Claiming that bushrangers had driven off his livestock, he proposed to change to kangaroo flesh. His unreliability annoyed the commandant, Andrew Geils [q.v.], whose complaints to Macquarie produced strict limits on Kent's activities. Unrepentant, Kent bought a house from Captain John Murray, and found that it belonged to the government. Later he built sheds and a store near Bridgewater on land that belonged to Robert Knopwood [q.v.]; he pestered Macquarie for a grant to recoup his losses but was refused, for by 1813 the governor had come to consider him a mischievous person and cautioned Lieut-Governors Davey and Sorell against his designs.

Kent got on well with Davey. They tippled together on Kent's imported rum and arranged for Kent to supply hay to the government at famine prices. Sorell was less amenable: he cancelled Kent's contracts for hay, flatly refused to pay old accounts, rejected his appeal for more convict servants as harvesters, curtailed his import of spirits and, when Kent officiously seized the *Lady Melville* for illicit trading in 1818, denied him legal protection. These buffets had little effect on Kent, who was busy with new speculations. In his roaming around Van Diemen's Land he had already found and tested a coal seam at Adventure Bay and experimented with burning seaweed to make alkali. In 1818 he made an establishment on the Huon River to produce a tanning extract by crushing and boiling wattle bark and evaporating the liquid into tar. In June 1819 he took two tons of this extract in four casks to Sydney, where successful tests by a local tanner attracted the attention of Simeon Lord, on whose advice the casks were sent to London in the *Surry*.

Kent returned to Hobart in October as a partner of Simeon Lord with some £800 to expand the new industry. The money was in the form of bills for woollen manufactures that Lord had sent to Hobart merchants without orders. The merchants refused to pay, so Kent took the goods and bartered some of them for provisions and wattle bark and the rest for cedar which he sold to pay his labourers. Commissioner Bigge [q.v.] showed great interest in the new industry, but Kent made little progress. Lord pressed him for another cargo and, when it was not produced, sued him for £1000. In 1822 Kent absconded to England in the *Lusitania*, Captain Langdon [q.v.]. They sailed by way of Macquarie Island, where Kent was recognized by sealers, to some of whom he was in debt. When news of his 'escape' reached Sydney, Kent's creditors issued writs against Langdon, who was duly fined £800 for a breach of regulations.

In London Kent signed a petition to the Colonial Office for the legal and commercial independence of Van Diemen's Land and in 1825 published a letter to Barron Field [q.v.], in refutation of 'hasty, inconsiderate and groundless assertions' made by Field in an address to the Agricultural Society to the prejudice of Tasmania, a name which Kent claimed to have coined. At the Colonial Office he gained the attention of Wilmot Horton, who asked the Society for the Encouragement of Arts and Science to report on the quality of Kent's new tanning substance. According to the society's committee of colonies and trade, it had been a timely discovery, for a mighty influx of South American hides had exhausted supplies of British oak bark and the tanners who tested Kent's extract found it a superior substitute. Next year the society awarded a gold medal to John Petchey [q.v.] for producing greater quantities of tanning extract, and Kent was given thirty guineas for his samples. In letters to Hobart Kent boasted his triumph and the *Colonial Times*, 1 June 1827, reported: 'What do you think of "mad Tommy Kent" now, with his boats, casks and extracts down the river. Everyone laughed at him for making it. But the tables are now turned, and . . . colonists should pay much closer attention to natural resources'. With unusual generosity the Colonial Office in 1828 added an order for 5000 acres, free freight for his machinery, and a promise of another 5000 acres when he produced 50 tons of extract.

In Sydney Lord had secured a judgment against Kent in his absence, and he arrived in 1828 to be arrested for debt. With creditors clamouring for his 5000 acres, Governor Darling did not issue orders for their demarcation until April 1831 and they were used to satisfy his creditors. Next January Governor Bourke ordered an unspecified area for Kent but in December 1831 the Colonial Office had given instructions that the grant be withheld. There is no record of a deed issued for either grant, although Dixon's map and Raymond's Calendar indicate that they were located west of Lake Bathurst. Kent died in a Sydney boarding house on 29 March 1832.

Kent was reputed to have married the widow of Captain John Murray of the 73rd Regiment and sometime commandant at Hobart. She returned to England after Kent's death and in 1846 her relations attempted to claim his land near Lake Bathurst.

HRNSW, 6; HRA (1), 6, 7, (3), 1-4; E. C. Rowland, 'Simeon Lord', JRAHS, 30 (1944); A. Jose, 'Kents galore', Forum, 19 Dec 1923; Hobart Town Gazette, 28 Feb 1818, 10 Dec 1824; Sydney Gazette, 16 Dec 1824; Colonial Times, 6 Nov 1829; MS cat under Thomas Kent (ML); CSO 11/40/964 (TA).

KENT, WILLIAM (1751-1812), naval officer, was born at Newcastle upon Tyne, England, the son of Henry Kent and his wife Mary, a sister of Governor John Hunter. He joined the navy in 1763 and became a lieutenant in 1781. In 1795 he was given command of the *Supply* which sailed with the *Reliance*, carrying Hunter as governor-elect to New South Wales, and reached Port Jackson on 7 September.

After the voyage Hunter reported that a survey had shown the *Supply* to be unseaworthy, 'a complete mass of rotten timber'; he praised his nephew's zeal and 'steady and active conduct', and proposed, in vain, that he be appointed to Norfolk Island and promoted commander. Despite the *Supply's* dangerous condition Kent willingly sailed her to the Cape in 1796-97, in company with *Reliance*, Captain Waterhouse [q.v.], to bring back livestock and stores. After Kent's return in May 1797, surveyors declared the *Supply* 'irreparable in this port or any other' and 'unfit to proceed to sea'. While in Sydney, Kent had occasion to comment adversely on the improper conduct of Judge-Advocate Dore [q.v.] in the civil court and to criticize the handling of the trial of Isaac Nichols [q.v.] in the criminal court. He received grants of 690 acres and a lease near the Tank Stream on which he built a house valued at more than £1500 and described as the best in Sydney. After the *Buffalo* arrived from England in May 1799 Hunter appointed Kent and his crew to her, sent them to the Cape and for the second time recommended Kent for promotion. After his return, Hunter appointed himself principle commander of the *Buffalo* and made Kent her second commander. Kent departed in her with Hunter in October 1800, after selling to the government his house for the 'reception and Education of the Orphans of this Country', and eleven cattle at £37 a head. He carried with him for Sir Joseph Banks [q.v.] emus, a water-mole in a keg and specimens of iron ore, but the last did not turn out well.

In October 1800 the acting governor, King, recommended Kent again for appointment as lieut-governor of Norfolk Island, but again in vain. In 1801 Kent complained to Banks of the neglect of his claims but next year he took the *Buffalo* back to Sydney with two nephews on board, Lieutenant William G. C. Kent [q.v.], and Lieutenant Bartholomew Kent, whose death was later falsely reported in the *Sydney Gazette*, 10 March 1805. When they arrived in October 1802 Kent senior was promoted commander. In April he was ordered to take the *Buffalo* with supplies to Norfolk Island and then to seek cattle in the East Indies and India. He proceeded along the west coast of New Caledonia where he found and charted 'one of the finest harbours in the world', Port St Vincent. He could not obtain cattle in the Indies but shipped 84 head, 4 mares and 2 stallions at Calcutta. In October 1804, four months after his return to Sydney, he took Colonel Paterson's [q.v.] party to form a settlement at Port Dalrymple.

In November 1802 Kent had been made a magistrate, and in March 1803 Governor

King appointed him a member of the council summoned to give advice on court-martial procedure following King's disputes with the officers of the New South Wales Corps. During these years in the colony Kent held about 1200 acres and ran some 350 sheep and a few cattle. On 23 May 1805 he left Port Jackson for the last time, after King had chosen him to take the *Investigator* to England with dispatches, since Kent was particularly well qualified to explain the circumstances in which a British privateer had seized two Spanish ships before war had been declared on Spain. In January 1806 he was appointed a post captain and in March Lord St Vincent suggested that he should go back to Australia to continue the survey begun by Matthew Flinders [q.v.], but Kent proposed to Banks that he be appointed assistant to the newly appointed Governor Bligh; however, Banks on this occasion was unable to persuade the Colonial Office to agree. In November 1808 Kent was given command of the *Agincourt*, and later was transferred to the *Union*, in which he died at sea off Toulon on 29 August 1812.

He married a cousin, Eliza Kent, and they had a son William (1799-1870) and two daughters, all born in Sydney. His wife died on 29 January 1810. In 1828 William junior sent a petition to the Colonial Office from Cheltenham, England, seeking rescue from 'dire pecuniary distress'. His father, he wrote, had died suddenly and without arranging his affairs, leaving him a friendless orphan. He was now a clerk, married with three children and, unable to take steps to regain his father's property which others were enjoying, sought a government post. In 1835-41 several farms of the elder Kent round Kissing Point were sold and presumably his children benefited. William, the son, visited Sydney from 12 December 1838 to 2 January 1839.

HRNSW, 3-6; *HRA* (1), 2-5; *Australian*, 21 July, 15 Dec 1835, 13 Dec 1838, 3 Jan 1839, 4 May 1841.

KENT, WILLIAM GEORGE CARLILE (b. 1788), naval officer, was born in Lanarkshire, Scotland, the second son of John Kent, who, after twenty years in the navy as a purser, in 1803 became steward of the Royal Naval Hospital, Plymouth. In July 1798 he entered the navy as a first-class volunteer in *Le Tigre* in which he served under Sir Sydney Smith in the eastern Mediterranean in 1799. In March 1800 he served in the *Theseus* at the blockade of Genoa. In 1802 he sailed to New South Wales in the *Buffalo*, commanded by his uncle Captain William Kent [q.v.]. He was appointed acting lieutenant in the *Buffalo* in August 1805 and in 1807 acting first lieutenant of the *Porpoise*. He commanded the *Lady Nelson* in 1807-08 when with the *Porpoise*, she removed some of the people from Norfolk Island to the Derwent.

When the *Lady Nelson* returned to Sydney in March 1808 Governor Bligh, who had been deposed in January, talked with Kent, 'conceived a favourable opinion of him' and handed Major Johnston [q.v.], the acting lieut-governor and leader of the rebels, a commission appointing Kent to the command of the *Porpoise*, vice Lieutenant Symons. When Johnston suspected that Symons was about to take the *Porpoise* to sea without bearing Johnston's dispatches to Lieut-Governor Paterson [q.v.] at Port Dalrymple, on 12 April he delivered Bligh's commission to Kent. A week later Kent sailed for Van Diemen's Land but found Paterson unwilling to come to Sydney, so Kent returned without him. When Lieut-Colonel Foveaux [q.v.] took over the government from Johnston, he permitted Bligh to communicate with the officers of the *Porpoise*. At his trial Kent said of Bligh that 'it is impossible for me to describe in adequate terms his Language, Tone and manner'. Bligh blamed Kent for not having reinstated him in his government and told him he 'should have blown down the town of Sydney about the ears of the Inhabitants'. In November Kent was sent to Port Dalrymple again and this time Paterson came back with him. On his return he was arrested, on Bligh's orders, by Captain Porteus, who had arrived from England to take command of *Porpoise*. Kent sought leave to go ashore because of his poor health, but Bligh would not trust him at large among the rebels. On 2 February Paterson granted the prisoner 1000 acres at Narellan, but Kent remained under arrest, though 'with the liberty of the ship', until released in November 1810 by the orders of the Admiralty, after Bligh had taken the *Porpoise* back to England. In January 1811 he was tried on the prosecution of Bligh, for various actions contrary to or without Bligh's orders; the court found that Kent 'under the extreme and extraordinary difficulties in which he was placed . . . was actuated by a sincere wish to perform his duty for the good of His Majesty's service . . . was justified in the conduct he pursued', and acquitted him. He was paid as captain of the *Porpoise* up to the time of the court martial.

Kent served in the *Union* under his uncle's command for six months in 1812, when he became first lieutenant in the *Sparrowhawk* on the Mediterranean Station.

There his eyesight was permanently injured, and in September 1814 he was promoted commander and put on half-pay. In 1816 he sought confirmation of the land grant made by Paterson, but this was refused.

On 30 December 1830 he married Susannah Elizabeth, third daughter of John Rankin, merchant, of Greenock, Scotland.

HRNSW, 5-7; HRA (1), 6, 7, 9; W. R. O'Byrne, A naval biographical dictionary (Lond, 1849); CO 201/88.

KENTISH, NATHANIEL LIPSCOMB (1797-1867), surveyor, author and editor, was born in Winchester, England, the son of Nathaniel Kentish, a naval surgeon. Trained as an engineer he became staff instructor in surveying and drawing at the Royal Military College, Sandhurst, in 1827. Dismissed after two years through retrenchments, he applied for a position in Upper Canada, but was appointed instead to the staff of the surveyor-general in New South Wales. He arrived at Sydney with his wife and two children in March 1830. Disagreements cost him his job in 1833, and in June he planned but never published a literary and religious magazine, 'Survevor-General'. Next year he sailed for England in the Sarah, left the 'leaky ship' at Cloudy Bay, New Zealand, and after five unhappy months returned to Sydney in the Hind.

In an 'unremitting endeavour to "Advance Australia"', Kentish began publication on 15 August 1834 of the Sydney Times, an independent, pro-emancipist, four-page semi-weekly. With sales rising to 1371 copies, his paper, though irregularly published, finally outstripped its four contemporaries. Kentish wanted to buy the Sydney Herald but his plans were upset by debts and by quarrels with George Cavenagh [q.v.] of the Sydney Gazette. The last 'Extraordinary' edition of the Times on 2 July 1838 contained the editor's 'Memorial to the Queen Upon Colonial Affairs'. Working next as an emigration agent and to this end publishing The Present State of New South Wales (1835) and The Political Economy of New South Wales (1838), Kentish advertised for employment as a civil engineer and surveyor. Friendly intervention gained him appointment in April 1839 as a senior surveyor in South Australia. Retrenched next year and unsuccessful in private practice, he took his family to Van Diemen's Land, where with credentials from Governor Gawler, he was appointed a contract surveyor on 18 November 1841. The surveyor-general Robert Power [q.v.] sent him to survey in the rugged north-west

of the island where he discovered Kentish Plains. Next year the Cornwall Chronicle printed his reports, as well as some of his verses and an Essay on Capital Punishment (Hobart, 1842) with a petition to the Queen urging abolition of the death penalty. From 1843 to 1845 he surveyed the road from Deloraine to Emu Bay. To escape 'intolerably severe duty in the bush' he then contracted to survey the town of Launceston in eight months for £260. He soon found his estimate wildly astray, but Power insisted on the terms of contract and dismissed Kentish when he appealed to Lieut-Governor Wilmot. The subsequent row went on for two years and involved the colonial government in voluminous correspondence. Kentish lost his contract but received £100 in compensation. Earlier he had dedicated a small privately printed collection of his verses to Gawler; now his laudatory verses to Wilmot appeared in the Colonial Times. As fire at the bookbinders had destroyed most copies of his poem The Bush in South Australia, he published a new version in several parts: Work in the Bush ... Thought in the Bush ... Life in the Bush of Van Diemen's Land (Hobart, 1846). In press, pamphlet and public meeting he continued to air his grievances against officialdom.

In June 1849 Kentish went to the Port Phillip District where he tried to float a Sheep and Cattle Mutual Assurance Co. for covering losses through catarrh and foot-rot. With forty-two prospective shareholders he announced in September that a public meeting would be called. When Cavenagh, now editor of the Melbourne Herald, attacked the assurance scheme, Kentish filed a libel suit. Incensed by further aspersions in the Herald, he attacked Cavenagh with a stockwhip and received a gaol sentence. On release, he planned three volumes on the Australasian Muse but the gold discoveries emptied the printing offices and the work never appeared. He celebrated the separation of Victoria from New South Wales with three anthems that appeared in 1850 and 1851, and shared with George Wright of Geelong the distinction of having the first literary work published in Victoria. Self styled 'Amateur Poet Laureate', in his second book, The Question of Questions ... (Melbourne, 1855), he published the anthems, some miscellaneous verse, including lines on the diggings and an essay. His last years were spent in Sydney where he died at Ashfield on 11 October 1867. His name is remembered in the municipality of Kentish, Tasmania. Although 'a man of honour and character, generally regarded as talented and enterprising, but neither judicious nor patient' his 'bizarre and paranoidal complaints against officials' tended to obscure the value of his exploratory and survey work. His writings were unnecessarily prolix, his verse over-decorated with worn-out illusions, his pamphleteering vitriolic. Egotistical and pedantic he was obsessed with the worth of his own achievements.

J. Bonwick, *Early struggles of the Australian press* (Lond, 1890); E. M. Miller, *Pressmen and governors* (Syd, 1952); *Victoria Colonist and Western Districts Advertiser,* 3, 10 Sept 1849; CSO 8/147, 148, 11/20/456 (TA); CO 323/134.   L. J. BLAKE

KERILLEAU; see HUON DE KERILLEAU

KERMODE, WILLIAM (1780-1852), merchant and settler, was born at Port Erin, Isle of Man, the son of Thomas Kermode and his wife Elizabeth, née Killey. As a youth he took up the sea as a career and is said to have made several voyages to India. In 1810 he married Anne Quayle, daughter of Rev. John Moore, vicar of Braddan, and Margaret, née Quayle, of West Hill, Castletown.

Kermode first arrived at Hobart Town in November 1819 as supercargo in the *Robert Quayle.* He went on to Sydney, where he had difficulty in disposing of his cargo and left it in the hands of agents. He sent his ship to the whale fishery and returned to England in the *Admiral Cockburn.* He made another voyage to Van Diemen's Land as supercargo in the *Mary* in 1821 and in June was granted 2000 acres on the Salt Pan Plains near Ross, but in Sydney, through mismanagement by his agents, he was declared bankrupt. He returned to England in 1822, taking with him a Tasmanian Aboriginal boy, George Van Diemen, at Lieut-Governor Sorell's request. In 1823 Kermode again visited Australia with a large cargo, intending to fulfil the settlement conditions of his land grant. In Hobart he was elected a director of the Sydney and Van Diemen's Land Packet Co. and became a founding shareholder of the Bank of Van Diemen's Land. In 1824 he was granted another 1000 acres and bought 2000 more, thus building up the property which he called Mona Vale, probably after Castle Mona, the original home of the dukes of Atholl on the Isle of Man. Kermode sailed for England in 1826 and returned next year with his son and George Van Diemen.

In June 1827 the land commissioners reported that Kermode was improving and cultivating his 'excellent Sheep Walk'.

After his wife and daughters joined him in May 1828 he was able to give the personal attention which was to make Mona Vale a show place. By 1834 his first modest timber house had been replaced by a substantial brick building; stone cottages and farm buildings were being erected and much of the estate laid out and fenced. According to *The Centenary History of the Midland Agricultural Association* (Launceston, 1938) 'Kermode was probably the most progressive of all the fine settlers who arrived in Sorell's time. He had vision and the energy and practical ability to bring his ideas into being'. With Saxon sheep from the Van Diemen's Land Co. he started his own stud in 1829 and later won many prizes for his sheep, horses and produce. The dry summers and negligible flow of the two streams which crossed the Salt Pan Plains led him to an early interest in water conservation. Both streams were dammed and hundreds of acres of irrigated pasture laid down to clover and grasses on hitherto useless land. Although the advice of such experts as H. C. Cotton [q.v.] on irrigation, and Count Strzelecki [q.v.] on soil analysis was not followed by the government, it was extensively used by Kermode who also gave generously of his time and energies to any practical proposals for improving farm production or standards.

These achievements showed his strength of purpose. He had been friendly with Sorell, but his very decided views led to an estrangement from Lieut-Governor Arthur. Kermode's need of land and convict labour was often supported at the Colonial Office by the duchess of Atholl, and in 1825 she even sought a government post for him. In that year, however, Kermode became involved in a threatened duel with his agent and Arthur refused him any further concessions. Two years later Kermode signed the protest against Arthur's restrictions on the press and was soon charged with harbouring runaway prisoners. Matters were not improved when the case was given much publicity by R. L. Murray [q.v.] in the *Austral-Asiatic Review,* February 1828. In 1835 more trouble arose over the alleged use by Kermode of stone cut by convicts in the government quarry and laid by a convict mason on the landing at Mona Vale. Kermode again proved his innocence, but the charges rankled and soon afterwards he published *Statement of Facts relating to the Recent Altercation . . .* (Hobart, 1836), a pamphlet vigorously supporting his friend, T. G. Gregson [q.v.], who had been imprisoned and fined for horsewhipping Arthur's nephew, Henry [q.v.].

With Sir John Franklin Kermode had better relations. Although he failed to win the lieut-governor's support for a land bank or mutual protection society to raise funds in London, he was appointed a member of the Legislative Council in 1842. When the financial crisis deepened he was one of the Patriotic Six who in October 1845 walked out of the council in protest against Eardley-Wilmot's handling of the annual estimates. Reappointed in 1848, Kermode again resigned, according to Lieut-Governor Denison, 'to create embarrassment for the Government'. But Kermode's health was failing. He retired to Mona Vale, where he died on 3 August 1852. His wife survived him by four months.

Of their three daughters, Anne was engaged to Sir John Jeffcott [q.v.] in 1836. After his death she married George Henry Moore, a Manxman who had been overseer at Mona Vale and later moved to New Zealand, where with substantial help from Kermode and Rev. John Lillie [q.v] he eventually became one of the largest landholders in North Canterbury.

ROBERT QUAYLE KERMODE (1812-1870), the eldest child and only son of William and Anne Kermode, was born on the Isle of Man and educated at Castletown. He arrived in Van Diemen's Land with his father in 1827, and was soon helping his father to enlarge their estate and improve farming methods. He was appointed a justice of the peace in 1843 and elected for Campbell Town to the Legislative Council in 1851. He took a leading part in political questions as an anti-transportationist. He served in the Legislative Council in 1856-57 and 1864-68, and the House of Assembly in 1857-59 and 1861-62; he was a minister without portfolio in the Weston and Smith administrations in 1857. He had liberal and enlightened views and contributed largely to the building funds of various churches and public institutions in the Ross district. He visited England in 1858-59 and New Zealand in 1863. In 1865 he commenced the third family home at Mona Vale; built of local sandstone, it had a tower and over fifty rooms, and is probably the largest private home in Australia. The duke of Edinburgh was entertained there in 1868.

At Longford on 10 November 1839 Robert Kermode married Martha, daughter of Thomas Archer [q.v.]; she bore him six sons and died in January 1853. On 16 June 1859 in London he married Emily, daughter of Henry Addenbroke of Cheltenham; they had a daughter and two sons. Kermode died on 4 May 1870 and was buried at Ross.

HRA (3), 3, 4, 6; G. A. Brown, Sheep breeding in Australia (Melb, 1880); P. L. Brown (ed), Clyde Company papers, 1-5 (Lond, 1941-63); R. C. K., Ross centenary (Hob, 1921); S. Butlin, Foundations of the Australian monetary system, 1788-1851 (Melb, 1953); Univ Tas, 'The Archer papers', Report on Hist MS Tas, 5 (1960); Newspaper indexes under W. Kermode (ML); MS cat under W. Kermode (ML); Correspondence file under Kermode (TA); CO 323/122, 124.

E. J. CAMERON

KERR, WILLIAM (1812-1859), journalist, was born in Wigtownshire, Scotland, the son of David Kerr, farmer, and his wife Anne, née McGammon. He migrated about 1837 to Sydney, where at first he worked as a tutor, becoming a journalist with the Colonist and then with the Sydney Gazette. In 1839 he moved to Melbourne, where he worked briefly with George Cavenagh [q.v.] on the Port Philip Herald before replacing Smith in January 1841 as editor of the rival paper, J. P. Fawkner's [q.v.] Port Phillip Patriot and Melbourne Advertiser. Originally this paper was the voice of the early settlers and big landholders, but after 1844, when Kerr and Fawkner quarrelled, Kerr changed its policy and it expressed the views of urban rather than rural Port Phillip. Superintendent La Trobe stated that it dealt systematically 'in abuse and gross misrepresentations of persons and facts'. Kerr even used his editorials to vilify its proprietor, Fawkner, who was driven to reply in the columns of the hated Herald. Soon afterwards Kerr left the Patriot and in 1846 started his own Argus, which became a daily in June 1849. The general tone of the Argus, lamented La Trobe, 'is quite as discreditable as that which distinguished the Patriot newspaper formerly'.

In 1848, as a result of damages arising from his libelling of Henry Moor [q.v.], registrar of the new Anglican diocese, Kerr became insolvent, and sold the Argus to Edward Wilson, but continued as editor. Under Kerr and Wilson the paper remained extremely radical. One of its slogans was 'Unlock the Lands', indicating its strong urban sympathies against the powerful squatting interest. Kerr spoke of the 'insatiable rapacity' of the squatters and of the support given them by 'this despicable abortion of a government'.

Another Argus slogan, representative of Kerr's strong views, was 'No Pollution'; this epitomized the opposition to convict labour of any sort, even to Pentonvillians and expirees. At a public meeting in 1844 Kerr thundered that 'he could not stand quietly by and see a whole community prostituted to get a little cheap labour for the squatter';

six years later the *Argus* was still condemning 'the insatiable cupidity of a few of the more greedy squatters who would sweep the bottomless pit to procure cheap labour'. Kerr was a member of the committee of the Anti-Transportation League and drafted the Convicts' Prevention Act in 1852.

Apart from his journalistic activities, which also included the publication in 1841 of the first Melbourne directory and of an almanac and directory in 1842, Kerr was active in local politics. In December 1842 he was elected as one of the twelve city councillors at Melbourne's first municipal election, and became one of the first four aldermen. He was Melbourne's second town clerk. In this capacity he served in 1853 on the first Commission of Sewers and Water Supply which was responsible for building the Yan Yean reservoir opened in 1857. Kerr was also influential in introducing the secret ballot in Victoria in 1856; indeed J. D. Lang [q.v.] insisted that credit for this should go to Kerr rather than to Charles Nicholson [q.v.]. Kerr was a protégé of Lang, with whom temperamentally he seems to have had much in common. It was partly at Kerr's urging that Lang stood for election as one of the Port Phillip members of the Legislative Council in 1850. Like Lang, Kerr was a keen advocate of separation, having been elected in 1840 as secretary of the Port Phillip Separation Association. Lang's influence may also be seen in Kerr's continual fermenting of the Catholic-Protestant feud, both as journalist and as provincial grand master of the Orangemen of the district. He resigned as town clerk in 1856 after some irregularities were shown in the accounts. He became stationmaster at Sunbury where he died on 25 May 1859, survived by his wife Caroline Amelia, née McCandlish, and four daughters.

Kerr was a man of many violent enthusiasms, and abounding energy despite a crippled arm. His language was unrestrained and during his twenty years in Port Phillip he quarrelled with most of the leading Melbourne citizens. He was given to stinging and sarcastic personal abuse of his opponents. Contemporary opinions of him range from 'thoughtless and thriftless' to 'generous and charitable'.

Garryowen (E. Finn), *The chronicles of early Melbourne*, 1-2 (Melb, 1888); W. Westgarth, *Personal recollections of early Melbourne and Victoria* (Melb, 1888), 83-91; J. Bonwick, *Early struggles of the Australian press* (Lond, 1890); H. G. Turner, *A history of the colony of Victoria*, 1-2 (Lond, 1904); A. D. Gilchrist (ed), *John Dunmore Lang*, 1-2 (Melb, 1951); R. D. Boys, *First years at Port Phillip*, 2nd ed (Melb, 1959); R. C. Seeger, 'The history of Melbourne's water supply', VHM, 22 (1947-50); R. M. McGowan, A study of social life and conditions in early Melbourne prior to separation, 1836-1851 (M.A. thesis, Univ Melb, 1951).

LYNDSAY GARDINER

KINCHELA, JOHN (1774?-1845), attorney-general and judge, was born at Kilkenny, Ireland, the second son of John Kinchela, merchant and bleacher, and his wife Rosina. After attending Dr John Ellison's Kilkenny College, he matriculated at Trinity College, Dublin (B.A., 1796; LL.B., LL.D., 1808). In 1798 he was called to the Irish Bar, practised in Dublin and in 1808 was admitted as an advocate in the 'Court of Prerogative and all other Ecclesiastical Courts'. By 1814 he had moved to Kilkenny where he became an alderman in 1817 and mayor in 1819 and also served in the Equity Courts and as county recorder. In 1824-25 he was in the West Indies as a commissioner of inquiry into the state of the captured negroes. On his return he moved to London.

At Dublin on 4 April 1796 Kinchela married Elizabeth Thornton, and after her death he married Anne Bourne on 19 February 1807. Although he inherited much property, out of kindness of heart he had mortgaged most of it by 1827. Afflicted by debt and increasing deafness he appealed to the marquess of Ormonde, lord lieutenant and keeper of the rolls of Kilkenny. In May 1829 Ormonde recommended him to the Colonial Office as an experienced lawyer or as a settler for the new Swan River settlement, and more urgently in June for 'any legal office' in the colonies, because 'his situation is truly distressing'. In August 1830 Kinchela was chosen to succeed A. M. Baxter [q.v.] as attorney-general in New South Wales at a salary of £1200 without the right of private practice. He was allowed £300 for his outfit but ran into more debt with a London tailor.

Kinchela arrived at Sydney in June 1831 in the *Renown* and his wife and three children followed in the *Curler* in August. They lived first in the Glebe at Hereford House, probably its first tenants, and then on the South Head Road at Juniper House, which he renamed Ormonde House. Kinchela was also granted two lots of four acres at Rushcutters Bay, but his application for a land grant for his son was rejected.

As attorney-general Kinchela found his office in great disorder. He applied successfully for a clerk to sort and file its records and soon gave evidence of 'his great anxiety to discharge his duty to the satisfaction of the Government'. He discovered arrears of unsettled actions accumulated over ten years, chiefly in unpaid debts for the purchase of government cattle and sheep. His activity resulted in large sums being paid into the Treasury, and proved more effective than his work on the commission of inquiry, ordered by the Colonial Office, into means of reducing the legal business of the government. In September 1831 Governor Bourke praised Kinchela's high principles, legal knowledge and great anxiety to give satisfaction, but complained that his extreme deafness hindered his work and rendered him inefficient as a member of the Legislative Council. Kinchela's colleagues also found him difficult: in 1833 the crown solicitor, W. H. Moore [q.v.], was suspended for insulting the attorney-general in a protest against the clerical duties that were delegated to him, and the solicitor-general, J. H. Plunkett [q.v.], claimed that, although he conducted nearly a hundred cases in the Criminal Sessions for the attorney-general, Kinchela gave him no assistance in the civil matters. Kinchela maintained that his advice had kept every department of the government free from legal embarrassment and had saved the Crown from defeat in every civil case. His frequent requests for an increase of salary were of no avail and creditors in Britain were persistent in pressing their claims, to the embarrassment of the Colonial Office. However, Bourke was sympathetic and in April 1836 when the chief justice, Francis Forbes [q.v.], went on leave, Kinchela was appointed acting puisne judge in the Supreme Court. His deafness caused some delays when he was sitting alone, but Bourke reported that 'in all the other duties of his office . . . his legal Knowledge and persevering research have been of essential service', and pleaded with unusual warmth for his permanent appointment, if not in Sydney, then to the bench in Van Diemen's Land. However, Glenelg was dismayed by Kinchela's long-standing debts and insisted on 'some temporary office' until a pension could be arranged. In September 1837 Kinchela was retired from the bench and appointed deputy-commissary in the Vice-Admiralty Court; a year later he was given additional work as advising Crown counsel at a salary of £500. In November 1840 he became master in equity at £800 a year, but within ten months he was 'attacked by Paralysis' and obliged to resign all his public offices, retiring on a pension of £500.

In 1838 Kinchela had to sell Ormonde House and his persistent Irish creditors were finally satisfied by his wife while he was unable to move. He died at Liverpool on 21 July 1845 aged 72, survived by his wife; her appeal to the Colonial Office for a pension was refused in 1848. One of his two daughters, Mary, married Thomas Gore on 3 August 1837. His son James Butler (b. 1815) became a clerk in the crown solicitor's office and at 22 through his father's influence was appointed police magistrate at Bathurst. Because of his inexperience other magistrates refused to sit with him, and when James Mudie [q.v.] returned to Sydney after ridiculing his father in The Felonry of New South Wales (London, 1837), young Kinchela publicly horsewhipped him and was fined £50. This was said to have been paid by public subscription, and soon afterwards he left the colony.

HRA (1), 15-24; Miscellaneous microfilm, FM4/1627 (ML); CO 201/421, 318/85, 87, 323/135; MS cat under Kinchela (ML).

KING, ANNA JOSEPHA (1765-1844), née Coombe, was born at Hatherleigh, Devon, England. On 11 March 1791 at St Martin-in-the-Fields, London, she was married to Philip Gidley King, who was a cousin; they sailed a few days later for Norfolk Island, the convict settlement where he had first been sent as commandant and superintendent in 1788.

King was the son of a draper and it is not likely that Anna Josepha was of any more distinguished parentage; but, whatever her background and education, at marriage she was able to step at once out of provincial life and take an effective place in a strange and adventurous world. Six weeks after she landed on Norfolk Island, her son Phillip Parker [q.v.] was born; in the next four years she had two daughters, one of whom died young. But even before her own son was born she had to care for Norfolk King, the elder of her husband's two illegitimate sons born during his earlier term on the island. During King's absence in England both boys had probably gone to Sydney with their convict mother; but in 1791 Norfolk returned to the island with his father. Later, both boys were sent to England, where King had them educated, and where as children they, Phillip, Maria and another daughter, Elizabeth (b. 1797), although under different roofs, played together when they met and sent each other their 'kind love' when apart. Cold sense of duty could have brought Mrs King to agree that something from her husband's small salary should be given to the care of his sons Norfolk and Sydney; but this loving-kindness between all his children could not have existed without a generous example from herself. Perhaps it was partly her acceptance of Norfolk's needs at the start of her married life that caused King's young secretary, W. N. Chapman [q.v.], to describe Mrs King as so good that it was a pleasure for any person to be near her.

For Mrs King's first fifteen months on the island she had for company the wife of Captain William Paterson [q.v.] of the New South Wales Corps, but after the Patersons' departure no other officer's wife came to share her exile until King's term was nearly ended. Her health was unreliable, the atmosphere on the island frequently discordant, food often short, communication with the outside world uncertain; she had a tempestuous, energetic, kindly, port-drinking and often ailing husband to care for, as well as her own infant children; but despite all difficulties she found and created happiness, for later, after-years of absence, she confessed to a longing to go back to the island to see her 'old friends' and her 'old dwelling' once more.

In 1796 they returned to England because of King's ill health. When King was appointed lieut-governor of New South Wales he and his wife sailed from England in the *Speedy* in November 1799. Mrs King kept a journal of this, her third voyage across the world. Only their youngest child, Elizabeth, sailed with them; Phillip and Maria, for their supposed educational advantage, were left behind, Maria with friends, the Enderbys [q.v.] of whaling fame, and Phillip with a tutor who was to let the parents have news of him *twice a year*. In the journal the anguish of the parting is plain, and does not fade. But it is not only for her children that Mrs King's heart aches, but also for humble people outside her own group and even for the convict women on board, battened down and 'they and their bedding getting as wet as drowned rats'. She labels herself a coward, being unable at first to rid herself of the fear of Napoleon's ships; storms and whales and fire-balls she dreads almost as much as the French; but mere discomforts she laughs at, and so loves a party that she persuades the reluctant King to stay an extra day at the Cape so that she may dance at the assembly in her new gold muslin dress.

In Sydney Mrs King found her husband and therefore herself on a stage much larger than that of Norfolk Island and presenting a more complex and important drama, involving a larger cast. She fully shared her husband's anxieties and labours; indeed, the influence she was thought to have over him earned her the nickname of 'Queen Josepha'. But one activity, strongly supported by the governor, was her own plan to mitigate the depravity of the Sydney scene by helping the hordes of neglected children that roamed its streets. The segregation and training of numbers of girl-waifs in what became known as Mrs King's Orphanage was the object of her daily attention and that of Mrs Paterson, her friend from Norfolk Island days and her friend again in Sydney whenever the quarrels of King and the military allowed.

In 1806 King, defeated by gout and opposition, was relieved by Captain William Bligh, and in a second sea-journal Mrs King described their nightmare nine-month voyage to England next year. King died in September 1808, leaving his wife and family in real need. The Treasury's meagre help was long in coming to his widow; but after a time she began to get financial relief from two sources in New South Wales: from cattle and from the land on which the cattle grazed, though her title to the first was vague and to the second illegal. The cattle were the flourishing descendants of a few beasts lost in the settlement's early days; two cows among them had belonged to Governor Phillip, who in 1801 remitted to King his claim on their progeny; her land was a grant of 790 acres made to her by Bligh in return for one, also illegal, made to Bligh by King. The ownership of Bligh's heiresses was challenged and their case was not settled until 1841; but Mrs King seems to have been left in undisturbed enjoyment of her grant at South Creek and the profits from both land and what Governor Macquarie described in 1810 as 'her fine numerous herds of horned cattle, of which she has upwards of 700 Head of all descriptions'.

Mrs King spent nearly twenty-four almost undocumented years in England before she was able to return, as she had long wished, to the colony where she had passed the most important part of her life. Two of her three daughters were settled there, Maria, wife of Hannibal Macarthur [q.v.] and Mary (b. 1805), wife of Robert Lethbridge; her distinguished son, Captain P. P. King, was about to settle there too. She sailed with him for Sydney in 1832 and on arrival was found by Elizabeth Macarthur [q.v.] 'as gay as ever' and 'very little changed'. At The Vineyard, Parramatta, the home of her daughter Maria, she was a valued part of an active family life until she died there on 26 July 1844. A stalwart member of the Church of England, she was buried in the graveyard of St Mary's, Penrith, formerly South Creek.

But for the accident of marriage, Mrs King, tall, dark-haired and vivacious, would never have appeared in the pages of British history; nor, although married to a colonial administrator, would she have counted in colonial records if she had been simply an anonymous wife. But the scattered references to her, as well as her own diaries in the Mitchell Library, Sydney, show that she was no cipher : a woman of sense and humanity, with a lively interest in persons and events, she takes her place as one of the more useful members of the difficult community of early New South Wales. A miniature of her is in the Mitchell Library, Sydney, and a portrait of the King family in 1799 by Robert Dighton is in the possession of Mr J. H. Goldfinch, Wahroonga, New South Wales.

M. Bassett, *The governor's lady, Mrs Philip Gidley King* (Melb, 1961), and for bibliog; Mme Vigant de Falbe, 'Reminiscences', *Bulletin*, 10, 17 Mar 1954; J. Baalman, 'Gubernatorial land jobbing', *JRAHS*, 48 (1962).   MARNIE BASSETT

KING, JAMES (1800-1857), merchant, manufacturer and vigneron, was the son of James King, a substantial farmer in Hertfordshire, England. His father suffered during the agricultural slump after the Napoleonic wars and in 1825, claiming a capital of £3000, applied for a land grant on one of the islands off Van Diemen's Land for the purpose of breeding rabbits. Nothing came of this application although he had already sent a shepherd and some prime merinos to the colony.

James, who had spent some years 'in the most respectable wool-stapling houses in Leeds' arrived in Sydney in 1827 and set up as a merchant. Soon after arrival he obtained a grant of 1920 acres near Raymond Terrace on the Williams River; he called it Irrawang, built a homestead, grew wheat, and raised cattle, and for ten years ineffectually complained to the government that he was properly entitled to a maximum grant of 2560 acres. His undertakings at Irrawang were supervised by overseers, as King spent most of his time in Sydney, where he shared in whaling and shipping ventures as well as carrying on general trade as an importer and purchaser of colonial produce.

Eager to explore and develop the resources of the colony, in 1831 he called the attention of the authorities to white sand deposits in the dunes along the South Head Road near Sydney. These, he claimed, were 'better suited for the manufacture of fine plate and flint glass than any found in England'. Manufacturers in England reported favourably on the sand for making both crystal ware and microscope lenses, 'a storehouse of philosophical power'. Since the colony badly needed payable ballast as well as exportable

materials and King claimed that he had spent £400 on exploiting his sand discovery, he asked for a grant of fifty acres either at Grose Farm on the Parramatta Road, now the site of the University of Sydney, or in the Domain, then a closely kept government preserve. The claim was refused, but in 1833 the Colonial Office recommended that King be allowed a remission of £100 on the price of any crown land he might buy. It was found in 1834 that charges for carrying the sand to England would make its price prohibitive, but in 1837 the London Society of Arts and Manufactures recognized King's discovery by awarding to him its silver medal.

About 1835 he settled at Irrawang, where he manufactured pottery and was praised by Governor Gipps for his ingenuity, enterprise and perseverance. King's main interest, however, was to develop the wine industry. At Irrawang in 1832 he had planted a vineyard, using Spanish, French and Portuguese vines. In February 1836 he made his first wine and began to extend the vineyard. Realizing that expert workmen were needed, he and twenty-two other producers decided to bring out German vine dressers; three of them came to Irrawang in 1848. From this time his wine gradually made its reputation in the colony; as a result of discriminating selection of vines, proper care and processing, the quality improved under continual supervision by King who rapidly learned the improved techniques. He confined his annual output to 2000 gallons and took special care in his cellar. In 1850 and 1852 he won the gold medal of the Horticultural Society of Sydney for white wines and light sparkling wines. In 1853 he helped to found the Hunter River Vineyard Association and was elected its first president. At the Paris Exhibition of 1855 he and other producers from the area, notably Mrs Maria Windeyer of Tomago, attracted favourable notice with their wines. King's entries won him a medal and some of his wine was served at the table of Emperor Napoleon III.

While in Europe for the exhibition of 1855 King visited the German chemist, Baron Justus von Liebig, who had earlier noted with approval the Irrawang experiments in blending and maturing wines. Von Liebig conducted King over some of the most famous German vineyards, and introduced him to such influential people as the grand duke of Nassau, who encouraged King by assuring him that the best Irrawang red wines were equal to the famous Assmannshausen vintages. This triumph probably led to King's publication in Edinburgh in 1857 of *Australia May Be an extensive Wine-growing Country.* A breakdown in health prevented King from returning to New South Wales. He died in London on 29 November 1857 aged 57.

He had married Eliza Elflida Millner (1812-1887) by whom he had three daughters and one son. His name is commemorated in the James King of Irrawang travelling scholarship, for which William Roberts of Penrith, who married King's widow, left £4000 to the University of Sydney in 1888. King was one of the first settlers to achieve reasonable success in viticulture, and his example, and the recognition he won, encouraged experiment by many of his neighbours.

Newcastle and Hunter District Hist Soc, J & Proc, 5 (1951).   DAVID S. MACMILLAN

KING, JOHN CHARLES (1817-1870), town clerk and politician, was born on 10 July 1817 at Dromara, County Down, Ireland, the son of Henry King, a landed proprietor and farmer. He was educated at the Belfast Royal Institute and Belfast College and was intended for the Presbyterian ministry. Deciding against this vocation, King sailed in 1838 for Australia. In Sydney he was so impressed with what he heard of Port Phillip that he returned to Ireland, married Elizabeth Johnston, of Annandale, Scotland, and sailed again for Australia with his parents and members of his family. He arrived in Melbourne in the *Salsette* in January 1841 and immediately set up as an auctioneer and commission agent in Elizabeth Street. Later he briefly served as government auctioneer.

When the Melbourne City Council was established in December 1842 King was appointed the first town clerk at £250 a year. He held office at a time when sectarian differences were strong and vocal. Although personally criticized, King served the council well, if unobtrusively, through its formative years. In March 1851 King resigned and was chosen to visit England as the agent of the Australasian League at a salary of £600. His primary task was to convince authorities in England that the colonists wanted the complete cessation of transportation of criminals to Australia; he was also to stimulate steam navigation between the two countries and to encourage the flow of capital and of emigration. His early report that Earl Grey was unalterably committed to continue transportation brought King much criticism, but Grey's loss of office in 1852 and the flood of capital and labour which followed the discovery of gold in Victoria soon combined to bring about all that was sought by the league.

The remainder of King's seven years in England were spent in lecturing and in acting as buyer and agent for the Melbourne City Council.

King returned to Victoria in 1857 and commenced business with his brother as an ironmonger in Collins Street. He also entered politics and was returned for Evelyn in the general elections for the Legislative Assembly in 1859. In October he was included in William Nicholson's cabinet as vice-president of the lands board and commissioner of public works, but in November his business failed and he resigned his portfolio and seat in parliament.

For the next five years he practised as auctioneer and agent, and in 1864 he became business manager of the *Argus*. In 1866 a chest illness began to trouble him seriously and his condition steadily declined. While returning from a health visit to Tasmania he died at sea on 26 January 1870; his death was attributed to chronic bronchitis and a liver complaint. He was buried in the Presbyterian section of the old cemetery in Queen Street. He was survived by his wife, two sons and three daughters, one of whom later married F. W. Haddon, editor of the *Argus*.

King was pale-faced, tall and spare, with mild looks that belied his determination and capacity. Opponents called him a master of intrigue, but others pointed to his gentlemanly demeanour, ready tact, and competence for public business.

Garryowen (E. Finn), *Chronicles of early Melbourne*, 1-2 (Melb, 1888); *Argus*, 29 Jan 1870; Haddon papers (La Trobe Lib, Melb); King papers (La Trobe Lib, Melb).

C. A. McCALLUM

KING, PHILIP GIDLEY (1758-1808), governor, was born at Launceston, Cornwall, England, on 23 April 1758. His family had long lived in the district and were not impecunious. His father, Philip, was a draper, his maternal grandfather, Gidley, was a local attorney; but though his origin shows that for men of humble birth it was easier to advance in the navy than in the army, it proved a handicap in New South Wales where some of his critics considered him 'not a gentleman'. For all that he was neither ignorant nor narrow in his interests, even if his references to the workings of Providence, his advice to his young son Norfolk, his views on alleged 'Republican sentiments' and 'seditious principles', and his reverence for the existing British constitution show that his religious and political opinions were clearly those of an orthodox naval officer.

King joined the navy as captain's servant

in H.M.S. *Swallow* on 22 December 1770. After five years in the East Indies he was moved to American waters in 1775, when fighting began against the rebellious colonies, and became a midshipman in the *Liverpool* in July. He was commissioned lieutenant in the *Renown* on 25 December 1778, after an examination the previous year when one of his examiners told King's mother that he was 'one of the most Promising young men I have ever met'. He returned to serve in the Channel Fleet from January 1780, and in the *Ariadne* he served under the command of Captain Arthur Phillip. In 1783 King sailed to India in the *Europe* with Phillip who formed a high opinion of his merits; on their return, since peace had been made, King was paid off. In October 1786, as soon as Phillip had been nominated to command the expedition then setting out to establish a penal settlement at Botany Bay, he chose King as second lieutenant in the *Sirius*, in which he was sailing himself. He took King with him when he transferred to the *Supply* in the hope of reaching their destination ahead of the main fleet, and a fortnight after they arrived selected him 'as a officer of merit . . . whose perseverance may be depended upon' to establish a subordinate settlement on Norfolk Island.

On 14 February King sailed for his new post with a party of twenty-three, including fifteen convicts. He discovered the difficulties in landing which were to harass the settlement there, but got ashore on 6 March. For two years he supervised this little establishment, organizing the clearing of land and the struggles against grubs, rats, hurricanes and occasionally troublesome convicts, but on the whole reporting favourably on its prospects. Despite the lack of a safe harbour, of lime and of any untimbered land, there was plenty of fish, the stock throve and the soil was good. It could maintain 'at least one hundred families', King told Phillip. Impressed by his work, the governor several times recommended his subordinate for naval promotion, but this would have raised difficulties because of King's lack of seniority; to solve the problem the secretary of state announced in December 1789 that King would be appointed lieut-governor of Norfolk Island at a salary of £250, and next month, in consequence, he was discharged from the *Sirius*; however, before this news reached New South Wales, King had sailed for England in March 1790 on Phillip's orders to report on the difficulties of the whole settlement.

King's visit to London was brief but successful. He arrived just before Christmas, saw Lord Grenville and Sir Joseph Banks [q.v.], discussed the problems of New South Wales, and on 2 March 1791 was promoted commander. On 11 March he married Anna Josepha Coombe [q.v.] at St Martin's-in-the-Fields and four days later sailed, with his wife and his young protégé, W. N. Chapman [q.v.], as a passenger, in H.M.S. *Gorgon* (Captain Parker) to return to Norfolk Island with his commission as lieut-governor. On the voyage he learned at the Cape of the continued shortages in New South Wales, so on his own responsibility he bought some livestock there; unfortunately many died before they reached Sydney and the reluctance of the Treasury to recognize such unwonted if highly warranted independent action by junior officials gave rise to a protracted correspondence on the question of paying for them. After five weeks in Sydney King landed on Norfolk Island early in November, and six weeks later Anna Josepha safely gave birth to a son, Phillip Parker [q.v.]; apart from this, King found much trouble on his hands.

During his twenty months absence the island had been under the command of Lieut-Governor Robert Ross [q.v.] and the population had grown to nearly one thousand. But Ross was not an easy commandant and convicts, settlers, soldiers and officials had become discontented under his rule. King found 'discord and strife on every person's countenance' and was 'pestered with complaints, bitter revilings, back-biting'. Tools and skilled labour were both very short. Thefts were common and there was still no criminal court on the island, despite the representations he had made in London on the need for better judicial arrangements. However, King's able and enthusiastic guidance helped to improve conditions. The regulations he issued in 1792 encouraged the settlers, who were drawn from ex-marines and ex-convicts, and he was willing to listen to their advice on fixing wages and prices and other things. By 1794 the island was self-sufficient in grain, and had a surplus of swine that it could send to Sydney. The numbers 'off the store' were high and few of the settlers wanted to leave, but unfortunately King had had no success in stimulating the growing of flax which so interested the British government. While in England he had persuaded the government to order Captain George Vancouver [q.v.], who was then setting out on a voyage of exploration in the Pacific, to bring native flax-dressers from New Zealand to Norfolk Island. Two Maoris were duly kidnapped, but when they arrived it was found that they knew nothing about flax-dressing: all that King could do was to take them home. This gave him the opportunity for a ten-day visit to New Zealand in November 1793, which earned him unmerited reproof from Lieut-Governor Grose [q.v.] and the duke of Portland for leaving his post without permission. Grose accompanied his reprimand in February 1794 with a criticism of King's treatment of the mutinous conduct of some of the New South Wales Corps on the island. This followed their unfounded allegations of the lieut-governor punishing them too severely and the ex-convicts too leniently when disputes arose between them, an argument between some soldiers and Mrs King's servants, and a drunken soldier's insolence to King himself. King, supported by most of the corps' officers, sent twenty mutineers to Sydney for trial by court martial, but Grose, probably imperfectly informed of the affair, sharply censured the lieut-governor's actions and issued orders which gave the military illegal authority over the civilian population. King implemented these instructions, though noting their impropriety; and in due course Portland ordered him to withdraw them and Grose apologized for the severity of his language. However, this precursor of conflict with the military which was to plague King later was followed by another portent of the future in his increasing ill health. He had become ill on the voyage to England in 1790 and in December 1795 was so sick with gout 'an almost fixed compression of the Lungs and Breast, with a difficulty of Breathing and a constant Pain in the Stomach' that 'much doubt was entertained of his Recovery'. Governor Hunter gave him leave of absence and in October 1796 King left Norfolk Island for England, carrying the customary plants for Banks.

In England he somewhat recovered his health and sought further employment. This he needed for financial reasons if no other, for, as he told Banks, his salary had been very small, he had 'neither kept a shop or sold drams', and his total worldly possessions were little more than £1500; if he were not given an appointment, he thought he would have to retire to farm in the west country. Phillip had wanted King to be appointed governor of New South Wales, had continued to advocate King's cause after Hunter had been preferred in 1794, and was partly responsible for his salary at Norfolk Island being raised to £450 in January 1795. Banks supported King too, and in January 1798 it was decided that he should return to New South Wales with a dormant commission to succeed Hunter in the event of the latter's death or absence from the colony, though at that time there was no question of his

being recalled. The commission was issued on 1 May, but King was to take out a new ship which was being built for the colonial service, whose design, as with James Cook's [q.v.] *Resolution* in 1772, was based in part on Banks's requirements for a 'plant cabbin'. It was utterly cranky and King's strenuous efforts to improve her while still satisfying Banks had no success; when she finally sailed in August 1799, she had to return to Portsmouth after her first encounter with rough weather to be condemned as unseaworthy. King was properly absolved of responsibility for her defects, but he had found the delay financially embarrassing and his 'cup of disappointment and anxiety' was 'compleatly overflowed' by the 'long detention'; however, he had the satisfaction of being commissioned post-captain on 5 December 1798, and when he sailed in the *Speedy* on 26 November 1799 he carried the dispatch recalling Hunter.

Authorized to assume office as soon as Hunter could arrange his departure, already irritated by the delays in England, anxious to set in motion radical reforms in the colony and worried about his pay, King showed none of the goodwill that had marked his earlier relations with his predecessor but displayed in a correspondence which each regarded as insulting an unseemly impatience for him to begone. King did not assume command until 28 September 1800, but long before then had assured Under-Secretary John King that his taking over was 'well-liked and anxiously looked for'. King wrote gloomily of existing conditions, insisted that 'nothing less than a total change in the system of administration' was necessary, and forecast that 'discontent will be general' when this took place. His task would be 'laborious and highly discouraging' but he would not be 'at all intimidated', and although he had no formal instructions until raised from the status of lieut-governor to governor in 1802, he improvised them for himself from the dispatches to Hunter and elaborated them in the orders he gave to Major Foveaux [q.v.] whom he appointed to replace himself as lieut-governor of Norfolk Island in June 1800.

King's first task was to attack the misconduct of monopolist traders and traffickers in liquor. In March 1799 the commander-in-chief had ordered Colonel William Paterson [q.v.], when he was leaving England to rejoin his corps, to inquire into his officers' trading activities, and this gave King the chance, even before Hunter had left, to ask Paterson to act. As soon as he assumed command King issued a host of orders which he had already prepared, including a new set of port and price regulations intended to curb exploitation and the liquor traffic. He felt compelled to allow Surgeons Balmain and D'Arcy Wentworth [qq.v] to sell 4359 gallons of spirits which they had on hand, but was able to reduce the rate of spirit imports to about a third that of the last months of Hunter's administration. He tried to persuade the government in Calcutta and British consuls in the United States to discourage the shipping of liquor to New South Wales and, to offer the colonists an alternative beverage, he began the construction of a brewery. It only began production in 1804, and in his efforts to reduce spirit drinking he faced the refusal of most convicts to work 'in what they . . . call their own time for any other mode of payment', but he cut spirit consumption per adult male in 1801-04 to about two and a half bottles a month. Unfortunately as time went on King found increasing difficulty in suppressing illicit local distillation, despite repeated orders against it, and although he imposed a duty of 5 per cent on imports to raise revenue, as Hunter had suggested in 1798, he did not anticipate the later policy of reducing the profits of illegal grog-selling by allowing unrestricted import subject to a moderately heavy duty.

In June 1800 King had protested to Hunter against the 'exorbitant demands of creditors' in the colony. He felt that the poorer settlers could best be protected by price control and by the 'establishment of a public warehouse', such as he had advocated for Norfolk Island in 1796 and Hunter had also referred to; but Hunter had not told the authorities in London what goods were needed. King's detailed requests were at once acted on, and merchandise was sold through it at a price only 50 per cent above cost to cover transport and selling charges. The increasing quantities imported commercially also weakened the monopolists' grip on the colony's economy and improved the colonists' means of obtaining supplies. King tried to control, though not always with success, prices, wages, hours of work, the employment of convicts, baking, butchers, interest rates, weights and measures and the value of all the many kinds of currency circulating in the colony; he tried to reduce forgeries by introducing printed forms for promissory notes, but they were usually ignored. He recalled all the officers' servants in excess of two each, and so reduced the number victualled by the Crown from 356 to 94; he increased the number of convicts on the public farms from 30 to 324, and had quadrupled their cultivated acreage by 1803; later he allowed them to decline, following orders from London and the increase in private agriculture. He helped the private farmers by land grants, by the issue of seed, tools, sheep and rations, by hiring oxen, by postponing—contrary to his instructions—the purchase of grain by tender and keeping its price up to 8s. a bushel, by ordering the government stores to buy direct from the grower and by distributing government breeding stock as a reward 'to those whose exertions . . . appeared to merit that encouragement'. He also increased the size of land grants and made reservations for pasturage adjacent to them. The upshot was that only 56 out of 646 farmers were 'on the stores' in 1806, compared with 110 out of 401 in 1800. The smallholders had done much better than before, particularly during the first half of his administration, and the colony seemed to be self-sufficient in grain, though the disastrous floods in 1806 destroyed King's hopes in this regard.

During King's administration the government's flocks and herds quintupled. He bought cattle from India to improve the quality of the government stock, and though disavowing the idea of the government concerning itself with 'fine-woolled sheep', and mindful of the importance to the small settlers of the 'weight of Carcase', he was able by careful breeding to produce 'a total change in Government Flock from Hair to Wool', and to distribute ewes to settlers in expectation of a general improvement in the flocks of the colony. He began the mining of coal, which he hoped would be a profitable export, was interested in timber cutting and encouraged experiments in growing vines, tobacco, cotton, hemp and indigo. Although in the opening sentence of the first journal of his experiences from 1787 to 1790, which was published with minor revision as an appendix to Hunter's *Historical Journal of the Transactions at Port Jackson and Norfolk Island* (London, 1793), King had affirmed the contemporary opinion that Botany Bay was being founded simply as a penal settlement, by 1791 he was expressing great hopes for it as a Pacific base for flax cultivation and for whaling. The flax was not a success but whaling was, and both it and later sealing owed much to King's encouragement. A friend of Samuel Enderby [q.v.], he advised the British government to allow the whalers to carry merchandise to New South Wales. He encouraged sealers to go to Bass Strait and whaling ships to visit New Zealand and the Pacific. In 1804 he encouraged Robert Campbell [q.v.] to make his experimental shipment of oil and skins in the *Lady Barlow* in contravention of the monopoly of the East India Co., which he had constantly urged the government to modify, and sought permission at the same time to open up trade between New South Wales and China.

As befitted a naval officer King's interest was attracted by the islands and the oceans in and around the Pacific. In 1793 he proposed a British settlement at the Bay of Islands in New Zealand. He continued to insist on the value of Norfolk Island, not least because it afforded 'the most ample Refreshment to our Whalers', and succeeded in 1807 in persuading the British government to reverse its decision to evacuate it. In 1801 he dispatched Lieutenant James Grant [q.v.] to complete the exploration of Bass Strait and to survey Western Port and then to examine Hunter's River; he sent two ships to Tahiti to try to open up a trade in pork, and Lieutenant John Murray [q.v.] on the voyage that led to the discovery of Port Phillip, where he urged that a settlement should be founded. In 1803 he sent Lieutenant John Bowen [q.v.] to establish a settlement on the Derwent River and next year sent Paterson to found one at Port Dalrymple on the Tamar. On land, he sent out Francis Barrallier [q.v.] on two expeditions, on the second enabling him to evade his military duties by instructing him in November 1802 to go on a mission to the 'King of the Mountains', and he encouraged the expeditions of George Caley [q.v.].

King could, of course, never forget that he was in charge of a convict colony. He had to keep the prisoners in subjection, but at the same time he could not ignore the growing number of emancipists, and firmly reminded Major Johnston [q.v.] that the British government had not intended the prisoners to be consigned 'to Oblivion and disgrace for ever'. King appointed emancipists to his bodyguard and enrolled them in the Loyal Associations, as had been done in the New South Wales Corps. Apart from the rather special case of appointing as military engineer, George Bellasis [q.v.], a former officer in the East India Co. who had killed an opponent in a duel, he placed men like Richard Fitzgerald, James Meehan, D. D. Mann, Andrew Thompson, Rev. Henry Fulton and Father Dixon [qq.v.] in administrative positions. He took firm measures to regulate the position of assigned servants, even if at first they were often disobeyed, and he laid the foundation of the future ticket-of-leave 'system by granting 'annual certificates' to prisoners deserving indulgence. Though he granted pardons to about 50 per cent more convicts every year than Hunter had done, he had about 30 per cent more to deal with and they included many political prisoners. Of these, especially the

Irish, King was at first perhaps unduly alarmed, though he had been in England in the dangerous years, 1797-99; however, after initial forebodings, in both 1801 and 1802 he was able to report their 'regular and orderly behaviour' and to compare their conduct most favourably with that of the military officers. He was again rather overexcited at the time of the Irish conspiracy in 1804, but he seems to have felt more secure after it had been suppressed and he had divided the ring-leaders between the different settlements, including Newcastle, which he re-established in 1804 largely in order to take them. That year, when the war with France had been renewed, to supplement the battery on Dawes Point King began to build the citadel at Fort Phillip, intending that it would also be a place of refuge in case of an internal rising; but it turned out to be rather a white elephant.

These and other public works were hampered by a shortage of convict labourers, until 1804 by their necessary employment on the public farms and afterwards by the very small numbers arriving. On the average King had few more than two hundred men working on buildings, but he was able to complete a granary, church and schoolhouse at the Hawkesbury, St John's Church, a gaol and brewery at Parramatta, a barrack at Castle Hill, saltworks, a guard-house, a printing office, wharves, mills, a bridge and a house for the judge-advocate at Sydney, as well as a tannery and a manufactory for canvas, sacking, blanketing and rope; he made progress with the fort and St Philip's Church, built boats and struggled, though not always successfully, to keep other buildings in repair.

King strove valiantly to satisfy the British government's never-ceasing demand to reduce the costs of the colony. The general success of his policies enabled him to cut the proportion of the population drawing government rations from 72 per cent in 1800 to 32 per cent in 1806 and the amount of their indebtedness to the government was reduced. Fortunately trouble with the Treasury over his expenditure when on Norfolk Island made him meticulous in his keeping of accounts, and he drew Treasury bills for stores at a rate about 20 per cent less than Hunter had done in 1796-98 for only three-quarters the number of people. In June 1802 King imposed a 5 per cent duty on imported spirits and on merchandise brought from east of the Cape and not of British manufacture; though legally unauthorized this was not questioned, and by using it for the gaol and orphan funds he began the appropriation of colonial revenue for local purposes. He was interested in the girls' Orphan School, and though he regretted that he could not establish a similar institution for boys, he took several day-schools 'under the protection of Government' and by apprenticeship taught convict boys to become skilled tradesmen. He asked the British government to send out supplies of smallpox vaccine, and so enabled the surgeons to perform the first successful vaccination in the colony. In March 1803 he permitted the government printer, George Howe [q.v.], to establish the *Sydney Gazette*, allowing him the use of the government press and type. He was sympathetic to the missionaries who visited the colony, welcomed Maori and Tahitian visitors to Sydney, and strove to keep peace with the Aboriginals. These, he told Governor Bligh, he 'ever considered the real Proprietors of the Soil'. He refused to allow them to be worked as slaves, tried to protect their persons and their property and to preserve a 'good understanding' with them; but he found them 'very capricious', often 'sanguinary and cruel to each other', and like his contemporaries failed to understand what he called their 'most ungrateful and treacherous conduct'.

He was an able and conscientious administrator, nearly always, as Phillip had said, 'labouring for the public and doing nothing for himself'. Yet this was not entirely true, especially as his health grew worse and his family increased. In 1779 he had been reprimanded for appointing, without authority, an agent to sell a prize on behalf of himself and the rest of the crew of the *Renown*. On Norfolk Island he acted as a broker for Treasury bills. In 1801 he arranged for the government store to buy the cargo of the *Britannia*, in which he had an interest, at a 50 per cent profit instead of the 30 per cent it was then paying for purchases from other ships, claiming in 1804 that he had received authority to raise the price, although in fact this only arrived three months later. He took, again without authority, 300 cattle valued at £5600 from the government herds to satisfy a claim to some of the 'wild cattle' which had strayed in 1788, and ignored orders to return them; he improperly granted 1345 acres to Bligh when he arrived in 1806 as his successor, and a week later allowed Mrs King with equal impropriety to accept 690 acres from Bligh, described, with delightful irony, as 'Thanks'. None of these actions was disinterested, but on eighteenth century standards they were not unusual; compared with most of his subordinates, he was a pillar of rectitude. His salary as governor was only £1000, half that of his successor, and when he died his property of £7000 amounted to little more than the current value of the cattle.

A more serious source of criticism was his hot temper which, if in part a professional attribute and intensified by sickness, severely handicapped him in New South Wales. If men like Banks, Phillip, Matthew Flinders, Nicholas Baudin and Rowland Hassall [qq.v.] held him in the highest esteem, others in the colony including Paterson, Captain Colnett R.N. and Joseph Holt [q.v.] found cause to complain of his 'violent passions' and the *Memoirs* of James Hardy Vaux [q.v.] portray a man at first benevolent, though mildly eccentric, becoming rather petty as well as irascible by the time of his voyage home in 1807. Though perhaps overfond of practical jokes he was not without a more sophisticated sense of humour, but as time went on he became overweight, heavy-eyed and strained, sometimes blustering and pompous, sometimes on the verge of breakdown, as he saw a widening gap between his hopes and his achievements. In the end he was defeated by the officers of the New South Wales Corps.

That he would have to fight them he knew when he arrived in Sydney in 1800, and even before he had assumed office he was regretting that Hunter had allowed Captain George Johnston to go home for his trial on charges of trading in spirits. Johnston was soon back untried, but trials in the colony were not successful, and King found the military arrogance which he had faced at Norfolk Island was now exacerbated by his economic policy. He badly needed capable law officers and a change in the personnel of the military force, the New South Wales Corps, but the British government ignored his requests for these things. He was faced with frequent disobedience and insolence which early in 1803, immediately after he had refused to allow a cargo of spirits to be landed from the *Atlas*, culminated in the circulation of libellous 'pipes' against him and his officials. The investigations and court martials which followed only revealed the animosity which existed between the governor and the corps; no wonder that King declared that 'for the prosperity of His Majesty's subjects in this territory . . . some change is absolutely necessary in our criminal courts'. With this Colonel Paterson entirely agreed, asserting that 'most of the disquiet that has agitated this settlement . . . is chiefly to be attributed to the unfortunate mixture of civil and military duties'. In November 1801 King had repeated Hunter's action and sent home an accused officer, John Macarthur [q.v.], charged with fighting a duel with his commander, Paterson, itself the result of a quarrel with the governor. But in July 1805 Macarthur returned in triumph. He had not been court-martialled, had resigned his commission, and had obtained an order for 5000 acres of the best land in the colony for his sheep-breeding. King had failed to receive support in England, just as when he complained of the proceedings of the local courts martial as vitally affecting the peace of the colony, the judge-advocate in London in January 1804 coldly told him that 'for the sake of harmony' he would 'pass over any seeming irregularity'. Owing to these disputes, in May 1803 King had asked to be given leave of absence while an inquiry was held into the state of the colony. In November the secretary of state at once accepted what he was quick to interpret as an offer of resignation, and after King received this reply in June 1804 his activities slowed down; but he was not relieved until August 1806 and in the interval he suspected that other critics, like Margarot, Henry Hayes, Michael Robinson and W. Maum [qq.v.], were blackening his reputation in England. For all that he had good friends in New South Wales, including Surgeon Harris [q.v.] and Rowland Hassall who managed his wife's farm, and who corresponded with him after his departure.

When he embarked in the *Buffalo* on 15 August for the voyage home he completely collapsed. He could not sail until 10 February 1807, and a stormy passage around Cape Horn delayed his arrival in England until November. He pressed the Colonial Office insistently for a pension, but before it was granted he died on 3 September 1808. He was buried in the churchyard of St Nicholas, Lower Tooting, London.

King had always aimed at promoting 'the prosperity of the colony, and giving a permanent security to the real interests of its inhabitants'. He knew he could not satisfy all, and had faced 'scurrility and abuse, clothed with darkness and assassination'. This abuse has apparently harmed his reputation, which stands today lower than is deserved. He worked hard for the good of New South Wales and left it very much better than he found it, but succumbed to sickness and the hard conditions of his service while still relatively young.

King had two natural sons, Norfolk (1789-1839) and Sydney (1790-1840), by Ann Inett, a convict from Worcestershire. They were born when their father was first on Norfolk Island, both were well cared for by him and rose to be lieutenants in the navy. His only legitimate son, P. P. King, married Harriet Lethbridge of Cornwall. Of King's four daughters, two settled in New South Wales: Mary (b. 1805) married her brother-in-law, Robert Lethbridge, in 1826 and Anna Maria (b. 1793) married Han-

nibal Macarthur [q.v.] in 1812. Elizabeth (b. 1797) who married an artist, Charles Runciman, remained in England, and Utricia (b. 1795) died as a child.

HRNSW, 1-7; HRA (1), 1-7, (3), 1; M. Bassett, *The governor's lady* (Lond, 1956); M. Roe, New South Wales under Governor King (M.A. thesis, Univ Melb, 1955); MS cat under P. G. King (ML).   A. G. L. SHAW

KING, PHILLIP PARKER (1791-1856), naval officer, hydrographer and company manager, was born on 13 December 1791 at Norfolk Island, the son of Philip Gidley King and his wife Anna Josepha, née Coombe. Young Phillip sailed for England with his parents in October 1796 in the *Britannia*. When his father left England in November 1799 to become governor of New South Wales, his sister Maria was left in the care of Mrs Samuel Enderby, and Phillip was placed under the tuition of Rev. S. Burford in Essex. In 1802 he was nominated to the Portsmouth Naval Academy. In November 1807 he entered the navy in the *Diana*. He became a midshipman and served for six years in the North Sea, the Bay of Biscay and the Mediterranean, being promoted master's mate in 1810 and lieutenant in February 1814.

There is no record of King's early surveying experience but according to family tradition Matthew Flinders [q.v.], a friend of the family, interested him in surveying and introduced him to Captain Thomas Hurd (1757-1823), hydrographer to the Admiralty 1808-23, who gave him careful training. In 1817 the British government decided that 'circumstances consequent upon the restoration of Peace . . . rendered it most important to explore, with as little delay as possible, that part of the coast of New Holland . . . not surveyed or examined by the late Captain Flinders', and appointed Lieutenant King to do this. Before he departed King married Harriet, daughter of Christopher Lethbridge, of Launceston, Cornwall. He arrived at Port Jackson in September 1817 in the *Dick* with instructions from the Colonial Office to Governor Macquarie that he was to be provided with the most suitable vessel and a carefully chosen crew. The 83-ton cutter *Mermaid* was bought for £2000 and the expedition sailed from Sydney on 22 December with a complement of nineteen including Allan Cunningham, J. S. Roe and the Aboriginal Bungaree [qq.v.]. By way of King George Sound they reached North West Cape where the survey began.

King had been instructed by the Admiralty to discover whether there was any river 'likely to lead to an interior navigation into this great continent', and by the Colonial Office to collect information about climate, topography, fauna, timber, minerals, and the natives and the prospects of developing trade with them. From February until June 1818 the expedition surveyed the coast as far as Van Diemen's Gulf and had many meetings with Aboriginals and Malay proas. In June the *Mermaid* visited Timor and then returned to Sydney the way she had come, arriving on 29 July. Next December and January King surveyed the recently discovered Macquarie Harbour in Van Diemen's Land and sailed in May 1819 for Torres Strait. He took John Oxley [q.v.] as far as the Hastings River, and went on to survey the coast between Cape Wessel and Admiralty Gulf. He returned to Sydney on 12 January 1820.

In Sydney Cove the *Mermaid* was careened, recoppered and caulked and then immersed for several days to destroy the cockroaches that infested the ship. However, both cockroaches and rats soon reappeared. Only two of the former crew volunteered to sail again and a new crew was formed, this time including a surgeon. The *Mermaid* sailed north on 14 June 1820. At Bowen she ran aground and suffered much damage. Surveys were made between Admiralty Gulf and Brunswick Sound on the north-west coast, but in September the ship began to leak badly. She was careened and ten days were spent repairing her. King then left the coast and sailed to Port Jackson where, after a narrow escape from wreck off Botany Bay, he arrived on 9 December.

King made his fourth and final survey in northern Australia in the *Bathurst*, 170 tons, which carried a complement of thirty-three, not counting a girl who had stowed away for love of the bos'n; in place of Bungaree King took another Aboriginal, Bundell. The *Bathurst* sailed on 26 May 1821 from Sydney by way of Torres Strait to the north-west coast. After a visit to Mauritius for rest and refreshment the *Bathurst* resumed the survey of the west coast. King arrived back in Sydney in April 1822. On these four voyages he made significant contributions to Australian exploration by establishing the insularity of several islands, by investigating the inner geography of many gulfs, and by giving the first report of Port Darwin.

When King reached Sydney he was ordered to return to England with his ship. On 27 July 1821 he had been promoted commander. In October 1822 he read a paper, 'On the maritime geography of Australia', to the newly formed Philosophical Society of Australia.

In April 1823 King reached England in poor health and thought of retiring to his Australian estates. In 1806 his father had granted him 660 acres on the South Creek, near Rooty Hill. Governor Macquarie had given him another 600 acres. He had 850 cattle, 40 horses, 1800 sheep, 100 pigs, and some forty men employed on his property by July 1822 when he sought permission to buy additional land at Rooty Hill. Governor Brisbane offered him instead a grant of 3000 acres. In 1824 King became a shareholder in the Australian Agricultural Co., newly established with a capital of £1,000,000 and a promise of 1,000,000 acres in New South Wales. He was appointed to the Australian Advisory Committee together with John Macarthur, his son James, his son-in-law Dr Bowman, and his nephew Hannibal [qq.v.], who was King's brother-in-law. According to Francis Forbes [q.v.] this cosy little family group contrived in its first year to defraud the company of more than £11,000, but King could hardly have played an active part, for he did not return to Australia for eight years.

King was now recognized as one of Britain's leading hydrographers and in February 1824 was made a fellow of the Royal Society. In London in 1826 he published his two-volume *Narrative of a Survey of the Intertropical and Western Coasts of Australia. Performed between the years 1818-1822*, partly illustrated by his own sketches. In May 1826 he sailed in command of H.M.S. *Adventure*, with H.M.S. *Beagle* in company, to chart the coasts of Peru, Chile and Patagonia. This arduous task lasted until 1830. Among King's subordinates were J. L. Stokes, J. C. Wickham and Owen Stanley [qq.v.]. There were narrow escapes from shipwreck and the two commanders were under great strain. In August 1828 the captain of the *Beagle* shot himself. When the expedition returned to England in October 1830 King, who had been promoted captain, was again in poor health. In 1832 he reached Sydney in the *Brothers*. In that year he had published *Sailing Directions to the Coasts of Eastern and Western Patagonia, and the Straits of Magellan and the Sea-Coast of Tierra del Fuego*. His journal of the South American survey is included in *Narrative of the Surveying Voyages of His Majesty's Ships, Adventure and Beagle . . . 3 vols (London, 1839), edited by Captain Robert Fitzroy, who succeeded to the command of the *Beagle* and in 1831-36 commanded the expedition.

In February 1829 King had been appointed to the New South Wales Legislative Council but, since he was absent from the colony, J. T. Campbell [q.v.] acted in his place. When Campbell died Hannibal Macarthur was appointed. In September 1832 a vacancy occurred in the council when John Macarthur was declared a lunatic. Governor Bourke did not appoint King because his brother-in-law was already on the council. In May 1837 the death of Archibald Bell [q.v.] created another vacancy and Bourke recommended the appointment of Sir John Jamison [q.v.]. King objected and claimed the seat. Bourke reported to London that he had chosen Jamison, a man of 'liberal principles' in preference to one 'well known to be opposed to those measures both in Church and State, which it has been the aim of my administration under the guidance of H.M.'s Government to introduce'. King persisted and wrote to the Colonial Office, but without success. However, in February 1839 Governor Gipps appointed King to the council and reported that 'though connected by family ties with what is here called the anti-emancipist party', he was 'liberal in his politics, as well as prudent and moderate in his general bearing'. Soon afterwards King was appointed resident commissioner of the Australian Agricultural Co.; he immediately offered to resign from the council but was induced to retain his seat until October when Gipps was advised to accept the resignation.

King was commissioner of the Australian Agricultural Co. for ten eventful years in its history. They saw the transition from mainly convict to mainly free labour, drought and depression in 1838-45, the abandonment of the company's claim to a coal monopoly, and the initiation of a plan to dispose of much of the company's land to small settlers. King took charge on 8 April 1834 at a salary of £1000. The company was then employing about five hundred men, including four hundred convicts, on its pastoral properties and one hundred convicts in the coal-mines, and sold 655 bales of wool and 21,200 tons of coal. The demand for coal was rising but skilled labour was scarce. In 1840 the company imported a hundred Irish Labourers, who proved unreliable, and forty Welsh miners, who proved troublesome. Between 1842 and 1845 sales of coal dropped from 35,000 tons to 23,000 tons. King often protested that coal was being mined elsewhere to the detriment of the company's monopoly. In 1845 James Brown was taken to court for opening a coal-mine near Maitland. Brown lost the case, but thereafter private coal-mines were not hindered and in 1850, with the company's consent, a proclamation cancelling the reservation of coal on all grants was issued. In 1842-45 the company, in common with other pastoralists, was in

difficulty; King and his officers asked that their salaries be reduced but the directors would not agree. By 1845 the company had obtained power to alienate 500,000 acres of its land and by 1847 all the company's properties had been freed from all conditions hitherto imposed and it was enabled to sell land as it wished. In 1849 King went to London in the *Hamlet* to plan the settlement of farmers on land sold to them by the company, and the establishment of towns and villages. The reduction of the company's holdings led to the abolition of King's post. There was some indignation when it was discovered that the only officer who obtained promotion in the reorganization was King's son, Philip Gidley (1817-1904).

In October 1846 the secretary of state called for annual reports on each observatory in the various colonies. King was appointed to the commission of inquiry and found the instruments and books in good condition at the Parramatta observatory but the buildings very dilapidated. On the commission's advice Governor FitzRoy ordered that the instruments be packed and placed in the ordnance store to preserve them from damage. As pastoralist and manager King kept up his interest in exploration and drawing. In 1837-38 he made an expedition to the Murrumbidgee and recorded his observations. In December 1838 and January 1839 he visited New Zealand and Norfolk Island in the *Pelorus*. His field books of surveys in the neighbourhoods of Parramatta, Newcastle and elsewhere in 1843-55 occupy eight volumes. In 1843 he made a survey of Port Stephens. He published articles in the *Nautical Magazine* and the *Zoological Journal* and printed some of his papers on a small private press. In 1844 Gipps placed King's name eighth in the list of nineteen persons considered eligible for a local order of merit.

King was seriously ill in November 1854. In 1855 he was promoted rear-admiral on the retired list. On the evening of 26 February 1856 he dined on board the *Juno* as the guest of Captain S. G. Fremantle. He was cheerful, but abstemious because of his poor health. He was put ashore and walked to his home in North Sydney, where he collapsed at the gate in an apoplectic fit from which he did not recover. His widow died at Ashfield, Sydney, on 19 December 1874. Of their eight children, the eldest, Philip Gidley, became manager of the Australian Agricultural Co. in 1854; the fourth Rev. Robert Lethbridge (1823-1898) was principal of Moore Theological College in 1868-78.

King was the first and for years the only

Australian-born to attain eminence in the world outside the Australian colonies. In 1836 Darwin described him as 'my beau ideal of a captain', but later commented that his journal abounded with 'Natural History of a very trashy nature'. G. C. Ingleton has described King as 'the greatest of the early Australian marine surveyors' and has written that his charts 'although not numerous, were of a quality not attained by any previous navigator in the Pacific'.

HRA (1), 9-11, 14, 16, 18-20, 22-26, (3), 2-6, (4), 1; J. Gregson, The Australian Agricultural Company 1824-1875 (Syd, 1907); G. C. Ingleton, Charting a continent (Syd, 1944); P. G. King, Letter-book 1797-1806 (ML); King family papers 1756-1903 (ML).

KINGSTON, SIR GEORGE STRICKLAND (1807-1880), engineer and politician, was born in Bandon, County Cork, Ireland, the son of George Kingston. After some training as an architect and civil engineer he migrated to England. He was employed in Birmingham in 1832. He took an active part in promoting the South Australian Act in 1834 and helped to lobby successfully for its passage through the House of Commons.

Kingston was appointed deputy-surveyor-general to the new colony and sailed with most of the surveying party in the Cygnet in March 1836. Because he detoured to Rio de Janeiro for cuddy supplies the Cygnet did not arrive at Nepean Bay until 11 September 1836, nearly a month after Colonel Light [q.v.], who was therefore left short-handed at a critical time. However, it was Kingston with John Morphett [q.v.] and Lieutenant Field who discovered the River Torrens, and the surveys of the city site were largely carried out under his supervision. At the ballot of town acres he selected several on behalf of Rowland Hill and for himself.

Kingston's ability as a surveyor was frequently questioned and it was he who was spared to return to England in August 1837 to ask for reinforcements for the Survey Department. The colonization commissioners sent him back next June with orders unpalatable to Light, who resigned with all his staff. Kingston proceeded with the country surveys almost single-handed but, soon after Governor Gawler's arrival in October 1838, he resigned. He established himself as a civil engineer, architect and surveyor, and in 1840 the Adelaide Municipal Council briefly engaged him as town surveyor. He was later engaged as inspector of public works and buildings. Among his works still standing

are the south-eastern corner of Government House (1839), the original section of the Adelaide Jail (1840), and the residence of Cummins at Camden Park (1841). He also designed the first monument to Colonel Light in Light Square (1843).

Kingston was prominent in forming the South Australian Mining Association to keep the mineral wealth of the colony from overseas speculators. With Edward Stephens [q.v.], he investigated copper finds at Burra in 1845, and then played a leading role in the 'snobs' party to defeat the 'nobs' for the mine. An original shareholder, he was appointed surveyor and architect of the mining association and with William Jacob carried out the Burra special survey of 20,000 acres. In April 1848 he was elected a director, deputy-chairman in October 1856 and chairman from 1857 until his death. In its first five years the 'monster mine' paid fifteen dividends each of 200 per cent.

In politics Kingston was a republican and a fiery supporter of civil and religious liberty. Elected for Burra and pledged by his constituents to radical reform, he entered the Legislative Council in 1851 and played a prominent part in winning for the colony a democratic Constitution with two elective chambers. In the first parliament under responsible government he was elected first Speaker in the House of Assembly. In 1857-62 he represented Burra and Clare, and Stanley in 1863-80. With one break in 1860-65 he was Speaker until 1880, holding the office competently, although unable to share the quarrels and factions which he earlier enjoyed.

Kingston was interested in the first volunteer movement and was once captain of the East Adelaide Rifles. He was also a member of the South Australian Lodge of Friendship and of the Statistical Society, keeping a valuable register of Adelaide's rainfall in 1839-79. He was knighted in 1870.

Kingston married three times: first in 1829 to Harriet (Henrietta) Ann Stuart (1807-1839), daughter of Captain Felix McDonough; second, in 1841 to Luduvina Catherina da Silva, daughter of Lieut-Colonel Charles Cameron [q.v.]; they had three daughters and three sons, the youngest of whom was Charles Cameron; and third in 1856 to Emma Mary Ann Catherine Berry, widowed daughter of Captain Lipson, first harbourmaster of South Australia. She also predeceased her husband. Kingston died at sea on 26 November 1880 on a voyage to India for his health. His funeral service was held at Trinity Church, Adelaide, where he had been a regular member.

The Public Library of South Australia and the South Australian Archives possess lithographic copies of a cadastral map of Adelaide, produced in London in 1842 after a plan made by Kingston in 1840-41, and registers of a rain gauge kept in Grote Street by Kingston 1839-60, and at West Terrace 1839-50. Parliament House, Adelaide, possesses a portrait of its first Speaker by A. MacCormac and the South Australian Archives has S. T. Gill's cartoons 'Heads of the People' including G. S. Kingston, and a portrait by Somes.

D. Pike, *Paradise of Dissent* (Melb, 1957); *Register* (Adel), 30 Aug 1869; Finniss papers (SAA).   JEAN PREST

KIRKLAND, KATHERINE (1808-1892), née Hamilton, was born on 23 February 1808 in Glasgow, Scotland, daughter of Archibald Hamilton (1772-1827), merchant, and his wife Agnes Anna, née Trokes. On 14 April 1836 at Glasgow she was married to Kenneth William, the seventh of eight children of John Kirkland and his wife Sybilla who was a sister of Sir Alexander Mackenzie, the Canadian explorer. Kenneth was then working in the sugar refining business inherited by his brother Alexander, but he became exasperated by Alexander's overbearing ways, and in June 1838 sailed from Greenock in the *Renown* with his wife and infant daughter Agnes, and with Katherine's brothers, James and Robert. The party arrived at Hobart Town in October and the men went to Port Phillip to select a farm. Kirkland chose one at Trawalla, 120 miles north-west of Melbourne, returned to Launceston, bought livestock, equipment and provisions, and in January 1839 took his family to Geelong.

Katherine's impressions of the journey through rugged country to her new home and of her two years of life there are recorded in the article *Life in the Bush* which, though published anonymously in *Chambers's Miscellany* in 1845, is undoubtedly the work of this intrepid woman. The publication is important because it gives the woman's angle on the social life of the rural community of the 1830s. She was distressed by the behaviour of many of the men, who prided themselves on the roughness of their dress and manners. Servants also were a problem, for they ran away if the settlers criticized their slovenly and dishonest practices.

Mrs Kirkland seemed to remain untouched by crude conditions. She graciously complimented her hostess on the damper when tasting it for the first time, and though barely settled in her new home managed to find accommodation for eight unexpected visitors. She went to Melbourne where her son, Kenneth William, was born on 16 September 1839, and returned in November. On New Year's day she served kangaroo soup, roast turkey, boiled mutton, parrot pie and plum pudding, all eaten at midday when the temperature was 100°, yet she could comment 'What good things we had in the bush'. The article also throws an interesting light on the early settlers' methods. She described her own activities in the dairy, and the work of the men, their troubles with wild dogs, Aboriginals and careless shepherds as they cleared their land and cared for their livestock.

The previous owners of the selection had abandoned it through fear of the Aboriginals; the Kirklands left after two years because Kenneth's family was concerned at his spending his life in manual labour. Katherine was pleased to move for the sake of her children. They went to a small farm at Darebin Creek but in April 1841 bushfires and illness drove them into Melbourne, where for six months her husband served as registrar of the Court of Requests at a salary of £150. Katherine opened a school but because of her health she sailed with the children on 10 September in the *Brilliant* for Glasgow. Her husband was forced to sell his estate, was declared insolvent in July 1842 and with the help of friends returned to Scotland. It is said that he later went to British Columbia and died there.

Katherine lived for some time with her mother and in December 1843 her third child, Isabella Christine, was born at Glasgow. Later she moved to Argyllshire and to Cheshire; she died on 10 June 1892 at the home of her granddaughter Ethel at Waterloo, Liverpool.

P. L. Brown (ed), *Clyde Company papers*, 3 (Lond, 1958); *Port Phillip Gazette* index (ML); Information from J. K. Wilson, Potten End, Herts.   JEAN HAGGER

KNATCHBULL, JOHN (1792?-1844), naval captain and convict, was probably the John Knatchbull baptized on 24 January 1793 at Norton, near Provender, Kent, England, the son of Sir Edward Knatchbull (1758-1819) and his second wife Frances, daughter of Thomas Graham, an American refugee. His father was a rollicking squire who married three times and had at least twenty children; John must have had a very casual upbringing before he was sent to Winchester School. He entered the navy as a volunteer in August 1804 and in the next years served in the *Ardent*,

Revenge, Zealand, Sybille, Téméraire, Leonidas, Cumberland, Ocean and *Ajax.* In November 1810 he passed his lieutenant's examination, served in *Sheerwater* until August 1812 when he was invalided home, and then in *Benbow* and *Queen.* In December 1813 he was commissioned to command *Doterel,* but missed the ship and was reappointed in September 1814. After Waterloo the navy was reduced and he retired on full pay until March 1818, when his pay was stopped by the Admiralty because of a debt he had incurred in the Azores.

At the Surrey Assizes on 21 August 1824, under the name of John Fitch, he was convicted of stealing with force and arms, and sentenced to transportation for fourteen years. He arrived in New South Wales in the *Asia* in April 1825 and was sent to Bathurst, where in November 1826 he was appointed constable to the mail service between Bathurst and Mount York. He was given a ticket-of-leave on 24 August 1829 after apprehending eight runaways. His ticket was altered to Liverpool when he became an overseer on the Parramatta Road. On 31 December 1831 he was charged with forging Judge Dowling's [q.v.] signature to a cheque on the Bank of Australia; he was found guilty and a sentence of death was recorded against him on 22 February 1832. This sentence was commuted to transportation for seven years to Norfolk Island, where he arrived late in 1832 in the *Governor Phillip* after several months on the hulk *Phoenix.* A conspiracy had been formed on the *Governor Phillip* to poison the ship's company, but the plot failed. In 1833 Knatchbull became partially paralysed. In January 1834, when a mutiny was planned, he claimed that he was unable to take part but offered to command a ship to South America if one could be captured. In the course of the mutiny's suppression by the guard under Foster Fyans [q.v.] Knatchbull turned informer. At the trials in Norfolk Island in July and August, after twenty-nine mutineers had been sentenced to death, Judge Burton [q.v.] severely reprimanded Fyans: 'Most improperly, Sir, did you act as a magistrate, in accepting a confession from Knatchbull; neither should any deposition have been taken from him. Throughout the trials his name has been connected in every case: he was the chief of the mutineers, the man you should have named first in the Calendar. You have saved his life, or prolonged it. He never can do good'.

After completing his secondary sentence Knatchbull returned to Sydney in May 1839 to serve the remainder of his original fourteen years. He went to Port Macquarie as an invalid and on 8 July 1842 received a ticket-of-leave, which was altered to Sydney in July 1843 to enable him to work on the coaster *Harriet.* On 6 January 1844 he was arrested for the murder of Mrs Ellen Jamieson, having been found with her money and pocket book on him, in the house where her body lay. He confessed to the crime and was brought to trial on 24 January. He was defended by Robert Lowe [q.v.], who for the first time in a British court raised the plea of moral insanity, but the judge and jury refused to accept it. Knatchbull was found guilty of murder and sentenced to death. He appealed unsuccessfully against the sentence on the ground that the judge had not directed that his body be dissected and anatomized after execution, thus making the sentence illegal. He was duly hanged on 13 February on a public gallows and has been credited by some with having 'died penitent'.

HRA (1), 13, 17, 23; H. Knatchbull-Hugessen, A *Kentish family* (Lond, 1960); C. Roderick, *John Knatchbull* (Syd, 1963); Sel cttee upon penal discipline, V & P (LA, Vic), 1856-57 (D.48), p 74; Col Sec, 1833-35, Norfolk Island, 4/2244.2 (NSWA); Executive Council minutes 1834, 4/1441, 1443 (NSWA); F. Fyans, Autobiography to 1843 (La Trobe Lib, Melb); MS cat under Knatchbull (ML); Newspaper indexes under Knatchbull (ML).

KNOPWOOD, ROBERT (1763-1838), cleric and diarist, was born on 2 June 1763, the third child and only surviving son of Robert Knopwood and his wife Elizabeth, née Barton of Threxton, Norfolk, England. He was 8 when his father died leaving debts of £10,000; part of the considerable family estate was sold to cover them, but Threxton itself remained and was worth £18,000 when Robert inherited it at 23. He was educated at Wymondham, Bury St Edmunds, and Newport, Essex; in June 1781 he was admitted a pensioner to Caius College, Cambridge, to study for the ministry. He graduated in 1786, but by this time had been borrowing substantially and was said to have become associated with the hunting and shooting set of the young Viscount Clermont. He was ordained deacon at Norwich in December 1788 and priest a year later. By this time he was so deeply in debt that he had to sell half of Threxton to Clermont; but he continued his heavy borrowing and in October 1795 was forced to sell the remainder of it. It is likely that he became chaplain to Clermont and later to Earl Spencer, through whose influence he was appointed chaplain in H.M.S. *Resolution* in 1801. He served in the West Indies and elsewhere until in 1803 he joined David Collins's expedition to Port Phillip.

From that date he began his famous diary and continued it until his death. At what is now Sorrento he conducted the first religious service in Victoria in October 1803 and, after Collins decided to abandon that settlement, the first service in Tasmania at Hobart Town in February 1804. In March 1805 he moved from his tent to Cottage Green, the house he had built at Battery Point, 'having been sixteen months three weeks and five days exposed to the inclemency of all weathers and continual robberies by convicts and servants'.

In addition to his 400-acre glebe at Clarence Plains (Rokeby), Governor King granted him 100 acres there and thirty acres in Hobart, Governor Macquarie granted him another 500 acres in 1815, and he also had a grant on the South Esk. But despite all this his ineptitude in money matters led to difficulties. By 1816 he was forced to accept an offer of £2000 for the Cottage Green property, though this fell through and in 1824 Lieut-Governor Arthur acquired it for £800. He served as a magistrate from March 1804 until 1828 and despite a reputation for kindliness showed no apparent concern at the severity of the sentences he felt called on to impose. He toured his huge parish on horseback, travelling as far as Port Dalrymple until Rev. J. Youl [q.v.] took up appointment there in 1819.

The near-illiteracy of his diary in the Royal Society of Tasmania, Hobart, is not borne out by his correspondence, and his letters show a man of finer qualities than those of the generally accepted sporting parson. The diary reveals that for many years he had a painful complaint, though his frequent indisposition was always ascribed to intemperance; but his liquor bills provide plenty of evidence of his conviviality. He entertained generously; Collins was a frequent visitor, and Knopwood often dined at Government House. The diary is a daily record of his own doings and those of the settlement; its value lies largely in the fact that often there is no other source for the period, and one wishes that he had devoted less space to the weather; he writes of his pride in his garden, and of his affection for Betty Mack, whom he had adopted as an infant when her mother was deserted by a marine. Henry Savery [q.v.], meeting Knopwood at Government House, saw him as 'an elderly parson in a straight-cut single breasted coat with an upright collar, a clergyman of the old school, remarkably

mild and placid countenance, manner easy and gentlemanly in the extreme, conversation lively and agreeable—a choice spirit'. However, he was no favourite of Macquarie, who frequently criticized his behaviour.

Knopwood's last years were saddened by sickness and poverty. In 1817 his salary of £182 was increased to £260; but in 1823 when he retired through ill health his pension was only £100, though he had his land at Rokeby. He ministered unofficially to his neighbours there until in 1826 he was appointed rector of the parish. He held this position until his death on 18 September 1838, harassed from time to time by his creditors. His grave was unmarked until Betty Mack's daughter, Mrs Stanfield, who had inherited his estate in Chancery, erected the present monument.

Rex and Thea Rienits, 'Some notes on the ancestry and life of the Rev. Robert Knopwood', *PTHRA*, 12 (1964-65); Correspondence file under Knopwood (TA).   LINDA MONKS

KNOWLES, CONRAD THEODORE (1810-1844), actor and manager, was born in England, the son of John Knowles, a Wesleyan minister. He had a sound classical education and some legal training. In April 1830 he arrived in Hobart Town where he seems to have spent some time as a tutor before moving to Sydney. Without any theatrical training or experience Knowles took a leading position amongst the performers when Barnett Levey [q.v.] opened his Theatre Royal in December 1832. During the first season he called himself Mr Cooper; from the second season onwards when he was made acting manager, he played under his own name many melodramatic, comic and tragic parts while singing and dancing in interludes. Since the beginning of his theatrical career Knowles's name was linked with that of the actress, Mrs Harriet Jones, who already in 1826 had appeared in Sydney amateur concerts; she called herself Mrs Love during the first season and from 1839 was generally known as Mrs Knowles.

Knowles was a firm favourite with Sydney audiences. He played two or three parts at every performance in the early years of the Theatre Royal and was Sydney's first Romeo, Othello and Shylock and Australia's first Hamlet and King Lear. Critics praised his deep voice, his figure and personal appearance, and the 'ease and elegance of the gentleman in his deportment' which distinguished him from any other local actor. He was very versatile, successful in comedy parts, even in the

French language, but especially in the characters of contemporary melodrama and domestic tragedy. The 'square and massive contour of his features' helped his characterization of old men. The strongest criticism brought against him was that he did not properly study his parts but the critics realized that he was permanently overburdened with far too many roles and frustrating managerial duties.

In May 1837 Knowles left for London to join his brother's legal firm but for health reasons returned to Sydney in October 1838; he made his début as Hamlet at the opening of the third season of the Victoria Theatre. His acting had become more refined since he had seen in London the great actors of his day, especially William Charles Macready (1793-1873), and his Sir Peter Teazle in *The School for Scandal* won special praise.

In 1840 he again became stage manager and his acting suffered from lack of study. When in February 1842 the Olympic Theatre opened in competition to the Victoria, Mr and Mrs Knowles with other leading players joined the new undertaking but were back at the Victoria three months later. There changes had taken place; a new leading player had appeared, F. Nesbitt

McCrone [q.v.], whose professional background gave him an advantage over the self-trained Knowles. The year 1842 also saw the introduction of 'colonial drama' in the Victoria Theatre. Knowles contributed *Salathiel*, a conventional and uninspired dramatization of E. Lytton Bulwer's novel *Leila; or the Siege of Granada* (London, 1838), which was performed twice. In May 1843 Knowles left the Victoria for another rival Sydney house, Joseph Simmons's [q.v.] City Theatre. It soon closed and Knowles, after a short tour of Tasmania, went to Melbourne; there in November 1843 he obtained a licence for the temporary theatre in Bourke Street, which he called the Victoria Theatre and unsuccessfully tried to run it on professional lines. He died after a short illness on 19 May 1844, aged 34.

According to the Sydney *Monitor*, 19 January 1838, 'Knowles was a candle lit at both ends, by nature and breeding a gentleman. His talents by nature were of the first order, but he was self-taught and overworked'.

C. Knowles, *Salathiel; or the Jewish chieftain: a drama in three acts* (Syd, 1842).

H. L. OPPENHEIM

L

LA BILLARDIERE, JACQUES-JULIEN HOUTOU DE (1755-1834), naturalist, was born at Alençon, France, on 23 October 1755. He studied botany at Montpellier before graduating as a doctor of medicine at Paris. After spending eighteen months in England examining plants brought from many parts of the world he botanized in the Alps, Cyprus, Syria and Mount Lebanon, Crete, Sardinia and Corsica. On his return to France he began to publish *Icones Plantarum Syriae rariorum descriptionibus et observationibus illustratae* (Paris, 1791), which he completed in 1812.

In 1791 he joined the expedition sent out under Bruny d'Entrecasteaux [q.v.] in *La Recherche* and *L'Espérance* to search for La Pérouse [q.v.]. On the voyage La Billardière collected not only plants but animals, fish and birds. He was a keen observer and his *Relation du Voyage à la recherche de La Pérouse* (1-2, and book of illustrations, Paris, 1800; English translation, London, 1800) contains valuable descriptions of the lands and peoples the expedition visited, including detailed accounts of the appearance and ways of the Australian Aboriginals. When, after the death of Bruny, the officers, mainly royalists, handed the ships to the Dutch in Java, La Billardière and a few other republicans were imprisoned from October 1793 until March 1795. Many members of the expedition died in Java and only 120 of the 219 who had set out from France survived to reach Mauritius.

When La Billardière arrived in France he discovered that his collections which contained more than 4000 plants, of which three-quarters were previously unknown, had been sent to England as prizes of war. He persuaded the French government to claim them. Sir Joseph Banks [q.v.] supported the claim and they were returned. In 1792 La Billardière had been made a corresponding member of L'Academie Royale des Sciences and in 1800 was elected to the Institut. He published *Nova Hollandiae Plantarum Specimen* (1-2, Paris, 1804-06), and many other works. He was aloof, independent and had a sharp tongue, but was evidently an active, versatile and devoted naturalist. He died in Paris on 8 January 1834.

According to Pierre Flourens (1794-1867), physiologist and member of the French Academy, La Billardière should be regarded as 'one of the first naturalists who made known the peculiar vegetation of the southern countries, which by their dissection and their classification, have added so much to botany'. His collections were bought by the English botanist, P. B. Webb (1793-1854), who bequeathed them to the grand duke of Tuscany; they are now in the museum of Florence. His name has been given to an Australian shrub (billardiera) of the *Apocynam* (dog's bane) family.

Nouvelle biographie générale, 28 (Paris, 1861); R. W. Giblin, *The early history of Tasmania*, 1 (Lond, 1928).

LAIDLEY, JAMES (1786-1835), deputy-commissary-general, was born in March 1786 in Perthshire, Scotland, the son of John and Sarah Laidley. He was appointed a deputy-assistant-commissary-general on 5 October 1810 and served in the Peninsular war. On 1 July 1814 he was promoted and sent to the West Indies, where he married Eliza Jane Shepheard of Barbados at Bridgetown on 10 August 1819. He then served in Canada and on 7 June 1825 became a deputy-commissary-general at Mauritius, where he stayed until ordered by the War Office to hold himself ready to proceed to New South Wales to replace William Wemyss [q.v.].

Laidley arrived in Sydney with his wife and five children in the *Orpheus* on 12 May 1827. He took charge of the commissariat in a time of deepening commercial and financial crisis. He was soon involved in local newspaper politics and on 25 July 1827 the *Sydney Gazette* accused the *Australian* of 'mawkish wheedling' to win his favour. He also made an impression on colonial society and was elected to the council of the Agricultural and Horticultural Society in October 1827, was conspicuous in attendance at social functions and in contributing to charitable causes, and became a foundation member of the Australian Racing Club in 1828. By this time Laidley was well established and had been granted five acres at Woolloomooloo Cove. He also had another six acres, four of which were cultivated, one horse and 150 cattle. Laidley gave evidence on behalf of Dr H. G. Douglass [q.v.] in a libel action in September. Next year he began his own action for libel against E. S. Hall [q.v.], and in June Laidley's Plains was named in his honour by A. Cunningham [q.v.].

In June 1827 on instructions from the Treasury Laidley began an inquiry into the administrative efficiency of the commissariat and concluded that the department had long been understaffed, causing undue delays in preparing and transmitting accounts and returns. Governor Darling agreed with these conclusions, the staff was augmented, and in August the commissariat was ordered to divide the colony's expenditure into three classes, 'Colonial, Military and Convict', with separate vouchers and requisitions for each section. A board was also appointed to regulate the accounts between the commissariat and the colonial Treasury, though Laidley never seemed to realize the importance of co-operation between these two departments. Nor did he seem aware that much distress in the colony was being caused by the export of coin to Mauritius, where the rating on silver made it a more profitable form of remittance than Treasury bills.

Laidley showed no initiative in making economic policy decisions, for he saw his duty mainly as the implementation of policy rather than its formulation. He concentrated on the administration of his department, and reported in 1830 that his staff of forty officers and clerks was not unnecessarily large because of the complexity and extent of commissariat obligations. Next year, however, the commissariat was reorganized; when the accounts branch was abolished the Audit Commission objected to Laidley's methods of cash accounting and a new system was instituted.

In 1832 Treasury bills became scarce because of large exports of whale oil and wool, and in January Laidley was forced to seek a loan of £10,000 from the colonial Treasury. Governor Bourke predicted to the Colonial Office that the military chest would probably fail unless the loan was granted, and Laidley was directed to retain a quantity of Spanish dollars, which he had been ordered to send to England.

In 1834 Laidley sought to be remunerated for unpaid duties in 1827-31 by being given the purchase money for 3840 acres; the Colonial Office admitted the justice of his claim but rejected his proposal and awarded him £825 10s. from colonial funds. He was also recommended for payment for his services on the committee superintending the construction and repair of all military and convict buildings in 1832-34. Frequent loans were made to the commissariat from the colonial Treasury in 1834-35, and Bourke had to direct that all Treasury bills be paid at par in an attempt to relieve both departments.

On 25 August 1835 Laidley was taken suddenly ill, and died five days later. He was buried with full military honours. He left a widow and eight children, but no will; as his property reverted to a son who was not yet 10, colonial observers forecast a hard time for the family. His wife died on 25 July 1860. One daughter, Theresa, married T. S. Mort at the church of St Lawrence, Sydney, on 27 October 1841, and another, Maria, married Henry Mort.

James Laidley was a competent and honest administrator, an affectionate husband and father, and a prominent member of colonial society. His tenure of office in the depression of the late 1820s and the pastoral boom of the 1830s displayed little constructive thought, and although his department was efficient in these troublous years he had very little personal influence on the economic progress of the colony.

HRA (1), 13-18; *Sydney Gazette*, 8 Oct 1827, 14 Mar, 15 Sept 1828; *Australian*, 9 Sept 1829, 13 Apr 1832; WO 58/116; Microfilm FM 1 (ML); Piper papers, v 2 (ML).

GEORGE PARSONS

LAING, CHARLES (1809?-1857), architect and surveyor, was born at Manchester, England, and appears to have been trained as an architect. He arrived in Melbourne in 1840 and after a brief period as a butcher set up practice in his profession. From 1845 to about 1850 he was city surveyor of Melbourne, without any interruption of his private practice. At least three maps of Melbourne drawn by Laing during that period are preserved.

His work as an architect ranged over ecclesiastical, institutional, domestic and business architecture and was fairly typical of the modest and unsophisticated style of the time. It included the still surviving stuccoed nave and tower of St Peter's, Eastern Hill (1846); a small church in Swanston Street, on the corner of Little Lonsdale Street, designed at half the usual fee for the penurious Free Presbyterian congregation (1847, demolished in 1863 to make way for the present church designed by Charles Webb); the Melbourne Benevolent Asylum in Victoria Street, North Melbourne (1850, now demolished); the English, Scottish and Australian Bank building on the corner of Elizabeth Street and Flinders Lane (1856, demolished in the 1880s, also attributed to Leonard Terry); a 31-room office block designed in 1856 for the solicitor Thomas Clark on the west side of Bank Place; the Royal Terrace for Hugh Glass in Brunswick Street, Fitzroy (1856, still standing with later accretions); and various other shops and houses in Melbourne and suburbs and in and round Geelong.

The best-preserved example of Laing's work is the house called Coryule, near Drysdale, in the Bellarine Peninsula. This was designed in 1849 for Miss Drysdale and Miss Newcomb [qq.v.], after the fashion of the picturesque phase of the Gothic revival. Part of Laing's plans and specifications for this house are preserved in the State Library of Victoria. The plans and specifications of three small cottages at Brighton, designed for Thomas Clark, solicitor, also survive in private possession.

Laing died at Brighton on 29 September 1857, at the age of 48, leaving his professional equipment to his son James, and the rest of his estate, which did not exceed £1000, to his wife Isabella, née Glasgow.

W. Bate, *A history of Brighton* (Melb, 1962); *Argus*, 17 Jan 1931.   J. L. O'BRIEN

LAING, HENRY (b. 1803), architect and surveyor, was a native of St Martin's, Westminster, England. On 23 March 1829 at Hereford, Laing was convicted of larceny to the value of £5 and transported to Van Diemen's Land in the *Thames*. His connexions were described as 'respectable', though his former course of life was listed as 'indifferent'. In the colony G. A. Robinson [q.v.] made immediate use of Laing's ability on some of his expeditions about 1830. In 1831 and 1833 Laing was tried for various misdemeanours even though by this time he had become a convict overseer. In March 1834 he was sent to Port Arthur and then became a clerk in the Colonial Engineer's Department, but in May 1836 he was back in Port Arthur because of several minor offences. Good conduct and useful service on Tasman Peninsula resulted in his appointment as constable on 10 September 1837.

Laing performed a variety of tasks during his four years on Tasman Peninsula. His most useful professional services included the preparation of numerous plans, elevations, sections and estimates of buildings, including the corn-mill and granary at Port Arthur, new barracks at Point Puer, and copies of buildings at the Salt Water River coal-mine and at Eaglehawk Neck. Laing was also responsible for the working drawings, plans and estimates of all the buildings that were erected while he was at Port Arthur. Some were ambitious structures but in all of them Laing demonstrated his competence by meticulous care and attention to detail. He also prepared a duplicate register of all buildings on the peninsula including plans, elevations and sections of each.

In November 1840 Laing was sent to the coal-mines to supervise the mining operations and held this position until an overseer was appointed. In 1841 he made sketches of parts of the bays on the peninsula as eligible sites for the new probation stations. In September Laing's appeal for a transfer from Port Arthur and professional employment by the government was supported by Booth, Lempriere [qq.v.] and Cart. It was not successful. In May 1842 Laing was granted a ticket-of-leave; he left no further record in Van Diemen's Land.

Correspondence file under H. Laing (TA).

ANNE MCMAHON

LAKELAND, JOHN (d. 1828), public servant, arrived in Van Diemen's Land in 1814 or 1815, 'with a view of establishing himself in the colony'. In 1816 he acted as provost-marshal when M. Tims [q.v.] was suspended and in July 1818 Lieut-Governor Sorell appointed him assistant to Major T. Bell [q.v.], engineer and inspector of public works in Hobart Town, at a salary of £75 with rations and three servants. In this post Lakeland became familiar with the general management of the convicts and with the procedure relating to their disposal and coercion. In 1820 he succeeded T. R. Crowder [q.v.] as principal superintendent of convicts and in 1825 resigned as assistant inspector of public works because the duties were too arduous to enable him to give full attention to his other office. As principal superintendent Lakeland was responsible for all matters concerning convict discipline and, after the arrival of Lieut-Governor Arthur, for putting into effect the policy of tightening up the control of the prisoners. During Lakeland's tenure office hours of work were lengthened, task work abolished, barracks opened, the payment of wages ceased, and the penal establishments of Macquarie Harbour and Maria Island were founded. In 1826, when the department was reorganized and the system of punishment by labour in chaingangs was begun, the position of some convicts was made more humiliating by the superintendent's recommendation that they be dressed in suitably conspicuous yellow clothing; the distillery at the Cascades was bought for use as a factory for the female convicts. On 26 November 1828, after a short illness brought on by assiduous application to his duties and the grievous effect on him of the death of a favourite daughter, he died at his residence at Pittwater.

Lakeland held land at Pittwater in 1818; he received 300 acres from Governor Macquarie in 1820 and 300 from Governor Brisbane in 1825. In 1830 his trustees received an additional 1960 acres near the River Styx. On 17 August 1818 Lakeland had married Mary Louisa, a daughter of Surgeon Thomas Arndell [q.v.] and sister-in-law of James Gordon [q.v.]. She survived him with two sons, James Gordon and John Thomas, and two daughters, Emily Elizabeth and Louisa. In 1831 Lakeland's widow married Thomas H. White; she died at her home, Macquarie Street, Hobart, in May 1835.

Lieut-Governor Arthur held Lakeland in high regard and in 1827 had supported his application for a further salary increase—it had been raised to £150 in 1825—to £400. He attended Lakeland's funeral, and in reporting his death declared that the government had 'been deprived of an intelligent and extremely indefatigable and zealous officer'. His office was the keystone in Arthur's administration and was exposed to temptation, but Lakeland filled it 'with great benefit to the Public Service'. The *Hobart Town Courier* declared that the convicts themselves lamented his loss 'with little less regret than those in the higher walks of life'.

HRA (3), 2-6; *Hobart Town Gazette*, 25 July, 29 Aug 1813, 1 July 1820; *Hobart Town Courier*, 29 Nov, 6 Dec 1828; *Tasmanian*, 28 Nov 1828, 8 May 1835; *Australian*, 18 Mar 1831; GO 33/24/837 (TA); CSO 1/301/7311, 1/354/8076, 1/558/12298 (TA).

L. L. ROBSON

LAMB, JOHN (1790-1862), naval officer, politician and merchant, was born at Penrith, England, the son of Captain Lamb of the East India Co.'s service. In recognition of distinguished conduct in saving his ship from a French privateer in 1798 Captain Lamb was given preferments for three of his sons in the navy. At 11 John became a first-class volunteer in the *Port Mahon* sloop commanded by his uncle, William Buchanan, on the Mediterranean Station, and within a year was a midshipman in the *Northumberland*, the youngest in the fleet at the capture of the fort of Alexandria in 1801. In 1803 he served in several ships patrolling the Channel and the Irish coast; in the *Warrior* he won the favour of Captain William Bligh who requested Sir Joseph Banks [q.v.] in April 1805 to transfer him to the ship bringing Bligh to New South Wales as governor. Promoted lieutenant in June 1808, he shared next November in the *Amethyst's* capture of the French frigate *La Thétis* off Lorient

after a furious contest of more than three hours. His last naval service was in the *Union* with the Toulon Fleet. He returned to England in August 1814 on half-pay and became associated with Buckles, Bagster & Buchanan. He sailed for them in September 1815 and June 1819 as master of the transport *Baring* with convicts to Sydney and in 1825-28 as master of the merchant ship *Palmira* on the Indian service.

A gratuity from the Patriotic Fund during his naval services provided him with a small capital, and with his cousin Walter Buchanan he formed the house of Lamb, Buchanan & Co. As its resident partner he arrived in Sydney with his wife and five children in the *Resource* in May 1829, expecting to remain at least ten years. Proving a capital of £2200 and claiming that he could triple it, he received in May 1830 a primary grant of 2560 acres which he selected in the County of St Vincent, and in 1838 he applied for a secondary grant.

Lamb soon became involved in public affairs. He was appointed justice of the peace in 1830 but rarely appeared on the bench. In 1836 Governor Bourke omitted his name and those of three other magistrates from the new Commission of the Peace, claiming that all four had acted on the bench in concert and 'used their power as Ministers of Justice to forward a political Intrigue'. Their strong protests were futile, for Glenelg approved Bourke's action. In 1844, however, Lamb was reappointed by Governor Gipps, a former acquaintance, and in September he was nominated to the Legislative Council. After it was reformed in 1851 he rejoined it until February 1853 as an elected member for the city of Sydney. In the legislature he was actively associated with at least ten select committees dealing generally with trade and economic matters and with communications. At the great protest meeting at Circular Quay in June 1849 when the convict transport *Hashemy* arrived he urged his fellow colonists to protect their adopted land 'from being again degraded and polluted by the name of penal settlement'; after moving the first of the anti-transportation resolutions he was appointed to the deputation that took the resolutions to the governor.

Lamb's greatest activity was in the commercial world. When his partnership with Buchanan was dissolved in 1834 he carried on business as Lamb & Co., woollen brokers and shipping agents. In 1837 he took Frederick Parbury as his partner. Lamb's commercial experience and business acumen were much in demand and he became a director of many large public companies, including the Sydney Alliance Assurance Co., the Australian Fire and Life Assurance Co. and the Sydney Railroad Co. He was a director and several times chairman of the Commercial Banking Co. of Sydney in 1834-50. In 1851-52 he was a founder and first chairman of the Sydney Chamber of Commerce and of the Royal Exchange.

His house, Spencer Lodge, was in the fashionable mercantile locale at Miller's Point, close to his wharf and stores in Darling Harbour. In 1855 he retired with a large fortune, returned to England leaving part of his grown up family behind, and built a house at Clapham Park, near London. After about two years he returned to Sydney and was again active in public affairs. In July 1857 he re-entered the Legislative Council as one of the first quinquennial appointments but resigned in 1861. As senior warden of the Light, Pilot and Navigation Board he conducted the inquiry into the loss of the *Catherine Adamson* and reported on Sydney's pilot service after the two great shipping disasters in 1857. He had accepted the rank of retired naval commander in May 1846.

In March 1823 at Islington, London, Lamb had married Emma Trant, daughter of John Robinson of Holloway, a London merchant and deputy-chairman of Lloyds. Of their eight sons and six daughters, a son and a daughter died in infancy. The eldest son Walter (1825-1906) became a director of the Commercial Banking Co. of Sydney and a legislative councillor in 1889-93; the second son Edward William (1828-1910) was secretary for lands in Queensland in 1867-68; the youngest son Alfred (1845-1890) represented West Sydney in the Legislative Assembly in 1889-90. John Lamb died at Larbert Lodge, Darlinghurst, on 17 January 1862 and his wife, aged 77, on 27 August 1880; both were buried in St Jude's churchyard, Randwick.

HRA (1), 9-10, 14, 16, 18-20, 23-24, 26; W. R. O'Byrne, A naval biographical dictionary (Lond, 1849); SMH, 12 June 1849; Sunday Times (Syd), 8 Sept 1907; J. Lamb, Letter-book, 1826-34 (ML); Land, 2/2093 (NSWA).

G. P. WALSH

LAMBE, DAVID (1803-1843), architect and farmer, was born in London, the second son of William Lambe (1765-1847) and his first wife Harriett Mary, daughter of Captain John Welsh of Plymstock, Devon. He came of an old Warwickshire family; his father, a well-known and much respected doctor, had moved to practise in Bloomsbury about 1803. David Lambe was educated at Charterhouse. In May 1823 he sought employment in Van Diemen's Land and in August a grant of land; this the Colonial Office promised since Lambe possessed the needed capital of £500. His motive for migration is unknown, though either his father's notorious eccentricities and vegetarianism or his sister's marriage to Saxe Bannister [q.v.], appointed attorney-general of New South Wales in October 1823, may have influenced his decision. He sailed in the *Adrian*, which also carried the newly appointed Lieut-Governor Arthur, and reached Hobart Town on 12 May 1824. A week after arrival Lambe wrote to Arthur seeking his 'protection' should a vacancy occur in either the architectural or surveying department, and on 3 June Arthur appointed him colonial architect at a salary of £150.

Lambe filled this office for three years and three months. In his own words 'he conceived his duty to be to draw out plans and specifications of all buildings proposed to be erected by the Crown, to inspect the progress of the work'. There is little evidence on which to assess the quality of his design work, but he is known to have inspected and reported upon works under construction including the nave of St John's Church at Launceston, St Matthew's Church at New Norfolk, the church and parsonage at Sorell, the stone bridge commenced by Major Bell [q.v.] and the courthouse at Richmond and the commissariat store at Launceston, now known as the Paterson Barracks. He reported upon the condition of St David's Church, Old Government House, the penitentiary and the parsonage in Hobart. At times he was associated with the surveyor, J. H. Wedge [q.v.], in making valuations of country properties and improvements. In January 1827 he was occupying a farm at Sandy Bay. Later that year he prepared drawings for the conversion of T. Y. Lowes's [q.v.] distillery at the Cascades into a female factory, but John Lee Archer [q.v.], immediately after his arrival, designed an amendment which the lieut-governor considered to be 'a very great improvement'. The appointment of Archer as civil engineer and colonial architect in August 1827 'unavoidably displaced Mr. Lambe'; from that time the records of his activity are meagre but show that he was largely concerned with farming and horticulture.

On 26 January 1832 at St David's Church, Hobart, he married Harriet Catherine, the sister of Saxe Bannister. In December he was living at Ivanhoe, New Norfolk, where he was a magistrate and appeared in the role of steward at the New Norfolk races. Both his married life and his period of apparent prosperity were brief. His wife died in May 1833, and in November 1838 Lambe applied without success to the colonial secretary for employment. In 1840 his farm of some twelve acres at Sandy Bay, known as Lambe's Gardens and planted with a great number and variety of fruit trees, was bought for £2150 by Thomas Wood Rowlands, a solicitor. Part of this property on which an early homestead stands is known as Ashfield. Lambe was living at Brown's River when a meeting of his creditors was called at the Hobart Court House in October 1842. He died at Brown's River of 'serious apoplexy' on 20 December 1843.

Lambe had the spirit of the pioneer and in the absence of more highly trained persons he coped with the architectural work of the colony in the early years of Arthur's governorship. Though his private enterprise had little success he appears to have been regarded with respect in the community and he is remembered principally for his connexion with some of Tasmania's oldest extant buildings.

HRA (3), 4-6; H. S. Wyndham, *William Lambe, M.D.* (Lond, 1940); *Hobart Town Gazette*, 14 May 1824; *Hobart Town Courier*, 28 Jan, 14 Dec 1832, 7 Oct 1842; *Independent* (Launceston), 1 June 1833; *Colonial Times*, 14 July 1840; *Cornwall Chronicle*, 23 Dec 1843; CSO 1 (TA); LSD 1 (TA); GO 33/1 (TA).

ROY S. SMITH

LANDALE, THOMAS (1795-1851), medical practitioner, was born probably in Scotland. He obtained a licentiate of the Royal College of Surgeons at Edinburgh, and attended medical schools in London and Paris. As surgeon in the *Midas* he arrived at Sydney in February 1821 and applied to Governor Macquarie for a land grant, claiming that he had goods worth £450 and £800 in cash. He was promised 800 acres in Van Diemen's Land, which he located near Campbell Town. In April he sailed from Hobart Town in the *Midas* for England, and returned in the *Christina* in January 1823. For at least a year he practised in Hobart 'near the bridge in Murray Street', and then moved to Launceston; on the banks of the North Esk he bought 'a fine farm', Elphin. There on 15 February 1825 he married Harriett, the eldest daughter of Richard Dry senior [q.v.]. In May 1829 he opened an apothecary's shop in Charles Street, Launceston; he was highly regarded as a medical practitioner and later practised with Drs Pugh [q.v.] and Grant as his partners. In 1840 Landale visited Britain with his family.

Landale became one of the most prosperous and respected citizens of Launceston. In 1828 he had been elected a director of the Cornwall Bank and later became a prominent shareholder in insurance companies and in such ventures as the Tasmanian Steam Navigation Co. He also acquired much property in town and country. Aged 56, he died on 3 June 1851, 'universally respected'.

Of his four sons, the eldest, Thomas, died in 1848 while returning from England in the *Rattler*. Three of his daughters married army officers.

Col Sec in letters, 4/1826 (NSWA); Correspondence file under T. Landale (TA).

P. H. WESSING

LANDOR, EDWARD WILLSON (1811-1878), solicitor, writer and pioneer, was born in England, a distant cousin of Walter Savage Landor, the English author. He apparently had some legal training in England and in 1834 his uncle gave him a junior partnership in his attorney's practice. He did not persevere in this and, accompanied by his two brothers, Henry and G. W., he emigrated to Western Australia for health reasons and arrived in the *Advocate* in August 1841.

The three brothers took up land near York but the youngest was left to run the property while Edward remained in Perth as a barrister and Henry practised medicine in York. In November 1842 Edward was appointed commissioner of the new Court of Requests in Perth, Guildford and Fremantle. He was granted leave in 1846 and resigned in 1847. He returned to England, where he married, and in 1847 published his partially autobiographical book, *The Bushman or, Life in a New Country*. It described his voyage to Australia and gave an entertaining and useful record of colonial life. It is valued as one of the few books on early Western Australia; according to Rev. J. R. Wollaston [q.v.], it gave the most accurate and just account of colonial policy which he had read. Landor returned to Western Australia in 1859 with his wife and three children, and resumed legal practice in Perth, now as a solicitor. He took a keen interest in the political life of the colony and as a journalist and lecturer was highly popular. He was a prolific contributor to the press using various pen-names, the best-known being Colonicus, under which he wrote often for the *Inquirer*. For a time he acted as editor of the *Perth Gazette*. In 1866 he gave up a good legal practice to become police magistrate for Perth. He was suspended from this office in 1872 by Governor Weld for partiality in committing L. C. Burges for trial on a charge of shooting an Aboriginal with intent to commit bodily harm rather than on a charge of murder. An account of the affair was published by Landor's friends, *The Case of E. W. Landor, Esq., J.P., Police Magistrate, Western Australia* (Perth, 1872). He was subsequently cleared and reinstated on instructions from the Colonial Office, and his dignified attitude to the affair earned him public respect. He continued in his office until his death on 24 October 1878. He left three daughters and a son, his wife having predeceased him by two years.

E. M. Russell, 'Early lawyers of WA', *JRWAHS*, 4 (1949-54).   M. MEDCALF

LANG, GIDEON SCOTT (1819-1880), pastoralist, was born on 25 January 1819 at Selkirk, Scotland, a son of Andrew Lang, a factory owner and writer to the signet. He left school at 16 and for the next five years worked in turn on a farm, in a counting house and in a bank. In 1839 his brothers, Thomas, a doctor, and William (1823-1877), trained as a farmer, migrated to Melbourne and took up land on the Saltwater River near Melbourne; in 1841 Gideon Scott Lang joined them. Finding shepherding monotonous he offered to build a toll-bridge over the Yarra, but a similar offer by other investors was accepted. Next he established a fishing venture but soon abandoned it for lack of reliable managers and because, he said, rivals encouraged unrest among his men and burned his nets and boats. He then rejoined his brothers and with them squatted on Heatherlea and later Narmbool in virgin country near Buninyong. Lang discussed the squatting problem in a treatise *Land and Labour in Australia . . .* (Melbourne, 1845) in which he proposed that a squatter should be allowed eight years of free occupation of as much land as his stock needed; at the end of that term his run should be surveyed and he should be allowed to buy enough land to carry his stock, including all land within three miles of permanent water, the price to be proportionate to the stock the land would carry and paid in fifteen annual instalments. Money paid by settlers was to be used to assist migration, chiefly of potential station hands.
At Narmbool the Langs succeeded in finding a peaceful solution to the problem presented by a large group of Aboriginals congregated on their run by making an agreement to feed some of them if no

attacks were made on their stock. As a result of this and later experiences he wrote *The Aborigines of Australia* (Melbourne, 1865) advising stern but consistent treatment of the natives, who should be given food by those who settled on their land. Lang's knowledge of their ways had been deepened by long overland journeys, always accompanied by Aboriginals, in search of good country: in 1845, for example, across the desert south-east of Lake Alexandrina; in 1846 from Bathurst, New South Wales, to Portland, Victoria.
In 1848 the Langs bought Mungadal in the Riverina and soon afterwards Pevensey. They bought other runs in this area, including Wanganella North, and eventually held a 30-mile frontage on the Murrumbidgee. For some years the later town of Hay was known as Lang's Crossing Place. In 1849 Lang edited *The Australian Merino* by Thomas Shaw [q.v.]. He was exploring in southern Queensland in 1850 but when the gold rushes made it difficult to retain enough stockmen the Langs overlanded their cattle from Queensland to their Riverina runs and G. S. Lang went to the diggings as a correspondent of the *Sydney Morning Herald*. Early in 1851 on the Darling Downs Lang had obtained information from Aboriginals about the death of Leichhardt [q.v.] and his party. Lang was eager to make a search and the Legislative Council voted £2000 for it, but because of drought the expedition was not sent. In 1856 he was elected to the Legislative Assembly for Liverpool Plains and Gwydir; when parliament was dissolved in December 1857 Lang did not seek reelection but took his family to Europe where he remained until 1862. While touring in 1859 he went to Como, where he had a conversation with Garibaldi, about whom he wrote admiringly in letters to *The Times*, 20 June 1859 and 1 June 1860. According to the *Sydney Mail*, July 1880, these letters 'attracted considerable attention, and his representations to the English Government led to its insisting on the Austrian Government treating Garibaldians as belligerents'.
In April 1863 the Riverina Association was formed, with Lang as president and George Peppin as vice-president, to protect the interests of Riverina landholders; the association advocated separation from New South Wales. In this period Lang bought land on the Darling River and a station near Wangaratta, Victoria. In 1866 he became first chairman of directors of the Commercial Bank in Melbourne and stood for the Victorian parliament without success. In 1879 he managed the agriculture and stock department of the International

Exhibition in Sydney; he died on 13 July 1880. In July 1854 he had married Elizabeth Jane, eldest daughter of William Cape [q.v.]. She died in April 1871, aged 39; they had three sons and a daughter.

Lang was an adventurous and enterprising pioneer always alert to the possibility of fresh avenues of profit in a new and expanding community. Versatile, assertive and cultivated, he was of a type not uncommon among men of means who settled on the Australian pastoral frontiers in the middle part of the century.

R. B. Ronald, *The Riverina, people and properties* (Melb, 1960); M. L. Kiddle, *Men of yesterday* (Melb, 1961); *SMH*, 7 Jan 1857; Sel cttee on the Riverine districts, Report, *V & P* (LA Vic), 1862-63 (42); D. E. Wilkie and F. Mueller, 'Report on white men's graves in the interior', *PRGSSA*, 16 (1914-15); N. F. Sizer, 'Gideon Scott Lang', *JRAHS*, 47 (1961).

LANG, JOHN DUNMORE (1799-1878), Presbyterian clergyman, politician, educationist, immigration organizer, historian, anthropologist, journalist, gaol-bird and, in his wife's words engraved on his statue in Sydney, 'Patriot and Statesman', was born on 25 August 1799 at Greenock, Scotland, the eldest child of William Lang, a small landowner who worked as a ships' joiner, and his wife, Mary Dunmore, who came from a similar background; she had formidable powers of moral indignation and such capacity for vituperation that in comparison her son's most savage strictures seemed but a mild remonstrance. Lang was educated for the ministry at the Largs parish school and the University of Glasgow, winning many scholarships and prizes (M.A., 1820). He later remembered the divinity professor, Dr Stevenson Macgill, as his most influential teacher, but was perhaps even more impressed by Dr Thomas Chalmers, then minister of the Tron Church in Glasgow. Thus Lang was brought up by Evangelicals who were beginning to challenge the prevailing moderatism within the Church of Scotland. He was licensed to preach by the Presbytery of Irvine in 1820 but, having an Evangelical aversion to the common system of lay patronage, considered emigrating overseas and, being assured by his younger brother in Sydney that a suitable field of labour there awaited him, he sailed in 1822, arriving in May 1823. He was the first Presbyterian minister in Sydney, although Rev. Archibald Macarthur [q.v.] had settled in Hobart Town in December 1822. The Scottish community in Sydney welcomed Lang as their minister. His first task was to build a church. Private subscriptions, he hoped, would be supplemented by a grant from the government which was both aiding Catholics and supporting the Church of England. An official refusal in insulting terms signed but not written by Governor Brisbane provoked Lang to a spirited defence of the Presbyterians; this sharp rebuke to the governor deprived Lang of support from influential sections of the community. Yet sufficient private funds were collected to begin Scots Church, which was finished in 1826.

Early in 1824 Lang's parents and their family arrived in Sydney. Soon afterwards Lang returned to England where he persuaded Bathurst to grant him an annual stipend of £300, obtained his doctorate of divinity and induced Rev. John McGarvie [q.v.] to become the minister at Portland Head. Back in Sydney friction between Lang and Dissenting Presbyterians was caused by personal conflicts, suspicion that Lang was insufficiently Evangelical and alarm at his readiness to challenge the civil authorities. This culminated in Lang's first polemical work, *Narrative of the Settlement of The Scots Church, Sydney, New South Wales* (Sydney, 1828), which was a violent attack on Deputy-Commissary-General Wemyss [q.v.], the leading Presbyterian layman, who had first befriended and provided hospitality for Lang but whose support for Lang's church had since grown cold. However, one of Lang's minor targets was James Elder [q.v.], who sued him for libel, claiming £300 for being described as a 'renegade missionary'; he was awarded damages of one farthing.

Lang, always eager to promote education, opened a primary school in 1826; John Robertson was one of its first pupils. In 1829, prompted by proposals to revive the Free Grammar School, Lang approached Archdeacon Broughton [q.v.], who was then planning The King's School, to see if he could co-operate with him in promoting secondary education. At first he thought this possible, but later feared that Presbyterians would not receive fair treatment in an Anglican school. He therefore appealed to Governor Darling to grant land for a Presbyterian school. This was refused, so in 1830 Lang joined, much to Broughton's disappointment, a group, predominantly Dissenting and emancipist, which was proposing to establish the non-denominational Sydney College. This venture provoked much sound criticism, not only from Broughton, as tending to produce irreligious education; but in the thinly settled colony the smaller denominations had little alternative. In 1830, however, before Sydney College was built, Lang inherited considerable properties from his father and, hiding his intentions from the governor and public, decided to abandon Sydney College and to sail again for England to make arrangements for a Presbyterian secondary school.

In England in December 1830 Lang was struck by the country's poverty and thought this might be relieved by emigration, while well chosen migrants might produce a moral reformation in New South Wales. Lang was alarmed by the gross wickedness produced by transportation, and free emigration complemented his plans for education. He persuaded the Colonial Office to grant a loan of £3500 for the establishment of a college on condition that an equal sum was subscribed privately. He obtained an advance of £1500 on this loan to take free migrants to Australia. Lang selected about 140 persons, Scottish tradesmen and their families. They agreed to repay their fares out of wages received when building the college. Lang recruited three schoolmasters and two more Presbyterian ministers. He also persuaded his 18-year-old cousin, Wilhelmina Mackie, to marry him. The wedding was to be at Cape Town to avoid opposition from Lang's mother, anticipated because of the difference in their ages. The marriage was happy and in all his public controversies Lang was comforted by a warmly harmonious family life, marred only by tragedies involving his children; of ten, five died in infancy.

Returning to Sydney in 1831 Lang was applauded for his patriotism and enterprise in bringing such valuable migrants, tradesmen better than any in the colony, who were to raise standards among Sydney builders. The Australian College buildings were commenced. But an intemperate attack by Lang on the Church and School Corporation, the lands of which, he suggested, could be sold to pay for immigration, led to a censure by the Legislative Council in 1832 which impaired his credit and lessened the public's financial support; so Lang was forced to use his own property to complete the buildings. Nevertheless the Australian College opened in 1831, and survived with ups and downs till 1854; at its best in the late 1830s it appears to have been run very efficiently.

In 1833-34 Lang again returned to Britain. As always on voyages, he wrote; this time it was his *An Historical and Statistical Account of New South Wales, both as a Penal Settlement and as a British Colony*, 1-2 (London, 1834) which ran to four editions. The *Westminster Review* suggested that its title should read 'The History of Doctor Lang, to which is added the History of New South Wales'; however, it was among the most widely read and fully informed accounts of Australia. In 1835 Lang commenced the weekly *Colonist*, which ran till 1840. The *Colonial Observer* (1841-44) and the *Press* (1851) were also Lang papers. Lang wished to use these journals to protect himself and the Australian College from newspaper attacks and to improve colonial morality. The upright young minister was always horrified by the licentiousness of the convict colony. Even his agitation for free immigration had a moral purpose, for he hoped the immigrants would behave better than convicts and emancipists and, by reducing colonial wages, lessen the workers' deplorable dissipation. He attacked fancy dress balls, Sabbath picnicking and alcoholic intemperance. A major target was the colonial press, especially that section run by convicts or emancipists. In June 1835 the emancipist, Edward O'Shaughnessy [q.v.] of the *Sydney Gazette* brought a libel action prosecuted by W. C. Wentworth [q.v.]. At the preliminary hearing Lang defended himself so ably that the case lapsed. Lang's sharpest journalistic attacks were made on sexual immorality; he was determined that none should enjoy the pleasures of matrimony without undertaking its responsibilities. He drove some offenders from society, one of whom later committed suicide. Lang recounted their sufferings with an implacable, hard impartiality.

In 1836 Lang again visited Britain, determined to recruit sufficient new clergy to outvote the backsliders and their abettors. The clergymen who had been recommended to him were often deemed suitable for the colony because they were unsuitable at home. Too many were over-fond of the bottle. Other members of the Presbytery of New South Wales, established in 1832, were far away in the bush, in ill health or insufficiently energetic to take action against this evil. He embarked in July, and before leaving Sydney Harbour wrote an article on the settlements at Twofold Bay and Port Phillip, which was sent ashore by the pilot for publication in the next issue of the *Colonist*. His recruitment of clergy in Scotland, northern Ireland and Germany was made easier by Bourke's 1836 Church Act which provided more liberal government support for religion. Lang obtained twelve Presbyterian clergymen, three Lutheran missionaries and ten German lay assistants, none too many, for he saw the Roman Catholic Church making every effort 'not only to rivet the chains of popery on a deluded people in the Australian Colonies, but to extend the reign of superstition over the neighbouring and highly interesting isles of the Pacific'. Lang also greatly stimulated Australian immigration by persuading destitute Scottish Highlanders, vainly seeking government funds to emigrate to Canada, to request government assisted passages to Australia. Over four thousand individuals were thus gained for New South Wales.

Lang returned to Sydney in December 1837 confident that 'McGarvie and his drunken party' would be 'done now and for ever'. But instead of relying on the increased numbers within the Presbytery of New South Wales to purify that court, he decided to establish, with the support of five new ministers mostly from Ulster, a new church court, entitled the Synod of New South Wales, which he hoped would soon embrace several presbyteries and quickly deprive the Presbytery of New South Wales of all influence. He miscalculated. McGarvie, a moderate, whose respect for civil authority approached Erastianism, retained the support of the government and the General Assembly of the Church of Scotland. So schism grew, for the Synod of New South Wales, while embracing the Westminster Confession of Faith, forbade appeals from its decisions to any church court overseas. The schism caused Lang's fifth trip to England in 1839 to secure the disallowance of an 1837 Presbyterian Church Act which recognized the Presbytery of New South Wales as the controlling body of the Presbyterian Church, to persuade the British government that colonial Presbyterians were independent of the General Assembly of the Church of Scotland, and to obtain for the Synod of New South Wales the hitherto withheld financial support implied by Bourke's Church Act. But the Colonial Office, advised by the General Assembly, refused to interfere with the Presbytery of New South Wales, and Lang failed to assert his clerical independence.

Early in 1840 he sailed for the United States to investigate how its churches managed without government support and, if possible, to raise sufficient money to make him independent of the General Assembly. In travels through eleven States from Massachusetts to South Carolina he was horrified by the wickedness of Catholic immigrants who both desecrated the Sabbath and formed an undue proportion of convicted criminals, was delighted by the evident moral and financial success of Presbyterian churches, and deeply impressed by the great merit of republican government based on the independent sovereignty of each State and a large measure of local autonomy. During Lang's absence the two Presbyterian groups in New South Wales combined to form the Synod of Australia in connexion with the established Church of Scotland. Lang returned from England in March 1841 and joined this body.

In October the synod agreed to accept suitable Australian College graduates as candidates for the ministry. This decision was important to Lang as it affected three of his great interests, the training of a native-born ministry, the future of the Australian College and the extension of the church. He immediately went to Port Phillip and Van Diemen's Land to raise funds for the college. With the approval of a congregational meeting, he was absent from Scots Church for five Sundays, arranging supply for his pulpit by Rev. Thomas Atkins [q.v.], a Congregationalist who had unsuccessfully applied to join the Presbyterians, but in November twenty-eight members of Lang's congregation formally complained to the Presbytery of Sydney of Atkins's unsuitability. In January 1842 the presbytery resolved generally on the undesirability of ministerial absences and referred the complaint about Atkins to synod, which admonished Lang to pay more attention to resolutions of church courts. On 6 February from his pulpit Lang denounced the Synod of Australia as 'a mere synagogue of Satan', actuated by 'a spirit of rancorous hostility' which 'could have emanated only from the Father of Evil'. He said he saw no abstract objection to a connexion between church and state, but that in New South Wales this meant state support of error, and, indeed, of the 'damnable delusion'. Moreover, within the Presbyterian Church it produced 'worldly-mindedness . . . lamentable inefficiency . . . clerical delinquency and . . . strife and contention'. He announced his resignation from Scots Church, intending to establish Presbyterianism in New Zealand. But his congregation wished him to stay and it was agreed that he should, and that Scots Church should renounce all state support and all connexion with the Synod of Australia. Lang's letter of resignation to the presbytery announced that he and the congregation would retain the Scots Church property. In October the synod ordered Lang to answer charges of slander, divisive action and contumacy. At the meeting Lang prepared to answer charges relating to his actions before 6 February, but refused to acknowledge synod's authority on or after that date. There were no charges for anything before 6 February so Lang and his supporters left the meeting, which proceeded to depose him from the Christian ministry, the heaviest sentence within its power. However, synod took no legal action in the civil courts at this time to obtain the Scots Church property. Lang could abandon the synod and renounce state aid because his congregation was perhaps as large and wealthy as all other Presbyterian congregations in the colony put together. He thus anticipated the disruption of the Church of Scotland and the subsequent formation of colonial Free Churches. But despite some similarity of principle Lang did not join with the Free Churchmen in New South Wales.

In June 1843 Lang was elected by the Port Phillip District to the Legislative Council in Sydney. In the next five months he served as chairman or member of nine select committees and made 184 speeches and statements and, irked by the £81,000 civil list, spoke of no taxation without representation, hinting that 100,000 free-born Australians, though now loyal to the Crown, would presently emulate the North American colonists. In August 1844 Lang moved for the separation of Port Phillip from New South Wales. He ably described the evident political and financial disadvantages suffered by the residents of Port Phillip and the gross injustice of holding them to New South Wales against their will. But the motion was supported only by members elected by the Port Phillip District. Lang later suggested to the Separation Committee in Melbourne that the members for Port Phillip should present a joint petition to the Queen. Lang prepared this petition which was favourably received and he became widely regarded, not only in Melbourne, as the author of separation. In 1844 Robert Lowe's [q.v.] select committee on education reported strongly in favour of a National system. Lang had earlier opposed this proposal, but now gave it his full support. Lowe resigned his seat before the report was submitted and Lang moved its adoption. The report was adopted, but Governor Gipps refused his concurrence and continued the denominational system.

In 1845, when the colony was recovering from depression and it seemed likely that assisted migration would be resumed, Lang decided to visit England again to encourage Protestant migration. He accordingly made two extensive tours in the Moreton Bay and Port Phillip Districts to gain information about Australia as a field for British emigration. He sailed with his wife and family in July 1846 by way of Brazil where he visited the University at Olinda and was afterwards elected an honorary member of the Literary Institute there. The next three years were among the busiest of Lang's busy life. He tried unsuccessfully to modify the Order in Council implementing the 1846 Squatting Act and to promote colonial railway and steamship companies. He published a pamphlet urging Irish Home Rule. But his main task was persuading people to migrate to Australia. Besides his books and pamphlets, some distributed free, he wrote many letters for the English press, including a weekly letter from March 1848 in the Evangelical *British Banner*. He made extended lecture tours beginning in the cotton manufacturing districts. He hoped to promote cotton growing in the Moreton Bay District and thereby add a valuable industry to Australia, provide employment for migrants and also undermine negro slavery, which he thought would collapse when free labour proved more efficient. By popular request he lectured widely, speaking in London, Bristol, Birmingham and many other English cities. He twice toured Ulster and spoke many times in the smaller towns as well as in the larger cities of Scotland. Despite a little money from well wishers in Australia he mainly supported himself and was often short of funds. Once he had to flee Edinburgh to avoid arrest for debt.

His continual theme was that the grinding poverty of Britain could be readily relieved by the boundless opportunities in Australia. He believed a prosperous Protestant peasantry in Australia would ease the evils of English industrialism. He gave many a desire to migrate to Australia; but the costs of transport remained an obstacle, especially when the fare to America was so much cheaper. Lang vainly tried to overcome this problem by founding emigration societies and joint-stock companies, and sought assistance from the government, which was then subsidizing approved migrants. He proposed that reputable migrants who paid their own fares should, in return, receive a free grant of crown land. Prolonged correspondence failed to secure this concession, so Lang visited Benjamin Hawes, under-secretary for the colonies, at his home in Brighton. According to Lang, Hawes twice verbally approved his plans, although Hawes later denied it. But Lang at once arranged for about 270 migrants to sail in the *Fortitude* in September 1848, on the assumption that they would receive free land in proportion to their passage money. This land, of course, was not granted. Lang attempted to co-operate with the emigration officials over his next three emigrant ships, but was so annoyed by them that he decided for his fifth and sixth ships, in 1849, to act independently. Three ships went to Port Phillip and three to Moreton Bay, taking more than 1200 migrants. Before returning on the last of his emigrant ships, Lang addressed an open letter to Earl Grey in which he criticized the whole administration of the Colonial Office, suggesting that assisted migration was a plot, through mixed marriages, to Romanize New South Wales. He bitterly attacked proposals to resume transportation and insisted that the Australian colonies be given control over their own affairs. After suggesting that Grey be dismissed and impeached he forecast the emergence of the United States of Australia.

In lectures delivered in Sydney in April 1850 Lang proclaimed his republicanism for the Australian colonies. This republicanism was due partly to his belief in the necessity of local self-rule, because he thought all government from a distance was bad government, and partly to his recent treatment by the British government and his dislike of aristocratic influences in English society and politics. Usually he chose to express his republicanism in his published writings, but ignored it at elections, preferring instead to cheer enthusiastically for the Queen when his opponent called for this show of loyalty. In 1850, however, he thought an Australian republic a serious possibility, for with aid from Henry Parkes, J. R. Wilshire and other radicals he founded the Australian League to encourage a sense of national identity, to resist any further convict transportation and to promote, by moral means exclusively, the entire freedom of the Australian colonies and their incorporation into one political federation. The Australian League made little impression, although Lang's republican ideals, as published later in *Freedom and Independence for the Golden Lands of Australia* (London, 1852) and *The Coming Event; or the United Provinces of Australia* (Sydney, 1850) were in considerable measure realized after the granting of responsible government and still more so in the twentieth century after the formation of the Commonwealth.

In July Lang was elected to the Legislative Council and sought a select committee to investigate Grey's charges against him of having selfish motives, deluding his migrants and attempting to deceive the New South Wales government. Without appointing a committee the council debated these charges and, while there was a bare quorum of thirteen, passed a motion censuring Lang. In February 1851 he published in the *Press* sketches of the 'De'il's Dozen' who had voted for his censure. The sketch of Thomas Icely [q.v.] alleged that in 1824 he had nefariously acquired the ship *Midas* and thereby heartlessly ruined its previous owner. This was untrue, as Lang apologetically acknowledged in a later issue; he had been deceived by a

rumour current for many years. Lang was convicted of malicious libel and sentenced to four months gaol and £100 fine, which was paid by a public subscription of 1s. a head. In the general election of 1851 Lang headed the poll for the city of Sydney, but did not take his seat as he was still in debt from his migration expenses and was being pressed by creditors. Some months earlier he had been gaoled in Melbourne until able to effect a compromise.

In February 1852 Lang sailed again for England. A public meeting in Brisbane had authorized him to seek separation and increased immigration for the Moreton Bay District. He also had business with his publishers. He spent a year in Britain, terribly lonely and desperately short of money. His emigration projects were snubbed by the Colonial Office, but some migrants were perhaps gained by the lectures he delivered as occasion arose.

In 1854 Lang was elected to the Legislative Council by the Moreton Bay District. He chose to stand for this district so that he could press for its separation. In December the council passed an address of farewell to Sir Charles FitzRoy. Lang, who alleged, probably correctly, that FitzRoy had got a girl in Berrima pregnant, moved an amendment, supported by five other members, criticizing the governor's moral influence as 'deleterious and baneful in the highest degree' and tending 'to alienate from Her Majesty the affections and respect of the Australian people'.

In December Lang's eldest son, George, was manager of the Ballarat branch of the Bank of New South Wales. He had been exceedingly lax in keeping records and submitting regular returns to headquarters. A senior bank official, Alexander Stuart, was sent to investigate and found deficiencies of about £9000. George Lang and the accountant, F. L. Drake, were charged with embezzlement, and sentenced respectively to five and four years hard labour. Lang refused to accept his son's guilt, and in January 1855 published a letter in the Melbourne *Argus* unhesitatingly and firmly denying the fairness of the trial, the impartiality of the judge, the criminality of the prisoners, the justice of the verdict and the equity of the sentence. Lang was charged with bringing the administration of justice into contempt. He spoke for two hours in his own defence and the jury unanimously and immediately acquitted him. Lang then published *The Convicts' Bank; or a Plain Statement of the Case of Alleged Embezzlement* (Sydney, 1855), in which he charged Stuart with 'malice prepense of the foulest character imaginable . . . and a degree of low-bred brutal malignity worthy only of an incarnate daemon'. At the instance of Stuart and the Bank of New South Wales Lang was charged with criminal libel and sentenced in July to imprisonment for six months. Despite 10,000 signatures on petitions for his release the sentence was served in full. In 1856 Lang petitioned the Victorian Legislative Assembly for a select committee to enquire into the conviction of his son and Drake. It reported in August 1857 that if evidence it heard had been allowed by the trial judge it was very questionable that the jury would have convicted. This evidence concerned a gold-buyer employed by the bank named James Burtchell who rapidly and mysteriously acquired a fortune and hurriedly left Australia just before the bank's deficiencies were discovered. The report, however, was equivocal, not definitely exculpating Lang and Drake, who nevertheless were released.

In December 1858 the Presbyterian minister at Shoalhaven invited Lang to preach in his church, which legally belonged to Alexander Berry [q.v.] who forbade Lang to use it. In January 1859 Lang wrote two letters to the *Illawarra Mercury* which were reprinted in the *Kiama Examiner*. Berry, said Lang, was the exact type of those antediluvian oppressors for whose enormous wickedness God was pleased to shorten the duration of human life; and he asked what would become of the world if creatures like Berry were to live for hundreds of years and reduce whole generations of Shoalhaven serfs to miserable vassalage and degradation. Five legal actions followed. Lang was twice acquitted of criminal libel. Berry got substantial damages from both newspapers. At a public meeting to raise funds to pay these damages, Lang read out the offending letter and was again charged with libel but acquitted.

In March 1860 Lang announced in a letter in the *Empire* that, following a recent English Divorce Act, a divorced husband with three Scottish names had married his adulterous concubine. Such marriages, Lang said, were abominable in God's sight, and he suggested that the parties concerned, instead of applying to a Protestant clergyman, might rather have approached the lessee of the parish bull, or the jockey who let out stallions for hire. Soon afterwards Lang was accosted in Hunter Street by a large muscular man, twenty years his junior, who thrashed him with a horsewhip and left his card entitled Malcolm Melville Macdonald. Captain Macdonald, a well-known Sydney sportsman, was fined £5 for assault.

In 1862 Lang piloted a bill through the Legislative Assembly to abolish primogeni-

ture in intestate estates. It was probably his most lasting legislative achievement. In May 1863 he libelled Rev. John West [q.v.] in the *Empire* and escaped with only £100 damages. In May 1865 Lang won £350 damages from the *Sydney Morning Herald*, after it alleged that he had been financially dishonest in 1840-41. This was the only time he abandoned his principle of never suing for libel.

After his rejection by the Synod of Australia in 1842 Lang had enlisted several ordained clergymen during his long stay in Britain in 1846-49, and in April 1850 he established the Synod of New South Wales, thus creating an ecclesiastical jurisdiction without which his voluntary Presbyterianism must have evolved into Congregationalism. He then devoted much time and energy to establishing and maintaining ministers of this synod in different parts of the colony. In 1853 the Presbytery of Irvine, on an application from the Synod of Australia, and, without even citing Lang to appear before it, declared he was no longer a minister of the Church of Scotland as he had since 1842 withdrawn himself from that church's recognized court in New South Wales. Strengthened by this decision the Synod of Australia commenced an action against Lang to obtain the Scots Church properties. After several years delay the Equity Court in October 1859, and the Supreme Court on appeal in July 1860, found for the synod. Despite opposition from his congregation Lang determined to appeal to the Privy Council and sailed for England in December 1860. Several complicated legal actions followed in the Presbytery of Irvine, the General Assembly and in the Court of Session, Scotland's highest civil court, before the presbytery in March 1863 reversed its previous endorsement of Lang's deposition from the ministry. Lang returned to Australia in July 1861. Eight months later the Privy Council found for him because he had occupied Scots Church twelve years before confirmation of the sentence of deposition was sought from the Presbytery of Irvine. In November the Synod of Australia, following the Scottish and English legal decisions, resolved that though Lang had been guilty of schism, slander and contumacy its sentence of deposition should be rescinded.

After several years negotiations between the four Presbyterian groups in the colony, the Synod of New South Wales dissolved itself in 1864 in preparation for the general Presbyterian union achieved in September 1865. Some, especially within the Synod of Australia, had wished to exclude Lang, but his position as senior Presbyterian clergyman in the colony and as a member of its legislature secured his inclusion. In December 1867 an Act was passed for the establishment of a Presbyterian college within the University of Sydney. Public subscriptions for its support were collected, the subscribers to elect the college council. Outmanoeuvered, Lang was restricted in the collection of subscriptions, and therefore of votes, to the more distant and thinly-settled parts of the colony. When the twelve councillors were elected in November 1870, Lang and only one of his supporters secured places, and there was no representative of those who had adhered to the established Church of Scotland. It was Lang's great ambition to become principal of the college. In July 1871 the Free-Church-dominated council voted against appointing Lang. In February 1872 it appointed Rev. John Kinross, but discovered that under the Act it was necessary to appoint as principal a member of the council, which Kinross was not. On 1 September Lang announced his resignation from Scots Church to devote himself to the training of a native-born ministry. On 24 September the council elected Rev. Adam Thomson as principal, but Lang, ever fertile in defeat, objected that this too was illegal, as Thomson's election meant there was a principal and only eleven instead of the statutory twelve councillors. He hoped, by referring the matter to parliament, that another tribunal might alter the arrangements whereby he was consistently outvoted in the council, but neither premier nor governor was impressed and the incorporation of St Andrew's College was duly proclaimed in the *Government Gazette*, 24 March 1873. Lang challenged the legality of the college in the Supreme Court, but in June lost the case and decided to appeal to the Privy Council. In October a public meeting was held to inaugurate St Andrew's. Uninvited, Lang attended to protest. His supporters reduced the proceedings to complete disorder, the pandemonium being so great that when members of the audience went across the street to the police station they found the constabulary had discreetly retired to avoid the necessity of assisting at the inauguration.

In December Rev. Dr Archibald Gilchrist was inducted to the charge of Scots Church. Earlier and not always happily, Lang had several colleagues at Scots Church but his position now was altered and subordinate. He retained the nominal status of senior minister but received only a retiring allowance and devolved responsibility and executive functions upon Gilchrist. In April 1874 he sailed for the last time for England, travelling by way of the United States.

In London he arranged for the fourth edition of his history of New South Wales and for his Privy Council appeal. This, however, was allowed to lapse. He returned in 1875.

In March 1877, when Archbishop Polding [q.v.] lay on his death-bed, John Robertson persuaded him to receive Lang, and Lang to visit him; both needed persuading as each thought the other would not agree to the meeting. The two clerics, antagonists for four decades, were alone together for about three-quarters of an hour while Robertson stood outside to prevent interruption. It is said that when Lang was driven home he had tears in his eyes and for once in his life remained silent. In May Gilchrist resigned to accept a call from North Melbourne. The Scots Church congregation was unwilling that Lang should resume full responsibilities but, with the support of the Presbytery of Sydney, he determined to do so. The congregation's officials then locked and boarded up the church to prevent entry by either minister or people, so Lang was reduced to seeking a policeman and a builder to gain access to the pulpit he had founded and then preached from for more than fifty years.

Lang died, after a stroke, on 8 August 1878. His widow, faithful to his memory, rejected a letter of condolence from the congregation as unfitting after their recent treatment of her husband, and also refused to accept a grant of £3000 from the government because the Legislative Assembly had voted against such expenditure while Lang was still alive.

Above all, Lang was a Presbyterian minister and always retained the Calvinism of his youth. Yet he co-operated willingly with other Protestant clergymen, especially Baptists and Congregationalists, often more cordially than with fellow Presbyterians, for his anger was most strongly aroused by those whom he felt had put their hands to the plough and then looked back. That he was responsible, even when elected moderator of the General Assembly in 1872, for divisions and tensions within the Presbyterian Church is obvious. But he was not alone responsible, for the history of Presbyterianism in Scotland and the other colonies was almost equally schismatic. Self-consciously an upright man he always castigated public immorality, but hundreds of the poor, homeless and bereaved remained deeply grateful to him as benefactor and friend. His belief in the authority of a literal interpretation of scripture, together with opinions about the imminent collapse of the Papacy, persuaded him that the end of the world was at hand. But neither this millenarianism nor his fundamental pessimism, which saw almost all men doomed to early and utter destruction, inhibited his continual activity for the temporal welfare of the unregenerate. His achievements in promoting education and immigration bear comparison with those of any of his contemporaries, but would have been much greater had his intense inner drive not been inextricably compounded with an irresistible impulse to hurt those who showed opposition or were even merely lukewarm towards his designs. Lang's political career, which finished in 1870, was marked by many electoral triumphs and he witnessed the achievement of almost all his political aims: the cessation of transportation, the separation of Victoria and of Queensland, the introduction of responsible and democratic government, radical land reform, National education and the abolition of state aid to religion. Was Lang influential in this long process which culminated in a liberal, democratic and secular society? Or, was he like a man in a boat, shooting over the political Niagara, and furiously whipping the water to make it go faster? He never took office, nor is it likely that any cabinet containing him would have lasted a fortnight. His penny postage and the abolition of primogeniture in intestate estates are meagre achievements when compared with Robertson's reform of the land laws or Parkes's reform of education. Lang was never a member of any of the factions which dominated New South Wales politics after 1856, and visitors were surprised to see how little notice the great Dr Lang excited in the Legislative Assembly. The failure of his republicanism also suggests a limited political influence, for he was quite powerless on this issue so dear to his heart. Yet it would be wrong to think that his advocacy of other causes was successful only because he was preaching to the already converted, for his was undoubtedly one of the most powerful voices extolling the virtues of liberal and secular values. His published works, whether of a polemical propagandist or more broadly educational nature, were not confined to his numerous books and pamphlets, for almost every day, it seems, he wrote an article for the press or at least a letter to the editor. His writings, though repetitious and egotistical, are nevertheless always vigorous and informative and often tinged with powerful sarcasm. These, together with innumerable lectures given in Sydney or in the bush on his never-ending colonial journeyings, must have had a large, though unmeasurable, influence in inculcating the colonial values which were dominant in Australia by the end of the nineteenth century.

A. Gilchrist (ed), *John Dunmore Lang*, 1-2 (Melb, 1951), and for bibliog; Lang papers (NL, Dixson Lib, Syd, Presbyterian Lib, Assembly Hall, Syd); Lang papers (in the possession of Sir John Ferguson, Syd).   D. W. A. BAKER

LANGDON, WILLIAM (1790-1879), naval officer and landowner, was born on 6 November 1790 at Montacute vicarage, Somerset, England, the fifth son of Rev. William Langdon. When 13, while at school at Beaminster, Dorset, he became inspired by the career of Admiral Hood (Viscount Bridport), obtained an interview with him and asked for an appointment as a midshipman. A few weeks later Bridport wrote to him directing him to join H.M.S. *Weymouth*, in which he became a first-class volunteer in April 1804. He sailed in her to Madras escorting East Indiamen. In September 1806 he was present at the capture of a French frigate off Rochefort; in 1806 he was transferred to the *Monarch* and in August 1807 to the *Champion*; he saw much action and when only 17 was sent to Plymouth in command of a French prize; in 1810 he joined the *Badger* and in August 1811 became acting lieutenant in the *Ringdove* in the West Indies, the promotion being confirmed in November. He was invalided from May 1812 to September 1814.

After the peace of Paris, seeing no prospect of speedy promotion, he retired, bought the *Lusitania*, 245 tons, and took her on a trading voyage to Sydney and Hobart Town, where he first landed in October 1821. On a second voyage he reached Sydney in May 1823. He exchanged the *Lusitania* for the *Hugh Crawford*, which reached Sydney in April 1825. In 1828 he bought the *Wanstead* and in 1829 the *Thomas Lawrie*. In November 1822 he was fined £800 for breaking the port regulations by giving a passage from Hobart to England to Thomas Kent [q.v.]

While still engaged in trading between England and the Australian colonies Langdon in 1823 received a grant of 1500 acres on the Clyde River near Bothwell. He added to this property, which he called Montacute, by purchase. In September 1834 Langdon arrived in Van Diemen's Land with his wife Anne, née Elliott, of Somerset, and their daughter Anne, to settle on his colonial estate. On his early voyages to Van Diemen's Land, and later, he introduced blackbirds, thrushes, goldfinches, pheasants and partridges to the colony. In September 1837 Langdon let his properties, totalling 6000 acres with 2000 sheep, for £1300 a year and in March 1838 returned to England, where he lived at Inwood

Lodge, near Sherborne, Dorset. There he entertained friends from Van Diemen's Land and encouraged many people to emigrate; then and later he paid the fares of some who emigrated and even had some educated at his own expense. On 14 June 1842 his only daughter Anne became the second wife of Sir Thomas Howland Roberts, third baronet, of Glassenbury, Kent.

On 20 May 1844 his wife died. In May 1846 he returned to Tasmania, with a second wife, Anne, née Chaffey, of Martock, Somerset. Thereafter he remained in Tasmania except during visits to England in 1857 and 1872. In 1853 he was promoted honorary commander in the navy, and was appointed to the Legislative Council. He was a devoted supporter of the Church of England and in 1856-57 built a church costing about £2000 on his own property; in 1860 he was a leader in establishing the practice of opening parliament with prayer. With the coming of responsible government he was elected to the Legislative Council in 1859 and remained a member until he retired in 1872. He made his home at Derwentwater, Sandy Bay, and died there on 23 May 1879. His obituary described him as 'a true friend, good master, and chivalrous Christian gentleman'.

His widow died at Hobart on 21 May 1902, aged 84. There were three sons and three daughters of this marriage.

W. R. O'Byrne, A naval biographical dictionary (Lond, 1849); R. W. Giblin, The early history of Tasmania, 2 (Melb, 1939); P. L. Brown (ed), Clyde Company papers, 1-3 (Lond, 1941-58); Hobart Town Courier, 16 Nov 1822; Church News (Hob), 1879.

LANGLANDS, HENRY (1794-1863), iron founder and politician, was born in London, a son of John Langlands, baker, of Dundee, and his wife Christian, née Thoms. His parents returned several years after his birth to their native town. He left school at an early age to become apprenticed to a linen-draper, a position which took him at 21 to Glasgow, where he became a traveller and eventually a partner of the business. During a thirty-year residence in this city he married three times: his first wife, Jessie Wilson, bore him one child; his second, Caroline Inches, added another five; the third marriage, to Janet Mitchell, was childless. He was also an active city politician and achieved some prominence as an opponent of slavery and protagonist of Catholic emancipation. Rivalling this interest was his active participation in the kirk, until his views changed and he became a Baptist in 1833.

Langlands, his wife and five surviving children left Scotland in 1846 to join his brother Robert, who with the help of another Scot, Thomas Fulton, had established the first foundry at Port Phillip some four years earlier. By the time he arrived on New Year's Day 1847 the partnership had dissolved and the two brothers took over its ownership. Several years later Robert retired and Henry became sole proprietor. From humble beginnings, a handful of men, one crude piece of machinery and a set of tools, the foundry prospered despite the additional hazards of high wages and the lack of raw materials. The products were of such high quality—castings for buildings, ornamental iron-work, wool presses, agricultural implements and mining machinery —that they competed successfully with any imported articles. By the time of his retirement shortly before his death Henry Langlands was one of the largest employers in the colony. His men were the first in the colony to cast a bell, and lamp-posts; they cast the boiler of the first train to run in Australia and they successfully launched the first cast-iron vessel, a river tug 109 feet in length, an event which was cheered by some 3000 spectators.

After six years in the colony Langlands stood for the Legislative Council, was narrowly defeated, but returned on a recount, only to be ousted from office some months later when the displaced F. J. Sargood successfully challenged the returns. His main claims to political recognition were that he was one of the twelve who each contributed £100 to the successful anti-transportation campaign and that he identified himself with the variegated anti-ministerial forces who favoured the introduction of some measure of democracy. But the Argus, the champion of democracy, branded him a moderate advocating 'half measures'. When he was returned fifth city representative to the Legislative Assembly of 1856, its contention was proved correct, for Langlands soon identified himself with a group of Nonconformists who were more concerned with the abolition of state aid to religion and with education reform than with democracy. It was this group which joined forces with the right to overthrow the first O'Shanassy ministry, a left-wing coalition.

Langlands died at his home at Jolimont on 21 June 1863 and his funeral took place at the Albert Street Baptist Church where he had been a senior deacon for many years. The business was carried on by his sons one of whom, Henry, had been one of the first pupils at Scotch College and dux for three successive years.

A hard-working but unspectacular politician, his main claim to recognition lies in the foundry and his persistent interest in every phase of colonial life. He chaired public meetings on numerous issues ranging from the Melbourne protest against government action at Eureka to the site of the museum. He was a generous supporter of charitable organizations, religious societies and temperance movements. His brother George, who migrated in 1849, was a pioneer of the Horsham district.

P. Just, *Australia* (Dundee, 1859); Garryowen (E. Finn), *Chronicles of early Melbourne*, 1-2 (Melb, 1888); G. Serle, *The golden age* (Melb, 1963); *Argus*, 7 June 1853, 23 June 1863; R. I. Cashman, Nonformists in Victoria in the 1850s (M.A. thesis, Monash Univ, 1962).
                                     R. I. CASHMAN

LA PEROUSE, JEAN-FRANCOIS DE GALAUP, COMTE DE (1741-1788), navigator, was born on 22 August 1741 at Albi, France. He entered the navy at 15 and when serving in the *Formidable* in the battle with Admiral Hawke off Belle-Isle in November 1759 was wounded and captured. Repatriated from England he was posted again to sea duties, where he perfected his techniques as a seaman and navigator and pursued his interest in oceanography. Promoted lieutenant in April 1775 and captain in 1780 after France joined the American war, he had opportunities to distinguish himself as a naval commander. His campaign against the British in Hudson Bay in August 1782 was a signal success, and he demonstrated his humanity by leaving with the remnants of the settlements enough arms and provisions to enable them to preserve themselves during the oncoming winter.

In 1783 the French government resolved to send an expedition to the Pacific to complete Captain Cook's [q.v.] unfinished work, and in particular to explore the passages in the Bering Sea, which had been a mystery to Europeans since the sixteenth century. King Louis XVI himself took a hand in drafting the plan and itinerary, a copy of which is in the Municipal Library at Rouen, France, and when La Pérouse was selected to lead the fleet gave him an audience before he sailed. In command of two ships, *La Boussole* and *L'Astrolabe* (Commandant de Langle), he left Brest on 1 August 1785 making for Brazil. Doubling Cape Horn he refitted in Chile, then sailed to the Sandwich Islands and thence to Alaska, where he turned south exploring and surveying the coast as far as California. After a short refit at Monterey, he sailed across the Pacific, discovered uncharted islands, and visited Macao and Manila. After six weeks

reprovisioning and refreshing he left on 10 April 1787 to survey the coasts and territories north of Korea, which had been described and commented on by Christian missionaries. He sailed up the Gulf of Tartary, naming several points on both its shores and discovered that Sakhalin was an island. In September he put in to Kamchatka to replenish his supplies. From there he dispatched an officer, Lesseps, overland to Paris with accounts of his discoveries, while he turned south making for New Holland. In December, at Tutuila, Samoa, which Bougainville had called the Navigator Islands when he explored them in 1767, natives suddenly attacked a party from *L'Astrolabe* seeking water and killed de Langle and eleven others. La Pérouse left without taking reprisals and sailed through the Pacific Islands to Norfolk Island and to Botany Bay. He was sighted off the coast there on 24 January 1788 but bad weather prevented his entering the bay for two days. By then Governor Phillip had sailed to Port Jackson, but Hunter had remained with the *Sirius* and the transports, and assisted La Pérouse to anchor. He established a camp on the northern shore, now called after him, and maintained good relations with the English during his six-week stay. He sailed on 10 March and was not heard of again. His disappearance led the French government in 1791 to equip another expedition under Bruny d'Entrecasteaux [q.v.] to look for him, but the search was fruitless.

As Franco-British relations deteriorated during the revolution unfounded rumours spread in France blaming the British for the tragedy which had occurred in the vicinity of the new colony. It was not until 1828 that the mystery was solved, when Dumont d'Urville [q.v.] ascertained that the La Pérouse expedition was wrecked at Vanikoro, Santa Cruz, north of the New Hebrides. In the meantime the revolutionary government had published the records of the voyage as far as Kamchatka : *Voyage De La Pérouse autour du Monde*, 1-4 (Paris, 1797). These volumes are still mines of cartographic and scientific information about the Pacific. Three English translations were published during 1798-99. An anonymous pamphlet *Fragmens du dernier voyage de la Pérouse* (Quimper, 1797), may have been the work of Père Receveur, a scientist on the expedition who died at Botany Bay on 17 February 1788.

On 17 June 1783 La Pérouse had married Louise-Eléonore Brander of Nantes. They had no children but since his name was taken in 1815 by the husbands of his two sisters, Dalmas and Barthez, it still survives in France.

Voyage de Lapérouse . . . enrichi de notes par M. De Lesseps (Paris, 1831); R. Maine, *Lapérouse* (Paris, 1946).

LESLIE R. MARCHANT

LARNACH, JOHN (1805-1869), settler, was born at Auchingill, County Caithness, Scotland, the son of William Larnach, naval purser, and his wife Margaret, née Smith. In July 1823 he arrived at Sydney in the *Andromeda* as a free settler. He became overseer first to John Bowman [q.v.] near Newcastle and then to James Mudie [q.v.] of Castle Forbes, Patrick's Plains, Hunter River. Later he became a partner of James Mudie and on 8 August 1827 at Newcastle married Emily, Mudie's eldest daughter. Larnach took up a near-by property, Rosemount, and lived there with his wife.

On the then remote Patrick's Plains transport was difficult, supplies were erratic and costs were high. Isolated settlers suffered from the frequent depredations of Aboriginals and runaway convicts. One of the shepherds on Bowman's station had been killed while Larnach was there, and in August 1826 he accompanied a party of mounted police when an Aboriginal guide was brutally treated and shot on suspicion of being involved in the spearing of two fencers. Larnach spent more time than Mudie at Castle Forbes, where some twenty assigned servants worked on heavy clearing and cultivation and were kept under rigid discipline. In November 1833 some of the convicts revolted, took to the bush and returned to plunder the property for food, clothes, guns, ammunition and horses. Larnach, who at the time was washing sheep in a near-by stream, was shot at but not injured, and he took refuge at the neighbouring home of Henry Dangar [q.v.]. A party of police and civilians including Larnach captured the absconders, six of whom were remanded to Sydney. After a dramatic trial in December 1833 three of the prisoners were executed in Sydney and two at Castle Forbes; the youngest was sent to Norfolk Island for life.

Accusations by the convicts at their trial caused such a public outcry that Governor Bourke ordered an inquiry by the solicitor-general, J. H. Plunkett, and the police superintendent, F. A. Hely [qq.v.]. They found that Mudie and Larnach had not been harsh or oppressive, but considered Larnach 'imprudent' in striking one convict and 'reprehensible' in bringing another before the local bench twice on the same day for the same offence so as to obtain two sentences of fifty lashes each. This report angered Mudie and Larnach who prepared a joint protest and asked Bourke to send it to London. Bourke refused because of its improper form, so in September 1834 they printed *Vindication of James Mudie and John Larnach, from certain reflections on their conduct contained in letters addressed to them . . . relative to the treatment by them of their convict servants*. They sent this pamphlet direct to the Colonial Office, where the governor's action was fully upheld.

Thereafter Larnach withdrew from public notice and after Castle Forbes was sold in 1836 carried on his agricultural and pastoral pursuits. He died at Rosemount on 10 February 1869, aged 64. His wife died at St Kilda, Melbourne, in April 1882 and was buried beside her husband in the Church of England cemetery at Singleton. Of their five daughters and four sons, William James Mudie Larnach became prominent in commerce and politics in New Zealand.

HRA (1), 12, 17; Newspaper indexes under Larnarch (ML); MS cat under Larnach (ML).

BERNARD T. DOWD
AVERIL F. FINK

LARRA, JAMES (1749-1839), Jewish emancipist and merchant, whose correct name was Lara, was a descendant of an illustrious Spanish-Jewish family. On 12 December 1787, aged 38, he was sentenced to death at the Old Bailey for having stolen a tankard worth £5. The sentence was commuted to transportation, and he arrived with the Second Fleet in June 1790 in the *Scarborough*. He was well regarded by the authorities, and the same year succeeded Constable John Harris [q.v.] as principal of the night-watch. In September 1794 he received a conditional pardon, and on 10 November married Susannah, née Wilkinson, the widow of a convict, John Langford. There was no issue of this marriage.

In May 1797 he received his first grant of fifty acres in the Field of Mars and devoted himself to farming, but next year decided to venture into the lucrative liquor trade. He became one of the agents of John Macarthur [q.v.], and on 19 September received one of the first liquor licences in the colony. On 4 June 1800 he was granted a free pardon, and about this time built his inn, the Freemasons' Arms, in Parramatta where in 1802 members of a French scientific expedition stayed for three months. François Péron [q.v.], in his account of this journey, was full of praise for Larra. He soon extended his activities to commercial enterprises, selling wheat and animal food to the government, and opening a well-stocked store on his premises. When the *Sydney Gazette* was deposited there in 1803 he became the first newspaper agent in Australia. He had enrolled in the Loyal Parramatta Association when it was founded in 1801, and in 1804 was promoted sergeant-major. In April 1804 he received a grant of 1000 acres in the Bankstown district, which he called Harris Farm; to this grant was added in 1809 a further 200 acres to be held in trust for his nieces Elizabeth and Hannah, the daughters of John Harris who had left the colony.

After the Rum Rebellion, Lieut-Governor Paterson [q.v.] granted Larra 600 acres at the Upper Nepean, and on 14 January 1809 appointed him 'vendue master for the District of Parramatta'. After his wife's death in June 1811, he married in September 1813 Phoebe, the rich widow of John Waldron, proprietor of the Duke of York inn at Sydney. Larra was then at the height of his career and so much estimated that some have called him 'the commercial nabob of Parramatta'; however, 1814 marked the beginning of his decline. After his wife died on 1 August rumour had him causing her death by 'improper sexual practices'. Tried on 5 September he was acquitted but his reputation had suffered so much that he was removed from office as auctioneer. He tried unsuccessfully to sell out and leave the country. He kept his liquor licence and tendered meat for government stores, but ran into financial difficulties and mortgaged his farms and the inn to Samuel Terry [q.v.].

On 18 March 1817 he married for the third time. His bride was a convict, Mary Ann Clarke, an English actress, and her exigencies led to his final ruin. In May 1821 Larra sent his wife to England to collect funds, but in June Terry had him declared bankrupt. Larra's wife returned in July 1822, but the pair soon separated, because she not only used the money for herself but made debts in his name for which Larra was thrown in the debtors' prison. Elizabeth Harris, whose second husband was Joseph Underwood [q.v.], rescued him and took him into her house. In 1828 he was still living with her at Ashfield but by 1837 he had moved to Parramatta. He died, aged 90, on 11 February 1839 and was buried in the Jewish section of the Devonshire Street cemetery in Sydney, unnoticed in the press.

James Larra was certainly the most prominent Jew in the earliest years of the colony, and one of the most colourful personalities and successful emancipists of his time. His downfall was not entirely undeserved, but he merited the epithet bestowed by James Holt [q.v.] 'James Larra, an honest Jew'. His name is preserved in the district where he had lived, by Larra Place at Telopea (Dundas) and Larra Street at Yennora (Guildford).

HRA (1), 3-8; G. F. J. Bergman, 'James Larra, the commercial nabob of Parramatta', *Aust Jewish Hist Soc J*, 5 (1959-64).

GEORGE F. J. BERGMAN

LASCELLES, THOMAS ALLEN (1783-1859), public servant and settler, was born on 29 September 1783 at Salisbury Street, Strand, London, the son of Michael Lascelles and Martha, daughter of Thomas Allen. According to his own account, he came of farming stock and was brought up on the land. He joined the 73rd Regiment as an ensign in 1811, became a lieutenant in 1813, finally reaching the rank of brevet captain. He went first to New South Wales in 1811, then in 1813 to Van Diemen's Land where in April he was appointed private secretary to Lieut-Governor Davey.

As Davey's creature, Lascelles antagonized most other people by his arrogance and frequent complaints were lodged against him. Governor Macquarie described him as 'generally very much disliked on account of his petulance, domineering manner, and assuming a degree of consequence quite incompatible with his subordinate station'. Like many other officials, Lascelles was anxious to profit from his office. In 1814 Davey assisted him by allowing him to help to seize some smuggled spirits and so to share in the spoil, which earned a reprimand from Macquarie. Later he managed to keep his assigned servants victualled by the government for more than the prescribed eighteen months, and from the stores 'borrowed' wheat which he bartered for rum.

When the 73rd Regiment left for India in June 1814 he remained behind; for allowing this Macquarie again reprimanded Davey severely. Lascelles resigned his commission in August but continued as Davey's secretary at 5s. a day until 16 November 1816. Lascelles then farmed a 1000-acre grant (later Frogmore) in the Pittwater district; in 1819 he received 800 acres in the district of Sussex. On 25 July 1820 he married Mary Ann, the widow of Denis McCarty [q.v.], née Mary Winwright (Wainwright). At this time he controlled Millbrook, a farm on the Lachlan River, and later a farm near New Norfolk. This estate was sold in the late 1830s, whereupon Lascelles' stepson, Edwin Lascelles, claimed the proceeds as McCarty's heir. Edwin later moved to Geelong where he associated with C. J. Dennys (Lascelles' nephew and eventual son-in-law) in founding the wool selling firm of Dennys Lascelles Ltd.

After holding no government position for a decade, in March 1827 Lascelles was appointed police magistrate for Richmond and a justice of the peace. From May he acted briefly as chief police magistrate, and was a member of the committee which that year investigated the robbery of the Treasury. He was relieved of office on 7 September 1829 for malpractices. In January he had appointed John Cooper to the police without the concurrence of his master. It was proved that Cooper had been taken from his master in the middle of harvest and then set to reaping Lascelles' crop. Although told to release Cooper immediately, Lascelles detained him until 26 March. Lascelles was never again a police magistrate, but must have been reappointed a justice of the peace almost immediately because his name appears in the almanacs until 1843.

In 1833-34 Lascelles was editor of the *Colonist*. He quarrelled with Thomas Mason [q.v.], police magistrate at New Norfolk when, contrary to government regulations, he lent an assigned servant to a neighbour in return for wheat and meat. This incident and another relating to the flogging of a convict named Greenwood which Mason ordered, led to both parties bringing libel charges against one another. Mason eventually dropped his, prosecuting instead the author of an article, 'The Wretched Greenwood', which appeared whilst Lascelles was editor of the *Colonist*. Lascelles won one case, though the attorney-general claimed that the verdict was contrary to the evidence, but lost the second when the jury also expressed 'their full conviction that the charge of perjury imputed to the Plaintiff [Mason] was wholly groundless'.

Litigious, corrupt and anti-social, Lascelles was beset by real as well as imagined difficulties. In 1847 he was declared insolvent. Hoping to mend his fortunes, he moved to Port Phillip about 1850. Late in 1852 he was appointed serjeant-at-arms and registrar of records to the Legislative Council of Victoria; for about three months he was also a justice of the peace. His wife ran a school in Hobart Town until the mid-1850s when she joined Lascelles in Victoria. He died of cholera at Geelong on 11 February 1859.

HRA (3), 2-5; Correspondence file under T. A. Lascelles (TA).   MARGRIET ROE

LATHAM, JOHN (1740-1837), ornithologist, was born on 27 June 1740 at Eltham, Kent, England, son of John Latham, a surgeon. He was educated at Merchant Taylors' School, studied anatomy under the radical surgeon John Hunter, and after completing his medical education at London hospitals practised medicine for many years at Dartford. After acquiring a considerable fortune he retired from practice in 1796 and settled at Romsey, Hampshire. In 1775 he was elected a fellow of the Royal Society and in 1796 received the degree of M.D. at Erlangen (Germany). He took a leading part in the formation of the Linnean Society of London in 1788. He was twice married, in 1763 and 1798. He died on 4 February 1837.

From early in life natural history and particularly birds were Latham's major interests and he became the leading English ornithologist of his day. The chief results of his studies were published in three works: A *General Synopsis of Birds*, 1-3, 1781-85, with supplements in 1787 and 1801; *Index Ornithologicus, sive systema ornithologiae* . . . 1-2, 1790, with supplement in 1801; A *General History of Birds*, 1-10, 1821-28. The illustrations were designed, etched and coloured by Latham himself. Apart from his major works he published papers in the transactions of learned societies, and contributed the descriptions of birds in *The Voyage of Governor Phillip to Botany Bay* . . . 1789.

The period of Latham's ornithological work coincided with Cook's [q.v.] voyages and the first years of colonization of eastern Australia, and as a result a large number of Australian birds were included in his books. He was a friend and correspondent of all the important English naturalists and collectors and thus was able to examine practically all specimens and drawings of birds which reached England. He was particularly interested in drawings and made copies of those which he borrowed. Sir Joseph Banks [q.v.] lent him the drawings made by artists on all Cook's voyages. A particularly important source of illustrations of Australian birds was the 'Lambert drawings' which he borrowed from Aylmer Bourke Lambert who apparently acquired them from Surgeon-General John White [q.v.]. A considerable number of these appear to be copies of some of the 'Watling drawings', the work of Thomas Watling [q.v.] and other artists in the infant settlement at Port Jackson. Although he does not mention Watling, Latham quotes notes on the habits of birds taken from drawings in the Watling set.

The birds described in the *Synopsis* and the first supplement were vernacular descriptions only and no scientific names were given. Johann Friedrich Gmelin published in 1788-89 a new enlarged edition of Linnaeus's *Systema Naturae* . . . and in that work rendered Latham's descriptions into Latin and gave them scientific names, thereby gaining the credit of being the first to describe and name scientifically the birds already brought to notice by Latham. In his *Index Ornithologicus* and the second supplement to the *Synopsis* Latham provided the first published descriptions and scientific names of many Australian birds, some common and well-known examples being the emu, white cockatoo, wedge-tailed eagle, lyre-bird and magpie.

Latham was essentially a compiler and his ornithology was not of a high standard even for his day; however, he made the first contribution of any importance to Australian ornithology, and it was not surpassed until John Gould [q.v.] embarked on his comprehensive and systematic study several decades later.

E. G. Allen, 'History of American ornithology before Audubon', American Philosophical Soc, *Trans*, 41 (1951); F. C. Sawyer, 'Notes on some original drawings of birds used by Dr John Latham', *Soc for Bibliog of Natural Hist J*, 2 (1949); H. M. Whittell, *The literature of Australian birds* (Perth, 1954).

                                                J. H. CALABY

LA TROBE, CHARLES JOSEPH (1801-1875), superintendent and lieut-governor, was born on 30 March 1801 in London, the son of Christian La Trobe and his wife Hannah, née Sims. His family was of Huguenot origin. His great-great-grandfather, Henri Bonneval La Trobe, had left France after the revocation of the Edict of Nantes to join the army of William of Orange and arrived in England in 1688; after being invalided out of the army he settled in Dublin and from there his grandson Benjamin went to England to train as a clergyman in the Moravian Church. Christian Ignatius, eldest son of the next generation, was also ordained in the Moravian Church and in 1787 became secretary to the Society for the Furtherance of the Gospel. As a missionary he travelled in South Africa in 1815-16 and in 1820 translated H. P. Hallbeck's *Narrative of a visit . . . to the New Missionary Settlement of the United Brethren* . . . An accomplished musician and composer, Christian was a friend of Haydn and is credited in Grove's *Dictionary of Music* as introducing recent European sacred music into England. Like his father he was active in the anti-slavery movement and had some contact with Wilberforce.

Charles appears to have been educated in Switzerland and intended to enter the ministry. He did not do so but taught for a time at the Fairfield Boys' Boarding School, a Moravian institution in Manchester. In October 1824 he went to Neuchâtel, Switzerland, as tutor to the family of the count de Pourtalès who was also of Huguenot extraction. He remained there until February 1827, becoming a noted mountaineer: a pioneer member of the Alpine Club, he climbed mountains and passes without the help of guides and porters. La Trobe's first book, *The Alpenstock: or Sketches of Swiss Scenery and Manners*, was published in 1829 and his second, *The Pedestrian: A Summer's Ramble in the Tyrol*, came out in 1832. As tutor or mentor La Trobe accompanied the dashing young Count Albert de Pourtalès during a tour of America which began in 1832. They visited the chief cities of North America and sailed down the Mississippi to New Orleans, and then toured the prairies with the American author, Washington Irving. Irving published an account of this journey, and La Trobe's *The Rambler in North America: 1832-1833* (London, 1835) was followed by *The Rambler in Mexico: 1834* (London, 1836). On his return from America La Trobe stayed at the country house of Frédéric Auguste de Montmollin, a Swiss councillor of state, and there became engaged to one of the Montmollin daughters, Sophie. They were married in the British Legation at Berne on 16 September 1835.

Possibly through the official contacts his family had made in the campaign for the abolition of slavery, La Trobe was sent by the British government in 1837 to report on measures necessary to fit the West Indians for freedom. He submitted three reports on negro education in the islands. In that year he also published *The Solace of Song*, short poems suggested by scenes visited on a continental tour, chiefly in Italy. In January 1839 he was appointed superintendent of the Port Phillip District; he arrived at Melbourne on 30 September with his wife and daughter, two servants and a prefabricated house.

La Trobe did not have the usual background of a colonial governor; he had no army or naval training, little administrative experience and, with his talents and interests, high principles and serious mind, he was a cultured gentleman rather than an intellectual or an executive. According to Washington Irving, 'He was a man of a thousand occupations; a botanist, a geologist, a hunter of beetles and butterflies, a musical amateur, a sketcher of no mean pretensions; in short, a complete virtuoso; added to which he was a very indefatigable, if not always a very successful, sportsman'. For such a man the district of Port Phillip provided great pleasure; 'I had from the first a passion for the plains and for my solitary hard rides across them, and retained it to the last'.

La Trobe did not come to administer an established colony, for the Port Phillip District was then a new and rapidly developing dependency of New South Wales. As superintendent all his decisions had to be approved by Governor Gipps, his senior who in Sydney controlled land sales, plans of public buildings and the appointment of officers; the revenue for Port Phillip administration was allotted by the New South Wales government. Gipps and La Trobe were on excellent terms of friendship and mutual respect, the governor acting as guide and mentor to the superintendent particularly in relationships with their mutual superiors at the Colonial Office. Gipps's large correspondence with La Trobe is pervaded by anxiety about Colonial Office reactions to his decisions and fear that these reactions will be adverse. This fear may have been contagious, for' La Trobe was charged with being indecisive and slow in action. Certainly he acted on Gipps's two rules: Keep your government out of debt and preserve the peace of the country.

Gipps had a steady and constant influence on La Trobe and when he retired in May 1846 penned a tribute to the younger man which must have propped up his always precarious self-confidence: 'I cannot call to my recollection a single instance in which anything approaching to complaint or dissatisfaction has been expressed by either of us towards the other. You have during the long period of more than seven years, been in the uninterrupted possession of my entire confidence; and I hope, trust and believe that you have entertained towards me the same kind and confidential feelings'.

La Trobe was content to be in a subordinate position to New South Wales but his colonists were not. Separation and convict transportation were two major issues of the superintendency. As early as 1840, when the population was only 10,000, a vigorous Separation Association had been founded. The principal grievance was the miserly allocation of revenue for public works in Port Phillip; a much needed bridge over the Yarra was long delayed, public highways were in shocking condition, there was no proper water supply and the first major public building was a massive gaol, more suited to the convict town of Sydney than the needs of Melbourne. Proceeds of crown land sales at Port Phillip were not spent on immigration to swell the labour force there but 'employed in supplying deficiencies in the revenue of the Sydney Government'. A part-elective Legislative Council was granted to New South Wales in 1843, and Port Phillip was allotted only six of the twenty-four elected members. It was an absurd measure, since few candidates could afford long periods in Sydney and they were easily outvoted when interests clashed. In 1844 the six representatives petitioned the Crown for separation, and in 1848 the colonists showed their contempt for absentee rule by electing Earl Grey to one of the positions.

La Trobe did not take the lead or campaign actively for separation, although he thought it 'the best thing that can, under the circumstances, happen to the district'. After 1847 he regarded agitation as unnecessary since Earl Grey had agreed to include separation in the reorganization plans which were being prepared for all the colonies. The Melbourne Town Council and the press, notably the Argus, led a fierce attack on La Trobe for failing to press Port Phillip's claims and needs strongly enough either in London or Sydney. He was specifically denounced for his attitude on the convict problem. On this matter public opinion was unfair. La Trobe strongly opposed the sending of convicts to Port Phillip and the proposed resumption of transportation, although he felt that 'exiles' might be acceptable and a useful addition to the always limited labour force and in 1844 was able to absorb several shiploads in the country districts. He showed his position clearly in 1849 when he refused to allow the Randolph to land its cargo of convicts at Port Phillip and sent the ship on to Sydney, thus defying the Colonial Office in response to a public outcry which was not likely to have stopped short of violence. For once La Trobe was the hero of the colony, in contrast to the preceding year when the Town Council had petitioned London for his removal. Claiming that it was the only organ for the expression of public opinion the Town Council charged La Trobe with a number of rather vague and trivial sins: he did not keep up a state befitting his official position; he permitted systematic mismanagement of public money; he neglected public works; he was 'faithless and insincere' in his relations with councillors. It is clear that they felt that not enough attention and importance was paid to their position by La Trobe, and their petty allegations were dismissed by Earl Grey. It is also clear from the public meeting held to demand his recall that La Trobe did not have the trust of the Melbourne colonists. His isolation from the separation movement made him suspect on other aspects of Port Phillip interests.

Soon after his arrival La Trobe had to institute relief works for the unemployed and stave off a strike when the speculative land boom burst in 1841. Severe depression continued for several years, with squatters forced to boil down their sheep for tallow since they could neither feed nor sell them. Government revenue was correspondingly curtailed, so that new officials were not appointed and Port Phillip estimates were reduced.

For four months in 1846 La Trobe acted as lieut-governor of Van Diemen's Land after the peremptory dismissal of Sir John Eardley-Wilmot by Gladstone, then secretary of state for the colonies. It was a difficult situation with Eardley-Wilmot still in the colony, vainly demanding specific charges to which he could reply; he died in the colony, smeared by the vague accusations regarding his moral character which Gladstone had privately given as the reason for his dismissal but would not particularize. In this shameful, unjust episode, La Trobe behaved well; many years later he commented, 'it was good Service, and prudently and delicately performed'.

The Australian Colonies Government Act of 1850 gave Victoria its own representative government in a Legislative Council of whose members two-thirds were elected and one-third nominated. In January 1851 when La Trobe was appointed lieut-governor he had an Executive Council of four, nominated by the Crown, and could veto or reserve bills of the Council, control the Civil List and the proceeds from the sale of crown lands, and initiate all budgetary legislation. Thus La Trobe was given considerable power, full responsibility and a constitutional arrangement in which conflict was inherent. The Legislative Council of Victoria followed the pattern of its counterpart in New South Wales in demanding greater powers. There were few able men from whom La Trobe could choose his executive and his council spokesmen. Only William Lonsdale [q.v.], first police magistrate of the district, was available to act as colonial secretary, a post for which he was not fitted. William Foster Stawell was appointed attorney-general, Alistair MacKenzie colonial treasurer and J. H. N. Cassell collector of customs. The people concerned in government, elected and government men alike, and the governor himself, were completely inexperienced in the new form of legislature or of politics, yet in their first year of office they had to cope with unprecedented crises.

In August 1851 La Trobe reported the discovery of gold at Ballarat. The government soon had to extend its rule over a wide area. Thousands of diggers were concentrated in places such as Ballarat, Omeo, Bendigo, hitherto isolated and the haunt only of sheep, cattle or kangaroos. Public works and land surveys ceased and police dwindled to a handful, but men had to be found to control the ever-shifting goldfield centres. La Trobe raised wages by half to keep his public servants, pleaded for military reinforcements to maintain order and men-of-war to protect the colony, and recruited commissioners to take charge of the fields. Almost every man in the colony went to the diggings at some time; La Trobe alienated most of them by following New South Wales in imposing a direct tax, the monthly licence fee to search for gold. It was ridiculous enough to attempt to collect the fee in September and October 1851 when few diggers could yet cover their expenses and when the government was unable to enforce its collection. It was a disastrous folly for La Trobe to raise the monthly fee to £3 from January 1852; well-organized and unified protest by the diggers and the press led to humiliating surrender by the government within a fortnight. La Trobe may have been persuaded by Stawell to raise the fee; certainly he was in urgent need of finance to pay the extra public service wages he had promised.

The Executive Council's attempt to control the goldfields and goldfields revenue led to friction with the Legislative Council, which refused to vote from the ordinary revenue any moneys for purposes arising from the discovery of gold. Ever timid in his relations with the Colonial Office, La Trobe did not take full responsibility himself in this crisis as a more experienced governor may have done, but waited for permission to give control of the goldfield portions of crown land and their revenue to the Legislative Council. Until this permission was received in September 1852 La Trobe was harried by hostile councillors, and he antagonized diggers by the imposition of direct taxation which bore no relation to ability to pay and which yielded no funds for amenities or services. He realized the disadvantages of a licence fee and preferred an export duty on gold. By the time such a duty could be substituted in September 1852, the Legislative Council was unwilling to do so and must thus bear the responsibility for later troubles.

By mid-1852 La Trobe's government was in full control again, albeit with a largely incompetent and corrupt police force. However, roads to the major fields had not been built and no provision had been made for the thousands of immigrants who were arriving from overseas, and no wharves were constructed to take the goods brought by the hundreds of ships soon to fill the harbour. It is possible that La Trobe under-estimated the magnitude of the discoveries, the staying power of their attraction, or the amount of revenue they would bring. His hands were full with the problem of establishing control. Crime increased greatly as Vandiemonians flocked into Victoria, uniting the citizens in a further attack on convicts and transportation. The council passed a harsh convicts' prevention bill and although it was clearly illegal La Trobe assented to it, thereby showing courage and an awareness of the strength of colonial opinion, and risking 'his office, his character and his prospects in Downing Street'.

On the vital land question La Trobe was also attuned to colonial feeling and may well have been influenced by Gipps's view. Leases under the 1847 Order in Council were never issued, since surveys of runs had hardly begun when gold was discovered. Soon the increased demand for farming land made it necessary to throw open some of the squatters' land for sale. La Trobe was anxious to anticipate 'the prospective wants of the community' by reserving land for agriculture but the weight of legal opinion was against him. The council became a battleground of the radical and urban forces against the squatters; when the issue came to a head in August 1852 La Trobe temporized. He referred the question to the Colonial Office, recommending that squatters be secured in their tenure only where the land was not wanted for purchase. Until a decision arrived La Trobe continued to reserve land for future sale in the pastoral areas and allowed squatters to buy their homestead blocks. It was a wise and fair decision, but La Trobe's delay in bringing small sections near the goldfields forward for sale aroused strong hostility from the diggers, who objected also to the high prices the blocks brought at auction.

By the end of 1853 both councils were becoming more competent and more co-operative in their duties. More efficient administrators were improving government activity and the Legislative Council had been given more power and responsibility. Public works had at last been put in hand, though with much wastefulness, inefficiency and expense. Financial returns from land sales and goldfields were declining by the end of the year but La Trobe had forgotten Gipps's dictum about keeping his government out of debt; he allowed the council to budget for a deficit so that a financial crisis loomed for his successor. Later he wrote, 'None can know how difficult [was the period 1851-52] but those who were in that fierce struggle for the maintenance of order under so many disadvantages'. Despite blunders and great difficulties during these times he made a profound achievement in keeping government functioning and in maintaining the rule of law. Eventually he coped with the immense and rapid physical and numerical expansion of his colony. The criticisms that must be made of him, his tardiness in providing for the onslaught and spread of population, his lack of initiative on the issues of goldfields control and licence fees, were due to his inexperience and continuing self-doubt as to his ability.

In December 1852 La Trobe had submitted his resignation but was not relieved until 1854; he sailed for England on 6 May. He was appointed C.B. in November 1858 and in 1864 was awarded a pension of £333, based on his period as lieut-governor. Sophie La Trobe was in ill health during their last years in Victoria and preceded her husband to Europe, where she died at her family home on 30 January 1854. On 3 October 1855 La Trobe married her widowed sister, Rose Isabelle de Meuron, thus excluding himself from another official appointment had he wanted one. Towards the end of his life his sight failed and he was unable to write the account of his Australian experience which he had planned under the title 'A Colonial Governor'. He died in England on 4 December 1875 and was buried at Litlington, near Eastbourne, Sussex, in the churchyard close to his last home, Clapham House. He left a son and three daughters by his first wife and two daughters by his second. His personal estate, coming mainly from the subdivision of his property in Melbourne, amounted to £15,905. His widow retired to Switzerland, where a small church, the Chapelle de l'Hermitage, was built as a memorial to La Trobe.

In his first speech in Melbourne La Trobe declared, 'It is not by individual aggrandisement, by the possession of numerous flocks or herds, or by costly acres, that the people shall secure for the country enduring prosperity and happiness, but by the acquisition and maintenance of sound religious and moral institutions without which no country can become truly great'. His active dedication to these values, in a society motivated almost entirely by materialistic acquisition, left a heritage and an influence which benefited future generations. La Trobe was an active supporter of the religious, cultural and educational institutions, often initiating their existence and straining his limited income for their benefit. It is he whom Melbourne must thank for their magnificent Botanic Gardens, and he gave leadership, prestige and support to the formation of the Mechanics' Institute, Royal Melbourne Hospital, the Benevolent Asylum, the Royal Philharmonic, the University of Melbourne.

G. W. Rusden, History of Australia, 1-3 (Lond, 1883); A. Gross, Charles Joseph La Trobe (Melb, 1956); G. Serle, The golden age (Melb, 1964); S. C. McCulloch, 'Unguarded comments . . . the Gipps-La Trobe private correspondence', Hist Studies, no 33, Nov 1959; La Trobe papers (La Trobe Lib, Melb); Dispatches to the secretary of state for the colonies, 1851-61 (La Trobe Lib, Melb); Executive Council minutes (La Trobe Lib, Melb).

JILL EASTWOOD

LAWLESS, CLEMENT FRANCIS (1815-1877) and PAUL (1817-1865), pastoralists, were born at Cloyne, County Cork, Ireland, the fifth and sixth children of John Lawless, Woodview, Cloyne, and his wife Mary, née Pyne. Both Clement, who was born on 22 February 1815, and Paul sailed for Australia from Liverpool in June 1840. After some experience of sheep farming on the Hunter River, the brothers bought cattle and drove them 600 miles to the Albert River in the Moreton Bay District, where in 1842 they took up the Nindooinbah run under a squatting licence. William Humphreys, who travelled with them, settled at Mount Martin (Mundoolun).

Seeking land more suitable for sheep Clement and Paul Lawless, with several others including Humphreys, Henry Herbert, Edward Hawkins and James Reid, rode up the Brisbane valley in 1846, taking with them as guide Jacky, a Brisbane River Aboriginal. They found fertile, well-grassed land watered by lagoons and deep creeks in the Burnett district. Thereupon Clement and Paul sold Nindooinbah and in 1847, with twenty shepherds, many sheep, some cattle and horses, and drays laden with supplies and tools, travelled through the Brisbane valley to the Burnett country. Nearing the end of their journey the Lawless brothers were attacked by Aboriginals who drove off numbers of sheep.

Clement and Paul Lawless took up Booubyjan, Windera and Boonimba, building their home on Booubyjan. These runs covered 281 square miles. In 1857 the brothers took up Bluff Plains and Bunya Creek in the Mary River valley, a run of thirty-four square miles which they named Imbil.

In 1855 Paul Lawless returned to Ireland, where in November 1858 he married Ellen, only daughter of William Nash, of Mallow, County Cork, and his wife Ellen, née Mahony, of Dunloe. In 1859 he returned with his wife to Australia. For the next six years they lived at Booubyjan, but Paul's failing health caused their return to Ireland where, soon after their arrival, he died at Youghal on 7 August 1865. His widow died on 27 July 1922; they had four children.

In 1859 Clement Lawless had returned to Ireland, where in September 1860 he married Henrietta Babington, daughter of Thomas Wise. He bought Kilcroan near Cloyne. His only child, Emmeline Anne, was born in 1866. With his wife and daughter he visited Queensland in 1867 and returned to Ireland next year. His last trip to Queensland was in 1873, when he sold his interest in Booubyjan and Imbil to Ellen, the widow of Paul Lawless. Clement died at Kilcroan, Ireland, on 22 May 1877 as the result of a hunting accident. Emmeline Anne married Warren Crooke (later knighted) who took the name of Lawless; she died in 1927, without issue.

The Lawless family is one of the few in Queensland who occupy in an unbroken line of descent the stations originally taken up by their pioneer forbears. Paul Lawless's elder son, John Paul (b. 1861), who in 1889 had married Mabel Gwynne Ethel, daughter of Thomas Evans, built his home on the Windera block, where seventy years later his widow and two daughters, Misses Ellen and Noel Lawless, still ran the property. When John Paul's brother, William Burnett, of Booubyjan, died in 1945 without children, he left Booubyjan to his nephews, Ivan Lawless of Goomally, Duaringa, and Burnett R. Lawless. Burnett bought his brother Ivan's share in 1955.

Cattle were well established on Booubyjan by 1872. Prizes for stud Durham stock were won at Maryborough and Gayndah Shows in 1876, 1877 and 1878. Later a Hereford stud was established at Windera. In 1888, most of Windera was resumed as well as parts of Boonimba and parts of Booubyjan.

M. J. Fox (comp), The history of Queensland, 2 (Brisb, 1921); Qld Women's Hist Assn, 1859 and before that (Brisb, 1960); Private information from Mrs B. R. Lawless, Booubyjan, Goomeri.   C. G. AUSTIN
CLEM LACK

LAWRENCE, WILLIAM EFFINGHAM (1781-1841), landowner, was the eldest son of Captain Effingham Lawrence, merchant and one of the corporation of the elder brethren of Trinity House, London, and his wife Catherine, née Farmer. With his brother Edward Billopp, Lawrence continued his father's business, mainly in shipping, with houses in London, Liverpool and New York. He was highly educated and deeply interested in scientific and constitutional developments. He was an intimate friend of Jeremy Bentham; when Lawrence, because of ill health and for economic reasons, decided to emigrate, Bentham wrote to Buenos Aires, 'Our excellent friend on his way to Australia is not without thoughts of touching at Rio de Janeiro: a worthier man, a more benevolent cosmopolite, never left any country; and very few better informed or more intelligent'.

Having arranged satisfactory terms with the British government for an Australian land grant in lieu of a Treasury payment in compensation for the loss of a ship, Lawrence bought the cutter Lord Liverpool (71 tons) and sailed for Australia in May 1822. Putting in at Rio de Janeiro for provisions and water, Lawrence found a political situation most attractive to his intellectual pursuits. Under the regent, Dom Pedro, Brazil was struggling for its independence from Portugal. Instead of remaining a few days Lawrence stayed for months and became a confidant of the chief minister, the distinguished Paulista, José Bonifacio Andrada, who wanted him to settle permanently in Rio. However, Lawrence sailed in November 1822 and arrived at George Town, Van Diemen's Land, next February. He carried instructions to Governor Brisbane that 2000 acres be granted to him and a similar area to his brother. Their lands were to adjoin, with provision for a reserve of 4000 acres to be given within five years upon cultivation and improvement of the original grant. Lieut-Governor Sorell authorized the grants and stipulated that they were to contain 8000 acres exclusive of waste land. Through this stipulation and the negligence of the deputy-surveyor-general, Lawrence's grant amounted to 12,000 acres, independent of a further 2000 acres reserved for his son. In 1824 Lieut-Governor Arthur questioned his right to acquire so much land and relations between them were strained until Arthur's recall.

Lawrence's grant, known as Formosa, was on the Lake River. He owned much land in and around Launceston including a town residence, Vermont (310 acres), an area known as Lawrence's Paddock (164 acres) through which Lawrence Vale Road now runs, the Punchbowl (924 acres) and Penquite (1832 acres). Later he bought more properties: Billopp (2000 acres) near Formosa, Point Effingham (9651 acres) and Danbury Park (3500 acres) on the Tamar

River. At his death he was one of the colony's largest and wealthiest landowners.

With his varied interests Lawrence was a prime mover in many schemes that benefited the north of Tasmania. In 1824 he and Thomas and Joseph Archer [qq.v.] were granted land on the marsh at Launceston on the condition that they drained, embanked and improved it. They abandoned their project and withdrew their claim to the marsh, after some citizens protested to the lieut-governor. By 1826 when many landowners had surplus stock for sale, a market was instituted at Ross Bridge, with Lawrence as chairman, for the disposal of stock and grain; it was similar to the fairs in English country towns. From this small beginning developed the Midland Agricultural Association.

Lawrence was also prominent in the field of education. In June 1826 he drafted a plan for establishing the Cornwall Collegiate Institution for the liberal and scientific education of youth, first in the school and later by lectures and physical experiments; the plan also included a botanical garden, chemical laboratory and a valuable and extensive library with a reading room for adults. Arthur granted fifty acres at Norfolk Plains and the institution was opened on 1 March 1828. Unfortunately it was not a success and soon became a private grammar school, but Lawrence did not lose interest in higher education. In 1838 he formed a committee, with William and James Henty and P. A. Mulgrave [qq.v.], to establish in Launceston a school based on the principles of the Church of England and under its supervision. He did not live to see this plan culminate in the opening of the Launceston Church of England Grammar School in 1846.

Lawrence played an important part in 1828 as a foundation director of the Cornwall Bank. In 1836 when the Bank of Australasia took over its affairs he became a director of the new bank, and remained on the board until his death. In 1832 he was a founder of the Tamar Steam Navigation Co., which bought the steam tug Tamar for sailing vessels on the Tamar River, and the Steam Packet (formerly Governor Arthur) for passengers and cargo between Launceston and George Town. Later they acquired the river steamer Gipsy. Until 1846 these ships were important in developing the Tamar valley.

Official recognition of Lawrence's merits was long in coming. However, Sir John Franklin quickly appreciated Lawrence's high character, great worth and commanding talent. R. C. Gunn [q.v.] considered him the cleverest and richest gentleman in the colony. In 1837 Lawrence was appointed a justice of the peace and next year a member of the Legislative Council. He retained his seat until his death at Launceston on 18 April 1841. According to his obituary, 'Mr Lawrence in his seat in the Council was foremost in advocating popular rights. He had a mind which soared above all petty notions of party politics or political manoeuvres. The colonists have lost a valuable friend, an able advocate, a disinterested patriot, by whom, through the constant and consistent exercise of independent principles—by pursuing an honest and honourable course of public life, aided by the possession of superior talents and abilities—he had rendered himself greatly prized and esteemed'.

In 1826 Lawrence had married a widow, Mary Ann George, née Smither, and he was survived by five sons and four daughters. His eldest son Robert William (d. 1833) was Tasmania's first distinguished botanist. Three sons continued in pastoral activities at Formosa, Billopp and Point Effingham; another held a commission in the 7th Dragoon Guards, and the youngest entered the medical profession, practised in Melbourne and was closely associated with the Melbourne Hospital from 1868 to 1878.

Correspondence file under Lawrence (TA).

BRUCE WALL

LAWRY, WALTER (1793-1859), Methodist missionary, was born on 3 August 1793 in Rutheren, near Bodmin, Cornwall, England. He was accepted as a candidate for the ministry by the British Conference in 1817 and was chaplain in the convict ship *Lady Castlereagh* which sailed from England and arrived in Sydney on 1 May 1818. As the colleague of Rev. Samuel Leigh [q.v.] he was stationed at Parramatta where he conducted services in the homes of Rowland Hassall and William Shelley [qq.v.]. In St John's Church on 22 November 1819 he married Mary Cover, daughter of Rowland and Elizabeth Hassall. On 29 October 1820 he conducted the first Methodist service west of the Blue Mountains in the Court House, Bathurst. The first Methodist church at Parramatta, dedicated on 20 April 1821, was built at his expense at a cost of £300. Next month a Sunday school was established, where he was able to gather regularly together some fifty young children, despite opposition from local clergy and church attendants. This highlighted the undercurrent of feeling between the British Conference, the Anglican clergy and the Wesleyan missionaries of New South Wales. For a time he was financially embarrassed, partly as a

result of paying for the church, but in 1821 was considerably helped by receiving a grant of 600 acres which Macquarie had previously promised him and which he forthwith sold.

On 7 April 1821 he received 'a large packet from England . . . wherein I see I am appointed to labour in the Friendly Islands'. When Leigh and his wife returned with Rev. William Walker [q.v.] to Sydney in 1821, Leigh informed Lawry that the British committee had appointed him to New Zealand. At a later local committee meeting presided over by Leigh it was decided that Lawry should proceed to Tonga. In order to do so he bought the *St Michael* for £1100. On 18 June 1822 he wrote 'We are now under sail . . . bound for New Zealand and Tonga. I leave New South Wales with a very heavy heart and much tempted to unbelief and discouragement relative to the new and venturous Mission. But I hope in God. The heavy debt which the purchase of this ship has involved me under is a great trial to me. I hope never to embark in another such affair'. After a brief visit to New Zealand, he went to Tonga and was assisted by William Singleton, a survivor from the *Port-au-Prince*, whose crew had been massacred by natives in 1804. Singleton acted as interpreter but, although sympathetic, was not prepared to accept Lawry's standards. The mission made little progress because of the persistent influence of the first white man in Tonga, Morgan, a runaway convict from Botany Bay. According to Lawry, 'to this day they remember Morgan's lies and believe them, consequently they detest our acts of religious worship more than anything we do or say, notwithstanding our efforts to convince them of their mistaken notions'.

Meanwhile Lawry received several letters of censure from the General Wesleyan Missionary Society's committee, and was ordered summarily to an appointment in Van Diemen's Land. Instead he returned to England, landing on New Year's day 1825. His interview with the missionary committee was satisfactory. A resolution was carried 'that the Committee cherish very warm sentiments of esteem for Mr Lawry with a high sense of his valuable services abroad'. He continued his ministry in England until 1843 when he was appointed general superintendent of the missions in New Zealand, which office he held for eleven years. In 1854 he retired because of ill health and went to Parramatta, where he lived until his death. He was buried on 30 March 1859 in the Wesleyan cemetery, Ross and Buller Streets. The Parramatta City Council commemorated his life and work by designating the area the Walter Lawry Methodist Memorial Park.

W. Lawry, *Friendly and Feejee islands: a missionary visit to various stations in the South-Seas, in . . .* 1848, ed G. Hoole, 2nd ed (Lond, 1850); A'sian Wesleyan Methodist Church, *Minutes* (Hob, 1858); J. Colwell, *The illustrated history of Methodism* (Syd, 1904); J. Colwell (ed), *A century in the Pacific* (Syd, 1914); *Spectator* (Melb), Jan 1932; W. Lawry, Diary (copy, Aust Methodist Hist Soc, Syd); Lawry papers (ML).   S. G. CLAUGHTON

LAWSON, WILLIAM (1774-1850), explorer and pastoralist, was born on 2 June 1774 at Finchley, Middlesex, England, the son of Scottish parents who had lived at Kirkpatrick. Educated in London, William was trained as a surveyor, but in June 1799 he bought a commission in the New South Wales Corps for £300. As an ensign he arrived at Sydney in November 1800 in the *Royal Admiral* and was soon posted to the garrison at Norfolk Island, where he married Sarah Leadbeater. He returned to Sydney in 1806, was promoted lieutenant and served for a time as commandant at Newcastle, a position he again occupied in 1809.

Like many of his fellow officers Lawson quickly began to acquire agricultural interests. About 1807 he bought a small property at Concord, where he kept 6 horses, 3 bulls and 14 cows. By 1810 this property had extended to 370 acres. As an officer he also acted on several courts martial, including those of D'Arcy Wentworth in 1807 and of John Macarthur [qq.v.] on the eve of the rebellion against Governor Bligh in 1808. In the interregnum after this, Lawson was appointed aide-de-camp to Major Johnston [q.v.] and received a grant of 500 acres at Prospect; here his wife lived when he was sent to England in 1810 as a witness at Johnston's court martial. Lawson was not very enthusiastic in the cause of the rebellion, and next year returned to Sydney in the *Admiral Gambier* before the trial took place. He accepted a commission as lieutenant in the New South Wales Veterans Company. From this circumstance, when his grant at Prospect was confirmed by Governor Macquarie, Lawson named it Veteran Hall. Here he built a fine 40-room mansion in early colonial style.

In 1813 Gregory Blaxland [q.v.] invited Lawson to accompany him and W. C. Wentworth [q.v.] on what proved to be the first successful attempt to find a route across the Blue Mountains. Lawson's knowledge of surveying made him a particularly valuable member of the expedition. His journal, with its accurate record of times and distances, enables the route to be precisely retraced. Macquarie rewarded each explorer with a grant of 1000 acres on the west of the ranges. Lawson selected his on the Campbell River near Bathurst. In 1819 he was appointed commandant of the new settlement of Bathurst, occupying this post until 1824 when he retired to Veteran Hall.

During his years at Bathurst Lawson undertook three journeys of exploration to find a practicable pass through the ranges to the Liverpool Plains. In this he was unsuccessful but his journeys helped to open up the rich pastoral district of Mudgee. Lawson attributed the discovery of the Cudgegong River to James Blackman [q.v.], but claimed that he himself discovered the site of Mudgee some ten miles beyond the farthest point reached by Blackman. On Lawson's advice George Cox [q.v.] occupied extensive lands in the Mudgee district, and his own family took up 6000 acres on the opposite side of the Cudgegong. Here Lawson built a homestead at Bombira Hill, which became one of the main centres for his pastoral activities, although he had many other extensive estates, including 25,000 acres on the Talbragar River, 6000 near Bathurst, 3000 in Roxburgh, 1500 near Springwood, his Veteran Hall property, and 160,000 acres in various other leases. In 1828 he owned 84,000 sheep, 14,750 cattle and 100 horses. He imported merino rams and ewes from England, as well as Shorthorn cattle and blood horses. His horses were famous throughout the colony in the coaching days.

Lawson not only helped to blaze the first pathway to the west, but he also had a leading role in opening up this country. He is reputed to have taken the first stock across the mountains in July 1815; he escorted Freycinet's [see Baudin] party of naturalists and botanists over the ranges in 1819; and in September 1822 he made the first discovery of coal to the west of the mountains at Hartley Vale. After his wife Sarah died on 14 July 1830 aged 47, Lawson spent most of his later years at Veteran Hall, leaving his sons Nelson and William to develop the inland stations.

A generous supporter of the Presbyterian Church, Lawson took an active part in the establishment of both Scots Church, Sydney, in 1824 and Scots Church, Parramatta, in 1838. As a magistrate he entered freely into public life and on 10 October 1825 signed a letter approving trial by jury. In 1841 he brought some labourers from Chile to work on his estates but found them unsatisfactory. He entered politics in 1843 as a member for Cumberland in the first partly-elective Legislative Council; he attended regularly until 1846, but took little part in its debates. At first he opposed the government, but did not share Wentworth's extreme views and in 1845 opposed him on several occasions. He did not support the squatters in 1844, and opposed a reduction of the price of land in 1846. After this his attendances became irregular and he did not seek re-election in 1848. On 16 June 1850 'Old Ironbark' Lawson died at Veteran Hall, and was buried in the churchyard of St Bartholomew, leaving most of his estates to his son William. His property at Prospect eventually passed into the hands of the Metropolitan Water Board, and is now largely covered by the Prospect reservoir. The house itself was demolished in 1926. A portrait of William Lawson is in the Mitchell Library, Sydney.

HRNSW, 4-7; HRA (1), 3-8, 10, 11, 13, 14, 16; H. Selkirk, 'Discovery of Mudgee', JRAHS, 8 (1922); C. H. Bertie, 'The Lawsons', Home, 1 Jan 1932; E. C. Lawson, Lawson of Veteran Hall (microfilm, ML); Farmer and Settler, 10 Dec 1954; W. Lawson's Journals, 1813, 1821-22 (ML); Bonwick transcripts, biography, v 3 (ML).   E. W. DUNLOP

LAYCOCK, THOMAS (1756?-1809), quartermaster, was enrolled as a sergeant in the New South Wales Corps in 1789 and arrived in Sydney in June 1790. He was promoted quartermaster in January 1791. Governor Phillip recommended Laycock for a vacant ensigncy in April 1792, but this was refused because he already held a commission. When Deputy-Commissary Thomas Freeman died in November 1794 Lieut-Governor Grose [q.v.] appointed Laycock to the vacant office. In 1796 Laycock was involved in the shooting of John Boston's [q.v.] pig and was ordered to pay damages along with other members of the corps charged with the offence. He resigned as deputy-commissary in December 1800 but retained his position as quartermaster. He had been granted 80 acres at Parsley Bay, later the site of Vaucluse House, in February 1793; 100 acres by the upper part of the harbour in September 1795; 160 acres at Liberty Plains in May 1799; and two other grants of which no record survives. By 1802 he held 448 acres by grant and had bought 900 more; by 1807 his total acreage was 1655 acres. He was praised for his part in putting down the Castle Hill uprising in March 1804, when he led the detachment of soldiers to Major George Johnston's [q.v.] aid in his encounter with the rebel leaders, and was afterwards a member of the court martial which tried the rebels.

Laycock's wife, Hannah (1758-1831), who arrived in the Gorgon in September 1791, left again for England about 1805. After her departure Laycock came under severe censure for his indecent behaviour and next year was found guilty of using mutinous language. In February 1808 he was replaced as quartermaster by the War Office but not entirely disgraced. In April Lieut-Governor Johnston appointed him to assist in making a survey of the government store, but John Macarthur [q.v.] advised against appointing him a magistrate and police officer. In October 1809 members of Laycock's family made representations to Lieut-Governor Paterson [q.v.] that he was labouring under mental derangement and unable to manage his affairs. After a report on his health by D'Arcy Wentworth [q.v.], Paterson appointed Laycock's sons William and Thomas [q.v.], his son-in-law Nicholas Bayly, William Broughton [qq.v.] and D'Arcy Wentworth to manage his estates and effects. He died on 27 December 1809.

In September 1810 Hannah Laycock returned to the colony and settled at King's Grove, the 500-acre grant she had received in 1804 from Governor King and which she had named after him. The present suburb of Kingsgrove includes the estate. The Laycocks had three sons and three daughters, including Sarah who married Nicholas Bayly, and Elizabeth who married a pioneer of the Hawkesbury district, Thomas Matcham Pitt, a relation of the earl of Chatham and Lord Nelson. Thomas Pitt's daughter Mary married her cousin, Thomas William Eber Bunker Laycock.

HRNSW, 2-5; HRA (1), 1-6; MS cat under T. Laycock (ML).

LAYCOCK, THOMAS (1786?-1823), soldier and explorer, was the son of Thomas Laycock [q.v.] and his wife Hannah, and came to Sydney with his mother in 1791. He entered the New South Wales Corps, and was its tallest officer when he was commissioned ensign in December 1795 and promoted lieutenant in 1802. After serving in turn at Sydney and Norfolk Island, he was sent to Port Dalrymple in 1806 under Captain A. F. Kemp [q.v.]. He was entrusted with dispatches for Lieut-Governor Collins in Hobart Town, and made the first journey across the island, with the object of obtaining relief for the famine stricken northern settlement. With a party of four men and three weeks provisions, Laycock went by way of the Lake River on 3 February 1807 and reached Hobart on 11 February, after penetrating the mountains past Wood's Lake (first known as Laycock's Lake) and descending the valley of the Clyde to the Derwent. After four days rest they made the return journey in less than a week but without help for the northern famine, as Hobart was equally short of food. For this service Laycock was rewarded with a cow, then greatly prized because of the shortages of food and livestock.

He returned to Sydney and in January 1808 was a member of the Criminal Court assembled to try John Macarthur [q.v.] whose behaviour led to the arrest and deposition of Governor Bligh. Laycock was the only casualty in the Rum Rebellion; while searching Government House he fell through a manhole on to his 'principal joint'. Partly because of his support for the new administration and partly as a reward for his exploration, he was granted 500 acres of land at Cabramatta by Lieut-Governor Foveaux [q.v.], but like all the rebels' grants it had to be surrendered when Governor Macquarie assumed office.

Laycock, newly married to Isabella, daughter of Eber Bunker [q.v.], returned to England with the corps in 1810, was promoted captain in the 98th Regiment in September 1811 and served in the American war. When his regiment returned to Britain Laycock sold his commission and in March 1817 reached Sydney in the *Fame* with his wife and two children. His wife died in May, and in July at St Philip's Church he married Margaret, daughter of John Connell, merchant, who bore him two more children. He set up a store, opened a hotel and was soon a large supplier of meat to the commissariat. In 1819 he was one of the leading citizens applying for trial by jury in the colony. He died on his estate at Bringelly on 7 November 1823, aged 37.

HRA (1), 6, 7, 9, 10, (3), 1; *Sydney Gazette*, 17 Oct 1812, 30 July 1814, 4 July 1818.

G. H. STANCOMBE

LAZAR, JOHN (1801-1879), actor and mayor, was born on 1 December 1801 in Edinburgh, the son of Abraham Lazar, stockbroker, and his wife Rachel, née Lazarus. When he arrived in Sydney on 26 February 1837, under the name of Lazarus, he claimed to be a tailor and also to have appeared on well-known London theatre stages. In May he began his Australian career as Shylock at the Theatre Royal in Sydney, his ten-year-old daughter Rachel, who later married the violinist Andrew Moore, becoming the principal dancer and main attraction during the last months of this theatre. In December Lazar was made manager of the Theatre Royal

until it closed in March 1838. He then was engaged at the new Victoria Theatre as actor and stage-manager. Attacks from the Sydney press on his limited acting capabilities and 'vulgar cockneyism' made him concentrate on management until the end of 1840 when he was engaged to appear in Adelaide at the Queen's Theatre, which had been built by Vaiben and Emanuel Solomon. By the standards of the time the theatre was large and well equipped and it opened on 11 January 1841 with Lazar playing Othello. On the same bill his daughter Rachel appeared in a farce and as a solo dancer. Lazar soon leased the Queen's Theatre and struggled valiantly amid the unpropitious early Adelaide atmosphere of puritanism, lack of general interest, and economic distress. Despite varied bills of Shakespeare, burlettas, innumerable farces and even some heroic attempts at opera he had to abandon his lease on 27 November 1842, and for a time he and his family again entrusted their theatrical fortunes to the more securely established eastern Australian cities. In May 1843, when the monopoly of Sydney's Victoria Theatre was threatened by the opening of the City Theatre, Lazar was brought back as manager until August 1844, and again in 1846. In these later years of his Sydney management he laid the foundations of opera and gave encouragement to local drama.

In 1848 Lazar returned to a more prosperous Adelaide and became associated with George Selth Coppin, who had successfully established the New Queen's Theatre in a building adjoining the old Queen's Theatre. This time Adelaide treated Lazar more kindly and he enjoyed considerable popularity. The climax of his theatrical career in Adelaide was his reappearance in 1850 at the old Queen's Theatre, remodelled and renamed the Royal Victoria Theatre. This time Lazar was highly regarded as a comedian and he enjoyed frequent praise in contemporary newspapers for his endeavours both as a manager and as actor. However, farces and racy productions of Shakespeare, often with songs and dances interpolated, required only a modicum of talent. Some of the comedy at the New Queen's Theatre was declared offensive and Lazar's management did little to encourage respectable audiences. Although not the first actor to play in Adelaide, John Lazar occupies an important place in the city's theatrical history since his was the first serious theatrical enterprise undertaken there.

In the 1850s Lazar's interest in the theatre lessened. He established a jeweller's and silversmith's business in Hindley

Street, Adelaide, and with this commercial background launched into civic affairs, becoming an alderman of the Adelaide City Council in 1853. He was mayor of Adelaide from 1855 to 1858, and he retired from the council in 1859. In 1863 he went to New Zealand where, somewhat surprisingly, he filled a number of purely administrative posts in various local government organizations.

John Lazar married Julia Solomon in London on 2 November probably in 1823. His sons Samuel and Abraham both became prominently associated with the theatre in Australia. He died in New Zealand on 8 June 1879. A portrait in oils is in the Freemasons' Hall, Adelaide.

G. L. Fischer, 'The professional theatre in South Australia, 1838-1922', Aust Letters, 2 (1959-60), no 4; G. L. Fischer, The Queen's Theatre, Adelaide, 1840-1842 (SAA).

G. L. FISCHER

LAZAREV, MIKHAIL PETROVICH (1788-1851), admiral and explorer, graduated from the Russian Naval Academy in 1803 and volunteered for further training service with the British navy. During the next five years Lazarev took part in voyages in the North and Mediterranean Seas, Pacific, Atlantic and Indian Oceans. On his return to Russia he took part in a battle against the Anglo-Swedish fleet in the Baltic, and in 1812 saw service in the brig Phoenix during its attack on Danzig. Between 1813 and 1816 he was in command of the Suvorov of the Russian-American Co. on a voyage around the world, in the course of which in 1814 he called at Port Jackson, and proceeding north from Sydney discovered and named the Suvorov group of islands. In 1819 he was appointed to command the Mirny, the second ship of the Russian Antarctic Expedition under the leadership of Captain F. F. Bellingshausen [q.v.] in the Vostok. This expedition twice visited Port Jackson. In 1822-25 Lazarev was in command on another round-the-world voyage in the Kreiser, with his brother Andrei in the Ladoga. They called at Hobart Town in 1823, and Andrei published an account of this voyage in 1832. In 1827 in command of the Azov, Mikhail Lazarev served with great distinction in the battle of Navarino. In 1833 he was promoted vice-admiral and appointed commander-in-chief of the Black Sea Fleet. He died in April 1851 in Vienna, where he was undergoing medical treatment.

A. Lazarev, Plavanie vokrug sveta na shliupe Ladoga (St Petersburg, 1832); N. Ivashnitsov, Obozrenie russkikh krugo-svetnykh puteshestvii (St Petersburg, 1850); A. V. Sokolov and E. G. Kushnarev, Tri krugosvetnykh plavaniia M. P. Lazareva (Moscow, 1951); M. P. Lazarev, Dokumenty, ed A. A. Samarov, 1 (Moscow, 1952); C. M. Hotimsky, Russkie v Avstralii (Melb, 1957); N. N. Baranovskii et al, Otechestvennye fiziko-geografy i puteshestvenniki (Moscow, 1959); Hobart Town Gazette, 31 May, 7, 14, 21 June 1823.   C. M. HOTIMSKY

LEAKE, GEORGE (1786-1849), merchant, was born in England, the son of Luke Leake and his wife Ann, née Heading. He married Anne Growse, who died in 1815 leaving him with one daughter, Ann Elizabeth. He sailed for the Swan River settlement in the Calista, arriving in August 1829. He was followed some months later by his mother, his daughter and his brother Luke. He brought with him six servants and considerable property which entitled him to 15,000 acres, most of which he selected on the Upper Swan. He was later granted a further 10,000 acres.

He set up in business as a merchant backed by large funds, and while the colony was struggling his sensible advice to Governor Stirling and financial assistance to settlers were a great asset. Lieutenant H. W. Bunbury [q.v.] noted in his diary in 1836 that Leake had it in his power to ruin two-thirds of the settlers by foreclosing his mortgages. Leake's public activities were many and varied. He was one of the initiators and an original director of the first Bank of Western Australia, formed in 1837. In 1839 he was one of four unofficial nominees to join five official members of the Legislative Council and retained his seat until his death. His commercial experience and ability to assess facts made him a practical legislator of great value. He was appointed a magistrate for the territory in 1839, the first to hold this position. In the same year he was chairman of the Perth Town Trust and later became chairman of the General Roads Trust. Also in 1839 he was appointed a commissioner to act as guardian to emigrant minors sent out by the Children's Friend Society. He was an early director of the Agricultural Society, an original member of the Central Board of Works constituted in 1847, and a large subscriber and member of the committee for building the Anglican church in Perth.

In 1840 he married Georgiana Mary Kingsford; there was no issue. He died on 31 May 1849, survived by his wife and daughter, who had married Richard McBride Broun in 1837.

W. St Pierre Bunbury and W. P. Morrell

(eds), *Early days in Western Australia, being the letters and journal of Lieut H. W. Bunbury* (Lond, 1930); A. Burton, 'George Leake at sea, 1829', *JRWAHS*, 1 (1927-31); *Perth Gazette*, 10 Oct 1840, 8 June 1849; *Inquirer*, 13 June 1849; P. U. Henn, Genealogical notes (Battye Lib, Perth).   M. MEDCALF

LEAKE, JOHN (1780-1865), pastoralist, was born on 5 December 1780, at Ellington near Ramsgate, Kent, England, the son of Robert Leake and his wife Sarah. His family were partners in the mercantile firm of Travis & Leake of Hull. Leake served as an ensign in the Hull Volunteers and saw action in the Napoleonic war before 1805, when he married Elizabeth (1786-1852), the daughter of William Bell, a Hull merchant, and his wife Jane. At the end of the war Leake took his family of six sons to Hamburg where he was soon well liked as the representative of many Yorkshire business houses and as a member of the committee for managing the affairs of the Church of England.

In 1822 he decided to emigrate and, with letters from the Colonial Office, William Wilberforce, General F. A. Wetherall and the British consul at Hamburg, he arrived at Hobart Town with most of his family and two servants in the *Andromeda* in May 1823. On the passage unhappy differences arose over the division of passengers at meals, and on landing Leake found it necessary to sue the captain (Muddle) for discriminatory treatment. For importing merchandise worth £3000 he was granted 2000 acres of land which he chose on the Macquarie River, near Campbell Town, adjoining that of other Hamburg emigrants. He established his family on this property, Rosedale, and left its management to his eldest son William, while he acted as accountant in the Derwent Bank in Hobart. By May 1828 he had a hundred Saxon sheep of the Steiger and Gadegast breeds, another highly improved flock of 1500, a nine-roomed stone and brick house, barns and other improvements. The government, pleased with his industry and profit from sales of wool and wheat, granted him an additional 2000 acres, part of which he located adjoining Rosedale and part at the Hunting Ground. In 1830 he took over the management of the farm and his son William replaced him at the bank. He later returned to banking, conducting the local branch of the Commercial Bank from its opening in 1838.

Made a justice of the peace in 1832, Leake acted as police magistrate at Campbell Town in the absence of the regular officer in 1834. In this capacity he handled disputes with kindliness and consideration and won from a critical superior the candid acknowledgment that his decisions were always right. Well liked for personal qualities and admired for his sagacity and successful industry, he was nominated to the Legislative Council in 1846 on the resignation of the Patriotic Six. Though not always in favour of Lieut-Governor Eardley-Wilmot's policies, he upheld his honour and personally appealed against his ill treatment to the secretary of state. When Sir William Denison had to reinstate the Patriotic Six, Leake lost his seat, but recovered it in 1848. Although a government nominee on the council until 1856, he took an independent line and did not always support the governor, but when he differed he registered his opposition responsibly and his dissent was constructive. He became a personal friend of Denison and one of his chief supporters for the continuance of transportation. Having himself had success in employing convicts by tempering careful management with encouragement and kindness, he advocated a policy of colonial assignment as an apprenticeship for rehabilitating prisoners after a period of punishment in England.

With the coming of responsible government in 1856 Leake retired to Rosedale, which had been restyled in the 1840s by James Blackburn [q.v.] into a stately Italian villa. His wife died here in 1852, and the management of his estate passed to his son Arthur, leaving Leake to spend his last years in fostering local projects. Earlier a member of the country committee of the Hobart Town Auxiliary Bible Society, he was a generous subscriber to the Campbell Town Church of England of which he was a churchwarden. He also endowed the hospital. In 1851-65 he was local commissioner of the Supreme Court of Van Diemen's Land. He died on 6 January 1865.

Two of his sons settled in South Australia, another became a successful doctor, and the youngest Charles Henry, was instrumental in organizing the Campbell Town water supply from the lake later named after him.

H. B. Stoney, *A residence in Tasmania* (Lond, 1856); K. R. von Stieglitz, *A short history of Campbell Town and the Midland pioneers* (Launceston, 1948); Correspondence file under Leake (TA).   A. RAND

LEARMONTH, JOHN (1812-1871), THOMAS (1818-1903), SOMERVILLE (1819-1878), and ANDREW JAMES (1825-1892), early settlers, were the sons of Thomas Learmonth (1783-1869) and his second wife, Christian Donald. They were grandsons of Margaret Livingstone, heiress to her grandfather, Alexander Mitchell, of Parkhall, Stirlingshire, Scotland, and her husband, John Learmonth, merchant, of Leith.

Thomas Learmonth senior's eldest brother, Alexander, inherited Parkhall, but died bankrupt in 1815, soon after Thomas, who had farmed the customs at Grangemouth, left for India to succeed the second brother, John, who had made enough at Calcutta to return and buy Parkhall when auctioned in 1820.

From India, doubtless influenced by Captain Charles Swanston and the Mercer [qq.v.] connexion, Thomas Learmonth senior moved to Van Diemen's Land, where by May 1835 he was a merchant in Hobart Town. Of his sons, John (M.D. Edinburgh) was married on 24 January 1837 to Anna, second daughter of Dr John Macwhirter, of Edinburgh; Thomas and Somerville began at Port Phillip as squatters in the following April. Andrew lived in Tasmania; in April 1845 he left for England with John's eldest son, John Franklin, who like himself became an ensign in the East India Co.'s army, but not before 1850, when Andrew returned to Australia, pending retirement after five years of service.

About 1845, shortly before he visited Britain, from which he returned in 1848, John Learmonth, whose headquarters had become Geelong, began to build a homestead which still stands, on freehold at Batesford acquired by his father in 1839 as successor with Swanston, Mercer, and John Montagu [q.v.] to the assets of the Port Phillip Association. This was called Laurence Park, after Thomas Learmonth senior's former holding near Falkirk. Here Andrew was in charge during 1854-55 when his brother was absent again; but by 1859 he was once more in Britain. His mother had died in Tasmania in 1841 and his father had suffered in that period's general financial collapse. By 1853, however, Thomas Learmonth senior was in Scotland with a third wife. There he remained, succeeding to the Parkhall estate in 1864, and taking the name of Livingstone before his own. All his sons left descendants, and all returned to Britain before or soon after his death.

Thomas and Somerville, acting first as agents for their father and brother John, led in the pastoral settlement of Port Phillip, and finally in wool production. They soon moved from Geelong to the Ballarat district, and from their Boninyong station took up the larger run of Borrumbeet. There, about 1859, with Andrew's help in the planning, they completed their Scottish baronial Ercildoun homestead, which apparently dates from 1854, the

year after Thomas responded from Boninyong to La Trobe's request for details of local settlement, and the year before the Boninyong station was let. Before they sold Ercildoun to Samuel Wilson in 1873 and left Australia, no woolgrower had better sheep than T. & S. Learmonth.

Thomas's report to La Trobe, with its accompanying map, sufficiently illustrates the partners' drive and intelligence. Ercildoun furniture in the Ballarat Art Gallery displays their taste. They were strict Presbyterians, whose departure has been attributed to their belief that they were unjustly treated in the notorious case of the Mount Egerton mine.

But, as heirs of Scotland and India, undoubtedly the brothers were versed in shrewd calculation and finesse. Despite their close attention to Thomas Shaw's [q.v.] Australian merino, they were essentially detached, investing sojourners, not inextricably entangled. Thomas junior, who finally possessed Parkhall, married in 1856 Louisa (d. 1878), youngest daughter of Major-General Sir Thomas Valiant, and in 1879 the fourth daughter of Lestock Reid (Mrs John Learmonth's uncle), of the Bombay Civil Service, whose second daughter married Somerville in 1860. Andrew's wife, whom he married in 1869, became Viscountess Portman in 1908.

T. F. Bride (ed), *Letters from Victorian pioneers* (Melb, 1898); P. L. Brown (ed), *The narrative of George Russell* (Lond, 1935); P. L. Brown (ed), *Clyde Company papers*, 2-5 (Lond, 1952-63); M. L. Kiddle, *Men of yesterday* (Melb, 1961); T. L. Mitchell papers (ML); Learmonth papers (SLV).   P. L. BROWN

LEE, WILLIAM (1794?-1870), settler, was born at Norfolk Island, probably the William Smith whose birth on 1 April 1794 was recorded there and probably son of the convict Sarah Smith who at her death in October 1804 was described as the wife of William Pantoney, alias Panton. He had arrived in the *Matilda* in August 1791, after being sentenced at Huntingdon to transportation for seven years on 11 March 1787. For many years William Lee was known as William Pantoney junior; he accompanied Pantoney to Port Dalrymple in 1805 and lived with him at Windsor in 1814. In 1812 William Lee's sister Maria married James Bloodsworth [q.v.] at St Philip's under the name of Maria Pantoney.

In 1816 William Pantoney junior was issued with government cattle and in 1818, under the name of William Lee and recommended by William Cox [q.v.] as a suitable settler, he was one of the first settlers at Bathurst and was given a grant of 134 acres at Kelso. Commissioner Bigge [q.v.] presented Lee with a ram as a reward for his industry, and recommended an increase in his grant, which Governor Brisbane later made, raising it to 300 acres. On 26 March 1821 Lee married Mary, the daughter of Thomas and Mary Dargin, at Windsor, and took his bride to Kelso. He became noted as a discoverer of good pastoral land and for introducing fine cattle to the district. He accompanied William Lawson [q.v.] on the first journey to Mudgee. In 1828 he built Claremont, and gradually acquired considerable property in the Bathurst district. He was granted 2430 acres at Larras Lake in 1830, and later took up stations on the Bogan, Lachlan and Castlereagh Rivers. At the time of his death his estate, sworn at £41,000, included 18,509 acres in the County of Wellington, and land at Lane Cove, Emu Plains, Bathurst, on the Lachlan River and O'Connell plains.

In July and August 1842 Lee occasioned a sharp clash between the squatters and Governor Gipps, when a public meeting of squatters at Bathurst protested against Lee being deprived of a depasturing licence for the Bogan district. Lee's stockmen had moved from the licensed area to a prohibited area; there the party was attacked by natives who had accompanied them from the Bogan and many were killed. The survivors summoned the police and a massacre of the Aboriginals followed. The squatters argued that Lee's men were forced to abandon the licensed station by drought, that Lee was not aware of the prohibited area, and that he was not given an opportunity of making his defence. Gipps replied that Lee was responsible for the unlawful action of his men and was morally responsible for the slaughter of the Aboriginals, and so refused either him or his son a licence for that district. The Australian, 26 August 1842, accused Gipps of failing to prove a case against Lee, but the Legislative Council rejected the squatters' petition for an amendment to the Crown Lands Occupation Act.

William Lee became a prominent Bathurst figure and in 1856-58 sat in the first Legislative Assembly as member for Roxburgh. He died at Kelso on 18 November 1870, aged 76; his wife Mary died on 15 September 1886, aged 87; both were buried in the Holy Trinity churchyard, Kelso. They had four daughters and six sons, of whom John, Thomas, William and George occupied stations throughout New South Wales. In 1938 a memorial was unveiled to William Lee at Larras Lake.

HRA (1), 23; G. S. Oakes, Kelso Church and the pioneers of the west (Syd, 1921); E. H. Brady, Short chapter of Australian family history (Syd, 1923); W. Lawson, Bathurst the golden, 1815-1938 (Bathurst, 1938); E. H. Brady, 'William Lee of Larras Lake', JRAHS, 25 (1939); W. G. Lee, 'A monument to William Lee', JRAHS, 24 (1938); Sydney Gazette, 22 June 1816; Australian, 3, 22, 24 Aug 1842; SMH, 26 Nov 1870; Norfolk Island victualling book (ML); MS cat under Lee, Pantoney (ML).   VIVIENNE PARSONS

LEICHHARDT, FRIEDRICH WILHELM LUDWIG (1813-1848?), naturalist and explorer, was born on 23 October 1813 at Trebatsch, Prussia, the fourth son and sixth of the eight children of Christian Hieronymus Matthias Leichhardt, farmer and royal inspector of peat, and his wife Charlotte Sophie, née Strählow. Leichhardt was educated at Trebatsch, a boarding school at Zaue, a gymnasium at Cottbus, and at the Universities of Berlin (1831, 1834-36) and Göttingen (1833). At Göttingen friendship with a fellow student, John Nicholson, who had studied medical science, aroused Leichhardt's interest in science, and he turned from his earlier study of philosophy and languages to the natural sciences. Leichhardt pursued knowledge for its own sake and not in preparation for any particular qualification or career; he ceased to follow a prescribed syllabus and no university degree was ever conferred upon him. The practice of addressing Leichhardt as 'Doctor' arose later out of recognition by his contemporaries that he was a man of learning dedicated to the pursuit of knowledge.

In 1837 John Nicholson's younger brother William, with whom Leichhardt studied at Berlin, returned to his home at Clifton in Gloucestershire and Leichhardt went with him. Until 1842 these two young men lived frugally on William's small income while they studied medical and natural science at the Royal College of Surgeons, the British Museum and the Jardin des Plantes, and by field observation in England, France, Italy and Switzerland. To enable Leichhardt to fulfil his plan to study the natural sciences in a vast new field William Nicholson paid his fare to Australia, provided clothes and necessities for the journey and gave him £200.

Leichhardt sailed from London in October 1841 in the Sir Edward Paget and arrived in Sydney on 14 February 1842. His expressed intention was to explore the inland of Australia. For six months he studied the Sydney district; he gave some lectures on its geology and botany. He hoped that Governor Gipps would establish a museum as a national institution and appoint him curator, or would appoint him director of the Botanical Garden, but he was not given any official position.

In September 1842 Leichhardt went to the Hunter River valley where he studied the geology, flora and fauna, and observed methods of farming and viticulture. Overland journeys undertaken alone between Newcastle and the Moreton Bay District occupied 1843 and early 1844. From May to July 1844 Leichhardt was in Sydney arranging his collections of plant and rock specimens and working upon the notes of his observations of the geology of the areas he had visited. He had hoped to accompany an overland expedition from Sydney to Port Essington which the Legislative Council had recommended and the surveyor-general, Sir Thomas Mitchell [q.v.], was willing to lead. Governor Gipps, however, refused to sanction 'an expedition of so hazardous and expensive a nature, without the knowledge and consent' of the Colonial Office. Leichhardt, irked by the delay and the uncertainty that an expedition financed by the government would be approved, decided himself, with the aid of private subscription, to lead an expedition of volunteers. Six including Leichhardt sailed from Sydney on 13 August 1844. In the Moreton Bay District four more joined the expedition, which left Jimbour, the farthest outpost of settlement on the Darling Downs, on 1 October. Two of the party turned back and on 28 June 1845 John Gilbert [q.v.] was killed in an attack on Leichhardt's camp by Aboriginals. The remaining seven reached Port Essington on 17 December 1845, completing an overland journey of nearly 3000 miles.

Returning in the *Heroine*, Leichhardt arrived in Sydney on 25 March 1846. As it was believed that his party had perished their unexpected success was greeted with great rejoicing. Leichhardt was hailed as 'Prince of Explorers' and his party as national heroes, and their achievement was rewarded by a government grant of £1000 and private subscriptions amounting to over £1500.

Leichhardt prepared his journal of the expedition from Moreton Bay to Port Essington for publication in England. He gave lectures on the 'Geology, Botany, Natural History, and Capabilities of the Country between Moreton Bay and Port Essington', and organized his next expedition, using to equip it part of his share (£1500) of the Port Essington reward. He planned to cross Australia from the Darling Downs to the west coast and to follow the coast south to the Swan River settlement. In December 1846 his party of eight including himself set out from the Darling Downs. Delayed by heavy rain and the straying of animals being taken for food, and weakened by fever, they were forced, after covering only 500 miles, to return in June 1847. After a fortnight's rest Leichhardt spent six weeks and covered 600 miles examining the course of the Condamine River and the country between Mitchell's route (1846) and his own route.

In August Leichhardt returned to Sydney to organize a second Swan River expedition. By February 1848 a party of seven including himself was assembled on the Darling Downs. He learned that Edmund Kennedy [q.v.] had returned from tracing the course of the river named the Victoria by Mitchell, and had reported that it was the upper part (Barcoo) of Cooper Creek. Believing himself again 'alone in the field' and confident that he could solve many problems about central Australia if he could skirt the northern limit of the desert he set out from the Condamine River in March 1848. By 3 April he reached McPherson's station, Cogoon, on the Darling Downs. After moving inland from Cogoon the expedition disappeared and no evidence showing conclusively what happened to it has been found.

Before Leichhardt's disappearance his contemporaries valued his work highly: in April 1847 the Geographical Society, Paris, divided the annual prize for the most important geographic discovery between Leichhardt and Rochet d'Héricourt, and on 24 May the Royal Geographical Society, London, awarded him its Patron's medal as recognition of 'the increased knowledge of the great continent of Australia' gained by his Moreton Bay-Port Essington journey. Prussia recognized this achievement by the king's pardon for having failed to return to Prussia when due to serve a period of compulsory military training. Geologists and botanists valued Leichhardt's collections of specimens and the records of his observations which, in an age accustomed to extravagant travellers' tales, were remarkable for their restraint and accuracy; he believed that as long as the traveller was truthful the scientist at home would be thankful to him. Leichhardt was a most dedicated servant of science and from this very dedication sprang a singleness of purpose which shaped his life, and made him somewhat ruthlessly regardless of all but his research. With perseverance, energy, courage and complete disregard of discomfort, and of the physical handicap of poor eyesight, he pursued his goals as 'an explorer of nature'. In Europe and Australia he found friends confident of his ability and the value of his work whose hospitality provided him with places to live while he studied. Yet Leichhardt, described by one of his hosts as 'the most amiable of men', was described by some, though not all, who accompanied him on his expeditions as jealous, selfish, suspicious, reticent, careless, slovenly, wholly unfitted for leadership, and 'very lax in his religious opinion'. Born into a Lutheran family, Leichhardt remembered with affection the church of his childhood, but grew independent of the teaching of any church, finding 'sufficient' the simple statement of faith 'I believe in Jesus Christ our Saviour'.

The contradiction between the admiration and affection for Leichhardt expressed by action and word during his lifetime and the adverse criticism which began about twenty years after he disappeared, makes any reliable assessment of his personal character wait upon the findings of research and the weighing of evidence.

An assessment of Leichhardt's work credits him with achieving one of the longest journeys of exploration by land in Australia, and one of the most useful in the discovery of 'excellent country available . . . for pastoral purposes', and in the collection of the data for the earliest map of the country covered by his route. Leichhardt left records of his observations in Australia from 1842 to 1848 in manuscript diaries, letters, notebooks, sketch-books, maps, and in his published works. These are: *Aseroe rubra*—description and drawing in 'Decades of Fungi' by M. J. Berkeley, *London Journal of Botany*, 3 (1844); 'Scientific Excursions in New Holland, by Dr Ludwig Leickhardt 1842-44; extracted from his letters to M. G. Durand, of Paris. Communicated by P. B. Webb, Esq.' *London Journal of Botany*, 4 (1845); 'Report of the expedition of L. Leichardt, Esq., from Moreton Bay to Port Essington', *Sydney Morning Herald*, 26 March 1846; *Lectures delivered by Dr. Ludwig Leichhardt, at the Sydney School of Arts, on the 18th and 25th days of August, 1846* (Sydney, 1846); 'Die heissen Winde Australiens' (Leichardt Schriftliche Mittheilung) *Froriep's Fortschritte der Geogr. u. Naturgesch.*, 2, 4 February 1847; L. Leichhardt, *Journal of an Overland Expedition in Australia, from Moreton Bay to Port Essington, a distance of upwards of 3000 miles, during the years 1844-1845* (London, 1847); *A detailed Map of Dr. Ludwig Leichhardt's route in Australia from Moreton Bay to Port Essington;* 'An account of a journey to the westward of Darling Downs, undertaken with the view of examining the country between Sir Thomas Mitchell's track and my own', *Sydney Morning Herald*, 11 October 1847; 'Ueber die Kohlenlager von Newcastle am Hunter von Ludwig Leichhardt in Australien'. Mitgetheilt von H. Girard in Ber-

lin (Taf. I), *Zeitsch. der deutschen geol. Ges.*, 1 (1849); 'Remarks on the Bones brought to Sydney by Mr Turner' by Ludwig Leichhardt in *Further Papers relative to the Discovery of Gold in Australia presented to both Houses of Parliament, December 1854* (London, 1855); 'Beiträge zur Geologie von Australien' von L. Leichhardt, herausgegeben von H. Girard, *Abh. naturf orsch. Ges. Halle*, 3, 1855 (1856); L. Leichhardt, 'Notes on the Geology of parts of New South Wales & Queensland, made in 1842-43', W. B. Clarke, ed., *Australian Almanac 1867*; W. B. Clarke, ed., 'Journal of Dr Leichhardt's Third Expedition', *Waugh's Australian Almanack 1860*; Sketch Map of the Balonne River and country he had ridden over done at Cecil Plains, August 1847 by Ludwig Leichhardt, in H. S. Russell, *The genesis of Queensland* (Sydney, 1888).

The Mitchell Library, Sydney, has a lithographic copy of a drawing of Leichhardt in 1846 by C. Rodius [q.v.]. The Heimat Museum in Beeskow has a portrait of Leichhardt which is a copy by Elisabeth Wolf in 1938 of a picture by Schmalfuss, 1855.

HRA (1), 24-26; C. P. Hodgson, *Reminiscences of Australia* (Lond, 1846); J. D. Lang, *Cooksland in north-eastern Australia* (Lond, 1847); E. A. Zuchold, *Dr Ludwig Leichhardt* (Leipzig, 1856); D. Bunce, *Australasiatic reminiscences* (Melb, 1857); J. Forrest, *Explorations in Australia* (Lond, 1875); G. Neumayer and O. Leichhardt (eds), *Dr Ludwig Leichhardt's Briefe an seine Angehörigen* (Hamburg, 1881); J. F. Mann, *Eight months with Dr Leichhardt, in the years 1846-47* (Syd, 1888); T. Archer, *Recollections of a rambling life* (Yokohama, 1897); A. Daiber, *Geschichten aus Australien* (Leipzig, 1902); C. D. Cotton, *Ludwig Leichhardt and the great south land* (Syd, 1938); A. H. Chisholm, *Strange new world* (Syd, 1941); L. L. Politzer (ed), *Dr Ludwig Leichhardt's letters from Australia . . . March 23, 1842 to April 3, 1848* (Melb, 1945); L. L. Politzer, *Bibliography of literature on Dr Ludwig Leichhardt* (Melb, 1953); A. C. Gregory, Expedition in search of Dr Leichhardt, PP (LA NSW), 1858, v 3; *Bulletin de la Société de Géographie*, 3 (1847); JRGS, 17 (1847); H. Hely, 'Expedition in search of Dr Leichhardt', PRGSSA, 16 (1914-15); E. E. Larcombe, 'The search for Dr Leichhardt', JRAHS, 12 (1926), 16 (1930); G. Krefft, 'Biographical sketch of youth and early manhood of Dr. Ludwig Leichhardt', SMH, 29 June 1866; J. H. Nicholson, 'Leichhardt and his friends', *Qld Daily Guardian*, 9 Aug 1866; Leichhardt diaries and papers (ML); L. Leichhardt, Letters (in possession of M. Aurousseau); W. Phillips, Journal (ML); J. Gilbert, Diary 18 Sept 1844-22 June 1845 (ML); E. F. Kunz, Report of Leichhardt papers in Mitchell and Dixson libraries, 1956 (ML).

RENEE ERDOS

LEIGH, SAMUEL (1785-1852), Methodist missionary, was born on 1 September 1785 at Milton, Staffordshire, England. He was thoughtful and studious, responsive to religious influences, and joined the Independent Church at Hanley, where he became a lay helper and preached in the adjacent villages. He attended a Congregational seminary at Gosport, Hampshire, but found that he could not accept its Calvinistic teachings and withdrew. He then joined the Wesleyan Society at Portsmouth, was accepted as a probationer by the Methodist Conference and appointed to the Shaftesbury circuit. Deeply conscious of his call as a missionary he offered for service abroad and was appointed to North America by the 1814 conference. This assignment was cancelled at the last moment and he was sent to New South Wales in answer to an appeal for a missionary by Methodists there.

Leigh arrived in Sydney in the *Hebe* on 10 August 1815, and presented his credentials next day. At first Governor Macquarie, distrusting 'Sectaries', gave Leigh scant encouragement, but the missionary's sincerity and singlemindedness gradually won his respect and support. The Anglican chaplains helped him consistently from the time of his arrival. His first service was held in a cottage in the Rocks area, where a Wesleyan Society had been meeting since 1812, but he soon turned his attention to the country and went to Castlereagh. He made contact with a farmer, John Lees, who was responsible for building there the first Methodist church in Australia. Leigh opened it on 7 October 1817. He then opened preaching places at Parramatta, Windsor, Liverpool and elsewhere in the district. On 13 September 1818 he laid the foundation stone of a chapel at Windsor, built on land given by Samuel Marsden [q.v.]. In January 1819 he laid the foundation stone of another chapel on land in Macquarie Street given by the governor and Thomas Wylde. In March he opened a small chapel which a retired soldier, Sergeant James Scott [q.v.], had built at his own expense in Princes Street. Thus Leigh established the first Methodist circuit, with some fourteen preaching places, which involved him in 150 miles of travel every three weeks.

He paid two visits to Newcastle, the first in response to a request from the Anglican chaplain, William Cowper [q.v.], the second at the express wish of Macquarie, and preached on both occasions. He was an active member of the Society for Promoting Christian Knowledge and Benevolence and helped to form the Colonial Auxiliary Bible Society in March 1817. But his strenuous work took heavy physical toll, and his friend Marsden generously provided him with a nine-month health trip to his mission of lay settlers at the Bay of Islands, New Zealand. When Leigh returned, it was obvious that a longer sea voyage was required to restore his health, and in 1820 he sailed for England. There he induced the conference to sanction a mission to New Zealand; and he married Catherine Clewes of Staffordshire. On the return voyage in 1821, the ship called at Hobart, where Leigh founded a mission and left it in the charge of Rev. William Horton, who had come from England with him. In February 1822 Leigh went with his wife to New Zealand where he established the first Wesleyan mission at Whangaroa. They returned to Sydney in September 1823 after being shipwrecked and suffering great privations. Despite indifferent health, Leigh continued to keep close touch with missionary activities. He was for a while acting superintendent of the Sydney circuit and later was appointed to Parramatta. There his wife died on 15 May 1831, and next year Leigh, saddened in spirit and broken in health, returned to England. He filled a number of circuit appointments, married Elizabeth, widow of Rev. William Kaye, in 1842, retired in 1845 and died on 2 May 1852, still earnestly commending the claims of missionary work in Australia and the South Seas.

The indefatigable labours, apostolic zeal and quiet courage that characterized all his undertakings give Leigh an honoured place in the history of Methodism. His memory is perpetuated in New South Wales by the Leigh Memorial Centenary Church, Parramatta, and the Leigh Theological College, Enfield.

A. Strachan, *Life of the Rev. Samuel Leigh* . . . 3rd ed (Lond, 1870).   R. H. DOUST

LEMPRIERE, THOMAS JAMES (1796-1852), public official, author and artist, was born on 11 January 1796 at Hamburg, Germany, the son of Thomas Lempriere, a British banker and merchant of Norman-Jersey descent, and his wife Harriet, née Allen. In 1803 he was interned by the French but, owing to his youth, was soon released to join his mother in England. His father, who had conducted a banking house at Calais, remained interned until the armistice of 1813, when he rejoined his family in England and resumed business there as a merchant.

In 1822 T. J. Lempriere emigrated to Van Diemen's Land in the *Regalia*. In Hobart Town on 29 May 1823 he married

Charlotte Smith; they had twelve children. He received a grant of land and became a merchant and foundation shareholder of the Bank of Van Diemen's Land. He was joined by his parents and sisters in 1825 when, with his father, he formed a merchant business in Hobart Town trading as Lempriere & Co., which failed in 1827. He left the company in 1826 for employment in the Commissariat Department as a storekeeper at the penal settlements on Maria Island and Macquarie Harbour. In 1831 he was transferred to the commissariat headquarters at Hobart as a clerk. He was promoted deputy-assistant-commissary-general on 20 January 1837 and assistant-commissary-general in December 1844. On 25 May 1846 he was also appointed a coroner for Tasmania. He was recalled to England in 1849 for immediate transfer as assistant-commissary-general in Hong Kong. After a brief service there he was invalided home in 1851 but died on the voyage on 6 January 1852. He was buried at Aden.

Lempriere was a regular diarist and gathered his observations of the convict stations at which he served for publication under the title 'The Penal Settlements of Van Diemen's Land'. This was published in part in the *Tasmanian Journal of Natural Science* during 1842 and 1846 and later issued in full by the Northern Branch of the Royal Society of Tasmania in 1954. His artistic talent was well known and he was commissioned to paint landscapes and the portraits of many prominent settlers. He also maintained a keen interest in natural history and was prominent among the early collectors who provided specimens of Tasmanian animals and plants for study in England.

HRA (1), 10, (3), 4, 5; A *monograph of the house of Lempriere* (priv print, 1862); W. Dixson, 'Notes on Australian Artists', *JRAHS*, 7 (1921); CSO 1 (TA); MS cat under Lempriere (ML); Burial records, St David's Park, Hob City Council.   W. F. ELLIS

LENNOX, DAVID (1788-1873), bridge-builder, was born at Ayr, Scotland. His wife having died in 1828, he took passage to Australia in the *Florentia*, arriving in Sydney in August 1832. He was a master mason and had already occupied responsible positions in Britain for more than twenty years, working on many bridges, including Telford's great suspension bridge over the Menai Straits and the 150-feet span stone-arch bridge over the Severn River at Gloucester.

In Sydney he was at first employed on day wages, cutting the coping stone for the hospital wall in Macquarie Street. His workmanship so impressed Surveyor-General Mitchell [q.v.] that he recommended Lennox to Governor Bourke as a person experienced in the construction of arches of the greatest magnitude in England, and thus secured his appointment on 1 October 1832 to the roads department at a salary of '£120 per annum but without any forage for a horse'. When Lennox was appointed superintendent of bridges in June 1833 Mitchell set him to work on a series of stone bridges, some of which are still standing.

Lennox's first bridge was on the main western road at Lapstone Hill. It is a graceful single arch of 20-feet span and 30 feet above water level, with a road width of 30 feet; it was constructed by a team of convicts using stone quarried near the site. By direction of the governor it was named Lennox Bridge and the keystones bear the name of its builder and the date 1833. It is the oldest bridge still standing on the mainland of Australia, and for ninety-three years it carried all the traffic from Sydney to the west; until 1963 it was still used by vehicles travelling up Mitchell's Pass on the initial climb over the Blue Mountains, although the main road was moved in 1926 to a better gradient by way of Knapsack Gully.

In January 1834 he fixed the site for a bridge over the Medway Rivulet on the main southern road three miles south of Berrima, now known as Three Legs o' Man Bridge; this was a timber structure supported on three masonry piers twenty feet apart. It was completed early in 1835 but was destroyed by flood about 1860 and later replaced. Lennox began the Queen's Wharf at Parramatta in March 1834 and finished it in January 1835; this masonry quay served as the terminal for vessels plying between Sydney and Parramatta. In the latter part of 1834 and throughout 1835 Lennox was engaged on one of his finest works: the Lansdowne Bridge over Prospect Creek on the main southern road near Liverpool, named by the governor in honour of the marquis of Lansdowne.

Lennox's design for the Lansdowne Bridge was for a single 110-feet span masonry arch, 30 feet wide and standing 30 feet above the water. Stone was quarried some seven miles away on the right bank of George's River. Work proceeded slowly because of the shortage of lime and of skilled labour, especially for the centring, and because the creek was subjected to heavy floods; but the bridge was opened by the governor with much ceremony on 26 January 1836. Lennox received a special bonus of £200 for this work and his salary was raised from £120 without allowances to £250 plus 2s. 6d. a day allowance. Lansdowne Bridge still carries traffic on the Hume Highway.

Lennox's 50-feet masonry-arch bridge over the Wingecarribee River at Berrima was opened in 1836 but destroyed by flood in 1860; Black Bob's Bridge, nine miles south of Berrima, was a single 30-feet span timber-beam bridge completed early in 1837, and replaced by the public works department in 1896 with a masonry arch; Duck Creek Bridge on the Parramatta Road thirteen miles from Sydney, originally designed by Lennox as a timber structure on stone piers, was built about 1837 as a semicircular brick arch of 30-feet span; and he produced a design for Bentley's Bridge at Rushcutters Bay, Sydney. At the same time, he constructed a dam across George's River at Liverpool, completed in 1836; and in 1839 erected the town boundary stones of Parramatta. As with all his structures, these works were carried out with convict labour.

The last bridge which he designed and built in New South Wales was over the Parramatta River in Church Street, Parramatta. Originally designed in 1835 as an elliptical arch of 90-feet span, it was built, after much controversy, as a simple stone arch spanning 80 feet and having a width of 39 feet. Construction began in November 1836, using the centring from the Lansdowne Bridge, adjusted to the new span, and the work was finished in 1839; it was named Lennox Bridge by the Parramatta council in 1867. The stone came from the Orphan School quarry, and lime was purchased at 1s. a bushel. This bridge remained unaltered until 1902 when a 10-feet width of the arch was strengthened internally to carry the Parramatta-Castle Hill tramway. In 1912 the parapet on the western side was removed and a cantilevered footway was added; and in 1934-35 the bridge was again widened on the western side by the construction of a stone-faced reinforced concrete arch alongside the original masonry span, and the eastern stone parapet was replaced with concrete.

Lennox was appointed district surveyor to the Parramatta Council in November 1843, but in October 1844 Governor Gipps appointed him to the Port Phillip District as superintendent of bridges, and he sailed from Sydney in November. For nine years he had charge of all roads, bridges, wharves and ferries, and acted as advisory engineer to various government departments. In this period he built fifty-three bridges, the most notable being the first Prince's Bridge over the Yarra River in Melbourne, a stone arch of 150-feet span, and the largest bridge

built by Lennox; it was completed in 1850 and lasted until replaced some thirty-five years later because of the necessity to provide for more traffic.

In November 1853 Lennox retired from the public service of Victoria; his salary had been raised to £300 in 1852 and £600 in 1853, and on his retirement parliament voted him a gratuity of £3000. He remained in Melbourne for nearly two years, returned to New South Wales in June 1855 and finally settled at 4 Campbell Street, Parramatta, in a house of his own design. Essentially a practical man, he amused himself in a small backyard workshop in his old age.

When he had sailed for Australia in 1832 he left behind two young daughters in the care of his sister, who afterwards married James Dalziel. In 1836 the Dalziels, with their own family and Lennox's two daughters, migrated to Australia, arriving in Sydney in the *Wave* in January 1837. The elder daughter Mary married George Urquhart, but died in 1841. Jane Lennox married Charles William Rowling; a widow when her father retired, she shared his home in Parramatta.

David Lennox died on 12 November 1873 and was buried in old St John's cemetery, Parramatta; by some oversight no inscription was placed upon his gravestone, so doubt exists as to the actual spot where his body lies. As a kindly taskmaster he sought mitigation of the sentences of convicts who gave good service and seldom had trouble with any of the hundreds of prisoners employed on his projects. Although retiring by temperament he showed quiet determination when his plans were opposed by others: for example, when Bourke in 1835 advocated a more elaborate design for Lennox Bridge, Parramatta. There is no doubt that, just as his arrival in New South Wales opened a new chapter in the bridge-building history of the colony, so did his departure close it. He was a pioneer of great skill and a master craftsman whose solution to the many technical problems brought him well-deserved and lasting fame.

M. Herman, *The early Australian architects and their work* (Syd, 1954); H. Selkirk, 'David Lennox', *JRAHS*, 6 (1920); W. L. Harvard, 'Mitchell's Pass, near Emu Plains', *JRAHS*, 19 (1934); MS cat under D. Lennox (ML).

J. M. ANTILL

LESLIE, PATRICK (1815-1881), pioneer and grazier, was born on 25 September 1815 at Warthill, Aberdeenshire, Scotland, the second son of William Leslie, ninth laird of Warthill and eighth of Folla, deputy-lieutenant, and his wife Jane, sister of W. S. Davidson [q.v.]. The Leslies were members of the Church of Scotland and Patrick was educated at a college in Aberdeen.

He sailed from London in December 1834 in the *Emma Eugenia* and arrived in Sydney next May. He spent most of a year learning flock management and colonial agriculture under the tutelage of the Macarthurs of Camden. In 1836 he went to manage the property of his uncle, Davidson, on the Krui River at Collaroi; by 1839, however, Leslie had rented Dunheved farm at Penrith and, when his brothers Walter and George arrived, he decided to look for new land north of the limits of settlement. In January 1840 he started with a large party for the Clarence River district, and then resolved to look at the Darling Downs discovered thirteen years before by Allan Cunningham [q.v.]. With one convict, Murphy, as a companion, he crossed and recrossed the southern and eastern downs and decided on the area that was to become Toolburra and Canning Downs for his first station. Walter Leslie and Ernest Dalrymple [q.v.] quickly followed with the flocks, and thus in 1840 the Leslies became the first settlers on the Darling Downs. Patrick returned to Sydney and on 9 September 1840 at Parramatta married Catherine, daughter of Hannibal Hawkins Macarthur [q.v.], and his best man was Stuart Donaldson.

The Leslies set about making Canning Downs a fine property, but had the misfortune to start its development during a depression. Despite a trip to Britain to see whether he could come to some arrangement with Davidson, to whom he was indebted, Patrick Leslie was ruined financially by 1844. Next year he bought thirty-four acres of land in Brisbane and built what became known as Newstead House, where he lived while pasturing his flocks on Canning Downs, now owned by his brothers. In 1846 he obtained a small property near Canning Downs and in 1847 he sold his Brisbane property to George Wickham [q.v.] in order to buy Goomburra on the Darling Downs. In that year, at the government's request, he selected the site for the town of Warwick, and next year bought the first lot in the land sales.

Until the 1850s Patrick Leslie and his brothers were the leading settlers on the Downs, being engaged in building up two very good properties as well as taking a prominent part in the political issues that affected pastoralists and in such transient schemes as the introduction of cotton and llamas. After selling Goomburra to the Sydney brewer, Robert Tooth, Patrick

Leslie returned to Britain, but he soon settled in New Zealand and bought land on the Waikato. He sold this estate in 1879 and retired to Milson's Point, Sydney, where he died on 12 August 1881. His son, William Norman, predeceased him in New Zealand in 1876, aged 35.

Patrick Leslie's chief claim to fame lies in his rediscovery of the Darling Downs and his pioneer work in settling the area. His exploration, with only one convict for company, was hailed by contemporaries as a feat of great merit. It was reported in the *Sydney Herald*, 1 May 1840, under the heading 'Important Discovery' and later generations have agreed that it was a fine piece of bushcraft. Of all the many sons of British landed gentry who did well under the adverse and strange conditions of the Australian bush, few adapted themselves so readily as Patrick Leslie. Roberts described him as 'absolutely fearless and something of a rough jewel, he was active and energetic, "hail-fellow-well-met" and "the prince of bushmen"'.

Leslie was a poor business manager, but his tenacity and courage enabled him to overcome financial reverses and to place himself eventually in a comfortable position. Politically he called himself 'a Rank Tory', which was understandable with his occupation, family connexions and friends. Rarely did a governor please him, though he dined with them all, yet Gipps, by allowing him to bring supplies through Brisbane, made certain the success of Downs settlement. Although an inveterate opponent of Rev. J. D. Lang [q.v.], he became a leader in the separation movement on the Downs, and represented Moreton, Wide Bay, Burnett and Maranoa in the first New South Wales Legislative Assembly in 1857. He could be a vigorous opponent or a staunch friend, and more than once backed his arguments with his fists. Outside his grazing and political interests, his main occupation was the breeding and, to a lesser extent, the racing of bloodstock. He can be regarded as the father of stud breeding in Queensland.

H. S. Russell, *The genesis of Queensland* (Syd, 1888); S. H. Roberts, *The squatting age in Australia 1835-1847*, 2nd ed (Melb, 1964); A. Morgan, 'Discovery of the Darling Downs', *Qld GJ*, 17 (1901-02); K. G. T. Waller, 'The letters of the Leslie brothers in Australia' (B.A. thesis, Univ Qld, 1956); Leslie family letters (ML).   K. G. T. WALLER

LEVEY, BARNETT (1798-1837), merchant and theatre director, was born in London, and arrived in Sydney in December 1821 in the *John Bull* to join his

brother Solomon [q.v.], a prosperous emancipist. Barnett Levey was the first free
Jewish settler in the colony. He established
himself as a merchant and in February
1825 opened a store at 72 George Street. In
June he married Sarah Emma Wilson, stepdaughter of Jacob Josephson, an emancipist.
In August 1825 he was appointed an
auctioneer in Sydney. As a general merchant he sold not only the usual goods
and spirits but also books; he established
one of the first lending libraries. Soon he
became interested in banking: in 1825 he
sold rupees for Colonel Dumaresq [q.v.],
and until the introduction of sterling currency issued the only rupee banknotes in
the colony. In January 1826 he was present
at the foundation meeting of the Sydney
Banking Co. In 1826-27 he erected behind
his store the Colchester warehouse, designed by F. Greenway [q.v.]. The laying
of the foundation stone in June 1827 was
associated with the opening of Masonic
Lodge No. 266, and of No. 260 of which
Levey was a member. He also built a flour-
mill, a wheat store and a windmill. The
erection of the windmill led in February
1827 to an acrimonious dispute with Governor Darling, whom Levey had displeased
in March 1826 when, after the governor's
direction that ticket-of-leave men should
not be licensed as publicans, Levey openly
offered to supply them with liquor. In 1827
he built Waverley House, a two-storey
residence in Georgian style near the later
Bondi Junction. Levey became one of the
first building promoters when in 1830 he
erected cottages in Waverley Crescent.

From 1826 Levey had interested himself
in the cultural activities of Sydney and had
sung songs at a number of concerts. He
now set about establishing the first permanent theatre in Australia. To finance
the building he founded a company in
November 1827, and next March a temporary theatre was erected at the rear of
his property. Because of this project he
neglected his business and in May 1828
had to mortgage his premises and mill to
Cooper & Levey for £4403. To gain more
money, he converted the front of his building into the Royal Hotel. In June 1829 he
obtained from Governor Darling a licence
for holding balls and concerts, but in January 1830 the government stopped his entertainments, 'our prison population being unfit subjects to go to plays'. This brought
Levey near to ruin. His financial situation
became so desperate that he tried to sell
the Royal Hotel. Unable to find a buyer
he evolved a scheme to sell it on the ton-
tine system, but the plan failed and the
hotel, the store, the granary and the mill
were sold by auction to Samuel Lyons

[q.v.] in December 1830. For a time Levey
went back to business, working as a
jeweller, watchmaker and estate agent, but
his determination to establish a theatre
was still strong. In 1832 he was permitted
to present four 'At Homes' at the Royal
Hotel to finance his theatrical plans and
on 22 December received the first theatre
licence granted in the colony. He prepared
a temporary stage in the saloon of the
hotel and, after having offered a silver
medal to the 'poets of Australia' for an
'approved opening address', he opened his
theatre on 26 December 1832 with Douglas
Jerrold's *Black-eyed Susan*. Governor
Bourke patronized his enterprise.

In August 1830 he received a grant of
640 acres in the Blue Mountains, and in
1831 70 acres in the suburb of Alexandria.
In 1835 he received 320 acres more in the
Blue Mountains; he called the mountain
grant Mount Sion, and on it the Pilgrim
Inn (Blaxland) was built.

The properties did not remain long in
his possession because he always needed
money for new ambitious plans. At last in
1833 Levey built, on land at the rear of the
Royal Hotel, the first real theatre in Australia, the Theatre Royal, seating about
1000 people. He secured a licence and it
was opened on 5 October with a presentation of *The Miller and his Men* and a
farce *The Irishman in London*. Levey was
now a theatre director indeed. Under his
direction not only melodramas and come-
dies were performed, but also some of
Shakespeare's plays and the operatic extravaganza *Giovanni in London*. However,
he was soon in trouble and in January
1834 he advertised for partners. Next
month he was joined by Joseph Simmons
[q.v.] who became part proprietor and
acting manager. Levey lost control of the
theatre to other lessees, though in 1836 he
briefly resumed the directorship. He still
kept some commercial interests, conducted
land sales in 1835 and in June 1836 was
appointed a director of the Australian Gaslight Co. In April 1837 he staged, as his
last great performance, with the assistance
of the 4th Regiment, a 'grand national and
patriotic pageant', but it was not a success.
He was now sick, tired, worn out by his
efforts to make the theatre pay. He died on
2 October 1837, leaving a widow and four
small children in poverty. When probate
was granted to his widow his estate did not
exceed £500. He was buried in the Jewish
portion of the Devonshire Street cemetery.
Barnett Levey was an idealist who sacrificed
his fortune and health but failed to reach
his goals; as the *Sydney Times*, 21 October
1837, acknowledged, 'to his spirit and
perseverance are the public indebted for

the introduction of theatricals into New South Wales'.

C. H. Bertie, *The story of the Royal Hotel & the Theatre Royal* (Syd, 1927); B. T. Dowd and W. Foster (eds), *The history of the Waverley municipal district* (Syd, 1959); *JRAHS*, 11 (1925), 306-08; A. W. Hyman, 'Barnett Levey', *Aust Jewish Hist Soc J*, 1 (1939-43); G. F. J. Bergman, 'Barnett Levey', *B'nai B'rith Bulletin*, 3 (1955).

                              GEORGE F. J. BERGMAN

LEVEY, SOLOMON (1794-1833), emancipist and merchant, was sentenced in October 1813 at the Old Bailey to transportation for seven years as an accessory to the theft of 90 lbs of tea and a wooden chest, a charge that he denied. He arrived in Sydney in the *Marquis of Wellington* in January 1815. He lost no time in starting his business career in Sydney, and was soon dealing in real estate and supplying the government store with various goods. On 8 February 1819 he received an absolute pardon and three days later married Ann, daughter of William Roberts, a wealthy emancipist who gave her a rich dowry of land and livestock. In November 1819 a son was born and in 1822 a daughter who died in childhood. The marriage proved a failure; Ann took a lover and ran away but died of maltreatment in February 1824. Levey never married again.

Levey prospered as store-keeper, ship-broker and agent and by 1825 claimed a turnover of £60,000 a year. He had sealing interests and a base at Tahiti whence he imported island products in his own ships; he was a partner in a water-mill at Liverpool, owned a rope factory, and had grazing properties and land grants in the Counties of Argyle and Cumberland. Soon after his pardon he became a proprietor of the Bank of New South Wales; he advocated lower interest rates and association with English banking firms. In December 1824 he joined other respectable citizens in a request to be admitted to jury duties. He was a generous supporter of benevolent and religious institutions and acted as a trustee for the Sydney Public Grammar School.

In June 1825 Levey joined forces with Daniel Cooper [q.v.]. They took over the Lachlan and Waterloo Co., formerly owned by Hutchinson, Terry & Co. By indenture of 6 May 1826 the firm Cooper & Levey was founded, each of the partners bringing £30,000 into the joint-stock enterprise. As importers, exporters, woolbuyers, ship-owners and shipbuilders, shipping agents, whalers and sealers and with their general store at the Waterloo Warehouse in George Street, Sydney, they had a large share of the colony's business. In March 1826 the firm acquired the properties of Captain John Piper [q.v.] in the eastern suburbs of Sydney. In 1828 Cooper & Levey were among the colony's largest owners of stock. The partners later acquired, by grant or purchase, most of the land in Waterloo, Alexandria, Redfern, Randwick and Neutral Bay. In 1826 Levey went to London to establish a buying office for Cooper & Levey and to raise money. In London he chartered several ships to take his merchandise to Sydney and acted as an ardent agent especially for Jewish emigration to New South Wales.

In December 1829 Levey was introduced to Thomas Peel [q.v.] and became his partner in a venture to establish colonists in the new settlement at Swan River. Under the name of Thomas Peel & Co., Levey was to act as director in London and Peel to manage affairs in Western Australia. Through mismanagement in the colony, the venture languished; Peel made no reports and even neglected to assure for Levey half of his land grant of 250,000 acres at Cockburn Sound. Although Levey had provided all the company's capital of £20,000 he continued to back the venture, selling land in Sydney to buy supplies for Peel and his settlers. By 1832 Levey was forced to seek information from the Colonial Office, thus revealing for the first time his share in the company. Although he lost a fortune in the venture he did not live to see its final failure. After a short illness he died in London on 10 October 1833.

Among bequests to his family and to benevolent institutions of various faiths, Levey left £500 to the Sydney College, which became the Sydney Grammar School. This sum, transferred after twenty years, made him the first benefactor of the University of Sydney.

Levey's real estate in New South Wales took ten years to liquidate and the estimated total value amounted to £14,332 10s. In 1843 his son John Levey-Roberts, who lived a life of leisure in Paris, settled the affairs of the partnership with Daniel Cooper and in 1851 came to an agreement with Peel in which Solomon Levey's share of 125,000 acres in Western Australia was assigned to him.

Solomon Levey was a man of upright character and great kindness. He was not only a shrewd pioneer businessman and able financier but an economist of great foresight and an outstanding immigration agent for Australia. When he trusted Thomas Peel, he was probably made incautious by the fact that an aristocrat and relation of Sir Robert Peel deigned to become the partner of a Jewish former convict. He had to pay dearly for this misjudgment.

G. F. J. Bergman, 'Solomon Levey', *JRAHS*, 49 (1963-64).   GEORGE F. J. BERGMAN

LEWIN, JOHN WILLIAM (1770-1819), naturalist and artist, was a son of William Lewin, a fellow of the Linnean Society and author of *The Birds of Great Britain* (London, 1789-94, second edition, 1795-1801). His sons John William and Thomas worked with him at Darenth in Kent and at Hoxton, London, during the preparation of this work; plates occur with their signatures and in his preface their father acknowledges their help in the compilation of the natural history observations.

About 1797 J. W. Lewin was anxious to visit New South Wales. He did not lack patrons. His first book, *Prodromus Entomology, Natural History of Lepidopterous Insects of New South Wales* (London, 1805) was dedicated to Lady Arden 'in grateful remembrance of that goodness which gave the Author an opportunity of employing his talents, as it were in a new world'. On 6 February 1798 the duke of Portland informed Governor Hunter that Lewin would sail in the *Buffalo* and that he should be allowed rations during his residence in the settlement. The entomologist, Dru Drury, who assisted many collectors, supplied him with an entomologist's outfit in payment for which Lewin engaged to send insects from New South Wales. Later Thomas Marsham, author of *Entomologia Britannica* (London, 1802) and Alexander McLeay [q.v.] united with Drury in sending money to Lewin in the colony.

By some mischance Lewin missed the *Buffalo*, although his wife was already on board. She was befriended by the captain and his wife, and after reaching the colony by Rev. Richard Johnson [q.v.] and his wife. Lewin arrived in the *Minerva* on 11 January 1800 and was immediately involved in a lawsuit in defence of his wife against an accusation of misconduct with the second mate of the *Buffalo*. She was cleared, but in September Lewin excused himself to Drury for not repaying his debt by delays caused by this 'unfortunate Business' and by his having been 'taken with the flux' during the winter.

From about September 1800 the Lewins lived at Parramatta. Lewin seized every opportunity of making expeditions to enlarge his collections. In March 1801 he received Governor King's permission to go with James Grant [q.v.] to Bass Strait, but

they ran into stormy weather and Lewin's *Bee*, a decked long-boat accompanying the *Lady Nelson*, was forced to return. A few months later he was with Colonel Paterson [q.v.] exploring the Hunter River and in November 1801 sailed for Tahiti in the brig *Norfolk*, commissioned to procure salt pork. When she ran ashore on Point Venus the ship's company took refuge with the mission there. The men were taken off in the *Porpoise*, and returned to Sydney on 19 December 1802.

In 1804 Governor King granted Lewin a 100-acre farm near Parramatta but it seems unlikely that he had the time or means to develop it. He was busy making expeditions to the Nattai River and the Cowpastures and engraving the plates for his two books on insects and birds. Conscious of his own lack of training in grammar and spelling, he tried to enlist the help of a well educated young man, John Grant [q.v.], who became his close friend in 1804, though it is not known if the requested help was given. Grant's verses praising Lewin, entitled 'Panegyric on an Eminent Artist', occur in a few copies of Lewin's *Birds of New Holland with their Natural History*. He became a member of the Parramatta Loyal Association, in which he rose to the rank of sergeant. He was among the settlers who supported Governor Bligh and was one of the signatories to a petition to Paterson in May 1808, expressing alarm at the governor's deposition.

The farm cannot have prospered for by November 1808 the Lewins were living in Sydney, first in Chapel Row (Castlereagh Street), and later at the Brickfields, on the eastern side of George Street. Both had licences to sell wines and spirits and Lewin advertised for orders for miniatures and portraits. He was paid from the police fund for various services including expeditions to contact Aboriginals and painting a coat of arms for the Supreme Court. In order to assure him some income Governor Macquarie appointed him coroner at Sydney at £40 a year, and doubled the salary in 1814. In 1811 and 1815 he executed 'transparencies' as decorations for the Queen's birthday ball at Government House. He was one of Macquarie's suite when the governor first crossed the Blue Mountains by William Cox's [q.v.] new road in May 1815. In 1817 and 1818 Macquarie commissioned drawings of plants collected during Oxley's [q.v.] explorations. The British government approved his appointment to accompany P. P. King [q.v.] on his explorations in the *Mermaid* but Lewin declined, pleading the difficulty of supporting his family during his absence.

While living in Sydney, Lewin seems to

have still hoped to own a farm. In 1809 Paterson gave him 200 acres in the district of Minto. Macquarie did not confirm this, but gave him 200 acres in Airds, which was perhaps a grant instead of it. In 1811 he sold the Parramatta farm. In 1817 he mortgaged the Airds farm and sold it for £100 next year. On 27 August 1819 he died. He was buried in the old burying ground now occupied by the Sydney Town Hall, but the remains were removed first to the Devonshire Street cemetery and thence, when the Central Railway Station was built, to La Perouse.

Lewin had hoped that the proceeds from the sale of his two books would enable him to return to England. Although this hope was not realized they greatly enhanced his fame and Drury secured his election as an associate of the Linnean Society in 1801. The books' plates are faithful and delicate representations of insects and birds which were then little known. *Prodromus Entomology*, published in 1805, appeared in a second edition in 1822 and the *Birds*, first printed in 1808, had two further editions in 1822 and 1838 as well as the variant published in Sydney in 1813. The texts of the London editions were edited by his brother Thomas with the help of eminent scientists. The collaboration of scientists and the issue of several editions, some reprinted, for watermarks later than imprints occur on plates, show the interest which these works aroused. All are rare today, especially the 1808 *Birds*. Only six copies of it are known, those of George III and five English subscribers. The consignment for Australia appears to have been lost and hence the curious Sydney 'edition' of 1813, with text by J. W. Lewin, perhaps using some descriptions by John Grant, and with plates made up of pulls from the engravings before the copper plates were sent to England, as well as one or two plates not in the London editions. The plates of the *Insects* and some of those in the *Birds* are the earliest copper plates known to have been engraved in New South Wales.

There is a collection of Lewin's paintings in the Mitchell Library, Sydney, and a number of natural history water-colour drawings in the Nan Kivell Collection in the National Library of Australia. His contemporaries esteemed him for his paintings of natural history subjects and of Aboriginals. Unfortunately few of the latter seem to have survived. His landscapes were not so much admired as those of artists adept in exact topography, but today they are historically valuable and have the merit of catching something of the atmosphere of Australian scenery.

All contemporary records bear witness to Lewin's engaging personality and unblemished character as well as to his talents. His wife, Anna Maria, was also gifted. She made drawings of plants and helped with the colouring of prints from the engravings. After Lewin's death Macquarie granted the George Street property to Mrs Lewin. She realized about £600 from the grant and returned to England with her son, William Arden, who had been born probably in 1808, after another child had died. She continued to promote the new edition of the *Birds* and reissues of both books, and from 1825 received an annual grant of £50 from the New South Wales government.

HRA (1), 2-4, 9; Linnean Soc NSW, *The Macleay memorial volume*, ed J. J. Fletcher (Syd, 1893); J. J. Fletcher, 'The Society's heritage from the Macleays', Linnean Soc NSW, *Procs*, 45 (1920); P. Mander-Jones, 'John William Lewin', *JRAHS*, 42 (1956-57); J. W. Lewin to Dru Drury (BM Natural History); MS cat under J. W. Lewin (ML).

PHYLLIS MANDER-JONES

LEWIS, MORTIMER WILLIAM (1796-1879), surveyor and architect, was born in London, the son of Thomas Arundel Lewis and his wife Caroline, née Derby. At 19 he was appointed surveyor and draftsman in the London office of the inspector-general of fortifications, and later as a private practitioner he spent eight years in surveying and building. He then received an appointment as assistant surveyor in the office of the surveyor-general of New South Wales.

Lewis left London in the *Dunvegan Castle* in September 1829 and arrived in Sydney next March with his wife Elizabeth, née Clements, whom he had married in 1819, three sons and one daughter. Another son was born in Sydney. Under the surveyor-general, T. L. Mitchell [q.v.], Lewis mapped the Dividing Range west of Sydney. Mitchell later appointed him town surveyor and in 1835 colonial architect in succession to Ambrose Hallen [q.v.]. Lewis held this post for fifteen years. His first design for the government was a lunatic asylum, which a century later was still part of the Gladesville hospital. More major works followed in 1837: the court-houses of Darlinghurst, Hartley, Berrima and Parramatta. The Darlinghurst court-house is an important example of the Greek revival style which Lewis favoured and used in many buildings. He was a prolific architect. After Government House, Sydney, was designed in London, he supervised its erection in 1838, and designed five gaols, three watchhouses, two police stations, three court-houses, a school, a customs house at Port Phillip and twelve churches, most of them in the Hunter River valley. As well as his buildings, many of Lewis's design drawings remain. They reveal him as a most competent and tasteful draftsman, meticulous in both the structural and pictorial aspects of his work.

The colonial architect's office was in a building, since vanished, attached to the eastern side of the Hyde Park barracks which now serve as the district courts, Queen's Square, Sydney. Lewis lived on the premises. Later he bought an estate at Bronte, where he began building a house which he sold half-finished to Robert Lowe [q.v.]. Soon afterwards Lewis lived at Adelaide Place, Darling Point.

He altered and added to the north wing of the hospital in Macquarie Street, Sydney, when it was converted into the Legislative Council chambers, but his work has since been vastly altered. His customs house at Circular Quay, Sydney, finished in 1844, is now so surrounded and embedded in the modern building that only vestiges can be discerned. Although Lewis was the leading designer in the Greek revival style in Australia, he was quite adept at Gothic revival, in which his most important building was the church of St John the Evangelist, Camden, consecrated on 7 June 1849. Its success is partly accidental, for its loveliest feature is the colourful brickwork of the walls which Lewis intended to plaster but was prevented by lack of funds. The spire is unusual in that it is brickwork, but its plastering over was essential. In the late 1840s he designed Sydney's first museum. Although estimated to cost £3000, some £5800 was spent before the roof was put on. Lewis came under attack from press and government and some legislative councillors wanted to abandon the whole project. Although enough money was granted to complete the museum, an official inquiry fixed the blame on Lewis and he resigned as colonial architect, an unfortunate end to a fruitful career. He was by no means ruined, for in 1850 he built himself a large house facing the Domain and called it Richmond Villa. It still exists as a part of the Parliament House installations, but the decadence of its Gothic revival design contrasts with the excellence of his previous work. He was fortunate that his activities coincided with the best period of Australia's colonial architecture, for by 1850 architectural taste was beginning to decay. It was also fortunate for his reputation that so many of his designs were of public buildings, which made their preservation more likely.

After twenty-nine years in retirement, Lewis contracted a kidney complaint and after an illness of two weeks died on 9 March 1879. He was buried in South Head cemetery, Sydney.

HRA (1), 15, 17, 19; J. Fowles, *Sydney in 1848* (Syd, 1848); C. H. Bertie, *Old colonial byways* (Syd, 1928); M. Herman, *The early Australian architects and their work* (Syd, 1954); *Heads of the People*, 2, 15 Jan 1848; MS cat under M. Lewis (ML); Lewis family papers (in possession of Mrs W. Lewis, Killara, NSW).   MORTON HERMAN

LEWIS, RICHARD (1789-1867), auctioneer and merchant, was born on 21 April 1789 at Oswestry, Shropshire, England, fourth son of Rev. David Lewis, vicar of Abernant and Conwil, Carmarthenshire, South Wales, and his wife Mary, née Lloyd, of Llandissilio in the same county. After some years with a firm of merchants in London he went to Hobart Town in 1815 and founded the business later known as R. Lewis & Sons which engaged in commercial and shipping pursuits. In December 1816 he was appointed government auctioneer, and by the time of Commissioner Bigge's [q.v.] inquiry he was a substantial merchant in the town. In 1823 he was one of the foundation proprietors of the Bank of Van Diemen's Land. His original land grant was at Plas y Dolan, Clarence Plains. In addition to his property at the corner of Collins and Argyle Streets where he carried on his businesses from the late 1820s until 1845, he acquired several others, including twelve acres at New Town, later known as Springvale Tea Gardens, and nine acres at Bellerive described in his will as 'an Inn formerly called the Highlander since known as the Devonshire Hotel and now known as the Retreat'; it is now owned by the Education Department. He acquired farms in the Cambridge district, including Milford (still occupied by his great-granddaughter Miss Margaret Louise Lewis), Llanherne (Hobart Airport), the Neck, the Bluff, Abernant and Cilwen.

On 23 October 1816 he married Isabella, fourth child of Captain Neil MacKellar [q.v.]. They had six sons and five daughters. In the 1840s he made his eldest two sons, David, later mayor of Hobart and colonial treasurer, and Neil, partners in his business. Apart from being made a justice of the peace, he did not take any active part in the political life of Tasmania, but apparently exercised much indirect influence on the community. He made three trips to England before he died at Hobart on 8 November 1867.

HRA (3), 2-4, 6; A. McKay (ed), *Journals of the land commissioners for Van Diemen's Land, 1826-28* (Hob, 1962); Family papers (in possession of author).   HUBERT C. LEWIS

LHOTSKY, JOHN (b. 1800), naturalist, was born on 27 June 1800 in Lemberg, (Lwów), Galicia, of Czechoslovakian parents. He was educated in Prague and Berlin, and joined the Bavarian Botanical Society and became a doctor of medicine in Vienna. The King of Bavaria bestowed a grant to assist his botanical and zoological research in South America and Australia, and after eighteen months in Brazil he arrived in Sydney in 1832.

Lhotsky unsuccessfully sought appointment as colonial zoologist in the museum in Sydney. In 1834 with government help he travelled to the Monaro district and explored its southern mountains. His *A Journey from Sydney to the Australian Alps*, incompletely published in Sydney in 1834-35, was his most important work. It introduced the Snowy River to geography and the prospect of a future city on the limestone 'Kembery' plains; he also envisaged rural development by artesian wells. Back in Sydney he exhibited his new specimens which were said to include gold, but his money was exhausted and his creditors began to press. He sold wood and vegetables for a living and with increasing vehemence kept on trying for a scientific post in the public service. Supported by Baron Bulow, the Prussian ambassador in London, he appealed to the Colonial Office in October 1835 for government help in another expedition to collect specimens for the royal museum at Berlin. When notified next April that his plea was rejected, he appealed again to be rewarded for his discoveries in the interior.

Disgusted with Sydney he went to Hobart Town in October 1836 in the *Francis Freeling*. Next month he was recommended by the surveyor-general, George Frankland [q.v.], to be appointed colonial naturalist. The acting lieut-governor refused, but allowed Lhotsky rations and three assigned servants to collect specimens to be delivered into Frankland's keeping. In less than two months he had more than 100 mineral specimens and 300 plants 'arranged as in European collections'. After Lieut-Governor Franklin arrived Lhotsky was appointed at 10s. a day to plan development of the coal-mines near Port Arthur by convict labour. He also made a complete geological map of Tasman Peninsula and at Hobart reported on a spring in the lime-kilns that Franklin wanted to use for improving the town's water supply.

After three months Lhotsky applied for an increased wage but lost his job. He turned to lecturing and journalism, with some initiative interviewing William Buckley [q.v.] and testing him on the geography of his travels and his knowledge of Aboriginal languages. He also applied for naturalization, but his debts continued to mount. He appealed to the government to buy his collection of natural history as the embryo of a national museum. Franklin was sympathetic but would not have it even at half-price; it was put up for private sale and the Legislative Council agreed to pay Lhotsky's remaining debts. In April 1838 he sailed for London in the *Emu*.

Lhotsky had acquired letters by Ferdinand Bauer [q.v.] written during the voyage of the *Investigator*, which he presented to the Linnean Society in London. A personal letter of recommendation from Franklin to Sir Roderick Murchison was less well received. Lhotsky eked out a living by lecturing and writing. He sank into dire poverty and his health deteriorated. The last record of him is a letter to John Dunmore Lang [q.v.] in 1861 proposing to apply to the Legislative Council in Sydney for alms as the first scientific discoverer of gold.

Lhotsky's newspaper articles are too numerous to list. The Royal Society's *Catalogue of Scientific Papers* shows his contributions to the proceedings of English and other European scientific bodies. His first Australian article was probably the anonymous 'Australian sketches, no 1' in the *Sydney Gazette*, 6 October 1832. Next year he conducted the natural history section of the *New South Wales Magazine*, and anonymously published *Illustrations of the Present State and Future Prospects of the Colony of New South Wales* (Sydney, 1835). His 'Song of the Women of the Menero Tribe' was 'the first specimen of Australian Music', and he also compiled an unpublished vocabulary of Tasmanian Aboriginals in 1836 and 1837 (Mitchell Library). Political and natural history articles appeared in the *New South Wales Literary, Political and Commercial Advertiser* and, from 1837, in *Information for the People* (Hobart). In London he continued to publish tracts and pamphlets: *Hunger and revolution* (1843); *On cases of death by starvation* (1844); *Life of Moses . . . a programme of European democracy* (n.d.); *Era Victoriae Humanae* (1847); *Regeneration of Society the only corrective of distress . . .* (1844), 2nd ed (London, 1845); and *Second Reformation* (1844).

Lhotsky was diligent in his scientific investigations; a genus of plants (*Lhotskia*) and another of fishes (*Lhotskya*) commemorate him. A volatile figure, he thought his years in Sydney came close to martyrdom, but much of the fault was his own. He was careless with money and too outspoken in criticism of those in high places. Rebuffs by officials drove him to despair and made him noisily hostile. Yet for all his tactlessness he was humane and imaginative towards helpless convicts and Aboriginals, reserving his medical knowledge for only the distressed poor. In London Murchison called him a mad Pole, but in Hobart a conservative editor refused to join thoughtlessly in the odium liberally thrown on this stranger and foreigner.

L. Paszkowski, *Polacy W Australii i Oceanii 1790-1940* (Lond, 1962); Tasmanian history pamphlets, 1 (SLV); J. H. Maiden, 'Records of Australian botanists', Roy Soc NSW, *Procs*, 42 (1908), 72-74; R. Etheridge jnr, 'Australian Museum, fragments of its early history', *Records* (Aust Museum, Syd), 1916, 1919; T. Iredale, 'Lhotsky's lament', *Aust Zoologist*, 3 (1922-24); G. P. Whitley, 'Some early naturalists and collectors in Aust', JRAHS, 19 (1933); CSO 5/72/1584 (TA); Lang papers, 7, 182-4 (ML); Calder papers (ML).

G. P. WHITLEY

LIARDET, WILBRAHAM FREDERICK EVELYN (1799-1878), hotel-keeper and water-colourist, was born on 17 July 1799 at Chelsea, London, the son of Wilbraham Liardet, an official in the Ordnance Department, and his wife Philippa, née Evelyn, widow of Major Houghton of the 69th Regiment and a direct descendant of John Evelyn, the diarist. The Liardet family was of Swiss origin.

Liardet entered the navy and served in the *Pelican*, but he transferred to the army, became a lieutenant in April 1825 and in September 1826 was retired on half-pay. About 1821 he had married his cousin Carolina Frederica, daughter of John William Tell Liardet, an officer of the Royal Marines. By 1839 they had had eleven children of whom five sons and four daughters survived infancy. In July of that year the family sailed for Sydney in the *William Metcalfe*.

The ship spent some three weeks in Hobson's Bay and Liardet decided to settle there. He left the family in the charge of his eldest son, Frank, 17, went on to Sydney with his second son, Frederick, and returned in the same ship a few weeks later. He settled by the water at what became Port Melbourne, hitherto occupied only by two fishermen, who lived in a hogshead cask. Liardet obtained a whale-boat and built a hut. He carried mail ashore from ships and by August 1840 was running a 'mail cart' to and from the town three times daily. In October he opened the

Brighton Pier Hotel and soon had a passenger coach service to Melbourne. Liardet had possessed a competence when he arrived but was a poor man of business. By December 1841 he had transferred his hotel licence to his son Frank and in 1845 was insolvent. Nevertheless the family enjoyed their life by the sea where Wilbraham was a leading net fisherman and entertained the growing community by playing the guitar and flute and singing to them. The hotel was extended and attracted pleasure seekers from town for whom Liardet organized horse races, regattas and archery. Liardet was a capable water-colour draftsman; in 1843 when Sir John Franklin visited Melbourne Liardet presented him with a view of Melbourne afterwards engraved and sold in London for a guinea a copy.

Frank married the widow of the licensee of the Albion Hotel, Williamstown, where they lived. Hector, the third son, went to sea for a time and then took over the Pier Hotel. John Evelyn, the fourth son, was sent to London where he studied law. About this time Mrs Liardet took the five younger children to England.

In 1850 Liardet resumed the licence of the Pier Hotel and then sold it and sailed to England. In a year or two he returned and he and his wife settled in a house on the Yarra River. As a result of the gold rush their sons were prospering as coach and steam-boat proprietors; in 1853 Frank and Hector combined to conduct the Chusan Hotel in Port Melbourne and in 1861 Hector opened a hotel in East Melbourne. In the early 1860s Hector, St Clere, the fifth son, and then Frank went to New Zealand, where their parents joined them and later spent several years and where one of the daughters married. Mrs Liardet was a sister of Captain Francis Liardet, R.N., who went to New Zealand in 1841 as agent at New Plymouth for the New Zealand Co.

In 1869, when the Royal Dockyard at Deptford, London, was closed, Liardet, now 70, went to England to claim part of the site on the ground that John Evelyn had granted the use of sixteen acres of his land at Deptford to enlarge the government dockyard on condition that the land should revert to his heirs if the government ceased to use it for ship-building. The claim did not succeed. In 1874 Liardet was again in Melbourne and soon was at work on a history of Melbourne illustrated with his own water-colour sketches. He made forty sketches of scenes in early Melbourne, but had not got beyond making notes towards the history when he died on 21 March 1878 at Vogeltown, Wellington, New Zealand, where he had arrived a few months before. His wife died in Wellington on 30 April 1882.

In the dedication of his uncompleted history Liardet wrote: 'The humble compiler of the drawings . . . of primitive buildings of the City of Melbourne deems it the highest consideration to dedicate his work to Sir Redmond Barry'. They depict Melbourne when it 'was dawning into a creditable township'. Drawings and notes are now in the La Trobe Library, Melbourne.

A. W. Greig, 'The Liardets of The Beach', *VHM*, 5 (1916-17).

LIGHT, WILLIAM (1786-1839), soldier and surveyor, was born on 27 April 1786 in Kuala Kedah, Malaya, the second son of Captain Francis Light (1740?-1794) and Martinha Rozells, traditionally a princess of Kedah but almost certainly a Portuguese Eurasian. His father, the illegitimate son of William Negus, a Suffolk landowner, and Mary Light, a serving girl, served four years in the navy, went to India in 1765 and became a trader in the seas around Siam, Malaya and Sumatra. While living on Junkceylon he urged the East India Co. to take over the island of Penang from the sultan of Kedah in return for protection. The company at last agreed to do this in 1786 with Light as the first superintendent.

William Light spent his infant years on Penang, but at 6 went to England to be educated by his father's friend, Charles Doughty, of Theberton, Suffolk. In 1799 he entered the navy as a volunteer, and left as a midshipman after two years. He became a civilian internee in France in May 1803 but escaped from Verdun on 5 January 1804. Next year he was in Calcutta at his sister's wedding on 9 March, and on 19 November was present when his brother-in-law, Major Welsh, fearing a massacre, disarmed a portion of his Indian regiment. He returned to Europe in 1806. In May 1808 he purchased a cornetcy in the 4th Dragoons, was promoted lieutenant in April 1809 while on the way to Spain and served with distinction throughout the Peninsular war. As an able linguist, who also drew well, reported accurately and showed great tact, he was frequently sent to confer with blood-thirsty guerilla bands. In November 1812 he became a junior staff officer at Wellington's headquarters, employed on mapping, reconnaissance and liaison duties. In spite of his daring and courage he went through more than forty actions without a wound.

On return from Spain he purchased a captaincy in the infantry in November 1814. On half-pay after Waterloo, which he just missed, he spent some time travelling in Europe. Four years later he was back on full pay, serving in the Channel Islands, Scotland, and Ireland. In 1821 he quitted the army with the brevet rank of major and on 24 May married E. Perois in Londonderry. Turning again to the Continent, he mixed in literary and artistic circles. In 1823 he became aide-de-camp to Sir Robert Wilson, who raised an international force to help the Spanish 'Liberales' in their constitutional struggle against King Ferdinand; Light serving in the Spanish revolutionary army with the rank of lieut-colonel. The campaign was a farce. The Liberales melted before the French army which came to aid Ferdinand, and Light was severely wounded in a scuffle for the possession of Corunna.

In 1824 he married Mary Bennet, a natural daughter of the third duke of Richmond. His wife's wealth was important to Light since his father's extensive estates on Penang had been filched by his father's friends from the ignorant Martinha. The couple travelled widely in Europe, Light making many sketches, some being published in *Sicilian Scenery* (London, 1823) and *Views of Pompeii* (London, 1828). In 1827 Light bought a yacht in England, sailed her first to Italy, and then cruised leisurely round the Mediterranean. At Alexandria in 1830 he became friendly with Mohammed Ali, then rising to power as the founder of modern Egypt. To recruit British officers for the Pasha's navy, Light sailed his yacht to England. He revisited Alexandria briefly in 1832 and in 1834 commanded the paddle steamer *Nile* on its voyage from England to join the Egyptian navy. The *Nile* was taken over by Captain Hindmarsh who on return to England in February 1835 was given by Light a letter of introduction to his friend Sir Charles Napier, newly resigned as governor of the proposed settlement in South Australia. This introduction indirectly led to Hindmarsh obtaining the post, although Napier had recommended Light.

In January 1836 Light returned to London and next month he was appointed surveyor-general of South Australia at £400 a year. Most of his staff and equipment had been selected already; Light made a few modifications, asked for two more assistants, and then unfortunately told the commissioners that 'he considered his staff sufficiently strong'. He fitted out the *Rapid* and, after a delay caused by his ill health, sailed in command of her with some of his staff on 1 May 1836. The main party under G. S. Kingston [q.v.], the deputy-surveyor, had left five weeks earlier in the *Cygnet*.

Light's instructions from the Colonization Commission set an impossible task. On his sole responsibility he was expected within two months to examine minutely 1500 miles of coastline, select 'the best situation' for the first settlement, survey the town site, divide 150 square miles of country into sections, and make reservations for secondary towns. He arrived off Kangaroo Island on 17 August 1836 and sailed straight to Encounter Bay, which he quickly rejected as unsafe and useless for a main harbour. Back at Kangaroo Island he found poor land, some South Australian Co. employees who had been there for a month, but no *Cygnet*. Before she arrived on 11 September, Light had started to examine the mainland coast. Rapid Bay, near the foot of Gulf St Vincent, impressed him favourably, but he sailed north to seek the harbour reported by the explorer, Captain Collet Barker [q.v.], and the whaling captain, John Jones. The harbour eluded Light, and settlers began to arrive two weeks before the entrance to the Port Adelaide River was found on 21 November.

The background of Mediterranean travel gave Light confidence in this small but safe harbour and in the adjacent fertile plains with the Lofty Ranges for water, as the site for his settlement. To accord with instructions, however, he had to visit Port Lincoln before deciding finally. He had returned to Gulf St Vincent and determined the actual city site by the time Hindmarsh arrived on 28 December 1836. Although pleased at first by the site, Hindmarsh demurred at it being six miles from the coast, and soon found other objections. Light pressed ahead with his survey of the town and laid out its 1042 acres by 11 March 1837. To appease Hindmarsh he later surveyed twenty-nine sections at Port Adelaide. Other surveys were impeded by dissensions among the colonists, and particularly the determined efforts, in which Hindmarsh was involved, to move the capital to Encounter Bay or Port Lincoln. When Light did commence the country surveys he found his staff inadequate in numbers and experience, their spirit sapped by poor pay, insufficient equipment and no provision for transport. Light and the resident commissioner, J. H. Fisher [q.v.], saw that the task would take several years. They decided to send Kingston to England to ask for more equipment and staff, and to urge the recall of Hindmarsh. Meanwhile Light struggled on with the survey and had 60,000 acres completed by December 1837, when Hindmarsh was still seeking from Lord Glenelg permission to move the settlement.

Some 150,000 acres were ready by June 1838 when Kingston returned with the commissioners' answers. Not only had Light's appeals been rejected, but his trigonometrical survey was to be replaced by 'running surveys' to speed up the work. If Light refused to carry out this temporary form of survey, Kingston was to do it while Light was to be relegated to the minor task of coastal examination. Light promptly resigned with all but two of his staff. Although his health was now particularly bad, he became the principal partner in a private firm of Light, Finniss & Co. Hindmarsh was recalled in July 1838. The new governor, Colonel George Gawler, arrived in October 1838 to find the survey department in confusion under Kingston, and he appointed Captain Charles Sturt [q.v.] as surveyor-general. Moves in London and Adelaide to have Light reinstated proved abortive because of his health.

In January 1839 Light set out for a survey contract north of Adelaide, but ten hours in the saddle proved too much for him and he was forced to return. Next afternoon his temporary dwelling was burnt down, and with it most of his lifetime accumulation of papers, journals, and sketches. He moved into his incompleted house, Theberton (Thebarton), living as an invalid, and nursed by Maria Gandy, who had come out with him in the *Rapid*. He was desperately poor and sold sketches to make a little money. With the aid of salvaged papers, he wrote and published at his own expense, *A Brief Journal of the Proceedings of William Light* (Adelaide, 1839). In May he took part in a search for a northerly route to the Murray, but returned from the trip in a severe fever. He died from tuberculosis on 6 October 1839 and was buried in the city square named after him.

Light separated from his wife in 1832 because, during his absence from Egypt, she had been living with another man, by whom she later had three children. These children were later given the name of Light. At his death Light appointed Maria Gandy his sole executrix and beneficiary.

Light was described as 'of medium height, sallow complexion, alert and handsome, with face clean shaven excepting closely cut side whiskers, black curly hair, brown eyes, straight nose, small mouth, and shapely chin'. He made friends readily and they remained loyal. One of them said that Light was 'a man of extraordinary accomplishments, soldier, seaman, musician, artist and good in all'.

In his *Brief Journal* Light wrote, 'The reasons that led me to fix Adelaide where it is I do not expect to be generally under-

stood or calmly judged of at present . . .
I leave it to posterity . . . to decide whether
I am entitled to praise or to blame'. B. T.
Finniss [q.v.], his friend and colleague,
said, 'If Colonel Light had not stood firm
. . . the first colonists would have been
ruined, the capital of the Company would
have perished, and public feeling would
have ruined the Commissioners'. Light gave
Adelaide its belt of parklands, a feature of
town planning ahead of the times. His fine
self-portrait is in the National Gallery,
Adelaide, and a portrait by George Jones,
R.A., is in the National Portrait Gallery,
London. In the Adelaide Town Hall there
is another portrait which is a copy of the
original held by descendants of the Light
family in England. A statue by Birnie
Rhind, stands on Montefiore Hill, overlooking the city he founded. A monument
over his grave, designed by Kingston and
erected in 1843, soon crumbled and was
replaced by a new one in 1905.

A. F. Steuart, A short sketch of the
lives of Francis and William Light, the
founders of Penang and Adelaide (Lond,
1901); T. Gill, A biographical sketch of
Colonel William Light (Adel, 1911); A. Grenfell Price, Founders and pioneers of South
Australia (Adel, 1929); M. P. Mayo, The life
and letters of Col. William Light (Adel,
1937); G. Dutton, Founder of a city (Melb,
1960).
                                    DAVID F. ELDER

LILLIE, JOHN (1806-1866), Presbyterian
minister, was the fourth son of David
Lillie, a Glasgow merchant. After some
education at the University of Glasgow,
he was licensed by the presbytery of that
city. Soon afterwards he became tutor to
the family of the duke of Argyll at Arden-
caple Castle, Dunbartonshire; the future
eighth duke was his pupil. Meanwhile the
congregation of St Andrew's, Hobart Town,
had asked the Church of Scotland to suggest a replacement for Archibald Macarthur [q.v.]. After some complication a
committee nominated Lillie late in 1836.
These moves coincided with colonial legislation to assist equally the Churches of
England, Rome, and Scotland. On arrival
at Hobart in September 1837, Lillie was
recognized at once as Presbyterian leader
by Lieut-Governor Franklin and by the
church after brief delay. Not only did Lillie
remain dominant during his frequent
terms as moderator, but as an effective
speaker and administrator he kept Tasmanian Presbyterianism united despite
church disruption in Scotland (1843) and
a querulous colonial society, a conspicuous
success when contrasted with the confusion
in contemporary New South Wales and in
Tasmania in later years.

Lillie's other great achievement as a
churchman was to uphold the equality of
his church with the Church of England.
From the outset he advanced James Thomson's arguments for multi-establishment
with a staunchness which clinched their
victory. This cause, combined with inclination, prompted Lillie to engage in politics.
Towards Franklin he was ambivalent,
sometimes critical, but the prime mover in
formal farewells; common antipathy to the
Anglicans linked him with Lieut-Governor
Eardley-Wilmot; his aggressiveness shocked
Lieut-Governor Denison, but won grudging respect. The outstanding issue on
which Lillie challenged Anglican claims
was education. He fought successively
Franklin's New College scheme, any system of denominational primary education,
and the grant of the Hutchins School site.
Generally he triumphed, sharing service on
the board which in 1853 effectually recommended non-denominational schools.

Education meant far more to Lillie than a
field in which to best the Anglicans. In
1838-54 he was president of the Hobart
Mechanics' Institute and his annual presidential addresses have properly won acclaim as 'the high-water mark of learning
publicly disseminated' in Van Diemen's
Land (Nadel, Australia's Colonial Culture,
Melbourne, 1957, 131). He was active in
the Tasmanian Society and in 1841 wrote
the introductory article in its admirable
Tasmanian Journal of Natural Science.
When the society split after Eardley-
Wilmot's arrival, Lillie went with the
lieut-governor's faction, which soon became the local Royal Society. He was a
foundation vice-president and secretary in
1845-48. He also helped to establish the
Hobart Town High School, acting as rector
in 1850-51 and setting it on a distinguished
course. Glasgow University granted him a
D.D. in 1848.

On 1 June 1838 Lillie married Mary
Gascoigne, daughter of John Burnett [q.v.];
she bore him several children. Lillie won
economic security by investing, in association with the Russell [q.v.] family, in the
sheep industry of Victoria's western district. After 1849 his only publications
were two funeral sermons. Suffering ill
health he went to Britain in 1856, lived
there for a few years, visited Hobart in
1858, and in 1861 migrated to Christchurch, New Zealand, where with W.
Kermode [q.v.] he had helped to finance
the North Canterbury pastoralist, G. H.
Moore. He revisited Hobart in mid-1862.
and died aged 59 at Christchurch on 15
January 1866, survived by his wife, three
daughters and a son.

His concern for education and science

suggests that Lillie was more a nineteenth century liberal than a traditional Calvinist. He was always sensitive to the heresy of exalting secular learning and human capacity, yet inexorably the optimism of contemporary liberalism overcame these scruples, causing him to posit a future 'in which the human spirit, freed from every disturbing and oppressive influence, shall realize the full evolution of its indefinite and most glorious capacities of both moral and intellectual improvements' (*Knowledge as the Means of Correcting Prejudice*, 34).

J. Heyer, *The Presbyterian pioneers of Van Diemen's Land* (Launceston, 1935); P. L. Brown (ed), *The narrative of George Russell* (Lond, 1935); P. L. Brown (ed), *Clyde Company papers*, 2-4 (Lond, 1952-59); Roy Soc Tas, *Papers*, 1913, 143; *Evening Star* (Christchurch), 3 Jan 1862; CO 280/70.

MICHAEL ROE

LINDESAY, SIR PATRICK (1778-1839), soldier and acting governor, was born on 24 February 1778 at Musselburgh, Scotland, the son of Lieut-Colonel John Lindesay. In November 1793, after education at the University of Edinburgh, he joined the army as an ensign and soon afterwards was gazetted lieutenant of the 78th Regiment.

Later he saw service in various countries, and in November 1827 as brevet colonel he arrived in Sydney to succeed Colonel William Stewart [q.v.] of the Buffs in command of the garrison at Port Jackson. He became a member of the Legislative Council soon after arrival and, when the post of lieut-governor was abolished, he virtually undertook the same duties. He was also, from April 1829, a member of the Executive Council, and from 22 October 1831, after the departure of Governor Darling, he served as acting governor until the arrival of Governor Bourke on 2 December 1831. He returned to England in 1836 and was then promoted major-general and knighted. He died at Portobello, near Edinburgh, on 14 March 1839.

Although the period of Lindesay's service in Australia was eventful, including as it did the struggle for representative government and various troubles encountered by Darling, his own experiences appear to have been relatively placid. He did not obtrude unnecessarily in controversial matters but devoted himself almost entirely to his military duties and to promoting natural history and explorations. It was partly through his influence that Charles Sturt [q.v.], who was a captain in his regiment, made during his great journey of 1829 along the Murray River a valuable collection of bird-skins which was sent by Lindesay to the Edinburgh museum. These and similar donations caused Robert Jameson [1774-1854], professor of natural history at Edinburgh, to write that Lindesay was 'a distinguished officer and a very active naturalist'. Moreover, in 1838 Jameson named the remarkable mound-building scrub-turkey of Australia *Meleagris lindesayi*, but the action was belated and the name could not be sustained.

Lindesay is commemorated by Sturt's naming of a tributary in South Australia the Lindesay River, and by similar tributes from the botanist-explorer, Allan Cunningham [q.v.], who originally applied the name Lindesay to a peak now known as Mount Barney near the border of New South Wales and Queensland, though in a readjustment the name was transferred to a neighbouring peak, and from the explorer, T. L. Mitchell [q.v.], who in 1831 gave his name to a dominating mount in the Nandewar Range, New South Wales.

HRA (1), 13-16; CO 323/135/423; MS cat under P. Lindesay (ML).   A. H. CHISHOLM

LITHGOW, WILLIAM (1784-1864), auditor-general, was born on 1 January 1784 in Scotland. He was educated at Edinburgh University and passed as a licentiate of the Church of Scotland, but in January 1808 he was appointed a clerk in the army commissariat and sent to Heligoland, where he also tutored the children of Commissary-general David Allan [q.v.]. In July 1812 Lithgow became deputy-assistant and was sent to take charge of the accounts branch of the commissariat in Mauritius. In April 1823 he was ordered to form and direct a similar branch in New South Wales.

Lithgow arrived at Sydney in May 1824 and soon impressed Governor Brisbane by his skill in introducing a system that simplified the work of the whole commissariat and brought useful economies. Lithgow acted at times as the governor's private secretary and on Brisbane's recommendation was given the additional post of auditor of colonial accounts so that he could have 'the entire financial state of the Colony under his eye'. Governor Darling also valued Lithgow's services and appointed him to the Board of General Purposes through which the colony's public administration was thoroughly, if somewhat autocratically, reorganized. Lithgow was appointed a magistrate and on occasions acted as clerk of the Executive Council and as private secretary to the governor. In 1826-27 he was a director of the old Bank of New South Wales; reappointed in 1829 he served the new bank for another twenty-three years. He sat on innumerable boards and inquiries and audited the accounts of many institutions as well as those of government and commissariat. In April 1827 Darling claimed that he had 'no more zealous officer in the government', but admitted that Lithgow, by attempting too much, was in arrears with his work. On the governor's recommendation Lithgow resigned as assistant commissary-general and was appointed auditor-general of colonial accounts at· a salary of £650.

Despite civil rank second only to the colonial secretary and a seat in the Executive and Legislative Councils he appears to have escaped most of the unpopularity of Darling and his 'creatures'. Governor Bourke thought Lithgow distinguished for liberal principles, employed him sometimes as private secretary and even hoped to make him colonial treasurer. But Lithgow's health was beginning to suffer; in spite of relief from auditing military accounts his duties were expanding greatly each year as new departments were created for the Port Phillip District, the border police, land sales and assisted immigration. Although he had won praise for the punctual dispatch of his financial statements in 1833, he was criticized thereafter by the Audit Board in London for arrears in his work and for failing to answer questions about his accounts. Each year the complaints mounted, culminating in a demand to the Colonial Office 'for effectual steps to enforce an immediate compliance'. In January 1842, warned by Governor Gipps that any delay would bring suspension, Lithgow exerted himself. His 'Accounts for the Year 1838' were sent to London in February and by June the annual reports for 1839-41. By October he had dispatched statements for the first half of 1842 and answered all outstanding questions on his accounts to the satisfaction of the Audit Board in London. Since the delays had not been entirely his fault, he had some solace in 1848 when he reported that the British Treasury had overlooked a substantial sum which should have been credited to the colony in the previous year.

With his office work in hand Lithgow gave more attention to his personal interests. He had always kept many private irons in the fire. From the grant of 2000 acres and a Sydney building allotment in 1824 he had built up substantial estates. He was a shareholder in the Bank of New South Wales and Bank of Australia and a trustee of the Savings Bank of New South Wales and the Australian Society for Deposits and Loans. He was a member of the Southern Cattle Association and served on the provisional committees of the British Australian Steam Navigation Co. and the Railway Association.

In 1848 Lithgow resigned from the Legislative Council after nineteen years service and on 30 April 1852 he retired as auditor-general with a pension of £339 3s. 4d. He died on 11 June 1864 at his home, St Leonard's Lodge, on the North Shore. Of his many bequests to friends, charities and institutions the largest, £1000, was for founding the Lithgow scholarships in the University of Sydney.

HRA (1), 11-26; WO 61/2 (PRO).

ALLAN HORTON

LITTLE; see DE LITTLE

LITTLEJOHN, ROBERT (1756-1818), gardener, was a Scot who, accompanied by his servant Thomas Littlefield, sailed as a settler in the *Ocean* with David Collins's expedition to Port Phillip and the River Derwent in 1803-04, with the promise of an immediate grant of land. They were so successful in cultivating their gardens that in December 1805-January 1806, Governor King granted them 100 acres each, to Littlefield at Stainsforth's Cove (New Town Bay), and to Littlejohn, at Miller's Bay, Glenorchy (Prince of Wales Bay), along the foreshore from New Town Creek to Humphrey's Rivulet.

Littlejohn died on 26 October 1818, 'a man of wealth of learning and a naturalist of repute'. He is associated with the *Veronica derwentia littlejohn*, figured and described in H. C. Andrews, *The Botanists Repository for new, and rare plants*, 531, (London, 1797-1814), and with plants and seeds sent to A. B. Lambert at Kew, and to Robert Brown [q.v.] at the British Museum. Although probate was granted to his nephew, Robert Ogilvie of Hobart Town, in March 1819, unfortunately the deeds for his grants were never issued, and the land commissioners disregarded them.

HRA (3), 1; *Hobart Town Gazette*, 28 Nov 1818.
JANET SOMERVILLE

LOANE, RO(W)LAND WALPOLE (d. 1844), merchant and settler, was descended from a family of English landlords residing in the south of Ireland. He claimed to have been a naval officer, but his name does not appear in the *Navy Lists*, among lieutenants' passing certificates or any other naval record. He arrived in Hobart Town in 1809 in his own ship *Union*, with a cargo of goods valued at £20,000. On her passage up the Derwent she was intercepted by H.M.S. *Porpoise*, under command of the deposed Governor Bligh. Loane sold Bligh 3½ tons of rice, 8 casks of meat, 3 hundredweight of sugar and 200 gallons of spirits before proceeding to Hobart. There he sold his ship and began business as a general merchant, using some of his capital for land speculation.

In 1813 the 133-ton brig *Campbell Macquarie* was built in Hobart to his order and taken to Sydney whence he operated as a merchant-trader. In 1818 he returned to Hobart with a cargo from India. Before departing for Sydney in 1813 he had bought a fifty-acre farm near Hobart, and leased it to the original owner. On his return in 1818 he found that the tenant had died, the land had been fenced for government purposes and the public was using a quarry on the property. He protested to the administration and was called upon to produce proof of his title. He was never able to recover the documents proving his ownership, and after long argument with the authorities, he lost his case, an experience which probably led to his subsequent retaliation against government and individuals. The loss or destruction of his account books during his absence from Hobart prevented the collection of large debts due to him. Altogether he believed that he had been robbed by unscrupulous persons and officials and that to progress in such a community he had to use weapons similar to those which had been used against him. According to Lieut-Governor Sorell, Loane was 'a person who always asserts that he is ill-used by the world collectively and individually. His hand is against everyone and everyone against him. Not a man in the colony would, I believe, rely upon his word or engagement for the most trifling thing'. He was an active and successful merchant in Hobart, but he seems to have been willing to let his cattle damage his neighbours' crops on the assumption that they would not be able to drive the beasts to the pound.

Loane had a land grant at Pittwater, and after 1818 purchased several areas in the country, including one at Eastern Marshes in the Oatlands district, and a number of small areas in Hobart on which he built houses and let them to government officers. In 1825 he completed a stone residence in Macquarie Street, named it Belle Vue and lived in it briefly before leaving for Sydney late in the year. He left in this house a caretaker, Mrs Hotson, a 'Woman of Color', whom he had found with several children in extreme poverty in Calcutta in 1823 and who was said to have been his mistress. Eager to extricate himself from this alliance he tried to persuade her to return to her husband in Mauritius, but she claimed that he had given her Belle Vue and would take nothing less. When she died in 1831 her daughter claimed the property. In his fight to regain the house, Loane was said to have consulted and quarrelled with every lawyer in Hobart. He finally took his case on appeal to England, but without success.

While in Sydney in 1827 he built a residence and acquired land in the town area. He then went abroad and was married in Ireland in 1828 to Mary Lee, daughter of a colonel of the Royal Marines. In 1830 he sailed for Tasmania with his wife and made his home on his property at Eastern Marshes, which he named Lee Mount. In 1834 he sold this property after an argument with the colonial government, during which he claimed, without a shred of evidence, that Lieut-Governor Arthur had a personal grievance against him and encouraged the pound-keepers and police to take his cattle. In 1839 he took his wife to England and there prosecuted his complaints in person, displaying a rancour, power of exaggeration and disregard of evidence that seem normal in his case but which did not impress the Colonial Office. In 1841 he returned to Hobart, where he died on 8 October 1844. Next year his widow married Major Oliver Dixon Ainsworth, promoted in 1848 to the senior military office in the colony; she died in 1853.

Completely absorbed with the promotion of his fortune from mercantile, distilling and shipping enterprises and the increase of his herds and landed estates, Loane became a byword in the colony for his unscrupulous and unceasing litigation. He took no part in the benevolent, religious and cultural societies that flourished in the community, nor was his name associated with the popular movements of the 1820s for increased civil freedom.

HRA (3), 2-3; CO 280/138; Correspondence file under Loane (TA); Arthur papers (ML).

F. C. GREEN

LOCHEE, FRANCIS (1811-1893), lawyer, editor and banker, was born on 8 March 1811 in London, one of identical twin sons of John Lockée, barrister, and his wife Louisa, née King. He was a descendant of a Huguenot family. His great-grandfather, naturalized by an Act which received royal assent on 8 May 1780, established the

Royal Military Academy, Little Chelsea, London, about 1770. After the early death of their parents the boys and an elder sister were left in the care of a guardian. It was their father's wish that the boys should enter a university and then train for a profession. Francis chose law, his brother Alfred medicine. Their vacations spent on the Continent added a mastery of French and Italian and some knowledge of Spanish to their formal classical training. In the 1830s Francis Lochée became interested in colonial affairs and particularly in the settlement at Swan River.

He sailed from Spithead in July 1838 in the Britomart and reached Fremantle in December. His fellow passengers were congenial and he established a lasting friendship with one of them, Dr Samuel Waterman Viveash, who was travelling with his family. Another passenger, William Tanner, who had large interests in the young settlement, was returning to the colony after a visit to England.

Well read, interested in politics, political economy and public affairs, a stimulating companion and an accomplished musician, Lochée was a welcome addition to colonial society. Governor John Hutt became a close friend and persuaded him to become the first Freemason initiated in the colony. He became a distinguished member of the lodges of St John and St George. Legal training, social background and personal tastes drew him into the circle of young lawyers who shared many of his ideas on colonial development. With William Tanner, landowner, farmer, banker, chairman of the town trust, he was a sleeping partner in a farming venture at Yandergine, ten miles east of York in the fertile Avon valley. Together they also started another enterprise more suited to Lochée's abilities: the weekly journal, the Inquirer: A Western Australian Journal of Politics and Literature, with Lochée as editor. The first number appeared on Wednesday, 5 August 1840. In June 1843, dissatisfied with its progress, Tanner withdrew his support. Lochée remained proprietor, editor and publisher until 1846.

As editor of the Inquirer he gave critical scrutiny to matters affecting colonists everywhere: crown land policy and prices, labour and capital supplies, the Colonial Office, Wakefieldian ideas and practices, and the policy of colonial governors. He was convinced that accurate information and cautious appraisal of prospects were necessary to encourage immigrants. In 1841 he published in Perth Report on the Statistics of Western Australia in 1840; with observations by the Colonial Committee of Correspondence. In May 1842 he became a member of the provisional committee of the Western Australian Society which aimed at attracting capital and making the colony widely known in Britain. He contributed to the funds of the Vineyard Society, set up in 1842 to establish a model experiment with the propagation of all types of vines; in 1845 he became a member of its committee and published its Manual for the Cultivation of the Vine and Olive in Western Australia. He also published the Journal of the Agricultural and Horticultural Society of Western Australia in 1843 and in 1842 The Record, or Pastorals for Guildford, a short-lived monthly journal edited by William Mitchell. With public spirit he shared with J. S. Roe [q.v.] the work of organizing the cathedral choir. He also joined the first Education Committee but resigned with two other members in 1856 when Governor Kennedy tried to make it an appendage of the colonial secretary's office. At Bishop Hale's request he joined the board of the bishop's new school. He also served as a member of the Town Trust, as a justice of the peace and, with Hutt, R. W. Nash [q.v.], and Vigors, in the activities of the Colonization Assurance Corporation. In 1846 Lochée was elected cashier (manager) by the shareholders of the Western Australian Bank established in 1841.

A man of definite ideas, but sparing no effort to inform his mind, his opinions influenced the board of directors. Their policy was often over cautious but the bank, entirely Western Australian in origin and ownership, proved very profitable to the shareholders and showed substantial earnings and capital appreciation over the years. Before his retirement Lochée saw the bank housed in permanent buildings, with branches opened at Fremantle, Geraldton and Bunbury.

On 27 August 1846 Francis Lochée married Emma, the sixth and youngest child of James Purkis, formerly of London. They had one son and seven daughters. He resigned from the bank in January 1889. His retirement was marred by ill health and impaired sight. He died on 22 November 1893. He was survived by his wife and three daughters: Charlotte Elizabeth Vigors, wife of Edward Shenton, Mary Ellen Landor, wife of Arthur Bridges Wright, and Constance, wife of Robert Edward Bush.

British Medical J, 10 May 1840; A. Burton, 'A versatile pioneer', JRWAHS, 3 (1938-48); Western Australian Bank records (Bank of NSW archives, Perth); Records (Honourable Soc of the Inner Temple).

MERAB HARRIS TAUMAN

LOCKYER, EDMUND (1784-1860), soldier and landowner, was born on 21 January 1784 at Wembury, Devon, England, the son of Edmund Lockyer, merchant, and his wife Joan. He entered the army as an ensign in the 19th Regiment in June 1803, was promoted lieutenant early in 1805 and acquired a captaincy in August. He was promoted major in August 1819 and in August 1824 transferred to the 57th Regiment. Most of his service had been in India and Ceylon. He arrived in Sydney in the *Royal Charlotte* in April 1825 with a detachment of the 57th; with him were his wife Sarah, née Morriss, and their children.

In August 1825 Governor Brisbane instructed him to proceed to Moreton Bay in the cutter *Mermaid*, 84 tons, and explore the Brisbane River as far as he could go 'with prudence', and report on the animals, birds, minerals and the 'nature, disposition, complexion etc. of the natives'. Lockyer set out on 1 September and, with John Finnegan, a former castaway who had guided Oxley [q.v.] in this district in 1823-24, explored the river in a small boat for 150 miles, about twice as far as Oxley had reached. He discovered the stream that bears his name and the Stanley River, and found coal near the present-day Ipswich. Since there was ample water over the bar the *Mermaid* was brought to Brisbane, the first sea-going vessel to enter the river. With a cargo of timber Lockyer returned to Sydney on 16 October 1825.

In March 1826 the British government, fearing that the French were planning to establish a colony on the west coast of Australia, instructed Governor Darling among other measures to have King George Sound examined as the possible site of a settlement. Lockyer was appointed by Darling to establish a settlement there and, should the French have already arrived, to land his troops and to inform the French that the whole of New Holland was subject to the British government. Lockyer sailed on 9 November 1826 in the *Amity*, with Lieutenant Festing, twenty-three convicts and a detachment of twenty of the 39th Regiment under Captain Wakefield, who was to take over the settlement when it had been established. The expedition reached the sound on Christmas Day and next day Lockyer and Festing landed. In a preliminary examination of the area one man was speared by Aboriginals but survived. By 10 January buildings had been erected, a garden dug and 'a quantity of amazing fine fish' caught. That day a boatload of sealers arrived. Lockyer arrested two of these, having evidence that they had committed outrages against Aboriginals,

and sent them to Sydney in the *Amity* when she departed on 24 January. From the sealers Lockyer learnt that Dumont D'Urville had surveyed King George Sound in November. On 12 February Lockyer with five others set out to walk to Swan River, but it rained heavily, a soldier fell ill and the schooner *Isabella* arrived on her way to Melville Island bringing instructions to Lockyer to return to Sydney and news that Captain Stirling in H.M.S. *Success* had already reconnoitred Swan River. Lockyer sailed for Sydney in the *Success* on 3 April, leaving Wakefield in charge.

In 1827 Lockyer sold his commission, having decided to settle in the colony. He was granted 2560 acres, which he named Lockyersleigh, in the Marulan district, and built a house, Ermington, on an estate near Ryde. By 1837 he had added 3635 acres to Lockyersleigh by purchase, and by 1853 the estate totalled 11,810 acres. In 1838 he leased and stocked Cavan, a run on the Murrumbidgee and Goodradigbee Rivers. Iron was found on Lockyersleigh and a beginning was made with mining, but the work was abandoned for lack of labour in the gold rush. However, the spade which was used to cut the first turf for the Sydney Railway Co. in July 1850 was made from Lockyer's iron.

Although a proficient artist and a devoted parent, Lockyer was easily imposed upon and dabbled in too many things to be a good farmer. In 1830 Lockyersleigh was said to be in great need of improvement and stocked with 'very miserable, coarse sheep' bred from 'old culls'. However, Lockyer was assisted by the occupancy of a variety of public appointments. When he retired from the army he had been appointed police magistrate at Parramatta. In 1828 Darling appointed him principal surveyor of roads and bridges at a salary of £600; but the secretary of state in May ordered that this office be abolished and the duties performed by assistants of the surveyor-general. Thereupon in December 1829 Lockyer became police magistrate at Parramatta again and from February to December 1830 superintendent of police there. In 1842 he was a member of the association formed to gain permission to import coolies from India. In 1852 he was appointed serjeant-at-arms to the Legislative Council and in 1856 usher of the black rod.

He died at his home, York House, Woolloomooloo on 10 June 1860 and was buried in the Camperdown cemetery. His first wife had died on 11 July 1853, aged 68. On 18 November 1854 he married Eliza Colston (Coulson). He was survived by his widow, eight children of the first marriage and three of the second. His son, Nicholas (1855-1933), became a leading New South Wales and Commonwealth public servant.

HRA (1), 12-16, 18, 19, 25, (3), 6; J. S. Battye, *Western Australia* (Oxford, 1924); R. Cilento (ed), *Triumph in the tropics* (Brisb, 1959); J. Jervis, 'Settlement in the Marulan-Bungonia district', *JRAHS*, 32 (1946); *Australian*, 26 Sept 1827, 9 Dec 1829, 24 Feb 1830); Lockyer papers (ML).

LOGAN, PATRICK (1791-1830), soldier, was baptized on 15 November 1791 at Coldingham, Berwickshire, Scotland, son of Abraham Logan, a farmer, and Janet née Johnston. He was descended from a noted Scottish family who could trace their ancestry for five centuries to the two representatives who were selected by Sir James Douglas to accompany him to the Holy Land. Logan joined the 57th Regiment as an ensign on 13 December 1810. He served in the Peninsular war, the American war of 1812 and with Wellington's army of occupation. He was promoted lieutenant in March 1813 but placed on half-pay in 1815. He rejoined his regiment in 1819 and in Ireland in 1823 was promoted captain and on 5 September married Letitia Anne O'Beirne at St John's Church, Sligo.

Next year the 57th Regiment was ordered to New South Wales and Logan arrived in Sydney on 22 April 1825. Next November he was appointed by Governor Brisbane to command of the convict settlement at Moreton Bay, which had been opened by Lieutenant Henry Miller in September 1824. As little had been done when Logan arrived in March 1826 he immediately started to develop the station by planting the flats (New Farm and Bulimba) with maize and carrying out an important programme of public works. Two of his buildings were still in use after 140 years: his commissariat store in William Street which became the lower floor of the State Stores, and his windmill, later the State Observatory. In 1827 he also established a branch station, a site that was later used as the Ipswich race-course.

Logan led several expeditions which added to geographical knowledge. In August 1826 he discovered the Logan River and next May the Albert River. In 1828, with Alan Cunningham and Charles Fraser [qq.v.], he succeeded in climbing Mount Barney, 5700 feet, then the highest altitude attained by a white man in Australia. In July 1830 he led an expedition to the headwaters of the Richmond River and on his return, since the regiment was due for transfer to India, he attempted to chart the windings of the upper Brisbane River. He never succeeded, for he was killed by Aboriginals on 17 October in the region of Mount Beppo.

He was survived by his widow and two young children. His son Robert Abraham followed his father's footsteps in the 57th Regiment and became a lieut-general. Logan's widow was recommended for a pension by Governor Darling, but by the regulations of 1829 the next-of-kin of army officers who died on colonial service were ineligible. However, after fifteen years of petitioning she was granted £70 a year.

Captain Logan is regarded by many historians as the true founder of Queensland, as he was an important explorer and the first to make any practical development. During his term as commandant of the convict settlement he showed a fine sense of duty, and no thought of personal gain in any of his activities. He was, however, reputed to be cruelly harsh to the convicts, the settlement was in continuous unrest and uprisings were frequent under his command. It has been claimed that his death was due to the convicts persuading the Aboriginals to avenge their wrongs, but according to Lieutenant G. Edwards of the 57th Regiment the Aboriginals themselves wanted to catch Logan on the expedition.

HRA (1), 13-16; G. J. N. Logan Home, *History of the Logan family* (Edinb, 1934); C. Bateson, *Patrick Logan* (Syd, 1966); R. M. Collins, 'Early explorations of the Logan', *PRGSQ*, 13 (1897-98); L. R. Cranfield, 'Life of Capt Patrick Logan', *JRQHS*, 6 (1959-61); *United Service J and Naval Military Mag*, 1831 pt 11; *Sydney Gazette*, 28 Apr 1825, 4 Mar 1826, 17 Aug, 21 Nov 1827, 16, 25 Nov 1830; MS cat under Logan (ML).

LOUIS R. CRANFIELD

LONSDALE, WILLIAM (1800?-1864), soldier and administrator, entered the British army as an ensign in 1819, became a lieutenant in the 4th Regiment in 1824 and arrived in Sydney in December 1831 with a detachment of troops guarding convicts in the *Bussorah Merchant*. During the next five years he served in Van Diemen's Land and in New South Wales. On 11 July 1834 he was promoted captain and on 6 April 1835, while stationed at Port Macquarie, he married Martha, the youngest daughter of Benjamin Smythe, civil engineer of Launceston. Like many of his fellow officers he also held civil office, first as assistant police magistrate, and from January 1836 as a justice of the peace.

Early in 1836 news of increasing numbers of unauthorized settlers in the south and of their outrages against the Aboriginals reached Sydney. Further attention was attracted in June when some inhabitants, led by John Batman [q.v.], petitioned for the appointment of a resident police magistrate. In September Lonsdale was chosen by Governor Bourke to be the first police magistrate at Port Phillip. His salary was £250 while he drew half-pay from his regiment; when he resigned from the army in March 1837 it rose to £300.

Lonsdale, his wife, children and two servants sailed in H.M.S. *Rattlesnake*, which anchored near the mouth of the Yarra River on 29 September 1836. Three surveyors, two customs officials, a commissariat clerk, Ensign King with thirty privates of the 4th Regiment, and thirty convicts followed in October. They found 224 residents in a settlement several miles up the Yarra. Lonsdale decided to establish the government centre there, although Gellibrand Point (Williamstown) would have been more convenient for the unloading of stores. The inland site, however, had the advantage of a plentiful supply of fresh water, and was, he reported, suited to the performance of his civil duties.

Lonsdale's duties were straightforward although his powers were less precise. Bourke's instructions conferred on him not only the ordinary jurisdiction of a justice of the peace, but also 'the general superintendence in the new settlement of all such matters as require the immediate exercise of the authority of the government' in accordance with the applicable laws of England and the acts of the governor and council. He was to send in returns and reports, take a census particularly noting land occupation, protect and conciliate the Aboriginals and try to induce them to offer their labour in return for food and clothing, employing as the medium of communication with them 'the European named Buckley' [q.v.].

Matters proceeded smoothly for the first few months. Lonsdale arranged the distribution of rations; and so plentiful and regular were supplies from Sydney and Van Diemen's Land that the issue to civilians was abolished within a year. Shelters were erected but it was not until November that Lonsdale could move his quarters from the ship to a cottage. Meanwhile he appointed a medical officer and required public house keepers to be licensed. He also wrote to the bishop of Australia deploring the lack of clergy, and reported that he read the service to soldiers and convicts and that the settlers held devotions in their houses. As instructed, he engaged William Buckley as constable and interpreter to the natives. When Governor Bourke visited Port Phillip in March 1837 he praised Lonsdale's ability,

zeal, activity and discretion, confirmed his choice of a site for the town, and named it Melbourne, though Lonsdale suggested Glenelg. In particular Bourke was pleased with Lonsdale's approach to the Aboriginals. The foundations of the new settlement had been laid and Lonsdale had contributed by conscientiously following instructions from Sydney and referring all decisions to his superiors.

In the next two years friction developed between Lonsdale and other civil officials who disputed his right to supervise their activities. The surveyors, Robert Russell and Robert Hoddle [qq.v.], would not recognize that he had any authority beyond that of a police magistrate, and Lonsdale complained that a missionary to the Aboriginals, George Langhorne, was subverting his authority. The *Melbourne Advertiser* and *Port Phillip Patriot* supported Lonsdale, while the *Port Phillip Gazette* criticized his administration. Lonsdale did not court public support nor answer public criticism but continued to carry out his instructions from Sydney.

Charles La Trobe, who arrived in Melbourne in October 1839 as the first superintendent of Port Phillip, relieved Lonsdale of all the disputed areas of responsibility. The people of Melbourne marked the occasion by presenting Lonsdale with an address and £350 for a silver service. Lonsdale continued to act as police magistrate until April 1840, when he was appointed sub-treasurer of Port Phillip by Governor Gipps at £400 with continued use of his house. He was the obvious choice for the post: Gipps praised his zeal, intelligence and integrity.

The district grew rapidly, and Lonsdale prospered with it. He was able to give security of £8000 when appointed sub-treasurer, and he joined in the mania of speculation between 1836 and 1841 to a degree which caused him to share in the general censure distributed by the first resident judge of Port Phillip, J. W. Willis [q.v.]. Gipps, in reporting this to the Colonial Office, acknowledged that Lonsdale was not altogether free from blame in purchasing bank shares from John Batman's estate, but did not consider his financial activities were, dishonest.

Lonsdale's relations with La Trobe were always good; indeed to his superiors he seemed reliable, conscientious and unpretentious. When La Trobe became the first patron of the Melbourne Mechanics' Institute, Lonsdale became its first president; in August 1842 La Trobe appointed him acting mayor of Melbourne until one could be elected under the new Corporation Act, and from October 1846 to February 1847 he acted as superintendent of Port Phillip while La Trobe was absent in Van Diemen's Land.

In 1851, when Victoria became a separate colony, Lonsdale was nominated by La Trobe as its first colonial secretary, at a salary of £900. This time he was not the first and obvious choice for the position, but was persuaded to accept it provisionally only from a sense of public duty. No one was more conscious of his shortcomings than Lonsdale himself; in particular he questioned his ability to take the leading political role in the Legislative Council expected of a colonial secretary. Nevertheless he held office and served in the Executive and Legislative Councils in 1851-53, the turbulent years of the gold rushes. It could not be said that he took a leading part but he gave no serious cause of complaint. He was probably relieved to hand over the colonial secretaryship to J. F. L. Foster, who arrived with a commission from Downing Street in July 1853. Lonsdale then became colonial treasurer at a salary of £1500. He continued to perform his official duties unobtrusively until July 1854, when he obtained eighteen months leave, and sailed for England. While he was away, responsible government was inaugurated in Victoria and Lonsdale retired on a pension. He died in London on 28 March 1864, survived by his widow and two sons.

The most noteworthy years of Lonsdale's long public career were 1836-39 when he supervised the founding of the new settlement at Port Phillip. By 1844 he was referred to as 'old Captain Lonsdale', and was associated with a past which seemed remote to those who knew only the prosperous and rapidly advancing colony of the 1850s. Lonsdale's high sense of duty and respect for authority made him a conscientious and hard-working servant of the Crown, and his ambitions never exceeded his abilities. Lonsdale Street, Melbourne, and Point Lonsdale were named after him, and Mount Martha after his wife.

HRA (1), 18, 20, 22-3, 25; H. G. Turner, *A history of the colony of Victoria*, 1-2 (Lond, 1904); R. D. Boys, *First years at Port Phillip*, 2nd ed (Melb, 1959); NSW Govt Gazette, 1836, 1, 395, 709; E. Scott, 'Capt Lonsdale and the foundation of Melbourne', VHM, 4 (1914-15); E. Scott, 'The administration of Capt Lonsdale', VHM, 6 (1917-18); *The Times*, 31 Mar 1864; CO 309/1.

B. R. PENNY

LORD, DAVID (1785-1847), landowner, was born probably at Halifax, Yorkshire, England, the son of James Lord (1757?-1824), a fustian maker at Bolton, and his wife Grace, née Haley. On 16 July 1801 his father was sentenced at Bradford to transportation for seven years. He sailed in H.M.S. *Calcutta* for Port Phillip, was removed to Van Diemen's Land, and after his emancipation accumulated a large fortune by unremitting industry, skilful farming, and shrewd trading, partly in spirits with and without licence, helped, according to the lands commissioners, 'by setting at defiance the Laws'.

David Lord and his family arrived at Hobart Town in the *Harriet* in March 1817. He engaged in business with his father and in 1819 he was appointed a member of the Lieut-Governor's Court. In 1817 he had been granted 100 acres and, after an application based on his possession of considerable property, he received a further grant of 700 acres in 1819.

When his father died on 4 August 1824, David inherited the estate, which Robert Knopwood [q.v.] said was worth £50,000. He continued to increase his holdings which soon included Blue Hills at Oatlands, Richmond Park, and land in the Sorell district, Kangaroo Point, Clarence Plains, Hobart and Sandy Bay. By February 1829 he claimed to hold 2000 acres by grants, at least one of which had been recorded as smaller than it was by the surveyor, 11,560 by purchase and 4150 by lease. In April 1827 the land commissioners recorded that Lord, 'the richest Man in the Island . . . knows not the extent of his Riches', and that his case exemplified the defects of the land system, under which 'those who have improved their farms the least, and who have set the regulations at defiance, are the only rich and . . . the only respectable Men in the Island. Riches, no matter by whom possessed or how acquired ensure Respect and Honors'. They reported that Lord's cattle roamed over eighteen and twenty miles, receiving attention only when they were to be marked or sold. In 1828 after Lieut-Governor Arthur ordered an investigation of the grants occupied by Lord, so that the government might interpose some check where the regulations had been violated, the surveyor-general reported in September that Lord had obtained control of large tracts of land in the Eastern Marshes by securing the waterholes in the area and that he had made practically no improvements on any of his holdings. One of his more notable land deals was his exchange in 1824 of ninety acres, which he had acquired as payment for a debt and which the government needed for Richmond township, for 1400 acres near Oatlands.

Lord was one of the foundation subscribers to the Van Diemen's Land Bank in

1823 and a director until his death. In March 1827 he was a member of a committee appointed to wait upon the lieut-governor with the first Tasmanian petition seeking 'Trial by Jury and Legislation by Representation' in order to secure an improved government which would ensure sound and secure conditions for land-owners. In November a number of colonists, including Lord, wrote to Arthur protesting against the promulgation of the recent Press Licensing Act and urging its repeal as an unconstitutional, unnecessary, degrading and oppressive ordinance.

Lord took an active interest in church affairs. Though he professed to be an Anglican, his interests appear to have been non-sectarian: in 1820 he was allocated a pew in St David's Church, Hobart; in 1822 he gave the land in Melville Street, Hobart, for a new Methodist chapel; and in 1823 he was a member of the committee appointed to seek the establishment of a Presbyterian Church.

After a protracted illness he died at his home in Macquarie Street, Hobart, on 12 April 1847. He was survived by his wife Hannah, née Morley, who died on 25 June 1867. They left two sons, James (1808-1881) and John (1814-1890), both of whom became members of the Legislative Council, and three daughters.

Portraits of David Lord are in the possession of the Misses Carr Lord of Sandy Bay, and of Mr John Lord of Launceston.

HRA (3), 2-6; A. McKay (ed), *Journals of the land commissioners for Van Diemen's Land, 1826-28* (Hob, 1962); *Hobart Town Gazette*, 22 Mar 1817, 23 June 1821, 5 Apr 1823, 2 June 1827; *Colonial Times*, 14 Dec 1827; *Hobart Town Courier*, 26 Oct 1832, 14 Apr 1847; Correspondence file under D. Lord (TA).   SUSAN ALLEN

LORD, EDWARD (1781-1859), officer of marines, commandant, pastoralist and merchant, was born on 15 June 1781 in Pembroke, Wales, the third son of Joseph Lord and his wife Corbetta, daughter of Lieut-General John Owen, brother of Sir William Owen, fourth baronet, of Orielton. Edward was gazetted a second lieutenant of marines on 12 September 1798 and stationed at Portsmouth.

In 1803 he joined the expedition of Lieut-Colonel David Collins to Port Phillip, and was in the first contingent which sailed thence to establish a settlement on the Derwent, Van Diemen's Land, in February 1804. In the same year he built the first private house in Hobart Town. In February 1805 he was granted sick leave to return to England, but after six months in Sydney he returned to Hobart with several ewes and a ram 'near the Spanish breed', the latter a gift from Governor King. He was appointed first lieutenant on 3 December 1805 and a month later received his first grant of 100 acres. By October 1806 he was the largest stock-owner in Van Diemen's Land; and within another year he was the senior officer there, subordinate only to Collins.

He again visited Sydney in April 1808, soon after the deposition of Governor Bligh, and from Lieut-Colonel Foveaux [q.v.] he obtained, among other favours, an appointment as magistrate and a grant of 500 acres, which he selected on the Derwent, towards New Norfolk. On 8 October 1808, soon after his return to Hobart, he married Maria Risely. He was an implacable opponent of Bligh while the deposed governor was at the Derwent from March to December 1809. Bligh complained that Lord and William Collins [q.v.] kept a shop, contrary to regulations, and monopolized 'the advantages of Trade to the great Injury of the Settlement'; for all that, in the same year Lord was appointed Naval Officer and inspector of public works.

When David Collins died unexpectedly on 24 March 1810 Lord took charge of the settlement and is said to have burned all the papers at Government House the same night. He applied to the secretary of state for the colonies to succeed Collins. Macquarie, who had a poor opinion of Lord, hastily sent Captain John Murray to take charge, relieved Lord of his offices and gave him leave to return to England. There on 20 October 1812, having learned that his application to succeed Collins had failed, Lord resigned his commission in the marines; next day through the influence of his brother John Owen, M.P. (who had changed his name on inheriting the rich Orielton estates near Pembroke) he received an order for a grant of 3000 acres. He took 1500 acres near Sydney and the other 1500 formed the nucleus of his Orielton estate in Van Diemen's Land, which grew to 3500 acres.

Lord returned to Hobart in March 1813 in his own brig, the *James Hay*, with goods worth £30,000, and was soon on intimate terms with Lieut-Governor Davey, although Macquarie had warned Davey that Lord was 'a dangerous and troublesome man'. One reason for Davey's recall was that in defiance of Macquarie he gave preferential trading concessions to Lord, and bought wheat from him at an excessive price. In 1817 Lord was suspected of smuggling from the *Kangaroo* which Captain Jeffreys [q.v.] had improperly brought to the Derwent and, when Lord charged Acting Commissary Broughton [q.v.] with improper trading, Lord refused to go to Sydney to prosecute at the court martial that Macquarie and Broughton desired. Judge-Advocate Wylde [q.v.] criticized both Lord and those officers in Hobart who had supported his accusations, and Macquarie exonerated Broughton, describing Lord as 'vindictive and implacable'.

When Sorell became lieut-governor, Macquarie named Lord first on his list of 'bad characters' at the Derwent. Despite this Lord and Sorell soon became close friends. When Lord returned to England late in 1819 he told Bathurst that he had been 'injured to an almost incalculable Amount' by Macquarie's 'harsh and unjust proceedings' and sought redress. Although his charges were refuted Bathurst gave him an order to Macquarie to grant him 3000 acres and recommended him to Sorell.

Having bought the *Caroline*, he returned to Van Diemen's Land in November 1820 with a large cargo of merchandise, and was at once appointed a magistrate. Soon afterwards he exchanged fourteen acres in Hobart for 7000 in the interior; these and his 3000 granted acres formed the nucleus of his noted estate, Lawrenny, on the River Clyde. At this time he was said to be the richest man in Van Diemen's Land, the owner of three ships, warehouses in Hobart and Port Dalrymple, 6000 cattle, 7000 sheep and 35,000 acres. When the Van Diemen's Land Agricultural Society was founded on 1 January 1822 Lord became its first president and he was also an original proprietor of the Bank of Van Diemen's Land. During 1822 he was accused of trying to bribe the head of the commissariat, but Governor Brisbane was prevented from investigating the matter by Lord's departure in the *Royal George* which he had chartered to carry wool to England. The ship was almost wrecked at Cape Town, which caused Lord 'serious Losses'. At this time he claimed assets in Van Diemen's Land of £200,000, and debts owing to him of £70,000. When in England, he asked Bathurst in 1823 to grant Van Diemen's Land independence from New South Wales, partly because of the difficulties in prosecuting in Sydney suits for the payment of debts; he also asked for a legislative council and the right of trial by jury in the colony. He returned to Hobart briefly in 1824, and again in 1827 when he signed a petition to parliament for 'Trial by Jury and Legislation by Representation'. His relations were far from cordial with Lieut-Governor Arthur. Governor Brisbane spoke of his sordid interests and proposed to remove him from the

magistracy. In 1828, leaving a manager in charge of his estates, Lord returned to England and settled at Downe, Kent. He visited Van Diemen's Land in 1838-39 and the tenacity of his character was revealed in 1846-47 when at the age of 65 he made his seventh voyage to the colony to press a claim for land in further compensation for a deficiency in the original survey of his Lawrenny estate twenty-five years earlier. Lieut-Governors Arthur and Denison had both rejected this, but despite opposition Lord ultimately won his claim in 1854.

He died at 12 Westbourne Terrace North, London, on 14 September 1859. His estate in England was valued at £2000, and he still held considerable property in Van Diemen's Land, though much of it was encumbered. In December 1824 Lord won a case against Charles Rowcroft [q.v.], settler, for criminal conversation with his wife, who had remained in Van Diemen's Land and died there two months before him. Lord was survived by one son and two daughters of this marriage, and by three sons and one daughter of an alliance in England.

While in Van Diemen's Land in 1846-47 two portraits of Lord were painted by T. G. Wainewright [q.v.]. A third portrait by an unknown artist is in the Tasmanian Museum and Art Gallery, Hobart.

HRA (1), 7-11, (3), 1-6; J. West, *The history of Tasmania*, 1-2 (Launceston, 1852); R. W. Giblin, *The early history of Tasmania*, 2 (Melb, 1939); M. C. I. Levy, *Governor George Arthur* (Melb, 1953); R. Crossland, *Wainewright in Tasmania* (Melb, 1954); Rex' and Thea Rienits, 'Bligh at the Derwent', PTHRA, 11 (1964); Hobart Town Gazette, 17, 24 Dec 1824; R. Knopwood, Diaries (Roy Soc Tas, Hob, & ML); Liverpool papers (BM).

THEA RIENITS

LORD, SIMEON (1771-1840), entrepreneur, was the fourth child of Simeon and Ann Lord of Dobroyd, Yorkshire, England. He was convicted at Manchester Quarter Sessions in April 1790 of stealing 21 pieces of cloth, 100 yards of muslin and 100 yards of calico from Robert Peel and associates; as the jury gave to the stolen material a nominal value of only 10d., Lord escaped with a sentence of transportation for seven years. He arrived in Sydney in 1791 and was soon assigned as servant to Captain Thomas Rowley [q.v.] of the 102nd Regiment.

Emancipated early and helped by his master, Lord seems to have begun his mercantile career as one of the shadowy figures who retailed spirits and general merchan-

dise bought in bulk by officers of the New
South Wales Corps. In September 1798 he
bought a warehouse, dwelling house and
other buildings on what is now the site of
Macquarie Place. In 1800 he was one of
the petitioners who sought the governor's
permission to buy merchandise direct from
the ship *Minerva* and so to by-pass the
officers' ring. Next January he was appointed public auctioneer, and captains
of vessels used him increasingly to sell their
wares and as a general agent. Profitable
though this was, Lord sought for years to
import his own cargoes, preferably in his
own ships. In 1799 he had bought a
Spanish prize, tactfully renamed her
Hunter, and sent her to India with oil, sealskins and New Zealand spars. Her master,
supposed to return with an illegal India
cargo, sold the ship and absconded. In 1801
the same fate befell another prize sent to
the Cape with coal; her captain, Hugh
Meehan, who was Lord's partner, also
absconded with the proceeds. During the
next twenty years Lord was a retailer,
auctioneer, sealer, pastoralist, timber merchant and ultimately a manufacturer, but
probably his most consistent success was
as a wholesale merchant and captain's
agent, buying some cargoes and selling
others on commission. Commissioner Bigge
[q.v.] commented favourably on Lord's
reputation as a captain's agent. He was
frequently given power of attorney by
New South Wales residents and acted for
Captain John Piper [q.v.] from 1802 to
1811, as agent and merchant banker.

In 1803 he began building the large
three-storey house by the Tank Stream
bridge which became a Sydney institution
as much as a residence. A boon to ships'
officers who wished to sleep ashore near
their merchandise, it was a rendezvous for
captains and supercargoes for the next
twenty years : in August 1804 one captain
left there merchandise worth £7000.

In January 1805 Lord formed a partnership with Henry Kable and James Underwood [qq.v.] who for some years had been
successful in boat building and sealing
while Lord had experience of the London
market and had a London agent Plummer,
Barham & Co. Robert Campbell [q.v.]
and Lord had been the first to export oil
and sealskins to England in 1803. These
valuable staples netted Lord, Kable &
Underwood more than £18,000. Lord's
share, when added to substantial sales on
his private account, brought him more
than £20,000. These totals would have been
considerably higher if Plummers had not
blundered badly. The partnership was almost defunct by the end of 1807 and ended
in a welter of lawsuits in which the judg-

ments favoured Lord. With mysterious ingenuity he contrived to prevent Plummers
from extracting £8000 in debts from the
defunct firm until at least 1819. Consignments of skins and oil established his
credit in London, and he bought the
Sydney Cove, which brought convicts to
Australia in 1807; the government may
never have known that an ex-convict
owned her, for the strict instructions on
behalf of the East India Co. to governors
against overseas trading by New South
Wales residents compelled her ownership
to be disguised, so Lord mortgaged his ship
to Plummers and registered her in their
name. Similarly Lord, Kable & Underwood
owned the *Commerce* in 1807, but carefully
had her mortgaged to Alexander Birnie &
Co. of London before permitting her departure from Sydney. In 1807 Lord also
secretly bought a share in the sealer
Brothers and in the Madras 'country' ship,
General Wellesley. His ambition was to
import English, Indian and China cargoes
on his own account, and clandestine ownership seemed to solve most of the English
and India problems. To obtain a China
cargo he first sought to join with Americans in the sandalwood trade, the one
staple he could provide which the Chinese
merchants valued.

A pioneer in the sealing industry, Lord
had early become interested in the wider
horizons of the Pacific. In 1803 his little
schooner *Marcia* brought the first cargo of
Fiji sandalwood to Sydney. In 1804 he
signed articles with Isaac Pendleton of the
American sealer *Union* for a sandalwood
voyage to Fiji; the wood was to be sold at
Canton and a China cargo obtained with
the proceeds and brought to Sydney for
sale on their joint account. However,
Pendleton was murdered and the *Union*
disappeared at Fiji. In 1805 Lord allied
himself with Captain Chase of the American sealer *Criterion* in a similar arrangement. Governor King sought to prevent
this illegal conjunction, and was furious
when his prohibitions were evaded and the
Criterion reappeared in Sydney with a
China cargo. Forbidden to land it, Chase
took it to America, where its sale netted
Lord 30,000 dollars. Later attempts to
evade the legal obstacles of a China voyage,
first with the *General Wellesley* and then
with a Spanish prize, were prevented by
circumstance or by Governor Bligh. In
spite of these frustrations Lord became
wealthy. He had astonishing financial re-
silience, but he often sought to evade
payment of his debts through litigious
time-wasting devices, and he also suffered
from the bad debts of others. In 1808 with
Thomas Moore and Dr John Harris [qq.v.]

he bought the prize *Pegasus* and sent her sealing, and next year chartered the *Boyd* to take skins to England. On the way her captain was to open a trade between Sydney and Cape Colony in which Lord would exchange coal, cedar and New Zealand spars for Cape wines. Lieut-Governor Paterson [q.v.] commended this illegal enterprise to the authorities at the Cape, but it did not survive the *Boyd's* destruction by Maoris. In 1810-11 the profits from sealing were declining, the London market was cold, and Plummers were attaching any consignments Lord sent to England to set off against his debts. So the man whose vessels had pioneered Foveaux Straits and the Penantipodes (Antipodes) Island abandoned the industry he had done much to establish.

Lord now took as his partner, Francis Williams [q.v.], who had married Lord's adopted daughter in 1806 and visited London and America on his behalf in 1807. After engaging in government contracts to bring rum, sugar and wheat from Calcutta along with similar merchandise on their own account, the partners sought to manufacture their own wares as overseas sources closed against them. These new ventures were launched in the teeth of severe financial reverses. In 1812 Lord lost five major lawsuits for a total of £11,500, and a further judgment of £8000 was given against the old firm in 1813; although he was awarded £12.000 against Kable, the victory proved fruitless. Next year he offered to sell his famous house to the government, as a combined court-house and residence for the judge-advocate and his clerks, but this was declined. Involved in Pacific ventures and manufacturing and other commitments he surrendered his auctioneer's licence to Robert Jenkins [q.v.] in 1813, but resumed it in 1816 after convicts had seized his brig *Trial*. His last export ventures seem to have been in the 1820s when, with Francis Shortt as partner, he was involved in large timber speculations, exporting cedar to England. Soon afterwards his trading activities seem to have ceased and he appears to have relied increasingly on his pastoral interests and the returns from his manufacturing business.

Unable to import the goods he wanted in the early Macquarie period, Lord had launched an ambitious scheme of manufacturing. In 1826 he told Governor Darling that he had employed twenty convicts for 'upwards of twenty years' in tanning and currying leather and in manufacturing hats, cloth, blankets, soap and candles. The hat-making had not begun until 1811 when Lord & Williams allied themselves with Reuben Uther [q.v.], a Lord employee who had mastered the craft. Uther withdrew in 1815 to launch his own business, and Lord's hat-making was thereafter managed by his stepson, John Black. In 1812 Lord & Williams formed a separate partnership with John Hutchinson, who may have claimed abilities he did not possess. They advertised for glass-blowers in May and a 'gross of perfect tumblers' had been produced by June. In 1813 the partners were seeking apprentices for weaving, spinning, pottery and dyeing. The firm dissolved in 1813, with the withdrawal of Williams to Van Diemen's Land and lawsuits between Lord and Hutchinson. Next year Lord built a factory at Botany and opened a fulling mill. His emphasis was now on shoes, hats, harness but especially textiles. In 1815 he was exporting to Tasmania, but lost two valuable cargoes, one in a wreck and the other in his brig *Trial*. He was employing sixty convicts and milling and dressing cloth for the government. In 1820 he showed Bigge samples of his textiles, hats, stockings and leather, which the commissioner estimated as a threat to British manufacturers. He also mentioned that he had produced shoes, candles and harness. These ventures have been described as premature, but they must have been reasonably successful since the factory was operating long after his death. In 1855 with a litigious pertinacity worthy of Simeon himself, his widow fought the commissioners of the city of Sydney to the House of Lords, winning compensation of more than £15,600 for the inundation of part of the Botany property and the loss of the stream which drove the mill.

Lord first acquired land about 1793 and by 1800 he owned about 400 acres at Petersham where he grazed 284 sheep with cattle, horses, pigs and goats. In 1805 he bought the 200-acre Brush Farm in the Field of Mars from William Cox [q.v.] and Sunning Hill Farm from Nicholas Bayly [q.v.]. He was then exporting wheat and maize to Hobart Town. In 1810 Lord held six grants and two leases, including 1140 acres granted him by Lieut-Governor Paterson to pasture his 300 cattle and 1000 sheep. He had formed a partnership in a pastoral business with John and Gregory Blaxland [qq.v.] in 1808, involving a joint ownership of 447 cattle and 2365 sheep. Some of the produce of his farms was probably sold to ships' captains to provision their ships. During the Macquarie period he acquired property in Tasmania and in 1820 sought permission to export 200 merinos there. In 1819 his real property outside Sydney included the 1500-acre Dobroyd estate between Long and Iron

Coves, a 700-acre tract between Liverpool Road and Cook's River, the 2300-acre Townson's Retreat on Botany Bay and the adjoining 620-acre King's Grove, the 2170-acre Lord's Folly, near South Creek, and a further 135 acres on Botany Bay, the site of his factory. He must have disposed of some land by 1822 when he was said to own a little over 5000 acres outside Sydney, only six Sydney residents holding more. In 1823 he was granted a further 600 acres adjoining his factory. Pressed by his creditors in the mid-1820s, Lord sought help from Governor Brisbane with a long list of grievances, which were ignored. Governor Darling proved more responsive. In compensation for the loss of the land and the buildings bought in 1798 and torn down after 1811 to make Macquarie Place, Lord was awarded £3000 in cash and £3562 10s. in land at 4s. an acre. Thus Lord found himself possessed in 1828 of an additional 17,813 acres scattered in substantial blocks from Sydney's outskirts to Orange. Some were sold to help pay off his creditors who had finally brought him to bay.

Lord's relations with the governors varied. King approved his sealing enterprise and his trading which helped to wreck monopolistic activities, but he violently disapproved Lord's ingenious evasions of the East India Co.'s monopoly and his close relations with men like M. M. Robinson [q.v.]. When King exiled Robinson to Norfolk Island in 1805, all Lord's threats and pleadings failed to get him back. When the governor left New South Wales Lord sued him for £5000 but was non-suited. Bligh, warned by his predecessor and with little sympathy for colonial enterprise, was soon at enmity with Lord and unjustly imprisoned him with Kable and Underwood in 1807. Lord's name was fifth on the requisition to Major Johnston [q.v.] to arrest Bligh in 1808. At loggerheads with John Macarthur [q.v.], a sealing and sandalwood competitor, Lord was on good terms with Lieut-Governors Foveaux [q.v.] and Paterson after Macarthur sailed for England. Macquarie particularly esteemed Lord, made him a magistrate in 1810, put him on the turnpike trust, and regularly had him to dine at Government House. A prominent subscriber to the race-course and active on several committees, he was one of the thirteen men whose deliberations in 1816 led to the formation of the Bank of New South Wales. He was an active member of the Auxiliary Bible Society, the Benevolent Society and the Waterloo Fund. In 1821 he resigned from the magistracy, but was prominent in the meetings which led to the petition to regularize past emancipations. He seems to have played little part in public life after 1821 when he leased his house and moved to a new home near his factory. His death on 29 January 1840 was barely noticed by the newspapers.

For all its dubious ethics, its controversies, quarrels, litigations, withered hopes and blighted ventures, Lord's career was no failure. If his plans were over-ambitious for the times or his own resources, he pioneered commerce in Australia and helped to transform a prison farm into a flourishing colony capable of attracting men of capital. With a few others, he strikingly demonstrated what emancipists could achieve in a new country. Like any good bourgeois, after he belatedly married the mother of his children in 1814, he wanted to establish his heirs in comfort and respectability. His family were left well provided for and rose to prominence. His eldest son, Simeon, was a Tasmanian and Queensland pastoralist and fathered two members of parliament, the founder of the Victoria Downs stations and a daughter who married a Queensland surveyor-general. Lord's second son, Francis, was a legislative councillor in 1843-48 and again in 1856-61 and 1864-92. Edward was city treasurer of Sydney and mayor of St Leonards. George William was a member of the Legislative Assembly after 1856, colonial treasurer in 1870-72, a legislative councillor in 1877-80 and a prominent company director. One of Lord's daughters took Dobroyd as her dowry, and another, ironically, married an East India Co. agent, Colonel Sir Alexander Dick. In addition a stepson was cashier of the Bank of New South Wales, and a stepdaughter married the Sydney merchant, Prosper de Mestre [q.v.], in 1821. Shrewd, unprincipled, impudent, a formidable litigant, a centre of controversy for many years, often generous, capable of bold and imaginative designs, perhaps Simeon Lord's most remarkable achievement was to found such a notable family.

HRNSW, 4-7; HRA (1), 2-10, 14-16, (4), 1; E. C. Rowland, 'Simeon Lord', JRAHS, 30 (1944,) 37 (1951); Supreme Court records (NSWA); MS cat under S. Lord (ML).

D. R. HAINSWORTH

LORD, THOMAS DAUNT (1783-1865), commandant of convicts and settler, joined the 62nd Regiment as an ensign in November 1800. Next year he transferred to the 2nd West India Regiment, and attained the rank of major in March 1820. He then became involved in the Bradley-Arthur dispute in Honduras and as a result agreed to sell his commission upon being granted six months leave to return to England. He changed sides and gave evidence on Arthur's behalf when in 1824 Bradley prosecuted Arthur for wrongful imprisonment. Later that year Lord applied for a land grant in Van Diemen's Land; he arrived at Hobart Town in the *Cumberland* in January 1825, accompanied by his wife Susan. In February he was made Naval Officer at £150 a year, but in July resigned to take up an appointment as commandant of the newly established Maria Island penal settlement, at 7s. 6d. a day. Lord held this position until the settlement was closed in November 1832. During this period Lord was three times accused of misappropriating government stores but each time he avoided prosecution and the accusers were punished. Under his control the settlement was firmly established and factories on the island produced tanned leather, shoes, cloth, and prisoners' clothing. About 100 yards of cloth were woven each week from yarn spun by women at the Female Factory at the Cascades, and about 1700 pairs of shoes were made each year. Several substantial buildings, were erected. A penitentiary measuring 186 feet by 25 feet was built in 1830 from 200,000 bricks made on the island; it was still standing in 1966.

Lord quarrelled with many of the officials who came and went during the seven years that Maria Island was a penal settlement under his command. But his bad personal record was offset to some extent by his practical achievements at this lonely outpost. If not brilliant, he was at least competent in shouldering his responsibilities.

Soon after his arrival in 1825 Lord had been granted 1000 acres at Point Bougainville opposite Maria Island. He later received a further 1560 acres because the first grant was of poor quality. He was appointed assistant police magistrate at Waterloo Point (Swansea) in December 1832, but was suspended in August 1834 for allegedly stealing and having in his possession cloth and other goods belonging to the government. He was acquitted in the Supreme Court on three charges of unlawful possession and several other charges against him were withdrawn but, when approval of his suspension was later received from London, his name was removed from the Commission of the Peace.

When he arrived in Tasmania Lord was obsequious to Arthur, but later became more confident and even arrogant. After his suspension he harboured much resentment against Arthur, whom he held responsible for all his troubles. He was not co-operative when Arthur asked him to refute further charges brought by Bradley, who was then in England, although the latter had described Lord 'as great a villain as any in Van Diemen's Land'.

Lord had one son, Wellington, and five daughters. His wife died on 7 September 1849, and in 1853 Lord tried unsuccessfully to sell his property, Oakhampton. He died there on 22 April 1865.

J. R. Morris, 'Early convict history of Maria Island', *PTHRA*, 11 (1964); Correspondence file under T. D. Lord (TA); Arthur papers (ML).   J. R. MORRIS

LOVELESS, GEORGE (1797-1874), Dorchester labourer and Tolpuddle 'martyr', was born in 1797 at the village of Tolpuddle, near Dorchester, in Dorset, England, where he worked as a ploughman, married and had three children. By 1830 he appears to have become respected in his own and neighbouring villages as a community leader and Wesleyan preacher. His writings and his part in the agricultural workers' movement of the 1830s indicate that he had read Robert Owen and was familiar with attempts then being made to establish trades unions in London, Birmingham and other districts. According to his own account he played no part in the agrarian disturbances that convulsed the southern counties in August-December 1830; but in the next two years he represented the Dorchester agricultural labourers in discussions with the farmers, who agreed to raise wages to 10s. a week. At Tolpuddle, however, farmers refused to pay more than 9s. and later reduced wages to 8s. and 7s., and threatened to reduce them to 6s. To protect their livelihood the labourers, advised by Loveless and two delegates from London, in October 1833 formed a Friendly Society of Agricultural Labourers, which charged an entrance fee of 1s. and a subscription of 1d. a week and began to meet at Thomas Standfield's cottage at Tolpuddle. Since 1824 it had no longer been illegal to form trades unions, but witnesses were found to testify that Loveless and his associates had bound their members by 'unlawful oaths', a felony under an Act of 1797, and for this offence the labourers' six leaders, George Loveless, his brother Henry, their brother-in-law Thomas Standfield, their nephew Thomas Standfield, James Hammett and James Brine, were found guilty at the Dorchester Assizes in March 1834, and sentenced to transportation for seven years to the Australian colonies.

James Loveless, the two Standfields, Hammett and Brine sailed in the *Surry* to Sydney, where they arrived in August 1834.

George Loveless was separated from his companions and sent to Van Diemen's Land in the *William Metcalfe*, reaching Hobart Town on 4 September. Lieut-Governor Arthur appreciated his sterling qualities and exemplary character and sent him to work on the domain farm at New Town as a shepherd and stock-keeper. Later he was employed by Major de Gillern [q.v.] at Glen Ayr, near Richmond; there he read in the *London Dispatch* of the great campaign that had been conducted in London for the prisoners' release and of Lord John Russell's order on 10 March 1836, that free pardons be issued to them. Loveless, however, had some months previously been persuaded to write to ask his wife Elizabeth to join him; when offered a free passage to England, he refused to accept it until certain that she had not already sailed. This delayed his departure for several months, but on 30 January 1837 he embarked in the *Eveline* and reached London in June. Meanwhile the authorities in New South Wales had been far more dilatory in conveying the government's instructions and offer to his companions. It was not until 11 September that James Loveless, Brine and the Standfields sailed from Sydney in the *John Barry*, reaching Plymouth in March 1838. James Hammett, who had been working in the interior of the colony, did not arrive in England until September 1839.

On their return the Lovelesses, Standfields and Brine settled on farms near Chipping Ongar in Essex, and migrated to Canada a few years later; James Hammett alone went back to Tolpuddle. George Loveless, like his companions, became an active Chartist; he wrote *The Victims of Whiggery* (London, 1837), a remarkable account of the Dorchester labourers' experiences and of the transportation system. He died on a farm at London, Ontario, on 6 March 1874.

W. M. Citrine et al (eds), *The book of the martyrs of Tolpuddle, 1834-1934* (Lond, 1934); Ac nos 2/159, 2/395 (TA).   G. RUDE

LOVELL, ESH (1796-1865), Wesleyan missioner, was the second son of a tenant farmer of Helperthorpe, East Riding, Yorkshire, England. He had a good education, became a staunch Wesleyan Methodist and married Anne Ousten. He was attracted by the promise of free land grants in Australia and sailed for Van Diemen's Land in the *Avon* with his wife and infant, Samuel. A second son, William Esh, was born at Mauritius on the voyage but died four years after they arrived in Hobart Town in July 1823.

Lovell brought with him an order from the Colonial Office to Lieut-Governor Sorell for a land grant proportionate to his capital, and was awarded 600 acres after showing that he had imported £135 in cash, £100 in sheep and £675 in merchandise and sundries. He did not at once take up his location order; instead he set up as a general merchant, and his wife as a milliner, in Melville Street, Hobart. Both became active members of the near-by Wesleyan Chapel and both conducted Sunday schools, Esh in Hobart and Anne at Kangaroo Point. A quarterly meeting in 1824 considered Lovell had excellent abilities for the pulpit : a deeply pious understanding, a firm attachment to Wesleyan discipline and a strong and healthy constitution. Although unordained he was appointed Methodist missioner in Launceston early in 1826, but his work was unsuccessful and next year he applied for a government post as schoolmaster and catechist. He was considered for the vacancy in Longford, but the appointment went to W. P. Weston [q.v.].

His strict sobriety and religious sincerity were qualities appreciated under Arthur's administration, and when the position of superintendent at the Female House of Correction at the Cascades became vacant in February 1828 he was appointed, with his wife as matron, at £150 a year. But he was not vigorous and systematic enough, and four years later a committee of inquiry into the factory found faults with his loose classification of women under punishment, the allocation of rations, and his wife's occasional employment of needleworkers to serve the needs of her own increasing family. Lovell objected to the committee's procedure, which gave him no chance to defend himself, and he resigned when the inquiry ended in December 1831.

For the next four years he conducted the Prospect Place Academy, a seminary for young gentlemen in Murray Street, continuing meanwhile his activities at the Melville Street Methodist Church and becoming one of the first trustees for its new building in 1835.

His wife died in 1834, leaving him with six children. In December 1835 he married Sophia Rebecca, a minor and the daughter of James Adkins of Hobart. By her he had eleven surviving children, but the marriage proved an unhappy one for the children of his first family, who, drawn closer together by the antipathy of their stepmother and the sternness of their father, all left home on reaching adulthood.

In September 1827 Surveyor Wedge [q.v.] had marked off a grant of 600 acres for Lovell near the Ben Lomond Rivulet, but he never occupied it and presumably sold it soon afterwards. In 1842 Lovell acquired a Richmond estate that included Carrington House, the property of former lieut-governors, and here the two daughters of his first marriage, Anne and Margaret, married the two eldest sons, Thomas and William, of his neighbour, William Kearney [q.v.] of Laburnum Park. Lovell died at Carrington on 16 May 1865.

J. R. Skemp (ed), *Letters to Anne . . . 1846-1872* (Melb, 1956); *Hobart Town Gazette*, 12 July, 2 Aug, 25 Oct 1823; *Hobart Town Courier*, 7 Jan 1832; *Cornwall Chronicle*, 9 Apr 1842; *Mercury*, 17 May 1865; CSO 1 (TA).   J. R. SKEMP

LOWE, ROBERT (1783-1832), grazier, was born on 29 August 1783 at Clerkenwell, London. He married Barbara Willard in Sussex on 2 October 1807, and arrived in New South Wales with his wife and two children in the *Mary* in May 1812. He brought an official letter testifying to his respectable connexions, and recommending him for a liberal land grant since he possessed property worth £1000; as a result he was granted 1000 acres at Bringelly in August 1812 and a further 500 acres there in September 1818. He named his house after Birling Gap on the Sussex coast near his wife's former home, and extended the property until in 1828 it amounted to 5600 acres. He also had 1280 acres at Liverpool.

Governor Macquarie made Lowe a magistrate in 1815 for the Bringelly and Cooke districts and in 1820 for the County of Cumberland. Lowe took an active part in the affairs of the Campbelltown district, was a member of the Agricultural Stock Club, vice-president of the Benevolent Society and a committee member of the Bible Society; he was sympathetic to the Aboriginals, supported the Native Institution and the Society for Promoting Christian Knowledge amongst the Aborigines of New South Wales. In 1817 he wrote warmly praising Macquarie's administration, moderation and philanthropy towards the convicts, but in July 1820 he told Commissioner Bigge [q.v.] that the prisoners were better reformed if employed in agriculture than if kept in town, that if unskilled convicts could not obtain such work they should be placed in road-gangs and that tickets-of-leave were too readily granted. He deplored the scarcity of mechanics in the country and condemned the system of agriculture in the colony on the ground that its successive grain crops tended to exhaust the soil and regretted that grantees of land across the mountains had done nothing to develop their properties.

In the 1815 drought Lowe had sustained large losses of sheep and cattle, and in December was allowed to take some of his flocks across the mountains to the Bathurst area. In October 1822 he sent a memorial to the colonial secretary requesting a land grant there on the grounds that he had improved the breed of sheep and cattle and incurred expense in building stockyards. He had also taken sheep and cattle as far as Mudgee, and there had erected stockyards in conjunction with William Lawson [q.v.]. Lowe and his sons later received considerable grants in Sidmeath valley, near Bathurst, and Lowe bought a property at Wilbertree, Mudgee.

His wife died on 21 February 1818, aged 38, leaving four sons and one daughter. On 5 November 1821 Lowe married Sarah Hazard, a widow, who bore him three sons and three daughters. Lowe died on 17 July 1832, and Sarah on 3 August 1878, aged 78; they were buried with his first wife at St John's, Parramatta.

HRA (1), 7, 9, 10; MS cat under R. Lowe (ML).   VIVIENNE PARSONS

LOWE, ROBERT, VISCOUNT SHERBROOKE (1811-1892), politician, was born on 4 December 1811 at Bingham, Nottinghamshire, England, the second son of Rev. Robert Lowe, prebendary of Southwell and rector of Bingham, and his wife Ellen, née Pyndar. An albino with defective vision, he led a sheltered childhood. When at 14 he was sent to Winchester, he suffered deeply from boyish ridicule of his physical peculiarities. In June 1829 he matriculated at University College, Oxford (B.A., 1833; M.A., 1836), where he made a name for himself as a scholar and as a speaker in Union debates. In 1835 he was awarded a fellowship at Magdalen, and enrolled at Lincoln's Inn. On 26 March 1836 he married Georgiana, second daughter of George Orred of Tranmere, Cheshire, and Aigburth Hall, Lancashire, and relinquished both his fellowship and plans for a legal career. In the years that followed he became one of Oxford's most successful private tutors, but he willingly left the drudgery of teaching in 1840 to return to Lincoln's Inn. In January 1842, when at the Bar, his eyesight had become so poor that doctors warned he would go blind within seven years. He resolved thereupon that in the seven allotted years of light he would seek his fortune in Australia.

Lowe arrived in Sydney on 8 October 1842 and nine days later was admitted to practise in the New South Wales Supreme Court. During the court recess in December and January severe headaches and a painful nervous tic of the eyes caused him again to seek the advice of doctors, who told him to give his eyes absolute rest; otherwise he might not only go blind but endanger his life. For the next nine months Lowe restlessly toured country districts with his wife. In October 1843 he decided to risk his eyes by resuming practice, but in those days of deep economic depression briefs were few. Governor Gipps lent a sympathetic ear and early in November, when he needed support in the Legislative Council, named Lowe as an unofficial nominee. From that vantage point Lowe was able to defend the government's position by voicing his deepest convictions: his belief in a policy of *laissez faire* and his faith in the utilitarian tenet that the only innovations desirable were those that would bring about better government. His first speeches electrified the the chamber as he attacked radical measures which Richard Windeyer and Wentworth [qq.v.] had proposed to meet the economic crisis. Lowe himself proposed that imprisonment for debt be abolished, a suggestion that was adopted by the council in diluted form in December 1843.

His brief success in the council bore fruit and, although the depression had worsened, his voice was heard regularly in the courts. In February 1844 he undertook the defence of John Knatchbull [q.v.], a convict who had senselessly murdered a young woman shopkeeper. Lowe's plea was novel for his time: that insanity of the will could exist apart from insanity of the intellect. He argued that Knatchbull had yielded to an irresistible impulse and could not be held responsible for his crime. The court, however, ruled otherwise. The Lowes subsequently adopted the murdered woman's two young children, Bobby and Polly Jamieson.

In March 1844 Gipps, confronted with large expenses for immigration, presented the Executive Council with a draft of squatting regulations that would raise the needed revenue. To Lowe, Gipps's move seemed incompatible with constitutional government. 'The power over the purse vested in the Legislature was perfectly useless', he was to declare, 'if the Government had at its entire command another resource derivable from the people, which it could raise without limit, and without reference to the assent or dissent of their representatives'. Simultaneous with his first major difference with the governor on public policy, there sprang up between them a private misunderstanding over the guest list at Government House, a dispute that contributed to the rupture of their friendship. In mid-March Lowe cast about for a constituency in Port Phillip, only to be rebuffed because, ironically, he was considered likely to support Gipps even from an elective seat.

Towards the end of April Lowe joined the Pastoral Association of New South Wales, which had been formed to combat the new squatting regulations. Gipps, angered by Lowe's desertion, sought to remove him from the council, but Lowe refused to relinquish his seat until he had completed a report on popular education, which recommended a state-supported, non-denominational system of schools. The council agreed to this suggestion, but Gipps, influenced by the strong protests of the Anglican bishop, by increasing ill health, and by personal bitterness towards his recalcitrant council, refused to carry out the council's recommendations. In the years that followed Lowe pursued the matter until, in 1847, Governor FitzRoy sanctioned the beginnings of a National school system.

After his resignation from the council in August 1844 Lowe, with the backing of the Pastoral Association, launched on 30 November a weekly journal, the *Atlas*, the declared purpose of which was to lobby for responsible government and for colonial control of colonial waste lands. 'This is the colony', Lowe wrote, 'that's under the Governor, that's under the Clerk, that's under the Lord, that's under the Commons, who are under the people, who know and care nothing about it'. During the first half year of publication he filled the pages of the *Atlas* with scathing articles and poems; as public duties came to occupy more of his time, he gradually relinquished control of the paper, until in 1847 he severed all connexion with it.

In April 1845 he returned to the Legislative Council. When news of the new land orders arrived in 1847, Lowe delivered five major speeches in which, with passionate sincerity, he disparaged the squatters' aims. In 1847 and 1849 he produced two masterful committee reports refuting the Wakefieldian theory of a high minimum price of land and advocating colonial control of colonial waste lands.

During his philippics on the land question in 1847 Lowe made his first direct appeal for popular support. In January 1848 when a Constitution involving indirect elections was proposed, he enhanced his popularity by an eloquent plea at a public meeting for passive resistance to any departure from the time-honoured principles of the British Constitution. At the general elections in June 1848 he was nominated by a committee of tradesmen for one of Sydney's two seats in the Legislative Council, and on 30 July was returned a close second to Wentworth in what the secretary of his election committee, Henry

Parkes, termed 'the birthday of Australian democracy'. In the following year, having come to believe that without convict labour the squatters could not succeed in their designs for land aggrandizement, Lowe was one of the leaders of popular resistance to an attempt of the British government to renew transportation. In June 1849, standing on the roof of an omnibus at Circular Quay, with the convict ship *Hashemy* anchored near by, he told the crowd: 'The injustice forced upon the Americans is not half so great as that forced upon this colony'. The British government made no further attempt to renew transportation to Sydney.

At the hustings in 1848 Lowe had expressed faith in the common people, provided they were educated, but he remained inalterably opposed either to class legislation or to manhood suffrage. He refused to join the Constitutional Association, a working class political organization which had grown out of the committee that had engineered his election. He also refused to help Sydney's unemployed to obtain relief from the government. But perhaps his crowning apostasy in the eyes of the working class was his support of the bounty immigration bill, which would have required assisted immigrants who subsequently left the colony to repay to the government the cost of their passage from Britain. When Lowe in November 1849, on account of his wife's increasing homesickness and ill health, unexpectedly announced his intended departure for England, there were few regrets, although his political supporters expressed annoyance at having to undergo the expense of another election. On 27 January 1850 the Lowes and the two Jamieson children sailed for home.

After a brief tour of the northern circuit Lowe, in August 1850, accepted an offer from a former pupil of his at Oxford, John Delane, editor of *The Times*, to join the paper's staff as a leader writer. For the next seventeen years, Lowe contributed an average of three leading articles a week, his last appearing in January 1868.

In July 1852 he entered parliament for the borough of Kidderminster. A series of appointments of increasing importance followed: joint secretary of the Board of Control, December 1852-January 1855; vice-president of the Board of Trade and paymaster-general August 1855-March 1858; vice-president of the committee of the Council on Education, June 1859-April 1864; chancellor of the Exchequer, December 1869-August 1873; Home secretary, August 1873-February 1874. While out of office in 1855, he strongly opposed the passing of the Australian Constitution bills as measures designed to help the squatters keep their monopoly of land. At the Board of Trade he brought in legislation that allowed joint stock companies to adopt the principle of limited liability. On the Education Committee, he introduced the revised code regulations in 1862 which provided for 'payment by results'. In 1864 he resigned office after charges that inspectors' reports had been unduly censored, charges of which the House subsequently exonerated him. Again out of office, in 1865 he led the opposition to extension of the borough franchise and next year to Lord John Russell's mild reform bill over which he managed to split his party and cause the fall of the government. As leader of what Bright called the political 'cave of Adullam', he was offered a post in the new Derby ministry, but refused. In 1867 he fought desperately to defeat the Tories' far-reaching reform bill. Although he failed, he so dominated the House of Commons by force of intellect, eloquence and conviction that he was spoken of as a future prime minister. After the passage of the 1867 Reform Act, he urged that greater attention be paid to the question of popular education. 'We must educate our masters', is a phrase attributed to him at this time. In 1868 he gave strenuous support towards the disestablishment of the Irish Church, and on 9 December 1868 entered Gladstone's cabinet as chancellor of the Exchequer. His first budgets were considered brilliant; in four years he took £12,000,000 off taxation and removed the last vestige of duty on corn, but after 1871 his finance came increasingly under criticism. In 1873 he was transferred to the Home Office where he remained until the Gladstone ministry fell in 1874. In 1876 in a speech at East Retford attacking the royal titles bill, Lowe tactlessly intimated that the Queen herself had been responsible for the bill's introduction. When the Liberals returned to power in 1880, Victoria made it clear that any ministry that included Lowe would be unacceptable to her. Lowe's active political life ended with his elevation to the House of Lords as Viscount Sherbrooke on 25 May 1880. Failing memory and near-blindness contributed to his political eclipse.

Georgiana Lowe, who had been ill for many years, died in November 1884; in February 1885, Lowe married Caroline, daughter of Thomas Sneyd of Ashcombe Park, Staffordshire. There were no children of either marriage. Lowe died at Warlingham, Surrey, on 27 July 1892. Among the honours he received were: Hon. LL.D. Edinburgh, 1867; Hon. D.C.L. Oxford, 1870; member of the senate of London University; trustee of the British Museum; fellow of the Royal Society; G.C.B., 30 June 1885.

A man of great intellect and integrity with a commanding power of eloquence, he was impatient of the lack of these qualities in others. Arrogant and inflexible, he did not bend to meet changing circumstances nor would he compromise with principle; conciliation was a word unknown to him. The effect of his efforts on the course of Australian political development was to broaden the base of its democracy, whereas in England he strove to maintain the narrow base of the reformed parliament of 1832. The seeming contradiction lay not in his attitude but in the differences in circumstances in the colony and the mother country. In the crucial decade of the 1840s in New South Wales no other single figure stands out more vividly both as antagonist to Gipps and the British government and as protagonist in the struggle for responsible government.

R. Lowe (Viscount Sherbrooke), *Speeches and letters on reform*, 2nd ed (Lond, 1867); A. P. Martin, *Life and letters of the Right Honourable Robert Lowe, Viscount Sherbrooke*, 1-2 (Lond, 1892); W. A. Gardner (Baroness Burghclere) ed, *A great lady's friendships* (Lond, 1933); *The history of The Times*, 2 (Lond, 1939); A. Briggs, *Victorian people* (Lond, 1954); R. L. Knight, *Illiberal Liberal: Robert Lowe in New South Wales, 1842-1850* (Melb, 1966).   R. L. KNIGHT

LOWE, WILLIAM (1805-1878), shipbuilder, was born on 21 July 1805 at Leith, Scotland, the second son of William Lowe, a 'landed proprietor', and Margaret, née Steel, of Stirling. The family descended from Huguenots who settled first in England and later in Scotland. At 14 William Lowe junior was apprenticed to the shipbuilding trade at the Royal Dockyard, Deptford. At 19 he was sent to Stettin, Prussia, to work on the building of several ships and there he stayed for nearly three years. He returned to Scotland, where his father gave him his share of his estate, a considerable sum. Thereupon Lowe sailed to South America where he visited Ecuador, Peru and Chile; from Valparaiso he embarked in the *Tiger* for Sydney, where he arrived in September 1828. On the voyage Lowe and a fellow passenger, James Marshall, were so useful in repairing damage suffered in a gale that the captain refunded their passage money.

In 1830 Lowe took up ten acres on the Williams River, where good hardwood and cedar were abundant. This land was adjacent to eleven acres owned by a Sydney merchant, Joseph Hickey Grose [q.v.]. Lowe, who was joined later by Marshall, made a wet dock, and by February 1831 they had built some small craft and were building for Grose a steam vessel, the *William the Fourth*, 54 tons, launched October 1831, which traded on the Australian coast for more than thirty years, and on the China coast for many years after that. The *William the Fourth*, the first coastal steamer wholly built in Australia, was eighty feet long and usually travelled at eight knots. In 1836 Lowe delivered the *Ceres* to the Hunter River Steam Packet Association. Next year his partnership with Marshall was dissolved but Lowe continued building vessels of high quality at the Deptford yards as he named them, until about 1860 when they were demolished. Four of the first twelve steamships built in the colony were Lowe's or Lowe's & Marshall's. From 1833 to 1836 Lowe was a director of a company that ran a steamer service to Parramatta, and from 1843 to 1852 his *Comet*, 50 tons, maintained a service to Parramatta, first in rivalry with and later in conjunction with Edye Manning's [q.v.] *Emu*.

In 1834 Lowe married Henrietta Blandford who died in 1846 leaving six children. In 1850 he married May Penfold, by whom he had eight children. Lowe died in May 1878; his wife lived until 1897.

H. Lowe, *William Lowe, pioneer shipbuilder of Clarencetown* (Raymond Terrace, nd).

LOWES, THOMAS YARDLEY (1798?-1870), distiller, merchant and auctioneer, arrived at Hobart Town from England in the *Thalia* on 27 April 1823, as a free settler, with his wife Anna Maria Theresa and infant daughter Mary Ann. He was joined by his parents in 1827.

Lowes received a land grant at Manor Owen, in the Lennox district, which he left unimproved and unoccupied for years. He was promised another 800 acres when he erected a distillery and malt house on another grant at Cascade Grove, Hobart, and began distilling in 1824. Because of the reduction of duty on foreign spirits in 1825 and the scarcity of grain he had to close his distillery, which was bought for £2000 in 1827 by the government for a factory and place of detention for female prisoners.

In 1825 Lowes was advertising as a general commission agent and three years later he was appointed cashier of the Bank of Van Diemen's Land. In 1832 he was actuary to the Van Diemen's Land Assurance Association, and became a licensed auctioneer in partnership with W. T. Macmichael; he also opened a wool mart in 1834. Later he acquired property at Lowes Park, Antill Ponds, and at Dairy Lands, Glenorchy, where he built Lowestoft.

Lieut-Governor Sorell spoke of Lowes as an industrious young man, and Lieut-Governor Arthur considered that disappointments over urban allotments and the unfulfilled promise of 800 additional acres had given a bias to Lowes's political principles and lost the government the benefit of his support.

His political activities began in 1824 when he was one of the signatories to a memorial to the King soliciting separation of Van Diemen's Land from New South Wales and its independence as a colony. In 1847 he took part in a public meeting on transportation, and spoke in favour of the continuation of transportation in a modified form. He was a member of the Legislative Council of Tasmania from 1856 until his death, a justice of the peace from 1862, one of the two members of the Bridgewater Commission, and a promoter of the Mersey and Deloraine Tramway Co. He was treasurer of the New Town Race Course in 1831-32, an early member of the Royal Society of Tasmania, and an original member, and captain in 1860-62, of the Buckingham Volunteer Rifle Corps. He was also a director of the Tasmanian Fire and Life Insurance Co. and a vice-president of the Manchester Unity Independent Order of Oddfellows.

His wife died in 1861. Their only child was married to Francis Oscar Tondeur on 21 October 1848. Lowes died at Lowestoft on 5 October 1870. He was buried in St Paul's Church of England cemetery, Glenorchy.

His obituary referred to him as a friend of the poor, somewhat eccentric, and a politician whose views were not of the most advanced order. A contemporary described him as 'a fine old English gentleman', generous, courteous, with a kindly wit, a success in business which he conducted with the highest integrity, and with a wide social circle.

Correspondence file under T. Y. Lowes (TA).
                                    E. M. GEDDES

LUCAS, JAMES (1792?-1853), pilot, was born at Norfolk Island, the son of Lieutenant James Hunt Lucas of the 102nd Regiment. There is a tradition that at an early age he was enlisted as midshipman in the *Porpoise* under Matthew Flinders [q.v.] and was in that ship when it was wrecked on the east coast of Australia in August 1803. He served for three years in the *Buffalo*, two years as second officer and chief officer in the *Kangaroo* and then four years as chief officer in the *Elk*.

In 1821 he was appointed harbourmaster and pilot at the newly formed penal settlement at Macquarie Harbour, and soon earned the reputation of being attentive to his duty, active, vigilant, bold and resolute and a man with whom prisoners could take no liberty. He was stationed at Cape Sorell and for eight years piloted across the shallow and treacherous entrance most vessels making for Macquarie Harbour. He was occasionally sent along the coast to search for escaping convicts and recaptured a number of them.

At Cape Sorell on 21 July 1828 he was married by Rev. William Schofield [q.v.], Wesleyan chaplain, to Margaret Keefe. His three children were baptized there. Next December, as he boarded the *James Lucas*, a small craft used to take supplies to the pilot station, the hatches were suddenly closed over him by convicts attempting to escape. He broke through the bulkhead and later captured two of the absconders near Circular Head. He applied for a less hazardous appointment and in November 1829 became a pilot at the Derwent, and was stationed at Point Louis in D'Entrecasteaux Channel. When he applied for land on Slopen Island he was refused by the Land Board on the ground that farming pursuits would be liable to divert a pilot's attention from his important public duties; later, however, he received 100 acres at Point Louis.

In August 1844 he boarded the *Angelina*, a ship carrying female convicts, was asked to produce his authority, but was not able to show his pilot's licence, which he seldom carried. Thereupon the captain abused him and, when Lucas showed resentment, lashed him to the rigging, and had the ship taken in by an unlicensed pilot.

In June 1853, after thirty-five years in government service, he applied for a pension. Some weeks later, always ready to help those in distress, he went to the assistance of the Dutch barque *Emilie*, aground at Halfmoon Bay. Lucas was severely injured when the warp line broke. He was taken to St Mary's hospital, where he died on 5 August 1853. Shops in Hobart closed and shipping in the port flew flags at half-mast when his funeral proceeded to St George's cemetery.

HRA (3), 4; *Hobart Town Courier*, 21 Oct 1842; *Colonial Times*, 27 Aug 1844, 13 Aug 1853; CSO 1/134/3237, 1/216/5209 (TA); GO 33/78/1161 (TA).
                                    E. R. PRETYMAN

LUCAS, NATHANIEL (1764-1818), joiner, carpenter and builder, was living in Red Lion Street, Holborn, London, in July 1784 when he was convicted at the Old Bailey of having stolen clothing from his neighbour; he was sentenced to transportation for seven years and sailed in 1787 in the *Scarborough* in the First Fleet. After his arrival in New South Wales, he and Olivia Gascoyne (Gascoigne or Gaskins), whom he later married, were among fifteen convicts specially selected for their character and vocation to pioneer Norfolk Island, where they arrived in the *Supply* on 6 March 1788. In 1791 he received a grant of fifteen acres, which he farmed, and in 1793 purchased another sixty acres from Charles Heritage, a former marine; apparently he was successful, for in August 1802 he sold wheat, maize and pork worth £450 to the government. On 11 June 1795 he had succeeded William Peate as master carpenter. He was suspended from 5 September 1800 to 13 March 1802. He was reappointed and held his post until the establishment was reduced in 1805. In April he returned with his family to Sydney in the *Investigator*. The ship carried materials for a government windmill which Lucas was to erect in Sydney, and he was allowed to carry materials for another windmill for himself; by June 1805 he completed the first post-mill to be erected in the settlement.

In Sydney Lucas became a private builder, but in 1808 after the rebellion against Bligh, he was appointed superintendent of carpenters at a salary of £50, with the extra privileges of victualling from the government stores and using assigned servants. In 1813 he was appointed superintendent of the government lumber yard, and had sixty-one men under him. Next year, when Governor Macquarie published Bathurst's order abolishing the privileges attached to this and many other offices, Lucas with many others petitioned the governor for their restoration, and Macquarie suspended the order. However, from this time Lucas gave increasing attention to building contracts. He had already been associated with the Rum Hospital in Sydney. In 1816 he was the builder of the parsonage at Liverpool and was associated with that at Parramatta (both demolished). In 1818 he gained the contract for building St Luke's Church, Liverpool, which Francis Greenway [q.v.] designed, and was present when Macquarie laid its foundation stone on 7 April. Greenway, who had quarrelled with Lucas over the hospital, quarrelled with him also over the foundations of the church, alleging that Lucas was much addicted to the bottle, and that he was using very poor stone at the church. On 5 May his body was found in the mud of the river at Liverpool; his death was said 'to have proceeded from his own act, owing to mental derangement'.

Lucas contributed twenty years service to Australian building. None of his work now remains except an unidentifiable portion of the Rum Hospital. He had thirteen children, eleven at Norfolk Island between 1789 and 1803, of whom two (twins) died in infancy, and two more in Sydney in 1805 and 1807.

HRA (1), 1-8; H. Rumsey, *The pioneers of Sydney Cove* (Syd, 1937); M. H. Ellis, *Francis Greenway*, 2nd ed (Syd, 1953); Norfolk Island victualling book (ML); L. Macquarie, Diary (ML).

MORTON HERMAN

LUTTRELL, EDWARD (1756-1824), surgeon, was the son of Major Southcott Hungerford Luttrell, whose father was Edward Luttrell of Dunster, Somerset, England. His grandmother Ann, née Hungerford, was descended from the lords of Irnham and other noble families. He married a clergyman's daughter, Martha Walters, and they had six sons and four daughters. In 1803 he was in private practice in Kent, England, when like some other settlers he was given permission to go to New South Wales; because of his family and his property he was thought likely 'to cultivate his land . . . with greater facility than most of the settlers who have preceded him' and Governor King was also instructed to give him a medical post when a vacancy occurred. In June 1804 Luttrell arrived at Port Jackson with his wife and eight children in the *Experiment*, Captain Withers, but soon afterwards his 'Feelings as a Father were much wounded', for one of his sons who had sailed twice with Withers deserted the ship in Sydney, and a daughter eloped with Withers when the *Experiment* sailed.

Luttrell was granted 400 choice acres near Mulgrave Place on the Hawkesbury, rations for his family and ten assigned servants, livestock, seed and tools. He soon had ten acres under wheat and bought some 400 sheep, but he was quickly disillusioned by the high costs, thefts, isolation and seasonal vagaries which, described at length in his letters to official friends in London, denied the fulfilment of his social ambitions and dreams. In June 1805 Luttrell was appointed assistant colonial surgeon at 5s. a day, with duties at Sydney and Parramatta. In 1807 he became friendly with Governor Bligh, and 'although unused to a Sea life, and being upwards of Fifty' he was appointed to H.M.S. *Porpoise* as a naval surgeon at 10s. a day and made five voyages in her. To his dismay he was superseded in November 1808 but, after applying to Lieut-Governor Paterson [q.v.] for reinstatement in his former position, he was appointed in February 1809 as acting assistant-surgeon in charge of the hospital for the sick of the military establishments at Parramatta, for which he was paid 5s. a day. Luttrell sought land grants for his eight children, and in August Paterson granted 125 acres in the Evan district to each. Governor Macquarie confirmed these, but in June 1813 he reported that he would not recommend Luttrell for promotion or additional pay since he was 'totally undeserving . . . deficient . . . in Humanity and in Attention to his Duty . . . sordid and Unfeeling and will not Afford any Medical Assistance to any Person who cannot pay him well for it'.

Macquarie had received many complaints of Luttrell's negligence and had more than once severely admonished him, and would have suspended him were it not for his large family. In April 1814 Luttrell was moved from Parramatta to Sydney, to be under the eye of the principal surgeon, D'Arcy Wentworth [q.v.]. Next year he was given a choice of retiring to his farm on a pension or of returning to the Parramatta Hospital, but in August he was appointed acting colonial surgeon at Hobart Town at a salary of £182 10s. He moved there in January 1816. He cleared himself of some charges by proving that he suffered from a severe rheumatic affection which often crippled him, but Macquarie told the Colonial Office that Luttrell, although 'not deemed deficient in professional Skill . . . is . . . Criminally inattentive to his Patients . . . extremely Irritable and Violent in his Temper and Very Infirm from Dissipation', and should be retired on half-pay. This for the time the office refused and Macquarie, thinking again of his large family, was reluctant to displace him.

In Hobart Luttrell was in constant trouble with Lieut-Governor Sorell for being a boon companion of Thomas Davey, for irregular attendance at the hospital and gaol and for negligence in submitting returns. He was censured for making false accusations, and repeatedly recommended for retirement. The Colonial Office in 1818 gave Macquarie permission to place Luttrell on half-pay, but not until June 1821, when James Scott [q.v.] was appointed, was it possible to replace him. Luttrell died at his home in Bridge Street on 10 June 1824 in his sixty-eighth year. His widow, after many appeals, was allowed a pension of £50; she died in May 1832.

HRNSW, 5-7; HRA (1), 5-10, (3), 2-6; V. Gibbs (ed), The complete peerage, 3 (Lond, 1913); Critic (Hob), 10 Feb 1922; LSD 1/7/514 (TA).

LYCETT, JOSEPH (b. 1774?), convict and artist, was born in Staffordshire, England. By profession a portrait and miniature painter, he was convicted of forgery at Salop Assizes on 10 August 1811 and sentenced to transportation for fourteen years. He sailed in the transport General Hewitt, in which Captain James Wallis [q.v.], of the 46th Regiment, an amateur artist of considerable ability, was coming out for a tour of duty. He reached Sydney in February 1814 and was soon appointed a clerk in the police office.

In May 1815 Sydney was flooded by hundreds of skilfully forged 5s. bills drawn on the postmaster. They were traced to Lycett, who was found in possession of a small copper-plate press. He was convicted of forgery and sent to Newcastle. Discipline there was strict and punishments were severe, but Lycett's lot appears to have become comparatively easy after Wallis became commandant in June 1816. Lycett drew up the plans for a church which Wallis projected and, when it was built in 1818, he painted the altar piece; he is said to have also produced the three-light window which still survives in the bishop's vestry of Newcastle Cathedral. He received a conditional pardon on Wallis's recommendation. In 1819-20 he travelled and drew extensively throughout New South Wales and Van Diemen's Land, and also executed many private commissions. In February 1820 Governor Macquarie sent to Lord Bathurst three of his drawings, including a large view of Sydney. It is generally believed that the absolute pardon which the artist received on 28 November 1821 was a reward for these.

Lycett, whose 'habits of intoxication' were 'fixed and incurable', according to Commissioner Bigge [q.v.], had possibly married in the colony, for in June 1822 he advertised that he intended to leave accompanied by his two daughters. They sailed together in the Shipley in September.

Lycett had already planned to publish in England a book of Australian views. There were to be twelve sets, published monthly, each with two aquatint views of New South Wales and two of Van Diemen's Land, with descriptive letterpress, and a supplement with maps of both colonies. By permission the series was dedicated to Bathurst. The parts began to appear in July 1824 at 7s. plain and 10s.6d. coloured, and when all had appeared they were bound together and sold as Views in Australia (London, 1825). Lycett announced that he intended to publish a natural history series along similar lines, but the project fell through.

Nothing is known of the rest of his life. A pencilled note in a copy of his *Views* in the Mitchell Library, Sydney, states that, when he was living near Bath, he forged some notes on the Stourbridge Bank. On being arrested he cut his throat, and when recovering in hospital he tore open the wound and killed himself. However, this is not confirmed.

Lycett was obviously a quick and prolific artist, and a large body of his work survives. There are many authenticated drawings in the Mitchell and Dixson Libraries (Sydney), the National Library and Nan Kivell Collection (Canberra), the Tasmanian Museum (Hobart) and in various private collections. Most are landscapes, but the Nan Kivell Collection has a series of thirteen watercolours of Australian flowering shrubs and three of trees, executed with great skill. One is dated 1820 and it is possible that all were drawn for Macquarie. Some of the surviving landscapes, notably a series formerly owned by the earls of Derby, are very freely and ably drawn in water-colour or wash, but many appear to have been working drawings from which he made his aquatints. At his best Lycett managed to capture something of the character of the Australian landscape, but his *Views*, although elegant and charming, retain none of this. They were obviously engraved to conform to what Lycett regarded as contemporary taste, and they look more like English parkland than antipodean bush scenes.

Bernard Smith, *Place, taste and tradition* (Syd, 1945); Bernard Smith, *European vision and the south Pacific 1768-1850* (Oxford, 1960); Rex and Thea Rienits, *Early artists of Australia* (Syd, 1963); C. Craig, *Old Tasmanian prints* (Launceston, 1964); W. Dixson, 'Notes on Australian artists', *JRAHS*, 5 (1919), p 242.   REX RIENITS

LYNCH, JOHN (fl. 1841-1848), stonemason and political agitator, was an Irishman, and probably came to Australia as a convict in the 1820s. For a time he was in business as a builder in partnership with Robert Hollingdale and Bernard Daley, a ticket-of-leave holder. This venture, which involved the partners in a complicated dispute with the emancipist distiller, Robert Cooper [q.v.], and his son, ended in insolvency and a short imprisonment for Lynch for contempt of court, early in 1844.

Lynch first attracted attention as a radical and hard-hitting speaker at the end of 1841, when the Sydney workmen were op-

posing a public loan for assisted migration. In the next three years of depression he spoke often at meetings organized by the operatives and their sympathizers, and occasionally at other public meetings. He advocated a broad franchise for the elective Legislative Council, supported the radicals' demand for municipal institutions, opposed the use of convict labour on public works and strongly criticized proposals for importing coolies. With other Roman Catholic radicals, such as W. A. Duncan [q.v.] and E. J. Hawksley, he played a part in Catholic lay affairs, and was a member of the Australian branch of the Loyal National Association. He was probably a member of the Mutual Protection Association formed in 1843, but seems to have played little public part in its proceedings, and after its disintegration his career as an agitator came almost to an end. He appeared again briefly at the end of 1848, when he delivered the stinging attack on Robert Lowe [q.v.] which marked the end of the alliance that Lowe had established with radical and working-class elements for the Sydney election in that year.

Lynch was an important figure in the operatives' political movement of the 1840s for two reasons. First, he was one of the few manual workers capable of speaking for the workmen; most of his fellow-orators who made public reputations were journalists such as James McEachern and Duncan or employers operating on a large scale, such as H. Macdermott [q.v.]. Second, he was perhaps the most class-conscious of all the radical spokesmen of the period. Appeals to his 'fellow operatives', references to them as 'the body that supported the whole of those called the upper classes', and the drawing of a distinction between those who 'lifted their hands to earn their bread' and the rest of the community, made up an important part of his speeches. The *Sydney Morning Herald* exaggerated when it described him as a 'leveller of the first water', but it was correct in perceiving that economic dividing lines and issues were never far from the surface of his thinking.

A. P. Martin, *Life and letters of the Right Honourable Robert Lowe, Viscount Sherbrooke*, 1-2 (Lond, 1893); L. M. Thomas, *The development of the labour movement in the Sydney district of New South Wales from 1788-1848* (Canberra, 1962).   L. J. HUME

LYONS, SAMUEL (1791-1851), businessman, was a tailor when convicted for theft in London on 16 February 1814. With a life sentence, he reached Sydney in the transport *Marquis of Wellington* in January 1815. He did not take kindly to convict discipline and in April absconded by ship and reached Prince of Wales Island, where he was detected and handed to Lieutenant Jeffreys [q.v.] who was returning in the *Kangaroo* from Colombo with other escaped prisoners. Back in Sydney in February 1816 he received corporal punishment and was again assigned as a servant. In August 1816 he was taken to Hobart Town in the *Kangaroo* and when she returned to Hobart in April 1817, he tried unsuccessfully to escape again with the help of Jeffreys. On 24 July 1819, for robbing government stores at Hobart, he was sentenced to receive 200 lashes and 4 years at Newcastle.

On 20 May 1822 Lyons married Mary Murphy according to the rites of the Roman Catholic Church. Next year he returned to Sydney and began life anew. He opened a small store in Pitt Street and in March 1825 he received a conditional pardon. In October 1831 he was recommended by Governor Darling as a 'man in good circumstances, industrious and respectable in business dealings'; he received an absolute pardon on 15 May 1832.

In 1825 Lyons set up as an auctioneer and vendue master at 75 George Street, where he lived with his wife and children. Within three years he had 'a tolerably fair share of the Public patronage' and was described as a man of integrity deserving what he acquired 'by his extraordinary application to trade'. In 1834 his sales of private land alone yielded £61,872, and he sent his three children to be educated in England. He also moved into new auction rooms and a new residence, built by the architect, John Verge [q.v.], at the corner of Charlotte Place and George Street. In 1835 he received a land grant in Fort Street and acquired properties in Bridge Street, Sydney, as well as at Bathurst and Newcastle. In 1836 he bought Apsley Lodge near Hyde Park, sold his George Street furniture, announced his retirement as an auctioneer and left for England. When he returned in March 1839 his resumption of business in Lower George Street caused much trouble with other auctioneers, but in January 1840 he had settled his differences with the Australian Auction Co. and regained possession of his property at Charlotte Place. There he recommenced auctioneering on a large scale, and his establishment was said to be second only to the Waterloo Warehouse of Cooper & Levey [qq.v.]. He cleared over £5464 a day.

Lyons had many other business interests. In 1842 he built Lyons Terrace, a sub-

stantial row of elegant houses, each costing £5000, in Liverpool Street opposite Hyde Park, and acquired many other properties, including a farm at Fivedock, where Lyons Road is named after him. In 1826 he helped to establish the Sydney Banking Co. and later acquired shares in the Bank of Australia and in the Bank of New South Wales. In 1827 he was joined by his brother, Saul, who arrived as a free immigrant, and some time later by another brother, Abraham. Samuel Lyons was also a substantial moneylender, which got him into temporary difficulties in the 1841-42 depression. His business brought him into touch with people of every class, and he won repute for being punctual, respectable and singularly clever.

Lyons was active in various public affairs. He served on the committee of the Sydney College, raised £1400 for it and in 1840 gave it £100 for a classical and mathematics library. He helped to found the Australian Patriotic Association, and joined the provisional committee for raising funds. He shared in petitions for trial by jury and taxation by representation, for the rejection of payment for public services not performed in the colony, for the wiser use of revenue from sales of waste land, and for the local government of Sydney. His conservative views and great wealth aroused antagonism, and in 1843 when W. C. Wentworth and Dr. W. Bland [qq.v.] won seats in the Legislative Council, he was credited with controlling their electoral machine and with using undue political influence. One editor claimed that Lyons wanted to limit the franchise to voters with at least £100 in property. In 1836 the *Sydney Herald* attacked the auctioneering system as corrupt, referring to Lyons as Mr 'L', the author of many enormities. Lyons took the *Herald* to court and was awarded £200 for libel. He denied allegiance to any political faction and, although other editors rallied to his defence, a riotous mob in November 1842 singled out his George Street residence for an attack. Clearly he had more political influence than he cared to admit.

In the 1828 census Lyons had declared himself a Protestant but after his wife died on 19 April 1832 he rejoined the Jewish community and became a prominent member of the York Street Synagogue and of many Jewish committees. His sons George and Samuel and his daughter Hannah were, however, brought up in the Christian faith. He never remarried.

Lyons died in Sydney on 3 August 1851, aged 60. He was buried in the Jewish portion of the Devonshire Street cemetery. In 1901 his tombstone was transferred to

Botany cemetery. His large property was left to his daughter and two sons. His elder son George Herbert (b. 1823) was a barrister in England. The younger son Samuel (b. 9 June 1826) took over his father's enterprises, and on 24 March 1853 at St James's, Sydney, married Charlotte Margaret Fuller; they had three sons and a daughter. He was twice returned to the New South Wales parliament: for Canterbury in 1859 and Central Cumberland in 1868, and was associated with Henry Parkes. Samuel became an 'official assignee' in the late 1870s, and died at Leura on 25 August 1910. His father's sister, Lydia, was the wife of Sampson Samuel, who died in London on 2 November 1820, a month before the birth of his son Saul. Lydia migrated in 1832 to Sydney, where Saul was later knighted.

HRA (3), 2; *Report of the committee of the Sydney Synagogue 1845-5605* (Syd, 1845); *Sydney Gazette,* 29 Dec 1825, 14 July 1828, 15 Mar 1834, 27 Jan 1835; *Sydney Herald,* 15 June, 21 Aug 1837, 5 Aug 1851; *Sydney Times,* 1 Oct 1836; *Australian,* 3 Feb, 21 Mar 1840, 1 Nov 1841, 28 June, 7 Nov 1842; W. A. Duncan, Autobiography, 1811-54 (ML); Record Book (Court House, Hob).

PAUL EDWIN LE ROY

LYTTLETON, WILLIAM THOMAS (1786?-1839), soldier and settler, was a distant connexion of the well-known Lyttelton family of Hagley Hall, Stourbridge, Worcestershire, England. He used the family crest on his silver, gave a family name, Westcote, to one of his sons, and the name, Hagley, to his property in Van Diemen's Land and to the near-by village. He entered the army as an ensign in the 73rd Regiment in April 1809. For five years he was wrongly listed as W. H. Lyttleton in the *Army Lists* and he even signed as 'W.H.' when he married. He was gazetted lieutenant in November 1810, but though known as 'Captain' Lyttleton in Tasmania, he never officially gained that rank. The regiment left Yarmouth in the *Hindostan* and *Dromedary* and arrived in Sydney in December 1809. In February 1810 a company under Major Gordon arrived at Port Dalrymple in the *Tryall,* and for a short time Lyttleton was attached to the Commissariat Department. In 1812 he was appointed Naval Officer at Port Dalrymple. On 4 January 1812 Lyttleton married Ann, daughter of Private James Hortle of the New South Wales Corps. In June 1814 the *Windham* took two companies of the 73rd Regiment from Hobart Town to Ceylon and in 1821 the regiment returned to England. Lyttleton was granted leave on grounds of ill health from February 1820 to January 1822 but in November 1824 he sold his commission and retired from the army. Claiming possession of 500 cattle in Tasmania, and a capital of more than £2000, he sailed from Leith in the *Triton* with his wife and family, and after arrival at Hobart on 4 October 1825, was granted 560 acres near Westbury and 800 acres in the Meander district. With William Archer he rented another 2560 acres at Norfolk Plains.

In November 1829 he was appointed police magistrate and deputy-chairman of Quarter Sessions at Launceston. In 1833 he convicted an assigned convict, Samuel Arnold, of cattle stealing and sentenced him to death, but after the trial suggested that 'another person' was the real culprit. This was taken to refer to Arnold's master, William Bryan [q.v.], who sent a friend to issue a challenge. Lyttelton declined and sent an account of the matter to the attorney-general. The challenger was prosecuted, and Lieut-Governor Arthur dismissed Bryan from the Commission of the Peace and recalled all his assigned servants.

Lyttelton is supposed to have built two notable late Georgian houses in Tasmania. He built probably only the western side of Hagley House, Hagley, but there is certainly evidence to connect him with Pinefield, at Longford, which the government bought for a parsonage in 1830, for Rev. R. R. Davies [q.v.], who in 1835 married Lyttelton's daughter. Lyttelton was also a talented amateur artist, two of his local paintings of 1811 and about 1830 are in the Mitchell Library, Sydney. He also drew the original picture from which was copied the well-known lithograph of Panshanger, the seat of Joseph Archer [q.v.].

In 1835 Lyttelton resigned his post at Launceston and on 14 January 1836 he sailed for England in the *Ann.* He died on 7 June 1839 in London and was buried at Kensal Green cemetery, where a tablet to his memory is in the chapel. His widow returned to Van Diemen's Land in 1843, then lived in New Zealand for some time, came back to Tasmania in 1863, died at Hobart in 1874 and was buried at St John's cemetery, Launceston, in the Davies's family vault. She had six other children, of whom the third son, Thomas Hamilton (1826-1876), was superintendent of police in Victoria. The novelist G. B. Lancaster (1874-1945) was a great-granddaughter and some of her characters are said to be modelled on Lyttelton.

HRA (3), 1; *Launceston Advertiser,* 31 Oct 1839; Correspondence file on W. T. Lyttleton (TA).

C. CRAIG

M

MACARTHUR, ARCHIBALD (d. 1847), Presbyterian minister, was sent by the Scottish Missionary Society to the University of Edinburgh, according to Rev. J. D. Lang [q.v.], but did not complete the course required for licentiates of the Church of Scotland. In December 1821, when the secessionist United Associate Presbytery of Edinburgh received a request from Scottish Presbyterians in Van Diemen's Land for a minister, Macarthur volunteered, and was ordained on 22 January 1822 as a missionary minister in Dr John Jamieson's Secession Chapel, Nicholson Street, Edinburgh.

Macarthur arrived in the *Skelton* at Hobart Town in December 1822, the first Presbyterian minister in Australia. He held his first service on 5 January 1823 in a room of the government factory. At a welcome meeting on 3 February 1823 the Presbyterian Church in Van Diemen's Land was officially formed, a committee of management appointed, and arrangements made to provide the minister's salary and to raise funds for a church. The government gave land and promised contributions equal to private donations for a church in Bathurst Street. The building, opened for services on 12 September 1824, was of plain design and soundly constructed in freestone, and in 1966 was still in use as a Sunday school. Macarthur was granted 1250 acres in the Bothwell district, which he later sold. He visited Sydney in 1825 and conducted services for Dr Lang, then in England. On 21 May 1828 he married Mary, née Geiss. They had three sons and a daughter, of whom there are records only of John, the third child. Macarthur's wife died on 2 December 1835 and was buried in the old Presbyterian cemetery on Trinity Hill, Hobart.

By 1834 a larger church was needed and sufficient funds were soon in sight to begin its erection. Meanwhile Macarthur's ordination was deemed irregular according to the practices of the Church of Scotland. In October 1835 the Presbytery of New South Wales sent Dr Lang to Van Diemen's Land to form a local Church of Scotland presbytery consisting of himself, Rev. John Mackersey [q.v.] of Macquarie and Rev. John Anderson of Launceston and, by its authority, to admit Macarthur as a *de facto* minister. Lang arrived in Hobart on 26 October to find that charges had been made against Macarthur gravely affecting his moral character, and that he admitted guilt. After conferring with Lieut-Governor Arthur and the Kirk session and after Macarthur had submitted his resignation, Lang declared the church vacant on Sunday 1 November. Some of the parishioners followed Macarthur when he tried to form a new congregation at Roxburgh House in Elizabeth Street, but on 8 June 1836 he left for England in the *Eldon* with his son John. Two weeks later the new church that his ministry had inspired was opened by Dr Lang. In 1842 Macarthur became minister of a new Congregational chapel at Barley, Herefordshire. In October 1843 at Chishall, Essex, he married Martha, daughter of Rev. James Dobson. He died at Bayswater, London, on 2 January 1847. His son John returned to Tasmania where he married Louisa Jean, a daughter of Algernon Burdett, and later Fanny Edith Jones, who was a daughter of A. F. Kemp [q.v.].

Macarthur was active in the Hobart community; he also established the Van Diemen's Land Missionary Society and was associated with the Temperance, the Infant School and the Auxiliary Bible Societies. Though he had no outstanding gifts, contemporary records show that he had determination and, despite hardships and prevalent low standards, exercised his ministry with devotion and vigour in a manner acceptable to his parishioners until the time of his moral lapse.

J. Heyer, *The Presbyterian pioneers of Van Diemen's Land* (Launceston, 1935); *Hobart Town Gazette*, 24 Dec 1822, 11 Jan 1823; *Hobart Town Courier*, 8 Jan 1836, 29 May 1847; GO 1/33/233, 33/19/614, 33/20/752.

S. M. MORTYN

MACARTHUR, ELIZABETH (1767?-1850), née Veale, was born in Devon, England. Her parents were Devon farmers apparently of some education and affluence. Elizabeth received an education which allowed her to write letters of eighteenth-century style and grace and which equipped her to manage the complicated affairs of her husband's business in later life. She married John Macarthur [q.v.] in October 1788. In June 1789 he joined the New South Wales Corps and Elizabeth accompanied him when he sailed to take up his position in the colony. Her letters to her family written during the journey to New South Wales are one of the outstanding records of early voyages on convict transports. A daughter born on the voyage did not survive, and Elizabeth landed in Sydney Cove on 28 June 1790 with her ailing eldest son Edward, born in Bath in 1789, to face the rigors of the foundation years of New South Wales.

As the first woman of education and sensitivity to reach the colony Elizabeth Macarthur had a specially privileged position in colonial life. From her arrival in the colony until her husband's departure in 1809 she held court amongst officers of the New South Wales Corps, naval officers and members of the colonial administration. The only governor who was free to enjoy her society was Phillip, for in later years her husband's political position was too controversial for any governor to seek the company of the Macarthur family. In these years four more sons, James (1793-1794), John (1794-1831), James (1798-1867) [q.v.] and William (1800-1882), were born and three daughters, Elizabeth (1792-1842), Mary (Mrs Bowman, b. 1795) and Emmeline (b. 1808). The cares of her increasing family and the anxieties of her husband's political role in no way dampened her spirits. Her letters to her family in England display an acute feminine intelligence quickly adapting to the circumstances of colonial life; through her husband and children she experienced remarkable happiness in the colony from the first years of her arrival. By 1794 the Macarthurs had their own house at Parramatta, Elizabeth Farm, 'a very excellent brick building'. The country, she wrote in 1798, held 'numerous advantages to persons holding appointments under Government . . . We enjoy here one of the finest climates in the world. The necessaries of life are abundant, and a fruitful soil affords us many luxuries. Nothing induces me to wish for a change but the difficulty of educating our children . . . Our gardens with fruit and vegetables are extensive; and produce abundantly. It is now spring, and the eye is delighted with a most beautiful variegated landscape; almonds, apricots, pear and apple trees are in full bloom; the native shrubs are also in flower, and the whole country gives a grateful perfume . . . The greater part of the country is like an English park, and the trees give to it the appearance of a wilderness, or shrubbery commonly attached to the habitations of people of fortune'.

Elizabeth Farm, though small, was one of the few in the colony in which the dignity of family life was maintained despite the extreme stresses of the colonial environment. The children received careful and painstaking education, both secular and religious, and the style of life was as near possible that of minor country gentry as they had known it in England. Within the Macarthur home order and harmony prevailed to an extent which equalled the chaos and violence of John Macarthur's public life. The rarity and the beauty of this family life within the context of the colonial situation so impressed even John's most extreme political enemies that it purchased immunity for his family. Elizabeth Macarthur, her ordered home, her carefully nurtured children always escaped any criticism which could be levelled against John, as they escaped from any possible reprisal for his part in the rebellion against Governor Bligh. The impressive achievement of feminine strength which this family life conveyed was enlivened by Mrs Macarthur's wit, high spirits and by her extremely charming personality. Her letters to Captain Piper [q.v.], a lifelong friend of the family, display this aspect of her personality, her delight in social occasions, her intelligent interest in the development of colonial society, and her humorous and uncomplaining acceptance of the deprivations of colonial life.

After her husband's enforced departure from the colony in 1809 Elizabeth's relatively carefree existence changed. Business partners administered the wide range of John's mercantile affairs during his absence, but his wife was responsible for the care of the valuable merino flocks, the Camden Park estate and the direction of its convict labourers, with the assistance only of her nephew, Hannibal Macarthur [q.v.], who was less experienced than she in colonial affairs. For eight years she managed the Camden Park establishment with conspicuous success. She visited it regularly, although this involved going to the limits of the known colonial world and placing herself in danger of the sporadic violence which occurred between settlers and Aboriginals. Without feminine company she travelled to visit the various merino flocks and to discuss the choice of rams, sales of sheep, the improvement of fleeces, and the care of all the valuable Macarthur stock with her one reliable convict overseer. After these journeys she wrote detailed reports of her inspections to her husband in England and on receiving his replies carried out to the letter his directions for the development of the flocks.

In these years, because of her remarkable ability in the management of the sheep, John Macarthur's enforced absence was converted into an advantage in the development of his plans for the colonial pastoral industry. His presence in England and Elizabeth's in the colony surmounted the otherwise almost insurmountable problem of communications in developing the colonial flocks at precisely the most delicate point in their growth. During these eight years under their joint direction the wool of the Macarthur merino flocks managed to enter competitively into the British market and to establish the reputation of the colony of New South Wales as a centre for wool-growing. A great part of the achievement was that of John, with his flair for publicity, his astute direction and his unfailing economic vision, but a significant proportion of it was Elizabeth's, since her determination and administrative ability overcame the first and most formidable practical obstacles, which were within the colony, to the export of wool. Her letters are neutral about the degree of pleasure she derived from the care of 'Mr. Macarthur's affairs'. If they were an insufferable burden of anxiety she never complained. If she enjoyed her masculine role she did not speak of it. She occasionally mentioned fatigue and apologized for her failures with stock records, but the emotional centre of her letters was always her concern for her children, the health and beauty of her daughters in the colony, and the well-being of her sons being educated under the care of their father in England.

The Macarthurs' marriage had a kind of eighteenth-century tone about it. The devotion of husband and wife for one another was of deep and moving intensity, yet Mrs Macarthur was able to endure the long years of separation from John without the stress which might have troubled a woman of less aristocratic temperament. She was an Anglican of more than formal piety and much comforted by faith. She had an energetic and educated appreciation of nature and took endless pleasure in describing the beauties of the colonial landscape, beauties which she perceived though few of her fellow colonists did, and she must have played a substantial role in making the country of their birth the centre of the affections of her sons James and William. During John's absence from the colony between 1809 and 1817 he frequently questioned the advisability of committing the family fortunes permanently to the colony, but though Elizabeth's letters to him have not survived it seems evident from his correspondence with her that she played an important role in reassuring him about his eventual return to the colony and about the success of their fortunes there.

After John's return to New South Wales in 1817 Elizabeth retired from active concern with the management of the family affairs. Her influence was, however, still very powerful. When the financial success of their grazing ventures seemed assured John Macarthur began to devote his energies to the building of a suitable family mansion on the Camden Park estate. It expressed his own vision of his family and its grandeur more than it was designed to please and delight his wife. During the mid-1820s Elizabeth spent more and more time in Sydney and Parramatta enjoying again a quiet social round now centred about the lives of her children. She was saddened by her husband's deep fits of melancholia and his obsessive and utterly unfounded fears that she had been unfaithful to him. His feelings of persecution became so violent that he could not bear to see his wife, and they lived the last few years of his life in virtual separation; though she suffered deeply from this rejection, her strength of character and extreme good sense kept the family together. She remained devoted to her husband until his death and encouraged her sons to deal with the difficult situation of caring for their father without allowing them to experience any sense of conflict in their relations with her. She died on 9 February 1850, having survived John by sixteen years, during which she lived to see the final amazing success of Australian wool exports in the mid-1830s and the fulfilment of every one of her husband's predictions concerning the economic development of the colony. Her influence on her sons cannot be overestimated. Both James and William were deeply devoted to her, and both owed their conservative and aristocratic temperaments less to their father's driving economic ambition than to their education and the influence and example of their mother.

Her portrait in the Dixson Gallery, Sydney, shows her to have been a woman of unusual beauty and taste in dress and deportment. In a small colonial society which delighted in petty gossip she was not touched by any. Scarcely another woman in the colonial world escaped criticism for some breach of taste in dress, manners or propriety. Impossible though it may seem she does not appear to have been mentioned by contemporaries except in praise. She did not use her undoubted position in the colony to mitigate any of its harshness. Though a sensitive and delicate woman, she did not leave any record of outrage at the brutality of the colonial world; perhaps she saw little of its extreme harshness since the Macarthur servants were always well housed and fed and not sternly punished by colonial standards. She chose instead to exercise her undoubted talents within the range of family and business life and was not provoked to efforts outside this sphere by the stimulus of the new and strange environment to which she became so deeply attached.

HRNSW, 2; S. Macarthur Onslow, *Early records of the Macarthurs of Camden* (Syd, 1912); M. H. Ellis, *John Macarthur* (Syd, 1955); J. Ker, 'The wool industry in New South Wales 1803-1830', *Business Archives*, 2, no 1 (Feb, 1962); J. Ker, 'The Macarthur family and the pastoral industry', *JRAHS*, 47 (1961); Macarthur papers (ML).

JILL CONWAY

MACARTHUR, HANNIBAL HAWKINS (1788-1861), pastoralist, politician and businessman, was born on 16 January 1788 at Plymouth, Devonshire, England, son of James Macarthur, who was the elder brother of John Macarthur [q.v.]. Persuaded by his uncle John to accompany him on his return to New South Wales he arrived at Sydney on 9 June 1805. In 1808 he returned to England by way of China and the Philippines, trading sandalwood unsuccessfully for his uncle. He arrived in England in 1810 and rejoined John, who had gone there in 1809 to help Lieut-Colonel George Johnston [q.v.] explain his part in the overthrow of Governor Bligh in 1808. In March 1812 John wrote to his wife Elizabeth that Hannibal was returning to the colony and would be able to help her, but added that he remained 'as blunt, honest and unsophisticated as when he left Parramatta'. This opinion had not prevented John from sending Hannibal in his *Isabella* with a cargo for disposal, which arrived in Sydney in August 1812. Hannibal's handling of this venture, shared by Keir, Buxton & Co. of London, did not come up to his uncle's exacting requirements, for in August 1813 John wrote critically and hoped that the affair would be a lesson to him. As late as July 1816 John was still complaining that he had hoped for a remittance from Hannibal but, 'God knows it would be very idle to hope for money from a man who will not answer my letters'. However, Hannibal had encountered a very severe commercial depression in the colony, which caused many merchants to fail. In the circumstances he handled the venture at least adequately and John's strictures reflected his own frustration and impatience.

As early as November 1812 Hannibal had seen the difficulties of combining trading with farming. But if he did not prove himself a lively business agent in John's opinion, he was at least useful to Elizabeth in looking after Macarthur's merino flocks during John's absence. In

1812 Hannibal had married Anna Maria, eldest daughter of the former governor, P. G. King, and next year he bought for £160 Captain Waterhouse's [q.v.] farm, The Vineyard, on the river near Parramatta, as a residence and settled down to help Elizabeth in the whole management of the flocks, including shearing, sorting, packing and shipping of the wool. He sought a land grant from Governor Macquarie but was disappointed, and when he complained to John he was told in June 1814 that his uncle could do nothing for him. However, he received some formal recognition in 1814 when he was made a magistrate, and he was given grants of land, including 1060 acres in the Cooke district, in August 1819. Next month he was promised 1000 acres 'in newly discovered country south of the cowpastures', an area opened by Charles Throsby [q.v.] in his south-western explorations in 1817-19. In 1820 Macquarie, in his tour to the south-west, noted that Hannibal had 1854 sheep and 165 cattle depastured on the Wollondilly River.

After John's return in 1817 Hannibal concentrated on his farming and business interests, which now included a store where, according to evidence given to Commissioner Bigge [q.v.], spirits were sold to unlicensed publicans. He had begun earlier to take an active part in community affairs centred on Parramatta; he joined the committee of the school for Aboriginals in 1814, and of the Female Orphan School in 1816, and in 1819 was reported to have conducted the district's first savings bank.

Although Macquarie thought him 'factious and dissatisfied', by 1821 Hannibal held a position of social prominence and financial security in the colony, reinforced by his family connexions, however the leader of the clan regarded him. He had naturally gravitated to the ranks of the exclusives, who sought a degree of political power commensurate with their own estimate of their social worth and economic power, a policy that had enlivened the penal colony virtually from its beginnings and was intimately linked with the Macarthurs, chiefly because of the exploits of John. A feature of this policy was the vilification and denigration of successive governors from Hunter to Macquarie. Sir Thomas Brisbane replaced Macquarie on 1 December 1821 and soon felt the familiar pressures, to be increased and diversified in the 1820s as legal reforms were effected and a Legislative Council established in 1824 under the provisions of 4 Geo. IV, c. 96.

In 1822 Hannibal played a leading part

in a sordid affair that reflected generally the aims of the exclusives, and particularly their resentment of Brisbane. The case involved charges of immorality against H. G. Douglass [q.v.], who was also a Parramatta magistrate, laid by James Hall [q.v.], a religiose naval surgeon. The upshot was the vindication of Douglass and the removal by Brisbane from the Commission of Peace of Hannibal, Rev. S. Marsden [q.v.], and three other magistrates concerned. Marsden then complained bitterly about Brisbane to his English patrons, causing Bathurst to initiate an inquiry into Douglass's career as a magistrate. Again Douglass was cleared. A final attempt to ruin Douglass was made by the Grand Jury, with Hannibal as foreman, by indicting him for sentencing a convict to daily flogging until he confessed where stolen goods were hidden. The Legislative Council investigated this charge and found that such sentences were not uncommon, having, indeed, been sometimes used by Hannibal and Marsden since 1815. Bathurst rebuked Hannibal for his part in the affair.

Hannibal's party activities prevented his restoration to the magistracy by Brisbane, but they did not hinder him from accumulating property and stock. He had told Bigge in 1820 that the production of fine wool should be one of the most important activities in the colony. By 1825 when he applied with his brother Charles for additional land he could tell Bathurst that he had purchased 300 sheep in 1813 and had 4600 in 1824; he claimed that the flock was 'the second in value and quality in the colony', and that he had surrounded his original grant of 1000 acres in Eden Forest, on the Wollondilly River, with 15,000 acres, to make 'the largest private establishment in New South Wales, so distant from any Township'. It transpired that Hannibal and Charles, who died in 1827, merely had permission to graze stock on the extra 15,000 acres, and in 1832 the Colonial Office declined to confirm the grant; instead Hannibal was ordered to buy the land on terms. He was interested in the export of timber as well as wool. By 1826 he had also developed banking interests, with other exclusives becoming a director of the Bank of Australia, which was able that year to help the government in relieving the difficulties of 'the Old Establishment' Bank of New South Wales.

The troubles of the Bank of New South Wales were indicative of economic depression for the colony in the late 1820s, aggravated by a severe drought in 1827 and 1828. These stringent conditions forced Hannibal and twenty-two others to seek relief from Governor Darling in May 1828 from the payment of 'Forty thousand pound which will become due on or before the month of August from ourselves and other respectable landed proprietors' for land bought during Brisbane's governorship. Darling made sympathetic concessions, thus reinforcing the instinct of 'the respectable people' to support the governor against 'the democratic rabble', among whom were W. C. Wentworth, E. S. Hall and R. Wardell [qq.v.]. This instinct found formal expression in 1829 when Hannibal and 114 other landed proprietors and merchants presented an address strongly supporting Darling, whose 'every measure', they said, had been 'grossly vituperated by licentious public writers in a manner calculated to inflame the minds of the lower orders of the community against Your Excellency's Administration'. This memorial suggested a new and accommodating phase of the exclusives' striving for political power, conditioned by the rise of articulate and influential emancipist leaders and a growing number of colonial-born and free immigrants. Colonial politics were becoming more complex, if not more sophisticated.

Hannibal himself was taking an active part in politics. In 1829 he was appointed an alternative member of the Legislative Council and in 1830 succeeded John Thomas Campbell [q.v.] on the council. There he was a principled representative of the exclusives, who prospered briefly in their paternalistic Tory phase under Darling, but wilted under Governor Bourke's Whig-Liberalism, with colonial society diversifying as the increased immigration of free settlers in the 1830s began to take effect and demands for representative government became pronounced. In 1830 Hannibal opposed strongly the inclusion of ex-convicts in juries, arguing that it would be 'destructive of that consideration for Virtue, Morality and good Faith, which cannot be too carefully inculcated or seriously impressed on the minds of the rising Generation of this mixed community'. His council activities included reporting on the observations of the Agricultural and Horticultural Society, which remained one of his chief interests, and acting on a sub-committee to examine the South Head Road bill in 1832. In 1836 with 426 others he signed the petition of the exclusives to the King and House of Commons, a response to the more democratic pressures exerted by the Australian Patriotic Association formed in 1835 by Sir John Jamison, W. Bland [qq.v.] and Wentworth. The exclusives argued that 'disorganising doctrines' were being propagated 'under the name of liberty', which 'would subvert the land-marks of Social order, and, confounding all just distinctions, sap the foundations of Society—all these are at stake'.

Meanwhile his farming, pastoral and business affairs continued to flourish. He had been appointed a member of the colonial committee set up in 1824 to control the Australian Agricultural Co. John Macarthur manipulated the three active members of this committee, his son and son-in-law, and his nephew Hannibal, who shared in the obloquy that fell on the family as the company ran into serious difficulties in 1827. Chief Justice Forbes [q.v.] reflected general opinion when he argued in a letter to Wilmot Horton that the resident committee had benefited itself 'at the expense of the employers', and had divided 'between eleven and twelve thousand pounds of the company's money' in the first year. But this was a temporary, and profitable, set-back. By 1835 Hannibal was chairman of directors of the Bank of Australia, and with his other financial interests and political activities he was one of the most prominent citizens of the colony.

The depression of the early 1840s brought a dramatic change to his fortunes as it did to many other colonists. The Bank of Australia failed and was liquidated in 1843. Hannibal lost a large part of his property and never fully recovered his financial status, though his political reputation remained. He was respected as one of the most intelligent and sincere of the conservatives who had now emerged in the increasingly democratic politics of the colony. He continued in the nominated Legislative Council until its end in 1843, when he was returned unopposed to represent Parramatta in the new part-elective council. He won recognition from Governor Gipps in 1844 as one of his enlightened supporters as the squatting crisis began. Hannibal retired from the council in 1848. In that year Captain P. P. King [q.v.], Hannibal's brother-in-law, writing from Port Stephens to his agent on 8 July, said that 'in consequence of the state of monetary affairs here', Hannibal had been 'obliged to bend to the storm and to pass through the Insolvent Court'. After this blow Hannibal retired to Ipswich, Queensland, where in 1852 he was appointed to the position of police magistrate on 1 January at £250 a year, raised to £275 on 1 July. His wife's death in September caused him such anguish that he had a physical breakdown. He applied for two months leave and on 30 October from Goomburra, the property of his son-in-law, P. Leslie [q.v.], sent in his resignation. He returned to England in 1853, where he

died at Norwood on 21 October 1861. Hannibal had six daughters and five sons, one of whom, George Fairfowl (1825-1890), was headmaster of The King's School, Parramatta, from 1869 to 1886.

HRA (1), 5-7, 9-12, 14-16, 18, 23, 24, (4), 1; M. H. Ellis, *John Macarthur* (Syd, 1955); King papers (ML); Macarthur papers (ML); MS cat under H. H. Macarthur (ML); Bigge Report, evidence, Bonwick transcripts (ML).

BEDE NAIRN

MACARTHUR, JAMES (1798-1867), landowner and politician, was born at Elizabeth Farm, Parramatta, the fourth child and fourth son of John Macarthur [q.v.]. He was educated privately at Parramatta by the Breton emigré, Huon de Kerilleau [q.v.], until March 1809, when he left for England with his father and his younger brother William. He went to a school in Hereford run by Dr Lindsay, classicist and Unitarian, until in 1813 he was apprenticed to a broker in a London counting house. From March 1815 to May 1816 he travelled with his father and William in France, Switzerland and Northern Italy. In September 1817 the three arrived in New South Wales. The elder John Macarthur had decided that his eldest son, Edward, should take up a military career in England, that the most intelligent son, John, should read law and represent the family's interests in England, while James and William administered the colonial holdings. For the next decade James devoted himself to estate administration, although he also served as unpaid magistrate in the first Court of Petty Sessions in the Camden district, and helped to establish churches, schools and other local institutions.

During James Macarthur's early manhood an important shift was occurring in the family holdings. While the original Camden Park estate was being intensively developed, further grants were successfully obtained through the Colonial Office and land was also bought at Sutton Forest, James's personal holding, and in the Taralga district, shared between James and William. The holdings proved very profitable and finally led to the Macarthurs becoming squatters on adjoining land. James's exertions as estate manager were more intense now than at any later stage and, although it was not his most important activity, he displayed great skill at it in association with William. William was unstable, liable to hysteria and fluctuations of mood, and tending towards brilliant but unsound plans. James was more a financier, a very sound book-keeper, who modified William's ideas to reality. He assisted

William in such schemes as the expansion of vine-growing, for which they had brought back cuttings and seeds from Europe in 1817, and a complicated but effective method of washing sheep before shearing to ensure that the wool would show well in the auction room. As an energetic explorer he was one of the first to go beyond Cookbundoon Range into the Taralga area. As an estate overseer he was a vigorous and hard master: while giving his convicts good food and clothing, he worked them for long hours, but had little faith in them, a feeling later reflected in his distrust of the working classes. He was vigorous also in such matters as insisting that tenants paid their rents during drought. He acquired much land but did not leave it idle: money and energy were devoted to its improvement, and in the late 1820s he worked out several technical devices such as mechanical irrigation. However, his strongest point was a knowledge of the international wool industry, gained in England before 1817 but particularly in 1828-30 in England and Germany. He knew the strength of the Saxon flocks that were the principal competitors of Australian wool, he understood the financial basis of wool-selling, and he imported overseas sheep which he crossbred to improve the quality. Under him Macarthur wool usually brought the best prices in the colony. A broad vision and rigorous standards were the striking features of his estate management.

Macarthur's major importance was the political role he played in New South Wales with varying intensity until his death. The significance of his influence is often underestimated because he preferred to work behind the scenes, seldom appealing to the public but depending on personal contacts and negotiation. Thus he presents an interesting contrast with W. C. Wentworth [q.v.], his famous contemporary, because the two differed greatly as individuals and used different methods, although in the 1840s and 1850s both often worked to the same end. Macarthur's influence depended on his powerful economic position in a colony relying heavily on the capitalistic expansion of pastoral activity, on his great personal ability and shrewdness, on his widespread British and colonial contacts, and on his consistent and frequently anguished concern for the welfare of New South Wales.

His political theories were expressed throughout his life in letters and occasional public statements. Those theories usually coincided with his economic interests, yet they were also connected with idealistic and rational motives. The core of his belief was social stability: change ought to be sanely and coolly considered. His views derived from certain features of eighteenth-century English aristocratic Whiggism and the classical virtues of discipline and order. His fear of social violence and upheaval may have been imparted by Huon de Kerilleau, a refugee from the French revolution, while the religious tolerance of the Enlightenment had influenced him strongly, especially through his old headmaster, Lindsay. He believed that in New South Wales political privilege should be given to those who by their wealth and respectability had a moral ascendancy over the lower classes. He believed that economic and social chaos would prevail if a hierarchy of respect were not preserved; on the purely economic level the colony's advancement was seriously hindered by the absence of an 'honest, industrious and orderly labouring class', for the colonial labour shortage allowed workmen to grow lazy and contemptuous of their betters. New settlers should be 'persons of respectability'. To him this key phrase implied important things: respect for society, for the effort that built it, for the tenuous bonds holding it together which 'wild democracy' could imperil. Constitutional safeguards should be maintained to prevent rash or sudden change, for liberty could only exist in a framework of order. These beliefs were held with great consistency all through his life. But the methods and tactics by which he tried to bring such beliefs to fruition were often deliberately veiled, and they altered greatly as the structure of colonial society and imperial policies changed dynamically from the 1820s to the 1860s. His conservative beliefs accorded with a conservative character: rational, steady, sane and often calculating. He became gloomy and disillusioned as he saw his ideal being undermined by an aggressive lower middle class.

Macarthur was appointed to his first important public office in 1824: senior member of the local committee of the Australian Agricultural Co. It occupied his attention for several years. The company failed in 1827 and Macarthur with others of his family attempted to keep this a secret. He went to London to explain matters to the directors, and in spite of much criticism he managed to escape any smear on his character. In London he gave evidence to the select committee on colonial expenditure; he broadened his knowledge of the world wool industry by travel in Europe; he continued or established family interests there, a process his father had begun and which his brother John, who had lived in England since 1802, had continued; on

15 December 1828 James visited 'the celebrated Gôthe', some of whose works he had read in Sydney. In April 1831 he returned to New South Wales. After his father's insanity in 1832 and death in 1834 he became the acknowledged head of the exclusive party and in 1836 he was entrusted with the presentation in England of the exclusive petition on transportation and immigration drawn up by a 'Committee of Merchants, Landowners and Free Inhabitants of New South Wales'. From this time he had great influence in public life.

In England Macarthur was very active. He supervised the publication of *New South Wales; Its Present State and Future Prospects*, which was ghosted for a fee of £80 by the author and librarian, Edward Edwards (1812-1886). Macarthur's extensive evidence in 1837-38 to the select committee on transportation was heard with great respect by Molesworth, Howick and Sir George Grey. He argued that convict transportation had been a demoralizing influence and had created in England a very unfavourable feeling towards New South Wales. However, the colony was now advancing and the time had come for a change: transportation and the use of assigned convict labour could now be decreased if Asian immigration were permitted and colonial land revenue were applied to free immigration. This direct method of attempting to influence colonial policy in London was continued in association with Charles Buller, the representative of the Australian Patriotic Association. They struck up a mutual liking; Macarthur was aware that representative government must come, but he managed to obtain Buller's agreement to far less radical changes than Buller's supporters in New South Wales wanted.

The most spectacular feat of his visit to England was his unromantic but most useful marriage to Emily Stone, daughter of a Lombard Street banker. Through her he became related to the Normans and the Barings. He was thus able to return to Australia with assurances of a greatly increased overdraft, and in the 1840s to lend money profitably at high interest, to complete his programme on the Camden estates, and to save the Macarthur interests from the depression which left his cousin Hannibal Macarthur [q.v.] and many others bankrupt. Political contacts were also made; the old Macarthur interests had been Tory, but now the family had access to a circle of rich, middle-class Liberals and aristocratic Whigs: the Bonham-Carters, the Cavendish-Bentincks, the Croziers, the Rices and Labouchere, a future secretary of state.

Unfortunately for Macarthur these interests were not to be as politically useful as he thought. In the 1820s, by personal contacts with the old Colonial Office, the Macarthurs had done very well in land grants and in opposition to the emancipists. But the politicians Macarthur knew had less influence with the new Colonial Office, for it was run by men of great independence: Merivale, Hawes, Elliot and especially James Stephen. Also it had increased in size and was more bureaucratic than in the days of personal patronage. In the next two decades the British government was to show increasingly less desire and ability to interfere in colonial affairs. The essential struggles affecting the colony were now fought in the colony, and there, as in England, Macarthur had many close contacts with the leading exclusive families, notably the McLeays, Kings and Bowmans [qq.v.]. These ties helped to give the conservatives great unity in the 1840s and 1850s.

Macarthur's policies for the rest of his life can only be understood on the basis of the radical change that developed in the family's landholding policy. Ever since John Macarthur had arrived in New South Wales the family's wealth had increased; by the period of James Macarthur's greatest activity, it was very considerable. By the early 1840s Camden Park was worth £200,000; James and William had 18,000 freehold acres at Taralga and other interests in the Nineteen Counties; they directed companies and they owned sixty valuable freehold acres in Sydney. Originally the Macarthur intention was to be a landowning family with consolidated and improved *freehold* estates after the aristocratic European model. Thus in the 1820s John Macarthur junior had battled in England for land grants near Camden, while at the same time James eagerly occupied and developed his own and the family's grants and purchases. After the Ripon regulations James and his brother continued to seek freehold estates by buying thousands of acres each year at the minimum upset price.

In London James spoke contemptuously of squatters to the Molesworth committee, but on his return in 1838 he found that William had begun a radical new policy of grazing on leased land, although the leases were still in the 'settled' Nineteen Counties. In 1839 James himself leased 9100 acres near existing Macarthur holdings, and in 1840 the two brothers had licences to squat beyond the boundaries of settlement. As James Macarthur became sympathetic to the squatter point of view, other factors were forcing him into uneasy alliance with Wentworth, who had posed as a tribune of the people to gain political aggrandizement but in the late 1830s was also becoming sympathetic to squatting. The coming together of these two men was the epitome of a larger process: men of similar capitalistic interests settled personal differences, and the long-standing emancipist-exclusive struggle changed into an alliance against, on the one hand, imperial policies on land, transportation, coolie labour and responsible government, and on the other, popular demands for more representative government. The Macarthurs and McLeays joined the Lords, Wentworth, Bland, Sir John Jamison [qq.v.] and men of that kind in a conservative alliance.

The process was gradual. It was assisted by the increase of free immigration and the pastoral boom in the late 1830s, by the cessation of transportation in 1840, by the removal of emancipist disabilities for service on juries, by the grave depression and by the 1842 Act granting the colony a measure of representative government. Macarthur ran for Cumberland in the stormy 1843 elections to the Legislative Council but was beaten by Charles Cowper. He then refused to enter the council as a nominee and did not return to official public life until 1848, but continued to intrigue and agitate in the conservative and squatting cause. In 1848 he was elected to the Legislative Council for Camden and retained his seat until the old Legislative Council was dissolved in 1856. The important part of his political life in these years was his growing alliance with Wentworth and the evolution of strong beliefs in a Constitution granting responsible government.

In 1842 Macarthur announced that he no longer opposed the constitutional aspirations of those emancipists whose industry had won them wealth and respectability. He and Wentworth gradually moved together because of common interests, but each generally disliked the other and the *rapprochement* was occasionally interrupted. For example, in the 1843 elections Macarthur did not run for the safe Camden seat; he left that to a conservative Roman Catholic, Roger Therry [q.v.], and contested Cumberland, evidently so as to increase the number of conservatives in the council. Therry was aided by the votes of Macarthur's servants and narrowly beat Cowper, of the popular party. Cowper then beat Macarthur, partly because Wentworth, seemingly to work off old personal grudges and resentments at Macarthur's greater social status, persuaded William Lawson [q.v.], who had been favouring Macarthur, to give his support to Cowper. The incident is most illuminating; it shows Macarthur's tolerance of Catholics, his

devious methods and his ambition, his arrogance in risking defeat and his use of his servants to swing the voting. A similar incident in 1849 showed petty spite freely flowing: connexions of Macarthur's successfully stopped Wentworth from obtaining the council Speakership for his friend Stuart Donaldson.

In spite of confused and personal politics Wentworth and Macarthur were brought together by the public events of the period. In the depression land sales were negligible, migration could not be financed, and an acute labour shortage developed. Wentworth and Macarthur both demanded a solution to this labour problem and both were condemned for inconsistency in supporting Earl Grey's proposal to send equal numbers of free immigrants and ticket-of-leave 'exiles' to the colony. In 1850 Macarthur vehemently denied any inconsistency, maintaining rightly that in 1838 he had not advocated the entire cessation of convict transportation, and defending Grey's proposal partly on humanitarian grounds and partly because any ascendancy of a convict population was no longer a danger.

In his years out of office Macarthur had consistently opposed the popular demand for representative government based on a wide suffrage. He had been thinking for years of an ideal conservative Constitution, but by the end of the 1840s had seen that the popular tumult could not be ignored; responsible government was inevitable. Accordingly he tried, together with Wentworth and other squatter leaders, to draft a Constitution which would be quickly effected by the British parliament before the popular party could object too much.

In the confused years after 1848 proposal after proposal was considered and the whole colony was in ferment. In 1852 the Legislative Councils of each colony were invited to draft new Constitutions and submit them to London for approval. Wentworth has received most credit for the draft sent from New South Wales, but Macarthur also played an important part. Both wanted conservative political institutions which could exist within the colony as permanent safeguards, unalterable either by the whim of any new administration at the Colonial Office or by popular local agitation. Macarthur shared in the proposal that made Wentworth notorious: a hereditary colonial aristocracy to sit in an upper House. Macarthur had been toying with this idea since the late 1830s, and Wentworth's letters from London in 1854 make frequent references to 'our bill'. The draft Constitution did not provide for the much ridiculed colonial aristocracy, but instead for a

Legislative Council of members nominated for life, an elective Legislative Assembly with a suffrage based on property qualifications, and a requirement of a two-thirds majority to change the Constitution. But it was still conservative, reflecting Macarthur's ideas of checks and balances. He showed his love of secrecy in 1850 when he publicly stated in the colony that he did not favour an upper House, yet wrote a memorial to Grey upholding the idea of a non-representative upper House. This memorial was sent without Wentworth's knowledge, and it suggests that Macarthur should receive more of the responsibility for the conservative Constitution.

The gold rushes had accentuated the trend to increase the power of the popular party. Macarthur was becoming increasingly disillusioned: in 1854 he felt like selling all his assets except Camden Park and going to England. He displayed some interest in education, supporting the foundation of the University of Sydney and becoming a member of its first senate. He continued his political activities, albeit with gloom. In 1856 he was elected to the new Legislative Assembly for Camden. To enable Donaldson to form a cabinet, Macarthur agreed to serve briefly as colonial treasurer, for certain conflicts could not otherwise be resolved. When Donaldson had the support he needed, Macarthur resigned his seat and the portfolio and was re-elected for West Camden. In 1859 his unhappiness reached its peak: he retired and refused Governor Denison's offer of a knighthood. In 1860 he returned to England, his whole life seeming wasted. In the 1820s he had opposed representative government. In the late 1830s he adopted delaying and compromising tactics so as to make the constitutional change of 1842 as moderate as possible. In the early 1840s his economic affairs were suddenly changed when he began squatting, and he found that imperial control of immigration and land policy conflicted with his new interests; he began to work with desperate hopefulness for a conservative Constitution, partly to obtain independence from Britain, partly to forestall the liberals. But his constitutional checks and balances had been reduced and the nightmare of his whole life, popular anarchy, appeared imminent.

In England on his fourth visit he represented New South Wales at an International Statistical Congress in 1860 and was a commissioner for New South Wales at the London Exhibition of 1862. Eventually he was attracted back to New South Wales partly by reports that extreme liberal opinions were in decline and that the Cowper-Robertson land legislation which appeared to endanger squatters' rights had led to far fewer selections of squatters' land than expected. However, the chief reason for his return in 1864 was that his daughter wanted to go back; he had also lost some of his revulsion for the revised Constitution. In June 1866 he accepted nomination to the Legislative Council and next March became president of the New South Wales Agricultural Society. He died, still a member of the Legislative Council, on 21 April 1867.

His career had been unsuccessful judged by the standards he set himself: his remarkable political talents had left nothing lasting behind them and his major policies had failed. Yet in the colony's sudden spurt towards political maturity his tenaciously held views and his leadership of the conservative squatters provided a reminder of the need for social stability and somewhat extreme methods in developing a primitive country. As an agriculturist and pastoralist he set an exacting standard in obtaining the best results from the land. His conservatism helped to temper the ideas of emancipists and liberals so that their views became more acceptable to the British government. Although his influence has been much underrated it contained a real truth, rarely noted and unpalatable: that society, especially in a rapidly changing colony, is a fragile thing and that few men are really properly equipped to hold political power. He was such a man; he often used his power for his own ends but he was also conscious that these ends coincided with the best interests of the colony.

HRA (1), 10-16, 18, 20-25; A. C. V. Melbourne, *Early constitutional development in Australia* (Oxford, 1934); M. H. Ellis, *John Macarthur* (Syd, 1955); MS cat under J. Macarthur (ML); V. R. de V. Voss, Notes (Hist Dept, Univ Syd).   J. D. HEYDON

MACARTHUR, JOHN (1767-1834), soldier, entrepreneur and pastoralist, was baptized on 3 September 1767 at Stoke Damerel, near Plymouth, England, the second son of fourteen children born to two expatriate Scots, Alexander Macarthur (formerly of Argyllshire) and his wife Katharine (d. 1777), who lived in the parish of St Andrew in Devonport. Alexander Macarthur was a mercer and draper in Plymouth, whose business was inherited by his eldest son, James. It was this background that later gave John Macarthur's enemies in New South Wales the excuse to lampoon him as 'Jack Boddice', a staymaker's apprentice. However, by 1782 enough influence had been secured to obtain an ensign's commission in Fish's Corps for the 15-year-old John. This corps, specially intended for the American war, was still being assembled in England when the war ended. When it was disbanded in 1783 Macarthur, on half-pay, retired to a farm at Holsworthy in Devon. There he remained in rural seclusion for almost five years, endeavouring fruitlessly to obtain military placement and in his discouragement toying with the idea of turning to law, for which he displayed an amateur but vigorous talent all his life. He returned to full pay in April 1788 as an ensign in the 68th Regiment (later Durham Light Infantry) stationed at Gibraltar since 1785. By 5 June 1789 he had dramatically enhanced his rank and opportunity by transferring as a lieutenant to the New South Wales Corps, then being enlisted for duty at Botany Bay.

At Bridgerule in October 1788 Macarthur had married Elizabeth [q.v.], née Veale, whose family of sturdy Cornish stock regarded her obviously ambitious but withdrawn suitor as 'too proud and haughty for our humble fortune'. When the New South Wales Corps sailed with the Second Fleet Macarthur was accompanied in the *Neptune* by Elizabeth and their first child Edward. After a quarrel that ended in a duel with the first master of the ship and another disagreement with his successor, Macarthur transferred his family to the *Scarborough* before the fleet reached the Cape of Good Hope. There he contracted a critical illness which, though he made an unexpected recovery, was to leave recurring symptoms throughout his life.

The family arrived in Port Jackson on 28 June 1790, nourishing hopes of quick promotion and a subsequent return to England. Next year Macarthur was posted inland to the Rose Hill settlement for four months. Incorrigibly haughty, he early trod a path strewn with minor hostilities which led to his withdrawal from all social intercourse at Government House after a reprimand from Governor Phillip. In 1792, under the benevolent aegis of his newly-arrived commanding officer, Major Francis Grose [q.v.], Macarthur returned to Parramatta as regimental paymaster with an added salary more than double his lieutenant's pay. This appointment, when combined in 1793 with the unpaid appointment by Grose, now acting-governor, as inspector of public works, gave him extensive and crucial control of the colony's rudimentary resources. Orders for the corps's regimental slops were by this time being placed with his brother James in Plymouth, while in combination with his brother officers Macarthur had already begun tentative commercial speculation within the colony.

Grants of land and gifts of stock from Grose helped to establish Elizabeth Farm which Macarthur began at Parramatta in 1793 on a 100-acre grant of 'some of the best ground that has been discovered'. With unrestricted access to convict labour Macarthur became the first in the colony to clear and cultivate fifty acres of virgin land, and this earned him another 100-acre grant. From this commanding position he soon became one of the foremost landholders in the colony, selling produce to the government, which even by 1794 returned several hundred pounds. Grose also lent his influence to compose serious differences between Macarthur and Captain Nepean [q.v.], to divert the menace of a court martial, and to intercede for a captaincy to which Macarthur was promoted on 6 May 1795.

By contrast with the accommodating acquiescence of Grose and his successor, Captain William Paterson [q.v.], tension grew between Macarthur and the new naval governor, Hunter, particularly when Hunter tried to modify the structure of military autocracy with which Macarthur chose to identify himself prominently. Consequently in February 1796 Hunter accepted Macarthur's resignation as inspector of public works 'without reluctance'. Further administrative disturbances, as well as bitter feuds with Richard Atkins and William Balmain [qq.v.], convinced Hunter of Macarthur's 'restless, ambitious and litigious disposition'. His official strictures on Macarthur ('scarcely anything short of the full power of the Governor wou'd be consider'd by this person as sufficient for conducting the dutys of his office') intensified when Macarthur, over his head, sent serious criticisms of Hunter's administration directly to the secretary of state and the military commander-in-chief. Despite the success of this campaign against Hunter, who was precipitately recalled, Macarthur at this time was strongly inclined to return to England himself. He proposed to the next governor, King, that he negotiate purchase by the government of Macarthur's entire colonial property which he valued at £4000, but before this matter could be decided Macarthur had committed himself to an extensive and subtle campaign intended to dismay and discredit King. The situation became unexpectedly critical for Macarthur when he failed to manipulate his commanding officer, Paterson, in an involved attempt to alienate his allegiance from the governor. Macarthur, challenged by Paterson, wounded his superior in an irregularly conducted duel on 14 September 1801. Macarthur, now openly flouting the governor, was put under immediate arrest by King, who was goaded to the point of regretting that official responsibility prevented him seeking personal satisfaction from 'this perturbator'. King, in the conviction that Macarthur's trial in the colony would merely yield a victory to Macarthur's interest, took the unusual step of dispatching him to England for court martial, accompanied by the observation that 'Experience has convinced every man in this colony that there are no resources which art, cunning, impudence and a pair of basilisk eyes can afford that he does not put in practice to obtain any point he undertakes'.

Macarthur sailed from Sydney in the *Hunter* in November 1801 accompanied by two of his children on a voyage which proved so devious that they did not reach England until December 1802. At Amboina Macarthur befriended the young British Resident, son of Sir Walter Farquhar, physician in ordinary to the prince of Wales. As a result of this propitious circumstance the father's considerable influence was to be exerted for many years in serious promotion of Macarthur's interests. In London the army's advocate-general reported that it was impossible to investigate Macarthur's case in England and recommended that he be remanded to New South Wales to join his regiment. Though official censure was scattered liberally over Macarthur as well as the administration at Botany Bay, it was made clear to King that the matter should be carried no further.

Before Macarthur left New South Wales some attention had already been directed to the colonial fleeces sent to Sir Joseph Banks [q.v.] by Governor King. These first examples of colonial potential had returned promising appraisal, and Macarthur carried with him to England some specimens of fleeces from his own flocks. It was incredibly propitious that Macarthur should return to England at the very time when war requirements, technical developments and the continental blockade were threatening a crisis in the British wool market. In July 1803 Macarthur was approached by two clothiers who, as deputies appointed to superintend the passing of a parliamentary bill relating to their trade, had seen samples of his wool which they declared to be 'of a very superior quality, equal to the best which comes from Spain'. From this meeting resulted the vision of the coincidence of

interest of the British woollen market and the wool producers of New South Wales, stimulated in Macarthur's imagination by the inflated wool prices of the Napoleonic war period. Within a week Macarthur had composed for government a *Statement of the Improvement and Progress of the Breed of Fine Woolled Sheep in New South Wales* (London 1803) which was supported by a memorial from the clothing interest to the Privy Council Committee for Trade and Plantations on the same subject. Investing himself with a sudden monopoly of authority and interest in this industry, Macarthur energetically canvassed support for an optimistic scheme of colonial wool production, to be developed under his personal supervision, which he maintained could free the British market from dependence on Spain. Though Banks was cautious and became increasingly sceptical, Macarthur's influence was sufficient to secure permission through Lord Camden for his resignation from the army and for his return to New South Wales to develop its wool industry. Official approval for his scheme was emphasized in a unique grant of 5000 acres of the best pasture land in the colony, to be increased by a further 5000 if tangible results were forthcoming, and by Macarthur's possession of rare Spanish sheep from the Royal flocks.

When Macarthur returned to Sydney on 8 June 1805 in the felicitously named whaling ship *Argo*, he faced unusual opportunity. With his now formidable patronage it had been simple to arrange part-ownership of the ship and commence as merchant. Governor King, with the best grace he could muster, described and accepted his project of sheep breeding and employing ships in the whale fishery as 'laudable and beneficial, exclusive of his being able to export the Wool of his increasing Breed to England . . . and returning with Articles of use and Comfort to sell the Inhabitants. Nor ought I to doubt, from his Assurances, that every expected Benefit may be derived from his exertions'. Hannibal Hawkins Macarthur [q.v.], accompanied his uncle to assist in these exertions. Also accompanying him as a hostage to fortune was W. S. Davidson [q.v.], the nephew of Sir Walter Farquhar, who carried permission for a grant of 2000 acres, which were taken up alongside the Macarthur lands and eventually incorporated in them.

The governor, though deferring to Camden's instructions 'whether right or wrong', still demurred at granting Macarthur his 5000 acres at the coveted Cowpastures, the best land in the colony.

Nevertheless it was arranged that both Macarthur and Davidson should occupy their grants provisionally while King argued his case with the British government. Macarthur soon had the assistance of thirty-four convict labourers to work his 8500 acres, though in 1806 his highly suspect proposal to manage the herds of wild government cattle at the Cowpastures was deferred with relief by King for the consideration of his successor, Governor Bligh.

Bligh, a protégé of Banks, had been commissioned by a new ministry to set the colony in order and was unimpressed by Macarthur's influence or his requirements. His will power if not his subtlety matched Macarthur's more equally than any previous governor's and with more dramatic results. Despite Bligh's terse rejection of Macarthur's requirements for his pastoral schemes and the undisguised personal hostility between the two, it was Macarthur's mercantile activities that provided a context for the events which ended in the rebellion that deposed Bligh. When Macarthur, resisting obligations incurred through his part-ownership of the schooner *Parramatta*, was committed for trial in January 1808 Bligh refused him the bail granted by an illegally constituted court. The commander of the New South Wales Corps, Major George Johnston [q.v.], thereupon ordered Macarthur's release, deposed Bligh and assumed the government of the colony. The specially created post of colonial secretary was bestowed on Macarthur who 'virtually administered' the colony until Lieut-Colonel Foveaux [q.v.] arrived in Sydney on 28 July and assumed command.

During this period of 'contending for the liberties of this unhappy Colony' the 'hero of the fleece' found his political energies too strong for his pastoral inclinations. Only his mercantile hopes persisted undiminished. In various partnerships, particularly with Hullett & Co. who supplied the ships, Macarthur dabbled in various Pacific enterprises including the whale and seal fisheries, and the sandalwood and pork trades. By 1808, with the aid of Davidson who later moved to Macao, the Macarthur trading interests were proposing with dubious legality to complete an ambitious Sydney, Canton, Calcutta cycle.

In 1809 Foveaux's successor as acting governor, Lieut-Colonel Paterson, authorized Macarthur to leave the colony along with other rebels intended to support Johnston in presenting his defence in England. Macarthur sailed on 29 March in the *Admiral Gambier*, after fruitlessly

offering his lands and stock for public sale. He left the ship at Rio in order to supervise the sale of a sandalwood cargo and reached Bristol on 9 October 1810. In the course of acting as agent for partnership concerns being juggled by Garnham Blaxcell [q.v.] in Sydney, Macarthur found that commercially 'the times are frightfully hazardous . . . and almost universal distrust and alarm prevails'. By November 1812 he revealed to Elizabeth that his mercantile adventures had swallowed up all the money he could command and left him considerably in debt.

In these two years accounts had been settled for the Bligh rebellion. Though Johnston had been cashiered after his court martial, which Macarthur attended, at Chelsea between April and June 1811, legal opinion was that none of the civilians involved could be tried for treason in England. Governor Macquarie received instructions from Lord Castlereagh that 'as Gov'r Bligh has represented that Mr McArthur has been the leading Promoter and Instigator of the mutinous Measures . . . you will, if Examinations be sworn against him . . . have him arrested thereupon and brought to Trial before the Criminal Court of the Settlement'. Macarthur's obvious course was to remain in England and exert every influence to have this obstacle removed. Because of the uncertainty of his position he was thrown into perplexity and doubt, toying with the idea of taking 'a small Farm of about a Hundred a Year' to help to balance his living expenses. At the same time he tried to resolve the problem of returning to New South Wales at personal risk and the alternative of withdrawing his family from 'plenty and affluence' in the colony to a life of 'pinching penury' in England. He became increasingly convinced that unless their colonial property would yield the £1600 a year necessary to support the family and educate and establish his sons he would have to return. Though he left the final decision to Elizabeth, he advised her to speak of leaving the colony as a settled thing because 'I have for some time spoken in that way here, and I am persuaded it has been beneficial'.

In this impasse his interest in wool revived as its value became more established and as other market prices in the colony had begun a sharp decline, 'it is obvious enough that the only marketable commodity will be the Wool'. References to wool and exhortations to Elizabeth and Hannibal to organize their methods at Parramatta and Camden increased, especially when Macarthur learnt to his chagrin that his wool was bringing only 20d. a lb. when his old rival, Samuel Marsden [q.v.] had received 45d. a lb. Macarthur turned his own attention to the English wool market, analysing production and processing techniques, and in 1815-16 went to the Continent· to investigate agriculture and the wine industry. Nevertheless in December 1814, depressed by accounts of colonial stagnation, he had returned to investment in trade, in the conviction that though wool was becoming yearly more valuable 'it will be but a scanty provision for us all unless we can do something in the Mercantile way'.

Though none of Macarthur's efforts in England served to clarify his position, the intention of returning to New South Wales had not been abandoned and was still the pivotal point of all his attempts 'to improve my fortune'. On the assumption that Macquarie was 'quite alive to the advancement of his own interest and Fortune', Macarthur wrote to Elizabeth in December 1814 and directed her to 'contrive to talk with Mrs Macquarie about our Sheep and take occasion to lament that the Flocks should remain Stationary. If this excite attention, you might cautiously hint at an arrangement that was on the point of being made with Governor King before he was relieved, which would have secured a splendid fortune for both our Families as he possessed the power to give me any quantity of Land and any number of Servants that might have been necessary. You might also say you have reason to believe that General Elliott, Lord Minto's Brother exerted all his interest to obtain the Gov'ship with a view to forward my plans'.

After protracted negotiations Macarthur received permission early in 1817 to return to New South Wales on condition that he should in no way associate in public affairs. With his sons William and James [q.v.] he reached Sydney in the transport *Lord Eldon* in September. Though he retired discreetly to Parramatta, he was soon out of humour with Governor Macquarie, who nonetheless had shown every consideration for his interests and many kindnesses to his household. Macquarie's refusal to grant more land in exchange for a monopolistic supply of pure-bred sheep and his rejection of the now traditional scheme for dealing with the wild cattle roused Macarthur to employ all his influence in London to destroy the governor's reputation in official circles and to precipitate his recall.

When Commissioner Bigge [q.v.] arrived in 1819 to investigate the administration of New South Wales Macarthur manoeuvred to influence his outlook. As an official witness he informed Bigge that he sold all the pure-bred merino lambs he did not require himself and had recently averaged £14 a head from a sale of forty-eight rams, but at the end of 1818 he had sent Walter Davidson a most pessimistic account of his attempt to introduce the merino which 'still creeps on almost unheeded', observing that he sold less than ten rams a year. His flocks of over 6000 at this time included some 300 pure merinos. The result of his careful cultivation of Bigge was the official promotion by the commissioner of Macarthur's vision of New South Wales as an extensive wool-exporting country controlled by men of real capital, with 'estates of at least 10,000 acres each', who would maintain transported convicts as their labour force and keep them landless and 'in proper subjection'. A colonial aristocracy would thus provide a necessary bulwark to the 'furious democrats' and their corroding influences.

Swiftly upon the official approval of the Bigge report came the sale of Camden fine wool in England for an unprecedented 124d. a lb., though one of Macarthur's sons 'could have desired that the general average had been higher'. In 1822 the Society of Arts in London presented Macarthur with two gold medals, one for importing 150,000 lbs. of fine wool from New South Wales, the other for importing fine wool equal to the best Saxon; in 1824 a larger medal was awarded for importing the largest quantity of fine wool. Amidst these tokens of success Macarthur successfully pressed his claim, confirmed in 1822, to the supplementary 5000 acres that he had been promised in 1804. They were also taken up in the Cowpastures. By the end of the decade Camden Park was 'the first agricultural establishment in the Colony', incorporating over 60,000 acres acquired by grant and purchase.

Governor Brisbane, under whose command Macarthur's son Edward had served, was impressed by Macarthur and his talents, and found his opinion reinforced by 'friends' in England. Brisbane's favour revived disturbance in New South Wales in 1822 when he made known his intention to appoint Macarthur to the magistracy. This proposal produced such opposition, culminating in an official protest from Judge-Advocate John Wylde and Judge Barron Field [qq.v.], that Brisbane had to withdraw his offer, but the reverberations of Macarthur's injured dignity and wrath reached as far as London, producing the suggestion from Bathurst that the magistracy be offered to one of Macarthur's sons should either feel anxious to undertake the duties of this office. Both declined and Field was pursued by Macarthur's vituperation till he left the colony in 1824.

In 1824 a scheme Macarthur had cherished since 1804 for a chartered company to organize the production of Australian wool was steered to completion by his favourite son John. A statute (5 Geo. IV, c. 86) secured the incorporation by charter of the Australian Agricultural Co., with a capital of £1,000,000, to be established on a 1,000,000-acre grant at Port Stephens with harbour rights at Newcastle. This inspired arrangement, richly subscribed in London, met a hostile reception in New South Wales, where it was regarded as a naked contrivance of the Macarthurs for their own aggrandizement that 'must entail inevitable destruction of the industry of every loyal subject in the Colony', but the company prospered so well· that soon Macarthur's colonial critics were waiting delightedly for him to appreciate that 'in proportion as the stock of the Company increases, just so are his stocks and herds deteriorating in value'. Four years after its establishment Macarthur suddenly and unconstitutionally asserted control in New South Wales and rumours of dislocation in the company's affairs soon resulted in its £100 shares being offered at £8.

His appointment in July 1825 as one of the three unofficial nominated members of the newly-created Legislative Council confirmed Macarthur as protagonist of the 'pure-merino' ultra-conservatives. Ironically, increasing outbursts of erratic temperament had already begun to destroy the remnants of his personal authority when, for the first time in his life, he was in a legitimate position to exercise it. His now automatic hostility towards governors was exposed early to Governor Darling and was converted into an extended dispute with the governor on the composition of the council. Macarthur's official appearances became infrequent and he ceased even to maintain communication with Darling, who perceptively doubted Macarthur's 'soundness', observing 'He is now a wayward child and remains at home brooding', and adding philosophically, 'but I expect is not altogether idle'. Macarthur's propensity for involving himself in public disturbances was unimpaired, and an application for the impeachment of Chief Justice Forbes [q.v.] followed a minor riot in which he was involved in 1828. His participation in

any public venture, such as the Agricultural Society, the Bank of Australia and the Australian and Sydney colleges, was punctuated automatically by disagreements. He was nevertheless appointed to the reformed Legislative Council in 1829 and remained until 1832 when he was removed at the request of Governor Bourke on the ground that he had been 'pronounced a lunatic', there being 'little hope of his restoration'. Macarthur died on 11 April 1834 and was buried at Camden Park, survived by Elizabeth, three of his sons and three daughters, two of his children having predeceased him.

Macarthur's serene and puritanical domestic life always offered the most striking contrast to his public life. His home was a reliable retreat, where deference, affection and encouragement flowed to his need. It was to this protective source, the check and balance of his turbulent spirit, that he owed all the strength to defend the material interests secured by his patron, Lord Camden.

Cultivated and sensitive in his aspirations, Macarthur's domineering and magnetic personality exhibited an apparently impregnable sense of personal superiority, but his arrogance concealed an anxious insecurity that contributed to the pursuit of unscrupulous ends and eventually gained control of his tormented mind. His abundant talent and eager involvement too often became distorted under the pressure of a determined but wholly undisciplined will. One of the more sympathetic of his critics believed he knew 'no medium between friendship and enmity'; humourless and a stranger to self-criticism, Macarthur had no gift for personal relationships and few resources to spare for friendship. Any contention in which he was involved released an uncontrolled vindictiveness, paraded in his boast to Governor Darling that he had 'never yet failed in ruining a man who had become obnoxious to him'. Subtlety and frustrated political acumen made Macarthur a dangerous adversary or subordinate, and as a disintegrating element in the administration and society of New South Wales he had no equal. Without access to sources of influence in England his significance would have caused Darling less puzzlement when he doubted if Macarthur was 'really entitled to that deference, which I cannot help thinking has been too generally and without due consideration conceded to him'.

A brilliant publicist and organizer, Macarthur's great service was to focus and promote English interest in colonial potential, to inspire and communicate the enticing vision of a great commercial staple. But his vision was a personal one, the necessary vehicle for a restless ambition whose dynamic energy was as likely to overset as advance it. Ultimately it was to the persistence and loyalty of his wife and sons that Macarthur owed the greater part of that reputation derived from his practical achievements with Australian wool.

HRNSW, 1-7; HRA (1), 1-17, (3), 2-3, (4), 1; S. Macarthur Onslow, *Early records of the Macarthurs of Camden* (Syd, 1914); S. J. Butlin, *Foundations of the Australian monetary system, 1788-1851*, (Melb, 1953); M. H. Ellis, *John Macarthur* (Syd, 1955) and for bibliog; H. B. Carter, *His Majesty's Spanish flock* (Syd, 1964); Newspaper indexes under J. Macarthur (ML); Macarthur papers (ML).

MARGARET STEVEN

McCARTY (McCARTHY), DENIS (d. 1820), farmer, was convicted at Wexford, Ireland, and arrived in Sydney in February 1800 in the *Friendship*. The ship carried no convict indents or records from Ireland, but most of the prisoners were captured rebels. McCarty was sent to Van Diemen's Land for disobedience in August 1803. In April 1808 he was appointed constable at New Norfolk where he built the first house. In June 1810 he was pardoned. On 30 November 1811 he presented an address of welcome to Governor Macquarie at Hobart Town on behalf of the New Norfolk residents. The governor had previously referred to the 'hearty rural and honest welcome' he had received when he and his wife had stayed for a night at McCarty's comfortable farm house.

Birch Grove Farm had grown from the five acres granted in 1808. From 1810 McCarty had been sending potatoes and other produce to Sydney and meantime had been appointed superintendent of stock. But he was not without his troubles. J. Ingle [q.v.] prosecuted him in January 1813, but as the proceedings were irregular the matter was dropped. Macquarie thought him 'too heavily engaged in private concerns' to be allowed to go back to his post as superintendent, but he did so, and at the end of the year Provost-Marshal Gore [q.v.] appointed McCarty as his deputy in Hobart as well. In 1814 he was arrested for smuggling, found guilty and sentenced to twelve months imprisonment in Sydney, but soon after he arrived there in July 1814 he threatened to prosecute Lieut-Governor Davey and other magistrates for trespass, stealing and false arrest. In February 1815 Ellis Bent [q.v.] told Macquarie that

the warrant committing McCarty was irregular and, since bushrangers had attacked his farm in his absence and stolen property worth £546 during the previous October, Macquarie used these losses as an excuse to remit the rest of the sentence. McCarty returned at once in his newly-purchased schooner *Geordy*, and when the bandits attacked the farm again in April and May he was there to resist them.

In November 1815 he sailed to explore the south-west coast, where the *Geordy* was wrecked. McCarty returned to the west coast in the *Sophia* next year, and at Macquarie Harbour found a safe channel through its treacherous entrance, explored it, discovered coal on its northern shore and brought pine from the Gordon River.

In June 1817 he was again in Sydney under arrest, this time to stand trial on a charge of assaulting M. J. Whitaker. Lieut-Governor Sorell told Macquarie that McCarty was 'one of the most turbulent and insubordinate Men in the Settlement'. McCarty admitted the assault, apologized for his 'outrageous conduct' and so persuaded .Whitaker to withdraw the prosecution.

After he returned to Van Diemen's Land in May 1818 he undertook to build a road, complete with bridges, from Hobart to New Norfolk, in return for 2000 acres of land. In June 1819 he reported that it had been completed, but when inspection showed that it was in a very bad state and Sorell refused payment, McCarty suggested that the government had made the contract really to compensate him for his losses from the bushrangers in 1814.

Early in 1820 his Birch Grove Farm was advertised for sale, possibly because he needed money but more probably because of some domestic tangle. On 25 March 1820 he was drowned, and rumours of foul play followed. The *Hobart Town Gazette* reported that 'he had been many years in the settlement, was of a speculative turn, had been the owner of three vessels, had acquired considerable landed and other property'. This was probably true, but the further claim that 'he was much respected at New Norfolk where he had chiefly resided', seems to have been exaggerated. His widow married T. A. Lascelles [q.v.] who had harassed McCarty in the past and soon dissipated the estate.

HRA (3), 1-3; L. Macquarie, *Journals of his tours in New South Wales and Van Diemen's Land, 1810-1822* (Syd, 1956); *Sydney Gazette*, 28 Aug 1803, 23 Dec 1815, Aug 1817; *Van Diemen's Land Gazette*, Apr 1814; *Hobart Town Gazette*, June 1816, Mar 1820; R. Knopwood, Diaries (Roy Soc Tas, Hob, & ML).

E. R. PRETYMAN

McCRAE, GEORGIANA HUNTLY (1804-1890), artist and diarist, was born on 15 March 1804, in London, the natural daughter of George, marquis of Huntly, afterwards fifth duke of Gordon ('Cock o' the North, ma Huntly braw'), and Jane, daughter of Ralph Graham of Rockmoor. She was educated in London at a convent school kept by noble French refugees from the Revolution and later at Claybrook House, Fulham, and the New Road Boarding School. She became an accomplished linguist; French was to her as a mother tongue and she was well grounded in Latin and Hebrew. She was a talented musician, but her strength was in pictorial art. She was taught drawing and painting by John Varley, John Glover [q.v.] and M. D. Serres, and miniature painting by Charles Hayter. She studied at the Royal Academy and in 1820-21 won medals for a miniature and a group of portraits in water-colours from the Society for Promoting Arts, Manufactures and Commerce.

After leaving school she lived for about seven years at Gordon Castle, where she was acknowledged and treated as the duke's daughter. Her romance with 'Perico' (Peter Charles Gordon of Wardhouse, a 'Spanish' Gordon and a Roman Catholic) was frustrated by the duchess, a bigoted Protestant, whose professions of goodwill to her were scarcely supported by her actions. Soon afterwards Georgiana went to live in Edinburgh, with high hopes, encouraged by her father's friends, of making a good income from portrait painting. A list in her handwriting, headed 'painted for "fame"—and money', shows that fifteen portraits were executed at Gordon Castle in 1827-29 and thirty-five at Edinburgh in 1829-30.

On 25 September 1830 at Gordon Castle Georgiana married Andrew Murison McCrae, a writer to the signet and a kinsman of the Gordons. Long afterwards she wrote in her Journal against the date of this anniversary 'left my easel and changed my name'. In 1834 they moved to London. Andrew practised at Westminster until, influenced by T. L. Mitchell [q.v.], he decided to emigrate, and sailed in the Royal Saxon. He reached Sydney in March 1839 and next year went to Port Phillip, where his brother, Dr Farquhar McCrae, with his wife and two children, his mother and two sisters, had arrived from Scotland in June 1839. Andrew began to practise law in Melbourne in partnership with James Montgomery.

Georgiana and her children were to have gone with Andrew, but she 'took ague' after the birth of her fourth child and it was deemed unwise for her to risk the sea voyage then. She did not embark with her four sons until October 1840 and in the Argyle they landed at Port Phillip on 1 March 1841. The family first lived in a wooden house in Bourke Street. In February 1842 they moved to Mayfield, on the Yarra River (near Studley Park), designed by her and described as 'one of the first superior houses erected in the Colony'. In 1843 Andrew took up the Arthur's Seat run near Dromana, and there built a house in which the family lived from 1845 to 1851. Probably because of the turmoil arising from the gold discoveries, Andrew abandoned squatting to become police magistrate at Alberton (Gippsland), then at Barrow's Inn, Hepburn, Creswick, and finally for seventeen years at Kilmore, where he was also warden for the goldfields, deputy-sheriff and commissioner of crown lands. He retired in 1866 and died in 1874. Georgiana did not accompany him in all these moves but lived with her children in Melbourne. She died in 1890. Of her eight children, the eldest, George Gordon, was a writer and the friend of writers, and the youngest son, Farquhar Peregrine, became inspector of the Bank of Australasia.

Georgiana does not seem to have painted many portraits after she came to Australia. On 8 February 1845 she wrote in her Journal: 'There is a living to be had here through my art of miniature painting, for which I have several orders in hand; but dare not oppose the family wishes that "money must not be made in that way"!' The Royal Australasian College of Surgeons in Melbourne has a fine oil painting of Dr Farquhar McCrae painted by her. At Mayfield and Arthur's Seat she did a large number of water-colours and drawings, many of which are in the possession of her descendants as well as some of her finest miniatures. She was a woman of strong character, exceptional education, wit, charm and cultivated taste, and was a significant figure in the early days of settlement in Victoria. It was said that her skill in managing the Aboriginals at Arthur's Seat was acknowledged by other runholders; she was as useful as a drover among cattle and horses, and was renowned as a 'medicine woman'. Mayfield and the homestead at Arthur's Seat were resorted to by people with literary and artistic leanings, and her visitors included Bishop Broughton, W. C. Wentworth, Benjamin Boyd [qq.v.], 'Orion' Horne, Henry Kendall, Adam Lindsay Gordon, Richard Birnie, Sir Oswald Brierly, Nicholas Chevalier, and Sir John Franklin. She was a close friend of Lieut-Governor La Trobe and his wife. According to an obituary by Alexander Sutherland, 'It was largely due to the influence of such women as Mrs McCrae that ideas of refinement and principles of taste were kept alive during the "dark ages" of our colonial history'.

In an English notebook Georgiana left recollections of her childhood and adolescence, a version of which was published by her grandson Hugh McCrae in several issues of *Southerly* in 1946-47. She kept journals during much of her life, which she rewrote in later years. One is known to have been destroyed by George Gordon McCrae under a promise which she had extracted from him. Another, covering the years 1838-48, was edited by Hugh McCrae and published in 1934 with the title *Georgiana's Journal*, and its illustrations included reproductions of her portraits and sketches.

NORMAN COWPER

McCRONE, FRANCIS NESBITT (1810?-1853), actor, was born in England. He arrived in Sydney in January 1842 and made his début at the Royal Victoria Theatre on 3 March in the title role of R. B. Sheridan's *Pizarro*. He appeared on the programmes as 'Mr Nesbitt from the Theatres Royal Edinburgh, Glasgow, Liverpool', and the critics were almost unanimous in their praise for 'his noble and commanding appearance, his full, rich and mellow voice, his graceful, appropriate and expressive action'. As Richard III and Shylock he soon established himself as favourite with the Victoria's audiences. In May he played Othello, considered his best part, and followed this with many of the leading parts from the repertoire of the tragedian in the classic tradition, e.g. *The Iron Chest* and *The Mountaineers* by G. Colman junior; *Rob Roy MacGregor* by I. Pocock; *Brutus* by J. H. Payne; *William Tell* by J. S. Knowles. Some critics warned that far too great demands were made on the strength of the 'best actor in the Southern hemisphere', especially since he was handicapped by lack of proper support from untrained local performers. But the management of the Victoria Theatre utilized Nesbitt's popular appeal to the utmost; this popularity remained unshaken by occasional disappointments when Nesbitt was too drunk to play.

For his benefit in February 1843 Nesbitt played *Ravenswood*, a dramatization of Sir Walter Scott's novel, for which he claimed authorship; there is reason to believe, however, that this play, performed only once, was written by Nesbitt's friend Edward Geoghegan, the convict author who also wrote for him the controversial tragedy

The Hibernian Father, first performed in May 1844.

In May 1843 Nesbitt left the Victoria Theatre for Joseph Simmons's [q.v.] short-lived City Theatre and a month later he sailed for Launceston where with other leading players from the Sydney and Hobart Town theatres he played for three months at the Theatre Royal Olympic under the management of F. B. Watson. In November he made his début in Hobart at Mrs Clarke's Royal Victoria Theatre; his initial success was great but fresh incidents of 'indisposition' led to his dismissal in February 1844. He returned to the Sydney Victoria Theatre, where he was warmly welcomed, yet a critic noted that 'his playing has decidedly not improved in his absence'.

In November 1844 after the first performance of *Coriolanus* Nesbitt suddenly left Sydney for Hobart. The next year saw him playing and, for brief periods, as manager at Launceston and at the Melbourne Pavilion and Queen's Theatre. In January 1846 he was back at the Sydney Victoria Theatre for a limited number of performances in his famous tragic parts; but public taste was turning away from the classical tradition towards a new realism in acting which contrasted sharply with Nesbitt's declamatory style. 'His greatest fault', wrote a critic now, 'lies in the uninterrupted employment of his powerful voice. He introduces no alteration of light and shadow . . . this soon becomes wearisome'. Of his Prospero was written that 'there is too much austere declamation—too frigid an elaborateness in the delivery . . . the impersonation was one unbroken monotony'.

With a steady influx of trained actors and with his own growing reputation for unreliability Nesbitt's days as the star of Australia's theatre were running out. He left for California in October 1849 and returned about two years later; while playing in Geelong he collapsed and died on 29 March 1853, aged 42. A tombstone in his memory was erected by 'a brother tragedian', G. V. Brooke.

F. Nesbitt, *Ravenswood: a tragic drama in three acts* (Syd, 1843); Plays submitted to the NSW Col Sec 1843-50 (NSWA).

H. L. OPPENHEIM

MACDERMOTT, HENRY (1798-1848), merchant and politician, was an Irishman. By his own account his family belonged to the Protestant gentry of County Roscommon, his father was an officer in the British army, and he himself, 'when very young', was an inspector of free schools in Ireland. He enlisted in 1820, came to Australia as a sergeant in the

39th Regiment in 1827, resigned as a sergeant-major in 1831 and settled in Sydney, where he became a wine and spirit merchant and invested in squatting, money-lending and land speculation. In 1837 he married Catherine Sarah, the eldest daughter of Lieutenant Francis Small, who later became superintendent of the Hyde Park Barracks. There were at least five sons of the marriage.

Macdermott's career as a politician began effectively in 1839, and by 1841 he had established himself as a spokesman for the political movement of the skilled workmen. In 1841 and 1842 he played an important part in the process which replaced the old conflict of emancipist versus exclusive with new divisions drawn on class and economic lines. By criticizing the proposals of W. C. Wentworth [q.v.] and his allies at public meetings called to demand or oppose the establishment of representative and municipal institutions in the colony, Macdermott brought out the conservative intentions of the leaders of the movement for colonial self-government and the conservative basis of the new alliance between Wentworth and James Macarthur [q.v.].

Macdermott's campaign won him popular support, but it alienated most of those who were endowed with political rights in the new Constitution and, as he soon saw, made it impossible for him to win a seat in the elective Legislative Council. He turned instead to municipal politics, and was elected councillor in 1842, alderman in 1843, and mayor in 1845. His term as mayor was undistinguished. By this time the Sydney City Council was already deep in the financial difficulties that led to its ultimate downfall. Macdermott seems to have been conscientious in attending to his mayoral duties, but he did nothing to solve the fundamental problems.

In the slump of the early 1840s Macdermott continued to speak at meetings organized by the operatives and, after August 1843, by the Mutual Protection Association. He supported in the City Council employment-creating policies, and gave anti-squatter evidence before both Lang's [q.v.] select committee on the extension of the franchise (1844) and the select committee on the Masters' and Servants' Act (1845). In 1844 he managed to draw political advantage from a much-publicized quarrel with Robert Lowe [q.v.]. But already in 1844 his association with the operatives was growing less close, and he soon surrendered the leadership of the movement. Unlike

some of his colleagues on the City Council he seems not to have taken a close interest in the internal affairs of the Mutual Protection Association. His relations with the operatives may have been affected by the controversy on education, for he strongly favoured the Irish National system, while many of the Catholics who had provided an important segment of his support were in 1844 demanding, under the leadership of the clergy, a fully denominational system. He remained an alderman until his membership of the council was cut short abruptly by his bankruptcy in September 1847. Treated generously by his creditors, he re-established himself in business, but his health had been poor for some time, and he died on 1 February 1848.

Macdermott was a man of fiery temperament, never hesitating to give or to take offence. In the eyes of some of his contemporaries he was 'a leveller, a chartist, a Robespierre, a rebel'. But although his radicalism was genuine, it was quite limited. He emphatically dissociated himself from talk about the Rights of Man, and he hesitated to advocate universal suffrage. He has attracted the attention of recent historians because of his association with the nascent labour movement, but it is equally appropriate to see him as a representative of the striving urban middle class, like Wilshire, Flood and others who served a political apprenticeship with him in the City Council.

A. P. Martin, *Life and letters of the Right Hon. Robert Lowe, Viscount Sherbrooke*, 1 (Lond, 1893), 216-20; L. M. Thomas, *The development of the labour movement in the Sydney district of New South Wales from 1788-1848* (Canberra, 1962); M. Roe, *Quest for authority in eastern Australia 1835-1851* (Melb, 1965); SMH, 2 Feb 1848; W. A. Duncan, Autobiography, 1811-54 (ML).

L. J. HUME

McDONALD, HUGH (1779-1819), soldier, was born on 20 April 1779 at Appin, Argyllshire, Scotland. After serving six years in the Breadalbane Fencibles he enlisted in the 46th Regiment on 9 April 1799. On 21 October 1803 he married Mary Ann Burrowes at Cork. He served in the West Indies in 1804-11 and was promoted quartermaster on 8 July 1813. He arrived in Sydney in the *Windham* with the headquarters and most of the remainder of the 46th Regiment in February 1814, and with his wife and one child. Three more children were born in Sydney.

In July 1817 Governor Macquarie sent

a long dispatch to the duke of York, commander-in-chief, complaining about the conduct of Colonel Molle [q.v.] and most other officers of the regiment, of whom some had ridiculed the governor, others had engaged in trading and farming speculations, and nearly all had refused to have any intercourse with emancipists. However, he listed eleven, including Quartermaster McDonald, who had displayed 'Uniformly Steady and Gentlemanlike Conduct', though since March 1814 McDonald had been ordering from London large consignments of softgoods and other items to retail in the colony. He did his business from premises in York Street and sent his private orders to Dickey, Shaw & Co., London, from whom he, as quartermaster, was accustomed to buy the regiment's clothing. The first of these orders included 144 dozen pairs of ladies' light-blue or white silk stockings, 4000 yards of linen check, 1000 yards of duck, 100 dozen knives and forks, 1000 balls of sewing cotton, and '6 of the Best Fashionable Straw Bonnets for Ladies with Trimmings'. Such orders continued but the London firm evidently kept itself well informed about the prospective movements of oversea customers, for in response to an order in June 1815 it sent him in May 1816 goods to the value of £471 11s. 5d.; 'much less than you give directions for — but we could not feel justified in increasing your order above your remittance as the Regiment is under orders to proceed to India'.

In September 1817 McDonald sailed for India with the regiment in the *Matilda*, leaving his wife and children in Sydney where his last child was born in June 1818. His wife was looking after his property, but soon after he arrived at Vellore he applied for twelve months leave to enable him to attend to his business affairs in Sydney and to take his family back to the regiment. Leave was granted and he reached Sydney probably early in 1819, but on 9 September he died, leaving an estate of £1500 to his wife and four children. On 6 June 1821 his widow married Matthew Bacon, a merchant; he carried on the business at York Street, and died on 23 August 1825. On 11 January 1828 Mary married Bernard Rochford, a farmer from County Galway, Ireland, who had arrived as a convict in the *Prince Regent* in January 1821. Rochford died on 11 August 1839 and his widow on 12 September 1855.

HRA (1), 9; H. McDonald, Letter-book, Feb 1813—3 Oct 1818, annotated by A. J. Gray (RAHS Lib).

MACDOUGALL, JOHN CAMPBELL (1805?-1848), printer, publisher and editor, was the son of John Macdougall (1781-1845), who after a court action over the insurance of a ship sunk in the North Sea in 1815 had sailed for Van Diemen's Land in 1821 and become a merchant and agent. J. C. Macdougall followed him in 1825, and next year established a store in Hobart Town. In 1827 he bought the *Tasmanian* from G. T. Howe [q.v.], and became its editor and publisher-proprietor, adopting a moderate attitude to the government. Toward the end of 1827 a series of articles appeared in the *Tasmanian* entitled 'Review of Colonel Arthur's administration', the authorship of which Macdougall acknowledged in 1842. R. L. Murray [q.v.] and Macdougall amalgamated their papers which became the *Tasmanian and Austral-Asiatic Review* in January 1829; Macdougall withdrew from the partnership toward the end of 1830. In 1832 he visited Sydney and in 1838 bought the *Trumpeter*, an advertising publication, from Henry Melville [q.v.]. Macdougall also became publisher-proprietor and later editor of the *Tasmanian*, but sold this paper to John Morgan [q.v.] in September 1839. In that year he bought the *Colonial Times* from Melville, and became its acknowledged editor, although Thomas Richards appears to have been in charge of the editorial work until 1847.

Early in 1841 Macdougall contemplated a business trip to England. He and his father became involved in a controversy with Edward Abbott of the *Hobart Town Advertiser* and W. G. Elliston and Thomas Macdowell [qq.v.] of the *Hobart Town Courier*. Macdougall assaulted Macdowell and was bound over to keep the peace. In 1842 Macdougall became involved in insolvency proceedings which were later satisfactorily adjusted; next year he was defendant in an action for libel against the Crown. Early in 1844 he was again involved in insolvency proceedings. In October he again became printer, publisher and proprietor of the *Tasmanian and Austral-Asiatic Review* for the editor, R. L. Murray. After its last issue on 26 June 1845 the *Tasmanian* was incorporated in the *Colonial Times* with Macdougall as editor and proprietor. After Eardley-Wilmot's death he defended the late lieut-governor's honour in the *Colonial Times*, 2 March 1847.

In May 1825 Macdougall married Sarah Oakes, widow of John Whyte, and a daughter was born in 1826. Sarah died on 29 December 1829 and in 1837 a son was born to his second wife Mary Ann.

After Macdougall died on 21 July 1848, aged 43, she carried on his printing business. The *Trumpeter* ceased soon after his death, but the *Colonial Times* remained under Mary Ann's management until February 1855 when it was sold to Henri James D'Emden, and she married Kenneth E. Brodribb of Melbourne.

E. M. Miller, *Pressmen and governors* (Syd, 1952); Correspondence file under J. Macdougall (TA).   E. FLINN

MACDOWELL, EDWARD (1798-1860), barrister, and THOMAS (1813-1868), newspaper editor, were the sons of John and Susan Macdowell of Marlton, near Wicklow, Ireland. Edward was called to the Bar at the Middle Temple in 1824 and served for some years on the Midland Circuit before he was appointed solicitor-general of New South Wales in 1830. He lost this position when he failed to take up his duties promptly, and had to accept instead the less remunerative solicitor-generalship of Van Diemen's Land. He held office from January 1833 to September 1837 when he succeeded Alfred Stephen as attorney-general. In December 1838 his brother Thomas joined him in Van Diemen's Land.

Thomas, who had worked in London as a reporter on the *Constitutional*, began his newspaper career in the colony early in 1839 as editor of the *Hobart Town Courier* under the conductorship of W. G. Elliston [q.v.]. In July 1841 he founded the *Van Diemen's Land Chronicle* and remained in charge until it ceased publication next December. Although both these newspapers enjoyed government patronage, the first loyalty of Thomas as their editor was not to the government but to the 'Arthur faction', with which Edward became linked by his marriage in June 1835 to Laura Jeanette, daughter of Charles Swanston [q.v.], the influential manager of the Derwent Bank.

From Thomas's arrival in the colony, the association of the Macdowell brothers was close and notorious. Many, including Gilbert Robertson and Lady Jane Franklin [qq.v.], suspected Edward of inspiring his brother's newspaper articles. In 1839 the *Hobart Town Courier*, with Thomas as editor, repeatedly attacked the solicitor-general, Herbert Jones, who had quarrelled with Edward and forced him to resign over the distillation issues bill. When these press attacks did not cease on Jones's handing back of the attorney-generalship to Macdowell after the bill had been

piloted through the Legislative Council, Jones was stung to make counter charges in a letter published in a rival newspaper, Gilbert Robertson's *True Colonist*. The dispute between the two law officers, each of whom appealed against the other to the Colonial Office, became a public scandal and in July 1841 both were dismissed.

The loss of his attorney-generalship left Edward free to devote his time to his legal practice, which became one of the most successful in the colony; one of its highlights was the defence in 1843 of the bushranger, Martin Cash [q.v.]. Freedom from office also allowed him and his brother more openly to support John Montagu [q.v.], the colonial secretary and leader of the 'Arthur faction', in his quarrel with Sir John Franklin. Thomas, as editor of the *Van Diemen's Land Chronicle*, was responsible for the first and most damaging of the attacks on Lady Franklin in the Tasmanian press. As a journalist, he excelled in invective: his jibes at J. C. Macdougall [q.v.], editor of the *Colonial Times* in 1841, and Thomas Gregson [q.v.] in 1848 struck home so effectively that the one attempted to whip him, the other to cudgel him in public; and of the critics of the Franklins, he was undoubtedly the most skilful and unrestrained.

After 1842 Thomas, although he continued to have an occasional interest in the *Hobart Town Courier* and in the short-lived *Spectator*, ceased to play an active role as a newspaperman. In February 1840 he had been elected manager of the Tasmanian Fire, Life and Marine Insurance Co., with which was associated the Hobart Town and Launceston Marine Insurance Co., and until his death devoted himself to running these two companies. On 28 April 1845 he married Jane Palmer at Hobart. She died in 1866, and two years later he left Hobart to establish in Melbourne a branch of the Derwent and Tamar Insurance Co. He died there on 18 December 1868, survived by five children.

After the recall of Franklin, Edward Macdowell began to make his way slowly back into official favour. In 1844 his successor as attorney-general was dismissed for having fought duels with Robert Stewart and Thomas Macdowell both, according to the *True Colonist*, provoked by Thomas Macdowell. This led to a series of promotions which left vacant the position of commissioner of the Insolvency Court to which in March 1845 Edward Macdowell was appointed. In December 1851 he was further charged with the duties of acting crown solicitor. In March 1854 his tenure of this position was made permanent. Next year he resigned and went with his children to Melbourne where he practised at the Bar until his death on 24 April 1860.

Although the role played by the Macdowell brothers in Tasmanian history was not attractive, they should not be dismissed merely as henchmen of the 'Arthur faction'. Men of undoubted capacity and ruthless ambition, they both found time during their stormy careers to defend not only their private interests but also the conservative and realistic political principles on which they held the Arthur administration had been based.

E. M. Miller, *Pressmen and governors* (Syd, 1952); *Hobart Town Courier*, 29 Nov 1839, 14 Feb 1840; *True Colonist*, 6 Dec 1839, 22 Mar 1844; *Mercury*, 21 Dec 1868; Correspondence file under Macdowell (TA).

LOUIS GREEN

McENCROE, JOHN (1794-1868), Catholic priest and archdeacon, was born on 26 December 1794 in Ardsallagh, near Cashel, County Tipperary, Ireland, son of William McEncroe and Mary D'Arcy. Two years later his father was killed in an accident. One of the children of his mother's second marriage was Teresa Walsh, later to become a Sister of Charity working in the same Australian mission as her brother. McEncroe was educated at Flynn's Grammar School. Wishing to become a priest he entered the seminary of Maynooth and was ordained in 1819. In 1822 he volunteered to go to the American mission with Bishop England of Baltimore, whose liberalism and enterprise had greatly influenced him. He was also deeply impressed by the striking contrast between American democracy and the repressive conditions he had known in Ireland. McEncroe became editor of England's *United States Catholic Miscellany*. Convinced by his American experience of the need of a Catholic press, he was later to establish in Sydney in 1850 the Catholic *Freeman's Journal*.

McEncroe returned to Ireland in 1829. In 1832, at the suggestion of J. H. Plunkett [q.v.], newly appointed solicitor-general to New South Wales, McEncroe became the official chaplain of the Catholics of Australia. Father J. J. Therry [q.v.] had recently been deprived of his official status because of his numerous clashes with the colonial government. It is a monument to McEncroe's patience, tact

and sympathy that he won and retained the friendship of the irascible pioneer priest until his death in 1864.

During his first ten years in the colony McEncroe spent much of his time and energy in caring for convicts, with whom he had considerable influence. He volunteered for Norfolk Island where he was chaplain from 1838 to 1842. Towards the end of his chaplaincy his concern for the convicts prompted him to write a number of letters to Governor Gipps describing the administration of the commandants from Anderson to Maconochie [qq.v.]. He hoped these first-hand descriptions would be a guide to Gipps and perhaps the Colonial Office. Though he admired Maconochie, he felt his system was a failure because he was too lenient and too easily deceived. Indeed, he was strenuously opposed to the entire system of transportation because it failed to reform the convict and brought social and political evils to the colony.

In Sydney McEncroe was a familiar figure on the public platform. In his forthright, racy style he advocated the rights of the working man and opposed the demands of the squatters on such issues as the Constitution, the revival of transportation, and land policy. He was a prominent member of benevolent societies, whether religious or secular, and a pioneer and apostle of the temperance movement; for many years the direction of Catholic education was his responsibility. His most valuable contribution in this field was the introduction of the Sisters of Mercy and the Marist Brothers into his parish schools. In securing the services of religious teachers he was paving the way for Vaughan's decision of 1879.

Within the church in Australia he wanted more priests and teaching orders, and above all the creation of new sees under Irish bishops. However, his friend and superior, Archbishop Polding [q.v.], dreamed of a flourishing colonial church under the care of his own order of English Benedictines. But the Catholic population in the colony was overwhelmingly Irish and these and the secular clergy resented the English Benedictines. The bitter struggle that ensued reached its peak in 1858-59, and the main medium for the Irish attack on the Benedictines, directed chiefly at the vicar-general, Abbot Gregory [q.v.], was the *Freeman's Journal*. McEncroe, no longer personally responsible for the *Journal*, condemned the offensive articles that appeared in it but refused to condemn the paper itself. This estranged him from his archbishop though fundamentally they remained friends. Throughout this struggle McEncroe never compromised his personal integrity and it was his line of argument that Rome eventually followed. He died on 22 August 1868 at St Patrick's, Church Hill, where he had been parish priest since 1861. He had one of the biggest funerals ever seen in the colony and his remains are interred with those of Therry and Polding in the crypt of St Mary's Cathedral, Sydney.

Two loves inspired McEncroe's life and directed all his energies: his church and his fellow-countrymen. In an age of bitter sectarianism and extreme nationalism, he was remarkable for his moderation and respect for opinions different from his own. These qualities, and his evident sincerity, won him the esteem and affection of Protestants and Catholics alike.

HRA (1), 16; J. Rigney, *An account of the life and missionary labours of the late Archdeacon McEncroe*, (Syd, 1868); P. Guilday, *The life and times of John England . . . (1786-1842)*, 1-2 (NY, 1927); R. Wynne, 'Archdeacon John McEncroe', *A'sian Catholic Record*, 21-23 (1954-56); R. A. Daly, 'Archdeacon McEncroe on Norfolk Island, 1838-1842', *A'sian Catholic Record*, 36 (1959); SMH, 18 Sept 1850, 14 Feb 1855; *Freeman's J*, 11 Sept 1858, 29 Aug 1868; McEncroe and Polding papers (Archdiocesan Archives, Syd); Therry papers (Canisius College, Pymble); Sister M. Stephanie, John McEncroe (M.A. thesis, Univ Syd, 1965).   P. K. PHILLIPS

McGARVIE, JOHN (1795-1853), Presbyterian minister and writer, was born in Glasgow, Scotland, and became a graduate of the university there. In answer to an appeal in 1825 for a minister for the church at Portland Head on the Hawkesbury River, New South Wales, he was selected by Rev. J. D. Lang [q.v.]. He arrived in Sydney in the *Greenock* on 22 May 1826 after a six months voyage from Leith. Met on arrival by Lang, he went straight to Portland Head as the first Presbyterian minister of the Ebenezer Church and remained there until 1830. In 1829 he contributed a series of biographical articles to the *Sydney Gazette* together with a number of his poems under such pseudonyms as 'M., Ananbaba', 'A.B., Marramatta' and 'C.D., Warrambamba'. When the *Sydney Herald* commenced in 1831, with his brother William [q.v.] as one of its three original proprietors, he contributed the editorials, and continued as leader writer for some years. He also appears to have chosen the paper's two mottoes, both from Pope: 'In moderation placing all my glory, while Tories call me Whig — and Whigs a Tory' and 'Sworn to no master, of no sect am I'. He was one of the founders in 1826 of the Sydney Dispensary, afterwards the Sydney Infirmary and Dispensary, and was its honorary secretary from 1836 until his death. He was also a founder of the Sydney School of Arts. On the establishment of the Australian College in 1831 he conducted the mathematics department and also lectured in natural philosophy and chemistry.

In 1832 he accepted an invitation to start a second Presbyterian congregation in Sydney and held services in the courthouse until St Andrew's Scots Church was ready 'for use of persons connected with the Established Church of Scotland.' Built in Kent Street near Bathurst Street, it was opened for divine service on 13 September 1835 and he remained as its minister until his death. McGarvie filled the pulpit at Scots Church in 1830 during Lang's absence abroad and two years later joined Lang and three others to form the first presbytery in Sydney. During the disagreements within the church connected with Lang, McGarvie seems to have taken an active part. In 1838 and again in 1848 he signed as 'Moderator'. He held many important offices in the church and took a fairly prominent part in the affairs of synod. In 1840 the University of Glasgow awarded him an honorary D.D. A volume of his sermons was published in Sydney in 1842. A list of his book purchases shows his wide range of reading and learning and his sermons were said to be distinguished for their literary merit. He died, unmarried, on 12 April 1853 and was buried at Gore Hill cemetery.

J. Maclehose, *The picture of Sydney* (Syd, 1838); J. Cameron, *Centenary history of the Presbyterian Church in New South Wales*, 1 (Syd, 1905); *A century of journalism. The Sydney Morning Herald, 1831-1931* (Syd, 1931); G. R. S. Reid, *The history of Ebenezer, Australia's oldest church*, 3rd ed (Petersham, 1951); C. A. White, *The challenge of the years: a history of the Presbyterian Church . . . New South Wales* (Syd, 1951); *Truth* (Syd), 26 Mar 1911; McGarvie papers (Presbyterian Lib, Assembly Hall, Syd); MS cat under J. McGarvie (ML).   JEAN F. ARNOT

McGARVIE, WILLIAM (1810-1841), journalist, bookseller and pastoralist, was born in Glasgow, Scotland. He was educated on classical lines, and worked for a brief period on the *Glasgow Herald* before following his brother John [q.v.] to New South Wales. He arrived in the *Comet* in 1828 and immediately took charge of the 'Australian Stationery Warehouse' which Robert Howe ran in conjunction with the *Sydney Gazette*. This shop in Lower George Street also had a circulating library; McGarvie's catalogue of its books was printed by the *Gazette* in 1829 and is today an important social document.

In 1831, with two other *Gazette* employees, Frederick Stokes and Ward Stephens [q.v.], he imported a printing press and they began publication of the *Sydney Herald*. McGarvie is credited with naming the paper after the *Glasgow Herald*. He stated its policy in the first issue, 18 April 1831 : the ideals were 'wholesome restraint' and 'reasoning founded on truth' as far as politics were concerned. Other guiding principles were loyalty to Britain, the dissemination of knowledge, the interests of literature and the advancement of education. In his first editorial McGarvie also paid a tribute to the native-born Australians and urged their advancement by the government. McGarvie edited the *Herald* for only half a dozen issues. He then sold his share to Stephens and Stokes and returned to Scotland. He came back again almost immediately in 1832, but in a storm was drenched in his cabin in the *Minerva*. His health had never been robust and he now suffered permanent damage to his lungs.

In Sydney he resumed bookselling at the Australian Warehouse, then under the proprietorship of Ann Howe, and issued another catalogue of its books in 1833. He then acquired a land grant of 320 acres at Port Macquarie to which he added another 100 acres by purchase. He named this estate Mount Pleasant, and after 1835 devoted most of his time to it. In 1841, after having been forced to spend six nights in the bush in wet weather, he contracted a severe cold and returned to Sydney. His health deteriorated quickly and he died in Sydney on 1 April 1841, aged 31, survived by his wife, Isabella, and a three-weeks-old son. His estate was valued at £3000. His widow later married Dr Frederick Mackellar, grandfather of the poet Dorothea Mackellar.

A century of . journalism. The Sydney Morning Herald, 1831-1931 (Syd, 1931); McGarvie papers (ML, Presbyterian Lib, Assembly Hall, Syd).   J. V. BYRNES

McGILL; *see* BIRABAN

MacGILLIVRAY, JOHN (1821-1867), naturalist, was born on 18 December 1821 at Aberdeen, Scotland, the eldest of twelve children of William MacGillivray (1796-1852), a famous British ornithologist and sometime Regius professor of natural history, Marischal College, Aberdeen. He studied medicine in Edinburgh but before his course was completed he was appointed by the thirteenth earl of Derby, a well-known patron of zoology, as naturalist under J. Beete Jukes [q.v.] in H.M.S. *Fly* commanded by Captain F. P. Blackwood [q.v.]. MacGillivray left England in the *Fly* in April 1842 and from then on spent the greater part of his life in Australia and the islands of the south-west Pacific. At Sydney in 1848 he married Williamina Paton Gray, a Scottish girl by whom he had a son and two daughters.

The *Fly* spent over three years around the Australian coast and New Guinea, engaged on a survey of the Great Barrier Reef and Torres Strait, and arrived back in England in February 1846. MacGillivray lost no opportunity to go ashore collecting when the *Fly* was in port, anchored off the coast or among the islands. Some idea of his activities can be obtained from Jukes's official *Narrative of the surveying Voyage of H.M.S. Fly . . .* (London, 1847) and his own papers in the *Zoologist* in 1846 recording his observations at Raine Island, Port Essington and other places.

MacGillivray again left England for Australia in December 1846 as naturalist in H.M.S. *Rattlesnake*, commanded by Captain Owen Stanley [q.v.]. Two other naturalists were on the staff, the assistant surgeon, T. H. Huxley [q.v.], later to become a famous biologist, and James Fowler Wilcox. The *Rattlesnake* reached Hobart Town in June 1847 and after its tour of duty arrived in England in October 1850. Most of the time was spent surveying between the Queensland coast and the Great Barrier Reef, the southern coast of New Guinea and the Louisiade Archipelago. Other places around the coast, such as Bass Strait and Port Essington, were visited, and the ship returned to Sydney between cruises.

MacGillivray stayed in England for two years while he wrote the *Narrative of the Voyage of H. M. S. Rattlesnake . . .* (1852). Later in 1852 he sailed as naturalist in H.M.S. *Herald*, under Captain H. M. Denham, on a surveying voyage to South America and the south Pacific. Between February 1853 and early 1855, when MacGillivray left the service, the ship was in Sydney or cruising among the islands of the south-west Pacific. Few details are known of the next few years of his life.

He read papers to the Horticultural Improvement Society in Sydney and appears to have been its secretary. In 1858-60 he was in the New Hebrides and returned to Sydney in 1861 after visiting Cape York. He worked for a time arranging the shell collection of Dr James C. Cox, a well-known conchologist. In 1862 and 1864 he published articles in Sydney newspapers.

In 1864 he settled at Grafton, an area noted for the richness of its fauna, and collected natural history specimens in a business partnership with J. F. Wilcox. About the end of 1866 he returned to Sydney and was again engaged by Dr Cox to help in preparing a monograph of Australian land shells. He was planning an expedition to Cape York when, at Sydney on 6 June 1867, he died suddenly of a heart attack, probably aggravated by an asthmatic condition. Other members of his family also migrated to Australia, notably Dr Paul Howard MacGillivray of Bendigo, Victoria, distinguished amateur naturalist specializing in the Bryozoa.

MacGillivray made large collections of specimens of all kinds of animals, especially birds and mollusc shells, and plants, which are still housed in the British Museum (Natural History), Kew Herbarium and other museums in England and Australia. Among his collections were the type specimens of many species described by John Gould [q.v.], George Bentham and others. His zeal and energy as a field worker were unsurpassed and it is obvious that he enjoyed collecting and observing in the field above all else. He had a remarkable facility for gaining the confidence of native peoples and took a great interest in them and collected vocabularies. His published work, notebooks, and the few surviving letters show him as a critical and intelligent observer and demonstrate an excellent knowledge of systematic zoology and animal distribution. Except for the *Rattlesnake* narrative his published work is essentially trivial, and it is surprising that he did not publish more substantial zoological papers and describe some of the new species which he discovered. Huxley found him an amiable companion on the *Rattlesnake* but later developed almost a contempt for him. Huxley's letters reveal his impatience with MacGillivray's dilatoriness in completing the narrative, which appears also to have been the despair of the publisher. An obituary notice records that MacGillivray's appointment in the *Herald* was terminated because of his intemperate habits, and there is a tradition among Australian naturalists that his career 'ended on a low rung'. His lapses have largely been forgotten, however, because of his great contributions to Australian natural history.

J. Huxley (ed), T. H. *Huxley's diary of the voyage of H.M.S. Rattlesnake* (Lond, 1935); T. Iredale, 'The last letters of John MacGillivray', *Australian Zoologist*, 9 (1937); J. H. Maiden, 'Records of Queensland botanists', *Report 12th meeting, A/sian Assn Advancement of Science* (Brisb, 1910). J. H. CALABY

McINTYRE, PETER (1783-1842), landowner, was born in Tomcairn, Perthshire, Scotland, the son of Donald (Daniel) and Mary McIntyre. In 1824 he was appointed the agent of Thomas Potter Macqueen [q.v.] who had received from the Colonial Office a free grant of 10,000 acres. McIntyre chartered the *Nimrod* and the *Hugh Crawford*, which he filled with emigrants, livestock, and supplies, and reached Sydney in April 1825.

He secured from Governor Darling a free grant of 4000 acres for himself and 4000 for his brother John and in May 1825 was possessed of land orders for 32,000 acres. Making verbal and written requests for various selections of land very vaguely defined to Henry Dangar [q.v.], the government surveyor, he put forward claims that conflicted with Dangar's for an area of rich alluvial at the junction of the Dart Brook and Hunter River. McIntyre accused his rival of improper and corrupt practices and secured his suspension. He was allowed a free choice after Dangar's prior claim on 1300 acres and secured Segenhoe for Macqueen and Blairmore (near Aberdeen) for himself.

McIntyre was an active superintendent and in 1826 offered farms to let; he opened a flour-mill in 1829 and was growing hops successfully in 1830. Nevertheless Macqueen sent out H. C. Sempill to replace him in 1830. In 1833 he was accused of perjury by Sempill but acquitted. In 1837, however, he and three other defendants were found guilty of malicious conspiracy to prevent fair competition at a crown land auction, and McIntyre was fined £100. About this time he was opening squatting runs in the Liverpool Plains and New England districts. In 1827 he had guided Allan Cunningham [q.v.] over the Liverpool Range and the explorer had named the Macintyre River in his honour. The runs of Peter McIntyre and his brother Donald in New England were Byron Plains, Waterloo, Falconer, and Guyra.

McIntyre died on 13 January 1842 at his estate of Pitnacree, Maitland. He left £2000 to his natural daughter Ann and the residue to his sister Mary. His main activities were to develop his estate, which he did by grant, purchases, and leases from the crown, and purchases from private individuals.

HRA (1), 13-15; G. N. Griffiths, *Some northern homes of N.S.W.* (Syd, 1954); *Australian*, 16 Aug 1833; *Sydney Gazette*, 5 Aug, 19 Sept 1837; J. F. Campbell, 'Discovery and settlement in New England', *JRAHS*, 8 (1922); MS cat under P. McIntyre (ML).

R. B. WALKER

MACKANESS, JOHN (1770?-1838), barrister and public servant, early became addicted to attending radical political meetings in and around London. He was called to the Bar of the Middle Temple in July 1794 and soon appointed recorder of Wallingford. In January 1824 through the influence of Baron Tenterden he was appointed sheriff of New South Wales at a salary of £1000, for which he was also to serve as coroner and provost-marshal. Soon after his arrival in the *Alfred* at Sydney in July 1824 Mackaness leased land at Hyde Park and bought 700 acres near Liverpool, where he later claimed to have spent £3000 on improvements and the cultivation of vines. In May 1825 Brisbane ordered that he be granted 2000 acres, but six months later this land had not been selected or surveyed.

In January 1826 Mackaness was petitioned to convene a public meeting of 'the Gentry, Magistrates, Merchants, Landholders, Farmers, Traders and other free Inhabitants' which approved an address to the newly-arrived Governor Darling advocating a part-elected legislative council and trial by jury. Darling was disgusted because Mackaness had chaired this radical meeting, but he sent the address to the Colonial Office, and the conservative Archdeacon Scott [q.v.] was so incensed that he hoped he would never see Mackaness again. At the same time the Sydney Grand Jury entertained Mackaness at a dinner and asked him to allow his portrait to be painted by Augustus Earle [q.v.] and hung in some public hall. On 26 January 1827 Mackaness convened another public meeting of 'Free Inhabitants', and was chosen to present their petition to Darling with Sir John Jamison and Gregory Blaxland [qq.v.]. That evening Mackaness was the only invited guest at an Anniversary Day dinner organized by 125 colonists who, Darling reported, were 'Emancipists and their immediate Connexions and Friends'. In March Darling noted that Mackaness was 'not well affected to the Government'; and was 'generally the leading Character at

all the Popular Meetings' and 'just the sort of Man to give a tone to such Associations'. Darling also complained that Mackaness had drawn on the public purse for travel expenses and a salary of £91 5s. as provost-marshal, and that although Mackaness disclaimed any obligation to visit the gaol, certain irregularities there would have been prevented if he had attended to his duties. In due course the Colonial Office approved Mackaness's travel expenses but disallowed his pay as provost-marshal.

Meanwhile the Colonial Office had another complaint about Mackaness. In 1823 an aged and infirm lady had surrendered the right to £1200 which Mackaness held as a trustee on condition that he paid her an annuity of £120, but by 1827 he had sent her only £90. Darling was asked to see that the arrears were promptly paid and future payments made half-yearly through the colonial treasurer. In November the governor told Mackaness that his services were no longer required because of his association with 'factious Individuals' and his failure to obey promptly a government order. In the same month Mackaness attended a dinner of the Turf Club, where the band played 'Over the hills and far away' when the toast of the governor was given. When Darling heard of this he promptly resigned as the club's patron, and in December a club meeting agreed to impertinent resolutions on Mackaness's casting vote as chairman and these were sent to the governor and the newspapers.

Mackaness claimed further grievances when his application to locate on the Goulburn plains the 2000 acres promised by Brisbane was referred to the Colonial Office. Mackaness appealed to the secretary of state, but in his covering dispatch Darling declared that he had 'as little pretension to the Character of a Gentleman of which he boasts, as he has to that of an honest Man', and had withheld the fees of his office instead of paying them into the Treasury.

In December 1827 Mackaness was admitted to practise in the Supreme Court as a barrister and attorney. Next February Chief Justice Forbes and Judge Stephen [qq.v.] testified to Mackaness's good conduct as sheriff, but within two weeks he was on trial in the Supreme Court for an allegedly drunken assault on the solicitor-general, was found guilty and fined £5. Although in October 1831 Mackaness was granted land in the parish of St Lawrence on the eve of Darling's departure, he continued to support the emancipists and talked of going to London to carry on the feud, but soon ceased to be a conspicuous leader. He died on 4 April 1838 and was buried in the Devonshire Street cemetery. The *Australian* described him as 'a warm and uncompromising advocate of the rights and liberty of the subject', but even his friends admitted that he was easily excited and often misguided in his judgments.

HRA (1), 11-15, (4), 1; A. Halloran, 'Some early legal celebrities', JRAHS, 12 (1927); *Australian*, 10 Apr 1838; MS cat under J. Mackaness (ML).

McKAY, ALEXANDER (1802?-1882), convict, explorer and farmer, was convicted in Glasgow, Scotland, on 25 April 1823 of robbery and sentenced to transportation for life. He arrived in Van Diemen's Land on 30 December 1824 in the *Sir Godfrey Webster*. His only offence after his arrival was to escape from a gang while clearing land for Dr Bromley [q.v.] on 20 August 1824 and to stow away in the *Ardent*; for this he received fifty lashes. In February 1827 he petitioned for a ticket-of-leave, saying that he had for two years been employed by the government under Captain Welsh [q.v.], on whose recommendation he had been assigned to the Van Diemen's Land Co. in April 1826 and had explored north-west Tasmania with the company's surveyors; he had gone round the island in an open boat examining every practicable harbour. Curr [q.v.] and Welsh testified to his good behaviour. However, Arthur refused to grant a ticket-of-leave as McKay had been in the colony only three years and had attempted to escape. In December 1829 McKay sought leave to go in pursuit of troublesome Aboriginals and Arthur decided that he should join G. A. Robinson [q.v.] and promised him emancipation in two years if his conduct merited it.

From January 1830 to April 1831 McKay worked under Robinson rounding up Aboriginals in the north-east. For thirteen weeks McKay was in charge of natives whom they had taken to Swan Island, while Robinson went to Hobart Town whence he returned in a government vessel and took the natives to Preservation Island. McKay claimed that he had tried to persuade the sealers not to molest the Aboriginals but Robinson declared that McKay had connived with the sealers and cohabited with the natives, even killing some of them. In 1830, however, he was granted a conditional pardon for his services in opening 'a conciliatory communication with the Aboriginal Tribes'.

In April 1831 G. Frankland [q.v.] asked for McKay's services at £1 a week to search for a lead-mine indicated by specimens McKay had been given by Aboriginals and in June asked for him again to mark out a road to Port Davey. However, Arthur was still chary of putting McKay in charge of such projects. In September, while in an expedition led by Robinson, he captured six natives and found the bodies of Captain B. B. Thomas [q.v.] and his overseer Parker who had been killed by Aboriginals near Port Sorell. As a reward Arthur gave him a suburban allotment and in November he was given a free pardon for meritorious conduct in capturing several natives in spite of repeated bold attempts by the tribes to rescue them. Frankland's request for McKay's services to explore in preparation for road-making was granted in April 1835, and by next January he had sixteen men under his charge on road work. While with the Survey Department he traced the River Mersey to its source, and explored round the Great Lake, Lake St Clair, and the Gordon River. In this phase he became acquainted with J. E. Calder [q.v.]. About 1864 McKay settled on forty-six acres at Peppermint Bay. He died there on 14 June 1882 in his eightieth year.

Frankland and Calder thought well of his work but there is evidence that he was a violent and untrustworthy man.

N. J. B. Plomley (ed), *Friendly mission* (Hob, 1966); Correspondence file under McKay (TA).

MacKELLAR, NEIL (d. 1802), military officer, was possibly a nephew of Colonel Patrick MacKellar of the Royal Engineers. He was commissioned an ensign in the New South Wales Corps on 21 April 1791 and arrived in the colony with the main body of his regiment in February 1792. He was a member of the court appointed by Lieut-Governor Grose [q.v.] to investigate King's actions during the disturbances at Norfolk Island in 1794. In June 1795 he accompanied Edward Abbott [q.v.] and a detachment of troops to protect the settlers against the Aboriginals at the Hawkesbury. In November he was promoted lieutenant. In October 1796 he joined Thomas Laycock [q.v.] and others as a defendant in an action brought by John Boston [q.v.] relating to the shooting of the latter's sow, but was acquitted. In 1797-99 he was in command at the Hawkesbury. On his return to Sydney he acted as adjutant until November 1800. As a member of the court which tried Isaac Nichols [q.v.] in March 1799 he took objection to Governor Hunter's request to make his vote public. In October he was a member of a court wherein five men were charged with the murder of two native boys. Under questioning he stated that orders issued for the destruction of Aboriginals whenever encountered, after they had committed outrages, had not been countermanded during his command at the Hawkesbury nor to his knowledge since.

In September 1800 he became secretary and aide-de-camp to Governor King, and was appointed an acting magistrate and a member of a committee to investigate an alleged conspiracy among the Irish convicts. On the grounds of internal security and the shortage of captains in Sydney, King appointed him to the local rank of captain in October. In April 1801 he was replaced by W. N. Chapman [q.v.] as secretary. In July Lieutenant Marshall, R.N., when on trial for assault, objected to MacKellar's membership of the court on the grounds that he had already prejudged the case. MacKellar took an active part in the later events leading up to the rencontre between Lieut-Colonel Paterson and John Macarthur [qq.v.], in which he acted as the former's second, so earning Macarthur's animosity. In March 1802 he prosecuted Nicholas Bayly [q.v.] on behalf of King for disobedience of orders relating to the trade in spirits. Soon afterwards he sailed for England in the *Caroline* with Macarthur's sword and King's dispatches concerning the duel, but the schooner was never sighted again.

A convict woman, Sarah Cooley, bore him three daughters and two sons in New South Wales, and his will in 1799 divided his property equally between Sarah and the four children who had then been born. His elder son, Lieutenant Duncan Mac-Kellar, R.N. (b. 4 December 1795), came to New South Wales with three children in the *City of Edinburgh* in 1825 and was granted land in the County of St Vincent.

MacKellar's actions in his last years can be ascribed to motives arising from expediency and patronage. His desire to take leave in England at that particular time, in spite of his apparent intention to return to the colony, can be attributed to a desire to avoid Macarthur's enmity. Although some of his actions may have indicated immaturity, they were consistent with certain principles: for example, his moral courage and loyalty in supporting Paterson and King, in spite of their obvious weaknesses in the face of strong hostility. MacKellar's display of independent character was in contrast to many other military officers. He did not trade in spirits, and was not unduly interested in obtaining landholdings or amassing a large fortune. Had he reached England he could well have profoundly altered Macarthur's career, and through this the course of Australia's history.

HRNSW, 2-5; HRA (1), 1-5; Piper papers (ML).

M. AUSTIN

McKENNY, JOHN (1788-1847), Wesleyan Methodist minister, was born at Coleraine, Ireland. He came of a Wesleyan family and began preaching in 1807. In the next year he was listed as a lay preacher, given full status in 1811 and accepted in 1813 as a member of Thomas Coke's mission to the East. McKenny's field was South Africa, where he worked for two years despite official discouragement. From 1816 to 1834 he served in Ceylon and then returned to England in poor health. There he was appointed by the conference to be chairman of the New South Wales mission. McKenny and his family reached Sydney by way of Hobart Town in April 1836.

McKenny found the local Methodists in a state of some confusion. There had been disputes about ministerial appointments and property management; there was indecision about the status of Methodism and its relations with the Church of England. Bourke's Church Act of 1836 did not solve these special problems, although it gave denominational equality and provision for government support. McKenny was not a dynamic or inspiring leader; his strength lay in the tactful management of affairs. He persuaded the government to give legal status to the Methodist connexion and secured full legal recognition for its marriage celebrations. The Wesleyan schools and immigrant ministers gained some Treasury support. By these means the Methodist dilemma of its former subservience to Anglicanism was gradually resolved.

McKenny had to combat the separatist tendency in Methodism, which the strengthening discipline and connexion with the State provoked into action. Revivalism had also to be harnessed to the general life of the Methodists. When he served at Parramatta (1840-43), McKenny directed several remarkable revival campaigns. During his superintendency, Methodist chapels multiplied in the urban areas and the settled districts. In Sydney the centenary chapel was completed after long delay in 1845, and a dozen new places of worship were built in the town and its suburbs. McKenny travelled widely to promote extension in the country, and spent as much of his time on administrative matters as on preaching and pastoral work. When McKenny was succeeded in 1846 by W. B. Boyce, Wesleyan Methodism in the colony had developed from the position of a semi-private religious society to that of a regularly constituted and accepted church. McKenny became a supernumerary in 1847 and died at Stanmore, Sydney, on 31 October of that year.

. J. Watsford, *Glorious gospel triumphs* (Lond, 1904); J. Colwell, *The illustrated history of Methodism. Australia* (Syd, 1904); Wesleyan Methodist Missionary Soc, NSW, Minutes (ML).   K. J. CABLE

McKENZIE, ALEXANDER KENNETH (1768-1838), banker and landowner, was born probably in Scotland. He had acquired much general knowledge and great experience in business by January 1797 when he married Mary Ann, sister of John Piper [q.v.]. They lived in London for many years and had six children when they emigrated in the *Admiral Cockburn* to Sydney. They arrived in December 1822 and next May McKenzie was appointed secretary and cashier of the Bank of New South Wales at a salary of £400.

McKenzie was soon active in the public affairs of the colony. In 1824 he signed petitions for a reduction of duties on timber exported to Britain and for government aid to Scots Church. In 1825 he became treasurer of the Sydney auxiliary of the Church Missionary Society, of the Religious Tract Society and of the Turf Club, and a collector of subscriptions for building a Roman Catholic chapel; he was granted 230 acres, which he located near Bathurst, where Governor Brisbane allowed him to purchase by instalments another 5000 acres at 5s. an acre. This estate McKenzie named Dochairn and left in charge of his eldest son, John Piper. They bought adjoining land and soon had 2000 acres cleared, 50 under cultivation, 250 cattle and 2500 sheep. To pay for this progress John McKenzie drew orders on his father; they passed through many hands and led to much inconvenience and occasional forgery, so A. K. McKenzie printed some three hundred £1 notes, payable at the Bank of New South Wales, and sent them to his son to use instead of orders. In due course these private notes came to the attention of the bank's directors and McKenzie was threatened with charges of negligence if not corrupt practice. The *Sydney Gazette*, 7 November 1827, interceded on his behalf and claimed that one

of the directors, Dr Redfern [q.v.], was eager to make his brother-in-law cashier in place of McKenzie. The charges were withdrawn but soon afterwards McKenzie resigned and became secretary of the Bank of Australia. He also resigned from the magistracy to which he had been appointed in July 1827, and withdrew from his benevolent activities.

In 1828 McKenzie had difficulty in paying the instalments on the 5000 acres he had bought from the crown, but as the pastoral boom gathered way in the early 1830s he sold part of the section to W. C. Wentworth [q.v.], and moved to Bathurst. After the Interest Act of 1834 he became active in financing pastoral expansion and helped to found the Bathurst Bank, which opened with him as its president. In 1836 he was reappointed to the magistracy, became treasurer of the Bathurst Bible Society and served on various committees. Next year he retired to Parramatta. He died there on 28 December 1838, aged 70, leaving an estate sworn at £10,000.

HRA (1), 11, 14; S. J. Butlin, *Foundations of the Australian monetary system, 1788-1851* (Melb, 1953); Newspaper indexes under A. K. McKenzie (ML).

MACKENZIE, DAVID (fl. 1834-1852), author, lecturer and landowner, graduated M.A. at Edinburgh University and claimed to have run a boarding academy at Hythe, near London, for six years before he was recruited by Rev. J. D. Lang [q.v.] in 1834 as a teacher in his Australian College, founded in 1831. In 1835 Mackenzie became senior master there and had charge of the boarders. The college grew from 12 pupils in January 1835 to 92 at the end of 1837. By 1838 the staff comprised Mackenzie, who taught mathematics and natural philosophy, and four others.

When Lang visited England in 1839-41 Mackenzie and the others officiated at Scots Church although they 'were only licentiates and not ordained ministers of the Church of Scotland, and consequently incompetent to solemnize baptisms and marriages'. Mackenzie also lectured at the Mechanics' School of Arts on the properties of matter, served on its committee and presided at its debating class and at discussions on spectres and ghosts. He professed astonishment at the colonists' thirst for reading, if only for books of 'a light and frivolous character', and at the comparative absence of social prejudices in Sydney. But in 1842 he and other leaders of the School of Arts were accused of being more eager 'to bring together the higher classes of society, and to gratify their polished taste, than to impart useful instruction to that body for whose exclusive benefit the Institution was founded'. The charge probably had substance, for Mackenzie was clearly trying to fill his purse by investing in livestock, taking up runs on the Namoi and Murray Rivers, and using Aboriginals to do his sheep-washing and shearing. He had also bought allotments cheaply in the new towns planned at Yass, Gundagai and Albury. When Lang returned and closed the college he complained that Mackenzie had become a 'clerical drover' and was 'absent three months together, visiting his stations, while the institution was left to take its chance'.

In 1844 Mackenzie visited Britain and on the voyage wrote *The Emigrant's Guide; or Ten Years' Practical Experience in Australia* (London, 1845). He soon returned to Australia to attend to his pastoral interests. The disposal of his rural town allotments involved much travelling between Sydney and Melbourne, but he had judiciously chosen his blocks on proposed street corners and they were all sold by 1850. Next year he bought sheep for 2s. each from an insolvent estate and made handsome profits after the discovery of gold. He also had his book republished in London in 1851, 1852 and 1853. By June 1852 he was in London where he published *The Gold Digger: A Visit to the Gold Fields of Australia in February, 1852*, dedicating it 'to the labouring classes of Great Britain and Ireland' and giving many useful hints from his 'own experience during the last ten years as a sheepholder', as well as a 'cheap and familiar guide' to those who 'may wish to try their luck at our Australian Goldfields'. He does not appear to have returned to Australia and his later career has not been traced.

G. Nadel, *Australia's colonial culture* (Melb, 1957); A. C. Child, 'Studies in the life and work of John Dunmore Lang', *JRAHS*, 22 (1936); Newspaper indexes under D. Mackenzie (ML); MS cat under D. Mackenzie (ML); Land papers 133 (NSWA).

MACKERSEY, JOHN (1789-1871), Presbyterian minister, was born at West Calder, Scotland, the son of Rev. Dr James Mackersey, Presbyterian minister of that parish. In November 1823 his elder brother, James, emigrated to Van Diemen's Land with property worth £1000 and received 1200 acres of land. Concerned that there was no clergyman resident near his son's property, Dr Mackersey suggested in 1824 that a young Scottish clergyman could be encouraged to emigrate if colonists guaranteed his salary. Two years later the Scottish settlers on the Macquarie River proposed to the Colonial Office that they were prepared to build a church and contribute £100 a year to a minister's salary if equal government assistance could be expected. This was agreed to and the head of the Scottish church was informed. In the colony the Macquarie settlers collected subscriptions for church, glebe and manse, acquired suitable land and began building.

John Mackersey, who had spent three years assisting his father as lay preacher in Scotland, was ordained with this colonial appointment in view, and duly sent out by the Edinburgh church authorities. He reached Hobart Town on 30 January 1829. The lieut-governor after their first meeting reported that Mackersey seemed well selected for his office, but regretted that the settlers were not prepared for his arrival. However, he had brought capital of £1220 and decided to rent Gaddesden at Campbell Town from April 1829, and to conduct a school there to supplement his clerical salary until the manse and church were ready. By putting much of his money into this venture, useful though it was, he reduced the capital available for improving land, and was therefore granted only 640 acres. As he had regarded his brother's original grant of 1200 acres as a minimum to compensate him for the Scottish clergy's superannuation allowance forfeited by his emigration, he was, within six months, a disappointed man, with a reputation among the government officials in Hobart as an abusive correspondent.

His difficulties were real. In November 1829 the convict labour on loan to the church building committee was withdrawn as funds were exhausted, with only the shell of the twelve-roomed manse completed and the church not even begun. All his attempts failed to enlarge his congregation, and so to increase funds; in the early 1830s seven families left the district, and depressed conditions made settlers reluctant to subscribe. Some were doubtful of the success of the venture; others disliked services being held temporarily in Mackersey's drawing room, and doubts as to the committee's title increased the problem. With his own future at stake, Mackersey lent the committee a large part of the money required to complete the buildings, and allowed the parish-paid half of his salary to fall into arrears so that the manse and church could be completed, a step which seemed basic to rallying his congregation. Kirklands Church was finally dedicated in October 1836, but confusion over the deeds and variation from the usual form of application for government assistance under the Church Act of 1837, prevented his reimbursement for some years. Still resentful at his meagre land grant, he applied for land in lieu, but was refused. Provident by nature, however, he lost no chance to acquire the personal security which lay in land ownership, and in 1842 bought a property he called Speedwell, at East Arm, on the Tamar River. As adjoining tracts came up for sale, he gradually added to his holdings there.

For twenty-five years he was a dominant figure on the Macquarie River, soon overcoming the initial setbacks and gathering together the nucleus of a congregation. Although his health finally suffered, he extended his parish to include Lincoln in the west and Cleveland and Epping in the north, holding services in the houses of scattered settlers until churches were built in those districts. For some years after moving to Kirklands manse, he continued to take pupils, and the lasting classical interest of some of those known to have studied under him is evidence of his equal success in this field, although an attempt in 1841 at running a school for girls also at Kirklands in partnership with Miss Ann Sylke, formerly a teacher at Ellinthorp Hall, proved unsuccessful.

In 1854 he relinquished his charge to Rev. Adam Turnbull [q.v.] and retired on a pension of £120. He continued to take an interest in church affairs, however, and so was drawn into the bitter controversies of the 1860s. In 1861 he was appointed to serve on a committee which attempted to make a definitive statement on Presbyterian doctrine. On its dissolution he was made convenor of a second committee. During its sittings the disagreements over doctrine had become public, and the committee was forced to censure Rev. Dr Storie for publishing virulent statements against persons involved in the dispute. The resulting report failed to please all the groups and was rejected by the presbytery. Three years later Mackersey was again thrust into the conflict, and with the moderator, Rev. C. Simson, was required to prepare further charges against Storie, who was found guilty by the presbytery. In time the quarrel subsided, Storie was reinstated and Mackersey returned to retirement. He died at Speedwell on 26 June 1871. Before leaving Scotland he had married Catherine Wallace; they had two sons and two daughters.

J. Heyer, The Presbyterian pioneers of Van Diemen's Land (Launceston, 1935); Correspondence file under Mackersey (TA).

LEX FINLAY

MACKIE, WILLIAM HENRY (1799-1860), advocate-general and senior magistrate, was born on 17 November 1799 at Cochin, India, the son of William Frederick Mackie, a surgeon in the East India Co., and his wife Elennora, née Hamilton. Sent to relatives in Londonderry, he attended a school conducted by R. B. Macklin and later another at Twickenham, Middlesex. At 15 he entered Trinity College, Cambridge (B.A., 1821), and was admitted to the Inner Temple in November 1822. He was not, however, called to the English Bar.

He arrived in Western Australia in the Caroline in October 1829 as a private settler, though possibly with hopes or even a recommendation for a legal position. In deciding to migrate he was probably influenced by his cousin, Captain F. C. Irwin [q.v.], with whom he was further connected by the marriage of his sister and Irwin's brother. The property Mackie and Irwin brought entitled them to a large land grant; they jointly took up 3240 acres at Henley Park on the Upper Swan, and another 7000 acres on the Avon between Beverley and York.

On 9 December 1829 Lieut-Governor Stirling appointed Mackie and seven other colonists justices of the peace, and formed a constabulary to preserve law and order. Although Stirling's instructions did not authorize criminal punishments, he thus provided for some continuity of the legal control to which migrants had been accustomed in England. These first measures, six months after the colony's foundation, had become necessary because of the increase of petty crime and drunkenness. Courts of Petty and Quarter Sessions were introduced, and Mackie was appointed their chairman as well as counsel to the local government. After their duties in the criminal courts, the next most important function of the magistrates was on the licensing bench of which Mackie became a member when it first met on 1 January 1830. In April that year the magistrates drafted jury rules and in July the first Quarter Sessions were held at Fremantle. Respect for the law was well established in the colony's first year.

In October 1831 Stirling received a commission from the Crown under which he established Legislative and Executive Councils, of which Mackie became a foundation member. Mackie was also appointed advocate-general. In February 1832 the first ordinance passed by the Legislative Council provided for a civil court under a commissioner with jurisdiction nearly equivalent to that of the superior civil courts in England. Until then Stirling had decided civil disputes himself, usually with advice from Mackie or another magistrate. G. F. Moore [q.v.] became first commissioner of the Civil Court, but in June 1834 he exchanged posts with the advocate-general, so that Mackie thereafter presided in both the civil and the criminal jurisdictions.

In Perth the courts sat in the rush-thatched church which served also as a schoolroom until replaced in 1837 by a new court-house that served the same three purposes for another few years; as Perth's oldest building, it was still in use in 1966. Although the law administered in the young colony was based on English law as it stood in 1829, Mackie appreciated the need for adapting it to local conditions and for simplification. With his support many legal reforms were made. Small debts and libel caused much litigation until 1836 when the Civil Court Ordinance and Rules were amended to limit the right of court practice to qualified persons. The justices of the peace were given jurisdiction in claims for small debts in 1836, and their duties were later increased by numerous statutes. The Small Debts Courts were especially useful in outlying settlements, and in Perth a similar Court of Requests was set up in 1842. Because labour was scarce in the colony's first two decades, the relationship between master and servant caused much concern. As early as March 1830 the magistrates met under Mackie's chairmanship to frame recommendations for the settlement of such disputes. An Act of 1842 provided further remedies, but the introduction of convicts in 1850 required more legislation, with heavy sentences for offences against property. Imprisonment in the stocks was stopped in 1851, the Grand Jury was abolished in 1855, and debtors were no longer imprisoned. In 1855 the first provision was made for the admission by examination of locally trained lawyers as practitioners in the Civil Court. Mackie interpreted the jurisdiction of the Civil Court very widely, although his successors, McFarland and Burt, were to doubt the court's competency in matters of equity and insolvency.

In his judgments Mackie quoted few authorities, for he worked with a meagre official library. His decision in 1836 to extradite a fugitive Tasmanian ex-official was probably wrong, and in 1853 he disagreed with a jury's decision in a case involving resumption of city land. Nevertheless he was universally respected

for his conscientious administration based on common sense and tolerance. A friendly patriarch, he was ideally suited to the conditions of the time. The position of advocate-general of South Australia was offered him by Governor Grey in 1841, but declined. In August 1842 Mackie became an unofficial nominee in the Legislative Council, although not without some criticism, which proved unjustified, that the nomination was designed to strengthen the government. When through illness he retired from his official positions in 1857, the Legislative and Executive Councils petitioned the Queen to honour him with 'some signal mark of royal favour'. The councillors spoke of his zeal, unimpeachable integrity and high intelligence. He enjoyed a generous pension until his death at Henley Park on 24 November 1860.

Mackie was also highly regarded in private life. At Whitehall, his town house in William Street near the river jetty, he had a much admired garden, and the Henley Park estate flourished largely through the work of his employee, Richard Edwards. He was on the committee of the Vineyard Society, which in the 1840s began the development of the botanical gardens in Perth now known as the Stirling Gardens. Well read, Mackie was secretary of the Western Australian Book Society in the 1830s. He played a leading part in the Western Australian Missionary Society which made an abortive attempt to found an Aboriginal mission at Upper Swan in 1836. He was a benefactor of All Saints' Church of England, which was built on land donated from the Henley Park estate, and in whose graveyard he was buried. Opened in 1839, the church was the oldest in the State still in use in 1966. A bachelor, he was survived by a cousin, John Coningham Mackie, who arrived soon after him in Western Australia to take up farming at York.

HRA (3), 6; F. C. Irwin, The state and position of Western Australia (Lond, 1835); G. F. Moore, Diary of ten years eventful life of an early settler in Western Australia (Lond, 1884); Civil Service J, 20 July 1929; E. M. Russell, 'Early lawyers of Western Australia', JRWAHS, 4 (1949-54); West Australian, 6 Mar 1937; W. S. Ferguson, Notes on early life of W. H. Mackie (Battye Lib, Perth); E. M. Russell, History of development of the legal system in WA (Battye Lib, Perth).　　　　J. H. M. HONNIBALL

McLACHLAN, CHARLES (1795?-1855), businessman, was born in Scotland and as a young man went to the West Indies, where he was employed as a plantation manager or a commercial agent by the Glasgow firm of Ewing & Reid. By 1822 he had returned to Scotland and obtained a position in the head office at Leith of the Australian Co., newly founded by a group of merchants and shipowners in Edinburgh and Leith with a view to organizing the first regular shipping service between Britain and the Australian colonies.

After the death of John Wyld, the company's principal agent in Australia, McLachlan was sent to Hobart Town to take charge. He arrived in October 1824 and, despite fierce competition in the shipping and importing business and a lack of exportable produce which would sell in Britain, he was able to carry on the company's affairs with some success until the depression of the late 1820s forced the board in Leith to wind up operations and dissolve the company in 1831-32. Under McLachlan the company brought out many hundreds of Scottish settlers, including many artisans. A prominent figure in the Hobart mercantile circle, McLachlan was appointed a justice of the peace in 1828 and was a promoter of the Hobart Exchange (1828) and of the Chamber of Commerce (1829). He became a director of the Bank of Van Diemen's Land in 1828 and was a leading member of the group which formed the Van Diemen's Land Assurance Co. in 1831-32. He acted as trustee and agent for merchants such as Walter Bethune [q.v.] and John Lord. In 1827 he joined in protests against Lieut-Governor Arthur's Press Licensing Act, and in 1828 he opposed the new import duties, though he was less critical of the administration than other merchants. In 1832 he was appointed to the Legislative Council and later served on several boards of inquiry into the colony's monetary problems. Henry Savery [q.v.] described him as 'a little undersized man, of very repelling features, a short, stout gentleman . . . whose temper was seldom ruffled, or his equanimity disturbed'.

McLachlan signed the petition for a Presbyterian minister in 1825 and later became treasurer of St Andrew's Church; he helped to found the St Andrew's Club, a welfare society, in 1826, the Mechanics' Institution in 1827 and the Agricultural and Commercial Association in 1829. Between 1825 and 1841 he obtained land grants totalling 3450 acres on the Blackman's River in the Salt Pan Plains, a whaling station at Southport, and several town allotments in Hobart. In the late 1830s he sent sheep to the Port Phillip District, had some interest in the Great Lake Co. and in 1840 bought land at Geelong. In the 1840s he was managing director of the Der-

went Bank and the Commercial Bank of Tasmania, both of which he had helped to found in 1827-29. He was a member of the Legislative Council from 1832 until 1842 when he left for England. After his return, in October 1847 he was chairman of the Hobart meeting which petitioned the British government to revoke the order for the removal of Sydney convicts to Van Diemen's Land. In 1842-46 and 1848-52 he lived in some style in Eaton Place, London, where he acted as unofficial agent for Van Diemen's Land. At Sydney in May 1829 he had married Isabella Dick, daughter of a Glasgow merchant; they had five daughters and three sons. He died in Melbourne on 16 April 1855. His widow died at Brighton, England, on 7 December 1882, aged 76.

McLachlan was one of the colony's leading businessmen, and it is doubtful if that premature Scottish experiment, the Australian Co. of Edinburgh and Leith, could have maintained its operations so long without his enterprising management in the colonies.

H. Savery, *The hermit in Van Diemen's Land*, eds C. H. Hadgraft and Margriet Roe (Brisb, 1964); Correspondence file under C. McLachlan (TA); MS cat under C. McLachlan (ML).   DAVID S. MACMILLAN

J. R. MORRIS

McLAREN, DAVID (1785-1850), company manager, was born at Perth, Scotland, the eldest son of David McLaren, a Glasgow manufacturer. He went to Glasgow College, where his parents wanted him to study for the Church of Scotland ministry. Instead he became an ardent Evangelical and seceded to the Congregationalists under Ralph Wardlaw (1779-1853). He married Mary Wingate, daughter of one of Wardlaw's deacons. In 1823 with his wife and other members he broke away on the question of infant baptism and formed a congregation of Scottish Baptists, for which he acted as elder. He was a powerful preacher and found regular Sabbath work a welcome relief from his many business anxieties.

After serving an apprenticeship with a Glasgow engineer McLaren had become an accountant and taken charge of many bankrupt estates. He also acted as an insurance and shipping agent, imported indigo and copperas, and struggled mightily for the souls of seamen in the Clyde ports. One of his clients was George Fife Angas [q.v.]; through fluctuations in the shipping trade they both suffered substantial loss, for which McLaren with over-sensitive conscience blamed himself. In 1832 he sought Angas's support in his application for the treasurership of the Glasgow Water Works at £300 a year. He was not successful, but in 1835 he accepted appointment by the South Australian Colonization Commission as emigration agent at Glasgow and Greenock, believing the post would bring 'publicity and honour'. Late that year he was also promised the Scottish agency for selling shares in the proposed South Australian Co. In July 1836 Angas's offer of the company's colonial managership caused McLaren much heart-searching. He did 'not need to leave Glasgow for a *sense of usefulness*' or for a livelihood, but his sense of debt to Angas made acceptance 'consistent with Duty'; in the same breath he complained that the salary was inadequate since his family must remain in Scotland.

With a salary of £600 and a seven year contract McLaren sailed in the *South Australian* and arrived at Kingscote, Kangaroo Island, in April 1837. Although the company's first colonial manager, Samuel Stephens [q.v.], scandalized McLaren by his conviviality and lack of piety he was not suspended until November. Thereafter because he knew his own limitations McLaren continued to exploit Stephens's skill as a judge of land and livestock. By 1841, in spite of bad luck in the ballot for country sections, McLaren had secured for the company more than 36,000 acres, assets that produced dividends for nearly a century. In other matters McLaren sedulously concentrated the company's investment. He gradually withdrew from whaling and shipping, regulated farm tenancies, and by hard dealing with overlanders stocked the company's land with cattle and sheep. By 1839 the Kingscote headquarters had been moved to Adelaide, where McLaren shrewdly began a road to the port and a wharf which bore his name for a hundred years.

McLaren's major contribution to the colony and the company was in banking. By cautious but well-placed loans he gained a commanding hold over many leading settlers and merchants and indirectly controlled much of Governor Gawler's heavy public expenditure. In the boom which followed McLaren carefully kept the company's land and trading accounts apart from its banking business, and with the onset of depression in 1840 was able to separate the company and bank in a manner that saved both from serious loss.

Through his canny deals McLaren became intensely unpopular but he found solace in religious activity. He acted as lay pastor to a group of Baptists and often preached to other congregations. Although he made generous loans to Dissenting chapels and schools he was the first to inveigh publicly against pretensions that the Church of England was established by law in the colony, and he discouraged attempts to found a Roman Catholic Church. By his unrelenting opposition to sins of the flesh he drove many less resolute men to excesses of frivolity and intemperance, yet despite his Calvinism he bitterly opposed capital punishment and believed in the redemption of Aboriginals. By business and belief he did his best to make Adelaide a strictly Protestant Evangelical preserve.

McLaren was offered the London management of the company when it was separated from its bank. Farewelled by more than a hundred leading colonists at a lavish luncheon he left Adelaide in January 1841 in the *John Pirie*. In Sydney his arrival was greeted by sneers from the press that the utopian experiment in South Australia had lamentably failed. In astute replies McLaren declared his esteem for Gawler, blamed the Colonization Commission for the colony's bankruptcy, and predicted that all public debts would be paid when South Australia became a Crown colony. He did not reveal that the company's loans to government were covered by special agreements or that its private debts were more than adequately secured by mortgages. In March McLaren sailed from Sydney in the *Louisa Campbell*. In London he was joined by his family from Glasgow. Though he suffered from 'impaired breathing' he managed the company's business with competence and profit and did much valuable work for the colony. He gave convincing evidence on the peculiar needs of Australian shipping to the select committee whose report led to repeal of the Navigation Acts in 1849. He died in London on 22 June 1850 and his gravestone proclaimed him 'steadfast, unmovable'.

Of his six children, the youngest, Alexander (1826-1910), became an outstanding Baptist minister at Manchester.

E. T. McLaren, *Dr McLaren of Manchester* (Lond, 1911); A. Grenfell Price, *Founders & pioneers of South Australia* (Adel, 1929); D. Pike, *Paradise of Dissent* (Melb, 1957); Angas papers (SAA).

McLEAY, ALEXANDER (1767-1848), public servant and entomologist, was born on 24 June 1767 in Ross-shire, Scotland, the son of William Macleay, provost of

Wick and deputy-lieutenant of Caithness. He was descended from an ancient family which came from Ulster; at the Reformation the family had substantial landholdings in Scotland, but by loyalty to the Stuarts suffered severe losses after the battle of Culloden.

Alexander had a classical education and went to London, where he became a partner of William Sharp as a wine merchant. On 15 October 1791 at St Dunstan's Church, London, he married Elizabeth, daughter of James Barclay, and in 1795 became chief clerk in the prisoners of war office. After the outbreak of war this office was linked with the Transport Board, of which he became head of the correspondence department and by 1806 secretary; when the board was abolished in 1815 he retired on a pension of £750. In these years McLeay acquired an enduring interest in entomology. He was elected as a fellow by the Linnean Society in 1794 and served as its secretary in 1798-1825. In 1809 he became a fellow of the Royal Society and joined its council in 1824. Among other public positions he was also a director of the British Fisheries Society and was associated with Thomas Telford's engineering projects in the north of Scotland. He prepared a monograph on the genus *Paussus*, and a variety of *Bocconia* was named *MacLeaya cordata* in his honour by Robert Brown [q.v.]. He also established the McLeay Collection, beginning with insects and enlarging it with varied purchases and acquisitions from Brazil, India, North Africa and Australia. By 1825 he was said to have the finest and most extensive collection of any private individual; as a noted scientist he was a corresponding member of several European societies and as a prominent public servant had served on many boards and given evidence in 1812 to the select committee on transportation.

In 1824 Earl Bathurst decided to end the friction between Governor Brisbane and Major Goulburn [q.v.] in the administration of New South Wales by recalling both officers and replacing them with General Darling and an experienced civilian assistant. After some persuasion by Bathurst McLeay was induced to accept appointment on 14 June 1825 as colonial secretary of New South Wales, at a salary of £2000. He also agreed to surrender the fees of his office on condition that his pension from the Transport Board was continued, though the British Treasury insisted on its payment from colonial funds.

With his wife, six daughters and his collection McLeay sailed in the *Marquis of Hastings* and arrived at Sydney in January 1826. Although John Macarthur junior had feared that he was too old and that his private pursuits would interfere with the duties of his office, McLeay was soon working twelve hours a day in conducting all the official correspondence, acting as 'the general medium of Communication' between governor and colonists and assisting in countless other details of government. In March he was made a magistrate and in July a member of the Executive and Legislative Councils. He became a member of the Board of General Purposes through which the colony's public administration was thoroughly reorganized and of the Land Board which implemented new regulations for the granting of land and the assignment of convict servants. He also served on many other public committees and inquiries, and became president of the Australian Museum, the Benevolent Society and the Sydney Dispensary, and vice-patron of the Agricultural Society. In 1826 he began a long association with the Subscription Library by chairing its first meeting; seventeen years later as president of its board he laid the foundation stone of the Public Library. A staunch Tory, he got on well with Darling, who commended him to the Colonial Office for labouring 'heartily and cheerfully, without intermission', and gave him such land grants as public servants were then entitled to. These included 54 acres at Elizabeth Bay and 2560 acres in Argyle County, at Byalla, to which he added 863 acres by purchase. At Brownlow Hill he bought 2000 acres in 1829, and 1663 acres of the old government cattle station were reserved for him by Darling and purchased in 1841. McLeay bought another reserve of 2560 acres at Ulladulla in 1840 and later he held the rights to several runs on the Murrumbidgee and Richmond Rivers.

To avoid repetition of earlier friction in high places in the colony McLeay had been specifically instructed to 'have no pretension to controul [the governor's] Judgement or to direct [his] decision in any particular case'. He obeyed this order but inevitably shared in the growing unpopularity of Darling. In 1826 when Sudds and Thompson were heavily ironed and drummed out of their regiment McLeay's veracity was doubted and his letter to the *Australian* was bitterly criticized. Next year his prominence in the unsuccessful attempt to restrain the 'Rascally News Papers' brought even more outspoken criticism and in Darling's presence he asked Chief Justice Forbes [q.v.] personally to hear a libel suit against the *Australian*, hoping thereby to persuade

Forbes to identify himself with the government. With judicial propriety Forbes rejected the suggestion and the case was dropped, but soon afterwards, when R. Wardell and W. C. Wentworth [qq.v.] sought to file a criminal information against McLeay, Forbes ruled that no public benefit could arise from it. On 27 September 1828 in the *Sydney Monitor* E. S. Hall [q.v.] took McLeay to task for accepting his Transport Board pension and choice land grants for himself and his family and doubling the costs of his department, and in March 1829 Wentworth's long impeachment of Darling purported to show the colonial secretary as the governor's accessory in a régime of 'fraud, falsehood and Cruelty'. These and other charges were carried to London and aired there by Joseph Hume. Although they were vigorously denied by Darling it was rumoured in Sydney that both Darling and McLeay were to be recalled. In the event Darling served his six year term and on his departure in 1831 reported so warmly on McLeay's competence and loyalty that the Colonial Office did not cut his salary in the general retrenchment after the Whigs took office, although Goderich ordered that McLeay's official residence was to be turned into government offices and that he must pay rent until his own house was built.

Under Sir Richard Bourke McLeay continued to work zealously. He shared the Whig governor's tolerance of Wesleyans and Quakers, but not his favourable attitude to emancipists, whom McLeay thought 'absolutely unfit to sit on any Jury on account of their ignorance and their drunken and immoral habits'. The press continued to criticize him as leader of the Tory or exclusive faction and in the Legislative Council members protested at his pension being charged to colonial funds; Bourke reported to London that strong and widespread feelings against it were revived each year when the estimates were debated. In July 1835, wearied by pinpricks but unyielding, McLeay told the council, 'it is not probable that I shall be long in office'. Bourke promptly reported to the Colonial Office that he supposed McLeay would publicly announce his retirement within a year, and nominated his own son-in-law, Deas Thomson [q.v.], to replace him, arguing that the reputation and personal ease of any governor were much influenced by the ability and confidence of his colonial secretary. In London Glenelg gazetted Thomson's appointment and sent instructions to Bourke to allow McLeay, in consideration of his long public service, to name his own date for retirement. Before this dispatch reached Sydney McLeay heard of Thomson's promotion from friends in England. At his request he was shown the relevant letters and then insisted that his words to council had been misrepresented and that he had no intention of retiring. At that time the colony was in uproar over the Bourke's National Schools bill. McLeay's determined hostility to it in and outside the Legislative Council was, according to Bourke, the cause of their final rupture. Notified that Thomson would assume duty in 1837 McLeay quitted his office on 2 January under protest. In bitter letters Bourke avowed a sincere respect for McLeay's private character but, to cover his own blunder, reported to the Colonial Office that he suspected McLeay of 'indifference and delays and perhaps the infidelities of office' in his release of official papers to the press; 'his constant intercourse and intimacy with the principal opponents of my Government may have led the Colonists to believe that its secrets were not best preserved nor its objects promoted in his office'. In return McLeay denied the truth of these suspicions but, while admitting that he had openly opposed the governor on three other issues beside National education, declared that he deserved credit for his moderation. The local press divided on the question, some supporting Bourke, others McLeay. The *Monitor* half-heartedly took Bourke's part 'on account of *political consistency*', dredged up unhappy memories of Darling's vengeful spirit, but concluded that honours were even.

In 1838, after Bourke was recalled, McLeay reprinted with more documents his pamphlet, *Correspondence between Major-Gen. Sir Richard Bourke . . . and Alexander McLeay*, first published in 1836 in Sydney. In April 1838 he sent copies of it to Governor Gipps and six months later claimed a compensation of £4000 for injurious misrepresentation by Bourke. To settle this claim the Colonial Office recommended a pension of £250 for McLeay. A majority in the Legislative Council thought this sum 'totally inadequate as a compensation for his loss of office' and proposed that he be given a gratuity equal to two years of his earlier salary. However, the Colonial Office accepted Gipps's recommendation that McLeay should receive £1750 in commutation of his colonial pension.

Meanwhile McLeay had completed his house at Elizabeth Bay in 1837 and his garden became famous for its rare plants. He continued to send specimens to the Royal and Linnean Societies, experimented in horticulture at Brownlow Hill, gave active support to the Sydney Botanic Garden and found time to serve on charitable committees and missionary societies. In 1842 he was presented with a silver 'candelabrum' by more than five hundred leading colonists to mark his 'great moral worth . . . integrity, ability and zeal'. It was inscribed with his family motto *Spes anchora vitae*, and was later presented to the New South Wales parliament by his descendants.

In November 1842 he stood for election to the first City Council in Sydney but was unsuccessful. In July 1843 he was returned for Gloucester, Macquarie and Stanley to the first part-elective Legislative Council. In August he was chosen as Speaker, much to the annoyance of Wentworth who commented severely on his age and debility, but his fellow conservatives considered him the elder statesman of the council. The Speaker's salary had been fixed at £750 but McLeay received only £500 because of the pension he had commuted. Another £250 was deducted from his Transport Board pension, the payment of which had reverted to the British Treasury in 1837. When McLeay resigned as Speaker in May 1846 the Treasury continued this deduction, but the Legislative Council appealed to the Queen and McLeay's full pension was restored with compensation for reductions while he was Speaker.

In December 1844 Governor Gipps had considered McLeay eligible for an order of merit, but regretted that he was understood to be in 'pecuniary embarrassment'. This was true, for he had found it difficult to reduce his costs after the loss of his salary as colonial secretary. Despite high prices for wool all his properties were mortgaged and only the arrival of his eldest son, William Sharp [q.v.], in 1839 saved him from insolvency in the depression of the early 1840s. William took over his father's liabilities and introduced the family to measures of economy which included the subdivision and sale of most of the Elizabeth Bay property. In April 1846 McLeay advertised for sale his library, 4000 of the 'best works on Theology, Biography, History, Botany, Medicine, Arts, Sciences, Mathematics, Education, and every branch of polite literature'. After his wife died on 13 August 1847, McLeay spent much time visiting his married daughters. After a carriage accident he died on 18 July 1848; his funeral at St James's Church, Sydney, was attended by many government officers.

Of his seventeen children, William Sharp was a noted naturalist, George [q.v.] an explorer and politician, and James Robert (1811-1892) secretary of the commission for the suppression of the slave trade in Cape Colony. Several of his daughters, with magnificent weddings, married into established colonial families : Margaret (b. 1802) to Archibald Clunes Innes [q.v.] in 1829; Christina Susan (b. 1799) to Colonel William Dumaresq [q.v.] in 1830; and Barbara Isabella (b. 1797) to P. L. Campbell [q.v.] in 1834. Through Rosa Roberta, who married Arthur Pooley Onslow in 1832, the Elizabeth Bay property passed into the hands of the Macarthur-Onslow family.

Alexander McLeay's reputation suffered from his zeal in carrying out the mandates of Darling and from his opposition to Bourke, and his unshakeable conservatism was later condemned by a few illiberal historians, although his competence and ability as a public servant were acknowledged by responsible contemporaries in London and Sydney. Long before he died public feeling had taken a favourable direction towards him and on his retirement as Speaker many grateful tributes were paid to him even by his former enemies, including Wentworth. He was loved and revered by his friends and inspired the loyalty of all who worked closely with him. As a man of science his name was respected far beyond the borders of New South Wales. His share in encouraging Australian exploration has been underestimated, though a river, mountain range, island and many streets bear his name. His scientific collection, augmented by his sons and nephew, was transferred to the Macleay Museum at the University of Sydney in 1890.

A portrait is in the Dixson Gallery, Sydney.

HRA (1), 11-26; J. J. Fletcher, 'The society's heritage from the Macleays', *Procs, Linnean Soc NSW*, 45 (1920); *Sydney Gazette*, 5 Jan 1826, 2 Jan, 7 Mar 1828; *Sydney Monitor*, 18, 20 Jan, 6 Mar 1837; *Australian*, 8 June 1841; *SMH*, 4 Nov 1842, 19 July, 2 Aug 1843; MS cat under A. McLeay (ML).

MACLEAY, SIR GEORGE (1809-1891), pastoralist and explorer, was born in London, the third son of Alexander McLeay [q.v.]. The McLeays, an old Caithness landed family, were connected by marriage with the Roses of Kilravock, and through this alliance with George Rose, Pitt's secretary of the treasury. George was educated at Westminster School, and came to Australia in the *Eliza* in 1827. The 1828 census recorded that he was a landowner with 3500 acres near Camden, but this was

probably the Brownlow Hill estate, owned
by his father.

In November 1829 George Macleay
accompanied Charles Sturt [q.v.] on his
expedition to the Murrumbidgee and the
Murray. He went 'as a companion, rather
than as an assistant', taking the place of
Hamilton Hume [q.v.], and he shared in
the hardships of that epic journey to the
sea and in the credit that redounded to the
discoverers of important waterways and
valuable tracts of good country. Sturt had
a high opinion of him, and wrote that
'amidst these distresses . . . [in April 1830]
Macleay preserved his good humour and
did his utmost to lighten the toil and to
cheer the men'. Macleay and Sturt became
close friends on this expedition, and thereafter kept up a regular correspondence.

From 1831 to 1859, except for a few
months in Italy in 1843-44, Macleay lived
on the Brownlow Hill estate, which he
farmed with considerable ability. He had
been granted 2560 acres for his services
with Sturt and in 1831-32 he established
a station on the Fish River, between Goulburn and Yass. In 1837 he formed a station
on the south side of the Murrumbidgee,
known as Toganmain; by 1857 its 212,000
acres adjoined the group of stations centring on Kerarbury owned by his cousin,
William John Macleay, who in partnership
with the Clarke brothers probably looked
after George Macleay's pastoral interests in
the district. Like many other settlers Macleay was hard hit in the depression of the
early 1840s, but he was clear of debt by
1850. By the 1860s occupation of his Murrumbidgee lands had made him very
wealthy. Apart from his inheritance from
his father, including Brownlow Hill, he
was the principal beneficiary under the will
of his brother William Sharp Macleay
[q.v.], from whom he inherited Elizabeth
Bay House, built by his father about 1836,
and the fifty acres of grounds and gardens
around it that were such a notable show-
place at the time.

In 1859 Macleay decided to live abroad.
He was in England until about 1870, and
thereafter in the south of France, whence
he returned briefly to Sydney in 1873 to
wind up his affairs. He travelled widely in
Europe and lived in style, winning repute
as a bon-vivant and owning a steam yacht
in which he voyaged among the Greek
islands, along the coasts of Turkey and
Syria, and to the northern shores of the
Black Sea. He was a prominent member of
the Australian circle in London which included such men as Sir Charles Nicholson,
W. C. Wentworth [qq.v.] and Francis
Merewether. In 1879 he set out on a trip

to the Nile and Jerusalem, accompanied by
two nieces, and Nicholson wrote to Edward
Deas Thomson [q.v.] in Sydney: 'Macleay's love for locomotion is, considering his
time of life, remarkable'.

His interests were wide throughout his
life, and they included politics, as befitted
the son of Alexander McLeay. In October
1831 he had signed the farewell address to
Governor Darling, and in 1836 the petition to Governor Bourke on education. In
1842 he was a member of the association
for obtaining permission to import coolies
from India, and in 1846 he was appointed
a magistrate. He was appointed a road
trust commissioner for Narellan in December 1849, and in September 1851 was elected
for the Murrumbidgee district to the Legislative Council, holding the seat until the
dissolution of February 1856; after responsible government he represented the same
constituency in the Legislative Assembly
from April 1856 to the dissolution of April
1859. In 1857 he declined appointment in
H. W. Parker's short-lived ministry. Like
W. J. Macleay, he was identified with the
opponents of Cowper and Parkes. A close
personal friend of his neighbour at Camden,
James Macarthur [q.v.] and of Macarthur's
brother, Sir Edward, he shared their conservative outlook in politics and corresponded
regularly with both. In 1855-60 he advocated the clearing of the Murray and
Murrumbidgee Rivers as an aid to
navigation.

Macleay shared the interest of his family
in the sciences. From his father he inherited
a keen enthusiasm for horticulture and he
was a zoologist of more than amateur
status. In 1836 he was appointed to the
committee of the Australian Museum and
Botanical Garden, and later became a
trustee of the museum. He was elected a
fellow of the Linnean Society of London,
and a member of its council in 1864. He
contributed specimens to the collections of
his brother and his cousin, which are now
housed in the Macleay Museum in the
University of Sydney. In 1846 he presented
fossils from the Murrumbidgee, collected
by himself, to the Australian Museum, and
he appears to have done other field work,
both on the Murrumbidgee and on his
European and near-East travels. In the early
1870s he assisted Sir Richard Owen with
the compilation of his book on the fossil
mammals of Australia, published in 1877.
Keenly interested in the arts as well as the
sciences, Macleay was responsible for recovering a fine fourth-century Greek statue
of Hermes from a river bed in Asia Minor.
This was presented by him to Nicholson,
who sent it out to the museum he had

founded in the University of Sydney. It is now known as 'the Nicholson Hermes'.

Macleay was appointed C.M.G. in 1869 and K.C.M.G. in 1875. He was a tall sturdy man with red hair; the Rufus River in south-western New South Wales was named by Sturt in his honour. He died at Mentone, France, on 24 June 1891.

Macleay was married twice, first to Barbara St Clair Innes in 1842 and, after her death in 1869, to Augusta Sams of Tasmania in 1890. His widow died in 1919. There were no children.

Hogan papers (ML); Sir William Macleay papers (Archives, Univ Syd); Riley papers (ML).   DAVID S. MACMILLAN

MACLEAY, WILLIAM SHARP (1792-1865), scholar and naturalist, was born on 21 July 1792 in London, the eldest son of Alexander McLeay [q.v.]. He was educated at Westminster School, where he distinguished himself as a classical scholar, and in 1809 proceeded to Trinity College, Cambridge (B.A., 1814; M.A., 1818). In 1818 he was appointed attaché to the British embassy in Paris and secretary to the board for liquidating British claims on the French government. In 1825 he became British commissioner of arbitration to the conjoint British and Spanish Court of Commission in Havana for the abolition of the slave trade; in 1830 he became commissary judge in that court, and by 1833 he was judge to the Mixed Tribunal of Justice. He remained in Havana until 1836, when he retired with a pension of £900. He arrived in March 1839 in Sydney where he spent the remainder of his life living at his father's home, Elizabeth Bay House, which he inherited in 1848.

His principal interest was natural history, for which he shared his father's enthusiasm. In Paris he had become acquainted with several distinguished scientists, including Georges Cuvier (1769-1832). Macleay published in London Horae Entomologicae; or, Essays on the annulose animals, pts 1-2 (1819-21) and another useful work, Annulosa Javanica; or an Attempt to Illustrate the Natural Affinities and Analogies of the Insects collected in Java by T. Horsfield, no. 1 (London, 1825). He continued his scientific observations and researches while in Cuba, and by 1837 he was sufficiently well known as a scientist to be elected to the councils of the Linnean Society of London and of the Zoological Society. At the meeting of the British Association for the Advancement of Science in Liverpool in September 1837 he was presi-dent of the section on natural history. In 1838 he published in London Illustrations of the Annulosa of South Africa and in Sydney he quickly developed a keen interest in the natural history of Australia, especially in the marine fauna in and around Port Jackson. The site of Elizabeth Bay House on the waterfront east of Sydney was convenient for such studies, and from about 1840 he began to build up a very large collection of specimens. Later he returned to his original scientific interest, entomology, and made a large collection of Australian insects. He was chiefly interested in the philosophical aspects of zoology, in investigating, as J. J Fletcher put it 'natural affinities and analogies, and in endeavouring to discover the natural system of classification'. His theories were hailed by his scientific friends, the ornithologists Vigors and Swainson, and he undoubtedly showed no small degree of originality. Professor Alfred Newton in his article on ornithology in the ninth edition of the Encyclopaedia Britannica, while critical of Macleay's theories, referred to him as 'a man of real genius'.

It was not only along the line of independent research and inquiry that Macleay's scientific bent developed, for he also interested many others in natural history, especially his cousin William John Macleay, and to a lesser extent, his brother George [q.v.]. He was keenly interested in the Australian Museum, and served on its committee before becoming a trustee in 1841, a position which he held until 1862. He was largely responsible for framing and introducing the Act establishing and endowing the museum. In his time Elizabeth Bay House became a regular meeting place for Sydney men with scientific interests, and visiting scientists were invariably entertained there, a tradition carried on by W. J. Macleay. Botany and geology were other fields in which he was absorbed from time to time, and in the 1850s the gardens at Elizabeth Bay became famous for the exotic shrubs and plants cultivated there under his supervision

Macleay's interests were not narrowly scientific. He was a man of broad culture and worldly experience, a fine classical scholar and an accomplished conversationalist. His circle of friends included Robert Lowe, Charles Nicholson, James Macarthur [qq.v.], and most of the intellectual circle in Sydney. Throughout his life he was studious, and he had the reputation of being shy and retiring, but his wide range of friends and acquaintances seems to belie this, and the belief may have grown up as a result of his gradual withdrawal into seclusion after 1860, when his health began to fail, partly as a result of his ten years residence in Cuba. Never openly involved in political controversies, he was widely respected in the Sydney community. For some years in the 1850s he was a member of the National Board of Education, and he served on the Executive Council under Sir William Denison in 1855.

Macleay was a fellow of the Royal Society and a well-known contributor to various scientific journals. According to his obituary notice in the Linnean Society of London *Proceedings*, 1864-65, his *Horae Entomologicae* 'contained some of the most important speculations as to the affinities or relations of various groups of animals to each other ever offered to the world, and of which it is almost impossible to overrate the suggestive value'.

Macleay died at Elizabeth Bay House on 26 January 1865. He never married and the heir to his estate and to Elizabeth Bay House was his brother, George. W. J. Macleay inherited his library and collection of specimens on the understanding that the bequest would be deposited in a suitable institution. In 1890 it was transferred to the Macleay Museum at the University of Sydney.

P. P. King, *Narrative of a survey of the intertropical and western coasts of Australia,* 1-2 (Lond, 1827); Linnean Soc NSW, *Macleay memorial volume,* ed J. J. Fletcher (Syd, 1893); *Calcutta J of Natural Hist,* July 1841; *Annals of Natural Hist,* 8 (1841), 9 (1842); *Tas J of Natural Science,* 3 (1849); Macleay papers (Archives, Univ Syd).

DAVID S. MACMILLAN

McMILLAN, ANGUS (1810-1865), explorer and pioneer pastoralist, was born on 14 August 1810 at Glenbrittle, Isle of Skye, Scotland, the fourth son of Ewan McMillan. He emigrated to New South Wales from Greenock in the *Minerva,* his journal on this voyage indicating intensely religious, narrow and intolerant views. He arrived in January 1838 with letters of introduction to Captain Lachlan Macalister, who made him a manager on Clifton station near Camden. McMillan was 'disgusted at the inhuman treatment of the convict labourers', and requested a transfer away from the settled colony. Macalister appointed him manager at Currawang in the Maneroo (Monaro) country and he began there in February 1839. In this year he learned much bushcraft, befriended Aboriginal tribes and after an eventful journey in May climbed Mount McLeod (The Hay-

stack) and glimpsed the plain and lakes country of Gippsland. On this journey his Aboriginal guide, Jimmy Gabber, attempted to murder him in his sleep and, realizing that the Aboriginal was terrified of the strange country, McMillan turned north to Omeo after nine days although he had provisions for six weeks.

Macalister, in the drought-stricken colony, received the news of prospective new pastures with enthusiasm and agreed to finance an expedition to explore the plains and seek a route to Corner Inlet from which stock and produce could be shipped.

With convict assistants, McMillan brought a bullock wagon from Currawang to Omeo in August 1839 and set up a station at Numbla Munjie (Ensay) with Monaro cattle and equipment ready for the summer expedition. After an abortive start in December 1839, he reinforced his party with two Omeo Aboriginals, Cabone Johnny and Friday, and moved down the Tambo River on 10 January 1840. His other men were Alan Cameron, Matthew Macalister and Edward Bath. They experienced little trouble, and Aboriginals did not attack them, but spoiled beef limited the explorations and lack of food forced a return after the Thomson River had been crossed. A few more miles would have given McMillan a view of the port essential to the new country. McMillan crossed the Tambo, Nicholson, Mitchell, Perry, Avon, Macalister and Thomson Rivers, realized the possibilities of the lakes system and reported enthusiastically to Captain Macalister on the quality of the country. In 1840 McMillan set up a station at Nuntin near the mouth of the Avon River for Macalister and selected his own property, Bushy Park, farther up-stream. He made two unsuccessful attempts, under leaders appointed by Macalister, to reach Corner Inlet, but finally found the way through the range with Tom Macalister and reached the port on 13 February 1841.

In March 1840 P. E. Strzelecki [q.v.] led his party through Numbla Munjie and, after Matthew Macalister had guided them, they followed McMillan's tracks through the new country and Strzelecki gave his own titles to salient features already named by McMillan. In his report to Governor Gipps and in a circulated pamphlet, Strzelecki made no mention that he had followed another man's trail and much of the credit properly due to McMillan was denied him. The two never met and McMillan remained hostile to 'the foreign imposter' until he died. He had called the area Caledonia Australis but Strzelecki's title Gippsland, in honour of the governor was preferred, although McMillan's other names were officially adopted.

McMillan settled at Bushy Park and until 1860 lived according to the social standards of the day. He engaged in the cattle trade to Hobart, grew wheat, bred sheep for wool and tallow, and at one time held leases over five properties. He smoked a pipe, enjoyed a convivial drink and raced horses against his neighbours' favourites. He entertained widely and was for many years president of the Gippsland Caledonian Society. His home became a haven for newly-arrived Scots to learn the language and aspects of the new life. McMillan took a sympathetic interest in the welfare of the Aboriginals. He was elected as the first representative for South Gippsland to the Victorian Legislative Assembly on 22 September 1859 but resigned after fourteen months. McMillan had invested heavily in cattle and his properties were deeply mortgaged. Disastrous fires and unsuccessful speculations depleted his resources and all his properties except Tabberabbera passed to mortgagees in October 1861. Frustration, disappointment and nagging illness were to accompany him through his last years.

In 1864, to his obvious delight, he was offered the leadership of the government's Alpine Expedition to open tracks in the mining areas of Omeo, Dargo and Matlock. He recruited his party at Stratford, and near the Crooked River in March his men discovered a rich gold deposit which they named the Pioneer. A rush to the area resulted in McMillan losing most of his original party by the end of May and he had difficulty in engaging new hands. Nevertheless over 220 miles of track were cut by the Alpine Expedition in the next twelve months. The work was arduous and at times McMillan blazed the route crawling on hands and knees through thick scrub. Early in 1865 his health deteriorated rapidly, he could not hold his men and he found difficulty in administration; details of his expenses were challenged by officials, who were unduly slow in approving wages and provision allowances. In May 1865 the party was disbanded and McMillan set out alone to complete the last task: blazing a trail from Dargo to the Moroka River. One of his pack-horses fell and rolled on him causing severe internal injuries. He set out for Bairnsdale but reached only as far as Iguana Creek, where he died in Gilleo's Hotel a few hours later on 18 May 1865.

He was buried in Sale cemetery after a Presbyterian service. He was survived by his wife Christina, née MacDougald, whom he had married in 1857, and by two sons, Ewan and Angus. They were left without sufficient means and a month after his death the government voted £2000 for their benefit.

McMillan pioneered Gippsland and spent the rest of his life contributing to its welfare. His popularity was testimony to the change wrought by the country in the narrow, bigoted young man who arrived in the colony. He died while extending the boundaries of the province he had discovered. Although he received little wealth from Gippsland and resented the credit given to Strzelecki as an explorer of the new district, his journals and letters and those of his contemporaries reveal him as courageous, strong and generous, with a great love for his adopted country.

A portrait in oils is in the shire of Alberton chambers, Yarram, Victoria.

T. F. Bride (ed), *Letters from Victorian pioneers* (Melb, 1899); R. Mackay, *Recollections of early Gippsland goldfields* (Traralgon, 1916); C. Daley, 'Angus McMillan', *VHM*, 11 (1926-27); Shillinglaw papers (La Trobe Lib, Melb).   THEO WEBSTER

MACONOCHIE, ALEXANDER (1787-1860), naval officer, geographer, and penal reformer, was born on 11 February 1787 at Edinburgh, the son of Alexander M'Konochie (the son adopted the present spelling in 1832) who was a legal agent and in 1791 succeeded Adam Smith on the Board of Customs for Scotland.

Brought up by a kinsman, Allan Maconochie, Lord Meadowbank, he received some legal training, but in 1803 entered the navy as a first-class volunteer, becoming a midshipman in 1804. He was on active service during the Napoleonic wars, and in 1810 was a lieutenant on the brig *Grasshopper* when it ran aground and surrendered to the Dutch. Handed over to the French, Maconochie was held prisoner of war at Verdun until Napoleon's abdication in 1814. He rejoined the navy and saw active service in the war against the United States at the capture of Washington and the assaults on New Orleans. After being in command of two vessels as a lieutcommander, he was paid off in 1815 and placed on the reserve list. In 1855 he was retired from the navy with the rank of captain. Between 1815 and 1828 he lived in Edinburgh, where in 1822 he married Mary Hutton-Browne. Seven children, of whom two girls and four boys survived, were born of the union.

Maconochie had not visited the Pacific Ocean, but he was interested in its countries, and in 1818 published A *Summary View of the Statistics and Existing Commerce of the Principal Shores of the Pacific Ocean, etc.* (London). About 1828 he settled in London with his family. He was one of the founders and the first secretary of the Royal Geographical Society in 1830, and in 1833 became the first professor of geography at the University of London. In 1836, as private secretary to his friend, Lieut-Governor Sir John Franklin, Maconochie left England for Hobart Town.

This appointment was intended to lead to a more important position in the administration of the colony, but the plan miscarried. He was soon in conflict with John Montagu [q.v.]. Maconochie wrote a *Report on the State of Prison Discipline in Van Diemen's Land . . .* (London, 1838), at the request of the English Society for the Improvement of Prison Discipline, and with the approval of the British authorities. It was sent by Franklin (who was aware that it was condemnatory of the system) to the Colonial Office, which transmitted it to the Home Office. With accompanying documents, it was published as a parliamentary paper and used by the Molesworth committee on transportation (1837-38). There is no justification for criticisms levelled at Maconochie over the publication of this report, but the storm it aroused in Hobart left Franklin with little alternative but to dismiss him. Maconochie claimed then, and often thereafter, that he arrived in Van Diemen's Land with no preconceptions against the convict system and no acquaintance with penological theories. This was true but, though he seems to have forgotten it, it is also true that in his 1818 work, A *Summary View*, he had formulated several propositions about 'penal science' in a discussion of the penal colony of New South Wales. Although some of these were contrary to the views he advanced from 1837 onwards, two remained always basic in his proposals: punishment should not be vindictively conceived but should aim at the reform of the convict, and a convict's sentence should be indeterminate, with release depending not on the lapse of time but on his own industry and exertions during incarceration. R. Gerard Ward considers this discussion in A *Summary View* scarcely sufficient to invalidate Maconochie's assertion that before his arrival in Van Diemen's Land he had 'not previously studied the subject of punishment'.

At the suggestion of the Molesworth committee Maconochie was appointed superintendent of the penal settlement at Norfolk Island and took up his duties in March 1840. Recalled by the Colonial Office he left the island in February 1844. During that period he formulated and applied most of the principles on which modern penology is based. Contrary to what is often asserted, the period of his administration was peaceful; on an unexpected visit to the island in March 1843 Governor Sir George Gipps found 'good order everywhere to prevail' (H.R.A. (1), 22, 617). Two grave happenings are sometimes held against Maconochie; one, an attempted seizure by convicts of the brig *Governor Phillip* in June 1842, resulting in six deaths and four executions, was not ascribable to any fault of his but to the carelessness of those in charge of the ship; and the other, a revolt which led to the execution of thirteen convicts, occurred in July 1846, more than two years after he had given up command. His claims that a high percentage of the convicts he discharged from the island did not offend again seem well founded.

Maconochie's notions of 'penal science' rested on the beliefs that cruelty debases both victim and the society inflicting it, and that punishment for crime should not be vindictive but designed to strengthen a prisoner's desire and capacity to observe social constraints. Criminal punishments of imprisonment should consist of task and not time sentences; instead of being sentenced to a fixed period of imprisonment, an offender should be sentenced to be imprisoned until he had performed an ascertainable period of labour, which should be measured by the number of 'marks of commendation' he earned, the scale of marks being devised to encourage habits of industry and frugality. A sentence should be served in progressive stages, one of which involved membership of a working party where each was held responsible for the conduct of the others. Cruel punishments and degrading conditions should not be imposed and convicts should not be deprived of self-respect. Although his proposals were commonly derided, they were favourably regarded by James Backhouse and G. W. Walker [qq.v.], and by Alfred Stephen.

Maconochie returned to England in 1844, but though officially it was insisted that the recall was in no sense unfavourable to his character (H.R.A. (1), 22, 691), there was no disposition in the Colonial Office to employ him. Charles Dickens thought well of his system and recommended it to Angela Burdett-Coutts, though he was mistaken in asserting (E. Johnson, ed., *Letters from Charles Dickens to Angela Burdett-Coutts*, 103) that Maconochie was appointed in 1847 to carry out his own proposal for using convict labour to construct a harbour at Weymouth. Maconochie expounded his theories in many pamphlets, and in 1846 he published *Crime and Punishment, The Mark System, framed to mix Persuasion with Punishment, and make their Effect improving, yet their Operation severe*, which has exercised an immense influence on the development of penology.

In 1849, through the good offices of his friend Matthew Davenport Hill, Q.C., recorder of Birmingham, he became governor of the new prison at Birmingham. He was unjustly dismissed in 1851, and in 1854 a Royal Commission, appointed because of the suicide of three young prisoners, which occurred after his dismissal, strongly censured his successor, Lieutenant Austin, and, while conceding Maconochie's humanity and benevolence, criticized him for resorting to illegal punishments. The events leading to the Royal Commission are the subject of Charles Reade's novel, *It's Never too late to Mend* (1856), in which Maconochie appears briefly as 'Captain O'Connor'. After dismissal he underwent a grave illness, but despite impaired health he continued to campaign for penal reform until his death at Morden, Surrey, on 25 October 1860.

Maconochie was a pioneer in penal reform, and suffered the fate of men in advance of their times. His concepts and many of his practical measures are now the basis of Western penal systems, and they were largely adopted in the *Declaration of Principles* at Cincinnati, United States of America, in 1870, embodying the fundamentals of modern penology. His contributions as a geographer before 1836 were, according to R. Gerard Ward, 'far ahead of those of most of his contemporaries'.

J. V. Barry, *Alexander Maconochie of Norfolk Island* (Melb, 1958); H. Mannheim (ed), *Pioneers in criminology* (Lond, 1960); P. Collins, *Dickens and crime* (Lond, 1962); *JRGS*, 31 (1861); S. C. McCulloch, 'Sir George Gipps and Captain Alexander Maconochie', *Hist Studies*, no 28, May 1957; R. A. Daly, 'Archdeacon McEncroe on Norfolk Island, 1838-1842', *A'sian Catholic Record*, 36 (1959); R. Gerard Ward, 'Captain Alexander Maconochie, R.N., K.H., 1787-1860', *Geog J*, 126 (1960).   JOHN V. BARRY

MACQUARIE, ELIZABETH HENRIETTA (1778-1835), was the youngest daughter of John Campbell of Airds, Scotland, and a relative of the earl of Breadalbane. Her sister married Maclaine of Lochbuy, a relation of the Macquaries.

Elizabeth's early life was probably like that of any other gently born Scotswoman without fortune. She grew up at Appin on her brother's estate. At 26 she met her distant cousin Colonel Lachlan Macquarie at the deathbed of Lochbuy. It was their first meeting as Macquarie had been seventeen years on military service in India. He was immediately attracted to his young kinswoman, who showed herself so helpful in trouble and had impeccable taste in gardens. The acquaintance ripened when he drove Elizabeth and Lochbuy's two sons to Edinburgh, a journey not without hardship. She would make, he told his diary, an admirable soldier's wife. Macquarie proposed to Elizabeth at her aunt's house in London in March 1805, making it clear to her that they could not marry until after his next tour of duty in India, probably in four years time, as he had made a solemn vow on the death of his first wife never to marry again in India or to take a wife to that country. Elizabeth accepted him and his conditions with 'notable candour'. Being posted to the command of the 73rd Regiment stationed in Perth, Macquarie returned much sooner than expected. The marriage took place at Holsworthy in Devon on 3 November 1807. The bride was 29, the groom 46. In September 1808 their first child, a daughter named Jane Jarvis after the first Mrs Macquarie, was born, but she died in December. In 1809 Macquarie was appointed governor of New South Wales. His wife accompanied him to the colony, although shortly before their departure she had a serious illness. She has left a vivacious journal of the seven months voyage.

They landed in Sydney on 31 December 1809. At Government House Elizabeth needed all her tact and sincerity. The colony was torn by factions and her husband's policy, especially with regard to emancipists, was controversial. Throughout she supported him loyally. She took a kindly interest in the welfare of women convicts and of the Aboriginals. She was intelligently interested in gardening and agriculture. With Mrs John Macarthur [q.v.] she is said to have pioneered haymaking in the colony. She had brought from England a collection of books on architecture which were useful to her husband and his architect, Francis Greenway [q.v.]. She also planned the road running round the inside of the Government Domain to the point which, like the road, was named after her.

Elizabeth accompanied her husband on several arduous journeys. In 1811 they went to Van Diemen's Land whither on the journey she showed herself, in her husband's words, 'a most excellent brave sailor'. In 1815 she journeyed by coach with him over the newly-crossed Blue Mountains. In 1818 she accompanied him to the Hunter River by sea in a brig named after her, Elizabeth Henrietta. Her second child, a boy named Lachlan, was born on 28 March 1814 to his parents' great joy.

Macquarie resigned his governorship in 1820. After his successor, Governor Brisbane, arrived on 7 November 1821 and assumed office on 1 December, the Macquaries paid farewell visits to many of their friends and made a final tour of the Illawarra in January 1822. They sailed for England on 15 February in the Surry.

The Macquaries now made their home at Jarvisfield, Macquarie's estate on Mull, which they reached in November 1823. The house had not been lived in for years and was poor, inadequate and far from weatherproof. Mrs Macquarie with her usual energy planned and supervised additions and repairs, but her husband was depressed and in poor health and when in 1824 he journeyed to London to finalize his colonial accounts she was overcome with foreboding. This was not groundless. She soon received a message that he was ill. Taking Lachlan, she hastened to London and was with him when he died on 1 July 1824. In a moving letter to her Australian friends Elizabeth recounted all the circumstances of his last days. This letter might serve as a portrait of a devoted wife.

The widow lived on at Jarvisfield. The government paid her a pension of £400 which at first she refused but was later persuaded by her friends to accept. She died on 11 March 1835. In 1836 she was posthumously granted 2000 acres in New South Wales. Like his father, Lachlan had entered the army, and served in the Scots Greys. He married Isabella Hamilton Dundas, third daughter of Colin Campbell of Fura, but was childless. Described as a 'dissolute drunkard', he died on 7 May 1845 as the result of a fall downstairs at Craignish Castle. A portrait of him dated 1823 in the collection of Mr E. A. Crome is on loan in the Mitchell Library, Sydney.

M. Barnard, Macquarie's world (Syd, 1941); M. H. Ellis, Lachlan Macquarie, 2nd ed (Syd, 1952); E. Macquarie, 'Letter', JRAHS, 16 (1930).   MARJORIE BARNARD

MACQUARIE, LACHLAN (1762-1824), governor, was born, according to a note in his own hand in a family Bible, on 31 January 1762 on the island of Ulva in the parish of Kilninian in the Inner Hebrides, Scotland. His father, Lachlan Macquarie, was a cousin of the sixteenth and last chieftain of the clan Macquarie. According to local tradition Macquarie senior was a carpenter or miller; certainly he was a tenant of the duke of Argyll, leasing the small farm of Oskamull in Mull which he was too poor to stock himself and therefore shared with two other tenants. His own part of the farm he shared with his son-in-law, Farquhar Maclaine, a tradesman. It is not known when he died, but in August 1785 Macquarie paid a mariner a pound to buy a headstone for his grave.

Macquarie's mother, Margaret, was the only sister of Murdoch Maclaine, chieftain of Lochbuy in Mull, and as a widow she farmed her pendicle of Oskamull, with her eldest son Donald and Farquhar Maclaine, until her death in 1810 at 82. Two letters from her exist, but it is doubtful whether she was literate; in 1803 when Macquarie wrote to her at her request, he asked his uncle, his normal correspondent, 'to cause some proper Person to read to her'. Of Macquarie's older brothers, Hector was a lieutenant in the New York Volunteer Regiment and died while prisoner of the American rebels in 1778; Donald who was described as possessing an 'infirm imbecile state of mind' died in 1801 at 50. Following his father's death Macquarie and his younger brother Charles, who died on 27 March 1835, came under the affectionate care of Murdoch Maclaine.

Whether Macquarie attended the Royal High School, Edinburgh, as tradition has it, is doubtful. What is certain is that in 1776 he volunteered and on 9 April 1777 obtained an ensigncy in the second battalion of the 84th Regiment, known as the Royal Highland Emigrants, commanded by a cousin, Colonel (later General) Allan Maclean. Murdoch Maclaine served as captain in the same battalion. Macquarie was posted first to Nova Scotia, where he landed on 31 October 1776, and then to New York and Charleston, but only on garrison duty. He was commissioned a lieutenant in the 71st Regiment on 18 January 1781. From Charleston Macquarie was posted to Jamaica and there made up his mind to try his fortune in the East Indies. Returning to Scotland in 1784 he was retired on half-pay when his regiment was disbanded. Three years later, through the patronage of Maclean, he was offered the senior lieutenancy in the 77th Regiment which was being raised for service in India, on condition that he found fifteen recruits for the colonel's company. On 28 March 1788, after several months of strenuous recruiting in Scotland, he marched from Dover Castle to Deal with the first division and embarked in the *Dublin* for Bombay. Macquarie was then 26. He had ten guineas in his pocket and left behind debts to his uncle and tradesmen.

Macquarie arrived at Bombay early in August and despite his gloom about prospects of promotion he fulfilled Maclean's prediction that he would get 'a step' within three months. On 9 November 1788 he was appointed a captain-lieutenant and considered himself 'a very lucky fellow'. Early in 1790 war with Tippoo Sahib seemed unavoidable and Macquarie was itching for battle, only praying that the war would last at least three years: 'in which time I think I shall be rather unlucky if I do not get a Company and make a few Hundred Pounds to assist my friends with'.

Three years later Macquarie was appointed major of brigade. By then he had not only paid off his debts but saved £1000 and sent home money to his family. Even more important, he was now in a position to propose to a West Indian heiress, Jane, youngest daughter of the late Thomas Jarvis, former chief justice of Antigua. She was living in Bombay with her sister and brother-in-law, James Morley, a wealthy, retired servant of the East India Co., and to Macquarie's joy ('Oh delightful glorious and generous girl!') accepted him.

They were married on 8 September 1793 in Morley's house, but the polite society in which Macquarie now moved proved expensive, and since the marriage settlement could not be touched he was soon in debt again. He was therefore relieved when his regiment was ordered to Calicut. In a bungalow there, which he named Staffa Lodge, Macquarie and his bride lived quietly but in content. He had paid off his debts by the time he saw further action, this time against the Dutch, taking part in the siege of Cochin (1795) and the capture of Colombo and Point de Galle (1796). There he stayed for nearly a month as governor, but hearing that his wife was unwell he obtained leave and hurried back to Calicut to find her in the last stage of consumption. Hoping desperately that sea air would help, Macquarie took her on a trip to Macao, but she died there on 15 July 1796 in her twenty-fourth year. Macquarie's profound grief was touchingly if verbosely expressed in the inscription on the ornate, black marble tombstone he raised over her grave in the Bombay

burying ground, and in numerous letters home. A letter by Jane, written to her mother-in-law to inform her of their marriage, suggests, as does the miniature portrait, a young woman of charm, sweetness and simplicity. She left her husband £6000 in English funds.

On 3 May 1796 Macquarie was promoted brevet major, and next year he added by purchase the office of deputy-paymaster-general of the King's troops in the Bombay presidency. That year he was in the expedition against the Pyché Rajah and in 1799, shortly after the engagement at Sedasere he was at the battle of Seringapatam, during which Tippoo was killed; this brought him £1300 in prize money. In April 1800 Governor Duncan of Bombay appointed him his confidential military secretary, though Macquarie generously stipulated that the emoluments of the office should continue to be paid to the previous occupant, a friend who was married and had small means.

On 18 September 1800 when he took office as president of the Sans Souci Club in Bombay he finally abandoned the black arm-band he had worn since his wife's death. Six months later General Baird asked Macquarie to accompany him as deputy-adjutant-general of the army of six thousand men he was taking to Egypt to help General Abercromby in expelling the French. Macquarie sailed for the Red Sea on 6 April 1801 and in Cairo learnt that Charles, now a captain in the Black Watch, had been seriously wounded at Aboukir. Their reunion took place at Alexandria in September 1801 and filled several ardent pages of his diary.

When the bulk of the British army left Egypt Macquarie became deputy-adjutant-general of all the remaining forces. As early as July 1801 he had word that he had been appointed at home to an effective majority of the 86th Regiment as from 15 January 1801, and on returning to Bombay in July 1802 he assumed command but was granted leave that year on the ground that he had urgent business at home. This was scarcely an exaggeration, for while in Egypt he had learnt that he had become a landowner in Mull.

Macquarie had for several years set his heart on acquiring part of the Lochbuy estate which his uncle was being forced by his creditors to sell. He told his uncle that he was willing to submit to any terms, but asked him to delay the sale until 1803, by which time he expected to be back in Britain and able to cash his fortune. Lochbuy, unable to wait, had bought 10,000 acres for Macquarie, and Macquarie's Bombay agents had provided security for the purchase money of £10,060. The Egyptian campaign had been so profitable that raising such a sum presented no difficulty; at the beginning of 1803 he estimated that he was worth £20,000 in money and land, twice the amount of his wealth only two years before. Understandably Macquarie was anxious to take possession of his estate. His principal motive in acquiring it, he assured his sister-in-law, Mrs Morley, was to perpetuate the memory of his late wife by naming it after her ('You will say—my beloved Sister—that I am romantick?—Be it so!') He was clearly also attracted to the idea of becoming a Highland laird and, indeed, for all his mourning, of having an estate to leave his heir. It was also perfectly natural that he should be homesick, especially as his uncle, now ailing, begged him to return.

He left Bombay on 6 January 1803 in the company ship *Sir Edward Hughes* after a farewell dinner presented by the governor. The ship sailed by the Cape and St Helena, and on 7 May Macquarie landed at Brighton, where he sat down at the Castle Inn to 'the most excellent comfortable English Dinner for the first time these 15 Years!' A week later war with France broke out again and in July the duke of York, as commander-in-chief, appointed him assistant-adjutant-general of the London district. Macquarie's rank was now lieut-colonel on the staff, the promotion being dated back to 7 November 1801.

These were strenuous days for him not only militarily but socially, for the 'awkward, rusticated, Jungle-Wallah', as he jocularly described himself, moved in the highest society. He was presented to the king ten days after his arrival and to the queen and all the princesses the following week, 'a grand and most pleasing Splendid Sight of the finest Women in all the World'. Equally flatteringly, Lord Castlereagh consulted him about Indian affairs.

Clearly Macquarie felt himself in his element despite the expense. This is the Macquarie of Opie's fine portrait in the Dixson Gallery, Sydney, the handsome, spruce young veteran of 41. In these circumstances he found it easier than might have been expected to reconcile himself to postponing his trip north and it was not until June 1804 that he was able to get away. His uncle was on his deathbed so the reunion was short. Macquarie had the melancholy task of breaking the news of Lochbuy's death to his mother at their first meeting since 1787. There was tragic irony here as elsewhere in his life. While at home Macquarie carried out his resolution to consecrate his new estate to his late wife under the name of Jarvisfield. He also

met there, and admired immensely, an amiable and accomplished kinswoman Elizabeth [q.v.], a Campbell of Airds, whom he was in due course to marry.

Macquarie's return to India could not be long delayed. He may have helped to precipitate this event by his foolish and unsuccessful attempt to deceive the duke of York about the age and whereabouts of two young relatives, the subjects of an anonymous letter which the duke had received from Mull. Though Macquarie protested that he had misrepresented nothing, he was lucky to avoid the ruin and disgrace which he himself feared would be the result of his 'bold fiction'; however, his application for a transfer to the guards was rejected out of hand and he was ordered back to India.

Macquarie left Portsmouth in the *City of London* on 24 April 1805, his heart lightened by the knowledge that Elizabeth had agreed to wait for him. His second tour of duty was comparatively brief. At Bombay in October he learnt that the duke of York had promoted him to the lieut-colonelcy of the 73rd Regiment which had already returned home. After serving in the north with his old regiment against Holkar Macquarie left India for the last time on 19 March 1807. This time he decided to take the overland route carrying dispatches. Taking ship to the Persian Gulf, where he narrowly escaped drowning, he and his companions went to the British factory at Basra; learning there that Turkey, at war with Russia, had broken off diplomatic relations with Britain, he decided to travel via St Petersburg. He picked up dispatches from the shah of Persia at Baghdad on the way, reached London on 17 October 1807, and was eventually rewarded with £750 by the government.

Seventeen days later he married Elizabeth Campbell in the little parish church of Holsworthy in Devon, and took her to Perth where his new regiment was garrisoned. By their first wedding anniversary they were also celebrating, with all the enthusiasm of belated parenthood, the arrival of a daughter, christened Jane Jarvis, but her death on 5 December 1808 threw a cloud over their lives which long lingered.

Dramatic distraction from grief was provided by the decision of the government at the end of 1808 to send Major-General Miles Nightingall and the 73rd Regiment to New South Wales to replace the deposed governor, Bligh, and the mutinous New South Wales Corps. Macquarie was to accompany his regiment, but the prospect of going abroad again so soon did not please him, especially as he reckoned that he was already the oldest lieut-colonel in the army and feared that the colony would be too remote to assist his further promotion. He therefore wrote at the end of March to General Sir David Dundas, the new commander-in-chief, reminding him of his thirty-two years service in the army and asking for promotion to colonel in the colony. More important, he applied to Castlereagh, secretary of state for the colonies, for the post of lieut-governor, and this appointment he received with the support of the duke of York and Sir Arthur Wellesley, the future duke of Wellington. When he heard that Nightingall had changed his mind about accepting the governorship, Macquarie boldly wrote to Castlereagh again, offer-offering his services as governor. At first this ploy appeared to have failed and on 26 April he duly attended a royal levée to pay his duty as lieut-governor; but the next day in Berkeley Square he met Castlereagh who told him he was to go as governor.

As the government was anxious about the situation in New South Wales the preparations for departure were hurried, but with characteristic canniness Macquarie wrote an effusive thank-you to Castlereagh ('Great men like these attentions—and they never do any harm') and a respectful letter to Sir Joseph Banks [q.v.], the colony's original patron, discreetly reminding him of hospitality the clan Macquarie had given him many years before. Banks was not well enough to see Macquarie but was favourably disposed. Macquarie also consulted T. W. Plummer, a lawyer, about the improvements desirable in the colonial government. A week before departure he received confidential Instructions in which Castlereagh emphasized that 'The Great Objects of attention are to improve the Morals of the Colonists, to encourage Marriage, to provide for Education, to prohibit the Use of Spirituous Liquors, to increase the Agriculture and Stock, so as to ensure the Certainty of a full supply to the Inhabitants under all Circumstances'. Macquarie's policy in the colony can only be understood in the light of this exhortation.

On 22 May 1809 Macquarie and his wife sailed with the regiment from Portsmouth in the storeship *Dromedary* escorted by H.M.S. *Hindostan*. During the seven-month voyage both of them kept a diary, his terse, hers lively. Also on board were Ellis Bent [q.v.], the newly-appointed deputy-judge-advocate, and his family. Thus the last of the autocratic, and non-constitutional, governors came to Australia with the first properly trained law officer.

At Rio de Janeiro Macquarie learned that Lieut-Colonel Johnston and John Macarthur [qq.v.], leaders in the deposition of Bligh, had just passed through on their way to England. This relieved him of the disagreeable duty of having to deal with them in the colony. Then after a light-hearted sojourn at Cape Town Macquarie and his party proceeded to New South Wales and entered Port Jackson on 28 December 1809. Macquarie was sworn in on New Year's Day 1810. Addressing the citizens at the ceremony he expressed the hope that the recent dissensions would now give way to a more becoming harmony along all classes. Officers displaced since Bligh's arrest were reinstated and all other acts of the 'revolutionary' government annulled. After Bligh arrived in Sydney on 17 January it required all the tact that Macquarie could muster to keep his relations with his predecessor more or less amicable until Bligh finally sailed for home on 12 May with Colonel Paterson [q.v.] and the New South Wales Corps. With the past out of the way Macquarie could devote his undivided attention to the present, and the future. Privately he had been pleasantly surprised to find the colony thriving and 'in a perfect state of tranquillity'. He was also pleased with the setting and the climate and hoped 'we shall be able to pass five or six years here pleasantly enough'.

The first year certainly passed pleasantly. By the time Macquarie was being congratulated on the first anniversary of his government the characteristics of his twelve-year administration had emerged. One was the new modelling of the public departments, including the commissariat, and the organization of the Police Fund as the basis of colonial revenue. Here he was able to draw on his experience as a staff officer, expertise the naval governors had largely lacked. Like his predecessors he levied customs duties without authority, and these had to be retrospectively confirmed by an Act passed in 1819. He opened a new market-place in Sydney in October 1810 and in March 1813 the first public fair held 'by regular authority' took place at Parramatta. In July 1813 the colony at last obtained a coinage in place of the notes of hand and barter previously used. At the end of 1816, despite the opposition of the British government, he encouraged the creation of the colony's first bank. But the most urgent problem, and an intractable one, was to increase agricultural production and livestock. Despite his efforts to encourage farmers to improve their properties alternate spectres of glut and famine continued to threaten the economy during most of his administration.

Macquarie embarked on his first tour of the outlying districts on 6 November 1810 and three days later was lost in the bush for several hours in the Bankstown district. He named Windsor and Richmond on this trip and paid some discreet compliments in calling new towns he marked out Liverpool, Castlereagh, Pitt-town and Wilberforce. This was the first of a series of tours including two visits to Van Diemen's Land in 1811 and 1821, three to Newcastle, one to Port Macquarie, which he founded in 1821, and one to the Illawarra in 1822. After the Blue Mountains had been crossed Macquarie set off on the new road across the range and selected the site of Bathurst on 7 May 1815. He encouraged so much exploration that by the time he left the colony the explored area was many times what it had been when he arrived.

Public works were another continuing concern. Despite Castlereagh's injunction about economy Macquarie was convinced that a new army barracks, a new general hospital, and a turnpike road to Parramatta and beyond could not be postponed. The barracks were completed by the end of 1810, the Parramatta road in April 1811. The hospital was built by D'Arcy Wentworth [q.v.], the principal surgeon, and two other colonists by a contract dated 6 November 1810, giving them a limited monopoly of importing spirits, the consumption of which Macquarie had found it impossible to prohibit. This was clearly a cheap way of obtaining an urgently needed building, and at a time when convict labour was very scarce it probably did not seem an altogether eccentric device to an old Indian officer; but it ran contrary to his own suggestion earlier that spirits should be freely imported, and it was strongly criticized in London. These undertakings were the first in an expensive building programme which transformed and still adorns Sydney, Parramatta and the new townships. In this he had the assistance of F. Greenway [q.v.] a convict whom he appointed civil architect. In 1822 Macquarie listed 265 works of varying scale which had been carried out during his rule.

All these projects were accomplished with the help of convict labour, which became embarrassingly plentiful as time went on. In 1819-21 the governor was unable to assign more than half the new arrivals, and had to recommence at Emu Plains the government farming operations which he had thankfully abandoned in 1811. For all that he reduced the average annual expenditure per convict by about two-thirds during his administration, even though the *total* doubled as the number of prisoners increased about tenfold. At the same time he tried to restrain the excessive use of corporal punishment by magistrates, tightened up the pass regulations, built barracks in Sydney, Parramatta and Windsor for the better control of the 'government' convicts and issued new regulations for the granting of tickets-of-leave.

Central to Macquarie's administration was his concern for public morality. In some of his earliest orders the prevailing habit of cohabiting without marriage was denounced, constables were directed to enforce laws against Sabbath-breaking, and a regular church parade was introduced for convicts in government employment. Already in October 1810 he claimed that 'a very apparent' change for the better had taken place in the 'Religious Tendency and Morals' of the inhabitants. Certainly church-going and the marriage rate increased. Closely connected with all this was his energetic establishment of schools in Sydney and elsewhere, his licensing regulations which reduced the number of public houses in Sydney alone from 75 to 20, and his seizure of clandestine stills. In 1811 he reorganized the Sydney police, appointing D'Arcy Wentworth superintendent.

As the strongest inducement to reform Macquarie decided that ex-convicts, when they had shown that they deserved the favour, should be readmitted to the rank in society they had forfeited. This was a new line of conduct, he recognized, though he believed it to be 'the benign Spirit of the Original Establishment of the Colony, and His Majesty's Paternal Instructions as to the mode of its Government'. Macquarie was clearly conscious of following the colony's founder, Admiral Phillip, whom he admired and corresponded with. A conscientious Freemason he was probably also influenced by his admiration of Wilberforce 'a true Patriot and the Real Friend of Mankind' and, perhaps above all, by his wife. Accordingly he made two emancipists magistrates in 1810 and invited them and others to his table.

This policy was approved by Liverpool as well as by Wilberforce and the select committee on transportation in 1812, but it aroused immediate indignation among immigrant settlers and military officers and alienated the very classes whose co-operation Castlereagh had advised him to foster. Early in 1810 the senior chaplain, Samuel Marsden [q.v.], refused outright to serve with the emancipist justices, Simeon Lord and Andrew Thompson [qq.v.], on the turnpike board for the new Parramatta

Road. In 1811 Macquarie flatteringly named a street in Parramatta after Marsden, but despite Wilberforce's attempts to mediate there was further controversy between them in 1814, and finally in January 1818 Marsden was summoned to Government House and denounced as a 'secret enemy'. Since the chaplain probably had more influential friends in England than any other colonist he proved a dangerous antagonist. So did J. H. Bent [q.v.], judge of the Supreme Court created under the new Charter of Justice granted in 1814. He kept his court closed rather than admit ex-convict attorneys to practise even though there was only one free lawyer in the colony. The governor's growing rift with both Bent brothers led to their recall. Ellis Bent died before this decision arrived, but his brother returned to England and assisted H. G. Bennet in mounting the campaign against Macquarie in the House of Commons which led to the appointment of a select committee on gaols and of J. T. Bigge [q.v.] as commissioner to enquire into the affairs of the colony. Macquarie's emancipist policy also led to his falling out with his old friend of Indian days, Colonel Molle [q.v.], who arrived with the 46th Regiment early in 1814 as lieut-governor. Macquarie's preference for ex-convict settlers was an extension of this policy, and by 1818 he went so far as to suggest the cessation for three years of all immigration apart from 'respectable Monied Men'. He had found many of the free immigrants unsatisfactory settlers and disapproved of their reluctance to fraternize with ex-convicts.

Macquarie's policy concerning the Aboriginals was an expression of the same humanitarian conscience. He organized the Native Institution (a school for Aboriginal children), a village at Elizabeth Bay for the Sydney tribe, an Aboriginal farm at George's Head and a sort of annual durbar for them at Parramatta. Orders of merit and even an old general's uniform were bestowed on deserving chiefs. The results of this naive policy were not very encouraging and in 1816, when the natives showed signs of ungrateful hostility, he organized a military drive to chasten them. But no other governor since Phillip had shown them so much sympathy.

More conventional piety was evident in his establishment of a male orphanage and other charitable institutions, and in his support of the Benevolent Society, the Bible Society and the Savings Bank. Yet Macquarie was no Puritan, witness his appointment of a convict, M. M. Robinson [q.v.], as poet laureate, his patronage of the first horse-races in Hyde Park, and his

tolerance of Lieut-Governor Sorell and other officials who were discreetly living in sin. Happily married himself there was in practice an easygoingness in Macquarie's attitude to private, as distinct from public, morality, which belonged more to the eighteenth than the nineteenth century.

In July 1811 Macquarie received official notification of his promotion to the rank of colonel a year before. On 25 November 1811 he was promoted brigadier-general, though he only heard about it eleven months later. In October 1813 he learnt that he had been a major-general since 4 June, but he seemed just as delighted to hear that his brother had at last married, and to an Edinburgh heiress at that. Macquarie had repeatedly urged him to come out to New South Wales, and concocted plans for his becoming collector of customs, lieut-governor, and even Macquarie's successor, but nothing came of them. Charles's son, the 'Hero Hector', and their young cousin, John Maclaine, the subjects of the 1803 episode, were both on Macquarie's staff in the colony; he was always ready to help his kin.

Undoubtedly the high moment of Macquarie's stay in the colony, and perhaps of his life, was the birth on 28 March 1814, following six miscarriages, of his son whom he gently allowed Elizabeth to name Lachlan after him. Their happiness on earth, he noted in his memorandum book, was now complete. For the last decade of his life Macquarie found a happy refuge from his worries in the role of doting father.

These worries accumulated during the second half of his reign. Castlereagh had told him before he left London that he would be given a pension if he stayed eight years as governor, and on 1 December 1817, within a month of that period, Macquarie tendered his resignation. This followed Bathurst's criticism of Macquarie's handling of the incident in which the American schooner *Traveller* had been seized without his authority. The governor considered the reprimand unjustified and its tone very insulting. Bathurst wrote a mollifying reply declining to accept the resignation until he heard further from Macquarie, but this dispatch went astray and was never received by the governor. Instead, though he reminded Bathurst of his resignation, he was informed of the appointment of Bigge, learning this only five days before the commissioner arrived on 26 September 1819.

Macquarie seems to have been genuinely pleased, in view of the parliamentary criticism, at the inquiry since 'his report *must* be favourable to my administration of the

Colony and highly honourable to my character'. But Macquarie and Bigge soon fell out over his 'absurd' public works policy and his appointment of the emancipist, Dr Redfern [q.v.], as a magistrate. This quarrel was patched up but another developed when Macquarie, who had been seriously ill, addressed his own questionnaire concerning his administration to all the magistrates in the colony. This contretemps in turn was settled in July 1820 on the emotional occasion of the solemn procession following news of the death of George III and after Macquarie had promised not to use the questionnaire while Bigge was in the colony. Ironically, the magistrates' replies were by no means wholly favourable to the governor. Meanwhile Macquarie had privately sent home a vigorous defence against Bennet's latest attack, which was published in 1821 as *A Letter to Viscount Sidmouth*.

At the end of 1820 Macquarie learnt with relief that his third application to resign had been accepted, but it was not until 12 February 1822, three months after his successor arrived, that he and his family embarked in the *Surry* with an arkful of Australian wild life for friends and patrons at home, cheered by a 'Harbour full of People'. They sailed three days later and arrived at Deptford on 5 July. The first part of Bigge's report had already been tabled in the House of Commons, so Macquarie lost no time in seeing Bathurst and submitting a detailed report of his administration. He had the satisfaction of receiving from Bathurst his assurance of the king's appreciation of his assiduity and integrity; he was 'most graciously received' on 5 August when presented to the monarch by Castlereagh. The same day Bigge's first volume was tabled in the Lords. Apparently it now began to circulate publicly, but with remarkable restraint Macquarie forbore to comment until the rest appeared. John Macarthur junior reported that 'the Governor bends his head to the storm like a true Scotchman, and calls on Mr. Bigge as if he was quite contented and at ease'. Unable to stand London, Macquarie went home to Scotland, and at the end of November, worried about his wife's health, he took her and Lachlan, with servants and a tutor, on a grand tour through France, Italy and Switzerland, spending two months at Hyères near Toulon. While abroad he received copies of Bigge's second and third volumes, for on the way back he stopped for twelve days at Fontainebleau to answer this 'false, vindictive and malicious Report'.

In London on 31 July 1823 he began a desperate attempt to salvage his reputa-tion and to secure his pension, but on neither issue was he able to obtain satisfaction from the government, and the sudden death of Castlereagh deprived him of a most influential patron. He had been defended by *John Bull* when Bigge's first volume was published, but Sydney Smith in the *Edinburgh Review* was so scathing that Macquarie even contemplated suing that journal for libel. In October he presented Bathurst with a 43-page commentary, but not until 1828 could his friends persuade the government to publish part of it as a parliamentary paper. Meanwhile the Treasury added to his worries, belatedly pestering him about the absence of receipts for £10,000 worth of dollars imported into the colony from India in 1812 and holding him answerable for this money.

Exhausted and sick at heart Macquarie sailed with his family for Mull in November, too poor now to travel by coach. In 1817 Charles had bought on his behalf part of the duke of Argyll's property on Mull. This had cost £22,000, all of Macquarie's fortune, and Elizabeth described the purchase as 'ruinous'. So it proved. Far from saving money Macquarie had been obliged to supplement his net salary (£1800) as governor from his own pocket, and he was now £500 in debt to his bankers. His earlier hopes of building a castle, a mansion or even a cottage on his estate had faded, and for a country seat they had to make do with the damp, draughty dwelling already there. Not only was it impossible to collect rent from the tenants but the land was virtually unsaleable.

In these circumstances obtaining the promised pension became urgent. So on 15 April 1824, accompanied by his faithful Indian manservant, formerly his slave boy, Macquarie set out to London and arrived on 24 April after a gruelling passage by steam-boat. Five days later he obtained an interview with Bathurst who confirmed that he would be paid a pension of £1000, twice as much as he had expected. He also received a letter in which Bathurst spoke reassuringly of Macquarie's 'able and successful administration', words which delighted the old man, though he complained to Elizabeth that he could not publish them, 'whereas this vile insidious Bigge Report is everywhere in the hands of everyone'.

The final irony was that Macquarie did not live to enjoy his pension. On 25 May he learnt that his application for a title had been rejected. On 11 June, having said a leisurely farewell to the king, the duke of York, Bathurst and others, preparatory to returning to Scotland, he woke feeling ill. He suffered much pain from his old bowel complaint and from strangury, and on 1 July died in his London lodgings. Elizabeth, who had hurried down from Mull, described the moment of his dignified death as 'the most sublime in my life'. Macquarie would have been pleased with the crowd of relations, friends and colleagues, including the duke of Argyll, the earl of Breadalbane and several generals who escorted his coffin up Regent Street and Portland Place, followed by forty coaches including those of the duke of Wellington, Bathurst and the earl of Harrington. His body was taken by boat to Mull and buried on his estate. The family tomb is now administered by the National Trust of Australia.

One of Macquarie's last errands in London had been to select 'a superb Vase' with the £500 the colonists of New South Wales had subscribed as a farewell gift. When news of his death reached Sydney at the end of October the *Sydney Gazette* and the *Australian* both carried fulsome tributes, elegaic verses were penned, and one colonist described him as 'the Howard or the Jonas Hanway of the Colony'. On 14 November, after a solemn procession, Rev. William Cowper [q.v.], an old friend, preached a sermon taking as his text the last verse of the 22nd chapter of Proverbs: 'Seest thou a man diligent in his business? he shall stand before kings; he shall not stand before mean men'. About £500 was quickly promised for a monument, but this plan was abandoned after a correspondent in the *Gazette* drily suggested that there were already memorials enough to this 'Grand Napoleon of these Australian Realms'. But the seed of the Macquarie legend, 'prince of men', had already been sown and was to prove the most enduring memorial of all:

> Early and late,—by day, by night,
> To serve mankind was his delight:
> Kind Ruler, Husband, Father, Friend,—
> What more can human nature blend?

In a will written in Sydney in 1815 Macquarie had settled the estate of Jarvisfield on his son, though providing an annuity of £300 out of it for his widow. His personal property was then valued at £22,000, but by 1824 this was probably largely illusory in view of the land market. Since Lachlan junior died childless Macquarie's fond ambition of establishing a line of lairds of Jarvisfield came to nothing.

Macquarie was a brisk and indefatigable writer of letters, diaries and memoranda, and the personality which emerges from these intimate sources is irresistibly attractive. Yet, though Macquarie was genial, generous and trusting, he was not really a simple man. For all his innocence and self-righteousness he was capable of deception and probably self-deception, and of considerable cunning in his strenuous pursuit of promotion, though by the standards of his contemporaries he probably had more integrity than most. His achievements in New South Wales during a longer administration than any other governor defy disparagement, and his prediction that '*my name* will not readily be forgotten after I have left it' has been richly fulfilled. Perhaps his most important accomplishment was to rescue dignity and respect for the vice-regal office after the sordid proceedings with Bligh.

But his failings were also palpable. In 1801 the future duke of Wellington called him 'an excellent man', but added that he had bad health and 'I think wants that decision in difficult cases which is the life of everything although he has habits of business'. In New South Wales he certainly mismanaged some cases; his rashly ordering three men to be flogged for trespassing in the government domain in 1816 was the most notorious instance. He himself wrote privately in 1810 that his talents and judgment were inadequate to the task of improving the colony 'or to that degree that the present backward State of everything would admit of'. Towards the end of his administration, as both health and temper failed, he became increasingly intolerant of criticism, including that of Bathurst and Bigge.

The fundamental issue between Macquarie and Bigge lay in their conception of the *raison d'être* of the colony. Macquarie always viewed it as 'a Penitentiary or Asylum on a Grand Scale' though he conceded that it 'must one day or other be one of the greatest and most flourishing Colonies belonging to the British Empire'. Bigge, more closely in touch with opinion in London and influenced by the ideas of John Macarthur, saw clearly its potentialities for free settlement and wool. Despite the governor's passionate plea Bigge's astute but conventional lawyer's mind was not impressed by the aim or the achievements of Macquarie's emancipist policy. That is hardly surprising; here Macquarie was ahead of his time, and indeed ahead of our own, and one can still wonder that an Indian army veteran, pillar of the established Church and an orthodox Tory in politics, ever came to father this extraordinary experiment. Certainly no other governor was so popular with both emancipist and convict: Andrew Thompson [q.v.], when he died in 1810, even left him a quarter of his estate. But he was unlucky to govern at a time when the authority of the governor still had no sound constitutional basis, when the pressure for economy was so strong, and when British policy was undergoing reappraisal.

Of Macquarie's personal characteristics it is worth emphasizing that he was far from humourless—a rather high-spirited and unvicious humour, witness his nicknaming his 'Royal Highland Camel' in Egypt 'the Laird of Kilbuckie'. Wherever he went he had an appreciative, if unoriginal, eye for 'romantick' landseape and historic places, and whether in London, St Petersburg, or Rio de Janeiro, enjoyed an evening at the theatre. Above all he was a man of strong family affections and, blessed in the person of both his wives, he proved a devoted husband and father, even agreeing to have the family's favourite old cow shipped all the way from Sydney to Mull.

L. Macquarie, *Journals of his tours in New South Wales and Van Diemen's Land, 1810-1822* (Syd, 1956); M. H. Ellis, *Lachlan Macquarie his life, adventures and times*, 4th ed (Syd, 1965); Macquarie papers (ML); Jarvis Collection (Lincolnshire County Archives); Lochbuie papers (Register House, Edinb); MS cat under Macquarie (ML, NL).

N. D. McLACHLAN

MACQUEEN, THOMAS POTTER (1791-1854), politician and colonizer, was born in Bedfordshire, England, at Segenhoe manor, Ridgmont, an estate which his father, Malcolm Macqueen, M.D., had inherited through his marriage to Mariana, only child of Thomas Potter. Thomas represented East Looe in parliament 1816-26 and Bedfordshire 1826-30. He joined the Bedfordshire yeomanry and reached the rank of lieut-colonel in 1820.

Macqueen read Commissioner Bigge's [q.v.] report with interest, and was attracted by the prospects of rural settlement in New South Wales. He evolved a plan whereby the colony might be developed by settlers with sufficient capital to employ convicts on their own account. English landed proprietors were to be encouraged to buy land in the colony and send out some of their dependants to ensure 'a wholesome population', although the effective capital would thus be invested by persons not living in the colony.

Through the good offices of Earl Bathurst, Macqueen in 1823 obtained a grant of 10,000 acres from Governor Brisbane with a provisional reserve of a further 10,000 acres. Next year he appointed Peter McIntyre [q.v.] as his overseer and entrusted to him the selection and development of his grant. A carefully chosen party

of mechanics, farmers and shepherds, equipped with farm machinery, stores, sheep, horses and stud cattle sailed in two chartered ships, *Hugh Crawford* and *Nimrod*, reaching Sydney on 7 April 1825. On Macqueen's behalf McIntyre chose as his grant 10,000 acres in the Hunter River valley, naming it Segenhoe after his employer's birthplace. Under McIntyre's guidance this quickly developed into a thriving agricultural estate. His work was continued by H. C. Sempill, who followed him as manager in 1830.

Macqueen's venture of 1824 was the first direct shipment of free emigrants to New South Wales and gave a great stimulus to agriculture in the colony. He introduced experienced farmers and artisans, bloodstock, and the capital necessary for progressive farming. Between 1825 and 1838 he spent at least £42,000 on plant, stock and improvements on Segenhoe, and firmly established the Hunter valley's reputation for efficient agriculture. During the drought in 1827-30 Segenhoe was the main source of grain for the whole valley. About 160 convicts were employed at Segenhoe, and Macqueen brought out some of their wives and families, numbers of them later becoming tenant farmers on the estate. Several of his employees, including the McIntyre brothers, Peter, John and Donald, Alexander Campbell, and Sempill, became pioneer squatters in the New England district. At the promptings of Macqueen the government laid out the township of Aberdeen in 1838, and the road to Segenhoe became part of the Great North Road.

Macqueen joined Thomas Peel [q.v.], Sir Francis Vincent and E. W. H. Schenley in November 1828 in presenting a request to the British government for a large land grant at Swan River in return for carrying there 10,000 settlers from the British Isles. The association hoped to reap financial benefits from the cultivation of tobacco, cotton, sugar, flax and drug-producing plants, and grazing horses, cattle and swine. Macqueen offered the management of his prospective Swan River estate to Robert Gouger [q.v.] but by the end of January 1829 all except Peel had withdrawn from the venture.

Macqueen continued to advocate planned emigration. In 1830 he was a member of the National Colonization Society, which made the first formal attempt to organize the doctrines of systematic colonization in London. He published two short political tracts: *The State of the Nation at the Close of 1830* (London, 1831) and *The State of the Country in*

1832 (London, 1832); both emphasized the poverty of the labouring classes and the severity of unemployment and advocated emigration, specially to New South Wales, as the solution.

In London throughout 1832 Macqueen tried to interest influential people in a joint whaling and banking enterprise; from this project sprang the Bank of Australasia. Thereafter he had little influence on its development although, in recognition of his initiating role, he was given a seat on the provisional board in London. He also helped to establish the Commercial Banking Co. of Sydney and became a director.

Meanwhile in 1831 a corruptly contested election had terminated Macqueen's political career. Having sold his English estate to the duke of Bedford, he went to New South Wales in July 1834. For the next four years Macqueen lived at Segenhoe and was a conspicuous figure in colonial society. He held office as a magistrate and had a town house in Darlinghurst. In August 1838 he sold his stock, leased Segenhoe, and returned to England where he published *Australia as she is and as she may be* (London, 1840).

At intervals between 1827 and 1841 he had been deeply in debt and there were suits against him in King's Bench and Common Pleas. In 1845 he was living at Caen, Normandy, perhaps to escape his debtors. By 1852 he had returned and was living at Banbury, Oxfordshire, but all his estates had been sold. He died of apoplexy, at the Queen's Hotel, Oswestry, on 31 March 1854.

At the New Church, Marylebone, on 26 October 1820, he had married Anne, sister of Sir Jacob Astley, baronet, of Melton Constable, Norfolk; they had two sons and three daughters.

HRA (1), 11-20, (3), 6; H. S. Russell, *Genesis of Queensland* (Syd, 1888); S. J. Butlin, *Australia and New Zealand Bank* (Melb, 1961); J. F. Campbell, 'Genesis of rural settlement on the Hunter', *JRAHS*, 12 (1926-27); Newcastle and Hunter District Hist Soc, *Procs*, 5 (1951), 158-60, 10 (1956), 117-18; *Scone Advocate*, 21 May 1920-6 Sept 1921.

E. W. DUNLOP

MACVITIE, THOMAS (1781-1833), merchant and banker, was born at Dumfries, Scotland. After some years in Cape Colony and Mauritius, he arrived in New South Wales in 1816 with a cargo of merchandise and set himself up as a merchant in Sydney. He was principally a wholesale importer but developed interests in whaling and in the export of timber. He appears to have established himself quickly in the commercial life of the colony, for he was one of the 'principal merchants' invited to the meeting which led to the formation of the Bank of New South Wales only a few months after his arrival. Governor Macquarie appointed him a magistrate in February 1821.

He decided to settle permanently in the colony and applied for a land grant in 1821, pledging to invest £2000 to £3000 in stock and improvements. He received 1000 acres in the Camden district as a new settler. In 1825 he bought 2000 acres of crown land near the Shoalhaven. He was a foundation member of the Agricultural Society of New South Wales, formed in 1822, and in the same year signed the memorial submitted by members to Bathurst protesting against the heavy English import duty on colonial wool. He became one of the few colonial shareholders of the Australian Agricultural Co., his one vote indicating an investment of more than £1000.

His association with members of the 'exclusive' party was important in his later career. After taking part in the initial moves in 1817 to establish the Bank of New South Wales and becoming an original shareholder, Macvitie was elected to the board of directors in 1821 and re-elected in 1823. He resigned from the board in 1826 when he was elected managing director of the new Bank of Australia, which opened for business at his house in Bligh Street in July 1826. The leading spirit behind this second bank in New South Wales was John Macarthur [q.v.] who, with a small group which included Macvitie, organized its formation; most of its first directors were shareholders of the Australian Agricultural Co. It was an 'exclusive' institution, 'the pure merino bank' in the words of the *Monitor*. No public offer of shares was made and it was said that at least half the shares went to 'settlers' and most of the remainder to civil and military officers.

Macvitie gave up his importing business to manage the new bank which entered immediately into aggressive competition with the older institution. It was not an easy period because of the dollar export crisis and the depression of the late 1820s. Macvitie was affected personally by the slump and drought, and in 1828 successfully sought postponement of payment on instalments due for land he had bought.

Macvitie was a vice-president of the Benevolent Society. As a leading Presbyterian he was active in the foundation of

Scots Church, and later became a trustee with Rev. J. D. Lang and David Ramsay [qq.v.]. His position as a prominent citizen was marked by his inclusion in the warrant of 1829 as one of the reserves for nomination to the Legislative Council in the event of a vacancy.

At Scots Church on 3 August 1826 Macvitie had married Ann, who was born in the colony about 1790, daughter of Joseph and Ann Jones; they had three sons and one daughter born between 1820 and 1825. He died on 3 February 1833, his wife surviving until 1875.

Whatever Macvitie's origins, in New South Wales, although not conspicuously wealthy, he seems to have been accepted as a person of sufficient social status and personal ability to become in a short time a leader of the mercantile community and a magistrate, and to have been well liked and respected. He took no prominent part in the political questions which agitated the colony in the 1820s. A sober and competent man of business, his most important achievement was his successful management of the Bank of Australia during its first years.

HRA (1), 10-16; MS cat under T. Macvitie (ML).   R. F. HOLDER

MAGAREY, THOMAS (1825-1902), miller and pastoralist, was born on 25 February 1825 in County Down, Ireland, the son of James Magarey and his wife Elizabeth. He spent most of his boyhood in Lancashire, and 'was brought up to the milling business'. At 17, with his brother James, he migrated to Nelson, New Zealand, paying his own passage. In the *Fifeshire* he became acquainted with a number of Dissenters, who as 'United Christians' built Ebenezer Chapel and started a Sunday school and temperance society soon after landing. Their unity was disturbed by the arrival of Anglican and Wesleyan ministers, and the Nelson settlement was deeply affected by economic distress. The Magarey brothers decided to try their fortune in South Australia, their interest aroused by the importation of wheat from Adelaide. They arrived in Adelaide in September 1845. Four years later they succeeded John Ridley [q.v.] as owners of the Hindmarsh flour-mill. The business later passed to Thomas, who built up extensive markets locally and overseas. As his first pastoral venture he leased in 1859 the Naracoorte run, its eighty-seven square miles being capable of carrying more than 20,000 sheep besides cattle and horses. He held two other smaller southeastern properties and more areas on Eyre Peninsula, including Tulkea at Sleaford Bay.

After his marriage Magarey made his home at Noarlunga, then moved to Hindmarsh, where in 1857 he was elected to the District Council. In 1860-63 he represented West Torrens in the House of Assembly, and then sat in the Legislative Council in 1863-65. As a legislator he championed the pastoral industry. He also advocated Bible reading in public schools. Before entering parliament he had strenuously opposed government grants to churches. He was an early joint proprietor of the *Register* and *Observer* and an original director of the Bank of Adelaide.

Magarey was reserved and severe. Indeed, to his grandchildren he seemed an alarming figure, unsmiling, with intense blue eyes under shaggy brows and with his grey hair worn long to protect an injury received in his early days at Nelson when a cart wheel damaged his head, setting up chronic neuralgia which lasted during his life. He was intensely religious. Converted to the idea of Christian unity in New Zealand, he was the first to introduce the teachings of the Church of Christ to Adelaide. With a breakaway group from the Scotch Baptist Church he had helped to found the first Church of Christ in Australia by 1849. He endowed chapels at Hindmarsh in 1854, and in Grote Street in 1856. In 1872 he joined the Plymouth Brethren, basing his 'conversion' on a reappraisal of the doctrine of baptism.

For his last thirty years he lived on his farm near Enfield, where he installed a telescope and studied the stars. In his home he had his own apartment sealed off by a baize door and seldom emerged except for family prayers. He died at Enfield on 31 August 1902.

In 1848 he had married Elizabeth, daughter of James Crabb Verco. They had eight children. The second son, Silvanus James, became prominent in the medical profession. He was in turn secretary and president of the newly formed South Australian Temperance Alliance, his pronounced views winning him a seat in 1888-97 in the Legislative Council, where he pleaded for the abolition of the liquor trade whenever he found opportunity. A grandson of Thomas Magarey presented the Magarey Medal, awarded annually for the best and fairest player in the South Australian Football League (Australian Rules).

Alfred Saunders, *Tales of a pioneer* (Christchurch, 1927); H. R. Taylor, *The history of*

Churches of Christ in South Australia (Adel, 1959); *Register* (Adel), 1 Sept 1902.

HERBERT R. TAYLOR

MAKINSON, THOMAS COOPER (1809-1893), Church of England clergyman converted to Catholicism, was born in October 1809 at Manchester, England, the son of Joseph Makinson, a cotton merchant, and his wife Mary, née Cooper. In January 1829 he was admitted to the Manchester Grammar School where Dr Jeremiah Smith was high master and on 8 July 1831 he enrolled as a sizar at St John's College, Cambridge (B.A., 1835). Makinson was ordained deacon by Bishop Bird of Chester on 16 August 1835, went to the curacy of St Ann, Manchester, and was priested on 17 July 1836. Jeremiah Smith was also rector of St Ann's in 1825-37, his ministry there ending with the fabric of the church dilapidated and the parish making an apparently negligible impact on a city that was desperately overcrowded and badly governed.

In 1837, at the instance of Bishop Broughton [q.v.], the Society for the Propagation of the Gospel appealed 'to the friends of the Church of England in behalf of their brethren in Australia', particularly for more clergy. Makinson, undoubtedly influenced by the depressed situation in Manchester, Smith's retirement from St Ann's, and his own marriage in 1837 to Sarah Ann Soulby (1815-1873), offered his services and was accepted. He sailed with his wife in the *Siam* and reached Sydney in January 1838, one of nine clergy who arrived in Sydney late in 1837 or in 1838 as a result of the society's appeal; each received a travel allowance of £150 and £50 a year in addition to the government stipend, and the local diocesan committee gave them each £50 to help in settling to colonial life.

Makinson soon took up parish duties at Mulgoa; his government stipend commenced on 13 February and his licence was issued on 31 March. In the parsonage he quickly established 'a most respectable boarding school', attended by twelve pupils. He celebrated divine worship every day in the church, and on Sundays after a service and a sermon, he went eleven miles to South Creek, until St Mary Magdalene's Church there was served from Penrith.

Thomas Whytehead, who visited Mulgoa in 1842, reckoned Makinson, his fellow collegian at Cambridge, 'the very picture of a parish priest: the clergyman at his parsonage-door habited in his black cassock, after the fashion of the olden times in England'. Whytehead found that Makinson was respected by the neighbouring clergy but was 'withal so humble and simple-minded, and such a picture of meekness that, while few know so much, few think they know so little'. In December 1842 Makinson assisted at the laying on of hands at the ordination of R. K. Sconce [q.v] in St James's Church, Sydney. During the 1840s he followed the activities of the Oxford Movement keenly and studied the tracts that were published. Presumably he discussed these tracts with Sconce when Sconce was minister at Penrith and South Creek.

Makinson continued as minister at Mulgoa until January 1848 when he moved to Sydney to take temporary charge at St Peter's Church, Cook's River. Sconce's doubts about the apostolic nature of the Church of England were becoming critical at that time; being dissatisfied by Broughton's explanations, he approached the Roman Catholic Archbishop, J. B. Polding [q.v.], who agreed 'with great joy of the heart' to see him and within a few days received him, his wife and family into the Catholic Church. At the same time Makinson, with his wife and family, who had precisely the same difficulties, was received into the church. The critical questions for both Sconce and Makinson were apostolic succession and the supremacy of the Pope. They resigned their licences as Anglican clergy on 21 February 1848, and five days later Broughton held a court at which sentences of deprivation and deposition from the ministry were pronounced against them; these sentences were read next day (Sunday) in the churches where they had officiated.

Many Anglicans in Sydney knew that Sconce was an advocate of 'Puseyism', but Makinson's conversion caused great surprise, partly because he had a country parish and was of a retiring nature, but chiefly by the rapidity with which he eventually acted; on 18 February he had consulted Broughton about a parish matter without giving any indication of a changing attitude, on the 20th he took the Sunday service at Cook's River, and on the 21st wrote to Broughton stating that he could 'no longer continue a minister or member of the Church of England'. Sconce's conversion seems to have influenced Makinson, whose decision was not made easier because he then had six children to support, the eldest being 8.

Polding employed Makinson and Sconce as teachers in charge of the lay school attached to St Mary's Seminary, at a salary of £150 each. Makinson also taught at St Mary's College, Lyndhurst, when it was inaugurated in February 1852 under the direction of Bishop C. H. Davis [q.v.]. In 1851 Makinson applied for appointment as the first lecturer in mathematics in the college that was intended initially to be the forerunner of the University of Sydney; he was placed second among the candidates, but the plan was altered and no appointment was made.

Soon after the death of Bishop Davis in May 1854, while Polding and Abbot H. G. Gregory [q.v.] were in Europe, Makinson took his wife and family to Belgium. For a time they lived at Liége where he earned a living by tutoring. About this time Polding appointed Makinson his secretary and on 26 January 1856 Makinson, his wife and family, with Polding, Gregory, and some other clergy arrived back in Sydney in the *Phoenix*. Makinson was secretary to the archbishop until March 1877 when Polding died. Until about 1860 he continued to teach at Lyndhurst, philosophy being one of his subjects. In 1858-85 Makinson was fellow of St John's College within the University of Sydney. He was on the sub-committee of fellows appointed to draw up letters to Pius IX, informing him of the college's founding, and to Newman, Wiseman, Ullathorne [q.v.], and Cullen seeking their assistance in the appointment of a first rector of the college.

The extent of Makinson's services as Polding's secretary awaits analysis, but it was generally accepted that he contributed to most of the archbishop's pastorals and that his personal position became more important after Gregory, with whom he later corresponded, had to leave the Australian mission. Polding indicated his reliance on Makinson when he wrote in December 1868: 'And now I am back in Sydney, to coldness, reserve and misery: not one except Makinson with whom I can speak unreservedly, and this is almost a safety-valve to me'.

When Polding died Makinson's eyesight was failing; he was allowed a liberal pension by Archbishop R. B. Vaughan and his active connexion with the archdiocese gradually tapered off to become an honourable sinecure. He lost his sight about 1883 and in his last years was mostly confined to his home in Gladesville, where he had lived since the early 1860s; he attended Mass regularly at the Marist Fathers' Church, Villa Maria, Hunter's Hill, almost to the time of his death on 7 November 1893. He was buried from Villa Maria in St Charles's cemetery, Ryde.

Makinson's wife died in 1873 and was also buried in St Charles's cemetery. Of their twelve children, three died young and six were born at Mulgoa, baptized Anglicans by their father and became Catholics with their parents in 1848. The eldest son, Henry Massey, taught at Lyndhurst before establishing a successful legal firm in Sydney. The youngest daughter, Miriam Josepha (1854-1896) married C. G. Heydon in 1880.

W. W. Burton, *The state of religion and education in New South Wales* (Lond, 1840); J. F. Smith (ed), *The admission register of the Manchester School*, 3 pt 2 (Manchester, 1874); T. Whytehead, *Poetical remains and letters* (Lond, 1877); H. N. Birt, *Benedictine pioneers in Australia*, 2 (Lond, 1911); SPG *Sydney Cttee Reports*, 1837-47; SMH, Feb 1848; Information from Canon E. Saxon, Manchester.

R. A. DALY

MANIFOLD, THOMAS (1809-1875), JOHN (1811-1877) and PETER (1817-1885), were the fourth, fifth and sixth sons of William Manifold and Mary, née Barnes, of Courthouse Farm, Bromborough, Cheshire, England. When the family decided to emigrate to Van Diemen's Land, Thomas was sent ahead. He arrived in Hobart Town on 23 January 1828 with £1500 and a letter of recommendation from the Colonial Office. On condition that he appoint a respectable free overseer, he obtained 1280 acres on the west bank of the Tamar River. John and Peter, with their parents and three sisters, arrived on 8 July 1831. Land grants had then finished, but William bought ninety acres next to his son's land, and on the combined properties the family built Kelso House.

Their holding was comparatively poor and, when news came of the Port Phillip District, Thomas lost no time in seeing it for himself in February 1836. What he saw made him hurry back to buy ewes and lambs, comprehensive stores, a horse and a dog. On 9 July, with one of his brothers, he put ashore what he claimed to be the first sheep ever landed at Point Henry, and proceeded to occupy both sides of the Moorabool River. Towards the end of the year Thomas returned to Van Diemen's Land, leaving John and Peter to run the new station. He went back, however, for several visits, during one of which the three brothers examined the country near Ballarat.

In December 1838, by penetrating the Stony Rises, John and Peter discovered Lake Purrumbete and the Mount Leura country. On 4 July Thomas had married

Jane Elizabeth, eldest daughter of Captain Walter Synnet, formerly of Ballinate, County Armagh, Ireland, and then of Van Diemen's Land. He hastened to join his brothers, and they occupied the Purrumbete run in January 1839. On this journey and later, they could not take their stock and drays through the Stony Rises, so went north of Lake Corangamite, discovering the neck of land between it and Lake Gnarpurt. By April the move from the Moorabool was complete. As yet they had no hut and were working day and night, but their delight in the new run was unbounded. John wrote to his mother: 'We are at last got to the land we wished for . . . it is a beautiful place, and cannot be surpassed by any I have ever seen'. The three brothers occupied Purrumbete together, breeding both sheep and cattle, until Thomas went to Grassmere run on the Merri River near Warrnambool in 1844. John and Peter soon gave up breeding sheep, but retained the well-known '3M' brand for the cattle. These were Shorthorns, derived from four bulls originally imported by the Bolden brothers [q.v.] and later improved by further importations, and were renowned for size and quality. By the time of the gold rush in 1851, John and Peter were breeding over 1000 head a year, as well as fattening stores.

The diggings disorganized Grassmere by drawing away Thomas's men, and Mrs Manifold took their two sons and two daughters to Europe for their education. Thomas gave up the property next year, went to England, and eventually brought his family back to live in Melbourne. At Purrumbete things were different. The brothers preferred black stockmen to white, so the discovery of gold upset them very little, while providing the very market they required. John was on his second visit to England when the rush started, and Peter went in his turn soon after John returned. On 2 September 1856 John married Marion Thomson, at Cormiston, Van Diemen's Land. They had four daughters and five sons, from three of whom, William Thomson, James Chester and Edward, the later generations of the family descend.

Through the years the brothers had contended with scab, fluke and footrot, depression, rabbits, bush fires and pleuro-pneumonia. In 1861 they appointed as manager Henry Manifold Matson, their nephew, who had already been with them for five years. Thomas died in Melbourne on 7 November 1875, John at Purrumbete on 3 January 1877 and Peter at Purrumbete on 13 July 1885.

Devout members of the Church of England, John and Peter gave generously towards building St Paul's Church, Camperdown, and guaranteed part of the vicar's stipend. Peter was a member of the Hampden and Heytesbury Roads Board from its inception, and carried on into the Hampden Shire Council when it was formed in 1864. However, it was not for public works that they were known, but for their personal example. In a new land where speculators and adventurers were all too common, the Manifold brothers were among those who intended it to be their home and their children's home. Industrious, unostentatious and hospitable, they were respected as men of the highest integrity.

J. Bonwick, Western Victoria; its geography, geology, and social condition (Geelong, 1858); T. F. Bride (ed), Letters from Victorian pioneers (Melb, 1898); P. L. Brown (ed), The narrative of George Russell (Lond, 1935); A. Henderson, Early pioneer families of Victoria and Riverina (Melb, 1936); I. Mead, Early settlement at Kelso in Van Diemen's Land (Launceston, 1961); W. Adeney, Diary (in possession of Mr A. W. Adeney, Middle Brighton, Vic); Family papers in possession of W. G. Manifold, Purrumbete, Weerite, Vic.   W. G. MANIFOLD

MANN, CHARLES (1799-1860), advocate-general, was born on 8 July 1799, at Syleham, East Suffolk, England, son of Charles Mann and his wife Sarah, née Moxon. After being articled to John Sheppard of Southwark he was admitted a solicitor in the King's Bench Division and set up practice in Cannon Street, London. He became associated with the South Australian colonizing movement, and in September 1835 read a paper to a well-attended meeting of the South Australian Literary and Scientific Association, answering the attacks by the Westminster Review on E. G. Wakefield's [q.v.] The New British Province (London, 1834) and other works on the colony. At the request of Captain Hindmarsh, and with the support of Lord de Saumarez, Mann was appointed the first South Australian advocate-general. He sailed in the Coromandel, arriving at Holdfast Bay on 12 January 1837.

Although he called himself a Whig, he seemed to believe that democratic spirit was the mainspring of emigration, 'the centrifugal force intended by Providence to overcome the cohesive effect of habit and civilized enjoyment; and send forth the burning democrat to the wilderness of nature with the Bible in the one hand and the axe in the other'. At the meeting on 10 February 1837 Mann supported Colonel Light's [q.v.] choice of the capital site and thereby won the enmity of Hindmarsh, whose attitude to the principles on which the colony had been founded drew further protests in April. In Mann's view the colony's success depended on preserving every power vested in the colonization commissioners by the Foundation Act (4 & 5 Wm IV, c. 95) on which the colony's land purchasers relied for their security and for government stability. In the disputes over the division of powers between governor and resident commissioner Mann acted as adviser to the latter, convinced that the former was seeking to undermine the statutory provisions. These views, expounded in the Council of Government, led to Mann's resignation from office on 13 November 1837. Next August he published an elaborate analysis of the powers of the various officials. On Hindmarsh's departure Mann considered himself *de jure* acting governor, though he made no bid for office. In London the crown law officers decided that Hindmarsh acted unconstitutionally in suspending Mann; Governor Gawler arrived in October 1838 with orders to reinstate him but, dismayed by Mann's candour, declined his administrative assistance. In an able series of articles in the *Southern Australian*, which they had helped to found, Mann and John Brown [q.v.] argued that Gawler's appointment as both governor and resident commissioner was contrary to colonizing theory and to the intentions of the colony's founders.

Mann built up a large private practice, and became master of the Supreme Court of South Australia in 1844 and acting judge in 1849. He was appointed crown solicitor in 1850, police magistrate and insolvency commissioner in 1856, and commissioner of the Court of Insolvency and stipendiary magistrate in 1858. He died at his home in Gilbert Street, Adelaide, on 24 May 1860.

Mann was described by an early settler as 'clever, agreeable . . . brimful of information on innumerable topics'. As well as winning a prominent place as a pioneer, he took an active part in many public movements. He was one of the first trustees of Trinity Church, although he later attended the Independent Church of Rev. T. Q. Stow [q.v.] and opposed state aid to religion. He was elected to Adelaide's first Municipal Council in 1840, gave popular lectures and supported claims for colonial self-government. He married four times: first to Bessie Sheppard, who died in England; second to Maria Josepha, sister of John Brown; third to Mary Cook; and fourth to Ann Malpas who, with three of his sons and two daughters, survived him.

His son Charles was born in Adelaide on 8 April 1838 and after education at the Collegiate School of St Peter and training in law was admitted to practise in 1860 and had a distinguished parliamentary career. In the House of Assembly he represented Burra in 1870-75 and Stanley in 1875-81. He served as attorney-general in five different ministries for a total of two years and as treasurer in Morgan's ministry for two years and a half. In 1875 he was appointed Q.C. and in 1879 awarded the title Honourable for life within South Australia. On 10 August 1865 he married Isabella Noble, the eldest daughter of W. H. Rowlands. He died on 13 July 1889.

G. H. Pitt, *The press in South Australia 1836 to 1850* (Adel, 1946); K. T. Borrow, *Charles Mann* (Adel, 1958).

MANN, DAVID DICKENSON (b. 1775?), clerk and author, entered the service of the duke of Northumberland and in May 1797 transferred to the household of Lord Charles Somerset, younger son of the fifth duke of Beaufort, as under-servant in charge of domestic affairs. On 21 September he was indicted for forging and uttering a false receipt for a sum of money due from Lord Charles to the household baker, Thomas Farmer, thereby defrauding both Somerset and Farmer, and was tried at the Old Bailey on 10 January 1798. He claimed that he had no intention of dishonesty, but had committed a great error owing to losses incurred through speculation. He was found guilty but his death sentence was commuted to transportation for life.

Mann arrived in Sydney in the *Hillsborough* in July 1799. He seems to have acted as a schoolmaster at Parramatta and in October 1800 he was appointed clerk assessor to the Naval Officer, to the Committee for the Erection of Jails and to the Orphan Committee, as well as having the duty of entering property agreements. On 13 September 1801 he married Elizabeth Wheeler in Sydney, and on 18 January 1802 he received an absolute pardon. In September the Orphan Committee allowed him 5s. a day for attendance on the committee and 2½ per cent for collecting money due to it. Mann was later employed at the secretary's office and in 1804 was directed to sign orders when Secretary Chapman [q.v.] went on leave, though Garnham Blaxcell [q.v.] was officially acting secretary. In December 1805 he was dismissed from the secretary's office and twice announced that he was going to England. However, he remained in the colony, holding a fourteen-year lease of a house on the Government Domain, which Governor King had given him in June 1804. In July 1807 Governor Bligh ordered him to quit along with others occupying houses improperly granted within government reserves, a fact which made him sympathize with the rebels when Bligh was deposed. In July 1808 the rebel government appointed him a clerk in the commissary's office. When Colonel Johnston [q.v.] left for England in the *Admiral Gambier* in March 1809, Mann accompanied him after his debts had been paid by the sale of his house to the rebel party. In 1811 he gave evidence at the court martial of Johnston and published in London *The Present Picture of New South Wales*, which he dedicated to Admiral John Hunter and illustrated with four large coloured views of Sydney by John Eyre [q.v.] and a plan of the colony. The book is a panegyric of Hunter's administration, but is most important as a statistical survey of the colony's development; it also suggests improvements to make it self-sufficient and less costly to the mother country. Nothing further is known of Mann's career.

HRNSW, 4, 6, 7; HRA (1), 2-7; *Proceedings of a general court-martial for the trial of Lieut.-Col. Geo. Johnston* (Lond, 1811); *Sydney Gazette*, 29 Dec 1805; MS cat under D. D. Mann (ML).   VIVIENNE PARSONS

MANNING, EDYE (1807-1889), merchant and shipowner, was born at Exeter, Devon, England, a son of John Edye Manning [q.v.]. He came to New South Wales with his wife, Fanny Elizabeth, and his eldest son, John Edye, in December 1831. He was a member of the provisional committee of the Australian Fire and Life Assurance Co. (1835), a director of the Australian Gaslight Co. (1836), and entered the embryonic steamship trade with the paddle-steamer *Maitland*, 103 tons, in 1838. Employing a method of salvaging wrecks that he originated, he raised the *Ceres* (Hunter River Steam Packet Association) with John Korff and built the fast *Victoria* around her engines in 1841. He tried without success to establish an 'Australasian Steam Navigation Co.' and to provide a steamer for the Sydney-Melbourne run after the 297-ton *Clonmel* sank near Wilson's Promontory, but in 1841 he entered the Sydney-Parramatta service with three small paddle-steamers, the *Emu*, the *Kangaroo* and the *Experiment*, in which he installed an engine to replace the horses previously used. Then, leaving the Hunter

River trade to the steamship company formed there in 1839, he bought the old paddle-steamer *William the Fourth* from J. H. Grose [q.v.], built the *Phoenix* around the engines of the old *Sophia Jane*, the first steamer imported from England, and started to trade with south coast ports and the Clarence River, where he bought Ramornie station in 1845. The south coast trade developed rapidly and in 1857 his company amalgamated with rival companies to form the Illawarra Steam Navigation Co. and in 1858 the Shoalhaven Steam Navigation Co. In that year he took over the management of the fleet and provided a Sydney wharf for it. On his retirement in 1862 he continued to trade in second-hand steamers on his own account and sold five ships to China and Japan between 1854 and 1863. His shipping interests were carried on by his son, John Edye Manning. He died at Wentworth Falls on 24 February 1889, leaving two sons and two daughters.

HRA (1), 22, 24, 26; R. Parsons, *Fleets of principal steamship owners registering vessels at Sydney prior to 1900* (Adel, 1959); R. Parsons, *Details of steamships registered at port of Sydney prior to 1900* (Adel, 1961); A. B. Portus, 'Early Australian steamers', JRAHS, 2 (1904-07); H. Kolsen, 'Company formation in N.S.W. 1828-1851', *Business Archives and History*, 1, no 6 (1959); J. Ginswick, 'Early Australian capital formation, 1836-1850', *Business Archives and History*, 1, no 6 (1959).   LOUISE T. DALEY

MANNING, JOHN EDYE (1783-1870), court registrar, was the second son of Rev. James Manning of Exeter, England, and his second wife, Lydia, née Edye. He married Matilda Jordan Cooke (1788-1860) on 1 May 1804 and about that time began practising law. In 1811 he became insolvent and executed a deed of assignment of his property for the benefit of his creditors. Between 1814 and 1823 Manning lived on the Continent; he returned to England in 1823 under the protection of the Insolvent Debtors' Relief Act and in 1824 sold his property.

Manning was appointed registrar of the Supreme Court of New South Wales in August 1828 on a salary of £800, and next May arrived in Sydney in the *Lord Melville* with his wife and five of his children.. His expectations were disappointed; on his arrival he complained to the Colonial Office that living costs were high and that the customary land grant and town allotment had not been immediately granted to him. Governor Darling was instructed to extend this indulgence to Manning and granted him two allotments at Rushcutters Bay in November 1831. Manning was also appointed curator of intestate estates by the judges of the Supreme Court, and despite his objections was obliged to lodge a security of £2000 to protect the public from loss. Since he could not raise this sum in the colony, his father and his elder brother, a barrister of Lincoln's Inn, entered into security in England on his behalf. In 1838 Manning again objected when the judges of the Supreme Court made new rules for the deposit of intestate money in the Savings Bank and for the quarterly audit of the registrar's accounts. Manning felt that these rules were inconsistent with the understanding on which he had accepted his position. He claimed that his official income had proved to be less than half the £2000 a year which he had been promised as the practical value of his office, and that, unless he could derive an indirect income through the custody of intestate estates, he would have to use his own salary to pay the cost of their administration, with consequent losses to the beneficiaries. However, these objections were waived by Glenelg who insisted that Manning had no reason for complaint or disappointment.

From his arrival in the colony Manning took an active part in public life; he was a member of the Stockholders' Committee, the Southern Cattle Association and the Sydney College Committee, a director of the Fire and Life Assurance Co. and the Sydney Ferry Co., and active in the formation of the Brisbane Water Steam Co., the Australian Navigation Co. and the Australian Mining Co. He was a member of the central committee of the Australian Immigration Association and a generous subscriber to religious and charitable funds. His large land holdings included houses and stores in Queen Street, Sydney, land at Brisbane Water, Melbourne, Carcoar, Goulburn and Wollongong, and a lease of Vermont near Camden.

In 1838 Manning opposed certain clauses in the bills of insolvent debtors and imprisonment for debt, claiming that they favoured the creditor and were inexpedient at a time when the colony was exposed to fluctuations in the English market. Late in 1841 he himself became a victim of the depression, for his property and stock were heavily mortgaged and his shares worthless. Manning told the judges of the Supreme Court that his financial difficulties prevented him from lodging the intestate estates money in the Savings Bank. He could give only a second mortgage on landed property as security for the payment of the balance of the trust money. In December 1841 his resignation was refused because he was under the control of the judges while he remained in office. In January 1842 Gipps decided to suspend him from office when the judges took out a writ against him. When Manning's town estate was sequestrated in March, his debts amounted to some £30,000, of which about £10,000 was trust money that he had failed to lodge with the Savings Bank. During the insolvency proceedings he admitted that his private and public funds had been kept in the same account. The judges claimed that he had been £1100 short in his balances at the 1838 audit and thereafter had evaded payment of the money into the bank by failing to collect trust funds, to advertise for creditors to claim their dues or to present the annual lists required by the British government.

Stanley charged the judges with responsibility for Manning's default because they had neglected to enforce their rules, and insisted that all claims for compensation be made in the colony. However, the British Treasury did obtain the £2000 lodged as security by Manning's family in England, although this sum, paid to the Colonial Treasury in 1846, did not go far in meeting the claims on Manning's estate by the beneficiaries of intestate estates. In May the Legislative Council petitioned the Queen to take steps to relieve those who had suffered through Manning's appointment to a position of trust despite a previous insolvency, but the British government refused to take action. Members of Manning's family in the colony offered to pay compensation for their father's default; their proposal was apparently disregarded, for in 1849 the Legislative Council passed an Act to provide for the payment of claims on the late registrar of the Supreme Court of New South Wales in respect of the Intestates' Estates Act (13 Vic. no. 44). Meanwhile Manning had returned to England, and again spent some time on the Continent. He appears to have received an annual remittance from the family of Lord Brougham, who had been instrumental in advancing the Manning family in New South Wales. John Edye Manning died in Bristol, England, on 16 January 1870; of his five sons and three daughters who survived infancy, Edye [q.v.] was a merchant in Sydney, and William Montagu had a distinguished legal career.

HRA (1), 14-16, 18-25; *Sydney Gazette*, 9 May 1829; *Australian*, 16 Oct 1841, 7 May 1842; MS cat under Manning (ML).

R. J. M. NEWTON

MANSFIELD, RALPH (1799-1880), Methodist missionary and newspaper editor, was born on 12 March 1799 at Toxteth Park, Liverpool, England, the son of Ralph Mansfield, manufacturer of earthenware, and his wife Ann, née Worthington. In 1820 he was ordained a Methodist minister, married Lydia Fellows, and sailed for New South Wales in the *Surry* to become a missionary. He arrived in September and soon became a leader in all Methodist activities, including the Auxiliary Wesleyan Missionary Society, of which he was secretary, and the *Australian Magazine*, which he edited and Robert Howe printed. Because of the small numbers of Methodists in the colony, the magazine was not exclusively religious but aimed at a blend of religion and literary interest. Despite its success, however, the Wesleyan Committee in London prohibited its publication.

Mansfield was moved to Hobart Town in July 1823, where he aimed to establish a seminary for young men in conjunction with a mission to Aboriginals. His plan found favour with Lieut-Governor Arthur, who allowed him the use of a house, helped to build a Methodist chapel, and invited him to nominate a Methodist chaplain for the penal station at Macquarie Harbour. He was transferred to Sydney in June 1825 and in 1826, when the first formal Methodist district meetings began, he became the corresponding secretary. Throughout these early years tension between the colonial missionaries and the British Committee was growing, and Mansfield himself was reprimanded for preaching during church hours and administering the Sacrament. He defended himself on the grounds that in his native Liverpool these privileges had been taken for granted by the Methodist Society. In 1828 his discontent came to a head when the committee restricted the family allowances to a level which the Sydney missionaries considered was inadequate for maintaining the same standard of living as their fellow preachers in England. Feeling that the impositions placed on him by the British Committee were too great Mansfield resigned as a missionary in October 1828, but proposed to continue as a local preacher. He later asked without success to be restored to an English circuit, but his religious zeal was not abated and he continued an enthusiastic member of his church and advocate of temperance to the end of his life.

Now that he had to find secular employment Mansfield became joint editor with Robert Howe of the *Sydney Gazette* on 1 January 1829. In the editorial of that day he declared that his policy would be neither directed against the established church nor exclusively religious, as he believed newspapers were not the place for theological debate, and that his political principles would be like those of Howe: attachment to the cause of government. A month later Robert Howe was drowned and Mansfield became sole editor.

Almost immediately he was thrust into the press conflict of Governor Darling's administration. He was found guilty of libel and fined £10 for publishing Darling's reply to the address of landowners and merchants when W. C. Wentworth [q.v.] threatened to impeach Darling. Judge Stephen [q.v.] found that although the libel, which was a personal attack on Wentworth, originated from high authority, this did not authorize Mansfield to publish it. Darling persuaded the Executive Council to pay his fine and costs, as he had merely acted under government orders. Mansfield's support of Darling brought criticism from Goderich who, imagining that Mansfield was a Church of England clergyman, thought that his character of a political partisan was unbecoming and that he should resign his editorship.

Mansfield remained editor of the *Sydney Gazette* until June 1832, and in 1831-39 contributed articles to the *Colonist*. In 1831 he printed the first issue of the *Government Gazette*, begun by Governor Bourke to replace the government notices in the *Sydney Gazette*. In 1836 he became secretary of the Protestant committee which opposed Bourke's attempt to introduce the Irish system of National education, for which he was severely denounced by the governor for being 'deeply, if not wholly engaged in secular pursuits of no very distinguished character'. By 1836 these secular pursuits included the duties of paid agent in the Land Commissioners' Court, director and secretary of the Australian Gaslight Co., director and treasurer of the Australian Steam Conveyance Co., joint-secretary of the Australian School Society with George Allen [q.v.] and book-seller. He was later secretary of the Sydney Floating Bridge Co. and the Royal Exchange Co. He opposed dismemberment of the colony in 1841, supported Indian immigration in 1842, and was the first secretary of the Baptist Church.

The broad scope of his interests and attitudes was recognized in 1841 when Charles Kemp [q.v.] and John Fairfax bought the *Sydney Morning Herald* and appointed Mansfield an editor. He was considered the dominant influence behind the paper, with its attachment to *laissez faire* principles, anxious lest the government become over-active, yet also critical of left-wing politics which might lead to social disruption. The paper opposed Governor Gipps's land regulations, the resumption of transportation and Wentworth's idea of responsible government, but supported the Church of England at crucial moments.

In 1847 Mansfield published an *Analytical view of the Census of New South Wales for the year 1846* and had earlier written a pamphlet on the 1841 census which was sent to the Colonial Office. These studies arranged the statistics of the colony to predict the progress of colonial society, his deductions being described by Gipps as 'curious and interesting'; in reality they were early attempts at demographical study.

Mansfield was not wealthy but had acquired Durham House, a property at Parramatta, and a cottage at Balmain. After his first wife died on 12 March 1831, he married Lucy, daughter of William Shelley [q.v.], on 5 April 1832. Of his first marriage only one daughter of seven children survived infancy, and of the second he had ten children of whom three sons and three daughters survived him. He died at Parramatta on 1 September 1880, aged 81, and was buried at Rookwood; a special train brought many friends from Sydney to attend his funeral. His widow died at Burwood on 5 October 1888.

HRA (1), 10, 15, 16, 18; J. Colwell, *The illustrated history of Methodism* (Syd, 1904); M. Roe, *Quest for authority in eastern Australia* (Melb, 1965); K. Palmer, 'Ralph Mansfield, Australia's first Baptist secretary', *Churinga*, Aug 1957; *Sydney Gazette*, 16 Sept 1820, 1 Jan, 3 Feb 1829; CSO 1/98/2310, 1/306/7355 (TA); MS cat under R. Mansfield (ML).   VIVIENNE PARSONS

MANTON, JOHN ALLEN (1807-1864), Wesleyan minister, was born on 17 August 1807 at Biggleswade, Bedfordshire, England, the son of Thomas and Jane Manton. At 15 he felt called to preach the gospel and in January 1823 was admitted into the Methodist Society on trial. He soon became a local preacher and in April 1830 entered the Christian ministry. Next January he was set apart for missionary service, and sailed in February for New South Wales in the *Surry*.

Manton's first appointment was at Parramatta. Six months later he replaced Rev. William Schofield [q.v.] in the penal station at Macquarie Harbour, Van Diemen's Land, whence he sailed in January 1833 for the new penal settlement at Port Arthur to become its first chaplain. At Sydney in April he married Anne Green from Spilsby, Lincolnshire. In addition to the usual clerical duties at Port Arthur, he organized and conducted schools for adult convicts and instructed some seventy convict boys at Point Puer, later receiving special thanks from Lieut-Governor Arthur for his faithful services. In 1834 he was transferred to Launceston where for three years he conducted a most successful ministry. This was followed by short terms in other settled parts of the colony. In 1841 Manton was reappointed to Port Arthur, where he remained until the government, unsettled by the influence of Bishop Nixon [q.v.], decided to withdraw Wesleyan chaplains from penal stations despite their long ministry of fourteen years. He then became superintendent minister at Hobart Town, and later moved to other centres.

At Campbell Town, in co-operation with Captain Samuel Horton of Somercotes, near Ross, Manton prepared to establish a Wesleyan school for boys in Tasmania, for which the captain offered a site of twenty acres and £1000 in cash. In 1855 the Wesleyan Methodist Conference in Sydney, the first in Australasia, decided to open a college named after Captain Horton in an uncompleted wing of the new school building; Manton was appointed its first principal. Two years later he asked to be relieved of its oversight and moved to New South Wales, where he suggested that a second Wesleyan collegiate institution should be established. In 1863 members of the Wesleyan Conference, of which he was elected president, supported him. Newington House, built in 1832 and owned by the Blaxland [q.v.] family, was inspected, leased and repaired throughout; with Manton as principal, it was opened in July as Newington College. He was never robust and his health failed altogether after fifteen months. He died at the college on 9 September 1864, survived by his widow and several children.

The *Tasmanian Messenger* said of him, 'He was a man of sound judgment and enlightened mind, a good preacher, a strict disciplinarian, a perfect gentleman, a thorough Wesleyan . . . Faultless he was not, but about him there was such a combination of tenderness and firmness, of sympathy and manliness, of Christian liberality and consistency, that his enemies were few and his friends were many'.

J. Colwell (ed), *A century in the Pacific* (Syd, 1914); *Launceston Advertiser*, 27 Nov 1834; *Hobart Town Courier*, 12 Apr 1855;

Tas Messenger, 1 Nov 1864; Manton papers
(copies in author's possession).

                                    E. R. PRETYMAN

MARGAROT MAURICE (1745-1815), a
'Scottish Martyr', was the son of a wine
and general merchant who operated between Portugal, France and Britain, and
was an ardent supporter of John Wilkes.
Educated at the university of Geneva, Margarot followed his father's business and
political interests. He was living in France
about 1789 and had acquaintances among
the revolutionary leaders. Returning to
England early in 1792, he joined the London Corresponding Society, which Thomas
Hardy (1752-1832) then led. Margarot
immediately dominated the society and became its president; in September he and
Hardy carried a *Congratulatory Address to
the National Convention of France*. Pamphlets from his pen urged fiscal and electoral reform, shorter parliaments and a
broader franchise. In November 1793
Margarot and Joseph Gerrald [q.v.] went to
Edinburgh to represent the society at the
British Convention of the Friends of the
People. The two stood out in debate and
authority selected them and William
Skirving [q.v.] to be charged with sedition.
Margarot's trial in January 1794 was distinguished by mob demonstrations in his
favour, by his own truculence and by the
judge's bias against the accused. Margarot
was sentenced to transportation for fourteen years and in April embarked in the
Surprize. He had remained as active as
possible in urging his followers to continued action.

Arrived in Sydney, Margarot at once
demanded his freedom from Lieut-Governor
Grose [q.v.], maintaining that the very
process of transportation discharged the
sentence. The plea failed; but though he
had to remain in the colony he was not
liable for compulsory labour; his wife had
accompanied him and he soon built a congenial life. In letters to friends and the
Colonial Office he criticized the officers'
economic power and urged that the British
government extirpate it. The officers said
he was seditious, and his name was mentioned apropos alleged rebellion in September and October 1800; but he had impressed
Governor Hunter and probably informed
him of political moves within the colony.

Margarot's relations with Governor King
were complex and mysterious. He warned
that he would scrutinize the newcomer's
behaviour and implied that he would report on it to the Colonial Office, yet he
seemingly became an informant for King
too. At the same time his home became a

centre for seditious elements, including radical 'gentlemen' convicts and United Irishmen. Margarot probably helped the Irish
to plan their rebellion on 4 March 1804.
Some months later King seized Margarot's
papers which he found to contain republican sentiments, evidence of conspiracy
with the Irish, denunciation of colonial
avarice and a forecast of Australia succeeding America as the world's chief power.
The military officers urged King to punish
Margarot, but the governor delayed, probably not only because of Margarot's useful
information but also for fear that the
convict was writing to the Colonial Office
about himself. However, in July 1805 Margarot was sent in turn to Norfolk Island,
Van Diemen's Land and Newcastle, where
he arrived early in 1806.

The following years are blank, but he
returned to England in 1810 and at once
began to lobby the Colonial Office. He
complained that he had been kept in New
South Wales beyond his term, and his
allegation that the officer junta which
seized power on 26 January 1808 had thus
avenged his long-standing hostility was
probably correct. He was a witness before
the 1812 parliamentary committee on transportation, where he pursued his campaign
against the officers and evidently influenced
the committee. He resumed his interest in
British politics. Two pamphlets, *Thoughts
on Revolution* (Harlow, 1812) and *Proposal
for a Grand National Jubilee* (Sheffield, nd)
propounded the old radical themes as well
as arguing how desirable it would be to
base the whole economy on the yeoman
farmer, and to restrict commerce to the
minimum. He died in London on 11 November 1815; his widow died some twenty
years later.

Most commentators have judged Margarot harshly, generally founding their
argument on his behaviour aboard the
Surprize, when he sided with the captain
in accusing T. F. Palmer [q.v.] of foment-
ing a convict mutiny. Rumours have alleged
that Margarot was a police spy among
British radicals; conceivably he reported to
Hunter and King on his apparent friends,
gentlemen radicals and United Irishmen, as
well as on his declared enemies, the officers.
Certainly Margarot was an arrogant, cantankerous man; he yearned for power and
lacked judgment. Yet Thomas Hardy, who
knew him well, remained loyal and Francis
Place, who studied Margarot's life story in
1837, discounted extreme criticisms of him.
This attitude was probably the wisest.
Margarot's feeling for social justice was
true and in him the intellectual 'left' came
to Australia.

HRNSW, 2-4; HRA (1), 1; Sel cttee on transportation, Report PP (HC), 1812. (341); M. Roe, 'Maurice Margarot: a radical in two hemispheres', Bulletin of the Institute of Hist Research (Univ of Lond), 31 (1958), no 83.
MICHAEL ROE

MARRIOTT, FITZHERBERT ADAMS (1811-1890), Anglican priest, was born on 27 May 1811 at Lincoln's Inn Fields, London, the second son of George Wharton Marriott of St Giles and Middle Temple, London, and his wife Selina Anne, the daughter of Archdeacon Adams of Huntingdonshire. He was educated at Charterhouse, and read classics at Oriel College, Oxford (B.A., 1829; M.A., 1836). After ordination in 1835 he was appointed to Cotesbach, a Leicestershire parish of which his uncle held the patronage. Chosen by Bishop Nixon [q.v.], a family friend, as his chaplain, he sailed with the episcopal party in the Duke of Roxburgh and arrived at Hobart Town in July 1843. Within a week, he was appointed archdeacon and soon had the added duties of surrogate.

After assisting for some time in busy northern parishes, he was sent to England by Nixon to make good the bishop's disputed authority over the chaplains in the Convict Department, raise money for the colonial church, and plead the cause of religious education for the colony. He made many contacts among churchmen and philanthropists in England and collected £5000 for Christ's College as well as an anonymous gift through the bishop of Ripon of £5000 for general expansion. Persuaded by the conciliatory attitude at Downing Street and by his own willingness to co-operate with Nixon, Marriott ignored his instruction and accepted the office of superintendent of convict chaplains, in hope that, while he also remained subject as archdeacon to the bishop's authority, Nixon would agree to abandon claims for complete authority over the chaplains and accept an indirect responsibility through himself. He returned in February 1846 and found that his assumption was wrong, for Nixon refused to ordain the twelve men brought out by Marriott until his responsibility for them was recognized. After much discussion the men were designated religious instructors and Marriott's position was changed to superintendent of religious instructors. He resigned this office in July 1846 and, when Nixon went to England to take up the issues himself, Marriott became vicar-general and special commissary.

On Nixon's return in 1847 Marriott was appointed chaplain to New Norfolk, where he remained until he left the colony on sick leave in February 1853. During the ritualist controversy he was a strong supporter of the bishop. Aware of Nixon's high regard, he was disappointed in not being transferred to St David's on the death of Dr William Bedford [q.v.], but the opposition of churchwardens and congregation to his ritualist stand would have made his ministry difficult. He was not expected to return to the colony and resigned his Tasmanian posts in September 1854, when he became curate of St Paul's, Knightsbridge, England. In December 1859 he was appointed vicar of Chaddesley Corbett, Worcestershire, a post he held until his death on 19 October 1890. On 26 September 1848 he had married Anne Julia, the second daughter of Major Charles Schaw [q.v.] and his wife Anne Frances, née Cockburn. She predeceased him by less than four months. They had two sons.

Marriott was a scholarly preacher and three of his sermons were published by request in Hobart: The Parochial System (1844), Is a Penal Colony reconcileable with God's constitution of human society and the Laws of Christ's Kingdom? (1847) and The Church of the Incarnation, our guide and refuge (1851). His Tasmanian career was marked by a succession of quarrels, both with the Evangelical clergy and with Lieut-Governor Wilmot whom he opposed strongly on the transportation question, (Letter Addressed to His Excellency . . . against the Renewal of Transportation, Hobart, 1847), and in the dispute over the bishop's authority. He was reputed to have spread rumours at the Colonial Office about Wilmot's private life which caused his dismissal. His responsible mission to England in the service of the colonial church won him wide esteem, and in 1856 his help to education was remembered in an honorary fellowship of Christ's College.

N. Nixon, The pioneer bishop in Van Diemen's Land 1843-1863 (Hob, 1954); Examiner (Launceston), 20 Oct 1847; Church News (Hob), Feb 1891; GO 33/55/766 (TA).
P. R. HART

MARSDEN, SAMUEL (1764-1838), chaplain, missionary and farmer, was born on 24 June 1764 at Farsley, Yorkshire, England, the son of Thomas Marsden, a blacksmith. He attended the village school, was then apprenticed to his father and grew up in an area and amongst a class much influenced by the Methodist religious revival. Well known locally as a lay preacher, Samuel gained the interest of the Elland

Society, an Evangelical group within the Church of England which sponsored the education for the ministry of promising but ill connected youths. Aged about 24, he went to Hull Grammar School, where he met the Milners, members of the Clapham sect, and through them William Wilberforce, doyen of humanitarian and missionary projects, who was to influence decisively the course of Marsden's life. In December 1790 the society sent him to Magdalene College, Cambridge, where he was admitted a *discipulus*. This career was cut short, for on 1 January 1793, after much persuasion, he accepted the appointment to which Wilberforce had recommended him as assistant to the chaplain of New South Wales. A proposal in March 1793 invited Elizabeth, daughter of Thomas Fristan of Hull, to take up the cross and share life's travails and pleasures with him across the seas. The couple were wed on 21 April; Samuel was ordained deacon on 17 March at Bristol and priest in May; on 1 July they left for New South Wales in the *William*. After a journey made memorable by Samuel's clashes with the captain and by the accouchement of Elizabeth as the ship was buffeted by a storm off Van Diemen's Land, they arrived in Sydney Cove on 10 March 1794.

In some significant ways the pattern of Marsden's life was set during his first year in New South Wales. As assistant to Rev. Richard Johnson [q.v.], after a brief visit to Norfolk Island in 1795, he was stationed at Parramatta. It was an important centre in the colony and Marsden remained there after Johnson's departure, although for some years he was the only Anglican clergyman on the mainland. He was promised the position of senior chaplain in 1802, but was much vexed at receiving only part of its stipend, and was not formally promoted until after his return from England in 1810. Governor Macquarie allowed him to live at Parramatta 'as being more convenient and centrical for the execution of his general superintending duties', and in September directed that Marsden should be regarded 'as the resident chaplain in that district'.

Marsden had quickly and deeply committed himself to farming, although he was inexperienced in it. By 1802 he had received 201 acres in grants, and had purchased 239 from other settlers; he had 200 acres cleared and grazed 480 sheep. Three years later he had over 1000 sheep, 44 cattle and 100 pigs on his farm which by then had increased to 1730 acres seven miles from Parramatta. In 1798, with Surgeon Arndell [q.v.], he had made a valuable report on the colony's agriculture; in 1803-05 he made several reports to Governor King and to Sir Joseph Banks [q.v.] on the prospects of sheep-breeding and wool-growing. King thought Marsden 'the best practical farmer in the colony', and when he visited England on leave in February 1807 he was recommended by Governor Bligh as one who had made the 'nature and soil' of the colony 'his particular study'. He concentrated on the development of strong heavy-framed sheep such as the Suffolk breed, which had a more immediate value in the colony than the fine-fleeced Spanish merinos imported by John Macarthur [q.v.]. In 1808 he had his own wool made up into a suit by the Thompsons of Horsforth in Yorkshire, and so impressed George III that he was given a present of merinos from the Windsor stud. Four years later more than 4000 lbs of his wool was sold in England at 45d. a lb. Marsden was an important promoter of the wool staple, even though his contribution to technology, breeding and marketing was far eclipsed by that of Macarthur.

Marsden satisfied his English correspondents that 'it was not from inclination' that he and Johnson first accepted Lieut-Governor Grose's [q.v.] offer of land, but from the duty to assist the colony to avert the threat of recurring famine. This explanation was wilfully misleading when published in An *Answer to certain calumnies in the late Governor Macquarie's pamphlet*, and the third edition of *Mr. Wentworth's Account of Australasia* (Lond, 1826), for in 1827, when his holdings totalled 3631 acres by grant and 1600 by purchase, his inclinations took him to Governor Darling with an unsuccessful request for permission to buy another 5000 acres of crown land. Undoubtedly the offer of land and convict servants to work it appealed enormously to Marsden, with his ox-like strength and restlessly active disposition. It brought financial security for a large family, and social acceptability and power to which he could not have aspired in England. Contemporary pietists placed great emphasis on an individual's own efforts, and Marsden, an apostle of personal conversion, believed that material advance was a proof of the genuineness of his personal sense of salvation. At the same time he was spurred by the temper of the colony on his arrival. The officers had begun their single-minded pursuit of wealth. Grose and Johnson were completely estranged and Marsden was soon complaining that Macarthur, the senior officer at Parramatta, frustrated his attempts to secure Sabbath observance by the convicts.

The eager materialism of this frontier society, the crude irreligion of his convict charges and their tendency to associate the chaplain with their other scourgers, helped to confirm Marsden's drift into worldly undertakings.

The advent of the more religiously inclined Governor Hunter in 1795 recognized the chaplain's efforts to reclaim the convicts' souls or at least to achieve an outward observance of moral and religious injunctions; but this effect was counterbalanced by Marsden's appointment as a magistrate and superintendent of government affairs at Parramatta. Clerical justices were common in England at the time but his magisterial posts kept him occupied with heavy temporal duties, and they also further estranged him as a clergyman from the convicts to whom he dispensed justice. No aspects of Marsden's activities did more harm to his pastoral work or to his historical character in Australia than his reputation for extreme severity as a magistrate. This was firmly set by September 1800 when, in the course of an inquiry into a suspected Irish uprising, Judge Advocate Atkins [q.v.] and Marsden had a suspect flogged mercilessly in the hope of securing information about hidden weapons. This particular action was scarcely defensible, but Marsden was not the only magistrate who ordered the infliction of illegal punishments. His general severity can be attributed to his high-mindedness, his passionate detestation of sin and his conviction that Parramatta was such a sink of iniquity that morality could be preserved only by the most rigorous disciplinary measures. For all that, the flogging parson, like the hanging judge, is commonly regarded as an unattractive character.

Meanwhile he continued to carry out his professional duties. He wrote to friends in England in 1799 of his exertions in opening a Sunday school and forwarding the building of a new church, St John's, Parramatta, which was opened in April 1803. He took an active and well-publicized interest in the establishment and administration of an orphan home and school, and declined to accept the fees due to him as treasurer. When in England in 1807-09 he was busy in drawing the attention of the authorities in church and state to the shortcomings of the colony's religious establishment, and was able to recruit additional assistant chaplains. Later he attracted the attention of Mrs Elizabeth Fry by his zeal for improving the lot of female convicts on the transport ships and in the colony, and he startled respectable people in England with his account of the immorality and crime that prevailed in Parramatta, which he thought largely due to the dilapidated condition of the female 'factory', though he did not mention his own prolonged lack of interest in its inmates. But it seems probable that his years as chaplain and magistrate confirmed his early doubts of the possibility of reclaiming the souls of the convicts, so steeped were they in vice and idleness, defeating the best of regulations with their 'invincible depravity'.

Feeling thus frustrated in evangelizing the convicts, Marsden looked elsewhere for professional fulfilment. He tried to civilize and convert the Aboriginals but his efforts were unsuccessful and, by the time Governor Macquarie founded the Native Institution, Marsden had abandoned all hopes of success with these people; by rejecting the material civilization of the European they baulked at what Marsden saw as the necessary first step towards conversion. 'The natives have no Reflection—they have no attachments, and they have no wants', he wrote. He had far more confidence in missions aimed at the people of the Pacific Islands, in whom he had become interested even before he was stimulated by the arrival in Sydney in 1798 of Rowland Hassall [q.v.] and a party of fugitives from Tahiti. He was able to combine evangelization with the promotion of trade with the islands, which he saw as a civilizing if also profitable activity. He had a chief's sons brought to live with him at Parramatta. After 1801 he had the local superintendence and financial management of the London Missionary Society, and was constantly concerned with the affairs of the Church Missionary Society and the British and Foreign Bible Society.

Marsden's absorbing interest as a missioner was in the Maoris of New Zealand, whom he described to Rev. Josiah Pratt during his visit to London in 1808 as 'a very superior people in point of mental capacity, requiring but the introduction of Commerce and the Arts, [which] having a natural tendency to inculcate industrious and moral habits, open a way for the introduction of the Gospel'. This English sojourn from early 1807 to May 1809 prepared the way for establishing the mission to the Maoris, in which enterprise Marsden displayed the qualities of courage, tenacity and resourcefulness that have made his name revered in New Zealand. Convinced from the first of the need to introduce industrious habits, Marsden engaged at his own initial expense craftsmen who were to return with him and teach the Maoris carpentry, shoemaking and ropemaking. His plans were interrupted by news of the massacre of the crew of the whaler *Boyd* at the Bay of Islands in 1809, but in 1813 he formed the New South Wales Society for Affording Protection to the Natives of the South Sea Islands and Promoting their Civilisation, and on 28 November 1814 set out with a party in the brig *Active*, which he had bought for £1400, to maintain the Maoris' contact with civilization.

This was the first of Marsden's seven voyages to New Zealand between 1814 and 1837. They yielded much in terms of self-realization but brought weighty problems of management, finance and discipline. Marsden found that the subordinates he left in New Zealand, no less than the missionaries he superintended in the South Seas, were very human men and women, peculiarly exposed in their tiny groups to rivalries, quarrels, pecuniary temptations and carnal desires that hindered their higher objectives. In April 1820 he reported that the missionaries at the Bay of Islands, heedless of warnings, had bartered muskets and powder for hogs and potatoes. Even the newly appointed superintendent, John Butler, and John Kendall had taken part in this traffic, so disturbing to the equilibrium of Maori society. Yet for all the abuses and the slow pace of conversion the missionaries 'stood between the Maori and the dregs of the oceans that congregated in the Bay of Islands'. Though Marsden regarded the establishment of an official settlement as most improbable, and even undesirable, 'as the Soldiers would be too much exposed to temptation from the Native Women', he suggested in 1830 that the posting of a naval vessel in New Zealand waters would 'prevent much mischief'. Certainly the missionary activities which he promoted paved the way for established government and organized European settlement soon after his death.

In the ten years before Marsden went to England in 1807 he enjoyed fairly cordial relations with the governors, his tranquillity being broken only by enmity towards John Macarthur and by such petty quarrels as that with George Caley [q.v.], whose dog worried the chaplain's pet rabbits. He was absent at the time of the Rum Rebellion, though in England he clearly showed his antipathy to the rebels and according to Macarthur did great mischief to their cause. But soon after his return to Sydney on 27 February 1810, signs of trouble appeared. The *Sydney Gazette*, 31 March 1810, informed Marsden of his appointment to the board of trustees of the Parramatta turnpike road, in company with two well-to-do ex-convicts. Considering this association derogatory to his sacred functions, Marsden declined, arousing Governor Macquarie to a fury which indicated that the latter's military training caused him to view an opposing opinion as insubordination. This was intensified when Marsden refused to read from the pulpit, as was customary, a proclamation directed against food speculators in the drought of 1814, a refusal which earned the chaplain a reprimand from the Colonial Office and the archbishop of Canterbury. Marsden, like Commissioner Bigge [q.v.] later and many other influential colonists, strongly opposed Macquarie's sympathy with emancipists, despite the attempts of his patron Wilberforce to mediate between the two and to modify the chaplain's apparent intolerance. In turn Macquarie developed an inveterate suspicion of Marsden that betrayed him into judgments which were sometimes illiberal and unfair. He suppressed Marsden's tentative use of an unauthorized version of the Psalms. He interpreted Marsden's well-justified demand for convict barracks at Parramatta as a criticism designed to discredit his administration. In November 1815 Marsden preached a funeral panegyric of Ellis Bent [q.v.] which seemed to many to be a criticism of the governor, who in turn blamed the chaplain for a further criticism sent to the Colonial Office early next year, though in fact its author was Nicholas Bayly [q.v.]. Soon after Macquarie received the dispatch asking for his comments on these allegations, he learned that Marsden had taken a deposition concerning his action more than a year before in ordering three men to be flogged for trespassing in the Domain. He summoned the parson to Government House and there in front of witnesses described him as '*the Head of a seditious low Cabal* and consequently unworthy of mixing in Private society' and commanded him to avoid his presence except upon public duty. Five months later, in May 1818, Marsden applied for leave to visit England for personal reasons and to recruit clergy for the colony. He had had considerable success in this on his previous visit in 1807-09, but Macquarie refused to allow him to go on the grounds that his services could not be spared. The governor probably feared, with some justification, that Marsden, through his many influential friends and patrons in London, would increase the growing opposition to Macquarie's policies; but it was quite untrue for him to add that Marsden 'had repeatedly visited his Native Country', when he had gone only once in twenty-four years. The antipathy between the two men sprang in part from different policies on various matters of public concern, especially the place of the emancipists in the community; it was intensified by the chaplain's wish that the separate character of the church in the official establishment should be recognized, as the colony was ceasing to be purely a penal settlement. This inevitably drove him to oppose the authoritarian governor, just as the law officers had shown a similar desire to assert the independence of the judiciary.

Equally disturbing to Marsden's peace were the attacks he suffered from the *Sydney Gazette*, which showed how much less saintly a figure he was in colonial than in English eyes. In March 1814 in a series of sarcastic letters he was taken to task for his failure to carry out what was said to be a promise he had made to donors in England that he was collecting books to establish a circulating library for adult education in the colony. Again, on 4 January 1817, an attacker, sheltering behind the *nom de plume* Philo Free, suggested *inter alia* that the chaplain's interest in the Pacific missions was aroused by hopes of material profits. In this case Marsden instituted libel actions which resulted in the conviction of the governor's secretary and official censor of the *Gazette*, J. T. Campbell [q.v.], who could only attempt to excuse his conduct as a natural reaction to the chaplain's snub to Macquarie's efforts to civilize the Aboriginals.

Public dispute and official disapproval continued to be Marsden's lot under Macquarie's successor. In 1822 Governor Brisbane suspended him, with other magistrates of the Parramatta bench, for refusing to sit with a colleague, Dr H. G. Douglass [q.v.], against whom they had brought a variety of charges, and in the next four years Marsden tasted humiliation many times. He was passed over when T. H. Scott [q.v.] was appointed archdeacon. His allegations against Douglass were unanimously rejected by a committee of inquiry, comprising the governor, Archdeacon Scott and Chief Justice Forbes [q.v.]. He was rebuked for his part in convicting a female convict, Ann Rumsby, against all the evidence brought forward and sentencing her to be transported to Port Macquarie. His name was publicly linked with the colonial practice of judicial torture of convicted prisoners; and Bathurst told him that he was unconvinced by his apologia on the matter. He was convicted of improperly allowing one of his assigned servants, James Ring, who sang in his choir, to 'be on his own hands', and was accused of intentionally not recapturing Ring when he later absconded to New Zealand and ran into Marsden there. In August 1826 Bathurst told Governor Darling that in the Douglass affair Marsden's behaviour was 'little becoming the character which he ought to maintain in the colony', and that in future Marsden was to 'repress that vehemence of temper which has too frequently marked his conduct of late, and which is as little suited to his Age, as it is to the profession to which he belongs'. Nothing daunted, Marsden published a *Statement, including a correspondence between the Commissioners of the Court of Enquiry, and the Rev. Samuel Marsden . . .* (Sydney, 1828). This, wrote Forbes, was 'a very incorrect account of the proceedings . . . Mr. Marsden seems to think that all who may happen to differ in opinion with him, must be influenced by impure motives'.

In 1826 Darling appointed him to the board of management of the Female Factory and made him one of the trustees of the Clergy and School Lands. He was one of the small superintending committee of the Church and School Corporation and of the committee which considered the plan of Archdeacon Broughton [q.v.] for the formation of an Anglican grammar school. He continued 'in the sole charge of a very extensive Parish' until 1831 when a regular assistant was first appointed. In 1834-36 he took charge of Church of England affairs during Broughton's visit to England, and in 1836 Broughton appointed him one of the three commissioners in the Consistorial Court he was then establishing. His early evangelicalism seems to have mellowed, and he did not oppose the anti-evangelical Broughton; but he did not shrink from controversy, publishing *A Letter from the Rev. Samuel Marsden to Mr. William Crook . . .* (Sydney, 1835) in answer to charges which J. D. Lang [q.v.] had made in his *An historical and statistical Account of New South Wales . . .* (London) the previous year, and in 1836, in keeping with the bitter anti-Roman Catholicism which had marked his whole career, taking a leading part in the opposition to Governor Bourke's proposal to establish National schools in New South Wales.

Three years after the death of his wife Marsden died on 12 May 1838 at St Matthew's Parsonage, Windsor, where he had gone in ill health for a rest. He was buried at St John's, Parramatta. Posterity has tended to judge him adversely on three counts: illiberality towards the emancipists, cruelty as a magistrate and undue materialism. On the first count he may be shown to have been more in touch with contemporary feeling than Macquarie. On the second, his colonial reputation was confirmed by Commissioner Bigge, who wrote that his character as a magistrate was 'stamped with severity'. Third, as Bigge pointed out, the variety of Marsden's activities and his temporal interests resulted inevitably in his ministry in the colony being somewhat overshadowed by that of some of his subordinates, like William Cowper and Robert Cartwright [qq.v.]. But other historians have laid greater stress on Marsden's Evangelical piety, though this caused some contemporaries to criticize him as 'methodistical'; his life, though often embittered by controversy, was relieved by substantial achievement and sustained by a confidence in the future of his adopted country. A son, Charles, and five daughters survived him.

HRNSW, 2-7; HRA (1), 1-18; O. Gregory, *Memoirs of . . . J. M. Good* (Lond, 1828); J. B. Marsden, *Life and work of Samuel Marsden*, ed J. Drummond (Christchurch, 1913); J. R. Elder (ed), *The letters and journals of Samuel Marsden* (Dunedin, 1932); S. M. Johnstone, *Samuel Marsden* (Syd, 1932); E. Ramsden, *Marsden and the missions: prelude to Waitangi* (Syd, 1936); M. H. Ellis, *Lachlan Macquarie*, 2nd ed (Syd, 1952); M. H. Ellis, *John Macarthur* (Syd, 1955); C. M. H. Clark, *A history of Australia*, 1 (Melb, 1962); M. Saclier, 'Sam Marsden's colony', *JRAHS*, 52 (1966); MS cat under Marsden (ML).

A. T. YARWOOD

MARTENS, CONRAD (1801-1878), artist, was born at Crutched Friars near the Tower of London, the son of J. C. H. Martens, a German merchant from Hamburg who had been appointed Austrian consul to London, where he married an Englishwoman. When his consular term expired Martens set up as a merchant in London. His three sons became artists. Conrad Martens received his training in landscape painting from Copley Fielding, who was the most popular teacher of his time. From him Martens learned the principles of picture-making which stood by him in his later isolation in Australia. After his father's death in 1816 the family moved to Exeter whence Martens practised his watercolour painting in the Devonshire landscape.

About 1832 Martens accepted an offer from Captain Blackwood [q.v.] of H.M.S. *Hyacinth* of a three-year voyage to India. Whilst at Rio de Janeiro he heard that Captain FitzRoy of the *Beagle*, leader of a scientific survey of Patagonia and Tierra del Fuego, wanted an artist to replace Augustus Earle [q.v.] who was leaving the expedition because of ill health.

Martens joined the *Beagle* at Montevideo, and became associated with a group of observant scientists which included Charles Darwin [q.v.]. Without losing his feeling for the picturesque, Martens now became more concerned with factual topography, but the varied interests of the expedition's members greatly widened his experience and had a very positive effect on his later work in Australia. That a lasting friendship developed between him and Darwin is shown by subsequent correspondence.

Probably because Captain FitzRoy was obliged to dispense with his second ship, Martens left the *Beagle* at Valparaiso in October 1834, and on 3 December sailed in the *Peruvian* for Tahiti, where he spent some time sketching. In March 1835 he sailed for New Zealand, and six weeks later arrived in Sydney, which became his home for the rest of his life. It had not been his intention to remain in Australia but he was soon at work and within six months had made sketching expeditions to the Illawarra, the Blue Mountains and Broken Bay.

His first residence was in Cumberland Street in the fashionable Rocks area, and from a Pitt Street studio he gave lessons in drawing and painting. In 1837 he married Jane Brackenbury, a daughter of William Carter, later master in equity and registrar of the Supreme Court. Their first child Rebecca was born in 1838, and the second daughter Elizabeth in 1839. A son, born in 1844, died in infancy.

Martens had a liking for the North Shore of Sydney with its panoramic vistas of the harbour and foreshores, and in 1844 built a house at St Leonard's. But the 1840s were lean years, and at one time he appears to have sought some financial help from his brother Henry in London. To augment his income he produced a lithographic 'view of Sydney from the North Shore', handcoloured prints of which sold for a guinea. Later, in 1850 he issued *Sketches in the environs of Sydney*, a series of twenty lithographs in five parts. For his watercolours Martens found his purchasers among the *élite* of Sydney's residents, and among the well-to-do landowners whose houses and holdings he painted. His landscapes show that he worked in New South Wales on the South Coast, and at Bong Bong, Lithgow, Scone and Walcha and in New England. He visited Brisbane several times, and in 1851 made an extensive sketching tour through the Darling Downs.

Apart from his travels the theme of Sydney Harbour occupied Martens consistently over a period of thirty-five years. He pictured the harbour under spacious skies, disposing lights and shadows over its headlands with rare compositional skill. He could command the wide sweep of harbour landscape enveloped in pearly atmosphere, yet take note of the characteristic sandstone formations interspersed with banksia and eucalypts in the foreground. His awareness of the European tradition of landscape, deriving from Claude, his curiosity about his new environment, and his reaction to its light all combined with his technical skill to create water-colour landscapes of an extremely high order. He stood alone in his period. His painting confirms principles propounded in a lecture on landscape painting that he delivered in Sydney in 1856. He advocated concentrating the strongest darks in the foreground, and using the highest lights and the deepest darks in such a way as to emphasize the principal objects.

As the rigours of a landscape painter's life began to tell on the ageing Martens, his friend Alexander Berry [q.v.] found a post for him in 1863 as a parliamentary librarian. Eight years later, in a letter to the architect and surveyor Robert Russell [q.v.], one of his earlier pupils, he wrote: 'I still continue to paint, and have several commissions, but have only a little time at my disposal as you may well suppose'. In his later years he developed an interest in astronomy and acquired a telescope from London. His notes and correspondence indicate more than a superficial interest and suggest that he carried his study to some depth.

He died on 21 August 1878 and was buried at St Thomas's Church, North Sydney, where the rest of his family are also buried. The font in this church, his place of worship for many years, is his handiwork. A portrait of Martens by Dr Maurice Felton is in the Mitchell Library, Sydney, which also houses a comprehensive collection of Martens's water-colours and oils. He is also well represented in the Dixson Galleries of the Public Library of New South Wales, and the National Art Galleries of New South Wales and Victoria. An impressive group of his landscapes is owned by Mr K. R. Stewart of Sydney.

L. Lindsay, *Conrad Martens, the man and his art* (Syd, 1920); Bernard Smith, *European vision and the south Pacific 1768-1850* (Oxford, 1960); J. Gray, Conrad Martens (B.A. thesis, Univ Melb, 1959); C. Martens, Correspondence and notebooks (Dixson Lib, Syd).   DOUGLAS DUNDAS

MASON, MARTIN (d. 1821), surgeon, magistrate and commander, arrived in Sydney on 18 July 1798 as surgeon in the *Britannia,* carrying female convicts. In May 1799 Governor Hunter appointed him acting surgeon in H.M.S. *Buffalo,* but King appointed him assistant colonial surgeon on 1 October 1800 and magistrate for the district of Parramatta and Toongabbie next January. Some months later he was sent to the Coal River to hold an inquiry, in conjunction with Ensign Barrallier [q.v.], into a mutiny. Corporal Wixstead had been in command there since the settlement had been established in June but he had not been able to hold the convicts in check; in September, after the inquiry, he was succeeded by Mason. Shafts were sunk to exploit better coal seams but the harsh methods which Mason employed against the convict miners provoked another mutiny and but for the intervention of Wixstead Mason would have lost his life. He was recalled to Sydney, left the Coal River on 8 December 1801 and next February returned to Toongabbie.

At the end of 1803 Mason was discharged as assistant surgeon and in 1804 began a practice at Green Hills (Windsor), probably the first private medical practice in Australia. On New Year's Day 1808 he signed an address to Governor Bligh requesting the 'privilege of Trade' and 'Trial by Jury of the People, as in England', but when the Rum Rebellion took place on 26 January Mason and his fellow settlers on the Hawkesbury sided with the deposed governor. In an address to Lieut-Colonel Paterson [q.v.] in April and in a letter to Bligh in August, they affirmed their loyalty to appointed authority and criticized Johnston, Foveaux and John Macarthur [qq.v.]. Mason was imprisoned for not obeying the officers now in control and was also charged with having an illicit still on his premises at the Hawkesbury. The evidence seems to show that he was innocent of the charge, and both Rev. Henry Fulton and William Gore [qq.v] contended that he was persecuted because of his sympathy with Bligh. When the deposed governor returned to England in 1810 the Hawkesbury settlers selected Mason and George Suttor [q.v.] as their representatives to give evidence for Bligh; their expenses were paid by public subscription until October, when with other witnesses they were allowed 15s. a day by the government. In letters to Lord Liverpool, Mason laid charges against Foveaux and Johnston, and alleged that they murdered his only son. He sought compensation from the British government for his imprisonment and loss of practice, and a grant of land for his loyalty and service. In August 1811 he was provided with a passage back to Australia in the *Mary*. He had married before coming out in 1798 and by this time appears to have had five children. He died before June 1821. His widow died at Parramatta on 24 May 1822.

Blunt and dogmatic, harsh yet efficient, Mason reflected, to a degree, the turbulent era of Australian history in which he lived. Though he lacked the subtlety to recognize such broader issues as autocratic rule and aristocratic pretensions in the developing colony, he was well aware of its penal character and of the role which appointed authority had to play in such a situation. As a magistrate, professional man and loyal private citizen he identified himself with that appointed authority and showed himself prepared to accept the consequences of his convictions.

HRNSW, 4, 7; HRA (1), 3-7; J. C. L. Fitzpatrick, *Those were the days* (Syd, 1923); W. J. Goold, 'The birth of Newcastle', Newcastle and Hunter District Hist Soc, *Procs*, 7 (1953).
                                                T. W. BLUNDEN

MASON, THOMAS (1800-1888), police magistrate, was born on 18 August 1800, the seventh of eight sons of Thomas Mason, a solicitor of Carlesley, near Coventry, Warwickshire, England. His father went to London in 1807 and in 1817 was appointed attorney-general at Tobago where he died. His maternal grandfather was Dr Fountain, a London clergyman and an able Greek scholar. At 7 Thomas went to the Merchant Taylors' School but the death of his father prevented him from going to Oxford and he joined the mercantile firm of Heath & Furze. There he learnt several foreign languages and continued to read in them until his death. Loss of his savings in a bank crash decided him to emigrate and in December 1829 he arrived in the *Thomson* at Hobart Town with no possessions.

His first ten months were spent with his brother-in-law, George Frankland [q.v.], who had encouraged him to come to Van Diemen's Land. He was made a justice of the peace and in March 1831 was appointed assistant police magistrate and muster master in Hobart. In October 1832 Mason applied for an allowance of lodging money and argued that the £100 paid to police magistrates elsewhere was supplemented by lodging allowances. As muster master he received £200 and had five clerks to help him but the salary of the

office had not increased since 1828. Lieut-Governor Arthur agreed that Mason deserved a rise and recommended his case to London, but without success.

In April 1834 Mason became involved in the case of the convict Joseph Greenwood who had absconded from a road-gang and then stabbed the constable who had tried to arrest him at the New Town race-course. Greenwood appeared first before Mason and another magistrate for the very prevalent offence of absconding and was sentenced to receive 100 lashes; he was then tried in the Supreme Court for his capital crime and found guilty, but before his execution on 16 April Greenwood petitioned Arthur, claiming that the flogging was a torture and disfigured him to meet his Maker. The petition was supported by fifteen citizens but Arthur backed the magistrates, although he expressed dismay at their summary proceedings. Greenwood's claim received much notoriety even in the London press and Mason became 'personally obnoxious' to the radicals in Hobart.

Mason was ·promoted in April 1835 to the police magistracy in New Norfolk, as Arthur explained, in 'approbation of the Zealous & independent conduct he has displayed' in Hobart. At New Norfolk Mason also served as coroner and commissioner in the Court of Requests. Again he met unpopularity even among his fellow magistrates, and in 1835 was grossly insulted in public by T. A. Lascelles [q.v.] whose assigned servant had been removed by Mason for absconding. Lascelles took his complaint to the Supreme Court, where he proved that he had only lent his servant to a neighbour and claimed that Mason had been influenced by feelings of malice since the Greenwood case. The court found for Lascelles, but J. T. Gellibrand [q.v.] thought Mason had a strong case for a new trial, and he was allowed to exchange offices for six months with Charles Arthur [q.v.] at Norfolk Plains. When retried, he was fully exonerated and his zeal was commended by Judges Montagu and Pedder [qq.v.].

From July to September 1837 Mason had further trouble on the bench when Major Gibson and Captain Armstrong claimed that his character had not been satisfactorily cleared; following a difference with Mason they resigned. Armstrong took the case to the Executive Council, but the resignations were accepted and Mason was honourably acquitted. In June 1841 he was insulted by the overseer of a road-gang. When Mason's complaints were ignored by Captain Cheyne [q.v.] he took them to the lieut-governor, who dismissed the overseer and criticized Cheyne for the improper employment of convict labour. After several other similar incidents it seemed clear to the lower classes at least that Mason was a ruthless 'hanging' magistrate. However, his career was not affected by his unpopularity and on 28 February 1844 he was appointed deputy-chairman of the General Quarter Sessions, only two weeks after being denounced by a fellow-magistrate, W. S. Sharland [q.v.], who was also treasurer of the New Norfolk Bridge Co. In July 1846 Mason temporarily became police magistrate in Hobart at a salary of £500 and next year returned to New Norfolk as police magistrate at £400 with allowances of £50. In April 1851 he was appointed police magistrate at Campbell Town at £450, and apart from five years at Oatlands held this post until his retirement. In 1862 his office was abolished and he retired on a pension. In 1868 he accepted the police magistracy at Launceston on half-pay in addition to his pension, and retired permanently in July 1879. He died at his home in Campbell Town in August 1888, leaving two unmarried daughters and a son Francis, who was archdeacon of Hobart.

Apart from his duties as magistrate, coroner and commissioner of the Court of Requests Mason was an administrator of charitable allowances, an examiner of the census and a returning officer without pay for three electoral districts, including Glamorgan from 1855. He is also said to have taken part in the Black war of 1830. On 25 April 1835 he married Abigail, third daughter of Major Harvey Welman of the 57th Regiment; she died in December 1852, aged 34.

Mason boasted in 1862 that he had never been absent from his post except to attend a levee at Government House. His energy was undoubted but it was exercised relentlessly in court and without tact towards his fellow officers. His unusually untidy writing once prompted the attorney-general to comment that he could not 'decipher the hieroglyphics of this profound artist'; Mason's pompous protest to the colonial secretary brought little balm to his vanity. The Colonial Times, 23 April 1833, conceded that 'Mister Muster Master Mason [had an] elegant and graceful seat on horseback', but chided him for appearing self important and 'big with the fate of the Colony'.

Colonial Times, 7 Jan, 22 Apr 1831; MS cat under Mason (ML); Correspondence file under Thomas Mason (TA).   A. F. PIKE

MASSEY, THOMAS (1759?-1858), police constable and settler, was a soldier in the 47th Regiment when committed for desertion and then convicted of burglary and sentenced to death at Chester, England, on 3 September 1789; reprieved on condition of transportation for life he came to Sydney in the Gorgon in 1791. Conditionally pardoned in 1800 on the ground of 'diligence and care exemplified in his conduct as a principal overseer and to enable him to become a settler', he received an absolute pardon in 1802 for good conduct. In 1804 he was a corporal in the Sydney Loyal Association, in October sailed with Colonel Paterson [q.v.] when the settlement at Port Dalrymple was established, and was appointed principal overseer and district constable there. Paterson commended his work, but in April 1809 he was dismissed. He took up farming and was granted 150 acres, but next year after a brief visit to Sydney, where he married Ann Simmonds and appealed to Governor Macquarie, he was reinstated, appointed superintendent of stock, and difficulties over his grant were settled. In January 1816 he was reprimanded for disrespect and disobedience, but apologized to the commandant, and next year was made superintendent of works at George Town and promoted chief constable of the district. In 1818 he was in trouble with the commandant again, and Macquarie ordered him to be dismissed entirely from the services of the government. After another apology he was restored, though described by Lieut-Governor Sorell as a 'turbulent and troublesome man'. He was granted 300 acres at the ford of the South Esk River in 1816 and in 1820 gave evidence to Commissioner Bigge [q.v.] about conditions at Launceston. That year he acquired a grazing licence, and during the 1820s supplied meat to the government. By 1829 he held, in association with his son who had been born in 1807, more than 4000 acres of land at Ellerslie, near Ben Lomond, five miles from Cleveland.

On 21 April 1830 Massey was committed for trial for attempting to shoot one of his servants, Bennett, with whom he had apparently been drinking before the fracas. In evidence it was said that he frequently quarrelled with his servants, and Mrs Bennett stated that he had tried to stab her as a result of an argument. As there is no record of the trial, the case was probably withdrawn and Massey returned to his property on the South Esk. He died in January 1858, allegedly aged 99.

HRA (1), 4, 5, 7, 8, (3), 1-3; L. S. Bethell, The story of Port Dalrymple (Hob, 1957);

Colonial Times, 30 Apr 1830; *Examiner* (Launceston), 7 Jan 1858.   C. G. BILLING

MATHER, ROBERT (1782?-1855), retailer, was born on 1 May 1782? at Lauder near Berwick upon Tweed, Northumberland, England, eldest son of Andrew Mather, blacksmith and farrier, and his wife Agnes, née Hamilton. He had little formal education but developed a sturdy, practical and independent character. At 14 he went to London, where he was apprenticed to a Scottish hosier for seven years and then set up for himself and became a member of the Weavers' Company and a freeman of the city. In the new Methodist movement his warm emotional temperament found a congenial atmosphere. On 16 October 1811 at St Luke's, Old Street, London, he married Ann, daughter of Rev. Joseph Benson and his wife Sarah, née Thompson; they had seven children, of whom one daughter and four sons survived infancy.

Mather became interested in emigrating to Van Diemen's Land because of representations from Rev. William Horton, Wesleyan minister at Hobart Town, to his coreligionists in England seeking to entice industrious and God-fearing men to emigrate. He was also influenced by the publications of W. C. Wentworth and Lieutenant Charles Jeffreys [qq.v.]. In October 1821 he sailed with his family in the *Hope*, but the ship was damaged at sea, put back to Ramsgate and was seized by the Customs for being overloaded. The family sailed again in the *Heroine* and arrived in Hobart on 10 September 1822.

Mather secured a house on Potter's Hill and set up in business, for the goods and implements in which he had invested his capital had reached Hobart before him. For a few months he was in partnership with Henry Hopkins [q.v.]. Early in 1823 Mather moved to London House, which he had built as a residence and place of business at the corner of Elizabeth and Liverpool Streets. In that year he was appointed a foundation trustee of the Wesleyan Church. His conscience did not allow him to apply for a land grant, because the residence conditions clashed with his wish to live in town where his children could be educated to his satisfaction. However, the regulations were changed in 1824 and he was granted 1200 acres at Muddy Plains; by later grant and purchase he held some 2000 acres which he called Lauderdale.

His wife died in 1831, and a few months later he closed his Hobart business and moved to his farm. At Muddy Plains he did all he could to encourage his neighbours and servants in religious observance. He held services in his home and established a Sunday school, with his family's help endeavouring to teach the children to read. In August 1832 and later, Lauderdale was visited by the Quaker missionaries, James Backhouse and G. W. Walker [qq.v.]. In 1834 Mather and some members of his family became members of the Society of Friends, and in 1840 Walker married Mather's daughter Sarah.

Mather's land was poor but he continued to sink large sums in unremunerative development of his farm; his financial position deteriorated and in February 1836 he was declared insolvent. Helped by friends, he made a fresh start in business in Hobart with his two elder sons. The business prospered, all his creditors were repaid and the moneys subscribed by his friends fully refunded. On 18 August 1842 he married Esther, sister of Captain James Dixon of the *Skelton*, who had published in London his *Narrative of a Voyage to New South Wales and Van Diemen's Land in the ship Skelton during the year 1820*.

Throughout his life Mather always tried to apply his religious principles in business. For his great integrity and generous and confiding nature, he earned widespread respect and affection. He died in Hobart on 26 March 1855.

J. Backhouse and C. Tylor, *The life and labours of George Washington Walker* (Lond, 1862); S. Benson, 'Memoir of Mrs Ann Mather', *Wesleyan-Methodist Mag* (Lond), Apr 1836; S. Benson, 'Letter to the editors', *Wesleyan-Methodist Mag* (Lond), Jan 1857; *Critic* (Hob), 22, 29 Sept, 7, 13, 20, 27 Oct, 3, 10, 17 Nov 1922; Walker papers (Univ Tas Lib); Mather papers (Univ Tas Lib and private possession of Misses E. & M. Robey, R. Mather, Hob).

ROBERT MATHER

MAUGHAM; *see* MAUM

MAUM (MAUGHAM), WILLIAM JAMES (1778-1850), Irish political prisoner, arrived in New South Wales in the *Minerva* in January 1800. According to one account he was a native of Charleville, County Cork, Ireland, and educated at Trinity College, Dublin, where he was placed by his uncle, Counsellor Kellor. He left the university at 18 and there is no record of his graduation. When transported for life three years later for an unspecified political offence he was a teacher of Latin and Greek. It has been said that he was involved in the Irish conspiracy in New

South Wales in September 1800 and under the name of Maughan was sentenced to receive 500 lashes, but the evidence of identification is not conclusive. In 1804 at St John's, Parramatta, he married Ann Diggins, a convict transported in the *Experiment* in 1803. He and Governor King were bitter enemies and when Maum made allegations against the governor's honesty King had him removed to Norfolk Island, together with 'those Incendiaries who have for some Years past been employed in promoting discord and fermenting Litigations'. King observed that Maum's 'principles and Conduct have changed as little as the others, Nor can Time or place have any Effect on such depraved Characters'. From Norfolk Island Maum sought in 1806 to return to Port Jackson as a schoolmaster; he claimed that he had never received an official sentence of transportation, and renewed his attacks on King, accusing him of accepting bribes and referring to the governor's 'cruelty and torture . . . in consequence of his suspicion that I wrote to some persons in power relative to his conduct in this territory'.

Maum was not allowed to go to Sydney, but was sent to Van Diemen's Land in the *Porpoise*, arriving on 17 January 1808, accompanied by his wife and two children. He told Lieut-Governor Collins that the character of delinquent given to him was very 'unmeritedly applied', and to a friend he wrote that it had been advisable to leave Norfolk Island after the way he was treated there. Collins had no post to offer Maum but promised him land at Herdsman's Cove. In 1810 he was made assistant in the commissariat at Hobart Town. After some difficulties he was granted a conditional pardon in 1813 by Governor Macquarie and briefly visited New South Wales before returning to Hobart. He was government store-keeper there from 1814 until September 1816, when he was dismissed after becoming involved in the embezzlements in the commissariat. A year later he was farming at Clarence Plains, where his haystacks were destroyed by fire, and he signed a memorial in Hobart in June 1818. He may then have returned to New South Wales, for a William Maughan of the right age, resident of Parramatta, was granted fifty acres in 1818. A year later he and his wife advised that they were leaving the colony for Europe and offered property for sale or lease, but apparently went no further than Hobart, for he gave evidence before Commissioner Bigge [q.v.] there in 1820. In 1828 he was a landholder, with an absolute pardon, living at Parramatta. Later he went back to Van Diemen's

Land and settled on his farm at Clarence Plains. In the Irish tradition he raced horses and had some success with his Galloway colt, Young Pompey, in 1841. He died at Clarence Plains on 26 September 1850; his second wife Sophia, daughter of Lieutenant William Bignell, died there five years later.

HRA (1), 2, 5, 8, (3), 1-4; *Sydney Gazette*, 27 July 1816, 25 Jan 1817, 20 Nov 1819; *Critic* (Hob), 8 Apr 1921; Col Sec in letters, 4/1847-48 (NSWA); CO 201/41; HO 10/21.

L. L. ROBSON

MEAGHER, THOMAS FRANCIS (1823-1867), Irish nationalist, was born at Waterford, Ireland, the son of a prosperous merchant, mayor of the city and its member in the British parliament. He was educated by Irish Jesuits at Clengowes in County Kildare and at Stonyhurst College in Lancashire. Returning to Dublin in 1843, he became a law student, joined the Repeal Association, and won an early reputation for silver-tongued oratory in the association's debates at Conciliation Hall. By 1845 he had attached himself to the militant Young Ireland wing of the association and in the critical disputes of 1846-47 joined John Mitchel and W. S. O'Brien [qq.v.] in breaking with the older 'moral force' leaders. In the spring of 1848 Meagher, as a rising young leader of the Young Ireland movement, accompanied O'Brien to Paris to present a congratulatory address to the newly formed French Republic; he was appointed a member of the committee of five who directed the abortive Irish insurrection that followed. After its defeat Meagher was brought to trial at Clonmel with O'Brien and his principal associates, and in October was sentenced first to death and later to transportation for life for his part in the affairs. With O'Brien, McManus and O'Donohoe he sailed in the *Swift* and arrived in Hobart Town in October 1849.

Meagher was soon granted a ticket-of-leave and allowed to live on parole in the Campbell Town district. At Ross he met Catherine Bennett of New Norfolk, whom he married on 22 February 1851. They lived in a cottage on Lake Sorell, where a son, Henry Emmet Fitzgerald, was born in February 1852 but died four months later and was buried in Richmond churchyard. Meagher had already planned escape from the island and in January had written to the police magistrate at Campbell Town surrendering his ticket-of-leave and withdrawing his parole. He sailed to Pernambuco and on to New

York, where he arrived in May 1852. Catherine joined him for a short while, but returned to Ireland and died on 12 May 1854 at Waterford.

Meagher married again in New York, was admitted to the Bar and became a United States citizen. He founded the *Irish News* which, like John Mitchel's *Citizen*, favoured the Southern cause. In the civil war he raised and commanded an Irish brigade, which fought on the Confederate side. After the Southerners' defeat, he became for a short while acting governor of Montana Territory, where his equestrian statue still stands. He died by drowning in the Missouri River on 1 July 1867. Meagher is remembered as a 'romantic hero' of the Young Ireland movement rather than for any practical qualities of leadership.

J. H. Cullen, *Young Ireland in Exile* (Dublin, 1928); D. R. Gwynn, *Young Ireland and 1848* (Cork, 1949); T. J. Kiernan, *The Irish exiles in Australia* (Melb, 1954); D. R. Gwynn, *Thomas Francis Meagher* (Dublin, 1961); Ac no 2/363 (TA).   G. RUDE

MEALMAKER, GEORGE (1768-1808), political transportee, was born on 10 February 1768 at Dundee, Scotland, the son of John Mealmaker, weaver, and his wife Alison, née Auchinleck. He came from a humble background but won modest affluence as a hand-loom weaver. He was a pioneer, active and extreme member of the 'Friends of Liberty' in Dundee early in 1791, a group formed to uphold the principles of the French revolution. In mid-1793 he wrote a broadsheet, inveighing against the 'despotism and tyranny' of the British government, and it was for publishing this that T. F. Palmer [q.v.] was transported. Mealmaker attended the convention at Edinburgh late in 1793, after which Margarot, Gerrald and Skirving [qq.v.] also met this fate. In the next months Mealmaker was secretary of the Dundee friends, who spread propaganda urging the militia not to fight against France. For this he was brought before the magistrates but no charge was laid against him.

Radical activity quietened in the next two years, although Mealmaker himself remained outspoken (*Sermon ... delivered in 1795*, London, nd); but he was quick to join the 'United Scotsmen', who in 1796 began to organize in imitation of their Irish namesakes. Indeed Mealmaker wrote the group's constitution, which asserted its 'whole aim' to be 'to secure Annual Parliaments and Universal Suffrage'; he also published *The Moral and Political Cate-*

chism of Man (Edinburgh, 1797), which expounded such radicalism at length. Authority reacted, and in January 1798 Mealmaker was tried for sedition and administering unlawful oaths. After a prejudiced hearing in which the two charges were not distinguished he was sentenced to transportation for fourteen years.

Mealmaker arrived in Sydney in the *Royal Admiral* in November 1800. He may at first have upheld his political interests, and in March 1802 rumours of convict rebellion involved him; but he denied the allegation and went unpunished. It was his craft, not his beliefs, which shaped his life in New South Wales. After becoming governor in 1800, King had tried to establish a weaving industry but found no suitable manager. In August 1803 he appointed Mealmaker for four years. Supervising the work at the Female Factory, Parramatta, he put four looms to work, and King's accounts of the industry tell a thorough success story. Mealmaker received a conditional pardon and generous emoluments. However, his life ended unhappily. Governor Bligh cared less about weaving than did King. In December 1807 fire partly destroyed the factory. On 30 March 1808 Mealmaker, destitute and apparently a drunkard, died from alcoholic suffocation and was buried at St John's, Parramatta. There his son by Mary Thomas had been baptized in 1805. Colonial life had ruined this forceful, self-assertive, interesting man.

On 23 November 1795 at Dundee, Mealmaker had married Marjory, daughter of John Thoms. She never left Dundee and died there on 16 November 1843, aged 68. An etching appears in John Kay, *A Series of Original Portraits and Caricature Etchings*, 1-2 (London, 1838).

HRA (1), 4-7; M. Roe, 'George Mealmaker, the forgotten martyr', *JRAHS*, 43 (1957).
                                    MICHAEL ROE

MEARES, RICHARD GOLDSMITH (1780-1862), soldier, settler and public servant, joined the army in 1808 and next year became a lieutenant in the Royal Fusiliers. In 1812 in the 2nd Life Guards he joined Wellington's forces at Lisbon and later served in Belgium, attending the duchess of Richmond's ball and distinguishing himself at Waterloo. In 1817 he was promoted captain and next year, on half-pay, retired to practise horticulture and sketching. In 1808 he married Eleanor Seymour of Newcastle upon Tyne. They lived at High Wycombe in Buckinghamshire and at Huish Cottage near Barnstaple in Devon.

With his wife and eight children, he arrived at Swan River in December 1829 with Thomas Peel [q.v.] in the Gilmore.

Before leaving England Meares had sold his commission and had given Peel £500 to be repaid in land and materials in the colony. Living at first in a carpeted marquee on Rockingham Beach and then at The Rocks, Clarence, he had great difficulty in feeding his family and seven servants while he struggled without success to make Peel fulfil his agreement. He revealed his plight to Lieut-Governor Arthur who in March 1831 urged the commandant at Launceston to find him good land for the maximum free grant available to a valiant soldier. Meares received permission next month to go to Van Diemen's Land, but he did not do so. In 1832 he moved to Guildford, where he was threatened in September with no further government rations unless he surrendered one of his horses. Appeals to London officials brought him brief appointment as district superintendent for Guildford in 1834 and a £300 remission certificate for his land purchases as an ex-serviceman. He sold the certificate to E. H. Pollard who used it to buy land in Van Diemen's Land. In 1837 Meares became a justice of the peace and in 1840-41 was government resident for the Murray district where he had 15,500 unproductive acres. At the same time he acquired land in the Avon valley and in September 1842 he moved to York as its government resident at a salary of £100. In addition to magisterial duties, he was registrar, statistician, collector of land fees and dog taxes, organizer of road repairing and bridge building parties and a member of the local school committee. He shared in founding the York Race Club and the York Fair. The opening of a convict hiring depot at York increased his responsibilities, but the district gained a court-house, hospital, good roads and an Anglican chaplain. His early administration was enlivened by squabbles with settlers, Aboriginals and neighbouring government residents, some being ventilated in the press to the embarrassment of Perth officials. But he mellowed with the years and became proudly patriarchal as his family began to marry. He resigned as government resident in 1859. His wife died on 20 January 1854 and Meares on 9 January 1862. He was buried in the old York cemetery

His Guildford home, Bower, and his residency at Avon, were furnished with great style and noted for conviviality befitting a dashing army officer. He was the first secretary of the club formed in 1839 for importing English thoroughbreds, and he also became an early director of the Western Australian Agricultural Society, had a fine garden and fruit trees at Guildford, and at York cultivated grape vines and introduced a new type of barley.

J. E. Deacon, 'Capt Richard Goldsmith Meares and his times', JRWAHS, 3 (1938-48); J. E. Deacon, A survey of the historical development of the Avon valley, with particular reference to York, Western Australia, 1830-1850 (M.A. thesis, Univ WA, 1947); CSO 1/508/11147, 1/876/18546 (TA).

MEEHAN, JAMES (1774-1826), surveyor, explorer and settler, was born in Ireland and sentenced to transportation for a part in the Irish rebellion of 1798; Commissioner Bigge [q.v.] later remarked that his offence was not serious. He arrived in Sydney in the Friendship on 16 February 1800 and in April was assigned as a servant to Charles Grimes [q.v.], the acting surveyor-general. In 1801 he accompanied Grimes and Barrallier [q.v.] on an exploration of the Hunter River and in 1802-03 went with Grimes and Fleming to King Island and Port Phillip.

While Grimes was on leave in 1803-06 G. W. Evans [q.v.] was appointed acting surveyor-general but most of the departmental duties were performed by Meehan, now conditionally pardoned; Grimes considered Meehan capable of carrying out the duties and commended his faithfulness and impartiality on his return. During this time Meehan measured farms to grantees and explored part of the Derwent (1803-04) and Shoalhaven (1805) Rivers. In 1806 he received an absolute pardon and in 1806-07 was again working in Van Diemen's Land.

After Governor Bligh's deposition in 1808 Colonel George Johnston [q.v.] sent Grimes to England with dispatches and the work of the Surveyor-General's Department again devolved upon Meehan, who was appointed acting surveyor of lands with a salary of £182 10s. Because of his part in overthrowing Bligh Grimes was not permitted to return to New South Wales and Meehan's appointment was confirmed by Governor Macquarie. After John Oxley [q.v.] assumed the office of surveyor-general in 1812 Macquarie appointed Meehan deputy-surveyor of lands, and in 1814 he became collector of quitrents and superintendent of roads, bridges and streets as well.

Since a great part of Oxley's time was taken up with exploration, much of the routine work of his department, particularly the measuring of grants, was undertaken by Meehan who told Bigge, 'I have measured every farm that has been measured' since August 1803. Macquarie held a high opinion of Meehan's knowledge of the country and included him in the parties which accompanied him on most of his tours of inspection in New South Wales and Van Diemen's Land. In 1812-13 Meehan was in Van Diemen's Land resurveying land and correcting previous mistakes there and in 1818 Macquarie sent him with Charles Throsby [q.v.] to seek a route from the Sutton Forest district to Jervis Bay. After parting from Throsby, who went downstream, Meehan followed the Shoalhaven gorge upstream; he failed to find a crossing place, but discovered Lake Bathurst and the Goulburn plains. Apart from fixing the boundaries of land grants Meehan made several contributions to the mapping of the colony, most notably a map of Sydney drawn in 1807, and he laid out the townships of Richmond, Castlereagh, Windsor, Pitt Town, Wilberforce, Liverpool and Bathurst in New South Wales, as well as Hobart Town in Van Diemen's Land.

In 1803 Meehan was granted 100 acres in the Field of Mars (near Ryde). This he sold five years later when Lieut-Governor Foveaux [q.v.] granted him 130 acres at Bankstown for 'His services and attention to his duty as Acting Surveyor in the Colony'; later he was granted 1140 acres at Ingleburn. These grants, like others made by the insurrectionary governors, were cancelled and reissued by Macquarie. Meehan named his Ingleburn farm Macquarie Field and there built a house which the governor referred to as Meehan's Castle.

In 1821 as a result of the 'Hardships, privations and Difficulties', endured during his early years in the colony and of his declining health he tendered his resignation and sought a pension. Acceptance of his resignation was delayed while he completed writing descriptions of the farms that had been measured, and collected the quitrents that were due, none of which had been collected since 1815 because Meehan had been wholly occupied with other tasks. His request for a pension was sent to England with glowing testimonies to his character and service from both Macquarie and Oxley, and in 1823 Governor Brisbane was authorized to grant him a pension not exceeding £100 when accounts were tendered for the outstanding quitrents, which he had by this time supplied. He retired to Macquarie Field where he died on 21 April 1826. His property passed to his son Thomas (b. 1809).

Meehan was one of that small group of emancipists who played an important part in the affairs of the colony during Macquarie's governorship and whose energy and ability justified Macquarie's belief that good conduct and reformation should enable a man to regain the place in society which he had lost when sentenced to transportation. He was one of those whom Macquarie invited to Government House, and in his *Letter to . . . Viscount Sidmouth* (London, 1821) Macquarie paid him this tribute: 'I have . . . had an opportunity of witnessing his indefatigable assiduity in the fulfilment of his arduous duties. I believe that no man has suffered so much privation and fatigue in the service of this Colony as Mr Meehan has done . . . His integrity has never, to my knowledge, been impeached; and I certainly consider him to be, both on account of his professional skill, and the faithfull and laborious discharge of his duty, a valuable man'.

HRA (1), 7-12, (3), 1-2; L. Macquarie, *Journals of his tours in New South Wales and Van Diemen's Land, 1810-1822* (Syd, 1956); B. T. Dowd, 'James Meehan', JRAHS, 28 (1942); MS cat under Meehan (ML).

T. M. PERRY

MEIN, JAMES (1761-1827), settler, was born probably at Melrose, near Galashiels, Scotland. He arrived in New South Wales accompanied by his wife Susannah in the *Coromandel* on 13 July 1802. He was one of a group of devout Presbyterians, including John Howe [q.v.], Owen Cavanough and J. Grono, who settled at Portland Head. There Mein received a grant of 100 acres dated 14 April 1803. His position in the Presbyterian Church is not entirely clear. Some have referred to him as an elder, others as a catechist. He certainly played the major part in the affairs of the Ebenezer congregation, leading at worship in the absence of a regular minister and lending his house for religious services until the erection of the church there in 1809, the first Presbyterian Church built in Australia. For this he earned the praise of Rev. J. D. Lang [q.v.] who described him as a 'venerable' man.

Together with the remaining *Coromandel* settlers and a number of other free settlers and emancipists he was a firm supporter of Governor Bligh in the Rum Rebellion. Personal antipathy towards some of the leading rebels, gratitude to Bligh for aid received after the great flood in 1806 and belief in the desirability of supporting the properly constituted authorities all played a part in shaping his attitude. On 18 April 1808 he joined in a plea to Lieut-Colonel Paterson [q.v.] to assume command and in an attack on John Macarthur [q.v.] and the other rebels.

At this stage his farming ventures were not particularly advanced. By late 1806 he had only 14½ acres under crop and owned 18 sheep and 8 hogs. Later he acquired an additional 50 acres but does not appear to have had more than moderate means. The 1821 muster showed him as having 27 acres under crop and owning 35 cattle and 35 hogs. On the other hand as he remained a public-spirited figure and a fairly regular and large supplier of meat to the commissariat, he must have been occupying other land. In 1816 he subscribed to the Waterloo fund, in 1817 to the relief fund for sufferers from the Hawkesbury River flood, and in 1819 to the Windsor Charitable Institution. A year later he joined the committee of the Windsor Bible Association and in 1826 served on juries at Windsor Quarter Sessions. He died on 13 July 1827.

HRA (1), 3; C. A. White, The challenge of the years: a history of the Presbyterian Church . . . New South Wales (Syd, 1951); Newspaper indexes under J. Mein (ML).

B. H. FLETCHER

MELVILLE, HENRY (1799-1873), journalist, publisher and author, appears to have been named Henry Saxelby Melville Wintle, but he always used the abbreviated form. He arrived in Hobart Town towards the end of 1827 or early in 1828. In March 1830 he bought the Colonial Times and later in the year printed and published Henry Savery's [q.v.] Quintus Servinton, the first Australian novel published in Australia. Early in 1831 he bought the Tasmanian from J. C. Macdougall [q.v.] and later in the year joined with R. L. Murray [q.v.] to produce the Tasmanian and Southern Literary and Political Journal, but withdrew his interests in May 1832. He married in February 1832 at New Norfolk, Eliza Romney, only daughter of Joseph Fisher of Philadelphia.

In May 1833 he began the Hobart Town Magazine, the first monthly magazine with definite literary pretentions to be published in Australia. Edited by Thomas Richards, it appeared in eighteen issues before its publication ceased in August 1834. Melville contributed a number of articles to it, including 'The Bushranger; or Norwood Vale'; when later

presented in Hobart, it was the first play with an Australian theme to be published and staged in Australia. He was also author of the anonymous Two letters written in Van Diemen's Land shewing the oppression and tyranny of the government (1835).

Between 1834 and 1837 Melville again united with R. L Murray to produce the Tasmanian and Austral-Asiatic Review. In 1835 Melville began publication of the Trumpeter, an advertising paper. About this time he was busily preparing a brief history of the colony's last ten years, which he hoped to publish in mid-1835 but the government disapproved the outlook of the newspapers he controlled and refused to supply him with statistical information.

Melville's article, 'A comment on the action of the Supreme Court in the case of R. Bryan' on a cattle-stealing charge, which appeared in the Colonial Times, November 1835, led to his imprisonment for contempt of court, but he was soon released. While in gaol he wrote 'A few words on prison discipline' and completed his history of the colony, which was a critical and descriptive account of Lieut-Governor Arthur's administration. These were printed in Hobart by Melville, smuggled in a ship and published in London under the title History of the Island of Van Diemen's Land from the year 1824 to 1835. He became involved in insolvency proceedings in 1838 and sold the Tasmanian to Maurice Smith, and the Trumpeter to J. C. Macdougall. The Colonial Times also passed to Macdougall in 1839.

Having given up business as a pressman Melville retired to his property, Murray Hall, at New Norfolk and pursued his studies in occult philosophy, astronomy and Freemasonry. He wrote letters to the Colonial Times in 1845-48, and in 1843 was engaged in controversy on the direction of movement of Lalande's comet. By 1847 his agricultural pursuits had become a financial embarrassment and in 1849 he left Tasmania, visiting other cities and fulfilling journalistic assignments before arriving in London where he published his Present state of Australia, with particular hints to emigrants in 1851. His last years were devoted to the investigation of occultism. He died on 22 December 1873. Next year Veritas, a work on the lost mysteries of Freemasonry, edited by Frederick Tennyson, brother of Alfred, was published posthumously: Melville had been working on it for forty years.

C. L. Barrett (ed), *Across the years* (Melb, 1948); E. M. Miller, *Pressmen and governors* (Syd, 1952); *Tas and Southern Literary and Political Mag*, 1 Mar, 7 June 1833; *Bib1io- news*, July 1951; *Hobart Town Courier*, 29 Nov 1833, 2 Feb, 27 Apr 1838; CSO 1 & 5 (TA).
                                                    E. FLINN

MENGE, JOHANN (1788-1852), geologist and linguist, was born on 24 January 1788 at Steinau, Hesse, Germany, the fifth of six sons of Nicholas Menge, a poor wheelwright, and his wife Anna Margaret, née Schmittin. He had little formal education after 13, but as a prodigy he soon became a private tutor on a near-by manor. At 17 he was engaged as a technical assistant by Privy Councillor Carl Cäsar von Leonhard, a lawyer of Hanau who collected and sold geological specimens. Quick to realize his technician's ability, Leonhard soon made him an associate in the business. Menge made a name for himself with papers on geognosy and fossils, and was elected a corresponding member of several learned societies. When Leonhard was called to the chair of geology at Munich in 1816 Menge began the travels that took him as far afield as Iceland and Siberia. Geology, however, was not his only love. At his base in Lübeck he came under the influence of the evangelist, Dr J. Geibel, who infected him with a passion for holy writ and faith in God to supply his worldly needs. At the same time he developed an amazing gift of tongues, mastering an encyclopaedic collection of languages. Legend had him offered an honorary professorship at Lübeck and a chair of Hebrew at Oxford. His most treasured possessions were polyglot Bibles and lexicons. At Lübeck he began publishing religious expositions of Hebraic oral tradition, a curious blend of linguistic science and mystical theology.

Menge married in 1810 and had three sons who later became Anglican missionaries in India. When his wife died in 1830 he moved to England where he taught languages, worked for the British and Foreign Bible Society as a translater and prepared a Chinese dictionary. In August 1836 he was engaged by the South Australian Co. as mine and quarry agent at £150 a year. At Kangaroo Island his eccentric ways made him an uncomfortable colleague and he was dismissed from the company in June 1838. He remained in the province, and by frequent excursions gained a curious knowledge of soils and minerals which, however exaggerated or ridiculous, was eagerly sought by land buyers and speculators with varying success. Menge rarely sought payment for his information and in 1840 even published his findings in *Mineral Kingdom of South Australia*. Once he refused an invitation to organize a mining company with British capital, because he was too busy planning a Chinese missionary college. His many other projects included the introduction of plant seedlings, intense interest in the Aboriginals, editorship of Adelaide's first German newspaper (1848), the use of irrigation and fertilizers, teaching Hebrew at the Lobethal Lutheran seminary, and the settlement of the Barossa Valley by German immigrants. A firm believer that all sickness derived from evil spirits, he tried to cure his own complaints by motion. One unusually long walk took him to the Victorian diggings in 1852; after notifying the lieut-governor of his arrival, he went to Forest Creek near Bendigo, where in the winter he died and was buried at the foot of a quartz hill.

F. S. Dutton, *South Australia and its mines* (Lond, 1846); W. A. Cawthorne, *Menge the mineralogist* (Adel, 1859); *Allgemeine deutsche biographie*, 21 (Leipzig, 1885); W. Präsent, 'Johannes Menge, ein Steinauer Naturforscher', *Unsere Heimat*, 1927; *Observer* (Adel), Feb-May 1844; D. Van Abbé, 'A German eccentric in South Australia, 1836-1852', *Hist Studies*, no 39, Nov 1962; L. A. Triebel, Outline biography of Menge from material in the Angas papers (German Dept, Univ Adel).
                                                    D. VAN ABBÉ

MENZIES, SIR CHARLES (1783-1866), officer of marines and commandant, was born at Bal Freike, Perthshire, Scotland, the son of Captain Charles Menzies of the 71st Regiment, and Sarah, née Walker. He was educated at Stirling, commissioned second lieutenant in the marines on 17 February 1798 and attached to Nelson's squadron off Boulogne. In December 1803 he was promoted lieutenant after he sailed to Australia earlier that year in the *Calcutta*. He commanded the detachment of marines which quelled the Vinegar Hill convict rebellion on 5 March 1804, and when Governor King decided on resettling the Coal Harbour, 'in conformity to my Lord Hobart's Instructions and . . . to Separate the Worst of the Irish sent here for Sedition from the others, as well as the great public advantage that Settlement will be of', on 14 March Menzies, signing himself C. A. F. N. Menzies, wrote offering his services to superintend the proposed settlement. King accepted his offer and gazetted him commandant of the settlement on 18 March 1804.

The expedition left Sydney on 28 March in the *Lady Nelson*, *Francis* and *Resource*, Menzies being accompanied by Dr James Mileham [q.v.] (surgeon), Isaac Knight (superintendent of convicts), John Tucker (store-keeper), Ferdinand Bauer [q.v.] (artist), George Cayley [q.v.] (botanist), eleven military guards and thirty-four convicts. The party arrived on 30 March and Menzies named the settlement Kingstown, but King's own choice, Newcastle, prevailed. Menzies' instructions were to use the convicts in 'getting as many coals as possible', cutting cedar, clearing ground for cultivation and 'to enforce a due observance of religion and good order'. In May Menzies discovered a convict plot to assassinate him and his small force, but he was able to arrest the conspirators and severely punish the ringleaders. During his term as commandant he had huts constructed for the military guard and the convicts, built a large stone wharf, established a coal beacon to assist navigation into the harbour, organized the cutting of cedar and the obtaining of salt from salt-pans at Collier's Point and reached satisfactory rates of production of coal. As King said 'Lieut. Menzies . . . fixed that Settlement and brought it to a forward degree of perfection'.

In July 1804 King sent Charles Cressy, a subaltern of the New South Wales Corps, to strengthen the military detachment at Newcastle and afford some relief to Menzies, but trouble soon arose between Colonel Paterson [q.v.] and Menzies on the question of military jurisdiction over the members of the corps stationed in Newcastle. Paterson argued that Cressy at no point came under Menzies' jurisdiction and could accept no orders from him. Ultimately Cressy challenged Menzies to a duel; Menzies ignored the challenge and arrested Cressy on a number of charges. After a court martial Cressy was cashiered. The case was referred to the judge-advocate-general, Sir Charles Morgan, who thought Cressy should, in view of his youth and inexperience, merely be reprimanded, for Menzies had 'conducted his command with a great want of Temper' and had brought three charges, which he could not substantiate, merely to aggravate the case. The episode sheds light on the status of the corps at this time and on King's apparent disinclination to deal strongly with it, for he had refused to intervene in the matter. In March 1805 Menzies

submitted his resignation to King to 'return to England to my duty in the Royal Marines'. He left soon afterwards and returned to active service.

Menzies played a notable part in the wars against Napoleon and was promoted captain in the Royal Marine Artillery in April 1813. He married Maria Wilhelmina, daughter of Dr Robert Bryant, physician to the duke of Gloucester and had five children. He commanded the Royal Marine Artillery from 1838 to 1844, progressing from major and lieut-colonel in 1837 to general in 1857. He was appointed aide-de-camp to the Queen in 1852, and created K.H. in 1831 and K.C.B. in 1856. He died at Hastings on 22 August 1866. Despite all this meritorious service his principal importance in Australia is as the founder of the first permanent settlement at Newcastle.

HRA (1), 4, 5; *Illustrated London News*, 1 Sept 1866; W. J. Goold, 'Lieut Charles A. F. N. Menzies', Newcastle and Hunter District Hist Soc, *Procs*, 4 (1950), 7 (1953); *Newcastle Morning Herald*, 17 Aug 1929).

E. FLOWERS

MERCER, GEORGE (1772-1853), GEORGE DUNCAN (1815-1884), JOHN HENRY (1823-1891), and WILLIAM DRUMMOND (1796?-1871) all shared in the settlement of Port Phillip, which the first never saw. He was of Dryden House, Midlothian, and 14 Moray Place, Edinburgh, and of the Gorthy and Tulchan estates, Perthshire, eighth and youngest son of William Mercer (1717-1785), of Pitteuchar and Potterhill—one of the 'black' Mercers of Aldie— and Elizabeth Swan (Mrs Mercer) a granddaughter of Charles II. The others were his second and fourth sons, and his only surviving nephew.

George Mercer sold his commission in the East India Co.'s marines to become a merchant in Calcutta, where Thomas Learmonth [q.v.] and others who moved to Australia also operated. On 12 September 1810, when his friend Dr John Macwhirter married the girl who became the future Dr John Learmonth's mother-in-law, Mercer married her sister, Frances Charlotte (1793-1862), daughter of Dr John Reid of the Bengal Medical Service. By 1833, when Mercer was a nabob based on Edinburgh, Captain Charles Swanston [q.v.] had persuaded him to invest in Van Diemen's Land, and had bought the Lovely Banks property, near Oatlands, on his behalf. Mercer sent David Fisher out as manager, planned for at least one son to follow him, and so in due course became a partner in the Port Phillip Association, its conscript but able advocate in Britain, and chief shareholder in the succeeding Derwent Co.

Lieutenant G. D. and Major W. D. Mercer reached Hobart Town from Calcutta in March 1838, having retired from the Bengal Native Infantry and 16th Lancers respectively. Both were soon at Port Phillip, exploring with Fisher, who held stations at Indented Head and Geelong, where he had already built the first weatherboard house. A similar bush homestead, unique among the slab huts, gave its name to the Weatherboard station, south of Golfhill, and this, with the Mount Mercer run and about 4500 of the 10,000 Gheringhap acres bought through remission by the Port Phillip Association, became George Mercer's in 1842-43, when the Derwent Co. was dissolved.

W. D. Mercer held the Warrambeen station, 1842-46, and Kanawalla, in partnership, 1850-51; but street names in Geelong and Malvern, Melbourne, attest his concentration upon town allotments. He sailed for Britain in 1841, but upon his return in 1846 was still remembered as the real 'Father of Separation'. He represented Port Phillip in the Legislative Council at Sydney in 1850-51, but before 1852 he was in South America on his way to Scotland. In June 1853, six months before George Mercer's death, he married the latter's eldest daughter, Anne Elliot. He then settled in Perthshire, as Mercer of Huntingtower.

G. D. Mercer succeeded John Gardiner [q.v.] as manager of the ill-fated Port Phillip Bank, 1841-42. He then took control at the Weatherboard, where J. H. Mercer, who emigrated when W. D. returned, replaced him in 1847-48, allowing him to visit home. From 1849, with G. D. back at the station, J. H. and W. D. evidently made their headquarters on the freehold in the crotch of the Barwon and Moorabool rivers, living at Tulchan homestead (now a bluestone ruin) until December 1850, when G. D. joined them to move into what they called Fyansford House, probably the original Fyansford Inn (1843), later the Swan Hotel, and today a farmstead.

In 1851-52 J. H. Mercer represented Grant in the first Victorian Legislative Council. He was in Scotland when his father died but was back in Victoria by July 1855, when he and G. D. secured probate for property valued at up to £50,000. Mount Mercer station had been sold in January 1853, and the Weatherboard eighteen months later. In 1856 G. D. Mercer returned to Scotland, where he died unmarried. J. H. remained near Geelong, where he busied himself as commissioner of insolvent estates and chairman of the water commission, and in 1857 had the Gheringhap freehold mapped as the Dryden estate. In February 1858 he valued the Golfhill station; but in 1861 he married in Scotland, where he eventually inherited Gorthy, as his grandson inherited Huntingtower upon the extinction of W. D. Mercer's family.

HRA (1), 18; W. Anderson, *The Scottish nation*, 3 (Edinb, 1863); J. Bonwick, *Port Phillip settlement* (Lond, 1883); P. L. Brown, *Clyde Company papers*, 2-5 (Lond, 1952-63) and for bibliog; S. J. Butlin, 'Charles Swanston and the Derwent Bank', *Hist Studies*, no 7, May 1943; Geelong & Dutigalla Association papers (Dixson Lib, Syd).   P. L. BROWN

MEREDITH, GEORGE (1777-1856) settler, was born on 13 February 1777 near Birmingham, England, the fourth son of John Meredith and his wife Sally, née Turner; his father was a prominent barrister and solicitor and descended from the ancient Amerydeth family of Devon and Wales. In 1796 Meredith was commissioned second lieutenant in the marines and later served in the West Indies, at the blockade of Ferrol in Spain and on the Mediterranean Station. At Alexandria in 1803 he made a daring ascent of Pompey's Pillar, a granite column 180 feet high, to fasten the Union Jack in place of a French cap-of-liberty placed there by Napoleon's forces. In 1805 when recruiting in Berkshire he met and married Sarah, the daughter of H. W. Hicks. Next year he retired on half-pay and commenced farming at Newbury; later the family moved to Haverfordwest, Pembrokeshire, and farmed there until 1819 when the post-war rural depression stimulated his interest in emigration. He then had two boys and three girls, the eldest being 13.

Meredith resolved to settle in Van Diemen's Land and applied to the Colonial Office for letters of introduction. In company with several partners he chartered a ship, but early in 1820 his wife died suddenly, thus jeopardizing the whole venture. By good fortune their former governess and companion, Mary Evans, consented to take care of the young family on the voyage. In July official permission was granted and in October the ship was loaded with personal possessions, extensive farm equipment and a small flock of merino sheep. An agreement had already been made to obtain additional stock from Edward Lord's [q.v.] flocks already on the island. The original partners, Meredith, Joseph Archer and T. G. Gregson [qq.v.], were joined by a number of passengers, including the Amos family [q.v.], John Kerr, Francis Desailly and John Meredith, a cousin of the family. Before embarkation George Meredith and Mary Evans were quietly married and on 8 November the expedition sailed in the *Emerald* and reached Hobart Town on 13 March 1821.

After settling the family in temporary lodgings Meredith presented his letters of introduction to Lieut-Governor Sorell and began to look for suitable land. He had already experienced the limited market outlets for inland farms in England and Wales, and was determined to secure coastal grants if possible. According to government surveys the most promising land lay at Oyster Bay, about 140 miles distant on the eastern coast, and a small party set out in a whale-boat to visit the district. Close examination proved the land to be greatly inferior to the official descriptions, but certain parts capable of development were selected and the party returned to Hobart on 24 April to lodge the formal applications.

Official permission was duly given to the whole scheme, which included the individual grants, and late in September, after the first livestock were dispatched overland, a small schooner was chartered to take the settlers to Oyster Bay. There they found part of the granted land occupied by William Talbot [q.v.], an emigrant Irishman who had already unsuccessfully sought inclusion in the group and now claimed that the land had been granted to him. Vigorously protesting he withdrew from the district but the dispute was finally decided in Meredith's favour in 1826.

Meanwhile the grants were developed and improved, both for seasonal crops and grazing stock; a tannery and flour-mill were established at the Meredith River, and bay whaling stations set up on near-by islands to try out whale oil for export. In a shipyard at Waterloo Point were built several trading vessels and also small craft for the use of sealing gangs on their visits to the Bass Strait islands. These enterprises required both skilled labour and special equipment and necessitated repeated visits to Hobart, so Meredith was able to maintain a close interest and participation in the public affairs of the free colonists. In 1824, after the declaration of a new Charter of Justice for Van Diemen's Land, Meredith and many other colonists met publicly to express their appreciation and to seek more benefits from the British government. In March 1827, after news that property owners in New South Wales were petitioning for an elective legislature, Meredith and other landowners arranged a public meeting to encourage similar efforts in Van Diemen's Land. A petition and addresses were prepared for submission to London by Lieut-Governor Arthur. Through misunderstanding the documents were delayed; copies were later sent privately to England but the whole matter lapsed because the Colonial Office disapproved of the colonists' attitude toward Arthur. Later that year Meredith and others again came into conflict with the lieut-governor over legislation to license the press, with which Meredith had strong connexions. Bitter official opposition toward Meredith continued throughout Arthur's term and constituted a severe restriction to his personal life and public spirit.

In the early 1820s many isolated settlements were under repeated attack from escaped convicts. In October 1825 the homestead at Oyster Bay was raided in Meredith's absence by the bushranger Matthew Brady [q.v.]. None of the family was injured but the house was ransacked and a servant taken hostage was later killed; fortunately the plate and other valuables were found buried near Hobart and returned. The family had first lived at Redbanks, a turf hut strengthened with timber, on the south bank of the Meredith River. About 1827 they moved into Belmont, a more spacious home lying about one mile further inland. About 1836 they moved into Cambria, a large dwelling designed by Meredith near the original home and surrounded by gardens which had been steadily developed since their arrival. From that time the management of the property devolved more upon the eldest sons, and they took the entire care of the estate when his wife Mary died unexpectedly in 1842. By his second marriage he had three sons and four daughters, of whom the second son John remained in charge at Oyster Bay until George Meredith died in 1856.

Several of Meredith's children became prominent in later years; his second son, Charles, was appointed colonial treasurer of Van Diemen's Land in 1857 and continued in high public offices for twenty years; the fourth son, John, was appointed a magistrate at Swansea in 1855 and contributed greatly to the welfare of the district; the fifth son, Edwin, migrated to New Zealand as a pioneer colonist in 1851, and the fifth daughter, Clara, married Richard Dry [q.v.].

George Meredith possessed qualities of endurance and strength which, coupled with his early experience at sea in command of men and subsequent farming life in England, resulted in a character eminently suitable for pioneer colonial life. The enthusiasm and encouragement of his wife Mary also contributed greatly to his successful career in public and private life.

HRA (3), 4-6; R. W. Giblin, *The early history of Tasmania*, 2 (Melb, 1939); A. D. Baker, *The life and times of Sir Richard Dry* (Hob, 1951); K. R. von Stieglitz, *Pioneers of the east coast from 1642* (Launceston, 1955); A. McKay (ed), *Journals of the land commissioners for Van Diemen's Land, 1826-28* (Hob, 1962); Correspondence file under Meredith (TA); MS cat under Meredith (ML); Meredith file (Roy Soc, Tas). DAVID HODGSON

MESTRE; see DE MESTRE

MIDDLETON, GEORGE AUGUSTUS (1791-1848), Anglican clergyman, was born on 31 August 1791 in London, the son of Charles Middleton. He was educated at Westminster School and at St John's College, Cambridge, and was later awarded a Lambeth M.A. After his wife's death he was ordained deacon and priest and in August 1819 commissioned as an assistant chaplain for New South Wales. With his son George Augustus he arrived in the *Prince Regent* at Sydney in January 1820. Almost immediately Middleton took charge of Parramatta and in December he was sent to Newcastle, where Christ Church had been built in 1817. He was the first chaplain appointed north of the Hawkesbury, although general spiritual oversight had been given by Rev. William Cowper [q.v.]. By December he claimed to have 'at length succeeded in introducing into the Town a degree of order to which under the present administration it had ever been a stranger' and also complained of the commandant's morals. In 1822 his application to return to England for 'some Private Family arrangements' was looked on favourably by Earl Bathurst but apparently he did not go.

Unhappy with conditions in the penal settlement Middleton became increasingly interested in the spiritual welfare of the free settlers in the Hunter valley. He regularly visited settlers on the Paterson and Williams Rivers, Patrick's Plains and as far as Segenhoe. This itinerant ministry led to the appointment of catechists to assist his work. Middleton also showed great interest in the Aboriginals. According to John Bingle [q.v.], who accompanied him 'with the whole tribe of up-

wards of one hundred' on a trip to Lake Macquarie, Middleton was 'an especial favourite with the blacks'. Middleton gave full support to Rev. L. E. Threlkeld [q.v.], accompanying him on his preliminary visit to Lake Macquarie in 1825. Like other clergy Middleton augmented his original land grant, and his 2400 acres at Glenrose, Paterson's Plains, earned him J. D. Lang's [q.v.] censure in the comment, 'every priest his own butcher'. According to Commandant Morisset [q.v.], his time was too much 'occupied in dealing in Cattle with the Convict Settlers: and I am sorry to say that my respect for that Gentleman has been much diminished by the reports I hear of his frequently dining with, and at the same table of people of that description'.

By 1826 Middleton's outspoken views had made him dangerous enemies. When reproved by Archdeacon Scott [q.v.] for treating a convict's family with 'cruelty and oppression', he asked unsuccessfully for an official investigation, and circulated letters seeking the vindication of his own clerical and private character. Scott had already decided to send him to the penal settlement at Port Macquarie as chaplain, but in May 1827 Middleton resigned in disgust, looking on the transfer as 'banishment'. He moved to Moore Park, on the Paterson River near Hinton, where he continued an unofficial itinerant ministry. From 1828 to 1830 he regularly visited and baptized in the district between Morpeth, Maitland, Branxton and Paterson, and was said to have kept a school at Phoenix Park near Morpeth. He also accompanied his friend, John Blaxland junior, on an exploratory journey when they discovered the overland route to Newcastle. After Bishop Broughton's [q.v.] pastoral visitation to the Hunter valley in 1837, Middleton was licensed to serve in the parishes of Butterwick and Seaham, and in April 1838 he was authorized to solemnize marriages in his house at Hinton, there being no church building in the area. In 1839 the Hinton parish was further limited to the lower reaches of the Williams and Paterson Rivers. Middleton also did much of the parish work in the ecclesiastical centre of Morpeth until failing health confined him to Hinton. He died there on 15 May 1848.

At Liverpool on 12 February 1824 he had married, as his second wife, Sarah, daughter of Robert Rose of London. His widow died at Tressingfield in March 1863; of their children Charles Richard became a police magistrate.

According to Threlkeld, Middleton was

'not Evangelical'. On his arrival he was said to be 'a great Gambler', and Samuel Marsden [q.v.] thought him 'a stranger to religion, but well read'. Although his interest in missions and itinerant work linked him closely with the Evangelical tradition, he was apparently the exception, both in educational standards and doctrine, of the colonial chaplains in the colony when Scott arrived. In 1826 the press, possibly with mild sarcasm, described him as 'unassuming, retired, devout, and unbusinesslike'. A window in his memory is in Newcastle Cathedral.

HRA (1), 10, 13-15, 21, 23; J. Bingle, *Past and present records of Newcastle* (Newcastle, 1873); A. P. Elkin, *Morpeth and I* (Syd, 1937); A. P. Elkin, *The diocese of Newcastle* (Syd, 1955); A. P. Elkin, 'Some early chaplains and churches in the Hunter River valley', *JRAHS*, 23 (1937); *Sydney Gazette*, 26 Aug 1826; MS cat under Middleton (ML).

NIEL GUNSON

MILEHAM, JAMES (1763?-1824), surgeon, was reputedly forced to emigrate from France because of the French revolution. He was given a commission as assistant surgeon in New South Wales by the British government in 1796 and arrived in the *Ganges* in June 1797, after nearly giving up the voyage because of ill treatment from one of the soldiers on board while the ship was in the Downs. He served at Sydney and Parramatta for some time and in October 1799 was ordered to relieve Thomas Jamison [q.v.] on Norfolk Island. He remained there until March 1802, but his salary for duty was collected by Jamison from their English agent and was not handed over to him, and he was refused an allowance for attendance on the troops because the commanding officer on Norfolk Island neglected to send a return of the detachment there. Harassed by his creditors, embarrassed by the failure of his agent in England, he had to sell 100 acres at Dundas which he had been granted in May 1799.

Mileham returned to Sydney in March 1802, where he did duty until being appointed to Castle Hill in January 1804 and to Newcastle in March, but by August he had been put under arrest by Lieutenant Menzies [q.v.] and brought to Sydney for disobedience of orders. In April 1805 he was found guilty by a court martial of refusing to attend a woman in child-birth and was sentenced to be publicly reprimanded. He was not on good terms with the principal surgeon, Jamison, whom he took to court

for assault in 1803, but he nevertheless supported Jamison in his stand against Governor Bligh in January 1808. He received a grant of 500 acres at Upper Nelson and 100 acres for his daughter from the rebel government in April 1809. Governor Macquarie regranted these in October 1811 and later granted him a further 700 acres at Illawarra with indulgences of convict labour and stock, but Mileham was obliged to sell these grants too, after the failure of his second agent, William Wilson, who had collected his pay before going bankrupt in 1810. He recovered part of the money from Robert Campbell [q.v.], Wilson's partner in trading ventures, but this was a blow from which his fortunes never recovered.

Mileham had been sent to the Hawkesbury in September 1808 and remained in the Windsor district until he retired. In June 1811 he was appointed a justice of the peace and magistrate for Castlereagh, and he took an active part in the public life of the district. He was a trustee of the Windsor Charitable Institution, treasurer of the Hawkesbury Benevolent Society and vice-president of the Windsor Bible Society; a Windsor street was named in his honour. In 1812 he rose to the rank of first assistant surgeon, but in 1816 declined an appointment in Van Diemen's Land. Two years later Macquarie refused to recommend his appointment as principal surgeon in succession to D'Arcy Wentworth [q.v.] on the grounds that his medical knowledge was defective, he was old and his eyesight was failing. In July 1821 he sought leave to retire on full pay because of his long service and poor health. Macquarie recommended that this request be granted and meanwhile gave him leave on full pay; as no reply was received from London Mileham continued on leave until he died.

Soon after his arrival in the colony Mileham formed an alliance with Elizabeth Price, by whom he had several children, but only a daughter Lucy (b. 1799), who later married Samuel Otoo Hassall, survived infancy. Elizabeth Price lived with Mileham until her death in July 1818 and was buried under the name of Elizabeth Mileham. On 2 June 1819 at St Matthew's, Windsor, he married Susanna(h), daughter of Henry Kable [q.v.] of Windsor. Mileham died on 28 September 1824, aged 61, at Castlereagh Street, Sydney; he was buried in the Sandhills cemetery and his remains were later reinterred at La Perouse. In announcing his death to Bathurst, Governor

Brisbane described Mileham as: 'a solitary instance of one who had continually resided in this colony nearly thirty years, and yet was in want'. Susanna Mileham received a pension of £100 a year until she died on 20 June 1885.

HRNSW, 3-7; HRA (1), 2-11; J. Steele, *Early days of Windsor* (Syd, 1916); *Sydney Gazette*, 8 June 1811, 19 Feb 1820, 25 Aug 1821, 30 Sept 1824.   VIVIENNE PARSONS

MILES, WILLIAM AUGUSTUS (1798-1851), commissioner of police and police magistrate, was ostensibly the eldest son of William Augustus Miles (1753?-1817), political writer, author of comic operas and holder of minor official posts, but currently believed a royal bastard. The rumours may have had some substance. William IV supported his application for the post of secretary of the Colonization Commission for South Australia in 1835 on the grounds that he was intelligent, well educated, and a protégé of the late King; on his gravestone in the old Camperdown cemetery was a crown and the words: 'Sweet nature gave a Prince but Fortune blind adorned him not whom nature had adorned'.

Miles held a number of civil appointments in England before coming to New South Wales: in the Privy Council office, as assistant commissioner of inquiry into the Poor Law, as assistant to the commission of inquiry into the state of the hand loom weavers, and as a commissioner of public charities. He had come into close contact with the commissioners of Metropolitan Police when assisting a committee of the House of Lords on secondary punishment, before which he gave evidence in 1834. In 1836 he printed a pamphlet in the form of a letter to Lord John Russell in which he advocated the establishment of a unified police force for England and Wales under the control of a single authority. As assistant commissioner to the Royal Commission on rural constabulary in 1836-39, he gained further knowledge of police matters. He was strongly recommended for the post of commissioner of police in Sydney by C. S. Lefevre, the Speaker of the House of Commons, who had been a member of the Rural Constabulary Commission, and was appointed in July 1840 by Lord John Russell, who thought him particularly well qualified for the post.

Parts of the Metropolitan Police system had already been introduced in Sydney in 1833, and Miles intended to make the Sydney police organization resemble the London one even more closely. Because of a shortage of suitable men and of funds he was unable fully to put into operation the organization he had planned, but he did insist that the Sydney constables should walk their beats at the regulation London pace of two miles and a half an hour, and that they should wear tightly buttoned tail coats similar to those of the London police. In addition to being executive head of the Sydney police Miles was a magistrate and found his work very heavy. There were frequent complaints that he was not active enough as commissioner and that he was not readily accessible to the public because he did much of his business from his home near Dawes Battery, instead of from the police office. In 1847 a board examined his accounts and found him guilty of carelessness. Next year the governor and Executive Council investigated charges against him of insobriety while on duty and wrongful dismissal of a police inspector. They found that the charge of insobriety was neither proved nor disproved, and reinstated the inspector who had been dismissed; they decided that Miles should exchange duties with Captain J. Long Innes, acting senior police magistrate. Payment of Miles's salary in this new post was bitterly opposed in the Legislative Council, and was passed only by the casting vote of the chairman of the committee of supply; next year his salary for 1850 was not sanctioned by the legislature and he went into enforced retirement. His claim to be compensated for loss of office was granted by the reconstituted Legislative Council in October 1851, after his death; during the debate he was warmly defended by W. C. Wentworth [q.v.], James Martin and others.

Miles appeared as a witness before various select committees of the Legislative Council, notably those on immigration (1842), the Water Police Amendment Act (1843), insecurity of life and property (1844), and police (1847). His interests were wide. He was a corresponding member of the Ethnological Society of London, of the Statistical Society, and of the *Muséum d'Histoire Naturelle* of Paris. Some of his drawings of Aboriginal rock carvings are in the Mitchell Library. In his later years he lived in Cleveland Street, Sydney, where he died on 25 April 1851.

HRA (1), 20-26; Ethnological Soc (Lond), *Journal*, 3 (1854); SMH, 19 Dec 1840, 9 Dec 1841, 2 Oct 1845, 31 May, 2, 8, 9 June 1848, 23 May 1849, 25 Apr, 22, 30 Oct 1851; H. King, Police organization and administration . . . NSW 1825-1851 (M.A. thesis,

Univ Syd, 1956); Executive Council minutes 1848-49 (NSWA); MS cat under W. A. Miles (ML); CO 323/175.

HAZEL KING

MILLER, ANDREW (d. 1790), commissary and governor's secretary, was the first commissary of stores and provisions for the colony of New South Wales. He was appointed probably on the recommendation of Governor Phillip, and in that capacity embarked in the *Sirius* in April 1787. On the way to New South Wales he stayed as a guest with Phillip at Rio de Janeiro and the Cape of Good Hope, apparently because his pay of 10s. a day was not adequate to meet his expenses. Miller's superior status had been recognized before he left England by his appointment as one of the members of the Vice-Admiralty Court, and after reaching Sydney he acted as secretary to the governor until replaced by David Collins in June.

His most important work was naturally that of the commissary. Because of the difficulties attached to the issue of provisions Miller sought the help of a trustworthy assistant, and in April the governor appointed Zachariah Clark. Even so, the position was not enviable; supplies were short and Miller had constantly to prepare lists of stores required from England. There was no coin or other medium of circulation and Miller had to issue notes on the Treasury to pay for the labour of free artificers.

In April 1790 he resigned. He had 'acted so unlike the commissary that he has lost his health and in three years has never made three shillings', wrote Phillip; if the government would give him a pension of £50, it would 'make an honest Man happy'. Miller left Sydney in the *Supply*, but after transhipping to a Dutch packet at Batavia he died at sea in August 1790. He was not a colourful administrator, but he displayed ability and courage, qualities which, like his honesty, were not common among commissary officers of this period.

HRNSW, 1 pt 2; HRA (1), 1; P. G. King, Letter-book 1788-89 (ML).

GEORGE PARSONS

MILLER, FREDERICK (1806-1862), Congregational minister, was born on 8 March 1806 at Hackney, London, the only son of Henry Miller, a librarian in the Bank of England. After attending Thompson's Academy at Cambridge Heath he studied with the intention of becoming an architect. Although confirmed in the Church of England at the Episcopal Jews' Chapel, in July 1825 he was greatly influenced by the prophetic preaching of Rev. Edward Irving at the Caledonian Church, Hatton Garden. He then attended Dr Burder's Independent Chapel, St Thomas's Square, became a member and at 22 entered Highbury College, Islington, as a candidate for the Christian ministry. When he learned that the London Missionary Society had received a request for a minister from Henry Hopkins [q.v.] of Hobart Town, he volunteered for service and with the college's approval accepted the invitation.

On 7 February 1830 at St John's Church, Hackney, he married his cousin, Elizabeth Miller. He was ordained in April and they left England together in May in the *Lang*, reached Hobart in September and duly took up residence in a house provided by Hopkins. Miller conducted his first service in October at Deane's Library, Elizabeth Street, preaching to some thirty people. He declined a salary of £200 offered by Lieut-Governor Arthur, considering such official support contrary to the ideals of Congregationalism, but he accepted a loan of £500 towards a new chapel. It was opened on 20 April 1832. The governor attended and personally contributed £25 to church funds. This chapel in Brisbane Street, Hobart, was the first Congregational or Independent church built and maintained in Australia, and Miller the first permanent minister of that denomination.

Miller was never robust but he laboured with a sincerity that won him general respect. Many local religious organizations originated with him and he laid himself out to foster their interests. He was an originator of the Colonial Missionary Society, assisted in re-establishing the Bethel Union for seamen and co-operated with James Backhouse and G. W. Walker [qq.v.] in the formation of a temperance society. A pulpit exchange for six months with the minister of the Independent Church in Collins Street, Melbourne, widened his activities, and three of his sermons and an address were published. In 1861, despite a long sea voyage taken on medical advice and with the financial assistance of his congregation, his health broke down completely. He died in Hobart on 13 October 1862. More than two thousand persons attended a memorial service in the Wesleyan Methodist Church, Melville Street. He was survived by his widow and seven children.

A. C. Nelson, *History of the effective establishment of Congregationalism in the Australian colonies and New Zealand* (Hob, 1930); E. Cox, *Life of the Rev Fredck Miller* (Hob, 1930); *Mercury*, 14 Oct 1862.

E. R. PRETYMAN

MILLER, GEORGE (fl. 1822-1833), clerk, arrived in New South Wales in the *Minerva* in October 1822, with introductions to Deputy-Commissary-General Wemyss [q.v.] and a recommendation from Robert Peddie, town clerk of Perth, Scotland, certifying that Miller had served as his apprentice for four years from October 1816, had been sober and industrious, and had shown considerable talents for business. Wemyss offered him a post in charge of cash payments, and in November 1823 he was appointed clerk in the Commissariat Department. When the settlement at Melville Island in Northern Australia was proposed he volunteered for duty there, hoping to gain promotion more rapidly. He was appointed to take charge of the commissariat there in August 1824.

After four years on Melville Island Miller's health became impaired under conditions which brought about the deaths of a third of those who had embarked with him. He was relieved in 1828 after a medical certificate had been sent to headquarters, and was granted two months leave. During his stay on Melville Island he visited Kupang, Timor, in 1826, in a vain attempt to establish regular communication and ensure a supply of provisions. In October 1828 he was sent to take charge of the commissariat at Port Macquarie, where he transferred from the store to the accounts branch to fill the vacancy caused by the removal of the senior deputy-assistant-commissary-general to Hobart Town. In answer to successive memorials to the Treasury he learnt that commissariat clerks engaged on the spot were to be considered only as temporary officials.

In 1833 Miller published a pamphlet entitled *The Patronage and Justice of the British Treasury Exemplified in a Plain Narrative*, in which he deplored the failure of the new Whig administration to stamp out the unjust patronage of the Tory period, citing his own case in the hope that publicity might lead to an inquiry.

It is not clear what became of Miller after this because his is a not uncommon name. It is impossible to know whether he was the same George Miller who became accountant of the Savings Bank and a director of the Sydney Banking Co. and Australian Gaslight Co. in the 1840s.

HRA (1), 12; *Sydney Gazette*, 18 Oct 1822, 27 Nov 1823.

VIVIENNE PARSONS

MILLIGAN, JOSEPH (1807-1884), surgeon, was born in Dumfriesshire, Scotland. He obtained the diploma of the Royal College of Surgeons of Edinburgh in January 1829 and in June 1830 was appointed surgeon to the Van Diemen's Land Co.'s establishment at Surrey Hills, where he arrived in February 1831. During his appointment as surgeon, and later surgeon-superintendent, he became interested in the natural history of the island, formed a close acquaintance with R. C. Gunn [q.v.] and collected specimens for W. J. Hooker.

In 1842 he left the company in February and settled briefly in Launceston. He was invited by Lady Franklin to accompany the overland expedition to Macquarie Harbour from March to May as medical attendant and naturalist. After his return he held a number of important government positions. In September he became inspector of convict discipline and member of the Board for Distributing Convicts. In March 1843 he married Eliza, second daughter of William Effingham Lawrence [q.v.] of Launceston. She died on Flinders Island on 31 July 1844 after giving birth to a son.

In December 1843 he was appointed superintendent and medical officer of the Aboriginals, a position which he occupied until 1855 except for the period April 1846 to May 1847 when he was visiting magistrate and medical officer at the short-lived second penal settlement at Macquarie Harbour. In October 1847 he supervised the transfer of the Aboriginal settlement, then totalling forty-six persons, from Flinders Island to Oyster Cove, where the numbers dwindled rapidly until in 1854 only sixteen remained. During this period of duty he compiled an extensive 'Vocabulary of the Dialects of Some of the Aboriginal Tribes of Tasmania' (Royal Society of Tasmania, *Papers*, 1859), with observations on native languages and customs.

Through his interest in natural history he became secretary of the Royal Society of Van Diemen's Land in 1848-60, its members and activities increasing under his guidance. In 1848 at Lieut-Governor Denison's request he surveyed the coal resources of the island and in April 1855 became chairman of the Douglas River Coal Mining Co. In 1856 he explored the eastern slopes of the western mountains for the Fingal Gold Exploration Co.

He was retired from government service with a pension in April 1860, and in June sailed for England with his son on eighteen months leave from the Royal Society. He did not return but at the exhibition of 1862 acted as commissioner for Tasmania. He died in London in 1884 leaving £350 as well as land at George Town and Bicheno to the Royal Society of Tasmania

Milligan's thirty years in Tasmania were marked by immense industry. His official duties were carried out with conscientiousness and good sense. J. D. Hooker called him 'one of the most indefatigable and able of Tasmanian botanists' and gave his name to the native lily genus *Milligania* and a number of species of other plants. He was elected a fellow of the Linnean Society in 1850. As a geologist he carried out surveys in all parts of the colony, discovering coal, copper and gold as well as numerous fossils. But perhaps his most notable work was his study of Aboriginal languages. This permanent contribution to knowledge, although not free from error, was a remarkable achievement for a man who was said to be unacquainted with any language but English.

E. M. Curr, *The Australian race*, 3 (Melb, 1887); A. Morton, *Register of papers published in the Tasmanian Journal and the Papers and Proceedings of the Royal Society of Tasmania* (Hob, 1887); W. Schmidt, *Die Tasmanischen Sprachen* (Utrecht, 1952); T. E. Burns and J. R. Skemp, *Van Diemen's Land correspondents* (Launceston, 1961); E. L. Piesse, 'The foundation and early work of the Society', Roy Soc Tas, *Papers*, 1913; Correspondence file under Milligan (TA).

W. G. HODDINOTT

MILLS, JOHN BRABYN (1808-1877) and CHARLES FREDERICK (1812-1855), whalers and pioneers, were born at the Officers' Quarters, Launceston, sons of Peter Mills [q.v.]; they were baptized by Rev. Robert Knopwood [q.v.]. They lived with their mother on the farm at Norfolk Plains, but early took to the sea. Long before permanent settlements were formed on the southern coasts of the Australian mainland sealing, whaling and kangaroo shooting on the shores and islands had their hey-day; wattle bark stripping began in the 1820s and all these pursuits were very profitable. The history of these ventures out of Launceston largely depends on tradition orally transmitted or written down by old men. However, there is enough evidence in reliable shipping and export records to accept the broad outlines of the story, in which the names of the

Mills brothers occur frequently with those of others such as Griffiths, Dutton [qq.v.] and Wishart, all men of fine physique, high nautical skill and courage, as much respected for their integrity as for deeds of daring.

According to tradition Captain James Wishart sailed the *Fairy* into Port Fairy, Victoria, on 25 April 1810; at some later date he gave his charts to John Mills, who with his brother Charles visited Port Fairy in 1826, and thereafter established shore bases on the southern mainland coast for sealing and whaling. The degree of permanence of these bases in relation to the well-organized settlement of the Hentys [q.v.] at Portland in 1834 has led to much discussion. Miss Olive Mills, a granddaughter of Charles Mills, claims that 'John and Charles Mills who settled permanently in Victoria in 1826 and remained there until the death of Charles Mills in 1855 and of John Mills in 1877 should have the right of being recognized as Victoria's First Settlers'. H. F. Learmonth, who made an exhaustive examination, summed up that 'it seems almost certain that at least one of the Mills Brothers was in Portland Bay as a temporary settler before the arrival of William Dutton' in 1828.

Captain John Mills, 'sailor, sealer, shipmaster, pelagic and port whaleman, port officer, pilot', after a wide experience in Australian and other waters suffered a financial loss in 1849 by the wreck of the brig *Essington* of which he was part owner, and soon afterwards retired from the coastal trade. In 1853 he was appointed harbourmaster at Belfast (Port Fairy) and in 1855 outport pilot as well. He retired on a pension in 1871 and died in 1877 at his son's home in Echuca. Charles Mills also left the sea and lived on his farm at Rosebrook, near Port Fairy, where he died after a sudden illness on 16 November 1855.

N. F. Learmonth, *The Portland Bay settlement . . . 1800 to 1851* (Melb, 1934); O. M. L. Mills, *Why should their honour fade?* (Melb, 1960); Mills papers (ML, La Trobe Lib, Melb, and in family possession).

CLIVE TURNBULL

MILLS, PETER (b. 1786), sailor, surveyor and settler, was born in Dublin. In February 1804 he entered the navy as an able seaman in the *Hazard* and soon transferred as a midshipman to the *Warrior* under Captain William Bligh. On 13 April 1805 Bligh, who had been appointed governor of New South Wales, told Sir Joseph Banks [q.v.] that he would like to take 'Mr Peter Mills, a young gentleman, 19 years of age', with him to the colony and asked for his discharge to be arranged. He arrived at Port Jackson with Bligh in 1806. There is no contemporary evidence for the legend that a Lieutenant Peter Bernard French Mills acted as secretary to Bligh and was recalled to London to give evidence at Major Johnston's [q.v.] trial after the governor was deposed.

In July 1807 Peter Mills was sent in the *Estramina* to Port Dalrymple to act as harbourmaster and deputy-surveyor. In the small community on the River Tamar Mills soon caused trouble between the civil and military officers, and was relieved of his duties as harbourmaster but allowed to continue as deputy-surveyor. On 23 January 1810 at Launceston he married Jennifer Ann, eldest daughter of Captain John Brabyn [q.v.]. Soon afterwards Mills was made superintendent of government stock by Brabyn, but the appointment was quickly overruled from Sydney. He had been granted 100 acres on the South Esk River but later discovered that the land had already been alienated. Although he was granted another 200 acres on Norfolk Plains in compensation for improvements he had begun, other mistakes in his surveys led to much litigation. In June 1812 he was suspended by Governor Macquarie but allowed to become a settler with rations for his family and assigned servants.

Out of office Mills's fortunes fell to 'so low an Ebb' that no one would trust him and in 1814 to escape his creditors he and the deputy-commissary, George Williams, and a few convicts formed a bushranging gang in emulation of Michael Howe [q.v.] who was then marauding in the area. In May Macquarie heard exaggerated accounts of their exploits and indignantly issued a proclamation for their arrest. However, Mills and Williams found little opportunity to 'support themselves by Rapine and Violence' and quickly tired of the discomforts of 'the Woods and retired Places'. In September they returned to Launceston, surrendered and were placed in custody. One October night Mills's wife brought rum to the guards and the prisoners escaped. Mills was soon found under a heap of straw in a stable. At his trial in Launceston he gave much information on the misuse of government stock by unfriendly officers and was duly committed to the Supreme Court in Sydney. His hearing there was delayed because the commandant at Launceston had failed to send the necessary papers and witnesses. Mills was therefore discharged after promising to behave. Macquarie had little hope of his reformation but 'from mere motives of humanity' let him return to his family in Van Diemen's Land. From Norfolk Plains

Mills moved to Hobart Town, whence he sailed in October 1816 in the *Adamant* and was reputed to have been lost at sea.

HRA (1), 7, 8, (3), 1-3, (4), 1; Correspondence file under Peter Mills (TA); Adm 36/16620, 17097 (PRO).

MILSON, JAMES (1783-1872), farmer, was born on 25 November 1783 at Grantham, Lincolnshire, England. He arrived in Sydney in the *Albion* in August 1806 and obtained employment on a farm at the Field of Mars (near Ryde). On 8 January 1810 at St Philip's Church, Sydney, he married Elizabeth Kilpack (1793-1850), his employer's daughter; he then described himself as 'servant and labourer'. By June 1820 he was living on a grant of 100 acres at Pennant Hills, where he ran 40 cattle. He had too little pasture for them and asked for more land. His request was supported by Robert Campbell [q.v.] who had been a fellow passenger in the *Albion*. In 1824 he was authorized to select 300 acres near Pennant Hills but when he was informed that this land had been granted to another he sought 50 acres at North Shore and 300 farther inland. By 1825 he was farming on the North Shore of Sydney Harbour; his house there was burnt down in a bush fire in November 1826 and the title deeds of his land at Castle Hill and Hunter's Hill were destroyed.

In the 1828 census he was recorded as a landholder, of Hunter's Hill, occupying 1600 acres, with 220 cattle; in his will, signed in July 1829, he listed 220 acres purchased at Castle Hill, 640 acres at Wallumbie (Wollombi), 50 acres granted by Governor Brisbane at North Shore, and 5 acres on Neutral Harbour (Bay). In 1823-24 Milson was employed as 'keeper' of Government House. In 1832 he built on the North Shore a reservoir for watering ships. In later years he acquired more land and was a keen yachtsman. He died in Sydney on 25 October 1872, survived by four sons and one of his two daughters.

His eldest son JAMES MILSON (1814-1903), was born on 25 November 1814 at the Field of Mars in Sydney and educated at Dr O'Halloran's [q.v.] school, which he left at 16 to serve his mercantile apprenticeship with the Sydney agency of the Liverpool firm of Aspinall, Brown & Co. On his majority, he became a partner in the firm of Robert Campbell junior [q.v.], his capital being provided by his father. Milson soon gained a wide knowledge of shipowning, importing and wool-buying, and won repute as one of Sydney's most progressive businessmen. The economic crisis in 1841-45 embarrassed the firm of Robert Campbell junior, its credit being over-extended and its bad debts numerous. It was wound up, and in 1846 Milson went into business on his own account. He built up a thriving mercantile concern in Sydney and in the 1850s embarked on pastoral ventures, especially in New England, where he bought Sugarloaf station in 1854. He began to interest himself in steam ferry services in Port Jackson and in September 1863 was one of the founders of the Milson's Point Ferry Co. which operated until March 1878, when it was sold and became the North Shore Ferry Co. In the 1860s Milson became a director of the Bank of New South Wales, the Colonial Sugar Refining Co., the Australian Gaslight Co., the Sydney Exchange and Assurance Co., and the Australian Steam Navigation Co. In 1868 he was deputy-mayor of East St Leonards and was the owner of Elamong and Cremorne estates. He acted as executor for his friend, W. C. Wentworth [q.v.], and was associated with several other conservative politicians. In the 1870s, with other members of the Milson family, he took up pastoral holdings in central Queensland in conjunction with Oscar de Satgé, as well as on the Diamantina and Gregory Rivers.

Keenly interested in charities of various kinds, Milson was a director of the Sydney Sailors' Home and of the Benevolent Asylum. In 1881 he founded the Oberlin Friendly Aid Society 'to give friendly aid to cultured persons now indigent'. Like his father he was an enthusiastic yachtsman from the 1830s onwards and in 1862 was first vice-commodore of the Royal Sydney Yacht Squadron and commodore in 1863. His 25-ton yacht Era was one of the best-known craft in Sydney in the 1860s. He was one of the first to see the possibilities of the Blue Mountains as a popular health resort. In his old age he opposed Federation.

Milson married twice: on 22 July 1852 to Marianne Grimes who died 5 November 1864, and on 24 November 1869 to Ann Stewart who died on 10 December 1888. He died on 13 January 1903, leaving three sons and three of his four daughters.

HRA (1), 16; R. H. Goddard, The life and times of James Milson (Melb, 1955); MS cat under J. Milson (ML).

DAVID S. MACMILLAN

MINCHIN, WILLIAM (1774?-1821), military officer and settler, was born in Ireland, probably in County Tipperary. Commissioned ensign and adjutant of the New South Wales Corps on 2 March 1797, he proceeded to take up his appointment in the female convict transport Lady Shore, in command of a detachment of troops which included French and Irish prisoners of war, deserters, and prisoners from the Savoy. The prisoners mutinied on 1 August 1797, and Minchin and his wife Ann, with twenty-seven others, were cast adrift on 15 August, making landfall at Port St Pedro (Rio Grande), Brazil, two days later. On his return to England he appears to have successfully answered charges concerning the mutiny, and in due course he sailed for New South Wales; on arriving there, he took up duty as adjutant from Neil MacKellar [q.v.] in November 1800. He was closely connected with the duel between Colonel Paterson and John Macarthur [qq.v.] in 1801. Next year he was a prime mover in the accusation that Nicholas Baudin [q.v.] was selling at great profit rum which he had bought as provisions for his voyage home. Arising from this episode, he and Surgeon John Harris [q.v.] were charged and acquitted of lying; however, one result was a loss of confidence in Minchin by some of his brother officers.

Because of Minchin's earlier artillery experience, Governor King appointed him engineer and artillery officer late in 1804, an appointment which involved training the Loyal Associations in the use of the 'great guns', and supervision of the construction of Fort Phillip. In March 1805 he was promoted lieutenant when MacKellar disappeared at sea.

Like his fellow officers Minchin was not enamoured of Governor Bligh. He was prominent in the rebellion in January 1808 and, while his part will never be fully clarified, at Colonel Johnston's [q.v.] court martial he was accused of removing the screws from the guns outside Government House and training those on the parade ground to fire in that direction. He accompanied Johnston from Annandale, was a member of the court which tried Macarthur both before and after the rebellion, procured spirits from the Jenny to celebrate the 'night of the illuminations', rescued Bligh from possible manhandling when he was arrested, and arrested Commissary George Palmer [q.v.], whose books and papers he seized, and Provost-Marshal Gore [q.v.].

Minchin carried Johnston's first despatches to the Colonial Office, arriving in England in September 1808. He returned to the colony next August and went again to England in 1810 by way of Cape Horn with the New South Wales Corps, now renumbered the 102nd Regiment, which thereby became the first regiment to circumnavigate the globe. An only daughter, Maria Matilda, was born during this voyage or soon afterwards. Minchin gave evidence at Johnston's court martial, applied for a captaincy in the Royal African Corps, which he did not receive because there was no vacancy, and then accompanied his regiment to Guernsey and to Bermuda, where it arrived in September 1811, two days after he had been promoted captain. He saw action in a few small skirmishes during the American war of 1812-14. In September 1813 the regiment moved to Halifax and in 1816 was stationed in New Brunswick where his brother George, later a member of its Legislative Council, was living.

In August 1817 Minchin retired and sold his commission; he returned to New South Wales with his wife and daughter in September 1818. In April 1820 Governor Macquarie appointed him principal superintendent of police, and treasurer of the Police Fund in the place of D'Arcy Wentworth [q.v.]. He became a director of the Bank of New South Wales, a member of the Bible Society, and was appointed a member of the Male Orphan, Female Orphan and Native Institutions. He died after a short illness on 26 March 1821. His widow was married to Eber Bunker [q.v.] in 1823, and his daughter to Henry Howey in 1826. Howey and his wife and family were lost in the Sarah in 1838.

Minchin did not trade in rum and his land holdings during his military service in the colony were small. During the interregnum Johnston made him a grant of 100 acres, and Paterson one of 200 acres to his wife; Macquarie cancelled both but in 1819 granted him 1000 acres which now forms part of the Minchinbury estate.

As a soldier Minchin was not outstanding. He apparently neither sought nor was he placed in a position to display any particular talent in his profession. His control of troops during the Lady Shore mutiny was weak and his judgment at fault, but it cannot be said that he was a traitor or that he lacked courage. He appears to have been reasonably conscientious as an adjutant, perhaps too much at times for his own good. While not without strength of character, he did not have the qualities necessary to influence markedly the course of events, but Macquarie thought him of superior intelligence and good moral conduct and considered his death a great public loss.

HRNSW, 3-7; HRA (1), 3-7, 10; J. Black, An authentic narrative of the mutiny on board the ship Lady Shore (Ipswich, 1798); J. G. Semple Lisle, The life of Major J. G. Semple Lisle (Lond, 1799); Proceedings of a general court-martial . . . for the trial of Lieut.-Col. Geo. Johnston (Lond, 1811); (L. Davoren), A new song made in New South Wales on the rebellion, ed G. Mackaness (Syd, 1951); Army letter-book 1816 (Legislative Lib, Fredericton, New Brunswick); WO 4/845, 17/2363; MS cat under W. Minchin (ML).

M. AUSTIN

MITCHEL, JOHN (1815-1875), Irish nationalist, was born on 3 November 1815 at Camnish, near Dungiven, County Derry, Ireland, the third son of Rev. John Mitchel, a Presbyterian minister, and his wife Mary, née Haslett. He was educated at Dr Henderson's school at Newry, where he began a lifelong friendship with John Martin, and at Trinity College, Dublin. He later described himself as a Unitarian Presbyterian. In 1837 he married Jane Verner of Newry, by whom he had three sons and two daughters. He was admitted a solicitor in 1840 and practised at Banbridge, near Newry, until the autumn of 1845 when, having been won for active support of the nationalist cause, he gave up his practice, moved to Dublin and became assistant editor of the Nation under Charles Gavan Duffy. Meanwhile he had joined the Repeal Association which, inspired by Daniel O'Connell, campaigned for the peaceable dissolution of the union with England; but he also became associated with the emerging Young Ireland movement, whose militancy and advocacy of physical force were leading to a collision between the older and younger leaders. The first open breach came in 1846 when Mitchel, W. S. O'Brien, T. F. Meagher [qq.v.] and others left the Repeal Association; but it was not complete until O'Connell's death a year later.

In December 1847 Mitchel broke with Duffy and the Nation and in February 1848 launched the United Irishman, a weekly newspaper that soon became the most influential of the organs propagating the militant views of the Young Ireland Movement. As conflict in Ireland sharpened, the authorities decided to take drastic action: habeas corpus was suspended and a new Treason Felony Act received the royal assent; under this new legislation Mitchel, having first been charged with sedition, was sentenced to fourteen years transportation for treason. Soon afterwards the other Young Ireland leaders, O'Brien, Meagher, Patrick O'Donohoe, John Martin, Terence McManus and Kevin O'Dogherty, were tried and sentenced for high treason at Clonmel and Dublin, and transported to Van Diemen's

Land. Mitchel was first committed to the hulks in Bermuda, and later sent to the Cape of Good Hope in the *Neptune*. The colonists refused to allow the ship to berth and, having lain at anchor for five months in Simon's Bay, she sailed to Van Diemen's Land and docked at Hobart Town in April 1850.

Mitchel, though the first to be sentenced, was thus the last of the Young Ireland leaders to reach Van Diemen's Land. He was granted a ticket-of-leave on parole and allowed to share a cottage near Bothwell with John Martin. He was also able to meet O'Dogherty and Meagher at Lake Sorell on the borders of their police districts. In May 1851 he went to meet his wife who was believed to be arriving at Launceston. For leaving the district without a pass he was arrested, but soon discharged. His wife Jane and children did not arrive in the brig *Union* until June, when they joined him at Bothwell. Two years later Mitchel successfully planned and carried through his escape from the island with the help of P. J. Smyth, who had come from New York as correspondent of the *New York Tribune* for the purpose. Having previously surrendered his parole and ticket-of-leave at Bothwell police station, he made his way to Hobart in June 1853, sailed for Sydney, and thence to Batavia, San Francisco and New York, where he received a hero's welcome in November.

In the United States Mitchel successively edited the *Citizen* and the *Southern Citizen*. His journalism won him many enemies: among Roman Catholics for his attacks on the temporal power of the Pope, and among abolitionists for his championship of the rights of Southern slave-owners. In 1860 he sailed to France, where he became the Paris correspondent of a number of American newspapers. Late in 1862 he returned to New York, made his way to Virginia and espoused the Southern cause in the civil war. Three of his sons fought on the Confederate side, two of them being killed in action. He quarrelled with Jefferson Davis, went to New York as the editor of the democratic *Daily News*, and spent five months in a fortress for criticizing the government. In 1868 he published *My Jail Journal, or Five Years in British Prisons*. In 1872 and 1874 he paid brief visits to Ireland, where he died on 20 March 1875, leaving a widow, a son and two daughters.

J. H. Cullen, *Young Ireland in exile* (Dublin, 1928); D. R. Gwynn, *Young Ireland and 1848* (Cork, 1949); T. J. Kiernan, *The Irish exiles in Australia* (Melb, 1954); Ac no 2/364 (TA).   G. RUDE

MITCHELL, JAMES (1792-1869), physician and industrialist, was born in Fife, Scotland, the fourth son of David Mitchell, farmer of Capledrae and Feuar in Aberdour, and his wife Margaret, née Low. Educated locally he joined the Army Medical Corps in 1810, and three years later qualified as a licentiate of the Royal College of Surgeons at Edinburgh. In the Napoleonic wars Mitchell saw active service in Spain, in America at the battle of New Orleans, and in the Netherlands. He was stationed at the British military hospital in Brussels during the battle of Waterloo. In June 1820 he was appointed assistant surgeon to the 48th Regiment then stationed in Sydney and arrived in November 1821 in the *John Barry*. He had made two earlier voyages to New South Wales, the first in 1817 as surgeon to the 48th Regiment which arrived in the transports *Matilda*, *Lloyds* and *Dick*, and again in 1820 as surgeon-superintendent in the *Neptune*.

In June 1823 he was transferred to the Colonial Medical Department as an assistant surgeon and posted to the Sydney Hospital. Mitchell later claimed that he was in charge of the hospital from 1825 until 1837, but he was not officially appointed surgeon until 1 January 1829. During the inquiry into the death of Joseph Sudds of the 57th Regiment Mitchell gave evidence that incurred the displeasure of Governor Darling. After being sentenced for petty theft and then heavily ironed by Darling's orders Sudds had died on 27 November 1826, according to Mitchell, as a result of 'inanition in conjunction with all the disturbing passions caused or connected with his unfortunate position'. However, a year later Darling recommended Mitchell's promotion to surgeon.

Mitchell continued to receive half-pay as a military officer until his resignation from the army in 1833. About that time he opened a private practice at Cumberland Place which he ran in conjunction with his duties at the hospital. He ran into trouble in April 1836 when on orders from London the Medical Department was placed under military regulations and reorganized by John Vaughan Thompson, deputy-inspector-general of hospitals. Thompson soon aroused the hostility of the colonial medical officers, especially Mitchell, by a series of petty and ill-timed orders and constant interference in established routines. In March 1837 Mitchell complained to the government, bitterly attacking Thompson's treatment of him, and his administration of the entire department. Thompson immediately brought counter-charges of disobedience against Mitchell;

this led to an official inquiry, after which Governor Bourke severely criticized Mitchell's actions and warned him against future disobedience. On 9 August Thompson issued an order making Mitchell directly responsible for medical duties at the convict barracks in Hyde Park. Implicit in the order was Mitchell's attendance at the barracks whenever corporal punishment was inflicted, a duty hitherto performed by his assistant. Mitchell's refusal to attend a flogging on 14 September led to his suspension. A court of inquiry found him guilty of disobedience and on 26 September his name was removed from the list of colonial surgeons. The next day a subscription was taken to present Mitchell with a service of plate in acknowledgment of his 'highly valuable professional services'. Almost immediately Mitchell prepared a fifty-two page defence which he entitled *Statement of the Case of Jas Mitchell, Esq. . . .* Thompson replied by a letter in the *Colonist* attacking Mitchell in harsh terms and leaving himself open to libel. Mitchell took action and won the case, being awarded £100 in damages and costs. For three years he pressed for a rehearing of his case, sending letters to men of influence in London and eventually a petition to the House of Commons, maintaining that his failure to attend the flogging was the result of a misapprehension. His cause was supported by some colonial newspapers and by friends such as Bishop Broughton and Judge Burton [qq.v.]. In October 1841, after a reinvestigation, Governor Gipps's recommendation that he be reinstated for one day and allowed to resign was approved by the Colonial Office.

Meanwhile Mitchell had continued his private practice which in 1841 Gipps described as 'extensive'. He had also developed an interest in agriculture. In 1822 he had been granted 2000 acres at Burragorang in the County of Camden, where he received much advice from the Macarthur family. In the next fifteen years he acquired many holdings in the Hunter district by grant and purchase, including the Burwood and Rothbury estates. Mitchell gained repute as an astute land dealer and was often asked to buy land for others. After his suspension he turned to the promotion of new industries, although he continued his private practice until the mid-1840s. His first industrial venture was a salt works at Stockton in 1838, but it soon failed. Between 1840 and 1843 he built a tweed factory at Stockton, equipping it with machinery from England. He leased it to Robert Fisher and Alexander Donaldson for a rent that was to be paid in tweed.

Among the workmen brought from Scotland for the factory were the miners, James and Alexander Brown, who later established the coal-mining firm of J. & A. Brown. Within seven years the tweed factory was producing seventy thousand yards of cloth a year and employing some three hundred men. It was destroyed by fire on 11 July 1851 and Mitchell lost more than £26,000.

Earlier he had suffered other loss through the failure of the Bank of Australia, of which he was a director and principal shareholder. The bank had been established in 1826 as an unlimited liability corporation, so the shareholders were liable for its debts. In the depression of the early 1840s the bank had lent large sums to settlers, taking mortgages on their properties as security. In 1843 it ceased operation, and two years later had liabilities in excess of £200,000, its assets consisting of unsaleable property. To enable the bank to dispose of these estates a lottery bill was passed by the Legislative Council in 1845, but it was refused royal assent, and in 1848 the shareholders were called upon to meet the bank's debts. Although Mitchell suffered from the bank's failure the extent of his losses is not known, and they may not have been as heavy as was generally assumed. In 1841 Gipps had reported that he was 'supposed to be in easy circumstances'. He had acquired a large fortune from his land and medical practice and held many shares in various companies. Throughout the 1840s he continued to invest money in such ventures as the Hunter River Steam Navigation Co. He donated a site at Stockton for St Andrew's Church and was apparently prepared to back the building of it; its foundation stone was laid in December 1845, but the building was never finished. Mitchell also continued to invest large sums in the development of local industries, thus indicating that his financial resources were far from depleted.

In 1846 he built a smelting works on his Burwood estate, importing copper ore for processing from South Australia and New Zealand. This venture was prompted by the discovery of rich coal resources on the estate by tenants. In the early 1840s he had leased portions of the estate and despite the monopoly of coal rights enjoyed by the Australian Agricultural Co. several of his lessees, including James and Alexander Brown and William Donaldson, were operating small coal-mines. In 1847 Mitchell gave evidence before the select committee inquiring into the Australian Agricultural Co.'s monopoly, and claimed that it hindered the progress of his smelting works by preventing the use of coal mined from his land. He also claimed that the monopoly inflated the price of coal and obstructed the development of Newcastle. Before the report was tabled the company surrendered its coal rights, and Mitchell was able to make full use of his coal in the smelting works.

To improve methods of shipping his coal he obtained permission from the government in May 1849 to erect a wharf and coal shoots on crown land by the Newcastle waterfront. In 1851 the Legislative Council passed a special Tram Road Act to enable him to build a railway from the estate to the wharf through the Australian Agricultural Co.'s land. In spite of the company's protests the Act was allowed to stand because Mitchell's works were thought to benefit the whole colony. In 1853 he established the Newcastle Coal and Copper Co., leasing to it the coal-mining and smelting works at Burwood. The company continued into the 1860s when labour disputes and financial crises led to its dissolution and Mitchell's re-acquisition of the land and works.

In 1865 Mitchell fell under the influence of a confidence man named William Ernest Wolfskehl, who represented himself as a member of a well-to-do banking family from Darmstadt. The two men became business partners, and their first venture, a glass and porcelain factory, proved a disaster, but they soon established the Burwood and Newcastle Smelting Co., bringing ore from the Currawang mine near Goulburn, Mitchell becoming Wolfskehl's guarantor for £15,000. When ore supplies became exhausted the company failed and Mitchell had to pay Wolfskehl's share. In November 1868 Mitchell tried to reopen the works with ore from South Australia, but through his ill health the project did not succeed.

Mitchell died at his home, Cumberland Place, on 1 February 1869. By a will made just before his death, Wolfskehl was named as his sole executor of an estate valued at more than £100,000. His family contested the will on the grounds of undue influence exerted by Wolfskehl, and pressed for an earlier will made in 1841 to be upheld. Though probate was delayed the family won the case in the Supreme Court. Mitchell's death terminated 'a long and useful career' in many spheres of colonial life. As a physician at the Sydney Hospital and in private practice he enjoyed much success and high public esteem. He was elected to the Medical Board in 1845 and became its president in 1852. In his long association with the board he did much to strengthen the medical profession and to

influence methods of treatment. Although many of his industrial ventures were costly failures, his continued faith in the Newcastle region greatly influenced its future development and the establishment of private industrial enterprises elsewhere. His interest in colonial industries also prompted him to assume an active role in a number of schemes for bringing skilled workers to New South Wales. In the 1840s he served as treasurer of the Australian Immigration Association. As well as being a director of the Bank of Australia Mitchell took a prominent part in many other commercial enterprises. He was a foundation member of the Sydney Banking Co. and served in the 1840s as a director of the Hunter River Steam Navigation Co., deputy-chairman of the Sydney Ferry Co., and a director and later chairman of the Australian Gaslight Co. He helped to establish the Mutual Provident Society and was a director in 1852-59 and chairman in 1860-65. He was an original proprietor of the Hunter River Railway Co. formed in the early 1850s to build a line between Newcastle and Maitland; it was taken over by the government in 1855.

In politics Mitchell actively opposed dismemberment of the colony in 1841 and in 1856-69 he was a member of the Legislative Council. However, he remained aloof from most of the political entanglements of his time and did not attach himself to any party.

Mitchell showed his interest in educational and cultural projects by acting as a trustee of the Australian Museum in 1853-69, a shareholder in the Newcastle Mechanics' Institute, and a generous benefactor to St Paul's College, to which he was elected a senior fellow in 1857. He was associated with the Australian Subscription Library, now the Public Library of New South Wales, as a committeeman from 1832 to 1853 and vice-president and president 1856 to 1869, and it was to this institution that his son, David Scott Mitchell, bequeathed his priceless collection of Australiana and an endowment to maintain it.

On 22 August 1833 at St James's Church, Sydney, Mitchell married Augusta Maria Frederick, only daughter of Dr Helenus Scott [q.v.] and his wife Augusta Maria. Of their three children, the eldest daughter, Augusta Maria, married Edward Christopher Merewether, later superintendent of the Australian Agricultural Co. in April 1860. Mitchell's high esteem and affection for the Scott family became evident in October when he assumed the surname Scott-Mitchell although he rarely used it, and was granted by the Lord Lyon in

Scotland a licence to bear and use the Scott family arms.

In 1827 Mitchell made barometrical observations for Allan Cunningham [q.v.] who was away from Sydney on an exploring party, and in gratitude the explorer named what is now known as the Namoi River after him.

HRA (1), 10, 11, 14, 19-21, 24; F. M. Bladen, *Public Library of New South Wales historical notes*, 2nd ed (Syd, 1911); W. J. Goold, 'Dr. Mitchell', Newcastle and Hunter District Hist Soc, *Procs*, 4 (1950); W. J. Goold, 'Stockton', Newcastle and Hunter District Hist Soc, *Procs*, 7 (1953); *Sydney Gazette*, 12 June 1823; *SMH*, 21 June 1844, 3, 4 Feb 1869; *Newcastle Chronicle*, 25 May 1869; *Newcastle Sun*, 20 Mar 1958, 31 Aug 1961; Sel cttee on coal, *Report*, V & P (LC, NSW), 1847; Merewether estate archives (Newcastle Public Lib); MS cat under James and David Scott Mitchell (ML); Information from C. E. Smith (Newcastle Public Lib).

ELIZABETH GUILFORD

MITCHELL, SIR THOMAS LIVINGSTONE (1792-1855), surveyor-general, was born on 15 June 1792 at Craigend, Scotland, the son of John Mitchell and his wife Janet, née Wilson. Though poor he was sufficiently educated to read widely in several languages and be proficient in several sciences. In 1811 he was gazetted a second lieutenant in the 95th Regiment and in the Peninsular war served at the battles of Ciudad Rodrigo, Badajoz and Salamanca. However, he was chiefly engaged with the staff obtaining topographical intelligence and came under the notice of Sir George Murray, the quartermaster-general, who selected him in 1814 to produce plans of the major Peninsular battlefields, a task which continued after the war. Mitchell obtained his majority in 1826 but was placed on half-pay. In June 1818 he had married Mary, the daughter of General Richard Blunt, and being incapable of inactivity, Mitchell in 1827 with Murray's support became assistant surveyor-general of New South Wales with the right to succeed Oxley [q.v.].

In 1827, when Mitchell and his family arrived in Sydney, the Survey Department was in an unsatisfactory condition. Surveying instruments were scarce and some surveyors were incompetent; their technical problems were rarely appreciated by the public or the government; moreover successive surveys of small areas were made without attempt to relate them to a general survey, so small errors accumulated till they became serious. Thus title deeds and the collection of quitrents were delayed and doubts and disputes arose about boundaries. Mitchell in 1828 started on the necessary but seemingly impossible task of making a general survey. Tent poles were used to measure a base line, and hill-tops, denuded of all trees save one, as trigonometrical points.

In 1828, on Oxley's death, Mitchell became surveyor-general, and in 1829 became responsible for the survey of roads and bridges. In 1830 he assumed sole responsibility for the Survey Department when the commissioners of survey were abolished in accordance with his wishes as expressed in a private letter to R. W. Hay at the Colonial Office. Mitchell frequently used such private communications direct to the source of power, a fact of great importance, especially in 1828-30 when his old patron, Sir George Murray, was the secretary of state for the colonies. By the end of 1830 Mitchell had made considerable changes in the roads from Sydney to Parramatta and to Liverpool; he had plotted a new road southwards through Berrima as far as Goulburn and had discovered and constructed a new western descent from the Blue Mountains towards Bathurst. These roads were substantially the same as those used today.

This successful road building led to a serious conflict with Governor Darling who feared that Mitchell's improvements might in time have to be superseded. Mitchell resented this implied criticism of his technical competence, and rightly confident that no better route existed, persisted against the governor's orders in building a new road down Mount Victoria. Darling retaliated by attempting to remove the Department of Roads and Bridges from Mitchell's authority. Mitchell officially, and unofficially through Hay, claimed authority, independent of the governor, directly from the Crown. In a dispatch of 28 March 1831 Darling stated bluntly that Mitchell should not be continued in the office of surveyor-general. His fear was that unless Mitchell were punished there would be 'an immediate end to all subordination and to the Government itself'. Meanwhile Murray had retired from the Colonial Office and his successor had determined on Darling's recall, so Mitchell, if not triumphant, at least survived. When Darling left the colony Mitchell at once persuaded the acting governor to send him exploring between the Castlereagh and Gwydir Rivers to test reports of the existence of a large river flowing to the northwest.

The expedition started in November 1831 northwards to Tamworth through known country. From Tamworth Mitchell explored to the Namoi and followed it down as far as Narrabri. He then cut across the plains to the Gwydir near Moree. Several weeks were spent charting the tributaries between the Gwydir and the Barwon without, of course, discovering the large river flowing to the north-west. In February 1832 after Aboriginals had killed two of his party and plundered the stores Mitchell returned to Sydney, not having disproved the existence of the mythical river, but rendering it, despite his hopes, much less likely.

During the 1830s the spread of squatting and the large number of free immigrants needing land greatly accentuated the problems of the Survey Department. On 15 June 1833, alarmed by the backwardness of the survey, Stanley wrote to Governor Bourke demanding that Mitchell provide an explanation. None was forthcoming till 5 May 1834 when Bourke transmitted from Mitchell a map of the colony divided into nineteen counties with a description of their boundaries, together with a memorandum emphasizing the necessity of a general survey before local surveys could effectively be made. On 10 October 1834 Bourke sent another more elaborate and very intemperate defence by Mitchell which was accepted by Stanley's successor, Glenelg, as satisfactory but with the pious hope that Mitchell would show no more insubordination.

In March 1835, excited as usual by prospects of glory, Mitchell began his second exploring journey. Its purpose was to trace the River Darling from the point where Sturt [q.v.] had left it in 1828, down to its junction with the Murray. It was assumed, but not certain, that these points were on the same river. The party went by easy stages to Boree station, just west of Orange, which was also the starting place for Mitchell's later expeditions. The route lay north-west to the Bogan which was reached in April. There the botanist Richard Cunningham [q.v.] wandered from the main party and despite a prolonged search was lost. It was later discovered that he had been killed by Aboriginals. Mitchell travelled down the Bogan to its junction with the Darling and then down the Darling till the vicinity of Menindee was reached on 9 July. The Darling Aboriginals had been 'implacably hostile and shamelessly dishonest' and, after an affray in which shots were fired and several Aboriginals killed and wounded, Mitchell decided to return home by the way he had come. The results of this expedition were slight. The course and terrain of a section of the Bogan and about

300 miles of the Darling had been charted. Mitchell had little doubt that this river was the same as that which entered the Murray but he had not followed it to this junction.

Mitchell's third expedition was intended to fill this gap. He was instructed to travel to Menindee, then down the Darling to the sea, if it flowed there; or, if it flowed into the Murray to go up the Murray to the inhabited parts of the colony. He was also empowered to follow the most promising stream flowing into the Murray. He set out in March 1836 vividly remembering a day exactly twenty-four years earlier outside the beleaguered towers of Badajoz. From Boree he went west to the Lachlan and followed that river until he reached the vicinity of Hillston on 20 April. Menindee was now about 200 miles almost due west. Lack of water in that direction persuaded Mitchell to follow the Lachlan to the south-west as the only practicable route. He reached the Murrumbidgee on 12 May and followed it to the Murray. While travelling along the Murray to its junction with the Darling, Mitchell's party on 24 May encountered a large body of Aboriginals who were at once recognized, according to Mitchell, as their old enemies from the Darling. Three days later near Mount Dispersion, fearing that his party might be subject to continual attacks and destroyed in detail, Mitchell set an ambush which was at once discovered. Firing broke out and, according to an Aboriginal with Mitchell's party, seven natives were killed; the remainder fled. At the end of May Mitchell reached the Darling and turned north upstream. He soon decided, while still about 130 miles in a direct line from Menindee, to abandon the survey of the deserts around the Darling and to use his resources to explore the more promising country along the Murray. For the second time he failed to complete the full exploration of the Darling.

Retracing his steps Mitchell went up the Murray till 20 June when he reached the junction of the Loddon where the country seemed so promising that he turned south-west into what is now Victoria and was so enchanted by the area he called it Australia Felix. Travelling chiefly west and south he reached the mouth of the Glenelg on 20 August and some days later, to their mutual surprise, he found the Henty brothers [q.v.] already established at Portland. He turned north-east, reached the Murray on 17 October and on 3 November arrived back in Sydney ahead of the main party. The rapid occupation of Australia Felix followed. Already settlers from Van

Diemen's Land were crossing Bass Strait and soon others were driving their flocks south-west along the tracks which Mitchell's heavy wagons had cut into the earth on their return to Sydney.

As on all his expeditions, Mitchell systematically surveyed as he travelled. After seven months his error, so he claimed, was only a mile and three-quarters. As a controversialist and thirster after glory, Mitchell was sometimes strangely blind to the truth; but he was a painstaking and competent surveyor, and his claim may be believed. In December 1836 the Executive Council conducted an inquiry into the killing of Aboriginals near Mount Dispersion. It regretted that Mitchell had not made sufficient efforts to conciliate the natives, but in view of their numbers and threatening aspect the council could not severely blame 'a want of coolness and presence of mind which it is the lot of few men to possess'.

On 19 May 1837 Mitchell left Sydney on eighteen months leave. He secured permission to publish an account of his explorations which appeared in 1838 entitled *Three Expeditions into the interior of Eastern Australia* . . . and he began a long correspondence with the Colonial Office to obtain a knighthood. Lingering doubts about Mitchell's behaviour near Mount Dispersion delayed this honour till 1839 when he was also distinguished by Oxford University's award of an honorary doctorate of civil law. In July 1838 Mitchell obtained a further twelve months leave for he was still working on the plans of the Peninsular battles. These were finished at the end of 1840 and, as published by James Wyld, are beautiful examples of Mitchell's skill as a draftsman. In March 1840 Mitchell requested a further six months leave, was granted three and ordered to leave England by 18 June. He nevertheless was arrested, narrowly missed being imprisoned for debt in London on 8 August and did not reach Australia till 1841.

The depression of the early 1840s had disastrous effects on the Survey Department. Its budget in 1842 was £26,000, but in 1844 only £12,000. Some of its members were at once transferred elsewhere. Others became licensed surveyors who received a third of their previous salary, but also the right to private practice; they were to be paid extra, according to a rather low scale of fees, for any government surveying they performed. This reduction in the department left it quite inadequate to undertake the survey of leases under the 1847 Order-in-Council and to meet the demand for land in the 1850s after the discovery of gold. There were too few surveyors and the licensed surveyors, in particular, were difficult to discipline and naturally preferred the higher emoluments obtainable from private practice.

In April 1844 Mitchell was elected to the Legislative Council at a by-election in Port Phillip. He had promised to support the separation of that district from New South Wales. Governor Gipps keenly felt the anomaly of a government officer sitting in the legislature and being free, and in Mitchell's case likely, to vote against government measures. Gipps ruled that 'the member for Port Phillip may act as he pleases, but the Surveyor General of New South Wales must obey and support the Government'. Mitchell had difficulty in separating his two roles and in August prudently resigned his seat.

In December 1845 Mitchell began his fourth expedition north-west from Boree in search of an overland route to Port Essington. By June 1846 he had established a depot on the Maranoa and for nearly four months explored around the headwaters of the Maranoa, Warrego and Belyando Rivers, still hopeful of finding a great river flowing north-west. On 25 September, near Isisford on the Barcoo, which he called the Victoria, when short of supplies and threatened by Aboriginals, he turned back, but only after his observations and his hopes had deluded him that he had at last found his great river to the northward. He reached Sydney ahead of his party on 29 December. On this tremendous journey he had not found a practicable route to Port Essington. Nor had he found his large northerly flowing river, although his quickly published account of the journey naturally suggested that he had. But he had charted an extensive area of unknown country in a major expedition lasting over twelve months without losing a man or suffering serious incident.

On 27 March 1847 Mitchell left Sydney on another twelve months leave, and early in 1848 made the usual attempts to obtain more, but secured only another month. He nevertheless took more and arrived back in Sydney about July 1848. He had had time to prepare his *Journal of an Expedition into the interior of Tropical Australia* . . . (London, 1848). In 1850 Mitchell published *The Australian Geography*, designed for the use of schools in New South Wales; a second edition appeared in 1851. This work must have been one of the first to place Australia at the centre of the world, but its pedagogic technique now seems greatly antiquated.

From 1848 to 1852 there was much correspondence between Mitchell, the governor and the colonial secretary in which Mitchell attempted to assert his independence of the local administration while Governor FitzRoy sought to ensure his subordination. Mitchell no longer enjoyed such powerful friends in high places. In 1851 FitzRoy recommended Mitchell's dismissal, but Grey ruled in 1852 that Mitchell would be dismissed only if guilty of further insubordination. Following an inaccurate public statement by Stuart Donaldson, Mitchell on 27 September 1851 fought a duel with him, one of the last in Australia. Each fired three shots; it was reported that one went through Donaldson's hat and another within an inch of Mitchell's throat.

In 1850 Mitchell read a paper to the Philosophical Society of New South Wales on the application of the principle of the boomerang to ships' propellers. In 1852 a successful trial of the new propeller on Sydney Harbour enabled Mitchell to obtain another twelve months leave. During the voyage he worked on a verse translation of The Lusiad of Luis de Camoens . . . (London, 1854). Mitchell requested official support for the development of his boomerang propeller. The Admiralty remained unimpressed, but trials of the invention seemed to vindicate it and Mitchell later declared that marine engineers were quietly adopting his proposals while denying him the credit. Mitchell was again reluctant to leave England and a threat of dismissal was necessary before he sailed in January 1854, five months after the expiration of his original leave.

In January 1855 an anonymous pamphlet was published in Sydney entitled To Bourke's Statue this Appropriate Effusion of Unprofitable Brass is Unceremoniously Dedicated, by Ichneumon, anxious to Instruct his Grandmothers in the Inductive Science of Sucking Eggs. There followed about thirty pages of satirical, scandalous and at times very witty doggerel attacking several prominent citizens. Mitchell was widely suspected of being the author and was urged by Sir Charles Nicholson [q.v.] and others to make a formal denial. He did so and may be believed, for he was one of those attacked and never otherwise displayed such a capacity for devastating self-criticism. There is a plausible family tradition that his eldest son, Livingstone, was responsible.

On becoming governor, Denison began an inquiry into Mitchell's work. Aware of his past record of determined insubordination he probably decided to be rid of him. On 4 July 1855 a Royal Commission, which included the Victorian surveyor-general and the professor of mathematics at Sydney University, was appointed to inquire into the Survey Department. Not only Mitchell believed that its real purpose was to secure his dismissal. Before its report was published Mitchell contracted a chill while surveying the line of road in the difficult country between Nelligen and Braidwood. He developed pneumonia and died at his home in Sydney on 5 October 1855. He was survived by his widow, but of his twelve children at least five predeceased him, two of them while employed in his own department.

The report of the Royal Commission severely condemned the methods and results of Mitchell's surveying and the administration of his department but is not a fair summary of his life's work. The criticism of his surveying technique is largely a priori and neglects both the substantial accuracy achieved, the inadequate and often primitive means at his disposal and the magnitude of the tasks he was required to perform. Mitchell was, however, a poor administrator. He had too many other interests and ambitions and was too often and too long away from his department either in England or exploring the interior. He had also a fatal inability to delegate responsibility to his subordinates with whom his relations were often very bad, and thus, despite enormous labours, he never got ahead of accumulating business. There was also insufficient supervision of surveyors in the field and consequently opportunities for the lazy and dishonest. But Mitchell was not responsible for the shortage of surveyors, the unrealistically large amount of work expected of them and, in particular, the division of the department into salaried and licensed surveyors which itself was a guarantee of inefficiency.

By 1855 the condition of the Survey Department was becoming a public scandal as its delays were preventing an increasing number of people from purchasing the land they wanted. Mitchell himself, however, was rarely blamed, and to the end retained great popularity. This was no doubt due in part to his well-known and repeated conflicts with governors; in part to his appreciation and fostering of those things peculiarly Australian, from an enlightened preference for convicts in his exploring parties to the retention of Aboriginal place names. Probably more important was his well-known belief, from as early as 1833 when he vainly resisted the acquisitions of the Australian Agricultural Co., that land should be readily available to small settlers and not monopolized by large landowners or squatters. Mitchell so pressed his views that after 1847 some squatters were hesitant to exercise their pre-emptive rights lest the land they selected immediately be declared government reserves. So the Tory surveyor-general (he had preferred to be fined rather than serve with emancipist jurors) who perhaps more than any other individual was responsible for delaying closer settlement, was distrusted by conservative squatters and admired by frustrated and radical settlers.

HRA (1), 13-26; G. E. T. Audley, *The public surveys of New South Wales* (Syd, 1866); J. H. L. Cumpston, *Thomas Mitchell* (Melb, 1954); V & P (LC NSW), 1854, 2, p 1137, 1858-59, 2, p 41; B. V. Couch, The administration of Thomas Mitchell 1826-37. A study of the man and his contemporaries (M.A. thesis, Univ Syd, 1963).

D. W. A. BAKER

MOFFITT, WILLIAM (1802-1874), stationer, bookseller and engraver, was born at Liverpool, England, where he served his apprenticeship as a bookbinder. Sentenced to seven years transportation in 1823 for stealing tea, he arrived at Sydney in the *Guildford* on 25 July 1827 and was assigned to the Engineer's Department. On 24 December 1829 he married Mary Anne Galliott, a free immigrant aged 16. Of their six children, three daughters married: Elizabeth Preston (b. 1834) to John Marks of Jamberoo; Mary Anne (b. 1836) to Robert Thorne of Sydney; and Sarah Jane (b. 1842) to James Marks of Jamberoo. Henry, aged 10, and Sophia Jane, 16 months, died of scarlatina in 1841, and another son died in infancy in 1832.

When his sentence expired Moffitt set up in business as a bookbinder, stationer, engraver and copperplate printer at 8 King Street, and in August 1833 moved to 23 Pitt Street. In 1831 he had two assigned servants, and five in 1832. The business prospered, and in March 1842 he made a trip to England with his wife and two daughters after selling thirty-two acres of 'rich forest land', with two cottages and an orchard, six miles from Sydney. On his departure he was presented with a silver snuff box of colonial workmanship by the Australian Lodge of the Independent Order of Oddfellows, which he and two others had founded in 1836. He was later for a time a director of the Australian Joint Stock Bank, and as early as 1846 supported a movement for the early closing of shops. In 1844 he stood unsuccessfully for the City Council but in general he avoided

public life, devoting himself to his business and to unobtrusive acts of private benevolence.

Moffitt published an *Australian Sheet Almanack* in 1834, 1835 and 1838, an *Australian Diary and Almanack* from 1837 to 1846, and the *New South Wales Calendar and General Post Office Directory* (previously published by Stephens & Stokes in 1832, 1833 and 1835 and by Anne Howe in 1836), for 1837, 1839, 1842 and 1846. Other publications included Lhotsky's [q.v.] *Illustrations of the Present State and Future Prospects of New South Wales* (1835-6) and William Burton's [q.v.]. *The Insolvent Law of New South Wales* (1842), though in these cases he may have acted merely as distributor, as he did for the engravings of the Society for the Promotion of the Fine Arts in Scotland. He was active as a bookseller, especially in the supply of school books but also regularly importing general literature such as the *Pickwick Papers* on its first publication, and at least twice advertising stocks of French and Italian books. His main business was, however, as a wholesale and retail stationer, and he was responsible for hundreds of engraved letter-heads and trade cards which found a market as far afield as Van Diemen's Land and the Bay of Islands, New Zealand, the decorative engravings on which, some from his own hand but many by other craftsmen such as W. Wilson and John Carmichael, comprise a unique record of the business life of the time. In the 1840s Moffitt also 'neatly executed' the first bank-notes for the New Zealand Bank.

Moffitt was very much the city tradesman. Unlike so many of his contemporaries he never felt the lure of squatting or broad country acres, but was content to invest shrewdly in city property. In 1845 his shop was said to be the handsomest in Sydney, and three years later Joseph Fowles [q.v.] noted the 'elegant design' of his row of four houses in Pitt Street. There he lived, near his shop, until his death, and there he could be seen on fine evenings sitting outside his front door chatting with the neighbours. In 1874 he handed over his business to T. R. Yeo, from whom it was purchased in 1886 by W. C. Penfold & Co. He died on 31 July 1874, survived by his three married daughters. He left an estate consisting of city freeholds, bank shares, mortgages and debentures valued at £230,000.

W. C. Penfold & Co. Ltd, A *century of progress in printing* (Syd, 1930); J. M. Forde ('Old Chum'), 'An old-time bookseller', *Truth* (Syd), 3 Jan 1926; MS cat under W.

Moffitt (ML); Newspaper indexes under W. Moffitt (ML).

L. F. Fitzhardinge

MOLLE, GEORGE JAMES (1773-1823), soldier and lieut-governor, was baptized on 6 March 1773, the youngest child of John Mow, of Mains in the parish of Chirnside, Berwickshire, a member of an old Scottish landed family. His mother Margaret, née Crow, died when he was young, his father in 1795. His brother William, a writer to the signet, adopted the name Molle in 1789. George joined the Scots Brigade (later 94th Regiment) in June 1793 as an ensign. He served in Gibraltar, the Cape of Good Hope, India, Egypt and Spain, and was regularly promoted until he attained the rank of lieut-colonel in September 1808. After a spell of garrison duty at Gibraltar he transferred to the 46th Regiment; when it was ordered to New South Wales in 1813, as its commanding officer he was appointed lieut-governor of the colony, where he arrived in February 1814. He was gazetted brevet colonel in June 1814. He and his wife played an active part in the colony's public and social life, for nearly two years being patrons of the Female Orphan School and members of the committee of the Institution for the Civilisation, Care and Education of Aborigines. He was an active Mason and took part in the first public Masonic ceremony in Australia, at the laying of the foundation stone of Captain Piper's [q.v.] new house on what is now Point Piper.

While in India Molle had met and become friendly with Governor Macquarie, who gave a dinner in his honour the month after he arrived; but the governor did not allow Molle the authority he considered was his due, and in his public activities he became an opponent of Macquarie.

Soon after their arrival Molle and his officers complained of high prices and asked for higher pay. They disliked the favour shown by Macquarie to the emancipists, whom they excluded from the regimental mess, even in cases when the governor looked on them with favour. In 1816 William C. Wentworth [q.v.] grossly insulted Molle in a 'pipe' or lampoon. Next year, during the investigation of its authorship, some of the officers of the regiment insulted Macquarie in his turn, and he felt that his 'old and Much liked Acquaintance' Molle, on whose 'Friendship and Candour' he had relied, had not seriously tried to check the opposition of his juniors to the governor. Molle insisted that D'Arcy Wentworth [q.v.], William's father, was responsible for his son's libels, and demanded that he be court-martialled. To end all this bickering, Macquarie asked that the regiment be removed. Fortunately in August 1817 the 48th arrived to relieve it, and Molle departed next month for Madras. In due course Judge-Advocate Wylde [q.v.] decided that D'Arcy Wentworth was not liable for trial by court martial for the offence Molle alleged he had committed.

Molle died at Belgaum, India, on 9 September 1823. His eldest son, William Macquarie, who was born on the voyage to Sydney in 1813, became the owner of the 'Molle's Maines' estate in New South Wales. The Molle Islands in Whitsunday passage are named after the lieut-governor.

HRA (1), 8, 9; MS cat under G. Molle (ML); J. Arnold, Journal, Aug 1810-Dec 1815 (ML).

David S. Macmillan

MOLLISON, ALEXANDER FULLERTON (1805-1885) and WILLIAM THOMAS (1816-1886), overlanders, pastoralists and members of parliament, were the sons of Crawford Mollison and his wife Elizabeth, née Fullerton. Alexander was born on 17 April 1805 in London. After some years in Jamaica and New York he arrived in New South Wales in May 1834. Two years later he visited Port Phillip, returned to Sydney and bought the rights of a pastoral run at Uriara on the Murrumbidgee River. In April 1837, attracted by Major Mitchell's [q.v.] account of Australia Felix, he set off in search of a run, taking with him two overseers, 49 servants, 5000 sheep, 634 cattle, 28 bullocks and 22 horses. After travelling some 400 miles he finally decided to settle on Tarringower on the Coliban, between Mount Macedon and Mount Alexander.

In 1838 Alexander was joined by his brother William, who was born in Sussex. Tarringower was subdivided and extended to Pyalong, which was occupied as a cattle station by the younger brother. An active worker for separation, Alexander had started by 1844 to take a keen interest in public affairs. In reply to a circular asking for suggestions sent out by the chairman of the Legislative Council committee on education, Sydney, he recommended a general school system for all classes and sects. He opposed compulsory attendance and considered that free education tended to demoralize and to be of less value than that which was paid for. In 1850 he organized the Merino Import Co. to import rams from Europe, hoping they would have 'a sensible effect on the whole flocks of

Port Phillip'. In 1851 he was an energetic member of the Committee of the Australian Colonists, who represented squatters of various colonies and worked to increase emigration from Britain to Australia. In that year he went to England where with fellow squatters in 1853 he presented to the duke of Newcastle their need for the pre-emptive rights provided by the 1847 Order in Council to be extended to the Port Phillip District. Except for a short visit to Victoria in 1859 Alexander remained in England until 1873, when he returned to live in Victoria.

William made his first appearance in public affairs when he was elected to the Legislative Council in 1853, after telling his constituents at Kyneton that he favoured liberal government, a National system of education for the country and a denominational one for the towns, and unlocking of the land with moderate compensation for squatters. In the Legislative Council he moved for an inquiry into the administration of justice upon the goldfields, probably being influenced by another brother, Crawford, sometime gold commissioner at Sandhurst. In 1856 William was elected to the Legislative Assembly, and in 1860 voted with William Nicholson's ministry on its land bill. He introduced the Oyster Fisheries Act, the Pleuro-Pneumonia Act, and the 1862 Scab Act. He retired from parliament in 1864, having been described by a contemporary as 'more than any other member, the exponent of the opinions entertained by the educated classes'. He gave £5000 for scholarships in modern languages at the University of Melbourne in 1884. He died in England on 9 November 1886.

'An honourable Christian gentleman' and 'a staunch supporter of diocesan institutions', Alexander died, after patiently suffering some years of ill health, at his home in Kew on 10 April 1885. His diary of the overland trips from Uriara to Port Phillip shows him to have been resourceful, of sound judgment, fair and just in his dealings and tolerant of others. The hopeful view he took of the future of the Aboriginal race was surprisingly modern.

T. F. Bride (ed), *Letters from Victorian pioneers* (Melb, 1898); *Argus*, 15 July 1850, 7, 21 June 1853, 11 Apr 1885; *Illustrated Melb Post*, 21 Mar 1863; C. Daley, 'Early squatting days', *VHM*, 9 (1922-23), no 1; A. F. Mollison, Diary of a journey made between 11 April and 6 December 1837, from Uriara on the Murrumbidgee to Port Phillip (La Trobe Lib, Melb).

GAEL THOMSEN

MOLLOY, GEORGIANA (1805-1843), amateur botanist, was born on 23 May 1805 near Carlisle, Cumberland, England, one of the five children of David and Mary Kennedy of Crosby Lodge. Both parents came of old Border families. In August 1829 she was married to Captain John Molloy [q.v.] and in October they sailed with their household possessions and eight servants to the new colony in Western Australia. After six weeks at Swan River they decided to settle some 200 miles farther south at Augusta at the opening of the Blackwood River on Flinders Bay, where her husband was appointed resident magistrate. Two other families with their servants accompanied them. Augusta lay in heavily timbered country and the settlement's early pioneering was lonely and hard. Three daughters and a son were born to Mrs Molloy, but the eldest daughter died at birth and the son at nineteen months, in tragic circumstances. In 1836 most of the settlers began to leave Augusta to look for land easier to develop. The Molloys themselves left in 1839 and moved to the Vasse River, sixty miles northward, where a homestead, Fair Lawn, was built, and two more daughters were born.

For relief from her arduous life of pioneering Georgiana Molloy turned to botanizing. She was a keen gardener but soon found greater enjoyment in observing the indigenous flowers which bloomed profusely in spring. At first she gathered, pressed and mounted them in a *hortus siccus*, but in 1836 Lady Stirling's cousin, Captain James Mangles, R.N., hitherto unknown to Mrs Molloy, wrote from England inviting her to collect and send him seeds of the native plants of the region. This she proceeded to do, accompanying them with written descriptions and with the albums of pressed flowers she had prepared. Most of their correspondence over five years has been preserved. The seeds she sent to Mangles were given by him to various botanical gardens in England, to such well-known private gardeners as Joseph Paxton, and to Dr Lindley, secretary of the Horticultural Society. Plants previously unknown were propagated and developed from them and were scientifically classified. Too often seeds and plants were poorly consigned from the antipodes and did not survive the shipping hazards; but Mrs Molloy's seeds from Western Australia became noted among English enthusiasts for their freshness and careful packing. Each *hortus siccus* she sent was remarkable for the precision both of mounting and description. Some of them are retained at Kew Herbarium. She won mention in

George Bentham's *Flora Australiensis* . . . (London, 1863-78) and in Britten and Boulger's *A Biographical Index of Deceased British and Irish Botanists*, 2nd ed (London, 1931). Had she lived longer she might have added to her botanical fame but soon after the birth of her sixth daughter she died at Fair Lawn, Busselton, on 8 April 1843. Her correspondence with friends, as well as with Captain Mangles, shows her to have had a most sensitive and interesting personality.

A. Hasluck, *Portrait with background: a life of Georgiana Molloy* (Melb, 1955); W. G. Pickering, 'The letters of Georgina Molloy', *JRWAHS*, 1 (1929); J. Mangles, Letter-books (Battye Lib, Perth); Molloy letters (WAA).

ALEXANDRA HASLUCK

MOLLOY, JOHN (1780-1867), pioneer and resident magistrate, was born on 5 September 1780 in London. His parentage is unknown, a tradition of the early days of the colony ascribing royal descent to him. As asserted by an early colonist, the Molloy from whom he took his name and his upbringing was Captain A. J. P. Molloy, R.N., a tyrannical captain dismissed from his ship for cowardice in 1795. Some colour of truth is lent to the first statement by Molloy's appearance and by the fact that he named his surroundings at Augusta by the various names and titles of Frederick, duke of York, second son of George III. He appears to have been educated at Harrow and Oxford, where his pocket money each year was £200, and on his majority was handed a cheque for £20,000 by a firm of London solicitors, who also purchased for him a commission in the navy. However, he transferred to the army in 1807, joining the 95th Regiment as a second lieutenant. In June 1809 as a lieutenant, he left with his battalion for the Peninsular war, fighting in all the major battles, and receiving the General Service Medal with eight bars. He later fought and was seriously wounded at Waterloo. Famous diaries of the time record that he was brave and well liked by his men. From 1820 to 1824 he was stationed in Ireland during the agrarian riots.

In 1829 he decided to emigrate to the new settlement at Swan River. With his wife Georgiana [q.v.] and household he arrived at Fremantle in the *Warrior* in March 1830. In April he was made a justice of the peace and in May founded a settlement 200 miles south of Fremantle called Augusta, where he was also resident magistrate. In 1839 he moved to the Vasse River, taking up 12,000 acres and making his home at Fair Lawn in Busselton. He spent much time developing his property, but his duties as resident magistrate were harder than at Augusta because American whalers frequented Geographe Bay, and the Aboriginals were troublesome. In 1841 a treacherous murder of one of his settlers had to be avenged, which Molloy did with the help of other settlers, in the way that his military training indicated.

In 1850 he visited London, meeting the duke of Wellington and other comrades of the Napoleonic wars; next year he was gazetted lieut-colonel. Western Australia had just begun the reception of convicts, and on his return he found a country convict depot installed at the Vasse, which increased his magisterial duties. In all his acts as magistrate he was equable and fair, an upright and honourable example to the district, his grand manner and distinguished appearance making him outstanding. He died on 6 October 1867. Of his surviving daughters, Sabina became the second wife of Bishop Hale, Mary married Edmund Du Cane, and Amelia married William Richardson Bunbury.

A. Hasluck, *Portrait with background, a life of Georgiana Molloy* (Melb, 1955); A. Burton and P. U. Henn (eds), *Wollaston's Picton journal* (Perth, 1948); Molloy letters (WAA).

ALEXANDRA HASLUCK

MONDS, THOMAS WILKES (1829-1916), miller, was born on 28 June 1829 in Launceston, Tasmania, the son of Thomas Monds and his wife Helena, née Roadside. His father, a descendant of a Huguenot family, arrived in Hobart Town in 1822 with his farming man, Rush, and went on to Launceston. Granted land at Tunbridge, he tried farming but was not successful. He then turned to business as a cooper in Launceston, opened a general store in Charles Street and later built a shop and dwelling in St John Street. He also made soap and candles, which hitherto had been imported from England. He died in 1838 after a fall. He was a gentle kindly man but he lacked the drive and initiative that were to characterize his son.

His wife was left with three children, Thomas, Helena and Benjamin, and very little means. In 1841 she married William Jones, a timber merchant. They moved to the Mersey and then settled at Don where they built a house in 1843. While splitting laths and shingles, young Monds was seen by John Guillan, who, after talks with him and his mother, offered to take the boy and teach him the business of millwright and miller.

Monds began his apprenticeship at the Supply Mills on the West Tamar River. His employers, Guillan and Symes, built the schooner *Dusty Miller* and traded with South Australia in wheat, flour, and farm produce; in 1844 she was wrecked and the cargo worth £10,000 was lost. As nothing had been insured, Guillan and Symes were declared bankrupt. In 1845 Guillan rebuilt the Albion Mills with modern machinery and gave Monds sole charge of it and the book-keeping. On finishing his apprenticeship he went for six months as foreman to the flour-mill of John Walker [q.v.] in Hobart, and thence to the Supply Mills, and to the Cataract Mills in Launceston. At 24 he doubled his capital in the paling trade at Forth and returned to Launceston to take charge of Button's Mill.

In 1852 he married Angelina Hall, by whom he had eight children. He built a house in Frankland Street, Launceston, so successfully that he set up as a builder for seven years and then returned to Albion Mills. Raising his first and last mortgage, he bought the stone mill at Carrick for £2100 in 1867, and moved into the cottage behind it with his family. His business flourished quickly and next year he was able to buy the steam mill of a bankrupt competitor.

In 1874 he built Hawthorn, a fine Gothic house with every modern convenience, and the adjoining farm of Hatton-dale, working its 1200 acres in conjunction with the mill. Later he took into partnership his second son Albert, who in 1898 married Fanny Robertson. The eldest son, who had been weakened by an accident at the mill, opened a store in Launceston.

After a world tour and much study of American roller mills and electricity, Monds moved to Launceston in 1885, but not to retirement. He completed thirty years as chairman and treasurer of the Carrick Road Trust, and nine years as an elected member of the Westbury Council, as well as serving as a territorial justice of Tasmania. In Launceston he became a director of the Tasmanian Permanent Trustees and Executors, the Equitable Building Society and the Mutual Insurance Society. He was also manager and trustee of the savings bank at Launceston. He published *Domestic and Other Pieces* (Launceston, 1903), *Autobiography* (Launceston, 1907), *Diary of our trip round the world* (Launceston, 1910).

Of a deeply religious nature, Monds had joined the Wesleyan Church and became superintendent of the Sunday school in Carrick. Under the pastorates of Revs W. Law and J. Massie in Launceston, he became an active member, deacon and treasurer of Christ Church. His wife died in 1905. Monds died in Launceston on 9 May 1916. A self-made man, his mill brought prosperity to himself and to Carrick.

M. K. Whishaw, *Tasmanian village* (Launceston, 1963); CSO 1 (TA).

MARY K. WHISHAW

MONTAGU, ALGERNON SIDNEY (1802-1880), judge, was born at Cambridge, England, the second son of Basil Montagu, legal and miscellaneous writer and philanthropist, and his second wife Laura, eldest daughter of Sir William Beaumaris Rush, of Roydon, Essex, and Wimbledon, Surrey. His father was a natural son of the notorious John Montagu, fourth earl of Sandwich. Algernon's mother died in 1806, and he spent much of his childhood in Westmorland, in the care of his father's intimate friends, William and Dorothy Wordsworth. He was educated at a private school in Ambleside. He was admitted to Gray's Inn in November 1817, and called to the Bar in February 1826. Two years later he applied successfully for appointment as attorney-general of Van Diemen's Land. With the wife and son of a gentleman-transportee, Henry Savery [q.v.], entrusted to his protection, he sailed in the *Henry Wellesley*, arriving at Hobart Town in October 1828. Montagu had scarcely taken office when he became embroiled in a quarrel with a solicitor, Henry Jennings, over a writ from Savery's creditors. Montagu's attitude was reasonable, but Jennings denounced him to the press and to the government. Both Lieut-Governor Arthur in Hobart and Sir George Murray at the Colonial Office thought the quarrel was private and declined to intervene. Despite this affair, and James Stephen's prediction that Montagu was 'very likely to give himself up to various affectations of sentiment, romantic feeling, and literary taste', Arthur learned to appreciate his new attorney-general. He conducted prosecutions with skill and fairness, and voluntarily abstained from private practice. By 1831 Arthur was 'perfectly satisfied' with his work, and anxiously hoped that he would be chosen to replace the puisne judge,

A. M. Baxter [q.v.]. Viscount Goderich agreed, and Montagu's elevation to the Supreme Court bench was gazetted on 1 February 1833, a very popular appointment.

Montagu soon became a controversial figure. His talents and his sound knowledge of law had won him acclaim as 'the disciple of Jeremy Bentham and Lord Campbell', but his eccentric ideas sometimes led to most indecorous behaviour. Once, after admonishing the attorney-general, Alfred Stephen, for undignified conduct in court, he was answered with sarcasm; his temper flared and prudence was thrown to the winds. Arthur had to warn both men against a repetition of the scene.

In 1834 Montagu incurred the enmity of the anti-Arthurite press, and was attacked as the 'mad Judge'. In his sturdy independence he was no respecter of high persons. In April 1840, on arriving in Launceston to hold a session of the Supreme Court, he found Lady Franklin in residence in the government cottage, which had traditionally been available for judges on circuit. Believing that the court was affronted when its privileges were waived in favour of vice-regal amusements, he wrote petulant letters to Sir John Franklin until rebuked by Lord John Russell and persuaded to apologize. In 1843, when Lieut-Governor Eardley-Wilmot ignored his Executive Council and reprieved a bushranger, Kavanagh, ten minutes before the time set for execution, Montagu angrily declared that such intervention could only be justified by the virtual abolition of capital punishment!

On 12 March 1832 in St David's Church, Hobart, Montagu married Maria Ann Adams, a free immigrant five years his senior. Thereafter he lived to the limit of his means. He bought Rosny, a comfortable home on the eastern shore of the Derwent estuary, and later extended the estate to more than 800 acres. He invested heavily in experimental farming and took to yachting on an impressive scale. In April 1841 he informed Franklin that he and the attorney-general, Edward MacDowell [q.v], wished to exchange offices; as the colony had no able barrister, Montagu believed he could make £3000 a year by private practice without neglecting his official duties. The proposal was coolly received but his brother, Alfred Otter Montagu, after hearing of the opportunities, sailed from England with his family in the Glenbervie. Arriving in Hobart in February 1843 he was soon admitted to the Bar and quickly built up a flourishing practice. His career was cut short in January 1849 when his yacht capsized in a sudden squall and he was drowned.

In the long depression of the 1840s Montagu's finances became precarious. In November 1847 he was sued by Anthony McMeckan for a debt of £283. Montagu obtained a summons from the chief justice, Sir John Pedder [q.v.], calling on McMeckan to show cause why his writ should not be set aside as illegal. When his summons was dismissed by Pedder, McMeckan complained through his solicitor, Thomas Young, to Lieut-Governor Denison, but as the Supreme Court was then constituted so that each judge was an integral part of it and could not be constituted without both of them, neither judge could sue or be sued in it. A week later, however, in their decision on Symonds v. Morgan, Pedder and Montagu declared a local dog tax invalid, thereby casting doubt on all the colony's revenue legislation. Denison, who was known at the Colonial Office to be lacking in 'temper and calm judgment', was much upset. Young had long nursed a grudge against Montagu and now had opportunity to attack. The ensuing allegations and rebuttals showed that Montagu was financially embarrassed and may have been involved in questionable transactions. On 31 December 1847 Montagu was amoved from office by an order of the lieut-governor and his Executive Council.

Stunned and demoralized, Montagu sailed in the Rattler with his family on 29 January 1848 and, on arrival in England, lodged an appeal to the Privy Council. It was dismissed in July 1849, even though the main charges against him were based on circumstantial evidence. Before leaving Hobart he had received flattering testimonials from all classes in the community. According to the Hobart Town Courier, 'He moved in an eccentric orbit; and if he terrified by those motions, he occasionally delighted us by the brilliant light which he cast around his path. Fresh, vigorous and original, his intellect always commanded respect and not unfrequently admiration'. Long after he left the colony it was hinted that he had seduced Mrs Henry Savery in 1828. The story seems improbable and its authors may have been influenced by news of the moral degeneracy of Montagu's later life.

In 1850 he was appointed resident magistrate in the Falkland Islands. He arrived in Stanley in July, leaving his wife, who had borne him two sons and a daughter, destitute in England, until the Colonial Office helped her to join him. Montagu acted as coroner, chairman of the magistrate's court and of the police court, and member of the Executive Council. He resigned in June 1854 and went to London where he was appointed registrar of deeds in Sierra Leone. His wife had been left in the Falklands where she opened a small school and eked out a bare existence. Montagu tried to repudiate responsibility for her but was officially forced to pay a regular maintenance. She returned to England and died there in March 1872.

Montagu had at least two illegitimate children in Freetown and, with his Creole mistress, was involved in some absurd scandals. Yet in spite of his lurid private life and quarrels with several governors, he did valuable work in Sierra Leone. He served as master of the Court of Records, clerk of the Crown and registrar of the Court of Chancery. He was permitted private practice and on occasions in 1856-67 acted as chief justice. In 1857 he published in London the Ordinances of the Colony of Sierra Leone; it was an immediate success and ran to seven editions. In 1874 he published in London similar collections of the laws of the Gold Coast and of Lagos. In 1880 he was given leave to visit England. He died of apoplexy on 22 June 1880, soon after arrival in London.

E. F. Moore, English Reports, 5 (Edinb, 1901), 379; C. Fyfe, A history of Sierra Leone (Lond, 1962); R. W. Baker, 'Early judges in Tasmania', PTHRA, 8 (1959-60); Correspondence file under A. S. Montagu (TA); CO 78/35, 268/46, 280/253.   P. A. HOWELL

MONTAGU, JOHN (1797-1853), soldier and public servant, was born on 21 August 1797 probably in India, the second son of Edward Montagu (1755-1799), lieut-colonel in the Bengal army and kinsman of the duke of Manchester, and his wife Barbara, née Fleetwood. He was sent to England and educated at Cheam in Surrey, Parson's Green in Knightsbridge, and by a private tutor. In February 1814 he joined the army as an ensign in the 52nd Regiment, fought at Waterloo, was promoted lieutenant in November 1815 and went on half-pay next February. In April 1819 he joined the 64th Regiment and returned to half-pay as a captain in November 1822. In April 1823 he married Jessy, daughter of Major-General Vaughan Worsley, and niece of

George Arthur, lieut-governor elect of Van Diemen's Land; in August he transferred to the 40th Regiment, companies of which were about to go to New South Wales.

Montagu and his wife sailed in the Adrian with Arthur's party and arrived at Hobart Town in May 1824. In November he was appointed secretary to the lieut-governor, and soon took over the books and papers at the colonial secretary's office. Under Arthur's direction he began a reform of the public accounts but in 1825 the Colonial Office disallowed his nomination as colonial secretary. In March 1826 he began to act as clerk of the Executive and Legislative Councils. This appointment was also rejected by the Colonial Office, but Arthur protested against the decision and kept him in office. Meanwhile Montagu served on many boards of inquiry and was active in tightening up colonial regulations. His zeal and forthright comments were not calculated to lessen the growing hostility towards Arthur's nepotism, and denunciations of the government by the press led to the controversial Newspaper Licensing Act in 1827. By that time rumours of the transfer of the 40th Regiment to India were afoot and Montagu hastily applied to London for retirement from the army. In January 1828 he applied successfully for a provisional grant of 2560 acres, Arthur noting that it was important for him 'to select land without delay as the most advantageous situations will otherwise be chosen'. Three months later Montagu was ordered with his regiment to India, but because no answer to his resignation had come from London he was allowed to take charge of military invalids who were being sent to England. Arthur gave him a year's leave from his clerical duties on half-pay. In London Montagu persuaded the Colonial Office to confirm his appointment as clerk of the councils on condition that he resigned from the army. He sold his commission in September 1830 and with a recommendation for another maximum land grant sailed with his wife in the Mermaid.

Back in Hobart in January 1831 Montagu resumed office in the councils and in June was gazetted a justice of the peace. He continued to enjoy the benefits of Arthur's patronage and in turn his diligence increased the efficiency of the administration. In December 1832 he became acting colonial treasurer and had much success in collecting quitrents. A year later he returned to his clerkship of the councils and in 1834 distinguished himself by reorganizing the postal department, an additional task for which he was paid

£50. At intervals he acted as colonial secretary while John Burnett [q.v.] was ill. In 1835 when Burnett became financially embarrassed Montagu persuaded him to retire on a pension, and in August was formally appointed colonial secretary.

Arthur was recalled in 1836 and left his personal investments in the hands of Montagu and two other executors. Montagu had borrowed from Arthur some £4000 for his home, Stowell, at Battery Point, and like Arthur had many land speculations in Van Diemen's Land and the Port Phillip District. He was also a director and the largest shareholder of the Derwent Bank; a few of his shares were in the names of his sons, but most were probably owned by Arthur.

Sir John Franklin, who arrived in Hobart in January 1837, had no experience of civil government. Faced by 'an independent party of great wealth and influence' entrenched in key positions throughout the colony, Franklin reported to the Colonial Office that he was determined to break it. However, he found it too powerful to resist and was inclined to leave the administration to Montagu while he pursued his own interests in exploration and science. Despite public hostility to the 'Arthurite Clique' the colonial secretary's office was said to run 'with the celerity of clockwork and courtesy was everywhere'. The first cloud on Montagu's horizon was the assignment of convicts, a system to which he and Arthur were strongly attached. Consulted at the Colonial Office in 1829 Montagu had opposed the use of convict gangs for public works and maintained that prisoners were a labour force best assigned to private contractors and settlers. Early in 1838, however, he showed how assignment could be abused when he secretly obtained a household cook who had been sentenced to secondary punishment for defrauding his employer, Alfred Stephen, the attorney-general. Franklin promptly sent the cook to a road-gang and rebuked Montagu, overruling his protests. The defeat rankled and in December Montagu applied for eighteen months leave, pleading urgent family affairs in England. In February 1839 he sailed with his family in the *Derwent*. Next year Montagu was again consulted when the Colonial Office was planning changes in the management of convicts following the reports of the Molesworth committee on transportation. This time he opposed Captain Maconochie's [q.v.] theory of reforming convicts in separate penal stations and advocated a ticket-of-leave system in stages that would 'create character and self-esteem' by exposing convicts gradually to the 'tempta-

tions of Society'. On a later visit to the Colonial Office in November 1842 Montagu had several interviews with high officials and elaborated in greater detail his 'Convict Probationary System', which Lord Stanley then ordered to be introduced in Van Diemen's Land.

In 1839 before leaving for England Montagu had sold his furniture for £5000 and tried to sell Stowell. When he had not returned to Hobart by June 1840 Franklin proposed to replace him, but Montagu's leave was extended. In London he spent much time seeking English investments for the Derwent Bank, thereby helping Charles Swanston [q.v.] to make it Tasmania's major loan bank; within three years it held more than two-thirds of the colony's mortgages of £400,000, the onset of depression increasing its 'thraldom' over many settlers and a large part of the press.

Montagu returned to Hobart in March 1841 charged with important private commissions and his reputation supposedly enhanced by the special confidence of the secretary of state. In April a ball was given in his honour and he was praised for having urged the British government to continue transportation to Van Diemen's Land. Soon afterwards he clashed with Lady Franklin over the site of Christ's College and with the lieut-governor over the dismissal of Dr Coverdale [q.v.]. The addition of an elaborate tower to St George's Church at Battery Point caused an open rupture; Montagu insisted that it had been approved by Franklin and, when contradicted, adopted an offensive policy of passive resistance. Mediation was attempted by Judge Pedder and Adam Turnbull [qq.v.], but failed when the Franklins were scurrilously attacked in the *Van Diemen's Land Chronicle*. Assured that Montagu controlled the paper Franklin called on him for an explanation. Montagu claimed that he denied the charge 'in the most solemn and sacred manner [of] a Christian gentleman', but he also insinuated that Franklin's memory was at fault. On 17 January 1842 Montagu was relieved of his office. Next day Franklin sent to London a mighty bundle of the relevant correspondence and a short statement giving five reasons for Montagu's suspension. Within two weeks the Hobart papers had the full story, 'authentic official information' supplied by Montagu. Before he sailed with his family in the *Calcutta* on 10 February he was given a testimonial signed by many leading colonists and money for plate to be inscribed *Magna est vis veritatis*. By June James Stephen at the Colonial Office had decided that the reasons given in Franklin's short statement did not justify Montagu's suspension. This opinion hardened as the dispatches from Hobart increased in volume, irrelevance and emotion. In contrast Montagu's letters and papers were impressive, with their air of injured innocence. When called to the Colonial Office on 28 August he was assured that no justifiable fault had been imputed to him, and next day he coolly told Stanley that Franklin 'was incapable of writing the letters signed by him . . . was little removed from an Imbecile . . . and had long been under the dominion of Lady Franklin'. He also accepted Stanley's offer of the colonial secretaryship at the Cape of Good Hope. On 13 September this news was sent to Franklin in a dispatch that questioned his judgment and relieved Montagu 'from every censure which infringes the integrity or the propriety of his conduct'.

Every relevant dispatch to and from Franklin was shown to Montagu and he sent copies of 'them to Swanston. Some appeared in the Hobart press, but the whole 'Manuscript Book' was circulated from the Derwent Bank with small show of secrecy. Franklin learnt of its existence from friends outraged by this underhand method of smearing the lieut-governor. His protest to London was sent to Montagu, whose last words on the case disclaimed any vindictive intention, vowed that the 'Book' was confidential, skirted around specific charges and contrived throughout to exalt the wisdom of the Colonial Office. Clearly Montagu had not outgrown the boyish disregard for truthfulness that had distressed his mother; even belated proof that he had lied about St George's tower failed to move him or the Colonial Office. Though historians disagree in interpreting the affair, it lost Montagu many friends in Hobart, and while it led to Franklin's recall, it effectively broke the power of the 'Arthurite Clique'.

In April 1843 Montagu assumed his duties at Cape Town. He worked in harmony with four governors, and in their many absences presided over the Executive and Legislative Councils. He had much success in reorganizing public finances, immigration and public works, especially the building of roads by convict labour, though his attempt to introduce stamp duties aroused much opposition. He applied his energies to the establishment of representative government in Cape Colony, strongly resisting any division of the colony and a franchise founded on wealth; according to one observer, 'by his flair for adapting existing administrative machinery to meet needs, he laid the soundest founda-

tions for a parliamentary structure'. In 1851 as acting-governor he reorganized the recruiting system that changed the course of the Kaffir war. Soon afterwards his health began to fail and his personal finances were in bad shape, although he had sold his properties in Tasmania and Victoria and repaid his debt to Arthur. In May 1852 he was granted fifteen months leave and returned with his family to England. A visit to the south of France did not improve his health and his leave was extended. He died in London on 4 November 1853, leaving an estate valued at £600. His wife was granted a pension of £300 and a public subscription in Cape Colony provided her and her three sons with some £3000.

HRA (1), 15, 18, 20, (3), 4-6; W. A. Newman, *John Montagu* (Cape Town, 1856); K. Fitzpatrick, *Sir John Franklin in Tasmania 1837-1843* (Melb, 1949); M. C. L. Levy, *Governor George Arthur* (Melb, 1953); A. G. L. Shaw, 'The origins of the probation system in Van Diemen's Land', *Hist Studies*, no 21, Nov 1953; J. J. Breitenbach, 'The development of the secretaryship to the governments at the Cape of Good Hope under John Montagu, 1843-52', *Archives Year Book, South African Hist*, 2 (1959); CO 48/351, 363, 280/ 158, 159; CSO 1/79/1767, 1/99/2388, 1/239/ 5782, 1/632/14281 (TA). JOHN REYNOLDS

MONTEFIORE, JOSEPH BARROW (1803-1893), merchant and financier, was born on 24 June 1803 in London, the youngest son of Eliezer Montefiore, merchant, of Barbados and London, and his wife Judith, née Barrow. As a scion of a wealthy Sephardi family he was educated at Hurwitz's school at Highgate and at Garcia's academy at Peckham. On leaving school he was articled to a firm of London tea brokers, thus continuing in the tradition of the Montefiores of Barbados, who made their fortune in colonial trade. In 1826 he became one of the twelve 'Jew brokers' in the city of London, buying the privilege for £1500. However, being young and enterprising and with a penchant for larger speculative ventures, he decided in June 1828 to emigrate to New South Wales, where he proposed to invest some £10,000 in the wool industry and the cultivation of drugs; he applied for a grant of 5000 acres.

Recommended by the Treasury as 'most respectable' and a valuable acquisition to the colony, he arrived in Sydney in February 1829 in the *Jupiter* with his wife Rebecca, née Mocatta, and their two children, his partner David Ribeiro Furtado and his wife, and his brother-in-law

George Mocatta. They established the trading firm J. B. Montefiore & Co., with an office in O'Connell Street. Montefiore acquired large tracts of land in New South Wales and by 1838 owned 12,502 acres by grant or purchase, including Nanima station, near Wellington. Though a landowner, he never became an 'agriculturist' as he had originally intended. In partnership with his brother Jacob (1801-1895), who in 1835-39 was a member of the South Australian Colonization Commission in London, he made a large fortune in real estate, helped to found the Bank of Australasia and was one of the channels through which English capital contributed to the pastoral expansion and speculative boom of the late 1830s. Joseph B. Montefiore was one of the sponsors of the bill, which became known as the Forbes Act of 1834, advocating interest rates free from statutory limits to encourage the flow of capital into the colony: 'restrict the rate of interest', he warned a sub-committee of the Legislative Council, 'and you at once destroy the stamina of the colony'. Early in 1841, when the depression set in, the Montefiore firm of Sydney and London went bankrupt and he returned to London.

By 1844 the Montefiore brothers, assisted by numerous friends and possibly the London Rothschilds, were back in business and Joseph B. Montefiore decided to try his luck in South Australia. He arrived in Adelaide from London on 27 July 1846 bringing with him his wife, nine daughters and two sons, two servants, 'a harp, a piano and 300 packages', and soon set up in business with his nephew Eliezer Levi Montefiore as importers and shipping agents. Joseph invested heavily in copper mines and served on the board of a number of mining companies, notably the Royal South Australian Mining Co. He was a member of the stock exchange, a committee member of the Adelaide Chamber of Commerce and an original trustee of the Savings Bank. In 1851 he stood for election to the East Adelaide seat of the Legislative Council as a 'good friend of free trade and moderate, unhurried reform and an opponent of state aid' but was roundly defeated. True to the Montefiore tradition he retired from business when still in his fifties and in 1860 returned to London where he was active for many years as one of the founders and stalwarts of the Jewish reform movement.

Montefiore was one of the earliest free Jewish settlers in New South Wales and was active in Jewish communal life from the start. He was the first president of the Jewish congregation of Sydney upon its official foundation in 1832 and helped to secure a land grant for a Jewish cemetery in 1835. In 1847, together with E. L. Montefiore, he pressed for a Jewish share in state aid to religion, by which means the nascent Jewish community of Adelaide meant to assert Jewish equality in South Australia. Likewise in 1851 he welcomed the General Education Act on behalf of the Adelaide Jewish community.

Enterprising, urbane, and noted for his wit and prodigious memory, he was perhaps the outstanding representative in the Australian colonies of the richly endowed Sephardi merchants, financiers and scholars of London, the vanguard of Jewish expansion into a new world and of the Jewish emancipation movement in the old. He died on 8 September 1893 in Brighton leaving ten daughters and three sons.

HRA (1), 14, 18; H. Munz, *Jews in South Australia, 1836-1936* (Adel, 1936); L. M. Goldman, *The Jews in Victoria in the nineteenth century* (Melb, 1954); L. M. Goldman, *The history of the Jews in New Zealand* (Wellington, 1958); D. J. Benjamin, 'The first Montefiore in Australia', *Aust Jewish Hist Soc J*, 2 (1944-48); A. Fabian, 'Early days of SA Jewry', *Aust Jewish Hist Soc J*, 2 (1944-48).

ISRAEL GETZLER

MOOR, HENRY (1809-1877), solicitor, was born at Greenwich, Kent, England, son of Henry Isaacs Moor and Elizabeth, née Remmington. After education at Rev. Charles P. Burney's school, Greenwich, he entered the legal profession. On 12 November 1831 he was admitted as an attorney, Court of Common Pleas, Lincoln's Inn. From 1832 to August 1841 he was in partnership in Furnival's Inn with John Simpson.

Moor arrived in Melbourne in February 1842, commenced business as a conveyancer, and was admitted as an attorney, solicitor and proctor in the Supreme Court of New South Wales in April 1843. Until November 1850 he was in partnership with Hugh John Chambers in a very successful practice. In December 1842 Moor was an unsuccessful candidate for the town clerkship of the corporation of Melbourne, but became a councillor for Bourke Ward in November 1843. From November 1844 to November 1845 he was Melbourne's second mayor, gaining wide popularity by stabilizing council finances, refusing his mayoral allowance, removing 'violent animosities' from the council and being a liberal chief magistrate. He was an alderman from November 1845 until April 1846, when he retired from the council. He was elected for Lonsdale Ward in November 1846 and had a second term as mayor to November 1847, in which time he was chairman of the provisional Committee for Anti-Transportation. He finally retired from the council in November 1849.

Moor was Port Phillip's most prominent lay Anglican, being the first registrar of the diocese of Melbourne from 13 February 1848 to 18 March 1854. In July 1849 he was elected by Geelong to the New South Wales Legislative Council. With the concurrence of Bishop Perry he introduced two highly unpopular Anglican Church bills for the Port Phillip District; his church temporalities bill sought wider powers for wardens and increased state aid, and his church discipline bill sought civil enforcement of decisions of the church court. Local petitioners attacked the bills as attempts to establish the church by law before Port Phillip was separated from New South Wales and a Victorian legislature established. Faced by J. D. Lang's [q.v.] opposition in the Legislative Council in Sydney, Moor withdrew the bills in August 1850.

Moor had pastoral holdings in Victoria, and was attacked for favouring the squatting interests in the debates on the Port Phillip electoral bill. In October 1851 he was defeated as a candidate for Portland in the elections for the first Victorian Legislative Council. It was known at the time that he intended leaving for England. The reason given was his disappointment over a libel suit in March 1851 against Edward Wilson and James Stewart Johnston, the proprietors of the Argus, for calling him a 'double faced and unprincipled schemer'. He won the verdict but damages of only one farthing. However, he won substantial damages in March and August 1848 against William Kerr [q.v.], editor of the Argus, who had lampooned Moor's activities as chief magistrate:

I'll frolic with the lasses
And feast my carnal sight
On the shameless work that passes
In a bawdy house at night.

In parochial Port Phillip Kerr and the Argus were seen as leaders of 'the Scotch Clique' and Moor as its main opponent with support from the Melbourne Morning Herald and Daily News.

Moor floated a Western Port Coal Co. in May 1850, his supporters including C. H. Ebden, J. B. Were, and G. Ward Cole [qq.v.]. From March 1849 to March 1851 he was first chairman of the Victoria Fire and Marine Insurance Co. The Argus attacked Moor for these enterprises, for his 'intimate association with banking' and his

friendships with Lieut-Governor La Trobe, Judge a' Beckett, and Bishop Perry. Moor appears to have been a talented and astute lawyer and businessman, stout in appearance and purse, jovial in manner and generous, but one whose liberal conservatism was not far removed from a less than benevolent despotism.

He left for England in January 1852, came back to Melbourne in December 1853, and returned permanently to England in March 1854. He had built a large fortune and retired at Brighton. He was defeated as a Conservative candidate for Brighton in July 1860, elected in February 1864, defeated in July 1865, and again defeated, as a Liberal Conservative, in November 1868. His first wife, Mary, died in 1870. He married Marion Wynton in 1871 and they had one daughter. He died in May 1877 at Teddington. He is thought to be the author of A Visit to Russia in the Autumn of 1862 (London, 1863). A portrait hangs in the Diocesan Registry, Melbourne.

F. J. Corder, 'A letter book of . . . Henry Moor, 1842-43', VHM, 29 (1959); Melb Town Council minutes (City Council archives, Melb).   F. STRAHAN

MOORE, GEORGE FLETCHER (1798-1886), lawyer, landed proprietor and diarist, was born on 10 December 1798 in Bond's Glen, Donemana, County Tyrone, Ireland, the second son of Joseph Moore and his wife Anne, née Fletcher. He was educated at Foyle College, Londonderry, and at Trinity College, Dublin (LL.B., 1820). After being called to the Irish Bar he practised for six years in the north-west circuit. His application for a legal position in the proposed Swan River settlement was refused by the Colonial Office, which felt that the governor should be free to make his own recommendations but gave him a letter to Stirling. Armed with this letter and another from his Irish legal colleagues, Moore made his own way to the colony in the brig Cleopatra. Accompanied by four servants he landed at Fremantle in October 1830 and obtained a grant, which he called Millendon, on the Upper Swan.

Farming gradually displaced his legal interests. He managed to buy 34 merinos and 10 lambs in 1832, and four years later he had 800 fine-woolled sheep and the lease of a farm at York. By 1884 he owned 24,000 acres of land, including valuable town allotments. From the time of his arrival he kept a journal and wrote lively and informative letters to his friends. These were later published as *Extracts from the Letters and Journals of George Fletcher Moore, Esq., now filling a judicial office at the Swan River Settlement*, edited by M. Doyle (London, 1834), and *Diary of Ten Years Eventful Life of an Early Settler in Western Australia . . .* (London, 1884). He revealed the difficulties encountered in developing his property, labour problems, the frequent food shortages and inflated prices. Many discouraged settlers left the colony, but Moore felt these were temporary reverses and refused to be depressed. He joined the Agricultural and Horticultural Society formed on 16 July 1831 and for a while was its secretary. Next September he attended the governor's first big ball, writing a song for the occasion and singing it during the evening

Less than a month after his arrival Moore accompanied the colonial secretary and party in search of Aboriginals concerned in a robbery. His sympathetic concern for the Aboriginals grew as he learned their language and listened to their stories, though 'he wished sadly that they would not steal his pigs'. He published *A Descriptive Vocabulary of the Language in Common Use amongst the Aborigines of Western Australia, with copious meanings, embodying much interesting information regarding the habits, manners and customs of the natives and the natural history of the country* (London, 1842), and *Evidences of an Inland Sea collected from the Natives of the Swan River Settlement* (Dublin, 1837).

Moore's observant nature and keen interest in the colony's progress found still another outlet for his abounding energy in exploration. He traced the course of the Swan River to its junction with the Avon. In 1831 he accompanied Ensign Dale when the York district was discovered. In 1835 Moore went northwards and in May 1836 discovered the river named after him. Later in the same year, with the colonial secretary, Peter Broun, and George Leake [qq.v.], he found grazing and agricultural land east and north of Northam. As a result of Lieutenant George Grey's reports of his 1839 expedition Moore was sent to examine the coastal district round Champion Bay and Point Moore (also named after him). His report was favourable but it was not till a more intensive search by the brothers Gregory in 1846 that this rich district began development. Moore also visited Houtman Abrolhos in 1839.

On 10 February 1832 the colony's first legislative ordinance (2 Wm IV, no 1) established a civil court. Moore was sworn in as commissioner on 17 February 1832.

Before this W. H. Mackie [q.v.] had become chairman of Quarter Sessions in 1830 and advocate-general in 1832. However, in 1834 the Colonial Office instructed the governor to combine the offices of chairman of Quarter Sessions and civil court commissioner in the person of Mackie. Moore was then appointed advocate-general. By virtue of this office he became an early member of the Legislative and Executive Councils and did very useful work as parliamentary draftsman. Although he also had the right to engage in private practice, there is no record of his having done so. He did, however, act as commissioner of works, roads and bridges, and with Surveyor-General J. S. Roe [q.v.] he waded among the 'Flats' of Perth waters in December 1834 and again early in 1838, probing about with sticks. Together they were responsible for determining the site of the original Perth Causeway across the 'Flats' to the south bank of the river.

In 1840 Moore was warmly recommended to the Colonial Office by Governor Hutt for leave to return to Ireland to see his ageing father. On his return he continued in office without interruption until 1846, when Governor Hutt was succeeded by Lieut-Colonel Clarke. Peter Broun, the colonial secretary, having failed in health, Moore was apointed to act for him in July 1846 and, after Broun's death in November, he discharged the duties of colonial secretary as well as his own legal duties till a successor was appointed. On 29 October 1846 Moore married Fanny Mary Jane Jackson (1814-1863), the stepdaughter of Governor Clarke. The next few months were particularly onerous for Moore and for Captain F. C. Irwin [q.v.], who acted as governor because of Clarke's illness which ended in his death in 1847. In 1852 Moore was again granted leave to visit his father. At the Colonial Office he discovered a misunderstanding over his absentee pay and a coolness towards his application for an extension of leave. He thereupon resigned and did not return to the colony; thus ended a distinguished public career.

Moore's later years were saddened by the chronic indisposition of his wife. On 16 June 1859 he wrote, 'I fear my chance of seeing Millendon again is feeble and remote'. After his wife's death on 24 October 1863, he lived in London and twenty years later wrote of his 'isolated unfriended position. Even in this great city I am almost alone in my eighty-fifth year'. He died at Kensington on 30 December 1886.

Moore was a religious man of strong convictions and upheld the custom of holding church services on his Swan estate.

In 1838 he had been appointed one of the trustees of Church of England property, including burial grounds; they also undertook the building of a permanent church in Perth. He was also a supporter of All Saints' Church, Upper Swan, on whose walls is a memorial tablet to him.

W. S. Ferguson, George Fletcher Moore: an Ulster pioneer in Western Australia, (Battye Lib, Perth); P. U. Henn, Genealogical notes (Battye Lib, Perth); G. F. Moore, Letters and journals (Battye Lib, Perth); CO 323/134.

ALFRED H. CHATE

MOORE, JOSHUA JOHN (d. 1864), grazier, was born at Horningsea, Cambridgeshire, England, the son of John Moore, a yeoman farmer. On 31 March 1813 he was commissioned an ensign in the Royal South Lincoln Militia. Promoted lieutenant in August, he transferred in September 1813 to the 14th Regiment, with which he fought at Waterloo. Soon afterwards he was placed on half-pay, and accompanied his brother-in-law, John Wylde [q.v.], newly appointed deputy-judge-advocate, to Sydney in the *Elizabeth*, arriving in October 1816. He was appointed clerk to the judge-advocate and registrar of the Governor's Court at a salary of £80. When the Supreme Court was established in 1824 he acted for a time as prothonotary, but when this post was abolished the following year he retired from official life to attend to his pastoral interests.

In 1819 he was granted by Macquarie 500 acres at Cabramatta near Liverpool which he called Horningsea, and here he lived until after the death of his first wife in 1839. In August 1821 he occupied land at Baw Baw, near Goulburn, where he was granted 600 acres in 1825 on leaving the public service, and where he lived during the later part of his life. On 21 October 1824 he took out a ticket-of-occupation for 2000 acres on what is now the site of Canberra, and on 16 December 1826 he applied to purchase 1000 acres already occupied by him 'situate at Canberry, on the E. bank of the river which waters Limestone Plains, above its junction with the Murrumbeeja, adjoining the grant of Mr Robert Campbell snr'. He had already built huts and stockyards on the ridge where the Canberra Community Hospital now stands and enclosed thirty acres for cultivation.

Moore had married first on 29 March 1825 at Liverpool Sarah Elizabeth, daughter of David Hollands of Bermondsey, Surrey, shipowner and shipwright. She died aged 53 on 27 September 1839, survived by one son, Frederick Thomas, and was buried at Liverpool. In 1841 at Goulburn Moore married Ann Augusta, daughter of Lieutenant John James Peters, by whom he had two sons and two daughters. He died at Baw Baw on 27 July 1864.

Moore was the first pastoralist to occupy land on the present site of Canberra, preceding Robert Campbell [q.v.] by about a year. It was, however, only an outstation formed by an overseer and a few convict stockmen. Moore himself never lived on the property, and took no part in the development of the district. In 1843 during the depression he sold it to Lieutenant Arthur Jeffreys, R.N., a son-in-law of Robert Campbell, who gave it the name Acton. Moore's property took in the present sites of the hospital, of Civic Centre and of the Australian National University.

HRA (1), 10, 11; F. W. Robinson, *Canberra's first hundred years*, 2nd ed (Syd, 1927); F. Watson, *A brief history of Canberra* (Canberra, 1927); L. F. Fitzhardinge, *St John's Church and Canberra*, 2nd ed (Canberra, 1959); MS cat under J. J. Moore (ML).

L. F. FITZHARDINGE

MOORE, THOMAS (1762-1840), sailor, farmer and philanthropist, was born in England of humble parents. He had little education, but was endowed with robust common sense and developed a character of great stability. He took to the sea and in October 1791 arrived in the *Britannia* in Sydney. There he may have met Rachel Turner who had arrived in 1790, but he continued to sail the Indian and Pacific Oceans for another five years. In May 1796 he berthed in Port Jackson again, went ashore as a free settler and next January was married to Rachel Turner.

In 1796 Governor Hunter had made him master boatbuilder in the dockyard at Port Jackson, and in 1798 he was a member of the Vice-Admiralty Court set up to try those accused of mutiny in the *Barwell*. In 1803 he was commissioned to survey and procure timber from George's River for ship building and naval purposes. He built his own cutter *Integrity*, and began to trade with Brisbane Water; he also engaged in general building. His heart was turning away from the sea and his eyes were on the rich new lands then being opened for farming.

In 1799 he received a grant of 470 acres, named Bulanaming, between Petersham and Cook's River. By 1804 he owned 1100 acres, and 1920 acres by 1807, mostly pasture land. He lived on a grant which he had been given beside the Tank Stream, on what became the southern side of Bridge

Street in Sydney. This was a three-acre orchard and the centre of his business activities. Moore was one of 833 persons who signed the 'Settlers' Address to Governor Bligh just before he was deposed by John Macarthur and Major George Johnston [qq.v.] in January 1808. He became a captain in the Loyal Sydney Volunteer Association in March 1808 and in March 1809 his name was listed among those whom Bligh forbade any shipmaster to assist to leave the colony.

In 1809 Moore gave up his post as master boatbuilder and withdrew from Sydney. He had received a large grant in the George's River district known as Moorebank, and the site which he chose for his home was to make him the first citizen of Liverpool. On 7 May 1810 he was gazetted a magistrate for George's River. He joined Macquarie on his tour of the district when the town site of Liverpool was proclaimed on 15 December. His last years were spent at Moorebank. He steadily added to his original grant by purchase and became one of the colony's largest landholders. He regularly supplied meat to the government stores in Sydney and his sources of income were wide and varied. He shared in the foundation of the Bank of New South Wales in 1817 and helped to open a savings bank at Liverpool in July 1819. He visited England in 1818 and in 1834 and went to Adelaide in 1839 to arrange for the sale and transhipment of 2000 sheep.

Moore was reappointed as magistrate for Liverpool each year until 1820 when his jurisdiction was extended throughout the County of Cumberland; in 1821 he became a magistrate for New South Wales. He contributed towards the building of a two-storey church school and a court-house opened in 1813, a Roman Catholic chapel in 1821 and a Presbyterian church in 1826. He helped to found an auxiliary of the British and Foreign Bible Society in 1817 and served on the Liverpool committee of the Wesleyan Auxiliary Missionary Society in 1824. It was natural that he should be called 'the King of Liverpool'. Although generous in his religious sympathies, Moore was primarily a devoted member of the Church of England. He was a constant friend of 'parson Marsden' and 'Mr. Cowper' [qq.v.], and used to worship at St Philip's, Church Hill. After he settled at Liverpool he would ride across to St John's, Parramatta, but the building of St Luke's, Liverpool, was begun in 1818 and it was used for worship in 1819 when the roof and four walls were up. In 1823 it still lacked pews and a gallery and Moore was active on the committee which sought

to raise funds to complete it. It was ready for dedication in 1824 and Moore became a member of its first committee. His home, with its habits of household prayers each day and of worship in St Luke's Church every Sunday, was a model of ordered piety and simple contentment.

On 13 November 1838 Rachel Moore died and Thomas was left without children or kinsfolk. He had formed a great admiration for Bishop Broughton [q.v.] and had given him land in the Rocks area of Lower George Street as a site for a future cathedral; the land was later resumed but the £20,000 received as compensation helped to build St Andrew's Cathedral. After his wife's death Moore determined to leave all his property to the Church of England in New South Wales. Next year his will was drawn up to give effect to this desire, and he died on Christmas Eve 1840. Under his will the rents and income from 2080 acres of Moorebank were to form an endowment for the see of Sydney; those from the remaining 4315 acres were to provide a fund to augment clergy stipends. His house and grounds at Liverpool were left for the foundation of a college for the education of young men of 'the Protestant persuasion'. The income from 700 acres at Minto and Liverpool were to provide an endowment for the college. On 1 March 1856 Moore Theological College was opened at Liverpool with Rev. W. M. Cowper (1810-1902) as acting principal and three students in residence. The college was transferred to a site in Newtown adjacent to the University of Sydney in 1891. A portrait of Moore hangs in the Chapter House in Sydney.

HRNSW, 3-7; M. L. Loane, A centenary history of Moore Theological College (Syd, 1955); Sydney Gazette, 11 Dec 1803, 1 June 1806, 15 May 1808; Oddfellow (Syd), 15 Oct 1924.
                                    M. L. LOANE

MOORE, WILLIAM HENRY (1788?-1854), solicitor, was the elder son of John Moore, a London solicitor, and his first wife Martha (Ann) Field. He served his clerkship with his father and in 1810 was admitted an attorney of the three superior courts at Westminster. For most of 1813 he acted as under-sheriff of London and Middlesex in place of his father who had died in January that year, and in February 1814 was recommended by J. H. Bent [q.v.] for appointment as one of the two unconvicted 'solicitors of the Crown' whom Bathurst proposed to send to New South Wales, to overcome earlier difficulties with ex-convict attorneys there. With Frederick Garling [q.v.] Moore was chosen and each was promised a salary of £300 from colonial funds as compensation for leaving England and undertaking the risks of practice in the colony. They were at first called 'stipendiary Solicitors', and later 'Crown or Government Solicitors', although they had 'no Public or Official Duty to perform' and were never considered 'as professionally retained in the service of the Colonial Government'.

Recommended to Governor Macquarie for 'every Privilege and Protection . . . extended to the Civil Colonial Officers of the Higher Classes', Moore sailed in the *Marquis of Wellington* with two sisters and a brother, and arrived at Sydney on 27 January 1815. On 11 May he was admitted to the courts as the first free solicitor in the colony. He showed a strong partiality for anti-emancipist politics. In February 1816 he joined Rev. Benjamin Vale [q.v.] in seizing the American schooner *Traveller* as a legal prize under the Navigation Acts, was suspended by Macquarie for 'insolence and insubordination' and denied every indulgence that had been extended to him. A year later Macquarie reported him to London as the 'Chief mover and promoter of a Memorial' to the House of Commons 'to convey Charges of the Most False and Malicious nature against me' and for forging signatures to this petition. After somewhat heated correspondence with the Colonial Office in November 1819 Moore apologized for his actions, and was then reinstated and given his indulgences and arrears of pay.

Under Governor Brisbane Moore was more cautious; though opposed to H. G. Douglass [q.v.] in his controversies with the Parramatta magistrates he avoided improper participation in the affair, and in September 1825 was appointed King's coroner or master of the Crown office with an additional salary of £300, but he narrowly escaped censure for organizing the exclusives' dinner to celebrate Brisbane's departure. Under Governor Darling Moore acted for nearly a year as attorney-general after the resignation of Saxe Bannister [q.v.] in October 1826, and he assured the governor that he had acted legally in the Sudds-Thompson affair; however, Darling was critical of his capacity and in December 1827 suspended him as 'Crown Solicitor' for supporting resolutions at a Turf Club dinner which the governor thought insulting. Moore's willing support for Darling's opponents seems out of character and he strongly protested his innocence. In a lengthy review of the disputes in the colony the secretary of state disapproved Darling's action in removing him. Moore's post of 'Crown Solicitor', in the sense in which the term was applied to him, was abolished, and the subsidy originally authorized by Bathurst was withdrawn. In 1852 Moore successfully petitioned the Legislative Council for compensation and was awarded £1800. In 1829 the office of crown solicitor in the modern sense of the term, previously held by Thomas Wylde, was revived, and Moore was appointed to it at a salary of £500, but without the right of private practice. In conducting the business of the Crown in the Supreme Court he was often outmatched by able opponents such as R. Wardell and W. C. Wentworth [qq.v.] and, though Moore sought the position of solicitor-general, Darling repeatedly stressed his incompetence, adding that he was 'certainly not disposed to serve the Government', was 'one of the most idle Men living' and urged his dismissal. In response to these mounting complaints of negligence, unnecessary delays and unintelligible reports, in June 1831 Governor Bourke was ordered to inquire into the solicitor's conduct. In January 1832 Bourke reported that Moore had been 'culpably neglectful on several occasions', but he hoped that the arrival of the new attorney-general, J. Kinchela [q.v.] would improve Moore's work. However, in 1834 the resentful letters which he wrote after being rebuked for refusing to prepare briefs led to his final suspension and his attempts to obtain an annuity were unsuccessful, though in 1842 he was appointed by the Supreme Court to examine persons applying for admission as attorneys.

Protected by Bathurst's promises and assured of a monopoly of private practice by Bent's refusal to admit ex-convict attorneys in court, Moore had built up a very lucrative private law office and by 1822 Commissioner Bigge could report to the Colonial Office that Garling and Moore had been 'very fully remunerated' for the expense of moving to the colony. At first Moore's brother, Thomas Matthews, had been his clerk and as a partner he had Edward Joseph Keith in 1825-27, his stepbrother Charles Dodwell Moore in 1828-34 and George S. Yarnton in 1841-42.

Moore had many other interests. In 1836-42 he was a director of the Commercial Banking Co. of Sydney, in 1837 became a shareholder in the Marine Insurance Co., a committee member of the Royal Exchange, and in 1842 chairman of the Union Assurance Co. In and around Sydney he acquired much land, some of it leased to tenants and some, at the corner of George and King Streets, he sold in 1834 at up to £55 10s. a foot. His chief farm, which he bought from Simeon Lord [q.v.] in 1824, was at the seven-mile post on the Liverpool Road. From his properties in County Camden in 1838 he sent sheep overland to Adelaide and went there himself to sell them.

In 1842 Moore offered himself unsuccessfully for appointment as town clerk of the new Sydney Municipal Council, claiming the special qualification of having had business associations with the Corporation of London. Next year, with liabilities exceeding his assets of £66,000, he was declared insolvent. Much of his country land had to be sold and his library of eight hundred volumes was offered at auction. His certificate of discharge is not officially recorded but it appears from recitals in a conveyance registered in 1853 that it was allowed by the Supreme Court on 8 July 1845. At his death on 13 October 1854 in College Street, Sydney, he left his remaining city land to his sister Ann, widow of William Cordeaux [q.v.], and some £2300 of goods and shares to his wife Mary, née Hanks, whom he had married on 13 August 1844 at St James's Church, Sydney, and who died on 5 November 1871, aged 65.

HRA (1), 8-17, (4), 1; M. H. Ellis, *Lachlan Macquarie* (Syd, 1947); C. M. Whittakers (comp), The Whittakers story (ML); Newspaper indexes under W. H. Moore (ML); Bigge Report, Appendix, Bonwick transcripts, Box 28/6710 (ML); MS cat under W. H. Moore (ML).   R. J. McKAY

MOREHEAD, ROBERT ARCHIBALD ALISON (1814?-1885), businessman, was born in Edinburgh, third son of Dr Robert Morehead, episcopal dean of Edinburgh in 1818-32, and his wife Margaret, née Wilson. The Moreheads of Herbertshire in Stirlingshire were an old landed family with strong Whig sympathies. His elder brothers entered the East India Co. service and Robert was sent to Glasgow, where after apprenticeship to an insurance broker he worked for James Finlay & Co. as bookkeeper and accountant and won their esteem. About 1837 he launched out on his own in Glasgow as a manufacturer of shawls and zebra cloth but ill health made him think of moving to a drier climate. In October 1840 he applied for the post of manager in Australia for the Scottish Australian Co., formed in Aberdeen in 1839-40, and was appointed on condition that he took 1000 shares and gave surety

for £5000. Morehead was cautious yet capable of quick decisive action, excellent qualities for a businessman arriving in Australia with investment funds in the depression of the early 1840s. When he reached Sydney in July 1841 with nearly £30,000 to invest, he discovered that by buying up mortgages and lending money at an average of 12½ per cent he was able to acquire some very valuable property in and around Sydney, in Melbourne and in such country centres as Maitland and Wollongong. By 'reaping this harvest of mortgages', as he put it, and his high rates of interest, he enabled his company to become the first really successful commercial venture based in Scotland and operating in Australia.

In 1843-44 Morehead became involved in the usury controversy raging in the colony. To counter W. C. Wentworth's [q.v.] proposals for an Interest Act, he wrote and published *Some Words for and to the Capitalists and Shareholders in banks and other moneyed companies connected with the Colony of New South Wales*, (Sydney, 1843), an indictment of the colonial speculators whom he termed the 'borrowcracy'. Having weathered the usury controversy and overcome disagreements with his directors in Scotland, who wanted him to be both cautious and daring, Morehead successfully launched out into commission and agency business and the advancing of money against produce, particularly wool. Other fields he entered were copper-mining in South Australia (1846), coal-mining at Newcastle (1858), and large-scale pastoral ventures in Queensland, particularly at Bowen Downs (1863), and in the Gulf country (1865-66) where his company was first to arrive, taking advantage of its holdings astride the route along the Thomson and Flinders Rivers. When he retired in 1884, Morehead had built up a great empire which included the largest pastoral station in Australia (Bowen Downs), holdings of city property on key sites, and some of the most productive mines on the northern New South Wales coalfield. The company's capital had increased from £30,000 in 1840 to over £600,000 in 1870.

Morehead's strong Whig and free-trade views were shown in his refusal to enter the coal vend in the 1870s and in his criticism of colonial politics. In the 1840s he opposed the claims of the squatters as 'would-be monopolists of the land', and later he gave no countenance to employers' associations or trade unions. Keenly interested in schools and more cultured than many of the businessmen of the day, he served on the Council of Education in the 1860s and was a trustee of the Public

Library. He died in Sydney on 9 January 1885, aged 71.

In 1841 Morehead had married Helen Buchanan Dunlop in Stirlingshire. They had two daughters and a son, Boyd Dunlop, who became premier of Queensland in 1888-90.

C. Morehead (ed), *Memorials of the life and writings of the Rev. R. Morehead, D.D.* (Edinb, 1875); D. S. Macmillan, *Bowen Downs, 1863-1963* (Syd, 1963); Scottish Australian Co. Records (Archives, Univ Syd).

DAVID S. MACMILLAN

MORGAN, JOHN (1792?-1866), soldier, public servant and publicist, was born at Petersfield, near Portsmouth, England. He received a commission in the Royal Marines on 25 July 1812 and soon served in Spain. His battalion sailed to North America in May 1813, first fighting in the southern United States and thence moving to Canada. Morgan acquitted himself with distinction. At the war's end he returned to England and half-pay. He married and had at least one child, named, as was her mother, Rebecca. In 1823 Morgan wrote *The Emigrant's Note Book and Guide . . .* (London, 1824). Surveying the major British colonies, he urged Canada's advantages. Events thwarted his own plans to settle there; instead he became agent in south Wales for the Canada Land Co. This post he forsook late in 1828 on appointment as store-keeper in the original establishment at Swan River.

At Perth he became also magistrate, justice of the peace, and barracks master. He wrote many letters to R. W. Hay describing the colony's progress. Hay's influence with Viscount Goderich won Morgan an offer of the police magistracy at Richmond, Van Diemen's Land, and he assumed this post late in 1834. Because Morgan believed that his debts disqualified him from paid offices, and hoped to earn more outside the public service, he resigned within three years as magistrate and a commissioner of the Court of Requests. But his position worsened, the sale of his land grant at Swan River fell through, and the British Treasury declared that his accounts as store-keeper showed a deficit of £800. Morgan argued that this 'debt' arose from the confusion inevitable in a colony's early years. However just his claim, the £800 shadowed his life henceforth. He sought many government jobs without success and finally the Crown resumed his Swan River land in compensation.

On leaving his official post Morgan be-came first a farmer, then a journalist. He was foundation editor of the *Hobart Town Advertiser* (1839), worked briefly on the *Tasmanian*, then began the *Tasmanian Weekly Dispatch* (1839-41). Meanwhile he had become secretary of the Hobart Mechanics' Institute, and of the Licensed Victuallers' Society, in whose interest he edited the *Morning Advertiser* (1841) and issued two directories (1840, 1847). He launched, with little success, a commercial exchange and an immigration agency. In 1846-51 he edited the *Britannia and Trades' Advocate* and for the next two years was secretary of the Hobart School of Arts. Intermittently he acted as agent for whatever business might offer.

As journalist and man of affairs Morgan expounded liberal-cum-transcendental ideas with variety, force, and flair. An advocate of colonial self-government, he was the litigant in 1847 in a test case wherein the local judiciary declared a dog-tax illegal, thus embarrassing the executive. He urged thorough reform of the British legal system and of the treatment of criminals. Thus he opposed transportation and denounced conditions in local gaols as well as in hospitals and lunatic asylums. Belief in the power of education showed especially in his connexion with the School of Arts. Morgan was unique among Australian contemporaries in his abuse of what he regarded as imperialist filibustering by Britain in the Middle East, China, India and New Zealand. He upheld the idea of a 'Universal Church', which would establish a new ethic of 'practical humanity'. His encouragement of benefit societies expressed this attitude and so did his dislike of episcopacy in both Anglican and Roman churches. Morgan fostered Hobart's Orange Lodge from 1846, and encouraged the supporters of J. J. Therry [q.v.] in that priest's dispute with Bishop Willson [q.v.].

Agriculture and anthropology were other studies that illuminated his Western Australian letters and his whole life. Morgan collaborated with his subject to write *The Life and Adventures of William Buckley . . .* (Hobart, 1852), in which he described the Australian Aboriginals as 'generally treacherous, cowardly, and mere creatures holding the link in the chain of animal life between the man and the monkey'. Morgan died at the Hobart General Hospital on 22 April 1866, in his seventy-fourth year.

J. Morgan, *Memorial to the . . . Lords . . . of the Admiralty and the . . . Treasury, the humble memorial of John Morgan* (Hob, 1849).   MICHAEL ROE

MORGAN, MOLLY (1762-1835), convict and landowner, was baptized as Mary Jones on 31 January 1762 at Diddlebury, near Ludlow, Shropshire, England, the daughter of David Jones, ratcatcher and labourer, and his wife Margaret, née Powell. She became a dressmaker after a brief period of schooling. On 25 June 1785 she married William Morgan, a wheelwright and carpenter from the village of Hopesay. On 8 August 1789 she was tried at the Shrewsbury Assizes and sentenced to transportation for seven years for having stolen hempen yarn from a bleaching factory. She arrived at Botany Bay in the *Neptune* with the Second Fleet on 28 June 1790 and was sent to Parramatta. There she was joined by her husband and, after she gained a ticket-of-leave, they opened a small shop. On 9 November 1794 she escaped in the store-ship *Resolution* with thirteen other convicts whose sentences had not expired. During the next few years there was some conjecture in the colony as to what had become of Molly Morgan, but she was working as a dressmaker in Plymouth, where she bigamously married Thomas Mears, a brassfounder. In 1803 their home was burnt down, and Mears accused his 'wife' of the crime; Molly was tried at the Croydon Sessions on 10 October 1803, found guilty and once again was sentenced to transportation.

She arrived at Port Jackson for the second time on 24 June 1804 in the *Experiment*. She soon acquired a protector in Thomas Byrne and became virtually a free agent. Several years later she was given land near Parramatta and a few cattle, but in 1816 she was found to have branded government cattle as her own, and was sent to the Newcastle penal settlement.

In 1819 she was one of a small party of well-behaved convicts given tickets-of-leave by Governor Macquarie and sent to establish a settlement at Wallis Plains (Maitland), where they were given a few acres of land. Molly worked her land herself and in a small way became a successful farmer. Near the river she opened a wine shanty, which became increasingly profitable as the settlement grew and river navigation extended. On 5 March 1822 she married Thomas Hunt, a young soldier stationed at the garrison at Wallis Plains. In November 1823 Governor Brisbane, impressed by her efforts at farming and her general resourcefulness, allowed her the lease of 159 acres (converted to a grant in May 1830) and the help of a convict clearing gang. She bought 203 acres at Anvil Creek and built the Angel Inn in the centre of her lease, which occupied the nucleus of the town of Maitland.

By the mid-1820s Molly had become a wealthy woman. Through her personality, Wallis Plains became known as Molly Morgan's and the track from the settlement to Singleton as Molly Morgan's line of road. The *Australian*, 23 January 1828, named her as one of the largest landholders on the Hunter River. As the settlement at Wallis Plains grew she subdivided her lease and sold small blocks as a quick means of making money, though irregularities in the sales and transfers were later to cause countless legal difficulties. Her wealth rapidly decreased and at her death the only property remaining in her name was mortgaged. Her last years were spent in retirement at Anvil Creek where she died on 27 June 1835.

Molly Morgan, the ex-convict with a long record of petty crime, immorality and self-indulgence, was also a woman of generosity and compassion for those in unfortunate circumstances. In 1827 she gave £100 towards the building of a school by the Church Corporation, and many other acts of generosity to the settlers have been recorded. She conducted a rough-and-ready hospital for the sick and is reputed to have ridden to Sydney more than once to intercede with the governor on behalf of convicts sentenced to execution.

At a time when the majority of women remained in the background of colonial society, Molly Morgan stands out as a colourful and rather remarkable personality, a pioneer of the Maitland district and one who successfully established her farm, built up trading interests, and impressed Governors Macquarie and Brisbane with her resourcefulness and ability.

D. Collins, *An account of the English colony in New South Wales*, 2 (Lond, 1802); J. Jervis, 'Genesis of settlement at Wallis Plains and the Maitlands', *JRAHS*, 26 (1940); W. J. Goold, 'Molly Morgan', Newcastle and Hunter District Hist Soc, Procs, 1 (1947); *Newcastle Morning Herald*, 17 Aug 1929, 8 Aug 1936, 5 Sept 1947; *Daily Mirror*, 27 Dec 1956; MS cat under M. Morgan (ML).

ELIZABETH GUILFORD

MORIARTY, WILLIAM (1792-1850), was born on 6 July 1792 at Dingle, County Kerry, Ireland, the son of Vice-Admiral Sylverius Moriarty. At 11 he entered the Royal Naval Academy and at 15 became midshipman in the *Nymph*. He took part in the siege of Copenhagen, and served on the Home, North American, Baltic and Mediterranean Stations. He passed his examinations at 18, was confirmed lieutenant in October 1813 and promoted commander in November 1822 for gallantry in an expedition to the Persian Gulf. He was locally known as captain, although he never attained this rank. He married Aphra, the daughter of Dr Crump of Tralee, County Kerry; they had three sons and three daughters.

Moriarty, his wife and two children embarked for Van Diemen's Land in the *Letitia* which was wrecked at St Jago, Cape Verde Islands. They were picked up by an American ship which took them to Rio de Janeiro, whence in the *Anne* they reached Hobart Town in June 1829. Moriarty lost all his possessions in the wreck and appealed to Lieut-Governor Arthur, who allowed him a maximum grant of 2560 acres on account of his naval rank; in March 1831 he received an additional grant of 1000 acres adjoining his original property, Dunorlan. He was gazetted a justice of the peace on 24 February 1830.

In July 1832 Moriarty was appointed port officer, first at Launceston and then at Hobart, at £300 a year. During his first three years in office he started the survey of the Actaeon Reef in the D'Entrecasteaux Channel where there had been several recent wrecks. He retired before the survey was completed but was soon asked to resume the work, although in October 1836 he had become assistant police magistrate at Westbury. He was appointed a coroner for Van Diemen's Land in April 1837 and, on the resignation of Captain King, resumed duty as port officer of Hobart at a salary of £500. In June 1841 the Legislative Council awarded him a gratuity of £1280 for his useful services as port officer and for his generous assistance to distressed passengers and crews.

In the Deloraine district Moriarty owned 4160 acres by grant and 2570 by purchase. In 1843, after trying to sell his Dunorlan estate, he leased it in small farms; three years later it was again put up for auction and bought by Henry Reed [q.v.].

Moriarty was a prime mover in forming the Merchant Seamen's Institution and a founder of the Hobart Town Infant School of which he was president for many years. He was also an active member of the Church of England. He died in office on 26 March 1850 and was buried in St George's cemetery, where a tablet was erected in his memory by the mercantile community of Hobart.

Next year his wife sailed with two daughters in the *Wellington* to England where she died in 1871, aged 70. A son,

Sylverius, first practised as a lawyer in Tasmania but later inherited an estate in Ireland, whither he went in 1877 and assumed by royal licence the surname Crump. Another son, William, became a commander in the navy. Captain Moriarty's sister Ellen, who died on 4 October 1849, lived for many years on her property Frogmore at Latrobe and was the first settler in that district. She was well known for her amiability of disposition and demeanour and for her kindness and charity to the poor; her name is preserved in the near-by township of Moriarty. Commander Merion Marshall Moriarty, R.N., a brother, was port officer of Sydney from 1842 until his death in 1847.

W. R. O'Byrne, *A naval biographical dictionary* (Lond, 1849); Correspondence file under Moriarty (TA).   JILL T. HANSEN

MORISSET, JAMES THOMAS (1780?-1852), military commandant, entered the army as an ensign in the 80th Regiment in February 1798. He became a lieutenant in November 1800, saw service in Egypt and India, and in December 1805 purchased a captaincy in the 48th Regiment. He fought in the Peninsular war and was wounded at Albuera. In 1817 he accompanied his regiment to New South Wales, and was promoted major in August 1819. On 24 December 1818 he had been appointed to relieve Captain Wallis [q.v.] as commandant at Newcastle, and made a magistrate. While at Newcastle he earned praise for his continuation of Wallis's work by improving the breakwater and building roads and barracks. In 1821 Governor Macquarie visited Newcastle, admired Morisset's work and named Morisset's Lagoon in his honour. Commissioner Bigge [q.v.] praised Morisset's attention to the prisoners, his attempt to adapt punishments to individual convicts, his superintendence of public works and his attention to their durability rather than their ornamentation. In November 1823 he was appointed commandant at Bathurst to relieve William Lawson [q.v.], and was commended by Governor Brisbane for restoring order after clashes with the natives had led to martial law being declared west of Mount York in 1824. He was relieved in January 1825 and next month returned to England on leave.

While in England Morisset reported to the Colonial Office on convict control in New South Wales and applied for the post of commandant at Norfolk Island which was about to be re-established as a penal settlement. Bathurst recommended Morisset to Governor Darling for the position, unless he preferred to retain Morisset in Sydney as superintendent of police. But Morisset remained in England and in August 1826 Bathurst told Darling that since Captain Rossi [q.v.] had been appointed superintendent of police, Morisset was to be made commandant of Norfolk Island at a salary of £600. He was promoted lieut-colonel on 19 December 1826 and placed on army half-pay.

On 2 May 1826 at New Church, Ryde, Isle of Wight, Morisset married Emily, the daughter of John and Louisa Vaux of Ryde. He arrived in Sydney in the *Harmony* in September 1827 with his wife and child. Darling objected to a married man being stationed at Norfolk Island and felt that Morisset's salary would cause jealousy among the other commandants who were not so highly paid; he argued that Morisset would be more advantageously employed as inspector of penal settlements and until some better arrangement could be made appointed him to act as superintendent of police in place of Rossi, whom he had made collector of customs. Morisset bitterly resented this arrangement, but the Colonial Office did not confirm Rossi's customs appointment, so Darling was forced to reinstate him as superintendent of police, and in February 1829 to appoint Morisset commandant of Norfolk Island, as originally planned.

He arrived there on 26 May, but the appointment did not come up to his expectations. He was dogged by ill health. He was refused a grant of 2560 acres, and the British government refused his claim for military allowances in addition to his salary. During his tenure on Norfolk Island the convicts made several attempts at mutiny, and Morisset later acquired a reputation for being a stern disciplinarian. He recommended importing a treadmill to Norfolk Island, but the British government objected on grounds of expense; this was a normal form of punishment at the time and Morisset does not appear to have been considered unnecessarily harsh by his contemporaries. Both Macquarie and Bigge approved his methods, as did later governors, and the *Sydney Gazette*, 28 November 1827, praised him for being upright and conscientious, and not frightened by daring offenders, while ironically lauding him as an opponent of capital punishment.

In August 1831 Morisset asked for a civil position in the colony, but no office was available. Early in 1834 he sold his commission in the army, declared his intention to resign and settle in New South Wales, and again sought appointment to any available civil office. Because of a violent nervous disorder he was given a year's leave in Sydney on half-pay.

When his leave expired he resigned his post and bought a farm at Winburndale Brook near Bathurst. There in May 1838 he was appointed police magistrate at a salary of £300, and in January 1841 commissioner of the Court of Requests. He lost heavily in the Bank of Australia's crash in 1842 and was forced to sell his property and devote part of his salary to paying off his debts. On 28 August 1841 the *Australian* described him as too ill and advanced in years to conduct the Bathurst bench properly, yet he continued in his post until his death on 17 August 1852, aged 72. He was buried in the old Kelso churchyard. Emily Morisset died at North Sydney on 7 March 1892, aged 89, and was buried at St Thomas's. They had four sons and six daughters, and in 1825 Morisset also had a son by Joanna Deasey. One son, Edric Norfolk Vaux Morisset, became commandant of native police in Queensland and superintendent of police at Bathurst, Maitland and Goulburn.

HRA (1), 10-17, 19; B. W. Champion, 'James T. Morisset', JRAHS, 20 (1934); *National Advocate* (Bathurst), 29 Jan 1929; MS cat under J. Morisset (ML); Newspaper indexes under Morisset (ML).

VIVIENNE PARSONS

MORPHETT, SIR JOHN (1809-1892), landowner and politician, was born on 4 May 1809 in London, a son of Nathaniel Morphett and Mary, née Gliddon, of Cummins, Ide, Devon. His father came from a Kentish family and was a London solicitor. After leaving school at 16 Morphett joined a London commercial office and at 21 entered the counting-house of Harris & Co., in Alexandria, Egypt.

Morphett returned to London in 1834 with his younger brother George and, through Dr Wright [q.v.], became interested in the South Australian Association, then pressing for the establishment of a colony in southern Australia, on the principles of systematic colonization advocated by E. G. Wakefield [q.v.]. On the passing of the South Australian Act (4 & 5 Wm IV, c. 95), Morphett issued a four-page circular, *Reasons for the Purchase of Land in South Australia, by Persons Resident in Britain; with a view to the removal of Labourers, and the profitable employment of Capital.* In this pamphlet he declared his intention of migrating and his readiness to act for purchasers of land. He also advertised in similar terms in the *Globe and Traveller*, 30 July 1835. In September 1834 he joined the South Australian Literary Association, and was soon elected to its committee. By 1835 he was one of the most energetic advocates of the new province.

Morphett sailed in the *Cygnet* and arrived in South Australia in September 1836. Two months later with Lieutenant Field and G. S. Kingston [q.v.], he discovered the River Torrens. He considered Kangaroo Island unsuitable for permanent settlement but reported favourably on the mainland after two visits, his letter being published in London in pamphlet form. At the crucial meeting on 10 February 1837 Morphett's votes were decisive in confirming the site of Adelaide. In July 1837 in support of the resident commissioner, J. H Fisher [q.v.], against Governor Hindmarsh, he joined the committee which established the *Southern Australian* and his report on these matters was published next year in London. Hindmarsh later complained that Morphett was largely responsible for his recall. In 1839 Morphett had a part in selecting six special surveys, mostly for his English friends and for the Secondary Towns Association. With his Mediterranean experience he believed that wool-growing was more suited than agriculture to South Australia, but he also knew that the colony needed men of capital. He threw his weight behind every good cause; in 1840 he became treasurer of Adelaide's Municipal Corporation, helped to found the Agricultural Society in 1844, gave support to the Collegiate School of St Peter and acted as attorney for the Society for Propagating the Gospel in foreign parts. He became a local director of the South Australian Banking Co., and served on the committee of the English Railway Co. His office on North Terrace was thronged by men seeking level-headed advice on land and commerce and he was a popular chairman at public meetings.

Morphett's political career was long and distinguished. In 1843 he became one of the first non-official nominees in the Legislative Council. In 1846 he was one of four who walked out in protest against the mining royalty proposals, but later he proposed the bill for state aid to religion. Next year he visited England, returning in time to oppose Earl Grey's federal plans and local moves for vote by ballot. When the Legislative Council was reformed he was again nominated and in August 1851 he was elected Speaker. In the first elec-

tions under responsible government in March 1857 he won a place in the Legislative Council. In 1861 he was chief secretary in the two short Reynolds' ministries, resigning because he was unable to support the moves to dismiss Judge Boothby. In 1865 he became president of the Legislative Council, and retained the post until his retirement from politics in 1873.

On 15 August 1838 Morphett married Elizabeth, the eldest daughter of J. H. Fisher. He was knighted in 1870, and died at his house, Cummins, Morphettville, on 7 November 1892, survived by six daughters and four sons. Portraits include a crayon drawing by Samuel Laurence in the possession of H. C. Morphett, Adelaide. As a prominent founder, his name figures large in South Australia's toponymy.

G. C. Morphett (comp), *The life and letters of Sir John Morphett* (Adel, 1936); A. Young, 'Thornton Leigh Hunt (1810-73) and the colonisation of South Australia', PRGSSA, 59 (1957-58).

MORRILL (MURRILLS), JAMES (1824-1865), sailor, came from Essex, England. He went to sea at an early age, and was carpenter's mate in the *Peruvian* when she left Sydney for China on 27 February 1846. In a cyclonic gale the barque was wrecked on Horseshoe Reef off the Great Barrier Reef. Twenty-two survivors took to the jolly-boat, on which they drifted for twenty-two days, often coming within sight of land but each time being driven off by contrary winds and tides. Morrill, an active and robust young man, did all he could to preserve the castaways by catching fish and even sharks, which were eaten raw, but despite such efforts only five people eventually survived the landing near Cape Bowling Green.

Of these, Miller, the shipwright, vanished in an attempt to bring rescue by paddling to civilization in an Aboriginal bark canoe found on the beach. An apprentice boy, White, succumbed to privations not long after the party was discovered by Aboriginals. This left the master of the *Peruvian*, Captain Pitkethley, his wife and Morrill; they were adopted into tribes of wandering Aboriginals, to whose habits of life they soon conformed completely. The Pitkethleys joined a tribe around Cape Cleveland but were both dead within two years. Morrill lived for seventeen years with a neighbouring tribe, centred on Mount Elliott and ranging between the Black and Burdekin Rivers. He was fairly well treated and adjusted himself well, but found his superior craftsmanship was useless as the Aboriginals took from him any tools or artifacts which he made himself.

With the opening of North Queensland for pastoral settlement in 1861 Morrill's isolation was at an end. News of the interlopers was followed by one or two unpromising contacts. A white horseman who murdered a native who was mourning his father was himself speared. But Morrill's wish to join his own people remained strong; his opportunity came on 25 January 1863 when he and a party of Aboriginals hunting for kangaroo came to an outstation of a sheep property. Overcoming great shyness, Morrill left his companions, washed himself as clean as he could and revealed himself to two astonished station hands with a cry of: 'Don't shoot, mates, I'm a British object!' He was recognized as a white, and his tribe reluctantly parted with him.

Lionized in Brisbane, he was presented at Government House, but does not seem greatly to have interested Governor Bowen. Appointed to the Department of Customs at Bowen, Morrill returned to North Queensland, where his knowledge and experience of the Aboriginals made him much in demand as interpreter and go-between and often promoted peaceful conciliation. His knowledge of the country and its seasonal variations was often consulted by squatters and explorers. In January 1864 he accompanied G. E. Dalrymple on the expedition to open the port of Cardwell, and in April 1865 he was in charge of the *Ariel* bringing the first cargo of bonded goods to the settlement on Cleveland Bay which later became Townsville. But his privations during his years of wandering had weakened his health, and on 30 October 1865 he died at Bowen. Aboriginals for many miles around came into town for a memorable mourning ceremony.

Morrill was married in 1864 to Eliza Ann Ross, a domestic servant employed by the police magistrate at Bowen. She remarried after his death, and died at Charters Towers about 1923. They had one son, whose descendants, in 1966, were still living in the Burdekin Delta district of North Queensland.

E. Gregory (ed), *Sketch of the residence of James Morrill among the Aboriginals of northern Queensland for seventeen years* (Brisb, 1866); M. A. H. Clarke, *Old tales of a young country* (Melb, 1871); F. Reid, *The romance of the Great Barrier Reef* (Syd, 1954); D. Jones, *Cardwell shire story* (Brisb, 1961); Bowen Hist Soc, *The story of James Morrill* (Bowen, 1964); *Port Denison Times*, 26 Mar, 2 Apr 1864, 1 Nov 1865.   G. C. BOLTON

MOSMAN, ARCHIBALD (1799-1863), merchant and pastoralist, was born on 15 October 1799, the elder of twin sons of Hugh Mosman, of Auchtyfardle, near Lesmahagow, Lanarkshire, Scotland, and his wife Agnes, née Kennedy. His father was convener of the County of Lanark and his eldest brother. Hugh, became deputy-lieutenant of Lanark. Archibald and his twin brother George, after spending some time growing sugar in the West Indies, arrived in Sydney in the *Civilian* on 24 August 1828. The ship appears to have been under charter to them; they brought with them their own clerk, W. Scott, and a recommendation to the governor from the Colonial Office. They at once launched into business. A warehouse was first established in George Street and in 1831 a small grant was obtained on the foreshore of Great Sirius Cove.

The sequence of events in Archibald Mosman's business career is certain but the dates are indefinite. Until 1832 the George Street warehouse was maintained doubtless to support general trade of the kind suggested by an announcement in the *Sydney Gazette*, 15 January 1829, that Messrs Mosman were agents for the *Mary* sailing to 'Liverpool direct' and that they would 'either purchase or make an advance on wool [in cash] consigned to their House in Liverpool'; perhaps connexions with Liverpool had been established during the years in the West Indies. The partnership between the brothers was dissolved in July 1829 but whether this was more than a business manoeuvre is uncertain. In practice the firm seems still to have been referred to as Messrs Mosman. In July 1832 the George Street warehouse was offered for sale and about that time Mosman built The Nest at Sirius Cove.

The brothers, like many Sydney merchants of the late 1820s, were interested in whaling, and Archibald planned to make Sirius Cove a centre for the industry. He bought out his competitor, John Bell, who had also been granted land at the cove for a whaling depot, and eventually extended his original grant to include a large part of the suburb which was given his name. In 1835 two whalers, the *Jane*, 221 tons, and the *Tigress*, 192 tons, were registered as belonging to the firm of Mosman; and in that year another vessel was bought by them, apparently for trade with New Zealand. The profits from whaling and from the berthing, careening and refitting facilities at Mosman's Bay appear to have been considerable; and in 1838 by arrangement, the precise nature of which is uncertain, Mosman's interests at Sirius Cove were taken over by Messrs

Hughes & Hosking [q.v.] in return for a fixed sum to be paid to Mosman annually. By August 1844, however, Mosman and Hughes & Hosking were bankrupt. Mosman lost not only his annuity but the whaling establishment as well. His other more speculative Sydney interests, the Floating Bridge Co., the Sydney Ferry Co. and the Australian Auction Co., seem all to have been abandoned; and it was probably soon after this that he acquired Furracabad station near Glen Innes. In the widely scattered information on Mosman little more can be found about his career. Presumably the initial cost of Furracabad was purely nominal and with the development of Glen Innes Mosman appears to have prospered sufficiently to remove eventually to Byron Lodge, Randwick, where he died on 29 January 1863.

He had married on 31 December 1847 Harriet Farquharson, who died on 24 August 1883. There appear to have been eleven children of the marriage, ten of whom survived. The eldest daughter married Sir Arthur Palmer and another married Sir Thomas McIlwraith. The eldest son, Hugh Mosman, was conspicuous in the development of the Charters Towers district, Queensland.

E. C. Sommerlad, *Land of the Beardies* (Glen Innes, 1922); E. A. Archer, 'Mosman's Bay', *JRAHS*, 2 (1906-09); J. H. Watson, Mosman newscuttings, MS, photographs (ML).

M. D. STEPHEN

MOUNTGARRETT, JACOB (1773?-1828), colonial surgeon, was probably the son of Rev. John Mountgarrett, curate of Drumbanagher, near Killeavy, County Armagh, Ireland. He was admitted as a member of the Company of Surgeons, London, on 17 May 1798, and thus qualified as a naval surgeon third rate, for he had been in the navy since 1790, and had seen service in the Mediterranean and at Cape St Vincent. After being paid off in 1802, he joined H.M.S. *Glatton* carrying convicts to New South Wales, as surgeon. He arrived in March 1803 and was immediately appointed surgeon to the new settlement proposed at the Derwent. He sailed with Lieutenant Bowen [q.v.] but when Lieut-Governor Collins arrived next February he told Mountgarrett that his medical staff was complete and gave him the opportunity to return to Sydney. Mountgarrett refused and asked that he should be considered a settler. He was the first to harvest wheat in the colony.

In August 1804 he was appointed surgeon to the new settlement about to be founded at Port Dalrymple by Lieut-Colonel Paterson [q.v.] and sailed with Paterson's party from Sydney in November. With Ensign Piper he undertook the early exploration of the country to the north-west of Port Dalrymple, and received a grant of 600 acres in Norfolk Plains on the South Esk River, for services which Paterson praised highly. He accompanied Governor Macquarie around the Port Dalrymple area in December 1811, and the governor and his wife visited his farm, seventeen miles from Launceston. But after the departure of Paterson and the death of Collins conditions throughout the island deteriorated and Mountgarrett became associated with many doubtful activities. He was accused of assisting Peter Mills [q.v.], surveyor and harbour-master, in his bushranging activities, and in 1815 was sent to Sydney for trial. He was acquitted but while in Sydney he had to have his arm amputated and sought permission to retire on a pension. When the pension was refused Mountgarrett returned to duty in December 1817, while Macquarie repeated his request for it to the Colonial Office. Next year it was approved, but by then Macquarie was unwilling to grant it and in September he recommended that Mountgarrett be dismissed. The surgeon was naturally handicapped by the loss of his arm, but Lieut-Governor Sorell had constantly complained of his neglect of duty. He was notorious as a bad debtor and was suspected of cattle stealing and misappropriating the stores and medicines for which he was responsible. Finally in 1821 he was succeeded as surgeon at Port Dalrymple by Robert Espie and was placed on half-pay. He died insolvent on 27 January 1828 and was buried in the old Church of England burial ground, Launceston. In 1811 he had married Bridget Edwards who was left destitute and died in April 1829.

HRA (1), 4-10, (3), 1-4; W. E. L. Crowther 'Mr Jacob Mountgarret', *JRAHS*, 34 (1948); Correspondence file under Mountgarrett (TA); MS cat under J. Mountgarret (ML).

ISABELLA J. MEAD

MUDIE, JAMES (1779-1852), officer of marines, landowner and author, was the son of John and Margaret Mudie of Forfarshire (Angus), Scotland. In May 1799 he was appointed second lieutenant in the 69th company of marines at Portsmouth and in 1800-02 served on St Marcouf Island in the English Channel, and in H.M.S. *Leda* in 1803-04. In 1805 he was promoted first lieutenant and ordered on recruiting service to Scotland, where he soon found himself in trouble over his accounts and was placed on half-pay. He returned to active service in July 1808 and joined the *Inflexible*, bound for Halifax, North America. By permission he exchanged with an officer in the *Samson*, which after some months returned to England. During his service he suffered periods of ill health which may have prevented further promotion. In 1809 he was ordered by the Admiralty to answer charges made against him in an anonymous letter to that office from Scotland. At first he denied the charges but finally had to admit they were true, and despite his many appeals was dismissed from the marines in August 1810.

Unemployed and short of money Mudie induced a bookselling firm to join him in a venture making commemorative medals of events and heroes in the Napoleonic wars; his engravings were included in *An Historical and Critical Account of a Grand Series of National Medals* (London, 1820). Through lack of support from the promised subscribers some £10,000 was lost in these ambitious schemes, and Mudie and the bookselling firm were forced into insolvency. Through the benevolence of Sir Charles Forbes and the Colonial Office Mudie, his three daughters and a stepdaughter were given free passages to New South Wales. They arrived at Sydney in July 1822. Mudie had an order for a land grant and was given 2150 acres on the Hunter River, which he named Castle Forbes after his patron. He also began a ladies' school at Parramatta; when it failed to win support he moved with his family to Castle Forbes.

Mudie acquired 2000 adjoining acres in 1825 and, with the assistance of many assigned convicts and his overseer, John Larnach [q.v.], who became his son-in-law and partner, Castle Forbes was turned into one of the finest agricultural establishments in the colony, producing substantial quantities of wool, meat and wheat. Mudie also boasted that his homestead was a fortress guarded by Newfoundland dogs and that his servants were severely disciplined under exacting rules. About 1830 he was appointed a justice of the peace by Governor Darling and served on the bench at Maitland, where he became greatly feared by convicts because of his excessive use of flogging for even minor offences. Mudie later claimed that he introduced this harsh policy to counter the lenient policy of Governor Bourke, who after his arrival in December 1831 took steps to reduce the magistrates' powers to inflict summary punishments. According to the *Sydney Herald*, Bourke's 'soothing system for con-

victs' was responsible for a great increase in crime. Mudie and a few other magistrates on the Hunter River shared this belief and secretly began to collect signatures for what their opponents later called the 'Hole and Corner Petition', copies of which, according to Bourke in September 1834, were sent to England 'for circulation in quarters where it is hoped an impression unfavourable to my Government may be produced'. Later that year the gross misstatements and inhuman attitudes of the petitioners were denounced in a pamphlet by 'An Unpaid Magistrate', thought to be Roger Therry [q.v.].

Meanwhile in November 1833 six convict servants at Castle Forbes had mutinied in Mudie's absence, robbed the stores and taken to the bush. An attempt to shoot Larnach failed and he escaped. The mutineers were arrested and remanded to Sydney, where they were found guilty; three were executed in Sydney and two at Castle Forbes; one was sent to Norfolk Island. Bourke appointed J. H. Plunkett and Frederick Hely [qq.v.] to investigate charges made at the trial against Mudie and Larnach for degrading treatment of their assigned servants. At the inquiry Mudie and Larnach were exonerated of ill treatment but criticized for the quality and quantity of the rations they supplied to convicts. Angered by the report the two men prepared a joint protest and asked Bourke to send it to London. The governor refused because of its improper form, so in September 1834 with help from E. S. Hall [q.v.], of the *Monitor*, they printed *Vindication of James Mudie and John Larnach, from certain reflections . . . relative to the treatment by them of their Convict Servants*. This pamphlet they sent direct to the Colonial Office. At the same time William Watt, a ticket-of-leave convict employed as a sub-editor in the *Sydney Gazette*, attacked Mudie for his cruelty to convicts in a pamphlet *Party Politics exposed*, signed by 'Humanitas'. Mudie in turn charged Watt with serious misdemeanours, and also attacked Roger Therry for defending the mutineers at their trial and Bourke for showing favouritism to convicts. Ineffectual in these tactics Mudie found revenge by inducing the colonial treasurer, C. D. Riddell [q.v.], to stand against the governor's nominee, Therry, for election to the chairmanship of the Quarter Sessions. Riddell's victory by one vote, later shown to be irregular, was upheld by the Colonial Office. Bourke regarded this ruling as a personal affront and decided to confirm the resignation he had already submitted.

In 1836 Mudie was not reappointed to

the Commission of the Peace; disgusted with colonial affairs, he sold Castle Forbes for £7000 and in March sailed for England determined on vengeance. In London in 1837 he published *The Felonry of New South Wales*, an attack on all whom he fancied had opposed him in the colony. He also appeared before the select committee on transportation; though much of his evidence was removed from the report, enough remains to reveal his distorted mind.

In 1840 Mudie returned to Sydney, where he found himself no longer welcome, for his vindictive comments had lost him old friends. John Kinchela, son of the judge who had been maligned in the book, publicly horsewhipped Mudie in Sydney, and when he was found guilty of assault the fine of £50 was promptly paid by a subscription in the court. In 1842 Mudie returned to London, where he lived until his death on 21 May 1852 at Tottenham.

His book, edited by Walter Stone, was republished in Melbourne in 1964.

HRA (1), 11, 16-18, 20, 21; P. Cunningham, *Two years in New South Wales*, 3rd ed (Lond, 1828); J. West, *The history of Tasmania*, 1-2 (Launceston, 1852); R. J. Flanagan, *The history of New South Wales*, 1 (Lond, 1862); R. Therry, *Reminiscences of thirty years' residence in New South Wales and Victoria* (Lond, 1863); *Sydney Gazette*, 9, 10 Dec 1833; *SMH*, 26 May 1875; *Australian*, index under Mudie (ML); MS cat under Mudie (ML); Col Sec in letters (NSWA); CO 201/113.   BERNARD T. DOWD
                                   AVERIL F. FINK

MUIR, THOMAS (1765-1799), lawyer and political reformer, was born on 24 August 1765 in Scotland, the only son of Thomas Muir, a prosperous Glasgow merchant. Educated at the local grammar school, he entered the University of Glasgow at the early age of 12. At first intended for the church, he came under the influence of the liberal-minded John Millar (1735-1801), a professor of law who collected into his circle the keener young men of his school. Muir entered warmly into college politics and showed a bent for satiric verse, often at the expense of the faculties. After graduating at Glasgow (M.A., 1782), he completed his studies at the University of Edinburgh and was admitted a member of the Faculty of Advocates in 1787. Although soon recognized as a fluent and eloquent speaker, his talent as a lawyer was not considered remarkable.

Radical opinion was then greatly influenced by the French Revolution, and Muir soon identified himself with the advocates of parliamentary and constitutional reform. In October 1792 he was elected vice-president of the newly formed Glasgow Associated Friends of the Constitution and of the People. In December 1792 a general convention of the Scottish Societies of the Friends of the People was held in Edinburgh at which Muir read an inflammatory address from the United Irishmen of Dublin. This action, together with evidence that he had distributed an allegedly seditious pamphlet by Thomas Paine resulted in his arrest in January 1793. Released on bail, he went to Paris with the quixotic but futile idea of interceding for the life of Louis XVI who was then awaiting execution; when he failed to return to Edinburgh for trial he was declared an outlaw and struck from the roll of advocates.

Muir obtained a French passport and decided to take refuge in the United States, but touching at Belfast on the way he rashly crossed to Scotland to make a clandestine visit to family and friends. Soon after landing at Portpatrick he was arrested, and brought to trial at Edinburgh on 23 August 1793. There, before a biased jury and the fearsome Lord Justice Braxfield, he was found guilty of sedition and sentenced to fourteen years transportation. The severity of this sentence evoked consternation both in Edinburgh and London where influential Whigs interceded on his behalf; but the Home Secretary, Henry Dundas, was adamant that an example be shown, and Muir, together with his fellow reformers, T. F. Palmer, Skirving and Margarot [qq.v.] sailed in the transport *Surprize* for New South Wales. This group, with Joseph Gerrald [q.v.], who was transported later, became known as the Scottish Martyrs.

Muir arrived in Sydney in October 1794. As a political prisoner he was freed from the usual convict restraint. He lived on a small farm he had bought across the harbour from Sydney Cove where he occupied himself with rural pursuits and prepared documents in exculpation of himself and fellow exiles.

Early in 1796 the American ship *Otter*, Captain Ebenezer Dorr, called at Sydney for refreshments while on a fur-trading voyage to the north-west coast of America. Urged by his companions Muir planned his escape with Dorr. On the night of 17 February he made his way out of the harbour in a small boat with two servants and was picked up by the *Otter* some miles off the coast. There is no evidence to support statements that President Washington arranged Muir's escape from the colony. After crossing the Pacific and reaching Nootka Sound, he learned that H.M.S. *Providence* was then in those waters. Fearing recapture, he transferred to the Spanish gunboat *Sutil* and in June 1796 reached Monterey, Spanish California, where he was hospitably received by the governor. Thence he wrote to Washington, Dr Joseph Priestley and others describing his escape and outlining his intentions of making his way to the United States. These letters were intercepted and are now in the Archives of the Indies, Seville.

Under the covert surveillance of the Spanish authorities he was allowed to go by sea to San Blas and thence by land to Mexico City and Vera Cruz. In November 1796 he reached Havana, but owing to the outbreak of war between England and Spain he was imprisoned there for four months and his original intention of reaching Philadelphia was frustrated. He was placed on board the frigate *Ninfa* sailing for Spain, but close to her destination she was intercepted by a British squadron under Sir John Jervis. In the subsequent engagement Muir was severely wounded in the face and lost his left eye, and though the British learnt he was on board they failed to recognize him because of his mutilation. He was sent ashore with the Spanish wounded to the hospital at Cadiz, whence news of his plight reached Paris; after some months he was released through the intercession of Talleyrand, the French foreign minister, and in December 1797 reached Paris. Here he was for a time a guest of the Directory and was consulted on proposals for an invasion of England, while the circumstances of his exile, wounds and disfigurement centred much public attention upon him. In two quarto volumes he prepared a manuscript, since lost, describing his exile and travels, and offered it to the French government as security for a small estate to which he could retire and recruit his shattered health. For months his petition remained unheeded; neglected by friends, pursued by poverty and enfeebled by his wounds, he drifted into obscurity. He died at Chantilly, near Paris, on 26 January 1799. His burial place is unknown.

HRNSW, 2; HRA (1), 1; *An account of the trial of Thomas Muir* (Edinb, 1793); *Histoire de la tyrannie du gouvernement anglais exercée envers le célèbre Thomas Muir, écossais* (Paris, 1798); F. Péron, *Mémoires du Capitaine Péron*, 1-2 (Paris, 1824); P. Mackenzie, *Life of Thomas Muir* (Glasgow, 1831); A. Savine, *Les débuts de Botany Bay* (Paris, 1911); J. W. Meikle, *Scotland and the French revolution* (Glasgow, 1912); J. Earnshaw, *Thomas Muir, Scottish martyr* (Syd, 1959); H. W. Meikle, 'Two Glasgow merchants in the French revolution', *Scottish Hist Review*, 8 (1911); M. Masson and J. F. Jameson, 'The Odyssey of Thomas Muir', *American Hist Review*, 29 (1923); H. W. Meikle, 'The death of Thomas Muir', *Scottish Hist Review*, 27 (1948); J. G. Lockhart, 'A skeleton in the cupboard', *Blackwood's Mag*, July 1950; MS cat under T. Muir (ML).

JOHN EARNSHAW

MULGRAVE, PETER ARCHER (1778?-1847), public servant, was superintendent of telegraphs in the Channel Islands in 1809-15 and had been wounded in action with a French privateer in 1810. In 1815 he resigned on a pension, but sought a position in the colonies. In 1820 he attended the Central School in London for instruction in the 'national' system of education which, founded by Dr Bell, was then much in vogue and, in the opinion of Lord Bathurst, was 'best adapted not only for securing to the rising generation . . . the Advantages of all necessary Instruction, but also in bringing them up in Habits of Industry and Regularity, and for implanting in their Minds the Principles of the Established Church'. In November Mulgrave was appointed superintendent of schools in Van Diemen's Land, soon after a complementary appointment had been made to Rev. Thomas Reddall [q.v.] in New South Wales. Mulgrave arrived at Hobart Town in June 1821, and in December reported to Lieut-Governor Sorell on the state of education in Van Diemen's Land, which he thought had been laid well enough to sustain the superstructure of the Bell system. In 1822 it was announced that a government school would open at the eastern end of Liverpool Street, Hobart, next to Mulgrave's premises; later that year he was made a magistrate, coroner and superintendent of police at Port Dalrymple; he also acted as superintendent of schools at Launceston, dividing the duties over the colony with Rev. William Bedford [q.v.] in a similar post at Hobart. In 1824 Mulgrave was appointed superintendent of police at Launceston. Next year he resigned as superintendent of schools and exchanged his land grant at Brighton Plains for one in Launceston. He earned high praise from Lieut-Governor Arthur for his work and in 1829 was appointed chief police magistrate. In December 1831 he returned to the north as chairman of Quarter Sessions and commissioner of the Court of Requests at Launceston, and held these positions until 1844.

Mulgrave had been the northern treasurer of the body formed to donate a present of plate to Sorell when he left the colony, and he joined with many others in urging the British authorities to separate the governments of New South Wales and Van Diemen's Land. He was one of the original directors of the Derwent Bank and was a director of the Cornwall Bank. He died in Launceston on 8 March 1847 'literally worn out in the Public Service'.

HRA (1), 10, (3), 4, 5; Hobart Town Gazette, 20 Apr 1822; Sydney Gazette, 28 Mar 1828; Australian, 16 Apr 1828, 30 Sept 1829, 30 Aug 1830, 13 Jan 1832; Examiner (Launceston), 8, 10 Mar 1847; CSO 1/110/2724, 1/348/7956, 1/885/18777, 5/174/4143; GO 33/47/690, 33/50/236 (TA).   L. L. ROBSON

MUNDY, GODFREY CHARLES (1804?-1860), soldier and author, was the eldest son of Major-General Godfrey Basil Mundy and Sarah Brydges, née Rodney, daughter of the first baron Rodney (1718-1792) who defeated the French Fleet under Comte de Grasse off Dominica in 1782.

Mundy entered the army as an ensign in 1821, was commissioned lieutenant in 1823, captain 1826, major 1839, lieut-colonel 1845, and colonel 1854. In 1825-26 he was decorated while serving in India as aide-de-camp to Lord Combermere at the siege and storming of Bhurtpore. He was later stationed in Canada and arrived in Sydney from London in the Agincourt in June 1846 as deputy-adjutant-general of the military forces in Australia. He left in August 1851 and during the Crimean war was appointed under-secretary in the War Office. On 4 April 1857 he was appointed lieut-governor of Jersey in the Channel Islands with the local rank of major-general. He died in London on 10 July 1860.

In 1832 Mundy published Pen and Pencil Sketches, being the Journal of a tour in India, and in 1852 Our Antipodes: or, Residence and Rambles in the Australasian Colonies. With a glimpse of the gold fields. He illustrated Our Antipodes with landscapes and lively scenes engraved from his own sketches. The first book went through three editions and the second four, not counting translations in German (1856) and Swedish (1857).

In Australia Mundy accompanied Governor FitzRoy, on several outback tours in New South Wales, and he visited Victoria, Van Diemen's Land and New Zealand. Aristocratic by birth and conventional in temper, he showed in his books a discerning eye, a lively pen, a keen sense of humour and a marked streak of sturdy common sense. Our Antipodes still makes entertaining reading and is an invaluable source of information for the Australian social historian. To read the book is to like the author.

JRAHS, 9 (1923), 163.   RUSSEL WARD
                                           KEN MACNAB

MURDOCH, JAMES (1785-1848), physician and farmer, was born on 14 July 1785 the son of John Murdoch of Craigow, Kinross-shire, Scotland, and his wife Mary, née Robertson. He studied medicine at Edinburgh and was appointed lecturer on midwifery and physician accoucheur to the Edinburgh New Town Dispensary. In November 1813 he married Grace, only daughter of James Beveridge, of Easter Balado, Kinross-shire. With his wife and son John he left for Van Diemen's Land in the Castle Forbes, arriving at Hobart Town on 1 March 1822. As an obstetrician and children's doctor he began a practice in Liverpool Street. In June he offered a course of instruction to midwives, and advertised his free attendance on the poor. He received a grant of 800 acres of land at Cambridge which he named Craigow. By 1829 he was living there and had bought a farm at Risdon where he established a medicinal garden and chemical still, reporting to the Royal College of Physicians, Edinburgh, of which he was a fellow, on the results of medicinal herb-growing in Van Diemen's Land. His cultivation of opium and aniseed and the production of sugar from beetroot were very successful. He had also made perfumes from the products of his Risdon garden.

His scientific interests were turned to further advantage in the extraction of salt from tidal pans at Pittwater on his Craigow property and in the mineralogical surveys of settlers' land on which he offered advice on the most advantageous method of cropping the soils and on the quality of coal, lime and metallic ore deposits found. In 1825 he had official encouragement in the analysis of the salt in the pans at Salt Pan Plains near Ross. Tenders were subsequently called for their lease.

Although reputedly convivial, he was highly respected for his medical skill throughout a widely scattered country practice on the east of the River Derwent. He died suddenly on 22 April 1848, his wife having predeceased him in 1841.

They had reared six sons and two daughters, of whom the most distinguished was John (1814-1878), who in 1840 established a corn-chandling business in Hobart and in 1858-64 served the city as an alderman. James Murdoch of Craigow (1852-

1925), more than twenty years member of the Legislative Council and warden of the Clarence municipality, was the eldest of John's seven sons and three daughters. Others of note were John Hugh Germain (1859-1923), merchant, director of the Australian Mutual Provident Society and member of the Chamber of Commerce; Peter (1865-1948), member of the House of Assembly, 1922; George (1873-1952), solicitor and founder of the Hobart legal firm which bears his name.

Hobart Town Gazette, 19 Oct 1822; Hobart Town Courier, 26 Apr 1828, 6 June 1834; Mercury, 1 Mar 1922; CSO 1/167/3885, 1/139/3392 (TA). A. RAND

MURDOCH, PETER (1795?-1871), public servant and settler, was descended on his father's side from a family powerful in Glasgow, Scotland, for nearly three centuries, and on his mother's from the Wallaces of Kelly. He was commissioned a lieutenant in the 35th Regiment in 1812 and was at Waterloo and in Paris during the occupation. In 1817 he was placed on half-pay and in 1821 accompanied his friend, Sir Thomas Brisbane, to New South Wales. He and James were the first of four brothers (John Wallace and Robert Wallace were the others) to come by way of New South Wales to settle in Van Diemen's Land.

Brisbane appointed Peter Murdoch superintendent of the government agricultural establishment at Emu Plains, New South Wales, in March 1822, and later defended him from retrospective allegations that he had connived at the prostitution of women convicts sent to work there. A board of inquiry dismissed the charges, finding his administration exemplary; Brisbane also gave him great credit for having made the farm yield a profit.

In January 1825 Peter, accompanied by James, arrived in Hobart Town to set up Lieut-Governor Arthur's new penal settlement on Maria Island. Brisbane recalled him to give evidence before the Emu Plains inquiry in September, and while he was in Sydney nominated him to the Commission of Survey and Valuation. Arthur appointed him second land commissioner in February 1826, and for two years he was Roderic O'Connor's [q.v.] companion, one might say crony, in the examination of the settled districts; Murdoch is responsible for two of the lively journals that resulted from their peregrinations.

In 1825 he had no intention of settling in Van Diemen's Land. He had been granted 2000 acres in New South Wales by Brisbane, who recommended him for another 2000 acres; but in 1827 Murdoch sought to take up this extension in the island. Darling would allow this only if Murdoch relinquished all his New South Wales land, and was surprised when he agreed. Murdoch transferred all his property to Van Diemen's Land, where he already had a farm at Broadmarsh, and took the 2000 acres at the Handsome Sugarloaf. He owned 4600 acres in 1831 when he sought an extension, and Arthur ordered a further 1000 acres in consideration of his services as land commissioner. By 1837 he was master of 6390 acres, including valuable land on Hunter Island.

In April 1834 Murdoch was appointed a police magistrate and stationed first at Richmond and then at Oatlands, where he resigned in 1835. Two years later he took his family to Scotland, and in December 1837 a son was born to his wife in Glasgow. She had had at least three children in Van Diemen's Land. He settled on an income at Todhillbank, Renfrewshire, 'interesting himself in country affairs and farming principally for amusement'. Murdoch seems to have been a competent and amiable man, who was widely mourned when he died at Capelrig, Renfrewshire, on 6 November 1871. His wife, whose Christian names were Barclay Brown, died at the same place some five weeks later.

HRA (1), 11, 12; Mercury, 19 Feb 1872; A. McKay (ed), Journals of the land commissioners for Van Diemen's Land, 1826-28 (Hob, 1962); Correspondence file under Peter Murdoch (TA). P. R. ELDERSHAW

MURPHY, FRANCIS (1795-1858), Catholic bishop, was born on 20 May 1795 at Navan, County Meath, Ireland, the eldest son of Arthur Murphy, brewer and distiller, and his wife Bridget, née Flood. After education at St Finian's College in Navan he matriculated in June 1818 at the ecclesiastical seminary founded and maintained by the Irish government under George III. At this seminary, called St Patrick's but officially the Royal College of Maynooth, he was ordained deacon in 1824 and priest in 1825. He was among the first to benefit from the Dunboyne establishment for advanced ecclesiastical studies, and completed courses in theology and sacred scripture with such conspicuous success that he won from his contemporaries the title of doctor.

Formal studies ended, he volunteered for missionary work in England and was sent to minister to the Irish Catholic workers in the Bradford woollen mills, and their families. He soon proved a sound administrator and an able controversialist, publishing the closely reasoned *Letter to . . . J. Taylor . . . in reply to his . . . attack on the dedicatory sermon preached by . . . Dr Barnes, on the opening of the New Catholic Chapel* (Bradford, 1827). In 1827 he was transferred to St Patrick's Church in Liverpool.

In 1837, influenced by Dr W. Ullathorne [q.v.], he obtained permission to go to Australia for five years. He arrived in Sydney in July 1838 with other priests whom he had induced to follow his example. Almost immediately, because of the impending departure of Bishop Polding [q.v.], he was appointed vicar-general with jurisdiction over the whole of Australia. In 1843 he was designated by Pope Gregory XVI to the new see of Adelaide. On 8 September 1844 he was consecrated in St Mary's Cathedral, Sydney, by Archbishop Polding assisted by Bishop Willson and by Archdeacon McEncroe [qq.v.], thus becoming the first bishop consecrated in Australasia.

The bishop sailed for Adelaide in the *Mary White* in October with one priest and two schoolteachers, calling at Port Phillip where he officiated at the first Pontifical High Mass celebrated in Melbourne. On 26 December he wrote from Adelaide, 'I found my Mission utterly destitute of church, chapel or school. The only priest in the Colony was obliged to celebrate Mass in a large storehouse'. Relief came unexpectedly with a gift of 500 rural acres and £2000 from William Leigh of Little Aston Hall, Staffordshire. With an annual subsidy of £490 from the Society for the Propagation of the Faith at Lyons and small subscriptions from his own flock who were mostly unskilled labourers, he was able to build a large schoolroom which was also used as a church called St Patrick's, and which was his pro-cathedral during his episcopate. He also built a stone house for himself and his clergy. In February 1846 he went to Europe in search of priests for his diocese and returned in July 1847. While in England he obtained from Charles Hansom, brother of Joseph of hansom cab fame, a model and plans of a cathedral for Adelaide. The foundation stone was laid on 17 March 1856. Many of his flock who joined the gold rush to Victoria sent their gold to him to sell and hold in trust or buy land for them. The return of these diggers brought some prosperity to the diocese.

Bishop Murphy was tall and sandy-haired with a fine sonorous voice that drew crowds, non-Catholic as well as Catholic, to hear him preach. His pulpit utterances about what Catholics did not believe amazed Protestants and led them to conclude 'that he would either become a Protestant or effect a union between the Romanists and the English branch of the Catholic Church'. His insistence on the pledge to avoid alcohol encouraged Protestants to revive their own temperance societies. He was naturally quick-tempered but easily appeased, and because of the warmth of his personality and the integrity of his judgment was highly regarded by his brother priests. It was partly through his exertions that the long-standing dispute between Bishop Willson and Father Therry [q.v.] was finally settled in 1857. He returned from a visit to Hobart Town in weakened health and died of pulmonary tuberculosis on 26 April 1858, and was buried in the unfinished St Francis Xavier's Cathedral.

Though always an ardent educationist Bishop Murphy will be better remembered as a church builder. In December 1857 his last report to Rome summed up his work: 'Twelve churches and six chapels have been built in the diocese, and two others are being built as well as a magnificent cathedral'.

F. Byrne, *History of the Catholic Church in South Australia* (Adel, 1896); H. N. Birt, *Benedictine pioneers in Australia*, 2 (Lond, 1911); F. Murphy, Journal (Archdiocesan Archives, Adelaide); Soc for the propagation of the faith, Archives (Rome, Fribourg); Benedictine Abbey, Downside (Archives); Therry papers (Canisius College, Pymble).

OSMUND THORPE

MURRAY, SIR GEORGE (1772-1846), soldier and politician, was born on 6 February 1772 at Ochtertyre, Crieff, Perthshire, Scotland, the second son of Sir William Murray, baronet, and Lady Augusta Mackenzie, daughter of the earl of Cromarty. He was educated at the Edinburgh High School and the University of Edinburgh and in March 1789 became an ensign in the 71st Regiment, from which he transferred to the 34th Regiment and thence in 1790 to the 3rd Foot Guards.

He served in Flanders in 1793-94 and the West Indies 1795-96, being promoted lieutenant and captain in 1794 and lieut-colonel in 1799. He saw active service in Egypt in 1801 and after holding a series of senior staff appointments at home and abroad was appointed quartermaster-general in Portugal under Sir John Moore in 1808. In March 1809 he became a brevet colonel and was appointed quartermaster-general on Wellington's staff in Spain and Portugal. He returned from Spain in 1811 and next year became quartermaster-general in Ireland and was there until September 1813 when he rejoined the army in Spain and remained with it until the Peninsular war ended. He had been promoted major-general in January 1812 and was appointed K.C.B. in September 1813.

In 1814 Murray was made governor of the Canadian colonies, but when war broke out again he obtained permission to join the army in Flanders and he remained with the army of occupation as chief of staff until 1818. In 1819-24 he was governor of the Royal Military College, Sandhurst, and in 1823 was elected to parliament. In 1825-28 he commanded in Ireland, being promoted lieut-general. From May 1828 to November 1830 he was secretary of state for the colonies in Wellington's administration. In his brief control at the Colonial Office, the colony of Western Australia was founded. By his lavish patronage of relations and friends in Perthshire, the Australian colonies gained some third-rate public servants and many first-rate settlers with capital. In his *Autobiography* (London, 1885) Henry Taylor, then a clerk in the Colonial Office, described him as 'an old soldier and a high-bred gentleman, whose countenance and natural stateliness and simple dignity of demeanour were all that can be desired in a Secretary of State, if to look the character were the one thing needful'. In 1832 he was defeated at the general election but gained in 1834 a seat which he soon lost. He was promoted general in November 1841. He died at Belgrave Square, London, on 28 July 1846.

He had married in 1826 Lady Louisa Erskine, sister of the marquis of Anglesea and widow of Sir James Erskine.

MURRAY, HUGH (1789-1845), grazier and merchant, was born in Edinburgh, the son of Hugh Murray, writer to the signet, and his wife Anne, née Young. In Edinburgh he married Jean, daughter of Andrew Carmichael, also a writer to the signet, and his wife Lillias, née Cross; they had eight children: Hugh, Andrew, Lillias, Anne, Margaret, Jane, Agnes and Elizabeth. Murray was one of a party which chartered the brig *Urania*, sailed from Leith in June 1822, and arrived in Hobart Town on 14 January 1823. He was accompanied by his wife and five children and a smith, ploughman and female servant. He brought capital of £2184 in goods and cash, and was granted 1760 acres which

he selected on the Macquarie River near Campbell Town and named St Leonard's.

His brother David, accompanied by his wife and two children, arrived in Hobart in the *Portland* on 10 September 1824, bringing with him a carpenter, cooper, farm overseer, and capital of £1456, and he was granted 800 acres near Campbell Town, which he selected between grants owned by J. P. Briggs and William Millikin. By some error this overlapped Briggs's grant and David Murray spent much time and energy endeavouring to settle the matter. He gave up his land to live in Launceston as licensee of the York Wine Vaults and died in 1837.

Hugh Murray applied for an additional grant in 1830, having improved his property by a dwelling house, outbuildings, two miles of four-railed fence and the cultivation of 100 acres. He had 1800 sheep and 25 cattle. He also expected to receive from £80 to £100 a year from the estate of his mother-in-law, who had recently died in Scotland. The police magistrate at Campbell Town reported that Murray was 'generally understood to have little surplus capital, being of rather expensive habits'. Nevertheless Murray was granted an additional 800 acres. He sold his property in 1831 to C. Baskerville Viveash, and it was renamed, or perhaps incorporated in a larger property, Baskerville. Murray moved to Hobart and established himself as a wine and spirit merchant, first in Liverpool Street and later in Collins Street. He also held the rights of a large sheep station at Port Phillip, where his eldest son Hugh, aged 23, had taken up land by Lake Colac in 1837 and was the first settler there. His brother Andrew joined him later in the year.

Hugh Murray was active in the Presbyterian Church. He helped to establish the first church, still standing, at Kirklands near Campbell Town, joined the petitioners for government aid for a minister for St Andrew's Church in Hobart, and helped to raise funds for the erection of Scots Church, Melbourne. He was one of the first trustees of the Hobart Savings Bank. He died at his home in Colville Street, Hobart, on 21 December 1845 and was buried in the Presbyterian cemetery. This was recently converted to a park, most of the headstones being set in the surrounding wall. Murray's headstone, however, was left in its original position, as were those of the first minister of the church and a few other dignitaries.

J. Heyer, *The Presbyterian pioneers of Van Diemen's Land* (Launceston, 1935); *Hobart*

Town Gazette, 18 Jan 1823, 10 Sept 1824;
Hobart Town Courier, 2 May 1829, 20 May
1836; *Colonial Times*, 15 May 1840.

H. M. MURRAY

MURRAY, JOHN (b. 1775?), seaman
and explorer, claimed to have been born
at Edinburgh, to have been 21 when he
joined the *Polyphemus* and to have begun
his career as an able seaman in the *Duke*
from June to December 1789, but in 1802
the Navy Board stated that all this was
incorrect. He had, however, served as a
midshipman in the *Polyphemus* from October 1794 to May 1797, as mate in the
Apollo from May to December 1797, as
second master and pilot of the *Blazer*
from January to July 1798 and as mate of
the *Porpoise* from October 1798 to July
1800, in which year he passed his lieutenant's examination. In November 1800
he came to New South Wales while serving
in the *Porpoise*, and next March Governor
King transferred him to the *Lady Nelson*
as mate. Murray was thus able to accompany Barrallier and James Grant [qq.v.]
on their visit to Jervis Bay and Western
Port, and on their survey of the Hunter
River in June. After their return to Sydney
Grant resigned his command and on 3
September King appointed Murray acting
lieutenant and commander of the *Lady
Nelson*. In October Murray took instructions to Lieut-Governor Foveaux [q.v.] on
Norfolk Island, and on his return was
ordered to complete Grant's exploration of
the south coast.

He set out for the Kent Group in Bass
Strait on 12 November but mistook his
destination and actually reached the Furneaux Islands. After returning to the Kent
Group he steered through the passage
separating the main islands, named Murray's Passage, and then began a survey of
Western Port, which he reached in December. On 4 January 1801 he sighted Port
Phillip but found the entrance dangerous
and decided to survey it later. He charted
the east coast of King Island, then returned
to Port Phillip on 31 January and sent
John Bowen [q.v.] into the bay in a
launch to examine it. Murray entered Port
Phillip in the *Lady Nelson* on 14 February
and anchored inside. He named various
landmarks: Arthur's Seat, Swan Island,
Point Paterson and Point Palmer. On 8
March he took possession of Port Phillip,
which he named Port King and which King
renamed later.

Murray arrived back in Sydney on 23
March, having made charts of the Kent
Group, King Island and Port Phillip; together with his journals they were sent to
England, with a recommendation by King
that Murray's lieutenancy be confirmed.
The *Lady Nelson* was badly in need of
new sails and caulking, but by the time
Matthew Flinders [q.v.] arrived on his
great voyage she appeared ready to accompany the *Investigator*. They left on 22
July 1802, but the *Lady Nelson* proved
unfit and on 17 October when they were
off the Cumberland Isles, Flinders ordered
Murray to return. Early in 1803 Murray
made another voyage to Norfolk Island
and to the Hawkesbury, but in April King
received a dispatch dated 5 May 1802,
informing him that the Navy Board had
refused to give Murray a commission or
pass him as an officer in the future because
he had given false details of service in
the *Duke* and had not been in service for
six years, as he claimed when examined
for his commission. King had to remove
Murray from his command but asked that,
if Murray should manage to clear his
name as he said he could, he be allowed
to return to take command of the *Lady
Nelson* again. King's good opinion of Murray was also shown in a letter to Sir
Joseph Banks [q.v.] recommending Murray
to his notice and expressing his desire that
Murray be allowed to return. Murray left
for England in the *Glatton* in May 1803,
and he appears as the author of charts
of the English coast made in 1804, 1805
and 1807, but he did not achieve his desire
to return to New South Wales.

HRNSW, 4, 5; HRA (1), 3, 4; F. P. Labil-
liere, *Early history of the colony of Victoria*,
2 (Lond, 1878); I. Lee, *The logbooks of the Lady
Nelson* (Lond, 1915); J. S. Cumpston, *Shipping arrivals and departures 1788-1825* (Canberra, 1963); T. W. Fowler, 'Flinders in Port
Phillip', *Vic Geog J*, 29 (1912); J. H. Watson,
'Early Port Phillip', *JRAHS*, 3 (1915-17); W. S.
Campbell, 'The Lady Nelson', *JRAHS*, 3
(1915-17); C. R. Long, 'Memorials to Victorian explorers', *VHM*, 4 (1914-15); Australian charts, 1795-1803 (ML); MS cat under
J. Murray (ML).   VIVIENNE PARSONS

MURRAY, ROBERT WILLIAM FELTON
LATHROP (1777-1850), landowner, soldier,
convict and journalist, was the only son of
Robert Lathropp and his wife Ann, née
Williams, of West Felton, Shropshire, and
Smith Square, London. Educated at West-
minster School and Cambridge University,
he was granted a commission in the 2nd
Royal Manx Fencibles in 1795. On coming
of age he assumed the additional surname
of Murray, claiming descent from a certain
Robert Murray who, as the son of Sir
William Murray, baronet, of Dynnyrne,
Scotland, had married into the Lathropp

family in 1630 and taken their name. A government announcement in the London *Gazette*, 3 April 1802, refers to him as Sir Robert Lathropp Murray, and this title was used in other periodicals of that time. He served in the Peninsular war, and the Army Lists from 1807 to 1814 show him attached to the 7th Foot, 1st Foot and from 1811, captain in the Royal Waggon Train.

In January 1815 he was tried for bigamy before the Recorder of London, and sentenced to transportation for seven years. It was alleged that he had married Alicia Marshall in Northern Ireland in 1797, and, during her lifetime, Catherine Clarke in 1801. He did not regard the first marriage as legal, and published his objections, a report of the trial, and a petition to the Prince Regent by his wife Catherine in a pamphlet entitled *An Appeal to the British Nation* 2nd ed (London, 1815). A plea to the House of Commons, sponsored by Sir Samuel Romilly, was rejected on 10 April 1815.

After his trial he appears to have omitted the final letter from his original surname, being known in Australia as Robert Lathrop Murray. His first mention is as clerk and constable of the Sydney bench, an employee of D'Arcy Wentworth [q.v.], in 1816. He was granted a pardon soon after arrival, and was recorded in the *Sydney Gazette* as principal clerk in the Police Office, and in 1820 assistant superintendent. He also engaged in outside business which took him to Hobart Town in 1821. In the next eight years he was given some large grants of land to the south of the town; he lived first at Dynnyrne Distillery in south Hobart and later built Dynnyrne House, which gave its name to a suburb. Across the Derwent, a mile beyond Kangaroo Point (Bellerive), was his country house, Wentworth.

In 1824 a number of letters signed 'A Colonist' began appearing in the press, violently criticizing the administration; at a public function on 7 April 1825 Murray acknowledged their authorship. He became editor of the *Hobart Town Gazette* on 8 July, and of the *Colonial Times* from 19 August 1825 to 4 August 1826. His attacks on Lieut-Governor Arthur continued, becoming in effect a war for the freedom of the press; but by 1828 when he returned to journalism, he had modified his attitude and tended to favour Arthur. Meanwhile he had been tried for an earlier financial irregularity and, after a confused verdict and a long-delayed judgment, received a pardon. Arthur had also been gratified, on moral grounds, by Murray's marriage

on 1 December 1827 to Eleanor, the daughter of Thomas and Sarah Dixon, of Ralph's Bay. He also became active in Freemasonry, being senior installing officer from 1828; he is recognized as the father of the order in the colony.

His second period of journalism began with the first issue, on 6 February 1828, of *Murray's Austral-Asiatic Review*. This continued under various names, sometimes amalgamated with the *Tasmanian* and sometimes with Murray in partnership or as editor under another owner until, as the *Tasmanian and Austral-Asiatic Review*, with Murray as editor and J. C. Macdougall [q.v.] as proprietor, it ceased publication on 26 June 1845. Murray's support of Arthur was to bring him into opposition to Lieut-Governor Franklin, who quarrelled with the officials of the Arthur faction. After the recall of Franklin, Murray defended his successor, Eardley-Wilmot, who encountered increasing opposition from a section of the colonists headed by the Patriotic Six. By the time Wilmot received notice of recall Murray himself was preparing to leave Van Diemen's Land.

Legislation passed at Westminster in 1842 on Irish marriages (5 & 6 Vic. c. 113) gave him hope that his conviction could be set aside, and by November 1847 he had his affairs sufficiently in order to leave for England. But old age and ill health had weakened his fighting spirit and he was unable to attain reinstatement in the army, which would have entitled him to a large sum in back pay. However, he was able to enter into possession of his estate at West Felton Hall where he died on 2 November 1850. His wife and her younger children had followed him to England; she proved her right to his property in the Vice-Chancellor's Court in December 1852. She then sold the English estate and in 1853 returned to Australia, dying in 1898.

Murray had children by each of his wives; a daughter by Alicia Marshall was living with Ann Lathropp when the latter made her will in 1803, and Catherine Clarke had a daughter who died in 1824. There was also a son, Edward Kent Strathearn Murray, whose mother, Mrs Lydia Marriott, was said to have been married to Murray in 1806; but no such marriage could be legal, as both Alicia Marshall and Catherine Clarke were alive in 1815. By Eleanor Dixon three sons and five daughters survived him, and their descendants all live in Australia.

Norwood Young (*Napoleon in Exile: Elba*, London, 1914, 287) claimed that 'a certain R. W. Murray' was received by the emperor at Elba, and 'being supposed to be a natural son of an English prince, his visit was regarded as evidence of an understanding between Napoleon and the Royal family'; on return to England Murray was transported for bigamy but 'the real offence was believed to be high treason'. If such were indeed the case, his transportation and prompt pardon in Australia suggest the protection of an eminent patron, who was himself sufficiently involved to wish Murray out of the way. The duke of Kent had maintained a correspondence with him on military matters, and was apparently godfather to Lydia Marriott's son; but neither he, nor any other son of George III could have been Murray's father, the eldest having been born in 1762. Murray himself made no such allegation, but claimed merely to be heir to a baronetcy as the son of Robert Lathropp.

Whatever his antecedents in England, it is by his life in Tasmania that he will be remembered. In the words of the Tasmanian historian R. W. Giblin, 'At a time when public opinion in England was still engaged in the strife, he was the man who put up the stoutest fight for Freedom of the Press in the island colony'.

A. C. Lowe, History of Tasmanian Operative Lodge no 1 (Hob, 1935); R. W. Giblin, The early history of Tasmania, 2 (Melb, 1939); M. H. Ellis, Lachlan Macquarie (Syd, 1947); E. M. Miller, Pressmen and governors (Syd, 1952); Shrewsbury Chronicle, 15 Nov 1850; Family papers (in possession of Dr Hugh Murray, Green Hills, Kingston, Tasmania).

C. R. MURRAY

MURRAY, SIR TERENCE AUBREY (1810-1873), landowner and politician, was born at Balliston, County Limerick, Ireland, the third and last child of Terence Murray and his wife Ellen, née Fitzgerald, of Movida. When Ulster was colonized the Murrays had been granted land in Antrim and Derry. The family belonged to the Roman Catholic Church and its loyalty to the Royalist cause in the seventeenth century brought it close to extermination. In 1811 Murray's father became paymaster of a brigade of Guards in Portugal, where his wife soon joined him. Young Terence was left with his grandmother. His mother became incurably ill on her return home and left again later for France, where she died. Paymaster Murray was transferred to the 48th Regiment in 1815. The 48th was then in Ireland and in 1817 was sent to New South Wales and thence in 1825 to India, where Murray became gravely ill. He was given sick leave to England where he re-

tired on half-pay and then decided to return to New South Wales, where his service entitled him to a free land grant. Leaving his elder son in Edinburgh to complete his medical studies, he sailed in the Elizabeth with his daughter and Terence. On arrival in Sydney in April 1827 he took his children to Erskine Park, a farm he had arranged to rent from the widow of his former commanding officer, Lieut-Colonel James Erskine [q.v.].

In September 1827 Murray was given authority to take possession of 2500 acres and located it north of Lake Bathurst and on the eastern banks of Mulwaree Ponds. While he remained at Erskine Park young Terence was left to supervise the assigned servants and to establish the new farm. After some months the government ordered the Murrays to move. They started again at another site west of Mulwaree Ponds, but were soon ordered to move again. Murray was angry but he was compensated by an additional grant in the name of his son Terence. About May 1829 a site was chosen in the broad valley north of Lake George. The son's land, adjoining his father's, was called Old Collector. His sister Anna Maria married Captain George Bunn in 1829; she wrote The Guardian (Sydney, 1837). His brother, James Fitzgerald Murray, on arrival in Sydney early in 1828, became a surgeon at the hospital, and in 1830 assistant surgeon to the penal settlement at Moreton Bay. Around 1835 he became superintendent of the Goulburn hospital. About 1839 he gave up active practice and built a homestead on land which he called Woden, granted to him in 1832 on the Limestone Plains. After her husband died in 1840, Anna Maria made her home with him; her two sons had already received early schooling at Goulburn.

In the solitude of his valley Terence continued his education alone, reading from well-chosen books until he knew long passages by heart. In Ireland he had attended the school of Rev. William White, an Anglican clergyman who gave him a respect for mathematics and a passion for Greek classics. Before leaving Dublin he had heard lectures by the Irish patriot, Daniel O'Connell (1775-1847), who impressed upon him indelibly that moral suasion was more successful than brute force for obtaining rights.

In 1832, after four years spent in improving the original Murray grants, Terence established another farm, called Ajamatong, in the south-west corner of the Collector valley. In 1833, during an outbreak of bushranging, Governor Bourke appointed him head of the police in the southern highlands. His appearance gave him natural authority. Strong and very tall, he had a serious manner, a fiery temper, sandy hair and penetrating, dark eyes. He was an intrepid horseman and rode long distances while carrying out his duties.

Paymaster Murray died in 1835, leaving his property in the Collector valley to his younger son. Murray bought land beside his inherited grant and on this property, Winderradeen, established a fine homestead in 1837. T. A. Murray and Thomas Walker [q.v.] bought from Francis Mowatt the promise of a grant at Yarrowlumla (Yarralumla), on the Limestone Plains.

The late 1830s were years of great drought. Lake George evaporated. At the height of the drought in January 1839, Murray, with two Aboriginal friends and two convict overseers, and Stewart Mowle, a schoolboy who had been brought out from England, rode into the mountains looking for fresh pastures on the high plains; he decided to set up a station at Cooleman for his starving stock. In 1841 Murray rode overland to Melbourne, meeting many Aboriginal friends in the mountains; he was back at Yarralumla within eighteen days. For the census of March 1841, 108 people were mustered at Yarralumla. A few months later in Sydney Murray told an immigration commission that he employed prisoners and as many free men as he could induce to work for him, but found it so hard to engage labour that he feared the colony would be ruined unless labourers were brought from India.

On 27 May 1843 at St James's Church of England, Sydney, Murray married Mary, daughter of Colonel J. G. N. Gibbes [q.v.]. He settled Yarralumla and part of Winderradeen on his wife, hoping thereby to save the properties if depression should cause his bankruptcy. She made a will, naming her father and brother as trustees. Murray, however, retained enough property in the Collector valley to qualify for election to the Legislative Council. In an advertisement in the *Sydney Morning Herald* he had already offered himself as a candidate who admitted no such distinction as Whig or Tory; his great objects were the welfare of the country, liberal and equal laws for all parties and all sects, and revival of the elements of prosperity and greatness that were lying dormant in the land.

Elected unopposed for the combined Counties of Murray, King and Georgiana he began his political life as a strong critic of the price of 20s. an acre for crown land. Within a week he proposed that a select committee should inquire into the sale of crown lands, and became its chairman. It reported that grazing was one of the most profitable pursuits in the colony but, of all occupations, the least likely to develop 'the active powers of the human mind' or the real resources of the country; since squatters had no enduring interest in the soil, the committee recommended the refund of fares to encourage English country gentlemen, clergymen, physicians, tradesmen and labourers, to emigrate as permanent settlers with their families and connexions.

In 1845 he was chairman of a select committee on the Masters and Servants Act. Its report advocated legal adjustments in disputes, and showed that the old convict system, though necessary in the colony's early years, had gone far to demoralize the employers as much as their free servants. For the same reasons he later opposed renewal of transportation to New South Wales. He also supported free trade within the empire, and the building of local railways, particularly a line to Goulburn, denouncing the Great South Road as the worst in the colony: his wool-drays, he said, were sometimes three months on the road to Sydney in wet weather. In 1846 he announced that he had given up squatting. While gold fever raged some years later Murray went fossicking among the Brindabella and Cooleman outcrops with scientific skill and detachment. At this time his sister left Woden to live at St Omer, since men working the property had gone to the diggings. She died there in 1889.

In the council Murray often spoke against capital punishment, describing it as a remnant of a barbarous state of society and no deterrent against crime. He opposed denominational education, declaring his favour of a general system on something like the Irish National system and his belief that those who resisted it were 'behind their age'. Though Catholic in upbringing, Murray's attitude to religion was liberal; once he startled the council by claiming to be a Unitarian, apparently thinking that this meant ecumenical. Murray was a member of W. C. Wentworth's [q.v.] committee that drew up the petition and remonstrance to the British government protesting against wrongs and insisting on the colony's undoubted rights. Later he sat on the select committee that drafted the new Constitution; at the outset Murray declared that the property qualifications for representatives were too high and excluded many talented men. Later he pressed for an inquiry into currency and banking. When trading banks assumed the right to issue money, he said, it was the duty of the legislature to dictate the terms; a national bank would give greater economic security.

Murray and his family left Yarralumla to make their home at Winderradeen about the beginning of 1855. His brother-in-law, Augustus Gibbes, took over Yarralumla and his parents went to live with him. Next year Murray was elected to the first Legislative Assembly. His brother, Dr Murray, was nominated to the Legislative Council and went to Sydney to take his seat, but soon became critically ill and died at Winderradeen on 24 June 1856.

Murray was not popular at first in the new Legislative Assembly; his aristocratic appearance and rather arrogant manner were against him. In the muddle of politics he was commonly ranged against the government, but in 1856 and again in 1857 he was appointed minister for Lands and Public Works under the leadership of Cowper, when the more conservative elements were in opposition. In November 1857 his first son, James Aubrey Gibbes, was born, after a succession of five daughters only two of whom survived infancy; his wife died on 2 January 1858, and on her death most of Murray's property in her name passed to the control of her trustees; this was to cause strained feelings between Murray and his relations-in-law.

In the late 1850s Murray and the young democrat, Daniel Deniehy, became staunch friends while making joint efforts to solve the land problem. Deniehy publicly declared that Murray was the only representative of the old territorial aristocracy to join the ranks of the reformers. Even his enemies recognized him as an authority on practical rural affairs, he said, and when Murray saw any attempt by the Tory squattocratic party to secure the prize of responsible government for perpetuating their own domination he became one of the most fearless, active and determined leaders of the opposition. Murray also became a friend of Henry Parkes, and they often caught the same train to the city.

After the defeat of the Cowper government in September 1859 Murray was commissioned by the governor to form a ministry but failed to do so. In the same month he proposed and became chairman of a select committee to inquire into the condition of the University of Sydney, which then had only thirty-eight students. It had been set up as a secular university, but the senate had introduced by-laws that, in effect, imposed religious tests on

students before they could be granted degrees. Murray supported an objection by some professors to these by-laws. He also thought the government was gravely mistaken in aiding the establishment of church colleges. In January 1860 J. H. Plunkett [q.v.] proposed Murray as Speaker of the Legislative Assembly, and he was elected.

In 1860 his sister Anna Maria, who had come to Sydney to care for his children, engaged Agnes Ann Edwards of Hammersmith, London, as a governess. She was a woman of great ability, wit and charm, and a cousin of W. S. Gilbert. Soon afterwards Murray proposed marriage to her. Although she was an Anglican and half his age, she accepted. They were married at Winderradeen on 4 August 1860, with two ceremonies, the first Catholic, the other Anglican. In December 1861 Agnes Murray gave birth to a son, John Hubert Plunkett, later Sir Hubert Murray, administrator of Papua. Her second son, born in January 1866, was George Gilbert Aimé, later Professor Gilbert Murray, Oxford.

In October 1862 Murray became president of the Legislative Council. He remembered his old friend, Stewart Mowle, who was appointed clerk in the council, and Mowle noticed a change in his boyhood hero: Murray had come to abhor the mountains he once loved and was quite won over to city life and the serenity of books. There were also financial difficulties. In September 1865 he was unable to pay his creditors. While the bailiff wept, Winderradeen was stripped of furniture. Murray and his wife then went in haste to Sydney for help. His many friends rallied with generosity and saved him from insolvency but his fine library had to be sold. In 1866-67 he became executive commissioner for the exhibit from New South Wales at the Paris Exhibition. He was also active as the president of the Society for the Abolition of Capital Punishment. In February 1869 he was knighted.

In November both his sons by his second wife were given a Catholic baptism by Dr John Forrest. However, in a codicil to his will in July 1871, Murray entrusted the religious education and spiritual guidance of all his children under 21 to his wife. Murray died on 22 June 1873, at Richmond House, Darlinghurst, after a long and painful illness. According to his instructions, he was buried at St Jude's Church of England, Randwick, but among the crowds who mourned him on his last journey was the Catholic archbishop of Sydney, who followed the funeral procession in his carriage.

'He served his country regardless of his own interests and died literally penniless', wrote Mowle; 'Those who knew him well, loved him with an unbounded love — he was the most faithful and best of friends'.

HRA (1), 13, 15, 20, 22, 23, 26; A. Mowle, Reminiscences 1822-51, by S. M. Mowle (ML); MS cat under E. B. Mowle and under George and Anna Maria Bunn (ML); Murray family papers (NL).   GWENDOLINE WILSON

N

NAIRN, WILLIAM (1767-1853), army officer, was born in England, commissioned in the 46th Regiment on 12 May 1800, promoted captain on 29 June 1809 and major on 30 August 1827. He married and had one son and two daughters. When his regiment relieved the 73rd in New South Wales early in 1814 Nairn was sent to Hobart Town in charge of a company. Governor Macquarie appointed him inspector of works on 1 April 1815 at a salary of £91, with rations and quarters. In this appointment he rendered outstanding service, and combined with it the task of hunting down the bushrangers then harassing the settlers in the outlying districts of the colony. He personally took the surrender of the notorious Michael Howe [q.v.] in 1817. Macquarie commended him, with others, in July 1817 for uniformly steady and gentlemanly conduct, whilst in the same dispatch castigating the officers of the 46th generally for engaging in trade and for disloyalty to the government. Lieut-Governor Sorell also praised his zealous co-operation and attention to duty in a dispatch to Macquarie in 1817 and in a General Order dated 18 January 1818. After relief by the 48th Regiment under Major Bell [q.v.] next June Nairn sailed with his detachment for India.

He had decided to settle in Van Diemen's Land when he retired from the army, and in 1832 returned to Hobart with his wife and family and a large consignment of stores and materials. He applied for land under the terms of the 1827 regulations allowing serving officers to receive grants from the Crown; since these regulations had expired in 1831, Lieut-Governor Arthur refused the application but recommended him for special consideration by the secretary of state. When the appeal was disallowed Nairn left in disgust for the new settlement at the Swan River, where his son William had taken up land in 1829. His capital entitled him to 8833 acres, which he selected near York, and he later acquired a further 3280 acres on the Canning River. In 1839 he was appointed one of the guardians to minors sent to the colony from the United Kingdom. He died at Fremantle on 8 June 1853, aged 86.

HRA (1), 9; *Inquirer*, 6 July 1853; Arthur to Goderich, 12 Mar 1832, CO 280/34.

E. M. DOLLERY

NASH, RICHARD WEST (1808-1850), advocate-general, was born in Dublin, the son of Richard Nash, rector of Ardstraw in the diocese of Londonderry. At 16 he entered Trinity College, Dublin (M.A., 1832), and was admitted to the Irish Bar. In 1839, after his marriage to Miss Schoales, he went to Western Australia where his brother-in-law, John Schoales, had settled in the previous year. Nash practised his profession but did not restrict his colonial activities to it. He became an enthusiastic farmer, acting as honorary secretary of the Agricultural Society in 1842-45 and publishing A *Manual for the Cultivation of the Vine and Olive in Western Australia* (Perth, 1845). For four months in 1846 he edited the *Inquirer* newspaper. He had served briefly as advocate-general in 1841 and was formally appointed to that position in November 1846, but journalism and agriculture remained his outstanding interests.

Nash was a lively controversialist and a member of the leading Church of England set in the colony. After the arrival in Perth of Bishop Brady [q.v.] with a party of priests and sisters early in 1846, a series of disputes developed between the local government and the Roman Catholic Church, in which Nash took a prominent part. He was secretary of the General Board of Education which was created in August 1847 and which originated Western Australia's state school system. In January 1849 he left the colony to become manager of the Colonization Assurance Corporation, founded in London to sponsor emigration, mainly to Western Australia. He published *Stray Suggestions on Colonization* (London, 1849). He died at Norwood near London on 22 December 1850.

E. M. Russell, 'Early lawyers of Western Australia', *JRWAHS*, 4 (1949-54).

DAVID MOSSENSON

NASH, ROBERT (1771-1819), miller, was born at Edenbridge, Kent, England, the son of a millwright. In February 1790 he was convicted at the Old Bailey, London, of breaking and entering a shop and stealing boots and shoes to the value of £14 10s. He was given a good character and his death sentence was commuted; transported for life, he reached New South Wales in the *Albemarle* in October 1791, and was sent to Norfolk Island. Before this he married Ann Hannaway, who in January 1789 had been sentenced to fourteen years transportation for receiving stolen goods, had come out in 1790 in the *Neptune* in the Second Fleet and been sent to Norfolk Island with her three children; later she bore him four daughters who went to Van Diemen's Land with their parents.

On Norfolk Island in 1795 Nash was commended by Lieut-Governor King for 'having ever behaved with propriety and advantage to the public'; in February 1796 he was conditionally pardoned, and received a grant of land. By the end of the year he was supplying pork to the government. In 1798 he was made master of the carpenters and built a house, which in 1801 he rented to Rev. Henry Fulton [q.v.]. Granted an absolute pardon in 1800, two years later he was made store-keeper, and soon afterwards a superintendent; as a 'deserving' character with a large family, Governor King gave him a cow from the government herd when he was 'discharged' upon the reduction of the settlement.

In 1808, when the Norfolk Island colonists were deported, Nash moved to Hobart Town and was given ten acres beside the New Town Rivulet. Here he built a flour-mill which in 1809 was carried away by a flood. Next year he built a second one on the Hobart Rivulet. As the food requirements of the settlement increased, wheat-growing extended to the rich lands towards Pittwater, where he was granted 200 acres. Like many of his neighbours he suffered from attacks by bushrangers in 1815, but in 1817 he was one of the largest contractors for the supply of wheat to the commissariat. In 1815, when he built a mill at 'his own expense', Lieut-Governor Davey asked Governor Macquarie to let him have a pair of millstones, which Macquarie sent down in December 1816. 'As an encouragement to his future industry', Nash was asked to pay only by grinding wheat for the government, when required, at not more than 1s. a bushel, until the debt was liquidated. On 8 February 1817 the *Hobart Town Gazette* reported with satisfaction that 'the first wind-mill erected in this Settlement' had begun operation.

Nash's health suffered from his continuous hard work under the primitive conditions of the early settlement, and he died at Sorell on 19 March 1819, aged 48.

HRA (1), 5, (3), 2-4; *Sydney Gazette*, 17 May 1817; *Hobart Town Gazette*, 29 May 1817; Correspondence file under R. Nash (TA).

F. C. GREEN

NATHAN, ISAAC (1790-1864), musician, was born in Canterbury, England, the eldest son of the Cantor Menehem Mona, a Polish refugee language master, who believed himself to be the son of Stanislaus II, last king of Poland. Isaac was so musically precocious that in 1809 his father apprenticed him to the famous London maestro Domenico Corri to learn singing and composition. In 1812 he eloped with a pupil, Rosetta Worthington, a minor novelist and the only child of an Irish army officer. In 1814 he persuaded Lord Byron to write a series of poems on Hebrew subjects, which he set to adaptations, made by himself, of ancient Jewish chants. *Hebrew Melodies* was highly successful, but Byron's flight from England in 1816 and the death of Nathan's pupil, Princess Charlotte, to whom he had dedicated *Hebrew Melodies*, deprived him of aristocratic patronage. In his ensuing financial difficulties he composed operettas such as *Sweethearts and Wives*; in 1823 he published in London *An Essay on the History and Theory of Music and on the Qualities, Capabilities and Management of the Human Voice*, subsequently called *Musurgia Vocalis*, which achieved a European reputation.

In 1824 his wife died, leaving two sons and four daughters, and in 1826 he married Henrietta Buckley. Under the stress of supporting his large family Nathan had apparently acted as secret agent for George IV, whose musical librarian he was; in 1837 William IV sent him on a mysterious mission, the nature of which remains unknown. But Queen Victoria's first prime minister, Lord Melbourne, whose wife had been Lady Caroline Lamb, one of Nathan's early patrons, refused to pay him the £2000 he claimed. He was financially ruined and the whole family left for Australia.

Nathan reached Sydney in April 1841 and immediately opened an academy of singing; he became choirmaster of St Mary's Cathedral and organized the largest concert of sacred music yet heard in the colony. He composed a 'solemn ode' *Australia the Wide and Free* for the inaugural dinner of Sydney's first Municipal Council (1842) and two 'choral odes', *Long Live Victoria* and *Hail, Star of the South*, for subsequent festivities. Henceforth he constituted himself musical laureate to the colony, celebrating the fifty-eighth anniversary of the founding of Sydney with *Currency Lasses* (1846), mourning the supposed death of the explorer Leichhardt [q.v.] with *Leichhardt's Grave*, and rejoicing in his return with *The Greeting Home Again*. He composed a setting of the Lord's Prayer for Bishop Broughton [q.v.] and sent his last composition *A Song to Freedom* (1863) as a gift to the Queen.

In May 1847 Nathan's romantic *Don John of Austria*, the first opera to be wholly composed and produced in Australia, was performed at the Victoria Theatre; it is one of his few manuscripts to survive. In 1849 he published, simultaneously in London and Sydney, his strange miscellany *The Southern Euphrosyne*. Its most interesting sections are devoted to the Aboriginals and their music, in transcribing which Nathan made pioneer experiments; the best known is *Koorinda Braia* (1842). Unfortunately, in his subsequent series of *Australian Melodies* he treated the native chants as Victorian ballads.

Nathan built Byron Lodge, a large house in Randwick. On 15 January 1864 he was killed while alighting from a city horse-tram. His second wife, three of whose six children had been born in Australia, died in 1890. His eldest son, Charles, an honorary F.R.C.S., was senior surgeon to the Sydney Infirmary and a pioneer in anaesthetics.

Isaac Nathan's influence on Australian musical history is hard to assess. His own music was of little worth but he probably contributed to the prevailing pseudo-Byronic and Romantic tone of Sydney's artistic life. He was certainly the first musician with a European reputation to settle in Australia, and the first to attempt a serious study of Aboriginal music. A portrait of Isaac Nathan, aged 25, is in the possession of the family of the late V. V. Nathan.

C. H. Bertie, *Isaac Nathan, Australia's first composer* (Syd, 1922); O. S. Phillips, *Isaac Nathan, friend of Byron* (Lond, 1940); F. Kelsey, 'Voice training', *Grove's dictionary of music*, 5th ed (Lond, 1954); F. Blume (ed), *Die Musik in Geschichte und Gegenwart* (Kassel, 1962); C. B. Mackerras, *The Hebrew melodist* (Syd, 1963).

CATHERINE MACKERRAS

NEALES, JOHN BENTHAM (1806-1873), auctioneer and politician, was born on 13 June 1806 in Plymouth, England. His father and his mother Elizabeth, a sister of Jeremy Bentham, both died when he was young, and he became the protégé of his famous uncle whose bequest financed his migration to South Australia. Neales arrived in Adelaide in June 1838 in the *Eden*. He promptly began business as an auctioneer and agent under the title of Neales Bentham, transposing his name to avoid confusion with another agent called Neale. Neales reverted to his correct name in 1842 when Neale left Adelaide.

In 1839 Neales bought land at Port Lincoln and became the first editor of the short lived *Port Lincoln Herald*, published in Adelaide. In 1841 he helped to form and manage the South Australian Mining Association that worked the Wheal Gawler silver and lead deposit newly discovered at Glen Osmond. Revived in 1845, the association acquired profitable copper mines at Montacute and at Burra, when Neales as an original shareholder made a substantial fortune. He inaugurated an unsuccessful search for gold in 1846, and ten years later advocated the mining of iron ore and local smelting. With this record he was often called the father of mining in South Australia.

Neales was prominent in advancing urban development to encourage investment and immigration. In the pit of depression in 1843 he risked unpopularity by resisting the importation of juvenile offenders from Parkhurst Prison and, as a member of the Board of City Commissioners in 1851 and later as a city councillor, he pressed energetically for new roads, water supply and sanitation for Adelaide. As early as 1846 he tried to establish a gas company and three years later subscribed heavily to the abortive City and Port Railway Co. When South Australia gained a part-elective Legislative Council in 1851 he won the North Adelaide seat by mild criticism of Downing Street's control of colonial land and strong advocacy of the possibility of the colony's untapped resources. Confessing High Church and Tory parentage he took a middle course between the radicals and conservatives and was appointed to the select committee that drafted the compromise Constitution of 1853. After responsible government he represented Adelaide in 1857-60, Stanley in 1862 and the Burra in 1862-70, serving twice as commissioner of crown lands and immigration. He was largely responsible for imposing taxes on the livestock of pastoral lessees in 1858 and in 1865 for empowering company formation and miners' associations with limited liability. Outside parliament he was prominent on the turf and as chairman of public meetings. His lively fluency and bustling enthusiasms made him a popular figure as well as winning him wealth.

In 1843 Neales married Margaret, the daughter of William Williams and Margaret, née Barnard, by whom he had two sons and three daughters. He died in Adelaide on 31 July 1873.

Papers in possession of Mrs D. L. Chapman, Adel.   H. J. FINNIS

NEPEAN, EVAN (1752-1822), civil servant, and NICHOLAS (1757-1823), marine and army officer, were the sons of Nicholas Nepean of Saltash, Cornwall, England. Evan entered the navy as a clerk and served as a purser in ships on the American coast during the rebellion of the American colonies. In 1782 he was appointed secretary to Lord Shuldham, port-admiral at Plymouth, and later that year became under-secretary of state in the Home Department. In this post he was concerned in the arrangements for the dispatch of the First Fleet and the administration of the newly established penal colony in New South Wales during its early years. In 1795 he was appointed secretary of the Admiralty, possibly through the influence of Admiral Sir John Jervis. He was created a baronet in 1804 and was a lord of the Admiralty in 1804-06. After six years out of office he was governor of Bombay in 1812-19 and died at Loders, Dorset, on 2 October 1822. He is remembered by Point Nepean, Victoria, and the Nepean River, New South Wales.

His brother Nicholas was baptized at Saltash on 9 November 1757 and joined the marines as a second lieutenant in December 1776. He saw action off Brest in July 1778 in the *Ocean*. He became a first lieutenant in December 1778, saw service in the *Triton* and *Britannia*, and was engaged in the recruiting service until February 1783. He remained in the marines until 1789, when he joined the New South Wales Corps as a captain on 5 June.

Nepean arrived in Sydney in June 1790 in the *Neptune*, in charge of the first detachment of the New South Wales Corps and, until the arrival of Major Grose [q.v.], he was the corps' commanding officer. During the voyage 'the fiery Nepean' had quarrelled with John Macarthur [q.v.], as a result of which Macarthur applied for Nepean to be court-martialled, but Grose succeeded in arranging a settlement of their dispute. From May 1791 Nepean was stationed at Parramatta, where Surgeon John Harris [q.v.] criticized his administration, accusing him of using his men for his own profit, and commenting that Nepean was discontented at not receiving promotion. In September 1793 Grose sent Nepean home in the *Britannia* because of ill health. When the ship called at Norfolk Island in November Lieut-Governor King directed Nepean to take charge of the island while he visited New Zealand. King asked Nepean to convey his impressions of Norfolk Island to the British government and gave him dispatches to take to England. Owing to the ship meeting pirates in the Malacca Straits he went to Batavia, where he stayed, very ill, until February 1794. Next year he was appointed major and in September joined the 93rd Regiment as lieut-colonel. Thereafter, interspersed with periods on half-pay, he served in Ireland 1795-96, Gibraltar 1802-03, and Canada 1807-10. He was not killed there, as has been stated, but was regularly promoted until he attained the rank of lieut-general in 1814. On 21 April 1784 he married Johanna Francina Carolina (1767?-1845), daughter of Major Wedikind of the 11th Hanoverian Regiment, at Stoke Damerel, Devon. They had four sons, all of whom followed naval and military careers. Nicholas finally retired on half-pay in June 1814, died at Newton Abbot, Devon, on 18 December 1823. His wife died on 4 June 1845.

HRNSW, 2; HRA (1), 1; MS cat under N. Nepean (ML).   VIVIENNE PARSONS

NESBITT; see McCRONE

NEWCOMB; see under DRYSDALE

NEWLAND, RIDGWAY WILLIAM (1790-1864), Congregational minister and pioneer, was born near Odiham, Hampshire, England. At 23 he began theological studies at Old College, Hoxton, and in 1817 he was ordained to the Congregationalist ministry at Hanley, Staffordshire, where he ministered for twenty-two years. Selected by the Colonial Missionary Society to form a settlement in South Australia, he sailed in the *Sir Charles Forbes* with some thirty colonists, including his second wife, née Keeling, an accomplished classical scholar, who cared for her three young children and five of Newland's first marriage. The party arrived in Adelaide in June 1839 and went on in the *Lord Hobart* to Encounter Bay, where a large area of land was taken up.

Newland pioneered with great gusto, helping his party to build houses that formed the township of Yelki. Under his initiative the small settlement became self-sufficient. From local clay he made jars and milk dishes, and, after advice from Hanley, burnt and crushed whale bones for export to the potteries. Crops flourished better than livestock on the coast; he lost sheep from footrot and cattle did not prosper. He worked with his people, clearing land, ploughing, harvesting, driving bullocks, breaking in horses and milking cows. By 1841 he had six wells and could report to Governor Grey that the Aboriginals were becoming as adept as Europeans in reaping his wheat, barley and oats.

Newland was also the unpaid pastor of the south, riding long distances to preach and minister to scattered settlers. His chapel at Encounter Bay was opened in 1846, and other places of worship were established by him. As a justice of the peace he took the lead in local causes, chaired all the local meetings, swaying public opinion at his will yet wounding no man's self-esteem. He supported his colleague, Rev. T. Q. Stow [q.v.], in opposition to state aid for religion and he gave evidence favouring secular schools to the select committee on education in 1851. More than once, he walked in a day the fifty miles to Adelaide carrying a bundle and wading through three rivers. As a district councillor he had much influence in opening a road and bridging the rivers. Returning from one preaching visit to Adelaide and Willunga, his coach capsized and he was fatally injured. He died on 9 March 1864. He was buried in a vault beneath the pulpit of his chapel and later reinterred in the Victor Harbor cemetery.

Although Newland published a sermon on 'Christian Liberality' at Hanley, he usually preached without notes or much preparation. He is remembered best as a fine example of muscular Christianity. His name is preserved at Victor Harbor by the Newland Memorial Church, Newland's Head and the Newland Bridge.

Observer (Adel), 11 Oct 1862, 12 Mar 1864, 30 Mar 1895; *Register* (Adel), 26 Mar 1864.

ALAN RENDELL

NICHOLAS, JOHN LIDDIARD (1784-1868), author and traveller, applied for permission to settle in New South Wales in 1812. An iron founder, of the Cannon foundry, New Gravel Lane, Shadwell, London, he promised that he and two partners would bring with them £10,000 in capital and equipment, including a steam-engine which they would be willing to sell to the governor for use in sawmilling. He arrived at Sydney in the *Earl Spencer*

in October 1813 with only one partner, John Dickson [q.v.]. The pair soon parted Nicholas claiming to be disappointed with Dickson's character. But Nicholas must have been disappointing as a businessman. Showing no enterprise, he spent his time sociably with Samuel Marsden and the Bents [qq.v.], becoming involved in Jeffery Bent's violent toll-gate incidents, though without imitating Bent in forcing his way through without payment.

In 1814 he accompanied Marsden to New Zealand on his missionary visit and in two volumes published a *Narrative of a Voyage to New Zealand . . .*(London, 1817). The book was well received and was translated into Dutch and German in 1819. Nicholas reported plainly and fairly on the voyage made in the brig *Active* between November and March, which resulted in the establishment of the first Christian mission to the Maoris and the first transfer of land to white men. On 24 February 1815, as one of two witnesses, Nicholas signed the deed of sale to the Church Missionary Society of 200 acres for twelve axes. He viewed the Maoris sympathetically and was pleased to meet two of them in England in 1818.

On his return from New Zealand Nicholas was granted 700 acres in the parish of Gidley, County of Cumberland, in October 1815 but he left the colony a month later in a ship bound for England by way of China, and in 1822 sold his land to Marsden for £300. Other glimpses of Nicholas, a report in 1820 that he was 'very comfortably off' and his own remark in 1838 that he was 'in no employment', confirm the picture of a man who preferred to live on his capital rather than venture it in commerce.

Nicholas supported Marsden in his disputes with the government and denied accusations by J. T. Campbell [q.v.] that the chaplain was abusing his office. He delivered to William Wilberforce and Elizabeth Fry copies of a letter from Marsden on the Female Factory at Parramatta; afterwards he assisted Mrs Fry in her attempts to improve conditions on female convict ships, and asked Marsden to comment on any observable results.

Nicholas died from senile decay at Reading, Berkshire, on 22 July 1868 and in the only indication of any occupation after his return to England, he was described as having been a 'Clerk to Charity Commissioners'.

HRA (1), 7; Sel cttee on the present state of the islands of New Zealand, Report, PP (HL), 1838 (680); MS cat under J. L. Nicholas (ML).

JOHN BARRETT

NICHOLS, ISAAC (1770-1819), farmer, shipowner and public servant, was born on 29 July 1770 at Calne, Wiltshire, England, the son of Jonathan Nichols, droget maker, and his wife Sarah. Found guilty of stealing, he was sentenced to seven years transportation at the Warminster Sessions, Wiltshire, in July 1790, and arrived in New South Wales in the *Admiral Barrington* in October 1791. After a few years in the country his ability, diligence and sobriety so impressed Governor Hunter and his aide-de-camp, George Johnston [q.v.], that the governor appointed him chief overseer of the convict gangs labouring round Sydney. On 20 December 1797 after his sentence had expired, Hunter granted him fifty acres in the Concord district, where he established a successful farm on which he was assisted by two convicts whose services he was allowed instead of salary as an overseer. Next year he obtained a spirit licence, the first of several, and opened an inn in George Street.

On 12 March 1799 Nichols was brought before the Criminal Court charged with having received stolen property. After a trial lasting four days he was convicted and sentenced to fourteen years on Norfolk Island. The three naval officers on the bench, Waterhouse, William Kent and Flinders [qq.v.], were all convinced that Nichols was innocent, but they were overborne by the judge-advocate, Richard Dore [q.v.], and the three officers of the New South Wales Corps, MacKellar, Lucas and Bayly [qq.v.]. Hunter was most dissatisfied with the trial, being convinced that the verdict was the result of perjury by the witnesses and prejudice on the part of Dore, so he suspended the sentence and referred the matter to England. There the papers remained pigeon-holed for nearly two years, but in January 1802 Governor King was directed to grant Nichols a free pardon.

In the meantime Nichols, keenly alert to the economic possibilities of the young colony, continued to prosper. Between 1797 and 1815 to his original grant at Concord he added further properties in the same district, at Hunter's Hill and at Petersham until his holdings totalled some 1400 acres. He leased half an acre in Sydney near the hospital wharf, which Lieut-Governor Foveaux [q.v.] converted to a grant. Here he built a substantial house and other buildings. He also established a shipyard, where in 1805 he built the *Governor Hunter*, 33 tons, which he used in the Newcastle, Hawkesbury and Bass Strait trade.

In the Bligh rebellion Nichols took the side of the insurrectionaries. In March 1809

he was appointed superintendent of public works and assistant to the Naval Officer; next month, to stop the practice of persons fraudulently obtaining mail from incoming vessels, he was made the colony's first postmaster, a position he held until his death. When Governor Macquarie arrived he too was impressed with Nichols, whom he described as 'a most zealous, active and useful man'. He appointed him principal superintendent of convicts in place of Nicholas Divine [q.v.], who was old and infirm. When Nichols sought leave to retire from this post in 1814 Macquarie spoke appreciatively of his great vigilance and unremitting attention to duty.

In his last ten years Nichols enjoyed the friendship and esteem of most leading people in the colony. His home was the scene of many social functions, including the Bachelors' Ball and the annual dinners to celebrate the foundation of the colony. He was a major supplier of meat to government stores and a generous subscriber to public causes. Everything he attempted was carried out with thoroughness and precision. When he died on 8 November 1819, the *Sydney Gazette* spoke of his devotion to his public duties, his worth as a farmer, his contributions to the improvement of colonial gardening, and of his activities as a shipowner.

On 11 September 1796 Nichols had married Mary Warren, and after her death by drowning in October 1804, he married Rosanna Abrahams, daughter of Esther Johnston [q.v.] on 18 February 1805. She bore him three sons, Isaac David (1804-1867), 'gentleman', George Robert (1809-1857) [q.v.], barrister and solicitor, and Charles Hamilton (1811-1869). Shortly before Isaac Nichols died he sent the two elder boys to England to be educated.

HRNSW, 3-7; HRA (1), 7, 8; *Sydney Gazette*, 17 Mar, 28 Apr 1805, 27 Aug 1809, 17 Oct, 14 Nov 1818.

ARTHUR McMARTIN

NICHOLSON, SIR CHARLES (1808-1903), statesman, landowner, businessman, connoisseur, scholar and physician, was born on 23 November 1808 in Cockermouth, Cumberland, England, the only son of Charles Nicholson, merchant and agent to Lord Egremont, and of Barbara Ascough, the daughter of a wealthy London merchant. Nicholson's mother died when he was 3 and his father a few years later, and he was brought up by a maiden aunt in Yorkshire. After private education by tutors, he went to the University of Edinburgh to study medicine. Having obtained his medical degree with distinction, being second in his year, he became an extraordinary member of the Hunterian Medical Society of Edinburgh. Nicholson graduated as doctor of medicine in 1833, after submitting a thesis in Latin on asphyxiation, its causes and treatment.

Later that year he sailed for Sydney with his aunt, Miss Ascough, and his cousin, James Ascough, to join his uncle, Captain James Ascough, a wealthy trader and shipowner, who had extensive landed property on the Hawkesbury River and the upper Hunter. Nicholson inherited most of his uncle's property on Ascough's death by drowning, and this was the foundation of his considerable fortune. For a few years after arrival he practised as a physician, gaining a local reputation in and around Sydney as a skilful obstetrician, but by 1840 he was devoting his attention to business affairs, buying land and stock and forming sheep stations. In the 1840s he also took an interest in establishing shipping and railway companies, and by 1850 he owned a fine estate and mansion at Luddenham, near Sydney, as well as the residence, Tarmons, at Potts Point, which he bought from Sir Maurice O'Connell [q.v.]. In 1836 he was prominent among the founders of the Australian Gaslight Co., in 1842 he was active in the movement to encourage immigration from India and throughout the 1840s he was a member of the Medical Board. By the early 1850s he was a trustee of both the savings bank and the Australian Museum.

In 1843 he was elected a member of the new part-elective Legislative Council as a representative for Port Phillip, and was soon recognized as one of the ablest speakers and men of business in the House. He was elected Speaker in 1846, and was twice re-elected to this office, holding it until the introduction of responsible government in 1856. Nicholson's ability to make friends among men of all political opinions, and his tact and moderation fitted him admirably for the Speakership, and often he was able to reconcile the discordant factions in the council. Generally in the 1840s he tended to align himself with the group headed by W. C. Wentworth [q.v.], and with the conservatives who looked to James Macarthur [q.v.] as their leader. In the usury question of 1843-44 and the land questions of the later 1840s he supported the policies of the Wentworth group. In 1855 he was appointed to the interim Executive Council which governed until the first administration under responsible government took over.

Nicholson was an unusual combination of man of affairs and scholar. He led a very active social life but was deeply interested in the classics, history and education, which he made one of his principal council interests. By 1845 he had already begun to collect rare books, antiquities, pictures and manuscripts, and was regarded as one of the most cultivated men in the colony. In 1849-50 he joined Wentworth in pressing for the establishment of a university, and in December 1850 was nominated a member of the original senate of the University of Sydney. As vice-provost from 1851 to 1854 and provost (later chancellor) from 1854 to 1862, he played an important part in working out the design of Australia's first university. His ideal was an institution patterned on Oxford and Cambridge but without the restrictions on entry that characterized those universities, and with the addition of new features in accordance with medical and scientific advances. Nicholson was a fellow of the senate until 1883 and until his death maintained a keen interest in the university, though he lived in England from 1862. He acted for some forty years as the university's agent in England, selecting staff and adding periodically to the library and to the museum of antiquities which he presented to the university in 1857. In 1855-58 he was in Egypt, where he visited archaeological sites and obtained a collection of early Egyptian art, then went to England, where, through his friendship with Sir James Clarke, the Queen's physician, he secured for the University of Sydney considerable publicity and a Royal Charter (1857) giving its degrees equal status with those of the old British universities.

On his return to Sydney in 1858 Nicholson was largely instrumental in securing the acceptance of Edmund Blacket's grandiose architectural plans for the completion of the university buildings. Finding that the whole political climate of the country had changed since 1856, he was reluctant to re-enter politics, but was nominated a member of the Legislative Council of the new colony of Queensland, and was prevailed upon by the governor, Sir George Bowen, to become president of the council. While in Queensland he acquired substantial land interests, especially in the Rockhampton district.

By 1862 he had decided to return again to England, where he found more scope for his cultural interests. He intended to return to Australia, but after his marriage in 1865 to Sarah Keightley, the talented and artistic daughter of a London solicitor, he settled in England, first on the country estate of Hadleigh, Essex, and from 1876 at Totteridge Grange, near Barnet, Hertfordshire. Nicholson soon became the central figure in the circle of Australian 'colonists' in London and was often consulted by the Colonial Office on Australian and other imperial problems. He became a leading member of the Royal Colonial Institute, the Royal Society of Arts, the British Association, and many other learned and cultural bodies. He pursued his archaeological interests with vigour and conducted excavations in the Channel Islands, Jutland and England in the 1860s and 1870s, and was later closely identified with the Egyptologists, Sayce and Petrie; he supported the Egyptian Exploration Fund. In the early 1880s he took up the study of Hebrew, and in 1891 he published a handsome volume entitled *Ægyptiaca, comprising a catalogue of Egyptian antiquities . . . now deposited in the Museum of Sydney.*

He published several pamphlets on Australia's resources and prospects, and was appointed to represent the interests of the Central Queensland Separation League in London in 1890. In the later part of the decade he expressed doubts as to the expediency of Federation. His business interests were considerable as chairman of the London, Liverpool and Globe Insurance Co., and a director of the Peninsular and Orient Steamship Co. He was also one of the first London businessmen to have financial interests in Persia. In 1901 fire destroyed Totteridge Grange and with it Nicholson's journals and correspondence. He died on 8 November 1903.

One of the outstanding men of his time in Sydney, Nicholson had strong humanitarian, religious and political views. In later life he opposed capital punishment, and described the horror he had felt at the multiple hangings he had witnessed in his early days in Sydney. A conservative who admired Gladstone, he also admired Dean Stanley, and rejected the doctrines of the Anglo-Catholics. He was a man of impressive appearance. He travelled as far afield as Russia beyond the Urals and had a wide range of influential acquaintances and correspondents. He was knighted in 1852, created a baronet in 1859, and held honorary degrees from the Universities of Oxford, Cambridge and Edinburgh. He had two sons, Charles Archibald, a distinguished ecclesiastical architect, who became the second baronet, and Sydney, a musician and composer of church music. The Nicholson Museum in the University of Sydney, and the Nicholson pictures there, including Lely's 'Lady in Blue',

commemorate his name. He has aptly been described as Australia's first great collector, and he was also a generous patron of the arts and sciences. The pre-Raphaelite sculptor, Thomas Woolner, whom he befriended in 1854, cast a handsome portrait medallion of him which is held in the archives of Sydney University, and in 1844 Ludwig Leichhardt [q.v.] named a mountain after him.

D. S. Macmillan, 'An Australian aristocrat', *Aust Q*, Sept, 1956; Nicholson papers (Archives, Univ Syd); Senate records (Archives, Univ Syd); MS cat under C. Nicholson (ML).   DAVID S. MACMILLAN

NIXON, FRANCIS RUSSELL (1803-1879), Church of England bishop, was born on 1 August 1803, the second son of Rev. Robert Nixon, D.D., F.R.S., of North Cray, Kent, England. He was educated at Merchant Taylors' School, London, and at Oxford (B.A., 1827; M.A., 1841; D.D., 1842). Graduating third class in classics he was made a probationary fellow of St John's College. After ordination he served as chaplain to the embassy at Naples and was then appointed one of the 'Six Preachers' at Canterbury Cathedral and chaplain to the archbishop. He next held the parish of Sandgate and the perpetual curacy of Ash next Sandwich. In January 1843, to provide funds for a chapel of ease at Ash, he published *Lectures, Historical, Doctrinal and Practical, on the Catechism of the Church of England;* it went through at least six editions. On 21 August 1842 Nixon was appointed first bishop of Tasmania and three days later was consecrated in Westminster Abbey with four other bishops. With his wife and children, their governess and Archdeacon F. A. Marriott [q.v.], he sailed in the *Duke of Roxburgh.* At Cape Town, where no Anglican bishop was appointed until 1848, he confirmed some four hundred persons, consecrated a church and ordained a priest. Arriving at Hobart Town in July 1843, he was received by civic and ecclesiastical leaders, took the oaths and was made a member of the Executive Council. His letters patent were read, creating Van Diemen's Land a separate diocese, St David's Church a cathedral and Hobart a city. A week later he was enthroned. His first official residence was in Upper Davey Street; after three years he moved to Boa Vista in Argyle Street (later part of the Friends' School), and in 1850 he bought Runnymede at New Town, renaming it Bishopstowe.

Nixon soon sized up the needs of his

diocese and within eighteen months sent Marriott to England for help; in particular he wanted men for more adequate spiritual ministrations; and money to build churches and schools. Most remarkable of all was his request for money to establish a college on English university lines for the higher education of colonial youth and for training them for holy orders. The archdeacon's mission was highly successful in obtaining both men and money: in 1846 the Launceston Church Grammar School was opened in May, the Hutchins School in Hobart in August, and Christ's College at Bishopsbourne in October.

Nixon was soon in collision with Lieut-Governor Eardley-Wilmot on the discipline of clergymen within the diocese. Wilmot acknowledged the bishop's control over colonial chaplains even though they were paid by the government, yet he continued to employ and pay two of them whose licences had been withdrawn by Nixon for unbecoming behaviour. His reason for thus thwarting the bishop was that these chaplains had not been 'tried and convicted', although he knew the bishop had no court. The problem of chaplains attached to the convict establishments was, however, more difficult. On 29 May 1844 Nixon put his case clearly in a letter to Lord Stanley; he refused to ordain, licence or have any official responsibility for chaplains to the convicts because they could be appointed, dismissed and restored without his privity and were therefore exclusively under civil jurisdiction. To avoid a clash, Wilmot called these chaplains 'religious instructors' and claimed that their ordination was not an essential qualification. After lengthy correspondence between Nixon, the lieut-governor, the secretary of state and the archbishop of Canterbury, a reasonable compromise was reached: the governor was to submit appointments and removals for the bishop's consent, and any disagreements were to be settled by consultation between Downing Street and Canterbury. Stanley hoped to ease tension by appointing Marriott 'superintendent of convict chaplains', but although the plan was supported by the archbishop of Canterbury, it angered Nixon as another instance of lay interference with episcopal authority. Through respect for Stanley and confidence in his archdeacon, he agreed to allow Marriott to act as superintendent, but only by his episcopal authority. Dissatisfied with this solution, Nixon went to England in 1846-48, but he got little support from the archbishop and none from the government. He was able, however, to denounce the convict system which was turning the

colony, he said, into 'the lazar house of the British dominions'. In 1847 he gave evidence before a House of Lords committee on the pitiable state of the convicts and the evils of transportation. His plain speaking contributed to the abolitionists' victory in 1853 and also helped to solve the problem of chaplains to the convicts.

Nixon had other difficulties with some of the clergy who had been in the colony before his arrival. Having tasted independence, they did not submit gracefully to his authority and looked on him as an interloper. The senior chaplain, Rev. William Bedford [q.v.] of St David's Church, was quite open in opposition. Three times he refused to produce his commission for inspection and, when Nixon insisted on using his cathedral for Lenten lectures, Bedford and his church wardens asserted their parochial rights over St David's, threatening to close the doors against him and to appeal to the civil authorities against his 'aggression'. The bishop's letters patent enjoined him to 'visit all Rectors, curates and chaplains' in the diocese 'with all manner of jurisdiction, power and coercion ecclesiastical', but they did not authorize the establishment of a consistorial court with power to compel the attendance of witnesses or to examine them on oath. Nixon sought this authority from the lieut-governor without success, for other denominations were suspicious. An appeal to London resulted in May 1849 in supplementary letters patent that omitted power to set up a court, and with no strengthening of his disciplinary power his difficulties were increased. The problem was not solved until, in consultation with his clergy and laity, the constitution of a synod was hammered out and given legal effect by the Tasmanian parliament on 5 November 1858. Next May the first synod met for thirteen days. One feature of it was that the laity shared equally with the bishop and clergy in management of the church's affairs. Its principal business was to pass acts for the trial of ecclesiastical offences, for the patronage of parishes and for a general church fund on a voluntary basis in preparation for the withdrawal of state aid.

In October 1850 Nixon went to Sydney for the historic meeting of the six Australasian bishops. Publication in Tasmania of the 'Minutes' of this meeting caused great controversy. The Oxford Movement and ritual questions were already disturbing the churches and in some quarters Nixon and a number of his new clergy were accused of Puseyite tendencies. This was far from true; in November 1844 in a dramatic scene at the cathedral Nixon had read a protest against the appointment of a Roman Catholic bishop in Tasmania and solemnly placed the document on the altar. In his visitation charge to the clergy in 1851, he clearly enunciated his 'full belief that soundness in the faith with regard to the sacraments of Christ is a probation against Romanism on the one hand and Puritanism on the other'. Nevertheless publication of the 'Minutes' brought addresses and counter-addresses to the bishop. The chief cause of unrest was the statement on baptismal regeneration, an aftermath of the Privy Council judgment on the Gorham case. Those who feared that the true faith was being undermined in the diocese formed an 'association of members of the Church of England for maintaining in Van Diemen's Land the principles of the Protestant Reformation'. Led by Rev. H. P. Fry [q.v.] they published a protest in the form of a 'solemn declaration', maintaining among other things the right of private judgment. With a high sense of his office and prerogatives, and of the need for discipline, Nixon maintained that private judgment in matters on which the church had declared her faith in the Book of Common Prayer and the Thirty-nine Articles was not consistent for any member of that church. He therefore refused preferment to anyone who had been a party to the protest. After long trouble and tension, his attitude mellowed, and on 1 June 1855 the *Tasmanian Church Chronicle*, reporting his third visitation, paid this tribute: 'we must be allowed to record our admiration of the perfect confidence and cordiality with which the Bishop placed himself in the hands of his clergy. His Lordship is better understood now than he seems to have been four years ago'. In recommending rather than enjoining the introduction of a weekly offertory to help the church to be self-supporting, he set a fine example by giving a tenth of his government income and other generous sums.

In the controversy between churches and government over subsidized education the bishop joined with vigour. Earlier, religious instruction of an Anglican type had a prominent place in the public day schools. In May 1839, however, a newly appointed Board of Education changed to a quasi-secular system, which provided for daily Bible readings but forbade denominational teaching, although allowing clergy the right to teach children of their church at convenient hours. Anglicans protested without avail against the spending of public funds on a system of religious education which denied the majority church the right to instruct her children in their own faith. The bishop urged clergy and people to repudiate state aid on these conditions, and to establish church schools financed by their own efforts, and where that was not possible, to organize Sunday schools.

Nixon never spared himself in the pastoral oversight of his large diocese, which included King Island, the Furneaux group and even Norfolk Island. In 1849 his yacht was stolen and never recovered, but he still contrived to visit the Bass Strait islands and northern Tasmanian settlements. His *Cruise of the Beacon*, published in 1854 with his own illustrations, records one such visit. At his home, between travelling, he had interviews, voluminous correspondence, administrative duties, reading and the preparation of sermons and lectures. Even so, he found time for his family and for music, sketching and painting.

In 1847 he was described as ' a remarkable man both in appearance and character, good-looking, coal-black hair . . . piercing black eyes, and full, rather thick lips; tenacious of his rights, extremely anxious to be correct with regard to costume and all other points of etiquette, devoted to the fine arts and a beautiful draughtsman'. But twenty years of pioneering took their toll. After illness in 1862 he went to England hoping to improve his health and to return next year. But he was no better and resigned from 19 August 1863, telling the archbishop of Canterbury that he could not conscientiously retain his office with satisfaction to himself or with efficiency to the church. He was given the important living of Bolton Percy, Yorkshire, but his health did not improve. In 1865 he retired to Vignolo on Lake Maggiore, Italy, which he loved. The milder climate brought benefit, although he was seldom free from his 'tooth-ache in the back'. He died on 7 April 1879, and was buried in the British cemetery at Stresa.

Nixon married three times. In 1829 he married Frances Maria Streatfield (d. 1834) by whom he had three children, Frances Maria, Robert and Harriet. In 1836 he married Anna Maria, daughter of Charles Woodcock; they had eight children. Anna Maria was a devoted wife who acted as his secretary. She also sketched and played the organ at St David's. Two years after Anna's death at Vignolo on 26 November 1868, Nixon married Flora Elizabeth Muller, who bore him two sons.

In the new cathedral in Hobart Nixon is remembered by a stained glass window and by the side chapel. A portrait in oils by Rev. J. Dixon is in the possession of

Holy Trinity Church, Launceston. A number of his water-colours are in the Diocesan Registry, Hobart, and others in private hands.

F. R. Nixon, *Charge delivered to the clergy of the diocese of Tasmania* (Hob, 1846, 1851, 1855); N. Nixon, *Pioneer bishop in Van Diemen's Land 1843-1863* (Hob, 1954); *Tasmanian Church Chronicle*, Jan 1852 - Dec 1856; N. Batt and M. Roe, 'Conflict within the Church of England in Tasmania, 1850-1858', *J of Religious History*, 1 (1966).

W. R. BARRETT

NOBBS, GEORGE HUNN (1799-1884), schoolteacher and pastor, was born on 16 October 1799 in Ireland; according to his own statements, he was the unacknowledged son of the marquis of Hastings and Jemima ffrench, the daughter of an Irish baronet. Nobbs's childhood was spent near Yarmouth with the farmer whose name he assumed. When 12 his mother's friend, Admiral Robert Murray, procured him a position in the navy and in 1813 he was appointed to the storeship *Indefatigable* in which he visited New South Wales and Van Diemen's Land. The following year he joined a ship belonging to South American patriots and, although captured by the royalists on three occasions, he continued to serve with the insurgent forces for six years, being commissioned a lieutenant in the Chilean navy in 1820 for his part in the capture by Lord Cochrane of the Spanish frigate *Esmeraldas* from under the Callao batteries.

In 1822 Nobbs returned to England at his mother's request and before her death later that year she urged him to settle in some remote part of the world where the wrong done her would be forgotten; her dying injunction was 'Go to Pitcairn Island, my son, dwell there, and the blessing of God rest upon you'.

After a period in the merchant service, including visits to West Africa as chief mate and captain of the *Gambia*, Nobbs accordingly left for Callao where he met an American, Noah Bunker, who possessed an eighteen-ton cutter in which the two sailed for Pitcairn. They landed on 5 November 1828 and were welcomed by John Adams, the aged patriarch who had largely handed over the spiritual and temporal care of his community to the Bristol shipwright, John Buffett. Though Buffett had been five years on Pitcairn Nobbs's superior education and stronger character enabled him to assume the position as pastor and schoolteacher, albeit not without friction, which continued after Adams's death four months later.

On 18 October 1829 Nobbs married Sarah, granddaughter of Fletcher Christian, and in 1831, when the islanders were removed to Tahiti, he asked to stay behind with his family. Deferring to popular pressure, however, he accompanied the community, and his ministrations at Tahiti, particularly to the many who fell sick, resulted in his being requested to return with them to Pitcairn 'as their sole teacher and minister'. Tahiti had weakened the community both morally and through the deaths of a fifth of its members, and after their return in September an anarchic period set in during which the distillation of spirits prohibited by Adams was recommenced, Nobbs's own position being weakened by his occasional lapses from temperance.

In October 1832 Joshua Hill, who arrived on Pitcairn claiming to be a representative of the British government, succeeded in supplanting Nobbs as pastor and teacher and in March 1834 forced him to leave the island. He thereupon settled as a missionary on Mangareva until, with Hill's exposure, the community requested him to return, which he did in October.

Although in 1838 Pitcairn was given a Constitution and code of laws, with an annually elected magistrate, Nobbs became in reality the leader of the community through his acknowledged talents and record of service. For over twenty years he taught the youth, ministered to the sick (augmenting by experience his rudimentary knowledge of medicine and surgery) and consoled the dying. In return he was spared many of the routine manual tasks of the islanders: as pastor his house was kept in repair; as surgeon he was given three acres of land for cultivation, and as schoolmaster 1s. a month for each scholar, from those who could afford it.

In 1852 Admiral Fairfax Moresby arranged for Nobbs to visit England, where on 30 November he was ordained as a priest and licensed as chaplain of Pitcairn Island by the bishop of London and appointed a missionary of the Society for the Propagation of the Gospel at a salary of £50; before returning he had an audience with Queen Victoria.

Four years later, and largely on the advice of Moresby and Nobbs, the community elected to migrate to Norfolk Island, where they arrived on 8 June 1856. Although Norfolk was a disappointment to many, Nobbs's exhortations and example prevented all but a few from returning to Pitcairn. He continued his former work as pastor and teacher until 1859, when Governor Denison sent Thomas Rossiter to act as schoolmaster and store-keeper and increased Nobbs's salary as chaplain by an annual grant of £50 from the island revenue. From about 1870, with increasing age and deafness, Nobbs gradually took a less active part in community life, though he continued to act as. chaplain. He died at Norfolk Island on 5 November 1884, leaving a widow, 10 children, 65 grand-children and 19 great-grandchildren.

Nobbs's arrival on Pitcairn was provi-dential for the community, arresting the demoralization and disintegration which followed the patriarchal rule of John Adams. He served the islanders with single-minded devotion both on Pitcairn and Norfolk, advising and guiding successive generations as they changed from a small adolescent and unsophisticated family to an adult community able to face the in-creasing pressures from the outside world with assurance. Though on Pitcairn he had to face criticism from island factions, especially from Hill's supporters led by Edward Quintal, and on his arrival at Norfolk from Bishop Selwyn, he received the constant support and friendship of Moresby and Rev. T. B. Murray, secretary of the Society for Promoting Christian Knowledge, and in his declining years en-joyed the honour and respect of the entire community.

G. H. Nobbs, A sermon . . . and an appendix containing some brief notices of Mr. Nobbs and his flock (Lond, 1852); T. B. Murray, Pitcairn: the island, the people, and the pastor (Lond, 1853); D. Belcher, The mutineers of the Bounty and their descend-ants in Pitcairn and Norfolk Islands (Lond, 1870); C. P. Lucas (ed), The Pitcairn Island register book (Lond, 1929); G. H. Nobbs, Papers 1836-79 (ML); Pitcairn Island Recorder, 1838 (ML); Minutes and correspondence (SPCK archives, Lond).   H. E. MAUDE

NORTON, JAMES (1795-1862), solicitor, was born on 27 July 1795, the third son of John Norton, of Hastings, England, and his wife Mary, née Bradford. He received a legal education and was admitted to practise as an attorney. He decided to try his fortune as a lawyer in New South Wales and sailed as captain's clerk in the Maria, which arrived at Sydney in Sep-tember 1818. He brought with him £800. Only four other solicitors were then prac-tising in the colony. His father, a brother and three sisters followed him to Sydney and the family received a large grant of land in the Mulgoa district with a six-mile frontage to the Nepean River where James Norton also was granted 950 acres, which

he farmed. The legal practice flourished and in 1826 he took William Barker into part-nership. Norton was counsel for the Crown in many big cases.

In his first year in Sydney he became an active member of a committee to form a savings bank. In May 1825 he became first registrar of the archdeaconry of Syd-ney, and served in it for thirty years. In 1834 he bought Elswick, a 100-acre property on the Parramatta Road. There he had an old-world garden with groups of roses, bamboos and gardenias, peacocks, a pond rich in eels, and an orchard. A row of cottages stood behind the house for the convict servants. He won several prizes for his flowers and plants at the Australian Floral and Horticultural Society Exhibition in 1841.

Norton was a shareholder in the Aus-tralian Agricultural Co. and a director of the Bank of Australia from April 1826 until its collapse in 1843. He was also director of the Bank of New South Wales from February 1823 until May 1826, when he resigned. He was nominated to the first Legislative Council under responsible gov-ernment on 16 September 1856 and framed many bills of a legal character. He took little part after 1859 because of ill health and his term of five years lapsed on 13 May 1861. Among his many pamphlets he published Essays and Reflections in Aus-tralia (Sydney, 1852) and Australian Essays on Subjects Political, Moral, and Religious (London, 1857). He declared himself un-deluded 'by the clap-trap of free trade', and wrote Facts for the Protectionists (Sydney, 1857) in refutation of J. D. Lang's [q.v.] article of the same name. In support of the Protectionists he also published Free Trade and Protection (Sydney, 1857) and The Condition of the Colony of New South Wales (Sydney, 1860).

On 10 January 1824 he married Jane, daughter of Alexander Kenneth McKenzie [q.v.], cashier of the Bank of New South Wales. They had eight sons and two daughters. His wife died on 23 March 1840 at Elswick and on 1 February 1843 he married Marian, only daughter of John Backhouse, of Ipswich, England, by whom he had three sons and two daughters. Norton died on 31 August 1862 at Elswick, and a few months later his widow sailed for England where she settled.

Norton had a rough manner and was very outspoken but was kind and conscien-tious and regarded with affection by those in close contact with him.

The Nortons of Sussex and New South Wales (Syd, 1912); A. Halloran, 'Some early legal celebrities', JRAHS, 10 (1924), p 322-28.

O

OAKDEN, PHILIP (1784?-1851), merchant, banker and social worker, was the son of Philip Oakden of Stydd, Derbyshire, England, and his wife Mary, née Huerdd. After a business failure in London he went to Hamburg in 1816 as a commission merchant in partnership with Osmond Gilles [q.v.] and by 1827, when he revisited England, he was able to repay all his creditors, who presented him with plate worth £100 inscribed with their testimony to his honour and moral rectitude. He finally left Hamburg in 1829 for Liverpool, where he joined the Wesleyan Society.

After the colonial success of other Hamburg merchants he emigrated to Van Diemen's Land in the *Forth* in November 1833, and next year was elected to the board of directors to organize the establishment of the independent Tamar Bank in Launceston. Competition from the new London-backed Bank of Australasia jeopardized the Tamar, which had considered closing until public opinion forced the Australasia to lend its rival enough funds to continue. However, in 1836, when Oakden heard through his friends in England of a scheme for establishing a United Banking Co. of Australia and Van Diemen's Land, the Tamar directors sent him to Liverpool empowered to negotiate an agreement with the new bank. Interest for the scheme was found, on his arrival, to be stronger among London financiers, who welcomed Oakden's proposal, his contacts in Liverpool and his success in interesting George Fife Angas [q.v.] to lend the weight of his name, influence and capital in the projected company. Oakden was chosen a director, and sent by the board to persuade Liverpool and Manchester interests to accept directorships. On his return to Launceston in the *Clifton* in April 1838 he helped to organize the taking over of the Tamar Bank and the formal opening of the Union Bank of which he became a foundation director. Sub-branches were formed in Campbell Town and in Melbourne and, with J. C. McLaren, Oakden opened a separate branch of the Union in Hobart Town.

Although his advice to business friends was sound and much sought after, his own ventures were not particularly successful. His land speculation in the Port Phillip District in 1840 was unprofitable. He founded the Launceston Shipping Co. and became its director and treasurer in January 1849, but disaster came with the wreck of its first ship, the *Philip Oakden*, in 1851. The properties he acquired from Launceston to Mole Creek (where the caves were first named after him as their discoverer) involved him in considerable litigation. He did moderately well with his flocks, which he improved by the import of pedigreed stock. In 1846 he was treasurer of the London Agency for Van Diemen's Land and in 1850 he was chairman of the Cornwall Fire and Marine Insurance Co.

His interest in charitable works was renowned. He was one of the early members of the Wesleyan Church in Launceston and a trustee of its first chapel, securing £600 for its completion in 1835. He was superintendent of the Sunday School, a promoter and member of the Board of Managers of the Launceston Bank for Savings, a trustee and for many years vice-president of the Mechanics' Institute, and a member of the committee of St John's Hospital, the Benevolent Society, and the Launceston Horticultural Society, a joint secretary of the Infant School and a member of the Westbury Road Trust. With more than usual truth, his obituarist could claim 'he was a man scrupulously just, candid, truthful and sincere'. He died at Launceston on 31 July 1851.

In October 1839 he married Georgiana, the daughter of George Cowie, an alderman of London. They had six children. A son Percy, an architect, designed the Methodist Church, Ross. A tablet was erected to Philip Oakden's memory in the Launceston Wesleyan Church, and his portrait hangs in the Australian and New Zealand Bank, previously the Union Bank, Launceston.

S. J. Butlin, *Foundations of the Australian monetary system 1788-1851* (Melb, 1953); S. J. Butlin, *Australia and New Zealand Bank* (Melb, 1961); *Wood's Tasmanian Almanack*, 1847-51; *Cornwall Chronicle*, 7 Apr 1838; *Examiner* (Launceston), 2 Aug 1851, 18 Aug 1962.   ISABELLA J. MEAD

OAKES, FRANCIS (1770-1844), chief constable, was born on 15 April 1770 at Foleshill, Warwickshire, England. A shoemaker by trade and a member of the Congregational Church, he volunteered as an artisan missionary to go to the South Seas in the *Duff* in 1796. He was stationed at Tahiti and was one of those who decided to leave the mission with Rev. J. F. Cover [q.v.]. On arriving in Sydney in 1798 he accepted a grant of 100 acres at Dundas and virtually abandoned his missionary vocation. He was one of the missionaries referred to by contemporaries as having dishonoured his calling by moral defection, though he later supported religious work in the colony.

Oakes remained on his farm until September 1805 when he was appointed chief constable for the Parramatta district. On 27 January 1806 he married Rebecca, the daughter of John and Mary Small; she was born at Sydney on 22 September 1789 and received some acclaim as 'the first or second Anglo-Australian to be married'. Regarded as 'a most useful officer', Oakes was involved in three of the cases leading to the overthrow of Governor Bligh. He gave evidence at the official investigation into the conduct of D'Arcy Wentworth [q.v.], was sent to arrest John Macarthur [q.v.] for refusing to attend an inquiry concerning the schooner Parramatta, and lodged a deposition against Macarthur, who had resisted arrest. His report resulted in the immediate criminal prosecution of Macarthur, who blamed Oakes for misconstruing his conversation. During the rebel administration Oakes was dismissed from office. He was one of the settlers who petitioned the Colonial Office in alarm at the condition of the colony; he was chosen by Bligh as a witness to attend Lieut-Colonel Johnston's [q.v.] court martial, and sailed to England with Bligh in May 1810. He returned to New South Wales in the Mary in May 1812 and resumed his duties. Besides being a police officer and farmer, he was also a baker, shop-keeper and contractor. His civic offices in the Parramatta district included inspector of slaughtering houses (June 1812), clerk of the public market (December 1812) and auctioneer (1814). In 1814-22 he was superintendent of the Female Factory at Parramatta. He was an honest steady citizen, though an index to his character is given in the story that when asked if he would swear to the truth of a certain statement, he replied, 'Oh, yes, I'll chance it'. He did not have the entire approbation of his religious colleagues, for W. Crook [q.v.] found him 'a bold rough creature', and J. D. Lang [q.v.] averred that he was known locally as 'a settler, a chief constable, an auctioneer and a scoundrel'. He died at Parramatta on 5 February 1844. His widow died there on 13 February 1883, having borne him fourteen children.

Two of his sons, George (1813-1881) and Francis Rowland became members of parliament, and a grandson, Archdeacon

George Spencer Oakes (1855-1932) was a noted Church of England clergyman in the west of New South Wales. Mary (1810-1880), the third daughter, worked among the female convicts. In May 1826 she married Rev. John Hutchinson (1793-1866), the first Wesleyan minister to be ordained in Australia. After working briefly as a missionary in Tonga, Hutchinson returned to Sydney in 1828 and in January 1832 he became superintendent of the Female House of Correction in Hobart. Mrs Hutchinson was appointed matron and according to Sir William Denison was 'virtually the superintendent'. When her husband was forced to resign through ill health in March 1851, Denison placed her in charge of the Female Factory in Launceston. She was noted for her efficiency and carried out her duties until she retired in August 1854, after the cessation of transportation to Tasmania. She died at North Hobart on 19 February 1880.

HRA (1), 2, 6-10, (4), 1; G. Paterson, The history of New South Wales (Newcastle upon Tyne, 1811), p 410, 570; R. C. Hutchinson, 'The Reverend John Hutchinson', PTHRA, 9 (1961); R. C. Hutchinson, 'Mrs Hutchinson and the female factories of early Australia', PTHRA, 11 (1963); MS cat under F. Oakes (ML).

NIEL GUNSON

OATLEY, JAMES (1770-1839), watch maker and settler, was a clock and watch maker of Stafford, England, when at the age of 44 he was convicted at the Southampton Assizes on 7 March 1814 and sentenced to transportation for life. He arrived in Sydney in the Marquis of Wellington on 27 January 1815. His wife Mary came free in the Northampton on 18 June, their eldest son being born on the voyage. Oatley set up in business as a watch and clock maker in George Street opposite the site of the present Town Hall. Governor Macquarie appointed him keeper of the town clock and commissioned him to make a clock for the turret of the Prisoners' Barracks being built by Francis Greenway [q.v.] in Macquarie Street; for this service Oatley was paid £75 in June 1819. He was also reputed to have made at least six grandfather clocks, and on 25 October 1821 was conditionally pardoned. He was granted 175 acres in the Hurstville district in October 1831, 300 acres in August 1833 and 40 acres in December 1835, the last having been ordered in 1824 by Governor Brisbane. The suburb of Oatley is named after him. He died on 8 October 1839 and was buried in a vault on his farm, Snugsburough, near Punchbowl.

His third son Frederick (1819-1890) took over the business in George Street. The second son James was born on 17 June 1817. He was apprenticed to a coach-builder and when 30 was licensee of the Sportsman's Arms Hotel at the corner of Pitt and Goulburn Streets. He was a member of the old City Council and, when it was reconstituted as the Municipal Council in 1857, he was elected an alderman and in 1862 mayor. He was member for Canterbury in the Legislative Assembly in 1864-69. He died on 31 December 1878 at his home in Bourke Street, Woolloomooloo, and was buried at Camperdown cemetery.

HRA (1), 10; *Jubilee history of the municipality of Hurstville, 1887-1937* (Syd, 1937); SMH, 1 Jan 1879; Newsletter, RAHS, June 1962.

O'BRIEN, HENRY (1793-1866) and CORNELIUS (1796-1869), pastoralists, were born at Holymount, County Mayo, Ireland, sons of Henry O'Brien, farmer, and Catherine, née Browne (d. 1837). After her husband's death Catherine married John Ward, and Henry, Cornelius and their brother Thomas were raised by their uncle, William Browne (1762-1833), of County Galway and Calcutta. In February 1814, 'being about to establish his family at Sydney New South Wales', Browne received permission 'to take with him to Bengal a labourer named Harry O'Brien for the purpose of taking charge of a quantity of rice and other articles which he may wish to send to New South Wales'. He then made arrangements for his sister, Catherine Ward, and her family to journey to New South Wales in the *Marquis of Wellington*. They arrived at Sydney in January 1815 and settled on a farm Browne had already acquired. Three months later Henry O'Brien arrived from India with letters of introduction to Governor Macquarie, who placed the family and their servants on the stores. In April 1816 Browne himself landed in the colony with his family in the *Mary*. In the next years the O'Brien brothers were closely associated with their uncle's activities and his properties at Abbotsbury, near Prospect, at Appin and the Illawarra. The management of the Illawarra property fell to Cornelius. Henry assisted with Abbotsbury and acted for his uncle during the latter's absences from the colony, besides making a number of trips to Calcutta himself. In 1820 Browne received permission for his son John and nephew Thomas O'Brien to take a thousand sheep beyond the Blue Mountains for better pasturage in the country that was rapidly being opened up. Other similar enterprises followed, and it was on one such journey to Bathurst in 1823 that Thomas O'Brien disappeared.

With youthful zeal Cornelius applied himself to the development of the Illawarra lands. In April 1821 he discovered a new line of road to the Illawarra, collected £60 by public subscription, and by January 1822 had cleared a track from Figtree to Appin. It was used that year by Macquarie on his Illawarra tour, for which Cornelius acted as guide. On 14 October at St Peter's, Campbelltown, Cornelius married Rebecca (1804-1888), daughter of William Broughton [q.v.]; they had no children.

Henry O'Brien concentrated his attention on the country being opened up beyond the Blue Mountains. He established a farm on the Bathurst plains, where he was granted 600 acres and three men in 1821. However, his rapidly increasing flocks forced him to look further afield for suitable pasturage, and finding the better country around the Lachlan River already occupied he turned towards the Murrumbidgee, taking up an estate that he named Douro on the Yass plains, and establishing the first sheep station on the Murrumbidgee at Jugiong. He became the largest stockholder in the district and a squatter of considerable influence. In 1829 his station was visited by Charles Sturt [q.v.], who was given sheep to take on his journey. In 1830 another visitor, William Edward Riley, commented on the efforts made by Henry O'Brien to improve the quality of his sheep by crossing them with pure merinos and Saxons, but complained of the lack of comfort at the Douro homestead, with draughts blowing through the log walls. By 1833 Henry O'Brien was reported as having some 12,000 sheep.

Cornelius, while managing his uncle's interests, also took up land on his own account, at the Five Islands and Bulli, a grant finally issuing in 1833. He developed trade in cedar as well as supplying stores to the military forces at Wollongong. In 1833, as an inducement for Cornelius to take a greater interest in the Yass district, Henry made over to him 100 acres adjoining Douro, now known as the Cooma estate. Cornelius eventually moved to Yass, selling his Bulli land in 1836. Later he took up the Hardwicke property and land at Bendenine. From 1837 both brothers held annual depasturing licences for runs on the Murrumbidgee and Lachlan Rivers.

On 25 July 1836 Henry O'Brien was married to Isabella, eldest daughter of Captain Macdonald of the 17th Regiment, first by the Presbyterian chaplain and then by a Roman Catholic priest. After Isabella died on 22 July 1838, aged 27, at their town residence in Upper Pitt Street, Sydney, Henry took a greater interest in public affairs, in both Yass and Sydney. In 1839 he was a member of the committee of the Subscription Library, associated himself with a memorial for the continuance of the transportation system, gave evidence on the Crown Lands Act, discharged his obligations as a justice of the peace and was commended for his efforts in pursuing bushrangers. On his land adjoining Yass he laid out the town of 'O'Connell', which was auctioned in August 1840. In that month he opened his new house at Douro with a ball and supper for 'the rank, beauty and fashion of the neighbourhood', for he was a member of the committee of the Yass hunt and a steward of the Yass races.

On 28 November 1840 at St Mary's Cathedral, Sydney, and afterwards at St Philip's Church, he married Elizabeth Sadlier (1803-1892), second daughter of William Cruden of Winchmore Hill, Middlesex, and Gategill, Kirkcudbrightshire, and his wife Elizabeth Sadlier, née Moody. He continued to achieve further prominence in public affairs. In 1842 he was a member of the committee for management of a petition for a representative legislature, he served as a commissioner of the Supreme Court and on the committee of an association to obtain permission to import coolies from the East Indies, and was proposed as a candidate for Gipps ward in the municipal elections. As one of the squatting authorities of the colony, he gave evidence at commissions of inquiry, at one such stating that he attributed 'the landed depression to the want of a market for surplus stock, the high rate of wages and the low price of wool in English and Colonial markets'.

In the midst of the depression in June 1843 he announced an experiment at his Fort Street premises in the process of boiling down sheep to ascertain the value of flocks. Wethers weighing 56 lbs were boiled down and an average of 27¼ lbs of tallow per sheep was obtained. Though not the first to see the advantages to be gained from boiling down and from smoking and salting mutton hams, Henry O'Brien made the process popular and thereby saved many pastoralists from bankruptcy. Sheep that were unsaleable in April and May 1843 were by July worth 5s. to 8s. each, 'for if they were melted down the tallow they produced would be worth that sum'. With brighter prospects for the pastoral industry, the brothers turned their attention to the improvement of their stock and holdings. Henry O'Brien in particular developed his sheep-breeding activities, importing some of the finest Negretti sheep then procurable.

Both Henry and Cornelius were members of the Yass District Council in 1844 and continued to serve as justices of the peace. On 25 December 1844, Elizabeth Sadlier O'Brien gave birth to a son, Henry, who was baptized on 23 January 1845 at St James's Church, Sydney. To provide for his son's education Henry O'Brien returned to England in 1856 with his family, entering his son at Eton. Whilst in England in 1859 he made his last will and testament, appointing Sir Charles Nicholson [q.v.] and his brother Cornelius as executors and trustees of his very considerable estate. Back in New South Wales he stood for parliament and was elected unopposed as member for Yass plains in December 1860. He assisted in the passage of the Robertson Land Acts, but because of ill health he was forced to resign in July 1861. His hopes for his son, who in May 1864 had obtained a commission of the 39th Regiment, were dashed when the latter died of paralysis on 12 August 1865. Intending to join his wife in England, he was winding up his affairs in New South Wales when he died at Douro on 27 January 1866, aged 73. Cornelius took over the management of the Douro estate, and on 4 July 1869 died at his property, Bendenine.

The O'Brien brothers left no direct descendants, but will be remembered for their pioneering activities in the pastoral industry: opening new country, developing the quality of their sheep and publicizing the boiling down process in a critical period for pastoralists. Though Henry was more prominent in public affairs, both contributed much to the advancement of the Yass district and to the administration of law and order. A memorial to Henry, a stained-glass window bearing the O'Brien coat of arms and motto, 'Nihil duce desperandum christo', is in St Clement's Church, Yass.

S. H. Roberts, *The squatting age in Australia, 1835-47* (Melb, 1935); J. Jervis, 'Illawarra: a century of history', *JRAHS*, 28 (1942); *Goulburn Herald*, 31 Jan, 3 Feb 1866, 10 July 1869; Newspaper indexes under H. and C. O'Brien (ML); William Browne letters (ML).

PETER SCOTT

O'BRIEN, WILLIAM SMITH (1803-1864), Irish nationalist, was born on 17 October 1803 at Dromoland, County Clare, Ireland, the second son of Sir Edward O'Brien, baronet, and Charlotte, née Smith. A Protestant, he was educated at Harrow and Trinity College, Cambridge (BA., 1826). He represented the Irish borough of Ennis in the unreformed British parliament from 1828 to 1831 and Limerick from 1835 until his exclusion from the Commons in 1849. For long an opponent of Daniel O'Connell, O'Brien joined his Repeal Association in 1843 and soon exercised an authority within it second only to 'the Liberator' himself. In the disputes dividing the Irish nationalist leaders in the 1840s O'Brien at first adopted a conciliatory role; and, although he walked out of the association with John Mitchel, T. F. Meagher [qq.v.] and other militants in July 1846, he continued to preach reconciliation until O'Connell's death in May 1847 completed the breach between the advocates of 'moral' and 'physical' force.

From this time he appears as the oldest, most experienced and respected, though by no means the most resolute or consistent, of the leaders of the militant Young Ireland or 'confederate' groups which, after the February 1848 revolution in Paris, urged the formation of an Irish national guard modelled on the French and a council of three hundred as the nucleus of an Irish national parliament; eventually after John Mitchel's arrest and condemnation in May 1848 he organized an armed insurrection. It was poorly led, ill equipped and unsupported, and proved abortive. Though O'Brien had long hesitated to engage in armed rebellion and refused to lend his name to the committee of five that directed it, he was recognized as its foremost leader, was arrested in August on a charge of high treason and at Clonmel in October 1848 was sentenced with T. F. Meagher, T. B. McManus and Patrick O'Donohoe to be hanged, drawn and quartered. The sentence was commuted to transportation for life; O'Brien and his principal lieutenants sailed in the *Swift* to Hobart Town, where they arrived on 27 October 1848. Three of O'Brien's humbler and lesser-known comrades-in-arms, Thomas Donovan, Thomas Wall and John Walsh, were sentenced at Waterford in July 1850 to seven years transportation for attacking the city's police barracks under O'Brien's orders and reached Hobart in the *Hyderabad* on 13 December 1850; a fourth, Cornelius Keeffe, sentenced at Waterford for a similar offence in March 1849, followed in the *Dalhousie* on 14 August 1852.

On arrival in Hobart O'Brien at first refused to give his parole in return for a ticket-of-leave and was in consequence denied the privileged treatment afforded to the other Young Ireland leaders. He was sent to Darlington station in the penal settlement of Maria Island; nine months later, after an unsuccessful attempt to escape to the United States in an American whaler, he was transferred to Port Arthur, where he was allowed to live in his own cottage (now a youth hostel). In November 1850 he was persuaded to give his parole, was granted a ticket-of-leave and settled first at New Norfolk and later at Avoca, where he acted as tutor to the children of a local doctor. Returning to New Norfolk he received a conditional pardon in 1854; he sailed for Europe and in Brussels was joined by his wife Lucy, née Gabbett, five sons and two daughters. In May 1856, following the intercession of 140 British parliamentarians, he was granted a free pardon which allowed him to return to Ireland. In 1859 he paid a brief visit to New York and in 1863 to Poland. He died at Bangor, Wales, on 18 June 1864.

J. H. Cullen, *Young Ireland in exile* (Dublin, 1928); D. R. Gwynn, *Young Ireland and 1848* (Cork, 1949); T. J. Kiernan, *The Irish exiles in Australia* (Melb, 1954); D. R. Gwynn, *Thomas Francis Meagher* (Dublin, 1961); Ac nos 2/306, 2/315, 2/363 (TA).

G. RUDE

O'CONNELL, SIR MAURICE CHARLES PHILIP (1768-1848), soldier, was born in County Kerry, Ireland, the son of Charles Philip O'Connell. A penniless younger son, he appears to have been dependent on the patronage and bounty of his kinsman General Count Daniel O'Connell (1745?-1833) of the Irish Brigade in the French Army. For some time O'Connell studied in Paris for the Roman Catholic priesthood, but in 1785 his father arranged his entry to a military school. In 1792 he became a captain in the French émigré forces serving on the French frontier under the duke of Brunswick and in October 1794, after the Irish Brigade had been reconstituted in the British Army, he was appointed captain in Count O'Connell's 4th Regiment. After a period on half-pay he was appointed in May 1800 a captain in the 1st West India Regiment, with which he served in Surinam, Grenada and Dominica. In January 1805 he was promoted brevet major and transferred to the 5th Regiment. He saw much action in the West Indies, and particularly distinguished himself at Roseau in Dominica in February 1805 when it was unsuccessfully attacked by greatly superior French forces. For his services in Dominica he was thanked by the House of

Assembly and presented with a sword worth 100 guineas, and the committee of the Patriotic Fund at Lloyds, London, gave him a sword worth £50 and plate worth £100.

In October 1806 he transferred to the 73rd Regiment of which he became lieut-colonel in May 1809. In December the 1st battalion of the 73rd with O'Connell in command, arrived in Port Jackson with Governor Macquarie; O'Connell was commissioned lieut-governor in January 1810. On 8 May at Government House he married Mary, daughter of the former Governor Bligh and widow of Lieutenant John Putland who had died on 4 January 1808. Bligh, who had planned to sail from Sydney with his family a few days later was distressed to leave Mary behind, but she was a headstrong young woman. Her dresses had shocked the more decorous members of the colony, and her hostility to her father's enemies soon began to embarrass the governor.

The day before the marriage Macquarie granted O'Connell 2500 acres, which he named Riverston; on 27 June he granted Mrs O'Connell 1055 acres in the district of Evan, adjoining Frogmore granted to her by Governor King; she now had 3000 acres, 7000 head of stock and £400 a year.

In May 1810 O'Connell was appointed a trustee of the Female Orphan Institution and from August was steward of the race-course. He became president of the Philanthropic Society in January 1814. In March 1810 Macquarie had recommended to the Colonial Office that O'Connell's salary of £250 be doubled to enable him to visit the outer settlements. This increase was never granted and by August 1813 Macquarie was urging the removal of O'Connell and the 73rd Regiment from the colony. Mrs O'Connell, he reported, 'naturally enough, has imbibed strong feelings of resentment and hatred against all those Persons and their Families, who were in the least inimical to her Father's Government . . . tho' Lieut. Colonel O'Connell is naturally a very well disposed Man, he allows himself to be a good deal influenced by his Wife's strong rooted Prejudices against the old Inhabitants of this country who took any active part against Governor Bligh'. Already arrangements had been made to relieve the 73rd and transfer it to Ceylon. O'Connell sailed with the main body of his regiment in the *General Hewitt* in April 1814.

In March 1815 Macquarie wrote to Bathurst that he had reason to believe that O'Connell, and Lieut-Colonel Geils [q.v.]

also of the 73rd, were each eager to obtain appointment to Van Diemen's Land in succession to Lieut-Governor Davey. Macquarie considered both very unfit for the post, O'Connell because of his 'illiberal national partialities and prejudices' and 'irritable temper and overbearing disposition'. Neither was appointed, nor was Macquarie's nominee, Joseph Foveaux [q.v.]. In Ceylon in 1815 O'Connell commanded the 73rd in the war against the King of Kandy. In August 1819 he was promoted colonel and in July 1830 major-general; in 1834 he was knighted. He returned to Sydney in the *Fairlie* in December 1838, having been appointed to command the forces in New South Wales. His military secretary was his son, Maurice Charles (1812-1879), a captain in the 73rd. On arrival General O'Connell was appointed to the Executive and Legislative Councils. It was not long before Lady O'Connell again made her presence felt. In August 1839 Governor Gipps reported to the Colonial Office that O'Connell was claiming on behalf of Bligh's heiresses 105 acres at Parramatta worth about £40,000 and including the sites of the Female Factory, the gaol, The King's School, the Roman Catholic school and chapel and many houses. His attorney had served notices of ejection on all occupiers of this land. Gipps directed attention to 'the extreme delicacy of the position in which this business has placed me' since O'Connell was the senior member of the Executive Council and, if the governor were to die, would succeed to the government. At length in February 1841 a settlement was reached whereby the heiresses surrendered their claim to the Parramatta land but their titles to other grants were confirmed. One of these, Camperdown, on the site of the present suburb of that name, was soon sold for more than £25,000.

In 1843-44 O'Connell was a nominated member of the partly-elected Legislative Council. In 1844 Gipps placed his name at the head of the list of nineteen persons considered eligible for a colonial order of merit; he was the only knight in the list. After Gipps departed in July 1846 O'Connell administered the government until the arrival of Governor FitzRoy in August. In November 1841 he had been promoted lieut-general, in December 1842 appointed colonel of the 81st Regiment and in January 1844 colonel of the 80th Regiment. He was succeeded as commander of the forces in New South Wales by Major-General Wynyard [q.v.] in 1847. He was about to sail for England when he died at Darlinghurst on 25 May 1848. He was given a full military funeral, the service being held at St James's Church. His widow lived in Paris for some years and then in London, where she died in 1864. There were two sons and a daughter. Maurice, after an eventful military career, settled in Australia.

HRA (1), 7, 8, 20-25, (3), 2; R. Cannon (comp), *Historical records of the 73rd Regiment, 1780-1851* (Lond, 1851); MS cat under O'Connell (ML).

O'CONNOR, RODERIC (1784-1860), public servant and landowner, was the son of Roger O'Connor and his first wife Louisa Anna, née Strachan. His father, descendant of a rich London merchant, was an eccentric Irish landowner whose sympathies veered from suppression of agricultural rioters to support of United Irishmen; by a second marriage he had two notable sons: Feargus, who became an erratic leader of English Chartists, and Francis, who won high military and political rank in Bolivia.

O'Connor's motives for emigrating to Van Diemen's Land can only be guessed, but the fact that he brought with him in his own ship *Ardent* his natural sons William and Arthur (Rattigan) may give the clue. They arrived in May 1824 and O'Connor, who had considerable capital, received a free 1000-acre grant on the Lake River. Here his experiences on his father's land and as a practical engineer were not wasted; bridges, weirs and farm buildings were among his early improvements. He lost no opportunity to increase his estate either by free grant or by shrewd purchase and in four years had trebled it.

Lieut-Governor Arthur, whose patronage and protection O'Connor was many times to enjoy, chose him to be third commissioner of survey and valuation. The commission had been set up in consequence of the British government's instructions to have the colony divided into counties, hundreds and parishes, and to have the waste lands of the Crown valued for purposes of levying quitrent; Arthur used them for many other purposes, such as reporting on the suitability of areas for towns, and surveying harbour facilities and the route for a north-south road.

O'Connor's journals point to the conclusion that he was the commission's most active member; in company with Peter Murdoch [q.v.] between 1826 and 1828 he examined all the settled districts of the island; what he saw is recorded in vivid and uncomplicated language that goes far beyond the usual limits of official reports. The journals give an entertaining picture of the landed community, exposing various stratagems to defraud the government of land and other assets, describing farming methods and improvements, recalling the humble and sometimes disreputable beginnings of many of the wealthy people, and fulminating against the unrighteous. They reflect a hot-tempered, outspoken, worldly-wise, contentious and egotistical Irish personality, but one possessed of wit and commonsense.

When his field work as commissioner ended, O'Connor was made inspector of roads and bridges, a post which gave him control of many hundreds of convicts on public works and put several major projects in his charge; these included the new wharf in Hobart Town, the Bridgewater causeway, as well as 'nearly all the finished parts of the Roads in this Colony'. He was also a magistrate and a member of the board for investigating disputed claims to land.

O'Connor left active public life when Arthur's governorship came to an end in 1836. But his many quarrels with officials and others, aired both in the courts and the press, insured him a place in the public eye; libel cases and lengthy and vigorous exchanges with his opponents in the newspapers, in one section of which he was influential, lent colour to his position as one of the largest landed proprietors in the colony. Lady Franklin [q.v.] told her sister that he was 'a man of immense estate . . . bound by ties of I know not what nature to the Arthur faction . . . but . . . a man of blasted reputation, of exceedingly immoral conduct and of viperous tongue and pen'. A large employer of convict labour on his estates, O'Connor was also from personal conviction solidly opposed to the anti-transportationists; this attitude probably influenced Lieut-Governors Eardley-Wilmot and Denison in nominating him for two terms, 1844-48 and 1852-53, in the Legislative Council.

The son of a professed atheist, O'Connor turned to the Roman Catholic Church very late in life; in the year of his death he gave it £10,000 for a cathedral in Hobart. In old age his irascibility became notorious, as from his Benham estate the 'red-hot Irishman' quarrelled with his neighbours and waged war on the local road trust. When he died in July 1860, he owned eleven properties totalling 65,000 acres and had 10,000 acres of leasehold. William had died in 1855 and Arthur inherited the estate.

A. McKay (ed), *Journals of the land commissioners for Van Diemen's Land 1826-1828* (Hob, 1962).   P. R. ELDERSHAW

OFFICER, SIR ROBERT (1800-1879), medical officer and politician, was born on 3 October 1800 near Dundee, Scotland, the son of Robert Officer, of Jacksbank, and his wife Isabella, née Kerr. In 1821 he obtained his diploma as a member of the Royal College of Surgeons, London. As ship's surgeon in the *Castle Forbes* he arrived at Hobart Town in March 1822. By May he was a supernumerary assistant surgeon at 3s. a day. On 25 October 1823 at St David's Church he married Jamima, daughter of Myles Patterson of Hunterston on the Shannon River. In 1824 Officer was moved to New Norfolk, allotted a district 'seven miles along the Derwent River', and given a forage allowance. By 1827 his district had increased to 'thirty five miles through populous districts'; he also acted as surgeon to the military garrison and their families and had charge of the New Norfolk Hospital, of convicts on many public works and of the gaol where he attended all corporal punishments. For these duties his pay was increased to 7s. a day and he was promoted district surgeon and appointed a magistrate. In 1831 he was criticized for sending convicts from roadgangs to New Norfolk for treatment, thereby interfering with their discipline; his reply was that he had 'no desire to be known as a mere slave driver'.

In 1826 Officer had been given a grant on the River Clyde. Soon afterwards he made a home for his family at Bothwell, where much property was held by the Pattersons and by Captain Patrick Wood, who had married Jane Patterson after resigning from the East India Co.'s service. In 1835 Officer moved with his family to Hobart, where he found time to distil oil from gum leaves; he recommended it to the lieut-governor as an article of export and was authorized to build a larger still and to provide samples of the oil for sending to England. In 1838 he sought promotion and was appointed to inspect the entire Colonial and Convict Medical Department. His report was well received by the Executive Council and the Colonial Office. Next year, when the military branch was separated on his recommendation, he was temporarily made colonial surgeon but his pay was not increased pending confirmation from London.

In 1838, against his wife's wishes, Officer had become infected by 'the mad Port Phillip transactions', and in partnership with his brother-in-law, Captain Wood, planned to send 3000 sheep to Geelong as a speculation. The first shipload left George Town in February 1839 but Officer thought it unwise to settle close to Geelong and engaged John Patterson and Matthew Gibb to find a run further afield. By August Officer was having an eight-roomed wooden house prefabricated for the new venture. In October he had 6500 sheep under offer at 22s. a head with a station thrown in, but did not buy because his wife was reluctant to move to the mainland. In November when she appeared to yield Officer and Wood ordered their agents to buy sheep and cattle, mostly on terms. On Gibb's advice Officer had also bought land and acquired the rights to several runs, some in conjunction with Wood. Granted leave to visit Port Phillip in December, Officer took his ready-made house, intending to settle permanently. Although Wood pleaded caution Officer continued to buy livestock at boom prices and because competent labour was scarce he undertook to pay £500 to bring workmen from Scotland. In 1840 he paid several visits to Port Phillip, but most of his business was left to the discretion of Patterson and Gibb. Suddenly the prospects became gloomy. He claimed land as bounty for importing labourers but was not permitted to locate it where he wished. When his workmen arrived they proved intractable and he braved his wife's wrath by sending for their two sons who were being educated in Edinburgh. In December he found that Gibb was exploiting him, for his wool had sold badly through poor preparation, so he resigned from the Medical Department intending to manage his own affairs. With the onset of depression he had begun to sell his livestock and some land. Through backing his brother-in-law, John Hugh Patterson, he was left with bills for at least £3000 but escaped insolvency and later salvaged enough property to establish his sons as pastoralists in Victoria.

In April 1841 Officer had tried without success to rejoin the medical service in Van Diemen's Land, but in June he was appointed health officer at Hobart with a salary of £150. He held this position until 1850. Each year he censured the city's insanitary condition, though with little effect; as Lieut-Governor Denison commented, 'foul smell is indeed a nuisance but many people consider it a much greater nuisance to be made to pay for the remedy'. Among many other duties Officer served in the Immigration Department, the Court of Medical Examiners, the committee for placing children from the

Queen's Orphan Schools in jobs, and as a trustee of the Infant School. In 1850 he resigned and retired to Hall Green, his home at New Norfolk. There he built up a private practice which he soon sold to his partner Dr James Agnew.

As an active supporter of Rev. John West [q.v.] on the anti-transportation issue Officer had become interested in politics. In October 1853 he was elected for Buckingham to the Legislative Council and next year shared in drafting the colony's Constitution for responsible government. In 1856 he was elected unopposed for Glenorchy to the new House of Assembly and after five years as chairman of committees was chosen as Speaker in 1861. He held this office with dignity and tact until forced by ill health to retire from parliament in April 1877. By that time he had also served as chairman of the New Norfolk Lunatic Asylum Commission, president of the Council of Education, member of the Hobart High School Committee, vice-president of the Royal Society of Tasmania, and a founding member and second president of the Tasmanian Club. As chairman of the Acclimatization Society and of the Salmon Commission he had shared in establishing Salmon Ponds near New Norfolk, which he showed to the duke of Edinburgh in 1868. In January 1869 he was knighted. With the years he acquired scattered property and when he died at Hall Green on 8 July 1879 he left an estate worth £6200. His widow died on 28 September 1881; they had six sons and seven daughters.

Officer's obituaries made much of his unostentatious benevolence to the poor, his earnestness and his personal piety. According to the Anglican *Church News* 'he was a Presbyterian who knew nothing of Presbyterian prejudices'. At Bothwell he had been a churchwarden and at New Norfolk he worshipped in the Church of England. He had often praised the Wesleyan missionaries for their work among the convicts and subscribed to various chapel funds in remote districts. In Hobart he was an elder of St Andrew's Church and treasurer of St John's, and a close friend of many Presbyterian ministers. In the Hobart Presbytery he was a prominent figure and at his death the oldest office-bearer. Officer College was established in Hobart in his memory.

HRA (3), 4; P. L. Brown (ed), *The narrative of George Russell* (Lond, 1935); J. Heyer, *The Presbyterian pioneers of Van Diemen's Land* (Launceston, 1935); P. L. Brown (ed), *Clyde Company papers*, 1-5 (Lond, 1941-63); Correspondence file under Officer (TA).

O'FLAHERTY, ELIZA (1818-1882), née Winstanley, was born in England, the elder daughter of William Winstanley and his wife Eliza, née Finch. She came to New South Wales with her family in May 1833 and made her first stage appearance in the leading role of *Clari, or the Maid of Milan*, a melodrama, at Barnett Levey's [q.v.] Theatre Royal, Sydney, on 31 October 1834. The occasion was a benefit performance for her father, a scene-painter at the theatre. Her younger sister, Ann (b. 1825), also took part in the programme.

The critics immediately recognized Eliza's strong natural talent, her remarkable speaking voice and her power of expression which triumphed over her lack of experience and faults of technique. She played a great variety of parts in the early days but it soon became clear that she was essentially a dramatic and tragic actress. In December 1835 she played Juliet, and Desdemona at the opening of the Royal Victoria Theatre in March 1838. Her sister Ann, a trained musician, gained great popularity in singing and dancing parts; she was engaged at the Victoria in November 1840 and after her marriage in 1841, as Mrs Ximenes, remained a popular performer for many years.

In February 1841 at St James's Church Eliza married Henry Charles O'Flaherty, a musician in the theatre orchestra; he made his acting début at her benefit in May. Later in the year she had played Portia, Lady Macbeth and other parts and was unanimously acclaimed 'in the southern hemisphere a star of the first magnitude'. After one of many disagreements with the management of the Victoria Theatre she left with her husband and had a successful season in Hobart and Launceston. In February 1842 they were back in Sydney, appearing in leading parts at the new Olympic Theatre; when it closed in May they tried to carry on with the management, Eliza once shocking the press by appearing as Richard III. Eliza returned to the Victoria, where in August she played the title role in *Isabelle of Valois; or, the Tyrant of Navarre*, written by O'Flaherty for her benefit, and appeared in many leading parts in the tragic and melodramatic repertoire of her day.

On 1 April 1846 the O'Flahertys sailed for England, where Eliza played Shakespearean roles in the provinces and appeared for a short season at the Princess Theatre in London. In 1848 she went to the United States, where she played Mistress Quickly to James Hackett's Falstaff at the Astor Place Opera House, New York. She returned to London and played leading Shakespearean and other roles for nine years with Charles Kean's company at the Princess Theatre. She appeared in several command performances before the Queen at Windsor Castle.

Her second career, as an author, began some time after her husband's death about 1854. Her first book, *Shifting Scenes in Theatrical Life*, was published in London in 1859. In 1860 her novel *Bitter-Sweet — So is the World* was serialized in the *Sydney Mail* under the pseudonym Ariele. She began to devote more time to writing, finally abandoning her dramatic career about 1864. Most of her stories were serialized under the name of Mrs Eliza Winstanley in the London Magazine *Bow Bells* and several were published in the series, *Dicks' English Novels*. In 1865 she became editress of the weekly *Fiction for Family Reading*, a subsidiary of *Bow Bells*. For themes she drew on her theatrical experiences, as in *Desmoro; or, the Red Hand* (1866) and *Entrances and Exits* (1868), and her memories of Australia. Among her Australian novels are *The Mistress of Hawk's Crag* (1864), *Twenty Straws* (London, 1864), *What is To Be Will Be* (London, 1867), and *For Her Natural Life: a tale of 1830* (1876). Although absent from Australia for more than thirty years, she wrote that she had fond memories of it, and in 1880 she returned. She died of 'diabetes and exhaustion' on 2 December 1882 in Sydney. Her grave is in Waverley cemetery.

The novels of Eliza Winstanley have curiosity value only, but the sum of her stage and literary activities conveys the picture of a gifted and vigorous personality. Although she was not, as legend had it for some time, a native-born Australian, she began her career in this country, and may fairly be described as the first Australian actress to succeed overseas.

N. M. ROBINSON

O'FLYNN (FLYNN), JEREMIAH FRANCIS (1788-1831), Roman Catholic priest, was born on 25 December 1788 in County Kerry, Ireland. He studied with the Franciscans at Killarney before entering a Cistercian monastery at Lulworth Abbey, Dorset, England, where he became a monk of the La Trappe reform, which had taken refuge there after its expulsion from France in 1790. In 1813 O'Flynn was ordained deacon and went with other Trappist monks to establish a mission in the West Indies. He quarrelled with the abbot but, when the mission was expelled from Mar-

tinique by the British governor, O'Flynn was allowed to remain as pastor of Santa Cruz. In April 1816 he was charged with intrusion and incompetence by Archbishop Neale of Baltimore, who held ecclesiastical jurisdiction over the Danish islands of the West Indies, and went to Rome to answer these charges. This he succeeded in doing and secured approval for an appointment to another mission in the West Indies. However, he came under the influence of Father Hayes, the representative of the Irish Catholic Association in Rome, whose brother, Michael Hayes [q.v.], a convict transported to New South Wales, had urged him to secure priests for the Irish convicts in the colony. O'Flynn was persuaded to seek appointment to a mission there; he was duly secularized, authorized as prefect-apostolic to 'Bottanibe' and given money for his expenses. He went to Dublin in November 1816 to seek additional help from the Irish bishops, and with two other Irish priests petitioned the Colonial Office for permission to proceed to New South Wales. When no reply was received O'Flynn left for London in January 1817 to plead his case, but Bathurst refused O'Flynn's request on the grounds of his insufficient education and poor command of English, an opinion with which Dr Poynter, the London vicar-general, concurred.

Undaunted, O'Flynn sailed in the *Duke of Wellington* and arrived at Sydney on 9 November 1817. He told Governor Macquarie that he had Bathurst's permission to serve as a priest in the colony, but since he had no proof Macquarie ordered him to leave in the same ship, feeling that he might incite the lower orders of Catholics to resist the government. By promising not to carry out his functions as a priest O'Flynn persuaded the governor to allow him to remain until he heard from London. He may have genuinely believed that his mission would be officially sanctioned, but meanwhile he did not keep his pledge, for he performed many baptisms and marriages as well as celebrating Mass secretly in private homes. Macquarie had suspected O'Flynn's story, and when he began to hear of many converts being made to Catholicism, and when the Catholic soldiers of the 48th Regiment petitioned that O'Flynn be allowed to stay, Macquarie again ordered him to leave, arrested him and placed him forcibly in the *David Shaw*. He sailed on 20 May 1818, though four hundred free Catholics and some leading Protestants petitioned Macquarie to allow O'Flynn to remain. When he reached London in November he again appealed to

Bathurst for permission to go to New South Wales, but was again refused.

O'Flynn returned to Ireland and thence to the West Indies. He was banished from San Domingo and in 1822 arrived in Philadelphia, only to become embroiled in schism. He went to San Domingo in 1823, was again expelled and returned to Philadelphia, where in 1825 he was invited to minister to Irish Catholics in Susquehanna County. There he spent his last years and died on 8 February 1831.

Simple but impulsive, Jeremiah O'Flynn managed to conflict with authority wherever he went, yet his clash with the Colonial Office helped to publicize the needs of Catholics in New South Wales and to influence the British government in 1820 in allowing the first official Roman Catholic missionaries to be sent to Australia.

HRA (1), 9; P. F. Moran, *History of the Catholic Church in Australasia* (Syd, 1895); E. M. O'Brien, *The dawn of Catholicism in Australia*, 1-2 (Syd, 1928); J. G. Murtagh, *Australia: the Catholic chapter*, 2nd ed (Syd, 1959); K. S. Inglis, 'Catholic historiography in Australia', *Hist Studies*, no 31, Nov 1958.

VIVIENNE PARSONS

OGILVIE, JAMES (1795?-1828), wine merchant, was 'a native of Banff, North Britain, of very respectable connexions, and no small pretensions to gentility'. He arrived at Hobart Town with his wife and family in the *Britomart* on 4 February 1822, bringing a letter of recommendation from Downing Street and some £1500 in goods and cash. Within a month he opened a shop at Harrington Street, Hobart, largely stocked with the merchandise he had imported. On 3 February 1823 he was elected to the committee for establishing a Presbyterian church in Hobart with Rev. Archibald Macarthur [q.v.] as its minister. He was an original shareholder in the Bank of Van Diemen's Land and signed the petition to the British government requesting that Lieut-Governor Sorell remain in office.

Ogilvie established the Derwent brewery before September 1823. Either it proved unsuccessful or he got into financial difficulty, for it was mortgaged to R. L. Murray [q.v.] before being sold to Peter Dudgeon and Frederick Bell on 2 January 1826. About 1823 Ogilvie built the British Hotel and Brandy (later Wine) Vaults in Liverpool Street, where he claimed that his goods were cheaper than elsewhere in town. Nevertheless he was soon eager to retire from the hotel trade. In January 1826 he offered the building to the government for offices; when rejected he renovated the premises and leased them in October to John Martin. He also had country property. In consideration of his assets he had been granted 1000 acres in the Hollow Tree district near Bothwell, but in 1823 tried to exchange this grant for land nearer town. He must have sold it soon afterwards, for in 1829 his widow was refused a second grant because he had got rid of his first one too quickly and with too little improvement. Ogilvie also owned a property, Eden, on the Big (Ouse) River. At his death his assets included the British Hotel and a 100-acre farm at Pittwater.

James Ogilvie died at his residence in Liverpool Street on 11 May 1828. His obituary in the *Hobart Town Courier* eulogized his private and public virtues and summed up his qualities: 'In short, he was a good member of society, and a worthy example of persevering industry'.

Ogilvie's widow Eliza first lived with and later married J. A. Thomson [q.v.], a convict builder and architect. On her second marriage certificate the additional Christian name Fordyce may have been her maiden name. It was doubtless Ogilvie's money which started Thomson on his prosperous career. In 1843-44 Thomson and his stepson Thomas Ogilvie were joint licensees of the British Hotel. Of Ogilvie's daughters, Eliza Ann married William Henry Windsor (1821?-1889), later under-treasurer of Tasmania, and Mary Grant married James Goodall Francis (1819-1884), sometime premier of Victoria. Eliza died in Liverpool Street, Hobart, on 5 December 1852, aged 51.

Correspondence files under J. Ogilvie and J. G. Francis (TA).

G. T. STILWELL

O'HALLORAN, THOMAS SHULDHAM (1797-1870), pioneer and commissioner of police, was born on 25 October 1797 at Berhampore, India, the second son of Major-General Sir Joseph O'Halloran, G.C.B., and his wife Lady Frances, a niece of the earl of Uxbridge. His father served in the British forces in India for more than fifty-three years; seven of his brothers served in the army and one in the navy.

O'Halloran entered the Royal Military College in 1808 and at 16 he sailed for India as an ensign in the 17th Regiment. He was promoted lieutenant in that regiment in 1817 and captain in the 99th Regiment in 1827. He returned to England after twenty years army service in India in 1834. Soon after his return he transferred to the Coldstream Guards where he was on half-pay until he joined the 97th Regiment in May 1837. Next year he sold his commission and sailed with his wife and two sons for South Australia in the *Rajasthan*. The family landed at Holdfast Bay in November 1838. O'Halloran had already bought a land order for four sections; these were taken at a place later known as O'Halloran Hill, where he moved with his family and started to build Lizard Lodge, named after a feature in his family arms. Five months after landing he entertained the governor and dined senior officials in his substantial new home. In 1839 he was gazetted major-commandant of the short-lived voluntary militia and in June 1840 Governor Gawler appointed him as the first commissioner of police. Instructed to reorganize the force, he weeded out inefficient police, enlisted recruits, enforced strict discipline, and created two divisions, one mounted and one foot, each under the command of an inspector. He led several police expeditions against warlike Aboriginals. The most important was against a Murray tribe which had murdered twenty-four survivors of the wreck of the *Maria*; two of the offenders were convicted by a drumhead court martial ordered by Governor Gawler and hanged in the presence of their tribe.

When Captain George Grey became governor he made drastic reductions in the police force, and proposed as part of his economy campaign in 1843 that O'Halloran should add to his duties as commissioner those of police magistrate. This O'Halloran was unwilling to do and he immediately resigned. On retirement he was presented with a silver snuff box by members of the mounted police and an illuminated address by the foot police. In 1854 he was gazetted lieut-colonel in the 1st Battalion, Volunteer Infantry. As a substantial farmer, horse-breeder and popular figure, O'Halloran was chosen to chair many important public gatherings, such as the well-attended breakfast given to Sturt [q.v.] at the start of his 1844 expedition to the interior.

In 1843 he was the first non-official member chosen by Grey for the Legislative Council. In 1846 he walked out with the other nominees in protest against Lieut-Governor Robe's bill for collecting royalties on minerals. He was active in founding Christ Church, O'Halloran Hill, which was consecrated by Bishop Short in 1848. He also served on the preparatory committees for the Collegiate School of St Peter, and became one of its first governors. His acquiescence in state aid for religion, how-ever, lost him the Noarlunga seat in the part-elective Legislative Council, although his supporters gave him dinners at Morphett Vale and Noarlunga after the election. With responsible government in 1857 he was elected to the Legislative Council at the head of twenty-seven candidates, receiving 3499 votes. He resigned on 9 June 1863. He died on 16 August 1870 and was buried in the family vault at Christ Church, O'Halloran Hill.

O'Halloran was first married at Dawlish, Devonshire, on 1 August 1821 to Anne, daughter of James Goss; she died at Calcutta in 1823, leaving two children. On 10 July 1834 at Newry, County Down, he married Jane, eldest daughter of James Waring, by whom he had three sons and one daughter.

Direct, forthright and uncomplicated, O'Halloran was a dashing officer with little time for the tortuous reasonings of theorists. His energetic action in subduing Aboriginals made the River Murray safe for overlanders and settlers but perturbed philanthropists. His independence prevented the Legislative Council from becoming a rubber stamp of governors or clamorous populace. His initiative as a farmer made him one of the first users of the Ridley [q.v.] harvesting machine and one of few successful large wheat-growers in the province.

WILLIAM LITTLEJOHN O'HALLORAN (1806-1885), brother of T. S. O'Halloran, was born in Ireland on 5 May 1806. He entered the army at an early age and served as an officer in India in the 38th Regiment until 1838, when he retired with the rank of captain. In 1840 he came with his family to South Australia. In 1843 he was appointed private secretary to Governor Grey and also clerk of the Legislative Council, where he held office until 1851, when he was appointed auditor-general. He remained in that office under several governments until 1868 and was highly regarded as an able and conscientious civil servant. He died at Glenelg on 15 July 1885.

On 15 December 1851 at Cork he married Elizabeth Minton Smyth, by whom he had five sons and three daughters. His eldest son, Joseph Sylvester O'Halloran, was secretary to the Royal Colonial Institute in London for many years.

J. W. Bull, *Early experiences of colonial life in South Australia* (Adel, 1878); A. Tolmer, *Reminiscences of an adventurous and chequered career at home and at the antipodes*, 1 (Lond, 1882); F. S. Dutton, *South Australia and its mines*, (Lond, 1846); T. O'Halloran, 'Journal, May 1841', PRGSSA, 7 (1903-04).   D. BRUCE ROSS

O'NEIL, PETER (1757-1846), Roman Catholic priest, was born on 29 June 1757, in the parish of Coona, County Cork, Ireland, a descendant of the O'Neil clan of County Tyrone. He attended a hedge school in Inch, studied classics at Kilworth, and then began ecclesiastical studies at the Irish College in Paris, eventually teaching Celtic language and literature there. He spent several years as a missionary in the diocese of Cloyne before receiving charge of the parish of Ballymacoda of which he had been an exceedingly popular curate. During the rebellion he was accused of sanctioning the murder of a United Irishman suspected of being a government spy; O'Neil refused, or was unable, to give information about it, was arrested, received 275 lashes without trial, and was threatened with another flogging unless he confessed. Distraught, he first wrote that he deserved his sufferings but later protested his innocence and decried the conditions under which he alleged that his confession had been extorted. He stated that he was allowed neither to be present nor to be represented at a court of inquiry on his case held in 1799 and that the court had failed to acquit him merely because of inaccuracies in his memorial. However, he was held in prison for two years before being transported in 1800 in the Anne which sailed from Cork a few days before an order arrived from the lord lieutenant to stop his departure.

On the voyage he helped to prevent a mutiny and so earned the approbation of the surgeon. Soon after he arrived on 21 February 1801 Governor King, who was then very disturbed by the Irish in the colony, sent him to Norfolk Island, as a priest 'of the most notorious, seditious and rebellious principles'. On the island he lived with Father Harold [q.v.]. In August 1802 Hobart recommended that all the priests be conditionally pardoned and that O'Neil be employed as a schoolteacher, but before his dispatch was written, instructions for O'Neil's release had been sent from Ireland on 30 May after another investigation of his case there. He was released on 15 January 1803 after a Government Order of 19 November 1802 had reached Norfolk Island. He sailed directly to Ireland, was reinstated as parish priest of Ballymacoda on 29 July 1803, and remained there until his death on 30 June 1846.

O'Neil's case provoked much controversy. His 'Humble Remonstrance' was published in The Catholic Question. Correspondence between the Right Hon. Lord Redesdale, Lord High Chancellor of Ireland, and the Right Hon. the Earl of Fingall (Dublin, 1804). The official justification was that the extraordinary action of the Irish military authorities was dictated by the desperate situation of the time. One of the unfortunate innocent victims of the emergency measures which the British government took in the Irish crisis, O'Neil carried the marks of his torture to his grave.

HRNSW, 4; R. R. Madden, The United Irishmen, their lives and times, 1, 2nd ed (Dublin, 1858); P. F. Moran, History of the Catholic Church in Australasia (Syd, 1895); Bonwick transcripts, biography v 4 (ML); P. G. King, Letter-book, 1797-1806 (ML).

VIVIENNE PARSONS

ORR, WILLIAM MORGAN (d. 1843), merchant and landowner, sailed from London in the Cyprus and arrived at Hobart Town via Sydney and Launceston in August 1825. With recommendations from the Colonial Office and assets of more than £3000 in goods, he was granted 2000 acres in the Hamilton district. His main business, however, was commerce and he rapidly accumulated great wealth. Although he was seriously disturbed by Lieut-Governor Arthur's administration and Press Licensing Act, he generally managed to keep out of colonial politics. As a merchant and shipping agent he had a store on the old wharf at Hobart. With small ships like the Richmond Packet and William IV he organized much sealing and bay whaling, and by 1831 he was shipping large quantities of whale-oil to London. By 1837 he had whaling stations at Recherche and Storm Bays and became prominent as an investor in large ships for the deep-sea fisheries. In 1838 his 289-ton Maria Orr was launched, the first full-rigged ship built in Hobart; the government presented a suit of sails and Orr's enterprise was applauded as a benefit to the colony. On 3 June 1835 at St David's Church of England he married Maria, the daughter of Michael Lackey of O'Brien's Bridge. They had a well-appointed home at Humphrey Rivulet near New Town.

Most of Orr's profits from trade and whaling were invested in land. His holdings increased by purchase and lease to some 80,000 acres in various parts of the island. When depression struck in 1841 he was one of the biggest and wealthiest merchants in Hobart. Caught with many bad debts, he had to solicit aid from friends to meet his commitments. When he was riding home one afternoon his horse was frightened by a gang of boys and bolted. It stumbled outside the Waggon and Horses

Inn; Orr had a violent fall and fractured his skull. He was unconscious for three days and died on 2 November 1843. His death spread a gloom over Hobart that was rarely equalled, for he was highly respected by all classes for his sincerity. Although his probate was sworn at £26,000, his death financially embarrassed some of his friends, but by 1846 all his creditors were fully paid after part of his land was sold by the sheriff for £20,000. His home at New Town was sold for £2400.

Orr was survived by two children and by his widow, who married Charles D'A. Lempriere on 13 May 1847. His brother, Alexander, who arrived in Hobart in November 1828, also became a merchant of wealth and high character; in 1846 he was nominated briefly to a vacancy in the Legislative Council. At St John's Church of England, Launceston, on 7 May 1839 he married Harriet Byron. In December 1855 Alexander Orr sailed for England in the *Heather Bell* with his wife and family.

HRA (3), 4, 6; *Hobart Town Courier*, 3 Nov 1843; *Austral-Asiatic Review*, 3 Nov 1843.

ORTON, JOSEPH RENNARD (1795-1842), Wesleyan Methodist missionary, was born on 10 October 1795 at Hull, England, a son of John and Eleanor Orton. While working for a ship chandler in London, he was befriended by a family named Wilkinson through whom he became active in Limehouse Wesleyan Chapel. He found a devoted wife in Sarah Jane Bragg whom he married in 1815. Of their twelve children, four died in infancy.

Entering the Wesleyan ministry in 1826, he was posted to Jamaica, where his concern for the slaves brought him into conflict with the local authorities and landed him in gaol. Eventually he was released, the case quashed and the local magistrates dismissed. But the damage was done. The foul conditions in the gaol seriously undermined his health and ultimately caused his death. To help him to recuperate, the church appointed him in 1830 to Bury St Edmunds in Suffolk. Next year he was sent to Australia where the critical state of Methodism called for strong leadership. Time proved him a wise choice. Arriving late in 1831, he began to infuse order and new life into the struggling church. His men were stationed as far apart as Parramatta and Hobart Town. Supervision involved weeks away from his home in Sydney and travelling was hazardous and exhausting. In 1832 he made the first of four journeys across the Blue Mountains to minister to the settlements springing up in the interior, preaching to all and sundry along the route, including the chain-gangs.

In 1833, on orders from England, he spent ten weeks in New Zealand, visiting mission stations. Fired by his spirit, Australian Methodism gained a new lease of life. Such was the growth that in 1835 Van Diemen's Land was made a separate district, with Orton at Hobart as first chairman. His pastoral visit to Launceston in 1836 was extended to the infant settlement across Bass Strait, where on 24 April he was the first clergyman to preach in Melbourne. Next year he was corresponding helpfully with the Methodists in the new colony of South Australia. Stirred by the fate of the Tasmanian Aboriginals, Orton published *Aborigines of Australia* (London, 1836), and pleaded with the new settlers to protect the native population. In their interests he made a special visit to Sydney to secure from Governor Gipps a grant of land for a mission. His next visit to Port Phillip in 1839 was to help Revs. Hurst and Tuckfield [q.v.] to establish the Buntingdale mission on the Barwon River, and to encourage the young Wesleyan Church in the fast-growing township of Melbourne. Although he was recalled to England in 1839 his departure was indefinitely deferred. He was sent to Tonga on a special mission but got no farther than New Zealand where he was stranded for months. At the end of 1840 he was back in Melbourne, tending the shepherdless flock until a permanent minister arrived. To the last he championed the case of the Aboriginals, conferring with the protectors, protesting against the travesties of justice he witnessed in court, and preparing reports to send to England. A very sick man, Orton sailed in 1842, but died on 30 April while still at sea. Later his family returned to Australia.

Orton is little known outside his own denomination; within it, he is almost a legend. His saintly spirit has left its mark upon his church. That he saved it, is widely agreed. Its early history in four Australian States is inextricably bound up with his name. More should be known of his gallant efforts on behalf of the coloured people, whose cause he espoused in Jamaica, Australia and New Zealand.

J. W. Miller, 'Joseph Orton', *A'sian Methodist Hist Soc J*, 7 (1939); Orton papers (ML).
J. RUSSELL ORTON

OSBORNE, HENRY (1803-1859), pastoralist, was born on 8 February 1803, the youngest of the ten children of Archie Osborne of Dirnaseer, County Tyrone,

Ireland. Two of his brothers had migrated to New South Wales and on the advice of one of them he sold his farm and other property for about £3000, invested this in a consignment of Irish linen, married Sarah, daughter of Rev. Benjamin Marshall of Dromore, County Down, and sailed for Sydney, where he arrived in May 1829. He sold his linen at a handsome profit and went to the property of Captain Thompson at Liverpool, where he gained some colonial experience before settling upon a grant of 2560 acres in the Illawarra near the present town of Dapto. This property, Marshall Mount, entitled him to some twenty-five labourers. He went in for dairying and at the same time bred large numbers of young cattle. In December 1839 he set out with one free settler, three convicts and three Aboriginals for South Australia, where he arrived four months later.

About this time Osborne began to acquire large holdings of land in the area between the Murrumbidgee and Murray Rivers southwards from Wagga Wagga. They included Barren Garry, Arejoel, and Brooking near Lockhart, all on the route which he had taken to South Australia. By the 1850s he owned very large holdings in the Illawarra, and in the Mount Keira and other coal-mines in the Maitland district, where an Act of parliament was required to deprive him of much of the land later occupied by the town of Maitland. He conducted an immense business in cattle in the Illawarra and also had large inland runs. It was to these that his descendants gravitated.

Henry Osborne became a member of the Legislative Council in 1851 and was elected to the Legislative Assembly in 1856. He died at Marshall Mount on 26 March 1859, survived by his wife, nine sons and three daughters. One son, Patrick Hill (1832-1902), was elected to the Legislative Assembly in 1864 and another, James (1845-1877), in 1869.

G. N. Griffiths, *Some southern homes of New South Wales* (Syd, 1952); P. J. B. Osborne, 'Some family history', Canberra Hist Soc, Papers, 1958; *SMH*, 30 Mar 1859.

P. J. B. OSBORNE

O'SHAUGHNESSY, EDWARD (1801-1840), journalist, poet and editor, was born in Ireland. His later work suggests that he had a sound education and a wide knowledge of literature. On 13 July 1824 he was convicted in Dublin of collecting taxes under false pretences and sentenced to seven years transportation. He probably committed the offence when in liquor, for there are many references to this weakness while he was in Sydney. He arrived in the *Asia* and was assigned as a reporter to Robert Howe of the *Sydney Gazette*. Until his sentence expired he lived at the *Gazette* office in Charlotte Street.

In the *Gazette* O'Shaughnessy published about thirty signed poems, mostly melancholy lyrics in the style of Thomas Moore. Later he showed that he could write satire in the manner of Byron equally well. His notices of Barnett Levey's [q.v.] dramatic ventures at the Theatre Royal were among the first dramatic criticisms in Australia. When he became editor of the *Gazette* he reprinted in it outstanding English poems and short stories from *Blackwood's Magazine*, thus continuing the tradition established by the founders, George [q.v.] and Robert Howe.

As far as can be discovered, O'Shaughnessy became editor of the *Gazette* on 1 June 1833 and continued for two years. This period covered the climax of the quarrel between Governor Bourke and the Tory magistrates on the question of convict discipline. The *Gazette* supported Bourke, but it is difficult to decide O'Shaughnessy's own views. The *Gazette's* traditional policy was to support the governor right or wrong, even though by 1833 it no longer relied largely on payment for the printing of Government Orders. O'Shaughnessy as an ex-convict was probably honest in his support of Bourke; the *Gazette* was referred to at this time as 'The Prisoners' Journal'. However, when he left the *Gazette* O'Shaughnessy wrote just as ably for the opposing party in the *Herald*.

O'Shaughnessy's editorship was marked by the bitter disputes over two political pamphlets issued by the *Gazette* in 1834. The first, *Party Politics Exposed* by 'Humanitas', the pen-name of William Watt, a sub-editor who later married the proprietress, Ann Howe, caused a storm of protest against O'Shaughnessy. The second, *Observations On the 'Hole and Corner Petition'* was by 'An Unpaid Magistrate', the pen-name of Roger Therry [q.v.], whose correspondence with O'Shaughnessy was later exposed by Major James Mudie [q.v.] in *The Felonry of New South Wales* (London, 1837). In the subsequent newspaper campaign for and against these pamphlets, O'Shaughnessy was attacked by J. D. Lang [q.v.] in the *Colonist*. Lang claimed that O'Shaughnessy, because he had once been a convict, was unworthy to edit a newspaper and stated that O'Shaughnessy's character was just as bad as when he had been 'lagged in Dublin'.

O'Shaughnessy sued Lang for libel but suddenly dropped proceedings. Although Lang claimed that O'Shaughnessy had been afraid to continue, the true reason seems to have been lack of money. Soon afterwards Mudie took Watt to court and O'Shaughnessy gave evidence against his former friend and colleague. Watt claimed that the *Herald* had paid O'Shaughnessy's debts in order to buy his evidence. Whether this was so or not, O'Shaughnessy certainly transferred to the *Herald* and was working on that paper when he died.

In 1838 Lang returned to the attack and stated that O'Shaughnessy, and not Ward Stephens [q.v.] was the true editor of the *Herald*. Although the *Herald*'s policy had not changed, Lang dubbed it 'The Convict Press'. O'Shaughnessy once more issued a writ for libel, but again the case did not reach the court. O'Shaughnessy continued to support all those aspects of convict discipline and colonial reform that he had previously denounced. He agitated for sterner convict discipline and the importation of coolie labour, justified the squatters who massacred Aboriginals, and expressed sectarian sentiments.

When he died in 1840 O'Shaughnessy's occupation was given as 'sub-editor', and his address as Princess Street, Sydney. He seems never to have married and left no will. He was buried according to the rites of the Church of England.

Freeman's J (Dublin), 1824; MS cat under O'Shaughnessy (ML); Newspaper indexes under O'Shaughnessy (ML).   J. V. BYRNES

OVENS, JOHN (1788-1825), soldier and engineer, was born at St Catherine, County Fermanagh, Ireland. Although educated for the church, he entered the army in 1808 as an ensign in the 73rd Regiment, went with it to New South Wales as a lieutenant in 1810, and was appointed engineer in general charge of public works. In October 1811 he returned to England on leave and transferred soon afterwards to the 74th Regiment, then serving in Spain under Brigadier-General Thomas Brisbane. He fought at Pampeluna, Orthes and Vittoria, where he was dangerously wounded on 21 June 1813. During the Peninsular war he became aide-de-camp to Brisbane and was promoted captain in 1819.

When Brisbane was appointed governor of New South Wales in 1821 he brought Ovens with him as aide-de-camp and made him acting chief engineer. Ovens now had general supervision of convict gangs. He improved the efficiency of the convicts employed on public works, supervised 'clearing gangs' with much success, and ultimately had fifty gangs preparing 'extensive tracts of land into a state for cultivation by the settler'. He also accompanied Captain Currie on an expedition to the upper Murrumbidgee and Monaro district in 1823, and helped John Oxley [q.v.] to survey Twofold Bay in October 1825.

'No public officer here', wrote Brisbane, 'has rendered me the same essential service, the Colony such general benefit, or imposed upon the Mother Country such a heavy debt of gratitude'. The governor made Ovens his private secretary when he was not finding Frederick Goulburn [q.v.] cooperative, and in 1824 in recognition of his services he secured his promotion to major in the 57th Regiment and obtained for him a grant of land at Longbottom (Concord). Ovens, who had been in poor health for some time, planned to retire to this estate, but died on 7 December 1825, six days after Brisbane's governorship ended.

By his request he was buried in the same grave as his friend Ellis Bent [q.v.] in the George Street burying ground. Later the bodies were reinterred, first at Garden Island, and finally at St Thomas's, North Sydney. The long inscription on the tombstone provides important biographical detail. Ovens's name was given to a river in Victoria and a mountain near Bathurst. Several writers have confused Major Ovens with Lieutenant John Ovens, also in the 57th Regiment at that time. Georgina Ovens was the wife of the lieutenant, and not of the major, who divided his estate among his brothers and sister.

HRA (1), 11-15; *Sydney Gazette*, 13 Dec 1825; *Truth* (Syd), 4 July 1909; *Army Lists*, 1821-1825.   E. W. DUNLOP

OXLEY, JOHN JOSEPH WILLIAM MOLESWORTH (1785?-1828), surveyor-general and explorer, was born at Kirkham Abbey near Westow, Yorkshire, England, the eldest son of John Oxley and his wife Isabella, who was related to the Irish Viscount Molesworth. He joined the navy in 1799 as a midshipman in the *Venerable*, and transferred in November 1801 to the *Buffalo*, in which as master's mate he sailed to Australia. Arriving there in October 1802 he engaged in coastal survey work including an expedition to Western Port in 1804-05. In 1805 Governor King appointed him acting lieutenant in charge of the *Buffalo*, and in 1806 he commanded the *Estramina* on a trip to Van Diemen's Land. Next year he returned to England where on 25 November he was commissioned lieutenant. He came back to Sydney in November 1808 to take up an appointment as first lieutenant in H.M.S. *Porpoise*, having sailed out as agent for the Transport Board in the convict ship *Speke*, in which he shipped goods worth £800 as an investment. He had obtained an order from the Colonial Office for a grant of 600 acres near the Nepean River, but Lieut-Governor Paterson [q.v.] granted him 1000 acres. Oxley had to surrender these in 1810, but Governor Macquarie granted him 600 acres near Camden which he increased in 1815 to 1000 acres again. This he called Kirkham.

When Paterson allowed the deposed Governor Bligh to leave Sydney in the *Porpoise* in March 1809 Oxley was aboard and sailed with Bligh to the Derwent. Next year he wrote a lengthy report on the settlements in Van Diemen's Land before sailing for England in the *Porpoise* in May. In London he applied for the post of Naval Officer in Sydney, and then, after paying C. Grimes [q.v.] to resign, according to John Macarthur [q.v.], he twice sought that of surveyor-general. Oxley denied that he had been a partisan of Macarthur when Bligh was deposed, but his letters show that he was on very intimate terms with the rebel leader. In 1812 he became engaged to Elizabeth Macarthur; this was broken off when her father discovered the extent of Oxley's debts. By that time, through the influence of Macarthur's friend Walter Davidson [q.v.], Oxley's second application for the surveyor-generalship had been successful. In 1811 he had retired from the navy, and in May 1812 sailed for Sydney in the *Minstrel* to take up his new duties.

During Governor Macquarie's administration Oxley was as much occupied with exploring as surveying. In 1815 his assistant, George Evans [q.v.], discovered the Lachlan River and reported good country south-west of Bathurst. In March 1817 Macquarie appointed Oxley to lead an expedition to explore this region and if possible 'to ascertain the real course . . . of the Lachlan . . . and whether it falls into the sea, or into some inland lake'. Leaving Bathurst on 28 April the explorers followed the Lachlan for more than two months until in July impassable marshes prevented further progress. Oxley then struck northward to the Macquarie River, which he traced back to Bathurst, where he arrived on 29 August. Macquarie highly praised Oxley's 'Zealous, Indefatigable and Intelligent Exertions' and recommended that he be given £200 for his 'Meritorious Services', which the secretary of state approved.

On 28 May 1818 Oxley led another expedition from Bathurst and followed the Macquarie River until it too disappeared into 'an ocean of reeds' (Macquarie marshes). From 6 July Oxley's party proceeded north-east until they discovered the Castlereagh River, then turning east they found the rich Liverpool Plains, reached and named the Peel River, crossed the southern part of the New England Range near Walcha, found the Hastings River and followed it to its estuary which was named Port Macquarie. A hazardous journey down the coast ended at Newcastle in November, some six months after the party's departure from Bathurst. The rich pastoral lands of the Liverpool Plains were quickly taken up by pastoralists, but Oxley failed in his primary object of tracing the Macquarie and Lachlan Rivers and formulated the mistaken theory of an inland sea. 'I feel confident', he wrote, 'we were in the immediate vicinity of an inland sea, most probably a shoal one . . . being filled up by immense depositions from the waters flowing into it from the higher lands'. Nevertheless his reports aroused great interest, and not only did his *Journals of Two Expeditions into the Interior of New South Wales* (London, 1820) give the first detailed description of the Australian inland, despite his grave doubts of the value of the lands he had traversed, but his discoveries paved the way for the later work of Charles Sturt and T. L. Mitchell [qq.v.].

Oxley's naval experience fitted him better for coastal survey work than for inland exploration. In September-December 1819 he made a trip by sea to Jervis Bay, where he thought the country did not offer 'the smallest inducement for the foundation of a Settlement on its shores, being . . . for the most part Barren and generally deficient in Water'. Earlier that year in the *Lady Nelson*, assisted by Phillip Parker King [q.v.] in the *Mermaid*, he had charted Port Macquarie, on which he reported favourably. In December 1820 he made a second survey of the district and reported in favour of establishing a new penal settlement there. In October 1823 he sailed north as far as Port Curtis, and on his return explored Moreton Bay and the Brisbane River, up which he sailed about fifty miles. His favourable report was again quickly followed by the formation of a penal settlement.

In 1820 Oxley had made several suggestions to Commissioner Bigge [q.v.] about the sale of land in New South Wales. Bigge accepted these and, when Governor Brisbane received his report, Oxley drafted in July 1824 specific regulations for sales at 5s. an acre, to be paid over three years; in 1825 and again in 1826 he drew up further regulations on land grants in accordance with the fluctuating orders of the Colonial Office. In 1825 he was appointed one of the three commissioners to carry out the thorough survey of the colony and its division into counties, shires and parishes which had been ordered from London; but this work was not easily accomplished. The duties of the survey office became very extensive as settlement expanded and Oxley was always handicapped by the lack of a sufficiently numerous trained staff. Governor Darling thought him 'very clever' but a man who would 'never submit to the Drudgery of carrying on the details of his Department'. He constantly sought increases in fees, salary and staff, but though both Macquarie and Brisbane supported his requests, the secretary of state was reluctant to incur the extra expenditure. In 1823 his salary was increased from 15s. to £1 a day; his fees had been increased in 1818 and between 1823 and 1828 brought him an average of nearly £1500 a year.

Oxley also had business interests. After he arrived in New South Wales in 1812 he acted as agent for Maude & Robinson of the Cape and Thomas & William Ward of London. He acted for the creditors of Garnham Blaxcell and Robert Campbell [qq.v.] and of the firm of Lord, Kable & Underwood [qq.v.]. He kept in touch with Walter Davidson at Canton, and acted for J. H. Bent [q.v.] with Alexander & Co. of Calcutta. In addition to these mercantile activities he was developing his properties and entered into partnership with Commissary Allan [q.v.] in raising cattle for the stores. Near his property, Kirkham, he received further grants of 820 acres at Minto in 1816 and 630 acres at Appin in 1817. After 1816 he sent cattle into the Bowral district and in June 1823 was granted 2300 acres there registered as Weston (probably a mistake for Westow). As a sheep breeder he took prizes at the shows of the Agricultural Society which he helped to found in 1822, though in 1824 John Macarthur criticized his 4000 crossbred sheep which, he said, Oxley sold as pure merinos to strangers; but Oxley and Macarthur were then on very bad terms. For a time Oxley was a director of the Bank of New South Wales, but in 1826 he was one of the founders and first directors of its 'exclusivist' rival, the Bank of Australia. He was a shareholder of the Australian Agricultural Co., which appears to have paid him for advice and assistance.

Oxley was keenly interested in the public and cultural life of the colony. He was

one of the first officers of the Bible Society when it was founded in 1817. In September 1819 he was appointed to the committee of the Female Orphan Institution, the Male Orphan Institution and the Public School Institution. In 1821 he became a foundation member of the Philosophical Society, and that December Governor Brisbane made him a magistrate. He subscribed to both St James's Church and to Scots Church where he was one of the congregation which in 1824 petitioned for government assistance for its minister. He was selected as one of the five members of the original Legislative Council in 1824, but was not reappointed when the council was reconstituted next year. He had always been a strong exclusive. Macquarie criticized him as 'factious and dissatisfied'. In 1812 John Macarthur wrote warmly of Oxley's 'good nature'; later he spoke in a very different vein after 'his unprincipled conduct made it necessary to drop his acquaintance'. Whatever his character his financial incapacity is clear, and this made him, in Macarthur's opinion, 'no more fit to make his way in the midst of the sharks among whom it will be his fate to live than he is qualified to be a Lord Chancellor'. Despite his investments, his fees and his land grants, when he died at Kirkham on 26 May 1828, he was so 'much embarrassed in his pecuniary circumstances' that the Executive Council felt compelled to recommend special assistance to his widow and children. The British government refused to sanction a pension but agreed to permit a grant of 5000 acres to Oxley's sons in recognition of their father's services.

On 31 October 1821 Oxley married Emma Norton (1798-1885) at St Philip's Church. They had two sons, John (b. 1824) and Henry (b. 1826), but earlier Oxley had had two daughters by Charlotte Thorpe and one by Elizabeth Marnon. He kept a substantial town house in Sydney, opposite St James's Church, and he built a fine country seat at Kirkham. He was aged only 42 when he died, but his constitution had 'been materially injured by the privations which he suffered during the Several Expeditions on which he was employed in exploring the Interior'. He was buried in the Devonshire Street cemetery in Sydney. A portrait is in the Mitchell Library, Sydney.

HRNSW, 6-7; HRA (1), 5-15; E. W. Dunlop, *John Oxley* (Melb, 1960); E. C. Rowland, 'The life and work of John Oxley', *JRAHS*, 28 (1942); J. Oxley, Field notebooks and reports (ML).　　　　　　　　　E. W. DUNLOP

P

PAGE, SAMUEL (1810-1878), publican, coach proprietor and pastoralist, was born on 30 March 1810 in London, the second son of George Page of Bermondsey, and his wife Sarah. His father, a Waterloo veteran, arrived in Hobart Town in January 1822 from England in the *Tiger*, settled at Bagdad and was later granted land at Lemon Springs although he claimed to have migrated without a shilling. His wife and three children, Samuel, John and Louisa, arrived in Van Diemen's Land in the brig *Belinda* in November 1823.

On 19 September 1833 at Hobart Samuel Page was married to Grace, daughter of Captain Harris, a master mariner. In 1835 he was granted the licence of the Glasgow Wine and Spirits Vaults at the north-east corner of Elizabeth and Liverpool Streets in Hobart, and two years later took over the Lake Dulverton Inn at Oatlands. In 1839 he moved to the Oatlands Hotel. With John Lord he became a coach proprietor in 1848. Next year he bought from the widow of John Edward Cox [q.v.] a coach service that had run between Hobart and Launceston for seventeen years. In 1853 Page took over the mail contract and after six years bought out John Lord for £8750. With three coaches daily each way, the service controlled most of the transport on the main road and required 300 horses and three main fodder stations. Fares ranged from 5s. for outside seats to £5 inside. Each mail coach carried an armed guard, and two when bullion was aboard. Although the service was never held up by bushrangers, Page himself was once stopped in Epping Forest by two of them, Ogden and Sullivan; he refused to take them seriously and was allowed to pass on, chiefly, he claimed, because one of them had worked for him. A more serious challenge came in 1873 when Alfred Burbury started a rival coach service, but within three years Hobart and Launceston were linked by railway.

During his coaching operations Page acquired many pastoral properties, including Northumbria, Anstey Barton, Woodlands. Kelvin Grove, Trefusis, Ellenthorpe, Stonehenge and Mount Vernon. At one time his landholdings and his flocks of 63,000 sheep were said to be the largest ever held by one person in the colony. Page was an enthusiastic breeder of race-horses and, with Sir James Agnew and James Lord, he helped to found the Tasmanian Racing Club in Hobart. He died at Hobart on 31 March 1878, and his widow on 9 August 1882. Of their four sons and six daughters, Alfred ran a stud farm at Melton Mowbray on a portion of Woodlands. Alfred's son, Charles Service Page, followed in his father's and grandfather's footsteps and served for twenty years on the committee of the Tasmanian Racing Club.

Correspondence file under Page (TA).

C. A. S. PAGE

PALMER, GEORGE THOMAS (1784-1854), landholder, was born on 26 April 1784 at Brompton, Kent, England, the son of John Palmer [q.v.], commissary of New South Wales, and his American wife Susan, née Stilwell. He joined the army in November 1800 and is reputed to have seen action against Napoleon. On 26 March 1805 he married Catherine Irene Pemberton (1787-1855) at Malta. In 1806 he came to New South Wales with her in the *Albion*, as a lieutenant in the 61st Regiment but with permission to settle as a free immigrant.

Between 7 May 1810 and 7 November 1811 he acted as provost-marshal while William Gore [q.v.] was absent in England. When Governor Macquarie dismissed John Jamieson [q.v.] from the position of superintendent of government stock, he appointed Palmer in his place from 1 May 1813 at an increased salary which he thought more commensurate to responsibility for government property valued at £40,000, and recommended Palmer at this time as 'a Young Man of good Education, high Honor & Integrity, active diligent & intelligent'. However, Palmer resigned the position within a year, set up his home at Pemberton Grange near Parramatta, and acquired extensive lands and stock, including 700 acres at Bringelly granted in August 1812. By 1828 he held Ginninderra Station in County Murray, where nearly 4000 of its 13,200 acres had been cleared and he ran almost 2000 head of cattle and 6000 sheep. He was a shareholder in the Australian Agricultural Co.

He was notably active in colonial public life. He was a magistrate for many years and, though one of those who preferred dismissal in August 1822 by Governor Brisbane to association on the bench with H. G. Douglass [q.v], was reinstated in November 1825. He was a member of the managing committee of the Female Factory in the late 1820s. In July 1829 he signed the address of landed proprietors and merchants in support of Governor Darling and in August 1836 served on the committee in opposition to the establishment of National schools. In 1829 his name was included in the list of those who might be nominated to the Legislative Council should there be a vacancy in that body. Later he returned to England and he died on 26 October 1854 at Bath, where he was buried. His wife and nine children survived him.

HRNSW, 7; HRA (1), 7, 8, 14, 15, 18; SMH, 22, 27 Jan 1855; MS cat under G. T. Palmer (ML).   MARGARET STEVEN

PALMER, JOHN (1760-1833), commissary, was born in England. He entered the navy as a captain's servant at 9, and appears to have been educated entirely in the navy, which maintained schoolmasters for such recruits. During the American war of independence he was serving in H.M.S. *Richmond* which was captured off Chesapeake Bay by a French squadron on 11 September 1781. In 1783, after his release as a prisoner of war, the dark, handsome officer married Susan Stilwell (1761-1832), daughter of an American loyalist family.

Palmer arrived in New South Wales with the First Fleet in 1788 as purser of Governor Phillip's flagship *Sirius*. The first commissary, Andrew Miller [q.v.], resigned in 1790 on account of ill health, and when the *Sirius* was wrecked off Norfolk Island Palmer was appointed commissary on 2 June 1791. In this post he was responsible for the reception and issue of all government stores, virtually the only supplies in the colony, and their supplement by purchase from private merchants. He negotiated payment for official business and was empowered to draw bills on the British Treasury. In effect he kept the public accounts and funds of the colony and was at once official supplier, contractor and banker to the settlement. The power and responsibility inherent in this office were wielded so discreetly and efficiently that Palmer enjoyed both official and private confidence. Though the duke of Wellington observed in 1810 that 'the prejudice of society against a commissary almost prevented him from receiving the common respect due to the character of a gentleman' Palmer, perhaps because of his naval background and the rather indirect way in which he had succeeded to this office, always carried the 'character of a gentleman' in the colony. His convivial nature and engaging personality combined with refinement and discretion to commend him to most of those with whom he came in contact.

By 1793 Palmer had decided to settle in New South Wales, though he had to wait three years before his application for leave was granted. In September 1796 he left for England in the *Britannia*, returning in November 1800 in the *Porpoise* with his wife and children, two sisters, Sophia (1777-1833) and Sarah (b.1774), and a naval brother, Christopher (1767-1821). In February 1793 Lieut-Governor Francis Grose [q.v.] had granted Palmer 100 acres at the head of Garden Island Cove, then known as Palmer's Cove. Here, set in an extensive orchard, Palmer built Woolloomooloo Farm, one of the colony's first permanent residences, where the Palmers lived and elegantly entertained the first rank of colonial society.

'Little Jack' Palmer was one of the most enterprising of the early settlers and acquired much knowledge of all aspects of the colony through his private speculations. Active and adventurous, he had early explored the interior of the colony, most of which he believed capable of cultivation. In 1795 Captain Waterhouse [q.v.] described him as one of the three principal farmers and stockholders in the colony and in 1803 Palmer was hailed as the first exponent of improved farming methods when he reduced the men employed on his 300-acre Hawkesbury farm from a hundred to fifteen. When giving evidence before the select committee on transportation in 1812 Palmer claimed, 'I had more ground than anybody else; I farmed more than any other person did'. By 1803 he owned several small colonial-built craft. Two, the *George* and the *John*, were employed sealing in Bass Strait and another, the *Edwin*, plied up the Hawkesbury River and along the coast with grain, timber and coals. In 1803 one of his employees discovered a new coal-mine at Hunter's River. On 17 September 1801 Palmer's sister Sophia had married Robert Campbell [q.v.], and during Campbell's absence in England in 1805 and 1806 Palmer acted as his agent. Palmer also owned a windmill on the margin of the Domain and a bakery near the present Conservatorium of Music. It is claimed that during the disastrous floods of 1806, when scarcity of grain inflated flour prices, Palmer ordered bread to be sold to the needy at lower prices than were then common.

In his judicial capacity as a magistrate, which he had been appointed by Grose in 1793, and as one of the principal civil officers, Palmer was familiar with most of the disturbances that occurred in the colony. In later evidence he revealed that he was no friend of John Macarthur [q.v.] or of most of the New South Wales Corps. He had been Dr Balmain's [q.v.] official second in 1794 when Macarthur had used the officers of the corps to insult the surgeon and avoid Balmain's challenge to a duel. When opposition to Governor Bligh became evident, Palmer engaged himself in the governor's cause. As a result he too became the butt of rebel hostility. Palmer was one of those dining at Government House on the night of Bligh's deposition. In a letter he later wrote to Bligh, Palmer reported what had happened after the governor's arrest: 'Immediately after this transaction they surrounded my Office, and not only seized upon the whole of my Public and private Books and Papers but also ordered the Keys of the Stores to be given up, and I was told . . . to consider myself under an Arrest; they then put seals on the doors of the Office, and placed a Centinel at each door. A few days after Mr Bayley, Mr John Blaxland, and Mr Garnham Blaxcell [qq.v.] broke the Seals of the Office, and ordered my Desk to be opened . . . they then seized my Ledgers, Books, and other Papers . . . I further beg leave to state that a Mr McArthur was appointed Colonial Secretary, a Situation never before known in the Colony, nor was ever permitted by Authority. Soon after he came to Act in that Situation he took from Major Johnston [q.v.] three Government Ledgers, and had them removed to his House'.

Although suspended by the rebels, Palmer embarrassed the new regime by persistently refusing, until instructed from England, to adjust claims made on the Commissary Department while he was in charge. He occupied himself in corresponding with Bligh about the alienation of government property, misappropriation of funds, and other malversations permitted under the rebel administration. After one of his demands for accounts was refused by Palmer, Macarthur accused him of insolence, contempt and disobedience and threatened that 'immediate measures will be resorted to, which, it is hoped, may bring you into a more temperate frame of mind'. In February 1809 Lieut-Colonel Paterson [q.v.] refused Palmer permission to leave for England until he settled these accounts.

On 18 March 1809 Palmer was committed by the rebel administration on a charge of sedition for having distributed, two days earlier, in company with Charles Hook [q.v.], ex-Governor Bligh's proclamation, declaring New South Wales in a state of mutiny. Palmer denied the competency of the court and refused to plead, but was found guilty and sentenced to three months imprisonment in Sydney gaol and directed to pay a fine of £50.

Palmer was reinstated by Governor Macquarie but failed to receive any official consideration for deprivations suffered in the rebellion and, indeed, received barest justice at the hands of authority. Though the secretary of state instructed Macquarie to examine the commissariat accounts and see that the office was placed on a proper footing, he observed that as the complaints against Palmer 'have been chiefly brought forward since the arrest of Governor Bligh, it is probable they are exaggerated by Party'. Palmer's examiners at the Comptroller's Office in London held that the charges 'seemed to have arisen as much from private pique as from zeal for the public service' and were too vague to justify a formal inquiry; however, they thought it inexpedient to restore Palmer because of his long tenure in office, and recommended the appointment of another commissary. On 25 July 1811 Palmer was demoted to assistant commissary and placed on half-pay, and next year the entire commissariat system was reorganized.

In 1810 Palmer had gone to England with Bligh as one of his chief witnesses against Johnston. During 1812 he gave valuable evidence to the select committee on transportation. In June 1813 he was reemployed in the commissariat and returned to New South Wales in May 1814. Soon afterwards a disagreement over the leasehold of five acres on which his windmill and bakery stood, which Macquarie claimed were in the Domain and which certainly overlooked Government House, resulted in the governor resuming them, albeit with compensation. In 1817 Macquarie recommended to London that Palmer be placed on half-pay, 'as he is of no sort of use whatever here nor never can be. He constantly resides at Parramatta, but does no duty there, and has had very little success in the recovering Payment of the Debts due to the Crown from individuals in this Country, for the recovery of which he was principally sent out'. In January 1819 Palmer was retired on half-pay.

On his return to the colony in 1814 Palmer had found his private affairs extremely straitened. The estate of Woolloomooloo, mortgaged for over £13,000, was eventually sold to Edward Riley [q.v.] for £2290 in May 1822, though the stock and furnishings were auctioned in 1816. In January 1818 Palmer was granted 1500 acres at Bathurst, which he named Hambledon, but he ran only a handful of stock. In the 1820s the family fortunes recovered.

Palmer received a grant in the Limestone Plains known as Jerrabombera, while at Waddon, near Parramatta, he farmed 3000 acres, one-third of which was cleared. By the 1830s he was running more than 3000 sheep and nearly 500 cattle.

From August 1803 to January 1824 he had been a member of the committee of the Female Orphan Institution. As a magistrate he sat frequently on the bench at Parramatta until dismissed by Governor Brisbane in the quarrel over the case of H. G. Douglass [q.v.] in 1822; he was restored to the magistracy on 3 November 1825 and continued to sit until within a year or two of his death. His reputation for discreet benevolence was enhanced by a friendly manner and cheerful nature. He was an adherent of the Church of England. When he died at Waddon on 27 September 1833, he was 'the last surviving officer of the first fleet that arrived in this part of His Majesty's Dominions'. His wife died in September 1832; she was survived by three sons, George Thomas [q.v.], John (1797-1839) and Edwin Campbell (b. 1802), and a daughter, Sophia Susannah (b. 1803), who had married Edward Close [q.v.].

HRNSW, 2-7; HRA (1), 1-11; G. Mackaness, The life of Vice-Admiral William Bligh, 2nd ed (Syd, 1951); H. V. Evatt, Rum Rebellion (Syd, 1955); Sydney Gazette, 5 Mar, 10 Apr, 1, 8 May, 3 July, 21 Aug, 4 Dec 1803, 19, 26 Mar, 8, 15 Oct 1809, 13 July, 10 Aug 1816, 7 Apr 1821; WO 61/1, 2; Adm 1/5319, 36/10978.   MARGARET STEVEN

PALMER, PHILIP (1799-1853), Anglican clergyman, was born at Landrake, Cornwall, England, the son of Jonathan Palmer and his wife Ursula, née Blake. After schooling at Landrake and Liskeard, he matriculated in 1824 and went to Trinity College, Cambridge (B.A., 1828; M.A., 1833). About 1830 he married Harriet, daughter of Rev. Jeremiah Owen, of Carmarthen, Wales; they had one daughter in May 1831 and another in April 1832. He was a curate at Langdon Hills, Essex, from 1831 to 1833. In response to a request from the Colonial Office, the bishop of London recommended Palmer, because of his piety and leadership qualities, for appointment as rural dean in Van Diemen's Land. In the William Bryan he arrived with his family at Hobart Town in June 1833, but to prevent the friction that might have arisen if Palmer had been put in charge of colonial clergy who were his seniors, Archdeacon W. G. Broughton [q.v.] limited his duties as rural dean to those of correspondence, the charge of Trinity and St

John's, New Town, and services at the penitentiary and hospital.

As rural dean he was given the seat in the Legislative Council formerly held by Rev. William Bedford [q.v.] and in 1834-36 served in the Executive Council where Lieut-Governor Arthur appreciated his co-operative nature after the delays arising from Bedford's contrariness. Resentful at being superseded, Bedford tried to frustrate the performance of the clerical duties for which Palmer was responsible. However, on the arrival in January 1837 of his brother-in-law, Archdeacon Hutchins [q.v.], Palmer ceased to be rural dean and lost his seat in the council. Although appointed acting archdeacon and Bishop Broughton's commissary on Hutchins's sudden death in June 1841, he was finally displaced on the arrival of Archdeacon Marriott with Bishop Nixon [qq.v.] two years later.

Continued ill health caused him to apply for a position in England. Disappointed on learning that he was not successful, he sought leave of absence for eighteen months, and sailed for England in February 1845. There he collected funds for the new Holy Trinity schoolhouse and residence. He returned in March 1847, far from well. After five more years of struggle with sickness, he became incapable of active work, planned a long leave to recuperate, and was preparing to resign from Holy Trinity when he died suddenly of apoplexy on 21 May 1853 at Hobart. He was survived by his widow and five children.

A man of strong evangelical views, Palmer came into conflict with Marriott and Nixon who described him as 'unfit for any post of trust or efficiency . . . weak in voice, deficient in zeal and active only in scattering the tracts of the Religious Tract Society'. For eleven years he was joint secretary of the undenominational British and Foreign Bible Society and had several disputes with the bishop during the 1840s for allowing the society to use Anglican churches for meetings at which Dissenting teachers criticized the lukewarmness and indifference of the Church of England. With other Low Churchmen, he signed the Solemn Declaration against Nixon in 1851, but ill health prevented him from taking further part in the ritualist controversy. In church development his greatest contribution was in the building of Holy Trinity Church and providing it with the first peal of bells in Australia. He took an interest in the transportation of convicts, and while in England suggested some expensive and impractical improvements in the separate housing of prisoners. He was an inspector of public schools, had a great affection for children, and established three Church of England schools in Hobart. During his term at Trinity, the debt on the building of the church was almost paid off. A marble tablet to his memory 'was erected in the church by his parishioners in 1854.

F. Bowden and M. Crawford, *The story of Trinity* (Hob, 1933); N. Nixon, *The pioneer bishop in Van Diemen's Land 1843-1863* (Hob, 1953); *Hobart Town Advertiser*, 24 May 1853, GO 1/33/321, 33/14/864 (TA); CO 280/167. 　　　　　　　P. R. HART

PALMER, THOMAS FYSHE (1747-1802), Unitarian minister and political reformer, was born in July 1747 at Ickwell, Bedfordshire, England, the son of Henry Fyshe of an ancient family who assumed the added name of Palmer by reason of an inheritance, and Elizabeth, daughter of James Ingram of Barnet. After receiving his early education under Rev. Henry Gunning of Ely, he spent five years at Eton and in 1765 entered Queen's College, Cambridge (B.A., 1769; M.A., 1772; B.D., 1781). He was ordained in 1771. At Cambridge seeds of doubt had been sown by his teachers and in 1783, after being curate at Leatherhead in Surrey for a short time, he became dissatisfied with certain doctrines of the Church of England, embraced Unitarianism, and for the next ten years preached that faith to Scottish congregations in Dundee and other Scottish towns. He displayed considerable Biblical learning by publishing in *The Theological Repository*, a series of tracts under the pseudonym Anglo-Scotus, and became acquainted with the celebrated Dr Joseph Priestley and his radical Birmingham circle. He was equally distinguished in his zeal for political reform, and became closely identified with a Dundee group, 'The Friends of Liberty', who were fervently advocating this cause. When George Mealmaker [q.v.], a Dundee weaver, wrote an 'Address to the People' on the subject of parliamentary reform, Palmer arranged for its printing and distribution. For this he was tried at Perth on 12 September 1793 on a charge of seditious practices, convicted, and sentenced to seven years transportation.

He sailed for New South Wales in April 1794 in the transport *Surprize*, which also carried his fellow Scottish Martyts, Thomas Muir, William Skirving and Maurice Margarot [qq.v.]. When in the tropics, Captain Campbell, master of the *Surprize*, acting on ill-founded charges of incitement to mutiny, confined Palmer and Skirving under conditions of extreme hardship, which were the subject of complaints laid before Lieut-Governor Grose [q.v.] on their arrival at Sydney on 25 October. A narrative describing his sufferings was taken back to England by Surgeon John White [q.v.] and published in 1797.

During his seven years of exile in Sydney Palmer was free from the usual convict restraint and engaged in various enterprises to supplement his private means. Apart from a farm which proved unproductive, he entered into a partnership with John Boston [q.v.] and James Ellis, two young free settlers who had also come in the *Surprize*; the latter was a son of a Dundee staymaker who had been Palmer's companion and protégé for several years and had given evidence at the trial. This partnership, known as Boston & Co., was one of the pioneer trading concerns in the colony. Their major undertaking was in shipbuilding. By August 1797, with the aid of an encyclopedia brought by Palmer from England, they built a small craft for the Norfolk Island trade. After this craft was lost at sea, a second vessel, the *Martha*, 30 tons, was built, and taken as far afield as Norfolk Island and the sealing grounds of Bass Strait. Little is known of these voyages, some of which were made without Governor Hunter's consent, but there is some evidence that they had reached as far as King Island before the end of 1798. Palmer was a close friend of Surgeon George Bass [q.v.], the explorer, who left his well chosen library of books in Palmer's care when he sailed for England in 1799; the two men exchanged information on the maritime exploration of south-east Australia, a subject of much comment in Palmer's letters to friends in England. Several of these letters were published anonymously as broadsheets by Rev. John Disney; one of them, severely criticizing Hunter's administration and lack of initiative in exploration, reached the duke of Portland who called on Hunter for an explanation. Hunter replied in his dispatch of 15 November 1799 and, while he did not openly name Palmer as the author of these charges, clearly indicated the friction then existing between the administration and Palmer and his associates.

When his sentence expired Palmer, Boston and Ellis bought the decrepit Spanish prize *El Plumier* and, with William Reid, a former seaman of the *Sirius*, as captain, sailed from Sydney for England in January 1801. After many troubles due to the need for repairs and a shortage of provisions, the ship, almost sinking, reached the Spanish island of Guam next January where it was condemned as unseaworthy.

Enfeebled by the hardships of the voyage, Palmer died there on 2 June 1802; he left his papers and effects to Ellis, who was then in Manila, but these were lost.

Some years later news reached England that because of Palmer's religious beliefs the Catholic friars had refused him a Christian burial and his body was interred on the seashore 'among pirates'. It lay there until May 1804, when the American ship *Mary* called at the island on a voyage from Sydney to Manila, and her master, Captain Balch, knowing something of Palmer's history, obtained permission from the Spanish governor to remove his remains. They were taken to Boston and a tablet was placed over his tomb in one of the churches of that city, though no trace of it can be found. A memorial to the Scottish Martyrs was later erected on Calton Hill, Edinburgh, and there his name is inscribed.

Palmer was probably the most cultured of those who came to New South Wales in the early years of settlement. Humane in sentiment and advanced in political opinion, he gained the friendship of the more liberal minded surgeons, White and Bass; but his radical views on politics and religion were looked at with suspicion in a penal colony and aroused the animosity of certain officers who accused him of being a 'leveller', and of Governor Hunter who described him as 'the dark and infamous assassin' because of criticism of his régime. Although he probably never left the immediate vicinity of the settlements he showed the keenest interest in the natural history of the country, the discoveries made on adjoining coasts and of the future prospects of the colony for which he held high hopes. His descriptions of the Aboriginals, with whom he lived for a short time, show a tender understanding of their mode of life, habits, and unspoilt gaiety, while he is equally vehement in his protestations at the outrages inflicted on them by the soldiery. He is to be remembered as one who cheerfully suffered exile for opinions now commonplace, and as a pioneer in trade, manufacture and shipbuilding in New South Wales.

HRNSW, 2, 3; *Trial of the Rev. Thomas Fyshe Palmer* (Edinb, 1793); G. Thompson, *Slavery and famine, punishment for sedition* (Lond, 1794); T. Belsham, *Memoirs of the late Reverend Theophilus Lindsey* (Lond, 1812); H. Paton (ed), *A series of original portraits . . . and illustrative anecdotes*, 1-2 (Edinb, 1838); H. Cockburn, *An examination of the trials for sedition . . . in Scotland* (Edinb, 1888); E. Im Thurn and L. C. Warton (eds), *The journal of William Lockerby* (Lond, 1925); *Mthly Mag* (Lond), Feb 1804; *Mthly Repository*, 1817; L. Baker-Short, 'Thomas Fyshe Palmer: from Eton to Botany Bay', *Trans*, Unitarian Hist Soc, 13 (1964); Lindsey-Millar correspondence (microfilm, ML); W. Haswell, Remarks on a voyage to Marianna Islands (microfilm, ML); T. Fyshe Palmer papers (Manchester College, Oxford, copy ML).
                      JOHN EARNSHAW

PAMPHLETT, THOMAS (1789?-1838), castaway, became a brickmaker at Manchester, England, and at 22 as James Groom was charged on 10 September 1810 at the Lancaster Assizes with stealing five pieces of woollen cloth and a bay mare in the County of Chester. He was found guilty and his death sentence was commuted to transportation for fourteen years. He arrived in Sydney in the *Guildford* in January 1812. In May 1814, for theft, he received 100 lashes and twelve months in irons in the gaol-gang, from which he absconded in October 1814 and May 1815. Subsequent good conduct earned him a conditional pardon on 31 January 1818.

In March 1823 with three other ticket-of-leave men, John Finnegan, Richard Parsons and John Thompson, he set out for the Five Islands (Illawarra) to cut cedar. Blown north by a storm in which Thompson died, the boat was wrecked on the outer shore of Moreton Island. After some hardships, mitigated by help from Aboriginals, they crossed to the mainland. Believing themselves south of Sydney they sought a northward route homewards. Aboriginals again helped them with food and directions and they soon came upon a large river (Brisbane). As it was too wide to cross they followed its banks upwards almost to the present site of Goodna. Finding a canoe they crossed the stream and returned along the opposite bank, again living with Aboriginals for some weeks.

In September 1823 Pamphlett and the Aboriginals attracted the attention of John Oxley [q.v.], who was then exploring in the *Mermaid* for the site of a new penal settlement at Moreton Bay. Pamphlett was taken on board and next day Finnegan was also rescued. Parsons was not found until the next year. Oxley was interested to hear of the large river and, with Finnegan as his guide, explored it as far as the point reached by the castaways. Oxley then took the two men with him to Sydney.

On 11 October 1826 Pamphlett was found guilty of larceny and sent for seven years to Moreton Bay. His tales of his earlier life among the Aboriginals encouraged others, including Davis and Bracewell [qq.v.] to seek relief from the hardships of the settlement, but Pamphlett's own behaviour was exemplary except for one day's escape in January 1833, all the more surprising as his sentence had almost expired. He left Moreton Bay in April, and lived uneventfully until his death on 1 December 1838 at Penrith.

B. Field (ed), *Geographical memoirs on New South Wales* (Lond, 1825); H. S. Russell, *The genesis of Queensland* (Syd, 1888); E. S. Jackson, 'Early visitors to Moreton Bay', *JRAHS*, 15 (1929-30); *JRQHS*, 3 (1937-47), 459-60; R. Cilento and C. L. Lack, 'Wild white men of Queensland', *JRQHS*, 6 (1959-62).

J. H. HORNIBROOK

PARKINSON, SYDNEY (1745?-1771), a natural history draughtsman, was born in Edinburgh, the younger of two sons of Joel Parkinson, a brewer and a Quaker. Although apprenticed to a wool draper, Parkinson's preference was for botanical drawing at which he showed great skill. About 1767 he went to London and was employed by Joseph Banks [q.v.] for whom he did some outstanding work; in 1768, when Banks formed his suite of 'scientific gentlemen' to accompany James Cook [q.v.] to the South Seas in the *Endeavour*, Parkinson went as botanical draughtsman. The death at Tahiti of Alexander Buchan, the topographical draughtsman, threw a heavy extra burden on Parkinson, but he bore it well and ably. During the voyage he made at least 1300 drawings or sketches, and compiled vocabularies of the natives of Tahiti and New Holland. On the way home, when the *Endeavour* called at Batavia for repairs, Parkinson was one of many who contracted dysentery, and he died at sea on 26 January 1771. In England later that year a dispute arose between Banks and Parkinson's brother, Stanfield. Banks had paid the latter £500 for balance of salary due and for Parkinson's papers and drawings. The papers were later lent to Stanfield Parkinson, who contrary to agreement had them transcribed for publication and was restrained by an injunction from doing so until the official account of the voyage had appeared. His book was published later in the same year, 1773, entitled *A Journal of a Voyage to the South Seas*, with a second enlarged edition in 1784. A result of the squabble was that although Hawkesworth, who edited the official account of the voyage, used Parkinson's papers and drawings freely he did not acknowledge them. Only two of Parkinson's illustrations in these books are of Australian subjects. His own contains a study of the two Aboriginals who opposed Cook at Botany Bay, and Hawkesworth has a view of the Endeavour River (Cooktown, Queensland). A third of a kangaroo, formerly attributed to Parkinson, is now known to have been from a painting by George Stubbs.

Parkinson was the first artist to set foot on Australian soil, to draw an authentic Australian landscape, and to portray Aboriginals from direct observation. A great quantity of his work survives. The British Museum has eighteen volumes of his plant drawings, of which eight, comprising 243 drawings, are of Australian plants, three volumes of zoological subjects, of which a few sketches relate to Australia, and many of his landscape and other drawings, mainly of Tahitian and New Zealand subjects. Parkinson was gentle, able and conscientious, noted, according to his brother, for 'his singular simplicity of conduct, his sincere regard for truth [and] his ardent thirst after knowledge'. Two portraits are known: a small head in oils in the British Museum (Natural History) and the engraved frontispiece to his *Voyage*.

J. Hawkesworth (ed), *An account of the voyages . . . for making discoveries in the southern hemisphere*, 1-3 (Lond, 1773); J. Britten (ed), *Illustrations of Australian plants collected in 1770 during Captain Cook's voyage* (Lond, 1905); Bernard Smith, *European vision and the south Pacific 1768-1850* (Oxford, 1960); Rex and Thea Rienits, *Early artists of Australia* (Syd, 1963); F. C. Sawyer, 'Some natural history drawings made during Cook's first voyage', *Soc for Bibliog of Natural Hist J*, 2 (1949); A. Lysaght, 'Captain Cook's kangaroo', *New Scientist*, 1 (1957).

REX RIENITS

PARRAMORE, WILLIAM THOMAS (1797-1854), public servant, was born on 30 September 1797, the eldest son of George Parramore and Patience, née Allen, of Wetmore Hall, Derbyshire, and received a legal training at Gray's Inn, London. His father, a farm-agent and mine-manager, decided to emigrate with his family in 1822 and William accompanied him in the *Woodlark*, arriving in Hobart Town on 8 July 1823. Land was chosen at Ross and at once George Parramore began farming his 1000-acre grant, Wetmore, assisted by his sons who obtained adjoining grants.

To increase the family income, William decided to return to law in Hobart as clerk in the office of the attorney-general, who advised him to practise on his own account. He was admitted as a solicitor and proctor in the Supreme Court in May 1824 but, finding the quarrelling of Van Diemen's Land settlers both distasteful and unprofitable, returned to government employment in April 1825 as clerk of the peace and registrar of the Court of Requests at £200 a year. Two years later Lieut-Governor Arthur, seeking a reliable and experienced colonist as private secretary, appointed Parramore at £300 a year. It was an arduous post and one demanding great discretion; Arthur's personal supervision of every department of the civil government involved his secretary for long hours in voluminous correspondence and in the assessment of convicts' records and settlers' claims for land and servants.

In November 1827 he married Thirza Cropper, formerly a schoolmistress at Caen, Normandy. Their only child, William, died in infancy. On the enforced resignation of James Gordon [q.v.] in 1832, Parramore, in poor health due to the close confinement of the previous five years, accepted the less onerous situation of police magistrate and coroner of Richmond, and went to live at Anglewood. However, in 1834, in deference to Gordon's protests at Arthur's choice of his former secretary as replacement at Richmond, it was thought advisable to send a new magistrate from England. Arthur regretted the loss of the 'competent firm and upright' assistance Parramore had given as police magistrate, and offered him the choice of the magistracy at Oatlands, reinstatement as private secretary, or the management of Arthur's Richmond estates. He chose the last, and two years later had to defend himself and his employer against charges made by T. G. Gregson [q.v.] that, before his resignation from Richmond, he had used government time for Arthur's private ends. He proved the falsity of the statements and forced Gregson to withdraw them publicly.

The friendship between Arthur and his former secretary continued long after the governor returned to England and greater honours, Parramore keeping him informed of developments in the system of convict discipline he had nurtured. A religious man, Parramore was one of the original subscribers to the building fund for St Luke's Church of England, Richmond, and a committee member of the Hobart Town Auxiliary Bible Society; he was also a member of the Royal Society. He spent the years after Arthur's departure consolidating his own estate at Richmond. After his wife's death in 1852, he planned to return to England, but on a farewell visit to his brother Thomas at Wetmore, Ross, he contracted pneumonia and died there on 31 July 1854.

E. M. Cooper, *Story of the Parramore family* (Yankalilla, SA, 1953); *Hobart Town Courier*, 6 May, 8, 22, 29 July 1846; *Hobart Town Gazette*, 7, 14 Apr 1832; Arthur papers, 27 (ML); GO 1, 25, 33 (TA); CSO 1 (TA).
MICHAEL C. I. LEVY

PARRY, SIR WILLIAM EDWARD (1790-1855), naval officer and explorer, was born on 19 December 1790 at Bath, Somerset, England, the son of a fashionable doctor, Caleb Hillier Parry, and Sarah, née Rigby. In 1803, after the brief truce in the French wars, he joined the navy and in the next thirteen years served in the blockade of Brest, in Baltic convoys and in America.

In 1817 he was chosen as second-in-command of Captain John Ross's naval expedition to Davis Strait and spent nearly ten years in exploring the Canadian Arctic in search of a North-West Passage. In the summer of 1818 Ross sailed around Baffin Bay and reported it to be landlocked. The Admiralty was unconvinced and next year sent Parry out again with two ships. Boldly traversing the pack-ice in Baffin Bay, he entered Lancaster Sound and found a broad channel which took him to long. 112° W., more than half-way to Bering Strait, in one season. He wintered there, his ships the first to winter deliberately in the Arctic, and, although intending to push farther west, he was defeated by ice. Many of the next generation of Arctic explorers sailed with Parry on this and two later voyages to the North-West (1821-23, 1824-25). In 1827 he attempted to reach the North Pole over the ice from Spitsbergen; he failed, but his record of lat. 82° 45' N. stood for fifty years. Parry was elected a fellow of the Royal Society in 1821.

In 1826 he married Isabella, daughter of Sir John Stanley, baronet, later first Baron Stanley of Alderley, in Cheshire, by whom he had ten children. In 1829 he and his friend John Franklin were knighted for their services to Arctic exploration. Meanwhile he had been appointed hydrographer to the Admiralty, but he found a sedentary life irksome and in 1829 accepted the offer of the Australian Agricultural Co. to go to New South Wales as commissioner in charge of their enterprises.

Parry landed in Sydney in December 1829 and was well received by Governor Darling. His first tour of the company's million-acre grant at Port Stephens convinced him that at least half of it was unfit for the prime purpose of raising sheep and would have to be exchanged. Fortunately the British government was amenable and Parry's chief task in his four years in Australia was to seek out new land and secure it for the company. A surveyor,

Henry Dangar [q.v.], had been engaged by the directors and Parry sent him first north of the Manning River and then west over the ranges to explore country known only to stockmen and from the accounts of John Oxley and Allan Cunningham [qq.v.]. Dangar reported favourably on the Liverpool Plains and in March 1832 Parry himself rode over these splendid pastures. In the meantime Darling had been succeeded by Governor Bourke, who received Parry at Parramatta. At this interview the governor was advised by the surveyor-general, T. L. Mitchell [q.v.], who had never concealed his suspicion and dislike of the company, a view shared by others in the colony. Since the size of the grant was limited, Parry laid claim to good land only in two regular blocks; Mitchell was determined that he should take good land with the bad and all in one block. Inevitably they clashed, and Bourke referred the question to the British government. Nearly a year later Parry was relieved to learn that his stand had been justified, and he saw the new land occupied before handing over to his successor, Colonel Henry Dumaresq [q.v.], in March 1834.

Parry had found the company's servants disaffected, the flocks dwindling, and the local proprietors willing to forfeit their shares rather than respond to calls for their money. All this was gradually changed. To his dismay the flocks continued to decline at first, because of the poor quality of the stock that had been bought locally and the prolonged drought that ended in 1830; but by 1834 losses had been more than made good and the flocks numbered 36,600. The company's estate was almost an *imperium in imperio* and Parry found himself commissioner, magistrate and minister to some 500 souls, half of them convicts; he not only started schools for the children but also baptized them. The local government's reluctance to take any responsibility for this large grant of land on the edge of the settled area, even for policing it, and the shortage of labour, were the subjects of copious official correspondence.

After his return to England Parry successively held the posts of comptroller of steam machinery at the Admiralty (1837-46), captain superintendent of Haslar Hospital, Gosport, and from 1853, on attaining flag rank, lieut-governor of Greenwich Hospital, the home for naval pensioners. In 1841, his first wife having died, he married Catharine, née Hankinson, widow of Samuel Hoare, by whom he had three children. In his last years he helped to organize the search for the lost Franklin expedition which finally ended the search for a North-West Passage. He died at Ems on 8 July 1855 and was buried at Greenwich.

Parry seems to have had all the qualities of leadership, including a gift for careful planning and management, infectious enthusiasm and trust in God; his evangelical piety increased with age. Contemporaries described him as tall and strikingly handsome.

Portraits include those by William Beechey (1819; on permanent loan to the National Maritime Museum), Samuel Drummond (1820; Royal United Services Institution) and Thomas Phillips (1827; Scott Polar Research Institute, Cambridge).

W. E. Parry, *Journal of the first, second and third voyages for the discovery of a North-West Passage*, 1-5 (Lond, 1828); W. E. Parry, *Narrative of an attempt to reach the North Pole . . . 1827* (Lond, 1828); E. Parry, *Memoirs of Rear-Admiral Sir W. E. Parry* (Lond, 1857); A. Parry, *Parry of the Arctic* (Lond, 1963); J. F. Campbell, 'The first decade of the AA Co', *JRAHS*, 9 (1923); W. E. Parry, Australian journal (ML).

ANN PARRY

PARSONS, CHARLES OCTAVIUS (1799-1863), pastoralist, was born on 7 May 1799 at Newton Hall, Monmouthshire, England, the eighth son of Rev. John Weddell Parsons, vicar of Wellington, Herefordshire, and his wife Frances, daughter and coheiress of David Morgan of Presteigne, through whom he was related to many distinguished Anglo-Welsh families. Of his brothers, Cecil (1786?-1876) was a deputy lieutenant and Guy (1769?-1834) high sheriff of Radnorshire. Four other brothers were killed in the Napoleonic wars.

Parsons arrived in Hobart Town in the *Princess Charlotte* in January 1823 with letters of introduction from people of influence, including the duke of York. He intended to settle on the land but was dissuaded by Major Bell [q.v.] and Affleck Moodie, upon whose recommendation to Lieut-Governor Sorell he was appointed commissariat store-keeper at Macquarie Harbour. Because of disagreement with Captain Butler [q.v.], the commandant, he was transferred to Maria Island in 1828, where his year's stay was characterized by mutual recriminations between himself and Major T. D. Lord [q.v.]. To restore harmony Parsons was dismissed; later events, however, proved Lord's dishonesty. Parsons returned to England, but came back to Van Diemen's Land in the *Thomas Laurie* in February 1831. At St David's

Church, Hobart, on 14 April 1832 he married Maria Jennings (1803-1881), and thus allied himself with a powerful coterie: Joseph Tice Gellibrand [q.v.] was his wife's first cousin and her brothers were important in the colony's legal and banking life. One of her sisters, Sophia Louisa, married Philip Russell [q.v.] of the Clyde Co. and another, Sarah Tice, married Rev. Joseph Beazley, well known as a Congregational minister at Green Ponds and later at Redfern, New South Wales.

On his return to Hobart in March 1831 Parsons requested reinstatement in public service. Lieut-Governor Arthur refused, but proposed putting the 'most liberal construction upon the report of the Land Board which the Regulations admit'. As Parsons had imported a capital of £2118 15s., Arthur allowed him 1560 acres with a conditional reserve of 1000 adjoining acres. Parsons took up his location at Clearlands (Cleveland), Ouse. In April 1832 he purchased New Grange, Swanport, but this soon passed to his kinsman, J. T. Gellibrand. However, Parsons was no business man and by March 1836 he was acting as overseer for George Scott. Soon afterwards he joined the party which went to Port Phillip to search for Gellibrand. In September 1837 he put up for sale his estates of Kimbolton, Cleveland, and Athol Brae, comprising 6120 acres in the Hamilton-Ouse district, stating that he was about to go to England. As only Kimbolton was sold this visit was abandoned, and soon afterwards he moved to Camden, near Richmond, which he sold in 1842 to go to Brush Farm near Runnymede. His great improvements with borrowed money alarmed his friends. In 1846 he became insolvent to the amount of £10,000 (the Clyde Company Papers claims that he lost £40,000) and once again he proposed to return to England for help from his relatives, but again he did not sail. Instead he leased Berriedale, Bothwell, from Philip Russell's estate on a wool rental. In 1862 when Bloomfield, the property still occupied by descendants, was acquired, the deeds were in his wife's name. In 1842 Parsons became a road commissioner at Prosser Plains.

High-spirited, impatient, and fond of horse-racing, Parsons was much liked by his contemporaries who in the time of his misfortune remembered his past generosity. These good qualities, however, did not make for success. He died at Berriedale on 14 April 1863, after a fall from his horse. He was survived by a widow, three sons and four daughters. The descendants of the second son, Cecil Joseph (1840-1928), continued to play an important part in Tasmanian pastoral life.

P. L. Brown (ed), *Clyde Company papers*, 1-3 (Lond, 1941-58); Correspondence file under Parsons (TA).   NANCY PARSONS

PATERSON, WILLIAM (1755-1810), soldier, explorer and lieut-governor, was born on 17 August 1755 in Scotland. As a boy he became keenly interested in botany and in 1777, through the patronage of Lady Strathmore, he was enabled to visit South Africa. He made four journeys into the interior; after he returned in 1780 he prepared an account of his experiences, entitled *Narrative of Four Journeys into the Country of the Hottentots and Caffraria*, which he published and dedicated to Sir Joseph Banks [q.v.] in 1789.

In 1781 Paterson became an ensign in the 98th Regiment. He served in India and next year wrote to Banks about specimens from the island of Johanna and his hopes of further finds on the Malabar coast. In 1783 he took part in the siege of Carour (Karur) and was promoted lieutenant. After the regiment was disbanded in 1785, he returned to England and in 1787 was transferred to the 73rd Regiment. In June 1789 he was gazetted captain in the New South Wales Corps, probably owing his appointment to Banks. After spending some months recruiting he sailed for Sydney and arrived in October 1791. He was immediately given command of the detachment on Norfolk Island, where he served from November 1791 until March 1793.

While there he collected and sent home botanical, geological and insect specimens for Banks, and in 1794 discussed with him the publication of his memoranda on the natural history of Norfolk Island. Meanwhile in September 1793 he had led an expedition to find a route through the Blue Mountains; he failed, but found and named the Grose River and discovered several new plants. He became second-in-command of the New South Wales Corps at the same time, and when Major Grose [q.v.] left the colony in December 1794 Paterson acted as administrator until Governor Hunter arrived nine months later. During this term he granted 4965 acres of land and made no attempt, either then or after Hunter assumed office, to check or to control the trading and farming activities of his officers or the propensity of the troops under his command to take the law into their hands when they felt aggrieved. In 1795 he was promoted major and next year went home on sick leave. While in England he advised Banks on plants and trees for the colony and in 1798 was gazetted lieut-colonel and elected a fellow of the Royal Society. In March 1799 he was ordered to return to Sydney, with specific instructions to investigate the officers' trading in spirits, to check this practice and so to restore the 'sullied' credit of the British officer.

He reached Sydney in November 1799 and became extremely critical of the last phase of Hunter's administration. He complained to Banks of the excessive importation of spirits, the high prices of commodities, and the threat of armed insurrection by the Irish convicts. When Governor King succeeded Hunter he appointed Paterson lieut-governor. In July 1801, in the controversies over the trial of Lieutenant James Marshall, R.N., Paterson supported John Macarthur [q.v.] and his officers, but disagreed with Macarthur's suggestion that the officers should break off social relations with the governor. A quarrel developed between Paterson and Macarthur, in which the lieut-governor alleged that Macarthur had disclosed information contained in a private letter written by Mrs Paterson to Mrs Macarthur [q.v.], and in September Paterson challenged Macarthur to a duel. Paterson was wounded in the shoulder, and Macarthur was sent to England under arrest. King complained that though Paterson was critical of Macarthur, and 'whenever he acts from his own sentiments he does what is justly right and honourable', he would not strongly oppose the officers of the regiment; as a result relations between the two deteriorated and, though they preserved an outward appearance of friendship for the sake of the government, they found renewed causes of friction in the behaviour of the officers towards Nicholas Baudin [q.v.] and in the publication of 'pipes' allegedly libelling the governor. At first Paterson had kept up his scientific interests, collecting plants from the Hawkesbury in 1799, seeking coal there in 1800 and exploring the Hunter River in 1801 with Lieutenant James Grant [q.v.], but his health steadily deteriorated and during the first half of 1803 he had to be relieved of his duties.

In May 1804 instructions were received from London that a new settlement should be founded at Port Dalrymple in Van Diemen's Land and that Paterson should be put in charge of it. After an attempt made abortive by bad weather, Paterson sailed from Sydney on 15 October with a detachment of soldiers and seventy-five convicts to found this outpost. He first selected a site at Western Arm, which he named York Town; in 1806 he formed a new settlement on the present site of Launceston but, though frequently there, he kept his headquarters at York Town. Paterson and his party experienced many difficulties, including shortage of supplies, and the hardships told on Paterson's health, but the commandant showed a keen eye for the natural resources of the island, as usual sent specimens to Banks, and noted the great outcrop of iron ore near Port Dalrymple, which he reported to King. 'If I had carts', he wrote, 'I could load the whole navy of Great Britain'. He believed that the new settlement, with its iron deposits, could become a special punishment colony for unruly convicts, 'by working them in irons, like they do in the mines in many parts of the world'. For lack of mining and quarrying tools nothing came of Paterson's suggestion, and he was not able to explore the outcrop further.

In February 1808 he received news from Major Johnston [q.v.], the officer commanding in Sydney, that Governor Bligh had been arrested. Paterson ordered H.M.S. Porpoise to proceed to Port Dalrymple so that he could sail for Sydney, but he was reluctant to become involved in the doings of the provisional government. Though he insisted on his right to office as lieut-governor, he used the excuses of his poor health, and the possible arrival of a successor from England, to postpone his departure for Sydney despite repeated and urgent requests from Lieut-Colonel Foveaux [q.v.] that he should take command. He finally left Port Dalrymple on 1 January 1809 and assumed office in Sydney nine days later. He refused to reinstate Bligh when pressed by him to do so, but he insisted that Bligh and Johnston should return to England. In poor health and drinking heavily, Paterson was a weak ruler. He spent most of the year at Parramatta as an invalid, and the clique which had overthrown Bligh had the real control of affairs. As Governor Macquarie reported later, Paterson was 'such an easy, good-natured, thoughtless man, that he latterly granted Lands to almost every person who asked them, without regard to their Merits or pretensions'. In this way 67,000 acres were disposed of, more than Governor King had granted in six years. Paterson was quite unsuitable for such a position in so difficult a time. After Macquarie arrived, Paterson sailed with the New South Wales Corps in the Dromedary on 12 May 1810, but died at sea off Cape Horn on 21 June.

Science was Paterson's chief interest. He maintained contact with Banks and other scholars in England, and sent specimens to them from India, New South Wales and Van Diemen's Land. As a member of the Royal Society, he met many of the leading scientists of the day during his sojourns in England, and his botanical collections are preserved in the Natural History Museum at South Kensington. He introduced several fruits into the colony, including a peach which did very well, and as early as 1794 he started a six-acre garden. Later he experimented with imported plants and trees on his 100-acre estate at Petersham, now a Sydney suburb. Unlike most of his colleagues Paterson neither participated in trading nor enriched himself while serving in the settlement, and he died a poor man.

About 1787 he had married Elizabeth Driver (1760?-1825), and she accompanied him to New South Wales in 1791. She took a prominent part in the life of the colony, helped to found the Orphans' School in 1800 and served on the committee of the Female Orphans' Institution in 1803. In 1809, according to John Oxley [q.v.], she did her best to restore unanimity in the settlement after the arrest of Governor Bligh. While her husband was in poor health Elizabeth looked after him with great care. She was a devoted and conscientious wife, described by Ralph Clark [q.v.] in 1791 as 'a good, cosy, Scotch lass, and fit for a soldier's wife'. Foveaux granted her 2000 acres in Van Diemen's land in 1808, and this was confirmed by Macquarie in 1810. However, when her husband died she was refused a pension and was ordered to repay some £200 that he had paid in public salaries without authority. In March 1814 she married Grose and took up residence at Bath, but her husband died in May. She remained a close friend of the Macarthurs, lived quietly in retirement and died at Bath in 1825.

HRA (1), 1-7, (3), 1; M. Bassett, *The governor's lady, Mrs. Philip Gidley King* (Melb, 1961); MS cat under W. Paterson (ML).

DAVID S. MACMILLAN

PEDDER SIR JOHN LEWES (1793-1859), judge, was born on 10 February 1793 in London, the eldest son of John Pedder of the Middle Temple. He was educated at Charterhouse, the Middle Temple, where he was called to the Bar in June 1820, and Trinity Hall, Cambridge (LL.B., 1822). He took up practice as a Chancery barrister and in 1823 he applied for the office of chief justice of Van Diemen's Land. His competitors enjoyed aristocratic patronage, but Pedder had testimonials from his academic and professional teachers, and was appointed in August. He sailed in the *Hibernia* with his wife Maria, daughter of Lieut-Colonel Everett, and on disembarking at Hobart Town in March 1824 was greeted with a salute of thirteen guns. The Supreme Court was opened on 10 May, with much rejoicing that Van Diemen's Land now had a court with full civil and criminal jurisdiction. Two days later Colonel Arthur landed to replace Colonel Sorell as lieut-governor. In 1825 an Order in Council granted Van Diemen's Land an independent government and extended Pedder's authority by abolishing the right of appeal from his decisions to the governor of New South Wales assisted in the hearing thereof by the chief justice of the Supreme Court of New South Wales. He was appointed a member of both the Executive and Legislative Councils.

Trial by jury was the most important question decided during Pedder's first years in office. The Act empowering the Crown to establish Supreme Courts in New South Wales and Van Diemen's Land (4 Geo. IV, c.96, s.6) provided that actions at law should be triable by a jury of twelve men if both parties concurred in an application to the presiding judge for such jury. In New South Wales Chief Justice Forbes [q.v.] construed s.19 of the Act to require that free men should be tried by juries of their fellows, but limited it to Courts of Quarter Sessions. In contrast Pedder ruled that the Act had introduced trial by jury in the Supreme Court only, and did not apply in inferior courts. The controversy which arose in 1825 in Hobart on this question branded Pedder as a member of the 'government party'.

Under the Act establishing the Legislative Council, local Acts of council had to be certified by the judge as being not repugnant to the laws of England. In 1827 Pedder certified a bill, enacted on instructions from Bathurst, for licensing the proprietors of newspapers. This approval shocked radical editors in Sydney, where a similar bill had been introduced, but Forbes had refused to certify its six licensing clauses. In Sydney the *Australian* denounced Pedder so scathingly that Governor Darling considered a criminal prosecution of its editor, Dr R. Wardell [q.v.], for libel, but the Newspaper Licensing Acts in both colonies were disallowed by the law officers of the Crown.

After this episode Pedder began to enjoy increasing popularity, which grew after his retirement from the Executive Council in 1836. His private life was beyond reproach. He never invested or borrowed in the colony, and thus avoided the possibility of scandals which embroiled his colleagues. He lived in the mansions, Secheron and, later, Newlands, rented for him by the government, although the chief justices in New South Wales had to pay rent for their official residences.

Pedder earned the respect of every lieut-governor from Sorell to Denison, but Arthur once impatiently remarked: 'Though a man of great talents and unbending integrity, of the purest intentions and a very safe adviser, he is so tedious and so minute that life is much too short to wait for his opinions and decision'. J. T. Gellibrand [q.v.] and Alfred Stephen complained of his rules of court through which he raised 'every technical objection that would prevail in England'. Pedder's judgments and reports to the Executive Council on capital cases show that he was appalled by the severity of the criminal code and diligent in giving prisoners the benefit of every possible doubt. In many cases, and often with difficulty, he succeeded in persuading the lieut-governor to pardon prisoners or commute their sentences.

In 1847-48 Pedder and the puisne judge, A. S. Montagu [q.v.], fell foul of Denison. The editor of the *Britannia*, John Morgan [q.v.], had refused to pay the dog tax levied under a local Act of 1846. He was proceeded against and fined. When the conviction was taken to the Supreme Court, it was quashed by Pedder and Montagu who ruled that the local Act was contrary to the imperial statute which, in establishing the Legislative Council, required that any enactment for levying a tax should also provide for the expected revenue to be devoted to some specific local purpose. Denison saw that four-fifths of the colony's revenue legislation could be challenged on similar grounds. He decided to vindicate the 'rights' of the local legislature. External issues were found for removing Montagu. When eight merchants launched proceedings to recover payments made under the Differential Duties Act, Denison persuaded his Executive Council that it was also necessary to prevent Pedder from further embarrassing the government. Denison accused Pedder of an illegal usurpation of power in Morgan's case, and enjoined him to take eighteen months leave while the doubtful laws were validated. With courage and integrity, Pedder refused this humiliation. He was then asked to show why he should not be suspended for neglect of duty in failing to certify

the invalidity of the Dog Act at the time of its passage. Pedder replied that he had considered the Dog Act constitutional until hearing the arguments of counsel in Morgan's case. The Executive Council resolved that this entitled Pedder to be acquitted of neglect of duty. Meanwhile Denison had summoned the local legislature, which purported to pass a validating bill. Though Pedder certified that it was beyond the Legislative Council's powers, the bill served its purpose until the imperial Australian Colonies Government Act removed the limiting stricture. Pedder and Montagu became heroes when their treatment by Denison became known, and the Colonial Office congratulated Pedder on his stand. In 1851, when the Legislative Council was reconstituted, Pedder retired from 'the disturbing arena of political strife'. Denison soon came to regret his handling of the Dog Act crisis, and in later dispatches revealed a positive admiration of Pedder.

While hearing a case on 19 July 1854 Pedder suffered a stroke, which temporarily deprived him of speech and the use of his left limbs, and he soon tendered his resignation. He retired on a pension equal to his salary of £1500. Much of his savings had been invested in English consols and he sold some 5000 sheep and his 15,000-acre grazing lease, Cupumnimnip, about forty miles from Melbourne. Meanwhile his wife had been stricken with paralysis. She died without issue on 23 October 1855. In 1856 Pedder returned to England. He died at Brighton on 24 March 1859. He had been knighted in November 1838.

Throughout his life Pedder was a convinced Anglican. His faith played a part in his deliberations in the Executive and Legislative Councils, for he dreaded 'any countenance being given to other sects, as injurious to the interests of the Established Church'. Thus he opposed grants and loans for building Methodist, Catholic or Congregationalist churches, and was critical of Catholic convicts who sought exemption from compulsory attendance at Anglican services.

HRA (1), 12, 13, 16, 18, (3), 4-6, (4), 1; Correspondence file under J. Pedder (TA).

P. A. HOWELL

PEEL, THOMAS (1793-1865), colonial promoter and landowner, was born in Lancashire, England, probably at Peelfold, near Blackburn, the second son of Thomas Peel and his wife Dorothy, née Bolton. His father, directly descended from the Peel who founded the family's cotton manufacturing fortunes, inherited the business.

When his elder brother entered the church, young Thomas showed no desire to follow his father in the family firm. After education at Harrow, he joined a firm of attorneys. About 1823 he married Mary Charlotte Dorking Ayrton, and after his children, Julia and Thomas, were born they moved to the estate of Carnousie in Banffshire, Scotland, where a second daughter, Dorothy, was born in 1827, and where he became master of the Turriff Hunt.

In 1828 Peel went to London and was planning to emigrate to New South Wales, when reports of the new free colony to be founded at Swan River changed his mind. He joined a syndicate of financiers in proposing to the government a plan whereby they would transfer ten thousand settlers with requisite stock and stores to the new colony within four years, and place them each on 200 acres of land, in return for which the syndicate wished to receive four million acres of land. The Colonial Office, however, was under pressure from Captain Stirling, who had explored the Swan River in 1827, either to grant him the right to develop the place under a proprietary charter, or to proclaim it a new crown colony of which he would be the governor. When Sir George Murray took charge at the Colonial Office in May 1828 he did not wish to grant a charter, or to incur the expense of forming a colony. The interest of Thomas Peel's association of investors seems to have been a deciding factor in persuading the government that the place could be a crown colony and at the same time be largely developed by outside capital. The government, however, felt it could not agree to the amount of territory the investors wished to receive, and could sanction only a grant of one million acres. At this, all the financiers interested withdrew, except Thomas Peel. While he hesitated, Solomon Levey [q.v.] proposed a ten-year partnership with him in the venture, to which he agreed. A deed of co-partnership was drawn up between them, a long and complicated document by which Levey was to finance the scheme and Peel, not being as wealthy as was thought, was to be the salaried manager of it in the colony, although he was to apply for the title deeds to the land in his own name, it being understood that these lands, with the exception of 25,000 acres, were in joint ownership.

Solomon Levey had amassed a fortune in property in New South Wales before he returned temporarily to England and thought he saw good potential in the new colony. Being both a Jew and a former convict, perhaps he considered it better not to appear as Peel's co-partner to the authorities. Their partnership, therefore, was concealed for many years from the Colonial Office, and from the general public for considerably longer. Peel appeared as the sole negotiator with the Colonial Office and as the sole investor and promoter of their emigration scheme. As a natural corollary he reaped the notoriety that resulted, first, when charges were made of favouritism on the part of his cousin, the Home Secretary, Robert Peel, in the granting of so much land; and second, when the scheme collapsed shortly after the emigrants' arrival in the colony.

By the agreement Peel negotiated with the Colonial Office he was granted priority of choice of 250,000 acres, which he chose on the southern banks of the Swan and Canning Rivers, with a further 250,000 to be allotted when he had landed four hundred settlers; after twenty-one years, if improvements and capital (which included the dispatch of emigrants) had been expended on the first 500,000, the remaining 500,000 acres would be allotted. But at the end of the negotiations in January 1829 the government suddenly stipulated that the first shipload of emigrants was to be landed before 1 November 1829, if priority of choice of land were to be retained.

Unfortunately, the *Gilmore*, the partnership's first ship bearing 179 emigrants, arrived six weeks late. Peel found his chosen land taken up, and had to accept 250,000 acres contiguous to it but farther south. In the next six months the *Gilmore* was followed by a small ship carrying stores, and two other emigrant ships. By Peel's arrangement with Levey, more stores and stock, paid for in London, were to be sent to Swan River from Sydney by the firm of Cooper & Levey. They never arrived. Peel was left, with inadequate funds and very little food beyond the flour and salt meat he had brought from London, to cope with 540 agitated settlers.

Peel was not impressed with the land allotted to him and, while he explored farther for better land and waited for Levey's promised stock and stores to arrive from Sydney, winter descended. Malnutrition and disease were rife among the emigrants encamped on the beach at the proposed town site of Clarence near Fremantle. Peel himself became ill and incapacitated from a gun-shot wound in the right hand, probably received in a duel with the captain of the *Rockingham*, his last ship, which was wrecked while anchoring in Cockburn Sound. This removed him from the scene at a critical time when his leadership was badly needed. His settlers became dissatisfied with conditions and with the promissory notes drawn on the firm of Cooper & Levey, with which they had been paid for the first few months, when Daniel Cooper [q.v.] announced his refusal to pay them. Many emigrants sought other employment, those who were good artisans finding it easily enough. They were to spend the next few years suing Peel for wages which he had guaranteed but for which they had not worked, while he sued them for repayment of passage money. Many workmen applied to the local court to be freed from their indentures; others followed Peel in an attempt to begin farming operations on his grant at the Murray River, forty-five miles south of Fremantle. Over this crucial time Peel had been advanced stores for their sustenance by the government, which held him responsible for the debt incurred.

After frequent attacks by Aboriginals most of the settlers at the Murray drifted back to Fremantle, leaving Peel almost alone. In 1833 his partner Levey died. The settlement scheme was by now a failure. Nevertheless in 1834 Peel claimed and received the title in fee simple to 250,000 acres, as the terms of the partnership obliged him to do. In that year his wife and children came out from England to join him.

Up to 1839, when the partnership with Levey or his heirs would cease, Peel was actively occupied in trying to develop his grant, partly by agriculture and partly by ventures such as whaling. When the General Road Trust was formed, he was made a trustee for Pinjarra; he also became a member of the Legislative Council. He resigned this honour fourteen months later, having made repeated protests that he received notices too late to attend meetings in Perth. He was active in pressing for a church near Pinjarra, giving 500 acres of land for it, but resuming it when the church was placed in the townsite. Instead he gave 1000 acres to the Bishop's fund.

In 1836 Peel had forwarded to Levey's executors various documents connected with the partnership and he also applied to the Colonial Office for the remaining 250,000 acres to which he considered himself entitled by his agreement. This was refused. In 1839 he managed to sell 13,770 acres of land. This enabled him to repay part of the debt to the Crown and to send his wife and daughters to England, hoping himself to follow soon to settle affairs with the executors and perhaps to make representations about the additional land he thought should be his. The years

passed, however, without his return. He made no further large sales and the debt was still a burden. In 1856 his elder daughter died in London and in the next year his wife, both of consumption. His younger daughter then returned to live with him.

In 1851 Levey's heir, John Levey Roberts (who had taken his mother's name) came to Perth, and articles of agreement between Roberts and Peel were made, to avoid litigation. The debt for stores contracted on behalf of the partnership became a first charge on the property, and subject to its payment the residue of the property was to be equally divided between Roberts and Peel. This amounted to 213,764 acres. In 1858 Roberts sold his moiety to the Colonization Assurance Corporation in return for 3747 shares in the company. Peel, however, retained his half until his death, when it was divided between his son Thomas and daughter Dorothy and his reputed son Frederick. Peel died at Mandurah on 21 December 1865 and was buried in the churchyard there.

As he grew older and poorer and crustier, and more withdrawn, he became a legend. Clad in a faded red hunting coat, he was often to be seen riding alone through the bush in his large domain. Governor Stirling and the first settlers had always given him the respect due to one who had made an immense attempt to aid in the foundation of the colony and whose failure was partly due to a series of unfortunate circumstances. His character has often been blamed for this failure, and it is true that he was hot-tempered, proud and often intolerant of stupidity. On the other hand he had vision, courage and strict standards of behaviour: almost unique among the early settlers, he never complained either about the country or his ill fortune. As one of his contemporaries and equals said, he 'displayed singular fortitude considering the severe losses he had sustained'.

A. Hasluck, *Thomas Peel of Swan River* (Melb, 1965) and for bibliog.

ALEXANDRA HASLUCK

PELSAERT, FRANCISCO (1591?-1630), officer of the Dutch East India Co., was born at Antwerp, Belgium, probably the son of Eberhard Pelzer. He was brother-in-law of Admiral Hendrick Brouwer. In 1618 he sailed for the east in the company's commercial service and two years later was posted to India as junior merchant. After travelling overland from Masulipatam to Surat, he was sent to Agra where he stayed for seven years, meanwhile becoming senior merchant. In 1626 he wrote an account of the Mogul Empire, which was translated from the Dutch by W. H. Moreland and P. Geyl, and published as *Jahangir's India. The Remonstrantie of Francisco Pelsaert* (Cambridge, 1925).

After a stay in Holland from June to October 1628, he left for Java in charge of three ships, but his own ship *Batavia* lost contact with the other two in the Atlantic. It was a difficult voyage with quarrelsome members among the crew, and there appeared some danger of mutiny before disaster struck: on 4 June 1629 the *Batavia* was wrecked at 28°40′ S. on a coral reef of the Houtman Abrolhos, about 45 miles off the present town of Geraldton. Leaving most of the crew and the passengers on two islets, Pelsaert set off on 8 June in the ship's boat with thirty men to look for fresh water in the neighbourhood. When this search proved unsuccessful he undertook the journey to Batavia. For eight days he followed the coast northwards as far as 22°17′ S, whence he made for the north-west, reaching the south coast of Java on 27 June and Batavia on 5 July. Ten days later Pelsaert left again in the small *Saerdam*, sailed to 30°16′ S. and reached the Australian west coast to the south of the Houtman Abrolhos on 3 September. It took another fortnight for the *Saerdam* to arrive at the Abrolhos. Meanwhile some of the survivors had mutinied and massacred 125 men and women. Pelsaert restored law and order and had the ringleaders of the mutiny tried. Seven were hanged on 2 October and two men were marooned on the mainland. After salvaging part of the *Batavia's* cargo Pelsaert returned to Batavia where he arrived on 5 December. Here the Court of Justice sentenced six more mutineers to death.

Pelsaert's health had suffered from the hardships, but nevertheless he took part in an expedition to Sumatra. Soon after his return to Batavia he died in September 1630. He does not seem to have taken his seat in the High Government at Batavia for which he had been selected as extraordinary member in 1629.

J. E. Heeres, *The part borne by the Dutch in the discovery of Australia 1606-1765* (Lond, 1899); *Biographie Nationale . . . de Belgique*, 16 (Brussels, 1901); F. W. Stapel, *De Oostindische Compagnie en Australië* (Amsterdam, 1937); A. Sharp, *The discovery of Australia* (Oxford, 1963); H. Drake-Brockman, *Voyage to disaster. The life of Francisco Pelsaert* (Syd, 1963).

J. VAN LOHUIZEN

PERON, FRANCOIS (1775-1810), naturalist, explorer and historian, was born on 22 August 1775 at Cérilly, Allier, France. His widowed mother made sacrifices to provide him with a sound education at Cérilly College, where the principal was impressed by the boy's ability and instructed him in theology as a possible future priest. War and revolution interrupted his studies. In 1792 he joined the army and served on the Rhine. He was wounded and captured at Kaiserslautern, and spent the idle months of his incarceration in Magdeburg fortress reading published accounts of voyages of exploration. Having lost an eye he was repatriated in 1794 and invalided out of the army. He spent three years at the Paris Medical School and also developed a growing interest in natural history from studying in the Paris Museum. Bad health and an unhappy love affair led him to forsake medical studies and seek a place in Baudin's [q.v.] expedition then preparing to leave for the South Seas. Thanks to the influence of Jussieu, professor of botany at the Jardin des Plantes, Paris, the committee of the Institute appointed him natural historian and anthropologist.

Péron's history of the voyage reveals his curiosity and indefatigable zeal as a scientist. He devoted himself to a rigorous research programme, including hydrographic surveys and a remarkable variety of scientific problems. His six-hourly records of meteorological information, and notes on surface and depth temperatures of the Indian Ocean complement the work done by Johann Forster during Cook's [qq.v.] exploration of the Pacific. His work on natural history, however, did not suffer as a result of other interests. As the result of death and desertion, by the time Baudin reached the Western Australian coast, Péron was the only remaining zoologist, with the exception of the fatally ill Maugé, of the five who had embarked. Working in co-operation with the artist Le Sueur, his devoted friend, he and his helpers collected 100,000 specimens of animal life. Although his early death prevented him from classifying his great collection, representing some 2500 species, in itself it made a fundamental contribution to Australian zoology and was the basis of later publications by Lamarck and the authors of the *Nouveau Dictionnaire d'Histoire Naturelle*.

Péron also interested himself in the 'noble savage'. He made observations on the indigenous inhabitants of the regions visited and left statistical records, especially from tests made with de Régnier's new dynamometer. With this instrument he measured the output of physical force of 'natural man' living in his natural state, comparing the result with 'civilized' European man, but his samples were too small to be significant. However, his observations on the Aboriginals, the value of which has still to be assessed, are of permanent importance in revealing the complexity of Australian types and cultures. He intended to use his material for a natural history of the types of man, but this was never completed. After his return to France in 1804 he was commissioned to write the official history of Baudin's expedition, *Voyage de Découvertes aux Terres Australes . . . sur les Corvettes le Géographe, le Naturaliste et la Goëlette le Casurina, pendant les Années 1800, 1801, 1802, 1803 et 1804* (Paris, 1807-16), which aimed to present a scientifically integrated but preliminary account of the expedition. His subsequently published papers revealed his grasp of detail and breadth of knowledge, and indicated his capacity as a scientist. However, his personality and training did not fit him for a lengthy voyage of discovery. He did not understand Baudin's problems, and his patriotism led him to upset Governor King and to make Matthew Flinders [q.v.] suspicious. He openly encouraged insubordination on the voyage and permanently blackened Baudin's work and character in the official history.

A chest complaint and old wounds caused him to give up writing the *Voyage* at volume 2, page 230, and it was completed by Louis de Freycinet [q.v. under Baudin]. Péron retired to his home village, where he died on 14 December 1810.

LESLIE R. MARCHANT
J. H. REYNOLDS

PEROUSE; see LA PEROUSE

PERRY, SAMUEL AUGUSTUS (1792-1854), soldier and surveyor, was born in Wales. He was appointed an ensign in the Royal Staff Corps in June 1809 and promoted lieutenant in 1811. He then served in the Peninsular war under Sir George Murray and was present at Badajoz, Nivelle and Nive. When the bridge over the Tagus at Alcantara was broken, he distinguished himself by filling the gap with a 'flying bridge' to carry the guns. On 12 April 1817 at St Paul's Church, Hammersmith, London, he married Caroline Elizabeth, daughter of James Johnson of Baker Street. In October 1819 he went on half-

pay, and in that year was appointed professor of topographical drawing at the Royal Military College, a position he occupied until 1823. In 1824 he went to Dominica as private secretary and colonial aide-de-camp to the governor, Major-General William Nicolay. Because of ill health he was compelled in 1827 to return to England where he lived on half-pay at Ampfield, Hampshire.

When T. L. Mitchell [q.v.] was appointed surveyor-general in New South Wales in 1828 he considered none of his juniors competent to succeed him as deputy-surveyor-general. Murray, now secretary of state, appointed Perry at a salary of £500 with allowances, and he reached Sydney in the *Sovereign* with his wife and six children in August 1829. Mitchell did not welcome the new arrival. In March 1831 Governor Darling reported to Murray: 'The jealousy of [Mitchell's] disposition prevents his permitting the Employment of any Person whom he supposes likely to deprive him of any part of the service. Thus, the Deputy Surveyor General was kept a perfect Cypher in Sydney for nearly 18 months after his arrival, not being permitted, even during Major Mitchell's absence, to see any but the Commonest Letters the others being selected for the Surveyor General by his Confidential Clerk'. However, when Darling suggested that Perry might take charge of the Road Department, Mitchell said that he could not be spared.

After Governor Bourke's arrival Under-Secretary Hay, having noted Mitchell's complaints about his staff, asked Mitchell for a confidential report on members of the survey department. In his reply on 22 September 1832 Mitchell complained that Perry was idle and insinuated that he might be happy to see the department's business going wrong. 'I am almost inclined to say', he added, 'abolish the situation and let me have the credit for doing all the duty; or, appoint a person who can and will assist me'. In April 1833 the Colonial Office ordered the removal of Perry and any other members of the department 'designated as objectionable' by Mitchell. However, Mitchell knew that he must have a deputy to lead the department during his long absences; Perry remained his deputy for twenty more years. During Mitchell's absences in the interior and in England between 1835 and 1841 the department was busy with surveys of towns, villages and allotments. Among the squatters who took up runs beyond the Nineteen Counties in this period was Perry's son, Thomas Augustus, who estab-

lished Llangollen (Llangothlin) and Bende-
meer in New England. In 1839 Perry
reported favourably on the Clarence River
district and in 1842 made a detailed survey
of it.

In 1844-45, during the depression, Perry
had eighteen months leave in England. In
1846 he accompanied Colonel Barney [q.v.]
on the investigation which resulted in the
proposal that Port Curtis should be the
centre of a new colony of North Australia.
During Mitchell's visit to England in
1847-48 Perry again conducted the department. When Mitchell returned he criticized
Perry so harshly that Perry complained to
Governor FitzRoy, who recommended to
the Colonial Office that Mitchell be
removed. The Colonial Office was aware of
the unfairness of Mitchell's insulting attitude towards Perry 'who has had to perform [Mitchell's] proper duties for him
whilst he has been spending whole years
in Europe bringing out lucrative books of
his own, or else indulging his taste in
exploring expeditions in the Colony'. However, Mitchell was not removed, and in
August 1852 Perry was given leave on the
ground of ill health. In April 1853 his
leave was extended but in July he felt
compelled to ask permission to retire, and
his retirement became effective in October.
He and his wife spent their remaining
years at Kiama, where Mrs Perry died,
probably late in 1853, and Perry on 15
January 1854. It is believed that they were
survived by nine children.

Perry was a loyal and capable administrator and a skilful surveyor. It was his
misfortune to serve under so objectionable
a superior as Mitchell, and greatly to his
credit that he seems never to have resorted to Mitchell's tactics in self-defence.

HRA (1), 14-22, 25, 26; N. Gray 'Samuel
Augustus Perry', *Descent*, 2 (1964).

BERNARD T. DOWD

PETCHY, JOHN (d. 1850), merchant, was
born at Romford, Essex, England, where,
as a labourer, in March 1810 he was found
guilty of receiving stolen goods and sentenced to transportation for fourteen years.
He arrived in Van Diemen's Land in the
Indefatigable on 9 May 1812. His subsequent conduct was evidently good, for
from 1816 to 1823 he was keeper in the
Hobart Town gaol; though sentenced to be
dismissed for neglect of duty in 1819, he
remained. While in this position of trust
he was granted 400 acres at Hollow Tree
on the South Arm peninsula. Though he
had frequent disputes with neighbours, the
holding apparently prospered; by 1825 he

had cultivated 150 acres and had 1000
sheep, 20 cattle, a substantial house, barn,
outbuildings, another 1000 acres under
lease and ten convict servants.

In June 1824 Petchy sailed for London
with a quantity of wattle bark extract in
which he hoped to interest the English
tanning trade. For this discovery he was
awarded a medal by the Society of Arts,
Commerce and Manufactures, though later
he claimed to have lost £2000 in trying to
establish a permanent trade. After his return to Hobart in May 1825 he embarked
on a variety of commercial ventures which
rapidly made him one of the colony's most
prosperous merchants. In the Hobart district he owned a brewery, tavern, store
and woodyard, though his most successful
enterprise was a licensed victualling and
cartage business at Kangaroo Point.

Petchy was best known for his seafaring
activities. He owned and operated three of
the eight Derwent River ferries plying
between Sullivan's Cove and Kangaroo
Point; his square rigged barque *Sir George
Arthur*, 389 tons, launched at Kangaroo
Point in 1838, was then the largest ship
built in the colony. From 1832 to 1839 he
was a prominent bay whaler and had three
shore stations at Recherche Bay hunting
the southern right whale. It was perhaps
fitting that Petchy lost his life at sea: in
December 1850 he was drowned with six
others, when the sailing boat in which they
were competing in the Hobart regatta capsized in a squall. Petchy left a widow
Elizabeth, née Callaghan, whom he married
probably in 1823 when she was assigned
to him as a convict servant. However, his
estate passed to his daughter by a former
marriage, Sarah Ann Russell.

Despite his lowly origins Petchy proved
himself a resourceful if not always a
scrupulous individual. His colonial life
amply illustrates the opportunities which
befell many an emancipist, and he himself
is typical of the vigorous entrepreneurs
who laid the firm economic foundations of
Australia's southernmost colony.

V&P (LC VDL), 1850 (22); *Hobart Town
Gazette*, 4 Dec 1819, 26 Nov 1825; *Hobart
Town Courier*, 4 Mar 1839; *Hobarton
Guardian*, 2 Dec 1850; CSO 1/298/7249,
1/337/7747; Correspondence file under J.
Petchy (TA).   W. E. GOODHAND

PETRIE, ANDREW (1798-1872), builder
and architect, was born in June 1798 in
Fife, Scotland, and trained in his craft in
Edinburgh. He was one of the Scottish
mechanics brought to Sydney in 1831 by
John Dunmore Lang [q.v.] as the nucleus

of a new force of free workers. Meeting much enmity from convict and emancipist workers, Petrie was glad to accept a post as clerk in the Ordnance Department. The quality of his work impressed Lieut-Colonel Barney [q.v.] so much that, when in 1837 there was an urgent appeal from Moreton Bay for a competent builder to repair crumbling structures, Petrie was sent there as clerk of works. His first important task was to repair the mechanism of the windmill which had never worked. His general duty was the supervision of prisoners engaged in making such necessities as soap and nails, and in building.

His charge took him to several convict outposts and gave him a taste for travel and exploration. His private journeys soon added to knowledge of the immediate environs of the settlement. When the convict station was removed in 1839 Petrie saw the opportunity at last of a free community, and with his family remained to contribute to its formation. In the new surroundings he was able to pursue two main interests: as builder and architect he was responsible for most of the important structures that arose; and he made many more journeys. He was the first white man to climb Mount Beerwah, one of the Glass House Mountains seen by Cook, and he was also the first to bring back samples of the Bunya pine. In 1842 with a small party in a boat he discovered the Mary River and brought back to the settlement two 'wild white men', James Davis or 'Duramboi' and David Bracewell or 'Wandi' [qq.v.].

In 1848 he lost his eyesight because of inefficient surgery after an attack of sandy blight. Such was his courage that he still kept control over his business: when plans were explained to him he ordered the necessary quantities of material and was even able to check the performance of his building workers; he used his cane if not satisfied. With advancing years he handed over more and more control to his eldest son, John, who became first lord mayor of Brisbane. His second son, Thomas, gained much knowledge of the Aboriginal tribes and their customs and languages.

The Petries' house was one of the social centres of Brisbane and readily offered accommodation to squatters coming from the outback, especially in the days before Brisbane had a few inns. Petrie was also generous to unfortunates, always being willing to help with food and work. He died on 20 February 1872.

H. S. Russell, *The genesis of Queensland* (Syd, 1888); C. C. Petrie (ed), *Tom Petrie's reminiscences of early Queensland* (Brisb, 1904); Thomas Dowse (Old Tom), *Brisbane Courier*, 31 July 1869; J. H. C. McClurg, Roy Hist Soc Qld, *Historical Miscellanea*, nos 3 and 10. A. A. MORRISON

PHILLIP, ARTHUR (1738-1814), admiral and governor, was born on 11 October 1738 in the parish of Allhallows, ward of Bread Street, London, the second child of Jacob Phillip, a language teacher who came to London from Frankfurt, and Elizabeth, née Breach, former wife of Captain Herbert, R.N., a relative of Lord Pembroke. It was possibly the influence of his mother that was instrumental in determining his future seafaring career. On 24 June 1751 he was enrolled on 'the establishment of poor boys' in the Greenwich school for the sons of seamen. Thus began a period of apprenticeship in the mercantile service that was completed in 1755 after two years at sea under Captain Redhead in the *Fortune*. During the Seven Years' war he saw active service in the navy, to which he had transferred. On 7 July 1761 he was provisionally appointed lieutenant, the promotion being confirmed a year later following an engagement resulting in the capture of Havana. With the coming of peace on 25 April 1763 he was retired on half-pay.

Save for the months between 13 November 1770 and 8 July 1771, when he served in H.M.S. *Egmont*, his connexions with the British navy in the next fifteen years were largely nominal. Probably much of his time was taken up with the properties known as Vernals Farm and Glasshayes which he acquired at Lyndhurst, Hampshire. There he had settled with his wife Margaret, the widow of John Denison, a prosperous London merchant. The marriage was celebrated on 19 July 1763, but could scarcely have been happy for by 1769 the two were separated. In 1774-78 Phillip served with distinction in South American waters as a captain in the Portuguese fleet, which he entered with the Admiralty's permission after the outbreak of the Spanish-Portuguese war. In 1778 he returned to the English navy. In November 1781 he was made a post captain and was given command of the 24-gun *Ariadne*; on 27 December 1782 he left her to take charge of the 64-gun *Europe*, taking with him his friend, Lieutenant P. G. King. His sealed orders sent him to India, but he saw no action in either vessel and was again retired on half-pay on 25 May 1784, after the signing of the peace treaties which ended the wars connected with the struggle of the British colonies in America for independence. He then spent a year in southern France and, when appointed the first governor of New South Wales on 12 October 1786, was engaged in survey work for the Admiralty.

By then Phillip was a man of mature years whose attainments, though not particularly outstanding, were solid. From inauspicious beginnings he had risen largely through his own merit, attracting favourable comment from those under whom he had served. The Portuguese authorities had described him as brave, honest, obedient and self-sacrificing. Experience had broadened without hardening or coarsening his somewhat sensitive nature and in a variety of ways prepared him for his new task. He was accustomed to command men and had even, while in the Portuguese navy, transported convicts from Lisbon to the Brazils. His naval training proved invaluable on the trip to Botany Bay and stood him in good stead when exploring the hinterland. Work on his Lyndhurst property had made him familiar with at least the rudiments of farming and added yet another dimension to his qualifications. How far these considerations weighed with the British government is difficult to say, for the circumstances surrounding both their offer and his acceptance of the governorship remain obscure. The first lord of the Admiralty had nothing to do with it, for Lord Howe, though prepared to accept the decision, stated that he personally did not think Phillip suited to the task. The governor's detractors maliciously claimed that he was chosen to rid the authorities of one pressing for preferment. It has also been suggested that Lord Sydney, faced with the need hurriedly to find someone for a mediocre post that no one else wanted, offered it to Phillip who was known to be reliable and trustworthy. Perhaps the most likely explanation is that the appointment was made on the advice of Sir George Rose, treasurer of the navy, who lived near Lyndhurst, knew Phillip and was impressed by him. Whatever the reason Phillip was presumably attracted by the prospect of returning to active service in a capacity that could satisfy his desire for adventure and his wish to command.

To the British government the new settlement was primarily to be an outlet for convicts whom it was undesirable to keep at home and impossible to transport elsewhere, but Phillip was inspired by the vision of a new outpost of empire growing up in the South Seas. He showed himself anxious to encourage free settlers to migrate, drew up plans for their reception, urged the extension of British law for their protection and resolved to insulate them from the contamination of convicts. 'As I would not wish convicts to lay the foundation of an Empire', he observed, 'I think they should ever remain separated from the garrison and other settlers that may come from Europe', even after their sentences were completed.

When these words were written Phillip was immersed in preparations for the sailing of the expedition and the planning of the actual settlement. His correspondence with the authorities between October 1786 and May 1787 revealed a sound grasp of administrative detail and a degree of foresight that confirmed the wisdom of their choice. In contrast to his superiors he displayed an awareness of the multitudinous problems inevitably involved in transplanting Englishmen to a little-known land on the far side of the globe. Not all his proposed solutions were accepted, but enough were incorporated to support the claim that he made a noteworthy contribution to the organization of the venture. Besides offering practical advice Phillip also enunciated some of the principles that were intended to guide his conduct. He proposed to treat the Aboriginals kindly and to establish harmonious relations with them. He resolved to try to reform as well as to discipline the convicts. In these respects his views were in keeping with the more advanced opinion of his age. Similarly his rational approach to life and indifference to religious fervour stamped him as a product of the eighteenth century and a not untypical member of the contemporary Church of England into which he had been baptized.

The First Fleet left England on 13 May 1787 and arrived at Botany Bay on 18 January 1788 after a voyage whose success again owed much to Phillip's care. The original site proved unsuited to settlement. Three days later Phillip discovered an appropriate spot at Port Jackson and on 26 January landing operations began there. All told 1030 persons went ashore, of whom 736 were convicts, including 188 women, the rest marines and civil officers, 27 with wives, and 37 children. These people formed the human material for a gaol and not surprisingly were placed under a form of government that gave an unusual amount of power to the governor. Phillip's first and second Commissions, dated 12 October 1786 and 2 April 1787, appointed him as the representative of the Crown in an area embracing roughly the eastern half of Australia together with adjacent Pacific islands. His responsibility was solely to his superiors in London and he was expected to carry out their orders as embodied in his first Instructions of 25 April 1787, his second Instructions of 20 August 1789 and official dispatches. Within these limits his powers were absolute. The Crown vested him with complete authority over the inhabitants and gave him the right to promulgate regulations touching practically all aspects of their lives. He combined executive and legislative functions and could remit sentences imposed by the Civil and Criminal Courts established under a warrant issued on 2 April 1787. Only the crimes of treason or wilful murder were exempt from this provision, but even here he could grant a reprieve while awaiting advice from London. Distance from Britain and the relative indifference of the Home Office towards the affairs of the infant colony enlarged even further the scope of the governor's initiative and increased his responsibilities.

The subordinate officers appointed to assist him proved of varied merit. Some worked diligently enough in their particular spheres and in addition made their mark as explorers or commentators on the contemporary scene. Several left behind journals of literary merit and historical value. Rarely, however, did they share Phillip's vision and enthusiasm, and most quickly came to despair of their mission, wrote home in gloomy tones of the hardships they were obliged to endure and urged the abandonment of the settlement. None felt more strongly on this score than the marine officers and their testy commander, Major Robert Ross [q.v.], who was also lieut-governor and Vice-Admiralty Court judge, and described New South Wales as the 'outcast of God's works'. The officers, construing their duties as being primarily military, caused Phillip much trouble. They refused to help in supervising the activities of the convicts even though, through the oversight of the British authorities, few suitable persons were available, and they objected to having to sit on the Criminal Court. Their discontent was heightened by the fact that unlike emancipists they were denied free grants of land and lacked the opportunity to secure any of the other perquisites traditionally associated with colonial service. Ross made matters worse by his high-handed actions, such as the arrest of five of his officers, which created friction in the mess and prompted Lieutenant Ralph Clark [q.v.] to describe him as 'the most disagreeable commanding officer I ever knew'. Although at first on reasonable terms with Phillip, Ross soon became quarrelsome, acting both as a focus of discontent and a major irritant. He supported and encouraged his fellow officers in their conflicts with Phillip, engaged in

clashes of his own, and complained of the governor's actions to the Home Office. Phillip for his part, more placid and forbearing in temperament, was anxious in the interests of the community as a whole to avoid friction between the civil and military authorities. Though firm in his attitude he endeavoured to placate Ross, but to little effect. In the end he solved the problem by ordering Ross to Norfolk Island on 5 March 1790 to replace P. G. King, the commandant there, whom he had previously decided to send to England to report personally on the establishment.

Far from being able to fall back on his aides in the initial trying years, therefore, Phillip had to struggle against widespread defeatism and occasional opposition. The attitude of the marine officers affected their men and possibly the convicts who had least cause of any to feel content with their lot. Partly to counter this attitude Phillip in his dispatches highlighted favourable developments and concealed the personal misgivings that constant tribulation must have led him to experience from time to time. Not the least of his accomplishments was to help to keep faith in the venture alive in official circles in London, and provide the optimism as well as the leadership without which morale in New South Wales itself might have crumbled completely.

Phillip's enthusiasm is all the more remarkable in view of the fact that during his five year term of office the colony assumed a shape that was not in accord with his wishes. Instead of the migrants whom he sought to encourage with grants of from 'five hundred to one thousand acres' and the assistance of 'not less than twenty men' maintained at government expense for two years, only convicts arrived. Nor was this surprising. When the Home Office finally dispatched Instructions to Phillip in August 1789 authorizing him to give grants to migrants it was on terms far less generous than he had contemplated. People leaving England lacked any real incentive to come to New South Wales and continued to sail for more accessible parts of the empire that were untainted by the stigma of convictism. Only thirteen venturesome souls departed for Sydney in the first five years and none of these landed until after Phillip's departure. The governor had expected a variety of advantages to flow from the presence of migrants; besides forming the basis for the kind of settlement he hoped would emerge, he thought they would also prove of practical value from the penal standpoint by assisting in administration and convict control, by employing the prisoners and by setting an example for them to follow. Inspired as they must be by the profit motive they would quickly make the settlement self-sufficient in basic foodstuffs. Their failure to materialize forced Phillip to depend on methods which he would have preferred to drop and which further increased his burdens.

Between 1788 and 1792 about 3546 male and 766 female convicts were landed at Port Jackson and handed over by the contractors to the governor, who faced the task of deciding how their sentences were to be served. Anxious to keep costs low the British government insisted that they be disposed of in such a way as to involve the Treasury in a minimum of expenditure. Previously, in the American colonies, settlers had taken them into employment, but in the absence of private employers in New South Wales most convicts remained in government hands throughout the first five years, and upon Phillip devolved the responsibility for directing their energies. The task was not made easier by the characteristics of the convicts themselves. Historians no longer regard them as the innocent victims of adverse social conditions and a harsh penal code. In dispelling this myth recent research has presented them as including a high proportion of professional criminals drawn from the more worthless element in society. Certainly they were for the most part unfit subjects for an experiment in colonization. Not unnaturally they resented being wrenched from their homeland and taken to a harsh, hostile and uncivilized land. Phillip found them lazy and anxious to escape work by any means possible. Few were mechanics or knew anything of agriculture, and each of the fleets that arrived up to 1792 contained a high proportion of aged and sick who were unfit for work. Worst of all was the Second Fleet which arrived in June 1790 after losing more than a quarter of its 'passengers' *en route* through sickness. Phillip's reports on the unscrupulous behaviour of the private contractors helped to produce improvements, but not until after the Third Fleet had arrived bearing convicts whose physical condition appalled him once more.

Matters were made even worse by continuing privation within the settlement itself resulting from the shortcomings of local agriculture and the failure of supplies to arrive on time from overseas. The crisis reached a peak in 1790 after the wreck of the storeship *Guardian* off the Cape of Good Hope; although the situation eased in 1791, it remained uncertain and even when the full ration could be issued it was generally unappetizing and often of poor quality. Under such conditions the health of the convicts deteriorated and they found prolonged manual labour difficult. Faced with a lack of suitable personnel to act as supervisors Phillip selected superintendents from among the better-behaved convicts, placed them under the few free men in the settlement, ex-marines, a few from the ships' crews, and some whose sentences had expired. He encouraged gardening. He had dispatched a party to Norfolk Island within a month of his arrival, and constantly reinforced it when he found that the island was more fertile than the land around Sydney. He exercised great care in distributing the ration and insisted on complete equality for all regardless of their standing. Some writers have attached the label communism to this egalitarian system. Such a term connotes a body of dogma completely foreign to Phillip and is highly misleading. The governor based his actions on no particular set of beliefs except a broad humanitarianism. By nature self-sacrificing he was not prepared to inflict greater suffering on others than on himself and he felt that gradations in the ration were unfair in time of scarcity.

Phillip's measures at best proved mere palliatives, but they helped to keep the settlement alive in its early years. In 1791 the marines were replaced by the New South Wales Corps. In the light of what was to come this may appear unfortunate, but Phillip's relations with the corps, though marked by occasional disagreement, were reasonably pleasant, partly because its officers had not then acquired the economic interests that led to conflict with later governors. The military commandant, Major Francis Grose [q.v.], was easygoing and affable; his only recorded disagreement with Phillip arose from his action in permitting his officers to charter a vessel to procure necessities from the Cape of Good Hope. Unlike Ross, Grose was highly impressed with the colony, and his attitude was shared by many of his officers and a number of the convicts, who showed an increasing tendency to settle after their sentences were completed. The more regular arrival of ships from overseas and the beginnings of trading contacts with foreign speculators lessened the feeling of isolation besides improving supplies. More important, however, by now much of the initial spadework had been completed and the outlines of a permanent settlement were becoming more firmly etched.

The community which, under Phillip's guidance, was gradually establishing itself, remained confined to a minute portion of the vast region over which his jurisdiction extended. The governor himself had from the outset been anxious to gain information about the hinterland of Port Jackson. Curiosity, the need to find areas of good soil, and a desire to escape tensions at headquarters all played a part in prompting his explorations. The difficulties of the terrain, the problems involved in provisioning a lengthy expedition through inhospitable country and the impossibility of being away long from the centre of affairs prevented him from penetrating very far inland. Nevertheless trips in which he took part resulted in the discovery of the Hawkesbury River and the gaining of detailed knowledge about the area between it and Port Jackson, including the Parramatta district. With his encouragement later expeditions were made that established the relationship between the Hawkesbury and Nepean Rivers and gained additional information about the quality of the soil. Meanwhile knowledge of the coastal area had been enlarged by whale-fishing and other sea-going parties.

Phillip opposed the settlement of the Hawkesbury because the area was too isolated and too little known, and 'proper people to conduct it' were lacking. The Parramatta region, on the other hand, he thought ideally suited because of its good soil, ready accessibility and proximity to water. There he moved many of the convicts from late 1788 onwards after the short-comings of Sydney for agricultural purposes had become apparent. In this area Phillip established a small township, which quickly emerged as the main centre of the colony's economic life; his naming one choice site within its bounds Rose Hill has been interpreted as additional evidence that Sir George Rose had been helpful in securing his appointment. Sydney, which he named and helped to design, and for which he planned broad streets, directed to suit the prevailing winds as well as the contours of its hills, remained important as a port and as the focus of social life, but its economic significance was slight until after the turn of the century, and his plans for its development had by then been abandoned.

Besides determining where the inhabitants should live Phillip also decided how they were to be occupied. At first he gave priority to the construction of necessary buildings, diverting most convict labour to this end; however, some public farming was carried on almost from the outset, originally at Farm Cove and later at Parramatta and Toongabbie. Its slow progress reflected the governor's inability to find adequate means of surmounting the many obstacles in his path. Poor seasons, the lack of suitable equipment and the difficulty of clearing and cultivating the thickly-wooded land added to his problems. By 1791 a mere 213 acres were under crop and the number of farm animals amounted to only 126 head, for some of the cattle brought out had strayed, while others had died or been slaughtered. The building programme, by contrast, had advanced more satisfactorily, resulting in the erection of dwelling places for the governor, the officers, the convicts and some of the troops, together with several store-houses. Having completed these and other essential tasks Phillip was able to give more attention to farming. The area cultivated by government labour expanded much more rapidly after 1791 and by October 1792 some 1017 acres were under crop on the public domain; although livestock was still scarce important advances had been made towards the attainment of self-sufficiency in grain. The community was still vitally dependent on overseas supplies for most of its needs, but no longer was survival thought to be impossible.

Providing for material needs formed only part of the task of running what was primarily a prison. Effective discipline was a vital necessity in an isolated community where convicts far outnumbered their gaolers and where it was impracticable to segregate them behind bars. Phillip housed the convicts in a series of huts so arranged that they could be policed at night; but the watch of necessity had to be drawn mainly from among the better convicts, and this caused further trouble with the marines who complained bitterly on the odd occasion when a convict policeman detected one of their number breaking the law. Offences committed within the colony were, if only minor, tried by the magistrates, or when more serious by the Civil and Criminal Courts. Phillip sat on neither bench, but he was able within limits to determine their composition and to vary their sentences, thereby influencing the course of justice. Before leaving England he had stated his opposition to the death penalty save for murder and sodomy, which crimes he felt best punished by handing guilty persons over to be eaten by 'the natives of New Zealand'. This harsh sentence was never imposed, but there were some executions, particularly for the theft of food in time of scarcity. More usual was the lash, then a standard punishment in the army and navy, or commital to a gaol-gang.

Phillip's discipline was firm, but by the standards of his time could not be considered unduly harsh or severe. Moreover he recognized the need to encourage good behaviour as well as to punish bad conduct. He rewarded signs of industry by personal commendation and sometimes by appointment to positions of trust, which carried various privileges. He granted twenty-six pardons to exemplary characters, including fourteen prisoners who had behaved well when the *Guardian* was wrecked. In a further effort to encourage the convicts Phillip made it clear that land grants would only be given to those who proved their worth while under sentence. These measures indicated his desire to reform his charges, an object to which the Home Office paid only lip service. How much success attended his efforts is difficult to say. Contemporaries as well as more recent writers, however, have paid testimony to the effectiveness of his rule. In general the convicts responded well to his guidance. Crimes against the person were rare and while thefts were fairly common many of these resulted from sheer desperation and hunger.

One of the offences Phillip refused to tolerate was ill treatment of the Aboriginals. In his Instructions he had been ordered to establish contact and maintain friendly relations with them and he took these humanitarian injunctions seriously. He interested himself in the life of the natives whose customs also attracted considerable attention from his fellow officers. He made them presents, placed two, Colebe and Bennelong [qq.v.], under his personal care, and did his utmost to win and keep their friendship. At first he seemed to have succeeded. The Aboriginals evinced no desire to drive the whites out and showed admiration for their power and their leader whose missing front tooth apparently possessed symbolic value. Friction later developed and matters eventually reached the point where Phillip was forced to take punitive action, though he continued to exercise restraint even after being wounded by a spear at Manly Cove. Throughout he sought to maintain harmony while gradually persuading the Aboriginals of the superiority of British civilization. Settlers who interfered with their pursuits remained liable to heavy punishment.

Although in 1788-92 convicts and their gaolers made up the bulk of the population there gradually appeared others who fell into neither category. As early as July 1789 a small batch of convicts sought their freedom, claiming that their sentences had expired. Through oversight Phillip had not been supplied with their records and being unable to verify their claims shelved them. Later this deficiency was remedied enabling the governor to liberate the growing number of convicts who each year completed their sentences. By 1792 some 350 persons, of whom the majority were men, had been restored to freedom. Some secured passages home but most were unable to do so and were obliged with diminishing reluctance to stay in New South Wales. There they found employment mainly on government works, but a minority struck out on their own and took up farming, introducing a new element into an economy dominated by public enterprise.

Phillip's second Commission dated 2 April 1787 had given him the power of granting land to approved persons, defined in his first Instructions as former convicts. The British government was anxious to encourage people of this kind to remain at Port Jackson and for this reason offered them small plots of land and full maintenance during the early months of operations. The Home Office also indicated its willingness to make grants to the non-commissioned officers and privates of the marines who might elect to remain after completing a tour of duty, and to any migrants who might arrive. Phillip was ordered to examine the soil, report on its quality and suggest terms on which it might be alienated. Without fully waiting for his advice, however, the secretary of state dispatched on 22 August 1789 fresh Instructions on the granting of land.

The only residents not permitted to own land were the civil staff and military officers, whose pleas for this concession were not satisfied until after Phillip had departed. The governor himself had viewed their requests with no great enthusiasm. While willing to allow them to grow foodstuff in time of shortage or run livestock on plots of crown land he was not happy at the thought of their becoming property owners. He feared their attention might be distracted from their duties. He realized that they would wish to employ convicts, and these he thought might be left too much to their own devices. Shortly before leaving England he stressed that insufficient convicts were available to make it possible for the officers' likely demands to be met. Phillip was also reserved in his attitude towards the issuing of land grants to emancipists, for he rightly felt that many would never succeed at farming.

Historians have been unable to agree as to the exact area he alienated. Judging by the Register of Land Grants, which has not been used by earlier writers, he granted 3440 acres on the mainland. At Norfolk Island he was obliged to recall some of the grants originally issued and by December 1792 had reallotted titles to a mere 49 acres, making a grand total of 3489 acres. This was considerably less than the area alienated by his immediate successors, a fact which resulted not from niggardliness but from the unwillingness of more than a handful of persons to try their hand at what was to most an unfamiliar occupation. Apart from James Ruse [q.v.] there were no requests for land until 1791 and by December 1792 only seventy-three persons occupied holdings on the mainland.

With characteristic thoroughness the governor did his utmost to ensure the success of a group whose activities might improve the food situation. He personally selected land for them in the vicinity of Parramatta close to water, protection, market and supplies. Where necessary he varied his Instructions in their interests providing them with aid for eighteen months instead of the year stipulated by the British government. Originally he had been ordered to reserve between each 150-acre block 'a space of ten acres in breadth and of thirty acres in depth'. Realizing the dangers of natives lurking in the undergrowth on such land and convinced of the need for farmers to live side by side so as to provide mutual aid he successfully recommended the abandonment of this injunction. To deter settlers from disposing of land he incorporated in the title deeds, whose wording he himself devised, a clause forbidding them to sell their grants until they had occupied them continuously for at least five years. On two occasions he took land away from men who had made little attempt to cultivate it. The progress of farming, however, was inevitably slow, for the settlers possessed few resources, inadequate tools and little experience. By December 1792 they had cleared little more than 517 acres, owned scarcely any livestock and were still mostly dependent on government aid for survival.

Although Phillip's reputation as an administrator must rest primarily on his work on the mainland of New South Wales, Norfolk Island also came under his control. In 1787 he had been ordered to settle this potentially useful spot to forestall occupation by any other power. On 12 February 1788 he made P. G. King the first commandant and two days later dispatched him to the island with a party of twenty-one, including fifteen convicts. Others were sent later mainly to ease the famine in New South Wales. By late 1792 the population totalled 1115 persons, and the island's activities which at first had been dominated by government enterprise, were diversified by settlers from the marines. Effort had also been made to grow flax though little had been accomplished. The real burden of controlling these and other developments fell on the rulers on the spot, successively P. G. King, Major Ross and Captain Paterson [q.v.]; nevertheless Phillip was in constant communication with them and as the person responsible for the island's management laid down some of the principles on which their actions were based.

On 11 December 1792 Phillip sailed for England in the *Atlantic* to seek medical attention for a pain in his side which had involved him in constant suffering. His work in New South Wales has been widely commended and, given the circumstances under which he was obliged to operate, it is difficult to see how he could have accomplished more than he did. Many of his hopes, including those for the encouragement of whaling off the coast which he recommended very strongly, were not realized. Despite these frustrations he retained his optimism to the end, displaying a fortitude and sense of duty that carried him through periods of great difficulty and physical pain. He left at a time when developments loomed which were to undo much of his work. One consequence of the discovery of the settlement by overseas merchants was that in increasing numbers they brought cargoes including liquor for sale. Phillip recognized the dangers of permitting the convicts to obtain spirits and the one occasion, in October 1792, when he allowed it to be sold to the other residents confirmed his fears, for there was widespread drunkenness and disturbance. The episode was not repeated but it must remain a matter of doubt whether, had he stayed much longer, Phillip could have countered the many problems that were to arise from the liquor trade. Similarly his departure preceded by only two months the arrival from London of orders allowing civil and military officers to own land, an event which provided these men with an opportunity to promote their interests and heightened the possibility of their conflict with a governor anxious to favour no single element in the community. It was perhaps fortunate that Phillip was unable to follow his original intention of returning to Port Jackson once his health was restored, but medical advice compelled him formally to resign on 23 July 1793. One of his first tasks upon returning to England was to raise an additional company for service with the New South Wales Corps; this was his last practical contribution to the settlement but he maintained an interest in its affairs and continued to be consulted on them for some time, though his recommendation of King as his successor was turned down.

By 1796 Phillip had sufficiently recovered his health to resume active naval duties. After successively commanding several ships, of which the last was the 98-gun *Blenheim*, he was given a shore appointment in 1798 as commander of the Hampshire Sea Fencibles whose purpose was to defend that county against invasion by Napoleon. Early in January 1799 he became a rear-admiral of the Blue and soon afterwards was given charge of the Sea Fencibles throughout England. This task fully absorbed his energies and involved him in much travelling and administrative work until he retired in 1805. The last nine years of his life saw him steadily advancing in the naval hierarchy while living in retirement at 19 Bennett Street, Bath, with his second wife Isabella, née Whitehead, whom he had married on 8 May 1794. He died on 31 August 1814 three months after receiving his last promotion to admiral of the Blue. He left an estate worth about £25,000 and was buried in the church of St Nicholas, Bathampton. A memorial to him is in Bath Abbey, and portraits are in the National Portrait Gallery, London, and the Mitchell and Dixson Galleries, Sydney.

HRNSW, 1, pt 2, 2; HRA (1), 1; G. Mackaness, *Admiral Arthur Phillip* (Syd, 1937) and for bibliog; M. Barnard Eldershaw, *Phillip of Australia* (Lond, 1938); MS cat under Phillip (ML); CO 201/1-9.

B. H. FLETCHER

PIDGEON, NATHANIEL (1803-1879), city missionary, was born on 16 August 1803 in Bellevue, County Wexford, Ireland, the only son of Richard Pidgeon, Church of England yeoman, of Ogle's Loyal Blues, and of Elizabeth Foley of Baladicken. James Bulger, an itinerant revivalist, won over the family to Methodism. After some years of casual worship Nathaniel was 'converted' and while active as a lay preacher met and married Eliza Proud, whose grandfather had assisted John Wesley in Ireland.

Pidgeon, his parents and thirteen other members of the family emigrated to Australia and arrived at Sydney in May 1841, excepting his father who died at sea. Pidgeon worked as a cabinet maker and lay preacher until 1850 when he decided to devote his whole time to evangelism and, in association with the Wesleyan Methodist Church, became the first city missionary in Sydney. About 1860 he felt the need for greater freedom of expression and separated from the Wesleyans. In 1861 he and his followers created an independent organization and successfully petitioned the government to register him as an Independent Methodist, with power to solemnize marriages. The new group built a brick chapel on a corner of Sussex and Liverpool Streets, but financial burdens soon proved too much for them. In 1868 five trustees of different denominations took over the responsibilities and maintained the chapel as an unsectarian place of worship for the poor of the city. Pidgeon continued his work with the chapel until accident and illness incapacitated him in 1875. He died at Milson's Point on 17 February 1879, leaving a widow, six sons and a daughter.

Pidgeon was a courageous and an apparently difficult character. Orthodoxy frowned upon his disregard for the form and gentility that made religion respectable. The very vehemence of his preaching offended the ears of the cultured ordained, although he often had 'the liberty', as he termed it. He prayed with, and exhorted against, the lowest elements of the city's degraded society. His generosity kept his family impoverished but often gained him unsolicited support for his work. A complex personality he was all things to all men: demagogue, bigot, scold and saint.

In 1859 Pidgeon published a *Camp Meeting and Revival Hymn Book for the Use of Christians of all Denominations*. In 1857 he wrote an autobiography, *The Life, Experience and Journal of Nathaniel Pidgeon, City Missionary*, which he expanded and republished in 1864.

W. E. PIDGEON

PINNOCK, JAMES DENHAM (1810?-1875), public servant and banker, was born at Winchester, England, the son of Timothy Denham Pinnock and his wife Maria, née Doswell. He became a temporary clerk in the Colonial Office, working in 1831 with the London Emigration Committee. In January 1835 he was appointed emigration agent in London, to scrutinize all would-be emigrants seeking bounties. His salary was £200 paid in equal proportions by New South Wales and Van Diemen's Land. In October Governor Bourke complained to the Colonial Office that Pinnock was not satisfying the wishes of the colonists: to have their confidence an agent needed an intimate acquaintance with colonial needs. However, Pinnock continued until he was appointed emigration agent in New South Wales, where he arrived in July 1838 in the *Amelia Thompson*. His salary was £500. In November he was one of a board of five to report on the care of emigrants in the *St George*. Their report strongly favoured 'bounty' ships, as distinct from 'government' ships, as being cheaper, healthier and otherwise more satisfactory. Pinnock continued to espouse the bounty system and criticize the agents in England. He was accused by the Land and Emigration Commission of making false statements intended to foster the bounty system in which 'large pecuniary interests are involved', and in July 1841 was replaced as emigration agent. According to Governor Gipps his removal 'caused a considerable sensation in the colony', he 'being generally considered a useful and trustworthy servant of the public, to whom the proceedings of the commissioners had been in many respects "extremely distasteful" '. James Stephen, on the other hand, described him as a man of 'light and unstable character'.

Transferred to Melbourne Pinnock became deputy-registrar of the Supreme Court at £450 a year, holding this office until the Port Phillip District was separated from New South Wales. He went to England in 1851 and on his return in 1854 served briefly as registrar, then as immigration agent in 1857-60 and land titles commissioner in 1862-63. After retirement he was elected to the Legislative Council by the Eastern Province. Earlier he had served as alderman in the Melbourne Town Council and on the committee of the Horticultural Society, but his chief interest seemed to be finance. In 1863 he became a director of the Bank of Victoria, of the Victorian Life and General Assurance Society, and in 1870 of the Melbourne Banking Corporation. As a churchman he served on the building committee of St Peter's, Melbourne, in 1846, and became a member of the Anglican Church Assembly in 1858. He died at his home in Wellington Parade, East Melbourne, on 20 May 1875, aged 65.

In 1844 Pinnock had married the eldest daughter of William Hull, and after her death he married Sibyl Herlock, daughter of John Chipperton, solicitor, on 21 June 1859. He had four children by his first wife and three by his second. Of his sons, James Denham became manager of the St Kilda branch of the Commercial Bank of Australia, and Robert Denham, M.D., (d. 1902), practised at Ballarat and in 1884 was commissioned a surgeon in the Victorian Defence Forces, retiring as a major in 1901.

HRA (1), 17-22; Argus, 21 May 1875.

PIPER, JOHN (1773-1851), military officer, public servant and landowner, was born on 20 April 1773 at Maybole, Ayrshire, Scotland, the son of Hugh Piper, a doctor. The Pipers were in the main an army family, and Scots only by adoption, having come from Cornwall and before that from Germany. Through the influence of his uncle, Captain John Piper, young John received a commission as ensign in the newly formed New South Wales Corps in April 1791, as his younger brother Hugh was to do in 1799. John sailed in the Pitt and arrived in Sydney in February 1792 when the infant settlement was still fighting for its life in the face of starvation. Piper was an immediate social success and became a close family friend of John Macarthur [q.v.].

In 1793 at his own request he was sent on duty to the even more primitive settlement at Norfolk Island, possibly because of an entanglement from which his more discreet friends were anxious to rescue him. While he was away they looked after his interests and secured him a land grant of 110 acres at Parramatta. On the island he received a liberal education in those savage military quarrels which beset the early days of the colony.

In 1795 Piper was promoted lieutenant and returned to the mainland. From 1797 to 1799 he was away on leave. In 1800 he was given the local rank of captain. In the struggle between the corps and Governor King, of which Macarthur was the ringleader, Piper stood with his friend, and in September 1801 acted as his second in a duel with Colonel Paterson [q.v.], his commanding officer. King arrested both Macarthur and Piper, but decided that Piper could be dealt with locally. At his court martial in 1802 he apologized and was acquitted, much to King's disgust.

In 1804 he was again detailed for duty on Norfolk Island. It was fortunate for Piper that he spent the next six years on the island and so was thrown clear of the troubles on the mainland, notably the Rum Rebellion. In September 1804 Lieut-Governor Foveaux [q.v.] left on prolonged sick leave and Piper became acting commandant, with the inadequate extra allowance of 5s. a day. His rule was mild. As one of his charges, Joseph Holt [q.v.], declared 'the new Governor had the good will and respect of everyone, for he had always conducted himself as a Christian and a gentleman'. He was promoted to the full rank of captain in November 1806.

By this time Norfolk Island had become an expense rather than an asset, and the British government was planning to close down the settlement and transfer its inhabitants to the mainland or Van Diemen's Land. The duty of beginning to carry out the frequently altered instructions fell to

Piper and in it he appears to have exhibited both tact and organizing ability.

In 1810 he returned to Sydney. It is probable that on Norfolk Island he met Mary Ann Shears, the 15-year-old daughter of a convict, and formed an attachment to her that lasted throughout his life. When he sailed for Britain on leave in September 1811 he took her with him, as well as their two little boys, and Sarah, the child of an earlier liaison. He faced a problem connected with both his family and his career, but he preferred Mary Ann and New South Wales to his regiment. Whereas his brother Hugh, now a captain, left the colony with his regiment to continue his army career, John resigned his commission and decided to seek civilian employment in the colony. In 1813 he was appointed Naval Officer in Sydney and arrived back in February 1814. On 10 February 1816 he married Mary Ann, by special licence. She had borne him two more sons while they were away and in due course they had nine more.

His duties included the collection of customs duties, excise on spirits and harbour dues, control of lighthouses and work which is now the province of the water police. The post was very much to Piper's taste and proved very remunerative: with a percentage on all monies collected, his income from it rose to more than £4000 a year. He bought the property now known as Vaucluse House. In 1816 he was granted 190 acres of land on Eliza Point, now Point Piper, for the site of his official residence. Here he built Henrietta Villa (also called the Naval Pavilion) at the cost of £10,000 and furnished it in the most luxurious style. It was completed in 1822 and became the scene of many sumptuous entertainments.

Piper was a close friend of Governor Macquarie, who in 1819 made him a magistrate. In 1825 he was chairman of directors of the Bank of New South Wales. He sat on the local committee of the Australian Agricultural Co., was president of the Scots Church committee and took part in many social and sporting activities. He owned much property, acquired by grant or purchase. Besides Point Piper he had 475 acres at Vaucluse, 1130 at Woollahra and Rose Bay, a farm of 295 acres at Petersham, 700 at Neutral Bay, 80 at Botany Bay, 2000 at Bathurst, 300 in Van Diemen's Land with various smaller farms, and an acre of city land in George Street. He was, however, not as solvent as he appeared and in 1826 he raised a mortgage of £20,000. When Governor Darling ordered an inquiry into the affairs of the Bank of New South Wales, confusion and favouritism came to light, and in January 1827 Piper resigned from the chairmanship. The previous October Darling had also ordered an inquiry into Piper's administration as Naval Officer. The following April he was suspended from his official position, when a deficiency of £12,000 was discovered. There was no question of peculation, but the collection of customs had been gravely mismanaged. Piper tried to drown himself but was rescued. Most of his property had to be sold. Values were low owing to the general depression, and the Point Piper estate, the land at Vaucluse, the city allotments, various farms and a parcel of shares brought only £5170 11s. However, his debt to government was paid in full and his other creditors were satisfied.

Piper retired with his family to the Bathurst property, Alloway Bank. Here he made cheeses, ran cattle and later sheep, and became an important figure in the town. He was a magistrate, worked for the Presbyterian Church, for the improvement of transport, patronized horse-racing and entertained many guests including Governors Darling and Bourke. But Alloway Bank did not thrive. By 1832 Piper was selling the remnants of his land in Sydney. In the drought of 1838 he mortgaged the property. Further impoverished by the depression, he was forced to sell it for only a few hundred pounds. Friends, notably W. C. Wentworth [q.v.], re-established the family on a 500-acre property, Westbourne, beside the Macquarie River, and tied it up for Mrs Piper and her numerous children. There John Piper died on 8 June 1851, and there Mrs Piper lived until her death twenty years later.

John Piper was a man of his times. He personified the colonial dream. In his sixty years in the colony he adapted himself to its development. During the military regime he was an officer; when Macquarie created a civil state he became a civil servant; when the race was to the pioneer he became one. He was honourable, generous, gay and so well loved that he was forgiven things which would have wrecked a stronger man. He was no business man, completely lacking the shrewdness which enriched so many of his brother officers. He was a master of the bright illusion.

A portrait in oils is in the Mitchell Library, Sydney.

HRNSW, 2-7; HRA (1), 1-13, 16; M. Barnard Eldershaw, *The life and times of Captain John Piper* (Syd, 1939), and for bibliog; Piper papers (ML).

MARJORIE BARNARD

PITCAIRN, ROBERT (1802-1861), solicitor, was born on 17 July 1802 in Edinburgh, where he was educated in law and became a writer to the signet. He arrived in Hobart Town from Leith in September 1824 as a settler recommended by the Colonial Office, and established himself on a grant near Bothwell. Soon persuaded to return to the legal profession he became the fourteenth barrister and solicitor admitted to the Supreme Court. His success brought modest prosperity. In September 1830 he married Dorothea Jessie, eldest daughter of Captain J. C. Dumas of the 63rd Regiment; they had a daughter and three sons, two of whom died in infancy. The home he built at New Town was known as Runnymede. In his early colonial experience his most important public service was as a member of a government committee set up during the depression of the 1840s to consider the law relating to insolvency. Their report, published in September 1844, recommended the abolition of imprisonment for debt and the protection of creditors of small sums, proposals which closely followed English legislation.

In 1845 Pitcairn became active in the cause for which he is chiefly remembered: the cessation of transportation, and its corollary the introduction of responsible government. His petitions to the British government were long and closely argued; although strongly contested by Lieut-Governors Eardley-Wilmot and Denison, they carried much weight both in Eardley-Wilmot's recall in so far as it was due to his mismanagement of convicts, and in the ultimate abolition of transportation. To Pitcairn the moral and social evils of the probation system and the exodus of thousands of free people to the mainland were to be cured only by the cessation of transportation, the introduction of representative government and the large-scale immigration of free families. These views brought him into close association with the Australasian League, which sought and gained the support of the mainland colonies for the cause of cessation. When transportation ceased in 1852, Pitcairn withdrew from public life. He died on 28 January 1861.

Pitcairn was a member of the Church of England, and the respect and affection in which he was held were expressed in a window to his memory in St David's Cathedral, Hobart, and a marble bust by Charles Summers unveiled by the chief justice in 1866 in the Supreme Court where, in a courtroom otherwise lacking ornament, it still stands as a memorial.

Correspondence file under Pitcairn (TA).

PETER CRISP

PITT, RICHARD (1765-1826), constable and settler, was born on 3 March 1765 at Tiverton, Devon, England, son of John Pitt and his wife Ann, née Cross. He married Jane Tanner (1768-1836) of Tiverton; they had four children. The eldest remained in England with Mrs Pitt when the father, with one daughter, Salome, and two sons, Philip and Francis, sailed as free settlers in the *Ocean* with David Collins's expedition which settled by the Derwent in 1804. In December he received a 100-acre grant from Governor King and began farming at Stainsforth's Cove (New Town), a district for which he was also appointed constable. Pitt made an unspectacular but sound job of each occupation. He grew wheat and barley, built up herds of sheep and pigs, and by 1809 he and his children were no longer victualled by the government. He leased grazing land at the Green Ponds (Kempton) district, where his children also located grants. A bushranger, William Martin, confessed on 21 April 1815 that he had stolen sheep 'from Richard Pitt at the Green Ponds Water Holes'.

Pitt retained his farming interests, but gave increasing attention to official duties as district constable at New Town. The *Hobart Town Gazette*, 27 December 1817, noted 'the vigilance and attention of this peace officer in apprehending absentee convicts'. On 14 February 1818 Pitt was appointed chief constable for Hobart Town. In recommending him to Governor Macquarie for the appointment, Lieut-Governor Sorell called Pitt one of the most respectable settlers. Pitt seized the opportunity of his new standing to ask for a free passage to the colony for his wife. Macquarie sent the request to London, but Mrs Pitt did not come. She died at Tiverton on 18 May 1836.

In evidence to Commissioner Bigge [q.v.] in May 1820 Pitt said his salary of £50 from the Police Fund was supplemented from fees on warrants at 2s. each, and summonses at 1s. each, although half the warrant fees went to the magistrate's clerk. He had fifty-two constables under his charge, but he personally examined goods and baggage in carts taken north to Port Dalrymple by free settlers, and every evening it was his duty to clear the inns of prisoners after bell-ringing at 8 p.m.

This old and most respectable colonist remained chief constable until his death at Hobart on 14 May 1826. He was buried in St David's burial ground and his tombstone was among those preserved to mark the jubilee of the Commonwealth of Australia in 1951. His character, reputation and sense of public responsibility were somewhat rare in the young colony.

The three children who came with him in the *Ocean* all settled in Van Diemen's Land.

HRA (1), 4, (3), 1-3, 6; *Hobart Town Gazette*, 27 May 1826.   JOHN REYNOLDS

PLATT, JOHN LAURIO (1782?-1836), sailor and settler, was said to have been born at Bashford, near Nottingham, England, the son of a Church of England clergyman, but no record of him or his father remains there. In October 1801 he joined the navy. He saw service in the Aegean Sea, the American war of 1812 and on the Gold Coast. In 1814 he retired and was appointed harbourmaster at Heligoland, where he remained until the garrison was removed. While there, he married Rosanne Dutton, daughter of the British consul at Cuxhaven, Germany.

Platt decided to settle in New South Wales, intending to erect a sawmill to be worked by horse power. He took a mill out with him in the *Providence* and arrived in January 1822 with a letter of introduction to Governor Brisbane and one from John Macarthur junior to his father. Platt received a grant of 2000 acres on the Hunter River in August 1822, one of the first made in the Newcastle district. He was the first of the original grantees to settle on his estate, which he named Iron Bark Hill. There he erected a homestead and windmill. He had hoped to export sawn wood to England, having been encouraged by the dealers in fancy woods there, but no evidence survives that he succeeded in doing so. He infringed the Australian Agricultural Co.'s monopoly by mining coal and shipping it on barges.

His affairs generally did not prosper. He suffered from chronic asthma. In 1831 his homestead was burnt down and two of his sons died in the fire. He built a new homestead on the road to Maitland, and tried to sell the estate but it needed development and he could not afford to make it profitable. His financial worries and concern for his family ended when he died in 1836, aged 54. He was held in much esteem in the district and was buried on 21 May in Christ Church cemetery. His wife also died that year and was buried on 22 October; their two remaining sons and five daughters were brought up by Lieutenant Close [q.v.], whose son Edward Charles later married Louisa Slade Platt. William Thompson Platt married a daughter of Dr George Brooks; her dowry was the area of land later known as Plattsburg. In 1838 Iron Bark Hill was sold to the Australian Agricultural Co.

W. J. Goold, 'John Laurio Platt', Newcastle and Hunter District Hist Soc, *Procs*, 3 (1949); *Sydney Gazette*, 11 Jan 1822; J. A. Braye, *History of Waratah* (ML); MS cat under Platt (ML).   VIVIENNE PARSONS

PLUNKETT, JOHN HUBERT (1802-1869), lawyer and politician, was born the younger of twins in June 1802 at Mount Plunkett, County Roscommon, Ireland. His family, which had aristocratic connexions, had kept some of its estates intact in 1703-78 and was thus well placed to take advantage of the relaxation of the penal laws against Catholics. John entered Trinity College, Dublin, in November 1819 (B.A., 1824), was called to the Irish Bar in 1826 and later to the English Bar. He won distinction and popularity on the Connaught circuit in 1826-32. Daniel O'Connell gave Plunkett the credit for the success of his candidates in Connaught at the 1830 general election which put the Whigs in power. Plunkett's reward was the solicitor-generalship of New South Wales at a salary of £800. He was the first Catholic appointed to high civil office in the colony, though R. Therry's [q.v.] appointment to a magistracy antedated his by three years. Plunkett arrived in Sydney with his wife and sister and four female servants in the *Southworth* in June 1832. Also in the ship was Rev. John McEncroe [q.v.].

John Kinchela [q.v.], the attorney-general, was deaf and Plunkett had to perform many of his duties. Thus from 1 August to 5 November 1833 he appeared for the attorney-general during the criminal session, conducting ninety-one cases and obtaining sixty-four convictions. In 1835 he published *The Australian Magistrate*, the first Australian practice book of its kind. It had great importance in effecting uniformity in the procedure of the inferior courts. In 1840 a second and revised edition was published by James Tegg [q.v.]. When Kinchela retired in February 1836 Plunkett was appointed attorney-general. He was given a double load, some said in hope that he would resign. As a Crown law officer he was largely responsible for the technical legal form and any technical legal defects of the legislation, which in these crucial years in New South Wales established the equality of all men before the law. Profound personal conviction went into his draftsmanship, beginning with the Magistrate's Act, which abolished summary punishment, the administration of justice in private houses, and the excessive use of the lash. Jury rights were first experimentally extended to emancipists at his instance. Ostentatiously he extended the protection of the law to convicts and assigned servants, and successfully used the Mudie [q.v.] case to argue the abolition of convict assignment. According to the *Sydney Morning Herald*, 'He exercised important influence on general legislation, and we believe that every measure tending to equalise the social conditions and promote civil and religious liberty amidst the various, and often hostile, elements of this Colony has either been framed or supported by him'. After the Myall Creek massacre in June 1838 he extended the same protection, with the same ostentation, to the Aboriginals, when he secured the condemnation to death of seven white men for the murder of a native. At the first trial Plunkett was defeated on a technical point: because a whole tribe had been massacred the remains of the Aboriginal in question could not be identified with sufficient certainty. Undeterred Plunkett brought forward a fresh charge and won his case. The action ensured his reputation for austere impartiality. Hence he was able to combine the offices of solicitor-general and attorney-general, engrossing those of grand jury and public prosecutor.

To judge from his later public utterances Plunkett considered the Church Act of 1836 the most important single achievement of his public career. It definitely disestablished the Church of England and established legal equality between Anglicans, Catholics and Presbyterians; its provisions were later extended to Methodists, and Plunkett himself would gladly have included Jews and Independents. Plunkett was the first president of the board set up to administer this Act in 1839. Like Governor Bourke he had wished to supplement the ecclesiastical provisions of the Act by the introduction of the Irish National system in schools, under which children of all religious bodies combined for secular education but separated for religious instruction. In Plunkett's mind, however, 'combined secular education' included the truths of natural religion, God, the after-life, and the Ten Commandments. The opposition of Catholic, Anglican and Noncomformist authorities, including McEncroe, though far from unanimous, sufficed to defeat this measure at the time. But in 1844 Plunkett supported the Lowe [q.v.] committee, of which he was a member, in advocating the National system, and when it came into force in 1848 Plunkett became the first chairman of the board.

From late 1841 to August 1843 Plunkett had been granted leave to attend to family affairs in Ireland. It is not possible to say exactly what contribution Plunkett made in England during the drafting, largely supervised by Stanley, of the 1842 Act for adding elected representatives to the Legislative Council of New South Wales. In 1837 he had, however, piloted the Market Commissioners' Act through the old council, establishing the first representative body in New South Wales, and within the limits of his office had been prominent in advocating extension of the franchise to include emancipists when the municipal council was incorporated in Sydney. His claim to have argued strongly with Stanley in favour of a wide franchise in 1842 is therefore credible. On his return he resumed duty as attorney-general, but not as solicitor-general, and in 1843-51 was one of the twelve official nominees in the newly-constituted council. But Plunkett was always a lawyer first. Although he preferred not to be elevated to the Supreme Court bench on uncertain terms when Judge Burton [q.v.] went on leave in 1837 he was an applicant for appointment as chief justice in October 1844. The post went temporarily to Alfred Stephen, who wrote to Governor Gipps expressing high regard for Plunkett and trusting that their rivalry would not 'disturb the friendly feelings between us . . . [as Plunkett] has many claims on . . . Government and country for . . . long, arduous and most faithful discharge of duty'.

Plunkett carried on as attorney-general in a political hurly-burly to which he was temperamentally unsuited, for he lacked eloquence, flexibility, and capacity for rapid decision. The reputation for genial sociability which he had brought from Ireland did not sit easily on him in the colonies, except with a few intimate friends, and he found himself increasingly isolated. He was at odds with many fellow-Catholics, including McEncroe and Archbishop Polding [q.v.], because of his views on education. The old O'Connellite could give only half-hearted support to the Catholic Association formed to promote church schools in 1851, and in 1853 he engaged in acrimonious public controversy with McEncroe on the education issue. He alienated extreme Protestant opinion, as represented or manipulated by J. D. Lang [q.v.], by the firm backing he gave to Caroline Chisholm [q.v.]. In the disputes on land tenure and squatting he fell foul of the anti-squatter party because he advised the governor that the crown had no power to break in upon licences already in operation and that the law did not permit the sale of licensable land once a licence had been applied for. Both Victorian and English legal opinion later backed him on these questions, and it was he who found a loophole for the executive in the provisions for reserving from lease, or resuming from lease, lands required for public use. But he also antagonized many of the squatter party by his opposition to any resumption of transportation. From 1843 to 1856 he was a member of the Executive Council, a key figure from the dawn of representative government until the granting of responsible government because of his unique experience of the law of the colony. His personal touch was most apparent in his stringent liquor legislation of 1856 and in the marriage bill of 1855 giving church weddings civil status. In 1849 he sat on the Wentworth [q.v.] committee to establish a university, and became a member of its first Senate. He made one crucial political mistake. Elected in 1852 to the drafting committee for the colony's new Constitution, he supported Wentworth's proposal for an hereditary upper house, and treated his critics with stubborn hauteur. The credit he earned by his other work on the Constitution was denied him because of this eccentricity.

In 1856 Plunkett retired from office on a pension of £1200. His impartial administration over a quarter of a century had won him widespread appreciation, and he decided to seek election to the first Legislative Assembly under responsible government. His political campaign leaned heavily on Irish national sentiment. Here he felt on strong ground, for each year when chairing the St Patrick's Day dinner, he always managed to break through his normal reserve. But against the background of the Crimean War Irish nationalism was an uncertain recommendation, and he was defeated for Sydney by a team led by Henry Parkes and Charles Cowper, who used Plunkett's Catholicism against him without scruple. He eventually won the country seat of Argyle, but felt unable to act as attorney-general under Cowper, since only the shortage of lawyers had prompted the invitation. In 1857-58 he was president of the Legislative Council.

In February 1858 Cowper, as premier, dismissed Plunkett from the presidency of the National Schools Board. It was a complex dispute, with personal and political overtones as well as important constitutional aspects on the relative powers of the reformed Council and of the board as a body corporate established by an Act of the superseded Legislative Council. Cowper correctly asserted the powers of the government generally, but acted vindictively in using the board's decision to publish its correspondence in the press as his reason for dismissing Plunkett. Public opinion strongly backed Plunkett, and the Legislative Assembly voted for him, but to no avail. As a result Plunkett resigned the presidency of the Legislative Council and all his many public offices. He now espoused the popular side in politics and used its methods. Defeated by the Parkes 'bunch' in 1856, in 1858 he 'bunched' himself with D. H. Deniehy for the electorate of Sydney. Only Plunkett won election. He sat in the Legislative Assembly from September 1858 into 1860, taking a democratic position on the land question, adult male suffrage, and the secret ballot, but did not resume his post on the National Schools Board or become attorney-general when invited in December 1859. Governor Young later appointed him to the Legislative Council and he held office in the ministry of James Martin in 1863-65. In 1865 at Young's instance he accepted the attorney-generalship in Cowper's cabinet and precipitated the fall of the ministry when he resigned from it. His health now required frequent absence from the council, and he eventually settled in Melbourne, coming to Sydney only for the parliamentary sessions.

Plunkett was an important leader of Catholic opinion in the colony. He publicly defended Polding when the archbishop left Sydney in 1854 and chaired the welcome gathering when he returned in 1856. He took the leading role in establishing St Vincent's Hospital, Potts Point, under the management of the Irish Sisters of Charity. He had been a generous benefactor to the sisters since they arrived in 1839. As treasurer of St Vincent's he consistently used his position to insist on the non-denominational character of the hospital. In 1858 he criticized the archbishop's control of the hospital's affairs which had contributed to the resignation of the head nun, Sister de Lacy, and thus joined the majority of prominent laymen who had been objecting for some time to the administration of the archdiocese. These protests resulted in Rome's recall of the vicar-general, H. G. Gregory [q.v.], in 1861. Plunkett became reconciled to Polding before 1869 when he acted as lay secretary to the second Provincial Synod in Melbourne. Meanwhile his attitude towards denominational schools had changed and prevented him from accepting William Forster's invitation to resume his seat on

the National Schools Board. The stand of
the Irish bishops against the National system was confirmed by the Australian
bishops late in 1862, and in the Legislative
Council Plunkett endorsed their action.

In his last years Plunkett devoted more
time to his lifelong recreation, the violin
and Irish folk music; on this subject he
gave many public addresses, which he
illustrated himself. He had become a Q.C,
and in 1863 published *On the Evidence of
Accomplices*. He was elected a founding
fellow of St John's College in June 1858,
and was vice-chancellor of the University
of Sydney in 1865-67. He died on 9 May
1869 in East Melbourne. His remains were
taken to Sydney and buried in the old
Devonshire Street cemetery, beside those
of Archpriest Therry [q.v.] and Archdeacon McEncroe. His widow survived him by
many years. They had no children, but
various kinsmen settled in Australia, including his twin brother.

A. Halloran, 'Some early legal celebrities',
JRAHS, 10 (1924); MS cat under Plunkett
(ML).   T. L. SUTTOR

POLDING, JOHN BEDE (1794-1877),
Catholic archbishop, was born on 18
October 1794 at Liverpool, England. His
father was of Dutch descent and his
mother came from the Brewer family, re-
cusants since the sixteenth century. His
family name was also spelt Poulden or
Polten. His parents died and at 8 he was
placed in the care of his uncle, Father
Bede Brewer, president-general of the
English Benedictine Congregation. Polding
was first taught by the Benedictine nuns
of the Convent of Our Lady of Consola-
tion of Cambray, who as refugees from
revolutionary France were located at
Much Woolton, near Liverpool. At 11 he
was sent to St Gregory's Benedictine College, at Acton Burnell, near Shrewsbury,
Shropshire. On 15 July 1810 Polding was
admitted to the religious community, taking the name of Bede. He received minor
orders in 1813 from Bishop Milner at
Wolverhampton, was ordained priest by
Bishop Poynter at Old Hall College on 4
March 1819, and on the 21st sang his
first mass at Downside.

Meanwhile he had undergone the rigorous juniorate of the Benedictines, excel-
ling in philosophy and theology. In 1814
the community transferred to St Gregory's
Monastery, Downside, where Polding remained for twenty years, filling various
offices in the school and monastery, and
in 1826-34 serving as secretary to the
president-general of the Benedictine Congregation. As prefect, Polding endeared

himself to the boys, one of whom was
to recall his prowess as a teacher of
drama, his patriotism, and his sympathy
for the Irish; 'though a thorough Lancashire man, he always identified himself
with Irish boys in their interest for their
country and her wrongs'. As became a
Lancashire man Polding also had a great
interest and some skill in cricket. His boyhood interest in the religious plight of
New South Wales took firmer shape when
he became novice-master in 1823.

The virtual absence of any Catholic
mission in Australia before 1818 reflected
the legal disabilities of Catholics in Britain
and the difficult position of Ireland within
the empire. Nearly all the Catholic convicts transported to New South Wales
were Irish; among them were three priests,
James Harold, James Dixon, and Peter
O'Neil [qq.v.], but they failed to found
an enduring mission. After 1815 policies
towards Catholics gradually became more
tolerant and the English Benedictines, who
had prospered moderately since their re-
establishment, were in a strategic position
to take advantage of the change. The
British government retained misgivings
about Irish Catholics, but acquired a
grudging appreciation of the English attributes of the Benedictines, dispositions
that were to play an important part in
Polding's career in Australia. Meanwhile
the predominant Irish interest in the colony
was illustrated in 1817 in the abortive
attempt of J. F. O'Flynn [q.v.] to establish himself as prefect-apostolic of New
Holland with the approval of Rome's Congregation for the Propagation of the Faith
(Propaganda). This case helped to clarify
the need for Propaganda to adjust its
policies to the novel post-1815 international
situation, especially in colonial areas. As
a result the vicar-apostolic of London,
rather than the Irish bishops, became the
link between Rome and the British government in relation to Australian affairs. The
O'Flynn case also impressed the government with the need for Catholic chaplains
in the colony. The formal colonial influence of the English Benedictines was accentuated in 1818 when the Cape of Good
Hope was erected by Papal Brief into a
vicariate and entrusted to them. In 1819
Polding's cousin, Bishop Edward Bede
Slater, was appointed vicar-apostolic with
jurisdiction over Mauritius, Madagascar,
the Cape, New Holland and Van Diemen's Land.

The Benedictines' inability to spare men
for all these missions was to remain a
continual check on their work in Australia.
In 1819 the government decided to add
two Catholic chaplains to the public

officers of New South Wales and two Irish volunteers, J. J. Therry and Philip Conolly [qq.v.], were accepted by Slater and appointed by Bathurst, with a salary of £100 each. Therry's immense energy, tactlessness, and missionary zeal led to his prominent association with groups opposed to official policies, to the withdrawal of his salary in 1826, and to the hardening of feeling against Irish priests both by the British government and the English Catholic authorities. In the 1830s the number of Irish Catholics in the colony continued to rise, though mainly they were convicts and working class people. After Catholic emancipation in 1829, however, a trickle of educated and politically significant Irish migrated to Sydney, notably Roger Therry and J. H. Plunkett [qq.v.], both of whom were appointed to high legal offices. John McEncroe [q.v.] accompanied Plunkett as an official chaplain, highly recommended by Archbishop Murray of Dublin.

In 1832 the Benedictine William Morris, who had replaced Slater as vicar-apostolic, appointed W. B. Ullathorne [q.v.] as his vicar-general in New South Wales, with British government approval. Ullathorne arrived, capably put the affairs of the church in order with McEncroe's help, and soon saw the need for episcopal control in Sydney. His representations to Rome and England had been anticipated in 1832 by McEncroe's recommendation to Archbishop Murray: 'There are 16,000 or 18,000 Catholics in this colony, not one half of whom hardly ever see a Priest . . . The Holy See should provide this place with a Bishop'. Rome responded to the Irish and English pressure by detaching Australia from the Mauritius vicariate. Negotiations were carried out with the vicar-apostolic of London rather than with the archbishop of Dublin, and the government was informed of each step. By Papal Briefs in 1834 Polding was appointed bishop of Hiero-Caesarea *in partibus infidelium* and vicar-apostolic of New Holland, Van Diemen's Land and the adjoining islands. He had declined earlier appointments for Mauritius and Madras but he accepted the Australian office on 14 June. Two weeks later in his private chapel Bishop Bramston, the vicar-apostolic of London, assisted by Bishops Griffiths and Rouchouze, consecrated Polding. On 20 February 1835 Governor Bourke was notified of the appointment and advised that 'it is very desirable that Dr Polding should be enabled to exercise a salutary influence over the Roman Catholic chaplains'. On 6 August Polding and his party arrived at Hobart Town, where he left a

priest and a student; and on 13 September at Sydney, with one priest, Father Corcoran, and five students, three of whom were Benedictines, including H. G. Gregory [q.v.]. In that month Polding's stipend was increased from £150 to £500.

New South Wales, although still formally a penal colony with convicts about 38 per cent of its total population of 71,662, was experiencing the effects of parliamentary reform in Britain. Bourke, a Whig appointee, gave practical form to the new order with able assistance from J. H. Plunkett. The British government, aware of the advantages of religion for an orderly society, was now prepared to allow other denominations to share in state aid which hitherto had been monopolized by the Church of England in New South Wales. Bourke's Church Act of 1836 gave effect to this new policy, much to the annoyance of W. G. Broughton [q.v.], the Anglican bishop, though Polding quickly adapted himself to the liberal changes of Bourke. He was now in middle age and had come from the upper ranks of English Catholic society. He belonged to an ancient order lately re-established in England after centuries of banishment but still uncertain of its role in English society, as were Catholics generally. Although his innate sympathy for the Irish was naturally accentuated by their common bond of religion, he nevertheless regarded them with at least a minimum of the disquiet felt by nearly all Englishmen of his class irrespective of creed. Though he did not owe his position to the British government, he had its approval and was paid from public funds. These were factors that had a pervasive influence on his long episcopate in New South Wales.

Polding was a man of deep and abiding sanctity, generous and warm-hearted though not without some reserve, and a born missioner who scorned every personal hardship to bring religion to his widely-scattered and underprivileged flock. His vicariate included the whole of Australia and in time he visited nearly all its major centres. In 1839 the *Weekly Orthodox Journal* quoted a letter from Sydney: 'His labors are incessant, his zeal unbounded, Protestants as well as Catholics revere him as a saint'.

On reaching Sydney Polding had seen the need for an intensive mission to the convicts and arranged with Bourke for all Catholics among the new-comers, about one-third and mostly Irish, to be put in his charge for a few days. Ullathorne later recorded that Polding took the leading part in instructing and giving the Sacraments to them; 'it was a touching sight', he wrote, 'to see the Bishop with one of his criminals kneeling by his side in the sanctuary, and by word and action, instructing all through one how to make their confessions, or how to receive the Holy Communion'. By 1841 some seven thousand convicts had undertaken these exercises. This example of pastoral care set an enlivening tone that was never absent from Polding's episcopate, even in times of conflict with members of his flock, clerical and lay.

With capable assistance from Ullathorne, Polding established a firm administration. He consecrated St Mary's as his cathedral and surveyed the need for more church buildings. He successfully directed J. J. Therry's energy into the Campbelltown area, and built up other centres at Parramatta, Windsor, Maitland and Wollongong. He also became involved in the control of schools; by 1836 he had thirteen primary schools, seven for boys, six for girls, all with government support, and had begun a steady programme to build and staff others. They never became as numerous or efficient as he wished and always provoked controversy of some kind, for colonial society was then peculiarly fluid, with settlement expanding and free immigration increasing. In consolidating his church Polding found his administrative duties a general trial and a restriction on his missionary work; more and more he came to rely on others for planning policy and organization, and gave much thought to starting an Australian Benedictine monastery that would train priests and provide culture and learning to a frontier society.

In 1836-38 Ullathorne went to Europe on a recruiting mission. He obtained only one Englishman out of fifteen priests and religious recruits. But he did win Rome's approval for Polding's monastery. Meanwhile Polding's zeal had aroused the Protestants, especially Broughton and the judges, W. Burton and J. W. Willis [qq.v.]; this opposition decided him to approach Rome to have the Australian mission reorganized, as suggested by Ullathorne especially, and W. A. Duncan [q.v], editor of the Catholic Australasian Chronicle. Polding was also anxious to obtain new priests, and to pay his ad limina visit to the Pope. The British government granted him leave and on 16 November 1840 he left Sydney with Ullathorne and Gregory.

The major event of his journey was Rome's approval on 5 April 1842 for the establishment of an Australian hierarchy. Sydney was made a metropolitan and archiepiscopal see; his later proposal that it be restricted to Benedictines was not approved. Adelaide and Hobart were separated from the original vicariate and made episcopal sees. Polding retained his status as vicar-apostolic and on 9 April was elevated to the archbishopric, with the title of 'Archbishop of Sydney and Metropolitan of Australia, Van Diemen's Land, and the Gambier Islands, etc.'. The British government gave tacit approval; before his departure Polding was received at the Colonial Office by Lord Stanley and given 'a grand dinner' by the earl of Derby. Polding's party of nineteen included four priests of the Passionist Order, who were to establish a mission to the Aboriginals, and three Christian Brothers. They reached Sydney on 9 March 1843. Two weeks later Broughton wrote to London protesting against Polding's assumption of the title of archbishop, but Stanley declined to discuss it. In 1847 Earl Grey advised Governor FitzRoy that since Irish archbishops and bishops could be addressed as 'Your Grace' or 'Your Lordship', colonial Catholic prelates should be similarly recognized.

Polding pursued tenaciously his idea of making his archdiocese Benedictine, with the priests and religious bound to him as superior of their order as well as archbishop. On 19 October 1843 he wrote, 'My residence has become a monastery . . . my desire is to establish two priests and a lay brother in each mission . . . Of course the Archbishop will be always the principal Superior. Thus the grievous inconveniences which have sometimes occurred from the meeting of two orders of clergy will be avoided'. This optimistic vision contrasted sharply with Ullathorne's realistic assessment in 1838 that Benedictinism had little hope in Australia, for Polding virtually ignored not only the increasing number of Irish secular clergy and Catholic population, but also the changing political and social conditions of the colony now that the convict transportation had ended. With a strong note of 'self-improvement' prevailing among the 'lower orders', politics had become the interest and prop of the many as well as the vocation of the few. The Irish, most of them Catholics, joined in with gusto, often stimulated by memories of Daniel O'Connell or the Young Ireland movement. Several radical newspapers reflected the ferment, among them Duncan's Weekly Register. Polding's English Benedictinism idea could hardly survive in these circumstances. It was part of the 'old' style Benedictinism, romantic and alien to a society conscious of its thrusting egalitarianism. But Polding held to his ideal against all portents and odds, including recruitment difficulties in New South Wales and England and the reform movement within English Benedictinism.

At the practical level Polding's episcopate continued auspiciously. On 8 September 1844 he consecrated Francis Murphy [q.v.] bishop of Adelaide, the first episcopal consecration in Australia, and in October he presided at the first Catholic Provincial Synod held in Australia, attended by Bishop Willson [q.v.] of Hobart, Murphy and senior priests from New South Wales, Van Diemen's Land, South Australia, the Port Phillip and Moreton Bay Districts, and Norfolk Island. Under Polding the Benedictine Monastery had some success; St Mary's was recognized as a monastic cathedral, and for about three years the monks lived the complete regular life, with full choral recitation of the Divine office at the canonical hours. But the pressure of his missionary work increased his reliance on Gregory who, as vicar-general and prior (later abbot) of the monastery, found difficulty in doing justice to both positions and was temperamentally unsuited for either. With ill discipline gradually spreading among the monks, Benedictinism appeared to breed inefficiency in archdiocesan affairs.

The Catholic laity displayed a talent for politics in the new democratic era ushered in by the part-elective Legislative Council in 1843: but they were not alone in this. As a religious minority suspected of a subversive bias towards the empire, they found certain prejudices operating powerfully against them and did not meet this opposition with a united front. The Catholic Church was anything but a political monolith during Polding's rule. One divisive issue was in Van Diemen's Land, where Willson for fourteen years held J. J. Therry personally responsible for a church debt of £3300. In 1844 Polding and McEncroe went to Hobart but failed to settle the matter. Next year Therry arrived in Sydney in hope of raising funds to pay the debt. Polding wrote to London about this visit: 'the people here are beginning to talk and canvass this unfortunate business; parties are again forming which we had well-nigh extinguished. The utmost prudence is required to steer aright. If I am kind to Therry, Dr. Willson will misinterpret it as upholding him in opposition; if I am not, all my people will lose confidence in me'. The parties thus formed were neither firm nor permanent, but the incident reflected a general lay instability which was related as much to general colonial politics as to ecclesiastical policy. The latter influence stemmed from Polding's enthusiastic but extemporized Benedictine experiment, now coming to be resented by increasing numbers of clergy and laity as promotions and full respect were denied the one, and outlying missionary service became more difficult for the other. A more discerning type of criticism could also be noted, well illustrated by Duncan, a complex Scot, erudite and cantankerous. Although loyal to Polding, he feared that the archbishop's policy might result in a completely subservient and inarticulate laity. By 1846 when he left Sydney for Moreton Bay, he had shown that the growing opposition to Polding was by no means wholly Irish. J. K. Heydon [q.v.], an English convert, began to press this same point after 1848.

Colonial politics inevitably overlapped religion. The Presbyterian, J. D. Lang [q.v.], railed against the Pope as 'the man of sin' and claimed to perceive in Caroline Chisholm's [q.v.] humane and ecumenical immigration work a Popish plot to take over Australia. Polding could be sure of Catholic and much Protestant support against such tirades, but not on 'the question of questions', as Lang aptly described education. Its deficiencies were forcibly driven home in 1844 by the report of a select committee: 'There are about 25,676 children between the ages of 4 and 14 years; of these only 7,642 receive instruction in public schools, and 4,865 in private schools, leaving about 13,000 children who, as far as your Committee know, are receiving no education at all. The expense of Public Education is about £1 per head; an enormous rate after every allowance has been made for the necessary dispersion of the inhabitants . . . a far greater proportion of the evil has arisen from the strictly denominational character of the private schools'. Polding had given evidence to the committee, and had crystallized the Catholic dilemma when he agreed with the chairman that, while salvation was man's fundamental objective, the ability to read and write contributed greatly to its attainment. The growing demands of salvation, efficiency and economy were to remain as basic governors of Catholic education policy. The problems they thrust up were deep and wide socially and politically, and mocked the overlapping Catholic divisions of minority Benedictines versus majority seculars, Irish versus English, and ex-convict versus free. Duncan and Plunkett favoured a National scheme of education as the most balanced solution; Polding and McEncroe favoured a denominational scheme. But other Catholics did not divide as laity versus clergy on this issue or any other.

Public opinion, despite Polding and Broughton, came slowly but firmly to support a National scheme.

With some relief Polding decided to visit Europe again. He needed a coadjutor bishop, more Englishmen for his monastery, and Benedictine nuns to complement the structure of his order. Another pressing need was to have Rome decide on the disagreement between himself and Bishop Willson of Hobart. Polding left Sydney on 16 February 1846 leaving Gregory, his vicar-general, to administer the archdiocese. For his coadjutor Polding hoped to recruit Ullathorne, but arrived in London to find that he had already accepted a mitre. Polding appealed widely for financial support for his seminary, stressing his goal of training native-born Benedictines. In a circular he stated that he had twenty-five clergy in his diocese, which altogether included 60,000 Catholics, 14,000 of them in Sydney. He succeeded in obtaining a group of Benedictine nuns from the Stanbrook convent. In Rome he failed to have his differences with Willson resolved, but won approval for the establishment of Melbourne as a separate see, and for a coadjutor bishop for himself. On 24 September 1847 Charles Henry Davis [q.v.] of the Downside Benedictines was appointed bishop of Maitland, but his duties were to be confined to helping the archbishop. Polding returned to Sydney on 6 February 1848. He brought with him two young English Benedictines, but within fifteen months they were sent back to England because, as Polding wrote, they 'disturbed almost to destruction the peace and well-being of my infant community'.

In Polding's absence Gregory in his high-handed and well-meaning way had eroded the prestige of Benedictinism. In order to raise funds to help to Benedictinize the archdiocese, he took up a plan, abortive and provocative, to tax the salaries paid by the government to Catholic chaplains. He tried to persuade the Christian Brothers and the Sisters of Charity to detach themselves from their congregations and to adopt either a form of Benedictine rule or the status of a diocesan organization. Both orders refused, the Christian Brothers returning to Ireland, and most of the Sisters of Charity going to Hobart in June 1847. These mistakes, for which Gregory was not rebuked by Polding, reflected the archbishop's deepening dependence on his vicar-general, and the indigence of his educational policy. The results were clear in the early 1870s when only about five schools staffed by religious orders were left in Sydney. Benedictinism neither produced a crop of eminent theologians in New South Wales nor encouraged the logical teachers of Catholic children, the teaching orders of sisters and brothers, to set down roots in the archdiocese. Polding was thus handicapped in promoting Catholic primary schools despite his objections to the religiously neutral National system. Although he encouraged the Benedictine nuns at Subiaco near Parramatta to establish a convent that would provide 'the better, that is, the richer classes of society with the means of education', its struggle for survival was as arduous as that of St Mary's Benedictine College, Lyndhurst, which was open for boys in 1852-77. Neither school fitted harmoniously into a society excited by gold discoveries and the growth of democratic government, and neither achieved Polding's élite designs. In 1850 the archbishop added his weight to the successful campaign against the proposal to exclude clergymen from the senate of the proposed University of Sydney. Polding was a member of the senate in 1856-77, and contributed considerably to the foundation of St John's College within the university in 1857-58 to counterbalance the contemporary 'conspiracy against [Christian] truth'.

By 1850 Polding's dream of Benedictinizing his archdiocese was fading. The experiment had brought him pain and accentuated dissension among his flock, but it was by no means the only cause. Dissension had been endemic since the colony's foundation in 1788 and the Catholics were no exception to the rule of strife. The quickening approach of responsible government gave new forms to colonial discord, but there were also unifying bonds in the colony and among the Catholics. Polding exemplified Catholic unity amidst the conflict; his sanctity and missionary journeys, continued at great strain and no small risk to himself as he aged, inspired a devotion to him personally, softened ill-feeling and obtruded the realities of Christian life irrevocably before all men. His relationship with McEncroe reflected the whole complex situation. The upper-class Englishman and the tough-minded Irishman understood one another; mutual affection and respect were the keynotes of their association, despite serious differences of opinion, and McEncroe's almost inspired capacity of correct analysis. So the progress of the Catholic Church in New South Wales, revealed in Gregory's 1851 report to Rome, points to the fundamental success of Polding in the important things, as far as statistics could reflect them: there were thirty-five priests, ministering to about 55,000 people, about half of them Irish born and most of the rest of Irish descent, in thirty-three parishes and thirty churches; in addition there were about fifty monks, nuns and religious students. The essential part of the remainder of Polding's episcopate from 1850 to 1877 was the consolidation of this successful ministry, yet marked by the conflict inherent in the movement that aimed at the appointment of Irish bishops to newly-erected country sees, the replacement of an English archbishop by an Irishman and the consequent attainment of harmony in a human situation vital to religion and all else, as the general English ascendancy declined.

This development demanded the end of the concept of a Benedictine abbey-diocese. The end came naturally from inner contradictions and social incompatibility, clear enough before 1850. While Gregory was in Europe in 1850-53 Davis took over the monastery. His efficiency and charitableness contrasted with Gregory's autocratic control, and for a time he seemed likely to restore at least tranquillity, even though he too realized, as he wrote in August 1850, that it would be 'some years before we shall be able to supply the wants of the mission from the monastery'. But the coadjutor's chronic ill health (he died in 1854) and Gregory's return in 1853 precipitated a climax. Several monks, headed by Patrick S. Farelly and J. Sheridan Moore, petitioned Rome to be allowed to leave the order to become secular priests. Their submission traversed the deficiencies of Benedictinism in New South Wales; they saw no hope of a native-born clergy, for none had yet been ordained, and claimed that monastic discipline created popular opposition and conflicted with missionary work. Above all, they complained about Gregory, his severity, his vindictiveness, his influence over Polding. In 1854 Rome decided that the abbey-diocese must go. Polding was in Rome to receive the decision. He had left Sydney abruptly with Gregory in March and had had a painful audience with Pius IX, at which Gregory appeared unexpectedly and broke down. In the upshot the archbishop resigned his see, but was appeased by the Pope. In January 1856 Polding and Gregory returned to Sydney. McEncroe had administered the archdiocese in their absence. Next year the Benedictine community was transferred from the cathedral to Lyndhurst, to be finally wound up in 1877.

In March 1851 McEncroe, with a clear realization of the Church's colonial needs, had written to Bishop Goold of Melbourne, seeking his help in Rome for a petition he was about to send to the Pope: 'It is obvious that the "Infant" Benedictine Monastery *cannot* [supply priests for the colony]. Irish students or priests will *not* come. In this state, thousands must perish. I suggest that two new Dioceses be formed . . . both to be placed under "Irish" Bishops who will soon get subjects from Ireland, the only country that can spare them'. Rome had been clearly impressed but, although no immediate steps were taken, events in Sydney together with more action by McEncroe, eventually contributed to the decisions that brought greater efficiency and harmony to the Catholic Church in New South Wales. McEncroe did not attempt to hide his work. He told Polding that he had written to Rome and emphasized that the great immigration after the gold discoveries demanded additional priests; 'otherwise the Catholic faith and Christian morals of the colony will be smothered in this cloud of gold dust'; and that these priests ought to be Irish.

Catholic laymen were inevitably involved in these vital adjustments. McEncroe had founded the *Freeman's Journal* in 1850. It played an essential part in the lively decisions and happenings affecting the Catholics in the following decade. McEncroe himself acted equivocally towards the *Journal*, even after he relinquished control to Heydon in 1857. Effectively if not harmoniously the *Journal* gathered together all the dissident elements: those who sought greater lay influence in church affairs, those who opposed the Benedictines or the English, and those who were simply disaffected. This mixed opposition was by no means entirely Irish. Duncan, for example, in 1857-58, made powerful criticisms of Polding and his administration, providing unmistakable evidence that beneath the undignified and uncharitable clamour lay a hard core of serious and necessary censure. However, the archbishop saw the criticism as a danger to discipline as well as to doctrine and on 11 June 1858, with the support of Goold and Willson, issued the salutary *Monitum Pastorale*, which pronounced against public discussion by the laity of matters properly belonging to church authorities. This checked the pressure but did not stop it, for clerics as well as laity were indulging in public criticisms.

On 26 July 1858 a number of laity met to accept Polding's invitation to systematize their grievances and submit them to him through J. J. Therry. A committee of seven prominent laymen was appointed. Their statement stressed the role of the laity in parish administration, the need for equality of secular and regular clergy and for competent religious and lay teachers. Polding was not responsive to it or to an appeal from a conference of secular clergy who cautiously sought equality in promotions with the Benedictines. But the force of change gathered momentum. The inevitable crisis was precipitated by the hapless Gregory, who appointed a Protestant to replace Plunkett on the Parramatta Catholic Orphanage Board. The appointment was quickly cancelled, but the outcry provided the occasion for a large meeting at the Victoria Theatre on 26 February 1859, at which all the resentments against Polding's policy found expression, with Gregory as the focal point. Polding acted firmly by demanding that the leaders of the meeting repudiate their behaviour or face excommunication. The case went on appeal to Rome. An anticlimax followed, but a vital one to Polding. In May 1859 it was reported that Sister de Lacy, the Irish head of St Vincent's Hospital, was returning to Ireland because Gregory, after the removal of copies of the authorized version of the Bible used by Protestant patients, had allegedly tried to discipline her in such a way that she resigned. She was supported by Plunkett in Sydney, and later by Archbishop Cullen in Dublin. Polding again backed Gregory; but he had shaken the confidence of most of his prominent laymen and at least some of the most influential bishops in Ireland.

Polding's vision of the archdiocese and his administration were now virtually shattered. His comments on the appeal of the leaders of the Victoria Theatre meeting were inaccurate in some details and tinged generally with an unwonted lack of charity. Yet the comments illuminated some of the essential Polding: his aristocratic aloofness and injudicious reliance on Gregory. The whole dispute had been paralleled by contemporary constitutional changes that substantially reduced British control in the colony. McEncroe inexorably gave Catholics the necessary impetus for change. In November 1858 he left for Europe. In Dublin he requested the bishops of Ireland to send priests and religious teachers to Australia and in Rome he won the personal interest of Cullen in his search for bishops and priests. In 1861 Rome's recall of Gregory without discussion with Polding showed clearly the extent of McEncroe's influence and the new trend of policy, with its doubts about the 'old' Benedictinism.

Polding had taken a leisurely view of the need for new sees in New South Wales. He was not opposed to them, rather he saw them gradually evolving and filling with bishops, preferably English Benedictines. As metropolitan of Australia he believed himself responsible for guaranteeing to the British government 'the loyalty and good feeling' of any bishop appointed in the province. In 1859 he wrote to Goold, who was in Rome, naming his choices for the proposed sees in the colony. However, when the four new dioceses of Maitland (hitherto titular), Goulburn, Bathurst and Armidale were erected in the 1860s, an Irish bishop was appointed to each.

These rebuffs had continued from Polding's visit to Rome in 1854. Though personally disheartening to him, they were related to the dynamic changes in colonial society since the introduction of representative government in 1843. The era of the paternal and benevolent representatives of the British government ruling by right had gone forever with the coming of responsible government in 1856. Polding belonged to that past era as his predominantly Irish flock continually reminded him. But the rebuffs were not meant to reflect on the quality of his ministry; nor could they, for the general religious progress of his archdiocese continued unabated. New forms of administration emerged but the strong bonds of affection stemming from Polding's zealous toil for his flock were strengthened by his trials. This was symbolized by his reconciliation with Plunkett, who died in 1869 soon after acting as lay secretary of the second Provincial Synod. In 1862 the New South Wales government withdrew its aid from all churches. Polding had been worried by voluntaryism; he now had full support from his flock. But he ignored the need for far-reaching changes in colonial education, and was unprepared for the Public Schools Act of 1866, which replaced the dual control of the National and Denominational Boards with a Council of Education. These alterations clearly foreshadowed the end of state aid for denominational schools, and could have been counteracted to some extent had Polding adopted a vigorous policy of recruitment of religious teachers. But he was now 72 and could not adapt himself to intensified and novel requirements in this vital field.

On 29 June 1865 St Mary's Cathedral was burned to the ground. It seemed like the final blow to Polding, but instead, it revealed to him not only the devotion of his flock, but also the respect and admiration of the colony at large, for the immediate response of Catholics to rebuild was matched by the generous support of all classes irrespective of creed. He left on his last visit to Rome on 22 November 1865; he failed to obtain a coadjutor bishop and in Ireland on a visit to Cullen was alarmed by Fenian activity. He returned to Sydney on 8 August 1867, where 'the Irish question' was playing some part in colonial politics. In October he wrote to Gregory, with whom he corresponded affectionately, that the so-called 'importation of Irish Bishops' had revived the ancient cry of 'No Popery!' Confusion was increased by a near-tragedy on 12 March 1868 when Prince Alfred was shot by 'a demented Fenian', Henry O'Farrell, at Clontarf near Sydney. The ensuing passionate excitement made Polding yearn for retirement in a monastery cell, although he was comforted by an invitation to visit the prince, who attempted sensibly to allay the bitterness.

On 6 January 1869 the temporary wooden structure at St Mary's was burnt down. Again the calamity was met with grim determination by Catholics and many others, to rebuild the cathedral, this time on a massive scale. But Polding was almost desolated; he confided to Gregory, 'I am completely bereaved, stript of all except two mitres and the stole the Pope gave me . . . I begin to consider myself a Jonah to be flung into the sea for the well-being of others'. He set out for the first Vatican Council on 9 October, but found the heat too much for him and returned from Aden.

He continued to press for a coadjutor. In 1871 he asked the Pope for an Englishman, 'because in a . . . See like this, which is the great [southern British] centre . . . and where there are such bitter animosities between the Irish and the Orange Societies, a man superior to all party spirit, and exalted by mental accomplishments and social virtues above the ordinary level, would be more acceptable, and, should difficulties arise, more conciliatory'. The British government agreed with the Pope's choice of Roger Bede Vaughan, a 'new' Benedictine, who arrived in Sydney late in 1873 as titular archbishop of Nazianus and coadjutor to the archbishop of Sydney. Polding slowly transferred the administration to the coadjutor; animated the archdiocese with a fresh spirit of dedication, and returned with renewed zeal to his missionary work, even travelling to Tasmania in January 1875. In 1874 he had the comfort of the heart-felt gratitude and devotion of Ulla-

thorne and his fellow-jubilarians, who recalled how he had inspired them at Downside, 'you pictured such missioners to us as trudging from place to place like St Paul, and carrying in a pack on the back whatever was needful for the Sacrifice and the Sacraments', and after reminding him of his teaching of mathematics, physical science and metaphysics concluded, 'the best of our teaching was the spiritual unction that flowed in happy moments from your heart to ours'. In the last stages of his fatal sickness in 1877 the compassion of the whole colony went out to him, symbolized perfectly by the tears of J. D. Lang as he left the archbishop's sick-room. Polding died at Sacred Heart Presbytery, Darlinghurst, in Sydney, on 16 March 1877. He was buried in Petersham cemetery, and his remains were transferred to St Mary's Cathedral on 17 March 1901.

HRA (1), 17-26; P. F. Moran, *History of the Catholic Church in Australasia* (Syd, 1895); H. N. Birt, *Benedictine pioneers in Australia*, 1-2 (Lond, 1911); T. L. Suttor, *Hierarchy and democracy in Australia, 1788-1870* (Melb, 1965); Gregory papers (Downside Abbey, copy Sancta Sophia College, Syd); Polding papers (Catholic Archives, Syd); M. M. Shanahan, Henry Gregory and the abbey-diocese of Sydney, 1835-1861 (M.A. thesis, Univ Syd, 1965).   BEDE NAIRN

POWELL, EDWARD (1762-1814), farmer and innkeeper, came from Lancaster, England, where he had been a farmer and fisherman. He visited New South Wales as a seaman in the *Lady Juliana* in the Second Fleet, and then returned as one of the colony's first group of free settlers. The party, which included Thomas Rose [q.v.] and was assisted by the British government after it had received urgent requests from Governor Phillip for free men, skilled labourers and farmers, sailed in the *Bellona* and reached Port Jackson on 16 January 1793. Eight days later Powell married Elizabeth Fish, a fellow passenger, who later bore him two sons and four daughters.

On 7 February Powell received the title to an 80-acre grant at Liberty Plains. Later, perhaps in the search for better soil, he moved to the Hawkesbury where by 1799 he had been appointed a constable. Hitherto an innocuous figure, in October 1799 he achieved notoriety when he was found guilty of being involved with four others in the murder of two Aboriginals, but the majority of the court thought that the case 'under all its peculiar circumstances' should be remitted to the

British government before any sentence was imposed. In January 1802 Lord Hobart recommended that they be given conditional pardons.

Meanwhile, although dismissed from the position of constable, Powell had been advancing his farming interests. By 1806 he owned 140 acres of which 32 were in cultivation, and a small quantity of livestock including two horses and two cows. Shortly before the Rum Rebellion, in which he supported Governor Bligh, he appears to have returned to the Liberty Plains district, and become an innkeeper as well as a farmer. His Halfway House, on the Parramatta Road between Sydney and Parramatta, was a landmark. In 1811 he was appointed poundkeeper for the area in which he gradually acquired additional property. He died on 19 October 1814, leaving his estate to his wife who administered it until her death in 1818. Control then passed into the hands of his son Edward, who at first let the inn and 500 acres, and then sold it to his brother-in-law, James Underwood [q.v.]. Another daughter of Edward Powell senior married Richard Siddins [q.v.].

HRA (1), 1-3; J. F. Campbell, 'Liberty Plains of the first free settlers, 1793', JRAHS, 22 (1936); Newspaper index under E. Powell (ML).   B. H. FLETCHER

POWER, ROBERT (1794-1869), military officer and surveyor-general, was born in Ireland, the second son of Edmond Power (1767-1837), sometime editor of the *Clonmel Gazette*, and his wife Ellen, née Sheehy. Two of his sisters married into the aristocracy: Marguerite (1789-1849) to Charles John Gardiner, earl of Blessington, and Ellen (1791-1845) to Charles Manners-Sutton, M.P., Viscount Canterbury. Robert was an ensign in the Leitrim Militia in September 1812 when he volunteered for service in the 91st Regiment. In 1815 he was commissioned lieutenant in the 73rd and in 1817 captain in the 20th. He resigned from the army in 1823 and became agent for the Tyrone estates. In 1829 by Blessington's will he inherited £1000 which helped him to keep 'his old reprobate of a father', his youngest sister Mary Ann, his own wife Margaret Ellen and his children. In 1837 he had to appeal for aid from Lady Blessington who sent him money and took charge of Mary Ann. Next year, through the influence of Edward Ellice, M.P., Power was appointed deputy-commissioner of crown lands and forests and deputy-surveyor-general in New Brunswick at a salary of £300. In 1840 his superior officer

resigned but Power was not appointed to the vacancy because the local inhabitants showed great jealousy of officers sent out from Britain. Since his position as deputy became redundant he was allowed a full year's salary and recommended by the local lieut-governor 'for any office in connexion with the Police Department either in Ireland or in any healthy Colony in Her Majesty's foreign possessions'. However, the Colonial Office decided to send him to Van Diemen's Land.

Power arrived in June 1841 at Hobart Town in the *Bombay*, accompanied by his wife, four children and two servants. Two daughters had been left with Lady Blessington in Paris to be educated. The eldest son, Charles John, a lieutenant in the Madras Army, died at Singapore on 13 November 1844. The second son married Anna Munro, daughter of George Hull [q.v.] on 10 August 1850.

In July 1841 Power was gazetted surveyor-general of Van Diemen's Land. Revenue from land sales was already falling off sharply because of the depression and his department was severely retrenched. The trigonometrical survey was stopped temporarily and most of the government surveyors were placed on contract work. As the depression lifted Power introduced a system of land leases which greatly increased revenue, although he also had to act as commissioner of crown lands without pay. These changes created much friction within the department and he was blamed for it by Lieut-Governor Denison. Through vice-regal patronage H. C. Cotton [q.v.] was made deputy-surveyor-general and placed in charge of the revived trigonometrical survey; Power was virtually relegated to administrative duties and his salary was reduced by £100. Although Power was always civil and obliging, Denison lamented to the Colonial Office that it was difficult to get rid of the head of a department without good reason.

On 12 December 1855 Power was advised that his retirement, on terms suggested by himself, would take effect from 1 January 1856. This arrangement broke down because after Denison's transfer to New South Wales Cotton had been removed from office and his successor as deputy-surveyor-general, James Sprent [q.v.], was too busily engaged in the supervision of field work. Power remained as nominal head of the department until 1 July 1857. In November he was appointed serjeant-at-arms of the House of Assembly and in July 1866 he became usher of the black rod. In 1857 he had been given a pension of £175, but it was increased in

1860 to £300 because he had been appointed from Britain. He died at Hobart on 15 February 1869.

M. Sadleir, *Blessington D'Orsay* (Lond, 1947); *Hobart Town Gazette*, 1841, p 596, 1857, p 1060; *Hobart Town Courier*, 2 July 1841, 28 Aug 1855; *Mercury*, 17 Feb 1869; GO 33/70/672, 818 (TA).　　A. R. LOVE

POWLETT, FREDERICK ARMAND (1811-1865), public servant, was born in January 1811 in Shropshire, England, the son of a chaplain to the Prince Regent and a descendant of the last duke of Bolton. In 1837 Powlett accompanied Sir John Franklin to Van Diemen's Land. After moving to the Port Phillip District he became a police magistrate. In November 1838 Powlett helped in the formation of the Melbourne Cricket Club and two years later became its first recorded president. Powlett was a pioneer of the plains around Bacchus Marsh and the upper reaches of the Werribee River, and for many years he had large pastoral interests in the Mount Macedon, Pentland Hills and Pyalong regions.

In 1840 he was appointed commissioner for the Westernport district and was still there when gold was discovered. He became the first gold commissioner in Victoria, his jurisdiction including Anderson's Creek, Ballarat and Castlemaine, but he soon relinquished the post. In October 1852, after the death of Alastair MacKenzie, Powlett was temporarily appointed colonial treasurer, with a seat in the Executive Council, holding office until J. F. L. Foster arrived from England in July 1853. Powlett next became chief commissioner of crown lands, but this post was abolished in 1860 while he was absent in England. Two years after his return to Victoria he became warden at the Buckland and later at Landsborough. In 1863 he was made police magistrate at Kyneton, an appointment which he held until his death.

Throughout his career Powlett served on various boards. After the Eureka Hotel riot of October 1854 he, with E. P. S. Sturt and Dr McCrae, conducted an inquiry into the administration of the Ballarat goldfield, at the direction of Sir Charles Hotham. In 1858 he was a member of the Church of England Assembly. Later he became captain of the Kyneton corps of the Castlemaine Rifles.

In 1850 Powlett had married Margaret, daughter of Dr William Thomsen and a sister of J. C. Thomsen, police magistrate at Gisborne. She died in 1853, and their only child, a daughter, was sent to England. Powlett died on 9 June 1865 after a short illness, and was buried beside his wife in the Heidelberg (Warringal) cemetery.

Powlett was a well known and much respected figure. He was a confidant of Lieut-Governor La Trobe and was agent for his property, as well as for Lady Franklin's [q.v.]. He had the tastes of an English country gentleman and, as a keen sportsman, was a renowned cricketer, race-horse owner, and huntsman. He had a high sense of honour, even fighting a duel to protect his reputation in 1842. He was fair and impartial, both as a lands commissioner settling squatting disputes and as a magistrate.

HRA (1), 21, 22; R. D. Boys, *First years at Port Phillip*, 2nd ed (Melb, 1959).

P. M. SALES

PRATT, JOHN JEFFREYS; *see* CAMDEN, SECOND EARL

PREISS, JOHANN AUGUST LUDWIG (1811-1883), naturalist, was born on 21 November 1811 at Herzberg am Harz, Germany. He attended university and received the degree of D. Phil. He arrived in the Swan River settlement in December 1838, became a naturalized British subject in 1841, but left for London in January 1842 and apparently spent the rest of his life in Germany. He settled at Herzberg am Harz in 1844 and died there on 21 November 1883.

Preiss was primarily a plant collector but he made extensive collections of natural history specimens of all kinds. In the course of his activities he visited most of the known parts of south-western Australia and several islands off the coast. He also bought specimens from local residents notably Johnston Drummond, son of James Drummond [q.v.], the naturalist. When John Gilbert [q.v.], the able collector employed by John Gould [q.v.], arrived in the colony in March 1839 he was dismayed to find Preiss there and in a letter to Gould complained that his rival had bought practically everything offering and was paying high prices. Gilbert informed Gould that in his dealings with the settlers he was endeavouring to overcome the foreign collector's established position by appealing to patriotic sentiments.

Preiss's very large collection of about 200,000 plant specimens was described by Johann Georg Christian Lehmann and a number of European collaborators, and published in Hamburg in parts in 1844-47 under the title *Plantae Preissianae sive enumeratio plantarum quas in Australasia occidentali et meridionale occidentali annis 1838-41 collegit L. Preiss* . . . Some plants collected by James Drummond and others from eastern Australia collected by T. L. Mitchell and J. Lhotsky [qq.v.] were also described in the work. Because of Preiss's thoroughness as a collector and the large number of species described and named for the first time in the *Plantae Preissianae*, it is an important reference work for the study of the Australian flora. Most of the collections of mollusc shells made by Preiss were dealt with by Carl Theodor Menke in a work entitled *Molluscorum Novae Hollandiae specimen* . . . published in Hanover in 1843.

Unfortunately for Preiss his large collections of mammals, birds, reptiles, insects and other material did not receive the treatment they deserved, and later workers received the credit for discovering new species which were undoubtedly first collected by him. He is known to have recorded extensive notes on his specimens but these do not appear to have survived. In October 1839 he offered to sell a large and important collection of bird skins to the government at Perth, but apparently the offer was declined. While in London he visited Gould and gave to him for description specimens of two kinds of kangaroos which had not until then come to Gould's notice. Preiss sold most of his specimens of animals to various European museums or dealers in natural history specimens, but most of them seem to have disappeared or cannot now be distinguished as having been collected by him. The only extant collection of Preiss's birds of any note seems to be that in the Municipal Museum of Halberstadt. Although so few specimens of mammals known to have come from Preiss can now be traced, dates and localities on labels attached to some specimens in European museums suggest that those specimens were collected by him. Had Preiss the backing of an ambitious and enterprising zoologist, as Gilbert had in Gould, it is certain that he would have been much better known today.

W. T. Stearn, 'Lehmann's "Plantae Preissianae"', *Soc for Bibliog of Natural Hist J*, 1 (1939), 203-5; H. M. Whittell, 'A review of the work of John Gilbert in Western Australia', *Emu*, 41 (1941); L. Glauert, 'The ornithological collecting of Dr L. Preiss in 1839', *WA Naturalist*, 1 (1948), 147-8; W. Meise, 'Notes on the ornithological collections of Preiss in the Swan River colony, 1838-1841', *Emu*, 51 (1951), 148-51.

J. H. CALABY

PRICE, CHARLES (1807-1891), Congregational minister, was born on 21 November 1807 in London, the son of John Price and Ann, née Seckerson. He attended schools in London and Coventry before becoming apprenticed to a silk weaver. As a teacher and lay preacher in the West Orchard Chapel, Coventry, he furthered his education under the guidance of his minister. In 1829 he entered Highbury College, London, and on completing his training consented to join a fellow-student, Rev. Frederick Miller [q.v.], in Van Diemen's Land. He was ordained in Coventry on 27 March 1832 and on 3 April married Catherine, daughter of John and Catherine Brogden. A week later they sailed in the *Princess Royal*, Price acting as chaplain to the women emigrants on board; on 23 August the ship was driven ashore in Frederick Henry Bay, and the Prices reached Hobart Town overland. There Price found his expected congregation dispersed, and moved to Launceston where Presbyterians and Wesleyans joined Congregationalists under his ministry in the Court House. News of the imminent arrival of a Presbyterian minister diminished the possibilities of continuance, and Price accepted the Congregational pastorate in Sydney.

The Sydney congregation, whose chapel Price opened on 15 February 1833, had two years previously made an unanswered application to London for a minister; seven weeks after Price began his ministry Rev. William Jarrett arrived. Price surrendered the pastorate and accepted the chaplaincy of the Australian Agricultural Co. at Port Stephens, for which its commissioner, Sir Edward Parry [q.v.], had vainly sought an Anglican clergyman. Price served there most acceptably from July 1833 to March 1836, an arrangement which led to an acrimonious correspondence between Archdeacon Broughton [q.v.] and Parry.

Price returned to Launceston on 29 April 1836 and, finding that Presbyterian and Wesleyan churches had been established, sought to found a Congregational church without undue call on Dissenting generosity. A church was formed on 26 October 1836 and the Tamar Street Chapel opened on 6 September 1837, but Price, who had established a grammar school in 1836, drew no stipend from the church until its building debts were settled in 1850. There was early disruption of the congregation when Rev. John West [q.v.] arrived in 1839 and drew away half the members to form a second church, but Price maintained an effective ministry for fifty-five years. He added chapels at Vincent Street (1848) and Inveresk (1858) to his pastorate. His qualities of leadership led to his election four times as chairman of the Tasmanian Congregational Union, and as the first president of the Congregational Union of Australasia. His death in Launceston on 4 August 1891 prevented assumption of the presidency. Of his four children, Charles Seckerson Yahrah was ordained in Launceston on 5 March 1861.

The Launceston community regarded Price as a founder of the temperance movement, the City Mission and the Bible Society. He lectured frequently on scientific subjects to the Mechanics' Institute, which he had helped to found, and it was claimed that 'he would have shone as a mechanic, as a teacher of languages, parliamentary debater, at the bar, or as a preacher of the Gospel'.

J. Fenton, *The life and work of the Reverend Charles Price* (Melb, 1886); C. S. Y. Price, *Reminiscences historical and characteristic of my beloved parents* (Melb, 1912); Broughton and Parry correspondence (ML).

G. L. LOCKLEY

PRICE, JOHN GILES (1808-1857), magistrate and penal administrator, was born on 20 October 1808, the fourth son of Sir Rose Price, first baronet, of Trengwainton, Cornwall, England. He was a pupil at Charterhouse in 1821, matriculated at Brasenose College, Oxford, on 21 May 1827, but left without taking a degree. Arriving in Hobart Town in May 1836, he took up farming in the Huon River district. On 12 June 1838 he married Mary, eldest daughter of Major James Franklin and the ward of Sir John Franklin, lieutgovernor of Van Diemen's Land.

On 1 January 1839 Price was appointed muster master of convicts and assistant police (stipendiary) magistrate. He acquired a thorough knowledge of the ways and cant language of the 'flash men' and confirmed criminals among the convicts, and is said by a critic, Rev. Thomas Rogers [q.v.], to have disguised himself as a constable and gone about Hobart at night in search of disorderly characters. In 1846 he suffered an illness the nature of which is not known but which was of sufficient gravity to lead Surgeon Bedford to state that Price should have leave of absence 'or else he will be laid up seriously'. Leave was approved, but in July 1846, before he could take it, he was appointed civil commandant of Norfolk Island, at a salary of £600, later £800, to take the place of Major Joseph Childs [q.v.], during whose administration, on 1 July 1846, a section of the convicts revolted and four minor

officials were murdered. Before his departure, at a public meeting of Hobart citizens, Price was given a service of plate valued at £300, and resolutions of regret at the loss of his services as a magistrate were carried. Leslie Norman (*Sea Wolves and Bandits*, Hobart, 1946, p. 165) asserts that Price was unwilling to take the appointment and did so only on the insistence of Lieut-Governor Sir John Eardley-Wilmot. He held the position of commandant from August 1846, when he arrived on Norfolk Island with his family, until January 1853. One of his first duties was to arrange for the trial of twenty-six convicts alleged to have been implicated in the murders during the revolt. Twelve convicts were hanged in two groups of six on 13 October 1846, and within the next three weeks five more convicts were executed, one for complicity in a murder during the revolt and four for other crimes.

Price's administration has been praised for its firmness and denounced for its harshness. A contemporary historian, John West [q.v.], asserted that he commenced it with a 'vigorous, summary, and, it is said, merciless exercise of his authority', and, noting that the charges against him had been disputed, commented, 'their substantial truth is, at least, rendered probable, by the accumulation of similar facts in the history of such settlements'. In February 1847 Price required the Anglican chaplain, Rev Thomas Rogers, to leave the island. Cogent evidence that Price was guilty of grave cruelty and abuse of power is furnished by Rogers in his *Correspondence etc.* and *Review of Dr. Hampton's First Report on Norfolk Island*, which were published in Launceston in 1849 while Price was still commandant, and by the Rt Rev. Robert Willson [q.v.], Roman Catholic bishop of Van Diemen's Land. Bishop Willson visited the island in 1846 when Childs was commandant, and twice during Price's administration, in 1849 and in 1852. He found conditions so much degenerated in 1852 that he wrote a long report to Lieut-Governor Sir William Denison, describing the plight of the convicts and the use of unduly harsh punishments. Before Willson's final visit the lieut-governor had required Price to explain the increased use of corporal punishments; Price defended his use of flogging, to which he professed great aversion, as necessary to enforce obedience to regulations, especially those controlling the use of tobacco.

The British government had in mind to abandon the island as a penal settlement and at his own request Price was given leave and in January 1853 returned to

Hobart. He was appointed inspector-general of penal establishments in Victoria in January 1854. The newly-established colony was confronted with grave problems arising from the explosive influx of gold seekers, who included many former convicts. The inadequate gaols were supplemented by hulks, moored in Hobson's Bay, on which conditions were appalling. Public disquiet forced investigations, and in 1856 the Legislative Council and the Legislative Assembly each appointed a select committee. The Legislative Council committee sat intermittently from 27 November 1856 to 29 July 1857, and the Legislative Assembly committee from 8 January 1857 to September 1857. Price gave evidence before both committees, but he was dead before either returned a report. On 26 March 1857 he visited Williamstown to investigate complaints about rations by convicts from the hulks employed there on public works. While he was listening to some grievances a party of convicts gathered around him. Missiles were thrown and one struck him heavily; as he turned away he was knocked down and severely battered about the head and body. On the next afternoon he died from his injuries. At the inquest fifteen convicts were committed for trial. They were tried in four groups, and seven were convicted and sentenced to death. Three were hanged on 28, three on 29, and one on 30 April 1857. Accounts of the trials leave the impression that some of the executed men may have been wrongly convicted.

Price's widow died at Malvern, Victoria, on 2 October 1894, and her death certificate states there were eight children of the marriage. When Price died six were living: John Frederick (b. 3 October 1839); James Franklin (b. 20 March 1841); Thomas Caradoc (b. 21 October 1842); Emily Mary (b. 5 October 1845); Anna Clara (b. 30 January 1846); and Jane de Winton (b. 1850?). John Frederick was among the early alumni of the University of Melbourne. He entered the Madras Civil Service and was appointed C.S.I. in 1893 and K.C.S.I. on his retirement in 1898. Known as Sir Frederick Price, he died at Trengwainton, Exmouth, on 12 June 1927. James Franklin was slain by natives on Mulgrave Island in Torres Strait in 1878 with three other members of the crew of the schooner *Gem*, captained by Francis Cadell. Thomas Caradoc served in the British army and later commanded the Victorian Mounted Rifles in the South African war, and was well known in Victoria as Colonel 'Tom' Price. He died at Warrnambool on 3 July 1911.

John Price became a legendary figure during his lifetime; after his death, 'Price Warung' (William Astley) made him the central figure in the story, 'John Price's Bar of Steel', in *Tales of the Old Regime* (Melbourne, 1897), and in the novel *For the Term of His Natural Life* (London, 1885) Marcus Clarke used Price as the foundation for 'Maurice Frere'. Clarke based his account of the conduct of Maurice Frere at Norfolk Island on Rev. Thomas Rogers's *Correspondence . . .*, from which he took almost verbatim extracts for use in the diary of 'Rev. James North', and his description of Frere's appearance accords with Price's. He was a man of great personal strength and considerable courage, and was capable of sentimental as well as merciless deeds.

J. West, *The history of Tasmania*, 2 (Launceston, 1852) 299; (T.L.B.), *Biographical memoir of the late Mr J. Price . . . with an account of the assassination, inquest and funeral, also a full report of the trial of the prisoners* (Melb, 1857); H. A. White, *Crime and criminals, or reminiscences of the penal department of Victoria* (Ballarat, 1890); J. Singleton, *A narrative of incidents in the eventful life of a physician* (Melb, 1891); G. J. de Winton, *Soldiering fifty years ago* (Lond, 1898); J. V. Barry, *The life and death of John Price* (Melb, 1964); Bishop Willson's letter, PP (HL), 1852-53, v 18, 88-95; Sel cttee on penal discipline, Report, V&P (LA Vic), 1856-57 (48); Sel cttee on penal establishments, Report, V&P (LC Vic), 1856-57 (D 13); CO 280/292.　　　　　　　　JOHN V. BARRY

PRIEUR, FRANCOIS XAVIER (1814-1891), merchant and author, was born on 8 May 1814 at Soulanges, Quebec, Canada, the son of Antoine and Archange Prieur. The family soon moved to the new settlement of St Polycarpe, where Prieur went to school. He then worked for a store-keeper at Soulanges for six years before setting up his own business at St Timothée in 1835. There he came into contact with the organization led by Louis Papineau to spread a spirit of nationalism among French Canadians. In 1838 he was sworn in as a 'castor' of the Association des Chasseurs, founded to drive the English out of Lower Canada. He appears to have been a leader of the rebellion in the St Timothée district. He was captured and tried at Montreal for treason between November 1838 and February 1839. He was first condemned to death, but later was among fifty-eight French Canadians whose sentences were commuted to transportation for life to New South Wales. They arrived in the *Buffalo* in February 1840. After his arrest and trial he kept a journal, later published as *Notes d'un condamné Politique de 1838* (Montreal, 1869); it gives a full account of the sufferings of the French Canadians in the *Buffalo* and their experiences in New South Wales.

Their first two years were spent at Long-bottom on the Parramatta River and then they were assigned to employers in 1842 at the height of the depression, but in addition to their language difficulties it was almost impossible to find work. Prieur worked in a confectioner's shop for a time and then was gardener for a Sydney merchant. After gaining a ticket-of-leave in February 1842 he set out with about ten compatriots to work at a Canadian sawmill on the Parramatta River, where he and his partner, Léon Ducharme, hired carters to transport timber to the river and then used a flat-bottomed boat to carry it to Sydney where it was sold for 20s. a thousand laths. A bush fire caused him to leave the sawmill, however, and with three other Frenchmen he began making candles, only to give this up because of impending failure. He rejoined Ducharme to work on the farm of a wealthy butcher, then set up a grocer's shop, bakery and blacksmith's forge with two former companions at Irish Town. It was here that he heard the first of their number had been pardoned. Prieur and Ducharme were both pardoned soon after, the news of their pardons being conveyed in Lord Stanley's dispatch of 29 February 1844.

Prieur had saved nothing for the journey home and took employment in helping a French merchant to wind up his affairs in Sydney. When the merchant left on the *Saint George* in February 1846 Prieur went with him and on his arrival in London found that a fund had been set up to pay their passages back to Canada. He sailed in the *Montreal* arriving in Quebec in September. He settled at St Martin in the parish of Chateaugay and ran a business there. He later established a business in English pottery and made several trips to England. In 1860 George Cartier made him superintendent of the Reformatory at Ile aux Noix and later he became superintendent of all Canadian prisons. He married Marguerite Aurélie Neveaux, and they had five sons and five daughters. He died on 1 January 1891, aged 76, and was buried in the cemetery of La Côte des Neiges, Montreal.

Léon Ducharme also published a journal of his experiences in New South Wales, *Journal d'un Exilé Politique aux Terres Australes* (Montreal, 1845), and although it is less detailed than Prieur's it gives more commentary on the colony. His account is otherwise much the same as Prieur's, but he describes Australia as possessing a pleasant climate, as being pastoral rather than agricultural, and deplores the numbers of poor immigrants and the shocking condition of the working class. The impressions of the French Canadians seem to have been highly unfavourable, especially as their stay was enforced and at a time of depression. Ducharme left for London in the *Achilles* in July 1844, and sailed to New York in the *Switzerland*, arriving in January 1845 and journeying thence to Canada.

Only one of the French Canadians settled in Australia: Joseph Marceau, a widower who left three children in Canada. He was pardoned in Lord Stanley's dispatch of 31 January 1844, and married Mary Barrett at Dapto on 9 October. He first took up shoemaking, then farmed at Dapto until his death on 8 June 1882, aged 77. He had six daughters and five sons.

Report of the state trials before a general court martial held at Montreal in 1838-39 exhibiting a complete history of the late rebellion in Lower Canada, 1-2 (Montreal, 1839); F. X. Prieur, *Notes of a convict of 1838*, tr G. Mackaness (Syd, 1949); MS cat under L. Ducharme, J. Marceau and F. X. Prieur (ML).   VIVIENNE PARSONS

PROUT, JOHN SKINNER (1806-1876), artist, was born probably at Plymouth, England, of Nonconformist parents. He was a nephew of the artist, Samuel Prout (1783-1852), whose renderings of medieval architecture were much admired by John Ruskin. About 1830 Prout married Maria, daughter of Stephen Marsh of Penzance, Cornwall; their first child was born at Plymouth on 31 August 1831. Prout acquired some knowledge of lithography and was largely self-trained as an artist. He spent much time in the west of England making topographical views of ancient monuments and in 1838 his *The Castles and Abbeys of Monmouthshire* was published in London. He visited the Wye valley and sketched the antiquities of Chester. He was also elected a member of the new Society of Painters in Water Colour. After two years of 'continued difficulties and harassment of mind' he sailed in the *Royal Sovereign* with his wife and seven children for Sydney, where his brother Cornelius had been under-sheriff since 1829. The family arrived on 14 December 1840, but the ship may have called at Melbourne, for Prout's *Journal of a voyage from Plymouth to Sydney* . . .

published in 1844, included a brief description of Port Phillip.

In 1841-42 Maria Prout, an able harpist, gave several concerts 'with peculiarly happy effect' at the Royal Victoria Theatre, but thereafter withdrew to domestic duties. Their eldest son, Victor Albert, attended the Normal Institution and won prizes for his intelligence. Prout had brought a lithographic plant and had it established by March 1841 when he reproduced drawings of the fire at the Albion Mills and its ruin. However, profitable work was scarce because of economic depression. In June he lectured at the School of Arts, but although the *Australian*, 25 November, declared that Prout 'not only understands painting but can clearly and popularly explain its principles', he was disappointed in December by the reception of his offer to give a series of six lectures at a guinea a ticket in the Grammar School, Phillip Street. In January 1842 he painted some 'elegant vignettes on the front of the boxes in the Olympic Theatre', and then had ample time to sketch many views of Sydney; for their reproduction he sought subscriptions in June, but publication was delayed while he attempted in vain to secure proper lithographic paper. With descriptive letterpress by John Rae, the first part of Prout's drawings appeared on 13 August as *Sydney Illustrated*. The second part followed in November and the fourth and last part was published in March 1844; a limited edition was reproduced in Sydney in 1948.

Prout visited Van Diemen's Land in January 1844. Much impressed he went back to Sydney for his family and arrived at Hobart Town in April. On 14 May the *Colonial Times* reported that his lectures were 'respectably attended . . . He sketches rapidly *with the brush*, and explains as he proceeds, showing the effects of light and shadow, and the great advantage it is to the artist his having a mind capable of chaste and correct composition'. On 14 June Prout announced a course of lectures 'on the cultivation of the fine arts, with practical illustrations'. They were well received and later in the year he published the first volume of *Tasmania Illustrated*, 'five grouped vignettes of Tasmanian scenes'. By the time the second volume appeared in 1846 Prout had toured the north of the island, where he was 'engaged by several gentlemen for the purpose of sketching their country seats, farms, and the country surrounding them'. In December Prout appears to have visited Norfolk Island and Sydney. In 1847 he spent three months at Port Phillip and six of his sketches there were published as *Views of Melbourne and Geelong*.

In March 1845 Prout's 10-year-old son, Frederick, had been killed by a falling stone. In March 1847 his second daughter, Matilda, married J. S. Dandridge at Hobart. In April 1848 Prout and his family sailed in the *Derwent* for London. In 1850 at the Western Literary and Scientific Institution, Leicester Square, he lectured and exhibited his dioramic views illustrating convict and emigrant life, and the habits of bushrangers and Aboriginals in Australia. In 1852 he published *An Illustrated Handbook of the Voyage to Australia* and in 1853 *A Magical Trip to the Gold Regions*; both works led to further exhibitions and ran to several editions. They also suggest that he may have revisited Australia, for he claimed that his sketches were made on the spot.

Prout died at Kentish Town, London, on 29 August 1876, leaving an estate of about £1500 to be invested for his two unmarried daughters. After Prout's death some of his drawings were used to illustrate E. C. Booth's *Australia* in 1876 and *Picturesque Antiquities of Bristol*, edited by E. Smith in 1893.

Prout was not very successful in Sydney, but his arrival in Tasmania greatly stimulated amateur painters. According to Mrs Meredith, 'landscape sketching and watercolour fever raged with extraordinary vehemence . . . The art that Mr. Prout taught and practised so well at once became the fashion'. Although the diarist Boyes [q.v.] complained that a drawing made for him by Prout was a 'poor washy thing not worth a frame', Prout had a fine taste for the picturesque, particularly in rural subjects, and delighted in the effects of mist and mountain, and free renderings of sea and shore. He was a strong champion of the right of the artist to interpret freely rather than merely to imitate the scene before him. He helped to organize the first Australian exhibition of paintings in 1845. His work is represented in the South Kensington Museum, the public galleries in Sydney and Hobart, and in the Mitchell and Dixson Galleries in Sydney. The National Library, Canberra, has forty-five of his Australian sketches and the Royal Society of Tasmania, Hobart, a portfolio of his Tasmanian and Victorian watercolours and pencil drawings. His best oil painting is considered to be 'A Waterfall', near Lake St Clair', executed while he was in Tasmania.

L. A. Meredith, *My home in Tasmania* (Lond, 1852); W. Dixson, 'Notes on Australian artists', *JRAHS*, 7 (1921); Newspaper indexes under J. S. Prout (ML); Correspondence file under Prout (TA).

V. W. HODGMAN

PUGH, WILLIAM RUSS (1805?-1897), medical practitioner, arrived in Hobart Town in the *Derwent* in December 1835, and reputedly walked soon after to Launceston, where the following May he married a fellow passenger Cornelia Ann, the daughter of G. A. Kirton, a London solicitor. He settled in Launceston and in July 1841 was appointed sub-agent for immigration and health officer for the port of Launceston. In this capacity he came into conflict with Henry Dowling's [q.v.] commercial hiring agency. When this position was discontinued in 1844 he took up private practice, and in June 1844 was nominated to the court of medical examiners. As a practitioner in Launceston he was courageous, aggressive and keenly interested in experiment. His great pride provoked hostility amongst Launceston doctors with whom he was reluctant to act in consultation. Once, when his ability was doubted, he retaliated by prosecuting a fellow practitioner who was unable to pay the fine for malicious persecution and was gaoled for twelve months.

With his partner, Dr James Grant, Pugh was continually engaged in experiments, and was quick to object to proposed legislation forbidding without exception the ownership of stills, essential to his medical and pharmaceutical research. Many of the drugs prescribed by Grant and Pugh were prepared from plants they had grown for the purpose. As early as 1842 he had installed lighting from coal gas in his house. An active member of the Tasmanian Society, predecessor of the Royal Society, he was a frequent visitor when the Franklins were at Government House, Hobart, and a friend of celebrated scientific men of his day. In 1846 he excited considerable colonial interest with an analysis of Tasmanian wheats for the Horticultural Society, confirming his friend Count Strzelecki's [q.v.] theory that the gluten content in colonial wheat had deteriorated through overcropping.

Reports of his ability as a surgeon appeared in the local press, and on 9 June 1847 notices of his successful attempts with ether, the first in Australia, using an apparatus copied from the *Illustrated London News*, 9 January 1847. In one operation he removed a tumour from a girl's lower jaw, and in another he removed cataracts from a man's eyes. The anaesthesia was successful, but in the Launceston *Examiner* Pugh discussed the difficulties associated with its use. Later that year he received an apparatus for administering ether from Bishop Nixon [q.v.] who was then in England.

Soon afterwards financial difficulties forced the closing of St John's Hospital, Launceston, with the administration of which Pugh had for many years been associated. He left the colony, taking with him testimonials of his unimpeachable character as a gentleman and skill as a surgeon from the mayor and aldermen of Launceston, and leading colonists. He had been in the Commission of the Peace since July 1843. He went first to Melbourne and later to Brighton, England, where his wife died in 1874. He died in London on 27 December 1897. Their only child had died in infancy.

H. Button, *Flotsam and jetsam* (Launceston, 1909); L. S. Bethell, *The story of Port Dalrymple* (Hob, 1957); W. Crowther, 'Introduction of surgical anaesthesia to V.D.L.', *MJA*, 8 Nov 1947; Correspondence file under Pugh (TA).

C. CRAIG

Q

QUAIFE, BARZILLAI (1798-1873), Congregational and Presbyterian minister, was born at Lenham, Kent, England, the son of Thomas Quaife, farmer, and his wife Amelia, née Austin. He entered Hoxton Academy, London, in 1824 and later served as teacher and minister at Collompton, Devon, at St Leonards-on-Sea, Sussex, and at other centres.

In 1835 he submitted to the South Australian Colonization Commissioners a 'Plan to provide the New Settlement of South Australia with the means of Religious instruction on the Congregational principle'. His own hopes of appointment under this plan were disappointed and a further offer of service in 1836 was declined by the Colonial Missionary Society. However, with help from George Fife Angas [q.v.] he reached Adelaide in September 1839, established a Bible and tract depot, and for six months wrote for Archibald Macdougall's *Southern Australian*.

Macdougall's offer of a partnership sent Quaife to Kororareka (Russell), New Zealand, where on 15 June 1840 he began to publish the *New Zealand Advertiser and Bay of Islands Gazette*. After twenty-seven issues it was suppressed when he attacked what he believed to be governmental transgression of Maori land rights. In February 1842 he became editor of the *Bay of Islands Observer* but soon resigned. His main work at Kororareka was the formation of the first Congregational church in New Zealand where he ministered from May 1840 until April 1844.

Intending to return to England, Quaife left for Sydney in May 1844. Delayed there, he preached in Parramatta and remained to form a Congregational church and erect a chapel. His relations with Rev. Dr Robert Ross [q.v.] of Pitt Street Congregational Church, Sydney, were uneasy; their connexions were severed when Quaife accepted a temporary appointment to Scots Church while Rev. Dr Lang [q.v.] was overseas. Quaife continued as supervising pastor of the Parramatta church until it closed in 1850, and his service to Scots Church was protracted until February 1847 when a Presbyterian minister arrived. Some members of the church, eager to retain Quaife's services, seceded and formed a church under his ministry, meeting first in the Macquarie Street Wesleyan Chapel and later in the old City Theatre, Market Street, and he ministered to it until 1850. To this point he regarded himself as a Congregationalist.

In 1850 Lang reopened the Australian College and appointed Quaife professor of mental philosophy and divinity. He became a foundation member of Lang's Synod of New South Wales (1850) and of the reunited synods (1865). His professorship lapsed when the college's work was restricted in 1852. From 1853 to 1855 he lived at Parramatta.

In 1855 Quaife moved to Paddington where he taught a school and ministered to a congregation in his home. In 1863 reconciliation with Congregational leaders was effected when he was invited to train three students for the ministry. He closed his school, merged his congregation with the Ocean Street Congregational Church, Woollahra, and, from 13 July 1863 until 30 September 1864, devoted himself to the tuition of his students; in October they were transferred to the newly-founded Camden College, but Quaife was bitterly wounded when he did not receive an expected tutorship in the college. Thenceforth ill health withdrew him from professional activity until his death on 3 March 1873.

In addition to his journalism mentioned above Quaife became leader-writer for the *Empire* (1852-57) and contributed articles to the *Atlas*, the *People's Advocate*, the *Press* and the *Illawarra Mercury*. He edited the *Christian Standard* in 1849 and both forms of the *Christian Pleader* from 1858 to 1864. Among other works he published *A condensed view of the proper design and uses of the Lord's Supper* (Parramatta, 1845), *The Rules of the Final Judgment* (Parramatta, 1846), and *Lectures on Prophecy and the Kingdom of Christ* (Sydney, 1848). His last publication, *The Intellectual Sciences*, 1-2 (Sydney, 1872), comprised lectures at the Australian College and has been claimed as the first serious philosophical work published in Australia.

Quaife was always conscious of his own rectitude. His colleagues acknowledged his integrity and ability, yet found themselves at odds with him. His self-vindication tends to obscure the faithfulness of his pastoral service. His students appreciated his erudition but felt that 'if teaching was his *forte*, omniscience was his foible'. He wrote didactically on many topics, but could be scathing in controversy; yet his journalism was influential in public and church affairs.

In 1836 Quaife married Maria Smith at St Anne's, Westminster; two of their four sons died in infancy and Maria died at Paddington, New South Wales, on 12 January 1857. On 29 May 1857 he married Eliza Buttrey, by whom he had a son and a daughter. Frederick Harrison Quaife, youngest son of the first marriage, graduated in the Universities of Sydney and Glasgow and practised medicine in Sydney, where he was a foundation member of the New South Wales Branch of the British Medical Association, its president in 1884-85, and a member of the New South Wales Medical Board from 1894 to 1915. He was a member and a vice-president of the Royal Society of New South Wales. William Francis Quaife, the son of the second marriage, graduated in the same universities and practised medicine in Sydney.

G. M. Meiklejohn, *Early conflicts of press and government* (Auckland, 1953); G. Nadel, *Australia's colonial culture* (Melb, 1957); Colonial Missionary Soc, Minutes (Lond); VDL Home Missionary and Christian Instruction Soc, Minutes (Congregational Union of Tas, Hob); MS cat under B. Quaife (ML).

G. L. LOCKLEY

QUIROS (QUEIROS), PEDRO FERNANDEZ DE (1563?-1615), navigator, was born at Evora, Portugal, but became subject to the King of Spain when the two countries were dynastically united in 1580. Quiros is the Spanish form of the name. He was a supercargo on Portuguese merchant ships and appears to have spent several years seafaring on the Pacific coasts of America. He was recognized as a competent and experienced navigator when in 1595 he was appointed chief pilot of an expedition of four ships under Alvaro de Mendaña setting out to colonize the Solomon Islands, which Mendaña had visited in 1567. They sailed from Callao, Peru, in April 1595 and in three months reached the Marquesas, which Mendaña at first thought were the Solomons. Quiros was most impressed by the natives, as was James Cook [q.v.] 180 years later; they were 'in all things so becoming that . . . nothing in his life ever caused him so much regret as the leaving of such fine creatures to be lost in that country'. However, they became importunate and many were killed, though Quiros thought 'such evil deeds' were 'not things to do, nor to praise, nor to allow, nor to maintain, nor to refrain from punishing if the occasion permits'. The expedition left the Marquesas in August and, after passing several small islands, on 8 September sighted a large one which Mendaña named Santa Cruz. There he proposed to establish a settlement; but the Spaniards again fell out with the natives, many of the crews were sick and discontent was rife despite Quiros's constant efforts to suppress disorder and support Mendaña's authority. In October Mendaña died and next month Quiros, who had taken over the command, decided that the place should be abandoned. He sailed WSW. for two days, but found no land and headed for Manila. He arrived on 11 February 1596 after a voyage in ships badly needing repair, against contrary winds, with a starving and dying company, and with difficulties intensified by the selfishness of Mendaña's widow. This was one of the greatest feats in the record of Pacific navigation and shows the great qualities Quiros possessed.

After eighteen months in the Philippines, he sailed for home. He reached Mexico in December 1597 and Spain next year. The expedition had given him the idea of discovering a great southern continent for Spain and for the church. He petitioned the king to send him on another expedition into the Pacific, and he took the opportunity of the jubilee of 1600 to go to Rome to seek Papal blessing for this enterprise. He stayed in Rome from September 1600 to April 1602, and in August 1601 had an audience with Pope Clement VIII. He greatly impressed the Spanish ambassador, the duke of Sesa, who told the King of Spain that 'his only excess was that he was over-zealous for the service of Your Majesty'. Otherwise he was a 'man of good judgment, experienced in his profession, hard-working, quiet and disinterested'; there were, Sesa thought, few pilots so skilled in making charts or who knew so much mathematics. Quiros had invented two instruments to aid navigation, both highly praised by distinguished mathematicians, one to ascertain the variation of the declination of the compass needle to the NE. and NW., and the other to determine latitude, and his *Treatise on Navigation*, first written as a letter to the king in 1602, showed a marked knowledge of the theory and practice of navigation.

At last, in March 1603, Quiros was authorized to undertake another voyage to convert the heathen and extend the Spanish dominions. He was delayed by being shipwrecked in the West Indies but reached Callao on 6 March 1605. In December he set out into the Pacific, intending to sail to latitude 30°S., then to criss-cross the Pacific between 10°-20°S. until he reached Santa Cruz, whence he would sail SW. to

20°S. and then NW., with the object of discovering a 'mainland' which he was sure existed 1000 leagues from Peru near the Marquesas Islands. However, when he first reached latitude 26°S. he changed his plan, unfortunately, for otherwise he might have discovered New Zealand, and sailed WNW. and W., and then NW., missing the Marquesas but discovering the Duff group and the Banks group, before reaching the New Hebrides or what he called Australis de Spiritu Santo on 3 May 1606. There, in 'a land more delightful, healthy and fertile' than any that could be found, he proposed to form a colony to be called New Jerusalem, with its capital Vera Cruz, but after a few weeks his ship, when returning for the second time because of contrary winds from attempted exploration to the south-east, was driven out to sea. Instead of trying to return his ship sailed for Mexico, possibly when the discontented among the crew seized an opportunity created by their captain's ill health. The second ship, with the pilot Luis Vaez de Torres [q.v.], was left behind.

Quiros reached Acapulco in November 1606 and Madrid in October 1607. For seven years he bombarded the king with memorials, at least sixty-five in number, asking to be sent on a third expedition, but the council thought that discoveries in the Pacific only weakened the mother country, and that Spain could not afford it. Quiros was employed as a cosmographer and the council forbade the publication of the memorials which reported his discoveries, lest other countries should benefit from them. At last in 1614 a new viceroy of Peru was told he could send out Quiros when he thought it convenient; Quiros sailed with him for New Spain, but died on the way in June 1615.

All who knew Quiros were impressed by his undoubted skill as a seaman and navigator, his sympathy with the natives of the islands, and his belief, in the last fifteen years of his life, in his spiritual mission; but though full of zeal and enthusiasm, he failed in the management of his men. Often weak and vacillating he had insufficient will power to control the turbulent and to cheer the half-hearted, and was by no means fitted for the task of forming new settlements.

In 1589 he married Dona Ana Chacon of Madrid, who bore him one son and one daughter.

J. Burney, A chronological history of the discoveries in the South Sea or Pacific Ocean, 2 (Lond, 1806); C. Markham (ed), Voyages of Pedro Fernandez de Quiros, 1595-1606, 1-2 (Lond, 1904); G. A. Wood, The discovery of Australia (Lond, 1922); J. C. Beaglehole, The exploration of the Pacific (Lond, 1947); Celsus Kelly, Pedro Fernandes de Queiros, the last great Portuguese navigator (Lisbon, 1961); C. Kelly, 'The narrative of Pedro Fernandez de Quiros', Hist Studies, no 34, May 1960; J. W. Forsyth, 'Clio etwas gebuckt', JRAHS, 49 (1964); E. Ortiz y Pi, Translation of Capt de Quiros memorials (ML).

R

RAINE, JOHN (1786?-1837), speculator and merchant, was the brother of Captain Thomas Raine [q.v.]. He was educated at Westminster School and articled to solicitors in Chancery Lane, London. Bearing a letter of recommendation from Lord Erskine, he arrived at Hobart Town with his wife, mother and brother in November 1819 in the *Regalia*, of which he said he was the 'principal freighter'. He went on to Sydney and there chartered the ship and equipped her for whale fishing from the Derwent. After the partial failure of this enterprise he sent her to Macquarie Island to collect sea-elephant oil, which in August 1821 he took to England in her, together with sixty-one bales of wool, the first exported from Van Diemen's land, where up to this time it had been badly neglected. Before leaving he had begun to run voyages with passengers and merchandise between Sydney and Hobart, and these he carried on with several ships until his death. He also received a grant of 2000 acres in the Derwent valley.

When Raine reached London, where he stayed in Coram Street, Brunswick Square, he received from the Society of Arts and Commerce their 1823 silver Ceres medal, for his efforts with the wool, and their large silver medal for the sea-elephant oil. He claimed that he deserved another for tanning leather and sought an allotment at Hobart on which to set up a steam-engine to run a flour and timber mill and to pump water from the Derwent for the town supply, but this was refused on the advice of Commissioner Bigge [q.v.]. However, in September 1822 he succeeded in his application to be made a notary public with permission to practise in British dependencies. He sailed for Sydney in his ship *Thalia* in May 1823.

For the rest of his life Raine lived chiefly in New South Wales, though making occasional visits to Hobart. In April 1825 he was granted twenty acres at Parramatta on which to build his much desired steam flour-mill. This he ran in conjunction with a bakery, a general store and a stage coach service to Sydney. His farm, though only fifty acres, was said to be a model and in 1827 he leased Samuel Marsden's [q.v.] Ranghaoo estate, changing its name to Westgrove. Though twice refused admission as an attorney Raine set himself up as a notary public with E. S. Hall [q.v.], was a Quarter Sessions juror, a subscriber to the Benevolent Society, the School of Industry and the Dispensary, and a supporter of the Parramatta races. But he was often involved in litigation both in Van Diemen's Land and in New South Wales and in 1828 was drawn into a quarrel over a dam which a neighbour built on Raine's land without giving him compensation. Raine threatened to divert the dam water and when John Macarthur [q.v.] sent a party to stop him 'acts of violence' followed. Raine sued Macarthur but though the court dismissed the case, for 'Raine was not free of blame', Macarthur, who had taken part in the riot and tried to shelter himself as a magistrate, was ordered to pay Raine's costs. In 1829-30 Raine suffered severely from the depression in the colony and had to sell much of his land and livestock and to transfer the mill to his mother. In 1834 a libel action led to his being briefly imprisoned. After this he resumed his seafaring activities. He made several voyages to the Derwent and died at sea on 20 December 1837 when his ship *Schah* was driven ashore by a heavy swell after a fierce gale; Raine's cabin-door could not be opened and the ship was abandoned. Reporting his death, *Bent's News* described him as a 'strange eccentric man . . . Liberal to the extreme, he expended several fortunes in speculation'. Raine was married and had at least one son John (b. 1817) and one daughter Elizabeth (b. 1820).

HRA (3), 3, 4; J. K. S. Houison, 'The Darling mills, Parramatta', *Parramatta & Dist Hist Soc J*, 3 (1926); Newspaper indexes under John Raine (ML); MS cat under John Raine (ML); CSO 1 (TA).
M. J. SHEEHAN

RAINE, THOMAS (1793-1860), mariner and merchant, was born on 21 June 1793, the youngest son of Richard Raine, barrister, and his wife Mary, née Beatty. He was educated at Westminster School and joined the merchant marine; when he sailed for Australia in 1814 as a junior officer in the convict transport *Surry*, an epidemic of typhus left him the only surviving officer. As acting master he sailed the ship to China for a homeward cargo and on the way examined part of the Great Barrier Reef, Raine Passage and Raine Island being named after him.

Confirmed as captain, Raine made five more voyages to Australia in the *Surry* between 1816 and 1823, four with convicts; his humane treatment of them earned him the commendation of Governor Macquarie. Between voyages he engaged in a variety of mercantile enterprises, establishing the first shore whaling station on the Australian mainland at Twofold Bay in 1818 and speculating in shipping elephant-seal oil from Macquarie Island to London and wheat from Chile to New South Wales. In 1819, with Macquarie's encouragement, he proposed to establish a packet service between England and Australia, but this proved abortive. On a return voyage from Valparaiso in 1821 he took off Henderson Island three survivors of the *Essex*, which had been sunk by a whale in mid-ocean. Later he made a second expedition to Macquarie Island and at the request of Edward Wollstonecraft [q.v.] drew up a detailed report on its resources.

In 1822, after he had taken Governor Macquarie back to England, Raine founded, in partnership with a ship's surgeon, David Ramsay [q.v], the Sydney firm of Raine & Ramsay, general merchants, shipowners and agents. Although he continued to act as captain of the *Surry* until 1827, she did not carry convicts again after 1823 and Raine became increasingly involved in the colony's affairs. He was a director of the Sydney and Van Diemen's Land Packet Co., and a prominent supporter of Sydney's benevolent and sporting institutions. He extended his business interests to include the timber trade, pork and coconut oil from Otaheite, sugar, spices and rum from Mauritius and the East, and flax and ships' spars from the establishment he formed at Hokianga, in the north-west of New Zealand, in 1828, the year after he had sent a trial shipment of Australian cedar to England. To finance these and other enterprises Raine & Ramsay were largely dependent on bills drawn on the Bank of New South Wales, on inadequate security according to a board of inquiry in May 1826, when they were the bank's largest debtors. This criticism was followed by Raine's resignation from the board of directors, to which he had been elected in December 1824. During the next eighteen months the intensifying general depression and the bank's restriction of credit increased the firm's difficulties, and in October 1828 the partnership with Ramsay was dissolved. In December Raine, who had been elected a director of the bank again in January, was one of those chosen by lot to retire and he did not seek re-election; early in the New Year he was bankrupt. However, in March an arrangement with his creditors was soon followed by his resumption of business at the New Zealand establishment, where in due course he built

three trading vessels which helped to restore his fortunes.

In 1831 his wife had settled near Bathurst, where seven years before Raine had been granted land. There in 1832 he built Rainbarn, now owned by the Boyd family, and engaged in wheat and dairy farming, built the first flour-mill in the district, and established Boree station farther out, whence Thomas Mitchell and Richard Cunningham [qq.v.] set out in 1835 on their expedition to the Darling River; during these years he gradually disposed of his mercantile concerns and was able to make further payments to his creditors.

While the combination of ship's captain and merchant adventurer was not uncommon in early Sydney, Raine stood out among his colleagues for his imagination in visualizing the commercial possibilities of new localities, products and trade routes and his technical ability to exploit them. His failure in business was caused through the lack not of enterprise or competence but of the necessary capital to carry his ventures over the difficult period of the late 1820s. Once bankrupt, Raine wisely realized his assets and invested what was left in country properties which he developed with success, becoming a well-known and respected figure in the Bathurst district. His accounts of Pitcairn and Macquarie Islands and journal of the *Surry* show him to have been an exceptionally accurate observer and recorder; that he was also a man of liberal and humanitarian principles is evinced by his behaviour towards his convict passengers, who on being disembarked after his first voyage as captain 'cheered repeatedly and expressed the liveliest gratitude for their good treatment'.

Raine had two children by Jane Wright at Parramatta in 1822 and 1825; at St James's, Sydney, on 30 March 1826 he married Fanny Eleanor, daughter of General Worsley; they had three sons and seven daughters. After the death of his wife and two of his children he returned in indifferent health to Sydney, where he died on 6 June 1860. He was an active Presbyterian and one of the founders of the Scots Church in Sydney in 1824.

HRA (1), 9, 10, 12-16; 'Captain Raine's narrative of a visit to Pitcairn's Island in the ship *Surry* 1821', *Australian Mag*, 1 (1821), 80-84, 109-14; R. H. Goddard, 'Captain Thomas Raine of the *Surry*', *JRAHS*, 26 (1940); *Aust Genealogist*, 4 (1942); Bank of NSW archives (Syd); Thomas Raine papers (Fisher Lib, Univ Syd).   H. E. MAUDE

RAMSAY, DAVID (1794-1860), medical practitioner and merchant, was born on 16 March 1794 in Perth, Scotland, the third son of John Ramsay, a prosperous corn merchant and miller, and his wife, née Pearson. He was educated in Perth and at Edinburgh University (M.D., 1817). Next year he sought a hospital appointment in London, but was unsuccessful. Reluctant to become a surgeon's assistant confined to a shop making up medicines with no opportunity of improving his medical education, he accepted the post of surgeon in the *Marchioness of Exeter*, at a monthly salary of £5, the use of the captain's table and liberty to trade a little. He made a modest profit on a voyage to the East Indies, but on his return to England in 1819 he found situations on ships hard to come by; after toying with the idea of furthering his professional knowledge at the University of Paris, early in 1820 he accepted a post in the *Surry*, Captain Thomas Raine [q.v.], going to New South Wales. After four months in Sydney he sailed for Valparaiso in the *Surry*. On the way Ramsay did useful natural history work on several islands, including Pitcairn; his description of the visit there is one of the most informative accounts of the islanders. In June 1821 he was back in Sydney, with which he was greatly impressed, but in February 1822 he embarked once more in the *Surry*, now taking Governor Macquarie and his family back to England.

Ramsay's appetite was whetted by what he considered the great commercial possibilities of New South Wales and, aided by some influential friends, he made arrangements to establish a 'House of Agency' in the import-export business with Raine as partner. Leaving England in the *Thalia* late in 1822 Ramsay reached Sydney in June 1823. With the establishment of the well-known house of Raine & Ramsay his career as a doctor appears to have ended, for there is no evidence available that he ever after practised medicine. Ramsay disagreed with Raine's expansionist policy and in 1828, when he complained that Raine was misappropriating large sums belonging to the firm for his personal use, the partnership was dissolved.

Although for a time short of funds, Ramsay continued to develop both his commercial and pastoral interests, including his grant of 2000 acres on the bank of the Fish River and his plant nursery at Dobroyd farm, a wedding present from his father-in-law, the wealthy emancipist merchant, Simeon Lord [q.v.]. Of some 480 acres about six miles from Sydney, it had been originally a grant to Nicholas Bayly [q.v.], who named it Sunning Hill farm; much of it is now covered by the suburb of Haberfield. Ramsay described it as 'one of the finest places in New South Wales, the oranges in the orchard alone being worth £100 per year'.

Ramsay took an active part in public affairs. He was treasurer to the Presbyterian Church in 1823, a signatory to its constitution drawn up in 1824 and a strong supporter of his fellow members in their efforts to build Scots Church in Sydney. In 1838 he was a mediator in the dispute between the synod and the presbytery and in 1845 was trustee to the congregation. He opposed Bourke's efforts to establish a National system of education in the colony, but his interest in education is shown by his election to the council of the Australian College, the brain-child of Rev. J. D. Lang [q.v.].

He had married Sarah Ann, eldest daughter of Simeon Lord, on 31 March 1825. He had ten children of whom the third youngest son, Edward Pearson Ramsay, was a noted ornithologist who for twenty years was curator of the Australian Museum in Sydney. David Ramsay died on 10 June 1860 and was buried on Dobroyd.

Upright but shrewd, dignified but warmly affectionate, Ramsay was a man of high principles. Deeply religious he followed all his life the strict path of Presbyterian orthodoxy. Although not possessed of great intellectual gifts, he was versatile enough to succeed as a doctor, as a student of natural history and as a man of business. He had as well some taste and talent for music. His letters reveal him as a dutiful son and a devoted father and husband.

I. Brodsky, *Dr David Ramsay* (Syd, 1960); R. B. Nicholson, *The Pitcairners* (Syd, 1965); R. H. Goddard, 'Captain Thomas Raine of the *Surry*', *JRAHS*, 26 (1940); MS cat under Ramsay (ML).

ARTHUR McMARTIN

RANKEN, GEORGE (1793-1860), farmer and pastoralist, was born on 10 April 1793 in Ayrshire, Scotland, the third son of George Ranken of Whitehill, Ayrshire, and Janet, née Logan, of Knockshinnock. The Ranken family was of Flemish origin, the founder of the Scottish branch having arrived in Scotland in the thirteenth century. Four brothers of George Ranken the younger were doctors, one a solicitor, one an army officer.

In May 1821 George Ranken married his first cousin, Janet Ranken Hutchison; they sailed in the *Lusitania*, and in October reached Hobart Town where Ranken took a house, and his wife wrote: 'A great many settlers have come out this season; all of them the grandest people I ever saw. They are surely come to spend not to make money'. Leaving his wife in Hobart Ranken went on to Sydney where he met Governor Brisbane and other grand people. In February he took his wife to Sydney where her first child was born, and where Ranken leased from Captain John Piper [q.v.] about 2000 acres at Petersham for £200 a year. The Rankens, with the help of a man from Cheshire, were soon successful cheese-makers, and when the Agricultural Society of New South Wales was formed in 1822 Ranken was elected to the district committee.

In 1822 the government made the first of a number of 2000-acre grants in the Bathurst district, where Ranken selected one for himself and named it Kelloshiel, one for Thomas Icely [q.v.] (Saltram) and one for Piper (Alloway Bank). Having found Petersham too close to Sydney—a stage for travellers and a drive for town people', Mrs Ranken complained—the Rankens moved out to Kelloshiel in 1823. The journey took a fortnight, Ranken and his wife riding, their child and his nurse travelling in a tilted cart and their possessions in two bullock drays. Mrs Ranken found only two other gentlewomen west of the mountains: the wife of the superintendent of convicts, T. F. Hawkins [q.v.], and the wife of the manager of the government farm. The settlers on these fertile plains were soon being harried by Aboriginals, and in August 1824 Brisbane declared martial law in the district and reinforced the garrison. After four months the Aboriginals' 'great and most warlike Chieftain' with most of his tribe sought pardon.

George Ranken's brother Arthur (1805-1892) arrived from Scotland in 1826, worked with George at Kelloshiel for some years and later settled at Glen Logan on the Lachlan River, where George also acquired a run of 4000 acres. He also discovered some fossil bones in the limestone caves of the Wellington valley and gave them to Rev. J. D Lang [q.v.], when he went to England in 1830, to hand to the University of Edinburgh. Ranken was a leader in the establishment of a Presbyterian congregation at Bathurst in 1832 and in July 1836 added his name to a resolution opposing National schools.

In the 1830s Ranken enlarged his estate by buying Saltram from Icely and obtaining additional grants until in 1836 he held 5424 acres at Bathurst as well as his Lachlan run. In 1837 he chartered the *Minerva* to import agricultural labourers and

mechanics with the help of the government bounty; in the same year he leased his Bathurst properties for four years, put a manager on the Lachlan run and in January 1838 sailed with his wife and nine children for Scotland where he rented an estate and whence he sent his four sons to Stettin, Germany, to be educated under a Lutheran pastor. However, a disastrous drought which began in New South Wales in 1838 cut short Ranken's stay and in 1841 he returned to Australia, bringing seven servants and three young would-be settlers. In the drought Ranken took the lead among Bathurst settlers in boiling down stock for tallow, and also exported salt beef to the islands. He had brought out five German vine-dressers and good vine cuttings, and they planted twenty acres at Kelloshiel where wine was produced until disease ruined the vines. He also grew hops, established a brewery and for a time was producing flour, cheese, wine and beer as well as running cattle and sheep. In 1855 he laid out the lower parts of Saltram in farm and village allotments which he sold for up to £30 an acre, and he built a bridge across the Macquarie River as part of this development plan. He named the village Eglinton after the earl of Eglinton. In 1859 Ranken went to England to patent improvements of the screw propeller and the paddle wheel for steamers, and these were made and tested at Portsmouth dockyard. By this time, however, he was suffering from serious affections of the liver, and he died at Woolwich, London, on 17 October 1860.

The next generation of Rankens produced writings of lasting interest. Mrs. W. B. Ranken, wife of George Ranken's second son, published *The Rankens of Bathurst* (Sydney, 1916), an intimate record of life on the western frontier; George Ranken (1827-1895), son of Thomas, the second son of George Ranken senior, who settled in Queensland, wrote a novel *Wyndabyne* (London, 1895) and books on land, stock and colonization; William Hugh Logan Ranken (1839-1902), son of one of George's doctor brothers, wrote *The Dominion of Australia* (London, 1874).

HRA (1), 11, 15; B. Greaves (ed), *The story of Bathurst* (Syd, 1961).   GAVIN LONG

RANSOM, THOMAS (1759?-1829), boat builder and publican, was convicted at Middlesex, England, on 9 September 1789 and sentenced to transportation for life. He arrived in Sydney in the *Scarborough* in June 1790. In September he was transferred to Norfolk Island, where he was employed on the repair of boats. He received a full pardon in September 1810. After the military commandant was withdrawn in 1814 Ransom and William Hutchinson [q.v.] supervised the evacuation of the remaining inhabitants in the *Kangaroo* to the River Derwent. At Hobart Town Ransom was appointed superintendent of boatbuilders and continued in that position until ill health forced him to retire. About 1817 he built the Joiners' Arms in Murray Street. Although his reputation was unimpeached and he was universally esteemed, his licence was revoked in June 1825 because 'it was discovered that the faithful and valuable female, who had for years borne his name . . . was unhappily unable to enter into the legal state of matrimony, in consequence of circumstances . . . which she could neither alter nor recur to, and which, until the prying eye of some persecuting hypocrite ferretted out, were before generally unknown'.

Ransom moved to Green Ponds where he had been granted 400 acres by Governor Macquarie in 1817. He spent some £1500 improving this property and in building the Royal Oak Inn. The land commissioners reported that he kept the best inn in Van Diemen's Land: 'nothing can exceed the civility and attention that the Traveller meets with here, an excellent larder, good beds, and capital stabling'. Ransom had also cleared and cultivated some of his land and was depasturing about 300 sheep and some cattle. In July 1828 Lieut-Governor Arthur granted him an additional 600 acres.

Ransom died at his inn on 6 February 1829 and was buried at Green Ponds. His property was bequeathed to his friend, Catherine Christiana McNally, who married Frederick von Stieglitz [q.v.] on 22 January 1830 and died in 1857 at Killymoon.

HRA (1), 7, 8, 10, (3), 3; A. McKay (ed), *Journals of the land commissioners for Van Diemen's Land 1826-28* (Hob, 1962); *Hobart Town Gazette*, 3 June 1825; CSO 1/10/159, 1/88/1947 (TA); MS cat under Thomas Ransom (ML).

RAPER, GEORGE (1768?-1797), seaman and artist, son of Henry and Catherine Raper, is thought to have come from Yorkshire, England. He entered the navy as a captain's servant on 20 August 1783 and on 22 December 1786 joined the *Sirius* in the First Fleet as an able seaman. He became a midshipman on 30 September 1787,

a few months before reaching Botany Bay in January 1788. In 1788-89 he sailed in the *Sirius* to obtain food from the Cape of Good Hope on a voyage that circumnavigated the globe. In March 1790 when the *Sirius* was wrecked on Norfolk Island Raper with most of his shipmates remained there. He returned to Sydney in the *Supply* in February 1791, left the colony soon afterwards in the hired Dutch ship *Waaksamheyd*, arrived in England on 22 April 1792, by way of the Duke of York Islands, Mindanao and Batavia, and was paid off on 16 May. On 27 June 1793 he was promoted lieutenant and later served in the *Cumberland*. Admiralty records show that he died in 1797, the note of administration describing him as 'Late Commander H.M.S. Cutter *Expedition*'.

Raper is known for his water-colour drawings of subjects mainly associated with the First Fleet, the foundation of the colony, the settlement of Norfolk Island, and his voyage home in the *Waaksamheyd*. He also executed numerous natural history paintings which are among the first done of the birds and flowers of Sydney Cove. Several of his drawings are of Norfolk and Lord Howe Island birds now extinct. The paintings by, or associated with, Raper are in three sets: a volume of 73 mounted sheets (one, no. 56, is now missing) of scenes, native implements, birds, flowers, fish and other subjects, in the British Museum (Natural History); two volumes in the Mitchell Library, Sydney, one of which contains 18 mounted sheets mainly of fish, the other 33 mounted sheets of flower paintings; and a volume of 66 water-colour drawings mostly of birds, in the Alexander Turnbull Library, Wellington, New Zealand. In addition a painting by Raper of the 'Settlement of Norfolk Island, May 1790', is in the Mitchell Library. Many of the bird paintings have accurate delineations of flowers or insects added as artistic decorations. Most of the drawings in the British Museum series are signed by Raper and seem to have been those broadly mentioned in his will: 'All other things, Drawings Papers and Books excepted, I desire may be sold at the Mast as is the Custom at Sea'. The paintings were eventually acquired by Osbert Salvin and F. Du Cane Godman and were exhibited to the Zoological Society of London in 1877. More recently Miss Eva Godman, daughter of F. Du Cane Godman, presented the volume to the British Museum (Natural History).

Only a few 'Raper' drawings in both the Mitchell Library and the Alexander Turnbull Library bear Raper's signature. Some of the unsigned paintings could be by him; others appear to be the work of contemporary artists and were probably collected by his associates.

K. A. Hindwood, 'George Raper: an artist of the First Fleet', JRAHS, 50 (1964), plates and for bibliog.   K. A. HINDWOOD

RAVEN, WILLIAM (1756-1814), master mariner and merchant, was born in October 1756, and entered the navy as master of the sloop *Tobago* on 24 March 1779. He enlisted in the West Indies, where he was probably serving in a merchant ship. Though the West Indian Squadron was then hard pressed for men, the fact that he was a master so young suggests considerable ability. In 1780 he was twice wounded when master of the *Albion*, which he had joined in Barbados the previous September. In February 1782 his son, William Thomas, who had been baptized at St Michael's, Barbados, on 3 February 1775 and later became a lieutenant, joined him as master's servant and served with him until May 1786. On 11 July 1783 examiners at Trinity House declared Raven qualified 'to take charge, as Master, of any of His Majesty's ships of the Third Rate', and he served as master of the *Grampus* for three years. In May 1786 he received a certificate for first-rate ships, but there is no further record of his services until 1791 when he was briefly master of the *Duke*.

In 1792 he sailed to New South Wales as captain and part owner of the *Britannia*, with stores and a three-year fishing licence from the East India Co. He left Sydney in October when his ship was chartered by the officers of the New South Wales Corps to procure provisions from the Cape of Good Hope in an effort to avoid the impositions practised by the captains of merchant ships visiting the colony. On the way Raven left the first sealing gang to operate on the New Zealand coast at Dusky Bay, under the charge of his second mate. He arrived back in Sydney in June 1793 with stock, provisions and spirits, and left again in September to procure provisions in Bengal for Lieut-Governor Grose [q.v.]. He relieved the sealing gang at Dusky Bay and then called at Norfolk Island, where Lieut-Governor King chartered the *Britannia* to convey himself and two Maoris to New Zealand. When Raven finally sailed for Bengal he was delayed by bad weather and encountered pirates in the Malacca Straits, and decided to try to buy his provisions at Batavia instead. He arrived there in February 1794, and after prolonged argument with the Dutch East India Co. over prices, made his purchases, but when he reached Sydney in June he found that store-ships had come from England with relief for the hungry colony. The officers then chartered the *Britannia* again, and in March 1795 Raven returned from the Cape with livestock and provisions for them. In June the acting governor, William Paterson [q.v.], once more chartered the ship to bring provisions from Bengal.

After Raven returned from Calcutta in May 1796 Governor Hunter engaged him in September to take 'a number of distressed invalids' back to England. He arrived there in June 1797 and asked the commissioners of the navy for time to arrange his accounts before receiving another posting. In December he was appointed master of the naval store-ship *Buffalo* and in May 1799 brought her to Port Jackson as a replacement for H.M.S. *Supply*. Hunter provided him with a passage home in the *Britannia* in December 1799, but he was captured by a French privateer off the Isle of Wight and taken a prisoner to France; however, he reached England in June 1800 and asked to be put on half-pay. Next year he asked that he be allowed to remain unemployed owing to 'very unpleasant circumstances of a private nature' and the need to settle still outstanding accounts from the *Buffalo*. On 6 November 1800 he had been admitted a Younger Brother of the Trinity House, and when war against Napoleon was resumed in 1803 he was commissioned lieutenant in the Trinity House volunteers; he served in the Thames flotilla, but reported in 1805 that the effects of the wounds received in 1780 made him unfit for more active service. He was elected an Elder Brother of Trinity House on 13 November 1806, and died on 14 August 1814.

Raven married Lucinda Wilson (b. 1752), daughter of the chief justice of Dominica; they had one daughter. In 1809 Raven stood godfather to his niece, Susan Mary, daughter of Admiral George Wilson. In 1795 he had been given a grant of 100 acres at Eastern Farms, and in 1799 received another 285 acres there and a lease in Sydney. Until at least 1822 these properties were managed for him by James Squires of Kissing Point. Although Raven had a modest estate when he died, his widow later applied for assistance to Trinity House, and she and her daughter received a pension until the middle of the century.

HRNSW, 2, 3, 4; HRA (1), 1, 2; R. McNab, *Historical records of New Zealand*, 2 (Wellington, 1914); J. S. Cumpston, *Shipping arrivals and departures Sydney, 1788-1825*

(Canberra, 1964); *Sydney Gazette*, 4 May 1811, 31 May 1822; MS cat under Raven (ML); Masters' Qualifications 1748-1805, Adm 106/2938 (PRO).

VIVIENNE PARSONS

RAYMOND, JAMES (1786?-1851), postmaster-general, was reputedly a landowner and magistrate in County Limerick, Ireland, who became involved in disturbances there and was forced to abandon his property when his life was threatened. When his lands became dilapidated in his absence, Raymond decided to emigrate. In July 1824 Henry Goulburn wrote on his behalf to Earl Bathurst, requesting a free passage for Raymond and his family to New South Wales because of their misfortunes in Ireland. Governor Darling was asked to provide Raymond with a suitable colonial appointment and, until it became available, to allow him the means of subsistence. With his wife Aphrasia and nine children, Raymond arrived at Sydney in the *Thames* in April 1826, and in May Darling made him coroner at Parramatta on a salary of £50, with additional allowances of £184 in place of rations and lodgings until a more suitable appointment could be found.

By September 1826 Darling was complaining to the Colonial Office that Raymond found his income insufficient and considered that the government should support him. Darling had intended to employ Raymond as police magistrate because of his supposed Irish experience, but Raymond denied this report, and his work as coroner proved that his education had been insufficient to equip him either for business or for public position. The Colonial Office replied that no other expectation had been held out to Raymond than the mere sufficiency afforded by a minor position, and that his allowances were to be only temporary. Meanwhile Darling had decided that Raymond's income was insufficient to maintain such a large family and had increased his allowance to £400. He was forced to withdraw this increase when he heard from the British government, and despite further appeals on Raymond's behalf no additional allowance was approved.

In September 1827 Darling, reluctant either to allow the family to starve or to be obliged to meet Raymond's debts, made him searcher and surveyor of customs. In April 1829 George Paton, the postmaster, died and Raymond was appointed to succeed him at a salary of £400; this was confirmed by Downing Street in September. Despite complaints that Raymond was dependent on his clerk

for the executive and legislative duties of his department and an accusation that he had unfairly dismissed the clerk, Darling upheld Raymond's conduct and later governors praised him as a meritorious public servant. In 1835 his title was changed to postmaster-general, and his salary had increased to £650 by the time of his death.

Raymond is noted for suggesting the introduction of stamped sheets to be used as envelopes, on the model of Rowland Hill's proposals; this suggestion was adopted by Governor Gipps in November 1838, anticipating the British penny postage in 1840. In 1839 Raymond bought Varroville, near Campbelltown, from Charles Sturt [q.v.] and there entertained extensively. He was also a keen follower of horse-racing and owned several horses himself. He died at Darlinghurst on 29 May 1851 aged 65, and was buried at St Peter's, Cook's River. His wife Aphrasia predeceased him on 1 September 1848; they had seven daughters and four sons, of whom James and Robert Peel held positions in the post office and William was a landholder at Bathurst.

HRA (1), 12, 13, 15-17, 19; R. C. V. Humphrey, 'The early postal and philatelic history of the colony of NSW', *JRAHS*, 25 (1939); *Sydney Gazette*, 12 Apr, 6 May 1826; *Australian*, 28 Apr 1829; *SMH*, 31 May 1851; MS cat under J. Raymond (ML).

VIVIENNE PARSONS

READ, GEORGE FREDERICK (1788-1860), merchant, settler and banker, was born on 29 September 1788 in London. He went to sea when 11 and was probably engaged in the East India Co.'s maritime service until 1808. Later he recorded in his journal that he visited the Derwent settlement that year and again in 1812, but was irritated by having his cargo commandeered and his crew placed on rations. He is believed to have brought the first merchant vessel through Torres Strait, and he continued to trade between Hobart Town, Sydney, Batavia, Calcutta and China.

In May 1814 as master and part-owner of the *Amelia* he brought tea, sugar, rum and tobacco from Calcutta to Sydney and returned with wine and whale oil. In 1816-18 he made voyages between Sydney, the Derwent, Batavia and Calcutta in his brig *Lynx*. In 1816 he was granted a town allotment in Sydney, but he suffered from asthma and in June 1818 moved to Hobart in the brig *Sophia*. He transferred his merchant establishment there and later formed partnerships with W. A. Bethune and Charles McLachlan [qq.v.]. In 1819 he was granted 800 acres at Redlands, Plenty, and four government servants. In 1822 he built a stone warehouse on Hunter's Island facing Sullivan's Cove (the old wharf) and was appointed a magistrate. He was one of the original proprietors of the Bank of Van Diemen's Land and its managing director from 1827 to 1849, living for some time in a 'comfortably fixed' villa on the Derwent. In 1829 he resumed the former business of Read & Bethune, and from then until 1852 acted as agent for John Ingle [q.v.].

He took a very considerable part in the development of the young colony, not least in its maritime industries, was one of the most important men in its formative years and contributed greatly to the community's welfare. He had interests in several ships trading to India, China and the Philippines, in which his third son, Henry (1828-1894), made several voyages as supercargo, and his ships took part in sealing and whaling. He was a good practical farmer, grew fine wheat, made bricks and helped to establish the salmon ponds at Redlands. He had other properties: Ivanhoe and Kinvarra, in the Plenty-New Norfolk district, Seton near Richmond, and Thornhill near Sorell. He also had a three-storied stone tea-warehouse in Salamanca Place, Hobart, other Hobart town property, and city sections bought at Melbourne's first land sale. He was versatile, enterprising and far-sighted. Lieut-Governor Sorell spoke highly of him, made him an assessor in the Lieut-Governor's Court and in 1822 appointed him a magistrate; however, he fell out with Lieut-Governor Arthur, protested against licensing the press, and was removed from the magistracy.

In 1816 at St Philip's, Sydney, he married Elizabeth Driver; they had one son, G. F. Read junior (1817-1854), a pioneer at Port Phillip, and two daughters. His wife died on 19 August 1821, and on 24 November 1824 at St David's, Hobart, he married Margaret (1800-1889), daughter of John Terry [q.v.], a flour-miller of New Norfolk. By his second marriage he had six sons and four daughters. He died at his home, Leyburne, New Town, on 23 July 1860.

Several of his letters to John Ingle were published under the title *Tasmanian Letters* 1824-1852 (Christchurch, 1945).

HRA (1), 10, (3), 2-6; A. McKay (ed), *Journals of the land commissioners for Van Diemen's Land, 1826-28* (Hob, 1962); G. F. Read, Papers (ML).   H. C. C. LANGDON

READ, RICHARD, 'Richard Read senior' (b. 1765?), artist, was born in London. In July 1812 he was sentenced in London to transportation for fourteen years and arrived in New South Wales in the *Earl*

Spencer in October 1813. He was granted a ticket-of-leave in December, and next January his wife Sarah and their daughter Lydia arrived as free settlers in the *Kangaroo*.

In November 1814 Read advertised in the *Sydney Gazette* the establishment of his drawing school, the first in Australia, at 37 Pitt Street, Sydney. In addition to offering lessons in the 'polite and elegant art of drawing in its most elevated branches', he had for sale designs for embroidery, drawings and paintings of 'various subjects' and announced his readiness to execute miniatures and portraits. In a notice of February 1821 he described the drawings as 'views of various parts of New Holland . . . drawings of Birds, Flowers, Native Figures, etc.' Read taught drawing, painted portraits and genre works, and decorated colonial mansions, including Piper Castle and Government House, until late in the 1820s when, according to a survey of 'The State of the Fine Arts in New South Wales', published in the *Sydney Gazette,* 28 July 1829, he relinquished his profession and took up farming.

In 1816 Read petitioned Governor Macquarie for mitigation of his sentence. He was conditionally pardoned in April 1819, and although he did not receive his absolute pardon until March 1825, he seems to have benefited from vice-regal patronage, and from commissions from wealthy settlers, for his petition of 1816 referred to 'indulgences received' and, he trusted, 'merited', at the governor's hands.

Richard Read gained a considerable reputation in the colony and by 1820 his talents were said to be 'too high to call for a panegyric'. He claimed that a series of portraits, framed and glazed, of Macquarie had been 'finished from the life'. Another portrait very well received was that of Michael Robinson [q.v.], the 'Poet Laureate' of the colony. The group portrait of 'Mrs. Piper and her Children' at Vaucluse House, Sydney, was thought to be the work of Read, but has since been attributed to Augustus Earle [q.v.].

All that is known of Read's artistic or social background before he arrived in the colony is that he had practised as a professional artist in London. In his first advertisement of 1814 Read pronounced himself 'History and Portrait Painter', but it was not until 1825 that he claimed to have been a pupil of Sir Joshua Reynolds. Read's assertion is difficult to accept, as in an advertisement of his drawing school, published in the *Sydney Gazette* in February 1821, he professed 'more than twenty-five years' experience of the Art', implying that his career had begun around 1796, four years after Sir Joshua Reynolds's death. Nevertheless Read's age at the time of his conviction—47 years—allows for the possibility that the artist had worked as an assistant in Reynolds's studio. The only known reference to an historical subject painted by Richard Read senior was made in 1819 in an anecdote published in the *Sydney Gazette*. Mr 'Reid' had presented a 'water painting' to an unnamed household in George Street, Sydney. The subject was taken from the eighteenth book of the *Iliad*, and happened to be placed above a teatray purchased by the mistress of the house which also depicted an incident from the *Iliad*.

Read was listed in the indent of the *Earl Spencer* as 'Read', and signed himself thus in his petition to the governor. The teller of the *Iliad* tale spells the artist's name as 'Reid' and so does the journalist who gave an account of decorations painted for the Bachelors' Ball by Read in January 1820. A notice of 1822 telling of Read's commission to execute a half-length portrait of Macquarie uses the spelling 'Reed', but the painter's use of the spelling 'Reid' in his professional advertisements does not appear until 1825. This may possibly have been his method of distinguishing himself from a fellow colonial artist, apparently no relation, Richard Read junior [q.v.], who had arrived in Sydney in 1819 as a free settler, and who also lived in Pitt Street at the same time as his older namesake.

It is probable that Read left the colony with his family after he was pardoned. No record of later work or of his death can be traced in New South Wales.

Rex and Thea Rienits, *Early artists of Australia* (Syd, 1963); W. Dixson, 'Notes on Australian artists', *JRAHS*, 5 (1919); *Sydney Gazette*, 6 Nov 1819, 8 Feb 1822; Convict indents (NSWA). JOCELYN GRAY

READ (REID), RICHARD junior (b. 1796?), artist, arrived in New South Wales in November 1819 in the *David Shaw* as a free settler. In February 1821 his first professional advertisement appeared in the *Sydney Gazette*. He described himself as a portrait and historical painter and miniature painter, offered for sale 'a most elegant collection of drawings consisting of Natives of New Zealand and New South Wales, View, Flowers, etc', and was ready to teach drawing 'on a most easy and entirely new plan'. In this first advertisement Read adopted the distinction 'junior',

drew attention to his address, 59 Pitt Street, and disclaimed any connexion whatever with any other person in the same profession, presumably a reference to Richard Read senior [q.v.], who also lived in Pitt Street. In an advertisement of April 1822 Read had dropped his claim to being an 'historical painter' but added landscape painting to his advertisement and offered to copy miniatures and portraits, and clean and restore oil paintings. In all later advertisements he described himself as a miniature and portrait painter who would also instruct in drawing and painting and clean and restore works of art. In the latest of these advertisements he gave his address as Somerset Lodge, Dowling Street, Surry Hills. From the same address Read contributed one miniature and four portraits to the 1849 exhibition of the Society for the Promotion of the Fine Arts in Australia; one portrait was of Dr Bland [q.v.] and another of Governor Bourke.

Very little is known of Read's personal life. On 30 May 1821 Richard Read, artist, was married by special licence at St Philip's Church to Eliza, aged 22, eldest daughter of Benjamin Hitchcock of George Street, Sydney. The age of the artist at this marriage was recorded as 25, but at the census of 1828, Richard Read, artist, who had arrived in 1819, gave his age as 29.

In July 1823 a Richard Read, who gave his address as York Street, Sydney, sent to Governor Brisbane a memorial seeking a grant of land in the Bathurst district, and asserted his readiness to 'take off and support three government men from His Majesty's Stores'. Richard Read, the artist, had indeed arrived in New South Wales 'free, about four years back', as was stated in the memorial, but his address before and after its submission, and until his removal to Dowling Street, continued to be Pitt Street. A professional advertisement published by Read in 1843 did, however, give two addresses: Dowling Street, and Willow Cottage, Pitt Street, so that it is possible that the artist retained a studio in Pitt Street and lived elsewhere.

The absence of his name from Sydney directories after 1851 suggests that Read and his wife may have left the colony. No record of his death can be found in New South Wales. The artist signed his memorial 'Read', and in the census of 1828 his name is also given as 'Read' as it is in the catalogue of the exhibition of 1849. Both 'Reid' and 'Read' appear in his professional advertisements.

W. Dixson, 'Notes on Australian artists', *JRAHS*, 5 (1919). JOCELYN GRAY

REDDALL, THOMAS (1780-1838), clergyman and educationist, was the son of Luke Reddall, of Aldridge, Staffordshire, England. He was educated for three years at Alban Hall, Oxford, in preparation for a colonial chaplaincy, was ordained on 19 December 1819, and next day appointed assistant chaplain to New South Wales. He did not leave immediately; from July 1819 he had attended the Central National School, London, to become proficient in the Madras system of instruction, and continued there till May 1820. As no schoolmaster was available to introduce the system into the colony, as had been determined as a matter of policy, Earl Bathurst appointed Reddall schoolmaster as well as chaplain with the salary of both, it being understood that he would resign 'when the System is Sufficiently established'.

Reddall arrived in Sydney with his wife, Isabella, and seven children on 14 September 1820. Two other daughters were born in the colony. Reddall immediately made a marked impression. His preaching was very highly praised. The change to the Madras system at the Male Orphan School was done so efficiently that it drew encomiums from both Governor Macquarie and Comissioner Bigge [q.v.]. His criticism of the building being erected near St James's Church as unsuitable for a school led to its being changed into a law court, and a new building, the Georgian School, in Castlereagh Street, was begun. At the end of 1820 Castle Meehan at Macquarie Fields was rented for him at the high figure of £180 a year. He opened a private school there and two of his first pupils were the son of Lachlan Macquarie and the son of Lieut-Governor Sorell, of Van Diemen's Land. In May 1821 he began duty as clergyman for the districts of Airds, Appin and Minto, and he was made a magistrate in August. In 1822 he became incumbent of the new Church of St Peter at Campbelltown. In January 1824 the Male and Female Orphan Schools and the Native Institution were brought under the joint administration of a committee of three, of whom Reddall was one. On 18 August 1824, on account of 'the languishing state of education', Reddall was appointed to the imposing position of director-general of all the government public schools, and the extra salary he received was greater than that of a chaplain. First Macquarie and then Governor Brisbane, sometimes in excess of their powers, were lavish in assisting him with land, cattle and finance. When Archdeacon Scott [q.v.] arrived in June 1825 as King's Visitor to the schools, Reddall was supernumerary but remained director-general until 6 February 1826. Next month all government schools passed under the control of the Church and School Corporation and Reddall's connexion with them ceased.

Reddall was commissioned to introduce the Madras system into the public schools of New South Wales, and he drew a salary as schoolmaster and director-general as well as his salary as chaplain for over five years. At the end of that period, however, the only schools using the system were the two in Sydney, the two orphan schools, and his own parish school at Campbelltown, and even these were not wholly the result of Reddall's efforts. It had taken only a brief period to complete a similar change in Van Diemen's Land. What promised to be a brilliant career ended in sterility. He was all too eager to rush into rural pursuits. He was using his glebe before there was a church. His private boys' school, begun so favourably, soon changed into a girls' school conducted by his wife and daughters. Instead of a parsonage he built his own home, Glen Alpine, two miles outside Campbelltown, and essayed a social status somewhat beyond his means. He overreached himself in his rural activities and ran into financial difficulties. A man of taste and refinement with a bright and active mind, an excellent conversationalist, cultured and capable, with a pleasing personality, he misused his talents. He died on 30 November 1838.

His eldest son John married Martha, the sister of W. C. Wentworth [q.v.]. His second son Thomas was educated at Corpus Christi College, Cambridge (B.A., 1838; M.A., 1841) and in 1859 became incumbent of his father's parish.

L. Macquarie, *Journals of his tours in New South Wales and Van Diemen's Land, 1810-1822* (Syd, 1956); MS cat under T. Reddall (ML).

V. W. E. GOODIN

REDFERN, WILLIAM (1774?-1833), surgeon, was born probably in Canada, and brought up at Trowbridge, Wiltshire, England, where his brother lived later. His letters show a command of English and acquaintance with the classics which suggest that he was well educated. In June 1797 after passing the examination of the London Company of Surgeons, the predecessor of the Royal College of Surgeons, he was commissioned surgeon's mate in the navy. He joined H.M.S. *Standard*, whose crew a few months later took part in the mutiny of the fleet at the Nore, which followed the success of the mutiny of the Channel Fleet at Spithead. In the course of the trouble Redfern advised the men 'to be more united among themselves', so he was included among the leaders to be tried by court martial. On 27 August a scrupulously fair court sentenced him to death, but because of his youth he was reprieved. He was kept in prison for four years until sent to New South Wales in the *Minorca*, on whose indent his name is bracketed with thirteen others as 'Mutineers'. On board he helped the surgeon and reached Sydney on 14 December 1801.

In May 1802 he commenced duty as assistant surgeon at Norfolk Island. He attracted the attention of Lieut-Governor Foveaux [q.v.] and soon received a conditional pardon; on 19 June 1803 he was given a free pardon by Governor King. For five years he worked hard there and gained a good medical reputation; when he returned to Sydney in 1808, Foveaux, then in command at headquarters, appointed him assistant surgeon, owing to 'the distress'd State of the Colony for medical aid' since 'his skill and ability in his profession are unquestionable, and his conduct has been such as to deserve particular approbation'. As he had no documentary evidence of his professional qualifications Surgeons Jamison, Harris [qq.v.] and William Bohan examined him in 'Medicine, Surgery and other necessary collateral Branches of Medical Literature'. They found him 'qualified to exercise the Profession of a Surgeon etc.'; the examination set a precedent followed for many years for testing anyone who wished to practise medicine in the colony. During 1809 Redfern attended John Macarthur's [q.v.] daughter and earned her father's deep gratitude for 'the skill he . . . manifested in discovering and applying an efficacious remedy to her extraordinary disease'. Macarthur promised to use his influence in Redfern's favour 'whenever Mr. Bligh's affair is settled', but by that time Governor Macquarie had recommended the confirmation of Redfern's appointment, and to this the secretary of state agreed.

Since 1808 Redfern had been working in the old and dilapidated hospital at Dawes Point. The building of an urgently needed replacement was one of the first tasks Macquarie put in hand. When it was completed in 1816 Redfern took charge of it, and D'Arcy Wentworth [q.v.], the principal surgeon, only occasionally visited the wards as a consultant. Redfern was assisted by his apprentice, Henry, son of Rev. William Cowper [q.v.], who after three years training was appointed assistant at the hospital. After two years in this post Redfern regarded him as a particularly well-trained practitioner. Cowper, as Redfern's apprentice, had succeeded James Shears who, commencing in 1813, was the first Australian medical student, but had died a year later. Occupation of the new hospital did not end the appalling conditions which had existed in the old place; there remained inadequacies of diet and sanitation, and the nursing care provided by the unreliable and often disorderly staff of convict attendants and nurses was very rough. Stealing was so rife that Redfern, having no trustworthy person on his staff—even Cowper was in trouble for supplying medicines, stockings and other items from the store to his friends—had perforce to issue all stores and supervise the making of medicines to check the theft of drugs.

In addition to his work in the hospital wards, Redfern conducted a daily outpatient clinic for men from the convict gangs. He also had the most extensive private practice in the colony, for he was the most popular doctor in the settlement and his services were widely sought. He was the family doctor to the Macarthurs and the Macquaries and attended the birth of Governor Macquarie's son. His professional skill was highly regarded by his colleagues and he had the reputation of being the best obstetrician in the colony.

Since Redfern was concerned with convict health it was natural that he should have been asked to investigate the heavy mortality suffered on the calamitous voyages of the convict transports *Surry*, *General Hewitt* and *Three Bees* in 1814. His report is one of the major Australian contributions to public health. His recommendations on the ventilation, cleanliness and fumigation of the ships, on the diet and clothing of the prisoners and the need for permitting them on deck were all important, but even more noteworthy was his insistence on the need for 'approved and skilful' surgeons in each ship and for defining clearly their powers *vis-à-vis* the ships' masters. To provide men for this service he recommended naval surgeons, 'Men of Abilities, who have been Accustomed to Sea practice, who know what is due to themselves as Men, and as Officers with full power to exercise their Judgment, without being liable to the Controul of the Masters of the Transports'. This advice was followed, and the appointment of surgeon-superintendents of convict, and later emigrant, ships put an end to most of the abuses of the past.

When D'Arcy Wentworth resigned as principal surgeon in 1818 Redfern expected to succeed him; but despite his previous promises to Redfern and a very strong recommendation from Macquarie, Bathurst appointed a naval surgeon, James Bowman [q.v.], probably because of his dislike of employing former convicts. Redfern thereupon resigned as assistant surgeon. On 14 October 1819 he left the government medical service, to which, declared Macquarie in a General Order, he had been 'so great and valuable an acquisition' thanks to 'his superior professional skill, steady attention and active zealous performance of the numerous important duties entrusted to him'. As a solace next month Macquarie appointed Redfern a magistrate, despite the warnings of Commissioner Bigge [q.v.] against doing so; next year Bathurst, expressing his disapproval of 'nominations of Convicts to the Magistracy', ordered his removal from the bench. Unfortunately Redfern had become a provocative symbol of the governor's emancipist policy.

Redfern always took an active part in the life of New South Wales. He was an honorary medical officer of the Benevolent Society, a member of its committee and that of the Aborigines' Institution. He was one of the first directors of the Bank of New South Wales. He and his wife had an estate of 100 acres which gave the name of Redfern to the Sydney suburb which later developed about it. In 1818 he was granted 1300 acres in the Airds district. This he called Campbell Fields in honour of Mrs Macquarie, and it was praised by Bigge as one of the best developed properties in the colony.

In 1817 the status of emancipists was shaken by a ruling of the King's Bench that persons freed by the governor's pardon, unlike those under pardons issued under the Great Seal in London, could not maintain personal action at law or acquire, retain or transmit property, and Judge Barron Field [q.v.] followed this in a decision in Sydney in 1820. At a meeting held in January 1821 it was decided to send Redfern and Edward Eagar [q.v.] to present a petition, appealing against this to the King. Redfern sailed for England on 27 October. The delegation was successful and the position was rectified by the New South Wales Act of 1823. While in England Redfern prepared an indictment against Bigge and a book criticizing his methods of inquiry, but did not publish it. After a sojourn in Madeira for his health he returned to New South Wales in the *Alfred* in July 1824, received a further grant at Campbell Fields and acquired land near Bathurst and Cowra. He lived at Campbell Fields and devoted more time to his farming activities, which included cultivating the vine as well as fine wool and cattle; he gradually withdrew from his medical practice, which he entirely gave up in September 1826. Two years later he took his son William to Edinburgh to be educated. Though he intended to return, he died there in July 1833. He left 23,190 acres in New South Wales, including 6296 at Airds and 11,362 at Bathurst.

When Redfern came from England in 1801 he was single. When he returned from Norfolk Island in 1808 in the schooner *Estramina*, according to the passenger list he was accompanied by his wife, but no other record of his marriage is known. On 4 April 1811 he married Sarah Wills of Sydney, and had two sons, William Lachlan Macquarie (b. 1819), who later lived in Edinburgh, and Joseph Foveaux (1823-30). In June 1834 Sarah married James Alexander of Glasgow and later returned with him to Sydney.

Redfern had great forcefulness and independence of character; Bigge, who found in him a proud and inflexible opponent, said he was the only person in the colony to resist his authority. He had kindliness and integrity, attributes that gained for him the support and enduring friendship of Macquarie, which was steadfastly maintained in the face of often bitter opposition from those who detested the rise of ex-convicts. He lacked a gracious bedside manner, but on his retirement the *Sydney Gazette*, 6 September 1826, commented, 'his experience and skill made ample amends for any apparent absence of overflowing politeness'. Disdained by many as an emancipist, Redfern was always ready to reply brusquely to men like Bigge and Bowman who were offensive to him. In 1827 he horsewhipped Robert Howe [q.v.] for attacking him in the *Gazette*, and was fined 30s. He was one of the greatest of the early medical practitioners of the colony, the first to receive an Australian qualification, the first teacher of Australian medical students, and the author of important reforms in the convict transports. Nevertheless, as a result of his youthful actions at the Nore, which, however justified, were naturally resented by the government, his later important services in New South Wales were ill requited.

HRA (1), 6-10; E. Ford, *The life and work of William Redfern* (Syd, 1953); N. J. Dunlop, 'William Redfern, the first Australian medical graduate', JRAHS, 14 (1928); E. Ford, 'Medical practice in early Sydney', MJA,

9 July 1955; *Australian*, 23 Jan 1828; Bigge Report, evidence, Bonwick transcripts (ML).
                                            EDWARD FORD

REDMOND, EDWARD (1766?-1840), publican, dealer and Catholic layman, was an uneducated Irish labourer who appears to have signed his name with a mark all his life. At 32 he was an Irish rebel of 1798, convicted in King's County in April and sentenced to transportation for life. He arrived in the *Minerva* in January 1800, described as McRedmond, the name Governor Macquarie used in 1813 when confirming his absolute pardon. Redmond had received a conditional pardon on 4 June 1803 and set up in business in Sydney. In January 1808 he signed the address expressing confidence in Governor Bligh, though also asking that the government grant freedom to trade and trial by jury to the free colonists of New South Wales. Next year the rebel government gave him a wine and spirit licence and 135 acres at Botany; on 1 December 1809 he received his absolute pardon which, like the grant and the liquor licence, Macquarie later confirmed.

Redmond married a widow, Winifred Duriault, née Dowling, on 15 October 1811. She had been convicted, with her sister Eliza, in County Kildare in 1801 and, sentenced to transportation for life, had arrived in the *Atlas* in July 1802, and in September had married François Duriault (de Riveau). He was a French vigneron who, together with Antoine Landrien, a fellow prisoner of war, had been sent out by the British government in 1801 to teach vine-growing to the colonists. In March 1804 Duriault was sent back to England because his work was unsatisfactory and Governor King suspected that he was implicated in the convict uprising at Castle Hill, but his wife remained in New South Wales with an infant son, who became known as John Redmond after she married Edward Redmond. She bore Redmond two daughters, Mary and Sarah.

Edward and Winifred Redmond seem to have become prosperous and respectable. In 1815 Redmond, in partnership with Patrick Cullen, leased the tolls between Sydney and Parramatta, and so was involved in the controversy which followed the refusal of J. H. Bent [q.v.] to pay them. In 1816 he became one of the original shareholders in the Bank of New South Wales. In 1819 he was one of the colony's business men who petitioned the British government to lessen the restrictions it placed on the carriage of goods to the colony in convict ships. In 1820 he was elected to the committee set up to arrange for building a permanent Roman Catholic Church in Sydney, after services had been begun in temporary buildings on Redmond's premises. During the 1820s he extended his activities as a landowner, though suffering from drought and depression in 1827-28. He died in 1840 and was buried in the Devonshire Street cemetery on 24 January. He was later reinterred at Botany. To his widow and children he left farms at Bathurst, Bingham, Annandale and on the Hawkesbury River, houses at Windsor and Liverpool, and Sydney houses in Essen Lane and Prince Street and on Brickfield Hill. He had risen from convict status to the ranks of respectability, and made a contribution to the establishment of the Roman Catholic Church in Australia.

HRNSW, 4; HRA (1), 2, 4, 7, 9, 10, 14; J. P. McGuanne, 'Old St Mary's', *JRAHS*, 3 (1915-17); MS cat under E. Redmond (ML).
                                        VIVIENNE PARSONS

REED, HENRY (1806-1880), landowner, shipowner, merchant and philanthropist, was born on 28 December 1806 at Doncaster, England, the youngest of four children of Samuel Reed (1773-1813), postmaster at Doncaster, and his wife Mary, née Rockliff. At 13 he was apprenticed to a merchant in Hull. At 20 he sailed from Gravesend by steerage in the *Tiger* and arrived at Hobart Town in April 1827 after a long hard journey that deepened his religious feeling. His goal was Launceston; with no conveyance available he walked the 120 miles with a shipmate, met J. W. Gleadow [q.v.] and obtained a position in his store.

Friendship with John Batman [q.v.], to whose marriage at Launceston he was a witness, made Reed quick to see the value of land and convict labour. He declared his assets at £605 and in January 1828 was given by Lieut-Governor Arthur a free land grant of 640 acres at the Nile rivulet. He soon acquired other properties near Launceston. He left Gleadow's store and with a partner traded as Reed & Duncan, general merchants. In 1830 the partnership was dissolved by mutual consent; Reed carried on the business under his own name and began his shipping ventures by chartering the *Britannia* with James Henty [q.v.] for a trading voyage to Swan River. Soon he had his own ships. The *Henry* was one of his first, followed by the *Socrates*. They were engaged in whaling, sealing and general trading out of Launceston to Hobart, Sydney, New Zealand and London. He had men at

Westernport for wattle bark, and at Kangaroo Island and Spencer Gulf for whales, and visited them often navigating and commanding his own ships. With William Dutton [q.v.] he established a whaling station at Portland Bay which he later sold to the Hentys. His enterprise on Australia's southern coast did much towards its later settlement.

In 1831 Reed sailed for England in the *Bombay*, and in London he married his cousin Maria Susanna Grubb. He also established an important business connexion with Henry Buckle & Co. Back in Van Diemen's Land in 1832 he was publicly thanked for helping to establish a lucrative whale oil trade at Launceston and for interesting British merchants in it. But he had little time for such pleasantries; when the *Socrates* arrived from London, he sent her to Port Phillip and thence to Mauritius for sugar, and he arranged settlement for Gatenby's [q.v.] wool which had been sold in France after consignment by Reed to Buckle's. In April 1833 he bought the whaler *Norval* and sailed in her for London with his family. Later in the year he sold the *Socrates*. The *Henry* paid several visits to the whaling grounds, and on a trip to Kangaroo Island the master, John Jones, sailed up the eastern coast of Gulf St Vincent and like Collet Barker [q.v.] found several rivers, some fine grass land and two good harbours; his report had some importance in the later settlement of South Australia.

In 1835 Reed returned to Launceston, took wheat in the *Norval* to Sydney and visited the first settlers at Port Phillip. His ships were soon busy carrying stores, livestock and migrants from Launceston. The *Henry*, on an early trip in May 1836 to Geelong, had her name given to Point Henry. Reed's enterprise helped the new settlement in many other ways, not least his loan of £3000 to John Batman. At the same time he did not neglect his activities in Van Diemen's Land, where he bought the attractive property of Native Hut Corner near Mole Creek, renamed it Wesley Dale and soon had thirty assigned convicts at work. In December 1835 he became an original director of the Bank of Australasia at Launceston and was appointed superintendent of the new Sunday school opened by the Paterson Street Methodist church.

With all his business ventures Reed found time for practical religion. By faith a Wesleyan and a fervent evangelist, he had ready sympathy for all unfortunates. At Port Phillip he spent some time up country with Aboriginals in hope of saving them from a fate like that of the Tasmanian tribes. He was reputed to have preached the first sermon on the site of Melbourne, his congregation being Henry and John Batman, William Buckley [q.v.] and three Sydney Aboriginals. To encourage the opening of a mission at the new settlement he offered £20 and annual subscriptions. At Launceston in November 1837 he had himself locked one night in the cells with condemned criminals who were to be executed next morning.

In politics Reed's experience was short and unpleasant. In 1845 when the Patriotic Six walked out of the Legislative Council in protest against increased taxation, Lieut-Governor Eardley-Wilmot had some difficulty in finding new nominees. Reed was persuaded to represent the northern mercantile interests, but after a few months of struggle against public opinion, he resigned his seat. The long depression that caused this rumpus was beginning to lift and prices for produce were rising. A business sensation was created in Launceston when Reed, as the agent of Buckle's, foreclosed on James Henty for the satisfaction of a large debt. Reed later helped Henty to re-establish himself and good personal terms between the two men were restored.

In December 1847 Reed sailed with his family in the *Lochnagar* for London. For the next twenty-six years he lived in England while his affairs in Launceston flourished and values appreciated. With Alfred Hawley he persuaded the London shipping firm of T. B. Walker to support trade with the River Tamar; in February 1852 the *Arnon* arrived in Launceston, the first of seven ships, one of which was named *Henry Reed* and another *Alfred Hawley*. Reed's major interest, however, was evangelical. He undertook many preaching engagements throughout the north of England and, dismayed by the widespread poverty he encountered, devoted himself to providing homes and assisting the poor with food and other necessities. In his native Doncaster he bought ten cottages for free occupation by aged Christians and arranged to pay all the rates and repair bills. For his own large family he built Dunorlan Villa at Harrogate in Yorkshire. Later he moved to Tunbridge Wells where, in spite of criticism by church associates, he built Dunorlan, an imposing residence in beautiful grounds; over the entrance his family crest showed a sheaf of wheat over the motto, 'nothing without the cross'.

Reed's wife died in 1860; she had borne him eleven children. In 1863 he married Margaret Sayres Elizabeth Frith of Enniskillen, Ireland, an ardent church worker, by whom he had five children. After his second marriage, his philanthropic interest increased. He became associated with General Booth and helped him with money and advice in the difficult formative years of the Salvation Army. Generous gifts were also made to other evangelical work such as the China Inland Mission and the East London Christian Mission. He helped to establish places of worship in the East End and schools on Bow Common. In 1869 he gave the first £1000 to Rev. William Pennefather for a church conference hall. He compiled *The Pioneer Hymn Book* (London, 1870) and published two tracts, 'Be filled with the spirit' and 'Incidents in an eventful life', *Dunorlan Tracts*, 1-2 (London, 1873).

In April 1873, while preaching in a Harrogate mission, Reed felt a call to return to Tasmania. With his family and attendants he sailed in the *Sobraon* and, after arrival at Launceston in December, settled at Mount Pleasant, which he bought next year from his friend John Crookes [q.v.]. Although he renovated Mount Pleasant making it the finest house in northern Tasmania, developed Wesley Dale and consolidated his other properties, his main concern was still evangelism. In 1875 he helped Rev. George Brown to establish the New Guinea Mission and bought for it the steam launch *Henry Reed*. In New Britain Brown named Henry Reed Bay in his honour. In Launceston he bought Parr's Hotel in Wellington Street in order to replace it with a mission church. The adjoining skittle alley was renovated and opened for worship in July 1876, but the Memorial Church on the site was completed in 1885 after his death, as were the near-by Dunorlan Cottages built in his memory to provide free housing with a sustenance allowance for elderly indigent women.

Reed spent much time with his family at Mountain Villa on Wesley Dale and was credited with discovering the Mole Creek caves. His health failed rapidly towards the end. He died at Mount Pleasant on 10 October 1880. His life purpose was outlined in a letter to a friend: 'I have been so much accustomed to put my whole heart into anything I have engaged in, and to do it in the best possible way, and never to be satisfied with anything but decided success whether in spiritual or temporal things, that it troubles me much when I see things half done or carelessly done, but I must ask the Lord to help me in old age to look over and pass by many things'.

Portraits of Henry Reed are in the possession of the Queen Victoria Museum and Art Gallery, Launceston, and of Mr H. D. Reed, Talinga, Hagley.

M. S. E. Reed, *Henry Reed. An eventful life, devoted to God and man* (Lond, 1907); Correspondence file under Henry Reed (TA); Family papers (in the possession of his grandchildren).   HUDSON FYSH

REIBEY, MARY (1777-1855), née Haydock, businesswoman and trader, was born on 12 May 1777 in Bury, Lancashire, England. She was convicted of horse stealing at Stafford on 21 July 1790 and sentenced to be transported for seven years. When arrested she was dressed as a boy and went under the name of James Burrow, but at her trial her identity was disclosed. The whole episode which resulted in her conviction as a felon at the age of 13 and transportation to New South Wales was probably no more than a high-spirited escapade attributable to lack of parental control, for her parents were dead and she lived with her grandmother. She arrived in Sydney in the *Royal Admiral* in October 1792 and was assigned as a nursemaid in the household of Major Francis Grose [q.v.]. On 7 September 1794 she married in Sydney Thomas Reibey, a young Irishman in the service of the East India Co., whom she had met in the transport and who had returned to Sydney in the *Britannia* that year.

Thomas Reibey (1769-1811) appears to have been the first free settler outside the military ring to trade. The first years of his married life were apparently spent on the Hawkesbury, where he acquired property and was engaged in the grain-carrying business; later he established himself near the waterside in what is now Macquarie Place and turned his former association with the East India Co. to advantage by importing general merchandise. He named his trading establishment Entally House, after a suburb in Calcutta. The scope of his business activity was indicated when in 1801 he became indebted to Robert Campbell senior [q.v.] for the sum of £160 10s., and in October 1803 he mortgaged to Campbell three Hawkesbury farms totalling 260 acres, their buildings, crops, livestock, and boats, along with certain other property and buildings in Sydney, for a further credit advance of £150 to enable him to carry on his business. By 1803 he also owned three small boats, *James, Edwin* and *Raven*, and traded to the Hunter and Hawkesbury Rivers in coals, cedar and wheat. He entered into partnership with Edward Wills (1778?-

1811) and was engaged in sealing in Bass Strait in 1805; in 1807 they bought the schooner *Mercury* for trade with the Pacific Islands.

During the great Hawkesbury River floods of 1806 Reibey did heroic work and saved the lives of several people. He was appointed a pilot in Port Jackson in March 1809 which suggests that he thought of giving up the sea, but in October he undertook his last voyage to China and India made necessary by losses suffered in New South Wales. He left Sydney in the *Lady Barlow* and returned a year later in the *Mary and Sally*. He died at Entally House on 5 April 1811 after a lingering illness, the origin of which was attributed to a *coup de soleil* which he suffered while in India. Reibey appears to have been an astute trader and kept apart from the squabbles of Governor Bligh and his antagonists.

On the death of her husband and his partner Edward Wills a month later, Mary Reibey was left with seven children and in entire control of numerous business concerns. She was a hotel-keeper, and already had had experience in assisting her husband and managing his interests when he was absent on voyages; she soon became a very prosperous member of the group trained in the tough school of competition with American, Chinese and Indian traders. Unlike many of her contemporaries she was not litigious but proved capable of conducting her business affairs with the utmost vigour. Perhaps she preferred her own more direct methods to enforce payment of debts, for in May 1817 she was found guilty of an assault upon one of her debtors, John Walker, at Windsor.

In the eyes of her contemporaries Mary Reibey gradually rose to respectability and affluence in the new emancipist society. She was a favourite of Governor Macquarie. She opened a new warehouse in George Street in 1812 and continued to manage her husband's ships and extended her operations by buying the *John Palmer* and in 1817 the brig *Governor Macquarie*. In 1816 she advertised for sale all her property, which included seven farms on the Hawkesbury, with the intention of returning to England. She was then said to be worth about £20,000, and by 1820 held 1000 acres of land, half of them by grant. In March 1820 in the *Admiral Cockburn* she took her daughters Celia and Eliza to England, and in Lancashire amid the scenes of her childhood she was received with interest and admiration. After her return to Sydney next year with her daughters, her affairs continued to flourish.

She made extensive investments in city property. By 1828 she had erected 'many elegant and substantial buildings in Macquarie Place, near the King's Wharf, and in the centre of George Street', and was turning her attention to Castlereagh Street. She gradually retired from active business and lived on her investments.

Mary Reibey, persevering and enterprising in everything she undertook, became legendary in the colony as the successful businesswoman. She took an interest in the church, education and works of charity. In 1825 she was appointed one of the governors of the Free Grammar School. Later Bishop Broughton [q.v.] commended her exertions in the cause of religion generally and of the Church of England in particular. On her retirement she lived in the suburb of Newtown until her death on 30 May 1855. The peace of her later years was disturbed a little by the publication in 1845 of Rev. Richard Cobbold's book on Margaret Catchpole [q.v.], which led to understandable rumours that she was the heroine of Cobbold's colourful story.

Thomas and Mary Reibey's three sons, who founded the Tasmanian branch of the family, all followed their parents' lead in mercantile and shipping ventures. The eldest son, Thomas (b. 6 May 1796), went to sea with his father and in November 1822 became a partner of his brother as a general merchant and commission agent at Launceston, trading under the name of Thomas Reibey & Co. He died at his estate, Entally, Hadspen, near Launceston, on 3 October 1842. The second son, James Haydock (b. 2 October 1798), was apprenticed in 1809 to John Campbell Burton, a merchant and agent from Bengal. In the 1820s he was trading in partnership with his elder brother and engaged in sealing and other coastal shipping activities. He was one of the first directors of the Derwent and Cornwall Banks in Van Diemen's Land in 1828. He originally settled near Hobart Town but later bought a property adjoining Entally and died in 1843. Of the four Reibey daughters, the youngest, Elizabeth Ann (b. 1810), married Captain Joseph Long Innes.

The surname was variously spelt as Raby, Rabey, and Reiby, but after the death of Thomas Reibey in 1811 Reibey was usually adopted by the family.

HRNSW, 5-7; HRA (1), 8, 10, 14, (3), 2-4; F. S. Eldershaw (ed), *The peaceful army* (Syd, 1938); J. M. Forde, 'Genesis of commerce in Australia', *JRAHS*, 3 (1915-17); P. Mander-Jones, 'Mary Reibey', *ABC Weekly*, Oct 1954; M. Reibey, Journal 1820-21 (ML); Supreme Court records (NSWA).   G. P. WALSH

REID, ALEXANDER (1783-1858), land-owner, was born in August 1783 in the village of Humbie, East Lothian, Scotland, the son of Alexander Reid, master brewer, and his wife Mary, née Gray (d. May 1810). His father farmed the old family property of Ratho, six miles from Edinburgh. This property was enlarged and enriched by the addition of several other estates, most notably that of Ratho Bank. However, there were ten other children in the family and Alexander had to fend for himself. By August 1805 he was a partner in the Leith mercantile firm of Liddell & Reid.

In December 1809 he married Mary Muirhead (b. 1789?), from the Clyde district in Scotland, and their first daughter, Jane, was born within a month of the firm's bankruptcy in mid-1814. After this failure Reid continued on his own with aid from relations and by February 1820 he was in a position to consider emigration. In August 1821 he sailed from Leith with his wife and two children in the *Castle Forbes*, and on 1 March 1822 they arrived in Hobart Town. They lived there for a short time until Reid was granted land on the Clyde River, nearly fifty miles from Hobart. The land was in two sections: 1400 acres which he called Ratho, and 600 acres, five miles downstream, which he named Humbie. The Reids moved to Ratho and lived in a mud cottage for three years until a more permanent homestead was built. At the cottage Mrs Reid had been held up by bushrangers while her husband was absent, but she showed characteristic self-control and coolness by handing over her keys so that her furniture would not be smashed.

As the near-by settlement of Bothwell grew, the Reids became active in the social life of the area and their farm began to prosper. In May 1830 Reid laid the foundation stone of the Bothwell Presbyterian Church and became a friend of Rev. James Garrett [q.v.]. In that year Reid took part in the 'Black War' against the Aboriginals. By mid-1837 Reid had 1000 ewes, 300 lambs and 20 cows and calves, and such success as a wool-grower that he had been able to pay off many of his debts within five years despite high colonial interest rates, and to assist his son-in-law with several large loans. In 1836, when the Clyde Co. was formed by his friend George Russell [q.v.], Reid showed interest in the venture but did not join it. However, he was both secretary and treasurer of the Cross Marsh Market Committee, later the Cross Marsh Agricultural Association. In mid-1837 Ratho was let for seven years to the Horne family at the high annual rent of £1000, and in April 1838

the Reids left Ratho and sailed for Scotland in the *Derwent*. One of Reid's first outings in Scotland was to visit the cattle show at Glasgow, and the family settled into a house in Edinburgh before moving to a rented property next to the Old Ratho Bank estate which was no longer in family hands. He prospered again in raising sheep and was active in the social life of the area: hunting, visiting relations and touring. The family was happy in Scotland but after lengthy consideration they returned to Van Diemen's Land and to their own Ratho in 1842. Reid eagerly set about with plans to improve the property and by 1844 his wool clips were surprisingly good. In 1858 Reid died, having suffered from chronic illnesses for about ten years.

Reid was popular, tolerant, kind and very emotional, but seemed to mask his strong feelings by wit and drollery in conversation and by dry understatement in his letters. His main interests were always economics and politics; he was honest but shrewd in business, and he was very strongly opposed to transportation and to Lieut-Governor Denison. He was always active in public affairs, as a justice of the peace, chairman of public meetings, and owner of horses in local races. He was not very religious and his wife and daughter, Jane, often criticized him for his spiritual unconcern.

He had four children: Jane, who in 1836 was widowed in India and spent many of the following years with her parents; Alexander (b. 1820), who had most of his father's characteristics and interests; Elizabeth, who was born on 10 October 1825 at Ratho and died a few weeks before the Reids returned to Scotland in 1838; and Mary who was born on 18 February 1829 at Ratho and died at sea on the voyage to Scotland, making a double tragedy for the family within a few months.

P. L. Brown (ed), *Clyde Company papers*, 1-5 (Lond, 1941-63).
A. F. PIKE

REID, DAVID (1777-1840), naval surgeon, was born at Aberdeen, Scotland. He entered the navy as assistant surgeon, was promoted surgeon in April 1799 and served at Trafalgar in the *Bellerophon*. As surgeon-superintendent of convict ships he went in the *Baring* to Sydney in 1815 and to Hobart Town and Sydney in 1819, and in the *Providence* to Hobart and Sydney in 1822. He settled in New South Wales in 1822 and in March received a grant of 1000 acres, which was increased to 2000 next January, in the Bungonia-Marulan district. By 1824 he was residing on his grant, which he had named Inverary Park, and by August 1856 had fifty-six acres under cultivation. He was appointed a magistrate, and commissioner for taking affidavits. In his district he was considered an efficient pastoralist, and 'one of the best practical agriculturists'. In 1829 his report on the activity of bushrangers led to the stationing of two military detachments in the area and later to the strengthening of the mounted police. On 25 June 1839 he was declared unfit for sea service and on 9 April 1840 he asked to be retired on half-pay, but not having been employed in naval service since 1822, was told that he had 'not the smallest claim' to a pension. He died on 7 July 1840 at Inverary and was buried in the Church of England cemetery at Bungonia. His wife Agnes, née Dyce, whom he had married in 1817, died in October 1860 and was buried at Wangaratta.

HRA (1), 10, 12, 13, 15, 18, 19; C. Bateson, *The convict ships, 1787-1868* (Glasgow, 1959); E. A. Mackay, 'Medical men as pastoral pioneers', *MJA*, 13 Oct 1934; J. Jervis, 'Settlement in the Marulan-Bungonia district', *JRAHS*, 32 (1947); Records (Soc Aust Gen, Syd). CHARLES BATESON

REID, THOMAS (1791-1825), naval surgeon and prison reformer, was born in Ireland and educated near Dungannon, County Tyrone. He entered the navy about 1811, passed examinations at the Royal College of Surgeons in London in 1813 and was admitted a member in November 1815. He was appointed a naval surgeon on 10 January 1814. At the instigation of Elizabeth Fry he made voyages as surgeon-superintendent of the convict ships *Neptune*, to Sydney in 1818, and *Morley*, to Hobart Town and Sydney in 1820, and both Governor Macquarie and Lieut-Governor Sorell reported on his conduct in these voyages with exceptional warmth; but Reid regarded transportation with repugnance, detested its brutalities and declined to make further voyages in convict transports.

After arriving in Sydney in the *Morley*, Reid accompanied Macquarie on his tour of inspection to Bathurst, and the governor described him as 'a most agreeable, good humoured and entertaining friend and associate'. Reid contemplated settling in New South Wales, but decided not to, perhaps because it was a penal settlement. He dedicated his *Two Voyages to New South Wales and Van Diemen's Land* (London, 1822) to Elizabeth Fry. He also published *Travels in Ireland, in the year 1822, ex-*

hibiting brief sketches of the moral, physical, and political state of the country (London, 1823). He died at Pentonville, London, on 21 August 1825. He was a capable surgeon, and a strong advocate of the employment of prisoners in a rational manner, believing this a necessary step towards their reformation.

HRA (1), 9-10, (3), 3; L. Macquarie, *Journals of his tours in New South Wales and Van Diemen's Land, 1810-1822* (Syd, 1956); C. Bateson, *The convict ships, 1787-1868* (Glasgow, 1959). CHARLES BATESON

REVELEY, HENRY WILLEY (1788-1875), civil engineer, was born in England, the son of Willey Reveley, an architect whose chief surviving work is the Church of All Saints at Southampton, and his wife Maria, née James. His parents were friends of such intellectual liberals as Jeremy Bentham, Thomas Holcroft, William Godwin and his wife Mary Wollstonecraft. When the last-named died soon after giving birth to a daughter, her infant was brought up for some years in the Reveley's home. This child later became the second wife of the poet Shelley and author of the novel *Frankenstein*. After Willey Reveley's death in 1799, his widow married John Gisbourne and the family went to live in Italy, where Henry studied mathematics and natural philosophy, distinguished himself by his scientific attainments, and graduated as a civil engineer at the University of Pisa, but had difficulty in obtaining employment. He became a close friend of Shelley, whom he saved from drowning in the River Arno in 1821. After the poet's death in 1822, Reveley returned to England, where he is reputed to have studied under John Rennie, the engineer and constructor of Waterloo Bridge. In 1827 he went with his wife Amelia, a sister of the artist Copley Fielding, to Cape Town as colonial civil engineer, but held this appointment for little more than a year.

When the barque *Parmelia* called at Cape Town in May 1829, Lieut-Governor James Stirling engaged Reveley as civil engineer to the Swan River settlement at a salary of £200 and the Reveleys continued the voyage with the founders of Western Australia. His first work after arrival was the building of huts at the temporary encampment on Garden Island. When the party moved to the mainland he was responsible for the design and construction of all public works. These included the first barracks, government offices, commissariat store, first Government House, the gaol at

Fremantle—a 12-sided building now known as the Round House—and the first court-house at Perth. He also superintended the cutting of a canal through the shallow flats in the Swan River near the later Cause-way, planned a breakwater and harbour at Fremantle, and as a private venture built in St George's Terrace the first water-mill in Perth on the Tuscan principle. Of the many buildings he designed in a simplified Georgian style, the only surviving ones in 1966 are the Round House, Fremantle (1831) and the Old Court House, Perth (1836).

In 1838 Reveley and his wife returned to England, where his continued interest in the colony was revealed by two articles: one written in 1844 from Parkstone, Dorset, on immigration policy and the other in 1873 from Reading on West Australian timber. He died at Reading in 1875. In spite of his varied attainments, Reveley's contribution to Western Australia seems to have been limited to his architecture. He is known to have tutored the son of at least one family, but the harsh con-ditions of early settlement left little opportunity for cultural and intellectual activity.

A. Hasluck, *Unwilling emigrants* (Melb, 1959); P. Hasluck and F. I. Bray, 'Early mills of Perth', JRWAHS, 1 (1927-31); *West Australian*, 22 June 1929.   RAY OLDHAM

RICHARDSON, JOHN MATTHEW (1797?-1882), gardener, was sentenced in England at the Sussex Assizes on 25 March 1822 to transportation for life. He arrived at Hobart Town in November and was soon transferred to Sydney where he was married at St Philip's Church on 13 July 1824 to Jane, née Nelson.

Richardson accompanied John Oxley [q.v.] on one or both of his expeditions of 1823 and 1824 and by 1825 if not earlier was employed in the Botanic Gar-den. In November 1825 Governor Brisbane, then organizing the settlement at Melville Island, arranged that a quantity of plants for culinary purposes should be sent to the new settlement in the *Philip Dundas* and that Richardson should accompany them to take charge of gardening there at a salary of £25. The *Philip Dundas*, with Richardson and his wife and child among the passengers, arrived at Melville Island on 22 February 1826. In March Richardson wrote a letter, probably to Henry Du-maresq [q.v.], protesting that he was not receiving rations for his wife and child and had not been provided with a dwelling. In January 1827 the commandant was in-structed from Sydney to allow rations for the wife and child 'from the time of his arrival at the Settlement'. In August 1826 Richardson had been sent in the cutter *Mermaid* to Timor whence he brought back some plants and seeds presented by the Dutch Resident. A daughter, Elizabeth Melville, was born to the Richardsons in March 1827. Later that year the wife, who was ailing, and children were about to return to Sydney in the *Amity* when Richardson got into trouble for having bought spirits from a visiting ship and retailed it to troops and prisoners; as pun-ishment the passages of the wife and child-ren were cancelled. When the decision was made in 1828 to abandon the settle-ment Richardson returned to Sydney in the *Lucy Anne* together with the troops and others.

Richardson served as botanical collector with Major T. L. Mitchell's [q.v.] expe-dition of 1836. Mitchell praised his 'inde-fatigable industry' and recommended him for a conditional pardon. It seems that a ticket-of-leave granted to Richardson in September 1829 had been withdrawn. How-ever, on 28 January 1837 Governor Bourke approved the grant of a conditional par-don. By 1852 Richardson had moved to Patrick's Plains: his wife had died and on 13 June 1852 he was married to Catharine Doyle at Singleton by a Catholic priest. Richardson died at Newcastle on 28 July 1882, and was survived by two sons and three daughters of the second marriage

MS cat under J. M. Richardson (ML).

RIDDELL, CAMPBELL DRUMMOND (1796-1858), public servant, was born on 9 January 1796, the son of Thomas Milles Riddell (d. 1796) and Margaretta, née Campbell. His grandfather was Sir James Riddell (d. 1797), first baronet, of Ardna-murchan, Argyllshire, Scotland.

Campbell Riddell matriculated in 1813 at Christ Church, Oxford, where his elder brother and his friend, Robert William Hay (1786-1861) graduated. Riddell did not graduate, but in 1819 was admitted to the Scottish faculty of advocates, of which he was still a member in 1829 when his re-lations and friends helped him into the colonial service, briefly as a commissioner of inquiry in Ceylon, and more perman-ently as colonial treasurer in New South Wales. In Colombo on 3 April 1830, he married Caroline Stuart Rodney, daughter of the government secretary in Ceylon, and arrived in Sydney with her in August 1830.

He began duty with grievances about his salary and soon had others : about a building allotment grant he did not get, about home leave and promotion he did not get soon enough, about extra duties for which he did not get extra pay. His salary was £1000 paid by the Colonial Office. Hay told him he was lucky and could not expect more in a period of economy, in which Hay himself was finally retrenched in 1836. On 15 December 1833 Hay wrote, 'My dear Riddell . . . I am always glad tò hear of your progress and wish heartily that you had no grievances to complain of, for I cannot remedy them and even to write at length and explain the reasons why I cannot do so is more than I can readily undertake'; and in 1834 he rebuked Riddell for telling tales about local politics and social life.

Although Governor Bourke thought him well paid for his financial work, he recommended additional payment for Riddell's service on the board for assigning servants but the British government refused; Bourke did not recommend additional payment when the duties of the collector of internal revenue were combined with those of the treasurer; and though Riddell did not please him in other respects Bourke praised him for his promptitude and benevolence in finding employment for female immigrants. Another duty which Riddell thought extra and onerous, but which Bourke and Hay thought within his duties as treasurer, was the custody of uninvested savings bank deposits. He came close to serious trouble when he was found to be holding these in an account of his own instead of in a Treasury account, but no misappropriation was proven or even alleged. He was just imprudent, and it was a major piece of imprudence which gave him a place in the political history of the colony. Bourke's consideration for Catholics and convicts had brought him into conflict with many of the honorary justices of the peace. In 1835, when they were to elect a chairman of the Quarter Sessions, Riddell asked Bourke if he had any objection to his being a candidate. As treasurer he was an executive councillor and Bourke replied that he could not with propriety take the chairmanship; Bourke saw advantage in the commissioner of the Court of Requests, Roger Therry [q.v.], becoming the chairman because he was a lawyer. But Therry was Catholic and Irish and regarded by most of the justices as either a tool of Bourke's or as his evil genius. Riddell appeared to accept Bourke's ruling that he should not stand, but did little to refuse or repudiate a nomination of himself against Therry and through him against the governor, and he was elected, by a disputed majority of one vote. He declined office but Bourke suspended him from the Executive Council and requested the Colonial Office to remove him from it.

He was compared both with a cabinet minister dismissed for publicly opposing his party and his premier, and with a public servant who had courageously exercised his rights as a citizen; in the days before responsible government public servant and minister were one. In particular he was an executive councillor, not as Riddell but as the treasurer. The secretary of state for the colonies, Glenelg, thought that he could not be removed from the council without being removed from the treasurership, and that in any case he had been sufficiently rebuked, and others admonished, by his temporary suspension. This dispatch, when shown to Riddell's brother, cleared Glenelg from criticism at home, but it did not satisfy Bourke, who insisted on either Riddell's removal from the council or acceptance of his own resignation. In a confidential reply to Bourke, Glenelg pleaded for Riddell and hinted that just as Bourke was entitled to obedience from his officers so the secretary of state was entitled to obedience from his governors. But Bourke's opponents won more through Riddell than they could have hoped for, and Bourke the great man went while Riddell the little man stayed.

In 1844 when a local order of merit was tentatively proposed, Bourke's successor, Gipps, put Riddell eleventh and Therry twelfth in a list of nineteen whom he considered deserving. Always aspiring to be colonial secretary, Riddell was appointed temporarily in January 1854, when Deas Thomson [q.v.] went to England with the draft of the Constitution for responsible government; he resumed the colonial treasurership in January 1856, but was retired under the provisions of the new Constitution on 5 June 1856. He was nominated to the Legislative Council in May 1856, but lost his seat in 1858 because of absence. He died in Britain on 27 December 1858.

One son, Thomas Milles Stratford, born on 22 January 1832, went to Gladstone, Queensland, as a member of the government resident's staff and died there on 16 September 1854. Another son, Rodney Stuart, born 7 November 1838, became the fourth baronet in 1883, and when he died on 2 January 1907 left no successor to the title. There were two married daughters. A portrait of Riddell in a kilt and one of his wife are in the Mitchell Library.

HRA (1), 15-26; R. J. Flanagan, *The history of New South Wales*, 1-2 (Lond, 1862); R. Therry, *Reminiscences of thirty years' residence in New South Wales and Victoria*, 2nd ed (Lond, 1863); G. W. Rusden, *History of Australia*, 2nd ed, 2 (Melb, 1897); J. W. Metcalfe, 'Governor Bourke—or, the lion and the wolves', *JRAHS*, 30 (1944); CO 201/255, 258, 324/87; Newspaper indexes and MS cat under C. D. Riddell (ML).

JOHN METCALFE

RIDLEY, JOHN (1806-1887), miller, inventor and preacher, was born on 26 May 1806 at West Boldon, near Sunderland, Durham, England, the son of John and Mary Ridley, who were cousins. His formal education was little more than that of a village school, but it was augmented by an insatiable love of books and a remarkable memory. Although baptized into the Church of England he came early under the influence of Wesleyan Methodism. He began preaching at 18 and at 23 was a recognized local preacher in the Sunderland circuit. At 15 he took over the milling business that his mother had managed since his father's death in 1811. After his mother's death in 1835 he married Mary Pybus, the daughter of a boarding school proprietor at West Boldon.

In 1839 Ridley left for South Australia in the *Warrior* with his wife and two children. Soon after arrival he lost a child through her clothes catching fire. He took over the flour-mill of the South Australian Co., installed a Watt's Beam steam engine, and began growing wheat on land he bought at Hindmarsh. With shrewd foresight he predicted that the heavy spending of Governor Gawler would bring depression and force colonists into rural production. When this happened he let his Hindmarsh farm and, as he toured the settled districts in search of grain for his mill, made many more land purchases. By 1843 the wheat crop threatened to expand beyond the capacity of the small labour force to harvest it. When a prize was offered in September for designs of harvesting machinery, Ridley did not compete because he was already building a reaper based on a woodcut in J. C. Loudon's *An Encyclopaedia of Agriculture* (3rd ed., London, 1835). Tested next month his machine failed; rebuilt with combs and beaters that swept off the heads of wheat, it was tried on his tenant's crop and proved successful, reaping seventy acres in a week at 5s. an acre. Next year he planned the manufacture and improvement of his harvesting machine; in 1845 he made seven and within five years over fifty were operating

in the province and others had been exported. Although it was claimed that the machine was invented in principle by John Wrathall Bull [q.v.], none disputed that Ridley was its first practical producer. In 1844 he was awarded a special prize by the Agricultural and Horticultural Society and in 1858 he was thanked by the South Australian parliament for a service that had helped to make possible the vast increase of wheat-growing in the province.

Ridley's returns from the harvesting machine were substantial but meagre compared with the dividends from his original shares in the Burra copper-mine, his flour-mill and his land investments. He left for Europe with his family on 18 March 1853 in the steamer *Melbourne* and after lengthy travel on the Continent, settled in England to devote his eccentric enthusiasm to invention and religion. At his own cost he had printed tens of thousands of copies of sermons and tracts that appealed to his principles and distributed them widely to grateful and ungrateful recipients. He was also an energetic lay preacher and made many gifts to evangelical churches and missions. Tall, spare and dignified, he was a venerable figure, particularly when his dark abundant hair whitened with age. He died in London on 25 November 1887.

His altruism and passion for practical improvement were sincere, and meant more to him than his own financial success. His self-reliance made him eschew government rewards in South Australia, where his memory is honoured by the Ridley memorial scholarship at Roseworthy Agricultural College, memorial gates to the Royal Agricultural and Horticultural Society's showground at Wayville and the electoral district of Ridley.

A. E. Ridley, *A backward glance* (Lond, 1904); G. L. Sutton, 'The invention of the stripper', *WA Dept of Agriculture Journal*, Sept 1937.
H. J. FINNIS

RILEY, ALEXANDER (1778?-1833), merchant and pastoralist, was born in London, the son of George Riley, a London book-seller of some education and prosperity, and his wife Margaret, née Raby. The family was from County Cavan and had a deep attachment to its Irish roots. Alexander's two sisters married Captain Ralph Wilson and A. F. Kemp [q.v.] of the New South Wales Corps, and it was their departure with their husbands for New South Wales which set Alexander thinking of emigrating himself. On 30 November 1803 he secured from the Colonial

Office permission to go out and a recommendation to the local administration. As one of the first free settlers to go to the colony he had no set pattern to pursue, but it seems clear from his family background that he expected to make his fortune in trade. He married Sophia Hardwicke on 30 October, two weeks before sailing in the *Experiment*, and they arrived in the colony in June 1804 with considerable expectations but few practical prospects.

Although he acquired a farm at the Hawkesbury in August he was appointed store-keeper and magistrate at Port Dalrymple, where his sisters and their families were settled; he quickly found favour with Colonel Paterson [q.v.], in 1805 became deputy-commissary there and rapidly grasped the economic possibilities of colonial trading and land cultivation. When Paterson was faced with assuming command of New South Wales after the deposition of Bligh, he asked Riley to go with him as secretary to the colony. Riley accepted, and reached Sydney in January 1809, but with a shrewd estimate of the eventual outcome of the rebellion he soon resigned and began to devote attention to his generous grant of land located at Liverpool. This he named Raby, and on it he began in a haphazard fashion to raise sheep.

He had at this time little farming experience but an excellent training in mercantile affairs, and it was in trade that he first began to prosper in the colony. His partner in New South Wales was Richard Jones [q.v.] and together they developed trading relations with Riley's younger brother, Edward [q.v.], in Calcutta, and with W. S. Davidson [q.v.] in Canton. The partnership of Jones & Riley continued until the 1820s, and they were the first to begin marine insurance in New South Wales. Riley was also one of the founders of the Bank of New South Wales in 1816, and briefly one of the original directors in 1817; but he had become a little disillusioned with colonial trade after the losses he incurred in the building of the Rum Hospital, and from 1812 onwards he had become more and more involved in the development of the pastoral industry and the wool trade. He purchased wool from settlers for export and developed his own flocks at Raby. His sheep had only the merest traces of merino blood, but in the inflated wool markets of war-time England their wool secured an extremely profitable price of 69d. a pound. Apart from the profit he liked life on the land. Years after he left the colony he wrote about his first sight of Raby with great emotion. Unlike other settlers who found the colonial landscape ugly and alien, Riley was deeply moved by the ownership of his land and by the beauty of its situation.

Suddenly in 1817 he decided to take his family home to England. He gave no explicit reasons for leaving, but they came in large part from the frustrations which all his ventures had met in the colony. He found the China trade difficult, the enforcement of the East India Co.'s monopoly seriously hampered his interests in whaling and sealing, and Governor Macquarie's new port dues threatened to reduce his margin of profit. His investments in wool had suffered from the collapse of the British wool market in the post-war depression. The advantage seemed to lie with colonial traders in London, and he planned to join them. He leased his land at Liverpool, left his commercial affairs in the colony to the direction of his brother Edward who had moved from Calcutta to New South Wales, bought the *Harriet*, and on 22 December 1817 sailed in her from Sydney Cove.

In London he gave valuable evidence on New South Wales to the select committee on gaols in 1819. He joined the firm of Donaldson, Wilkinson & Co., agents for the colonial trade, a successful and highly respected business with connexions in South Africa, India and more recently New South Wales; but he had not been in his new position long before he began to realize the future value of his land in New South Wales and to understand the most efficient methods by which colonial wool production might be developed. In collaboration with Edward he undertook to import into New South Wales an entire flock of Saxon merino sheep, a breed which had the most highly developed fleeces in Europe, with wool better than that of the Spanish merinos then in the colony and more adapted to what Riley correctly guessed would be the future technological developments of the British cloth trade; he expected them to flourish in the mild colonial climate and produce wool at a fraction of the cost of European competitors.

Despite these expert insights the venture was highly speculative. The flock cost between £10 and £11 a head; transport was expensive and very risky. However, he chartered the *Sir George Osborne* in August 1825, and the sheep, better housed on the journey than many of the human passengers, reached New South Wales in excellent condition. Riley's nephew Edward (b. 1806) had supervised them on the voyage and it was intended that he would hand over the direction of the venture to his father, Edward Riley senior; but since they arrived after the father's death they remained in the care of his young and inexperienced son. As a result the direction exercised by Alexander Riley from London was of crucial importance, and he spent great energy in writing detailed instructions on their care and management, fulfilling a role in their development similar to that played by John Macarthur [q.v.] in the improvement of his merinos some years before.

Riley had little but faith to sustain him during the depression of the mid-1820s. No sooner had he strained every source of credit to launch the pastoral venture than the financial collapse and the decline of the wool market made it seem unwarranted, and serious droughts in 1826-28 threatened the entire plan. However, by 1830 the design had been carried through to success and the Raby Saxon merino flocks were returning a handsome profit for their owners, Alexander and his young son. The sheep eventually formed the basis of the most important merino strain in the development of the Australian merino and their importance to the Australian pastoral industry is probably greater than that of any other single flock.

Riley was often tempted to return to New South Wales. He frequently longed for the company of colonial friends and the old ways of his Sydney life, the busy days at his warehouse in Pitt Street, his spacious home in Burwood and the exceptionally beautiful countryside of Raby. In 1824 he apparently received from the secretary of state an oral promise of a grant of 10,000 acres of land, similar to that given to Macarthur, as a reward for the successful importation of a new strain of merinos into the colony, and the last years of his life were devoted to agitation to secure it. Eventually he succeeded and in 1831 occupied a grant in beautiful country just beyond Yass, bordering on the limits of location. He called it Cavan, after the family's Irish home, and there after ten years of effort the speculation began to reap the dreamed-of rewards.

Riley was a shrewd and capable businessman, but also excitable, emotional and highly imaginative, tormented by fits of dreadful anxiety, and a little uncertain of his relations with others. His family life was conventional and his marriage apparently happy, but his real emotional investment lay in the highly speculative activity which was his chief contribution to colonial life. He escaped involvement in the bitter factions of New South Wales. His temperament was to negotiate rather than to confront difficulties outright. His economic insights and his real passion for the land were communicated to his son and namesake with whom he was the mildest of parents. His own plans and all his most detailed advice to his nephew and son on the management of their affairs were posited on a highly individualistic economic activity, never on a rich pastoral society dependent on forced labour. His correspondence hardly hinted at a penal society except for the returns of assigned servants and their wages. Like most settlers of his status he supported the Benevolent Society and Society for the Propagation of the Gospel, but these were merely the conventional good works of his conventional Evangelical piety. In his declining years ill health prevented the fulfilment of his desire to see the colony and his land once again, and he died in London on 17 November 1833.

J. Ker, 'The wool industry in NSW 1803-30', *Business Archives and History*, 1 (1956-61), 2 (1962); J. Ker, 'Merchants and merinos', *JRAHS*, 46 (1960); Riley family papers (ML).   JILL CONWAY

RILEY, EDWARD (1784-1825), merchant and pastoralist, was born on 30 January 1784 in London, younger brother of Alexander Riley [q.v.]. He was the first of the family to be fascinated by colonial life and he went to Calcutta to engage in the colonial trade. There in 1805 he married Anne Moran, who bore him three sons and a daughter. He dealt in every possible kind of shipment to Canton and to the Australian colonies. In the trade with New South Wales he dealt with his brother and Richard Jones [q.v.], shipping to them regular cargoes of rum, clothing and food. He enjoyed Anglo-Indian life despite violent fluctuations in his fortunes, and acquired in Calcutta a taste for splendid living, but he was not really gifted in business matters and came to rely more and more on the judgment of his elder brother.

After the death of his wife in Calcutta on 13 May 1810, he experienced such deep fits of depression that his brother began to urge him to settle in New South Wales, which he visited several times between 1811 and 1814. Always mercurial, Edward then suddenly rallied and took a second wife, Anne Wilkinson, the daughter of a colonel in Calcutta. In 1816 he went to Sydney to settle and quickly became one of its leading citizens. Governor Macquarie gave him a grant of land and soon made him a magistrate. In 1818 he was a director of the Bank of New South Wales. He took the largest house available in the colony, Surgeon Harris's [q.v.] Ultimo House, and began to live there in a style and degree of luxury little known in New South Wales. Advertisements for cooks, butlers and well-trained servants appeared in the *Sydney Gazette* to the amusement of experienced colonists acquainted with the ways of convict servants. All did not go well. His second wife bore him three sons and three daughters but his business affairs fluctuated; after one serious reverse his effects at Ultimo House went up for sale while the family moved to a smaller house at Woolloomooloo where he had secured a large tract of land. In the early 1820s his brother Alexander, then in London, confidently relying on his brother's business ability, began to urge a plan for introducing Saxon merinos to the colony, but Edward seems to have been too sunk in melancholy to confide in his brother his fears concerning his business affairs. Edward rallied and suddenly made a long trip into the interior to search for good grazing land, and wrote enthusiastically about the new country around Yass and Goulburn, but his health began to deteriorate and the alterations in his moods became more and more violent. He suffered severely from gout, and this together with his irritation at the limitations of colonial life brought on deep fits of depression. On 21 February 1825 he retired to his room after dinner, placed a shotgun barrel in his mouth, and blew out his brains.

He had considerable charm and engaging honesty, and was devoted to his family. His failures were more imagined than real for, after his death, confusion about the validity of two conflicting wills which he left involved an immense litigation about the settlement of his estate, which proved to be of substantial value. The Riley land and buildings at Raby had been very neglected under his care. His own land was not developed, although it was supposed to support some of the Saxon sheep already on their voyage out to Australia. In mercantile ventures he had not managed to develop the insights into the future economic growth of the colony which brought such success to other merchants. Indeed in his few years residence in the colony he had little personal effect on events. Yet he was an important link in the chain of family command which worked so effectively to introduce Saxon merinos to the colony, and in his role in India the family relationship had served well to bring success to the partnership of Jones & Riley. After his death his eldest son, Edward, who was born in India on 20 July 1806, succeeded in carrying out the pastoral venture which Alexander and Edward Riley senior had begun.

J. Ker, 'Merchants and merinos', *JRAHS*, 46 (1960); Riley family papers (ML); Riley estate papers (Uncat MS 222/1, ML).

JILL CONWAY

RITCHIE, THOMAS (1789-1851), naval officer and landowner, was born at Rhynd, Perthshire, Scotland. At 15 he entered the navy as a first-class volunteer in the sloop *Diligence*. Later in the *Combatant* he served in the English Channel and Baltic until captured by the Danes in September 1807. He was exchanged in 1809 and joined the *Courageux*, accompanied the expedition to Walcheren, served again in the Baltic in the *Victory*, and in 1812 became acting lieutenant in the *Ariel*. He spent the last three years of war in the *Cherokee* at Leith. In 1814-15 he obtained leave from the Admiralty, purchased the brig *Greyhound* and traded between India and Australia.

In February 1818 he arrived in Hobart Town, advertised his mixed cargo for sale and later sailed for Sydney. There as he was leaving a waterman brought out a passenger, Hannah Harris, a free native of New South Wales. Ritchie took her to Ceylon and married her in 1831. However, when he returned to Sydney in April 1819 he had to face charges brought against him by the government for abducting her from the colony without the governor's consent.

Ritchie was fined £500 with £250 costs, and he attributed the severity of the sentence to Governor Macquarie's pique at Ritchie's having had in his possession a 'Book . . . found to contain in Manuscript all of what were considered the best satirical fugitive pieces of the day at that time forming a principal amusement of the best educated colonists'. His property reduced to about £2500, Ritchie sold the *Greyhound* and left Sydney for Hobart at the end of 1820 to claim property left to him on the death of his brother, Captain John Ritchie, who had been commandant at Port Dalrymple in 1812-14. He went on to Port Dalrymple, where he began shipping grain to Sydney; but he lost a full cargo in the *Commerce*, and decided to go on the land. Macquarie, remembering the 'Book', as Ritchie said, would give him only 700 acres, but he bought extensions and Lieut-Governor Arthur granted him 1300 acres. Ritchie felt that his capital and rank entitled him to much more, and in 1830 he went to England to press his claim, which ultimately failed. Yet by 1832 his land amounted to 3630 acres, widely scattered in Northern Tasmania. In 1833 his new flour-mills on his Scone property, Perth, were praised by the local press. Powered by a water race from a weir across the South Esk River at Perth, they served a wide hinterland.

In the 1840s Ritchie was elected president of the St Andrew's Club, a benevolent society which became an active immigration agency; he was also a strong opponent of transportation to the colony and a promoter of horse-racing. In April 1845 he was appointed a justice of the peace but otherwise took little part in public affairs, devoting his energies to the improvement of his breeds of cattle and sheep which became widely renowned under later owners of Scone. He died at Perth on 9 February 1851 after a long illness, leaving a family of seven sons and two daughters. His widow Hannah survived him more than thirty years, dying at Longford on 25 August 1882. The eldest sons inherited the estates of Scone and its mill, and Cairns Mount, Chudleigh; another son founded the legal firm of Ritchie Parker, and others acquired farms in the Perth district.

W. R. O'Byrne, A *naval biographical dictionary* (Lond, 1849); Correspondence file under Ritchie (TA).

ROBE, FREDERICK HOLT (1802-1871), soldier and administrator, was the fourth son of Colonel Sir William Robe and his wife Sarah, the daughter of Captain Thomas Watt of Quebec. At 15 he joined the army, was gazetted ensign in 1817 and promoted lieutenant in the 84th Regiment in 1825 and captain in the 87th Regiment in 1833. With the Anglo-Turkish force in the Syrian campaign of 1840-41 he took part in the advance on Gaza and the affair before Askalon and received the war medal and the Turkish medal. In 1841 he was promoted brevet major for services in the field. He was assistant military secretary at Gibraltar in 1845 when he was ordered to take the place of Governor Grey in South Australia. Robe went reluctantly, for he had no administrative experience except as an army officer. He arrived in Adelaide in the *Elphinstone*, which soon went on to New Zealand with Grey, to whom Robe had been instructed to look for advice and assistance.

Robe was sworn in as lieut-governor of South Australia on 25 October 1845 and soon found his position difficult. Grey's administration had been adjusted to an impoverished colony; now wheat and copper were changing the economy from penury to comparative affluence. Robe was conservative and a High Anglican, accustomed by training as a soldier to obey his superiors and to expect obedience from his inferiors. These attributes made him ill-fitted to control aspiring colonists who demanded independence and an increasing share in their own government. In the Legislative Council Robe could count on his three senior public servants but constant opposition of the four non-official nominees forced him frequently to use his casting as well as his deliberative vote. He was responsible for giving South Australia its first Education Act but most of his actions made him unpopular. He enjoyed giving balls and entertainments at Government House, yet as a bachelor he had to appoint a hostess, and his choice was often criticized. When labour became scarce with rising prosperity, employers clamoured for Chinese coolies and scorned his plan for introducing the families of ex-servicemen. When shipping congested the harbour, his proposal to pay for a steam tug was condemned by merchants as a violation of their free port. However, Robe's administration was bedevilled by two large issues, both of which were largely initiated by instructions from Downing Street.

The first was the royalty question. Before Robe's time no mineral rights were reserved to the Crown when land grants were made. After the discovery of copper Grey proposed in 1844 to withhold from sale any crown land known to contain minerals, and one private tender for a section was actually refused. Disgruntled settlers prepared a petition to the Queen; with 700 signatures, it was carried to Government House on 29 December 1845 by a deputation. Robe's brief reply was that he would forward the petition. Next March regulations were gazetted reserving a royalty of one-fifteenth of all minerals from crown lands sold after that date; this resulted in another petition to the Queen. Sales of land continued, but in May 1846 Robe, on the instructions of Lord Stanley, withheld from sale for a year any land suspected of containing minerals. Robe's bill to facilitate the collection of mineral royalty dues was carried on its second reading on 2 October 1846 by his casting vote, after which the council had to adjourn because the four non-official members walked out, leaving it without a quorum. They returned a week later and Robe forced the bill through committee by his casting vote, thus vindicating his authority: he then withdrew the bill.

The second bone of contention was state aid to religion. Robe's own inclination was to confine this to the Church of England, an attitude in direct conflict with that of many of the colony's founders and early settlers. The scheme adopted by Robe gave state aid to religious denominations according to their numbers; in July 1846 the grant-in-aid to carry it into effect was proposed by John Morphett [q.v.] and sanctioned with the strong support of Anglican members in the Legislative Council. The measure was noisily opposed by a large number of voluntaryist Dissenters, many Anglicans, and some Catholics whose bishop had fallen out with Robe. The South Australian League for the Maintenance of Religious Freedom was promptly formed and a petition in protest with 2000 signatures was presented to Robe who commented stiffly, 'I have no remark to make'; this petition was sent to England and the news of its rejection by the Queen reached Adelaide in October 1847. Meanwhile other petitions flooded the Legislative Council, but in July 1847 Robe, in accordance with directions from England, introduced an ordinance in which *per capita* grants were replaced by limited subsidies to churches in proportion to the amounts subscribed by each congregation. This ordinance was also bitterly opposed by voluntaryists in the council and throughout the colony, but in 1848 it came into operation for three years. During Robe's term grants of land were also made to the churches of England, Scotland, and Rome and to the Wesleyans and some Lutherans; other churches rejected all state aid. Bishop Short, who, on arrival in 1847 stayed with his family at Government House for a month, was also granted portion of Victoria Square in Adelaide as the site for a cathedral; in 1855, however, the Supreme Court of South Australia decided that this grant was invalid.

Robe was a cultured man; he suggested, without avail, the formation of an 'Adelaide Art Society' and he was patron of the Mechanics' Institute which was reopened in 1847. He regularly attended meets of the Adelaide Hunt Club. Early in 1846 he went in the government cutter to examine the south-east coast, and the town of Robe on Guichen Bay bears his name. Even his bitterest enemies admitted that he was honest and straightforward. If not wholly a success as governor, he failed through duty too rigidly applied to a society in ferment. He also found his position distasteful and after only six months

in Adelaide he applied for transfer. In 1847 he was appointed deputy-quartermaster-general at Mauritius, but could not leave South Australia until Sir Henry Fox Young arrived in August 1848. Although in farewell Robe told the Legislative Council that he looked to his Sovereign alone for 'any expression of approbation', warm tributes were paid to him by many colonists. He was promoted lieut-colonel in 1847 and in 1848 was made C.B. He did not return to Australia; he was promoted colonel in 1854 and major-general in 1862. He never married. He died at 10 Palace Gardens Terrace, London, on 4 April 1871.

E. Hodder, *The history of South Australia*, 1 (Lond, 1893); RGSSA, *Centenary history of South Australia* (Adel, 1936); D. Pike, *Paradise of Dissent* (Melb, 1957); Robe letters (SAA).

E. J. R. MORGAN

ROBERTSON, GILBERT (1794-1851), editor and agriculturist, was born on 10 December 1794 at Trinidad, West Indies, the son of Gilbert Robertson, who had large possessions in Demerara, British Guiana, and died at Edinburgh on 10 March 1840.

Robertson served a four-year apprenticeship in agriculture in Scotland and took a farm, but lost it when the Corn Law caused prices to fall. He migrated to Van Diemen's Land in 1822 with his wife and child; five other children were born in the colony. He was granted 400 acres and rented another farm but was unable to carry out his plans with only two assigned servants. When a partnership failed, his farm was sold and he was in the debtors' prison at Hobart Town in 1824. He petitioned Lieut-Governor Arthur in 1825 for employment on the government farm at New Town and was its superintendent for five years. When his services were dispensed with, he was granted land, which he named Woodburn, in the Coal River district, Richmond. As Richmond's chief constable he volunteered in 1829 to lead an expedition against marauding Aboriginals. This and a later expedition were unsuccessful, although they helped Robertson to appraise the agricultural possibilities of land he traversed. He outspokenly defended the Aboriginals. In February 1832 his convict labour was withdrawn and he was dismissed from the police force for supplying his assigned servants with wine for a harvest celebration, after which a man was found dead in the neighbourhood. He protested, however, that they were innocent of the murder.

Robertson was engaged as editor and reporter of the *Colonist*, first issued on 6

July 1832, owned by T. G. Gregson and George Meredith [qq.v.] and printed by Andrew Bent [q.v.]. This arrangement did not last, and on 5 August 1834 Robertson published the *True Colonist and Van Diemen's Land Political Despatch and Agricultural and Commercial Advertiser*. From 2 January 1835 this paper became Tasmania's first daily, but Robertson was soon imprisoned for libellous charges of maladministration and accounting against Lieut-Governor Arthur and a Hobart attorney, W. T. Rowlands. Although helped by Andrew Bent, he could not bring out the paper daily from prison; after 20 March 1835 it reverted to semi-weekly and sometimes weekly publication. His defence against the alleged libels was that they were published for the public good, in hope of an inquiry into the colony's affairs. The last issue of the *True Colonist* appeared on 26 December 1844 when Robertson left to become superintendent of agriculture at Norfolk Island. He resigned in 1846 after a quarrel with the commandant, soon afterwards becoming a station overseer at Colac, Victoria. He was editor of the *Victoria Colonist and Western District Advertiser* when he fell from his horse in a fit of apoplexy and died at Geelong on 5 September 1851.

Robertson was a fiery opponent of the Arthur regime and his greatest influence was exerted through his vigorous, although one-sided, *True Colonist*. Most contemporary newspapers quarrelled with him, although the *Britannia* admitted that he was the first to show the colonial applicability of the Act of James I securing the rights of the subject against arbitrary ejectments by the Crown. He also published many scientific articles on farming, was interested in agricultural societies, and lectured on agriculture and colonization to the Hobart Town Mechanics' Institute, of which he was a prominent member.

H. Melville, *The history of the island of Van Diemen's Land from 1824 to 1835* (Hob, 1835); E. M. Miller, *Pressmen and governors* (Syd, 1952); *True Colonist*, Jan-Mar 1835; *Britannia*, 20 Aug 1846; *Colonial Times*, 19 Jan 1847; *Hobart Town Courier*, 17 Sept 1851; *Mercury*, 1 Apr 1872; CSO 1 (TA).

MARGERY GODFREY

ROBINSON, FREDERICK JOHN; see GODERICH, VISCOUNT

ROBINSON, GEORGE AUGUSTUS (1788-1866), protector of Aboriginals, was born on 22 March 1788 probably in London, a younger son of William Robinson, a builder in Boston, Lincolnshire, and his wife Susannah, née Perry, of Yeovil, Somerset. His youth was probably spent in London with his family at Islington. He had little formal schooling but educated himself by reading widely. He was employed for some years in the Engineers' Department at Chatham, and was connected with, and possibly superintended, the building of some of the martello towers on the east coast of England. On 28 February 1814 in London he married Maria Amelia Evans. Some jottings among his papers show that he was then in the building trade and interested in religious activities.

Early in 1822 Robinson was considering emigration. His first choice was America, and he seems to have booked his passage to the Poyais settlement in Nicaragua. News reached England about June 1823 of the fraudulent nature of that enterprise, and Robinson decided to emigrate to the Australian colonies instead. Leaving his wife and five children behind he sailed from Leith in the *Triton*, travelling steerage. His journal on the voyage shows him as serious and religious, thoughtful in conversation yet companionable and sharing in quiet conviviality. He arrived in Hobart Town in January 1824 and soon set up as a builder. Within a year he was employing several men and had accumulated some £400, but in spite of this rosy picture he could not persuade his wife to join him with their children until April 1826. In Hobart Robinson became secretary of the Seamen's Friend and Bethel Union Society, joined the committee of the Auxiliary Bible Society, visited prisoners and the condemned in the gaol, and helped to found the Mechanics' Institute.

At the time of Robinson's arrival, relations between Aboriginals and settlers had almost reached the stage of open hostility, a result partly of the usurpation of the natives' hunting grounds, partly of cruel treatment and killing of natives by shepherds, stockmen, bushrangers and sealers, partly of the kidnapping of native children. Relations continued to deteriorate and Lieut-Governor Arthur increased punitive measures in an attempt to solve a problem which, from the viewpoint of the settlers, seemed to require either the extermination of the Aboriginals or their removal from lands that the settlers wanted to possess. Many colonists spoke of conciliation but little was done, although Arthur never wholly gave up the idea. The successful rationing of Aboriginals on Bruny Island, begun in May 1828, induced the government to advertise next March for a steady man of good character to effect an intercourse with the natives. Robinson believed that conciliation was possible, applied for the position and was appointed.

On 30 March 1829 Robinson left Hobart for Bruny Island. He spent a few weeks in getting to know the Aboriginals and in looking for a suitable spot for a settlement where he hoped to civilize them and teach them Christian principles. His native village was to have huts, a school and a potato ground; the Aboriginals were to be prevailed upon to settle down, adopt European habits and till the soil, with their children learning trades. English was to be the language of the settlement and Bell's system was to be used in the school. However, the scheme had scarcely begun when Robinson realized that he must become well acquainted with the customs and language of the Aboriginals. By June he was proposing that he should visit the tribes of the south coast to acquaint them with Arthur's humane intentions. On 27 January 1830 he left Hobart for Port Davey, where he explored and met a party of Aboriginals. He then went up the west coast, for a time in their company, and reached Macquarie Harbour on 20 April. After a few days rest he continued north arriving at the Van Diemen's Land Co.'s settlement at Cape Grim on 14 June. Moving east he reached Launceston on 2 October. For the rest of 1830 and most of 1831 Robinson was in north-eastern and eastern Tasmania and on the islands in Bass Strait seeking information about the sealers. From October to December 1831 he was in central Tasmania searching for the feared Big River and Oyster Bay Aboriginals, but when he finally came up with them only sixteen remained. His return to Hobart with the captives was deemed a Roman triumph. From February to November 1832 Robinson was in north-western Tasmania, from December 1832 to October 1833 round Macquarie Harbour, and from December 1833 to August 1834 in the north-west again. He had circled the island and visited all the existing tribes, but although he had seen as much of the country as any of his contemporaries, his observations did not influence exploration or open new areas for settlement. He recorded his journeys minutely in his journals, but there the information remained: he was interested only in the natives.

The pattern of each expedition was much the same. Robinson had his two elder sons, an escort of convict porters and servants, and a following of at least a dozen friendly natives; a boat was used along the coast.

When first approaching a tribe the Europeans kept in the background while the friendly Aboriginals went forward, made contact and persuaded the tribe to come to Robinson, who would give them presents and food. At first Robinson concentrated on establishing friendly relations with the tribes, but in the second expedition he began persuading them to come into captivity, promising them a place where they could live unmolested by the settlers and be fed and clothed. Those giving themselves up were sent to Bass Strait where, after several changes, a permanent settlement was established on Flinders Island.

Robinson had begun his work from motives of compassion: hoping to help the Aboriginals and improve their conditions, he readily sacrificed financial security and the comforts of his home. As his plans succeeded, however, he became less patient with the natives and more interested in financial rewards. With natural vanity he came to think that he alone had worthwhile ideas on the treatment of Aboriginals, alone had their welfare at heart, alone had been responsible for their capture. These views were largely true, but they did not win him friends.

By August 1834 the Aboriginal problem, as the colonists saw it, had been settled, since all but about a dozen natives had been removed from the mainland to the Flinders settlement. This had its beginnings on Swan Island in November 1830. Although under Robinson's general superintendence, it was largely managed by commandants who had little interest in their charges and behaved like gaolers. Mortality had been severe, and by 1835 the Aboriginal population, estimated at about 4000 before European settlement began, had shrunk to fewer than 150 natives, of whom about half were the survivors of those sent by Robinson to Flinders Island. Introduced disease was now rapidly reducing the number of survivors.

When Robinson himself took control at the Flinders settlement in October 1835 he first set out to provide adequate food supplies and to improve housing; but his greatest change was to root out Aboriginal culture and to attempt its replacement with a nineteenth century peasant culture. Schools were established in which the natives were taught to read and write. Catechetical religion took a prominent place in all the instruction. The teachers were drawn from the Europeans in the settlement and from those native children who had learned to read and write at the Hobart Orphan School. Attempts were made to 'civilize' the natives in other ways: markets were held where they were taught to buy and sell in hope that they would come to realize the value of property; they were given new names and taught to elect their own native police. The experiment failed, partly because the natives were dying off rapidly, but chiefly because no culture can be uprooted without being replaced by an adequate and acceptable substitute.

Robinson's work among the Tasmanian Aboriginals had more than a local interest, because Arthur, once he had seen that conciliation could prevent the inevitable clash between the colonizing power and the native inhabitants, was anxious that it should be tried in the newer Australian colonies to prevent a recurrence of what he had experienced in Tasmania. As early as 1832 Arthur suggested that Robinson might practise the principles of conciliation at Spencer Gulf or Swan River, and in February 1835 he was asked to undertake such work at Portland Bay. This scheme came to nothing, but in August 1836 Robinson was offered appointment as protector of Aboriginals in South Australia; he refused it because the salary was less than he thought he deserved. Some two years later he was offered the chief protectorship at Port Phillip, and as he considered the salary adequate he accepted.

Robinson left Flinders Island for Port Phillip in February 1839. His departure marked the end of a vision, the saving of the Tasmanian race. He spent nearly eleven years at Port Phillip, but his work there was not impressive. Unlike the Tasmanian tribes the Victorian Aboriginals, on whom he tried to thrust his idea of civilization, were free to come and go as they pleased. His handling of the affairs of the protectorate was weak, anything of value coming from his sub-protectors, although he made several noteworthy overland journeys to South Australia, New South Wales and the Murray valley, the day-to-day record of these in his journals giving valuable information about the tribes and the state of the country he traversed.

The Port Phillip protectorate was abolished on 31 December 1849 leaving Robinson free to do as he wished. He was well off and had a pension. His wife had died in September 1848; except for his daughter Cecelia his family was grown up. He could afford to live in comfort. In May 1852 he sailed in the *Medway* for London. There on 4 June 1853 he married Rose, daughter of J. B. Pyne, a well-known artist; five children of this marriage survived. The Robinsons lived on the Continent, mostly in Rome and Paris, until about June

1858, when they returned to England and next year settled in Bath. The sojourn in Europe and particularly at Bath, brought to Robinson much of what he wanted: comfortable living and social acceptance, as well as a place among the followers of the arts and sciences. He died in Bath on 18 October 1866.

N. J. B. Plomley (ed), *Friendly mission* (Hob, 1966) and for bibliog.

ROBINSON, JOSEPH PHELPS (1815?-1848), banker and landowner, was a Quaker who arrived in Sydney in the steamship *Cornubia* in June 1842 as a partner of Benjamin Boyd [q.v.] and resident manager of the Royal Bank of Australia. With Boyd he set up an office at Church Hill and soon acquired land at Eden and many large runs in the Monaro. In 1843 banking business took Robinson to Port Phillip, where he became a keen supporter of the separation movement and was elected to represent Melbourne in the New South Wales Legislative Council in 1844-48. Opponents called him the 'member for Boyd' but conceded his unusual ability.

In Sydney Robinson joined the Australian Club, and in the Legislative Council he advocated that each session should be opened with prayer. His concern for savings banks and mechanics' institutes, his service on the select committee on education and later as treasurer of the National School Society, and his placing of the *Cornubia* at the disposal of the Sydney Bethel Union, all helped to win him the title of 'Humanity Robinson'. He was also zealous in presenting claims for roads, bridges and other improvements in Melbourne, and as treasurer of the Pastoralists' Association he gave evidence to the select committee on land grievances. On his own account Robinson imported and exported goods and in 1844 acquired depasturing licences for the runs of Yarrowick in the New England district and Clifton on the Darling Downs, thereby escaping bankruptcy when Boyd and the Royal Bank crashed. In 1846 he gave sheep to H.M.S. *Bramble* during her visit to Brisbane and bullocks to Leichhardt's [q.v.] ill-fated expedition. Aged 33 he died of scarlet fever on 13 August 1848 at his cottage, Clee Villa, on the north shore of Sydney Harbour.

MS cat under J. P. Robinson (ML).

ROBINSON, MICHAEL MASSEY (1744-1826), convict, public servant and poet, was born probably in the south of England, where he attended the University of Oxford and later practised law. He also wrote poetical quips, one of which was the cause of his transportation to Australia. It no longer exists but is known to have been an attack on James Oldham, an ironmonger and alderman of the city of London. In it Robinson revived an old, disproven charge against Oldham of having murdered a former employer; he attempted to extort money from his victim by threatening to publish the verse, whereupon Oldham prosecuted him for blackmail. Robinson was convicted and sentenced to death at the Old Bailey in February 1796, but was reprieved at the prosecutor's request, and transported to New South Wales. On the voyage to Sydney in the *Barwell*, which arrived in May 1798, his superior manners won him the special consideration of the captain; he was permitted to take his meals with the petty officers, a bottle of wine and a dinner being sent to him daily from the captain's table.

Travelling by the same ship was Richard Dore [q.v.], to take up office as deputy-judge-advocate of New South Wales. Dore was a sick man and Robinson ingratiated himself with him by attending to his comfort and amusing him in talk; as soon as Dore opened his commission in Sydney he appointed Robinson, with the governor's sanction, as his secretary. With his legal training, he was probably better fitted than any other man in Sydney for the position. He acted only nominally and was paid no salary, but the emoluments were considerable to a man as tactful as Robinson, and possession of the office gave him moderate status. A fortnight after landing in Sydney Robinson was granted a conditional pardon. In November 1800 he was appointed officer for the registration of agreements, thus beginning the registration of all legal documents in the colony, exclusive of land grants. In December 1800 Dore died, and since Richard Atkins [q.v.], who was appointed to succeed him, knew little law Robinson virtually ran the office. All movement permits were issued by him and it was easy for him to forge Atkins's signature and pocket the 'consideration' offered by the grateful recipient of an order.

For some time Robinson got away with this jobbery, but on 18 September 1802 he was convicted of 'wilful and corrupt perjury', after having 'most unjustifiably and oppressively demanded' a gallon of rum as a fee for the delivery of a bail bond. He was sentenced to Norfolk Island, but he had been making himself useful as a general agent and adviser to Simeon Lord [q.v.] and other merchants, and a number of the most respected gentry in Sydney petitioned for his pardon. Governor King, seeing that the culprit was indispensable in his office, held the sentence in abeyance and restored Robinson to his post. Some time later his forgery of movement permits was discovered, and he had to be ordered 'never to interfere in any circumstances respecting law transactions in private or public'.

In 1805 he was associated with Maurice Margarot and Sir Henry Grant Hayes [qq.v.] in 'promoting discords' in the settlement and making complaints to England, so in August he was sent to Norfolk Island to serve his sentence. Next year Captain Piper [q.v.], commandant at Norfolk Island, permitted him to return to Sydney, though Governor Bligh censured him for doing so. Robinson was allowed to land in December 1806. Soon afterwards he married Elizabeth Rowley, and at 64 became the father of a son, and later of another boy and a girl. In April 1810 he was appointed chief clerk to the secretary's office under Governor Macquarie and for eleven years thereafter composed the birthday odes for which he is best remembered, one for the King's birthday and one for the Queen's. In 1818 and 1819 he was granted two cows from the government herd 'for his services as Poet Laureate', but after Macquarie resigned, Robinson was retired by Governor Brisbane, the odes stopped and were followed by several ballads lamenting the departure of Macquarie and referring scornfully to his successor.

Robinson was not the first writer of verse in Australia. Earlier 'pipes' against King had been common, and in 1809 a satirical verse on the Rum Rebellion, 'A New Song made in New South Wales' was written, almost certainly the work of an Irish convict attorney, Laurence Davoren, who had been convicted in Dublin in February 1791 and was transported to Sydney in the *Boddingtons* in 1793. Bligh made a holograph copy of this verse during his imprisonment, but Robinson's was the first verse published here, and the first that can be ascribed with absolute certainty. All Robinson's odes except one were published in the official *Gazette*, and it became the author's practice to recite his new verse at each birthday levee at Government House. They are stilted and rhetorical in style and lack true imaginative invention, but are not without pathos; they appealed to Robinson's contemporaries through their stimulation of memories of what it meant to be a convict, and they expressed the ardent community spirit which informed Macquarie's Sydney.

Robinson was one of the original shareholders of the Bank of New South Wales, where he had a very comfortable balance in 1820. The previous year he had been appointed deputy-provost-marshal; in 1821 he became principal clerk in the Police Office, a post he occupied until his death on 22 December 1826.

HRA (1), 4-10, 12; E. M. O'Brien, *The hostage: a miracle play* (Syd, 1928); M. M. Robinson, *Odes*, ed G. Mackaness (Syd, 1946); L. Davoren, *A new song made in New South Wales on the rebellion*, ed G. Mackaness (Syd, 1951); *Gleaner*, 5 Apr 1827; MS cat under M. M. Robinson (ML).

DONOVAN CLARKE

RODIUS (RHODIUS), CHARLES (1802-1860), artist, was born in Cologne, Germany. Inscriptions in French on some of his drawings suggest that his background was French rather than German. He went to England and acquired an easy command of the English language. In 1829 he was convicted at Westminster on a charge of stealing a reticule and sentenced to transportation for seven years. He arrived in New South Wales in December 1829 in the *Sarah*.

On arrival Rodius was assigned to the Department of Public Works, where he was employed without salary in instructing civil and military officers in drawing. As a draughtsman he was also engaged by the colonial architect to produce plans of 'every building throughout the Colony' and to formulate plans of projected buildings. His service was considered invaluable, and his seniors were reluctant to uphold Rodius's application for a ticket-of-leave which would exempt him from compulsory government service.

In addition to regular attendance at the department Rodius, as soon as he arrived in the colony, was engaged to teach drawing and perspective to the children of reputable gentlemen in Sydney. These included children of Chief Justice Forbes [q.v.], of whom there is a small crayon-and-wash portrait by Rodius in the Dixson Collection, Sydney; W. Foster, chairman of the Courts of Quarter Sessions, and J. E. Manning [q.v.]. All three testified on the artist's behalf to his good conduct and regular attendance when, in November 1831, he applied to Governor Darling for a ticket-of-leave. A ticket-of-exemption, with the requirement that he remain in the district of Sydney, was granted to Rodius in July 1832, a ticket-of-leave in February

1834, and a certificate of freedom in July 1841.

Rodius's ticket-of-exemption records his calling, before conviction, as 'artist and architect', and he is believed to have made engravings of buildings in Paris for the French government. In a notice published in 1839 advertising that he was giving lessons in drawing and perspective, Rodius described himself as a 'Pupil of the Royal Academy of France'.

In 1831 the first of his lithographed portraits of Aboriginal 'Kings' and their wives was published, and the series was completed in 1834. In addition he executed portraits in 'French crayon' and oils, and the first of his landscape paintings to be engraved, a coloured view of Port Jackson taken from Bunker's Hill, was sold in 1834. Other lithographed works included a view of the Lansdowne Bridge, 1836, a second series of Aboriginals' portraits, 1840, and illustrations of the Kennedy [q.v.] expedition of 1849. Rodius contributed a small number of works to the exhibitions of the Society for the Promotion of the Fine Arts in Australia in 1847, 1849 and 1857. To the last he sent a portrait of Ludwig Leichhardt [q.v.].

From his professional activities as art teacher, portraitist and landscape painter, Rodius must have made a fair living, for in 1835 he paid £45 for a block of land in Campbell Street, Sydney, and was able to support a wife and child. The parish of St James records the birth of a son, Charles Prossper, to Charles Rodius, artist, and Maria Bryan, seamstress, on 27 August 1834. This wife presumably died, for he remarried. The death of his second wife, Harriet, took place on 14 December 1838. The notice of Harriet's death gave her age as 'in her 17th year', but the tombstone which Rodius engraved for her, 'sculptured by her afflicted husband as a last tribute his affection can give' (removed from the Devonshire Street cemetery to La Perouse) gives her age as 18. In July 1841, soon after receiving his certificate of freedom, Rodius sailed for Port Phillip, but the length and purpose of his stay is not known.

During the late 1850s Rodius suffered a stroke which paralysed one side, and on 9 April 1860 he died 'of infirmity' at the Liverpool Hospital. The record of his death indicates that he was a Roman Catholic, and that at the time of his death nothing was known to the hospital authorities of his family in Australia or of his parents.

Rodius signed his name 'Rodius' and it was spelt thus on his certificates of exemption, leave, and freedom. The spelling

'Rhodius' was used in newspaper notices of his work, and in communications concerning the artist's activities in the Department of Public Works.

W. Dixson, 'Notes on Australian artists', *JRAHS*, 5 (1919); Convict indents (ML).

JOCELYN GRAY

ROE, JOHN SEPTIMUS (1797-1878), naval officer, surveyor and explorer, was born on 8 May 1797 at Newbury, Berkshire, England, the seventh son of Rev. James Roe, rector of Newbury, and his wife Sophia, née Brookes. His boyhood wish to become a teacher was frustrated by lack of money for his education, but his father secured for him a place at Christ's Hospital, London, where he became a pupil of the mathematical school. At school Roe formed the habit of writing to his parents lengthy letters about his doings and his thoughts and he continued to be a devoted diarist throughout his life. The earliest letters show the struggle his parents had to keep him at school and the boy's determination not to fail them.

Roe was appointed a midshipman in the navy on 27 May 1813 and sailed in the *Rippon* which was employed in the blockade of the French coast. Adventure came immediately, with the capture of a Spanish galleon, and soon young Roe came under notice for a carefully drawn chart of Brest Harbour. When the *Rippon* paid off in August 1814 Roe spent several months in the *Horatio*. On uncomfortable convoys relieved by short periods of surveying, he found satisfaction with his log-book, charts and sketches of places visited. After brief service surveying in the Channel Islands the *Horatio* sailed for the China Station in July 1815 and did not return to England until January 1817. Places visited by his ship were recorded in Roe's log-book, and as often as he could he wrote to his parents recording such incidents as the chase of Portuguese ships, riding out gales, a brush with Malays and the prostration of the ship's company by tropical heat.

Soon after the *Horatio* paid off at Deptford in 1817 Roe passed examinations in mathematics and navigation and was posted as master's mate to the surveying service in New South Wales then under the command of P. P. King [q.v.]. In his letters Roe referred to his task as the completion of the work done by Matthew Flinders [q.v.], the interruption of whose exploring, Roe wrote, 'had left in much, and indeed almost total geographical uncertainty, the whole of the western, north-western and northern coasts of Australia, comprised between Cape Leeuwin and the Gulf of Carpentaria, with much of the north-eastern coastline from Torres' Strait to Breaksea Spit, a knowledge of the whole of which could not but prove highly beneficial both to a rising colony and its parent state'.

Roe sailed for Sydney in the *Dick* in February 1817 and arrived in September. No ship was immediately available for the survey work, and for a short time he had the unusual experience of moving socially in Government House circles. His letters home at this period are a quaint mixture of awed respect for the quality and restrained enjoyment. To fill the wide gaps noted by Roe the *Mermaid*, 85 tons, was commissioned in Sydney by King and on 21 December 1817 Roe sailed in her on the first of three coastal surveys. On this voyage of 5000 miles the *Mermaid* circumnavigated Australia and surveys were made of sections of the coastline, chiefly north of Exmouth Gulf. In December 1818 the *Mermaid* was used in a brief survey of the Derwent River, and on 8 May 1819 Roe again sailed in her on a survey voyage to the northernmost part of Australia expected to last eight months. Roe wrote that this voyage was to make a proper survey of the coast which had never been explored since Captain Cook's [q.v.] superficial examination. The report of this voyage contained much information about the waters of the Great Barrier Reef and the coast westwards from the Gulf of Carpentaria to the Bonaparte Archipelago on the west coast. Roe's third voyage in the *Mermaid* was nearly the last for the ship's company. The little teak ship leaked badly. She met heavy weather and, after a hazardous and uncomfortable voyage along the northern coastline, limped back to Sydney, where she was laid up for extensive repairs.

Roe transferred to the brig *Bathurst*, 170 tons, whose mission was to continue the survey of the west coast of Australia. She left Sydney in May 1821, and on 30 June Roe fell from the masthead fifty feet to the deck, receiving bruises and a very deep wound over the right temple; to this fall Roe later attributed the loss of sight of his right eye. Those in the *Bathurst* surveyed along the west coast of Australia as far as Roebuck Bay and, having replenished stores at Mauritius, returned to survey the coast between Cape Leeuwin and Cape Levêque. The *Bathurst* returned to England on 10 May 1823, and Roe sought from the Admiralty an appointment as lieutenant, a rank in which he had acted in the *Bathurst* on the instruction of King. This appointment was made on 1 June 1823, and his pay as a lieutenant was backdated to 25 April 1822.

Roe was afloat again in February 1824 as lieutenant in the *Tamar* bound for Sydney. Under Captain J. G. Bremer [q.v.] the *Tamar* sailed from Sydney to Port Essington and there on 20 September 1824 established a settlement and took possession of the northern coast of Australia. Roe read the proclamation when this ceremony was repeated at Melville Island. Later the *Tamar* sailed for the India Station, where the ship's company saw action in the war against Burma and Roe was awarded the Burma medal. He prepared three charts of portions of the Arabian and African coasts where the *Tamar* cruised on convoy duty, and made scores of sketches and swift surveys in his own log-books. He handed these surveys to the Admiralty on his return to England late in 1827 and was delighted to be appointed to the Hydrographic Office to work on sailing directions for publication in *The Australia Directory* (London, 1830).

Roe's service on the India Station had affected his health. He was recuperating from a severe illness when he was offered the post of surveyor-general at the new settlement to be established at Swan River. To enable him to accept the position the Admiralty gave him two years leave, later extended for over forty years. From the time he arrived in the transport *Parmelia* in June 1829 until his death, Roe was influential in the development of Western Australia. He made surveys of the sea approaches to the Swan River, surveyed the sites of Fremantle and Perth, and 'with one sickly assistant' superintended the marking of the town lots and land taken up by the pioneer settlers. He was responsible for drawing up most of the land regulations. As surveyor-general he became a member of the Executive and Legislative Councils. He was interested in civic development and was the sponsor of many early moves in the progress of Perth. Additional duties, such as that of registrar of brands, he accepted with reluctance but dutifully carried out.

He was active in founding the Swan River Mechanics' Institute and was its president for many years. This became Perth's first cultural centre. His collection of botanical specimens won him membership of the Linnean Society; later he extended his collection to include zoology and mineralogy, and thus laid the foundations of what became the Perth Museum. The claim has been made that Roe was responsible for setting aside for public use King's Park, a reserve in which Perth takes particular pride. Roe certainly noted as early as 31 December 1830 that 'the neighbourhood of Mt Eliza [King's Park] is reserved for public purposes'; but others, notably Governor Weld, Sir John Forrest and Sir Malcolm Fraser, were more closely associated with the moves that created the reserve in perpetuity.

Roe left records of sixteen journeys of exploration. The first eight, between 1830 and 1835 were comparatively short trips to the south and the south-west. In 1836 he went east of Perth for about 180 miles and then north for 100 miles. Three years later he led a party north to succour men from Captain George Grey's expedition. His final expedition in 1848-49 occupied five months and took him to Russell Range east of Esperance. The privations he suffered in this arid region and the fatigues of the journey caused him to note that he was past the age for such work.

Historians have called Roe 'the father of Australian explorers'. This title takes into account not only the survey work he did on the Australian coast and his inland expeditions but the inspiration he gave to such younger explorers as John and Alexander Forrest, who were with him as surveyors, and the Gregory brothers, who also worked with him. Roe's capacity for work, his ability to apply himself, his careful keeping of records, and his will to succeed earned the respect of all who were closely associated with him. His was not a warm character but one that commanded respect and admiration.

In 1860 Roe revisited England but did not remain long. While there he applied for promotion to commander, but three years passed before the rank was granted, 'with no extra emoluments'. He retired in August 1870. One of the last entries in his diary read: 'I have not been an idle man in my generation'.

In January 1829 by special arrangement Roe had married Matilda Bennett, of the Isle of Man, a few weeks before he sailed from Portsmouth in the *Parmelia*. His letters at that time display an unsuspected tenderness: he wooed his Matilda with importunate ardour and pestered officials so that they could marry in the short time between his appointment and the departure of the *Parmelia*. The first of their thirteen children was born on Christmas Day 1829 and was among the first born at Swan River. Several of their sons were prominent in public life in Western Australia. Roe's name is perpetuated in several places in Western Australia, such as Roebourne.

Roe died on 28 May 1878. His wife had predeceased him by a few years. According to his obituary in the Perth *Inquirer and Commercial News*, 'His hands were clean: he never used the privileges of his post unduly to his own advantage or the advancement of his numerous family'. In public tributes to his long service to the colony regret was expressed that he had not received all the honours he deserved.

P. P. King, *Narrative of a survey of the intertropical and western coasts of Australia*, 1-2 (Lond, 1827); F. R. Mercer, *Amazing career: the story of Western Australia's first surveyor-general* (Perth, 1962); *West Australian*, 31 May 1878; P. U. Henn, Genealogical notes (Battye Lib, Perth); Roe papers (Battye Lib, Perth).   MALCOLM UREN

ROEMER, CHARLES WILLIAM (b. 1799), merchant, was a native of Leipzig, Germany. For many years he lived at Cheapside, London, as an importer of German wool. Early in 1832 he emigrated to New South Wales to grow and export Australian wool. In February 1836 he petitioned for letters of denization to give him legal title to the crown land he had already bought in New South Wales; his request was granted in August. Roemer bought land including 847 acres in the Port Phillip District in 1840-41 and property at Moreton Bay, Scone, Raymond Terrace, Clarence Town, Mudgee, Yass and Queanbeyan, but he continued to live in Sydney as a merchant. He imported some rare wine in 1841 but most of his activity was in the export trade.

In 1834 he had opened the Sydney Bank in Charlotte Place, on a plan that was original, but too cautious for his associates. In November 1836 he was elected director of the Commercial Banking Co. of Sydney, and in December was appointed auditor for the Fire and Life Assurance Co. By January 1840 he was a director of the Australian Auction Co., but mostly he operated as an individual financier. He was charged in the Sydney Police Court on 10 November 1840 with obtaining £522 15s. under false pretences from J. T. Hughes and was committed for trial but acquitted in February 1841. In January 1839 Roemer, a short, fair man with a round face, chaired a meeting in Sydney in support of a German mission at Moreton Bay, and in January 1841 he subscribed to the building of Christ Church St Laurence in Sydney. He was also a member of a committee appointed in July 1842 to report on the suitability of Broulee as a shipping port on the south coast of New South Wales.

Roemer sailed from Sydney in the *Shamrock* on 16 September 1844. In October 1854 he gave a power of attorney to S. K. Salting [q.v.] of Sydney and Bielby Hawthorn of Melbourne to enable them to dispose of his property in the mainland colonies, New Zealand and Van Diemen's Land. None of his later activities or his death have been traced.

HRA (1), 18; S. J. Butlin, *Foundations of the Australian monetary system 1788-1851* (Melb, 1953); Newspaper indexes under Roemer (ML).   A. F. PIKE

ROGERS, THOMAS GEORGE (1806-1903), religious instructor, was born probably in Dublin, the son of Thomas Rogers. After admission to Trinity College, Dublin, in November 1823, he held permanent curacies at St Paul's, Walsall, in 1826-39, Holbeck, near Leeds, in 1839-44 and Stainland, near Halifax, in 1844. About 1834 he had married Sarah Smyth, of Dublin. Finding his endowments too small for a growing family he accepted an offer by the Society for the Propagation of the Gospel to go to Norfolk Island as a religious instructor of convicts at a salary of £250 with a living allowance. He was appointed in November 1844 and given £125 by the society and £250 by the Colonial Office to take out his wife and six children, but left them in the care of the vicar of Halifax, promising to remit a third of his salary for their maintenance.

In the *Bussorah Merchant* Rogers arrived at Sydney in June 1845 and in July went on to Hobart, where Bishop Nixon [q.v.] refused him a licence because religious instructors in the convict department were outside episcopal control. In September Rogers reached Norfolk Island, where the chaplains also maintained that he was in an unecclesiastical position, and the convicts soon discovered the anomaly. In October he complained to the commandant, Joseph Childs [q.v.], that his duties were not clearly defined. Childs misunderstood the complaint and for months letters between the two men went back and forth each day, Childs insisting on discipline and Rogers professing increasing outrage at the inhumanity and irreligion of the commandant. In January 1846 Rogers proposed to report Childs to Nixon and the Colonial Office and in May asked for leave to put his case to the lieut-governor in Hobart. When refused he wrote to the superintendent of religious instructors, Archdeacon F. A. Marriott [q.v.], who assured him from Hobart that his complaints would be investigated. In August

John Price [q.v.] replaced Childs as commandant. Rogers was soon in trouble and Price, in a 200-page dispatch on his misdemeanours, recommended his removal from the island. In Hobart the acting lieutgovernor, La Trobe, and the comptrollergeneral of convicts, J. S. Hampton [q.v.], agreed that Rogers should be recalled because 'he was deficient in temper and discretion'. He left Norfolk Island in February 1847.

In Hobart Lieut-Governor Denison refused to see him, wrote to London about his neglect of his family, and removed him from the convict department. Marriott was more sympathetic, offered him temporary curacies at New Norfolk and at Windermere near Launceston, but lost patience when Rogers stayed in Hobart, bombarding Denison and Downing Street with long rebuttals of Price's charges. When Bishop Nixon returned from England in 1848 Rogers was admitted to deacon's orders and went to Windermere. Publication at Launceston in April 1849 of *Correspondence relating to the Dismissal of the Rev. T. Rogers, from his Chaplaincy at Norfolk Island* brought him angry reproof for daring to print official documents without government sanction. Unabashed, Rogers published in October a statement from his churchwardens, with laudatory testimonials from six Launceston citizens and from Fielding Browne [q.v.] who had witnessed the 'faithful, fearless, yet affectionate performance of his clerical duties' at Norfolk Island.

In December Rogers heard through the bishop that his wife had died in Dublin, her death hastened by the long silence of her husband who had sent only £75 in four years, and his six children left destitute. In January 1850 Rogers sought leave to return to Ireland for them and sailed in the *Philip Oakden* on 28 February, but friends had already subscribed to send them to Melbourne and according to family tradition he passed them on the way.

In London in July 1858 he gave evidence to the parliamentary committee on the petition of William Henry Barber, a wrongly convicted solicitor whom he had befriended on the island. Until 1860 Rogers's name remained in clergy lists as chaplain of Norfolk Island, but he became a Roman Catholic before he returned to Australia, where he worked as a tutor and under the name 'Peutetre' contributed many religious articles to the *Advocate* in Melbourne. He died at Malvern on 17 January 1903 aged 98.

Of his children, two daughters married at Launceston; a son, John William Foster, born at Leeds on 16 July 1842, was edu-

cated in Melbourne, had a school at Ballarat in 1870, became headmaster of the Melbourne Hebrew School in 1878 and was married at St Kilda in 1881.

Rogers's account of the evils of the Norfolk Island penal settlement may have helped to inspire the founding of the Anti-Transportation League at Launceston; it was given a much wider impact by Marcus Clarke, who with some fictional licence used him as the prototype of Rev. James North in *For the Term of his Natural Life*.

J. West, *The history of Tasmania*, 2 (Launceston, 1852), p 299-302; J. V. Barry, *The life and death of John Price* (Melb, 1964); T. Rogers, Letter-book 1844-46 (ML); W. F. Rogers, *Man's inhumanity—being a chaplain's chronicle of Norfolk Island in the 'forties* (ML); Correspondence file under Thomas Rogers (TA).

ROSE, DAVID (d. 1826), farmer, arrived in Sydney from London in 1810 as a lieutenant in the 73rd Regiment. In April he was transferred to Port Dalrymple in the *Trial* and continued his successful army career there. In 1812, when Major Gordon of the 73rd Regiment at Launceston 'had sunk into mental debility', Rose was one of several officers who performed Gordon's duties. Rose was also one of the officers towards whom Major Stewart was antagonistic and this may have encouraged his resignation in August 1814.

While still a lieutenant Rose had begun an apparently successful public service career. In January 1812 Gordon, with Governor Macquarie's approval, appointed Rose inspector of government herds and livestock at Port Dalrymple at 5s. a day. During his term of office he served on the inquiry in May 1813 into the case of Edward Woolly who was accused of maiming cattle. In April 1820 when examined by Commissioner Bigge [q.v.] Rose admitted that he had not always acted according to instructions, but he explained that his assistants were too few, his pay too meagre, and his instructions unrealistic. He was a witness in the examinations of Frederick Drennan's [q.v.] charges against Lieut-Colonel Cimitiere [q.v.] for malversation of government stores and herds. Drennan accused Rose of wrongfully being allowed assigned servants and rations as a magistrate, but more serious were depositions about discrepancies in Rose's stock returns. However, Rose was able to account for the irregularities. It was also revealed that Rose had had to buy stationery with his own money, and to build government stockyards for which he had not been paid for over a year; and he had been instructed to separate the government stock from privately owned cattle, an absurd order for that unfenced country. He was said to have been exchanging cattle with the notorious William Field, but these charges had little effect on Rose's career and until his services were no longer required he was given wider powers. In November 1820 when the herds were consolidated under one central superintendent he resigned, after chairing a committee during his last month of office to draft proposals for disposing of the government livestock.

Rose had become a farmer on his retirement from the army and seemed to be modestly successful as a wheat-grower and meat contractor. He was granted land, which he named Corra Lynn, on the North Esk River near Launceston. In 1814 he was also granted six cows from the government herds on three years credit and was promised six assigned servants when they became available. On his discharge from the public service in 1820 he increased his landholdings by grant and purchase. His other activities included brick-making and in 1818 he sold 3000 to the commandant at Port Dalrymple.

An old friend of Macquarie, with whom he had long served in the same regiment, Rose was a supporter of the local Bible Society and seemed to be of excellent character, although in 1820 Drennan wildly accused him of being 'a Drunkard and illiterate'. His death on 6 July 1826 was hastened by a wound from a dog bite.

HRA (3), 1-3.

ROSE, THOMAS (1749?-1833), farmer, was born at Blandford, Dorset, England. There he married Jane Topp, who bore him three sons and one daughter before 1792. In August that year, as the result of repeated requests by Governor Phillip for the dispatch of intelligent and experienced farmers, Thomas Rose and his family together with four other free settlers sailed in the *Bellona* for New South Wales. Rose and his companions were the first free and independent settlers to reach Australia. They arrived in Sydney on 16 January 1793, when David Collins noted that Rose was 'the most respectable of these people, and apparently the best calculated for a *bona-fide* settler'. The new arrivals chose land about seven miles west of Sydney, which they called Liberty Plains, now the Strathfield-Homebush district, where Rose received first 80 and later 120 acres. Why they settled there is uncertain, for the soil was poor, and without manure was quickly exhausted, but possibly Lieut-

Governor Francis Grose [q.v.] wanted to establish settlement between Sydney and Parramatta for the safety and convenience of the travelling public. Rose soon decided that they had 'made a hasty and bad choice of situation' and according to family records he soon afterwards moved to Prospect, where he was made an overseer in charge of the government farm and stock, and where his second daughter, Sarah, was born. He appears to have stayed at Prospect for some twelve years. He and his family then moved to more fertile lands along the Hawkesbury River where they purchased the 30-acre grant of William Mackay near the later-named Wilberforce, which Grose began to settle in 1794. There he spent the rest of his life and became a well-known and highly respected figure, surrounded by a growing army of descendants. A son and a daughter had been born in the colony. He died on 15 November 1833 and was buried in the cemetery of St John's, Wilberforce. His wife, who predeceased him in 1827, was, according to the *Sydney Gazette*, the first woman to attain the status of great-grandmother in the colony since its establishment.

Quiet, homely, unassuming and industrious, Thomas Rose belonged to that humble band of men who, in a rough and licentious age, helped to lay the foundations of ordered social life in a new country.

HRA (1), 2-6; D. Collins, *An account of the English colony in New South Wales*, 1-2 (Lond, 1798-1802); J. F. Campbell, 'The dawn of rural settlement in Australia', JRAHS, 11 (1925); *Windsor and Richmond Gazette*, 21 Aug 1925; MS cat under T. Rose (ML).

ARTHUR McMARTIN

ROSE, THOMAS (d. 1837), baker, publican and water conservator, of Newport, Shropshire, England, was convicted of housebreaking at Shrewsbury on 19 March 1793 and sentenced to death. The sentence was commuted to transportation for life and he arrived at Sydney in the *Barwell* in May 1798. About 1804 he set up in Sydney as a baker, which had been his former occupation. On 13 April 1806 he married Elizabeth, whose father Thomas Bartlett had been a fellow-convict in the *Barwell* and whose mother Ann Bartlett had followed with her daughter in the *Nile* in 1801. They had six children. In the month of his marriage he received a publican's licence. He was conditionally pardoned on 4 June 1806, and on 1 December 1809 Lieut-Governor Paterson [q.v.] gave him an absolute pardon, which Governor Macquarie later confirmed, and land at the corner of King and Castlereagh Streets, fronting what was then known as Chapel Row. There he had built a bakery and alongside it the Rose and Crown Inn, both of which were opened for business in 1810. He gradually increased his holdings in this part of town until he gained possession of the entire block now bounded by King, Elizabeth, Market and Castlereagh Streets. Together with Charles Thompson, another Sydney baker, Rose rented John Palmer's [q.v.] windmill from June 1813 to June 1814; next May he put his bakehouse on the market.

In 1816 his grant of forty acres in the Evan district, located for him in 1813, was cancelled, apparently because he had procured signatures to the petition against Macquarie, supposedly written by J. H. Bent and Benjamin Vale [qq.v.]; for the same reason he failed to retain his liquor licence between 1817 and 1820. In 1819 he clashed with the governor again when Macquarie decided to build St James's parochial school on part of Rose's block; however, in exchange for the school site he was granted 300 acres on the main southern road east of Campbelltown. About the same time he bought a 400-acre farm on the Appin Road, named Mount Gilead, which had been originally granted to Reuben Uther [q.v.]; later he gradually added to this Campbelltown estate, which by 1828 was estimated at 2460 acres.

For some time Rose had been quite a public figure as a Sydney businessman, being a stockholder in the Bank of New South Wales, a trustee of the Sydney Public Free Grammar School, and treasurer of the Sydney Reading Room; he acted as clerk of the Sydney race-course until 1827, promoted the first races in Sydney and owned many successful race-horses. On 1 November 1826 his wife died, and next year he moved to Mount Gilead. There he lived for the rest of his life and won fame for his experiments in water conservation. He had begun these on a small scale in 1824 and next year had built a larger dam, with a stone embankment, holding nearly 120 million cubic feet. In 1829 he built a smaller and cheaper dam near the main road, for the relief of his hard-pressed neighbours in the 1829 drought; later this so impressed Governor Bourke that in 1833 he gave the people of Campbelltown a plot of ground for building a reservoir by public subscription. In July 1835 Rose asked the British government for a free grant in acknowledgment of his services in supplying water to his neighbours; though this was refused, the undaunted Rose next year built a sixty-foot windmill, all of ironbark timber, including shaft and gear wheels.

On 21 September 1829 Rose married again, and his second wife Sarah Pye, the daughter of an old Baulkham Hills settler, bore him five children. He died on 3 March 1837 and was buried at Mount Gilead; later his remains were transferred to St Peter's, Campbelltown. He left a large estate, including farms on the Nepean, at Airds and Botany Bay, houses in Richmond and Windsor, as well as property in Market and Castlereagh Streets, Sydney, and the estate at Mount Gilead. His wife Sarah died on 20 June 1869.

Possessed of great drive, energy and an excellent business sense, Thomas Rose was one of those enterprising men who arrived in the colony as convicts and went on to win wealth and respectability in the tough economic society of their new land. He is remembered as a colourful figure in the early commercial and sporting life of Sydney, and as a pioneer of the Appin-Campbelltown district.

HRA (1), 16-18; *Sydney Gazette*, 13 Apr 1806, 17 Dec 1809, 8 Sept 1810, 16 Mar 1811, 27 July 1815, 12 May 1821, 9 Oct 1823; *Australian*, 15 July 1826, 8 May 1835; *Windsor and Richmond Gazette*, 14 Aug 1925; MS cat under T. Rose (ML).

VIVIENNE PARSONS

ROSS, HUGH COKELEY (1795-1869), lawyer, came of an Episcopalian family of Aberdeen, Scotland. He received his primary education at Morden Academy, Morden, Surrey, England, and later qualified as barrister, solicitor and conveyancer at the Courts of Westminster. He reached Hobart Town in the *Regalia* in December 1822, was admitted to the Lieut-Governor's Court on 1 April 1823, and next day to the Supreme Court of Civil and Ecclesiastical Jurisdiction for New South Wales. In June he entered into partnership with George Cartwright, and together they acted as solicitors to the Bank of Van Diemen's Land on its formation in August. In October 1824 he applied for a land grant and, on the strength of his capital of £7500, received 1000 acres at Bothwell, on which to graze livestock received in payment for legal services.

When Alfred Stephen, solicitor-general and crown solicitor, took leave of absence in 1832-33, Ross acted at first in both positions and later as crown solicitor only. He continued his private practice, until

given onerous duties with the commission
inquiring into the titles of land, the remuneration for which was always in arrears
and poor compensation for that of his
private practice. On the dismissal of H. J.
Emmett [q.v.], Ross became clerk of the
peace, confirmation of the appointment
being strongly recommended by Lieut-
Governor Arthur, who expressed himself
very satisfied with his past services to the
government. Later Ross was given the additional duties of conducting jury cases at
the Quarter Sessions, until such cases were
discontinued. At the suggestion of Stephen,
then attorney-general, he was appointed
crown solicitor at a salary of £500. Until
the arrival of Herbert Jones as solicitor-
general, Ross acted competently in his positions but his inability to work harmoniously with Jones brought complaints of his
attitude and efficiency.

Ross was in financial difficulties in 1840.
His family was increasing, his salary fell
by £100 and his large residence in Hobart
was sold for £1000 less than its value in
the depressed colonial economy. Ross found
it necessary to borrow from Crown debts
which it was his responsibility to sue for,
but not collect. Hoping to find more remunerative work in Port Phillip, he asked for
leave, and when refused, absented himself.
Not until six days after his departure was
the extent of his defalcations realized. Warrants immediately sent to other colonial
ports, determined Ross on taking a ship
for Singapore. He went from there to
Batavia, and in May 1841 appeared in
Western Australia, whence after some difficulty with an extradition warrant he was
brought back to Hobart in custody, to the
regret of the colonists who sympathized
with Ross's difficulties and those of his wife
and family. He was committed for trial on
8 March 1842, charged with embezzlement
of £2021 belonging to the Crown. Edward
Macdowell [q.v.], formerly attorney-general until he too had disagreed with the
solicitor-general, shattered the prosecution's
case on a legal point and won a verdict
of not guilty. Ross then free, sailed with
one son for Sydney and New Zealand,
where he set up as a lawyer in Lambton
Quay, Wellington, that year. In February
1844, after a legal dispute, he mortally
wounded a fellow lawyer, W. V. Brewer,
in a duel. Ross served as a lieutenant in
the militia during the disturbances in the
North Island in 1846. In the early 1850s
he retired from his legal practice and
settled at Cokeley, on the Rangitikei
River, where his wife died in September
1853. He died on 27 August 1869, aged
73.

Ross was twice married. Left with four
small children on the death of his wife
Sarah in 1825, he married Anna Maria,
daughter of James Boteler Wood, in 1829,
and by her had four sons, three of whom
survived.

L. E. Ward, *Early Wellington* (Wellington,
1928); Correspondence file under Ross (TA).
                              HUGH D. ROSS

ROSS, JAMES (1786-1838), teacher and
editor, was baptized on 4 January 1787
at Aberdeen, Scotland, the third son of
Alexander Ross, writer to the signet, and
his wife Catharine, née Morrison. He was
educated at Marischal College, Aberdeen
(M.A., 1803; LL.D., 1818) and conducted a
school first at Sevenoaks, Kent, and then at
Sunbury, Middlesex, where he married
Susannah, née Smith. He won great esteem
as a schoolmaster but by 1822 was in
financial difficulties and in poor health. He
decided to emigrate to Van Diemen's Land
and make a home there for his rapidly
growing family, to farm and to teach a
few pupils.

Supported by a recommendation from
Macquarie to Lieut-Governor Sorell and
with a capital of £1309, including books
worth £100, he arrived at Hobart Town in
the *Regalia* in December 1822 and in January was granted 1000 acres on the River
Shannon; he named this property the Hermitage. In 1824 he discussed with Sorell
the possibility of establishing a school and
for this purpose sought a grant near
Hobart. In 1825 he became the tutor of
Lieut-Governor Arthur's children and his
own. By this time he was discouraged by
losses caused by bushrangers and a fire at
the Hermitage and in May 1825 was appointed jointly with G. T. Howe [q.v.]
government printer and editor of the
Hobart Town Gazette at a salary of £300.
They published the first issue of the *Gazette*
on 25 June. In January 1827 the partnership of Howe & Ross was dissolved; Ross
was appointed to sole charge of the government printing office in February and in
March Howe began publishing the *Tasmanian* in Hobart. Under the new arrangement the *Hobart Town Gazette* was an
official weekly paper containing government announcements but no comment or
discussion. In October Ross began to publish weekly also the *Hobart Town Courier*,
an independent newspaper, but one which
consistently supported the government. In
1828, instead of his salary, Ross was
given a contract to print the *Gazette* for
£5 a week with a monopoly of government

printing. In 1829 he began producing the annual *Hobart Town Almanack*, and in February 1833 the short-lived *Hobart Town Chronicle*. In 1835 he edited and published four issues of the *Van Diemen's Land Monthly Magazine*, in which appeared verse, literary articles, and articles on natural history. In 1832 he was granted 312 acres, Paraclete, on Knocklofty.

In January 1834 he wrote to the colonial secretary, John Montagu [q.v.] charging Andrew Bent and Henry Melville [qq.v.] with conspiring to take his work away from him; Melville, he said, had informed Ross's clerk that he would persevere in public attacks on the government and Ross until he had succeeded in removing him from office. Ross's claim that he made only a modest profit was confirmed by the auditor. Earlier he had declared that his work had increased but not his emoluments; he had to teach his children himself and had been unable to afford to send any of them to Britain. Ross and R. L. Murray [q.v.] frequently attacked each other in the columns of their newspapers and in November 1836 Ross had an angry controversy with Gilbert Robertson [q.v.]. In 1836, with government approval, Ross disposed of his printing, bookbinding and stationery establishments to G. W. Elliston [q.v.] for £12,000, and bound him to fulfil his engagements as government printer. He then retired to Carrington in the Richmond district.

After Ross's retirement Franklin, supporting his request for a secondary grant of land, wrote: 'If I were called upon to name the person who had in the greatest degree contributed to the welfare of Van Diemen's Land in the last twelve years I should certainly name Ross. His knowledge is most various and extensive and he has the gift of conveying it in the most simple, pleasing and popular manner . . . But in doing good he overlooked his family'. As an editor Ross had 'frequently quite embarrassed the Government by his support. Politics were evidently not his forte, and often on perusing his Paper might I have exclaimed "Save me from my friends"'. Ross published *An Essay on Prison Discipline* (2nd ed., Hobart, 1833). In the *Penny Magazine* (London), 31 March, 5 and 12 May 1832, he described his experiences in Van Diemen's Land under the heading 'An Emigrant's Struggles'. Some of his articles in the *Hobart Town Almanack* were used by Marcus Clarke in *For the Term of His Natural Life*.

He died of apoplexy at Carrington on 1 August 1838, and was buried in St Luke's cemetery, Richmond. Next year his widow, left with thirteen children, announced that she would open a boarding school at Carrington. In 1842 Carrington was sold to Esh Lovell [q.v.] for £2750 and the school moved to Paraclete. Mrs Ross married Robert Stewart, solicitor, of Hobart, and died at Battery Point on 12 May 1871, aged 75.

HRA (3), 4, 6; P. L. Brown (ed), *Clyde Company papers*, 1 (Lond, 1941); E. M. Miller, *Pressmen and governors* (Syd, 1952); GO 1/30/64 (TA); CSO 1/89/1987, 1/114/2847 (TA); CO 201/113; MS cat under James Ross (ML).

ROSS, ROBERT (b. 1740?), officer of marines and lieut-governor, was born probably in Scotland. In June 1756 he joined the marines as a second lieutenant, and in 1757-60 served in North America, being present at the siege of Louisburg and the capture of Quebec. He was promoted first lieutenant in October 1759, captain in March 1773 and brevet major in March 1783. In the American war in 1775-76 he saw action at Bunker's Hill. While he was returning to England in H.M.S. *Ardent* in August 1779 the ship was captured and he became a prisoner of the French until exchanged. In 1781-82 he served in several actions in the Mediterranean and West Indies. He was appointed lieut-governor of New South Wales on 24 October 1786 and sailed in the *Scarborough* with the First Fleet. Ross owed this appointment to his acquaintance with Sir John Jervis and Evan Nepean [q.v.], with whom he had served in the *Foudroyant* in American waters.

From the foundation of the colony, Ross and Captain Arthur Phillip were at odds, and David Collins expressed his 'inexpressible hatred' for the major. Ross considered that the marine officers' status in the settlement was not elevated enough. He supported Captain James Campbell when the latter objected to being compelled to sit as a member of the Criminal Court, and he tried to persuade the other officers to take a similar attitude. He opposed Phillip's schemes for organizing the convicts and refused to allow the officers to help to supervise the prisoners. He criticized the governor for not building fortifications, while at the same time complaining that his officers had to remain under canvas and later throwing difficulties in the way of Phillip's efforts to have barracks built. Certainly he missed no opportunity of embarrassing and hindering Phillip and at one stage placed five officers under arrest after a trivial disagreement about the sentence of a court martial, suspended two more, had two others asking to be relieved, and the adjutant and quartermaster under his displeasure. He was, wrote Ralph Clark [q.v.] 'without exception the most disagreeable commanding officer I ever knew'. These quarrels naturally made Phillip's task of carrying on the administration more difficult, and later Ross encouraged friction between the marines and the convict guards.

Ross never adapted himself to life in the colony and he had no faith in its future. He was, in addition, worried about his 'very small tho' numerous family' in Britain, who seem to have been in poor circumstances. In 1788 he stated: 'I do not scruple to pronounce that in the whole world there is not a worse country than what we have yet seen of this. All that is contiguous to us is so very barren and forbidding that it may with truth be said, here Nature is reversed'. Ross was critical of Phillip's choice of a site for the settlement, which he declared would 'never answer'. The British government gave him scant sympathy, and in due course decided to recall the marines; but before this was made known in New South Wales, Phillip sent Ross in March 1790 to take charge of Norfolk Island, probably to avoid an open quarrel. Soon after his arrival the *Sirius*, which had brought him to the island, was wrecked and Ross proclaimed martial law, which remained in force for four months. In this he apparently exceeded his authority. He lost many of his personal possessions on the island, and more about the same time when the *Guardian* which was carrying them was wrecked near Cape Town. He worked out a scheme by which the convicts should grow most of their own food, but this entailed the clearing of more land and the heavy work increased the convicts' discontent. The scheme was abolished by Ross's successor.

Relieved on Norfolk Island, where he had quarrelled with his officers as vigorously as he had at Port Jackson, Ross reached Sydney on 5 December 1791. A few days later he fought a duel with Captain Hill, in which both participants escaped unscathed. On 13 December he embarked with the marines for England and resumed his military career. First employed as a recruiting officer, he served in H.M.S. *Director*, 1796-1800, for some time under Captain Bligh, *St Albans*, 1801-02, and in the East Indies in *Sceptre*, 1803-08. His son, John, who went out with him to New South Wales as a 'volunteer', without pay, was given by his father a commission as second lieutenant in 1789.

Ross was not a success as second-in-command of the new colony. He was conscientious and efficient but hankered after more active duty with prospects of promotion, and these the colony could not supply.

HRNSW, 1, pt 2; HRA (1), 1, 2; MS cat under R. Ross (ML).

DAVID S. MACMILLAN

ROSS, ROBERT (1792-1862), Congregational minister, was born on 15 August 1792 at Leith, Scotland, the son of Robert Ross, candle manufacturer, and his first wife Johan, née Scott. After education at Heriot's Hospital, Edinburgh, he was employed by legal firms in 1806-14. In 1813 he began studies for the ministry and embarked on a medical course (M.D., 1818). He married Marina, daughter of John Haldon, on 26 January 1818. He was ordained to the ministry of the Church of Scotland next March and, under appointment with the Edinburgh (from 1819, the Scottish) Missionary Society, went to Russian Tartary. At Orenburg (1818-21) and Astrakhan (1821-25), he served with distinction and was specially commended as a medical practitioner and linguist. Political changes closed the mission in 1825 and Ross returned to Edinburgh. On 29 August 1827 he became minister of the Kidderminster Congregational Church, Worcestershire, and remained there for twelve years. His wife died on 3 November 1829, and in 1832 he married Sarah Grafton. During his pastorate he helped to form the Colonial Missionary Society in 1836 and was a director of the London Missionary Society in 1837-38.

In 1839 he was invited to Sydney as minister of the Pitt Street Congregational Church and as agent of both the Colonial and London Missionary Societies. On arrival in February 1840 he found that dissension had largely dispersed his congregation, but he soon gathered an influential group, erected a new chapel, and established the church firmly. Unfortunately the necessary concentration of his energies and his congregation's resources on the town chapel hindered an early expansion of Congregationalism in the colony. However, Ross won deserved repute, not only for a notable ministry and effective missionary agencies, but also for community service given through the Bible Society, the Religious Tract Society, the German Mission to Aborigines, the Infirmary, the Benevolent Asylum, the Australian School Society, and the Australian Subscription Library. In 1854 he suffered partial paralysis and resigned his pastorate, but continued to give his colleagues such assistance as he could until his death at Edgecliffe on 2 November 1862. He was survived by his wife, who died in 1878, and by their two children, and by four children of his first marriage.

Portraits in oils are held by the Kidderminster and the Pitt Street Churches.

Scottish Missionary Register, 1-5 (1820-25); *Congregational Mag*, 10 (1827), 12 (1829), 22 (1839); *Evangelical Mag*, 9 (1863); *Congregational Year Book*, 1864; LMS archives (Westminster); Colonial Missionary Soc, Reports (Lond); Ross papers, 1818-25 (copies held by Mrs D. Lamb, Turramurra, NSW).

G. L. LOCKLEY

ROSSI, FRANCIS NICHOLAS (1776-1851), soldier and public servant, was born in Corsica, France, the son of Philippe François Antoine, Comte de Rossi, who, through aiding the British occupation of Corsica in 1795, lost his possessions when the island was surrendered to France in 1796 and was compensated with a pension by the British government. Rossi entered the British army in 1795 as ensign in an Anglo-Corsican battalion. In 1798 he transferred to the 69th Regiment and served in Holland. Next year as lieutenant in the 5th Regiment he served in Gibraltar and was favourably noticed for conspicuous ability.

In April 1803 he joined a regiment formed to serve in Ceylon and was promoted captain in January 1807. In 1811 he was appointed aide-de-camp to Sir Robert Townsend Farquhar who in 1812 became governor of Mauritius, where Rossi also held the civil posts of deputy-secretary to the government and collector of registration and mortgage dues. Sent to Bengal in 1815, he arranged for the transportation to Mauritius of Indian convicts. He carried dispatches to England in 1816 and in 1817 was appointed general superintendent of the convict department in Mauritius. Through fear that the scattered working parties of convicts might incite the slaves to rebellion, Rossi enforced rigorous discipline. In 1822 he married Antoinette Geneviève Sornay, by whom he had two sons, Francis Robert Louis (b. 1823) and Alexander Philip (b. 1828). Rossi left Mauritius when Farquhar's governorship ended in 1823 and in August 1824 accepted the post of superintendent of police in New South Wales, offered him by Earl Bathurst.

Rossi took up his duties in Sydney on 19 May 1825, replacing D'Arcy Wentworth [q.v.]. He reorganized the Sydney police on a system somewhat similar to that of the Bow Street police office in London. Through his own tireless efforts he made the force more efficient, although continuously hampered by inadequate funds and recruits of poor quality; even worse, control of the colony's police forces was divided between the benches of magistrates outside Sydney, the officers of the mounted police, and the head of the Sydney police. In appointing Rossi, Bathurst intended to carry out a recommendation of Commissioner Bigge [q.v.] that the police of the whole colony should be under one central authority. However, Governors Brisbane and Darling postponed change. Rossi remained, therefore, executive head of the Sydney police only, although he had authority to correspond directly with the rural benches of magistrates and was himself a police magistrate. He felt the weight of his duties and in May 1827 was temporarily appointed to the less arduous post of comptroller, and in December acting collector of customs in Sydney. Despite Darling's earnest request, this appointment was not confirmed and in 1829 Rossi resumed duty with the police. In 1833 the Sydney Police Act (4 Wm IV, no 7 NSW) introduced a new system, the application of which Rossi felt was too onerous for his health, already impaired by heavy duties. He obtained a year's leave during which he was permitted to sell his army commission on condition that he retired from the police.

After retirement in November 1834 he lived on his property Rossiville in the Goulburn district. He had long believed himself a British subject, first because George III had assumed the crown of Corsica in 1794, and second because of his long service in the British army. In 1843, however, he found that he was still an alien in the eyes of the law and became anxious about his right to own land. On the representation of Governor Gipps in May 1844, the Colonial Office authorized the issue of letters of denization to Rossi. When the legal competency of denizens and naturalized aliens to hold land in the colony was questioned in 1845, Rossi's case was noticed by the governor as one of particular hardship. To relieve the situation, an amending Act (11 Vic. no 39 NSW) was passed by the Legislative Council in September 1847 and given royal assent in October 1848. Rossi died on 26 November 1851.

Throughout his career in New South Wales, Rossi was surrounded by discreditable rumours. However groundless, they adversely affected his status as a magistrate and his influence on the Sydney police. For example the House of Commons was told in 1826 that he had instructed soldiers in Mauritius to ignore any indications of slave-trading; he was exonerated after a board of magistrates in Sydney examined the accusations and heard his explanation. Another harmful rumour was that his appointment in Sydney was a reward for personal services to George IV. Rossi, it was alleged, had been sent to Italy in 1819 with the secret commission to obtain evidence for the royal divorce and, under the pseudonym 'Majorca' or 'Majocchi', had been an important witness against Queen Caroline. No firm evidence substantiated the rumours but they persisted in Sydney, and the words 'non mi ricordo in Queen Caroline Trial' were noted against his name in a members' list of the Australian Club compiled by P. P. King [q.v.] in 1844. Rossi was involved in a local scandal when allegations of malpractice as a magistrate were brought against him in the Supreme Court in 1826. In giving judgment, the chief justice absolved Rossi from corrupt motives, but because his conduct had been irregular he was not allowed costs.

Some critics thought him unsuited for his post in Sydney because of his foreign origins and accent, and his inability to understand the nature of English law and customs. Bathurst himself seemed to doubt Rossi's suitability and gave Darling authority to transfer him to another post if he saw fit. However, Darling was well satisfied with Rossi's conduct, and Brisbane and Bourke commented favourably on his zeal and energy. In suggesting eligible names for a proposed local order of merit in 1844, Gipps included Rossi and bore high testimony to his character and to his long, honorary service on the Goulburn bench.

HRA (1), 11-18, 23, 24; *Sydney Monitor*, 7, 28 July, 11 Aug 1826; *Sydney Gazette*, 23 Jan, 15 Feb, 5, 22 July, 5, 9, 12 Aug 1826; A. Halloran, 'Some early legal celebrities', *JRAHS*, 10 (1924); H. King, Police organisation and administration in . . . NSW, 1825-1851 (M.A. thesis, Univ Syd, 1956); Darling to Bathurst, enclosed statement of F. N. Rossi, 7 Dec 1826, CO 201/174; Dispatches to the governors of NSW, 1834 (ML); Rossi papers (ML); King papers (ML).   HAZEL KING

ROUS, HENRY JOHN (1795-1877), naval officer, was the second son of John Rous, Viscount Dunwich and first earl of Stradbroke of Henham Hall, Wangford, Suffolk, England, and his second wife,

Charlotte Whitaker. He was educated at Westminster School and entered the navy in 1808 as a first-class volunteer in the *Royal William* at Plymouth. Transferred to the *Repulse* in 1809, to the *Tonnant* in 1811 and to the *Bacchante* in 1812-14, he took part in three attacks on enemy convoys in the Adriatic, boarding and capturing one vessel from the ship's yawl. Complimented for his bravery and promoted lieutenant in 1814, commander in 1817 and post-captain in 1823, he was given command of the frigate *Rainbow* on the East India Station in 1825 and arrived in Sydney in February 1827.

In April he organized the first regatta in Sydney Harbour. When sent on a duty voyage to Moreton Bay in June he took the unprecedented step of inviting Governor Darling to accompany him and was honoured in the naming of Stradbroke Island, Dunwich, Rainbow Reach, and Rous Channel. His inherited interest in horse-racing led him to seek the improvement of colonial-bred horses and he imported the stallion Emigrant, and sent thoroughbred stock to Launceston, Van Diemen's Land, where he formed a company. Recalled to India on 29 July he returned to Sydney on 1 May 1828, bringing the thoroughbred mare Iris, and received a grant of 2560 acres on the Molonglo plains (Canberra) with permission to buy another 9240 acres. On 14 August he left in the *Rainbow* to explore the northern rivers of New South Wales. Prevented by heavy surf from entering the undiscovered Clarence River he charted the Tweed River which he named the Clarence, unaware that it had been discovered and named in 1823 by John Oxley [q.v.]. On his return journey he was the first government official to investigate an indentation of the coastline in Captain Flinders' [q.v.] chart five leagues south of Cape Byron and on 26-27 August he entered and explored a river which he named the Richmond and the north headland Lennox, after Charles, the fifth duke of Richmond of the Lennox line. After publishing a report of his discoveries in the *Australian Quarterly Journal of Theology, Literature and Science*, 1828, he returned to England in 1829 and retired on half-pay. Returning to the active list in 1835 he commanded the *Pique*, which grounded on the Labrador side of the Strait of Belle Isle in September. Without keels, rudder or pumps he made the 1500-mile journey to England where he was acquitted, but not commended, at a court martial. He was promoted rear-admiral in 1852 and admiral in 1864, but never went to sea again. In

1836 he married Sophia Cuthbert and in 1838 he was elected steward of the Jockey Club. He won the Westminster seat in the House of Commons against strong opposition in 1841 and, although created first lord of the Admiralty by Sir Robert Peel in 1846, he retired and devoted the rest of his life to the turf. Following the publication of his *The Laws and Practice of Horse Racing* (London, 1866) he became a recognized authority as honorary handicapper of the Jockey Club and author of the weight-for-age scale. He died without issue in 1877.

H. Hoste (ed), *Memoirs and letters of Capt. Sir William Hoste*, 1-2 (Lond, 1833); G. H. Hoste, *Service afloat; or the career of Sir William Hoste* (Lond, 1887); T. H. Bird, *Admiral Rous and the English turf, 1795-1877* (Lond, 1939); *Sydney Gazette*, 30 Apr 1827, 5 Sept 1828; P. Willett, 'Admiral Rous', *British race horse*, v 14 no 4, v 15 no 2; *Log of H.M.S. Rainbow* (PRO); H. J. Rous, *Letters to CSO*, 1827-28 (NSWA).

LOUISE T. DALEY

ROUSE, RICHARD (1774-1852), public servant and settler, was born on 26 February 1774 in Oxfordshire, England, the eldest son of Richard Rouse and his wife Elizabeth, née Taylor. He married Elizabeth Adams on 6 June 1796 and, with a letter of recommendation from the duke of Portland, arrived in the *Nile* at Sydney in December 1801 as a free settler with his wife and two small children, one of whom had been born on the voyage. In March 1802 Governor King granted Rouse 100 acres and he was soon well established on a farm at North Richmond on the Hawkesbury River. In July 1805 he was appointed superintendent of public works at Parramatta. He moved to a house opposite the gates of Government House, Parramatta, and Margaret Catchpole [q.v.], a convict servant of the family on the voyage and in the colony, was left as overseer at the North Richmond farm.

In 1806 Rouse welcomed Governor Bligh as a man strong enough to protect the settlers from the despotism of the Rum Corps and was one of the governor's staunchest supporters. He signed several memorials sympathizing with the governor and was named by Bligh as one of the witnesses he wished to take to England. However, the trip did not eventuate as Bligh changed his mind.

This loyalty had cost Rouse his position as a public servant, but he turned his attention to his farms; on 14 January 1810 he was reinstated by Governor Macquarie and in October 1814 was appointed auctioneer at Parramatta. He superintended the construction of many buildings, toll-houses and turnpikes in the vicinity of Parramatta, Windsor and Liverpool, including the renovation of Government House, Parramatta, in 1815 and the erection of the Parramatta Hospital in 1818, and gave evidence before Commissioner Bigge [q.v.] on these building activities.

On 8 October 1816 Rouse was granted 450 acres near the site of the battle of Vinegar Hill, in the Bathurst district of Sydney; at the suggestion of Macquarie the grant was named Rouse Hill. The actual possession of the land had taken place a few years previously, as the *Sydney Gazette* had first mentioned Rouse Hill on 27 November 1813, and the homestead was begun soon afterwards. It took a few years to build and was a two-storey, twenty-two room house, which has been occupied by members of the Rouse family ever since.

In 1822 Rouse sent his sons in search of good pasturage in the area north-west of the Blue Mountains which had just been thrown open for settlement; in 1825 they took up land for him ninety miles north of Bathurst at Guntawang on the Cudgegong River near Gulgong, which had recently been relinquished by George and Henry Cox because of the hostility of the Aboriginals in that region. This grant of 4000 acres was gradually increased, and became two stations, Guntawang and Biragambil, which were inherited by his sons Edwin and George. Both properties prospered and the Rouses were connected with progressive movements in the towns of Mudgee and Gulgong for many years. Rouse also acquired Ewenmar on the Castlereagh River, Gillendoon near Warren, Cobborah near Wellington and other land at Bathurst as well as the properties at Penrith and Richmond. By 1828 he possessed about 10,000 acres, but by then he had retired to Rouse Hill. There he devoted his time to the raising of sheep and cattle, the breeding of thoroughbred horses and the management of his various properties. He became well known for the quality of his stock, which he improved from time to time with imported sires, and he was the original owner of the 'Crooked R' brand, which was afterwards used by his sons.

Rouse was the type of pioneer that the colony needed, a devoted family man, a loyal member of the Church of England, a hard-working and honest public servant and a very efficient grazier. His many properties ensured the future of his three sons and four daughters who survived childhood, including Mary, the eldest, who married Jonathan, son of the missionary Rowland Hassall [q.v.]; Jane who married Alfred Kennerley, premier of Tasmania in 1873-76; Eleanor who married first John Terry of Box Hill, son of Samuel Terry [q.v.] and after his death, Major Thomas Wingate; George, the second boy enrolled at The King's School, Parramatta, when it opened in 1832; and Elizabeth Henrietta who married Robert, son of Richard Fitzgerald [q.v.] of Windsor.

In 1847 W. Griffiths of Parramatta executed crayon drawings of Richard and Elizabeth Rouse, both then aged 73, and these are still at Rouse Hill. A copy of the portrait of Richard Rouse is hanging at the Australasian Pioneers' Club, Sydney. Mrs Rouse died in December 1849 and Richard on 10 May 1852. He was buried in a vault at St Peter's Church, Richmond.

HRNSW, 5-7; HRA (1), 3-11; *Sydney Gazette*, 7 July 1805, 14 Jan 1810; G. H. F. Cox, *History of Mudgee* (ML), p 46, 56; Title deeds for Rouse Hill (in possession of Mrs George Terry, Rouse Hill); MS cat under Rouse (ML).   MARJORIE LENEHAN

ROWCROFT, CHARLES (1798-1856), novelist, was born on 12 July 1798 probably in London, the eldest son of Thomas Rowcroft, an East India merchant and London alderman, and his wife Jannett, née Guest. His father became British consul-general in Lima, Peru, and in December 1824 was mistaken for one of Bolivar's revolutionary supporters and shot.

Charles was educated at Eton in 1809-11. In August 1821 he arrived at Hobart Town in the *Grace* with his brother Horace, and took up a grant of 2000 acres at Norwood, five miles north of the present town of Bothwell on the Fat Doe (Clyde) River. In 1822 he was made a justice of the peace. He was a member of the committee of the Agricultural Society of Van Diemen's Land and an original shareholder of the Van Diemen's Land Bank. In 1823 he unsuccessfully sought the position of colonial secretary. In December 1824 he was the unsuccessful defendant in a case in which E. Lord [q.v.] sued him for a criminal conversation, and damages of £100 were awarded against him. By this time he was almost a pauper. His land was poor so, after hearing of his father's death, he left Van Diemen's Land in the *Cumberland* in September 1825, and sailed by way of Sydney to Brazil. The nine children and Jane, the widow of

Thomas Oakley Curling, who had died in Hobart in March, sailed on the same ship; on 16 December Rowcroft married Mrs Curling at San Sebastian on the Rio de Janeiro.

Rowcroft returned to England and in 1827 bought a boarding school at Streatham, in London. Some time afterwards he conducted the *Courier*. In 1843 he published in London his first novel, *Tales of the Colonies, or, the Adventures of an Emigrant, Edited by a late Colonial Magistrate*. This is the first Australian novel of the emigrant genre of any stature and in a lengthy preface Rowcroft explains the advantages of taking up land in the colonies. The most valuable parts of the novel are those which are descriptive of the typical experiences of a new settler. On this has been superimposed a sensational and melodramatic tale of blacks, bushrangers and white settlers in Van Diemen's Land in the 1820s.

In 1845 when Thomas Hood retired Rowcroft became editor of *Hood's Magazine and Comic Miscellany*. To this he contributed during 1846 his second Australian novel, *The Bushranger of Van Diemen's Land*, a work much inferior to his first, set in the wilds of south-east Van Diemen's Land and written, according to his preface, to deter those who contemplated taking to crime in England in the belief that transportation was a passport to opportunity, wealth and ease. He gave up his editorship in 1846. Five further novels by Rowcroft were published between 1846 and 1852, only one of which, *George Mayford: An Emigrant in Search of a Colony* (1851) was connected with Australia. He also wrote *Confessions of an Etonian* (1852).

On 1 July 1852 he was appointed the first holder of the post of British consul at Cincinnati, United States, but was expelled after controversy with the American government over his alleged attempts to recruit some of its citizens for the British army in the Crimean war, charges which Rowcroft said were concocted by dissident Irish 'to vex and thwart the British government' by entrapping him into 'a violation of the neutrality laws'. He sailed for London from New York in the *Cherubim* on 17 August 1856, and died, somewhat mysteriously, at sea on 23 August. He left two daughters and three sons, and a widow who was granted a civil list pension.

HRA (3), 4; F. Boase, *Modern English biography* (Lond, 1901); *The Times*, 11 Oct 1856; MS cat under Rowcroft (ML); Correspondence file under Rowcroft (TA).

J. C. HORNER
CECIL HADGRAFT

ROWLEY, THOMAS (1748?-1806), soldier and landholder, was appointed adjutant of the New South Wales Corps in 1789 and promoted lieutenant in April 1791. His background is unknown but the singularly poor grammar and spelling in his letters indicate that he could not have been well educated. He arrived at Port Jackson in 1792 and was promoted captain on 21 June 1796. He served in Sydney until 1799 when he left for a tour of duty at Norfolk Island. The premature departure of the commandant, Captain Piper [q.v.], in November obliged Rowley as the senior officer present to take charge of the island's affairs. His rule lasted until July 1800 and, according to his own account, was sufficiently creditable to earn the praise of the settlers and of Governor King, though it involved him in severe and unexplained financial losses.

In 1802 he resigned his commission. He probably found it difficult to combine full military duties with his other pursuits, for he was one of those officers who had always sought to supplement their pay by other means. He set up his one-time servant Simeon Lord [q.v.] in business, and it is possible that he engaged in trade himself. Certainly he became a farmer after receiving his first grant in 1793. Thenceforth he accumulated land at a fairly steady rate, principally at Bankstown, Petersham and near Concord. In 1801-02 he bought livestock from Colonel Foveaux [q.v.]. By 1805 he owned 1975 acres, which he used mainly for grazing 519 sheep. He owned some Spanish sheep acquired from Captain Waterhouse [q.v.] but made no effort to breed from them; interested only in meat production, he paid no attention to woolgrowing.

Rowley acquired most of his land during the King period, an era which appears to have been quite a happy one for him. He managed to avoid becoming involved in the recurrent quarrels between the governor and officers and seems to have lived on good terms with King. In October 1802 he was given responsibility for the management of the civil and military barracks and became captain of the Sydney company of the Loyal Association. He displayed an active interest in its work and in April 1804 was promoted commandant. In the same month he was sworn in as a magistrate. He died of consumption on 27 May 1806, leaving his property in trust for his three daughters, two sons, and Elizabeth Selwyn, a former convict who had arrived in the Pitt in February 1792 after being convicted at Gloucester, and who was the mother of four of these children.

HRNSW, 1-4; HRA (1), 1-4; MS cat under T. Rowley (ML).

B. H. FLETCHER

RUMKER, CHRISTIAN CARL LUDWIG (1788-1862), astronomer, was born on 18 May 1788 at Stargard, Mecklenburg-Strelitz, Germany, the son of J. F. Rümker, court-councillor. He showed a talent for mathematics, and his father sent him to the Builders' Academy at Berlin where in 1807 he passed the state examination as a master builder. He was disinclined to follow this trade and, after working for about two years as a teacher of mathematics in Hamburg, went to England in 1809. From 1809 to 1811 he served as a midshipman in the East India Co. and then entered the merchant navy, where he became a helmsman. Seized by a press-gang in July 1813, he accepted a position as teacher of sea cadets with officer's rank and served in H.M.S. Benbow, Montagu and Albion. In 1816 he took part in a punitive expedition against Algiers. During his Mediterranean service he made the acquaintance of Baron Franz-Xaver de Zach, an Austrian astronomer, who induced him to pursue the study of astronomy. His first publications about observations at Malta in the Edinburgh Philosophical Journal of 1819 drew the attention of other scientists to his work, with much effect on his career.

Discharged from the navy in 1819 he returned to Hamburg, where he was employed as teacher at the school of navigation. Recommended to Sir Thomas Brisbane by Captain Peter Heywood, under whom he had served in the Montagu, Rümker was engaged as the newly appointed governor's private astronomer. He arrived in Sydney with the official party in 1821 and worked at Brisbane's private observatory at Parramatta where on 2 June 1822 he rediscovered Encke's comet. For this achievement Rümker was awarded a silver medal and £100 by the Royal Astronomical Society and a gold medal by the Institut de France. The grateful governor bestowed on Rümker a grant of 1000 acres at Stonequarry Creek (Picton). Disagreements with Brisbane over private and professional matters, as well as animosity towards his collaborator in the observatory, James Dunlop [q.v.], led in June 1823 to Rümker's retirement to his farm which he had named Stargard after his birthplace. There, on Reservoir Hill he continued his observations and discovered two comets in the constellation Lion.

In London Captain Heywood had pleaded his case with Alexander McLeay [q.v.], the new colonial secretary who, after Brisbane's departure, recalled Rümker to Parramatta where he recommenced work in May 1826 and in September discovered a new comet in the constellation Orion. On 21 December 1827 Governor Darling appointed him government astronomer; he was the first to hold that title in Australia.

In 1828 Rümker received a second land grant of 1000 acres at Stargard and later acquired another 200 acres by deed. In February 1828 the Senate of Hamburg elected him director of its school of navigation, but Rümker did not even answer the senate's letter as he did not wish to relinquish his Australian position. In January 1829 he went to London to obtain new instruments for the Parramatta observatory and to induce the Royal Society to print his *Astronomical Observations made at the Observatory at Parramatta in New South Wales*. These were published in 1829 as a supplementary volume to the *Philosophical Transactions* at government expense. His return to Parramatta seemed assured when, through the animosity of Brisbane, he became involved in a quarrel with Sir James South, president of the Royal Astronomical Society, who used his influence to have Rümker finally dismissed from British government service in June 1830. Rümker returned to Hamburg, where in 1831 he became director of the school of navigation and in 1833 also director of the Hamburg observatory. In 1831 Rümker published in Hamburg, *On the Most Effectual Means of Encouraging Scientific Undertakings*, a bitter pamphlet about his dismissal, but later he became reconciled with Brisbane. He dedicated to Brisbane his *Preliminary Catalogue of Fixed Stars intended for a Prospectus of a Catalogue of the Stars of the Southern Hemisphere included within the Tropic of Capricorn now Reduced from the Observations made in the Observatory at Parramatta* (Hamburg, 1832).

In later years Rümker displayed great scientific activity. *The Catalogue of Scientific Papers* (1871), compiled by the Royal Society of London, lists 233 papers by him in various scientific journals. Many learned societies honoured him with membership and fellowship. In 1850 the King of Hanover conferred on him his gold medal for arts and science. The greatest satisfaction in his life came in 1854 when the Royal Astronomical Society gave him its gold medal. In 1857 he was granted permanent leave for health reasons. He went to Lisbon, where he continued to reduce his Parramatta observations. In

Hamburg Professor George F. W. Rümker, the illegitimate son of his housekeeper, became his successor as director of the Hamburg observatory. In 1848 Rümker had married a spinster, Mary Ann Crockford of Clerkenwell, Middlesex; they had no children. He died at Lisbon on 21 December 1862 and was buried in the churchyard of the English church at Estrella.

Rümker was a man of great integrity and indefatigable diligence, but he was headstrong and of a somewhat violent character. When awarding the gold medal of the Royal Astronomical Society to Rümker, the astronomer royal, Sir George Biddell Airy, said that Rümker's dismissal was 'the greatest misfortune that happened to Southern Astronomy', a comment that did less than justice to James Dunlop, Rümker's associate and successor at Parramatta.

Some of Rümker's work was published over the name Charles Stargard Rümker, his land was granted to Charles Luis Rümker and the Royal Astronomical Society presented its medal to Dr P. Karl Rümker.

G. F. J. Bergman, 'Christian Carl Ludwig Rümker (1788-1862), Australia's first government astronomer', JRAHS, 46 (1960), and for bibliog; Rümker letters, 1825-49 (Dixson Lib, Syd); Correspondence with Dr John Lee (La Trobe Lib, Melb).

GEORGE F. J. BERGMAN

RUSE, JAMES (1760-1837), pioneer and smallholder, was born at Launceston, Cornwall, England. At the Cornwall Assizes in 1782 he was convicted of burglarious breaking and entering; his capital sentence was changed to transportation to Africa for seven years. During the next five years while the government was searching for ways of solving the convict problem Ruse spent much of his time in the hulk *Dunkirk* at Plymouth. When it was decided to establish a penal settlement in New South Wales he was sent out in the First Fleet in 1787 in the *Scarborough*. In July 1789 he claimed that his sentence had expired and soon afterwards he asked for a land grant, inspired by the desire to take up farming, an occupation to which he had been bred. Lacking evidence that Ruse was entitled to his freedom, Governor Phillip did not at once give him a grant, but in November permitted him to occupy an allotment near Parramatta, withholding the title until his capacity as a farmer and his right to freedom had been proved. The governor made this concession partly because he knew Ruse to be industrious and partly because he was anxious to discover how long it would take an emancipist to become self-sufficient.

Although not the first person to cultivate land in the colony on his own behalf, Ruse was the first ex-convict to seek a grant, for other emancipists displayed no inclination to take up agriculture. Undeterred by famine, drought and the depredations of convicts Ruse applied himself diligently to his task, helped by Phillip who provided him with provisions, clothing, seed, implements, livestock, a hut and assistance in clearing a small area of land. He proved not only a hard worker but also, by local standards, an enlightened farmer who made quite effective use of the limited means at his disposal. By February 1791 he was able to support both himself and his wife, Elizabeth Perry, a convict whom he had married on 5 September 1790. In April 1791 he received the title to his land, the first grant issued in New South Wales.

Besides justifying the faith placed in him Ruse had also scotched the belief held by many contemporaries that a smallholder could never maintain himself in New South Wales. This was not his only contribution to the expansion of private farming. He left Parramatta in despair at the quality of the land and in October 1793 sold his farm to Surgeon John Harris [q.v.] for £40. Having spent the proceeds, originally intended to pay his passage to England, he was obliged to seek a fresh grant and in January 1794 he became one of the twenty-two settlers responsible both for opening the Hawkesbury River area and for demonstrating its superiority as an agricultural centre over all other known regions. Why he chose a region hitherto regarded by many as unsuitable for farming is uncertain, but he made it his home for the next few years. At first he appears to have fared quite well and in June 1797 received the title to an additional forty-acre grant; nine months later when poverty was acute among smallholders, he sold his original grant for £300, which suggests that it must have been well developed. Before 1800 he had bought an additional twenty acres but he mortgaged them in March 1801.

In 1797 he had been brought to court on charges of running a gambling school on his premises, but since no details of the trial are available, there can be no certainty that he engaged in a pastime enjoyed by many of his fellow settlers. In the next decade he still owned some land at the Hawkesbury, but his name appears on none of the available lists of settlers. In 1806 his wife was recorded as farming

fifteen acres at the Hawkesbury and she later signed the petitions extolling Bligh, but of Ruse himself there was no mention. The only evidence of his presence was an agreement dated May 1801 apprenticing his son James as a mariner in the firm of Kable & Underwood [qq.v.]. It has been suggested that he found employment on local vessels himself, for on several occasions the *Sydney Gazette* listed a James Ruse among the crew members of such ships, but these references were probably to his son.

In 1809 Ruse successfully requested a grant at Bankstown, for the recent Hawkesbury floods had caused him heavy losses. He retained contact with the Hawkesbury throughout the Macquarie period and in 1819 received a 100-acre grant at Riverstone. The muster of that year, however, showed him as owning only 45 acres in the Windsor district of which 20 were cleared and 19½ under crop. In addition he owned 3 horses, 2 cows and 7 hogs. Subsequently his fortunes seem to have declined for in 1825 he was recorded as owning a mere ten acres of land, all in the Windsor district, and twelve hogs. Since this small property could scarcely have sustained him, it comes as no surprise to find that by 1828 he was working as an overseer for Captain Brooks at Lower Minto. In 1834 he was living at Macquarie Fields. Two years later he was received into the Roman Catholic Church, though there is no evidence that his wife or seven children followed his example. His death on 5 September 1837 brought to a close the career of one whose importance in New South Wales history has been unduly exaggerated and romanticized. Although his early achievements were noteworthy, he soon faded into the background and led an existence that scarcely distinguished him from many of his associates.

HRNSW, 1, pt 2; HRA (1), 1; D. Collins, *An account of the English colony in New South Wales*, 1-2 (Lond, 1798-1802); W. Tench, *A complete account of the settlement at Port Jackson in New South Wales* (Lond, 1793); C. Tolchard, *The humble adventurer: life and times of James Ruse* (Melb, 1965); I. K. Sampson, 'The first grain', JRAHS, 25 (1939); A. C. MacDougall, Australia's first independent farmer (ML).

B. H. FLETCHER

RUSSELL, FRANCIS THOMAS CUSACK (1823-1876), Church of England clergyman, was the only son of Rev. Thomas Russell, rector of Killarney, County Kerry, Ireland. Both his parents died when Russell was only an infant and he was brought up by his uncle, Sir William Smith, chief baron of the county. In 1841 he was admitted to Trinity College, Dublin, intending to study medicine but he changed to law (B.A., 1846).

With his close friend, Peter Teulon Beamish, Russell offered himself to the Society for the Propagation of the Gospel for service in New South Wales and soon after their arrival in the colony they were both made deacons by Bishop Broughton [q.v.] in September 1847. Russell was appointed to St Mark's, Alexandria (Darling Point), whilst Beamish was stationed at Singleton. Within six months the staunch Protestant feelings of these two young Irishmen led them openly to criticize Tractarian teaching at St James's Theological College and Russell wrote a strongly worded protest to Broughton, virtually accusing the bishop of laxity in doctrinal standards after the secession of Revs R. K. Sconce and T. C. Makinson [qq.v.] to Rome. Sympathy for Beamish, whom he believed to have been badly treated on another issue by Broughton, possibly made Russell more outspoken than he might otherwise have been, but the result of this criticism was that both the friends were suspended for three months and were refused ordination to the priesthood. In spite of protests from Russell's parishioners and a number of prominent citizens including members of the Legislative Council, Broughton remained adamant and the two deacons offered their services to Bishop Perry in Melbourne. At first Perry refused to take them without the sanction of the bishop of Sydney, but in 1850, believing that the necessary permission had been given, he sent Russell to itinerate along the Wannon River; Beamish was stationed at Warrnambool, where he later became archdeacon.

For the next twenty-five years Russell worked ably and faithfully in this pastoral area, earning a name as the 'Apostle of the Western District'. His parish included Heywood, Digby, Henty, Sandford, Casterton, Hamilton (the Grange), Harrow, Balmoral and Coleraine. Having no vicarage at first, he visited each district in turn, travelling continually and sleeping at station homesteads, often holding services under the trees by the roadside. Russell bought land at Hamilton at his own expense which was later repaid by his sympathetic parishioners, and eventually a parsonage was erected on the Tahara estate, between Coleraine and Merino, through the generosity of Samuel Pratt Winter who, in spite of his agnosticism, was a warm friend and admirer of Russell.

Energetic and purposeful, Russell was responsible for the first churches at Caster-ton, Merino, Henty, Digby, Branxholme and Hamilton. At the same time he found time to read for his Doctorate of Laws and his cultivated mind, combined with a sympathetic understanding of people, attracted him to a much wider circle than his own parishioners.

In 1866 Bishop Perry ordained him priest. More than once Russell declined preferment, being content to remain at his vicarage on the Wannon. In 1875 he was granted leave and his parishioners subscribed a total of £1500 for a trip to England, but his health had been broken by the strenuous years of pioneering and he died on 7 February 1876 in the *Hampshire* whilst returning to Victoria.

His portrait hangs in the dining-room at Murndal, the station of the Winter family, whose friendship he enjoyed throughout his ministry.

M. L. Kiddle, Men of yesterday (Melb, 1961); R. Border, Church and state in Australia 1788-1872 (Lond, 1962); J. Barrett, That better country (Melb, 1966); K. J. Cable, 'Religious controversies in New South Wales in the mid nineteenth century', *JRAHS*, 49 (1963); Church of England Messenger (Vic), 13 Apr 1876; S. Smith, An apostle of Western Victoria (Mollison Lib, St Paul's Cathedral, Melb); Turnbull papers (Geelong Hist Soc).

SYDNEY H. SMITH

RUSSELL, HENRY STUART (1818-1889), pastoralist, explorer and historian, was born on 16 March 1818 at Halliford, Middlesex, England, the son of an East India Co. officer, whose twelve years of service brought him wealth and social position. After education at Harrow and Oxford, Russell travelled extensively in France and Italy. At 22 he migrated to Australia. On arrival in Sydney he was welcomed by Arthur and Pemberton Hodgson, his second cousins and associates at Harrow, and stayed for some time with Arthur Hodgson on his New England station. In September 1840 Hodgson and Gilbert Elliott established Eton Vale on the Darling Downs where Russell became their guest. Next year with his brother Sydenham he took up Cecil Plains on the Darling Downs and occupied it until 1849.

In May 1842 Russell joined a party which sailed in a whale-boat up the coast from Brisbane on an exploring expedition to Wide Bay in search of sheep country. The party, which included Andrew Petrie [q.v.] and Captain Joliffe, discovered the river later named the Mary, on which the city of Maryborough now stands. They also found and brought back to Brisbane with them two runaway convicts from the penal settlement, James Bracewell and James Davis [qq.v.], 'wild white men' who had been living with the Aboriginals of Wide Bay for a number of years. In November Russell with his brother Sydenham and William Glover, son of a Norfolk archdeacon, made another expedition to the Wide Bay country. Travelling overland he discovered and named the Boyne River, which was later proved to be the head of the Burnett. This expedition resulted in Russell taking up Burrandowan station, Davis having told him of fine pastures in the locality. On this journey Russell met J. C. Bidwill [q.v.], the botanist, and assisted him in finding several specimens of the Bunya Pine (*Araucaria bidwillii*), three of which Bidwill sent to the London Botanical Society. In 1844 the explorer Ludwig Leichhardt [q.v.] visited Cecil Plains.

Russell sold Burrandowan in 1847 to Philip Friell. Although Cecil Plains was occupied by James Taylor as his partner, Russell's pastoral career ended in 1849. He visited England in 1850 and returned next year to settle in Brisbane. In 1853 he was elected to the Legislative Council of New South Wales. He resigned in 1855 and again travelled to England, where he actively supported the agitation to separate the Moreton Bay District from New South Wales. He never saw Queensland again. In 1859, when his interest in Cecil Plains was sold to Taylor, he returned to Sydney and lived elegantly for seven years at Mosman Bay. He then suffered financial reverses and in 1888 sailed again for England. He died at Ottery St Mary, Devon, on 5 March 1889.

Russell was married in 1851 to Charlotte, sister of Philip Pinnock, senior police magistrate and sheriff of Queensland. His second wife Selina, née Oakes, whom he married in 1874, survived him with five sons of the first marriage, and a daughter of the second. Two of his sons, John R. Stuart Russell and W. G. Stuart Russell, travelled to the Gulf country in 1878 and took up country which they later abandoned. W. G. Stuart Russell owned Yelvertoft station for many years. Russell is best remembered for his *The Genesis of Queensland* published in 1888; although inaccurate in some details it is a valuable record in lively and picturesque language of the early settlement and the growth of the pastoral industry.

J. E. Murphy and E. W. Easton, *Wilderness to wealth* (Nanango, 1950); F. W. S. Cumbrae-Stewart, 'Some Queensland memoir writers', JRQHS, 2 (1920-35); Russell papers (ML).

C. G. Austin
Clem Lack

RUSSELL, Lord John, first Earl Russell (1792-1878), statesman, was born on 18 August 1792 in Mayfair, London, the third son of John, sixth duke of Bedford, and his first wife, Georgiana Elizabeth, second daughter of the fourth Viscount Torrington. Educated at Westminster School (1803-04) and Edinburgh University (1809-12), he began in 1813 that Whig political career for which his family connexions prepared him. He sat in the Commons almost without a break until 1861, when he was created first Earl Russell of Kingston Russell, Dorsetshire.

Russell was more important as a British than an imperial statesman. He was in the forefront of the movement for the Reform Act of 1832. In Lord Melbourne's government (1835-41), he was the most powerful minister; and he was himself twice prime minister. He presided over the Colonial Office in 1839-41 and from February to July 1855.

The problems of Canada took up much of Russell's energies during his first term at the Colonial Office. The most important part of his Australian policy was the issue of an Order in Council, 1 May 1840, to stop convict transportation to New South Wales on 1 August that year. Russell had sat in the select committee on transportation (1837-38) and thought that New South Wales, with its large free population, should cease to be a penal station. His Order in Council was issued precipitately and caused resentment in the colony among those who wished for convict labour, and concern in England to those troubled by the difficulties of providing for the convicts elsewhere. Believing that there was no longer any need to fear the emancipists as a separate political force in New South Wales, Russell tried to liberalize its Constitution. In July 1840 he introduced a New South Wales bill designed to increase self-government by establishing a part-elective Legislative Council; the bill had no stipulations against emancipists, but it did provide for the separation of new colonies out of New South Wales. Russell abandoned it almost immediately because of his own doubts and the opposition that it raised.

Russell intended also new measures of settlement. In December 1839 he dismissed the incompetent South Australian Commission. A month later he approved the appointment of a new board, the Colonial Land and Emigration Commission, to exercise wider functions throughout the empire as a whole, particularly in Australia. When he consulted them about land sales policy they advised him that all crown lands in

New South Wales outside the Nineteen
Counties and the towns already established should be sold at a uniform fixed
price. In a dispatch of 31 May 1840 Russell
proposed to divide New South Wales into
three districts: the Northern including
Moreton Bay, the Middle, and the Southern
including the Port Phillip area. Land in the
Middle District was to be sold by auction
at a minimum upset price, and in the
Southern District at a uniform fixed price
of £1 an acre, except in new towns. No
immediate arrangements were made for
the Northern District.

All Russell's measures for New South
Wales aroused strong opposition. Governor
Gipps thought the Constitution too liberal
and preferred sales by auction to sales at
a uniform fixed price. Powerful interests
wished to retain convict labour. The Middle
District did not wish the colony to be dis-
membered. In addition, South Australia
was still in confusion; Van Diemen's Land
was running down economically and, partly
because transportation to New South
Wales had ceased, was suffering from too
many convicts. Russell resolved on retreat.
In August 1841 he cancelled his instructions
for the division of New South Wales and
the alienation of crown lands. In addition
to ending transportation to New South
Wales and appointing the land and emigration commission Russell made a significant contribution in two other matters:
he was responsible for the appointment of
Captain George Grey as governor of
South Australia, and in 1840 he had disallowed an Act of the Legislative Council
of Western Australia that permitted the
evidence of Aboriginals to be accepted
without oath in criminal cases and provided
that summary corporal punishment might
be inflicted on people of this race.

During Russell's first prime ministership
(1846-52) imperial policy underwent great
changes which he did little to promote and
less to initiate. The third Earl Grey, who
held the Colonial Office during those years,
settled the government's policy on all important matters of empire, including the
Australian Constitutions, land and immigration policy, and convict transportation.
Russell objected privately to Grey's obstinate attempts to force convicts on the colonies, was lukewarm about his Federation
proposals and thought Grey too active in
policy-making. In none of these matters
was his influence decisive.

In 1855 Russell was at the Colonial Office
when some of the Australian Constitution
bills were sent home. He decided to return
the South Australian bill, which had been
pushed through the Legislative Council of

that colony to the annoyance of public
opinion. By amending the New South
Wales Constitution he defeated the attempts of that colony's conservatives to en-
trench their political position and persuaded parliament to pass an Act authorizing the Queen to assent to the New South
Wales bill as amended. Because the Tasmanian bill was unexceptionable Russell at
once obtained an Order in Council to put
it into force, as allowed by the Australian
Colonies Government Act of 1850. To complete the bargains made with the Australian colonies by Sir John Pakington and
the duke of Newcastle, while they were
secretaries of state for war and the colonies, parliament in 1855 passed 18 & 19
Vic. c. 56, which gave the colonies control
of their own land policies.

Russell declined in 1855 to act on suggestions from New South Wales, Victoria
and the General Association for the Australian Colonies, a private body in London,
that the new Constitutions should be
crowned with a federal assembly. Britain,
he declared, would not federate the Australian colonies except at their official request.

Russell died at Pembroke Lodge, Richmond Park, Surrey, on 28 May 1878. He
often doubted whether self-governing colonies would remain in the empire, but, so
far as Australia was concerned, he nearly
always supported the liberal side.

The National Gallery, London, has portraits by G. F. Watts and Sir Francis Grant,
and a marble bust by John Francis.

J. Russell, *Recollections and suggestions,
1813-1873*, 2nd ed (Lond, 1875); R. C. Mills,
The colonization of Australia 1829-42 (Lond,
1915); W. P. Morrell, *British colonial policy
in the age of Peel and Russell* (Oxford, 1930);
J. M. Ward, *Earl Grey and the Australian
colonies, 1846-1857* (Melb, 1958).

JOHN M. WARD

RUSSELL, PHILIP (1796?-1844) and
GEORGE (1812-1888), pastoralists, were
half-brothers, sons of Philip Russell (1766?-
1834), a tenant farmer in Fife, Scotland,
who married his first cousin, Isabella Russell (d. 1807), and then his paternal aunt's
granddaughter, Anne Carstairs (d. 1826).
Their father's position and resources ensured them sound basic schooling, religious,
social, and agricultural training, but not
independent holdings in Scotland.

Philip Russell emigrated to Van Diemen's
Land in 1821 with Captain Patrick Wood,
formerly of the East India Co., to manage
Wood's prospective farming concerns. He
thus helped to establish the Dennistoun

estate near Bothwell, but relinquished immediate control when his elder brother, William, arrived in 1839 and became Wood's tenant. Philip then concentrated upon his own property, Strathbarton, near Apsley. George Russell joined Philip in 1831, and farmed for five years under his supervision. He followed John Batman's [q.v.] exploratory lead to Port Phillip in March 1836, and returned there in October as manager of the pastoral Clyde Company, a joint stock concern formed in Scotland by Captain Wood, with Philip Russell as resident Australian partner. In 1839 George Russell moved his headquarters from the Moorabool River at Batesford, near Geelong, westward to the Leigh River, where in 1842 he secured his Golfhill homestead by purchase from the Crown. Philip, who married Sophia Jennings, first cousin to J. T. Gellibrand [q.v.], died there childless in July 1844. George was by then a partner in the Clyde Company. In 1846 he extended its operations to Terinallum, near Mount Elephant.

The company was dissolved in 1857-58. Its sales showed a final return of £258,000 for £78,000 invested. George Russell, whose share was a sixth, bought the central Golfhill freehold of 8500 acres, which he eventually enlarged to 28,000, or about two-fifths of the former licensed run. He had other pastoral properties, but lived at Golfhill, and died on 3 November 1888 in the present homestead. Euphemia Carstairs, the first cousin whom he married in Scotland in 1852, died in its predecessor in 1867, leaving seven daughters and a son. The bachelor son inherited Golfhill, but arranged for the youngest child, Janet, later Mrs John Biddlecombe (1866-1954), to take over before his death in 1898. Mrs Biddlecombe ran Golf Hill, as it was later spelt, substantially intact, with a celebrated Hereford stud, until her last years, then accepted its subdivision for soldier settlement.

George Russell—'The Governor' to his disciples—first followed his brother Philip. Both were sagacious, high-principled, hardworking, helpful breakers of new ground. 'What numbers of young men there are all more or less connected with the Russells!' wrote Philip's widow from Sydney in 1855; 'What results have followed from one or two acting as pioneers!' Robert Russell, founding minister of Evandale, Tasmania, and Alexander Russell, of Mawallock station, Victoria, were George's full brothers. William Lewis of Stoneleigh, and Philip Lewis of Elderslie, Victoria, were Philip's full nephews. Philip Russell of Carngham, Victoria, and his brothers Thomas of Ba-

runah Plains, and John of Native Creek No. 2, were first cousins of both pioneers. Robert Simson of Langi Kal Kal and his brothers, James, John, and Colin, all of Victoria, were their first cousins once removed.

There is a joint memorial in George Russell's autobiography, and in the Clyde Company papers that he began to assemble while Philip was still his mentor. These are accessible through Mrs Biddlecombe's decision to sponsor their publication as representative records.

P. L. Brown (ed), *The narrative of George Russell* (Lond, 1935); P. L. Brown (ed) *Clyde Company papers*, 1-5 (Lond, 1941-63); Private information.   P. L. BROWN

RUSSELL, ROBERT (1808-1900), surveyor, architect and artist, was born on 13 February 1808 near Kennington Common, London, the son of Robert Russell, merchant, and his wife Margaret, née Leslie. After a sound education Russell went to Edinburgh in 1823 and was articled for five years to the architect William Burn, who had been a pupil of Sir Robert Smirke. Later he worked in London with two minor architects, and then in the office of John Nash during the alterations and additions to Buckingham Palace.

Ten months employment on the ordnance survey in Drogheda, Ireland, in 1830-31 gave Russell a preference for surveying, as allowing greater leisure, and curiosity about Australia led to his emigration and arrival in Sydney in the *Sir John Rae Reid* on 24 September 1833 with letters of introduction to T. L. Mitchell [q.v.]. He was appointed to the Survey Department as acting assistant to the town surveyor on 22 October, much of his work being concerned with crown land grants. Like his father Russell had been an amateur artist and collector and became in 1835 one of the first pupils of Conrad Martens [q.v.], with whom he corresponded until 1871.

On 10 September 1836 Russell was appointed surveyor to the infant settlement at Port Phillip and he arrived with a group of officials in the *Sterlingshire* on 5 October, accompanied by his assistants, Frederick Robert D'Arcy as draughtsman and William Wedge Darke as chainman; he was also to be commissioner of crown lands. Russell's first surveys were in the Geelong and Werribee areas, but in general his work was not considered to be characterized by enough alacrity. A topographical feature survey of the Melbourne site was produced (and later lithographed in

England) on his own initiative, but his horses were unready for further expeditions. On this survey Robert Hoddle [q.v.] drew the standard grid plan, after he superseded Russell upon his appointment as surveyor-in-charge on 1 March 1837. Russell was obliged, after one false start overland, to return to Sydney to complete surveying commitments and while there he made a series of drawings of the city's environs in the style of Martens. He returned to Melbourne about 30 March 1838, as clerk of works with architectural responsibilities. A contentious and discordant government career continued until 18 June 1839 when he was removed from office. Amid discontent on both sides Russell entered into more remunerative practice as architect and, primarily, surveyor.

Russell's career from this time is somewhat obscure: his work involved marking out allotments in Melbourne and the interior, advising purchasers, settling disputes and acting as commission agent and speculative investor, in the early years from an office in Melbourne Chambers, Bourke Street. An offer to survey Melbourne by contract in December 1841 was rejected, but amongst work in the interior and particularly Gippsland is recorded his surveying expedition to Port Albert and the Wilson's Promontory area in April-May 1843, which produced a sequence of topographical studies and drawings. Russell had been unsuccessful in the ballot of five equally competent applicants for appointment as town surveyor on 24 December 1842, but later he received temporary official employment: for some months after August 1851 he became assistant to W. H. Wright, commissioner of crown lands, and in October-December 1866 he was mining surveyor on the goldfields in the Taradale district.

Despite his distinguished background Russell's architectural work was limited. He is assumed to have been responsible for his office as clerk of works, a small brick and shingle construction said to be the first durable government building utilizing plans and elevations (1838), and a watch house (1839); the first formal stone government building, the Customs House (1839-41, demolished 1858) was commenced under his supervision upon the basis of a design from the Sydney colonial architect's office. Russell was architect also for the austere, stone Bank of Australasia (1840-41, now demolished), and at least one contemporary domestic commission, a house for Lyon Campbell, is recorded. The only documentable work remaining is St James's Old Cathedral, built basically under his super-

vision in 1839-42. The slender pyramidal spire of his original design was omitted, and an octagonal domical termination, added in 1851 by Charles Laing [q.v.], is alien to the Regency classicism of the concept. The church, consecrated in 1853, was moved to King Street near Flagstaff Gardens in 1914 with considerable alteration to the substituted tower design.

Russell left for England with his wife and children in the *Kent* in June 1856, and returned in the *Norfolk* in May 1860. While in London he appears to have acted as guide to art exhibitions for visiting colonial friends. After his return he worked from offices situated variously in Collins, Swanston, Little Collins and Elizabeth Streets. His private address also moved around the city proper: Fitzroy, East Melbourne and Richmond. Russell's last home was a cottage at 283 Burnley Street, Richmond, where he died on 10 April 1900; he was buried in the Melbourne general cemetery. On 17 December 1839 at an Anglican ceremony in Melbourne Russell had married Mary Ann Collis Smith. He was survived by five of their seven children; one daughter, Helen Cunard, received some local fame as a singer.

The range of Russell's interests was considerable. His letters provide a valuable and vivid description of early Victorian settlement and his own surroundings. He was well read in literary, technical and philosophical works and wrote articles, highly romantic poetry and verse dramas, an unpublished novel (The Shipwreck), and translations from the French. An inveterate experimenter and inventor, with interests in the graphic arts, he was the pioneer lithographer and etcher in Victoria, his etchings showing the influence of Salvator Rosa and Claude Lorraine. He also interested himself in the *cliché-verre* or glass-print, heliogravure and the dageurreotype, about which he had been informed by Strzelecki [q.v.], and believed that such processes would supersede copper engraving for reproductive purposes; glass-prints by him reproducing etchings by Rembrandt exist. Russell achieved some local fame as a connoisseur of old-master paintings and as a print collector. By 1889 his collection contained a comprehensive selection of the great names of etching and engraving.

His topographical delineations include landscapes of Sydney, Melbourne and environs, and the coastal and inland areas of Victoria. The famous first views of the Melbourne settlement from 1837 onwards were also lithographed by Russell, and he produced painted replicas of them until the last decade of his life. Apart from occasional head and figure studies and copies from old masters, his other work was intensely romantic in feeling: idyllic picturesque fantasies and dramatic imaginary landscapes under the strong influence of J. M. W. Turner and, perhaps, Francesco Guardi. Dating largely from 1870-90, after his return from Europe, these were often in experimentally mixed media with many original effects, and invariably on a very small scale, despite their freedom and unusual colour combinations. This prolific output, intended sometimes for sale but primarily as gifts, is represented in many private collections, in the National Library of Australia (Nan Kivell Collection), the Dixson and Mitchell Libraries, Sydney, the National Gallery of Victoria and the State Library of Victoria, which possesses a portrait by Alice Panton painted late in his life.

T. O'Callaghan, 'Scraps of early Melbourne history, 1835-1839', VHM, 3 (1914), 7 (1919); E. Scott, 'Captain Lonsdale and the foundation of Melbourne', VHM, 4 (1915); A. W. Greig, 'The official foundation of Melbourne', VHM, 7 (1919); A. W. Greig, 'Who selected the site of Melbourne?', VHM, 11 (1927); H. S. McComb, 'Surveyor Hoddle's field books of Melbourne', VHM, 16 (1937), 17 (1938); H. Preston, 'Robert Russell, the father of Melbourne', Roy Vic Institute of Architects *Bulletin*, Mar-Apr 1956; *Evelyn Observer*, 28 Dec 1888; *Table Talk*, 13 Sept 1889; *Argus*, 12 June 1897, 26 Apr 1899.

HARLEY PRESTON

RUTLEDGE, WILLIAM (1806-1876), merchant, banker and settler, was the eldest son of James Rutledge, of Ballymagirl, near Bawnboy, County Cavan, Ireland, and Martha, née Forster, of Langford. On reaching Sydney in the *Harriet* in December 1829 Rutledge set up as a contractor for government supplies, and after five years was assigned six convicts. In 1834 his address was the Field of Mars, Parramatta, and later he acquired land at Kissing Point and Eastwood. In 1837 he bought two blocks of 640 acres on the Molonglo River near Queanbeyan. He gave evidence before the select committee on the 1839 Squatting Act, and became a director of the Commercial Banking Co. of Sydney and a justice of the peace. After establishing himself he brought out two sisters and four of his five brothers: Thomas, who remained at Carwoola near Queanbeyan, Richard and Lloyd who later went to Port Fairy, Victoria, and John who moved to California.

In 1838 Rutledge took sheep overland to Port Phillip. He bought several lots at the early Melbourne land sales and entered into a partnership with Benjamin Baxter, whom he financed to build cottages in the Port Phillip area at £650 each. At Kilmore he established a tenant community on a special survey which he never took up, although he became known as the town's founder and gave land for a Roman Catholic Church. In 1841 he applied for another special survey at Corner Inlet but decided against settling there. He moved back and forth between Sydney and Port Phillip; he was in Sydney on 18 August 1840 for his wedding at St James's Church, to Eliza, daughter of Richard Kirk (they had two sons and five daughters), and for the Lord Mayor's dinner in 1842; he became an early member of the Australian Club in 1839.

In 1843 he visited Port Fairy and immediately bought a mercantile firm started by John Cox. In partnership with Horace Flower and Francis Forster, he founded the firm of William Rutledge & Co. They shipped wool, tallow and, later, gold to England, and imported a wide variety of goods, using their own ships and wharf. They also issued their own notes and tokens, and by facilitating credit, fostered the early intercolonial cattle trade. The company flourished until 1862 when it went bankrupt with debts of some £117,000. Within a year the partners won an honourable discharge.

In 1843 Rutledge, with four partners whom he gradually bought out, took up a special survey of 5120 acres, known as Farnham, near Koroit, Victoria, the imprecise boundaries of which were to involve him in lengthy correspondence with Superintendent La Trobe, ending in a stern rebuke. Farnham was worked by tenants from the first, Rutledge bringing out Irish families at his own expense. Reputed a kind and considerate landlord he furnished his tenants with rations, seed and implements. Until 1865 he lived at Port Fairy, but after the crash he eschewed commerce and moved to Farnham where he made another fortune by breeding Lincoln sheep. His stud was begun and maintained by purchases from the flock of J. R. Kirkham of Lincolnshire, for he strongly favoured inbreeding. Like all the men of his family a great lover of horses, he bred thoroughbreds, Clydesdales and Shetland ponies.

Called 'Terrible Billy' by Edward Henty [q.v.] for his explosive temper and unreserved use of 'the language of a centurion' and liking to have a finger in every pie, he had frequent quarrels, some of them with the authorities. In 1844 as a magistrate he began a turbulent career on the Port Fairy bench. In 1851 it was interrupted by an acrimonious dispute with a police magistrate, William Mair. Both parties bombarded the unfortunate La Trobe with complaints. Mair accused Rutledge of partiality in dispensing justice and of 'violent, arbitrary and tyrannical conduct'. Rutledge accused Mair of being dictatorial and using police horses for his private purposes. The disputes with Mair ended when Rutledge was charged with assault by his own court and fined £5. Mair was moved to Alberton; Rutledge was relieved of his magistracy but reinstated in 1857.

Rutledge had been appealing in vain for years for emigrants to be sent direct to Port Fairy to ease the shortage of farm labourers and domestic servants. In 1858, when the emigrant ship *Runnymede* came unexpectedly into Portland Bay, he sent his brother Lloyd, armed with blank forms of agreement, to board the ship. Despite Rutledge's complaints of 'obstruction and malversation' when Police Magistrate Blair [q.v.] tried to prevent these doubtful activities, Lloyd got away with seventy souls.

In 1851 Rutledge was elected for Villiers and Heytesbury to the first Victorian Legislative Council. He told his constituents that he was in favour of squatting and commercial interests, state aid to all the Christian churches, education, and liberal expenditure in the pastoral districts, while he was strongly opposed to sinecures, all other wasteful public expenditure, and the appropriation of large sums for works in and round Melbourne. He sat in the first Victorian Legislative Assembly from 1856 to 1859 and remained a 'roads and bridges man'. His parliamentary career was surprisingly quiet except for a violent attack on Earl Grey in 1852 and for the election he fought in 1861. Although aware that he was 'disqualified' as a government contractor, he stood against Richard Davies Ireland and defeated him. Ireland appealed against his return and, after heated debate in the Legislative Assembly, was declared duly elected and promptly sworn in as attorney-general. In 1854 Rutledge had resigned from the Legislative Council to take his children to England to be educated. He was commissioned by the government to organize steamship mails, and was present at the launching of the colony's first warship, *Victoria*. He was also honorary secretary to the General Association for the Australian Colonies. He again visited England in 1861-62.

Rutledge was very active in local affairs; he was a trustee of the Savings Bank and president of the Villiers and Heytesbury Agricultural Society when it held its first show in 1854. He was responsible for the local jockey club, being its steward, starter and judge, as well as always having horses running. From 1868 to 1873 he was a member of the Warrnambool Shire Council and Roads Board. He was an Anglican and served his church well, being on the building committee in 1848 and first vice-president of the vestry in 1859. He died at Port Fairy on 1 June 1876.

William Rutledge was inextricably entwined with the early history and prosperity of Port Fairy, for he instigated many of its activities. His wife was 'beloved for her kindness and hospitality' and together they kept open house: their dinners, balls, musical evenings, and parties for the races were at the heart of the district's social life. He was warm-hearted, courageous, generous and outspoken, with a vigorous and energetic personality, which became a legend in the Western District. Despite his explosive temper he was loved and respected, if not always respectable. Charles Pasley, the colonial engineer, wrote to his father in 1854: 'I am glad you have met "Billy" Rutledge . . . as he is a man whom I like. He is thoroughly honest and straightforward, although a little queer and hot tempered, and is a fair specimen of a Colonial who has raised himself from poverty to competence, if not wealth, by honest, energetic and persevering industry'.

J. Bonwick, *Western Victoria; its geography, geology and social condition* (Geelong, 1858); R. Osborne, *The history of Warrnambool* (Prahran, 1887); A. Sutherland, *Victoria and its metropolis*, 1-2 (Melb, 1888); R. Boldrewood (T. A. Browne), *Old Melbourne memories*, 2nd ed (Lond, 1896); W. Earle, *Port Fairy* (Port Fairy, 1896); M. L. Kiddle, *Men of yesterday* (Melb, 1961); M. Rutledge, 'William Rutledge—pioneer', VHM, 36 (1965); A. M. Baxter, Diary, 1844-49 (Dixson Lib); W. Rutledge, Letters (Dixson Lib, NL, La Trobe Lib, Melb).

MARTHA RUTLEDGE

RYAN, THOMAS (1790-1846), soldier, was born on 26 August 1790 in County Fermanagh, Ireland. At 15 he joined the 104th Regiment as an ensign and became a lieutenant in the 50th Regiment in October 1808. He was promoted captain in September 1819 and major in August 1830. He served in the Walcheren expedition in 1809 and later in the Peninsular war where he received several wounds at Fuentes De Onoro. After ten years service at Jamaica, he was appointed K.H. and went to Van Diemen's Land with his wife and son in the *George the Third*, which struck a reef near the southern entrance to D'Entrecasteaux Channel on the night of

12 April 1835 and became a total wreck; only 161, including 81 convicts, were saved out of the ship's complement of 295.

In December 1835 he was appointed to command the troops in northern Van Diemen's Land and made a justice of the peace. He remained in command there until 1839, interested himself in the building of the Ross Bridge and, when he departed, was given a farewell address by the northern residents and cheered by the convicts for his just administration. In 1838, while in temporary command of the Hobart Town garrison, he administered the oath of allegiance to Lieut-Governor Franklin on the accession of Queen Victoria. Next year he superintended the building near South Port of a monument to those lost in the wreck of the *George the Third*.

In June 1839 he joined the headquarters of his regiment in Sydney. Franklin was not sorry to see him go. 'I am heartily glad Major Ryan is going away not I trust to return . . . He got into a sad scrape at Launceston . . . through some intrigue with a man's wife and the story says was thrashed. He certainly had the marks of a Black Eye when he dined on the *Pelorus* . . . What an old Debaucher he must be'. Ryan was commandant at Norfolk Island from September 1839 to March 1840 when Captain Maconochie [q.v.] succeeded him.

He left for India with his regiment in January 1841, was promoted brevet lieut-colonel in April 1844, and fought at the Maharajpore in December 1843. On 10 February 1846 he was severely wounded at the battle of Sobraon, and died from his wounds before hearing that he had been appointed C.B. in April. On a monument at Canterbury Cathedral his name headed the list of officers and men of the 50th Regiment who fell in the Sutlej campaign.

A. E. Fyler, *The history of the 50th or (The Queen's Own) Regiment* (Lond, 1895); G. Mackaness (ed), *Some private correspondence of Sir John and Lady Jane Franklin*, 1-2 (Syd, 1947); *Hobart Town Courier*, 8 Mar, 5 July 1839; *Cornwall Chronicle*, 9 Apr 1839; WO 25/794.

S

SADLEIR, RICHARD (1794-1889), naval officer, schoolmaster and pamphleteer, was born on 6 May 1794 at Cork, Ireland, the fourth son of James Sadleir, who became a landowner and manufacturer near Bandon. Sadleir was educated privately and at Bandon Classical School. His earliest aspiration was for the church (he had a life-long devotion to the Protestant cause) but in February 1808 he joined the navy. He served on the European, African and American Stations and was promoted lieutenant on 21 May 1819; his only other advancement was as commander on the retired list on 9 April 1875. Sadleir became interested in the colonies when he was on duty on the American Lakes and on his return to Ireland in 1821 he was concerned in emigration schemes to Canada.

In 1825 Sadleir went to New South Wales and on the recommendation of Archdeacon Scott [q.v.] undertook an official tour to investigate the condition of the Aboriginals and their relations with the settlers. Sadleir's study was long and thorough, and his concern for the natives remained active. He gave evidence on the subject before a Legislative Council committee in 1838 and, late in life, published a short book on the *Aborigines of Australia* (Sydney, 1883). In 1826, having £1000 of capital, he was granted 2650 acres in the Hunter River valley.

Sadleir was not a rich man and his interests were religious and educational rather than agricultural. In October 1826 he was appointed a catechist for the Church of England in the Upper Hunter and ministered there for more than two years. Twenty years later he considered securing ordination from Bishop Perry of Melbourne but this intention was frustrated. Sadleir became master of the Male Orphan School at Liverpool in succession to Rev. Robert Cartwright [q.v.], whose daughter Ann (1810-1870) he married in December 1829. He remained there until 1851 and exercised an effective, if highly individual, mastership.

When Sadleir's official duties came to an end he took an active part in political controversy, contested unsuccessfully the constituency of St Vincent in the first elections under responsible government, and was elected in the radical interest for the Lower Hunter in 1861. His parliamentary career ended in 1864 but he continued to write on the land laws and constitutional reform for another twenty years. He produced a steady stream of pamphlets, petitions and articles on topics ranging from railway extension and the city water supply to the homoeopathic system of medicine and the production of non-combustible light; he wrote against Henry George on single tax and Bishop Broughton [q.v.] on baptismal regeneration. He sent more letters to newspaper editors than anyone else of his time.

Religious matters were the object of Sadleir's constant concern. He was an ardent Evangelical and an opponent of what he considered to be clerical autocracy. As joint secretary of the Church of England Constitution Defence Association in 1852, he organized with skill and some success a lay protest movement against Bishop Broughton's plan for colonial church government. He argued against Tractarianism in the 1840s and Anglo-Catholicism in the 1880s. His convictions, though expressed with a singular lack of moderation, were sincere and often coherent.

Sadleir's later activities were not solely polemical. He was energetic in local affairs as a justice of the peace, member of denominational school boards and mayor of Liverpool. Church administration took much of his time and so did charitable and philanthropic work. He remained vigorous in debate and action and quick to espouse new causes until his death at Liverpool on 6 March 1889.

HRA (1), 13-15; *Town and Country J*, 2 Apr 1887; A. P. Elkin, 'Some early chaplains and churches in the Hunter River valley,' JRAHS, 23 (1937); Church of England Constitution Defence Assoc, Minutes (ML); Sadleir papers (ML).   K. J. CABLE

SALMON, THOMAS (1780?-1847), merchant and landowner, born in Gloucestershire, England, became an architect in London and lived at Gloucester Terrace, Stepney. According to his own account he first visited Hobart Town in 1812 in the *Atlanta*, in which he had a third of the ownership. As the cargo had not been inspected at Sydney his venture proved costly, for he was not permitted to sell his wine, spirits and porter except in limited quantities to civil and military officers. Nevertheless in 1816 he returned to Hobart with his wife, three children and his brother, James, in the *Adamant*. As he also brought goods worth £1500 and had paid more than £500 for passages and freight, he was granted 200 acres at Humphrey's Rivulet (Glenorchy). In 1817 he received another 300 acres near Oatlands, although he then had a general store in Macquarie Street. In 1820 he bought two rams from the government and that year was appointed a member of the Lieut-Governor's Court.

In 1824 when Lieut-Governor Arthur arrived Salmon applied for an additional land grant, claiming that he had insufficient pasture for his cattle. Although he had cleared and cultivated 70 of the 90 acres of Stethorn farm, bought at Prince of Wales Bay, New Town, his application was refused because only 15 of his 500 granted acres had been improved. Salmon then complained of a conspiracy against him; his house and store had been raided by convict road-gangs and his assigned servants had been withdrawn. Some restitution was made but in 1827 he again complained: 'Mine is a Losing Farm and I have 38 cattle from which I supply many of the Inhabitants of Hobart Town with Milk and have not a servant left'. An inquiry revealed that his three convict servants had been arrested for disorderly behaviour and placed in a chain-gang. Finally the report reached Arthur who rejected the appeal: 'I may be mistaken, but this person Salmon is a character I continually meet with riding furiously and exceedingly drunk . . . a most improper master to have a convict servant'. Salmon continued to acquire small properties but little fortune. He died in Hobart on 12 May 1847 and his widow Elizabeth survived him for two years.

Their eldest son Thomas (1807-1868) was granted 100 acres near Oatlands in 1826, became chief police constable there and later tried his hand as a surveyor and poundkeeper. The second son, Charles Frederick (1808-1844) became manager of the Steamboat Store at New Norfolk, and died insolvent. Another son, Joseph, was a farmer at Oatlands. He died in 1846, crushed by a wagon wheel.

HRA (3), 2, 3; CSO 1/89/2007, 1/107/2588, 1/370/8423 (TA).   K. R. VON STIEGLITZ

SALTING, SEVERIN KANUTE (1805-1865), merchant and landowner, was born at Copenhagen of Danish parents. He gained experience as a merchant in London with Thomas Wilson & Co., and about 1822 went to India as a trader. In London in 1833 he married Louisa Augusta, née Fiellerup, whose Danish parents had lived for years in India. Salting sailed with his wife in the *Charles Eaton* and arrived at Sydney in July 1834. With C. J. Garrard as his partner he set up a marine store and ship chandlery and soon acquired additional interests. He was elected a director of the Fire and Life Insurance Co. in May 1836, served as a local director of the Union Bank of Australia from January 1839 to November 1844, and was appointed a trustee of the Savings Bank of New South Wales in November 1841. In 1842 he dissolved his partnership with Garrard and joined Philip William Flower, with John Henry Challis as a junior partner, in the new firm of Flower, Salting & Co., of Hunter Street, Sydney.

In November 1843 Salting petitioned for letters of denization; they were granted next year on the recommendation of Governor Gipps who knew him as 'a gentleman of great respectability'. Salting gave evidence to several select committees on financial questions and at the inquiry into the minimum price of crown land he condemned the squatters for their greed. In October 1848 Governor FitzRoy appointed him and John Lamb [q.v.] to investigate surcharges in the accounts of the collector of customs.

Salting's two sons were born in Sydney, George on 15 August 1835 and William on 18 January 1837. They attended a local school and in 1848 went with their parents to England, where George went to Eton and William to Brighton College. In 1853 the family returned to New South Wales, and the boys entered the University of Sydney. Both graduated in arts in 1857 and their father founded the Salting Exhibition for boys educated at Sydney Grammar School. In 1858 Salting took his family to England, where his wife died on 24 July. After travelling on the Continent Salting made his home at Silverlands, near Chertsey, Kent. He died there on 14 September 1865 and was buried in the same grave as his wife at Brompton cemetery. The grave is now maintained by the earl of Haddington, whose mother was the daughter of Salting's son, William.

Through his firm, sheep stations, sugar plantations, and wide investments Salting had become very wealthy. He left an estate in England valued at £90,000 and another in New South Wales worth £85,000. His chief beneficiaries were his sons. George won international repute as a collector of works of art and Chinese pottery and died in London on 12 December 1909. William died on 23 June 1905.

HRA (1), 23, 26; Newspaper indexes under Salting (ML); MS cat under Salting (ML).

A. F. PIKE

415

SALVADO, ROSENDO (1814-1900), Benedictine monk, missionary and author, was born on 1 March 1814 at Tuy, Spain, the son of Peter Salvado and his wife Francisca Rotea. The Salvado was a long-lived and musical family. Wealth at home favoured Salvado's musical bent, but he pledged his vigour and talent to a higher cause. At 15 he entered the Benedictine abbey of St Martin at Compostela, was clothed in the habit on 24 July 1829, and took his three religious vows a year later.

In the new monk music found more than a dilettante. The distinction won after a two-year course in organ-playing secured for him the post of first organist at St Martin's in 1832. He was also an accomplished pianist and a composer. None of his music was printed but there are extant some of his sacred compositions written for his Western Australian Aboriginals and for convicts in Fremantle gaol, and a major work *Fantasia*, with variations and finale.

At 18 he added the study of liberal arts and philosophy to his duties as organist. The repose of the cloister was disturbed by the Spanish revolutionaries, who in 1835 decreed the closing of convents and the secularization of monks. Three years of patient waiting saw no end to the conflict, so in September 1838 he set out for Naples to be incorporated with the abbey of La Cava. There he was ordained priest in February 1839, and was instrumental in giving the abbey an organ which for mechanism, range and tone could rival the best in Europe.

This was the prelude to Salvado's great epic. His philanthropy prompted him to flee his organ and its glory and to choose instead the retreat of a distant mission field. The Sydney mission under Bishop Polding [q.v.] was first proposed, but Dr Brady's [q.v.] consecration in Rome for the new see of Perth led to a change of mind. Salvado and his Benedictine confrère, Serra, were assigned to the bishop's missionary party. They sailed from London in the *Elizabeth* and landed at Fremantle in January 1846.

Salvado was dedicated to what he believed the highest ideal in life, the reclaiming of souls. Monk first and apostle second, he wanted to use his talents on behalf of a raw colony where things had to be created. As an apostle he set up a system of Aboriginal education that surprised learned men, and as a monk he poured out his heart in prayer and applied the Benedictine Rule that made labour a duty of existence.

With Serra, whose main associate he was, he wound his way along a hundred miles of bush track to a spot in the Victoria Plains, where on 1 March 1846 he established a mission for the training of Aboriginals; it was first named Central as the centre of proposed outlying Aboriginal missions, and later New Norcia, after Norcia, Italy, the birthplace of St Benedict. Hunger soon drove him back to Perth to give a one-man piano concert for which he was paid £1 from each of his audience of seventy music lovers. That saved his mission, but all through the formative years of New Norcia, 1846-67, he lived by 'the sweat of his brow'. Dressed in dungarees, he looked nothing like the Catholic prelate of Protestant imagination. He drove his bullock cart, felled trees, ploughed, sowed and planted to turn the desert into a land rich in corn, wine and honey. Through his Rule he became a mystic, but a sociable one, fervent in seeking the Aboriginals, roaming with them and sharing their bush life. With a physique 'enduring as marble' he set hard standards that only Serra, out of a party of five, could share. But Serra too had to quit when he was appointed to the see of Port Victoria in 1848 and next year coadjutor in the diocese of Perth, and Salvado was left to shape anew the mission.

The change from nomadic to settled life started with the building of an abbey, round which the village came to be built. Here he gathered his Murara-Murara, Victoria Plains Aboriginals, and set about teaching them to work and to be Christians. By the method of inference he built ideas on ideas, his Western culture upon Aboriginal culture. Through their spears and boomerangs he taught the value and meaning of property and ownership. Soon his pupils were adept in husbandry, handicrafts and stockwork, many of them becoming first-class ploughmen, teamsters and farm workers. However, their poor physical strength and indolence hindered them from developing into responsible farmers.

According to Florence Nightingale, it was in Salvado's school that 'the grafting of civilizing habits on unreclaimed races was gradually accomplished'. The stone-age man had held his own against his surroundings; when the nimbleness, skill, endurance and rhythmical motion of the race were guided from the corroboree to the bat and ball, to brass and string music, the Murara-Murara became the heroes of the cricket field and of the music room. Salvado's Aboriginal colony supplied Mivart with the strongest argument to refute his opponent Darwin [q.v.] on 'the essential bestiality of man'. It also gave to the world the first two black post-mistresses and telegraph operators, the one half-caste, the other full blood.

From the beginning Salvado believed that progress at New Norcia was checked by dependence on the bishop of Perth. Sent to Europe in 1849 to raise funds he also pressed the case for New Norcia's home rule. In August he was consecrated bishop of Port Victoria in the Northern Territory. The closing of the garrison settlement deprived him of subjects before he left Italy and, while he waited in Naples for new orders from Rome, he wrote his *Memorie storiche dell'Australia particolarmente della Missione Benedettina di Nuova Norcia* (Rome, 1851); the first part was historical but the second and third dealt *con amore* with New Norcia and the Murara-Murara. This large work was published in Spanish in 1853, French in 1854, but never in English. Contemporary reviews judged it 'a liberal book appealing to the mind and to the heart'.

In 1853 Salvado was sent back to Western Australia. He administered the see of Perth while Bishop Serra was absent in Europe. Four years later he returned to New Norcia with renewed zeal to pursue his purposes for the mission of which he was named temporary administrator in 1859. But his prayer for home rule was not answered until 12 March 1867 when a papal decree gave Bishop Salvado of Port Victoria the additional title of Lord Abbot of New Norcia for life.

With greater freedom the mission entered a second period, 1867-1900, in which Salvado gave wider expression to the part of agriculture in monastic labour and took a leading part in shaping legislation on behalf of the Aboriginals. He and his monks had grown their daily bread by labour; now his journeys across a far-flung wild country looking for pastures and water and opening new tracks were to be as important for colonial expansion as for the mission. His efforts in seeking legal equality for whites and blacks in matters where the two races were equally concerned influenced the amendment in 1875 of the 1871 Bastardy Act and the addition of clause 5 to the 1874 Industrial Schools Act; the one could be invoked to enjoin an Aboriginal child's maintenance on its putative white father, and the other ensured the education of an Aboriginal minor by enabling mission managers to become the child's lawful guardians. His election as protector of Aboriginal natives in June 1887 was a deserved distinction and it made legal what had long been accepted in practice.

Never content with his empty title of bishop of Port Victoria, Salvado was relieved when it was changed to the titular bishop of Adriana in March 1889. In the work of reclaiming some seven hundred of his uncircumcised Murara-Murara and providing them with a means of living, he finally broke through tribal boundaries and won over to him 101 of the circumcised across the border. He loved them all to the end. After securing the future of his mission, he died in Rome on 29 December 1900, calling his distant piccanninies one by one. His remains were brought to Western Australia in June 1903 and re-buried in the tomb of Carrara marble behind the high altar in the church of his beloved New Norcia.

F. Nightingale, *Sanitary statistics of native colonial schools and hospitals* (Lond, 1863); J. Flood, *New Norcia* (Lond, 1908); H. N. Birt, *Benedictine pioneers in Australia*, 2 (Lond, 1911); Roy Com on condition of the natives, Report, PP (WA), 1905 (5), evidence 2021-93; R. Rios, History of New Norcia (Archives, New Norcia); Salvado papers (Archives, New Norcia). Dom William

SAMSON, LIONEL (1799-1878), pioneer and merchant, was probably the son of Michael Samson, a member of one of the old established and wealthy families of English Jewry. He read at Magdalen College, Oxford, and later became a member of the London Stock Exchange. With his friend George Leake [q.v.] he became interested in migration to the colonies. Legend has the two friends meeting Captain Stirling who persuaded them to turn their eyes from Canada towards Western Australia.

Samson arrived at Fremantle in the *Calista* in August 1829 with personal effects and much merchandise. He took up several land allotments in Perth and Fremantle. Within a year of his arrival he had set up his business as a wine and spirit merchant, importer and auctioneer. His brother William, who had accompanied him, was associated with the venture but after some years moved to Adelaide. Samson maintained his original business interests throughout the rest of his life, adding whaling and other projects to his activities; from 1830 to 1832 he was postmaster-general. In 1842 he returned briefly to England, where he married Frances Levi; they had three sons and three daughters.

Samson was a prominent figure in the public and business life of Perth and Fremantle. With his wit and charm and his commercial integrity he achieved a respected and prominent position in society. He was a member of the Fremantle Town Trust. He died on 15 March 1878.

The business which Samson started in Fremantle passed to his sons. It has remained in the family's hands ever since, Western Australia's oldest family business. His descendants have also remained closely identified with the commercial and civic life of the city of Fremantle.

J. G. Wilson (ed), *Western Australia's centenary, 1829-1929* (Perth, 1929).

DAVID MOSSENSON

SAUNDERS, JOHN (1806-1859), Baptist minister, was born on 7 October 1806 in London. At 17 he became a member of the Baptist Church, Cold Harbour Lane, Camberwell, under the ministry of Rev. E. Steane. He was articled to an attorney and became a solicitor. When 19 he began to prepare for missionary service. He studied at the University of Edinburgh, was ordained to the Baptist ministry and became responsible for the formation of churches at Mason Court, Shoreditch and Ball's Pond. In 1834 while minister at Stoke Newington, London, he declined an opportunity to enter parliament.

The request for a pastor from the Baptists of Sydney came while he was considering missionary service in India. With his wife Elizabeth he sailed as chaplain in the *George Hibbert*, a ship carrying female prisoners, and arrived in Sydney in December 1834. No obligation for his passage or work in Australia was undertaken by the Baptist Missionary Society of England, for its charter was 'to go only to the heathen'. Baptist services were begun immediately, first in York Street, then in a room attached to St James's Church of England, known as the Court House Room. Services were held also at South Head lighthouse. Finally in 1836 the first Baptist chapel was built on land in Bathurst Street granted to a congregation of Baptists under the leadership of Rev John McKaeg who, before the arrival of John Saunders, led a small group of Baptists under a somewhat erratic ministry, too irresponsible to call for recognition. The Bathurst Street chapel was described as a Particular Baptist church which provided for open communion and open fellowship. John Saunders ministered there for thirteen years. He visited Melbourne in 1844 and 1845 and Van Diemen's Land in 1846. He opposed the transportation system and crusaded tirelessly for its abolition. When a petition for cessation of transportation with 6765 signatures was presented to Governor FitzRoy in 1846, Saunders was among those deputed to present it.

His opposition to the rum traffic earned for him the name of 'the Apostle of Temperance'. By constant journeying over the colony as far as the Blue Mountains he obtained thousands of signatures for total abstinence. At the conclusion of one lecture in Sydney Governor Gipps, who had chaired the meeting, led the way in the signing of the pledge.

In 1847 John Saunders announced his return to England because ill health had made a continuance of his ministry impossible. The attorney-general, J. H. Plunkett [q.v.], chaired his farewell meeting; Saunders was given a testimonial of £300. In spite of illness he resumed practice as a solicitor and served as pastor in suburban churches of London. He died on 1 May 1859. When news reached Sydney that his widow had been left destitute the *Sydney Morning Herald* opened a subscription list and £650 was sent to her.

HRA (1), 18, 25; *Baptist Mag* (Lond), 28 (1836); A'sian *Baptist Mag*, 1 (1838-39); *Aust Baptist*, 13 Aug 1946, 1 Apr 1959; J. Saunders, Letter-book (ML).   B. G. WRIGHT

SAVAGE, ARTHUR (1798-1852), naval surgeon, gained the diploma of the Royal College of Surgeons in London and became an assistant surgeon in March 1820 and surgeon in July 1826. As surgeon-superintendent he went in the convict ships *John* to Hobart in 1833, *Norfolk* to Hobart in 1835 and *Captain Cook* to Sydney in 1836, and in the emigrant ship *Magistrate* to Sydney in 1838. His conscientious and capable work in the convict service earned him selection by the New South Wales government as an emigration agent in the United Kingdom. In 1837 he selected the Irish emigrants for the *William Jardine*, but although he obtained permission to take his wife and two daughters, with a view to settling permanently in New South Wales, he did not sail in that ship. He and his family arrived at Sydney in 1838 in the *Magistrate*. In January 1839 he was registered by the New South Wales Medical Board to practise his profession. When John Dobie [q.v.], who had proposed the appointment of a health officer for Sydney in August 1838 and who had been appointed to that post in December, resigned, Savage succeeded him on 5 November 1839. He capably held the post until his death on 19 July 1852.

C. Bateson, *The convict ships, 1787-1868* (Glasgow, 1959); V & P (LC NSW), 1838, p 886-90; Col Sec in letters, 4/2408, 1838, (ML).

CHARLES BATESON

SAVAGE, JOHN (b. 1770), surgeon, was born on 20 October 1770. At 26 he obtained his certificate of competence as a surgeon and served in the *Melville Castle* in 1796-97. For some years thereafter he was a lieutenant and assistant surgeon in the 1st West York Militia under the command of Lord Fitzwilliam, who in July 1802 procured his appointment as one of the assistant surgeons in New South Wales. Savage arrived with his wife in the *Glatton* in March 1803. In November he was appointed assistant surgeon at Norfolk Island but did not go there; in May 1804 he was appointed to Port Dalrymple but again did not leave Sydney. Most of his duty was at Parramatta, where in January 1804 he was appointed assistant surgeon and magistrate for the County of Cumberland, and in March captain of the Parramatta Loyal Association. In April he bought three farms in the district and by 1805 held 330 acres.

Savage was a member of the Royal Jennerian Society, established in 1803 to assist the proper spread of vaccination, and from the time he arrived in Sydney he experimented with cowpox; in May 1804 he successfully vaccinated a child for the first time in the colony. He later claimed to have vaccinated or provided the material for vaccinating nearly a thousand children. He also claimed that his success alienated the principal surgeon, John Jamison [q.v.], whose own attempts at vaccination had been unsuccessful. In June 1805 Jamison had Savage tried by a general court martial for neglect of duty in refusing to attend the wife of a settler when in child-birth. Savage stated that midwifery was not part of his duty, but was found guilty and sentenced to be cashiered. Governor King, who thought highly of Savage, reported the matter to England, and, since Savage was necessarily suspended from duty, gave him leave to return home. Next month he sailed with his wife, carrying the dispatches which the governor entrusted to him, and leaving his cattle and farms in charge of Samuel Marsden [q.v.]. In England Savage's sentence was set aside, for the alleged offence was not a military one within the Mutiny Act or the Articles of War, and King was directed to restore the surgeon to his former duty. However, Savage did not return. In November Edward Jenner sought a post for Savage in any regiment where there was a vacancy, and in December 1807 Governor Bligh was informed that Savage had been engaged by the East India Co.

While in London he published *Some Account of New Zealand, particularly the Bay of Islands, and surrounding Country . . . with a description of the Religion and Government, Language, Arts, Manufactures, Manners and Customs of the Natives, etc.* (1807). He had collected material for this book when the *Ferrett* stopped at New Zealand on the way to England, and dedicated it to Fitzwilliam. It received favourable notice in the *Edinburgh* and *Eclectic Reviews*, and *Annales des Voyages, de la Géographie et de l'Histoire*, 19 (Paris, 1812), praised it as the first work published on New Zealand since Cook's [q.v.] account.

In March 1808 Savage took up his duties as assistant surgeon in Bengal, and in June 1823 he was appointed surgeon. In 1835 he was back in London in ill health. He had lost his savings through the incompetence of his agents, and he wrote to Marsden thanking him for the sale of his farms in New South Wales and asking him to sell the remainder of his property. In August he retired from the Indian Medical Service.

HRNSW, 4, 5; HRA (1), 3-6; A. D. McKinlay, *Savage's account of New Zealand in 1805* (Wellington, 1939); *Sydney Gazette*, 15 May 1803, 29 Jan, 8 Apr 1804.

VIVIENNE PARSONS

SAVERY, HENRY (1791-1842), businessman, forger, convict and author, was born on 4 August 1791 at Butcombe, Somerset, England, the sixth son of John Savery, a Bristol banker, and may have been educated at Oswestry Grammar School. He served an apprenticeship to business in Bristol, where he engaged in sugar refining, through which he became bankrupt, and newspaper editing. On 14 October 1815 he married Eliza Elliott, daughter of William Elliott Oliver, of Blackfriars, London. A son, Henry Oliver, was born on 30 June 1816.

Returning to sugar refining he entered upon commitments beyond his firm's resources, forged fictitious bills, fled, was pursued by his partner Saward, and was captured on board the *Hudson* at Cowes within half an hour of sailing. Brought back to Bristol, he pleaded guilty on the advice of a magistrate, was condemned to death on 4 April 1825, but the day before the hanging was to take place his sentence was commuted to transportation for life.

He arrived in Hobart Town in the *Medway* early in December 1825 and was employed as a clerk in the colonial secretary's office and then in the colonial treasurer's. In 1827 he was assigned to Captain B. B. Thomas [q.v.], superintendent of the Van

Diemen's Land Establishment. Early in 1828 Eliza Savery sailed in the *Jessie Lawson*, was saved from the wreck of that ship, and later in the *Henry Wellesley* arrived at Hobart in October to find Savery still bond and threatened by a writ for debt. His distress was probably heightened by doubts of the relationship between his wife and Algernon Montagu [q.v.], the attorney-general, to whose care her parents had entrusted her on the voyage. Savery attempted suicide by cutting his throat but was saved by the attentions of Dr William Crowther. After her husband was imprisoned for debt Eliza Savery left Hobart in mid-February 1829, never to return.

While in prison Savery wrote sketches of Hobart life for the *Colonial Times*, from June to December 1829, under the title of *The Hermit in Van Diemen's Land*, using the pseudonym Simon Stukeley. They formed the first volume of Australian essays; published in Hobart in 1829 they were the subject of a libel suit in May 1830. After his release Savery wrote *Quintus Servinton*, the first Australian novel. It was published in three volumes in Hobart in 1830-31. Both works are now extremely rare, only four or five copies of each being known to exist.

For some years after this Savery prospered somewhat. In June 1832 he was granted a ticket-of-leave which was withdrawn for some months in 1833 because of a law suit in which he served as an innocent victim; he engaged in agriculture, was granted a conditional pardon early in 1838, and even had one or two assigned servants. Then, falling into debt, he once again forged bills, was arrested, and in October 1840 was condemned by his wife's former protector, Montagu. Savery was sent to Port Arthur, where he died, possibly from a stroke, on 6 February 1842.

Though his literary fame rests mainly on his priority in time, his sketches have some life and vividness, and his novel, in part autobiographical, gives an insight into business life in England and convict life in Tasmania.

H. Savery, *Quintus Servinton*, ed. C. Hadgraft (Brisb, 1962); E. Morris Miller, *Pressmen and governors* (Syd, 1952).

CECIL HADGRAFT

SCHAFFER (SCHAEFFER), PHILIP (d. 1828?), farmer, was born in Hesse, Germany, and served as a lieutenant in a German rifle corps under British command in North America. In 1789, at Governor Phillip's suggestion, the British government recruited nine farmers and others to be superintendents of convicts. One of these was Schaffer, then a widower with a daughter Elizabeth, aged 10; he was described as 'accustomed to farming'.

They sailed in H.M.S. *Guardian* in September. After she was wrecked off the Cape of Good Hope, Schaffer and four other superintendents were taken aboard the *Lady Juliana* at the Cape and reached Sydney in June 1790. Schaffer could not speak English well and, instead of remaining a superintendent, was established on 30 March 1791 as a farmer on 140 acres at Parramatta which he named the Vineyard. He was provided with a hut, tools, seed grain and two sows, and two acres were cleared for him. He and his daughter and four male convicts allotted to him were rationed from the public store for eighteen months. Thus, with William Reid and Robert Webb, seamen from the *Sirius*, he was one of the first three men who came free to New South Wales and were granted land. The deeds for grants to these three and to James Ruse [q.v.] were each signed on 22 February 1792, although the grants had been made earlier. By October Schaffer had twenty-seven acres under maize, two acres under wheat, one acre of garden, one under vines and eight acres cleared for planting. The only other vines then recorded were on three acres in the governor's garden at Parramatta.

His later achievements did not match his early promise. In December Phillip granted him occupancy of an 100-foot allotment in Sydney. In August 1797 Captain Waterhouse [q.v.] bought the Vineyard for £140, and, though in 1806 Schaffer held sixty acres granted at the Field of Mars in 1794 and sixty acres of purchased land at Redbank, he had only eighteen acres under grain crops. On 14 October 1811 he married Margaret McKinnon, according to J. D. Lang [q.v.], a former convict from Skye, who had arrived in the *Royal Admiral* in 1791. In 1814 Schaffer was still farming at Parramatta. He was a recipient of government cattle and in 1816 was granted fifty acres at Narrabeen. In November 1825 he and his wife were granted a hundred acres 'for their natural lives'; however, Lang wrote that 'old age, poverty and intemperance' caused Schaffer to sell his land piecemeal. He died about 1828 in the Benevolent Asylum, where his widow was also an inmate.

HRNSW, 1-3; HRA (1), 1; J. D. Lang, *An historical and statistical account of New South Wales*, 2nd ed (Lond, 1837), 45-48; Land grant registers (NSWA).

SCHAW, CHARLES (1785-1874), soldier and police magistrate, was born on 10 October 1785 in Jamaica. He was educated at Eton and at 17 entered the army. After ten years service in England and the West Indies he became captain by purchase in the 60th Regiment, and served in the Peninsular war. On the formation of a new corps of officers for the 85th Regiment he was appointed captain in January 1813 and was present at the siege of St Sebastian. In America he again acquitted himself with honour and in 1824 was appointed major of brigade in Honduras. Gazetted brevet-major in 1830, he returned to England. He transferred to the 21st Regiment and went to Van Diemen's Land in 1833 with his wife, seven daughters and a son. On arrival he was nominated coroner and deputy-chairman of Quarter Sessions by Lieut-Governor Arthur and sent to Bothwell as assistant police magistrate. He sold out of the army in April 1835.

Schaw administered the district of Bothwell for eight years. He bought a new house for £850, called it Schawfield, and farmed on its ten acres. Within three years his additions to the house gave it thirty-seven rooms and cost £4000. He furnished it lavishly and lived in great style, once giving a grand dinner and ball to Sir John and Lady Franklin. Though popular at first his family soon became disliked for their haughty manners. Living on the verge of insolvency Schaw became quarrelsome with his neighbours and particularly with Rev. James Garrett [q.v] under whom he was a churchwarden; Garrett once impounded the major's pigs and found himself charged with cruelty to animals. Complaints about Schaw were numerous: it was claimed that he usurped crown land and that his magisterial decisions were influenced by the past history of each person appearing before him. It was also said that his strong prejudices deterred any other magistrate from sitting with him on the bench. Although John Clark, a justice of the peace and honorary magistrate, and Garrett supported these complaints, Lieut-Governor Franklin refused to take action, even after a public meeting and a petition had brought an official inquiry into Schaw's conduct.

In 1841 Schaw was promoted to the full police magistracy of Richmond where he remained for fifteen years. There again complaints were made against his autocratic temperament, his favours to friends and his readiness to take offence at the smallest slights. His attempts to damage his enemies in official eyes by repeating harmful gossip and irrelevant details was con-demned by Lieut-Governor Fox Young in March 1855. With the decision next year to amalgamate the police districts of Richmond and Sorell, Schaw retired. He returned to England with a pension from the colonial government, settled at Torquay in 1858 and devoted the remainder of his life to the Church of England. He died on 5 March 1874. His eldest daughter, Frances Sarah, married William Sharland [q.v.] at Bothwell in 1835, and his son, Charles, went to Western Australia after digging gold at Bendigo.

Schaw's resolution as a soldier was appreciated in the army but won him few friends as an administrator. His autocratic methods and short temper lost him the co-operation of his colleagues, and his imperfect notion of a magistrate's duties, particularly at Bothwell, made him callous to colonial opinion.

P. L. Brown (ed), *Clyde Company papers*, 1-5 (Lond, 1941-63); *Mercury*, 9 May 1874; Clark-Weston papers (Royal Soc Tas, Hob); CSO 1, 8, 11 and 24 (TA); CSD 1 (TA).

JULIE CARINGTON SMITH

SCHMIDT, KARL WILHELM EDWARD (d. 1864), missionary, was born at Stargard, Pomerania (Poland). After education at the Universities of Halle and Berlin, he was the first theological student at the missionary seminary of Rev. Dr J. E. Gossner, minister of the Bethlehem Bohemian Church in Berlin and later founder of the Evangelical Union for the Spread of Christianity among the Heathen. Schmidt was recommended as the clerical leader of a party of nine artisan missionaries also trained by Gossner for service with an English society. In 1837 Samuel Jackson, London manager of the Union Bank of Australia, and friend of Gossner, brought them to the attention of Rev. J. D. Lang [q.v.] who was seeking recruits for a Presbyterian-sponsored mission to the Aboriginals at Moreton Bay. The party consisted of five married artisans, Ambrosius Theophilus Wilhelm Hartenstein (1811-1861), Johann Gottfried Haussmann (1811-1901), Johann Peter Niqué (1811-1903), Franz Joseph August Rodé (1811-1903), Johann Leopold Zillmann (1813-1892), and four single artisans, August Albrecht (b. 1816), Ludwig Dögé, Friedrich Theodore Franz (1814-1891) and Johann Gottfried Wagner (1809-1893). Lang engaged them to conduct a mission somewhat on the Moravian plan.

Schmidt married, and was ordained by the consistory of the Prussian Church at Stargard. Lang also engaged a married missionary surgeon, Moritz Schneider, from the Missionary Society of Leipzig. The missionaries were designated at the Bethlehem Church on 9 July 1837 and at Greenock, Scotland, they were joined by Rev. C. Eipper [q.v.]. The missionaries, their passages paid by the British government, arrived in Sydney in January 1838 in the *Minerva*. Schneider, who had attended the typhus fever victims on board, died in quarantine, and his widow later married Franz. Schmidt, with Eipper, was admitted as a member of the Presbyterian Synod of New South Wales. Although leader of the mission he did not sail to the station but ministered to a German congregation in Sydney and helped to incorporate the New South Wales Society in aid of the German Mission to the Aborigines, which was to support the mission in conjunction with government funds. On arrival in Brisbane in June 1838 Schmidt found that the first party had selected a site which they called Zion Hill (Nundah).

In 1840 the missionaries were reported to have fired upon the Aboriginals. Seeking an explanation, Lieutenant Gorman, commandant at Moreton Bay, learnt from Schmidt that the missionaries fired their guns only to frighten Aboriginals who raided their gardens and menaced their families. By July 1841 Schmidt reported progress in his school for Aboriginal children. In 1842 Governor Gipps threatened to withdraw support unless the mission site was changed. In June 1842 Schmidt, with nine Aboriginals, explored the country round the Bunya Mountains in the Wide Bay district; his reports and published extracts from his journal drew attention to the belief that Aboriginals were being poisoned by the squatters in the area beyond the limit of authorized settlement. In a later controversy it was alleged that the missionaries had not followed up their suspicions through fear of the squatters. Schmidt made a journey to Toorbul in December 1842 and January 1843, and soon afterwards entertained Leichhardt [q.v.], who was favourably impressed by the mission.

When both government and the Sydney committee withdrew support because of general lack of funds and the apparent failure to 'civilize' the Aboriginals, Schmidt became dissatisfied with the mission's organization and the 'most shameful, treacherous, backsliding work' of supporters in Berlin and in Sydney. He decided to accept a call to a Lutheran church in New York State, but changed his mind and stayed at Zion Hill until 1845, despite Lang's attempts to persuade him to form a congregation in Sydney.

In 1846 Schmidt and his wife returned to England. After ministering to a German Lutheran congregation in London, he applied to the London Missionary Society and in 1848-57 served as a missionary in Samoa. His wife died at Falealili, Upolu, on 25 May 1855. In 1857 Schmidt resigned and conducted a free school for children of foreign residents at Apia. Also in 1857 he married Salaneta, a Samoan by whom he had one son. He died at Apia early in 1864. Though somewhat difficult and querulous Schmidt was dedicated to his calling. Disillusioned at the spiritual results of missionary work both in Queensland and Samoa, he devoted much time to the collection of vocabularies, translation of portions of the Bible into the local Aboriginal dialect, and the translation and revision of the Samoan Bible.

Before Schmidt left the mission, a second party from the Gossner society arrived in Sydney in January 1844; its four artisans had been designated as missionaries for the New Hebrides at the Bethlehem Church on 21 August 1843, but on Lang's advice two of them, Carl Friedrich Gerler (1817-1894) and Johann Wilhelm Gericke, decided to reinforce the mission at Zion Hill. Although the missionaries now had to support themselves, the mission temporarily revived, and a branch station was begun at Burpengary near Caboolture. In keeping with their policy of assimilation to the Australian community they had anglicized some of their names. By 1850, however, there were few Aboriginals at Zion Hill, and some missionaries left to pioneer other districts.

Godfrey Wagner was the first of the lay missionaries to extend his work to other areas. In Sydney on 7 February 1850 he married Anna Catharine Weiss, who bore him five children. After working as a catechist in the southern districts of New South Wales he was ordained by the Presbyterian Synod in October 1850, served in Tumut for a year, and then returned to Nundah on account of his wife's ill health. In 1856 he was appointed to an itinerating ministry embracing Ipswich, the Burnett district and the Darling Downs.

After the abandonment of the mission Godfrey Haussman entered the Australian College and was ordained by the synod in December 1851. He was appointed itinerant chaplain to the English and German settlers in 'the Northern district'. For eighteen months he was stationed at Maryborough and ministered to the settlers in the Burnett and Dawson districts. There in 1853 missionary work among the Aboriginals was recommenced by Rev. W. Ridley with Haussman as his assistant. In July 1855 Haussman moved to Victoria where he was pastor of Germantown (Grovedale, Geelong) until 1861 when he became pastor of the Nazareth Lutheran Church in Brisbane. In 1863 he began services in the Beenleigh district. He never completely abandoned his missionary calling and in 1866 established the Bethesda Aboriginal Mission at Beenleigh, conducting it with help from other Gossner missionaries until the mission property was sold in 1883. He died at Beenleigh on 31 December 1901.

Haussman was a man of great energy and dedication. His 'unconfessional' Lutheranism brought him into dispute with the more orthodox Gossner missionaries and Lutheran ministers, but he extended the Lutheran cause among both German and English settlers, and won regard as the patriarch of the German settlers in Queensland. One of his sons, Rev. John Haussman received a university education in Germany before returning as a Gossner missionary to join his father in 1866. He served at Rockhampton and Mackay and later joined the Presbyterian Church.

Gerler, whose educational and personal qualifications assured his leadership of the remnant of the mission, was ordained to be their pastor by Rev. Matthias Goethe on 28 October 1856. He was a pioneer viticulturist in the district and remained the leading figure of the mission until his death at Nundah on 14 December 1894.

Peter Niquet and J. W. Gericke were both ordained by the Synod of New South Wales on 4 November 1856. They had been recruited by Goethe for mission work on the Victorian goldfields. Niquet served as Evangelical Lutheran pastor at Ballarat (1856-64), Light's Pass (1865-88) and Adelaide (1891-92). He died at Mount Gambier in March 1903. Gericke ministered to the Germans at Bendigo until 1857. He later became a settler in the Gympie district in 1867.

Of those who remained at Nundah, Franz and Zillman became pioneers of the Caboolture district. Rodé and Zillman both gave evidence before the select committee of the Legislative Assembly on the native police force in 1861. Zillman took an active part in Lutheran, Methodist and Baptist churches. His second son, Rev. Dr Leopold Zillman (1841-1919) was successively a Methodist, Congregational and Anglican minister and a chaplain of prisons in New York; he married five times and wrote an autobiography and several works of history, fiction and verse.

J. D. Lang, Appeal to the friends of missions, on behalf of the German mission to the Aborigines of New South Wales (Lond, 1839); J. D. Lang, Cooksland, or the Moreton Bay district of New South Wales (Lond, 1848); J. J. Knight, In the early days (Brisb, 1895); H. J. J. Sparks, Queensland's first free settlement 1838-1938 (Brisb, 1938); F. O. Theile, The Lutheran Church in Queensland (Brisb, 1938); W. N. Gunson, 'The Nundah missionaries', JRQHS, 6 (1959-61); Newspaper cuttings (Oxley Lib, Brisb); Lang papers (ML).

NIEL GUNSON

SCHOFIELD, WILLIAM (1793-1878), Wesleyan missionary, was born on 17 June 1793 at Dudley Hill, near Bradford, Yorkshire, England. He began work in a commercial house. His family had no connexions with Methodism but Schofield came under its influence in 1814. In January 1819 he was put on trial as a local preacher and in 1826 was accepted by the Wesleyan Methodist Conference as a minister. At the suggestion of Lieut-Governor Arthur of Van Diemen's Land the British government asked the conference to supply missionaries for the penal establishments in Van Diemen's Land. Schofield was selected and in April 1827 sailed for Sydney in the Alacrity. On arrival in October he re-embarked in the Harvey for Hobart Town where with some reluctance he accepted appointment as the first missionary chaplain at Macquarie Harbour. He sailed from Hobart in the Derwent and, although distressed by what he saw and heard on arrival, he was not dismayed.

Schofield's first service with the convicts at Macquarie Harbour was held on 30 March 1828. A large room was provided for later meetings and, although attendance was compulsory, it was soon evident that some of the men and boys were influenced by his message. The penal settlement already had a small Methodist class meeting which Schofield continued; he added weekly meetings for religious conversation, regular evening lectures and singing classes, and a night school, all with voluntary attendance. In these projects he was helped by the commissariat clerk, T. J. Lempriere [q.v.], and others, including young convicts who tried to teach old convicts to read. The results of this work impressed the commandant and his officers, but Schofield was not deceived by signs of religious revival; he warned his successor, Rev. J. A. Manton [q.v.] to be cautious in recommending apparently pious convicts to the governor for removal to less isolated prisons.

At Arthur's request Schofield extended his term at Macquarie Harbour to a fourth year, during which the Wesleyan Committee in London appointed him to the mission at Tonga. Schofield objected to this transfer because of the difficulty of learning a new language at his age, and the district committee amended the decision by sending him to Parramatta, New South Wales. There, from 1832 to 1834, and in later circuit appointments at Windsor (1834-38), Sackville Reach (1838-39), Sydney (1839-42), Melbourne (1842-45), Parramatta (1845-47), Windsor (1847-50) and Goulburn (1850-51), he ministered faithfully and acceptably. In 1851 he became a supernumerary minister but continued to preach. Released from a fixed station he became associated with the church's acquisition of York Street House as a depot for Methodist literature.

Schofield died at Waverley on 9 June 1878. He left an estate of nearly £50,000, of which £40,000 went at his wife's death to the Wesleyan Methodist Church of New South Wales to establish 'The Rev. W. Schofield's Free and Perpetual Loan Fund'. Against the background of early commercial experience in Yorkshire, his letter-book reveals his first minor financial transactions in Van Diemen's Land in 1831; it appears that his fortune was gradually amassed by thrift and careful investment. In 1849 he acquired from the Hawkesbury Benevolent Society its Mooki River cattle-run. On his death he bequeathed about £9000 to relatives, most of whom he had never met. His ability to endow a substantial fund was an unusual outcome of a normally ill-paid vocation. Although an astute financier he had in his circuits a well-earned reputation for untiring industry, pastoral concern, judicious counsel and carefully prepared expository preaching. His devotion to duty was perhaps most marked at Macquarie Harbour, where his remarkable gifts of prayer and leadership were much in evidence.

Schofield's first wife Martha, whom he married on 15 March 1827, was the daughter of Roger Milnes of Horton. After her death on 30 April 1849 he married Kezia, widow of Lancelot Iredale; she died on 24 April 1863. His third wife, Ellen, the widow of James Barker, survived him, and died in November 1893. She had means of her own as well as those inherited upon Schofield's death and used them generously in support of the Methodist Church. Her name is commemorated in Schofield Hall, Methodist Ladies' College, Burwood, New South Wales, for the construction of which she provided £2800 in 1886. No children were born to Schofield by any of his marriages.

HRA (3), 6; *In Memoriam, Rev. W. Schofield* (Newtown, nd); W. Moister, *Missionary worthies* (Lond, 1885); J. Colwell, *The illustrated history of Methodism* (Syd, 1904); C. I. Benson (ed), *A century of Victorian Methodism* (Melb, 1935); Rev. W. Schofield, Journal 1827-63 and letter-book 1827-39 (ML); J. A. Manton, Inward letter-book (copy, E. R. Pretyman, Hob).

G. L. LOCKLEY

SCONCE, ROBERT KNOX (1818-1852), Church of England clergyman converted to Catholicism and schoolteacher, was born on 12 June 1818 at Rochester, Kent, England, the son of Robert Clement Sconce (1788-1847), purser in the navy and later secretary to Admiral Sir John Duckworth, and his wife Sarah, only daughter of Rev. Dr Vicesimus Knox (1752-1821), writer, theologian, preacher and headmaster of Tonbridge School, 1778-1812. His great-grandfather, Vicesimus Knox (1729-1779), was headmaster of Tonbridge in 1771-78, and his uncle, Rev. Dr Thomas Knox (1784-1843), in 1812-43.

Sarah Sconce died five days after her son was born, leaving him and two young daughters. Her husband remarried and for some years was chief commissary of the navy at Malta. R. K. Sconce lived there until 1829 when he entered Tonbridge School, where he was head boy in the sixth form in 1835 and won exhibitions to Brasenose College, Oxford (B.A., 1840). After graduation he was eligible for a fellowship but instead on 11 August 1840 he married Elizabeth Catherine, third daughter of Rev. Edward Repton (1783-1860), a canon of Westminster and chaplain to the House of Commons.

Sconce and his wife, his sister Sarah Susanna and her husband Captain Richard Bunbury, R.N., and the Bunbury's one-year-old son embarked at Plymouth in the *Argyle* and landed at Port Phillip in March 1841. In August he and Bunbury were appointed magistrates of the territory by Governor Gipps. However, Sconce's sister-in-law, Miss Repton, prevailed on Rev. Edward Coleridge of Eton College to write to Bishop Broughton [q.v.], introducing Sconce and adding that he was 'going forth with the spirit of a missionary and the deepest reverence for the Church of England'. Georgiana McCrae [q.v.], a fellow-passenger in the *Argyle*, later sketched Sconce's portrait for Miss Repton and summed him up as 'introspective, a careful and precise speaker'. His wife, however, was something of a foil, 'so playful and artless she seems'.

Broughton was short of clergy and, as the government had decided to pay no more fares for immigrant clergy, he had an added reason for inviting Sconce to

Sydney for ordination, a request which Sconce did not seek but did not feel it right to refuse. He reached Sydney in November, passed a 'very satisfactory' examination before Broughton and Rev. R. Allwood [q.v.], and was ordained deacon in St James's Church on 19 December. Broughton then sent him to St Stephen's, Penrith, and St Mary Magdalene's, South Creek, which he considered one of the best preferments he could offer. Broughton was also attracted by Mrs Sconce's personality: 'I was pleased . . . with the spirit of so young a woman, making no objection of any sort to all the roughnesses which at first they will have to encounter . . . So I begged her to take care of the girls in the school and lent her two books of Psalmody . . . and sent her off as happy a parson's wife as is is to be met with in the Universe'.

Sconce was priested by Broughton on 18 December 1842 in St James's Church at the largest ordination ceremony so far held in Australia: five priests and two deacons. Rev. T. C. Makinson [q.v.] was among the priests assisting the bishop in the laying on of hands.

Sconce continued at Penrith and South Creek in 1843, and in that year prepared a pamphlet Answers to the question, why do I submit to the Teaching of the Church? In 1844 Sconce was moved to St Andrew's parish, where he used a temporary church while work on the cathedral proceeded slowly. As minister at St Andrew's, Sconce occupied a prominent position in Sydney church affairs, and in January 1846 Broughton, lamenting the condition and small numbers of his clergy, noted that 'Myself and Sconce . . . are the only two thoroughly sound'. In 1845-47 Sconce was one of the clergy who lectured at St James's College which Broughton inaugurated for training local postulants. The college was moved in 1847 to Lyndhurst, James Bowman's [q.v.] property in Glebe, but enrolments fell away after 1848 partly, as alleged later, because Sconce taught the Tridentine doctrine of justification and advocated other Catholic doctrines to the students. By 1852 Lyndhurst was bought by the Catholic Church and St Mary's College was established there under Bishop Davis [q.v.].

Sconce's doubts about Anglican doctrines reached a critical stage in February 1848. Finally unable to accept Broughton's explanations of problems of ecclesiastical history, he spent 'ten days in prayer . . . and earnest thought; ten nights in hard struggles and tears' before his mind was clear. On 21 February

Sconce and Makinson resigned their licences as Anglican priests; five days later Broughton held a court at which sentences of deprivation and deposition from the ministry were pronounced, and Sconce's sentence was read the following Sunday in the St Andrew's parish church.

Sconce gave some details of his conversion in a pamphlet published in April, Reasons for submitting to the Catholic Church, in which, and in later published controversy between Broughton and himself, he described how he had taken his difficulties to Rev. W. H. Walsh, of Christ Church in St Lawrence's parish, and then to Broughton. Neither, however, was able to persuade him that the Catholic tenets of apostolic succession and papal supremacy were incorrect. Broughton was deeply touched by Sconce's conversion and in 1848 wrote that Sconce 'was among the most able and zealous of my helpers and though I had seen with regret during these last two years certain tendencies taking possession of him and an attachment amounting to a morbid enthusiasm impelling him to Mr Newman's person and opinions both, yet to the very last I would not give up my confidence in him. The blow therefore came more heavily upon me, and I will not affect to deny has made a greater breach in my happiness than any occurrence during many a year has done'. In order to dissuade any parishioners who might have been inclined to follow Sconce's lead, Broughton personally assumed charge of St Andrew's from March to November 1848.

Apparently it was during his 'ten days in prayer' that Sconce first approached Archbishop Polding [q.v.], who agreed 'with great joy of heart' to see him, and within a few days, Sconce, his wife and children became Catholics. Polding employed Sconce and Makinson as teachers in charge of the lay school attached to St Mary's Seminary at a salary of £150 each. Sconce continued at the seminary until 1851, and then began to study for admission to the Bar. However, he contracted scarlet fever and died on 28 March 1852. He was buried from St Mary's Cathedral.

His wife died at Brighton in England in 1898. Of their two boys and three girls, born between June 1841 and December 1847, one boy and one girl died young. Madeline, Elizabeth and Edward survived their mother.

Sconce's and Makinson's were considered the two most important conversions in Australia related to the Newman-Manning wave of conversions in England.

Sconce's conversion had a more resounding effect in the colony, for he had held prominent positions, whereas Makinson came from the relative obscurity of a country parish. One result of their defection from Anglicanism was the development of a critical attitude towards Broughton, who was considered to hold some Puseyite sympathies, and generally the conversions appear to have had a part in fostering the Low Church tradition of the Church of England in Sydney.

T. Whytehead, *Poetical remains and letters* (Lond, 1877); H. N. Birt, *Benedictine pioneers in Australia*, 2 (Lond, 1911); H. McCrae (ed), *Georgiana's journal* (Syd, 1934); M. L. Loane, *A centenary history of Moore Theological College* (Syd, 1955); SPG *Sydney Cttee Reports*, 1841-47; *Atlas* (Syd), Feb-Dec 1848; *SMH*, Feb 1848; Broughton papers (microfilm, NL).

R. A. DALY

SCOTT, DANIEL (1800-1865), harbourmaster, was born in Liverpool, England, the son of Daniel Scott and his wife Janet, née Campbell. His father was a flagmaker for the navy and merchant service. As a boy Daniel ran away to sea and at 21 was captain of a small cargo ship that plied between the Gold Coast and the West Indies. On one voyage he rescued three men adrift in an open boat and was commended by the Royal Humane Society.

On 5 August 1829 he arrived in the *Calista* at Fremantle, where he was appointed deputy-harbourmaster and pilot at a salary of £100. He soon found time for commercial ventures. At Fremantle he built his own jetty and used it for his lightering business. Several of his boats traded up and down the coast and his *Mary Ann* was commissioned by Governor Stirling to transport provisions from Garden Island to the early mainland settlement. Scott was largely responsible for having the first sea-going vessel built in the colony; its launching as the *Lady Stirling* in May 1836 was a gala occasion. He was also part-owner of the whaler *Napoleon* in the 1840s and commanded her on one whaling voyage in 1842. In Fremantle he was assigned several blocks which he developed in different ways. On one he built a well for watering ships, and on another a warehouse for wool and grain; it was later used as a convict prison.

With enormous energy Scott supported the pioneers who opened up the colony and he acquired land in several districts. However, he showed little desire to settle as a farmer and his chief interests were centred on Fremantle. An active leader in pressing for local government, he was elected the first chairman of the Fremantle Town Trust in January 1848 and held the position three times in the next ten years. He was also an honorary member of the local volunteer company and he strongly supported the local Church of England. His religious convictions had been strengthened by experience as a young sailor and he became a guarantor of the first church built in Fremantle.

In spite of all these time-consuming public and private activities Scott continued to give good service as harbourmaster, often using his own boats and equipment on government duty. Through injury to an arm he had difficulty with his pilot duties, and he resigned his official position in February 1851. Free to devote all his time to commerce, he concentrated on the Geraldton area, urging the government to open the district for mining. In 1864 he formed the Geraldton Smelting and Mining Co., but it lapsed after his death at Fremantle on 20 February 1865.

Seven months after arrival in Western Australia Scott married Frances Harriet Davis; they had eight daughters and three sons. The eldest son, Daniel Henry, carried on his father's business.

J. K. Hitchcock, *The history of Fremantle . . . 1829-1929* (Fremantle, 1929); P. U. Henn, Genealogical notes (Battye Lib, Perth).

P. J. COLES

SCOTT, ELLIS MARTIN (1799?-1829), merchant, arrived in Sydney from Leith, Scotland, in October 1825 in the *Triton* to take up the position of agent for the Australian Co. of Sydney and Leith, in conjunction with A. Warren. Under the name of Warren & Scott they set up business in George Street. Scott took an active part in the business community, being on the committee of the Chamber of Commerce, a member of the Agricultural Society and a director of the Bank of New South Wales from December 1826 to December 1828. He was appointed magistrate for the town of Sydney in September 1827. In July 1829 he signed the address of the landed proprietors and merchants in support of Governor Darling. By this time he had acquired property in the colony, including a grant of 2000 acres at Patrick's Plains on the Hunter River, and in addition had bought 1500 acres on the Williams River, 215 acres on the Liverpool Road and 10 acres on Parramatta Road.

He died on 3 November 1829 of a 'lingering consumption', aged 30, leaving his property in New South Wales and a fourth share in the brig *Tigress* to his mother Mrs Mary Scott of Musselburgh, Scotland.

HRA (1), 14, 15; *Australian*, 20 Oct 1825, 6 Nov 1829; *Sydney Gazette*, 31 Aug 1827; MS cat under E. M. Scott (ML).

VIVIENNE PARSONS

SCOTT, JAMES (d. 1796), sergeant of marines, was a member of the marine detachment in the First Fleet, and arrived in New South Wales as one of three sergeants in the *Prince of Wales*. He had had little formal education but was already an experienced and competent non-commissioned officer when the fleet sailed. On 26 October 1786 he had married Jane Boxell at St Mary's Church, Portsea, now a suburb of Portsmouth, both being of that parish. A daughter, Elizabeth, was born in the *Prince of Wales* in Rio de Janeiro on 29 August 1787 and a son, William Boxell, in Sydney on 4 June 1790.

Scott and his family embarked in H.M.S. *Gorgon* in Sydney on 31 October 1791. They sailed for England on 18 December and all survived the voyage despite the illness and deaths on board. Scott was discharged at Spithead on 21 June 1792 and from next October until March 1796 he served as a squad sergeant or second squad sergeant on shore at Portsmouth at £20 a year. He died towards the end of March 1796 and was buried at Portsmouth on 2 April.

Scott is chiefly notable because of his diary, which covers the period from May 1787 to May 1792, and is one of the few surviving contemporary accounts of the first settlement of Australia by a member of his class. It was published in Sydney in 1963 under the title *Remarks on a Passage to Botany Bay, 1787-1792*. His life both as a marine and as a family man was otherwise undistinguished and blameless. He was a loyal member of his corps conscientiously performing the duties of his rank, commanding the quarter guard, assisting in a routine inspection of the powder in the magazine, or searching for a marine lost in the bush. Whether in this or in keeping pigs and poultry in Sydney he was sober and industrious, interested in the novelty of his experiences but lacking either in imagination or in the ability to reveal it in his diary

G. D. RICHARDSON

SCOTT, JAMES (1790-1837), surgeon, was born at Inchdrewer Castle, Banffshire, Scotland, the eldest son of Thomas Scott.

At 19 he received the diploma of the Royal College of Surgeons, Edinburgh, and after service in the navy he resumed his studies at Edinburgh University (M.D., 1815). In January 1820 he arrived in Sydney as surgeon-superintendent in the convict transport *Castle Forbes* and went on with it to Hobart Town. In May he gave evidence on conditions at the Hobart Hospital before Commissioner Bigge [q.v.]. Next month he obtained a permit to settle in New South Wales and an order for a land grant of 800 acres, which he transferred to Van Diemen's Land when in December 1820 he accepted temporary appointment at Hobart as colonial surgeon and controller of medical services in the southern part of the island. Bigge had criticized the house, hired for a hospital in Hobart, and proposed changes in the plans of the new hospital. Scott implemented these changes and obtained equipment, but he had to send his reports and requisitions to the principal surgeon in Sydney. In 1824 with Lieut-Governor Sorell's help he appealed successfully for permanent appointment, which he held until 1835. His journal in the possession of the Royal Society of Tasmania gives a vivid picture of medical conditions in a young colony. As well as serving the hospital and the civil establishment he was permitted to engage in private practice, said to be worth £2000 a year.

Scott became a magistrate in 1824 and soon had to inquire into the escape of two convicts from a transport at Rio de Janeiro. He also joined other justices in complaints about the extreme unfitness of the buildings used as a police office and as a female factory. When as a public servant he added his name to a petition for repeal of the Press Licensing Act, Lieut-Governor Arthur reported him to Downing Street for behaviour 'long considered very improper'. On 25 June 1821 Scott married Lucy, the only child of Lieut-Governor Davey. Governor Macquarie attended the wedding and gave Lucy a grant of 1000 acres for her own exclusive use; it was located at Bothwell and named Rothiemay. Scott held an estate at Scottsdale near New Norfolk, extensive property at Bothwell, land at New Town on which he built Boa Vista and Roseway, and the Constantia brewery. He was an original proprietor of the Bank of Van Diemen's Land, and he joined the committee of the first Presbyterian church in Hobart. He was also keen on natural history and collected specimens and wrote articles on his work. For a time he had in his employ the convict artist, W. B. Gould [q.v.]. He died on 26 July 1837 and was buried in the old St David's cemetery, leaving four sons and two daughters. His wife survived him for ten years.

Scott was a confident surgeon and a sound physician. By nature autocratic, he quarrelled both with medical officers in his department and also independent practitioners and at one time refused their students entry to his operations. He was, however, an able administrator and highly respected by his colleagues.

HRA (1), 10, (3), 3, 4; R. W. Giblin, *The early history of Tasmania*, 2 (Melb, 1939); A. McKay (ed), *Journals of the land commissioners for Van Diemen's Land, 1826-28* (Hob, 1962); W. E. L. Crowther, 'Practice and personalities at Hobart Town 1828-1832, as indicated by the day book of James Scott', *MJA*, 20 Mar 1954; CSO 1/606/14062 (TA).

G. H. STANCOMBE

SCOTT, ROBERT (1799?-1844) and HELENUS (1802-1879), settlers, were born at Bombay, India, sons of Dr Helenus Scott and his wife Augusta Maria, daughter of Colonel Charles Frederick. After thirty years of outstanding medical service in India their father's health failed; with his sons he sailed from England in the *Britomart*, planning to spend four years in New South Wales, but died suddenly at sea on 16 November 1821 and was buried at the Cape of Good Hope. His sons arrived at Sydney, where each received a land grant of 2000 acres. Their combined estate, Glendon, on the Hunter River near Singleton, was enlarged by later purchases to about 10,000 acres. The brothers bred blood horses and by 1832 had more than 300 at Glendon. Toss, a Bourbon stallion imported in 1829, Trumpet (1830), Dover (1836) and Akbar, an Arab (1841), as well as colonial-bred stallions and dams of high quality, established the Scotts' reputations as stud-masters. Although the Glendon horses were dispersed in the 1840s they laid sound foundations for the first of the great Hunter valley thoroughbred studs.

Robert, who had been educated at St Andrews, Scotland, and later at Lincoln's Inn, entered fully into the social and political life of the colony's exclusivists. Appointed a magistrate in 1824, he frequently presided at local courts, actively supporting and often initiating attempts to reduce the depredations of Aboriginals and bushrangers. His 'superior education and acquirements' were favourably noticed by Governors Brisbane and Darling; he became a director of the Commercial Banking Co. of Sydney and served on many committees. In 1838, however, after his injudicious and somewhat arrogant defence of the Myall Creek murderers, he was removed from the magistracy; according to Governor Gipps, 'The station, which he held in Society, made it the more necessary to mark the disapprobation of the Government'. Measuring his wealth by quantity rather than quality of land, and totally unskilled in farm management, Scott spent lavishly for small return, but as host to artists, explorers, clergy and scientists he made Glendon a cultural centre unique in its place and time. He died unmarried at Glendon on 30 July 1844.

Helenus preferred life at Glendon to the cavalry cadetcy proffered by relatives. His soundness of character and devoted service as magistrate and district warden of Patrick's Plains weighed more heavily than did his family connexions when Governor Gipps recommended him in 1844 for a colonial order of merit. His brother's early death, the depression of the 1840s and his family's involvement in the failure of the Bank of Australia left him almost penniless. He was appointed a stipendiary magistrate and, after service in several country towns, sold Glendon and settled permanently in Newcastle with his wife Sarah Anne, née Rusden, an accomplished linguist and scholar. He died on 24 August 1879 at the Newcastle police barracks and was buried at Glendon; he was survived by eight children, of whom the most notable was Rose Scott.

On 17 November 1840 Dr Scott's widow, Augusta Maria, died at her home in Cumberland Street, Sydney, aged 65. Her death brought together in New South Wales her six surviving children, of whom only Patrick, the youngest, returned to England, where he died at Glendon, Surrey, in 1887. Another son, David Charles Frederick (1804-1881), who was educated at Woolwich Academy, became a captain in the East India Co.'s service in 1824 and arrived in New South Wales in 1835. He resigned his commission in 1840 and lived for a few years on his grant, Bengalla, near Muswellbrook, before moving to Sydney, where in 1848-49 he edited the short-lived but ambitious *New South Wales Sporting Magazine*. In 1849 he was made a stipendiary magistrate and from 1860 until his death was police magistrate for Sydney. Truly benevolent, Scott used his public office to lend weight to his work for the destitute and his private means were spent freely in many individual cases of need. He was a considerable student of Arabic and Persian and a competent artist, as was his wife Maria Jane, née Barney. Predeceased by his two sons, he died on 16 May 1881 at his home, Lisgar, named after his cousin John Young, Baron Lisgar.

Augusta Maria (1798-1871), the only daughter of Dr Helenus Scott, accompanied her mother to New South Wales in 1832. A voluminous letter writer, she preserved almost intact a century of family correspondence. She shared her mother's informed pleasure in painting, sculpture and the theatre, and before reaching New South Wales she acquired a keen interest in natural history. In 1833 she married Dr James Mitchell [q.v.], with whom she had corresponded for some years.

The Scott brothers came to New South Wales eager to make quick fortunes and to return home. They failed in this ambition and left no concrete contribution to the colony's progress save their thoroughbred stud, but the family's influence on the cultural life of New South Wales was strong and enduring.

HRA (1), 12, 19, 23, 24; D. M. Barrie, *The Australian bloodhorse* (Syd, 1956); SMH, 17 May 1881; Scott family papers (ML); James Mitchell papers (ML).   NANCY GRAY

SCOTT, THOMAS (1800-1855), surveyor and landowner, was the son of George Scott of West Morriston, Earlston, Berwickshire, Scotland, and his wife Betty, née Pringle. After education as a surveyor he came to Hobart Town in 1820 in the *Skelton* and temporarily became superintendent of government stock. Next year he was appointed by Governor Macquarie as assistant surveyor under the deputy-surveyor-general, G. W. Evans [q.v.]. Scott was active in his profession and responsible for surveying much of the early settlements. Between 1822 and 1824 he explored parts of the east coast, laid out the town of Bothwell, and published his chart of Tasmania which showed much more detail than earlier maps. A variant entitled 'A Military Map' was prepared in 1826 but not published. During the 1820s he took up Mount Morriston at the Macquarie River near Ross, to which he and his brother George later added.

In 1824 Evans applied for permission to retire and Scott applied for the vacancy, but when Governor Darling called at Hobart on his way to Sydney he appointed his brother-in-law, Edward Dumaresq [q.v.], as acting-surveyor-general. Lieut-Governor Arthur confirmed the appointment, but reported that he was satisfied with Scott's zeal and abilities and asked that his salary be increased. The Colonial Office then appointed Scott as surveyor-general, but Arthur changed his opinion of Scott's accuracy and honesty, partly because Roderic O'Connor [q.v.] refused to

serve as a land commissioner under him. More important, Scott had become implicated in accusations against Evans, who had accepted bribes to measure holdings in excess of areas granted. In 1826 the Executive Council inquired into these charges and reported that both surveyors were at fault, but excused Scott for acquiescing in the errors of his senior officer. As a result George Frankland [q.v.] was appointed surveyor-general, Dumaresq acted as chief land commissioner and Scott continued as assistant surveyor.

In 1826 Scott took a party to Adventure Bay and South Cape to explore coal seams, but reported that the shaft and the road to the mine were too arduous undertakings. His party established friendly relations with the local Aboriginals. In 1828 he examined Port Arthur as a place for settlement. Next year he accompanied Arthur on a journey from Hobart to Mole Creek and through the Van Diemen's Land Co.'s land at Middlesex Plains, Surrey Hills, Hampshire Hills and Emu Bay. The company's proposed grants were based on Scott's map, but it misled the manager, E. Curr [q.v.], who deduced from it that the north-western country was isolated from other settlements by several days travel through impassable mountains.

In 1829 Captain Edward Boyd [q.v.] was appointed deputy surveyor-general, despite Scott's protests, but although still third in the department he was promoted senior assistant surveyor in 1830. In 1832 he became surveyor for the County of Cornwall. About this time he took up residence at Bowhill, Glen Dhu, Launceston; he also gave the town of Deloraine its name, taking it from the *Lay of the Last Minstrel*, by his kinsman, Sir Walter Scott. In the same year his plan of Launceston was published for the *Hobart Town Almanac* by James Ross [q.v.]. In 1833 Boyd was sent to Launceston to open a branch of the survey office and Scott was moved to George Town. In 1835 he married Ann Reid. Next year he obtained two years leave to visit Scotland, and arranged for his brother James to be his deputy, each to share equally his annual salary of £350. Soon after his return he resigned and devoted himself to his own land and business interests. On his death at Earlston in 1855 he had amassed a fortune estimated at £107,800.

JAMES SCOTT (1810-1884) arrived in Hobart in the *Ann Jamieson* in 1832. He was trained as a surveyor by his brother Thomas and worked with him, and on his resignation in 1838 joined the staff of the Survey Department. The appointment was short-lived. Next year when contract surveying was introduced he was approved as a surveyor to be paid on piecework. Of strong physique and an excellent bushman, he became the chief surveyor in the north. In 1845 he married Agnes Mathie McGown, by whom he had eleven children. He made his home at Bowhill.

James Scott is best known for his explorations of the north-east. In April 1852 he was engaged by the government to find a bridle road for stock from the last settlement on St Patrick's River to Cape Portland, a vast area not previously crossed by white man. He went up St Patrick's River, passed north-west of Mount Maurice to what he thought was Forester's River, over a tier to the Ringarooma River, which he followed south-east of Mount Cameron to Cape Portland, and then returned to Launceston along the coast. He reported adversely: any track would be very costly and devoid of resting places for stock. He proposed instead a line by way of Piper's River, across the Little Forester about three miles above Bowood and then north-east to the Tomahawk and Ringarooma Rivers. In October 1852 he marked out this road. Next January he applied for government assistance to open up a line of communication from St Patrick's River along his former route to the Ringarooma River. He was promised £40 for this task but declined on the ground of ill health and other business. However, both he and his brother George applied for land on the Ringarooma River at what is now Legerwood, and by November 1853 he reported that he had completed a bridle road and that the land supposed to be on the Great Forester's River was on the main branch of the Ringarooma River. A little later he found fertile land in the near-by Scottsdale district, which was named after him.

For most of the 1850s Scott was the only surveyor in Launceston. In 1853 the department ceased to give him work, but not for long as no other surveyors could be found. When again offered a government post he refused it and continued to work on contract. He did much of the early survey of Port Sorell and Devonport. When the lands of the Cressy Land Co. were broken up about 1854 he did the survey. He did not like 'teaching young men who might oppose me later', but in 1856 when Thomas's two sons arrived he trained the elder, James Reid Scott. After 1860 he restricted his activities as a surveyor. He owned many properties and an interest in a coal mine at the Don River, was a director of the British and Tasmanian Charcoal Iron Co., and a foundation

director and later chairman of the Mutual Fire Insurance Co. He was appointed a justice of the peace in 1862. He served on the Launceston City Council, and in 1879 was chairman of the Launceston General Hospital Board. For some years he was chairman of the Paterson's Plains Road Trust. Independent of any political party, he was a member of the House of Assembly for George Town in 1869-77 and for South Launceston from 1878 until his death in 1884.

Hobart Town Gazette, 22 Feb 1839; *Examiner* (Launceston), 3 July 1855; S. M. Franks, Land exploration in Tasmania, 1824-42 (M.A. thesis, Univ Tas, 1958); GO 1/3/228 & 357, 1/5/402, 1/11/183, 1/29/57 & 148 (TA); GO 33/3/201 (TA); CSO 1 & 5 (TA); LSD 1 (TA); Scott letters (Queen Victoria Museum, Launceston).   G. H. CRAWFORD

SCOTT, THOMAS ALISON (1777?-1881), pioneer sugar grower, was born in Glasgow, Scotland, the son of Thomas Scott, merchant, and his wife Elizabeth, née Rhodey. He claimed to be the brother of Admiral Sir James Scott. He was first sent to his uncle Thomas Rhodey, a merchant and insurance broker of Liverpool, for training in business, and was then taken to St Thomas in the West Indies by Sir James Bonstein, who procured the appointment of customs searcher and waiter for him. In 1797 he went to Antigua where he managed his father's estate for several years. After visiting sugar plantations in Louisiana he called at Sydney about 1816 on his way to Calcutta. Impressed with the potential of New South Wales for sugar growing, Scott decided to stay.

In 1820 he went to Tahiti to establish a sugar plantation, having been engaged by Edward Eagar [q.v.], but stayed only a few months because the necessary machinery was at Raiatea. He was then asked by Rev. John Williams to establish sugar production at Raiatea in 1822; for this he was paid by the London Missionary Society. Major Goulburn [q.v.] learnt of his success there and in December 1823 engaged him to grow sugar and tobacco at Port Macquarie, at a salary of £250. The sugar he produced there in 1824 appears to have been the first in Australia, and large quantities of his sugar and tobacco were sold at the commissariat store in Sydney. The venture was not an unqualified success, for in 1825 Scott was suspended, and a commission of inquiry in 1828 commented unfavourably on his work. Governor Darling reported in 1830 that before the commission was set up Scott had been found unqualified for the management of such an establishment, and he had subsequently been dismissed and the production of sugar abandoned because no one could replace him.

Scott received an order for a land grant of 1280 acres, but exchanged it for 320 acres which he considered highly suitable for sugar growing, only to find it had been set aside for the township of Gosford. He was allowed to retain 25 acres and select another 640 acres elsewhere. In 1837 he applied without success for compensation for the loss he claimed to have sustained in this transfer. On his land, which he named Point Clare, Scott established a model sugar plantation, but he lacked the capital to buy the machinery needed for commercial success. He supplemented his income by government employment, being postmaster at Brisbane Water in 1836-40, clerk of petty sessions in 1836-43 on a salary of £100, and also poundkeeper and coroner for a time. He raised tobacco and bananas, for which he won prizes at the Floral and Horticultural Society shows in 1840 and 1841.

For many years Scott carried on a vigorous campaign for the introduction of sugar on a commercial basis in the colony. He later claimed to have directly influenced the beginnings of the industry at Kiama and on the Manning River, and to have supplied Captain Hope, who began sugar growing in Queensland, with plants and instructions. He exhibited sugar at the Melbourne and Paris Exhibitions. In 1866 he petitioned the Legislative Assembly for a reward for his public services and his case was taken up by Rev. J. D. Lang [q.v.]. A select committee was formed in 1869 to decide his case, and Scott gave evidence of his pioneering work carried out at a financial loss. Many of his claims were denied by Rev. Edward Holland, who also claimed to have pioneered the industry, but the committee nevertheless agreed to Lang's motion to present Scott with a gratuity of £1000. He was eventually granted a pension of £240 instead, much to his disappointment, for he feared his family would soon be left destitute.

Scott married Mary Anne Crone of Port Macquarie on 17 December 1827 at Scots Church, Sydney; they had seven daughters and five sons. He died at Point Clare on 16 October 1881, aged 105, and was buried at Point Frederick. Mary Anne Scott died on 19 August 1905, aged 94.

HRA (1), 15, 19; C. Swancott, *The Brisbane Water story*, 4 (Woy Woy, 1955); A. G. Lowndes, *South Pacific enterprise* (Syd, 1956); J. Jervis, 'T. A. Scott and the genesis of the sugar industry', *JRAHS*, 26 (1940); *Sydney Gazette*, 25 Aug 1821; MS cat under T. A. Scott (ML).
VIVIENNE PARSONS

SCOTT, THOMAS HOBBES (1783-1860), Church of England clergyman, was baptized on 24 April 1783 at Kelmscott, Oxford, England, one of the youngest of eight children of James Scott, sometime vicar of Itchen Stoke, Hampshire, and chaplain ordinary to George III, and his wife Jane Elizabeth, née Harmood. Of his four brothers, three matriculated at Oxford, and of his three sisters, Jane Elizabeth was married to Edward Harley, fifth earl of Oxford, Charlotte to Thomas Hanway Bigge, and Mary to William Ord, M.P. for Morpeth. When his father died in 1794 T. H. Scott received no inheritance, but he went to France, became a vice-consul at Bordeaux and was reputed to have been a wine merchant. At 30 he matriculated and entered St Alban's Hall, Oxford (B.A., 1817; M.A., 1818).

In 1819 when his brother-in-law J. T. Bigge [q.v.], was appointed commissioner to investigate the affairs of New South Wales Scott was appointed his secretary, with the right to succeed Bigge if he died or was incapacitated. He returned to England with Bigge, was consulted at the Colonial Office and submitted plans for chaplains and schools in the colony. He was ordained deacon in 1821, advanced to the priesthood in 1822 and appointed rector of Whitfield, in the diocese of Durham. The British government reconstituted the ecclesiastical affairs of the colony by creating, under letters patent, an archdeaconry of New South Wales in the diocese of Calcutta. On 2 October 1824 through William Ord's persuasion Scott accepted appointment as archdeacon of New South Wales with authority in the dependencies of New South Wales, including Van Diemen's Land, at a salary of £2000 with allowances. He was given almost complete control of ecclesiastical matters in the colony and the archdeaconry was constituted a body corporate with perpetual succession. He took rank and precedence next to the lieut-governor, and was an ex officio member of the Legislative Council.

As an administrator Scott was tireless and exacting. He visited every part of his archdeaconry and made two long visits to Van Diemen's Land, where Lieut-Governor Arthur was an admired friend and adviser. No detail of church management was too small for this bachelor dignitary. He appointed teachers, sextons and clerks, negotiated for sites of churches and schools, and demanded exhaustive returns and reports from his chaplains, of whom there were, when he arrived, nine on the mainland and two in Van Diemen's Land. Although he reprimanded most of them from time to time, he remained on good terms with the senior chaplain, Samuel Marsden [q.v.]. In his official visits to churches and schools he investigated affairs thoroughly and sympathetically. He had great concern for the pastoral welfare of the people and he constantly appealed for more clergy, new buildings, equipment and money. He reported in detail to his bishop and sent him copies of direct correspondence with the Ecclesiastical Board for the Colonies, the archbishop of Canterbury and the bishop of London, but communication between India and Sydney took so long that the administration of the archdeaconry from Calcutta proved impractical and in some subjects Scott became independent of his bishop.

Scott was appointed King's visitor of schools by the Colonial Office and thus became virtually responsible for the colony's public education. His educational policy was guided by the principle that the church and education were inseparably connected, the funds to sustain them being administered by the same trustees. Since this view was shared by the Colonial Office, Bathurst in March 1826 erected the Corporation of the Trustees of Church and School Lands granting one-seventh of the lands of New South Wales to the corporation for the purposes of the Church of England and education in the colony. Scott was ex-officio vice-president. He placed special importance on his work for education and set out, as visitor, to build schools throughout the colony, establish teacher-training centres, inaugurate secondary education, and encourage mechanics' institutes. He set up a School of Industry for training servant girls and helped the work of the male and the female orphan schools. But despite this considerable effort and some progress in setting up schools the development of education facilities was slow. The corporation was too big in conception, impractical and unwieldy, and delay in the surveys denied quick access to resources. Nevertheless Scott made a major contribution by drawing attention to the need for public financial support of colonial education, its proper control, and an adequate supply and training of teachers. He kept the governor and Colonial Office well informed on educational matters, and his advice and findings had considerable influence. Scott had been in-

structed to pursue the civilization and conversion of the Aboriginals. In 1826 he appointed Richard Sadleir [q.v.] to conduct a peaceful mission to the natives in the County of Argyle and established a school of reading, carpentry and needlework for Aboriginals at Blacktown. He deplored the brutal treatment of the Tasmanian Aboriginals.

Scott was a Tory and unpopular with the progressives of the colony. He was a friend and admirer of John Macarthur [q.v.] and in 1829 won high praise from Governor Darling who wrote, 'his zeal in the performance of his professional duties, as well as in the discharge of those which are attached to him as a member of the Government has been unabated'. However, Darling had written to Under-Secretary Hay in October 1826 that Scott's connexion with Bigge and his 'Constant Association' with the Macarthurs deprived him of any chance of popularity in the colony. Inevitably Scott was persistently abused by the *Australian* and E. S. Hall's [q.v.] *Monitor*. The shortcomings of the Church and School Corporation were laid at his door. He was criticized as a supporter of Darling, for holding shares in the Australian Agricultural Co., for opposing the establishment of a theatre, for having been a merchant, for receiving so large a salary. Many of the attacks were mere abuse and innuendo. The combative and uncompromising archdeacon became involved in many lawsuits, some trivial and some important. He expressed his anger with Hall by locking his pew in St James's Church against him. Hall forced the lock, whereupon Scott had the pew decked over. On one occasion Hall and his family sat on the steps at the altar rail. Legal actions followed: Hall was found guilty of trespass and criminal libel; in a third action Hall obtained damages from Scott, which were later paid by the government. Scott also had several disputes with the Roman Catholic priest, J. J. Therry [q.v.] and was frequently under attack from J. D. Lang [q.v.] whom he described as his 'slanderer-general'.

Scott apparently found little satisfaction in his position as archdeacon, for he had not contemplated a long stay in the colony and had left a curate in charge of his English parish. In October 1826 Darling reported that Scott appeared 'very ill at ease' and spoke of returning to England. In July 1827 he wrote to Arthur that he daily wished for release from his duties and in 1828 his brother-in-law, William Ord, reported to the Colonial Office that Scott would willingly give up his £2000 a year for £200 at home. However, he did not resign until 16 September 1829, when he was replaced by Archdeacon W. G. Broughton [q.v.].

On his return voyage to England in H.M.S. *Success* the ship struck a reef off Fremantle in November and Scott was marooned at the new Swan River settlement. For the first two months he was the only ordained minister at Perth. With help from settlers and particularly the garrison, he built a temporary church, where he held the colony's first Christmas service and the first Holy Communion. When the colonial chaplain, J. B. Wittenoom [q.v.], arrived Scott gave him brotherly assistance and unofficial advice, and won such popular regard that the village of Kelmscott was named after his birthplace. He sailed for England in the *William* by way of Batavia, where in November 1830 he opened an English chapel.

In England Scott resumed his parish at Whitfield, was appointed archdeacon there in 1841 and became an honorary canon of Durham Cathedral in 1845. His property in Sydney, Parramatta and County Argyle was a source of constant anxiety especially in the depression of the 1840s, and helped to retain his interest in the progress of New South Wales. He was also deeply concerned with British politics and in 1836 wrote to Arthur, 'I feel confident that the only chance of avoiding a revolution in Church & State is to reform the gross & barefaced abuses in both; & instead of the former being an overgrown & most partially paid & ill supplied medium thro' which pure religion is administered to the country . . . we should have an efficient ministry & something more than temporalities to look after'. Scott died, unmarried, on 1 January 1860 at Whitfield, leaving an estate valued at less than £800, and bequeathing his family Bible, his gun and his specimens of art to his relations.

Although arbitrary and autocratic, Scott made an energetic and honest endeavour to fulfil his spiritual mission. His work in New South Wales was significant because of the attempt to 'establish' the Church of England in New South Wales. Although opposition to the 'establishment' led to its abandonment by 1836 when the Church Act was passed, Scott's systematic organization helped to make possible the erection of an episcopate.

HRA (1), 10-16; W. W. Burton, *The state of religion and education in New South Wales* (Lond, 1840); R. A. Giles, *Constitutional history of the Australian Church* (Lond, 1929); E. C. Rowland, *A century of the English Church in New South Wales* (Syd, 1948); Ross Border, *Church and State in Australia 1788-1872* (Lond, 1962); F. L. Wood, 'Some early educational problems', *JRAHS*, 17 (1931); A. Burton, 'Notes on three archdeacons', *JRWAHS*, 2 (1932-36); R. T. Wyatt, 'A wine merchant in gaiters', *JRAHS*, 35 (1949-50); MS cat under T. H. Scott (ML).

ROSS BORDER

SEAL, CHARLES (1801-1852), merchant, pastoralist, shipowner and whaler, was born at Whissonsett, Norfolk, England, the second son of Richard Seal and his wife Sarah, née Pressley. He arrived in Van Diemen's Land in the *Regalia* in January 1823, bringing property worth £796 and received a grant of 600 acres on the Lower Clyde. He established himself as a merchant in Hobart Town in partnership with Edward Rand and took general cargo to Mauritius by way of the Swan River settlement in 1830. He visited England in 1826 and again in 1830, when, on 2 December at South Creake, Norfolk, he married Phillis, tenth child of Henry Goggs and Martha, née Buscall. In 1835 he became sub-tenant of his brother-in-law Matthew Goggs and rented Maria Island at £180 a year, establishing there two whaling stations and depasturing 2400 sheep. He was in England in 1839 when his lease expired and his agent bid for a five year lease at a total of £513, but the government claimed this was an annual rental. After protests extending over two years the matter was settled in Seal's favour.

In the 1830s he had a short partnership with Judah Solomon and a shop in Murray Street. He was on the Hobart committee of the Bank of Van Diemen's Land and a trustee of the Hobart Town Savings Bank. In 1846 he was elected a town commissioner. He was on the local committee of the London Agency for Van Diemen's Land and, from 1845 onwards, of the Regatta Association.

By 1850 he owned the biggest whaling fleet in the colony, with his shipping office at 20 Salamanca Place, Hobart. Among his ships were the *Highlander*, *Sussex*, *Southern Cross*, *Cheviot*, *Litherland*, *Pacific*, *Dundee Merchant*, *Prince Leopold*, *Pride* and *Maria Orr*. His *Eamont*, under Captain Lovitt, is thought to have made the first known contact between Australia and Japan; wrecked off Akkeshi on the island of Hokkaido in May 1850, the ship's crew was kept under guard through the winter and then transferred to Nagasaki where, after much questioning on the English and trade, they were taken in October to Batavia by a Dutch ship and thence to Adelaide. Seal's *Prince Regent* had been William IV's yacht, and his *Aladdin* had seen action as the *Mutine* in the battle of the Nile.

Seal died in Hobart at his residence, St Kilda House, 13 Macquarie Street, on 9 November 1852, well liked for his genial character and the honesty which characterized his business dealings. By his will he left property worth £33,000 to his family. He was survived by his wife and five of their ten children; a daughter Phillis married Charles, eldest son of George Carr Clark [q.v.] of Ellenthorpe, Ross.

J. E. Philp, *Whaling ways of Hobart Town* (Hob, 1936); *Hobart Town Gazette*, 29 July 1826; *Colonial Times*, 1 Jan 1830; *Hobart Town Courier*, 15 Mar 1851, 18 Nov 1852; CSO 1/187/4495, 8/31/321 (TA); Private papers in possession of Sir William Crowther, Hob, and the author.   PATRICIA FOSTER

SECCOMBE, WILLIAM (1796?-1864), surgeon, was born at Plymouth, England, the son of a surgeon. He became a member of the Royal College of Surgeons in 1818 and next year a licentiate of the Society of Apothecaries.

In May 1824 he arrived in Hobart Town in the *Adrian* as surgeon to Lieut-Governor Arthur and his suite and was immediately appointed assistant surgeon at Pittwater with the privilege of attending the Colonial Hospital, Hobart. Next year he attended the military garrison. He took leave of absence in April 1829, caring for military invalids travelling with him to Chatham in the *Mermaid*. In England he had his leave extended to assist his father in a cholera epidemic in Plymouth and in 1833 received a presentation from Plymouth for his help.

On return to the colony he took charge of the Colonial Hospital in Launceston where, despite heavy responsibilities with the penitentiary, factory, house of correction and the military, he was allowed private practice as well. It was as head of this hospital that he was first criticized for neglect of duty when a prisoner died of pneumonia. Seccombe's evidence only incriminated himself and his assistant was cleared of the charge of manslaughter. Much indignation was felt therefore when Seccombe sat as judge that year in the Court of Quarter Sessions.

After this episode Seccombe was transferred to the Hobart Town Hospital in 1840. Because the salary was inadequate he applied next year for appointment as immigration and health officer for the port of Hobart, but was unsuccessful. He was therefore relieved when the lieut-governor supported his right to charge for profes-

sional attendance to the family of a half-pay officer, Major Welman, who had challenged his account. In 1842 he joined colleagues in appealing for larger salaries since the increase in convict department duties no longer permitted supplementary private practice. They won improved standing and, with sixteen years service, Seccombe's salary was increased from 10s. to 15s. a day.

Encouraged by this success and temporary appointment as principal medical officer in 1844, he asked that his title be changed from assistant colonial surgeon to colonial surgeon. His request met no encouragement. An application for the position of Hobart Town coroner at this time was equally unsuccessful. In June he was appointed to the Court of Medical Examiners. A squabble in 1845 with a fellow surgeon, C. G. Casey [q.v.] who, egged on by two malicious women patients, reported Seccombe's neglect and later denied it, was investigated by a board. Seccombe was cleared of the charge, but ill feeling continued. In April insolvency added to his worries.

From July 1846 to September 1851 he was surgeon to the gaol and police in Hobart, but another charge of neglect and irregular performance of duty, this time from the principal medical officer, led to his transfer as medical officer to the Impression Bay convict station. There misunderstandings arose with the superintendent of the station, and in March 1853 Seccombe was brought back to the Hobart Town Hospital. He was appointed to the Commission of the Peace, coroner and then senior colonial surgeon; in 1855 he was sent to Port Arthur as resident medical officer.

After his marriage in March 1827 to Sophia, the second daughter of A. F. Kemp [q.v.] and his second wife Elizabeth, née Riley, Seccombe received land in Hobart and built Tremayne in Macquarie Street. He had acquired 2000 acres at Melton Mowbray, but it was to Hobart that he retired, and in Hobart that he died on 6 November 1864. His wife predeceased him in July 1860. Of their family, Fanny Maria married Sir Valentine Fleming as his second wife, and Ella Georgina married the Rev. F. B. Sharland.

That he should have continued in the government service for forty years, despite a lack of responsibility and an uncooperative nature, surely supports his obituarist's high estimation of his surgical skill.

Correspondence file under Seccombe (TA).

J. BRUCE HAMILTON

SEYMOUR-SYMERS, THOMAS LYELL (1797-1884), sea-trader, generally known as Symers, was born in Brechin, Scotland, the eldest son of Thomas Seymour-Symers, Presbyterian minister, and his wife, Clementine, the daughter of James Carnegie, a younger son of the earl of Southesk. Educated by his father, he entered the East India Co.'s service and was second mate in the *Blenden Hall* in 1821 when wrecked on Inaccessible Island in the South Atlantic. Later at Coringa in India he built the *Caledonia* in which he traded between India, China and Australian ports, and explored the southern coast of Australia for harbours. In 1830 he married Mary Johnstone, a Madras banker's daughter.

Four years later he settled in Albany, Western Australia. There he explored, inaugurated the first regular shipping service, and imported cattle and horses from India and sheep from Van Diemen's Land. On a trading voyage to Sydney in 1840 he became involved with the French whaler *La Ville de Bordeaux*; its seizure by Robert Richard Torrens in Adelaide, for a suspected breach of the navigation laws, caused years of litigation and Symer's bankruptcy. Losing the *Caledonia* for debt, Symers returned to Albany, determined to mend his fortunes and seek 'justice'. With his family's help he made money, but was permanently soured by a final, no-claim French court decision concerning *La Ville de Bordeaux*. Perforce now a land-lubber, he stood for the Town Trust and took active, and sometimes violent, part in such local affairs as the harbour, roads, timber industry, whaling and copper-mining. He died at Albany on 23 November 1884. He had four sons and three daughters. A dynamic, wide-visioned, controversial, aggressive figure, his papers and family records tell the progressive, pioneering story of Albany district.

R. Glover, 'Captain Symers at Albany', *JRWAHS*, 4 (1949-54); R. Glover, Captain Symers, trader (M.A. thesis, Univ WA, 1952), and for bibliog; Symers collection, family papers and documents 1821-75 (WAA); Papers relating to the seizure of *La Ville de Bordeaux* (SAA).
RHODA GLOVER

SHADFORTH, THOMAS (1771?-1862), soldier and company director, was born in England, the son of Henry Shadforth, a landed proprietor. He became a lieutenant in the 47th Regiment in September 1798 and was transferred to the 57th Regiment as captain in May 1802. In 1811 he was wounded at the battle of Albuera in Spain and promoted major. About 1801 in Bermuda he had married Frances, née Hinson.

Shadforth, who had been promoted lieut-colonel in August 1819, arrived in Sydney with the 57th Regiment in the *Mangles* in February 1826, accompanied by his wife and their daughter Frances. Their eldest son Henry John Tudor, a lieutenant in the 57th, had arrived in the *Minstrel* in August 1825, and the second son, Thomas, who had been made an ensign in the 57th in 1825, arrived probably about the same time. Another son, Robert William, after completing his education in England, arrived at Sydney in the *Sovereign* in May 1835.

In June 1828 Governor Darling appointed Shadforth president of a board to check and destroy commissariat notes in the military chest, to list those still in circulation so that they could be called in, and to destroy the plates from which they had been struck. These tasks were promptly carried out. When the 57th Regiment was ordered to India in 1831 Shadforth, then 60, decided to resign and settle in New South Wales. He bought Ravenswood, 640 acres, at Mulgoa, and for the next thirty years was a leader in the commercial and social life of Sydney. In January 1833 he became honorary secretary of the Australian Subscription Library, established in 1826, and the precursor of the Public Library of New South Wales. In June he was appointed a director of the reorganized Bank of Australia and remained on the board until the bank failed in March 1843. In 1835 he became president of the Australian Wheat and Flour Co. and of the Australian Union Benefit Society, in 1836 deputy-chairman of the Australian Gaslight Co., and a director of the Fire and Life Assurance Co., in June 1839 a trustee of the Illawarra Steam Co. and in 1841 a trustee of the Savings Bank of New South Wales. In 1842 he was a member of the association formed to seek permission to import labourers from India.

He died at Eveleigh House, Redfern, Sydney, on 4 August 1862; his wife had died at Ravenswood on 6 October 1850, aged 79. Their son Henry became the first serjeant-at-arms of the New South Wales Legislative Assembly in 1856-60 and usher of the black rod of the Legislative Council in 1860-83; he married on 10 March 1828 Mary Anne, daughter of Judge Stephen [q.v.] of the Supreme Court of New South Wales, and died on 21 September 1890. Thomas became a lieut-colonel in November 1854 and was killed at Sebastopol in the Crimean war, leaving a widow and four daughters. Frances married on 12 May

1829 Francis Stephen, fifth son of Judge Stephen.

HRA (1), 12, 14, 18, 20, 21, 24, 25; *Australian*, 2 Dec 1831, 28 June 1833, 13, 17 Mar 1835, 19 Apr, 31 May, 5 July 1836, 22 Jan, 6 June, 29 Aug 1839, 18 Nov 1841; MS cat under T. Shadforth (ML).

SHARLAND, WILLIAM STANLEY (1801-1877), surveyor, was the son of John Sharland, surgeon, and his wife Mary Jane, née Culley. John Sharland made a 'moderate fortune' in India, where he was on the staff of the governor-general, Sir John Shore, later Baron Teignmouth (1751-1834). On his return to England he bought land at high post-war prices and began farming. In the 1820s he fell on difficult times and, with a recommendation from Teignmouth, emigrated to Van Diemen's Land where he arrived with his two sons William and John Frederick (1797?-1870) in the *Elizabeth* in July 1823. He settled on some 1800 acres near Hamilton. His wife, Jane, and daughter, Anne Jane, joined him in April 1825. In 1829 he was appointed surgeon at Bothwell and in 1835 was gazetted a justice of the peace for the territory. In 1836 his wife died. In 1853 he retired from practice, and he died at Hamilton on 6 November 1855, aged 93.

Soon after his arrival William Sharland joined the Survey Department under G. W. Evans [q.v.] as a copying clerk. He soon became an acting assistant surveyor at a salary of £100. When E. Dumaresq [q.v.] took charge of the Survey Office he gave Sharland more responsible work and in February 1827, supporting a recommendation by the Executive Council that Sharland's salary be raised from £100 to £200, praised his zeal and perseverance and commended his survey and plan of Launceston, his line of road across the island, and his plan of streets and areas of Hobart Town; he did as much work as any two assistants. The Colonial Office approved the increase in August 1828. Sharland explored the sources of the Derwent River and claimed to have discovered Lake St Clair in 1827. He laid out New Norfolk, Hamilton, Oatlands, Bothwell and Brighton. Despite his protests he was retrenched from the Survey Department in 1839 after the arrival of G. Frankland [q.v.] and employed as a contract surveyor.

Meanwhile Sharland had become a large landholder. When he arrived he was granted 400 acres adjoining his father's land. By June 1828 he had 1000 acres and 1250 sheep, and employed a free overseer at £40 a year and two assigned servants. In June 1828 he was granted an additional 1000 acres and by 1831 had leased 2200 acres at New Norfolk and been granted 560 more. By 1828 he was also a pioneer hop-grower and in 1847 imported 50,000 sets from a nursery in Kent.

In 1832 he was engaged in a dispute with Edward Abbott about the ownership of 460 acres which Sharland claimed but which a tribunal granted to Abbott. In July Abbott averred that Sharland had dealt in land while in the Survey Department and was occupying 3000 acres adjoining his own grant without paying rent, to the exclusion of other settlers. Sharland replied that he had never bought or sold a grant; his land was all granted by the government and improved under his father's expert direction; the 3000 acres referred to was in fact 1800 acres rented by his father until the government put them up for sale.

Sharland was a constant visitor at Government House in the days of Franklin, Denison and Young, and in 1849 he was appointed to the Legislative Council. After responsible government he was elected to the Legislative Council in 1857-60, and then represented New Norfolk in the House of Assembly in 1861-72. In 1835 he had married Frances Sara, daughter of Major Schaw [q.v.]; they had six sons and eight daughters. After her death in March 1859 he married Margaret Fyfe, of Mount Nodd. He was a devoted member of the Church of England and for many years a member of synod. He died on 23 October 1877 and was buried at New Norfolk.

John Frederick, the elder brother, returned to England where he qualified as a surgeon. Back in Van Diemen's Land in 1828 he again received a grant and was appointed a district surgeon at 3s. a day. He practised at Bothwell until 1838 and then at Hamilton, winning great respect and affection. In April 1835 he was a foundation member of the Bothwell Literary Society, and in June married Mary Jane, the youngest daughter of Major James Culley. Later he sat in the House of Assembly from 1861 to 1865. Anne Sharland opened a school at Woodlands, Hobart, in 1825, moved it to Roxburgh House, Liverpool Street, in 1827, and in July 1830 married William Barnes [q.v.]. After his death in 1848 she married in 1856 Captain Edwin Whiting, of Kelso, Tasmania.

HRA (3), 4-6; P. L. Brown (ed), *Clyde Company papers*, 1-5 (Lond, 1941-63); Correspondence file under Sharland (TA).

SHAW, GEORGE (1751-1813), naturalist, was born on 10 December 1751 at Bierton, Buckinghamshire, England, son of Rev. Timothy Shaw. He was educated by his father until 1765 when he entered Magdalen College, Oxford (B.A., 1769; M.A., 1772). He was ordained deacon in 1774. Because of his love of natural history he abandoned the church as a profession, studied medicine at Edinburgh for three years, and then returned to Oxford as deputy-lecturer in botany. In 1787 he was admitted to the degrees of M.B. and M.D., after which he began practice in London. He took part in founding the Linnean Society of London in 1788 and in 1789 was elected a fellow of the Royal Society. In 1791 he was appointed to the natural history section of the British Museum, and in 1807 became keeper, a position he retained until his death on 22 July 1813.

Shaw's life as a professional naturalist coincided with the early years of the colonization of eastern Australia. The colonists were very interested in the novel fauna which they encountered, and specimens of the strange creatures were sent to Sir Joseph Banks [q.v.] and other savants in England. Many of the novelties came into the hands of Shaw and he published the first descriptions with scientific names of several of the common and best known Australian animals, for example, the platypus, echidna, wombat, budgerigar and black snake. He provided the well-known generic name (*Macropus*) for the common grey kangaroo.

Shaw could not conceal his scepticism when describing so extraordinary a creature as the platypus and was not entirely convinced that the specimen was not a fake. It was the only one known at the time and is still preserved in the British Museum (Natural History). Among the many animals first made known to science by Shaw was the remarkable Australian musk duck, described from a historic specimen collected at King George Sound in 1791 when that place was discovered and named by George Vancouver [q.v.].

As was common among naturalists of his day Shaw covered a wide field and the subjects of his accounts include mammals, birds, reptiles, fishes and some invertebrates. The chief works in which he described Australian animals are: *Zoology of New Holland* (1794), *The Naturalists' Miscellany* : . . 1-24 (1789-1813), and *General Zoology*, 1-8 (1800-12). He also contributed part of the account of the animals in John White's [q.v.] *Journal of a Voyage to New South Wales* . . . (1790).

The majority are contained in the *Naturalists' Miscellany*, and are accompanied by coloured engravings by Frederick Polydore Nodder. The descriptions are brief and some of the subjects cannot be identified without Nodder's mediocre illustrations. Shaw's standards were typical of his day, however, and it was not until later, when intensive exploration of the non-European world brought to light such a wealth of previously unknown creatures, that detailed critical descriptions were found to be a necessity.

J. H. CALABY

SHAW, THOMAS (1800?-1865?), wool expert, was born in Yorkshire, England. He started work as a woolsorter in boyhood, and later became a woolbuyer and preparer of wools for various manufacturers. His attention was early drawn to wools from Australia, and he noticed 'inexplicable' changes and deterioration in their quality. When, therefore, his employers, J. T. Simes & Co., London, who already recognized a time of crisis and of opportunity, responded to a request from Robert Campbell [q.v.] & Co., Sydney, for 'a competent person as buyer and sorter and instructor of sorters', Shaw arrived with his second son, Thomas, aged 15, in September 1843, determined 'to get as speedily as possible amongst sheep and try to . . . clear up this mystery which so much puzzled us'.

He travelled extensively through the eastern Australian colonies and New Zealand, observing climatic, soil and working conditions, noting the casual, unselective methods of sheep-breeding current on many properties. In 1849 at Melbourne, helped by G. S. Lang [q.v.], he published a pamphlet, *The Australian Merino*, which began a sharp controversy. Shaw urged Australian growers to consider precisely what English buyers wanted, to breed sheep fit for the purpose, and to prepare their wool better, particularly by washing it more carefully before shearing. The 'Pure Australian Merino' should be the target, but as yet there was little promise and much backsliding. Australian growers, Shaw declared, 'know nothing whatever about wool'; by haphazard breeding they had produced 'a mongrel breed, in which may be found every shade between the real Australian Merino and the dried-up Leicester, mixed with myriads not fit to class as respectable goats'; their disregard of environment exposed their flocks to disease or 'the transmutation of . . .

fleeces into scrubbing brushes'. Natural protests were led by one 'Ignoramus', who in the Melbourne *Morning Herald*, 1 August 1849, condemned Shaw as a mere new-comer and claimed that the squatters were doing as well as possible, considering their shortage of funds and labour. But Shaw had gained welcome publicity: improvement of wool by wiser breeding and management was brought very much to the fore.

In 1850 Shaw 'was very influential in forming the Merino Import Company', as he then believed that occasional infusions of new blood might improve the acclimatized sheep. This project failed and in 1860 from the Darling Downs he produced as a Sydney publication his *Practical Treatise on Sheep Breeding and Wool Growing*, based on his original principle, 'suit the breed to the character of climate and pasture'; he urged: 'import no more foreign sheep of any description, but breed entirely from the Australian merino'. Especially in the Western District of Victoria, leading men, impressed by his logic and will to help them, had gradually adopted his methods. Flocks bred without crossing had become resistant to disease, and their wool 'Australian' in character. J. L. Currie of Larra believed that to Shaw was due 'the formation of the Australian merino'. But Shaw warned, 'it would take but a short time to spoil it; one cross with any foreign sheep, and the character of the offspring is changed, the Australian qualities spoiled'. He was a tough, aggressive little man, who throve on argument and opposition. By his work with such leaders as Currie, the Learmonths of Ercildoun and Philip Russell of Carngham [qq.v.], he converted many sceptics.

In 1823 Shaw had married Ann Turner, by whom he had two sons and five daughters, who all settled in Australia. Jonathan, the elder son, became the leading sheep classer of his day. Thomas Shaw junior worked with his father for a time, and was so like him in character and interests that they are often confused. Both were apt to wander about Australia. But the son was teetotal, and anchored himself to his Wooriwyrite station. The father seems to have had no settled home; what money he had, he spent on drink. He is supposed to have died in the late 1860s in New South Wales, but his death is not officially recorded there.

P. L. Brown (ed), *Clyde Company papers*, 4 (Lond, 1959); M. L. Kiddle, *Men of yesterday* (Melb, 1961); *Port Phillip Gazette*, 15 Apr 1843.   LYNDSAY GARDINER

SHELLEY (SHELLY), WILLIAM (1774-1815), missionary and trader, was born on 29 May 1774 at Hanley, Staffordshire, England, where his family had long been associated with the local potteries. He was apprenticed to a cabinet maker at Leek, joined the Congregational Church in 1794 and volunteered as an artisan missionary to the (London) Missionary Society. He was one of the party which sailed in the *Duff* in 1796 with Rev. J. F. Cover [q.v.] and was a member of the original mission to Tonga. When the Tongans killed three missionaries in 1799 he escaped and next year went to Sydney in the *Betsy*, in company with the *Anna Josepha*, navigated by Rev. John Harris [q.v.]. Shelley took up his residence with Rowland Hassall [q.v.] at Parramatta, commenced his own trade, and helped in the religious work of the settlement.

In March 1801 he left for England in the *Royal Admiral* in the hope of reopening the Tongan mission, but after arriving at Tahiti decided to join the mission there. He returned to Sydney to marry Elizabeth Bean, daughter of a free settler, which he did on 7 October and returned to Tahiti next month. While in the colony he impressed Samuel Marsden [q.v.] with the dangers to the mission of establishing a government colony at Tahiti and proposed that the pork trade should be conducted by the Missionary Society. Shelley was deeply impressed with the need of a ship to support the mission by trade and, being dissatisfied with the organization of the mission, determined to work independently. He returned to Sydney in the *Lucy* in April 1806, taking with him about forty gallons of rum made secretly at the mission still to use for barter. Soon he entered into a commercial arrangement with John Macarthur and Garnham Blaxcell [qq.v.], and engaged as supercargo in the *Elizabeth*, which had been bought to open trade in sandalwood with Fiji. However, Shelley sailed to Tahiti in the *Harrington* in January 1807. There he built the *Halcyon*, which he sent to Sydney with a cargo of pork, and in May he joined the *Elizabeth*, returning to Sydney in June and again in November, estimating that his own share was upwards of £1000. Convinced that a trading ship was essential if the mission was to prosper, and with plans to reopen the Tongan mission, he sailed for London in the *Albion* in November 1808, but he could not convince the directors that he was right, even though he had the help of Marsden, who was then in England.

Early in 1810 Shelley returned to New South Wales and next year opened a general store in York Street, Sydney. In August 1812 he was granted 400 acres at Cabramatta and a town lease at Cockle Bay, but early in 1813 he closed his business and sailed from Sydney in May as master of the *Queen Charlotte*. In the Tuamotus the ship was seized by Raiatean pearl divers, three men were murdered and Shelley narrowly escaped with his life. He recovered the ship at Tahiti and returned to Sydney in February 1814 with a large cargo of shells and 'as large a quantity of pearls as has ever yet been procured by a single vessel'. It was probably during this voyage that Shelley left a European artisan at Tongatapu preparatory to reopening the mission there.

Resettling at Parramatta, Shelley conducted Congregational services in his house and commenced work among the Aboriginals. He attempted to learn the language, took some children into his own family and addressed Governor Macquarie on 'the practicability of civilizing' them. He was invited to draw up plans and in December was appointed superintendent and principal instructor of the Native Institution at Parramatta, the first of its kind in the colony. However, after establishing the school, he died on 6 July 1815.

According to Marsden, with whom he was on intimate terms, Shelley was a man 'of very comprehensive mind'. Macarthur described him as 'respectable and intelligent'. Captain House found him an over 'busy' person, whilst to W. P. Crook [q.v.], he was 'bustling and active', with his heart 'set on this world'. Macquarie described him as well qualified and a 'Moral, Well Meaning Man'.

Mrs Shelley continued the work of the institution, but despite Macquarie's interest it met with little success and was closed in 1826. Shelley's plans to reopen the Tongan mission were also abandoned, but later Mrs Shelley persuaded Rev. Walter Lawry [q.v.] to reopen it. She died on 20 September 1878. Two of their sons, William (1803-1845) and George (1812-1852), were among the pioneers of the Tumut district, taking their herds beyond the Nineteen Counties in 1829.

HRNSW, 6; HRA (1), 7, 8, 10; G. L. Lockley, An estimate of the contribution made in NSW by missionaries of the LMS . . . between 1798 and 1825 (M.A. thesis, Univ Syd, 1949); E. Robarts, Journal . . . with a vocabulary of the Marquesan language, 1824 (NL Scotland, microfilm NL); MS cat under W. Shelley (ML); W. House, Transactions on board of the former colonial brig Norfolk at Otaheita 1801-02 (ML).

NIEL GUNSON

SHENTON, GEORGE (1811-1867), chemist and merchant, was born on 2 January 1811 at Winchester, England, a son of William Shenton of Buriton Manor and his wife Anna Marie, née Young. At 15 he was articled to a Portsmouth druggist, a pious Wesleyan who strongly influenced his character. After completing his professional training he set out for Western Australia in the hope of improving his health and his fortune. He arrived in the *Cygnet* on 27 January 1833 and joined his cousin William Kernot Shenton, an engineer who had preceded him in October 1829. Sixteen months later he had sole charge of his cousin's flour-mill at South Perth when it was attacked by Aboriginals. Although Shenton himself was unharmed, 980 lbs of flour were stolen; together with other depredations the attack prompted Governor Stirling to retaliate and the 'Battle of Pinjarra' followed in October 1834.

Shenton established himself as the first chemist and druggist in Perth and quickly prospered; in 1838 he moved to more capacious premises in Hay Street. He soon extended his trade and built up a flourishing general merchandising and agency business, employing Francis Armstrong as manager and confidential clerk. Taking a lead in the colonists' efforts to overcome the depression of the early 1840s and to boost exports, Shenton sent a sample shipment of jarrah and sandalwood to England in 1845. Timber quickly became a major export. In 1847 he advertised that he would buy 'sandalwood, wool, oil, wheat, gum and all other colonial produce'. Offices and warehouses were built on the waterfront behind his St George's Terrace home, Rose Hall, and the main shipping department was later transferred to Fremantle.

From 1848 Shenton played an important part in opening the Geraldton district. With other Perth businessmen he invested in a succession of mining ventures. The output of these copper and lead mines around the lower Murchison River and Northampton fluctuated considerably, partly because of the caution of the directors and managers. Minerals, however, provided a valuable export, vieing with sandalwood for second place to wool after 1859. The exploitation of the Geraldton district's potential for wool and wheat quickly followed. In 1852 Shenton exchanged his own farm at Wanneroo, near Perth, for land on the Greenough River flats. He established a store at Geraldton and gave experience in management there to his eldest son George, when he came of age. From it the mining settlements and convict road parties were victualled. In this and other districts

Shenton set many a farmer and grazier on his feet, but he had less success as one of the promoters of pastoral settlement at Roebuck Bay (Broome) in 1864. His commercial career culminated in his election as a director of the Western Australian Bank from 1847 to 1867, and he was chairman at the time of his death.

Shenton supported many public enterprises and activities. A man of high ideals and liberal principles, he saw his own fortunes synonymous with Western Australia's progress. As agent for various shipping companies in 1848 he joined in pressing the government to encourage overseas steam communication. He opposed the suggested introduction of female convicts. Elected a member of the Perth Town Trust in 1847, he served as chairman from 1853 until 1858 when he guided its transformation into the Perth City Council. In 1858, when the nominated members of the Legislative Council reflected landed rather than commercial interests, he joined a deputation to advocate representative government.

Shenton was a trustee of the Swan River Mechanics' Institute and of the Western Australian Total Abstinence Society, and as a keen gardener was a committeeman of the Vineyard Society. Cape lilac trees which he provided were planted along the western side of St George's Terrace in 1857. Of firm religious convictions, he served the Wesleyan Methodists as secretary and trustee, lay-preacher, particularly at Fremantle, Sunday school superintendent and class leader. He was a strong supporter of the church's missions to the Aboriginals at York and Wanneroo, and he gave generously towards the building of Wesley Church, Perth.

On 29 November 1838 Shenton married Ann Catherina (1821-1904), daughter of John Cousins, retired officer of the merchant marine. Of their eleven children, three sons, George, Edward and Ernest, followed their father into commerce, and seven daughters married into well-known Western Australian families.

Though frail of body, George Shenton was energetic, persevering and perceptive. His honourable and successful career was cut short on 25 March 1867 when, on an intended business visit to Bunbury, he was drowned in the wreck of his schooner Lass of Geraldton near Mandurah.

Swan River News, 2 (1843)—4 (1847); Western Australian Almanack, 1849; Civil Service J, 20 July 1929; West Australian, 30 Oct 1847, 29 Mar, 12 Apr 1867; G. J. Kelly, 'History of Mining in the Geraldton District', JRWAHS, 6 (1962-65); P. U. Henn, Genealogical notes (Battye Lib, Perth); Shenton letters (Battye Lib, Perth).

J. H. M. HONNIBALL

SHEPHERDSON, JOHN BANKS (1809-1897), schoolmaster and magistrate, was born on 22 May 1809 at East Heslerton, Yorkshire, England, the son of George Shepherdson (1774-1838), a devout Wesleyan Methodist. He was educated by Rev. Thomas Farrow, of West Heslerton, and his uncle, Rev. Jabez Banks, vicar of Bempton. Although his parents wanted him to study for the church, he went to sea in 1824 and spent about three months in Jamaica. On returning to England he did some teaching, and in 1827 he married Marianne Craike, of Hovingham.

In 1836 the South Australian School Society was founded in London and Shepherdson was chosen as its colonial director. He was sent by George Fife Angas [q.v.] first to the training school of the British and Foreign School Society and then to further study in a school at Lindfield in Sussex where boys were taught farming, gardening, tailoring, shoemaking, etc. in addition to ordinary subjects. With free passages for himself, his wife, daughter and three sons, Shepherdson sailed in the Hartley, arriving at Adelaide on 25 October 1837. He set about enlisting the support of leading colonists. On 25 January 1838 at a public meeting chaired by Governor Hindmarsh it was resolved to form the South Australian School Society in connexion with the London society. On 28 May Shepherdson opened his school in the parklands near Trinity Church in a wooden house with separate departments for girls and boys. Fifty children soon strained his accommodation, but although he won praise for successful teaching, his earnings were small. In September he was offering evening classes for adults, but next month he was asking Angas for a passage back to England, which was refused. To get enough to live on he also acted as secretary of the South Australian Cattle Co.

In November 1839 he resigned through ill health and moved to Echunga. In 1840 he took up Craike Farm, Hawdon Vale, near Nairne, where he struggled against pests and low prices. In 1847 at Mount Barker he was appointed postmaster and clerk of the bench and in 1850 clerk of the local court. He also kept cattle and in 1849 he acquired a portable sawmill. He had so much to do that his work as postmaster suffered, and official rebukes led to his resigning that position. As clerk of the court, however, he won high praise from the four local justices. In 1855 he applied for the position of second inspector of schools, but did not receive the appointment. He wrote *The Practice of the Local Courts of South Australia* (Mount Barker, 1858). He was commended by some forty prominent residents for his ability and uniform kindness when in 1861 he was made a justice of the peace and appointed special and stipendiary magistrate for Yorke Peninsula. He resided first at Kadina, but soon moved to Wallaroo where, except for a year's visit to England in 1875, he lived at Weymouth House for the rest of his life. He retired in 1887.

Shepherdson was a member of the Church of England: at Mount Barker he served as organist and at Wallaroo he was largely instrumental in establishing St Mary's Church; he was for twenty-two years a member of synod, and a lay reader until his eyesight failed. He died on 24 May 1897. His first wife, by whom he had eleven children, died in 1859. He later married Sarah Kelleway Gray, who died in 1902.

G. C. Morphett, *John Banks Shepherdson, pioneer schoolmaster and a stipendiary magistrate* (Adel, 1947).   A. C. HITCHCOX

SHERBROOKE, VISCOUNT; *see* LOWE, ROBERT

SHERWIN, ISAAC (1804-1869), merchant, was born on 24 April 1804 at Burslem, Staffordshire, England, a son of John Sherwin (1780?-1853), merchant, and his wife Elizabeth. After education in England he went at 12 to Germany, where he had five years experience in merchandising. He arrived with his family in Van Diemen's Land in January 1823 and lived on his father's grant, Sherwood, on the River Clyde near Bothwell. He went to England and Germany in 1825 and returned to Van Diemen's Land in July 1829. Next year the Sherwin home was burned to the ground by Aboriginals, and his brother John Sargent Sherwin was granted 500 acres for leading the four men who pursued the marauders.

In 1831 Isaac Sherwin helped to establish Cook & Sherwin, merchants in Charles Street, Launceston. In 1838 despite risk of attack by bushrangers he rode on horseback 120 miles from Hobart Town with money and papers to establish the Launceston branch of the Commercial Bank of Tasmania and was for some years its manager. He suffered heavy losses in the depression of the 1840s and retired in 1845

to Sherwood where, with much initiative and enterprise, he installed one of the colony's first irrigation systems. A tunnel, 150 yards long, was cut with pick and shovel through a sandstone hill above the River Clyde and the waters irrigated some 240 acres. In March 1850 with several millers, landholders and other settlers on the Clyde he petitioned successfully for regulation of the waters of Lakes Crescent and Sorell. Back at Launceston in 1855 he was appointed the first agent in Tasmania for the Australian Mutual Provident Society. At a public meeting called to form the Launceston Gas Co. in 1858 he was elected secretary *pro tem* and, after the company's first meeting, a director. He was also a director of the Bank of Van Diemen's Land and an agent for the Van Diemen's Land Insurance Co.

As well as establishing many business enterprises Sherwin was an active philanthropist, with deep religious convictions. In 1831 he bought some ten acres on Colonial Hill where he built Alice Place, to which he brought his bride next year. The Quaker missionaries Backhouse and Walker [qq.v.] were frequent house guests and held many meetings at the home of this 'thoughtful young couple'. As an enthusiastic Wesleyan, Sherwin gave a corner portion of his land for the Margaret Street chapel, built in 1838. He was one of the six founders of the Launceston Benevolent Society in 1834 and next year an original trustee of the Launceston Bank for Savings, becoming its first paid actuary in 1843-44. He was also an original trustee of the Hobart Savings Bank founded by G. W. Walker in 1845. Sherwin helped to establish the short-lived *Teetotal Advocate* in 1843, and on retirement as president of the Tasmanian Teetotal Society in 1845 he received a presentation in token of respect and esteem for his zealous and successful exertions in the cause. In June 1854 he was nominated a trustee and secretary of the Cornwall Free Hospital and, when it became the Launceston General Hospital, he was the first chairman of its board in 1865-69. He was also secretary of the Launceston Horticultural Society from 1857 to 1864. He died on 27 June 1869 and was buried in the Charles Street cemetery, Launceston.

In February 1832 Sherwin married Catherine Taylor of Sydney; they had four sons and three daughters. Other members of his family in Van Diemen's Land were his uncle, James Sherwin, who arrived in May 1828 and at Kangaroo Bottom set up an earthenware manufactory, known as the New Town Pottery, and his brother, George

Green Sherwin, an early settler on the Huon, whose daughter Amy later became known as the 'Tasmanian Nightingale', and was Prima Donna Assoluta at Covent Garden Opera House in 1885.

Correspondence file on Isaac Sherwin (TA).

ANN FYSH

SHOOBRIDGE, WILLIAM (1781-1836), hop-grower, was the son of Richard and Susannah Shoobridge of Tenterden, Kent, England; he came from a long line of farmers and hop-growers. He married Mary Jenkins (1784-1822) and on 20 August 1821 applied from Mottingham, Kent, for a grant of land in Van Diemen's Land. In September 1821 he received a letter of recommendation from the Colonial Office to Lieut-Governor Sorell. He sailed in the *Denmark Hill* with his wife and eight children. Another child was born on the voyage but did not survive, and Mary Shoobridge and two other children also died on board.

Shoobridge arrived in Hobart Town on 18 May 1822 with goods and cash totalling £798. Sorell persuaded him to accept the post of superintendent of the timber yard, and he was granted twenty acres at Providence Valley, where he built Kent Cottage in 1823. There in 1824 he was shot at by a convict, John Logan. A metal rule in his pocket saved him from serious injury; Logan was executed in 1825 for attempted murder. Shoobridge resigned after a few years to devote himself to the production of hops at Providence Valley from sets he had brought from Kent. In this he had some success, the first marketable crop being produced in 1825, 453 lbs in 1826, 362 in 1827 and 1043 in 1828; all was sold locally. In 1827 he was placed in charge of a near-by government limekiln at £40 a year, to encourage his hop-growing. He held this position until 1830.

A local brewer, Henry Condell, later first mayor of Melbourne, was involved for several years in a dispute with Shoobridge over the main access to Providence Valley, which Condell had fenced. Shoobridge also acquired a farm of 700 acres in the Drummond district, now Tea Tree, and was half-owner of a mill at Battery Point. His fortunes fluctuated and only with the assistance of A. F. Kemp [q.v.] and others did he remain solvent. When he first arrived in the colony he was a Methodist, and in 1823 was on the Wesleyan Methodist Schools' Committee for Hobart and assisted with the Methodist Mission. Later he became a close associate of James Backhouse

and G. W. Walker [qq.v.] and supported the Society of Friends. He gave the society half an acre of Providence Valley as a burial ground and was the first person buried there when he died in 1836. In 1833 he had married Harriet Shaw. His son, Richard, carried on the farm at Providence Valley until 1864 and another son, Ebenezer, grew hops at Richmond and later New Norfolk.

Although Shoobridge is generally credited with being the first to grow hops in Van Diemen's Land, the claim of Richard Clarke to have done so in 1810 appears hard to dispute. The Shoobridge family continued the tradition of hop-growing and built up one of public service. Today his descendants remain leading hop-growers in Tasmania.

Correspondence file under Shoobridge (TA).

J. R. MORRIS

SHORTLAND, JOHN (1739-1803), naval officer, was born near Plymouth, son of John Shortland, the senior member of a remarkable west of England family, six members of whom were associated with the colonization of Australia and New Zealand. In 1755 he entered the navy as a midshipman and served under Boscawen off Newfoundland, under Byng off Minorca and under Rodney in the West Indies, being present at the reduction of several islands. On his promotion to lieutenant in 1763 he was engaged in the transport service between England and America. In 1782 he was in command of the transports taking reinforcements to the relief of Gibraltar and in 1786, after returning with troops from Halifax, was appointed naval agent to the transports of the First Fleet. This was an important and responsible post because he was charged with the oversight and proper fulfilment of the contracts for transport. The masters of all the transports were under his command, and he directed the provision of bulkheads and cabins for the accommodation of the soldiers and convicts. As Governor Phillip was detained in London until 11 May 1787, two days before the fleet sailed, attending to the other manifold details connected with the welfare of the projected colony, a large part of the credit for the success of this voyage was due to the vigilance and efficiency with which Shortland discharged his responsibilities. He had also procured appointments on the expedition for his sons, John [q.v.] and Thomas George (1771-1827).

After leaving the Cape of Good Hope Phillip transferred to the *Supply* and in company with three of the fastest transports in charge of Shortland sailed ahead of the rest of the fleet as an advance party. Shortland's squadron, the first to reach Botany Bay, arrived on 17 January 1788. Shortland remained at Port Jackson until 14 July, when he sailed for England in the *Alexander*, carrying the first dispatches of Governor Phillip to the secretary of state. The *Alexander* was accompanied by the *Borrowdale*, *Prince of Wales* and *Friendship*, the last being later abandoned. On the voyage by way of Batavia Shortland discovered and charted many islands and reefs, including the dangerous Middleton Shoal, sighted but did not identify the Solomon Islands, and after a most adventurous voyage arrived back in England in May 1789. During his absence he had kept a full journal of transactions which was highly valued by the authorities. He strongly urged the Admiralty to have the eastern coast of Australia properly charted and was thus, to some extent, responsible for the subsequent dispatch of Matthew Flinders [q.v.] in the *Investigator*. He was promoted commander in 1790 and after further active service finally retired to Lille in France where he died in 1803. He was survived by his widow, two sons and two daughters.

Shortland, a fine seaman, a capable and experienced officer and an affectionate father, has on two important occasions been confused with his more famous son, John: first on the celebration of the son's discovery of the Hunter River, and second, on the 150th anniversary of the same event, when the postal department issued a stamp which showed the face of the father instead of the son.

HRNSW, 1-4; HRA (1), 1, 2; J. Hunter, *An historical journal of the transactions at Port Jackson and Norfolk Island* (Lond, 1793); W. Tench, *A narrative of the expedition to Botany Bay* (Lond, 1789); *Naval Chronicle*, 24 (1810); Bonwick transcripts, biography (ML).

ARTHUR MCMARTIN

SHORTLAND, JOHN (1769-1810), naval officer, was born on 5 September 1769, the eldest son of John Shortland [q.v.]. In 1781 he joined the navy as a midshipman and went to Quebec in a transport commanded by his father. From 1783 to 1787 he served in the West Indies, first in the *Surprize* and then in the *Latona*. In 1787 his father secured his appointment as master's mate in the *Sirius* when the First Fleet sailed for Australia. Shortland spent nearly five years in Australia, including

eleven months on Norfolk Island where the *Sirius* was wrecked in 1790. In 1792 he returned to England with Hunter and next year was promoted lieutenant in the *Arrogant*.

In 1794 he returned to Australia with the new governor, Hunter, in the *Reliance* as first lieutenant. In this capacity he was too busy to join his shipmates, Bass and Flinders [qq.v.], in their expeditions, but on 9 September 1797, while on his way to Port Stephens in pursuit of some runaway convicts who had seized 'the largest and best boat, belonging to Government', he entered the estuary of the Hunter River, where William and Mary Bryant [q.v.] and their party had probably sheltered briefly when they escaped northwards in 1791. During his brief stay Shortland named the river, though for some years it was often referred to as the Coal River, made the first chart of the harbour in the form of an eye-sketch and collected some samples of coal; in a later letter to his father he predicted that his discovery would prove 'a great acquisition to the settlement'.

In 1797 he was granted twenty-five acres at Liberty Plains and in 1800 received from Hunter another 300 acres at Bankstown. However, the steady round of naval duties and service as a member of the Criminal Court at Sydney were for Shortland no substitute for the action and excitement of the naval war in Europe, and in 1800 he returned to England in the *Reliance*. Soon afterwards he went to Egypt as agent for the troops under Abercromby, served in the *Dolphin* and the *Trompeuse*, and was then ordered to the Guinea coast where through the death of the captain he became commander of the *Squirrel*. In 1805 he joined the Halifax Station under Admiral Warren as post-captain in the *Junon*, a captured 40-gun French frigate fitted out partly at his own expense. On 13 December 1809 he fought a gallant but hopeless action against two 48-gun and two 20-gun French ships. He was very seriously wounded and his ship so badly damaged that the enemy was compelled to burn her. His mangled body was taken by the French to the hospital at Guadeloupe where he died on 21 January 1810, 'firm in his attachment to the Protestant faith'. He was buried with full military honours at Basse Terre. He was unmarried.

Skilful and devoted to his profession, Shortland had also proved a dutiful son, an affectionate brother and a good master. Active, diligent and courageous, his career was an epitome of all the best in the naval officer of the period. His name is commemorated in a suburb of Newcastle, the city whose site he had explored in 1797.

HRNSW, 1-4; HRA (1), 1, 2; *Naval Chronicle*, 24 (1810); MS cat under J. Shortland (ML).   ARTHUR MCMARTIN

SIDAWAY, ROBERT (1757?-1809), a watchcase maker, was sentenced to transportation for life at the Old Bailey in 1782 for housebreaking, and arrived in New South Wales in the First Fleet transport *Friendship* in January 1788. Although Ralph Clark [q.v.] mentioned in his journal that Sidaway, a 'daring and villainous fellow', was put in leg irons for a month on the way out, apparently he behaved better after his arrival, for he received a conditional pardon on 29 November 1792, an absolute pardon on 27 September 1794, and was given a contract as baker for the troops. In January 1796 Sidaway opened the first theatre in Sydney. It had been built by convicts under the management of John Sparrow. It was in Bell Row and was used until 1798, when Governor Hunter ordered that it be closed as it was a corrupting influence, probably because of the robberies taking place on theatre nights. It operated again for a time in 1800 and then ceased altogether.

Sidaway held a 130-acre farm, partly purchased and partly leased, at the Field of Mars, on which he grew maize and wheat. He was one of those settlers permitted by Hunter to buy goods at moderate prices from the *Minerva* in 1800. He kept a public house and in 1805 obtained a wine and spirit licence. He died on 13 October 1809, aged 52, described by the *Sydney Gazette* as a philanthropist and a respected member of society. He had formed an alliance with Mary Marshall, who had been sentenced to transportation for life at the Old Bailey on 23 February 1785 and had arrived in the First Fleet in the *Lady Penrhyn*. As Sidaway's residuary legatee, she sent Governor Macquarie a memorial applying for a renewal of the lease on Sidaway's property in Sydney, but this was refused. She continued in Sydney as a publican.

HRNSW, 2, 3; HRA (1), 1; P. McGuire, *The Australian theatre* (Melb, 1948); J. Kardoss, *A brief history of the Australian theatre* (Syd, 1955); *Sydney Gazette*, 3 Nov 1805, 15 Oct 1809; MS cat under R. Sidaway (ML).   VIVIENNE PARSONS

SIDDINS, RICHARD (1770?-1846), master mariner, pilot and lighthouse keeper, first came to New South Wales in the crew of the whaler *Alexander* in May 1804.

For many years he took part in trading voyages between Calcutta and the islands of the South Seas, calling periodically at Port Jackson. He arrived in 1806 in the *King George*, in 1808 in the *Mercury*, in 1809 as master of the *Mercury* and in 1810 as master of the *Endeavour*. In 1811 he became master of the *Campbell Macquarie*; on 10 June 1812 she ran aground at Macquarie Island and went to pieces, but Siddins and his crew were saved and he was given a passage home in the *Perseverance*. In 1813 he again called at Sydney as master of the *Elizabeth and Mary* on his way to the sealing islands, and in June 1814 arrived as master of the new *Campbell Macquarie* on his way to the Society Islands and Fiji in quest of a cargo of sandalwood. From 1814 to 1818 Siddins was master of the *Campbell Macquarie*, calling at Sydney with general merchandise from Calcutta, then leaving for the whale fishery and sandalwood of the South Seas and the islands, and calling again on his way home to Calcutta to take on spars and coal. Dr Joseph Arnold [q.v.] described him as having been long in the sandalwood trade and well acquainted with the Fiji Islands, even understanding their language.

In Sydney in 1816 Siddons married Jane, daughter of Edward Powell and Elizabeth Fish, of the half-way house at Parramatta. He had previously fathered a son by Catherine Keenan and a daughter by Eleanor Cooper, both of Sydney. Siddins continued his trading voyages, becoming master of the *Lynx* in 1819 until July 1823, when he returned from Macquarie Island. He then settled in the colony, becoming one of the Port Jackson pilots. In August 1824 he was granted 600 acres on the Williams River and in September 1834 3½ acres at Watson's Bay. In 1832 he was compelled by ill health to exchange his situation as pilot with the superintendent of the South Head lighthouse. He died on 2 July 1846, aged 76. His wife died on 9 February 1883 and was buried at Richmond cemetery; they had two sons and nine daughters. A son, Joseph Richard (1823-1891), became a pilot at South Head.

HRA (1), 7; J. S. Cumpston, *Shipping arrivals and departures, Sydney, 1788-1825* (Canberra, 1963); *Sydney Gazette*, 31 Oct 1812; *Australian*, 13 Apr 1832; MS cat under Siddins (ML).   VIVIENNE PARSONS

SIDNEY, SAMUEL (1813-1883), journalist and author, was baptized Samuel Solomon in Birmingham, England, the son of Abraham Solomon, M.D. He was educated for the law and practised briefly as a solicitor but soon turned to journalism, adopting the pen name of Sidney. His principal and lifelong interest was in agriculture. He visited and wrote about agricultural exhibitions in England and on the Continent and was hunting correspondent for the *Illustrated London News*. In 1859 he was an unsuccessful candidate for the secretaryship of the Royal Agricultural Society but next year was appointed secretary of the Agricultural Hall Co. His *Book of the Horse*, first published in London in 1873, was very highly praised.

From about 1847 to 1855 Sidney became very interested in Australia, perhaps because of the shrewd observations of his younger brother, John (b. 1821), who had been in New South Wales for some six years from about 1838. In 1847 Samuel Sidney published in London *A Voice from the Far Interior of Australia*, by 'A Bushman', relying on his brother's material; he admitted the ghosting in the preface to the second edition of *The Three Colonies of Australia* (London, 1853). In August 1848 *Sidney's Australian Hand-Book* appeared, written by both brothers; sub-titled, 'How to Settle and Succeed in Australia', it was an immediate popular success, seven 1000-copy editions being sold in five months. Of particular interest in this *Hand-Book* is the anti-Wakefieldian espousal of the general values of squatters, who were called 'the heart's blood of Australia'.

The success of the *Hand-Book* led the brothers to begin *Sidney's Emigrant's Journal*, which was published weekly from 5 October 1848 to 12 July 1849. When John returned to Australia Samuel edited the new monthly, *Sidney's Emigrant's Journal and Traveller's Magazine*; six issues appeared in 1849-50. At a high standard of reliability the journal offered assorted fare: letters from emigrants, queries from would-be emigrants, stories and book reviews.

Samuel Sidney's *The Three Colonies of Australia* was published in London in September 1852. More than 5000 copies were sold in the first year, and by 1854 German and American editions were in print. The book is of considerable importance, both for its anti-Wakefield attitudes and for its outspoken 'pro-Australian' sentiments. Like Wakefield, Sidney never set foot in Australia, though he was very well informed about the colony's affairs. His colonial interest brought him into touch with many notable people in England and he made it his business to acquaint himself with the works of Caroline Chisholm and Alexander Harris [qq.v], from both of whom he quotes. In all, the book's documentation is most impressive, and Sidney's writing is both finely pointed and graceful. On

major issues, he was anti-Bligh, in favour of cheap land, an ardent champion of colonial self-government, and against continued transportation. Samuel Sidney died on 8 June 1883.

STANLEY TICK

SIMMONS, JOSEPH (1810?-1880?), actor and manager, arrived from England in Sydney as a settler in May 1830 and became an auctioneer at 61 George Street. He claimed to have been connected with English provincial theatres and minor London houses since he was 12 and may have been one of the amateurs who appeared at Barnett Levey's [q.v.] early concerts. In 1832 Simmons left for England; while in Hobart Town in November he gave a concert under the name of Joseph Ray and stated his intention of bringing a theatrical company to the colonies.

Back in Sydney in January 1834 Simmons opened Paddington House, a 'fancy bazaar' in George Street. At this time Levey was advertising for a partner with capital for his young Theatre Royal, specifying that 'such only as are prepared to give their personal attention to the management of the concern can be accepted'. In February Simmons became part-proprietor and manager of the theatre and also made his début as actor. The critics praised his first-rate talent as comic performer, especially in Irish characters, but he played a much wider range of parts and was Sydney's first Macbeth; his best Shakespearian parts were Mercutio and Iago. As manager, however, Simmons was less successful; 'the warmth of his temper and the impetuosity of his disposition' led to constant friction and litigation and the partnership with Levey ended in February 1835. Simmons continued his business activities and there were persistent rumours of his planning to start a second theatre in Sydney. But he was one of the six lessees who in April 1835 took over the Theatre Royal and he once again became its manager. In November the other partners withdrew, leaving Simmons as sole lessee and manager until May 1836. After another furious row with Levey he left for Launceston and Hobart where he gave several concerts and dramatic readings, this time under his own name. His stay in Hobart coincided with the shareholders' meeting which was to decide on the letting of Hobart's new Theatre Royal; Simmons was considered as a lessee but he returned to Sydney as partner in the new firm of Simmons & Marks, auctioneers and ironmongers. When the partnership dissolved in September 1837 Simmons gave concerts and dramatic readings in Sydney; in July 1838 Joseph Wyatt [q.v.], one of his fellow-lessees of the Theatre Royal, engaged him for his new Victoria Theatre. In March 1839 Simmons became licensee of a public house but he remained at the theatre until October. In 1841-42 he made several unsuccessful applications for a licence to open a second theatre in Sydney but he missed the opportunity and an outsider opened the Olympic Theatre in February-May 1842. In April Simmons was back as manager and performer at the Victoria Theatre and soon afterwards achieved the greatest success of his career as actor and singer. A burletta, *The Mock Catalani in Little Puddleton*, for which Charles Nagel claimed authorship although it was the adaptation of an older German play, offered in its title part full opportunity for Simmons's special talents as comic actor and counter-tenor; already he had delighted audiences with a 'Mock Italian Aria'.

In September Simmons left the Victoria to concentrate on preparations for his own theatre. The government still was disinclined to allow a second theatre but a new power had arisen: the City Council of Sydney backed Simmons's application to open his City Theatre in 'Mr Burdekin's large store, at the corner of Market Street'. With his partner, James Belmore, a highly skilled machinist from the London theatres, who had worked in the Sydney theatres and had been important in the building of Hobart's Theatre Royal, Simmons converted the store into a beautiful little theatre and most of the Victoria's leading players joined his company. Yet the small City Theatre, which opened in May 1843, could not compete with the Victoria and had to close after a few weeks.

Back at the Victoria Simmons enjoyed great popularity as an actor, especially in comedy parts. For his benefit in August 1844 he presented his own drama, *The Duellist*, which he claimed to be 'the first truly original drama ever produced in the Colony'; it was performed only twice. A month later he became owner of the Tavistock Hotel at the corner of King and York Streets and there he gave free concerts three nights every week. He still appeared occasionally in comedy parts at the Victoria Theatre until his final row with Wyatt in April 1845. 'My theatrical career in New South Wales is ended', Simmons wrote in a letter to his public with whom he had been so popular for eleven years.

Heads of the People, 6 November 1847, in an article, 'The Country Storekeeper',

with portrait drawing, tells of a later phase in the life of Joseph Simmons; 'in every circle where his name is mentioned, it carries with it an idea of fun and good humour'. Almost half a century after his first arrival in Sydney, in June 1879, a Grand Complimentary Benefit was given in Sydney's Theatre Royal to Joseph Simmons senior, 'the old favourite actor and manager'. He played one of his early parts, Benjamin Bowbell in *The Illustrious Stranger*; a critic wrote that 'notwithstanding that he is not so young as he once was, he made a very amusing portraiture'.

H. L. OPPENHEIM

SIMPKINSON DE WESSELOW, FRANCIS GUILLEMARD (1819-1906), naval officer and artist, was born on 26 May 1819 in London, the son of Sir John Augustus Francis Simpkinson, barrister and later Q.C., and his wife Mary, née Griffin, who was a sister of Lady Jane Franklin [q.v.]. In March 1832 he joined the navy as a first-class volunteer in H.M.S. *Britannia*, in which he served, apart from twenty-eight days in October 1833 in the *Rainbow* with his uncle, Sir John Franklin, until February 1835 when he was transferred to the *Jupiter*. Ten months later he joined the *Sulphur*. In 1836 this surveying ship under Captain Edward Belcher began a seven year voyage around the world. In various places Simpkinson helped to take synchronous pendulum observations, and in Belcher's *Narrative of a Voyage around the World* (London, 1843), he is mentioned as one of the two midshipmen who accompanied Belcher on a visit to the vice-consul at Tepic, Mexico. Simpkinson's own diary from 28 March to 25 August 1837, now in the Mitchell Library, Sydney, describes the ship's progress up the west coast of America especially from Panama to Mexico, and thence to Hawaii, where he thought Belcher's attempt to restore order with the help of a French frigate was very badly handled. Simpkinson did not complete the world voyage, for in June 1838 he was transferred to the *Harrier*. In the early 1840s he is said to have been admitted to the Royal Naval College and, after serving in the China war as gunner's mate, to have been placed on half-pay.

In May 1844 he was restored to full pay and ordered to Van Diemen's Land to place himself under the orders of Lieutenant J. H. Kay [q.v.] at the magnetic observatory in Hobart Town. Simpkinson arrived in September in the *Pestonjee Bomanjee* and was allowed double pay for his services at the observatory even after he was promoted lieutenant in December 1845.

Simpkinson was an accomplished artist and in Hobart he painted a number of landscapes, some of which now belong to the Royal Society of Tasmania and are in the Tasmanian Museum and Art Gallery. Some water-colours by Simpkinson were hung among the 276 works displayed at the first public exhibition of paintings in Australia; it was held on 6 January 1845 in the Legislative Council chambers.

In 1849 Simpkinson left Hobart in the *Calcutta* for England, where he returned to half-pay. His last commission was in the *Fisgard* from March 1854 to March 1855 on surveying duties. He was retired as a lieutenant in April 1870. At St Leonard's on 14 December 1858 he had married Emily, daughter of George Henry Malcolm Wagner. They were living at Westminster in November 1869 when Simpkinson added de Wesselow to his surname by deed poll. Later he lived at Cannes where he acquired much property. He died in London on 4 December 1906 and his estate was sworn at more than £70,000.

W. R. O'Byrne, A *naval biographical dictionary* (Lond, 1849); *The Times*, 18 Nov 1869, 24 Dec 1906; G. T. W. B. Boyes, Diary (Roy Soc Tas, Hob); Adm 24/106, 119, 37/7930, 8301, 38/9116, 107/75.

V. W. HODGMAN

SIMPSON, JAMES (1792?-1857), public servant, arrived in Van Diemen's Land from England in April 1825 in the *Elizabeth*. He immediately received an appointment as superintendent of government stock at Ross bridge. In March 1827 he was made police magistrate at Norfolk Plains and later at Campbell Town. In 1832 he removed to Hobart Town as commissioner of the Land Board. Dissatisfied with his prospects in Tasmania, Simpson joined the Port Phillip Association and in February 1836 offered his resignation to Lieut-Governor Arthur, who reluctantly reported to the Colonial Office that Simpson 'had been infected with the Port Phillip mania'.

Simpson arrived at Melbourne in April 1836 in the barque *Caledonia*. As a member of the Port Phillip Association he had been allotted an area of land between the Werribee River and Station Peak, but held this for only a short time. On 1 June 1836 the leading settlers of Port Phillip held the first public meeting at the township and by popular decision appointed Simpson as arbitrator in all disputes between individuals, except in questions relating to land, with power to impose and collect fines. The meeting also agreed to petition Governor Bourke in Sydney for the appointment of a resident magistrate, and in September 1836 Captain William Lonsdale [q.v.] arrived to take up that post. In April 1837 Simpson was also officially made a magistrate and, when Lonsdale was made sub-treasurer, Simpson in June 1840 became police magistrate of Melbourne and held office for a year.

A succession of official positions followed: chairman of the market commissioners (1841), warden of the district council of Bourke (1843), temporary sub-treasurer (1846), commissioner of crown lands (1849), sheriff (1851) and president of commissioners of sewers and water supply (1853). At the same time Simpson was in the forefront of the business, cultural and charitable life of the community as vice-president of the first savings bank, president of the Mechanics' Institute, president of the Pastoral and Agricultural Society, a director of the Bank of Australasia, managing director of the Steam Navigation Co. and a first trustee of St Peter's Church. While his name and prestige were given to these and many other sound and worthy enterprises, he consistently refused to be associated with the many controversial activities which the ferment of the times produced in the growing city.

Throughout the 1840s Simpson lived in Little Flinders Street, but later moved to a new house in Wellington Parade, East Melbourne. There he died, of an abscess on the liver, on 17 April 1857, aged 65. He was buried in the Church of England section of the Melbourne general cemetery.

Contemporary references were unanimous in paying respect to Simpson as one who exercised a natural authority without losing the regard of his fellows. Edmund Finn [q.v.], who knew him well, described him thus: 'There was a something stern and slightly forbidding in his sallowed face; but it was only skin deep: and, if one could not admire him outwardly, the honesty of purpose which seemed to actuate him, never failed to ensure for him one's respect', adding that he was 'the best liked man in the province'. With increasing years, Simpson largely withdrew from public life, but his funeral procession was reported to be more than three-quarters of a mile in length, testifying to the affection and esteem in which he was held.

HRA (3), 4, 5; Garryowen (E. Finn), *The chronicles of early Melbourne*, 1-2 (Melb, 1888); R. D. Boys, *First years at Port Phillip*, 2nd ed (Melb, 1959); A. S. Kenyon, 'The Port Phillip Association', VHM, 16 (1936-37); *Herald* (Melb), 21 Apr 1857; Kenyon index of pioneers (SLV); Correspondence file under J. Simpson (TA).   C. A. McCALLUM

SIMPSON, STEPHEN (1792?-1869), homoeopath and public servant, was born at Lichfield, Staffordshire, England. He joined the army as an ensign in 1813 and after service with the 14th Light Dragoons he resigned in 1817 to qualify in medicine and then to travel extensively in Europe as personal physician to a member of the Russian nobility. He became a disciple of Samuel Christian Friedrich Hahnemann, the founder of homoeopathy, and he practised the new science in Rome for a number of years. Returning to England with the duchess of Sutherland's son, whom he had successfully treated, he tried to set up a practice in London and there he published in 1836 A *Practical View of Homoeopathy, Being an Address to British Practitioners,* the first English book on the subject. However, because of opposition and ridicule from the medical profession, he abandoned homoeopathy and left for New South Wales after marrying a woman to whom he had been engaged for twenty years.

He arrived in Sydney in the *Wilmot* in January 1840, with a recommendation to Governor Gipps from the Colonial Office. His wife died shortly after their arrival. Next July he sailed in the *Speculator* to Moreton Bay, where in May 1841 he was appointed acting colonial surgeon in the absence of Dr D. K. Ballow [q.v.], but thereafter never practised again. With the end of military government and the removal of Owen Gorman from office in May 1842, Simpson was appointed commissioner of crown lands for Moreton Bay and also acting administrator until the arrival of J. C. Wickham [q.v.] next year. His report to Gipps on Petrie's [q.v.] excursion north of Moreton Bay contains an account of Davis and Bracewell [qq.v.], whom he afterwards employed on his property, and in his report on the state of the Aboriginals in the Moreton Bay district on 1 January 1844 he described his expedition into the bunya country with Rev. C. Eipper [q.v.], four mounted policemen and six prisoners in March and April 1843. He sat in the first court of petty sessions in September 1843 and remained a justice of the peace until 1861.

Simpson first lived in one of the empty cottages of the former female penitentiary at Eagle Farm but he later moved to Redbank where J. D. Lang [q.v.] reported dining with him in a slab hut. About 1846 he built a substantial house in a luxuriant garden at Woogaroo (later Wolston and now Wacol). Wolston House, still standing, proved a welcome overnight stop for Benjamin Glennie and others who travelled from Brisbane to Ipswich and the Darling Downs, and J. Watts avowed that Simpson's stud of horses was the best in the colony. From 1851 Simpson made substantial land purchases in this area and there his nephew, J. M. Ommaney, after whom a near-by mountain was named, was killed by a fall from a horse in 1856.

Simpson was appointed a trustee of the Brisbane General Hospital in 1848, a returning officer in the 1851 elections, police magistrate for the Moreton district in 1853. He retired from government office in 1855. In May 1860 he became a life member of the first Legislative Council in the popular interest but attended only once before he left for Sydney in the *Yarra Yarra* in December and thence in the *Jeddo* for England. Although his non-attendance was questioned in parliament he was granted leave until September 1864. He died at Portland Square, London, on 11 March 1869.

Stephen Simpson was known as 'the most respected man in the colony'. When Henry Mort asked an Aboriginal 'Who is God?' he received the reply 'Carbon white fellow, like it Doctor Simpson, sit down here'.

HRA (1), 22, 23; H. S. Russell, *The genesis of Queensland* (Syd, 1888), 211, 247; E. V. Stevens, 'Stephen Simpson', *JRQHS*, 5 (1953-57); D. Gordon, 'Men of medicine at separation', *MJA*, 7 July 1962; *Brisbane Courier*, 8 Aug 1846, 3 Jan 1861, 22 May 1869.

JUDITH ILTIS

SINGLETON, BENJAMIN (1788-1853), settler and miller, was born on 7 August 1788 in England of Scottish parentage. His father, William, then a warehouse porter in London, was sentenced at the Old Bailey on 8 June 1791 to transportation for seven years. With his wife Hannah and two sons, Benjamin and Joseph, William arrived at Port Jackson in the *Pitt* on 14 February 1792. Five years later the family settled on a ninety-acre grant at Mulgrave Place, where another son, James, then aged 30, joined them in 1808.

James and Benjamin built excellent water-mills, the first at Kurrajong, where they ground wheat for the government stores, a second at Lower Portland Head and a third on James's fifty-acre grant at the Hawkesbury. Benjamin accompanied William Parr on part of his exploration of the present Bulga Road in October 1817 but, realizing the advantages to be gained by discovering a trafficable route to the Hunter valley, he withdrew and led a private expedition in April 1818. This, like Parr's, was a failure, but the experience proved useful when two years later as a member of John Howe's [q.v.] party, he finally reached Patrick's Plains. The town of Singleton is built on part of Singleton's 200 acres, granted on 31 March 1821 as a reward for his share in this successful expedition.

Cattle on agistment from the Hawkesbury were soon grazing 'at Singleton's' and in February 1823 Major Morisset [q.v.] appointed him district constable, on the recommendation of E. C. Close [q.v.] who thought Singleton 'a very trustworthy man'. In the same year he fell foul of James Mudie [q.v.], who refused to accept his instructions concerning the employment of convicts on Sundays and their attendance at musters. Singleton appealed successfully to Close, the nearest magistrate, to uphold his authority 'or else the District will be no better than bushrangers'. In 1825 his application for additional land, granted in 1828, was supported by the four major landholders of the district.

Farming he found 'but a poor employment'. He was grazing stock on Liverpool Plains in 1827, his mill and inn at Singleton being managed by relatives. With his brother Joseph he built a water-mill at Boatfalls, near Clarencetown, in 1831 and then embarked on a new venture. He commissioned from Lowe's [q.v.] yard at Clarencetown a horse-drawn vessel, aptly named the *Experiment*, to be used in the Parramatta trade. Neither horses nor passengers took kindly to the novelty, and in December 1832 he offered it for sale 'for want of funds to propel her by steam'. Want of funds also forced the subdivision, sale or mortgage of much of his property during the 1830s and his insolvency in 1842, but did not prevent him making the first gifts of land to the Anglican and Presbyterian churches in Singleton. His unique contribution to education was to plough a furrow from the town to the schoolhouse at Whittingham, so that the children would not lose their way. He died on 2 May 1853, aged 65, and was buried in the Whittingham (Singleton) cemetery. He was survived by his wife Mary (1796-1877), daughter of Thomas Sharling of the 102nd Regiment, whom he had married on 7 February 1811, and by their ten children.

Adventurous, energetic and trustworthy, he retained the affectionate regard of his friends and well deserved Mudie's unconscious tribute—'Singleton is on a perfect footing of equality with his convict servants, mine or any he comes in contact with . . . in a word *Ben* Singleton (as they call him) is a fine fellow'.

William Parr, Journal (ML); B. Singleton, Journal (ML); Col Sec in letters, 19-21, Newcastle, 1823 (NSWA). NANCY GRAY

SKIRVING, WILLIAM (d. 1796), political reformer, was the son of a farmer at Libberton, Lanarkshire, Scotland. At first intended for the church, he was educated at the old and famous grammar school at Haddington and at the University of Edinburgh. Later he abandoned his hopes of the ministry and became tutor to the family of Sir Alexander Dick of Prestonfield. Inclined to agriculture he then leased a farm at Damhead in Fife, and soon afterwards in January 1775 married Rachel, daughter of Andrew Abercrombie, merchant of Kirkcaldy. Later he took possession of the farm of Strathruddie in Fife which was the property of his wife and to which he applied himself with great aptitude. In 1792 he moved to Edinburgh where he published the first volume of his *The Husbandman's Assistant*, and unsuccessfully sought the chair of agriculture at the University of Edinburgh.

Always a man of firm liberal opinion, he was drawn to the more radical groups which, under the influence of the French Revolution, were then strongly advocating constitutional reform, and in December 1792 was appointed secretary to a convention of the Societies of the Friends of the People then being held in Edinburgh. Alarmed at the growing clamour for reform and the republican sentiments expressed by this group, the government took strong repressive action which resulted in the Scottish sedition trials of 1793-94. Undeterred by the sentence of transportation passed on his fellow reformers Muir and Fyshe Palmer [qq.v.], Skirving continued his active work for the Friends of the People; for this he was brought to trial on 6-7 January 1794 and was sentenced to transportation for fourteen years. Together with Muir, Fyshe Palmer and Margarot [q.v.] he sailed for New South Wales in the transport *Surprize* in May 1794.

During the outward voyage he and Fyshe Palmer were subjected to brutal ill treatment by the master, Captain Campbell, on a trumped-up charge of conspiracy to mutiny, but on their arrival at Sydney in October these charges were dropped, and as a political prisoner he was freed from the usual convict restraint. He was allotted a small house on the eastern bank of the Tank Stream and allowed to purchase a farm of about 100 acres in the present district of Petersham, which he named New Strathruddie after his old home in Scotland. To this farm he applied himself with his usual diligence but, disheartened by unproductive soil and distressed by the separation from his wife and two sons, his health declined. He was removed to his house in the main camp and, although attended daily by Surgeon George Bass [q.v.] of the *Reliance*, he died on 19 March 1796.

Skirving was a man of high principle and unblemished personal character who sacrificed much for his ideals of political reform, all of which have long since been accomplished. His only epitaph in Australia is a marginal note on the burial entry in St Philip's register, 'a seditionist, but a man of respectable moral conduct', but his name is perpetuated on a monument erected to the Scottish Martyrs on Calton Hill, Edinburgh, in 1844.

HRNSW, 2, 3; HRA (1), 1; *The trial of William Skirving* (Edinb, 1794); T. F. Palmer, *A narrative . . . on board the Surprise transport* (Cambridge, 1797); T. J. Howell (ed), *State trials*, 23 (Lond, 1817); H. W. Meikle, *Scotland and the French revolution* (Glasgow, 1912); *Fife Free Press*, 2 Mar 1895; MS cat under Scottish Martyrs (ML).

JOHN EARNSHAW

SLADE, ERNEST AUGUSTUS (1805-1878), superintendent of convict barracks and police magistrate, was born on 30 June 1805, the son of General Sir John Slade (1762-1859), baronet, and his first wife Anna Eliza, née Dawson. His father distinguished himself during the Peninsular war at the battles of Busaco and Fuentes de Oñoro and received the thanks of parliament and a gold medal for his services.

Slade was an unruly and extravagant youth and his father hastened to get him into the army so that he would be under discipline and preferably out of England. A commission was bought for him for £450 and he joined the 54th Regiment as an ensign on 1 August 1822 and was promoted lieutenant in May 1825; in 1828 he transferred to the 40th Regiment and saw service in the Australian colonies and India. He retired from the army in 1831 and returned to New South Wales in 1832 with a letter of introduction from the Colonial Office to Governor Bourke expressing the wish that he be placed in any office which happened to be vacant when he arrived. In February 1833 Bourke appointed Slade superintendent of the con-

vict barracks at Hyde Park with a residence within the barracks and a salary of £150; next October he was appointed also to the part-time office of third police magistrate for Sydney for which he received an additional £100 a year. He held these appointments until 1 November 1834 when he became involved in court proceedings which received wide publicity. Because of the scandal to which these proceedings gave rise, Bourke told him that he could no longer hold his appointments; he was allowed to resign. Slade complained to the Colonial Office that he had been summarily and unjustly dismissed from his appointments; he admitted the irregularity of his own domestic establishment, but alleged in extenuation that many of the most respectable and useful justices of the peace of the colony were living in a state of concubinage with female servants.

He returned to England and in July 1836 applied to the Colonial Office for another appointment; he was told that it was unlikely that one could be offered to him in the foreseeable future. As a witness before the select committee on transportation in 1837 he gave a lurid picture of the moral depravity of the convict population in New South Wales; he also claimed that he had devised the type of cat then in general use in the colony and boasted that, if punishment were administered with it under his own supervision, it never failed to break the skin in four lashes. He alleged that Bourke had used the disclosures on his moral conduct merely as a pretext to deprive him of office, and that the real reason was that his severe treatment of convicts ran counter to the governor's own policy of leniency. He was re-examined by Sir George Grey on another part of his evidence in which he made allegations damaging to the character of the governor's son, Richard Bourke; the allegations were shown to be false and were expunged from the records.

Slade was twice married and had one daughter. He died at Boulogne, France, on 5 March 1878.

HRA (1), 11-15, 17, 18; *Statistical returns of the colony of NSW*, 1833, 1834; Sel cttee on transportation, Report 1837, PP (HC), 1837 (518); CO 202/27, 35; CO 201/246; WO 31/516; Bourke papers (ML).

HAZEL KING

SLOMAN, THOMAS MARTIN (1811-1902), banker and pastoralist, was born on 29 May 1811 at Exeter, England, the eldest son of Samuel George Sloman. He was educated at Ottery St Mary's with the intention of entering the ministry of the Church of England. However, he changed his mind and became a midshipman with the East India Co. In November 1833 he arrived in Sydney in the *Ann*, bringing letters of introduction to Rev. Samuel Marsden [q.v.].

For nine months he worked at Rev. Thomas Hassall's [q.v.] station at Jerry's Plains, and then entered into partnership with Sydney Jamieson Watson on the cattle station, Kill-me-cat, on the Tumut River. He dissolved this partnership in 1835 and next year, when he went to Bathurst to inspect sheep owned by Hassall, he was persuaded to accept the position of accountant in the Bathurst Bank. In 1840, when the Union Bank took over this bank, he was offered the position of manager, but declined. He had an interest in the business of John Lipscombe until 1840, when he joined J. J. Ashe in the firm of Sloman & Ashe. Four years later this partnership was dissolved and he made a trip to England, returning in 1846. He then became a partner with an auctioneer, Tress. In 1848 he bought half shares in Meadows Station, near Wellington, and Belaringar and Dundallamal on the lower Macquarie River. He later sold these interests to David Baird. When All Saints' Church, Bathurst, was completed in 1849 he organized a fund for a peal of bells. In 1851 he dissolved his partnership with Tress, went to England, and watched the casting of the bells at Loughborough; he returned in 1852.

In September 1855 he married Amelia Tregenna Henning at St Paul's Church, Chippendale. In 1858 he was a partner of Thomas Woolley [q.v.] in an ironmonger's business in Sydney. In the 1860s he held several properties in the Wellington district, and made trips to New Zealand with loads of cattle. He returned to banking in 1872 when he became manager of the Bathurst branch of the Savings Bank of New South Wales, a post he filled for twenty-five years; the branch was popularly known as Sloman's Bank. During those years he took an active part in the public life of Bathurst. He was a trustee of All Saints' Cathedral, a churchwarden, one of the original council of trustees of All Saints' College (1873-84), an alderman, and a worker for most charitable movements.

As a young man he was a fine athlete. All his life was guided by Christian principles, and he was scrupulously honest in his varied business activities. His work for the Bathurst cathedral was outstanding,

and his name is on the foundation stone. On his ninetieth birthday he was presented with an illuminated address by the citizens of Bathurst. He spent his later years writing of the events and worthy citizens of that town. He died at his son's home at Dubbo on 3 August 1902. There were nine children.

G. Wilson (ed), *Official history of the municipal jubilee of Bathurst 1862-1912* (Syd, 1913); R. Henning, *Letters* (Syd, 1952); W. A. Steel and J. M. Antill, *The history of All Saints' College Bathurst 1873-1951* (Syd, 1964); Sloman papers (in possession of Miss M. W. Sloman, Bathurst).

BERNARD GREAVES

SMITH, HENRY GILBERT (1802-1886), merchant, was fifth of the eight children of Thomas Smith (1767-1833), of Great Houghton and Quinton, Northamptonshire, England, and his wife Frances, née Flesher, of Towchester. In August 1827 he arrived in Hobart Town in the *Lang* with his brother Charles (1804-1849). Henry went on to Sydney but Charles was disgusted with Australia and returned to England in September. Henry was impressed by prospects in New South Wales and bought 2560 acres on the Molonglo plain. In 1829 he went to England and returned in June 1830 to set up the importing and mercantile firm of Smith Bros in Macquarie Place, Sydney, with his brother Thomas (1795-1842) who arrived in November. Acting with great energy and initiative, they built the first steam-ferry in Sydney using an engine they had brought out with them. This 25-ton ferry, the *Surprise*, ran between Sydney and Parramatta, but it was not successful and in 1832 was sold in Van Diemen's Land. The firm was amicably dissolved in 1832 and Thomas turned to accountancy, while Henry continued as a merchant. In 1833 he took his 9-year-old nephew, Thomas Whistler Smith [q.v.], into his office as a clerk, and gradually the business began to prosper and expand. In July 1835 Henry was elected a director of the Commercial Banking Co. of Sydney and in 1853 chairman of its board of directors. Also in 1835 Henry became the virtually independent Sydney agent of the Bathurst Bank; when he sailed for England late in 1836 Thomas took over the agency and continued to conduct loans in Sydney for the bank until it closed in October 1840. By 1846 Henry was back in Sydney and in February was appointed provisional director of the proposed railway association; later he was one of the three government directors of the Sydney Railway Co. From May 1856 to August 1858 he was a member of the Legislative Council. In 1848 Henry retired from his firm with the hope that Eustace Smith, a younger nephew, would take his place, but Eustace refused and the business was left to T. W. Smith.

In England in January 1839 Smith married Eleanor, of the Whistler family which was closely associated with the Smiths in business as well as in marriage. Eleanor died in October. By 1846 Smith was living at the Octagon in Darling Point, Sydney, in what he called a 'bachelor tower'. After another visit to England he lived at Fairlight, which he had built at Manly on a large area of land stretching from Sydney Harbour to Ocean Beach. There he was struck by the prospects of Manly as a seaside resort and he built cottages, a hotel, church, school, 'Vauxhall Gardens', and baths. He placed the stone kangaroo on the cliff above Manly facing the ocean and had much to do with planting the first Norfolk Island pines on the ocean front. Smith family names have been given to many streets in the area. In 1856 he donated the land for a Congregational church to be built in Wollongong. Also in 1856 Smith married Anne Margaret Thomas at Brisbane. After she died in 1866 at Manly he went to England, where he married his third wife Anna Louisa Lloyd (d. 1893). He died at Brighton on 1 April 1886, leaving an estate valued at more than £66,000. His three sons, Henry Stinton, Gilbert Flesher and Eustace Alfred, lived in England and in 1889 took the surname of Smith-Rewse.

K. W. Street, *Annals of the Street family of Birtley* (Syd, 1941); S. J. Butlin, *Foundations of the Australian monetary system, 1788-1851* (Melb, 1953).   A. F. PIKE

SMITH, PHILIP THOMAS (1800-1880), lawyer and landowner, was born in August 1800 at Faversham, Kent, England, the son of a landowner. After education at Rochester Mathematical School, he joined the navy as a midshipman and served in the Channel Fleet. He soon left the sea and became articled to Dawes & Son of Angel Court, Fleet Street, and in due course was admitted to the Bar as a solicitor. Deciding to emigrate, he sent £5000 to Van Diemen's Land, sailed in the *Royal Admiral* with a letter of introduction to Lieut-Governor Arthur, some valuable horses (lost in stormy weather) and unassembled

parts of a steam-boat, and arrived in Hobart Town in April 1832.

Smith was admitted to the rolls of the Supreme Court, but within two months bought some 28,000 acres of the government reserves near Ross. After the deposit was paid he sailed for England, having persuaded the government to defer further instalments until he could raise more money. He returned in the *Lonach* in October 1833 with his brothers Arthur and Lewis. The property was divided. Philip built Syndal on his section where he lived with Lewis, who soon returned to England. In 1838 Philip was joined by his wife and daughter from England; the latter, still alert in mind and body at 103, died in 1931, and her diaries from 1842 to 1900 survive. Arthur took 8000 acres, and at St David's Church, Hobart, in May 1836 married Jane Jeffreys, the youngest daughter of Michael Dobson of Gateshead, Durham; they built Beaufront and lived on the property until they returned to England in the 1850s, when it was sold.

At first Philip Smith continued his legal practice but, with some of the best land in the colony, he soon devoted all his time to Syndal. He resigned from the Commission of the Peace, charging the magistrate at Campbell Town with irregularity in a trial, and publishing his angry letters in two solid pages of the *Hobart Town Courier*, 24 November 1837. He sent stock to the new settlements at Adelaide and Port Phillip, and was active in founding the Midland Agricultural Association. Unlike many others he survived depression in the early 1840s, although he sometimes talked of selling out and making a fresh start as a lawyer. In 1843 he was appointed a justice of the peace and soon after became an ardent anti-transportationist, writing and speaking fearlessly for the cause. He also contributed to the London Agency of J. A. Jackson [q.v.] through which the colonists hoped to hasten responsible government. When it came he represented South Esk in the Legislative Council in 1856-57, but his interest in politics dwindled.

In 1861 Smith visited England with his family, but his impatient activity allowed no retirement. Back in Hobart he turned vigorously to social reform and philanthropy. A fervent Anglican, he was a generous donor to the church. A staunch teetotaller, he canvassed fearlessly and even attended the licensing court to oppose each new extension. He was also an irascible critic of the honorary Board of Education, believing that its lack of responsibility had saddled Tasmania with inferior and incompetent schoolmasters. With constructive zeal in 1874 he offered parliament £1000 for a teachers' training college, and repeated the offer in 1875. Next year he told a select committee that he wanted paid management of the education board, although his offer was not dependent on it. Parliament demurred at the cost and questioned his advanced views, but his principles did not waver. In 1877 when he left with his family for England, he invested £1000 in a trust for the sole purpose of training teachers. This fund, supplemented by £500 from his daughter, was alienated to the cost of the Philip Smith Training College opened in January 1911 on the Hobart Domain. He died at Nice on 14 March 1880. His portrait, painted in Florence, is in the possession of the college.

Journals (HA Tas), 1876, no 3; G. T. Stilwell, 'Ross reserve', PTHRA, 10 (1962); Mercury, 19 Mar 1880; Smith papers in author's possession.   J. B. PONDER

SMITH, THOMAS WHISTLER (1824-1859), businessman and banker, was born on 26 September 1824 at Hornsey, Middlesex, England, the eldest son of Thomas Smith and his wife Penelope, née Whistler. At the invitation of his brother Henry Gilbert Smith [q.v.], Thomas Smith brought his family to Sydney in November 1830 and went into partnership with his brother as Smith Bros., importers, agents and merchants; they had a warehouse and residence in Macquarie Place. At 9 young Thomas entered Smith Bros as a clerk. After his father's death in 1842 and his uncle's retirement in 1848, he took over the business and entered into partnership with John Croft, under the name of Smith, Croft & Co. The partnership was dissolved in 1858 when T. W. Smith decided to go to England.

On 29 June 1847 he married Sarah Maria, second daughter of John Street and his wife Maria Wood, née Rendell; and they lived at Ecclesbourne, Darling Point, until 1850, when they moved to the family home, Glenrock, on the site of the present Ascham School. Public spirited and a zealous churchman, he was the original warden of St Mark's, Darling Point, the first vice-president of the Union Club, director of several companies, and a member of the Legislative Assembly representing the North Riding of Cumberland from 1857-58. He was a founder of the Royal Exchange and at 27 the youngest man to be elected to its board of directors, of which he was deputy-chairman for some

time. He was a director of the Commercial Banking Co. of Sydney, the Australian Gaslight Co., the Australian Trust Co., the Australian General Assurance Co., the Australian Steam Navigation Co., and the Sydney Exchange Co. In 1859 he resigned his directorates and went to London to open the first office of the Commercial Banking Co. of Sydney there and to act as managing director of its board. Previously he had been a director of the bank from 1850 to 1851 and again from 1857 to 1859, when he became deputy-chairman.

During his stay in London he had intended to study politics to prepare for his return to the colonial parliament, but these ambitions and his brilliant business career came to an abrupt end, when he caught diphtheria and died on 12 November 1859. His family returned to New South Wales; his widow Sarah Maria died in 1892; they had four daughters and two sons.

K. W. Street, Annals of the Street family of Birtley (Syd, 1941); W. J. Lyons, 'Prominent business figures of Sydney in the 1850s', Business Archives, 1, no 3 (May 1957); The Commercial Banking Co. Syd Ltd, Half-yearly reports 1848-1910 (Syd, 1911); MS cat under T. W. Smith (ML).   VIVIENNE PARSONS

SMYTH, ARTHUR BOWES (1750-1790), surgeon, was born on 23 August 1750 at Tolleshunt D'Arcy, Essex, England, the seventh child of Thomas Smyth, a surgeon. He lived at Tolleshunt D'Arcy and practised there at least between 1778 and 1783. In 1787 he was appointed a surgeon in the Lady Penrhyn in the First Fleet; he took charge of the prisoners when the convicts' surgeon on board, Dr Alltree, fell ill at Tenerife. Under the name of Arthur Bowes, as he was known in the colony, from 22 March 1787 to 12 August 1789 he kept a journal which included a record of the events of the voyage and the first weeks in New South Wales. While still in Sydney, on 19 March he reported on the birds of Lord Howe Island where Lieutenant Ball [q.v.] had landed from the Supply on the way back from Norfolk Island.

Smyth left Sydney in the Lady Penrhyn on 20 April, and the journal is most significant for its descriptions of bird life at Port Jackson and Lord Howe Island, where the ship called on her way to China. He collected curios and natural history specimens on his excursions at Port Jackson, in a way typical of the non-scientific collecting done in the colony before George

Caley [q.v.] arrived in 1800. Bowes must have been one of the first white men to see an emu, of which he made a drawing. While on Lord Howe Island he made the earliest known drawing of the now extinct white gallinule, and observed the bell magpie or currawong and four now rare or extinct birds, which have been identified as the Lord Howe Island pigeon, the booby, the Lord Howe Island rail or woodhen, and an extinct species of parrakeet. He died soon after his return to England and was buried at Tolleshunt D'Arcy on 31 March 1790. A copy of his journal is in the Mitchell Library, Sydney, but the original is probably the one acquired from a descendant of Sir William Denison, which in 1964 was offered for sale by Francis Edwards Ltd, of London.

HRNSW, 1 pt 2, 2; K. A. Hindwood, 'An historic diary', *Emu*, 32 (1932); MS 995 (ML).

SNODGRASS, KENNETH (1784-1853), soldier and administrator, was born in Paisley, Scotland, the son of a Presbyterian minister. He became ensign in the 90th Regiment in 1802 and lieutenant in the 52nd in August 1804. In 1806 he accompanied the regiment to Sicily and two years later to Sweden. He was promoted captain on 20 October 1808 and from 1809 to 1814 fought in the Peninsular war, entering the Portuguese army in which he was appointed a major in November 1812. He commanded a corps of 400 grenadiers at the battle of Vittoria.

At the siege of San Sebastian he distinguished himself on 30 August 1813 by fording the River Urumea at night and eluding the French sentries in order to reconnoitre the scene of the next day's successful assault. In the course of storming the convent redoubt and outworks of the fortress he was himself wounded and two-thirds of his 'forlorn hope' were killed within fifteen minutes. He was again wounded during the battle of the Nive on 11 December 1813, and suffered a severe head wound in the battle of Orthes in February 1814. He received decorations for his part in five major actions and was appointed C.B. in 1815. On 21 June 1817 he was promoted lieut-colonel; he remained in the Portuguese army until 1822.

When an army medical board, considering his old head wound, ruled him unfit for service in the East or West Indies, which was tantamount to retiring him from active duties, he decided to accept appointment as major of brigade in Sydney,

in the hope of settling in Australia. With his wife and six children he reached Sydney in December 1828.

On 1 January 1829 he was appointed commandant of the mounted police and placed in charge of the Ordnance Department. He applied for a land grant and an allotment in Sydney, but both applications were rejected as regulations forbade grants to serving military officers, and from this time on he complained increasingly, although governors continued to praise his devotion to duty. He pointed out that he had come to New South Wales fully expecting to be able to settle his family comfortably and had performed extra duties without payment. The refusal of his requests was the harder to accept as civil officers were being granted town allotments while he had been forced to devote one-eighth of his salary to the rent of an unsuitable house.

Although he gave up command of the mounted police in October 1830, he continued to occupy unpaid offices as a member of the Executive Council from July 1832 and of the Legislative Council from November 1833. With the departure of Colonel Arthur from Van Diemen's Land he was selected to be lieut-governor until the arrival of Sir John Franklin, from 28 October 1836 to 5 January 1837. He was acting governor of New South Wales from 5 December 1837 to 23 February 1838, between the departure of Governor Bourke and the arrival of Governor Gipps.

In Van Diemen's Land he had successfully pursued his professed desire 'to continue the state vehicle in its due and regular motion, free from upsets on one side or the other'. In Sydney, however, he was condemned by J. D. Lang [q.v.] when he withdrew the salaries of six Presbyterian ministers who supported Lang's establishment of a synod free from the Church of Scotland. The payment of stipends depended on a certificate from the moderator and this had not been granted, but Lang saw in the act a proof of previous 'obtuseness of moral feeling'. Adverting to the fact that the acting governor had employed as tutor a convict transported for attempted murder, Lang concluded that it was an outrage upon the Presbyterian community to entrust their interests to a man 'who had spontaneously delivered over his own children to the guardianship of an assassin'. Gipps, on arrival, found that Snodgrass had been drawing the full salary allowed to the governor and it was then realized that the same had occurred in Hobart Town a year earlier. The Colonial Office ruled that in both cases he was entitled to only half the salary, but Snodgrass refused to repay anything, claiming instead that he should be paid for the earlier duties which he had performed for nothing. After more than two years the controversy was settled only by the grant of £755 for the extra duties, the money being retained by the government in satisfaction of its own claims.

In 1839 Snodgrass sold his commission and retired to his estate, Eagleton, near Raymond Terrace. There he soon became involved in a dispute with his neighbour, James King [q.v.] of Irrawang, over the breaking of a boundary fence which King had erected. When Snodgrass finally wrote a hot letter, offering to 'give the usual explanation', he was charged with attempting to provoke a duel and fined £100 in the Supreme Court in July 1842. The fine was remitted by Gipps in consideration of his important services and honourable career. A series of disputes between the neighbours continued. At one stage, King claimed, Snodgrass instituted an attempt to open an unfenced public road through Irrawang, and in 1851 he sought to use a proposed National school as a further means of gaining a right-of-way through King's property.

Meanwhile Snodgrass had been elected to the Legislative Council in 1848 as representative for the Counties of Gloucester, Macquarie and Stanley, an area stretching from Raymond Terrace to Brisbane. His policy, following the middle course of his Tasmanian administration, was so framed that it was impossible to define what he supported. In the council he played no very active part and resigned in 1850.

By his wife Janet, née Wright (1790-1845), whom he had married in Scotland in May 1814, he had a large family which included Peter [q.v.], who became a member of the Victorian Legislative Council, and John, an officer in the 96th Regiment. Snodgrass died at Raymond Terrace on 14 October 1853.

Snodgrass was at his best as a soldier, and achieved little outside active service. He had the affection of his military colleagues: to them his gallantry and devotion made him 'a friend of sterling merit, never mentioned by those who knew him but with united esteem and respect'. To civilians he could show contempt and intransigence, which were partly attributable to the head wound which had incapacitated him. James King's opinion of him was that military men should hold no civil appointment and were 'utterly dangerous' when they added 'cunning and intrigue to their other qualities'.

HRA (1), 14-21, 24; *Maitland Mercury*, 7 Sept 1850; *Examiner* (Launceston), 3 Dec 1853; Supreme Court records (NSWA).

E. J. LEA-SCARLETT

SNODGRASS, PETER (1817-1867), pastoralist and politician, was born on 29 September 1817 in Portugal, the third son of Lieut-Colonel Kenneth Snodgrass [q.v.]. He arrived at Sydney with his parents in December 1828. From New South Wales he overlanded to the Port Phillip District in 1838; he himself gave the date as 1837 but memory played him false. His first property was Murrindindi, near Yea, on the Goulburn River. His timing was unfortunate because the depression of the early 1840s brought him and many others to insolvency. However, he battled on and for the rest of his life was interested in other stations, sometimes on his own account and sometimes in partnership. As a young man he was adventurous, high-spirited and a reckless horseman. On 1 January 1840 in Melbourne he figured in a duel with another young squatter, William Ryrie, on the site of the present Spencer Street railway station; after Snodgrass fired precipitately and grazed his own toe, honour was satisfied. On another occasion when bushrangers were active beyond Eltham, he was among a group of young squatters whose help Superintendent La Trobe sought for the police. Snodgrass and other volunteers were sworn in as special constables, issued with firearms and captured the gang.

In 1851 he was elected to the first Victorian Legislative Council and retained his seat until responsible government. He was then elected member for Anglesey in the Legislative Assembly and in 1864 member for South Gippsland, a seat which he held until his death. He was not a good speaker and his main activity in parliament was the advancement of the squatters' interests.

His public activities included that of a trustee of Scots Church, Collins Street, Melbourne. On the visit of the duke of Edinburgh in November 1867 he went by steamer to Queenscliff to witness the arrival. On his return he suffered pain and, soon after reaching his home at South Yarra, died suddenly from aneurism of the heart.

In 1846 he had married Charlotte Agnes Cotton who survived him with six sons and three daughters. One daughter married Major-General F. G. Hughes. The eldest daughter, Janet Marian, married Sir William Clarke.

Garryowen (E. Finn), *Chronicles of early Melbourne*, 1-2 (Melb, 1888); C. S. Ross, *Colonization and church work in Victoria* (Melb, 1891); T. F. Bride (ed), *Letters from Victorian pioneers* (Melb, 1898); M. L. Kiddle, *Men of yesterday* (Melb, 1961); *Argus*, 26 Nov 1867; F. J. Corder, Case book of Henry Moor (copy, Roy Hist Soc Vic).

ALAN GROSS

SOLANDER, DANIEL (1733-1782), naturalist, was born on 19 February 1733 at Piteä in Norrland, Sweden, the son of Rev. Carl Solander and Magdalena, née Bostadia. Although baptized Daniel, Solander later adopted his father's name with the suffix 'son' as an extra Christian name and he recorded his signature accordingly. It is likely that he received much of his education from his father before enrolling at the University of Uppsala in July 1750. Solander studied languages and the humanities and attended lectures delivered by his uncle, Daniel Solander, who was professor of law. The professor of botany was the celebrated Linnaeus (Carl von Linné) who was soon impressed by young Solander's ability and accordingly persuaded his father to let him study natural history. In 1756 Solander edited Linnaeus's *Elementa Botanica*.

Advised by Linnaeus to go to England, Solander arrived in London in June 1760 with letters of introduction to two leading naturalists, John Ellis and Peter Collinson. He did not return and so did not present his doctoral thesis, although long before the *Endeavour* voyage he was referred to as 'Dr Solander'. Towards the end of 1761 Linnaeus advised Solander that the chair of botany at the Academy of Sciences, St Petersburg, was offered to him, but on the advice of Collinson and other English friends he declined the post. He also declined to succeed Linnaeus at Uppsala. On Collinson's recommendation Solander was engaged to catalogue the natural history collections in the British Museum and on his appointment as assistant librarian in 1763 was able to promote effectively the Linnaean system of classification. In the following year he was elected a fellow of the Royal Society, and by 1765 he was working on a descriptive catalogue of the vast private museum of the duchess of Portland.

Solander's work and social activities led him to meet Joseph Banks [q.v.] who in 1768 invited him to join the scientific staff of the *Endeavour*. Engaged at £400 a year, Solander assisted Banks to make a large collection of natural history specimens, including many from the east coast of Australia. After his return to England in July 1771 Solander became Banks's secretary and librarian. He was presented to George III in August, and in November he received the honorary degree of doctor of civil law from the University of Oxford. To Linnaeus's dismay Banks and Solander seemed more eager to organize further expeditions than to complete the arrangement and classification of the collections already made. In 1772 they explored the Isle of Wight, the western highlands of Scotland, and Iceland, and returned with much material ranging from Icelandic plants to specimens of lava from Mount Hekla. Next year Solander joined Banks on an expedition to Wales, and he was also appointed keeper of natural history at the British Museum. He lived with Banks in London, amid the books, herbarium specimens and natural curiosities in his care. He died on 13 May 1782, after a stroke. He was buried in the Swedish Church, London, and in 1913 his remains were moved to the Swedish churchyard in Woking.

Daniel Solander was a rather short, plump man of some thirteen stone, jovial, fond of company and much in demand in London society; he had a ready welcome for any Swedish visitors to England. Deeply affected by the marriage in 1764 of Linnaeus's eldest daughter, Elisabeth Christina, he became a confirmed bachelor. He was a popular conversationalist and 'a philosophical gossip'; notoriously forgetful and careless about his appearance, except for a weakness for elaborate waistcoats, he was a most uncertain correspondent. Though accomplished in Swedish, Dutch, English and Latin, he published little, for his full programmes at Soho Square and the museum were intensified by social obligations. However, he left much manuscript material relating especially to the *Endeavour* voyage and the expedition to Iceland. Banks proposed to publish an ambitious botanical work for which many beautiful copper plates were prepared. Solander contributed the Latin descriptions of the plants depicted, and happily these ultimately appeared when the trustees of the British Museum authorized publication of the plates in *Illustrations of Australian Plants collected in 1770 during Captain Cook's Voyage round the World in H.M.S. Endeavour*, edited by James Britten (London, 1905). When Gustavus Brander (1720-1787) presented to the British Museum a collection of fossils in clays from Hordwell and Barton, the specimens were described by Solander in *Fossilia Hantoniensis collecta, et in Musaeo Britannico deposita a Gustavo Brander* (London,

1766), a finely illustrated work. Solander also published 'An Account of the Gardenia' in *Philosophical Transactions*, 52 (1761-62) and another on a parasitic worm in *Nova Acta Societas Scientiarum Upsalensis*, 1 (1773). Another work, published posthumously, was *The Natural History of many . . . uncommon Zoophytes, collected by John Ellis* (London, 1786).

The naturalist has been commemorated by Point Solander, the south headland of Botany Bay; a monument at Kurnell, Botany Bay, erected by the Swedish community in 1914; the tropical American plant genus *Solandra*; a few Australian plant species; an island off the south of New Zealand; and the 'Solander case', a book-box for carrying notes and specimens. The Linnean Society, London, and Brigadier C. H. Vaughan have portraits.

J. H. Maiden, *Sir Joseph Banks* (Syd, 1909); J. Britten and G. S. Boulger, *A biographical index of deceased British and Irish botanists*, 2nd ed (Lond, 1931); H. C. Cameron, *Sir Joseph Banks* (Lond, 1952); J. C. Beaglehole (ed), *The Endeavour journal of Joseph Banks, 1768-1771*, 1-2 (Syd, 1962); R. E. Fries, 'Commemoration address', *Swedish Roy Academy of Sciences Year-book*, 1940, and for bibliog.

L. A. GILBERT

SOLOMON, ISAAC (IKEY) (1787?-1850), convict and dealer, was born one of a family of nine children in Gravel Lane, Houndsditch, London. He married Ann, daughter of Moses Julian, coachmaster, of Aldgate. Solomon first had a shop at Brighton, but later opened what was ostensibly a jeweller's shop in Bell Lane, London, where he carried on business as a receiver of stolen goods.

In 1810 he was arrested for picking pockets, tried at the Old Bailey in conjunction with Joel Joseph and sentenced to transportation for life. Solomon went no farther than the hulks, where after three or four years he managed to escape from the hulk *Zetland*. He continued his business as a fence and achieved such notoriety that, when again arrested, three pamphlets containing highly exaggerated accounts of his criminal activity were published about him. At his arrest on 25 April 1827 he was charged with theft and receiving, the goods involved being 6 watches, 3½ yards of woollen cloth, 17 shawls, 12 pieces of Valentia cloth, lace, bobbinet, caps and other articles. He was committed for trial and lodged in Newgate prison. On a writ of habeas corpus he was taken to the Court of King's Bench, but the application

failed and he was led to a hackney coach to be conveyed back to Newgate. Unknown to his captors the coach was driven by Solomon's father-in-law, whom the turnkeys permitted to make a detour through Petticoat Lane. At a prearranged place some of Solomon's friends overpowered the guard and released him.

Solomon fled the country, going first to Denmark and then to the United States. A reward was offered for his capture and his wife was arrested for receiving stolen goods. Ann Solomon was sentenced to transportation for fourteen years. She had two grown-up sons, John and Moses, two younger sons aged 9 and 3, and two daughters aged 7 and 5. Ann was transported in the ship *Mermaid* and arrived at Hobart Town in June 1828 with her four youngest children. She was assigned as a servant to Richard Newman, an officer of police; her sons John and Moses migrated to Van Diemen's Land to live with her.

Solomon meanwhile moved to Rio de Janeiro whence he sailed in the *Coronet* to Hobart, travelling under the assumed name of Slowman. However, Hobart was the enforced home of many of his old colleagues and customers and he was soon recognized. He bought real estate in Hobart and opened a shop. Quarrels broke out in the Newman household, Mrs Solomon's assignment was revoked and she was placed in the Female House of Correction. Isaac applied to have his wife assigned to him. It was notorious that Solomon was a fugitive from justice, but Lieut-Governor Arthur could then do nothing to apprehend him because he had no warrant, although on 17 October 1828 he had written to the Colonial Office asking for one. After repeated requests had been made for Ann Solomon's release, Isaac entered into a £1000 bond to guarantee that she would not escape from the colony, and a number of local publicans and merchants, including John Pascoe Fawkner [q.v.] entered into sureties of £100 or £200 each. Arthur relented and allowed Mrs Solomon to be assigned to her husband.

When the *Lady of the Lake* arrived in Hobart in November 1829 it brought warrants for Solomon's arrest, and these were immediately executed. Solomon's counsel, however, had him brought before the court on a writ of habeas corpus and, because of a technical fault in the warrants from London, the application for his release was sustained by the court. The judge fixed bail at £2000, with four sureties of £500, and Solomon's friends found it difficult to raise so much money. Arthur was in a dilemma, and finally issued a warrant in his own name against Solomon and had him placed in the *Prince Regent* for England.

Sydney and Hobart newspapers denounced the governor's refusal to abide by the principles of habeas corpus. Thomas Capon, the chief constable, was put in charge of his special prisoner because the master of the ship had refused to guarantee his safe arrival.

Solomon was tried at the Old Bailey on eight charges of receiving stolen goods, found guilty on two, and sentenced to transportation for fourteen years. He arrived at Hobart in the *William Glen Anderson* in November 1831 and was sent to Richmond gaol, where in 1832 he became a javelin man. In 1834 he was transferred to Port Arthur and in 1835 was granted a ticket-of-leave on condition that he lived at least twenty miles from Hobart. He took up residence at New Norfolk and was reunited with his family, although the two elder sons seem to have left Van Diemen's Land by that time. His family had now become estranged from him and there were violent quarrels. Most of the children took their mother's part and he turned them out of his house. Mrs Solomon was sent to the Female House of Correction again as a result of some of these altercations, and her daughter Ann had to write numerous petitions before her mother was released in September 1835. The elder Ann Solomon was granted a ticket-of-leave in November 1835 and a conditional pardon in May 1840. Isaac lived apart from his wife after this, remaining in New Norfolk till 1838; he was living at New Town when in 1840 he was granted a conditional pardon. He received the certificate of his freedom in 1844.

Solomon died in September 1850 and was buried on the 3rd of that month. His estate did not exceed £70.

GO 2/5, 33/5-7 (TA); Executive Council 2/1 (TA); CSO 1/354/8078, 1/430/9642, 1/849/17494, 5/131/3131 (TA); Convict Records 31/39, 40/9 (TA).   R. C. SHARMAN

SOLOMON, JOSEPH (1780?-1851), merchant was in partnership with his brother Judah (1777?-1856) as Jewish shopkeepers in London when in August 1819 at the Kent Assizes they were convicted of hiring burglars to repossess unpaid goods. They arrived at Sydney in the *Prince Regent* next January and were sent in the *Castle Forbes* to Hobart Town, where they landed in March. By January 1821, trading as J. & J. Solomon, they had a general store at the corner of Liverpool and Argyle Streets. In June they were acquitted on a charge of selling spirits without a licence, though similar charges later cost them £50 in fines. In 1823 both brothers were foundation subscribers to the Bank of Van Diemen's Land. By 1825 they had a new store in Argyle Street and had begun dealing in town and country land; Joseph had moved to Launceston, where he opened the Tasmanian Store in Cameron Street. He received his conditional pardon seven years later and his free pardon in 1836. By that time the brothers had opened a second business in Launceston, and a branch at Evandale which was soon raided by bushrangers, but the two brothers were drifting apart. Another store was opened at Campbell Town in 1838 and next year Joseph announced his withdrawal from the partnership, though it was not formally dissolved for three years.

Both brothers had left wives and families in England but, unlike Judah, Joseph had abandoned the Jewish faith and was joined by his lawful children, though his wife had died. At St John's Church, Launceston, in July 1833 his son Lion Henry married Frances, daughter of Edward and Ann Symonds from Wolveton, Dorset, and on 17 November Joseph Solomon married Eliza Backas (Backhouse), the widowed daughter of Sharpland Graves of County Wicklow, Ireland. His three daughters also married: Mary to William Roberts in 1835, Sarah to Benjamin Walford in 1838 and Frances to Anthony Cottrell, who had been chief constable at Launceston and as a member of John Batman's [q.v.] syndicate looked after Solomon's speculations at Port Phillip. Solomon soon withdrew from his investments in Melbourne and with help from Lion was content to consolidate his business interests in Launceston, surrounded by his family. As his health declined he spent more time on his property near Evandale, where he had built his country home, Riverview. There he died on 14 May 1851, aged 71, and was buried in the Anglican churchyard at Evandale. He was survived by his wife, four children and thirteen grandchildren. He had left his estate in order, even making an annuity of £25 to an aged aunt in England, 'this being the amount I have hitherto been in the habit of remitting to her'.

Solomon had no son named Joseph. In M. Gordon, *Jews in Van Diemen's Land* (Sydney, 1965), Joseph Solomon has been credited with a son of that name. This is a wrong identification. The Joseph who went to Port Phillip in 1839 and lived for a time at Saltwater River may have been the son of Judah who contested the Huon electorate in Tasmania in 1880.

HRA (3), 4; J. Fenton, A *history of Tasmania* (Hob, 1884); Correspondence file under J. Solomon (TA); H. J. Solomon, The queer colony (in author's possession).

H. J. SOLOMON

SORELL, WILLIAM (1775-1848), soldier and lieut-governor, was born probably in the West Indies, the son of Major-General William Alexander Sorell and his wife Jane. His official correspondence shows both a cultivated mind and a competence in writing. As the son of a senior officer and a suitable candidate for a commission in keeping with the common practice of the times, he joined the army and in August 1790 was appointed an ensign in the 31st Regiment. Promoted lieutenant in 1793, he fought in the West Indies, where he was severely wounded. In 1795 he was promoted captain and acted as aide-de-camp to Lieut-General Sir James Pulteney. He took part in the expedition to North Holland in 1799 and next year was present at minor attacks on Spanish naval ports. When war against Napoleon was renewed Sorell served at home. Promoted major in 1804, he took part in the special training of Sir John Moore's Light Brigade. In 1807 he went to the Cape of Good Hope with the rank of lieut-colonel and was deputy-adjutant-general of the British forces there until 1811.

He married Louisa Matilda, daughter of Lieut-General Cox, and had seven children, but in 1807 arranged a separation from her. While at the Cape he commenced a liaison with the wife of Lieutenant Kent, who was stationed there, at the same time as he earned a well-deserved professional reputation as a very able administrator amid the confusion that followed the British capture of the colony from the Dutch. After his return to England he was promoted major in the 46th Regiment in 1812 but next year resigned from military service.

On 3 April 1816 Sorell was appointed to replace Lieut-Colonel Davey as lieut-governor of Van Diemen's Land in the hope that he would be able to restore order and bring direction and organization into the government of that colony. He sailed in the transport *Sir William Bensley* and reached Sydney on 10 March 1817. During a brief stay there Sorell impressed Governor Macquarie before going on to Hobart Town.

On 9 April he assumed office and at once proceeded to try to reform the abuses prevalent on the Derwent. He found much disorder in the administration, government activities were not co-ordinated and peculation was common. The convicts were under little control; bushranging had almost reached the proportions of open armed revolt against authority. Sorell knew that his powers were severely limited and his authority in most matters was confined to carrying out instructions received from Macquarie; he was not allowed to allocate land to settlers or to employ government funds or prison labour without sanction and he was required to submit details of public expenditure to Sydney. Colonel Cimitiere [q.v.], the commandant at Port Dalrymple, shared with him the power to grant prisoners tickets-of-leave and, although Sorell was lieut-governor and Cimitiere had to report and make returns to Hobart, the latter also acted under direct instructions from Macquarie. By 1820 Cimitiere had so obstinately resisted Sorell's orders that there was an open quarrel between the two. When Commissioner Bigge [q.v.] investigated charges of corruption against Cimitiere, he suggested that the controlling power of the lieut-governor in Hobart should be strengthened.

Sorell firmly met the challenge of Michael Howe [q.v.], the leader of the bushrangers and self-styled 'Governor of the Woods'. Well planned and executed military operations quickly ended Howe's career and sent most of his followers to the gallows. The stern warning was not lost on those runaway convicts who sought to emulate Howe. The 'Old Man', as Sorell was known, probably on account of his white hair, was rightly feared as nobody in the colony before him. Sorell's 'campaign' did not end when his captives swung on the public gallows as a warning to others. He knew that large-scale bushranging was only made possible by help given by outwardly law-abiding free colonists, and told Macquarie that he was doing his utmost to detect Howe's accomplices and abettors. In less than eighteen months after taking office Sorell had arrested all the known sympathizers of the bushrangers and those who assisted them.

With law and order restored, Sorell was able to carry out the reforms and plans he had formed for the development of the colony. Organizing a proper personal staff and successfully employing his considerable diplomatic skill, he secured the essential co-operation of the newly appointed Deputy-Judge-Advocate Abbott [q.v.], the senior chaplain and the commanding officer of the troops. The duties of each public officer were clearly defined and a proper system of accounts, records and correspondence installed, so that Sorell can be regarded as the founder of sound administrative systems in the colony.

From 1817 onwards free colonists began to arrive in increasing numbers. Sorell personally carried out investigations of land which seemed suitable for grants. His journeys into the unknown country in the upper Derwent valley and along the Clyde River give him a place in the history of the island's inland exploration. Although there are no records of his having been engaged in farming in England, he showed a very practical concern in expanding production from the land. All through his letters and dispatches are references to the care of livestock, the proper selection of seed for grain crops and their proper harvesting and storage. A community which ten years earlier had faced famine became a producer of surplus crops which were exported to Sydney and even abroad. Sorell recognized the value of the Midland plains for pastoral production. With Macquarie's co-operation he was able to arrange for the importation of several hundred merino sheep from the famous Camden flock, and these laid the foundations of the Tasmanian fine-wool industry. Commerce increased as a result of stable conditions and land development, but the chaotic condition of the currency was a source of embarrassment and loss to all concerned with trade. Sorell could not withdraw the debased coins and promissory notes in circulation, or abolish the custom of the use of rum for exchange, but 'he constantly endeavoured to keep all official values expressed in sterling, despite the fact that the Spanish dollar was the commonest coin', and he made an important contribution to commerce by taking steps, with the aid of leading merchants, to establish a bank, the Bank of Van Diemen's Land.

Recognizing that the British government regarded the colony principally as a community for the reception, punishment and wherever possible the reclamation of prisoners, Sorell was at pains to organize governmental agencies for these purposes. Over the convicts he established a 'system of perpetual reference and control', through regular musters, the strict issue of passes and a full series of registers. He built convict barracks in Hobart which were first occupied in 1822. He tried to assign prisoners only to reputable employers and to guard against the lax granting of tickets-of-leave by restricting them to convicts who gave evidence of good behaviour, apart from a few with special skills. For reconvicted prisoners he established the penal settlement on Sarah Island in the then remote Macquarie Harbour. Later generations, with small knowledge of the conditions of the times and the lack of humanity in his generation's attitude to crime and punishment, have severely criticized Sorell for the conditions there. However, he had no funds or authority to establish a proper penal settlement or to build costly prisons, and he had to deal with many desperate men whom other gaolers had gladly sent to Tasmania.

Sorell's policies were so successful that the colony's conditions and prospects became well known and favourably regarded in Britain. The ready availability of land suitable for sheep-breeding and wool-growing and of cheap assigned labour attracted a considerable number of former army and navy officers who brought their families, household goods, agricultural implements and in many cases substantial capital with them. Sorell was also extremely mindful of his social responsibilities. The plight of the Aboriginals who were losing their hunting grounds and their fisheries troubled him and he did what he could to prevent their exploitation by the settlers. He took firm steps to prevent the enslavement of native children. The plight of abandoned white orphans, an early problem in the colony, attracted his notice; before leaving office he took steps to establish an institution for their care, although many years were to pass before this humane intention was carried out. Such was the satisfaction with Sorell's government that in 1821 the free settlers took the most unusual step in early Australian affairs of presenting him with plate valued at 500 guineas.

Unfortunately Sorell's private affairs never ceased to intrude upon his public duties. In July 1817, a few months after assuming office in Van Diemen's Land, he had to pay £3000 damages to Lieutenant Kent for criminal conversation with Kent's wife. Next year Bathurst admonished him for leaving his own wife and family of seven young children in England without support. Sorell explained that this was partly due to his wife's refusal to agree to reasonable proposals for the children's education, but in January 1819 he instructed that an allowance of £200 a year be paid to her 'out of the Moiety of my salary issued in England'. He did not deny his responsibility but pleaded that 'pressure of affairs alone prevented that claim being put upon a footing beyond contingency at an earlier period'.

Meanwhile Mrs Kent, who bore Sorell several children, went to Tasmania and took up residence at Government House. This situation did not long escape the attention of A. F. Kemp [q.v.], who had played an unworthy part in the deposition of Governor Bligh and was living as a farmer and merchant in Tasmania. When Kemp found Sorell would not defer to his unreasonable demands he commenced a vindictive campaign against him. He complained of Sorell 'now living in open Adultery with Mrs Kent, publicly parading about in the Government carriage, and introducing her . . . as Mrs Sorell . . . the Lieutenant Governor living in a public state of concubinage to the evil example of the Rising Generation'. Macquarie seems quite properly to have ignored Kemp's charge, but Bathurst asked Commissioner Bigge to investigate it. Bigge examined Kemp in Hobart. He stated that Kemp's charge 'is founded in Truth' but added the opinion of Deputy-Judge-Advocate Abbott, who did 'not admit that it has produced any restraint upon the limited circle of their society'; his examination of Major Bell [q.v.], the commanding officer in the colony, shows that Kemp's attacks had been made only after he had been convicted by a bench of magistrates for refusing to make police returns of persons in his employ. Bigge clearly had little patience with Kemp and paid Sorell the unusual tribute of telling Bathurst how impressed he had been by Sorell's 'great and distinguished merit'. Bigge felt that in the circumstances he could not visit Government House socially, but Sorell never allowed this 'to have the slightest effect upon our private or public intercourse'. After Bigge's inquiry Sorell wrote directly to Bathurst about 'an Accuser who has been incessantly employed in traducing my acts and my administration, and The Judges, The Magistracy and public Functionaries of The Settlement'. He referred to Kemp's character in New South Wales and his arrest of Governor Bligh and said that as Kemp proposed as a magistrate to call a public meeting of free settlers to discuss Sorell's acts, he suspended him. 'With regard to myself', concluded Sorell, 'I am conscious that if . . . I can lay claim to unimpeachable Conduct in the discharge of my publick duty, and to guarded and prudent Demeanour, I have yet to interest, Your Lordship's indulgent Consideration, because I did in one instance incur the Censure of The World'.

Bigge also reported that the lieut-governor, who received only £800 a year, was grossly underpaid, and in 1823 his salary was raised to £1500. This was a short-lived benefit to Sorell, for in August Bathurst wrote that he had decided to recall him. 'In communicating to you the painful necessity, under which I have found myself placed, of appointing a Successor to you in Van Diemen's Land, I shall not feel it necessary to detail the reasons, which you will know, have compelled me to a measure which, on other accounts, I should have wished to avoid', he said, thus evading the cause of what amounted to dismissal. When this became known unofficially in the colony a representative meeting of protest was held at Hobart. A memorial was prepared and signed by all the free settlers of standing, including his erstwhile accuser, Kemp. It did not reach London in time to be considered by the secretary of state, but it is unlikely that it would have altered the government's decision. However, Under-Secretary Horton wrote to assure Sorell 'that his Lordship fully appreciates the zeal and ability with which you administered the Government of Van Diemen's Land and that it will afford his Lordship much satisfaction whenever circumstances may permit of his availing himself of your further Services', and the British government authorized the payment to him of £500 out of colonial revenue so long as he remained unemployed in any public capacity.

Sorell's term of office ended on 14 May 1824. Whilst waiting to leave the colony he wrote for his successor, Lieut-Governor Arthur, a lengthy, well-balanced, lucid and valuable report on the state of Van Diemen's Land. When he reached England he was well received at the Colonial Office, a fact which might be thought to raise the question why he was relieved of his post; but Bathurst clearly distinguished between Sorell's administrative ability and the effect the example of his private life would have on colonial society. Sorell was not employed again as an administrator and died at Marylebone, London, on 4 June 1848. His small estate was left to his widow. His son William [q.v.] remained in Tasmania, where his descendants became prominent.

No evidence has yet been produced to refute the contemporary judgments that Sorell was a wise and unusually capable civil and military administrator. To his task of restoring order and encouraging progress in settled social conditions he allied an unshakeable firmness with skill, tact and patience. Contemporaries recorded his 'personal charm' and 'friendly manner' which made official relations easy between governor and governed. No Tasmanian governor has received the public marks of esteem and affection shown to Sorell. There was a long-lived legend, perhaps based on fact, that Sorell used to spend some of his day standing at the Government House gate, Macquarie Street, Hobart, talking to passers-by and listening to their views and petitions; however, it must be remembered that his popularity was perhaps enhanced in retrospect on account of the widespread dislike of his successor.

His character was complex. In official dealings he was just and honourable, and unlike many of his gubernatorial contemporaries he made no attempt to avail himself of legal opportunities to add to his private fortune. He was negligent in his family obligations, and his failure to recognize the social conventions was by deliberate choice. For this he was apparently prepared to pay. He damaged the official career to which he was certainly dedicated, but the majority of the influential free Tasmanian colonists of his period seemed to have overlooked unconventional conduct or impropriety and saw Sorell as a wise, fatherly ruler.

HRA (1), 9-11, 13, (3), 2-6, (4), 1; R. W. Giblin, *The early history of Tasmania*, 2 (Melb, 1939); R. M. H. Garvie, 'The journal of William Sorell', PTHRA, 9 (1961).

JOHN REYNOLDS

SORELL, WILLIAM (1800-1860), registrar, was the eldest son of Lieut-Governor William Sorell who, when taking his appointment in Van Diemen's Land, had left his family in England. Sorell junior resented his father's disregard of his career and wrote in 1822 to Commissioner J. T Bigge [q.v.] stating his determination to go to the colony to assert his claims on his father's attention in person. To save the lieut-governor this embarrassment, Bigge appealed on the son's behalf to the Colonial Office. There his resentment was appeased and, with the blessing of Earl Bathurst and a recommendation to the notice of Colonel Arthur, Sorell reached Hobart Town in December 1823. Next month he received 1000 acres of land in the Hamilton district and in 1828 a town allotment. On the sudden death of the officer chosen by the Colonial Office to be registrar of the new Supreme Court of Van Diemen's Land, Sorell senior suggested his son to Lieut-Governor Arthur and to Governor Brisbane. His qualifications and capacity for the position were approved by Chief Justice Pedder [q.v.] and as nominee he duly read the royal charter when the Supreme Court, separated at last from the court of New South Wales, was first opened on 10 May 1824. His appointment at £600 was confirmed by the Colonial Office in December.

In the next thirty-six years his worth in the public service was shown in the variety of his additional posts. In 1836 he was appointed registrar of deeds and master of the Supreme Court. Four years later he became commissioner of the Supreme Court and commissioner of insolvent estates. From 1847 to 1854 he was on the commission investigating titles to land. For some time he was a member of the Board of Education and from 1847 to 1859 was a commissioner of the Bridgewater bridge. In 1849 he served on the boards for disposing of crown waste lands by sale and licence and for creating a fund to provide retiring allowances to officers in the colonial service. A year later he joined the board formed to inquire into the Registrar-General's Department. In 1852 he became registrar of the Vice-Admiralty Court, in 1854 curator of intestate estates, and in 1856 member of the board that reported on colonial revenue. In 1857 he was made registrar of births, deaths and marriages and deputy-registrar for the Hobart district. He was well liked by all members of the legal profession and their respect for his judgment brought him many commissions as an arbitrator. On his death on 17 November 1860 the public offices were closed in respect. He was a member of the Church of England and was buried in the family vault in St David's Park cemetery.

In 1825 Sorell had married Elizabeth Julia, the daughter of Captain Anthony Fenn Kemp [q.v.] of Mount Vernon, Kempton. They had five children, one of whom, Julia, married Thomas Arnold [q.v.]. A man of great integrity, Sorell's domestic life was very unhappy because of the collapse of his marriage, the removal of his children to Paris and his worry in achieving their return to him.

W. Sorell, Diary, Aug 1823-Aug 1825 (in possession of Sorell family, Hob); Correspondence file under Sorell (TA).

R. M. H. GARVIE

SOUTHWELL, DANIEL (1764?-1797), naval officer and diarist, joined the navy in May 1780 as a first lieutenant's servant. He embarked as a midshipman in the *Sirius* in 1787 and was made a mate on the voyage to New South Wales. He kept a journal from the time of sailing until May 1789 and also corresponded with his mother, Jane Southwell, and his uncle, Rev. Weeden Butler of Chelsea. These letters are in the British Museum and transcriptions made by James Bonwick are in the Mitchell Library.

In 1788-89 Southwell was in the *Sirius* when she went to the Cape of Good Hope for stores. About March 1790, against his will when *Sirius* was sent to Norfolk Island, Southwell was placed in charge of the look-out station on South Head.

Southwell's journal and letters record details of the journey and the establishment of the settlement, provide an insight into the hopes and fears of a young naval officer in the colony, and reflect the attitudes and moods of some of the settlers. He comes to the conclusion that the colony will be a 'long-continued heavy expence to the m'r country', and his high regard for Governor Phillip changes: at first he had written of him as 'very kind and considerate' and 'one of a thousand', but by July 1790 the governor is one of those 'people whose ill-nature sometimes get the better of their understanding', and Southwell confessed to be 'rather vex'd at myself for being so very lavish in my encomiums formerly'. The letters have much to say of the Aboriginals and include a brief vocabulary of their language. On 28 March 1791 Southwell sailed from Sydney in the *Waaksamheyd*. On 11 February 1794 he was made a lieutenant. He was wounded off Portugal and died in Lisbon Hospital on 21 August 1797 aged about 33.

HRNSW, 2.   ALLAN HORTON

SPAIN, WILLIAM (1803-1876), attorney, was born on 14 March 1803 at Cowes, Isle of Wight, England, the son of George Spain, master mariner and shipowner. Educated for the law, he was admitted to the King's Bench as an attorney in 1823. In May 1825 he married Mary Elizabeth, daughter of Sir Henry White, mayor of Portsmouth. He took an active interest in politics, once acting as private secretary to Lord Palmerston, by whom he appears to have been admired. Sir George Staunton and Lord John Russell also spoke well of him, the latter being responsible for his appointment, in January 1841, as commissioner to examine the land claims of the New Zealand settlers under the recently signed treaty of Waitangi. Leaving England with thirteen members of his family, Spain reached New Zealand in December after a hazardous voyage which included a mutiny and a shipwreck. For three years he carried out his duties as commissioner, but his thorough and careful methods aroused opposition from both the New Zealand Co. and some of the Maori sympathizers. The latter believed his procedures were too slow to meet the immediate difficulties arising from disputed claims.

Leaving New Zealand for Sydney he practised as a solicitor from 1845 to 1851 when he accepted the newly created position of inspector-general of police and entered the Legislative Council of New South Wales. In his endeavour to create an adequate police force, as empowered under 14 Vic. no 38 NSW, he aroused much criticism from the press and from some members of the council, who attacked him for his apparent delay in organizing the outer police districts. His determination to master the facts of a confused situation before making vital decisions again told against him; furthermore the discovery of gold in New South Wales soon after he had taken office placed an impossible burden upon his resources and created 'difficulties of a most extraordinary nature'. On the grounds that hostile public criticism had destroyed his influence over his subordinates, Spain resigned his office on 11 December 1851, although both Governor FitzRoy and Deas Thomson [q.v.] expressed their complete confidence in him. The 1862 Police Act, which established the present system, owed much to Spain and his successor Captain William Colburn Mayne. Spain then returned to private practice in Sydney. In 1856 Governor Denison appointed him to the new Legislative Council, set up under the Constitution Act, a position he held until 1858. Upon his retirement he built a family home at Waverley, which he named Palmerston after his former patron. He died on 5 April 1876.

William's eldest son, David, joined the navy and reached the rank of rear-admiral after service which included a period in New Zealand during the Maori war. William Spain's descendants have continued to provide active members of the legal profession in Sydney.

HRA (1), 26; J. S. Marais, *The colonisation of New Zealand* (Lond, 1927); J. Miller, *Early Victorian New Zealand* (Lond, 1958); SMH, 15 Oct, 2, 20 Nov, 8, 15, 20 Dec 1851; New Zealand papers, 1838-46 (ML); Spain papers (in possession of Ian Spain, Castle Hill, NSW).
                              J. BACH

SPARK, ALEXANDER BRODIE (1792-1856), merchant, was born on 9 August 1792 at Elgin, Scotland, the son of a watchmaker. He had a literary education at Elgin, studied French and acquired an interest in astronomy. After some experience in business he went in June 1811 to Tod's counting house in London, where he also started a small literary society. Though aiming at 'that Scottish modesty united to

English confidence which is the character I admire', he found living difficult on £50 a year and sought parental help. In reply he was lectured for overspending and for bad grammar in his letters, but won his father's favour by finding supplies of low-priced watches and a design for a 'Patent Warning Clock'. In 1817 he was still with Tod, captivated by his work in the shipping department. In 1820 he went on a continental tour, during which he spent some days with William Wordsworth and the poet's wife and sister.

Confident that he could do better with a business of his own, Spark obtained a letter of recommendation as a free settler, sailed in the *Princess Charlotte* and arrived at Sydney in April 1823. He took over a store in George Street and was soon selling sugar, drapery and wines, and supplying salt meat to the commissariat at Sydney and Parramatta. By 1825 he was chartering ships for coastal trading and having the *Sydney Packet* built for him. Next year he started a shipping agency, selling incoming cargoes, sending stores to Hobart Town, colonial produce to Calcutta, and the first of his many wool consignments to London, backloading when possible with merchandise. He also acted as agent for country settlers, selling their produce and supplying them with livestock, stores, overseers and ploughmen. Although he owned more than 6000 acres on the Hunter River and a nine-acre grant at Woolloomooloo his passion for buying and selling had extended to land.

However pressing his business, Spark had found time to serve in Sydney on the Grand Jury, becoming its foreman in 1826 and a justice of the peace in 1827. He also joined the committee of the Agricultural Society and the Chamber of Commerce, subscribed to such worthy causes as Scots Church, the Benevolent Society and the Female School of Industry, and readily signed petitions for the maintenance of law and order and congratulatory memorials to the governors. Despite two unsuccessful attempts to be elected a director of the Bank of New South Wales he joined the first board of the Bank of Australia in 1826 and became its managing director in 1832. By then his business activities had increased, especially his wool exports. He continued his court work and land dealings, and in 1836 became the first treasurer of the Australian Gaslight Co., a director of at least two insurance companies and an active investor in several stream navigation companies. Although Spark had several houses in Sydney, the site that pleased him most for a country residence was his farm, Tempe, at Cook's River. There in 1831 he had begun a garden, planted an orchard

and vineyard, and carefully planned a new home. By 1836 it was a rendezvous for bankers, merchants and large landowners, among them James Mudie [q.v.] and other magistrates whom he also met on his regular visits to the Hunter River. Through this association Spark incurred the wrath of Governor Bourke and narrowly escaped removal from the Commission of the Peace. Unrepentant, he became the private distributor of Mudie's *The Felonry of New South Wales* when copies arrived next year.

Disturbed by divisions among the Presbyterians in Sydney, Spark turned to the Church of England and actively supported the building of St Peter's Church at Cook's River. It was consecrated in 1839. In that busy year he entertained 778 visitors at Tempe, was agent for twenty-two ships, had a third share in the steamer *Victoria*, won prizes at the Horticultural Show, extended his land dealing to Melbourne, continued his court work, imported stallions for his Hunter River stud, became agent of the South Australian Co., vice-president of the Commercial Banking Co. of Sydney and a director of the Australian Loan Co., and attended meetings of the Savings Bank trustees each month, concerts, dances, theatres, races, innumerable auction sales, and a Government House ball, where he met Lady Franklin [q.v.], whom he thought 'by no means the Amazon supposed, but a gentle affable woman'. He also patronized the arts, played golf, cards and chess, read widely, undertook works of benevolence, fished and bathed in Cook's River, visited outlying centres, and passed huge quantities of produce and merchandise through his stores; his only complaint was his rheumatism.

In 1840 Spark bought land in New Zealand and took pastoral leases in the New England district, although he already had more than fifty title deeds to land. On 27 April at St Peter's Church he married Frances Maria, née Biddulph, the widow of Dr Henry Wyatt Radford, who had owned Ravensfield station on the Hunter River. But the halcyon days were over. By September drought and the running down of the pastoral boom had created nervousness in the money market. Spark had guaranteed loans for friends who now became bankrupt. To find cash to help them he mortgaged, for the first time in his life, a town property, Tusculum, for £6000. He also had to sell some of his land, shares and ships to meet bills of £21,000 that fell due in March. His diary records at length the melancholy he felt at this divine judgment for his sins, but his first son was born in April and he could not fail his wife by reducing the establishment at Tempe, where he employed thirty-five servants. Unable to collect his own debts he continued to sell his assets and in 1844 he was certified insolvent. He recovered slowly and in 1846 was shipping copper ore to England and horses to India, although his fortune and his place in society were chiefly re-established by successful speculation after the discovery of gold in 1851. He died at Tempe on 21 October 1856 from a heart complaint, survived by his wife, two sons and three daughters.

Despite his activity in public affairs Spark was too patronizing to make much impact on colonists less wealthy than himself. His severe judgments on wrongdoers were rarely matched by self-criticism and his oft-expressed piety seemed meaningful only when he was distressed. His knowledge of shipping and commerce was undoubtedly a boon to New South Wales, but his personal detachment prevented any deep identity with his adopted country.

HRA (1), 11-12, 14-21, 24, (3), 4; E. de Selincourt (ed), *Journals of Dorothy Wordsworth* (Lond, 1841); A. B. Spark, Diaries and family papers (ML).

SPENCER, SIR RICHARD (1779-1839), naval officer and settler, was born on 9 December 1779, the only son of Richard Spencer, a London merchant. At 14 he entered the navy as a midshipman, serving in Channel patrols and later on North American and West Indian Stations. Transferred to the Mediterranean at 21, he was promoted lieutenant in the captured French *Guillaume Tell*. In the brig *Camelion* he commanded a unit of a gunboat patrol for some years, once guarding a flank of the British army at Aboukir Bay. He was appointed by Nelson to command the captured French schooner *Renard*, aptly renamed *Crafty*; in her for five lively years he harassed enemy shipping, intercepted dispatches, captured sulphur cargoes, and rescued thirty Maltese captives who rewarded him with a hundred-guinea set of plate. He suffered severe head wounds in action against two Spanish 24-pounders, and on one shore leave he swam storm-swept Valetta harbour to save the *Crafty* from destruction by the *Eagle*, adrift from her moorings. Early in 1808, he was appointed commander of the corvette *Samarang* on the East Indies Station, where his service in the subjection of Amboina and adjacent islands brought promotion to command the *Blanche*, and post rank early in 1812. Soon afterwards he went on half-

pay until June 1815 when he was appointed captain of the *Eurydice* on the Irish Station. In that year he was appointed C.B. A typical product of Nelson's school, his knowledge of naval strategy, his initiative and his charm of manner inspired loyalty in subordinates and gained advancement from superiors.

On 31 August 1812 Spencer married Ann Warden Liddon of Charmouth, Dorset. When his naval career ended in 1817 he settled with his wife on a farm at Lyme Regis, Dorset, for seventeen years, during which nine of their ten children were born. In 1833 he was appointed K.H. and government resident of Albany, Plantagenet district of Western Australia, on the recommendation of Sir James Stirling. Spencer and his family sailed in the storeship *Buffalo*, in company with his chartered *Brilliant*, loaded ark-like with plants, livestock, farm implements, stores and servants. In September they reached Albany, where he found seventeen civilians, a few soldiers, dilapidated buildings and a moribund economy.

Albany's development in the next six years was largely due to Spencer's administrative skill, energy and determination. As well as performing his judicial duties as local representative of the government he superintended public works, native welfare, police, and surveys. Records tell of official duties performed with the efficiency, zeal and probity born of his naval training which often irked some settlers. His own affairs also prospered. On arrival he bought Strawberry Hill; to its six cleared acres he added 1400 virgin acres and the existing wattle and daub dwelling he enlarged with two-storied additions. Within two years good progress had been made with all his agrarian and livestock plans. The needs of his sheep prompted the purchase of pastures thirty miles north-west of Albany on the Hay River. Soon afterwards two-storied additions in granite were made to his homestead. His leadership and insistence on the need for a church won posthumous reward in October 1848 when Bishop Short consecrated St John's Church at Albany.

Spencer died suddenly at Strawberry Hill on 24 July 1839. His grave, as he wished, overlooked King George Sound. He was survived by his wife, who in spite of a reduced income contrived to maintain great style and gracious hospitality. She had much difficulty with her headstrong sons. In 1843 she took three of them to England for education, but later one was drowned, another was sent to New Zealand and a third was killed by a falling tree. Of their daughters, Eliza Lucy was married to Captain George Grey on 2 November 1839, and Augusta was married to George Edward Egerton-Warburton, a pioneer settler near Mount Barker. Lady Spencer died in 1855.

J. Marshall, *Royal naval biography*, 3 (Lond, 1829); W. H. Fitchett, *Nelson and his captains* (Lond, 1902); H. Colebatch (ed), *A story of a hundred years: Western Australia 1829-1929* (Perth, 1929); G. E. Egerton-Warburton, 'Albany, past and present', (Newspaper cuttings, WAA); Spencer papers (copies in author's possession).

ROBERT STEPHENS

SPODE, JOSIAH (1790-1858), landowner and public servant, was the grandson of Josiah Spode of Stoke Lodge, Stoke-on-Trent, England, founder of the famous Staffordshire pottery. He served in the navy, first as a midshipman and then in 1809-10 as an officer. He retired from the navy to manage the family pottery, but on the birth of a first cousin he was no longer the heir and decided to leave England. He married the daughter of the wealthy Garner family and sailed in the *Brixton* for Hobart Town, where he arrived in 1821. With declared assets of £821 16s. 9d. and credentials from the Colonial Office, he was given a grant of land near Hamilton, about thirty miles from New Norfolk. He later exchanged it for land at Macquarie Plains which he leased after making sufficient improvements to earn an additional grant of 1000 acres at Shooter's Hill, eight miles from New Norfolk.

His interest in farming was secondary to his aspirations in the colonial service. In 1828 he was appointed muster master with charge of convict records and assistant police magistrate for Hobart. In 1829 he also became coroner. In 1832 he was promoted principal superintendent of convicts, and in 1839 became chief police magistrate and also a member of the Legislative Council, where he upheld the existing convict system in the face of Alexander Maconochie's [q.v.] criticism. Two years later he resigned from the council when reappointed principal superintendent of convicts. In 1844 this office was abolished and next year he retired with an annual pension of £220 from the colonial service, in which he had for seventeen years been a most efficient officer. In the meantime he had built at New Town a town house known as Stoke Cottage. He continued to live there but still owned the Shooter's Hill property where in 1846 he had bought

an additional 640 acres. In 1851 he advertised his intention to lease this property, which included a new house with 2137 acres of land, 100 of them under cultivation. In 1854 he sailed for England with his wife and two youngest sons in the *Antipodes*. He died on 1 November 1858 at Grange Villa, Tring, aged 68. Of his many children the eldest son, Josiah, studied medicine in England and returned to practise in Melbourne.

Spode received his colonial appointment under Lieut-Governor Arthur's administration, and the satisfaction he gave his demanding chief is comment on his efficiency. Scrupulously honest in a situation he could have used to his own advantage, his assignment of the available convict labour among grasping settlers was executed with great fairness. He prided himself on the accuracy of the extensive records he had to keep and during his long term of office became so familiar with the thousands of convicts under his charge that his advice to Arthur on the treatment of particular men was invaluable. Although thorough and conscientious, he lacked generosity; for all his dependability he appears as a humourless, slightly arrogant and colourless civil servant.

L. S. Bethell, *The valley of the Derwent* (Hob, 1961); Correspondence file under Spode (TA). F. C. GREEN

SPRENT, JAMES (1808-1863), surveyor, was born at Manchester, England, the son of a publisher from Glasgow. After education in local schools he went to Glasgow University (M.A., 1825) and to St John's College, Cambridge. He sailed from Liverpool in the *Norval* and arrived at Hobart Town in May 1830, bringing 'a large investment in books, engravings and stationery' worth £1260. In Liverpool Street he soon opened 'a public school for young gentlemen', where he taught foreign languages, English grammar, geography, arithmetic, geometry, mensuration, trigonometry and 'all those parts of Natural Philosophy connected with these subjects'. In 1832 he began classes for young ladies and adults after school hours, and lectured on astronomy at the Mechanics' Institute. Early next year he moved his academy to his cottage at Mount Pleasant. Soon afterwards it closed, for his application for a free land grant had been rejected by the Colonial Office in spite of his capital and his claim that when he left England his ultimate intention was to establish himself on the land.

In August 1833 Sprent was appointed a temporary assistant surveyor at a salary of £200. For 'attainments of a high order' he was placed on the trigonometrical survey. Within three years he had triangulated much of the south-eastern half of Van Diemen's Land and established many observation stations for accurately measuring sections in the settled districts. In this arduous performance he and his men had suffered many privations; hidden and almost forgotten in rugged mountains and heavy forests their tents and clothes fell to pieces and they were often obliged to eat 'carnivorous quadrupeds'. Although the work was stimulating and involved no clashes with settlers, Sprent was still on the department's lowest rung and in August 1836 he sought promotion. The surveyor-general, George Frankland [q.v.], testified to his zeal and skill, but could do little more since work on the trigonometrical survey was about to be suspended. In March 1838 Sprent was made a permanent assistant surveyor at £300 a year. In the department's retrenchment next year, when other government surveyors were reduced to casual contracts at fixed rates, he and James Calder [q.v.] were the only assistants retained on the permanent staff. For 'their great personal activity and large share of scientific skill' they were each given a salary of £450 from which they had to pay their labourers and all other expenses. With the onset of depression land sales fell off and Sprent's work became varied. In 1841 he was ordered to Hobart for special duty for a month and returned to Eastern Marshes to find his camp and equipment burnt to ashes; for this loss he was compensated. Later that year he marked out three roads from the settled districts to prospective harbours on the east coast, and in 1842 he began surveying the sections of the Van Diemen's Land Co. in the north-west of the island. About this time Sprent married Susannah Hassall, fifth daughter of Francis Oakes of Parramatta; in July 1843 he recorded anxiety about leaving 'his family in the power of drunken ruffians' at Circular Head.

In 1847 Sprent joined the Bridgewater Bridge Commission, was appointed a first-class assistant surveyor at £500 a year and given charge of the newly-resumed trigonometrical survey. This time he had eleven men and sometimes used a schooner to move his camp. Again he encountered terrible hardships and rough terrain, especially on the west coast, but the survey was completed in 1853 with the establishment of 206 observation stations at a total cost of some £20,000. Sprent then retired

from active field-work, although he later reported on the proposed Launceston-Deloraine railway and submitted a plan for maintaining the flow of the River Clyde in summer.

In September 1855 the select committee on the Survey Department paid tribute to his skill, perseverance and exceptional knowledge of the colony, and recommended him for appointment as head of the department. Next year, through the economies of the first parliament under responsible government, Robert Power [q.v.] was allowed to retain office as surveyor-general and Sprent became his deputy at £350 a year. In June 1857 he was appointed chief surveyor and acting surveyor-general and his salary was increased in half-yearly stages to £600. Although handicapped by lack of funds he divided the colony into districts each with its own surveyor to bring his local map up to date and to prepare land for sale and lease. In this way his own map of Tasmania was completed by 1859 in great detail. Coloured and mounted on rollers it was in such demand that thirty copies had been supplied to courts and government offices by 1860 and only one remained at the Survey Department.

Early in 1859 Sprent's health became impaired. He ceased duty as surveyor-general and commissioner of crown lands on 1 September and was given a pension of £217 11s. 10d. He died of apoplexy at his home in Warwick Street, Hobart, on 22 September 1863, aged 55. Of his seven children, three died in a scarlet fever epidemic in 1853, and the only surviving son, Charles Percy, after education at Hobart High School, followed his father's profession and did much exploration work. From 1882 until his death he was administrative head of the Tasmanian Lands and Surveys Department.

Sprent was resourceful, intelligent and an excellent bushman. According to Edward Boyd [q.v.] he was 'a man of too rigidly correct principles to swerve from the strict line of his duty at the instance of any living man'. Among his wide interests was an observatory which he set up in his home, and he was a close friend of Rev. John Lillie [q.v.] whose first will named him as an executor.

Sel cttee on Survey Dept, Report, *Journals* (LC, Tas), 1855 (56); GO 33/11/173 (TA); Correspondence file under Sprent (TA).

SQUIRE, JAMES (1755?-1822), brewer and farmer, arrived in the *Friendship* in the First Fleet, having been convicted at Kingston, Surrey, England, on 11 April

1785 and sentenced to transportation for seven years. He was one of the earliest, if not the first, to brew beer in the colony and the first to cultivate the hop plant in Australia successfully.

At first Squire lived in Sydney where he brewed small amounts which he sold at 4d. a quart; he also brewed privately for Lieut-Governors Grose and Paterson [qq.v.] from English malt. In July 1795 he was granted thirty acres at Kissing Point (Ryde), where he built his brewery and tavern which developed as a haven for river passengers between Sydney and Parramatta. Near his brewery he began his hop plantation; from a single vine produced in 1806 it grew to five acres producing 1500 lbs by 1812. Squire, 'the Whitbread of New South Wales', gave detailed written evidence on his brewing techniques and materials to Commissioner Bigge [q.v.] in December 1820, by which time he had enlarged his brewery and had an output of forty hogsheads a week nearly all the year round. Peter Cunningham [q.v.] recorded the virtues of Squire's famous colonial solatium and mentioned an epitaph in Parramatta churchyard which, he claimed, the jocose brewer took pleasure in quoting: 'Ye who wish to lie here Drink Squire's beer!'

Because of the vagaries of the local grain market and the import trade Squire could not depend on one activity only for a livelihood; his brewery was an integral part of a large farming and grazing property and he was one of the largest regular suppliers of meat to the commissariat. By 1822 he had about 1000 acres at Kissing Point which included many of the original small grants in the area, acquired from impoverished or dissolute settlers.

Squire was industrious and community-spirited, a popular figure amongst the emancipist class. He was district constable for many years and acted as a banker for many of his poorer neighbours. He was a friend of the Aboriginals; Bennelong [q.v.] was buried on his farm. Squire died on 16 May 1822. According to the artist and fellow emancipist, Joseph Lycett [q.v.], 'He was . . . universally respected and beloved for his amiable and useful qualities as a member of society, and more especially as the friend and protector of the lower class of settlers. Had he been less liberal, he might have died more wealthy; but his assistance always accompanied his advice to the poor and unfortunate, and his name will long be pronounced with veneration by the grateful objects of his liberality'.

After Squire's death the brewery was carried on by his son James until his death on 7 March 1826, aged 29. It was then closed but was reopened for a time in 1828 by Squire's son-in-law, Thomas Charles Farnell; after this time the celebrated half-way house to Parramatta receded in the memory of its once noisy and grateful patrons.

Squire had left a wife, Martha, two sons and a daughter in England. In the colony he had one son, James, and seven daughters by Elizabeth Mason, who also arrived in the First Fleet and who died on 10 June 1809. Squire's youngest daughter, Mary Ann (b. 1 August 1804) married T. C. Farnell (1800-1834), a free settler, on 6 March 1824 : the eldest child of this union, James Squire Farnell (1825-1888), was premier of New South Wales in 1877-78.

HRA (1), 10; J. Lycett, *Views in Australia* (Lond, 1824); P. Cunningham, *Two years in New South Wales*, 3rd ed, 1 (Lond, 1828); *Sydney Gazette*, 21 Mar 1812, 3 May 1817; Bigge Report, Bonwick transcripts (ML); Wentworth papers (ML); Information from J. K. Lavett, Dulwich, SA.   G. P. WALSH

STACKHOUSE, ALFRED (1811-1876), Church of England clergyman, was born on 24 July 1811 at Camberwell Grove, London, the son of John Stackhouse (1776-1849), of Surrey, and his wife Frances Mary (1780-1849), the elder daughter of Thomas Rashleigh of Blackheath. After preliminary schooling he went to Lincoln College, Oxford (B.A., 1834; M.A., 1837). He was made deacon in June 1835 and after ordination to the priesthood in March 1838 was appointed a chaplain to the East India Co. in the presidency of Bombay. After various short appointments in India he was given two years leave in March 1840 to recover his health in Van Diemen's Land. As Rev. R. R. Davies [q.v.] was in England Stackhouse took his place at Longford and Perth. When Davies returned in July 1841 Perth petitioned Lieut-Governor Franklin to make Perth and Breadalbane a separate parish with Stackhouse as incumbent. Franklin was so slow in deciding that Stackhouse left for India in February 1842, but when Franklin's approval did reach him he resigned his post and returned to Van Diemen's Land.

He resumed work at Perth in January 1843 and soon spread his activities to Franklin village. Sermons preached in these parishes he published later. An inveterate pamphleteer in support of his convictions, he published in Launceston, *A Message from God* (1853) and *Darkness made Light or the Story of 'Old Sam' the Christian Jew* (1859); in strong support of the temperance movement he produced

Religious Objections to Teetotal Societies, Considered in connexion with Christian Duty (1846). The awakening of interest in eschatology in the 1840s greatly influenced his thinking. In *Eight lectures on the Signs of the Times* (1849) and other pamphlets he piled up evidence, ranging from recent earthquakes and wars to the growth of Chartism, to show the imminence of the second coming of Christ.

By his sincerity Stackhouse retained Bishop Nixon's [q.v.] respect, though he was a leader in the Low Church attack on Nixon after the first meeting of the Australian bishops in 1850. His differences with the bishop were expressed in *The Gorham Heresy and the Non-natural Explanation of the Articles of the Church of England* (1851), and *The Divine Right of private judgment in matters of Religion* (1852). Stackhouse had a lively interest in missions and acted as secretary for several societies. He took part in the movement to establish a Tasmanian synod but shocked it by opposing state aid to churches. In politics he was a strong opponent of transportation.

When Longford fell vacant in 1860 Stackhouse was offered the parish and he remained there until ill health forced his resignation. Not long before his death on 25 May 1876 he had published an *Address to young persons who are of age to be confirmed*, a work considered highly by the metropolitan of Sydney who bought 500 copies. His most successful pamphlet, *Family Prayers* (Launceston, 1845), ran to a third edition.

On 17 May 1843 he had married Ellen (1824-1898), the second daughter of Thomas Archer [q.v.] of Woolmers, Longford. Their children were Frances Mary (1851-1933), Rev. Alfred Rashleigh (1854-1896), Melville Archer (1856-1901), Ernest Valentine (1859-1916) and Cecil Arthur (b. 1863).

An obituary described him as a 'sincerely pious, honest, large-hearted Christian who could have been a counterpart of Goldsmith's Vicar of Wakefield had he been placed in some secluded part of England, and not had his loving nature disturbed by coming into contact with British and British-Indian politicians, camps, wars and rumours of wars during his residence in India'.

Cornwall Chronicle, 29 May 1876; *Church News* (Hob), Sept 1898; Correspondence file under Stackhouse (TA).   P. R. HART

STANFIELD, DANIEL (d. 1826), marine and settler, was reputed to have come from an English naval family. He arrived at Port Jackson with the First Fleet as a private in the marines. He was promoted corporal and on 15 October 1791 at St Philip's married Alice, widow of Thomas Harmsworth who had died at Sydney in 1788. In less than a month Stanfield was on duty at Norfolk Island. By 1794 he was discharged from the marines, sworn in as a constable, had begun to farm at Little Cascade and received two goats from Lieut-Governor King, who described him as a deserving settler. In March Stanfield was robbed and with other islanders petitioned Lieut-Governor Grose [q.v.] for restoration of the arms of which they had been deprived by government order. Stanfield also talked of enlisting in the New South Wales Corps, and in November he sailed in the *Daedalus* for Port Jackson. Next October he returned to Norfolk Island in the *Supply* with his wife, four children and the promise of a sixty-acre land grant. By 1804 he had five children, 30 sheep, and of his 120 acres 35 were under cultivation. When the evacuation of Norfolk Island was planned, Governor King suggested that Stanfield with his children should remain and encouraged him by offering additional land from expired leases on the island. However keen and determined, Stanfield did not find life easy; he sailed with his family in the *City of Edinburgh* and arrived at Hobart Town in October 1808. Next month he took up land at Green Point near Bridgewater and built a weatherboard house which he valued at more than £2000 and which stood for over a century. There Stanfield's industry and enthusiasm brought him better results than in Norfolk Island: by February 1825 he had been granted 1200 acres in widely separated areas, had purchased 890 more and claimed to have 1000 cattle, 800 sheep, 10 horses, a flour-mill and other capital. His only grievances were that Michael Howe [q.v.] had raided his stockyard and other bushrangers had plundered his properties, though he was sometimes compensated for these deprivations by more land. In 1826 he was summoned to Hobart to give evidence against the receivers of goods stolen from him, but he died there suddenly on 4 February, leaving 'a very numerous and opulent family'.

His eldest son DANIEL STANFIELD was baptized on 25 April 1790 at St Philip's, Sydney. He inherited a full measure of his father's energy and acquisitiveness, and a great deal of property. But he was not entirely reliant on his father. By 1825 he could claim 450 cattle, 600 sheep, 7 horses and other capital. His land grants included 410 acres from Governor Macquarie, 300 from Governor Brisbane, and

300 from Lieut-Governor Arthur, and he had bought 830 acres at Green Lagoon. His brothers also had land and stock and in 1827 the land commissioners reported that the Stanfields, 'a large Clan altogether, have had immense Herds of Wild Cattle roaming all over this quarter of the Island, finding themselves limited, they have driven off many hundreds to the Sea Coast'.

Stanfield improved his properties and became well known as a stock-breeder. In 1828 he was one of the first in Van Diemen's Land to export apples to Britain; one specimen was a foot in diameter, but the shipment did not carry well. Like his father he had trouble with bushrangers and by 1825 had been to Sydney twice to give evidence at the trials of some culprits. Again like his father he had a large family: in Hobart in January 1816 he married Maria Kimberley (d. 1851), the daughter of a transported convict; according to one report, they had eight children by 1831. He died on 28 March 1856.

HRNSW, 2; HRA (1), 5, (3), 2, 3; P. G. King papers (ML); *Colonial Times*, 3 July 1829; *Tasmanian Mail*, 17 Oct 1908; CSO 1/288/6887, 1/289/6899 (TA).

STANLEY, EDWARD GEORGE GEOFFREY SMITH, fourteenth EARL OF DERBY, (1799-1869), politician, was born on 29 March 1799 at Knowsley Park, Lancashire, England, the son of Edward Smith Stanley, thirteenth earl, and his cousin Charlotte Margaret, daughter of Rev. Geoffrey Hornby. He was educated at Eton and Christ Church, Oxford (hon. D.C.L., 1852), and was M.P. for Stockbridge 1822-26, Preston 1826-30, Windsor 1831-32 and North Lancashire 1832-44. He was undersecretary for war and the colonies under Canning and Goderich in 1827-28 and secretary for Ireland under Earl Grey 1830-33. In 1831 he brought in the Act which created a Board of National Education in Ireland and provided that children of all denominations were to be admitted to schools receiving a government grant and that the instruction was to include religious teaching of an undogmatic kind. He transferred to the Colonial Office in March 1833 until June 1834, carrying through the bill for the abolition of slavery drafted by James Stephen. He resigned in 1834, being opposed to the Irish disendowment proposals, and joined Peel and the Conservative opposition in 1835. He was called to the House of Lords as Lord Stanley of Bickerstaffe in 1844. As secretary of state for war and the colonies from September 1841 until his resignation in December 1845 on the question of the repeal of the corn laws, he elaborated and organized the 'probation' system of convict administration in Van Diemen's Land. Autocratic and conservative, he frequently disregarded James Stephen's recommendations or acted without consultation, and was vehemently opposed to any increase in colonial expenditure. Although reluctantly accepting the protectionist leadership in 1846 he declined to form a ministry, but became prime minister in February-December 1852, 1858-59 and 1866-68. He succeeded to the earldom in 1851. He was chancellor of Oxford University in 1852 and the Derby scholarship was founded to commemorate him in 1870. He published miscellaneous works including a version of the *Iliad* (1864; privately printed, 1862). He married in May 1825 Emma Caroline, second daughter of Edward Bootle Wilbraham (later Lord Skelmersdale), by whom he had two sons and a daughter, and he died at Knowsley Park on 23 October 1869.

In his *Autobiography* (London, 1885) Henry Taylor (1800-1886), who was a clerk in the Colonial Office, described Stanley as 'a very able . . . man; he had force, energy and vivacity; and he was an effective speaker, always clear and strong, sometimes commonplace, but not seldom brilliant. He had the gifts of a party politician . . . playing the game of politics with more of party than of public spirit'.

STANLEY, OWEN (1811-1850), naval officer, was born on 13 June 1811, the eldest son of Edward Stanley, bishop of Norwich, and Catherine, daughter of Rev. Oswald Leicester, rector of Stoke, Shropshire, England. His brother was dean of Westminster and his uncle Lord Stanley of Alderley. Owen entered the Royal Naval College at 15 and after training shipped as a volunteer in the frigate *Druid* in January 1826. Two months later he became midshipman in the *Ganges* and spent the next four years on the coast of South America, serving chiefly in small ships on surveying work; in 1830 he was employed under P. P. King [q.v.] in the sloop *Adventure* on a survey of the Straits of Magellan. He passed his examination for promotion to lieutenant in June 1830, returned to England five months later, and next May was commissioned lieutenant while serving in the *Belvidera* with the Mediterranean Squadron. For five years on this station he again served in small ships on surveying work, this time in the Greek archipelago. He then joined the

Arctic expedition which left the Orkneys in June 1836, sailing in the *Terror* and having charge of astronomical and magnetic observations during the voyage towards the North Pole.

As a lieutenant at 26 he received his first independent command, the brig *Britomart*, in which he sailed in 1838 for the East Indies Station and Australasian waters, chiefly on surveying work. When the expedition to establish a northern colony at Port Essington sailed in September 1838, the *Britomart* accompanied it, Stanley being made a magistrate and a commissioner of crown lands for the purpose. He visited the new colony again in 1841, and described the settlement in November as 'all well, and on the best possible terms with the Natives', and its commandant, Captain John Macarthur, as the victim of official incompetence and naval interference. Stanley was not solely engaged upon surveying work, however, for his duties took him in 1840 to New Zealand where, under the orders of Lieut-Governor Hobson [q.v.], he was sent in July to the Banks Peninsula where French emigrants were expected to form a settlement upon land bought by Captain Langlois from the Maoris of Akaroa. Stanley, taking with him a police magistrate to station there, preceded the French arrival and succeeded in establishing good relations with the French commandant, Lavaud, who saluted the British flag. For his behaviour in a delicate situation Stanley was highly commended by the Admiralty, having already been promoted commander in April 1839.

In 1841 Stanley was at Singapore on his way to the fighting in Burma and thence returned to England, where in 1844 he achieved post rank as captain and two years later received command of another surveying ship, *Rattlesnake*, destined for the East Indies Station. In December 1846 he was ordered from England to Australia to survey the region of Harvey's Bay in a new project for establishing a colony in that part of North Australia. This plan was abandoned, but Stanley sailed from England, taking with him the naturalists, T. H. Huxley and J. MacGillivray [qq.v.], under orders to survey New Guinea waters. November 1847 found him on the Australian coast at Port Curtis, surveying the harbour which he thought a very good anchorage, before setting out in the next year northward to New Guinea. In June 1848 he offered protection and assistance to the ship which carried Kennedy's [q.v.] expedition to Cape York and then proceeded to the Louisiade Islands off south-east New Gui-

nea to make a survey of the archipelago. Upon this mission which lasted throughout 1849 he contracted an illness of which he died in Sydney in March 1850.

Stanley's achievement was principally scientific. Made a fellow of both the Royal Society and the Royal Astronomical Society for his surveying and observation work, he charted considerable sections of the north-east Australian coast, made a track of the Arafura Sea, and charted the channels and islands of south-east New Guinea. He was admired as a careful and competent seaman by MacGillivray and was a warm friend of Sir John Franklin, but he was condemned by Huxley for cowardice because of his reluctance to land on New Guinea shores for fear of conflict with the natives; however, Huxley was angry not to be able to collect specimens ashore and made no allowance for the disease with which Stanley was then afflicted. His work is commemorated in the name of the Owen Stanley Range in New Guinea.

HRA (1), 19-22, 25, 26; W. R. O'Byrne, *A naval biographical dictionary* (Lond, 1949); J. MacGillivray, *Narrative of the voyage of HMS Rattlesnake . . . 1846-1850*, 1-2 (Lond, 1852); J. Huxley (ed), *T. H. Huxley's diary of the voyage of HMS Rattlesnake* (Lond, 1935).
                                                    FRANCIS WEST

STAPYLTON, GRANVILLE WILLIAM CHETWYND (1800-1840), surveyor and explorer, was the youngest son of Major-General Granville Anson Chetwynd Stapylton and his wife Martha, only daughter of Henry Stapylton of Wighill, Yorkshire, England. His paternal grandfather was the fourth Viscount Chetwynd.

Stapylton married Catherine Bulteel of Fleet, Hampshire, in 1825, and in November 1828 was appointed an assistant surveyor in New South Wales. He carried out a number of difficult surveys near Sydney and in 1831 was with a party which traced the Abercrombie River from Bathurst towards the Lake George area. In 1833 his work found favour with the surveyor-general, T. L. Mitchell [q.v.]. In 1834 he was praised by the Colonial Office and recommended to Governor Bourke for promotion. In 1836 Stapylton was appointed second-in-command of Mitchell's overland expedition to Australia Felix. In this he did a valuable job, but was very critical of his leader and irked by having to take frequent charge of the base camp and thus prevented from sharing the excitement of making new discoveries. A copy of Stapylton's journal of this expedition is in the La Trobe Library, Melbourne.

Stapylton was sent to Port Phillip to work under the direction of Robert Hoddle [q.v.]; he travelled to Melbourne overland, arriving in April 1838. About this time he appears to have fallen a victim of intemperance, for the administrator at Port Phillip, Captain Lonsdale, wrote to the colonial secretary on 5 October 1838, that Stapylton had been so drunk that the chief constable had been forced to confine him, and on another occasion he had found him drunk under his dray.

He was suspended from duty by Lonsdale but later reinstated by Governor Gipps and sent to work under Robert Dixon [q.v.] at Moreton Bay. He was engaged in surveying the coast south from Brisbane on 31 May 1840 when Aboriginals attacked his camp. Stapylton and an assistant, William Tuck, were killed, and another member of the party was severely injured. Tuck's body was buried on the spot but Stapylton's was taken to Brisbane.

HRA (1), 14, 15, 17; J. H. L. Cumpston, *Thomas Mitchell* (Melb, 1954); VHM, 7 (1919), p 12-13; *Australian*, 15 Apr 1829, 30 Dec 1831, 1 Apr 1836, 25 Aug 1840, 15 May, 15 June 1841; PP (GB), 1841 (85), appendix B.   Louis R. Cranfield

STEPHEN, GEORGE MILNER (1812-1894), public servant, geologist, barrister and faith-healer, was born on 18 December 1812 at Wells, Somerset, England, the sixth son of John Stephen [q.v.] and his wife Mary Anne, née Pasmore. At Honiton Grammar School he topped every class and was said to have memorized the entire *Eton Latin Syntax*. He arrived at Sydney in the *Prince Regent* with his father in July 1824. Within a year he won the silver medal for classics at Sydney Grammar School and became a commissariat clerk. In 1829 he went to Hobart Town, where his brother Alfred was crown solicitor and in September 1830 was appointed a clerk in the Supreme Court at a salary of £200. In January 1832 he also became registrar of the archdeaconry, where he was praised for preparing a register of births, marriages and deaths, 1804-1822, but received no pay and resigned in June 1834. Next year the Executive Council refused to publish his 'small manual for police officers and a digest of colonial laws'. Thus denied the fruits of his labours he fell into dissolute ways, to the embarrassment of his patrons, who recommended him for twelve months leave

to care for his father's estate in Sydney. He left Hobart in March 1836 and soon entered the legal office of his brother Francis in Sydney. When Francis died in February 1837 George's leave was extended and he applied to the Supreme Court for admission as an attorney to look after his brother's clients. Since he was untrained the judges refused his request and he returned to his clerkship in Hobart.

Although Stephen's relations in London and Australia were numerous and powerful, his prospects of professional advance were not bright, and his next opportunity was unexpected. In South Australia the advocate-general, Charles Mann [q.v.], had resigned in November. Governor Hindmarsh, hearing from Sir John Jeffcott [q.v.] that Alfred Stephen had resigned his office in Hobart, appealed to Sir John Franklin for help and enclosed a letter inviting 'Mr Stephen' to accept the vacancy in Adelaide. Franklin added the name 'Alfred' to the addressed letter and sent it to the Supreme Court, but was soon startled by a request from George for three months leave to visit Adelaide to consider the offer on the spot, and for an advance of £100 to buy law books. The Hobart press was also amazed. *Bent's News*, 31 March 1838, admitted that George 'wrote a fine hand and made good figures' but wondered how 'a raw, inexperienced young man . . . with neither educational qualifications or pretensions' could advise a government on points of law.

George sailed on 3 February 1838 with a congratulatory memorial from sixteen members of the Bar in Hobart and Launceston, and on the 9th was appointed advocate-general and crown solicitor in Adelaide. Seeking confirmation from the Colonial Office, Hindmarsh sent a copy of the memorial and explained to James Stephen: '*his very connexion with yourself* and his being abused by such people as do so convinces me that he is a good loyal subject', a comment which the under-secretary thought 'unimportant'.

Between daily dinners and chess with the governor and parties at Government House, where he tuned the piano and played the flute and guitar, Stephen studied hard and drafted some useful ordinances. He helped to arrest several 'dangerous Ruffians', prepared their indictments and prosecuted them successfully at the Quarter Sessions, where after advice from Alfred he also won two civil actions and a chancery suit. Since the resident commissioner, J. H. Fisher [q.v.] had absented himself from the Council of

Government before Hindmarsh sailed for England on 16 July, Stephen was left as the senior council member and so became acting governor. His opening address was modest and dignified, though frank about the empty treasury. When Fisher refused to pay the civil service from the land fund Stephen made a loan of £200 from his own pocket to support the police. He also began the allotment of country sections to settlers. In October when Governor Gawler arrived Stephen was appointed colonial secretary, and received an address with 229 signatures praising his liberality and ability, though he refused to allow a protest meeting against his land speculation.

Stephen's meteoric public career in Adelaide ended unhappily. With a loan from Alfred he had already bought shares in Hindmarsh's land investments and had assisted Mrs Hindmarsh to sell several sections very profitably. With her help in February 1839 he bought for £4000 a special survey of 4000 acres on the Gawler River. He openly boasted of the value of this fertile section and in March it was rumoured that he had sold half of it for £20,000. The *Southern Australian* promptly reported that the sale was a hoax. Stephen successfully sued the printer for libel, declaring on oath that the price was £10,000 and denying that he had ever said it was £20,000. The printer then brought action against him for wilful and corrupt perjury, and produced a letter from Stephen to George Stevenson [q.v.] stating that the land had been sold for £20,000. Judge Cooper [q.v.] ruled that the letter could not be used as evidence since it had not been produced at the earlier trial. Stephen was acquitted, but several magistrates refused to sit on the bench with him. Stephen then sued the printer of the *South Australian Gazette and Colonial Register* for libel. At the trial much attention was given to the letter to Stevenson. Against a vast amount of circumstantial evidence Stephen affirmed that he had written £10,000 and that the '2' was a forgery. He lost the case, but later some members of the jury signed an affidavit 'that they had never noticed the tail of the "1", sworn by Governor Gawler and Captain Sturt [q.v.] to have existed, on their first seeing the note, and which tail had been erased'.

Stephen at once resigned all his public offices, but stayed in Adelaide, helped to edit the short-lived *Guardian*, sold more land for himself and Mrs Hindmarsh, gave drawing lessons to her daughters and at Trinity Church on 7 July 1840 married Mary Hindmarsh. A month later he arrived with her at Sydney and sailed in the *Louisa* for England in December. Their first child was born in Penzance and in September 1841 Stephen was elected a member of the Royal Geological Society of Cornwall. Soon afterwards he became government secretary to his father-in-law at Heligoland. There Stephen painted portraits of many European notables and was so well rewarded that he thought of making painting his profession. In 1844 he changed his mind when a disgruntled citizen on the island complained to the Colonial Office about his perjury record. Stephen promptly applied for admission to the Middle Temple, where the benchers examined the papers sent from Downing Street on his Adelaide trials. In 1845 he was congratulated by the Colonial Office for 'having received the public and unequivocal vindication of his character'. He was duly admitted to the Middle Temple, kept his terms and was called to the Bar.

In 1846 Stephen returned to Adelaide, but although he had been recommended by Lord Stanley for appointment as advocate-general he was not given a government post. He was admitted to practise in the Supreme Court and in March 1849 when Judge Cooper took sick leave, he applied for appointment as puisne judge and later as chief justice. However, the Colonial Office decided to appoint a barrister from England and thought of offering Stephen a judgeship at Otago, but the reports on him were 'not very favourable'. In July his old enemy Stevenson published a story that Stephen had found iron ore in the Lofty Ranges, bought the section and in violation of the vendor's reserved rights begun mining and smelting on the property. This implication of false pretences led to a libel action which Stephen won with damages of one farthing. After gold was discovered in Victoria Stephen claimed to have found a payable deposit near Adelaide and offered to lead the way to it. One hot December day in 1851 large crowds with shovels and tin dishes climbed the range, but neither Stephen nor his mine could be found. Soon afterwards he moved to Melbourne. In 1853 he was admitted to the Bar, became first vice-president of the Royal Geological Society of Victoria, visited the goldfields and sailed for Europe. From Heligoland in 1854 he sent notes to the Colonial Office on the island's geology covering a confidential report on its defences and international plots hatched at its gaming tables. He was elected a fellow of the Royal Geological and Geographical

Societies in London and in 1855 a member of the Geological Society of Germany and the Natural History Society of Dresden. For presenting samples of his precious stones collected in Australia to the museum at Dresden he was given a gold box by the King of Saxony.

In London he helped to found the British Australian Gold Mining Co., and as its chief manager returned to Melbourne in 1856. Although he resumed his legal practice and on occasion assisted the parliamentary draftsman he spent much time on the goldfields. In June he offered himself to the diggers of Talbot for election to the Legislative Council. Revived assertions that he was a perjurer were rejected by the miners and on 12 July he defended himself in a long autobiography in the Age. On 20 August the Argus repeated the insinuations. Next February Stephen brought an action against the proprietors for libel but the jury could not agree, and in March 1857 eighty citizens unsuccessfully petitioned the Supreme Court to disbar him for acting as counsel for prisoners charged with the murder of John Price [q.v.]. Next year the Argus repeated its earlier slanders against him; they were copied by the Herald, but its editor promptly apologized after an interview with Stephen. In 1859-61 he represented Collingwood in the Legislative Assembly. Although his political career was undistinguished he conducted some important cases in the courts and continued his geological searches. He sent samples of his precious stones to the governor, Sir Charles Darling, in 1863, to the Melbourne exhibition of Australian gems in 1865 and to the intercolonial exhibition, where he was awarded a medal in 1867.

In September 1862 Stephen had applied ineffectually for a district court judgeship in New South Wales and had then moved to the mining district of Beechworth, warmly farewelled by fellow practitioners and friends who complimented him on 'outliving all animosity'. Early in 1864 he went to Sydney, where he was admitted to the Bar. He still had investments in mining companies and in 1870 invented two gold-washing machines for which he was awarded medals. Two years later he was elected a fellow of the Royal Society of New South Wales, presented a paper 'On the gems of Australia' and exhibited his collection. In March 1877 he was appointed parliamentary draftsman. By that time he had developed strong views about social ethics and began to dabble in spiritualism. On a visit to Victoria he discovered that he had the

gift of faith healing. His fame spread rapidly and he was soon treating over fifty patients a day. His legal practice suffered, he lost his parliamentary office and his family fell into financial straits. Fortunately one of his patients was Lady Parkes and, after an appeal to her husband, Stephen was appointed crown prosecutor in 1879. He soon had to resign because this position required much travelling and he was beset wherever he went by sufferers eager for healing.

By touch, breathing on affected joints, red flannel, 'magnetised' water in which his hands had been washed, and ordering away pain Stephen was reputed to have lengthened short limbs and to have cured blindness, deafness, rheumatism, St Vitus dance and consumption; even cancers were cured by sending his will power each morning to patients up to 250 miles away. He gave 'free days' at the Temperance Hall in Sydney for the poor, and his rooms in Phillip Street were always thronged. Letters attesting his healing powers appeared in many newspapers, though the Sydney Bulletin, 17 July 1880, mocked his powers and he was attacked in the anonymous pamphlet Mediums and their Dupes (Sydney, 1879). This pamphlet was promptly repudiated by Stephen's eldest son, Harold, who also published George Milner Stephen and His Marvellous Cures, about 1880. In 1887 Stephen went to London, where his wife died on 27 December and where he was said to have treated the prince of Wales. He returned to Melbourne in 1889 still active as a healer. Paradoxically he suffered terribly himself from 'an internal affliction' and after an operation he died on 16 January 1894 at his home in Brunswick. Of his nine sons and four daughters, only three sons survived him.

G. R. Smith (comp), The Australian healer (Reading, 1889); C. H. Fitts, 'Lines of communication', Medico-Legal Soc Procs, 6 (1953-54); G. M. Stephen, Diary and papers (ML); Correspondence file under G. M. Stephen (TA); CO 13/10, 62.

STEPHEN, SIR JAMES (1789-1859), public servant, was born on 3 January 1789 at Lambeth, London, the third son of James Stephen (1758-1832; M.P. 1808-15; Master in Chancery 1811), and his first wife Anne, née Stent. His father was a close friend of William Wilberforce, whose sister he married after his first wife's death, and a leading campaigner for the abolition of slavery. Like Wilberforce he belonged to that group of evangelical Christian philanthropists designated by Sydney Smith, the Clapham Sect, to whose ideals his son gave lifelong loyalty.

In 1806 James Stephen entered Trinity Hall, Cambridge (LL.B., 1812). He was called to the Bar at Lincoln's Inn in November 1811 and entered practice in the Chancery Court. In 1813, at Bathurst's nomination, his long service with the Colonial Office began. At first he acted as part-time counsel, reviewing colonial acts at £3 3s. a time. His advice on general colonial questions was increasingly sought, and in 1825 at considerable financial sacrifice he decided to give up private practice and accept the position of permanent counsel to the Colonial Office and Board of Trade.

As his admiring colleague, Henry Taylor, put it, Stephen entered the Colonial Office because he 'hoped to get a hold upon the policy of the government in the matter of slavery', and his success 'raised the first outcry against him'. The duke of Wellington was not alone in wishing, in June 1830, that Stephen would confine himself to questions of law 'instead of . . . Questions of Policy with which according to my Notions he ought to have nothing to do'. However, suspicions that this dedicated son of a prominent abolitionist must be partisan in professional judgment were unfounded. It was not by moral argument but by meticulous and soundly based legal criticism that Stephen demonstrated the iniquity of slave laws. His success in this was crucial in securing abolition.

In 1834 Stephen was appointed assistant under-secretary in the Colonial Office, and in 1836 permanent under-secretary, holding this position until his retirement in 1847. Throughout this period the Colonial Office was faced with rapidly expanding responsibilities for which its staff, in numbers and talent, was largely ill equipped. Direction was nominally in the hands of the secretary of state for war and the colonies, but this office had small attraction for politicians, for the House of Commons showed but fitful and fractious interest in colonial affairs. Moreover political instability resulted in rapid changes in holders of the office. It was therefore inevitable that successive ministers should depend upon the under-secretary as 'the depository of all that knowledge of which the Secretary of State must daily avail himself'. It was for precisely this role, unprotestingly subordinate and greatly experienced, that Stephen's character and talents fitted him, making him one of the greatest civil servants of the nineteenth century; but it inevitably exposed him to the charge of ruling the Colonial Office and the award of such sobriquets as 'King Stephen', 'Mr. Over-Secretary Stephen' and 'Mr. Mother-Country'.

Undoubtedly Stephen tried to give direction and consistency to colonial policy and to lift it above the level of what seemed expedient in the short run; but Taylor's remark that for more than a quarter of a century Stephen 'more than any one man virtually governed the British Empire' is misleading. It overestimates Stephen's influence on his chiefs, and seriously underestimates the degree of freedom extended to colonial governors.

Stephen made three particular contributions to colonial policy. First, he insisted that in a growing colony the mother country had a positive duty to guard the weak. 'The desire to extinguish the freedom of action of those on whose labour the profit of Capital depends is a passion always at work', he wrote; he feared that colonial settlers avid for quick profits would exploit the natives and the poor. This fear underlay his opposition to E. G. Wakefield's [q.v.] theories of colonization, particularly in New Zealand; their details he further criticized as vague and impracticable. His conception of the mother country's role is clearly illustrated in his minute, 12 September 1843, in which he opposed the introduction of cheap coloured labour into Australia; its key sentence stresses the duty to 'watch over the welfare of the many rather than the present advantage of the few'. 'I entirely concur', noted Stanley; and the proposal was vetoed.

Second, Stephen believed that colonial governors and officials should be given a large measure of freedom and trust. If his repeated stress on the superior knowledge of the man on the spot led him into estimates of particular individuals which now seem wrong, it was wiser than constant meddling in local affairs.

Third, Stephen favoured the development of colonial self-government. He was much involved in its establishment in Canada, and was convinced that 'the course we took in relation to Canada was the only right one . . . that of cheerfully relaxing, one after another, the bonds of authority, as soon as the colony itself desired that relaxation'.

Stephen had small appetite for imperial expansion. His remark in a private letter in 1839 that most of England's colonies were 'wretched burdens which in an evil hour we assumed and have no right to lay down again' has been much quoted, but is uncharacteristically gloomy; he concluded that the British annexation of New

Zealand was 'if not an expedient, at least an inevitable measure'.

Within the Colonial Office Stephen was indefatigably hard-working. He was not the first to attempt administrative reform; nor did all his reforms, the most important being the perfection of a system of minuting, work like charms. R. B. Pugh believes that Stephen's insistence on formality 'decelerated the machine'. He was not good at delegation; his distaste for conference inclined him 'to engross work into his own hands and not to be much helped'. Painfully shy, he found relationships with all but a few intimates difficult. He did not suffer fools gladly; nor could he bring himself to compromise with men who, like Wakefield, he found 'wanting in truth and honour'. Such criticisms are, however, outweighed by what Bell and Morrell acclaimed as 'the wisdom, the experience, the essential righteousness of Stephen'.

Stephen was deeply religious, of latitudinarian sympathies. He found religious literature of surpassing interest and from 1833 regularly contributed articles to the *Edinburgh Review*, published in 1849 as *Essays in Ecclesiastical Biography*. His style, both in minutes and essays, is lucid and graceful, and his sense of humour keen. He was ascetic by temperament; it was typical of him that he 'once smoked a cigar and found it so delicious that he never smoked again'.

Stephen resigned office in 1847 because of ill health. He was knighted and made a member of the Privy Council. He was still consulted on colonial questions and played an important part in drafting the report of the Privy Council committee on the Constitutions of the Australian colonies. In 1849 he was appointed regius professor of modern history at Cambridge, and published his *Lectures on the History of France* in 1851. At Cambridge he disliked both dons and undergraduates, and was accused of heresy for disputing the meaning of eternal damnation. He had been wont to envy the life of the scholar or recluse; but it is likely that Stephen exercised his talents and fulfilled his ambitions at his desk in the Colonial Office as he could have in no other way.

On 22 December 1814 Stephen had married Jane Catherine, daughter of Rev. John Venn, rector of Clapham. Family life afforded him great pleasure: 'the real thing', he once remarked, 'is domestic society'. He died at Coblenz on 14 September 1859, and his widow in 1875. Of their five children, Leslie (1832-1904) was first editor of the *Dictionary of National Biography* and father of Virginia Woolf. Stephen's paternal uncle, John Stephen

[q.v.], and several other relations held government offices in Australia.

A bust of Stephen by Marochetti is in the National Portrait Gallery, London.

H. Taylor, *Autobiography* (Lond, 1885); L. Stephen, *The life of Sir James Fitzjames Stephen* (Lond, 1895); C. E. Stephen, *The Right Honourable Sir James Stephen* (Gloucester, 1906); K. N. Bell and W. P. Morrell (eds), *Select documents on British colonial policy* (Oxford, 1928); P. Knaplund, *James Stephen and the British colonial system* (Madison, 1953); D. M. Young, *The Colonial Office in the early nineteenth century* (Lond, 1961); J. C. Beaglehole, 'The Colonial Office, 1782-1854', *Hist Studies*, no 3, Apr 1941; E. T. Williams, 'The Colonial Office in the thirties', *Hist Studies*, no 7, May 1943; R. B. Pugh, 'The Colonial Office', *Cambridge Hist British Empire*, 3 (1959); J. W. Cell, 'The Colonial Office in the fifties', *Hist Studies*, no 45, Oct 1965; H. T. Manning, 'Who ran the British empire 1830-1850?' *J British Studies*, Connecticut, 5 (1965).   J. E. EGERTON

STEPHEN, JOHN (1771-1833), judge, was the son of James Stephen, of Aberdeen, Scotland, and Sibella Milner, of Poole, Dorsetshire. Some of the children of this union and some of their descendants were to secure to the Stephen clan a very distinguished place in the legal history of England and several of her colonies. The most influential of them in British colonial history was James Stephen junior, who from 1836 to 1847 was permanent undersecretary of state for the colonies. John Stephen was his uncle, and to his nephew he owed the appointment that brought him to New South Wales in August 1824.

In early manhood John Stephen built up a lucrative practice as an attorney and barrister in Basse Terre, St Kitts, West Indies. Having acquired a competency there, he returned to England about 1808, and in 1810 bought a beautiful little estate near Wells, Somersetshire. Unfortunately for him and his family, he speculated unprofitably, and in 1815 was obliged to resume his practice at Basse Terre. But he was unable to regain his previous footing and, as his son Alfred recorded, 'dear mother was compelled to be frugal in all things'. Relief came from nephew James. A legal office requiring a man of Uncle John's qualifications had been created at Sydney by the New South Wales Act of 1823 and, at the request of James Stephen, Earl Bathurst 'enabled' John Stephen, in his nephew's words, 'to change the land of slaves for the land of convicts'.

On 20 January 1824 Bathurst informed Governor Brisbane that 'His Majesty [had]

been pleased to nominate John Stephen, Esqre., Barrister at Law, the late Solicitor General of the St. Christopher's Government, as the Commissioner of the several Courts of Requests which are to be at present established in New South Wales'. His Majesty had overlooked the fact, however, that the New South Wales Act, section 20, provided that the said Courts of Requests were to be held by a commissioner appointed by the governor of the colony. This power was so promptly exercised by Governor Brisbane that, several months before Bathurst's dispatch was received, Dr H. G. Douglass [q.v.] had been appointed to the position. In the result he was given another post at a higher salary, and on 7 August 1824 John Stephen entered on duty. Fortune now favoured him. On the day following his appointment as commissioner of the Courts of Requests, His Majesty had appointed him solicitor-general of New South Wales. He was thus the first to hold that office in the colony. No salary was attached to it, but as he had the right of private practice it enhanced his status at the Bar and he was soon in receipt of fees for assisting Attorney-General Bannister [q.v.]. Moreover within twelve months his official salary was raised from £600 to £800.

One of the first, if not the first, briefs held by John Stephen in 'the land of convicts' arose out of the opinion which he had given certain justices of the peace, that Bannister was in error in holding that, under section 19 of the Act of 1823, free persons arraigned in Courts of Quarter Sessions must be tried before an ordinary jury of twelve of the citizenry. The issue was determined by Chief Justice Forbes [q.v.] on 14 October 1824. He upheld Bannister's contention. A month later, on the motion of D'Arcy Wentworth [q.v.] who declined nomination for the position, John Stephen was unanimously chosen as chairman of the Courts of Quarter Sessions. After 'the experiment', as Brisbane described it, of trial by a civil jury in criminal cases in such courts had been in operation for a year, the governor asked Stephen to give him his opinion as to the success or otherwise of it. 'I have found in the Juries of this territory', replied the commissioner, 'as much attention to regularity and regard to their duty, as in any Juries in England or in any part of His Majesty's Dominions. I am persuaded that the Institution of Juries in this Colony in all cases would be highly beneficial'.

In November 1824 Forbes accompanied Brisbane on a tour of inspection, by way of Port Macquarie, to the Brisbane River. In his absence Stephen, under a commission issued by the governor, acted as chief justice. On 17 August 1825 the Legislative Council, in Forbes's absence through illness, resolved that, in view of the multifarious and heavy duties of the chief justice and their obvious effect upon his health, provision should be made without delay for the appointment of an assistant judge in the Supreme Court, and *instanter* they passed a short Act authorizing the governor to do this. Within the hour Brisbane appointed John Stephen to the position. He thus became the first puisne judge of the Supreme Court of New South Wales. There was grave doubt, however, as to whether this Act, 6 Geo. IV, no 16, was *intra vires* the Legislative Council. Under the New South Wales Act the power to make any such addition to the bench of the Supreme Court was reserved to the Crown. This doubt was never resolved. By a warrant under the sign manual, 1 April 1826, Stephen was formally appointed puisne judge, and in due course the secretary of state directed that his salary of £1500 as such should be backdated to 17 August 1825. In February 1826 Governor Darling appointed him to act as chief justice during the absence of Forbes on sick leave for about three months. 'I trust', wrote the governor, that 'the necessity, which has caused the arrangement, will not exist for any length of time, as I apprehend, from Mr. Stephen's general health and constitution, that he would prove unequal to the burthen, which Mr. Forbes's absence has just now imposed upon him'.

'As [Stephen] laboured under considerable infirmity at the time of my arrival, and resigned office in consequence soon afterwards', wrote Governor Bourke in 1834, 'I am not able from personal observation to communicate anything respecting his usefulness as a Judge in this Colony; but I understand he was previously considered a person of considerable professional knowledge and ability'. It may be assumed that this understanding derived from Chief Justice Forbes. With some hesitation because of Stephen's intemperance, in respect of which the latter gave him accepted assurances, but upon which Colonel Dumaresq [q.v.] dilated in a letter to Under-Secretary Hay, Forbes had commended his appointment as puisne judge to Brisbane, and he was in friendly relations with him as a colleague for seven years.

'Mr. Stephen . . . poor Man', Governor Darling informed the secretary of state in July 1828, 'is a Tool in the hands of the Chief Justice, who works with him as best answers his immediate object'. John Macarthur senior [q.v.] conveyed the same opinion to his son John, but in more opprobrious terms. No specific evidence was adduced by either of these gentlemen in support of this charge. Neither Forbes nor Stephen was acquainted with it, still less given an opportunity to answer it. It is true that, after the manner of the judiciary, Stephen frequently concurred with the chief justice when they sat together, but it is no less true that on occasion he differed from him, as he did in the leading case of R. v. Farrell and Dingle, and in the notable appeal case of Wentworth v. Mansfield [qq.v.] when Stephen delivered the minority judgment.

When roused, as when his precedence vis-a-vis Dowling [q.v.] was in question, Stephen showed that he was not of the stuff of which tools and dupes are made. So, too, when he deemed that Darling was encroaching upon the province of the judiciary, or concluded that the legal rights of accused persons were being infringed by superior authority, he independently asserted himself with unmistakable energy. Indeed his unrestrained condemnation from the bench of the practice whereby a military jury was empanelled to try cases in which the governor was, in reality, the prosecutor, contributed to a radical amendment of the law in this respect.

Stephen could be blunt to the point of rudeness. He disregarded the secretary of state's instructions relating to official correspondence in a manner very discourteous to the governor. He allowed Wentworth unusual latitude in cases that came before him touching the honour and dignity of Darling and Archdeacon Scott [q.v.]. At times he expressed himself from the bench in terms that must have grated on the ears of his learned brethren. On several occasions he was sternly admonished by the Colonial Office for being indiscreet, one of the more severe of these censures being written by his nephew James although dispatched over the signature of the secretary of state. 'If I have anything to reproach myself with, in regard to Mr. Justice Stephen', wrote Darling in July 1831, 'it is the forbearance I have shewn in not reporting his unfitness for his Office. I abstained in order to promote the wishes of His Majesty's Government', meaning thereby, it is apprehended, the wishes as conceived by the governor of the judge's very influential relation in the Colonial Office.

The 'unfitness' to which the governor alluded was in part physical. When Mr Justice Dowling first saw Stephen in February 1828 he appeared to him 'very infirm, shattered and in bad health.

[He] seemed to be marked down for another world'. Repeated and protracted attacks of gout kept him off the bench for months on end, and thus added to the already heavy burdens of the chief justice and of Dowling, the second puisne judge. Yet Stephen clung to his seat. In October 1831 when, according to his son, he was 'so infirm in body and in memory that he [was] incompetent to the discharge of his public duties', he tendered his resignation to the secretary of state conditional on receiving a retiring allowance of £750 a year. Viscount Goderich fixed the figure, however, at £500, and in consequence Stephen was still in office when his successor, William Burton [q.v.], reached Sydney in December 1832. Ten days later under pressure from Bourke and on the understanding that his salary was to continue until the end of the month, Stephen, grumbling the while, resigned. He died on 21 December 1833. His widow died in 1863 in her eighty-ninth year.

Any sketch of the life of Mr Justice John Stephen would be inadequate without some reference to the Stephen ménage. He and his wife Mary Anne, née Pasmore, had six boys, one of whom died aged 10, and three girls. His fourth son, Alfred, was appointed a puisne judge of the Supreme Court of New South Wales in 1839, and was chief justice in 1844-73. Of the other children, John and Francis, and the eldest daughter Sibella, by reason of her marriage to Captain Robison, were often in Darling's mind. John gave him abundant cause to dismiss him from the public service. Robison, for much less cause, Darling cashiered and successfully prosecuted in London. Francis was a lively young spark who hobnobbed with Wentworth, Wardell, Mackaness [qq.v.] and other Adullamites whom Darling detested. He and Edward Smith Hall [q.v.] were the leaders in organizing a final, but abortive demonstration against the departing governor. It follows, therefore, that Darling's name must have been a byword at Ultimo House, the town residence of Mr Justice Stephen. It is extremely likely that this home was the source of some of the leakages to the hostile press for which Darling blamed Chief Justice Forbes. Stephen resented the imputations, and his dislike of the governor, which was avowedly shared by his nephew in Downing Street, became the more intense.

HRA (1), 11-17; R. M. Bedford, Think of Stephen: a family chronicle (Syd, 1954); MS cat under John Stephen (ML); Newspaper indexes under John Stephen (ML); CO 201/ 195/450, 229/320.   C. H. CURREY

STEPHENS, ALFRED WARD (1804-1852), printer, editor and pastoralist, was born at Portsmouth, England. He was probably a journeyman printer before he arrived in Sydney in the *Resource* on 6 May 1829, travelling steerage with his wife Eliza. Stephens found employment on the *Sydney Gazette* under the editorship of Rev. Ralph Mansfield [q.v.] and there he met Frederick Stokes and William McGarvie [q.v.]. With the intention of establishing a general printing business they combined to import a press from London but, orders being fewer than they expected, they decided to publish a newspaper instead. This paper first appeared on 18 April 1831 as the *Sydney Herald* (later the *Sydney Morning Herald*). McGarvie withdrew after six weeks and, although Stephens and Stokes were joint proprietors, Stephens seems to have been the acknowledged editor.

Before the *Herald* appeared, the Tories in Sydney and the Hunter River district had no newspaper to express their political and economic opinions. The *Herald* filled this gap. Thus in 1832 Stephens & Stokes printed the protest of John Bingle [q.v.], a Hunter River magistrate, against the laxity of convict discipline under Governor Bourke: *Letter to the Right Honourable His Majesty's Principal Secretary of State for the Colonies.* This was the first shot in a bitter campaign against Bourke that reached a climax in 1835. Stephens and Bingle were supported by a group of rebellious magistrates most of whom were wealthy landholders and squatters. Stephens later purchased Bingle's Hunter River property, Puen Buen.

After the convict rebellion at Castle Forbes in November 1833 Stephens gave powerful support to James Mudie [q.v.], the owner of that property. The *Herald* was also involved in libel actions and accused of using underhand methods to score off its opponents. In July 1834, for example, Edward O'Shaughnessy [q.v.], editor of the *Sydney Gazette*, accused Stephens of having in his possession a stolen copy of a pamphlet, *Party Politics exposed*, printed anonymously by the *Gazette*; Stephens retaliated by accusing its sub-editor, William Watt, of inciting James Hay, a *Herald* compositor, to steal copy from the *Herald*, and giving him 10s. for it. Stephens lost the case but soon afterwards acquired O'Shaughnessy's services for the *Herald*.

In 1836 Stephens had 'a little difference' with Stokes and bought his share in the paper. As sole editor and proprietor Stephens for the next five years exerted a strong influence on colonial affairs with O'Shaughnessy as his leader writer. He took an active interest in public life and supported representative government, and demands for the cessation of transportation, appropriation of colonial funds for emigration, lower land prices, security of tenure for the squatters, and open discussion in the Legislative Council. In 1839 Stephens became a director of the Hunter River Navigation Co. and began to devote all his energies to grazing. He sold the *Herald* to Stokes and invested his money in land in the Hunter River district. At the same time he sent overseers to depasture his stock on land in New England. Reliable immigrants, mainly married couples, were selected to work on his properties, which included Runnymede, Lismore and Stratheden. His stations were among the finest in the district but he visited them rarely and took no part in the meetings of neighbouring squatters.

Stephens's pastoral activities were dogged by bad luck from the start. Drought and depression between 1840 and 1843 caused him to go insolvent and he was forced to sell land as cheaply as 1s. 3d. an acre and to sacrifice his stock. In 1841, for example, he sold 12,000 sheep at 1s. 6d. each, 1100 cattle at £1 a head and 50 horses at £14 each. Runnymede station, of 128,000 acres, proved a tragic investment: it was acquired for his son, who in 1842 was accidentally shot while stooping to drink from a waterhole. Runnymede also dealt the final blow to Stephens's financial hopes: in 1847 he was prosecuted by Shaw and Leycaster for allowing stock to trespass on what is now known locally as 'Disputed Plain'. Although Stephens won the case, Leycaster finally carried the dispute to the Privy Council, where he lost, but the legal costs were so heavy that both he and Stephens were ruined. The loss of his son and this second insolvency affected Stephens's health and he was inactive for the last years of his life. He died in Sydney in July 1852 and left effects worth only £20.

Stephens was an able man but somewhat eccentric. Many amusing stories are told of his squatting life, especially during the hard times of 1842-43 when employees were paid in what was known as 'Calabash' orders, drawn on consignments of sheepskins, wool, tallow or hides; these orders were frequently dishonoured even after the consignments had reached the consignee.

A century of journalism. The Sydney Morning Herald, 1831-1931 (Syd, 1931); V & P (LC NSW), 1844-47; *Government Gazette*, 1838-48; J. Mitchell papers (ML).

J. V. BYRNES

STEPHENS, EDWARD (1811-1861), bank manager, was born on 19 October 1811 in London, the tenth son of Rev. John Stephens (1772-1841), sometime president of the Wesleyan Methodist Conference, and his wife Rebecca Eliza, née Raynor. Among his brothers was John Raynor Stephens (1805-1879), who became a Wesleyan minister, but was suspended for political activity in 1834, arrested in December 1838 for disturbing the public peace as a Chartist and sentenced to imprisonment for eighteen months. Edward was a clerk and assistant cashier in the Hull Banking Co. from 1833 until 1836 when he was appointed cashier and accountant of the South Australian Co. He sailed for South Australia with his wife Emma, née Harrison, in the *Coromandel* and on 17 January 1837 arrived at Holdfast Bay. There he set up his office in a tent but at first business was slight. He was induced to sign a letter to Governor Hindmarsh asking for a public meeting to reconsider the site of Adelaide. Although in February the meeting decided in favour of Colonel Light's [q.v.] choice Stephens did not hesitate to buy eight city acres when they were auctioned, and later became very friendly with Light. Stephens fell foul of Hindmarsh and was rebuked by George Fife Angas [q.v.] for dabbling in politics, but he became more judicious under David McLaren [q.v.] and was appointed a justice of the peace. In 1840 when the company's business was divided Stephens became the Adelaide manager of the South Australian Banking Co. He steered it 'tactfully and forcefully' through the depression, although he lost the government account by refusing to comply with Governor Grey's demands. When mineral ores were discovered Stephens was quick to send to England samples of silver-lead and copper for testing, and he was one of the first to visit the Burra copper deposits; his own investment in the area was small but the bank profited greatly from his energetic promotion of it.

As a zealous Wesleyan Stephens was active in establishing Methodism in Adelaide. The first Methodist sermon had been preached in his tent at Holdfast Bay and the first class meetings were held in his home on North Terrace. He was largely responsible for building the first two Methodist chapels in Adelaide and providing them with ministers. He was also chairman of the League for the Preservation of Religious Freedom, a strenuous position in 1846 when state aid to churches was introduced. Acceptance of aid by the Wesleyans so shocked Stephens that he withdrew and formed the short-lived Representative Methodist Church.

In 1849 the South Australian Banking Co. made a profit of £15,000 and declared a dividend of 6 per cent on its paid up capital of £180,000. Two years later Stephens visited England with his wife and thereby missed the crisis over the Bullion Act. On his return to Adelaide he stood as a conservative candidate for West Adelaide in the Legislative Council election in 1853; although defeated he was compensated with a seat as a government nominee. He served on the civil list committee but took little part in revising the colony's proposed constitutional bill. In 1855 he toured the colonies of eastern Australia and returned to London. There he continued to serve South Australia on committees for conferences, reunions and exhibitions. He died on 28 February 1861, and his wife on 4 December 1871, at Howard Lodge, Maida Vale.

G. F. Holyoake, *The Life of John Raynor Stephens* (Lond, 1881); D. Pike, *Paradise of Dissent* (Melb, 1957).

STEPHENS, JOHN (1806-1850), newspaper editor, was born on 30 September 1806 at North Shields, Northumberland, England, the seventh son of Rev. John Stephens and brother of Edward [q.v.]. He was educated at a Wesleyan academy and at a grammar school in Leeds. Through helping his father distribute church magazines he became a 'precocious bibliopolist' and after apprenticeship in the book trade opened his own shop in London. There he married the only daughter of William Fleming, an active Wesleyan. In 1832 Stephens helped to found the *Christian Advocate* as a Methodist journal, but it soon became the recognized organ of the anti-slavery party. After emancipation he used his editorials to attack the conservative Wesleyans and lost his job. For some time he worked on various newspapers and about 1838 George Fife Angas [q.v.] employed him to write emigration propaganda. Stephens's first notable work was *The Land of Promise*, republished in 1839 as *The History of the Rise and Progress of the new British Province of South Australia*. In that year his exposure of absurdities in T. Horton James, *Six Months in South Australia* (London, 1839), ran to three editions. He also edited the *South Australian Colonist*, on which Angas lost heavily; it was replaced in 1841 by the monthly *South Australian News* at a cheaper rate. Meanwhile Stephens found time to send trenchant articles to various newspapers.

By 1842 his first wife had died and he

had remarried. He emigrated with his wife to Adelaide, where he arrived in January 1843. In July he began the *Adelaide Observer* and soon afterwards acquired the *South Australian Register*. His career as a colonial journalist was punctuated by storms and scandals. Apart from his reputation as a 'Johnny Drinkwater', his discreet championship of small farmers and his advocacy of religious liberty, he was not narrow-minded as to what appeared in his papers, or from what creed, party or person it emanated. In his opinion 'certain moral felonies were punishable only through the medium of the press', and in his uncompromising exposures scarcely a week went by without an appeal to redress some local injustice. These attacks won him acclaim as the champion of independent journalism but lost him advertisers. To raise funds in 1846 he published *The Royal South Australian Almanack and General Directory* and in 1847 a *Voice from South Australia*, an appeal to the starving millions of the United Kingdom to emigrate, and next year the first number of *The Adelaide Miscellany of Useful and Entertaining Knowledge*. In 1848 his presses were seized for debt and a rival obligingly printed two issues. Although his plant was then returned, anxiety played havoc with his health and for months he had to leave the paper to subordinates. In attempts to imitate their master they involved Stephens in at least eight libel actions in 1849. Next year the *Register* became a daily, but the strain on Stephens proved too great. Grieved by the lack of any love for literature in a population of 50,000 he died in his brother Edward's fine home, Seacombe, at Brighton on 28 November 1850. He was survived by his wife, three infant daughters and a son.

G. H. Pitt, *The press in South Australia 1836 to 1850* (Adel, 1946); D. Pike, *Paradise of Dissent* (Melb, 1957).

STEPHENS, SAMUEL (1808-1840), company manager, was born in England, the eighth son of Rev. John Stephens and brother of Edward [q.v.]. He was connected for some time with a Birmingham commercial house but after a quarrel with his minister over the powers of the Wesleyan Conference, was censured by a circuit meeting and lost his job. In May 1835 he appealed to George Fife Angas [q.v.] for an assistant surveyorship in South Australia. Although unsuccessful he was appointed Angas's London agent, helped to form the South Australian Co.

and became its first colonial manager. He sailed in the *Duke of York* in February 1836 and on 27 July was the first of the new settlers to step ashore at Nepean Bay, Kangaroo Island. He had a seven year contract and wide discretionary powers which he exercised with exuberance. After sketchily settling the company's headquarters at Kingscote he turned to the mainland, where he bought many sections for the company at the original auction of Adelaide and reserved others at the port. He gave generous advances to settlers and involved the company in the import of foodstuffs and livestock. In the van of every project, he was too busy to write careful dispatches, and in less than a year his outlay of £14,000 and poor accounting alarmed the directors in London. Angas was scandalized by reports of disorder and drunkenness among the company's indentured labourers on Kangaroo Island. In April 1837 David McLaren [q.v.] arrived as the company's commercial manager and Stephens was demoted. He was suspended in November after a fracas at the company's whaling station in Encounter Bay, where he was charged with killing a sailor from a rival fishery.

Out of office Stephens's character deteriorated and he became excitable and intemperate, but his excellent judgment of soil and stock was in constant demand by exploration parties and landbuyers, including the company. He was returning from an expedition to the River Murray on 18 January 1840 when he recklessly raced his horse over a steep hill and was killed. He was buried in Adelaide, survived by his wife Charlotte Hudson, née Beare, whom he had married in the *John Pirie* at Nepean Bay on 24 September 1836. She lived in retirement, for a time supported by her brother-in-law Edward, until her death in 1875 at the age of 93.

A. J. Perkins, *South Australia: an agricultural and pastoral state in the making* (Adel, 1939); D. Pike, *Paradise of Dissent* (Melb, 1957); I. A. Diamond, *History of South Australian Co: the first decade* (M.A. thesis, Univ Adel, 1955).

STEVENSON, GEORGE (1799-1856), editor, was born on 13 April 1799 at Berwick upon Tweed, Northumberland, England, the son of a gentleman farmer, who died when he was 12. He went to sea in an East Indiaman, returned to Scotland and briefly studied medicine. He then worked on his brother's ranch in Canada, visited Central America and the West Indies, and returned to England in 1830.

He claimed that in 1835 he became joint editor of the *Globe*; more probably he was only a travelling correspondent, and he was heavily in debt to the owner, Colonel Torrens [q.v.]. Next year he was appointed secretary to the governor and clerk of the council in the new province of South Australia. He also applied to Lord Glenelg for appointment as protector of Aborigines, because of his experience with North American Indians and his benevolent character. On 12 May 1836 at St George's, Hanover Square, London, he married Margaret Gorton, née Hutton, of Chester, one of the witnesses being Henry Lytton Bulwer. His wife was the widow of John Gorton, who had been an assistant editor of the *Globe*; she had helped to prepare his *A General Biographical Dictionary* published in London in 1828.

Before leaving England Stevenson gave evidence before the select committee on the disposal of waste lands in the British colonies. Although claiming that 'incessant engagement in political warfare was not consonant to his taste', he entered into an agreement to produce a newspaper in the colony, with Robert Thomas as manager and printer, and himself as editor. The first number of the *South Australian Gazette and Colonial Register* appeared in London on 18 June 1836, announcing that 'the intention of publishing its second number in a city of the wilderness of which the site is yet unknown, may appear to many more chimerical than interesting'. Stevenson sailed in the *Buffalo*, with Governor Hindmarsh, and arrived on 28 December 1836 at Holdfast Bay where he read the governor's first proclamation to the assembled colonists. Stevenson won the confidence of Hindmarsh and was sent to report on the lawless state of Kangaroo Island. He then joined the opposition to the capital site chosen by Colonel Light [q.v.], and later to supporters of the resident commissioner, J. H. Fisher [q.v.]. After the second number of the *South Australian Gazette and Colonial Register* appeared in Adelaide on 3 June 1837, Stevenson's fiery articles aggravated antagonism to the governor, and after the third issue J. H. Fisher, Light and others began planning a second newspaper, the *Southern Australian*, edited by Charles Mann and John Brown [qq.v.]. After Governor Gawler arrived, Stevenson resigned his official appointments and his exposure of G. M. Stephen [q.v.] soon led to separation of the *Government Gazette* and the *Register*. Later criticism of Gawler lost him a share in the government printing. In 1840 he became associated with the Port Lincoln

special survey. He was twice elected to the Municipal Corporation of Adelaide, serving as alderman in 1840-41.

Although Stevenson withdrew from the *South Australian Register* in 1842 he returned to journalism three years later and revived the *South Australian Gazette and Colonial Register*, changing *Colonial* to *Mining* in October 1847. Although a Presbyterian, he had some part in founding the Collegiate School of St Peter. In 1849 his inveterate exposures brought him public blows from R. R. Torrens, but he later won a Pyrrhic victory in court. In March 1852 his newspaper ceased publication, and after a brief visit to the Victorian goldfields he was appointed coroner in Adelaide. He died at his home, Lytton Lodge, in Finniss Street, North Adelaide, on 18 October 1856. He was survived by one daughter who married E. V. De Mole, and two sons, one of whom, George John William, became member for East Torrens in the House of Assembly in 1871-75 and attorney-general in the Ayers ministry in 1872-73.

Stevenson was an enthusiastic horticulturist and often lectured on the subject. He helped to form the local Natural History Society and his own garden and orchard were among the best in early Adelaide, his experiments proving of great value. As a journalist he was never pompous or pedantic, but his strong opinions were expressed with fearless vigour and provoked much controversy.

J. Bonwick, *Early struggles of the Australian press* (Lond, 1890); G. H. Pitt, *The press in South Australia 1836 to 1850* (Adel, 1946); *Advertiser* (Adel), 12 Nov 1936; G. Stevenson, *Journal* (Angas papers, SAA); Stevenson to Glenelg, 23 Apr 1836, CO 13/5.

STEWART, WILLIAM (1769-1854), soldier and lieut-governor, was the son of William Stewart of Caithness, Scotland, and grandson of Donald Stewart of Appin, one of Prince Charles Edward's officers. Stewart joined the 101st Regiment as an ensign in 1794 and was transferred to the 3rd Regiment in 1796. He served in the West Indies, notably at Grenada, St Vincent, St Lucia and St Eustatius until 1802, and on the Peninsula (1808-12). In Portugal Stewart took part in severe fighting, was wounded, decorated, and promoted lieut-colonel in August 1810. He commanded the 3rd Regiment in America in 1814 and in the army of occupation in France in 1815-18. He became a colonel by purchase in 1819.

In 1821 the 3rd Regiment was sent to New South Wales. Stewart disembarked at

Sydney in April 1825. Before leaving England he had obtained a commission as lieut-governor but on 1 January 1825 this was amended by instructions that he was to associate the two senior members of the Legislative Council in any government of his. Stewart was senior military officer in the colony and a member of the Legislative Council. Governor Brisbane held a poor opinion of him, and, although he had been authorized to leave Sydney any time after May, Brisbane delayed his departure, claiming that he could not trust the administration to the lieut-governor. The reasons for Brisbane's hostility are not clear but it is likely that he suspected Stewart's humanitarian and liberal views. Brisbane departed on 1 December 1825, and Stewart governed the colony for eighteen days until the arrival of Governor Darling. His only important proclamation was on the fixing of postal rates. He also formed a small mounted police force and pardoned some convicts whom Brisbane had left under capital sentence.

Darling regarded Stewart highly and employed him in various duties, making him a member of the Land Board, the Board of General Purposes, and an inquiry in 1826 into the administration of the Female Orphan School. Conflict between the two men occurred only once, after the drumming-out of Privates Sudds and Thompson in November 1826. Stewart claimed that Darling had promised that the heavy irons used on the offenders would be worn only during the parade, but they were not removed until later. When Stewart discovered this after the death of Sudds he rebuked the governor for his failure to keep his promise.

In 1827 Stewart relinquished his position as lieut-governor when he went to India to command his regiment. He was promoted major-general in July 1830 and returned to New South Wales in 1832 to live in retirement near Bathurst on Mount Pleasant, an estate of 3200 acres granted by Darling in 1826. After retirement Stewart took little part in public life, although he chaired a meeting at Bathurst in 1850 to protest against the proposed revival of transportation. He died on 8 April 1854 and was buried on his property.

Stewart married Sylvia Anne, née Wolfe, and was survived by three daughters and one son, James Horne Stewart. A portrait by an unknown artist is owned by a descendant, Mrs S. Jamieson, of Strath, Bathurst.

HRA (1), 12; *Major-General William Stewart* (priv print, copy in possession of Mrs S. Jamieson, Bathurst); Stewart papers (Bathurst Hist Soc); Newspaper indexes under William Stewart (ML).

THEO BARKER

STIEGLITZ; *see* VON STIEGLITZ

STILES, HENRY TARLTON (1808-1867), Church of England clergyman, was born on 24 June 1808 at Bristol, England, a son of Carter and Sophia Stiles. According to family tradition he was intended for the Indian army. His strong Evangelical upbringing led him to the Church Missionary Society's college at Islington though 'his constitution [was] not considered calculated to withstand the effects of a Tropical Climate'. Stiles had scholarly interests—he hoped at one time that the Bristol Clerical Education Society might sponsor him at Oxford—and served as tutor in several important families, including that of James Stephen of the Colonial Office. It may have been Stephen who prompted him to look to Australia, where the authorities had decided to recruit clergy and were having difficulty in securing an Englishman as master of the Female Orphan School. Stiles was appointed to this position in 1832 because of very high testimony to his peculiar fitness 'for the education and superintendance of Youth'. He was ordained deacon on 23 December 1832 and priest on 20 January 1833 by Bishop Blomfield of London. On 11 February he married Jane, the eldest daughter of Charles and Grace Hole, of Kingsbridge.

Stiles sailed in the *Warrior* and reached Sydney in July. He had been promised the first vacant chaplaincy in addition to the Orphan School mastership; alternatively, he might receive the charge of a parish. Within a month he was sent temporarily to St Matthew's, Windsor, and the appointment was made permanent before the year ended.

As an Evangelical with missionary interests, Stiles became a close friend of Rev. Samuel Marsden [q.v.], who sent him to Norfolk Island in August 1834 and December 1835 to minister to condemned felons. In November 1836 he sent evidence to the proposed committee on transportation stressing the need for drastic reform of the penal system at Norfolk Island. These were to be Stiles's only excursions outside Windsor. He settled down to the duties of his parish, which included Richmond until 1842, Kurrajong and Clydesdale, and where the Hawkesbury River, the mountains, bad roads and the scattered population made pastoral visitation 'a work of great fatigue'. However, the parish was well-equipped with churches, schools and a rectory, and had wealthy influential parishioners.

After Marsden died Stiles was influenced by Bishop Broughton [q.v.] and by Tractarian teachings, and preached and wrote against the Methodists, who were numerous in the Hawkesbury area. Stiles's friendship with the Sydney adherents of the Oxford school of theology involved him in the disputes which followed the secession to Rome of Rev. R. K. Sconce [q.v.] in 1848. Broughton withdrew an offer to Stiles of Sconce's vacant cure of St Andrew's, and Stiles, alarmed and perplexed by the bitter controversy, refused a second offer. Broughton had secured for him a Lambeth M.A. in 1843, but his later promise of a canonry was not carried out.

The Sconce affair was Stiles's last, though involuntary, venture into public debate. Thereafter he devoted himself to his parish, where he tried to uphold the Tractarian tradition, despite opposition from some members of his congregation. The arrival of the Evangelical Bishop Barker in 1855 put Stiles's school of churchmanship on the defensive and increased his concentration on local affairs. But Stiles supported Barker in founding the Diocesan Church Society and in seeking synodical government by legislative enactment. He remained on good terms with his bishop, although he could not be in the circle of his advisers.

After 1860 Stiles was in poor health and in June 1866 his regular ministry ceased. On 21 June 1867 a great Hawkesbury flood occurred while Stiles lay dying. He directed that the church be opened to the homeless; the Methodist minister was one of the first to take refuge there. Stiles died on 22 June and his wife on 24 March 1868. There were four sons of the marriage and a daughter, Mary Emma, who married Rev. C. F. Garnsey, Stiles's curate and successor at Windsor and later rector of Christ Church St Laurence, Sydney.

Henry Stiles held no high office in the church, headed no cause and remained in the one district for the whole of his colonial career. His change from Evangelical missionary and teacher to High Church parish clergyman was typical of his time, but Stiles was unusual in the extent to which he carried it. The settled character of his parish helped in his transition. Bishop Barker considered him 'intellectual and gentlemanly and in conversation most agreeable', and he had a reputation for kindliness and, except where principles of churchmanship were involved, of ready accommodation to the views of others.

HRA (1), 16; C. F. Garnsey, A *sermon* . . . *for the occasion of the death of the Rev.* H. T. *Stiles* (Windsor, 1867); Sel cttee on clergy stipends, V & P (LC NSW), 1854, 1; Stiles papers (ML).   K. J. CABLE

STIRLING, SIR JAMES (1791-1865), governor, was the fifth son and the eighth of the fifteen children of Andrew Stirling of Drumpellier, Lanarkshire, Scotland. His mother, Anne, was his father's first cousin, being the daughter of Admiral Sir Walter Stirling and the sister of Sir Walter Stirling, first baronet, of Faskine.

At 12 Stirling entered the navy as a first-class volunteer, embarking on the storeship *Camel* for the West Indies. He was fortunate at first in having the patronage of his uncle, Rear-Admiral Charles Stirling. Soon after arriving in the West Indies, young James was transferred to the *Hercules*, and in 1805 he went to serve in his uncle's flagship *Glory*. He saw action off Cape Finisterre against the French and Spanish fleets, and later served in the *Sampson* and the *Diadem* in the operations on the Rio de la Plata. After watching the fall of Montevideo and being incorrectly reported as killed in action, he served for a time on the Home Station, and on 12 August 1809 was promoted lieutenant in the *Warspite*. In 1811 he was flag lieutenant to his uncle, who was then in command at Jamaica, and on 27 February 1812 received his first command, the sloop *Moselle*, and soon afterwards the larger sloop *Brazen*, in which he was employed during the American war in harassing forts and shipping near the Mississippi. Later Stirling was sent to Hudson Bay, the North Sea, the Gulf of Mexico and the West Indies. Meanwhile his uncle had been court-martialled on a charge of corrupt practices and was prematurely retired from the service. However, it was not the loss of his uncle's patronage but the final defeat of Bonaparte which dimmed Stirling's prospects. On 7 December 1818 he was promoted to post rank and placed on half-pay.

In 1818 Stirling had no qualifications for shore employment although he had a tidy sum from prize money and a small but secure income from the Treasury. For a while he travelled in Europe and moved in London and county society. At Woodbridge, Surrey, he became acquainted with the Mangles family, whose wealthy head had extensive interests in the East Indies, had been high sheriff for Surrey in 1808, was a director of the East India Co. and in 1832-37 represented Guildford in parliament. His third daughter, Ellen, attracted Stirling's attention. The couple were married at Stoke Church, Guildford, on 3

September 1823 on Ellen's sixteenth birthday; they had five sons and six daughters.

The Stirlings toured the Continent, and after their return lived at Woodbridge until renewed naval activity by the French brought a welcome change in Stirling's prospects. The politicians at Westminster and the administrators in New South Wales had already been alerted to the possibility of French colonization in the Pacific, and had taken steps to forestall any such move by posting garrisons at several places in the north and south of Australia. One of these, on Melville Island, had been badly sited and it was decided to move the garrison to a better place. In April 1826 Stirling was given command of the new *Success* with instructions to take a supply of currency to Sydney and then to move the Melville Island garrison. On arrival at Sydney he joined an inland expedition and received a grant of 2500 acres from Governor Darling. Darling had already sent a garrison to King George Sound, but Stirling persuaded him that, as the monsoons prevented immediate transfer of the northern garrison, and as a French expedition was already acting suspiciously in Australian waters, he should be allowed to examine the west coast of Australia to see whether it provided a suitable site for a garrison or for another settlement to open trade with the East Indies. Stirling sailed in 1827 and during a fortnight's visit was much impressed with the land in the vicinity of the Swan River. So also was the New South Wales government botanist, Charles Frazer [q.v.], whose report added weight to Stirling's political and commercial arguments in favour of its immediate acquisition and Stirling's appointment to establish a new colony there. Both opinions were supported by Darling, though not by the colonial administrators in London, who were loth to assume a further territorial burden and who, in Stirling's words, 'trembled at the thought of the expenditure involved'.

Stirling completed his assignment in the *Success* and then joined the East India Squadron for a tour of duty. However, a severe stomach ailment caused him to be invalided home on half-pay, thus giving him a good chance to press for a new settlement in Western Australia. In London his persistent arguments attracted the attention of investors and speculators, who joined him in badgering the Colonial Office to grant them government sanctions and land concessions. Stirling himself was not committed to any particular form of colonization, having a 'bounty of ideas' on the subject, many of them no doubt inspired by conversations with the Mangles family at Woodbridge. At one time he favoured floating a syndicate like the Australian Agricultural Co., and at another the formation of an association such as had founded Georgia and Pennsylvania, but he was always insistent that no convicts should be sent out with the settlers. In May 1828 a change in the British government brought Sir George Murray, a friend of the Stirling family, into charge of the Colonial Office; his parliamentary assistant, Horace Twiss, was also a friend of the Stirlings. After some delay it was decided to establish a colony in New Holland under the direct control of the British government, and superintended initially by Stirling: a bill would soon be brought before parliament to provide for its government; private capitalists and syndicates would be allotted land in the proposed settlement according to the amount of capital and the money they spent on fares and equipment; priority of choice would be given only to those who arrived before the end of 1830, and no syndicate or company would be the exclusive patron and proprietor of the settlement.

On 2 May 1829 Captain C. H. Fremantle of the *Challenger* took possession, at the mouth of the Swan River, of the whole of Australia which was not then included within the boundaries of New South Wales. Stirling, who arrived later with his family and civil officials in the storeship *Parmelia*, proclaimed the foundation of the colony on 18 June. No other arrangements had been made to establish the settlement, apart from the dispatch of Captain F. C. Irwin [q.v.] with a detachment of the 63rd Regiment in H.M.S. *Sulphur*. None of the country had been explored and surveyed and the coastal waters were virtually uncharted. It was left to the ingenuity of the settlers and the untried administrative capacity of Stirling to surmount all difficulties.

Stirling administered the Swan River settlement from June 1829 until August 1832, when he left on an extended visit to England where he was knighted, and again from August 1834 until December 1838. His first official designation of lieutgovernor was superseded by that of governor in November 1831, after the tardy arrival of the official documents constituting his office and appointing him to it, as well as establishing the permanent organs of government and justice. He was therefore not only the founder of the colony but for almost a decade its ruler and patriarch. At no time were his powers to govern the colony seriously impaired either by instructions from London or by obstruction from officials or settlers in the colony itself. In February 1832 an Executive and a Legislative Council met for the first time, with identical membership, but the governor presided over both bodies and other colonists had no say in government.

In his early administration Stirling took a leading part in exploring the coastal districts near the Swan, Murray, Collie, Preston, Blackwood and Vasse Rivers, and the first settlements were sited there in preference to the areas east of the Darling Range. It was some time before his chief aides, Peter Broun [q.v.], the colonial secretary and keeper of the accounts, and Lieutenant J. S. Roe, R.N. [q.v.], the surveyor-general, were able to set up proper departments in Perth, and most routine decisions were made by the governor. On legal matters he sought the advice of W. H. Mackie [q.v.], the advocate-general. Stirling personally welcomed the early settlers, made it easy for any of them to obtain an audience with him and acted as a polite rubbing-post for their multitude of petty grievances. He was also attentive to the complaints of the lower orders.

The main problem in the colony's early days was to get enough food to prevent starvation, and this largely depended on finding good soil in the right position. Clearing the virgin bush and building weather-proof homes called for much effort, adaptation and improvisation. While the settlers were establishing themselves, Stirling had to buy emergency supplies from the Cape and Van Diemen's Land. The burdensome economic troubles of this ill-planned little colony and the recurrent hairbreadth escapes from famine were not permitted to interfere with the due observance of British law and justice. Honorary magistrates were appointed to see that the lower orders kept their places and fulfilled their obligations: pioneering anxieties were not to interrupt the genteel style of living of the middle and upper orders in this colony of transplanted Britons. The governor expected his guests to dress formally for dinner, even if meals were taken under canvas in oppressive summer heat, or at his country seat of Woodbridge, near the little town of Guildford. The musical evenings and the outdoor recreations of hunting and picnicking were designed to make any new settler from the English counties feel almost at home. Public worship was officially recognized by the appointment of colonial chaplains; the colony was predominantly English and Anglican. Stirling was not deeply religious but he realized the value of the churches in helping to maintain moral standards and public order.

The small Aboriginal population in the vicinity of the first settlements was sometimes troublesome. In company with his settlers, Stirling patronized those who succumbed to the ways of the white man and became persistent beggars, but he ordered summary punishments for those who became persistent thieves. Several natives responsible for killing white settlers were captured, tried and executed. In October 1834 the governor personally led a posse of twenty-five police, soldiers and settlers to punish some seventy natives of the Murray River tribe in retaliation for several murders and 'the pertinacious endeavours of these savages to commit depredations of property'. This one-sided encounter between bullets and spears became known as the 'Battle of Pinjarra'. Fourteen Aboriginals and one police superintendent were killed.

The credit rightfully accorded to Stirling for his part in founding the colony of Western Australia and for his vision, tenacity and enterprise in guiding its early development must be balanced by the colony's obvious failure to make much material progress. At no time during his ten year term did the settlers number more than 3000 men, women and children. When he left in 1839 the flag had been well and truly planted to warn off ambitious French naval officers or other marauders, but little else had been achieved. The land near the Swan was very poor and on the south-western coast was heavily timbered and very difficult to clear. Good land was more scarce than even Stirling was prepared to admit in unguarded comments to friends and relatives in England. Because of the poor quality very little land was bought after sales were introduced in 1832; no grain was effectively harvested until 1835, and experience proved the sandy soils of the inland more suited to grazing sheep than to intensive agriculture. Viewed as a strategic operation, Swan River was probably of some significance; in any event, the British government was always most reluctant to abandon any land which it had added to its empire. But as a commercial and agricultural enterprise, it was a failure. A Mangles-inspired scheme to plant a settlement of Anglo-Indians near Albany on the south coast and to develop trade with India collapsed when the first vessel was lost in 1833 with all hands.

As governor and general administrative factotum, Stirling's personal responsibilities were heavy, and the constant anxiety borne by this colonial Solon, prompted by the uncertain future of the colony, must have outweighed the occasional excitement of finding new country or of launching the colony on some new venture. He had knowingly embarked on an undertaking with only slight support from the British government, the protection of a distant navy, and the salaries of a few officials. Stirling himself received a grant of 100,000 acres of land in the colony and repayment of his expenses, but the government was always reluctant to accept the slightest financial responsibility for his or the colony's success.

Stirling's repeated requests for succour were fruitless. So also was his visit to England in 1833-34, which had originally been inspired by the need for 'an agreeable leave of absence' but was at the last moment sanctified by the consensus of opinion among settlers that a personal deputation was likely to do them more good than any more letters or petitions. Captain Irwin was left to administer the colony in his absence. However, the British government was not well pleased at seeing this truant governor on its doorstep, and Stirling was lucky to escape censure for leaving his post without permission. He was saved mainly by his obvious sincerity on behalf of a group of settlers who had long since ceased to welcome new shiploads of either capitalists or workmen. For nearly two years Stirling doggedly explained to officials and politicians in London the necessitous circumstances of the colonists, but to no avail. He returned to the colony more than ever apprehensive about its future, and in the next four years was able to effect few improvements. He had, however, to combat the persistent opposition of legislative councillors to his proposal for financing a mounted constabulary from local funds, and their objection to the British government's proposal to add several nominated, not elected, representatives to the Legislative Council.

The whining of frustrated speculators grew loud in 1837-38, the colonists inconsistently demanding both increased public expenditure and decreased taxation. Stirling had also to cope with the deliberate falsifications in the British press by the Wakefieldians, who cited the Swan River as the best example of the worst type of colonization, in order to back their propaganda for the founding of a new type of colony in the south of Australia. They eagerly seized on the failure of the grandiose land settlement scheme of Thomas Peel [q.v.], which they misguidedly identified with the whole colony, and whose failure they wrongly and maliciously attributed to faults in government policy rather than to the calibre of its promoter or to the deficiencies of nature. Stirling gave Peel no priority in the choice of his land and he was not responsible for Peel's financial difficulties.

At various times Stirling was strongly criticized for his inept administration, for his aloofness or domineering attitude towards his civil officers, for his lack of humour, for his occasional acts of nepotism in the public service, and for his erratic and blundering land policies. In the voluminous public correspondence, in the columns of the colonial press, in the surviving papers of private settlers, and even in the governor's own matter-of-fact dispatches, there is ample evidence that Stirling tried to do too much, and much of what he did was badly done. Some historians have thought his governorship merely a congenial and profitable diversion from his naval career. It is true that many early settlers had been misled by the enthusiastic reports of Stirling and Frazer, and that during the first eighteen months much land was unwisely distributed, either in very large blocks, which tied up its development, or to speculators with no intention of cultivating it. Stirling also allowed his robust and somewhat irrational enthusiasm, which flowed strongly after his discovery of each new piece of attractive countryside, to influence his official judgment. He could never distinguish clearly between his personal profit and the public advantage, and he constantly changed the location of the various portions of land which were to form his own grant of 100,000 acres. Finally he never fully realized the inevitable consequences of the settlement's three most obvious deficiencies: an exposed anchorage in Gage Roads and Cockburn Sound, an unnavigable river between port and capital, and an extreme shortage of good farming land. He recognized their existence but grossly underrated their influence in aggravating the privations which plagued the settlement for the first twenty years. Indeed, Albany on the south coast, which had been settled as a convict garrison in December 1826 and became part of the new colony in March 1831, was the colony's chief port for seventy years.

Stirling once wrote that it was a dangerous experiment to colonize an unknown land and that he was exceedingly apprehensive about its ultimate success. But his public policies belied the sincerity of his private correspondence, and in some official dispatches he unjustifiably slighted the calibre of men who quickly summed up the true situation, packed their belongings and left for other colonies. Nevertheless he was always as much a settler and investor as the settlers whom he governed, and this helped to soften the edge of carping criticism when despondency was widespread, especially in 1837-38. So also did the dignified bearing of his youthful and charming wife, whose gracious manner amidst her recurrent pregnancies, endeared her to wives in the settlement.

Stirling resigned in October 1837 when his relations with the leading settlers were severely strained, and when the Aboriginals were once more troublesome. Glenelg's acknowledgment of his dispatch reached Perth in December 1838. Stirling left Fremantle on 5 January 1839, a few days after welcoming his successor, John Hutt, a well-known Wakefieldian. A short time before Stirling sailed he had lamented that the colony advanced 'steadily but somewhat slowly for want of a greater public expenditure'. In January 1839 the settlers still had only a tenuous hold. They had developed a sort of farm economy which provided most of their necessities, and they sent a few hundred bales of wool a year to England from their 20,000 sheep. In exchange for barrels of whale oil obtained by barter from passing American whalers in need of provisions, the colonists imported clothing, tobacco and spirits. Wheat and flour had still to be imported from Hobart Town. Flour-milling, boatbuilding and brewing were the only other important industries. The white population in 1839 was estimated at 1302 males and 852 females. A few hundred Aboriginals lived on the outskirts of the towns of Fremantle, Perth and Albany, and around the camp sites of Guildford, Kelmscott, Bunbury, and York. The total government expenditure was £11,462.

Stirling had every cause to be despondent, and his resignation was probably motivated as much by his frustrations as by his desire to resume his naval career. His wife was also eager to go home, being tired of the restricted social round and apprehensive about the education of her elder children. The leading settlers were honestly pained to see Stirling leave. He had been their mentor and had shared their speculations in a great adventure. His tall and dignified bearing, his commanding presence, and his responsiveness to public esteem had enabled the settlers to face an uncertain future. Now, it seemed, they had been handed into the custody of their detractors.

After his return to England Stirling toyed with the idea of a further colonial appointment. He was only 48 and doubly qualified as naval commander and civil administrator. However, in October 1840 he was appointed to command the Indus on the Mediterranean Station, where he remained until June 1844. After another three years ashore he was appointed to the Howe, which he commanded in the Mediterranean from April 1847 to April 1850, when he was knighted by the King of Greece. At no time did he lose interest in his languishing little colony in the antipodes, always ready to join deputations to the Colonial Office or to add his signature to memorials seeking more favourable treatment from the British government. He was not only willing to help the colony as a whole, but also his erstwhile fellow colonists as individuals. He also campaigned with great zest for more land to be added to his grant in the colony because of his own capital investment in it. He was unsuccessful. His nephew, Andrew Stirling (d. 1844), who had looked after his colonial interests, had much difficulty in putting his affairs in order. This difficulty, however, was trifling compared with the task which the Lands and Surveys Department had in disentangling the complexity of Stirling's land grants. His main business deal in later years was the sale of most of his Australind grant to the Western Australian Co. in 1840-41, which was responsible for a short-lived Wakefieldian sub-colony near Bunbury.

In July 1851 Stirling was promoted rear-admiral and next year served at the Admiralty. At exactly the same time the British government was arranging to export some thousands of convicts to Western Australia as the only feasible means of saving the little colony of 6000 people from perpetual bankruptcy and stagnation. From January 1854 to February 1856, Stirling was commander-in-chief of the naval forces in China and the East Indies, and he was promoted vice-admiral in August 1857, the year in which his youngest son, Walter, was killed at Cawnpore in the Indian mutiny. Stirling became an admiral in November 1862, and died in comfortable retirement at Guildford in Surrey on 22 April 1865. His wife survived him by nine years and lived to see her eldest son, Frederick, take command of the naval squadron in Australian waters.

W. B. Kimberly, History of West Australia (Melb, 1897); R. C. Mills, The colonization of Australia 1829-1842 (Lond, 1915); J. S. Battye, Western Australia (Oxford, 1924); M. Uren, Land looking west (Lond, 1948); F. K. Crowley, Australia's western third (Lond, 1960); P. J. Boyce, The role of the governor in WA, 1829-1890 (M.A. thesis, Univ WA, 1961); Stirling papers (Battye Lib, Perth).
F. K. CROWLEY

STOKES, JOHN LORT (1812-1885), explorer and hydrographer, was the son of Henry Stokes. He entered the navy in the Prince Regent in 1824 and was soon transferred to the brig Beagle, in which he served for eighteen years, becoming midshipman in 1825, mate and assistant surveyor in 1831, lieutenant in 1837 and commander in 1841.

After marine surveys of South America in 1826-32 and the voyage around the world described by Charles Darwin [q.v.] in 1833-36, the *Beagle* was sent under Commander J. C. Wickham [q.v.] to survey Australian waters, arriving in December 1837. During the survey of the Timor Sea in 1839 Stokes was several times entrusted with the closer examination of what is now the Northern Territory coast. He was the first to discover and name the Victoria River and Port Darwin, commemorating his old shipmate. While examining Point Pearce in October 1839 Stokes was speared in the shoulder by Aboriginals, but recovered from his wound and in March 1841 succeeded Wickham in command of the *Beagle*. Between June and August of that year he surveyed part of the Gulf of Carpentaria, indulging whenever possible 'the exquisite enjoyment of discovery' by making excursions inland. He named the Flinders and Albert Rivers, and between them the Plains of Promise, whose pleasing appearance prompted him to foretell the spread of 'many christian hamlets' throughout the area. Stokes had not allowed for the fluctuation in northern seasons, and 120 years later the area was still largely unoccupied but for cattle stations. A later piece of prophecy was no more fortunate. In December 1841, while the *Beagle* was off the coast of Western Australia, Stokes was requested to inspect Port Grey, a site proposed for the Australind settlement on the basis of enthusiastic reports by Captain George Grey. Arriving in midsummer, Stokes was not impressed, and the Western Australian Co. accordingly decided to retain the site near Bunbury originally proposed for its settlement. Within ten years the Port Grey-Champion Bay area was settled and later became one of the earliest successful wheat-growing areas in Western Australia. Stokes's doubtful judgment as a land explorer could not obscure his merits as a marine surveyor. Many of the hydrographic maps prepared by Wickham and Stokes during their North Australian cruises, and later while Stokes was examining Bass Strait in 1842, were still in use during World War II.

After returning to England he published in two volumes *Discoveries in Australia* (London, 1846). He rose high in the service of the Admiralty, ending as admiral on the retired list in 1877. He spent his retirement on an estate at Haverfordwest, Pembrokeshire, and died on 11 June 1885. An enterprising and efficient officer, Stokes was a man of genial personality, with considerable ability as a vivacious writer.

He was married twice, first to Fanny Jane, née Marlay, and second to Louisa French, née Partridge, widow of H. J. Garratt.

G. C. Ingleton, *Charting a continent* (Syd, 1944); J. L. Stokes, Letters, 1848-53 (Dixson Lib, Syd).
                                        G. C. BOLTON

STONE, GEORGE FREDERICK (1812-1875), attorney-general, followed his older brother, Alfred Hawes Stone, solicitor, to the Swan River in 1831 and became his partner, though unqualified by examination. By dint of hard study and perseverance, the self-taught scholar became one of the soundest legal advisers in the colony. In July 1833 he was appointed notary public and next year acting sheriff, the appointment being confirmed in 1839. In 1841 he became registrar of births, marriages and deaths and took the first systematic census of the colony in 1848. His other appointments were chairman of the Board of Works in 1842, member of the Education Committee in 1846 and inspector of weights and measures in 1851. He was made acting crown solicitor in 1852 (confirmed 1853) and held the office till 1859 when he was appointed advocate-general. The Supreme Court Act of June 1861 having changed the title to attorney-general, his position was again confirmed and he held it until he was superannuated in 1870 through chronic ill health, worn out 'by frequent responsibility for vital courses of action'. He died at Rose Hill, Perth, on 18 August 1875.

He had been elected to the Agricultural Society in 1841 and was a director and temporary secretary of the Western Australian Bank established in June 1841.

On 6 September 1838 Stone married Charlotte Maria, daughter of Captain F. Whitfield, resident magistrate of Toodyay. Of their nine children, the second son Edward, born on 9 March 1844, later became chief justice.

Twentieth century impressions of Western Australia (Perth, 1901); E. M. Russell, 'Early lawyers of WA', JRWAHS, 4 (1949-54); P. U. Henn, Genealogical notes (Battye Lib, Perth).
                                        ALFRED H. CHATE

STONOR, ALBAN CHARLES (1817-1866), barrister, was born in Oxfordshire, England, the son of Charles Stonor, a colonel in the Spanish army, and his wife Mary, daughter of Charles Butler, a prominent advocate of Catholic emancipation. In the best tradition of his old Catholic family he was called to the Bar, at Lincoln's Inn.

Stonor arrived in Sydney in January 1842 with a royal warrant as crown solicitor in Van Diemen's Land at a salary of £250. In Hobart Town he claimed the additional position of clerk of the peace at £250, insisting that the Colonial Office had promised him both posts in order to relieve him of the need for private practice. When Lieut-Governor Franklin refused the dual appointment, Stonor appealed successfully to Downing Street. He was granted leave from September 1843 to January 1844 and on his return applied for the vacant position of solicitor-general, claiming to have discharged his difficult and laborious duties with efficiency and to be eligible by precedent for promotion. Lieut-Governor Eardley-Wilmot admitted his diligence but, having no faith in his eminence at the Bar, he did not recommend Stonor for the post.

On 18 November 1844 at Christ Church, Longford, Stonor married Eliza Anne, the eldest daughter of A. R. Truro. Next year he spent some months as crown prosecutor in the Criminal Court of Norfolk Island. Back in Hobart as editor of the *Spectator* he supported the unpopular Eardley-Wilmot and in 1846, prompted by the establishment of Christ College, 'the noble seminary of native talent', published his *Poetical Fragments*, translations from Lucan's *Pharsalia*, Hesiod's *Theogony*, Cleanthes' *Hymn* and other extracts. The local press had no sympathy with his politics, but admired the beauty of his poetry, praised his cultivated mind and proclaimed his work as 'far surpassing any colonial production we have yet seen'.

In January 1847 Stonor and his wife left for London on leave at half-pay. He gave evidence before the House of Lords committee on transportation in May 1847, but his chief aim was to arrange a trust fund for his mother. He stayed in England for eighteen months, partly because of his own and his wife's ill health and partly because he could not get a suitable passage. During his absence the senior legal posts in Van Diemen's Land were reshuffled. Stonor found himself promoted to solicitor-general at a salary of £600, but his duties were too much for his precarious health. After two months at New Norfolk in 1851 he was examined by the Medical Board, who found him 'labouring under melancholy' and recommended at least two years leave. In 1852 he returned to England, leaving his wife in Hobart. When asked to resign in December 1853 he applied for a pension, supported by the duke of Newcastle and Lieut-Governor Denison, who warmly praised his zeal and legal skill, attributed his illness to anxiety in the performance of duty and lamented his mental collapse. After long demur the Treasury granted him a gratuity of £425, equivalent to one month's salary for each year of service exclusive of leave, poor recompense for his integrity in office that exposed many frauds by contractors and landgrabbers. He died in 1866, without issue.

Correspondence file under Stonor (TA).

STORY, GEORGE FORDYCE (1800-1885), medical practitioner, was born on 4 June 1800 in London, the son of George Story, Wesleyan minister. He received his early schooling in London and, after three years apprenticeship to a chemist in Aberdeen, studied medicine in Edinburgh, received his diploma in 1824, and practised in London. On the death of his widowed mother in 1828, he sailed for Sydney as surgeon in the *Mary* with his childhood friend, Francis Cotton [q.v.].

Wearied by the long voyage and attracted by his first Australian landfall, he stayed in Van Diemen's Land. In April 1829 he took up the duties of district assistant surgeon at Waterloo Point Military Station, where he had to attend all floggings of prisoners and soldiers, perform post-mortems, vaccinate, inspect the gaol and road-gangs, and make weather reports. Along a sparsely settled sixty miles of coastal strip he treated families and their assigned servants for their illnesses, accidents and injuries sustained from attacks by Aboriginals and bushrangers. Though his own life was often endangered when fording flooded rivers, travelling on horseback in all weather or at night on precipitous unmade tracks, and penetrating alone into hostile territory where even soldiers had to go in pairs, he was paid only 3s. a day. His few private fees barely covered the cost of horses and medicines, and to supplement his income he became store-keeper at Waterloo Point. He also received a land grant but lost it because his onerous duties and unaggressive ways prevented him from improving it and defending his claim. His home became Kelvedon, with the Cotton family.

When the convict department was reorganized the store-keeping post ended. In 1844 Story became secretary of the Royal Society of Tasmania at a salary of £200 and superintended the development of the Botanical Gardens. Next year the government grant for this project was not renewed, and he returned to Kelvedon and the medical profession.

An observant and intelligent naturalist, he sent minerals to Lady Franklin [q.v.], bird skins to her husband, ferns to James Backhouse [q.v.] and botanical specimens to Mueller. In his isolation he tried to keep up with the latest scientific discoveries and experimented with new drugs, chloroform and photographic chemicals. His skill in diagnosis and prescription, and his gentle touch made him unusually successful in saving lives, and kept him in demand even in his last eleven years when he was blind with cataracts. Although studious and retiring he gave long service to his community as a temperance worker, electoral officer, a founder of the Glamorgan Library in Swansea in 1862, and member of the local school board in 1869.

During the journey of Backhouse and Walker he became a Quaker, attended the small Kelvedon, and short-lived Launceston Meeting, and travelled around the island and to South Australia, Victoria and New South Wales to encourage other struggling Meetings.

He died on 7 June 1885, mourned by every family on the east coast, and was buried at Kelvedon next to Anna Maria and Francis Cotton. Early pioneers owed much to his skill and devotion.

J. Backhouse, *A narrative of a visit to the Australian colonies* (Lond, 1843); J. Backhouse and C. Tylor, *The life and labours of George Washington Walker*, (Lond, 1862); Mthly Meeting minute books (Soc of Friends, Hob); G. F. Story, Journals and correspondence, Cotton papers (Univ Tas); CSO 1 & 5 (TA).   MARY BARTRAM TROTT

STOW, THOMAS QUINTON (1801-1862), Congregational minister, was born on 7 July 1801 at Hadleigh, Suffolk, England. He was descended from an old Suffolk farming family of Stowmarket, near Hadleigh. He began preaching at 17 and later studied at the Missionary College, Gosport, under Dr David Bogue, a theologian of great repute and a founder of the London Missionary Society. Stow was minister at Framlingham, Suffolk, in 1822-25, at Buntingford, Hertfordshire, and at the Old Independent Church, Halstead, Essex, in 1832-37. At Framlingham he married Elizabeth, daughter of William Eppes of Bristol and his wife Elizabeth, née Randolph, a descendant of an old American family in Virginia. By 1836 he had published in London *Memoirs of Rowland Taylor, LL.D.* and *The Scope of Piety.*

On 12 October 1836 Stow was accepted for service in South Australia by the newly formed Colonial Missionary Society. In an announcement to his people, published at Halstead in 1836, he proved that his decision was not hasty: 'Six years ago I wrote a piece in the Congregational Magazine, recommending the formation of this very society which now commissions me with its affairs in Australia'. With his wife and four young sons he sailed from Gravesend in the *Hartley* and arrived in South Australia in October 1837.

Stow pitched his marquee and preached his first sermon in it in November. Next month, with ten others, he formed the first Congregational Church in South Australia and was elected pastor. Early in 1838, on North Terrace, he helped to build a temporary place of worship with gum-wood posts, pine rafters and reed thatch. At the request of some leading colonists he opened a daily classical academy, thus beginning higher education in the colony. In December 1839 the foundation stone of a new Congregational chapel was laid in Freeman Street. Opened in November 1840, it had a heavy debt, which caused Stow much embarrassment during the depression years. He supplemented his income by farming a property on the River Torrens which he named Felixstow.

Stow was responsible for forming many new churches and for recruiting and training several ministers. He was the first chairman of the Congregational Union of South Australia in 1850, and he did much to foster friendly relations between all denominations. He was appointed to the first board of education in 1846 and served on many other public committees, always ready to promote moral, social and intellectual progress. As the outstanding preacher in early Adelaide, his firm stand against state aid to religion had a powerful influence from 1846 until the grants were abandoned in 1851. Several of his sermons were published. His strenuous activities took their toll and his health suffered. After a ministry in Adelaide of nineteen years, Stow was obliged to resign his pastorate in September 1856. In February 1862 he went to Pitt Street Congregational Church, Sydney, on a temporary engagement. He died there on 19 July at the home of John Fairfax. He was buried in West Terrace cemetery, Adelaide, on 7 August, mourned by the whole city: parliament and banks closed for the occasion. Public subscription gave him a costly headstone and in 1867 Stow Memorial Church in Flinders Street became his best known memorial.

Stow's widow died in Adelaide on 8 July 1867. Of their four sons, Randolph Isham, Jefferson Pickman and Augustine made their mark in South Australia. The youngest son, Wycliffe, studied law and spent most of his life in other states.

F. W. Cox and L. Robjohns, *Three-quarters of a century* (Adel, 1912); G. C. Morphett, *Rev. Thos. Quinton Stow* (Adel, 1948); *Advertiser* (Adel), 8 Aug 1862, 17 Apr 1867; B. L. Jones, *History of Stow Memorial Church* (Stow Memorial Church).

BRIAN L. JONES

STRACHAN, JAMES FORD (1810-1875), merchant, woolbroker and politician, was born at Montrose, Scotland, the fifth son of John Strachan and his wife Isobel, née Smith. In 1832 he arrived in Van Diemen's Land with his widowed mother and two sisters. By 1835 he was in business in Argyle Street, Hobart Town. Later he partnered one John Johnson, until the latter withdrew in August 1840. By that time Strachan was concentrating on Port Phillip, which he first visited in March 1836. Before 1837, from 'one little wooden box' in what became Market Street, Melbourne, through his deputy, Francis Nodin, he worked as a squatters' provider.

Strachan bought two lots at the first local land sale, and in 1838 made one the site of Melbourne's first brick building, which still stands. That year he opened a store at Geelong. In October 1839 a schooner built to his order for the Port Phillip run was launched at Hobart, called the *Lilias*, after his bride, who was the eldest daughter of Hugh Murray [q.v.].

Point Lilias, at the entrance to Corio Bay, was named after Strachan's schooner. Lilias Strachan was partly drawn to Geelong by the fortunes of her brother Hugh, who was one of the first settlers around Lake Colac, and had written to her four months before he penetrated as far, in May 1837: 'No spear wound or anything of the sort to recount to you, but live a quiet, peaceable, sober, monotonous, pleasant life, without bothering anybody or anybody bothering me. I can bake a damper, wash a shirt, put on a patch, grease a pair of boots, cook a dinner, with any man in Port Phillip . . . The sheep are thriving beautifully. The country is ideal for a sheep-run; beautiful scenery, lovely hills, softly gliding streams—you never saw such grass'.

Strachan believed that Geelong would suit him best. Early in 1840 he finished its first stone building, a house and store facing the bay on the corner still occupied by Strachan & Co. Ltd. February found him living there, but his wife did not move until 1843. She joined him during a period of great depression, which caused him to relinquish his business in Hobart and Melbourne but, with the return of prosperity, Strachan again advanced. In 1849, he commissioned Charles Laing [q.v.], architect, to build a stone mansion on twenty-one acres of freehold fronting Corio Bay. Called Lunan, after the bay south of Montrose, this house is now controlled by the Victorian Education Department, and is classified 'A' by the National Trust. Here Strachan lived until his death on 14 April 1875.

Like many contemporaries of equal status, Strachan developed first-hand pastoral interests. He owned part of Mount Gellibrand station, now Mooleric. But probably his best course was the one he followed steadily: that of the mercantile middleman setting new standards of commercial usage.

Politically Strachan began as a worker for separation. In 1851 he represented Geelong in the first Victorian Legislative Council. In 1854, when his firm denounced a map purporting to show that Melbourne was closer than Geelong to Ballarat, Hotham appointed him to the goldfields commission. He joined the outspoken majority, and with responsible government was elected for the south-western province to the new Legislative Council. He was minister without portfolio in the second Haines ministry in 1857-58, but during the later battle on the tariff and Darling grant 'tacks' he resigned his seat to win the western province against McCulloch's supporter, Henry Miller. He remained a member until 1874.

Strachan was concerned with the establishment of the Geelong Botanical Gardens, of the state-aided Geelong National Grammar School (now the Matthew Flinders School), and of St George's Presbyterian Church, Geelong. The eldest of his three sons was one of the first Australians to row for Cambridge (1870); the second published some useful reminiscences. All followed their father's lead in the sphere of pastoral production and primary mercantile business.

T. F. Bride (ed), *Letters from Victorian pioneers* (Melb, 1898); H. M. Strachan, *Some notes and recollections* (Melb, 1927); A. Henderson, *Early pioneer families of Victoria and Riverina* (Melb, 1936); P. L. Brown (ed), *Clyde Company papers*, 2-5 (Lond, 1952-63); W. R. Brownhill, *The history of Geelong and Corio Bay* (Melb, 1955); L. J. Blake, 'Lunan's story', *Educational Mag*, 14 (1957), no 11.

P. L. BROWN

STRANGE, FREDERICK (1807?-1873), artist, was born at Nottingham, England. By trade he was a portrait painter and house painter. On 22 June 1837 he was tried at the Quarter Sessions, Colchester, Essex, for stealing a watch and sentenced to imprisonment for life. He was transported to Van Diemen's Land in the *Neptune* and in January 1838 arrived at Hobart Town, where he became a government messenger. In 1841 he obtained a third-class pass and went to Launceston where he painted portraits and gave lessons in drawing but made a miserable living. One of his pupils was Robert Dowling, who became a well-known portrait painter; another was Henry Button, later owner and editor of the Launceston *Examiner* and mayor of Launceston.

In 1848 he moved to Hobart and for some time worked in a paint shop there. On 4 December 1848 Strange received a conditional pardon. He returned to Launceston and in 1851 exhibited views of the town and surrounding landscape at the Launceston Art Exhibition. He advertised lessons in landscape drawing and offered to make portraits in oils or daguerreotype. A painter by preference, by 1862 he was either unwilling or unable to compete with the cheaper and then more fashionable daguerreotype portraiture and his premises were taken over by a photographer. Strange then took up the trade of grocer in Charles Street, Launceston, where he died on 31 March 1873. He was a Dissenter and unmarried.

His careful attention to topographical and architectural detail provided a valuable record of the early colony. His work was characterized by good drawing and delicate water-colouring. Thirty-five works have been located.

C. Craig and I. Mead, 'Frederick Strange—artist', Roy Soc Tas, *Papers*, 1963.

ISABELLA J. MEAD

STRUTH, JOHN (1804-1886), mechanical and marine engineer, was born on 1 January 1804 in Berwickshire, Scotland, of a farming family that had come from Holland in the fifteenth century; one of his ancestors was Admiral Struth and another Sir Nathaniel Struth. After an engineering apprenticeship with Messrs Murray of Chester-Le-Street, Durham, he remained with them as a tradesman until he migrated to Sydney in the barque *Mountaineer*. On his arrival in September 1832 he was employed by Thomas Barker [q.v.], a pioneer of steam flour-milling. Seven years later Struth had his own flour-mill, and in the following year he bought land on Darling Harbour at the foot of King Street, where he built a wharf, known for many years as Struth's Wharf. He undertook casting in iron and brass, blacksmithing, machining, building of agricultural machines, meat salting injectors and ships' steam engines. His letterhead engraving shows a small paddle steamer at the quay, busy workshops beyond, and a steep ramp to a dwelling at street level.

In 1847 Struth told a select committee of the Legislative Council that he used 400 tons of Newcastle coal a year for his smithy and for burning to coke for foundry purposes. He had erected machinery at many coal-mines in England, and thought the Australian mines 'more advantageously situated for working at trifling expense'. He complained that the general management at Newcastle was much too expensive, and the coal too dear at 12s. a ton alongside his wharf. He concluded, 'we are now paying forty pounds a ton for some descriptions of iron, which in England would not cost above ten pounds a ton'. His evidence to another select committee in 1848 disclosed that his wife and three children had died during the previous two years and a half while the family lived in Sussex Street. He attributed his loss to the miasma from slaughter houses and piggeries, and to the filth washed down from higher levels. About this time he built for Sir Thomas Mitchell [q.v.] a 'bomareng' twelve feet in diameter, intended to drive a boat by means of an air propellor.

Struth's establishment was bought by Napier & Postlethwaite in 1854, and in the following year Struth, wealthy but in poor health, took his 13-year-old son to England. In 1866 he returned to Sydney, where he died at 95 Phillip Street on 12 January 1886. He had married in 1829 Alison Hislop Lockie. Of their seven children a son and two daughters survived.

Struth was a consistent member of the Presbyterian Church, and after his retirement he gave large sums to charities. A man of robust constitution, he devoted his skill and energy to building up his fortune at a favourable time when the colony needed steam navigation and manufactures that could not easily be brought from England.

N. Selfe, 'Annual address to engineering section', Roy Soc NSW, *Procs*, 34 (1900); *Illustrated Sydney News*, 15 Feb 1886; Sel cttee on coal, Report, V & P (LC, NSW), 1847; Sel cttee on slaughter houses, Report, V&P (LC NSW), 1848.   ARTHUR CORBETT

Strzelecki

STRZELECKI, Sir PAUL EDMUND DE (1797-1873), explorer and scientist, was born on 20 July 1797 at Gluszyna, near Poznan, Western Poland, the son of poor gentry, without land or title. As Poznan was then under Prussian control, he was a Prussian citizen. He left school without matriculating, spent a short time in the Prussian army, and left Poznan after an attempt to elope with a young neighbour, Aleksandryna (Adyna) Turno, to whom he wrote for many years. He may have visited the mines in Saxony and Mount Vesuvius in Italy, whence he returned to Poland. In 1830, after a charge of misappropriation of funds by the son of his employer, Prince Sapieha, he left Poland. From then on, lending some colour to the charge, he had a small income from investments in Russia. There is no conclusive evidence of his participation in the 1830 insurrection, though he later hinted at it to Tasmanian friends.

He had no formal training in geology, a science then in its infancy in England, but was probably, like his English contemporaries, self taught. He was using the title Count in London by 1833, and next year left for North America, where he travelled widely, analysing soil, examining minerals (tradition claims he discovered copper in Canada), and visiting farms to study soil conservation and to analyse the gluten content of wheat. In South America in 1836 he visited the most important mineral areas and he went up the west coast from Chile to California. During this time he became a strong opponent of the slave trade.

As a guest in H.M.S. Fly he visited a number of Pacific islands; in Hawaii he climbed Kilauea; in the Marquesas Islands he studied native languages, though it is not probable that, as H. Bartel Frere claims, Strzelecki introduced the jury system to Tahiti. In 1839 he was the guest of James Busby [q.v.] in New Zealand, and reached Sydney in April, with letters of introduction to Governor Gipps who treated him with some reserve, and to P. P. King [q.v.] and Stuart Donaldson, who became his close friends.

In August 1839 he told Adyna Turno that he planned a geological survey of the country, and in December, after a visit to the Bathurst-Wellington district, stated to the geologists, W. B. Clarke and J. D. Dana [q.v.], that the local mineralogy was 'very tame', a surprising statement in the light of later events. The field-work for his geological map took him in zigzags across New South Wales, and to the Australian Alps, where alone he ascended what he considered the highest peak, calling it after the Polish democratic leader, Tadeusz

Kosciuszko. Thence he and his party travelled through Gippsland, already crossed by McMillan [q.v.], and arrived at Westernport weary and starving. Strzelecki then went to Van Diemen's Land, where he became a close friend of the Franklins and did important work as explorer, geologist, and scientific farmer, and like the earlier Lhotsky [q.v.] made analyses of coal deposits. He left Sydney for Singapore in April 1843, reached London in October, and found most of his private means lost in a French bank failure. He invested what remained in an annuity and seems to have found work; he lived as a well-to-do man.

In 1845 he became a British subject, and published in London his Physical Description of New South Wales and Van Diemen's Land, for which he received the founder's medal of the Royal Geographical Society. The book laid the basis of Australian palaeontology. Strzelecki thought it would be an important aid to the immigration of capital and men. In 1847-48 he was in charge of distributing in parts of Ireland famine relief funds collected by the British Relief Association and did outstanding work; some of the principles of relief he laid down have become standard procedure. In recognition of his work he was commended by both Houses of Parliament and appointed a C.B.

The discovery of payable gold by Hargraves and others started Strzelecki on a long struggle, ably supported by friends in Sydney, to prove his own priority of claim. After publication of his Gold and Silver (London, 1856), his scientific priority was acknowledged; McBrien's discovery was probably still unknown, but no credit was given to Lhotsky, who in 1834, before Strzelecki had left England, had gold extracted from his specimens in Sydney.

In his last years he interested himself in emigration to Australia. After the Crimean war he visited Russia with Lord Lyons. His honours included fellowships of the Royal Geographical and Royal Societies, an honorary D.C.L. from Oxford, and, through Gladstone, the K.C.M.G. (1869). He died of cancer in October 1873, leaving a will which ordered the destruction of his papers and the burial of his body in an unmarked grave. This took place in the Church of England section of Kensal Green cemetery. Recently his wish has been disregarded and an inscribed stone now marks the grave.

Strzelecki was a complex character. He was energetic and ambitious, a capable and thorough scientist, an excellent administrator, a man with a gift for friendship, but resentful of injury and not quick to forgive those, like his sister, who he thought had treated him badly. Had he wished, he might have reached a high position in Australia (as Lord John Russell believed) but had apparently antagonized Gipps; he was deeply disappointed when W. B. Clarke was commissioned to survey for minerals in 1851. His final break with his fiancée and his resentment towards his fellow-countrymen because of their earlier treatment of him left him without any ties with his old life.

His work brought him success and praise; identification of himself with the country of his adoption brought him lasting satisfaction, though his renunciation of marriage and the loss of his early faith are perhaps reflected in the pessimistic terms of his will.

B. Strzelecki, *Biography of Count Paul Edmund de Strzelecki* (NY, 1935); G. Rawson, *The count. A life of Sir Paul Edmund Strzelecki* (Lond, 1954); W. Slabczynski, *Pawel Edmund Strzelecki* (Warsaw, 1957); P. E. Strzelecki, *Pisma wybrane*, ed W. Slabczynski (Warsaw, 1960); H. M. E. Heney, *In a dark glass* (Syd, 1961), and for bibliog; N. Zmichowska, 'O Pawle Edmundzie Strzeleckim wedlug Rodzinnych i Towarzyskich Wspomnien', *Athenaeum* (Warsaw, 1876, copy, Fisher Lib, Syd); W. L. Harvard, 'Sir P. E. de Strzelecki', *JRAHS*, 26 (1940); P. E. Strzelecki, Letters to Adyna Turno, 1839-51 (ML); MS cat under P. E. Strzelecki (ML); Franklin papers (ML, Scott Polar Res Institute, Cambridge); P. E. Strzelecki, Journal, 1840 (Dixson Lib, Syd).
HELEN HENEY

STURT, CHARLES (1795-1869), explorer, soldier and public servant, was born on 28 April 1795 in India, eldest of eight sons and one of thirteen children of Thomas Napier Lennox Sturt, a judge in Bengal under the East India Co. Although his Sturt and Napier ancestors were both Dorsetshire families of some standing, his father had reached India too late to share in the golden harvest reaped by many early officials and his life is described by Sturt's biographer as '45 years of clouded fortunes'.

Charles was sent at 5 to relations in England and at 15 entered Harrow. His father's economic difficulties prevented his entry to Cambridge and in 1813 he procured, through the intercession of his aunt with the Prince Regent, a commission as ensign in the 39th Regiment. He served in the Pyrenees late in the Peninsular war, fought against the Americans in Canada and returned to Europe a few days after Waterloo. He spent the next three years with the army of occupation in France and in 1818 was sent with his regiment to Ireland on garrison duties. On 7 April 1823 he was gazetted lieutenant and promoted captain on 15 December 1825. In

December 1826 after a brief sojourn in England he embarked with a detachment of his regiment in the *Mariner* in charge of convicts for New South Wales and arrived at Sydney on 23 May 1827. In Sydney the two main subjects of discussion among intelligent people were politics and the mysteries of Australian geography. The savagely personal nature of local politics did not attract Sturt but the great unknown did. John Oxley and Allan Cunningham [qq.v.] had charted a series of rivers, their courses directed towards the centre of the continent; the inference was that an inland sea lay beyond the horizon. Sturt and others longed for the honour of discovering it.

Soon after his arrival Sturt was appointed, possibly because of a family connexion with Governor Darling, military secretary to the governor and major of brigade to the garrison. With these offices he could have taken an active part in politics, but preferred to interest himself in exploration and by November 1827 was able to write to his cousin, Isaac Wood, that the governor had agreed to his leading an expedition into the interior. Because Darling had few officers on whom he felt that he could rely, he did not formally authorize the expedition for nearly twelve months. Meanwhile Sturt had, perhaps naively, discussed the proposal with the newly-appointed surveyor-general, T. L. Mitchell [q.v.], who felt that he had been slighted, and argued with some justice that Sturt, who had no qualifications, was being pushed by influence into a task which offered the prospect of honour, and which was his *ex officio*. Darling rejected this contention out of hand and Sturt acquired a lifelong enemy in Mitchell.

On 4 November 1828 Sturt received approval to proceed with his proposal to trace the course of the Macquarie River. Prudently he selected as his assistant the native-born Hamilton Hume [q.v.], who had already shared leadership of a major expedition to the south coast. With three soldiers and eight convicts Sturt left Sydney on 10 November. Hume joined them at Bathurst and, after collecting equipment from the government station at Wellington Valley, they moved on 7 December to what became virtually the base camp at Mount Harris. On 22 December the expedition started down the Macquarie through country blasted by drought and searing heat. Having unsuccessfully tried to use a light boat, on 31 December Sturt and Hume began independent reconnaissances in which Hume established the limits of the Macquarie marshes and Sturt examined the country across the Bogan River. They then proceeded north along the Bogan and on 2 February came suddenly on 'a noble river' flowing to the west; Sturt named it the Darling. Unhappily its waters were undrinkable at that point because of salt springs. They followed the Darling downstream until 9 February, then returned to Mount Harris and from there traced the Castlereagh northward until it too joined the Darling. They then returned to Wellington Valley down the eastern side of the Macquarie marshes, having sketched in the main outlines of the northern river system and discovered the previously unknown Darling River. The expedition, however, had discovered no extensive good country. Although Sturt was ill on his return to Sydney he was scrupulous in recommending the convicts in his party for such indulgences as the colonial government could grant. Darling granted some remissions of sentence and in his dispatches commended Sturt's patience and zeal.

The Darling River had offered a new challenge and Sturt soon sought permission to lead another expedition to trace the Darling to its assumed outlet in the inland sea. However, it was decided instead that he should investigate the Lachlan-Murrumbidgee river system discovered by Oxley and proceed to the Darling only if the Murrumbidgee proved impassable.

On 3 November 1829 the second expedition left Sydney. In Sturt's party were George Macleay [q.v.], son of the colonial secretary, Harris, Hopkinson, Fraser and Clayton, who had all been in his first expedition, and several soldiers and convicts. They moved through country which was partly settled until 28 November when they left Warby's station near Gundagai which was then the limit of settlement and set off into the unknown country. After many crossings of the Murrumbidgee to find suitable tracks for the drays they moved down the north bank of the river and on Christmas arrived at its junction with the Lachlan. There difficult marshes raised the question whether they should follow the governor's instructions or go to the Darling. Since the Murrumbidgee was still fairly clear Sturt decided to use the whale-boat which he had brought with him and to build a small skiff from local timber. On 7 January 1830 he set out with seven men in the two boats on the Murrumbidgee.

Apart from the complete loss of the skiff soon after embarkation the journey was uneventful until 14 January when the rapid current of the Murrumbidgee carried them to a 'broad and noble river' which Sturt later named in honour of Sir George Murray, secretary of state for the colonies.

Further down the Murray they had two threatening encounters with Aboriginals, and on 23 January came to a new large stream flowing in from the north. After rowing up it for a few miles Sturt was convinced that it was the Darling and returned to the Murray. An uneventful voyage brought them on 9 February to Lake Alexandrina whence they walked over the sandhills to the southern coast. They reached the channel where the lake entered the sea but were dismayed to find it impracticable for shipping. Depressed by failing to find either an effective inland waterway or the ship which Darling had promised to send from Sydney, Sturt now faced the appalling prospect of rowing more than 900 miles against a strong current with his weary men and certain food shortage. They began the return journey on 12 February and on 23 March arrived at the Murrumbidgee depot only to find it deserted by the base party which had been left there. The starving crew struggled on until 11 April when Sturt abandoned the boat and sent two men to seek the relief party which he believed to be near. A week later the two men returned with supplies and the revived expedition reached Sydney safely on 25 May.

Although an interim dispatch carried by Macleay in advance of the main party had been published in the *Sydney Gazette* Darling did not report to England on the expedition until February 1831. Meanwhile Sturt, after a short illness, had been sent to Norfolk Island as commandant of the garrison. There he took part in the rescue of the occupants of a wrecked boat and, though active in quelling a convict mutiny, had nevertheless earned the respect even of the mutineers for his generally humane outlook. In July he was relieved by F. C. Crotty, captain in the 39th Regiment.

Sturt's return to Sydney was delayed by illness until October; already there had been proposals to send him to New Zealand as Resident or on another journey to the Darling, but his health was so bad that he was immediately granted leave to go to England. On the voyage his eyesight, which had been failing, broke down completely leaving him totally blind. While undergoing crude but moderately successful treatment for his condition he published an account of his two journeys and after many petitions to the Colonial Office was promised a grant of 5000 acres in New South Wales on condition that he sold his commission and renounced all other rights arising from his military service. On 20 September 1834 he married Charlotte Greene, the daughter of an old family friend.

Sturt sailed with his wife and arrived at Sydney in mid-1835. With intentions of settling down to country life he located his grant at Ginninderra (near Canberra) in June and in August bought 1950 acres at Mittagong, where he lived for two years. In this time he was appointed a justice of the peace, became a passive member of the governing body of the Australian Museum, was recommended unsuccessfully for appointment to the Legislative Council, and christened his first child Napier George. Early in 1837 he bought 1000 acres at Varroville between Liverpool and Campbelltown, where he soon established another home.

In 1838 financial difficulties forced him to sell his Mittagong property and induced him to join in a venture for overlanding cattle to South Australia. Although in the process he was able to add something to knowledge of the Murray River, the journey almost ended in disaster. Breeding cows in the herd delayed the party and it ran short of supplies and had to be rescued by his friend, E. J. Eyre [q.v.]. The venture was also a financial failure. Sturt was greeted in Adelaide by flattering attention which brought balm to his pride injured by recent failures. Incautiously he became associated with an attempted land transaction which some colonists thought was questionable. On 30 October he returned to Sydney to learn of the birth of his second son, Charles.

In Adelaide he had been invited to join the South Australian public service and on 8 November 1838 was formally offered the position of surveyor-general. Despite his lack of technical qualifications and some doubts about Governor Gawler's power to make the appointment, he accepted, sold his property in New South Wales and sailed with his family for Adelaide on 27 February 1839. In spite of sickness and continuing financial worries all seemed to go well. The first shattering blow came in September when Lieutenant Frome [q.v.] arrived from London with a commission as surveyor-general. Gawler, in a loyal attempt to help Sturt, appointed him assistant commissioner of lands, though at a reduced salary. In November he and his wife joined Gawler in what was intended to be a short excursion up the Murray valley. On this expedition a young man lost his life and the governor was placed in serious danger. Although Sturt was not responsible the tragedy affected him deeply.

In 1841 Sturt was offered the resident management of the South Australian Co., but refused. Soon afterwards he committed what was probably the most serious error of judgment in his life: when news

arrived that Captain George Grey was to replace Gawler as governor, Sturt wrote to the Colonial Office complaining of Grey's youth and offering himself as an alternative candidate for vice-regal office. Grey, who could not tolerate opposition, never forgave him this clumsy affront.

From that time Sturt's affairs worsened. Grey confirmed his provisional appointment as assistant commissioner, but later refused him the office of colonial secretary on the grounds that his sight was too poor. The Colonial Office then decided to abolish the assistant commissionership, leaving Sturt with the inferior post of registrar-general at a much lower salary. To a man of Sturt's temperament the situation was now intolerable. He was at loggerheads with the governor, deeply in debt, inadequately paid, and could see no hope of improving his prospects. He petitioned the Colonial Office for financial compensation or transfer to another colony. When refused, he decided that the only course left to him was to establish by some bold stroke a claim on the government for special consideration. His best chance of doing this was in exploration and, since he still believed in the existence of an inland sea, he prepared a grandiose plan for exploring and surveying, within two years, the entire unknown interior of the continent, and in 1843 forwarded it to the Colonial Office through his old friend, Sir Ralph Darling. While waiting for a reply he and Grey had a series of minor clashes which culminated in Sturt's censure by the Executive Council for an incautious letter. In May 1844 the secretary of state rejected Sturt's original plan but approved a more limited proposal to penetrate the centre of the continent in an attempt to establish the existence of a mountain range near latitude 28°S.

On 10 August 1844 Sturt left Adelaide with 15 men, 6 drays, a boat and 200 sheep. In eight days the party reached Moorundie and then followed the Murray River to its junction with the Darling, and up the Darling to the vicinity of Lake Cawndilla, where they camped for two months making several scouting expeditions into and beyond the Barrier Range. In December the party was short of water and some of the men showed signs of scurvy but they moved further north into the Grey Range. There they made a camp on permanent water fortunately found at Depot Glen on Preservation Creek. By that time summer heat had dried up all other water within reach and from 27 January 1845 to 16 July they were literally trapped in inhospitable country; men and equipment suffered terribly from the heat and

Sturt's second-in-command, James Poole, died of scurvy.

In July they were released by heavy rain. Sturt moved his party in a north-westerly direction to Fort Grey, whence he made a series of reconnoitring expeditions culminating in a 450-mile journey towards the centre of the continent. Repulsed by the sand dunes of the Simpson desert he at last reluctantly abandoned the idea of an inland sea.

Sturt and his party returned exhausted to Fort Grey and after another trip to the Cooper's Creek area from 9 October to 17 November they found the waterhole was rapidly drying. Return to the River Murray became imperative but nevertheless Sturt proposed that the main party should go home, while he and John McDouall Stuart made a do-or-die trip towards the centre. The surgeon, J. H. Browne, resisted so strongly that these heroics were dropped and the whole party went off together. At this point Sturt then succumbed to a serious attack of scurvy and Browne took command through the most difficult part of the journey. By using Aboriginal foods Sturt had almost recovered when the expedition reached Moorundie on 15 January. He arrived at Adelaide on 19 January 1846 ahead of his party, which followed a few days later.

In his absence Grey had been replaced by Major Robe and Sturt had been appointed colonial treasurer. His position was now more comfortable and early in 1847 he applied for leave. He left for England on 8 May and arrived in London just too late to receive personally the gold medal of the Royal Geographical Society, but was able to complete a published account of the expedition. On his return to Adelaide in August 1849 he was soon appointed colonial secretary but unfortunately his sight began to fail and at the end of 1851 he retired on a pension of £600.

Sturt had often expressed his love for Australia and his determination never to return to England, but the need to secure the future of his children forced him to change his mind and he left Australia on 19 March 1853. He spent his last years peacefully at Cheltenham, being widely respected and continually consulted about Australian affairs, particularly the preparations for the North Australian expedition of 1854. He applied unsuccessfully for the governorship of Victoria in 1855 and of Queensland in 1858. In 1869 at the instigation of his friends he sought a knighthood, but died on 16 June before the formalities were completed. Later the Queen permitted his widow to use the title Lady Sturt. He was pursued to the end by financial difficulties and it was said that had his old friend George Macleay not come forward, there would not have been enough in his estate for a decent burial.

Although Sturt probably entered his career as an explorer through influence, his selection was justified by results. He was a careful and accurate observer and an intelligent interpreter of what he saw, and it was unfortunate that much of his work revealed nothing but desolation. He prided himself with some justice on his impeccable treatment of the Aboriginals, and earned the respect and liking of his men by his courtesy and care for their well-being. Indeed his capacity for arousing and retaining affection was remarkable; it made him an ideal family man but a failure in public life. Without toughness and egocentricity to balance his poor judgment and business capacity he had little chance of success in colonial politics. In this sphere he might well be described as a born loser. He remained throughout his life an English Tory gentleman with an unshakeable faith in God. Despite his passionate interest in Australia, his inability to appreciate the attitudes of the colonial community was shown by his proposal in 1858 for a colony of Asiatic convicts in the north. He will always be remembered, however, as the first to chart the Murray River.

HRA (1), 14-18; N. G. Sturt, *Life of Charles Sturt* (Lond, 1895); J. H. L. Cumpston, *Charles Sturt* (Melb, 1951); H. J. Finnis, 'J. H. Browne journal', *South Australiana*, 6 (1966); Newspaper indexes under C. Sturt (ML); MS cat under C. Sturt (ML, NL, SAA); CO 13/11, 14, 15, 38, 15/1-3, 201/126, 244, 323/169, 171.

H. J. GIBBNEY

SUTTOR, GEORGE (1774-1859), settler, was born on 11 June 1774 at Chelsea, then on the outskirts of London, the third son of a Scottish market gardener and his wife, née Thomas. He went to school in Milman's Row, Chelsea, and then to Leith's Academy in Paradise Row until he was about 14, when he began work in his father's garden. His first ambition was to be an actor, but after reading accounts of the voyages of Captain Cook and Sir Joseph Banks [qq.v.], he became interested in settling in New South Wales. Possessed of a wild and romantic imagination, Suttor dreamed of converting the wilderness into a fruitful garden and building a new life with his childhood sweetheart Sarah Maria Dobinson. He also seems to have felt that there was little opportunity in England for a younger son.

Through the auspices of George Aufrère, for whom Suttor's father had originally worked, he gained an interview with Banks in February 1798. Banks warned him of the difficulties of settling in New South Wales without capital, but arranged for him to take charge of a collection of plants being sent to the colony as a replacement for those lost in the *Guardian*, in return for a free passage for himself and his wife and the usual land grant and indulgences given to settlers. In August Suttor began preparing the plants for shipment in the *Porpoise*. He married Sarah Dobinson on 2 August at the Church of All Saints, London Wall; their families helped to fit them out for the voyage and Banks presented them with £30. On the way to Portsmouth the *Porpoise* was nearly wrecked off Margate, and when the ship sailed in September she was disabled in a gale in the Bay of Biscay and again had to put back to port. A Spanish corvette was commissioned to take her place and renamed the *Porpoise*; in her the Suttors finally left England on 17 March 1800, arriving in Sydney in November. Many of the plants failed to survive the voyage but some were replaced at the Cape. Banks commended Suttor for his care and, on his recommendation, Suttor received a five guinea reward from the Treasury.

Suttor went first to Parramatta, where his family lived while he selected his grant, 186 acres at Baulkham Hills, which he received in March 1802. He was disappointed in his prospects in the colony and wrote to Banks asking for a civil appointment. For many years the family struggled, held back by lack of capital and high prices, although Suttor did have a limited success with his orangery, grown from trees presented to him by Colonel William Paterson [q.v.]. Before Governor King left he promised Suttor another 200 acres, but he did not receive it, and a grant promised by Governor Bligh was forestalled by the rebellion. Suttor was a firm supporter of Bligh and a leader among the settlers. In May 1808 he was instrumental in drawing up an address of welcome to Paterson, anticipating his arrival in Sydney and asking him to take action against the rebels; but as Paterson did not come it was not presented. In November Suttor drew up another petition to be sent to the Colonial Office and with Martin Mason [q.v.] was chosen for a mission to London to explain the abuses in the colony and ask for the reinstatement of Bligh. In the meantime, however, Suttor was imprisoned for six months for failing to attend Lieut-Governor Foveaux's [q.v.] general muster and for impugning his authority.

In 1810 Bligh took Suttor with him in the *Hindostan* as a witness against the rebel leader, Colonel Johnston [q.v.]. While in England Suttor approached Banks for help but, impatient at Banks's delay, he wrote to the Colonial Office himself. His appeal was rejected and he returned to the colony in the *Mary* in May 1812. He found his family well, but he had incurred considerable debts and again appealed to Banks. When Samuel Marsden [q.v.] began to undertake his missionary voyages to New Zealand he recommended that Suttor replace him as superintendent of the Lunatic Asylum at Castle Hill. Suttor was appointed in August 1814 at a salary of £50, with quarters and rations for his family and the use of the government land there. Suttor quarrelled with Parmeter, the surgeon in charge of the asylum, about the extent of their respective authorities, and in December 1818 charged him with neglect of the patients. Suttor's and Parmeter's depositions were heard before Hannibal Macarthur [q.v.], who concluded that both men had neglected their duty. One of the main charges against Suttor was that he had used the lunatics to labour on his farm at Baulkham Hills, and as a result of this inquiry in February 1819 he was dismissed.

He returned to his farm, but in 1820 he sought an additional grant, since his stock were dying and his land was cut by the roads to Windsor and Castle Hill. The caterpillar plague ravaged his farm and he began to think of settling beyond the Blue Mountains. Knowing that Governor Macquarie was not likely to grant him anything more than the 100 acres he had received at Eastern Creek, he waited until Governor Brisbane arrived and then applied for a grazing licence at Bathurst. He selected land on the Bathurst plains and applied for a grant in 1822, having taken his stock across with the help of his sons. The station was granted to someone else, but Suttor selected another, eventually establishing Brucedale at the junction of Winburndale and Clear Creeks, and there the family found the prosperity they had sought so long.

In 1825 Suttor was a member of the notorious Parramatta Grand Jury which, led by Hannibal Macarthur, criticized H. G. Douglass [q.v.]. After 1833 Suttor lived in Elizabeth Street, Sydney. In March 1839 he and his wife left for Europe in the *Laura* and toured the Continent, where Suttor obtained information on vineyards and wine-making. In 1843 he published in London *The Culture of the Grape-Vine, and the Orange, in Australia and New Zealand*, and during his stay there was elected a member of the Linnean Society. After his wife died at Rouen on 17 August

1844, Suttor embarked in the *Thomas Lowry* for Sydney. He arrived in November 1845 and in 1851 acquired Alloway Bank, Bathurst. In 1855 he published at Parramatta *Memoirs Historical and Scientific of the Right Honourable Sir Joseph Banks* (reprinted, Sydney, 1948). On 5 May 1859 he died at Alloway Bank and was buried at Kelso, near Bathurst. He had five sons and three daughters, of whom William Henry was a pioneer squatter and member of the Legislative Council. His grandsons, William Henry Suttor and Sir Francis Suttor, later became members of the Legislative Assembly.

HRNSW, 4-7; HRA (1), 2, 6, 7, 9, 11, 15; G. S. Oakes, *Kelso Church and the pioneers of the West* (Syd, 1923); H. V. Evatt, *Rum rebellion*, 1st ed (Syd, 1938); C. H. Bertie, 'The Suttors', *Home*, March 1930; MS cat under G. Suttor (ML).   VIVIENNE PARSONS

SWANSTON, CHARLES (1789-1850), banker and merchant, was born at Berwick upon Tweed, Northumberland, England, the son of Robert Swanston and Rebecca, daughter of Johnston Lambert of Mordington and Margaret Handyside of Tweedmouth. At 16 he was commissioned a lieutenant in the Madras establishment of the East India Co.'s army. After some time at the Military Institute at Fort St George he joined the Madras army in the field against the rajah of Travancore and was later employed in the survey of that state. In 1810 he was a member of an expedition which obtained the capitulation of Mauritius and he was immediately appointed to make a military survey of the island, including the soundings of its harbours, bays and coastal waters, and to report on its defences. As a reward for this work, the duke of York offered him a commission in the Brigade of Guards but he declined.

In May 1814 Swanston left England and returned to duty in India with dispatches to the governor-general. This journey was undertaken overland from Scutari to Baghdad, a distance of 1500 miles, and was accomplished in 48 days entirely on horseback. In September 1817 he was ordered to raise 1000 men for the Poona Auxiliary Horse, and was appointed its commandant after six weeks of successful recruitment. In command of these troops he was involved in several actions and three times wounded. In 1818, after a forced march of seventy miles performed in eighteen hours with his whole division, he captured Trimbackjee Dainglia, an agitator on whose head the government had placed a price of £10,000. This reward was never paid, as a proclamation withdrawing it had been issued just before his capture.

In January 1819 Swanston was promoted captain, but a year later lost his command because of great reductions in the army. In 1821 he was offered appointment as assistant quartermaster-general of the army but declined, accepting instead the office of military paymaster in the provinces of Travancore and Tinnevelly, a position he held for six years. In September 1828 he was granted a year's leave to Van Diemen's Land on account of ill health.

He arrived at Hobart Town in H.M.S. *Success* on 4 January 1829 with his wife Georgina, née Sherson, and family. Although on leave, he evidently decided to settle in the country, for he soon bought Fenton Forest, an estate on the River Styx, and Newtown Park at New Town. He also acquired land at Kingborough and some 4200 acres in the County of Westmorland. He returned briefly to India in 1830 at the expiration of his leave and, having resigned his army appointment, left again for Van Diemen's Land in May 1831. Now finally settled in the colony he became closely acquainted with Lieut-Governor Arthur and his chief officials, especially Captain John Montagu and Captain Matthew Forster [qq.v.].

In November 1831 Swanston was appointed managing director of the Derwent Bank, which was established as a partnership by a group of Hobart citizens, including several officials, and first opened for business in January 1828. Although the bank at first had seven directors, a meeting of shareholders in March 1830 agreed to reduce the number to three, one of them to be a full-time salaried managing director. The first managing director of the bank was W. H. Hamilton [q.v.], who soon returned to London as the bank's representative. Charles Swanston was appointed to succeed him; on 26 November 1831 he signed a covenant with the other two directors, Hamilton and Stephen Adey [q.v.], that each should hold forty of the bank's 200 shares, and should not acquire a greater number or sell shares without first offering them to the other two. When Adey went to England Swanston bought more shares, thereby gaining a majority of votes and undivided control. Under his management the Derwent Bank prospered, attracting large amounts of overseas capital for investment at high rates of interest. He was responsible for introducing the overdraft system into Australian banking in 1834, in which year he established the Derwent Savings Bank. His influence in the colony increased when he was nominated to the Legislative Council.

In addition to the bank he conducted a

big business as import and export agent, investment agent and wool broker. He imported rum, tea and other goods in quantity, acting as agent for Jardine, Matheson & Co. of Canton and for firms in Madras, Mauritius, Calcutta, Manila and the Netherlands Indies, whose goods he distributed not only in Hobart but in Sydney and Adelaide. On behalf of many officers and officials in India he also invested money in Van Diemen's Land in mortgages and bank shares. His largest investor was G. D. Mercer [q.v.] of Edinburgh. In 1835 when John Batman [q.v.] sought support for his proposal to colonize Port Phillip, a syndicate called the Port Phillip Association was formed with Swanston and J. T. Gellibrand [q.v.] as leading members. Swanston's role was to obtain the necessary finance and to act in effect as its commercial manager. He included Mercer in the association.

In 1835 Batman's expedition landed at Port Phillip and bought some 600,000 acres, including the future sites of Melbourne and Geelong. Recognition of the title to this land was refused by the government in Sydney and London despite strenuous efforts of the Port Phillip Association to press their claims. Settlement of Port Phillip was finally carried out under the regulations in force in New South Wales, most of the rural land being put up for auction in Sydney. An agent for the Port Phillip Association bought 9500 acres near Geelong for £7919 7s. 7d., and as an act of grace a remission of £7000 towards their expenses was allowed. Most of the members of the original association had by this time dropped out, Swanston and Mercer were the sole remaining shareholders. In 1844 Swanston, in partnership with his son-in-law Edward Willis, began trading as a merchant in Geelong. The firm, which lasted until 1854, held the pastoral properties Murgheboluc, Paywit, Ocean Grove, Point Lonsdale, Gnawarre and Native Creek No. 3 in the Geelong district, and in 1846 near Harrow, a station of 112,000 acres, later subdivided into several smaller runs, with Swanston & Willis retaining the Koolomurt section after the others were sold.

In October 1841 Swanston had converted the Derwent Bank into a mortgage bank. As the depression of the 1840s deepened the flow of overseas investments to the bank greatly diminished, the value of the land over which the bank held mortgages dropped disastrously, the price of wool fell and debtors to the bank found difficulty in meeting interest payments. He managed to keep the Derwent Bank going for another five years, latterly with the financial assistance of the Bank of Australasia and the Union Bank but, when in 1849 these institutions withdrew their support, he resigned and the Derwent Bank went into liquidation, John Walker [q.v.] being appointed liquidator. The bank's affairs and Swanston's had not been kept separate, and his liabilities were £104,375, of which £58,504 was due to the bank. Finally his creditors received 10s. in the £. In 1850, tired and worried, he sailed for America but stayed there only briefly. On his return voyage to Australia he died on 5 September and was buried at sea.

Charles Swanston had five sons and three daughters. The eldest son, Charles Lambert, took over his father's interest in Swanston & Willis in 1850 and continued the management of the properties near Geelong. He was largely responsible for the endowment of Geelong Grammar School. Later, with his brother Kinnear, he held a large sheep station, Otama, in the South Island of New Zealand from 1864 until 1877. Two other sons, Oliver and Nowell, joined the Indian army, both retiring as major-generals. The fourth son, Robert, became British consul in Fiji. Of his three daughters, Caroline, married Edward Willis.

Throughout his life in Tasmania Swanston was a controversial figure, conducting the affairs of the Derwent Bank with an autocratic hand and influencing the colony both by his financial dealings and by his intimate contact with colonial administrators. His association with the governor through his membership of the Legislative Council was friendly while Arthur held office, but sometimes bitter during Sir John Franklin's rule. In 1845, when Eardley-Wilmot was lieut-governor, Swanston was one of the Patriotic Six, led by T. G. Gregson [q.v.], who walked out of the council leaving it without a quorum.

Swanston foresaw the great potential of the future Victoria but accepted the defeat of his Port Phillip scheme with good grace. He was unfortunate that economic circumstances beyond his control finally caused the failure of his bank and his own ruin.

Statement of services of Captain Charles Swanston (Uxbridge, 1891); H. G. Turner, *A history of the colony of Victoria*, 1 (Lond, 1904), 102; P. L. Brown (ed), *Clyde Company papers*, 2-3 (Lond, 1952-58); S. J. Butlin, 'Charles Swanston and the Derwent Bank', *Hist Studies*, no 7, May 1943; W. H. Hudspeth, 'Rise and fall of Charles Swanston', Roy Soc Tas, *Papers*, 1948.

CHARLES SWANSTON

SYMERS; *see* SEYMOUR-SYMERS

T

TABER, THOMAS (1763-1842), teacher and parish clerk, was born on 10 May 1763 in London, where he later married Frances Sarah Medhurst. He arrived in Sydney on 2 June 1797 with his wife and three children, Deborah, Frances Sarah and Thomas. Two other children, James and George, were born in the colony.

Although a watch-finisher by trade he was immediately employed as a teacher at the school established in his church by Richard Johnson [q.v.], and was an instant success. His consistent and satisfactory work won the appreciation of Johnson and an award of £10 a year from the Society for Propagation of the Gospel in Foreign Parts. After the church was burned down in October 1798, the school was conducted under very unsatisfactory conditions, first in the Court House and then in 'an old Store House, very cold and damp'. Taber carried on steadfastly and was rewarded with the additional position of parish clerk in 1800. In 1802 he was transferred to Parramatta, but was back in Sydney in 1805. Taber reopened the school in rented premises; it was given some government assistance, but in every other way was a private school. Governor Macquarie gave teachers the full status of government employees; this enabled Governor Brisbane to grant Taber's request in 1824 to retire and to fix a pension for 'your unremitting attention to your duty as Schoolmaster in this colony upwards of twenty-five years' at £50 with an additional £20 for services as parish clerk. As the schools passed out of government control soon afterwards, Taber was one of the very few teachers to draw a pension. He did so till he died on 1 May 1842.

Thomas junior assisted his father and then was in charge of St Philip's Infant School for many years. Thomas senior and his sons James and George received grants of land near Liverpool and successfully pioneered the Menangle district.

J. J. Moloney, *Early Menangle* (Newcastle, 1929); MS cat under Taber (ML).

V. W. E. GOODIN

TALBOT, WILLIAM (1784?-1845), pastoralist, was the youngest son of Richard Talbot of Malahide Castle, County Dublin, Ireland, and his wife Margaret, the daughter of James O'Reilley of Ballinlough, Westmeath, whose family belonged to the Milesian princely house of Breffney, and who was later created Baroness Talbot of Malahide. In 1796 he was sent to the Manchester School and in 1814-17 travelled in Europe and the Middle East. In November 1820 he arrived in Hobart Town in the *Caroline*, went on to Sydney where he disposed of his investment to Edward Lord [q.v.] and on the strength of his assets of £6057 received a location order for 2000 acres. Returning to Van Diemen's Land next April with six convict servants, he heard of George Meredith's [q.v.] discovery of good land at Great Swan Port on the east coast, and asked him if he might share in its proposed settlement. He received permission from Lieut-Governor Sorell on the understanding that Meredith had prior right of choice. Ignoring this proviso, Talbot selected land, built a hut, began farming, and was firmly established when the deputy-surveyor-general came to measure off the east coast grants. It was then discovered that Talbot had taken land chosen by Meredith. Sorell supported Meredith's claim to the land and favoured compensating Talbot with extra land elsewhere, but fifteen months passed before the Sydney authorities agreed. Sorell's successor, Colonel George Arthur made the final decision to reinstate Meredith, giving Talbot six months to vacate the land and choose 3000 acres elsewhere. Further compensation for his vacated premises, a five-roomed house, dairy and fencing, was refused, though the government did allow him to choose a very extensive river front at Fingal and supplied convict labour to re-establish Malahide there.

As a wool-grower his success was remarkable. He invested most of his capital in stock, and only two years after taking up residence at Swan Port, he owned more than 3000 sheep and over 300 cattle. Too far from a market to grow crops profitably at Fingal, he concentrated on improving his flocks. By 1827 his Saxon and merino fleeces brought prices well above average on the London market and yielded him a profit of £1000. With extensive use of adjoining crown lands, the advantage of the first settler in the district, his flocks increased to 7000 by 1829 and his cattle numbered 1000. As a reward for his contribution to the wool industry despite the setback of a false start he was granted an additional 1500 acres.

William Talbot's success enticed other members of the family to emigrate. In 1830 his nephew Samuel Robdard John

Neil Talbot arrived; too late for a grant, he began buying land in the Fingal neighbourhood. Other nephews came out later, served apprenticeships to sheep farming at Malahide and managed the property while William Talbot visited England and made extensive tours through the Australian colonies. He died unmarried on 22 December 1845.

Samuel Talbot inherited Malahide, which soon afterwards was reckoned to include 40,000 acres. Although he had brought members of the anti-government party to court for challenging him to a duel not long after his arrival, he took no further part in public affairs. Well informed, kind hearted and affable, he was well liked in the colony where his success was the admitted result of sound judgment and judicious economy. On his return to Ireland, Malahide was managed by another nephew, Richard Gilbert Talbot, who was appointed in 1852 to the Legislative Council by Lieut-Governor Denison whose transportation policy he supported.

R. M. Hartwell, *The economic development of Van Diemen's Land 1820-1850* (Melb, 1954); Correspondence file under Talbot (TA).

A. RAND

TASMAN, ABEL JANSZOON (1603?-1659), mariner, was born at Lutjegast, near Groningen, in the Netherlands. He received a sufficient education to enable him to express his ideas clearly in writing and to become a skilled navigator. He married Claesgie Meyndrix, by whom he had a daughter. After his wife died, he married Joanna Tiercx in January 1632. Soon afterwards, as a sailor before the mast, he sailed for the East Indies, where he was a first mate in February and a skipper in May 1634. In that year in a minor exploration he had a narrow escape from death, when in an incautious landing several of his companions were massacred by people of Ceram. After spending some time in warlike and anti-smuggling operations he returned to Holland in 1637.

He sailed for the Indies again in 1638 as skipper of a flute, taking his wife with him. From the outset he was treated as one of the most reliable skippers there. He was at first employed in military and trading voyages, but in 1639 was appointed second-in-command, under Quast, of two ships which set out in June to find islands believed to lie east of Japan. He returned in November from this search. Despite a disastrous death-roll on it, he offered to repeat the search, but was sent instead on trading voyages to Japan and Cambodia.

In 1642 he was appointed to command two ships to explore southern and eastern waters. Sailing in August he discovered Van Diemen's Land, New Zealand, the Tonga Islands and some of the Fiji group, and re-explored part of the north coast of New Guinea. On his return to Batavia in June 1643 he was chosen to take part in an expedition to form a settlement in the Tonga Islands from which the Chilean coast was to be raided; while this expedition was preparing, he was ordered to find whether there was a passage into the South Sea between Carpentaria and De Witt's Land. For this purpose he set out with three vessels at the end of January 1644 and, following the coasts from Cape Valsche round to Cape Cloates, satisfied himself that, except perhaps at Endeavour Strait, there was no passage. He was rewarded after his return in August 1644 by confirmation in the grade of commandeur, with a substantial increase in pay dated back to the beginning of his voyage in 1642.

The plan to raid Chile was abandoned, and Tasman was appointed to the Council of Justice at Batavia. In mid-1647 he was sent on a mission to the King of Siam and was granted precedence over all Dutchmen in the kingdom. After that mission, he was given command of a fleet of eight vessels which sailed in May 1648 against the Spaniards. His conduct in this operation was unsatisfactory and, after his return in January 1649, proceedings were taken against him for having, when inflamed by liquor, treated one of his sailors in a barbarous way; as a result he was removed from office during the governor-general's pleasure. He was formally reinstated in January 1651, but not long afterwards retired from the service and became a merchant in Batavia. He died there in affluent circumstances in 1659. His daughter by his first marriage had married first Philip Heylman, and later Jacob Bremer. In 1661 permission was given for his widow to marry Jan Meyndert Springer.

Tasman was a member of the Reformed Church. He was a brave and energetic mariner, a humane and properly cautious explorer, and a conspicuously able commander, though over-hasty on one occasion at least. Reflections which have been cast upon his courage are the fruit of ignorance. There are two supposed portraits of him: one owned by the Royal Commonwealth Society in London, the other in the National Library in Canberra.

J. E. Heeres (ed), *Abel Janszoon Tasman's journal of his discovery of Van Diemen's*

Land and New Zealand in 1642 (Amsterdam, 1898); R. P. Meyjes, *De reizen van Abel Janszoon Tasman en Franchoys Jacobzoon Visscher* (The Hague, 1919); *Winkler Prins Encyclopaedie*, 17 (Amsterdam, 1953); W. Forster, 'An early chart of Tasmania', *Geog J*, 37 (1911); J. W. Forsyth, 'Clio etwas gebuckt', *JRAHS*, 49 (1963-64).   J. W. FORSYTH

TAYLOR, GEORGE (1758-1828), farmer, was born at Balvaird, near Abernethy, Scotland, and in March 1791 married Mary Low of the same parish. With their eight children they occupied Balvaird Farm, leased by his family from the earl of Mansfield since the seventeenth century. In 1822 Taylor emigrated to Van Diemen's Land with most of his family, arriving in the *Princess Charlotte* at Hobart Town in January 1823. He brought with him the usual letter of recommendation from the Colonial Office and capital of £890, and received an 800-acre land grant on the Macquarie River, which he named Valleyfield. Three of his sons Robert (1791-1861), David (1796-1860) and George (1800-1826) each brought a letter of recommendation and capital of £700, and each was granted 700 acres on the Macquarie south of Valleyfield.

In November 1824 George Taylor senior was a signatory to the address soliciting separation from New South Wales. A staunch Presbyterian, he was chairman of a meeting in January 1826 to consider the establishment of a Presbyterian church in the district; the church was built ten years later. In July 1824 the family successfully defended their home against a gang of seven bushrangers led by James Crawford, and including Matthew Brady [q.v.] and McCabe. The Taylors' defence was so vigorous that the bushrangers were forced to withdraw leaving behind their stores and ammunition. Crawford and another of the gang were captured and later executed in Launceston. Writing to Taylor later in 1824 Lieut-Governor Arthur highly commended the family's spirited defence of their home and held it as an example to other settlers. To lessen the inconvenience of the family's isolated situation Taylor paid the passage of fourteen Scottish labourers who were indentured to him; he also imported a large quantity of blacksmith's tools.

Taylor died on 19 April 1828, aged 70. His widow married Henry William Gage, and died in July 1850, aged 85. Robert, the eldest son, inherited the 2100 acres of Valleyfield; in addition to his original grant, he had already acquired some 2500 acres and several town allotments

in Perth and Campbell Town, and was renting another 2000 acres. In 1838 he married Margaret, the daughter of George and Margaret Stewart of Stewarton, Macquarie River; they had eight sons and two daughters. The second son, David, sold his grant to Robert and bought Winton from Dr Adam Turnbull [q.v.]. He married Nancy, daughter of Andrew and Hannah Gatenby [q.v.] and in the early 1840s with Robert, bought Kenilworth from the Forlonge [q.v.] family, and half their outstanding Saxon merino flock. This was the origin of the later well-known Taylor stud.

George, the third son, after receiving an extra 500 acres in compensation for losing the use of an arm in the fight with bushrangers, was killed by Aboriginals in November 1826. John (1804-1850), the youngest son who arrived in the *Greencock* in January 1828, received 500 acres by grant, and bought the near-by property of an Indian settler Rum John Conn, naming his estate St Johnstone.

Three of the four daughters married settlers in the district; the eldest later settled in the Portland district.

Correspondence file under G. Taylor (TA).
                 A. W. TAYLOR

TEGG, JAMES (1808-1845) and SAMUEL AUGUSTUS (b. 1813), booksellers and publishers, were born in Cheapside, London, sons of Thomas Tegg, bookseller, and his wife Mary, née Holland. Thomas Tegg had been orphaned early and boarded out in Scotland, where he was apprenticed to a country bookseller, from whom he ran away and after a number of adventures came to London in 1796. Later he established himself in Cheapside, where he built up a very large business as a publisher of cheap reprints and as a dealer in remainders. He described himself as 'the broom that swept the booksellers' warehouses'.

James Tegg was born on 16 January 1808 and arrived in Sydney with Samuel in 1834. In January 1835 they opened as 'wholesale and retail book merchants' in George Street, where they announced that 'all orders intrusted to them will be executed with promptitude and correctness, and at London prices'. There were then three booksellers in Sydney (McGarvie, Moffitt [qq.v.] and Evans) and a fifth (Lane) set up at about the same time.

By December Samuel had returned to England, presumably to collect stock for Van Diemen's Land. James soon launched into publishing with *Tegg's Monthly*

Magazine (March-July 1836). This bold
venture 'devoted to general literature,
avoiding the stormy arenas of politics and
polemics, and combining amusement with
instruction' contained extracts from English
magazines and contributions by local
writers, whose dilatoriness in delivering
copy, according to Tegg, caused its demise.
The first number included the story of
Fisher's ghost, and an anonymous sketch
of early days on the Hawkesbury attributed
in the Mitchell Library copy to Dr Lang
[q.v.]. A later venture, *The Literary News;
A Review and Magazine of Fact and
Fiction, The Arts, Sciences, & Belles Lettres*,
was published weekly from August 1837
to February 1838. Though short lived these
optimistic ventures served to advertise
their publisher and to establish a connexion
in the literary world of Sydney. Other
publications by Tegg included, besides his
New South Wales Pocket Almanac,
which appeared yearly from 1836 to
1844, such works of colonial literature
as James Martin's *Australian Sketch
Book* (1838), *Legends of Australia*,
a novel issued in four parts (1842) and
Henry Parkes's *Stolen Moments* (1842);
curiosities like *Psellus' Dialogue on the
Operation of Daemons; . . .* by Marcus
Collisson (1843) and William Lee's *Brandy
and Salt; being an effectual remedy for most
of the diseases which afflict humanity*
(1842); and new editions of Hovell and
Hume's [qq.v.] *Journey of Discovery to
Port Phillip, New South Wales, in 1824
and 1825* (1837); Lady Darling's *Simple
Rules for the Guidance of Persons in
humble life . . .* (1837) and J. H. Plunkett's
[q.v.] *The Australian Magistrate* (1840).
His name also appears, with his brothers',
in joint imprints on some of his father's
publications, such as his *Handbook for
Emigrants* (1839 and later editions).

In 1837 Tegg added printing to his
activities, carrying on business as J. Tegg
& Co., at the Atlas Office and Book
Repository, George Street. Until the establishment of a government printer in 1840
he shared the government printing with
the *Herald* office and others. In 1842 he
disposed of this business to D. L. Welch,
who later published the *Atlas* newspaper
from this office. Tegg, however, was
primarily a bookseller, regularly advertising
a wide range of books, many of which were
probably drawn from his father's remainder
stock, and from time to time issuing cata-
logues, one of which, for 1842, the *Colonial
Observer* thought comprised 'a greater
amount of light and trashy reading than
we like to see', but hoped that Mr Tegg of
London would continue to send out a
liberal supply of his cheap editions of

standard works 'to improve the taste of
our colony, and to form our colonial youth
to vigorous thinking'. On 16 December 1836
Tegg married Eliza Rebecca Silvester of
London; they had two daughters. In August
1844 he sold out to W. A. Colman on
account of ill health. He died on 16 May
1845, leaving an estate valued at under
£100.

Samuel Augustus Tegg had accompanied his brother to Sydney in 1834, but
soon returned to London, whence he
arrived in Hobart Town in the *Wave* in
December 1836. In February 1837 he married Caroline, second daughter of W. Lewis
Wilson of Hobart. He set up as a bookseller and stationer in Elizabeth Street. In
January 1839 he opened the Derwent Circulating Library and in May 1845 the
Wellington Bridge Stationery Shop and
Library, which at the end of that year he
sold to James Walch. He had taken premises
at Brisbane Street, Launceston, in November 1844, and carried on business there
until he sold out in October 1847. After
visiting Sydney, where he was his brother's
executor, he returned to London. On leaving Tasmania he advertised that he would
continue to act as agent for the Launceston
business, and that 'orders for books etc,
executed personally in London, [would be]
delivered in V.D.L. at the published prices'.

Even more than his brother, S. A. Tegg
was venturesome in encouraging local
writers. Among his publications were James
Knox's *Poetic Trifles* (1838), David Burn's
[q.v.] *Plays and Fugitive Pieces* (1842),
James Bonwick's *Geography for the Use of
Australian Youth* (1845), and N. L. Kentish's [q.v.] *Essay on Capital Punishment*
(1842) and *Work in the Bush* (1846).

The importance of the Teggs as booksellers lay in their connexion with the
London trade. They offer the first example
of an attempt to exploit the colonial market
through a chain of interconnected businesses with their centre in London. As
publishers both brothers made a significant
contribution to Australian writing in its
embryonic stage. Neither seems to have
inherited the hard-headed acumen and
persistence by which their father accumulated a fortune. James had a strain of
optimism and enterprise, with perhaps a
leaning to extreme Protestantism, and
Samuel a restlessness that drove him to
build up and sell out one business after
another.

T. Tegg, *Memoir of the late Thomas Tegg*
(Lond, 1870); *Parish Registers of St Mary-
le-Bow* (Harleian Society), v 44; Newspaper
indexes under Tegg (ML); MS cat under Tegg
(ML).
                                    L. F. FITZHARDINGE

TENCH, WATKIN (1758?-1833), officer of marines and author, was born between May 1758 and May 1759 at Chester, England, the son of Fisher Tench and his wife Margaret (Margaritta). His father, a native of Chester, was a dancing master and proprietor of 'a most respectable boarding school', which was no doubt the source of Tench's very sound education and of the influential contacts, especially with the Wynne Williams family, which helped to launch him on his career. The year before Watkin's birth Fisher Tench became a freeman of Chester on the nomination of the mayor. Several children born before Watkin had died in infancy; only two, John and Watkin, survived their father, who died in 1784.

On 25 January 1776 Tench entered the Marine Corps as a second lieutenant. During the war for American independence he served off the American coast, first in the *Nonsuch* and then as first lieutenant in the *Mermaid*. When the *Mermaid* was driven ashore he spent three months as a prisoner of war in Maryland and then from October 1778 to March 1779 served in the *Unicorn*. He was promoted captain-lieutenant in September 1782 but, with the war over, was placed on half-pay in May 1786.

Towards the end of the year he volunteered for a three-year tour of service with the convict settlement about to be formed at Botany Bay. He sailed in the transport *Charlotte* on 13 May 1787 as one of the two captain-lieutenants of the marine detachment under Major Robert Ross [q.v.], and arrived in Botany Bay on 20 January 1788.

After the transfer to Port Jackson and the formal establishment of the settlement Tench was occupied with his military duties and with routine tasks. In March 1788, with four other officers, he was placed under arrest by Ross for refusing to alter the sentence of a court martial of which he was president, but they were soon released. Apart from this, he seems to have maintained good relations with everyone in the little community, being especially intimate with Lieutenant William Dawes [q.v.], whose observatory provided a quiet refuge and whose interest in the Aboriginals Tench shared. Tench was a keen explorer and much of his leisure was spent as a member or as leader of expeditions to the west and south-west of the settlement, discovering the Nepean River and tracing it to the Hawkesbury, and penetrating as far as the Razorback. It is clear that he felt the fascination of the bush, of its strange solitude and of its informal camp-fire nights, but he had also a keen

practical interest, noting the absence of water and taking samples of the soil wherever he went. Apart from this his main relaxations seem to have been observing the life about him for description in his journal, for which he seems to have arranged publication before leaving England, studying the Aboriginals and watching the first struggling attempts at agriculture.

Tench sailed for England with the marines in the *Gorgon* in December 1792. Promotion to brevet major awaited him on his return, and with the outbreak of war with France he was soon at sea again. In November 1794 his ship, the *Alexander*, 74 guns, under Admiral Rodney Bligh, was captured after a desperate battle with three French 74s, and Tench spent six months as a prisoner of war, mostly on parole at Quimper as interpreter to Bligh. Here he turned some previous knowledge of France and his observant eye to the study of the effects of the revolution in that remote corner of Brittany, and his *Letters from France*, published after his return, display the same qualities as his better known Australian journals. After being liberated by exchange, he served for the rest of the war in the Channel Fleet in the *Polyphemus* and *Princess Royal*, being promoted brevet lieut-colonel in 1798. From March 1802 he served in various shore depots with regular promotions until he retired on half-pay as major-general on 1 January 1816. Three years later he returned to the active list as commandant of the Plymouth Division, retiring with the rank of lieut-general on 18 July 1821.

Some time after his return from Australia Tench married Anna Maria, daughter of Robert Sargent, surgeon, of Devonport, who was five years his junior. They had no children, but in 1821 they adopted the four orphaned children of one of Mrs Tench's sisters and her husband Captain Bedford, R.N. Two of the boys became captains in the navy and one a bank manager at Penzance; the fourth child, a girl, died at Penzance in 1832. Tench died at Devonport on 7 May 1833; his wife, aged 82, on 1 August 1847.

Tench's claim to remembrance rests on the two books in which he described the voyage to and the early years of the settlement in New South Wales, at once the most perceptive and the most literary of the contemporary accounts. Less detailed than David Collins, less matter of fact than Arthur Phillip or John White [q.v.], Watkin Tench was the first to mould Australian experience into a work of conscious art. To a sound eighteenth-century style—he had read Voltaire and

Gibbon—he added an interest in the novel, the picturesque and the primitive which foreshadows romanticism. His eye ranged over the convicts and the Aboriginals with a mixture of shrewd common-sense and sympathetic tolerance, and his reaction to the country itself shows the same qualities. His notes, made while the events were fresh, were no doubt polished at leisure and were then selected and arranged to bring out the main themes, and his writing combines the freshness of immediately recorded experience with more elaborate set pieces and reflections.

Tench published three books: A *Narrative of the Expedition to Botany Bay: with an account of New South Wales, its productions, inhabitants &c* (London, 1789, three editions; also Dublin and New York editions and translations into French, German and Dutch); A *Complete Account of the Settlement at Port Jackson, in New South Wales, including an accurate description of the situation of the colony; and of its natural productions; taken on the spot* (London, 1793; German and Swedish translations); and *Letters written in France, to a friend in London, between the month of November 1794 and the month of May 1795* (London, 1796). The *Narrative* was reprinted in Sydney in 1938, and the *Narrative* and the *Complete Account*, with introduction, notes and bibliography, under the title *Sydney's First Four Years* in Sydney in 1961 (revised ed., 1964).

HRNSW, 1 pt 2; J. Hemingway, *History of the city of Chester*, 2 (Chester, 1831), 32-33; G. C. Boase, *Collectanea cornubiensia* (Truro, 1890), 64, 975; G. A. Wood, 'Lieutenant William Dawes and Captain Watkin Tench', JRAHS, 10 (1924); L. F. Fitzhardinge, 'The origin of Watkin Tench: a note', JRAHS, 50 (1964).   L. F. FITZHARDINGE

TERRY, JOHN (1771-1844), pioneer, was the son of Ralph Terry of The Mill, Redmire, Yorkshire, England, in which county the family had also milling and other interests at Bedale, Forcett and Askrigg. He married Martha, daughter of Thomas Powell of Hornby Castle, and for a number of years carried on the family business of milling. In 1818, presumably because of economic conditions, he left England for New South Wales, arriving in Sydney in March 1819 with his family, in the *Surry* with a letter from the Colonial Office to Governor Macquarie, to whom he appeared 'a good worthy man'. He was apparently dissatisfied with New South Wales and soon sold the livestock, house and three acres that he had bought at Liverpool. After a preliminary visit to Van Diemen's Land he sailed for Hobart Town in the *Prince Leopold*, arriving on 6 December 1819 with his wife, eleven children, two servants, 'a pair of millstones and a variety of utensils for the purpose of erecting a water mill'. This mill he proceeded to build at Elizabeth Town (New Norfolk), near the Derwent River, and within a year he was grinding wheat. He also took up a grant of 1400 acres at Macquarie Plains, 'about 10 miles up the country' and this property he named Askrigg. There is a charming account by Terry in a letter home (1822) of his early labours in creating a mill, farm and orchard in idyllic surroundings: 'I threw off my coat and rose with the sun, wrought at all that came to hand. I now thank God and consider myself and my family in a very comfortable position . . . Wild duck in great numbers, as many as 300 to 400 rise at once. Black swan and land quail, wild pigeons coloured like a peacock, and fish in great plenty . . . Hunt the kangaroo. Trees here cast a shell of bark, not leaves. Wood, when cut green, sinks in the water like a stone. Your shortest day is our longest and your Summer our Winter. The cuckoo cries in the night and mostly in our winter; the man in the moon has his legs upward'.

Governor Macquarie inspected the mill in June 1821. In 1826 Terry told the land commissioners that his output was more than six bushels an hour and that his mill race required all the water of the Lachlan River for six months each year. He had much help from his grown-up sons and had also cleared most of his farm. Terry sought government compensation for alleged injury sustained by the formation of the New Norfolk watercourse. Although the colonial secretary, John Montagu [q.v.], protested that Terry had predated correspondence by two years to make good his claim, his appeal was accepted in 1841, even if not in the form presented. In 1835 he was also involved in a dispute over a land boundary. A jury decided that both land grants were equally valid and that the error was the fault of the surveyor-general; in due course the Colonial Office ordered that Terry be granted another thirty-six acres elsewhere. Despite these and other vicissitudes Terry achieved his ambition of creating a patriarchal establishment in what is probably the most English-appearing part of Australia. He died at his home on 8 July 1844. His numerous descendants have intermarried with colonial families all over Australia.

HRA (3), 3; A. McKay (ed), *Journals of the land commissioners for Van Diemen's Land*

1826-28 (Hob, 1962); *Sydney Gazette*, 11 Oct 1819; *Colonial Times*, 10 July 1844; GO 1/26/647-9 (TA);. Correspondence file under J. Terry (TA); Family papers (in possession of C. A. J. Swan, Caulfield, Vic).

CLIVE TURNBULL

TERRY, SAMUEL (1776?-1838), merchant, landowner and 'The Botany Bay Rothschild', was a labourer at Manchester, England, when on 22 January 1800 at the Salford Quarter Sessions, Lancashire, he was convicted of the theft of 400 pairs of stockings and sentenced to transportation for seven years. In June he was transferred to the unsalubrious hulk *Fortunée* at Langstone Harbour, and thence to the transport *Earl Cornwallis* in which he arrived at Sydney in June 1801. He worked under Samuel Marsden's [q.v.] direction in a stonemasons' gang on the Parramatta female factory and gaol, and he helped to cut stones for the church; he was both flogged for neglect of duty and rewarded for his industry. Before his sentence expired in 1807 he had served as a private soldier, been self-employed as a stonemason, and had set up a shop at Parramatta. By 1808 he was not only one of the 'proprietors of landed property' who asked Governor Bligh for 'privileges of trade' and trial by jury, but also listed as a favoured recipient of government cattle; by 1809 he had a farm on the Hawkesbury River.

Terry moved to Sydney, became an innkeeper, and in February 1810, when liquor licences were curtailed, his was one of the twenty granted The next month he married the widow variously known as Rosetta (Rosata) Marsh or Madden, née Pracey, a woman of some importance, whose background is as elusive as her age. She had come free to the colony in 1799 in the disease-ridden *Hillsborough* on which a third of the convict complement had died. It seems probable that she came as the wife of the convict Edward Madden who died in the *Hillsborough* at Cape Town, and that she later became the widow of another convict, Henry Marsh. She was an innkeeper herself when she married Terry, and he acquired both her Pitt Street property and her three children.

The Terrys prospered rapidly, first through their inn and store but soon by speculation in city and pastoral properties. By 1815 Terry had established a farm, Mount Pleasant, on the Nepean River and also had Illawarra properties; in 1817 Governor Macquarie, who granted him city allotments, described him as a 'wealthy trader'. Terry was also an important sup-plier of flour and fresh meat to the government. Between 1817 and 1820 he held more than a fifth of the total value of mortgages registered in the colony, a higher proportion than that of the Bank of New South Wales. Commissioner Bigge [q.v.] reported that in 1820 he had 1450 cattle, 3800 sheep, and 19,000 acres, almost exactly half of the land held by former convicts. He was also one of the largest shareholders in the bank, but when he stood for election as director in 1818, 1819 and 1820 he was unsuccessful; when elected in 1822 he was refused his seat on the pretext that, as an expiree, he was not 'unconditionally free'.

The means by which Terry prospered were the subject of public gossip but they have never been carefully assessed. Certainly he acquired wealth first by frugality and shrewdness; his enemies were quick to add charges of unscrupulous extortion. The Bigge report gives the gist of the charges, based largely on Marsden's hostile evidence, that were amplified in the distorted moral homilies of 'A.L.F.' (*The History of Samuel Terry, in Botany Bay . . .* London, 1838) and Rev. Thomas Atkins [q.v.] and in later irresponsible journalism. Bigge alleged that officers and small settlers, after becoming intoxicated at Terry's public house, signed away rights to their possessions as security for debts. By this means, according to Bigge, Terry accumulated considerable capital, and land second only to D'Arcy Wentworth's [q.v.]. Edward Eagar [q.v.] dismissed such charges as 'mere naked assertions, unsupported by any fact or any evidence', and cited the 'approbation of his good Character' by Macquarie, who had known Terry for twelve years. Neither his detractors nor his supporters were disinterested.

Terry was a litigious man and had brought at least twenty-eight actions in the Supreme Court by 1821. Though he apparently acted within the law and though his misdeeds were exaggerated by the emancipists' enemies, public bitterness towards him suggests that he was relentless in his business dealings. But those were litigious times, and some cases brought against him speak less well for his adversaries than for Terry.

In the 1820s Terry consolidated his wealth; he established a bloodstock stud on Illawarra land granted him by Macquarie, built the vast Terry's Buildings opposite his residence in Pitt Street, established a country seat, Box Hill, and developed his farming properties at Liverpool, on the Nepean, and later at Yass and Bathurst, as well as flour-mills and breweries. When again elected to the board of the Bank of New South Wales in August 1828 by 308 votes to 83 he took office only until December. By that time he had become a leading philanthropist, contributing *inter alia* to the Benevolent Society, Auxiliary Bible Society, Sydney Public Grammar School, and later to Sydney College, on whose committees he served actively. He supported the Wesleyans and became a trustee for them in 1822.

In the late 1820s Terry was firmly established as a public figure, though still often censured for his methods and for his material success. He became increasingly identified with the political aspirations of the emancipists and at times their spokesman: for example, as treasurer of the committee formed in 1821 to defend their rights. In 1827, 1830 and 1831 he was a leader in organizing petitions for trial by jury and a house of assembly, and also in expressing patriotic feeling through Australia Day celebrations; he was in the chair at the fortieth anniversary dinner in 1828 and again in 1831 as first president of the 'Australian Society for the Promotion of the Growth and Cultivation of Colonial Produce and Manufactures'. In 1826 he became president of a Masonic Lodge and was prominent in its activities in the following years of his life. Despite criticisms and snubs he had attained a position of public eminence and often of public responsibility.

Terry was also now the patriarch of a large family which he liberally supported, but any dreams of a financial dynasty were to be largely dispelled. His son and principal heir, Edward, died childless soon after Terry himself. Some of the family's fortune was dissipated in the speculations and bankruptcy of the mercantile firm of Hughes & Hosking. A daughter, Martha, married John Hosking [q.v.] and a stepdaughter, Esther Marsh, married Terry's nephew, John Terry Hughes. At a ceremony performed by Marsden himself, a son, John Terry, married into the respected Rouse [q.v.] family in 1831, and his children were to be active in the colony's political life.

When Terry died on 22 February 1838, three years after a paralytic seizure, he was buried with Masonic honours and the band of the 50th Regiment led the procession. The funeral, described as the grandest seen in the colony, may be taken as the summation of his life's striving. He left a personal estate of £250,000, an income of over £10,000 a year from Sydney rentals, and landed property that defies assessment. His will was eventually published by the government as a public document. His wife lived until 5 September 1858. The family sold to the government the land now occupied by Martin Place and the General Post Office, Sydney.

The Terrys, Samuel and Rosetta, may be seen in retrospect as two able, singleminded early colonists who resolved to reverse their unfavourable, brutalizing early fortunes—and succeeded.

J. T. Bigge, Report . . . into the state of the colony of NSW, PP (HC), 1822 (448); P. E. LeRoy, 'Samuel Terry', JRAHS, 47 (1961); Bonwick transcripts (ML); Information from Mrs M. F. Lenehan, Lane Cove, NSW.

GWYNETH M. DOW

THERRY, JOHN JOSEPH (1790-1864), Catholic priest, the son of John Therry, of Cork, Ireland, and his wife Eliza, née Connolly, was educated privately and at St Patrick's College, Carlow. Ordained priest in 1815, he was assigned to parochial work in Dublin and then Cork, where he became secretary to the bishop, Dr Murphy. His interest in Australia, aroused by the transportation of Irish convicts and the publicity surrounding the forced return of Father Jeremiah O'Flynn [q.v.] in 1818, came to the notice of Bishop Edward Bede Slater, whom Pius VII had appointed vicar-apostolic of the 'Cape of Good Hope, Madagascar, Mauritius, and New Holland with the adjacent islands'. At the same time the Colonial Office had consented under the pressure of radical demand, the increasing influence of the Irish hierarchy and the somewhat diffident promptings of Bishop Poynter, vicar-apostolic of the London district, to send two official Roman Catholic chaplains to New South Wales. Recommended by his own bishop as a capable, zealous and 'valuable young man', Therry sailed from Cork under a senior priest, Father Philip Conolly [q.v.], in the *Janus*, which carried more than a hundred prisoners. They arrived in Sydney, authorized by both church and state, in May 1820.

Therry described his life in Australia for the next forty-four years as 'one of incessant labour very often accompanied by painful anxiety'. Popular, energetic and restless, he appreciated from the beginning the delicacy of his role. He had to be at once a farseeing pastor making up for years of neglect, a conscientious official of an autocratic British colonial system, and a pragmatic Irish supporter of the democratic freedoms. Though respectful of authority and grateful for co-operation, he was impatient of any curtailment of what he considered his own legal or social rights as a Catholic priest in a situation governed by extraordinary circumstances.

The immediate tasks of instruction, visitation and administration of the Sacraments went ahead, and Governor Macquarie's initial attitude of executive peremptoriness combined with abrupt, detailed regulation gave way to a gruff but friendly trust. Commissioner Bigge [q.v.] was courteous and helpful. In 1821 Father Conolly, an eccentric temperamentally incompatible with his companion, went to Van Diemen's Land, leaving Therry for five seminal years the only priest on the mainland. Articulate and thorough, he set himself the task of attending to every aspect of the moral and religious life of the Catholics. He travelled unceasingly, living with his scattered people wherever they were to be found, sometimes using three or four horses in a day. His influence was impressive among the Protestant settlers and outstanding among the convicts. His correspondence shows the trust they placed in him. For the rest of his life he was banker, adviser and arbitrator to many of them as well as spiritual director and community leader. He also early formed a lasting interest in the Aboriginals, who became very attached to him. He pleaded the cause of their education to Governor Darling and in 1834 wrote to the governor's private secretary renewing his offer of services and accommodation.

The building of a church in Sydney, planned from the first days of the chaplaincy, was one of Therry's main preoccupations. The assistance or substantial tolerance of the leading colonists was assured, and on 29 October 1821 Governor Macquarie laid the foundation stone of St Mary's Church on a site he had assigned at the edge of Hyde Park, near the convict barracks. Greenway [q.v.] made himself available for consultation on the architecture and construction. J. T. Campbell, John Piper and Frederick Goulburn [qq.v.] were regularly involved in the organization of subscriptions. Government help was promised, but Therry was criticized for the elaborate design and size of the building, and the project quickly got out of hand financially. His accounts, never very coherent though always scrupulously maintained, became progressively more chaotic as his charities multiplied and the financing of schools and churches in Sydney, Parramatta, and the outlying townships involved him in attempts to raise funds by farming and stock-breeding. The scattered and casual nature of his dealings, the absence of a reliable and able book-keeper and his own sanguine character made financial crisis inevitable. His failure to separate private and public matters hampered and indeed later

crippled his apostolate. But demands for his services came from the hospital, gaols, farms, the government establishments, his own day and Sunday schools, and from road-gangs and assigned convicts. He went, whenever summoned, to Wollongong, Goulburn, Maitland, Bathurst and Newcastle.

Oppressive behaviour by officials or settlers towards the soldiers or convicts angered him, particularly where religious issues were involved. He was bitterly resentful of his exclusion from certain government institutions, especially the Orphan School, where he was unhappy about children whose parents were Catholic being baptized and instructed by the Anglican chaplains. By 1824, however, the patronage of Governor Brisbane and his own growing experience encouraged him to hope for impartiality and support. He was confident that, with the arrival of new priests to share his work, a remarkable expansion of Catholic practice and activity was possible. With the aid of his committees, trustees and friends, and the advent of what he termed 'a free, liberal and talented press', he began to feel secure. He had even been held up by the governor as a model of discrimination and good judgment to the zealous and horrified Presbyterian pioneer, the recently arrived Dr J. D. Lang [q.v.].

When the British government decided on a major religious adjustment to ensure the stability and increase the influence of the straining overseas branches of the state Church, Therry along with other Dissenters found himself fighting once more for permission to carry out vital services of his ministry. In New South Wales the appointment of Archdeacon Scott [q.v.] was accompanied by the creation of the Church and School Corporation in 1825. In its provisions the Church of England was overwhelmingly favoured. Therry was proud of his friendship and contacts with non-Catholics and irenical rather than sectarian by conviction, but found it hard enough to cope with the demands of the ten thousand Catholics for assembly, instruction and burial without the added unwelcome prospect of perpetual disputes with the privileged Anglicans over precedence, registration, fees and access to colonial funds. Already a rallying point for religious grievance, he now became prominent in a possible opposition party. On 14 June 1825 the *Sydney Gazette* misquoted him as having but 'qualified' respect for 'the other Revd. Gentlemen of the Establishment'. The incident was magnified in a time of tension. Bathurst was shocked at Therry's pragmatic approach to those regulations he regarded as unjust or petty and at his open assault on religious monopoly. He was removed from his official situation as chaplain and his salary was withdrawn soon after the arrival of Governor Darling. Despite frequent and general protest he was not reinstated until 1837. However, Therry had grown accustomed to fend for himself and saw that the generosity of his friends and his countrymen would enable him to carry on much as he had done. He decided to stay and to represent his claims. His criticisms were enthusiastically taken up by Wentworth and Wardell [qq.v.] in the *Australian*, and E. S. Hall [q.v.] in the *Monitor*. Darling distrusted Therry's influence among the convicts, but decided to ignore rather than to expel him, chiefly because his removal 'would in all probability have called forth some expression of the public opinion in his favour'.

The withdrawal of government approval involved Therry in continual disabilities and hindrances in the exercise of his priestly functions, especially in the visitation of the sick and dying in gaols and hospitals, and in the performance of marriages. But even after the arrival of Father Daniel Power as official chaplain in December 1826 Therry remained the chief influence. The two priests had more work than they could deal with, but Therry's impetuosity and Power's inadequate health led them into a series of collisions, particularly when the building of St Mary's came to a standstill and Therry demanded more vigorous action. Father Power died in March 1830 and Therry was again left alone with his mounting debts and worries. His genius for publicity and organization is illustrated in the repeated representations made on his behalf by the principal officials and magistrates, and supported in March 1830 by over 1400 householders. Grudgingly he was permitted to act as chaplain without status or salary. His popularity and energy made it impossible for Father Dowling, who arrived in September 1831, to replace him in the public estimation, much to the chagrin of both newcomer and governor.

The arrival of Governor Bourke, the news of Catholic emancipation, the collapse of the Church and School Corporation, and the appointment first of Roger Therry [q.v.] as commissioner of the Court of Requests in 1829 and of J. H. Plunkett [q.v.] as solicitor-general in 1832, both loyal friends of Therry, offered new opportunities for Catholic progress. Yet Therry was still frustrated and unrecognized when Father McEncroe [q.v.] landed in June 1832. McEncroe was quite capable of

managing the indomitable but stubborn veterans and making them lifelong colleagues and confidants. A dispute about the St Mary's land had become deadlocked through Therry's obstinacy, and disastrous litigation was in prospect when Bishop Morris, Slater's successor, appointed the English Benedictine, Father William Ullathorne [q.v.], as his vicar-general in the colony. Despite his youth, Ullathorne's confidence and ecclesiastical authority enabled him to take over the reins from Therry when he arrived in February 1833. The first bishop, J. B. Polding [q.v.], came in 1835 and Therry went willingly as parish priest to Campbelltown, with an area extending beyond Yass as his immediate care. By Bourke's Church Act of 1836 the principle of religious equality had been accepted in the colony, and in April 1837 he was restored to a government salary.

In April 1838 he was sent by Polding to Van Diemen's Land as vicar-general. It was intended also that he should visit Port Phillip on his way, but he did not do so, going to Launceston and thence to Hobart Town, where Father Conolly had become estranged from his people, and the usual difficulties had arisen about jurisdiction, salaries and the deeds of church land. Therry reconciled Conolly before the latter's death in August 1839. He visited the interior and attended to the convicts. His church building at Hobart and Launceston was assisted by Sir John Franklin's spasmodic patronage, but on St Joseph's, Hobart, and on the schools demanded by the free settlers, he overreached himself. Loneliness, responsibility, illness and debt pressed heavily on him and he found himself again struggling for justice and religious equality in the government institutions. In July 1841 he visited Sydney briefly to get help and to try to clear up some of his business entanglements. There he was consulted by Caroline Chisholm [q.v.], whom he was able to help and advise about her first plans to work among the emigrants. Though sick, he was thinking of a mission to New Zealand and perhaps the Pacific Islands, and formed an interest which in 1860 prompted him to implore Governor Denison to put an end to the Maori wars and to offer his own services as mediator.

Dr Willson [q.v.], the first bishop, arrived in Hobart in May 1844. He had not expected the church debts to be so great or so complicated, and the two men fell out. A long and dreary dispute arose, especially about the St Joseph's property. Neither man had much humour, and not all the goodwill they certainly possessed, or the good offices of Polding, McEncroe,

Charles Swanston [q.v.] of the Derwent Bank, the colonial secretary or Rome itself could bring an end to the quarrel, which smouldered for fourteen miserable years. The affair became an *idée fixe* with Therry, who stayed on for fear that his lay trustees would be victimized or that his debts would not be met in a time of depression. In September 1846, however, he went to Melbourne as parish priest in the place of Father Geoghegan who had founded the church there. He remained until April 1847.

Therry was at Windsor in New South Wales as parish priest until June 1848 when he returned to live in Van Diemen's Land for six years. His efforts to settle affairs there were unsuccessful and, after a period of adjustment in New South Wales, he went in May 1856 to Balmain where he spent the rest of his life. Mellowed and serene, he continued to be an energetic pastor, watching the growth of the church in whose establishment he had played such a definitive part, the coming of the religious Orders, and the completion of his own church at Balmain and the first St Mary's, generously contributing whenever he could to every new development. He became spiritual director to the Sisters of Charity at St Vincent's, and in 1858 was made archpriest, taking precedence after the vicar-general. In 1859 he was elected a founding fellow of the council of St John's College within the University of Sydney. He had been given or had bought a number of properties which he tried to develop for the provision of more schools and churches for the growing Catholic community. Notable among these were his farms at Bong Bong and Albury, a property which is now the suburb of Lidcombe, and 1500 acres at Pittwater, where he tried unsuccessfully to mine coal.

Simple and unselfish, a firm democrat and a zealous priest, Therry was a man of large notions and considerable achievement. He was an unsophisticated man with no clear ideas of social systems or political reform. Yet his energy and persistence proved a continual source of trouble to those who opposed his ideas of what was right or possible. Of the middle class, gentle, 'pious, zealous, and obstinate', he admired but lacked the education and ability of his more vivid contemporaries. But despite his peculiarities and limitations he undertook many obligations and responsibilities which would in the circumstances have crushed greater men. His enthusiasm and sincerity assure him of a firm place among the founders of the Catholic Church and in the history of civil liberties in Australia. He firmly believed

in a distant future for which he built, often regardless of existing conditions. A legend in his own lifetime, he died on 25 May 1864, and his funeral was 'certainly the most numerously attended' ever seen in Sydney to that date. His remains are now in the crypt of St Mary's Cathedral, where the Lady Chapel was erected as his memorial.

Correspondence relative to St Joseph's Church, Hobart Town (Hob, 1850); P. F. Moran, *History of the Catholic Church in Australasia* (Syd, 1895); H. N. Birt, *Benedictine pioneers in Australia,* 1-2 (Lond, 1911); E. M. O'Brien, *Life and letters of Archpriest John Joseph Therry,* 1-2 (Syd, 1922); E. M. O'Brien, *The dawn of Catholicism in Australia,* 1-2 (Syd, 1928); J. H. Cullen, *The Catholic Church in Tasmania* (Launceston, 1949); J. H. Cullen, 'The dispute between Dr Willson and Father Therry', *A'sian Catholic Record,* 28 (1951), 29 (1952); Therry papers (Canisius College, Pymble).

J. EDDY

THERRY, SIR ROGER (1800-1874), judge, was born at Cork, Ireland, and educated at Clongowes College and Trinity College, Dublin. In 1822 at Dublin he became secretary of the National Society for the Education of the Poor in Ireland; he was called to the Irish Bar and actively associated with Daniel O'Connell in the campaign for Catholic emancipation. In 1827 he was called to the English Bar. In the next year he edited *The Speeches of George Canning,* and wrote a memoir on the life of that statesman. On 9 August 1827 at Dublin he married Mrs Ann Reilly, née Corley. In April 1829 he was appointed commissioner, with the right of private practice, of the Courts of Requests (small debts) in New South Wales. He arrived in Sydney with his wife in November.

To his commissionership Therry brought a thorough knowledge of law and legal procedure, good humour, and an understanding of the mainsprings of human action. In 1834 Chief Justice Forbes [q.v.] testified that he had 'formed a high opinion of [Therry's] knowledge as a lawyer and of his talents as an advocate'. Mr Justice Dowling [q.v.] bore witness that, in his conduct as a barrister, Therry 'sustained that gentlemanly carriage and high tone of honourable integrity, which ever distinguished the British Bar'. From March 1841 to August 1843 he acted as attorney-general and, as such, sat in the Legislative Council. In June 1843 he stood for election to the new part-elective Legislative Council as the representative of Camden. His opponent was Charles Cowper, a staunch Anglican. The religious issue was raised.

James Macarthur [q.v.], who on principle rejected the contention that a man's religion should, in itself, be a disqualification, threw his weight behind Therry who was elected. He vacated his seat in January 1845 but returned to the legislature in May 1856 as a nominee member of the first Legislative Council under responsible government.

In December 1844 he was appointed resident judge at Port Phillip. There he administered justice with the goodwill of Superintendent La Trobe, the legal profession and the public until February 1846 when he was transferred to the Supreme Court of New South Wales. In 1850 he presided at the first sitting of the Supreme Court, on circuit, at Brisbane. He was the primary judge in Equity, and no decree of his in that jurisdiction was reversed. When the Supreme Court sat *in banco* he occupied the bench with Alfred Stephen and John Nodes Dickinson, both sound lawyers, and was frequently content to concur in their judgments.

Each of the three governors under whom Therry served before his elevation to the bench commended him to the Colonial Office. 'He has on all occasions since his arrival', reported Governor Darling, 'conducted himself in a manner to merit the approbation of this Government'. Governor Bourke described him as 'a barrister of character . . . whose zeal and ability in forwarding the views of His Majesty's and of the local Government entitle the fullest consideration'. 'During the time that I have held the Government', wrote Gipps in 1838, 'I have had ample cause to form a very favorable opinion of his discretion and ability'. This, apparently, was also the opinion of men of commerce, for late in 1834, Therry was elected to the first board of directors of the Commercial Banking Co. of Sydney.

In Gipps's rating, Roger Therry and J. H. Plunkett [q.v.] were 'the two most distinguished barristers' then in the colony. They were also the two outstanding Catholic laymen. 'The circumstance of Mr. Plunkett and Mr. Therry being both Roman Catholics', reported the governor, 'has, without any undue bias on the part of the Government, necessarily, on more than one occasion, proved disadvantageous to the professional advancement of the latter'.

According to the Catholic historian, J. G. Murtagh, 'Therry found the Catholics of the Colony in a sad plight . . . During the first thirty years, [they] formed a quarter of the population, but their religion was unrecognised and their spiritual needs unprovided for'. In May 1820, however, John Joseph Therry [q.v.] arrived as one of two Catholic chaplains. In him his co-religionists found a devoted and indomitable missionary and General Darling an uncompromising stickler for their claims to religious freedom. Roger Therry was his close friend and exerted himself on his behalf in influential quarters.

In January 1830, to remove any doubts as to the application to New South Wales of the British Catholic Emancipation Act of 1829, it was adopted by the local Act 10 Geo. IV, no 9. During the next decade Roger Therry was assisted in his campaign for the more equitable treatment of his co-religionists by men of the calibre of J. H. Plunkett, Vicar-General Ullathorne, Father McEncroe, Bishop Polding and W. A. Duncan [qq.v.], editor of the *Australasian Chronicle*. His most formidable antagonist was Archdeacon Broughton [q.v.] whose denunciation of subscriptions by Protestants to the building of a Catholic chapel evoked, in 1833, a letter from Therry to Edward Blount, M.P., for which he was admonished by the Colonial Office. He may have been indiscreet but his protest did him credit. Bourke's Church Act of 1836, 7 Wm IV, no 3, and his plan for undenominational public schools embodied principles that Therry espoused. His regard for the governor bordered on idolatry, and he was the secretary of the movement which resulted in the erection of an arresting monument in recognition of Bourke's services.

Therry never hid his light under a bushel and the energy and success with which he pressed his advancement exposed him to charges of pluralism and cupidity. Furthermore, as counsel, now for the defence, now for the prosecution, in several inflamed cases, and as an eloquent advocate in matters highly controversial, he incurred the bitter enmity of some of his opponents. Two of these, James Mudie and Richard Jones [qq.v.], encompassed his defeat when, in 1835, he sought election, by the benches of magistrates, to the chairmanship of the Courts of Quarter Sessions. The success of the other candidate, C. D. Riddell [q.v.], the colonial treasurer, and the support given the latter by the Colonial Office led to Bourke's resignation.

When he resigned his judgeship in 1859, Therry retired to England. There in February 1863 he published his *Reminiscences of Thirty Years' Residence in New South Wales and Victoria*. The edition was limited to a thousand copies, three hundred of which were sent to Sydney. In the United Kingdom the reviews of the book were so favourable and the demand for it so insistent that the publisher suggested a second edition. This was published in April 1863. In it Therry corrected the most egregious, but by no means all the factual errors that blemished the first, and added a few pages and a map. By October 1863, however, he heard that his book had been so adversely criticized in New South Wales that it had become unsaleable in Sydney. Thereupon he arranged with his publisher for the return of all the unsold copies there. 'The best evidence I could afford that I had no intention at least of awakening painful feelings', he remarked on 25 March 1865, 'is that I suppressed the book when I learned that I had done so. The cost was no serious inconvenience to me and annoyed me less than the lesson I have learned of the valuelessness of some friendships on which I had relied'.

The *Reminiscences*, or vetted recollections, should be read in conjunction with Therry's letters from 1851 to 1866 to James Macarthur, who contributed material for the book and helped in the correction of the first edition. In this correspondence is to be found *inter alia* the explanation of Therry's misleading account of the Rum Rebellion and of Hannibal Macarthur's [q.v.] part in the case of Henry Bayne, and of his own silence in respect of Gipps's relations with Robert Lowe [q.v.]. Factually, even the second edition has to be corrected again and again: names and dates are awry. Yet, as a descriptive narrative of places, natives, dramatis personae and events, it is a very readable, useful piece of work devoid of rancour and disclosing deep human sympathies.

Therry was always politically minded, and, as a member of the several Legislative Councils, he was in close touch with leading men and measures in an exciting period of Australian history. His deep and active interest in the promotion of education at all levels was lifelong. On 24 December 1850 Sir Charles FitzRoy, with the advice of the Executive Council, nominated and appointed him one of the sixteen original members of the senate of the University of Sydney. His intense hostility to voting by ballot, manhood suffrage and E. G. Wakefield's [q.v.] views on the upset price for crown land were shared by many eminent men of his generation.

Therry was knighted in 1869 and died at Bath in May 1874. Of his children, a son became a captain in the army in India, one daughter married a British naval officer and another entered Subiaco Convent.

HRA (1), 14-25; J. D. Lang, *An historical and statistical account of New South Wales*, 3rd ed, 1-2 (Lond, 1852); J. G. Legge (ed), *A selection of Supreme Court cases in New South Wales, from 1825 to 1862*, 1-2 (Syd, 1896); J. G. Murtagh, *Australia: the Catholic*

chapter, 2nd ed (Syd, 1959); Diary of Thomas Callaghan, 1838-1845 (RAHS Lib, Syd); Macarthur papers, v 34 (ML); MS cat under R. Therry (ML).

C. H. CURREY

THOMAS, DAVID JOHN (1813-1871), medical practitioner, was born on 13 September 1813 near Llangadock in Carmarthenshire, Wales, the eldest son of seven children of William and Ann Thomas. After an apprenticeship at Swansea Infirmary and further medical studies at University College Hospital, London, notably under Robert Liston, he became a licentiate of the Society of Apothecaries and a member of the Royal College of Surgeons in 1838. After a short period as house surgeon to the Royal Lying-In Hospital, Golden Square, he signed on as ship's surgeon in the *Louisa Campbell*, commanded by an old school friend, Captain Buckley, for the round trip to Van Diemen's Land.

After leaving Launceston the ship called at Port Phillip in January 1839. Thomas's arrival was as unconventional as were many of his later escapades and numerous practical jokes in the colony; he swam ashore from a swamped boat, walked six miles through the bush in the dark to a hut, was attacked by a watchdog, and escaped in a boat down the river to arrive at 'Fawkner's Pub, where no doubt his troubles ended'. Thomas was prevailed upon to leave the ship and begin practice in Port Phillip, then a settlement of about 2000 people with four or five doctors already established. That year Dr Farquhar McCrae arrived at Port Phillip with members of his family, and in December 1840 his sister, Margaret Forbes, was married to Thomas, who also entered into partnership with McCrae. Thomas was a member of the staff of the Melbourne Hospital, or its precursors, from its beginnings in 1841, and was the first surgeon in Victoria to perform a variety of operations, notably for arterial aneurysms, and including perhaps the first deliberate laparotomy for an intestinal tumour in Australia. His greatest achievement, requiring initiative and courage in so isolated a community, was to introduce ether anaesthesia to Victoria on 2 August 1847, less than a year after its discovery in America; he painlessly amputated the forearm of a shocked patient in forty seconds, two minutes after the ether inhalation had been commenced. The patient had travelled a hundred miles in three days after a shooting accident, and four weeks later rode back unaided. In reporting his experiences with ether in September 1847 to the Port Phillip Medical Association, of which he was a foundation member in 1846 and sometime committeeman and vice-president, he showed an awareness of its value which was not shared by many of his contemporaries both in Australia and abroad, referring to it 'as one of the greatest blessings bestowed on mankind', the use of which would in due course become general. The manuscript of this paper, the third presented to the association, was prepared for publication in the *Australian Medical Journal*, but as this journal became defunct it remained unpublished until 1934 when the manuscript was brought to light. Thomas also claimed to have been the first to use chloroform in Melbourne. In 1850, after McCrae's departure for Sydney, Thomas entered into partnership with Edward Barker, who represented the firm on the goldfields.

In 1853 Thomas sold his home and furniture and went with his family to England, accompanied by a testimonial and public expression of goodwill and regret. He took his doctorate in medicine by examination at the University of St Andrews, Scotland, obtained the fellowship of the Royal College of Surgeons, London, and studied surgery, anatomy and microscopy at the principal medical centres in Britain and on the Continent, where his work was highly commended. On his return in 1859 Thomas, always casual about income and expenditure, found himself in financial difficulties after the general fall in land values. These problems, accentuated by the need to re-establish his practice after a long absence in the face of increased and sometimes unethical competition, culminated in his bankruptcy in 1864. None the less, he succeeded in once more becoming the leader of the profession, for in the same year he was elected president of the Medical Society of Victoria. Ultimately he was compelled by pressure of work to limit his practice to surgery, of which he was a deft and able exponent. In 1860 he had been re-elected to the staff of the Melbourne Hospital at the top of the poll, and in 1865 he was chairman of staff. He was appointed examiner in anatomy and physiology at the newly established medical school in the University of Melbourne in 1862, receiving its doctorate of medicine *ad eundem gradum*. Among other appointments, he was an official visitor to the Kew Asylum, honorary physician to the Deaf and Dumb Institute, and member of the Medical Board of Victoria, as he had been before his departure overseas. An ardent Welshman, he was president of the annual Ballarat Eisteddfod in 1867. He

contributed over forty papers, mostly case reports, to the *Australian Medical Journal*, of which the most important was his valedictory address in 1865 as president of the Medical Society of Victoria. Thomas was a small man of boundless energy and good humour, partial to a good dinner and a convivial gathering, but no less afraid of controversy, 'a delightful combination of Puck, Peter Pan, Fluellen'. Never averse to a wager, he was a keen follower of horse-racing, and was himself noted for his horsemanship. Thomas's leadership of the medical profession in two different eras of the colony's history was recognized by his colleagues in 1869 when he was presented with a signed testimonial, illuminated on vellum, by the Medical Society of Victoria. On 1 June 1871 he died of a 'stroke', after several premonitory episodes, at 58, and it is perhaps characteristic that he should die not only poor but intestate. He was survived by a wife and four daughters. Two sisters and his youngest brother Charles migrated to Port Phillip in 1840; Charles Thomas's recollections of his childhood and family and of his pastoral ventures include some references to his brother. D. J. Thomas is sometimes confused with J. Davies Thomas, who practised chiefly in Adelaide and who also wrote on anaesthesia.

Garryowen (E. Finn), *The chronicles of early Melbourne*, 1-2 (Melb, 1888); H. McCrae (ed), *Georgiana's journal* (Syd, 1934); D. M. O'Sullivan, 'David John Thomas', MJA, 30 June 1956 and for bibliog; C. Thomas, Reminiscences (Museum of Medical Soc, Vic).

BRYAN GANDEVIA

THOMAS, EVAN HENRY (1801?-1837), editor and lawyer, was born in Antrim, Ireland. He arrived in Hobart Town in August 1822 in the *William Shand*. His first year was spent variously as teacher, as an agent to assist clients through minor legal difficulties, as a dealer in property, as an innkeeper and as a pastry manufacturer. His poems, a 'Sonnet', unsigned, and 'The emigrant', by E. H. T., in the *Hobart Town Gazette*, 12 and 19 October 1822, were the first to appear in print in Van Diemen's Land.

In June 1824 Andrew Bent [q.v.] appointed Thomas editor of the *Hobart Town Gazette* without the sanction of Lieut-Governor Arthur. Thomas's editorials expounded his ideals of a free press and of a colony of free settlers instead of convicts. When Arthur claimed that the *Hobart Town Gazette* was government property Thomas was sent to Sydney to represent Bent before Governor Brisbane. Brisbane's verdict was in favour of Bent. On his return to Hobart, Thomas's editorial on 8 October 1824, known as the Gideonite article, openly criticized the government. The attorney-general, J. T. Gellibrand [q.v.], declared this article libellous, but for six months Arthur delayed proceedings against Bent as proprietor of the newspaper. When the trial took place in July and August 1825, Thomas had already resigned as editor of the *Gazette*. When called as a witness he affirmed full responsibility for the Gideonite article and other editorials, but Bent was found guilty by the military jury.

The Albion Hotel, which belonged to his wife before her marriage, was sold in May 1827, and Thomas moved with his family to Launceston where he became a commission agent and auctioneer at the Albion mart. He visited England between March 1830 and June 1831 to settle his share in an inherited estate and on his return to Launceston announced his appointment as a notary public and conveyancer for Van Diemen's Land and New South Wales. He practised as an attorney before the bench of magistrates and at the Quarter Sessions in Launceston.

Thomas supported the Launceston amateur dramatic association and on 14 October 1835 the Cameron company successfully produced his three-act play the *Bandit of the Rhine* in the Launceston theatre. This was the first original single play to be wholly written and published in Australia, although no copies of the publication have survived. The play was staged in the Theatre Royal, Hobart, on 22 October 1836. Thomas planned another romantic play, the 'Rose of the Wilderness, or Emily the Maniac', but it was never written. While in Launceston Thomas took little part in politics. As editor of the *Hobart Town Gazette* he encouraged literary writings although his own poems were neither distinctive nor inspiring. His prose works were more successful. It has been suggested that Thomas was connected with the satire *The Van Diemen's Land Warriors* . . . written anonymously by Pindar Juvenal and printed by Bent in 1827.

Thomas died on 26 December 1837 aged 36 and was buried in the old Cyprus Street cemetery, Launceston. In May 1823 he had married Sarah, née Divine, the widow, first of William Wilson, and then of Richard Wallis, licensee of the Cat and Fiddle Hotel, Hobart. A daughter was born in March 1824, and a son, James Montgomery, in July 1828.

R. W. Giblin, *The early history of Tasmania*, 2 (Lond, 1939); E. M. Miller, *Press-men and governors* (Syd, 1952); *Hobart Town Gazette*, 24 Aug, 23 Nov, 21 Dec 1822, 10 May, 6 Sept 1823, 18 June, 2 July 1825, 18 Nov 1826; *Colonial Times*, 24 Mar 1826, 6 Dec 1828; *Cornwall Chronicle*, 8 Aug, 3, 17 Oct 1835; *Bent's News*, 30 Dec 1837; CSO 1/170/4096, 1/190/4523 (TA).   E. FLINN

THOMAS, JOCELYN HENRY CONNOR (1780-1862), public servant and landowner, and BARTHOLOMEW BOYLE (1785?-1831), soldier and settler, were the sons of Rev. Bartholomew Thomas, D.D., rector of Cloydagh and squire of Everton, Queen's County, Ireland, and his wife Anna Jocelyn, née Davidson. Jocelyn was educated at Eton, and so probably was Bartholomew; both certainly went to Trinity College, Dublin.

Bartholomew entered the army as a cornet in the 17th Light Dragoons on 13 June 1805, transferred as a lieutenant to the 9th Light Dragoons on 26 May 1809, and was later in the 100th Regiment, the 4th Garrison Battalion, and finally the 18th Regiment, from which he resigned by sale of his commission in 1814. He later served under Bolivar in South America. He married in 1811; his wife's name was Louisa, and they had no children. When Bartholomew's youngest sister Marianne Burrell died, Louisa mothered her four young children.

Jocelyn was married on 11 April 1808 to Charlotte, daughter of Henry Partridge, chief justice of Ely. In Ireland he became agent for the estates of Lord Stanhope and Lady Portarlington. In 1813 Jocelyn in association with his brother and others leased 'the entire slobs in the harbour of Wexford' for the purpose of reclaiming 1100 acres from the sea, but 'on the eve of completion an unprecedented high tide destroyed in one hour the labour of more than seven years' with a loss of £40,000. He felt it better to be elsewhere while poor, so after a short time in France he emigrated to Van Diemen's Land with his wife and seven children, three servants and their two children; they arrived in the *Derwent* on 2 February 1824.

Jocelyn first accepted without inspection a grant of 1000 acres on the South Esk River south of Snake Banks (Powranna), but finding the clear land subject to flood he made a deal with Donald Campbell for 500 acres near Evandale with a house on it, and named it Everton. His son Bartholomew William was granted 500 acres on the South Esk. This became Milford. Jocelyn later acquired several blocks to the east of Milford till his holdings there totalled about 8000 acres when sold in 1833.

Eight months after arrival Jocelyn was appointed acting colonial treasurer by Lieut-Governor Arthur, and the appointment was confirmed on 4 July 1825. The duties included receiving moneys once a quarter from the collector of customs, W. H. Hamilton [q.v.]. The two new officers quickly increased the collections from customs, earning Arthur's praise but displeasing merchants and others who preferred 'the convenience' of Dr Bromley's [q.v.] earlier methods. However, Earl Bathurst disallowed Arthur's selection of Hamilton, and instead appointed a quite unqualified man, Rolla O'Ferrall.

When Van Diemen's Land became independent of New South Wales and acquired an Executive Council Jocelyn became one of its five members. His experience as magistrate and agent in Ireland and his 'air of authority', combined with a pleasing manner of speech, doubtless contributed to his fitness for this position. His home was Roseway Lodge, a property of some ten acres on New Town Rivulet, three miles out of Hobart Town. There two more daughters were born.

The two brothers met again when Bartholomew arrived at Hobart in the *Albion* on 3 May 1826. He brought with him men, livestock, machinery and stores for the New South Wales and Van Diemen's Land Establishment, a partnership formed in England in 1825 by Thomas and five others, with an initial capital of £24,000. On the voyage more than half the horses and many of the cattle and sheep died.

More loss soon followed. Bartholomew went on to Sydney in the *Albion* on 27 May, having accepted Arthur's location of land in Van Diemen's Land on the Ringarooma River, and arranged for his establishment, under Henry Widowson, to proceed there in the schooner *Sally*. The little ship was wrecked near its destination on the night of 30 June 1826 with the loss of thirteen lives and much of the company's machinery and stores, which were not insured.

He returned from Sydney eleven days later. The Ringarooma location was given up but a grant of 10,000 acres was soon secured, with a reservation of a further similar area, and a farm with some buildings bought all together in one block on the west side of the Lake River. He named the place Cressy, after the battlefield where his ancestor had been created Knight Banneret. The partnership became known as the Cressy Co. or Horse Breeding Co.

The report of 13 August 1827 to the colonial secretary, J. Burnett [q.v.], of operations at Cressy for about ten months records impressive achievement in developing the holding, but financial matters and accountancy were neglected or ignored and became the subject of action by the sheriff. 'Relying on information that later turned out to be inaccurate, the home directors dissolved their partnership with B. B. Thomas', by a press notice, 28 June 1828. Lieutenant Thomas Dutton, R.N., succeeded as manager.

Bartholomew became the 'first settler in Devon' by taking over from absentee owners two adjacent locations west of Port Sorell totalling 2200 acres, with financial help from Jocelyn. In his three years there he achieved a notable success by establishing friendly relations with the local tribes, while over most of the island there were frequent killings of whites by the dispossessed blacks. In company with his 'faithful friend' and overseer, Parker, he was speared to death by a hostile tribe from the south on 31 August 1831. Jocelyn became the owner of North Down, his brother's property at Port Sorell. Bartholomew's widow died at Stoke Damerel, Devon, England, on 12 April 1862.

During the late 1820s Jocelyn had been worried about his financial position, having borrowed too deeply in order to buy land. The situation exploded when a snap audit on 23 October 1832 disclosed a serious shortage in the Treasury chest. It was first estimated at £7112 6s. 1d., but in 1834 the official finding was £10,627 10s. 5¼d., a figure which Jocelyn disputed, claiming that actual receipts were less than the warrants issued. He admitted a shortage but not misappropriation, and asserted that there had been frequent robberies, most of which he had not reported because he had found it was useless to do so unless he could name the suspects. This, understandably, was not accepted as a valid explanation. He was dismissed from office, as also was O'Ferrall, as evidence of collusion between them emerged. The event made Jocelyn Thomas, first colonial treasurer, a controversial figure in history. According to John West [q.v.] 'It appeared that capital had been borrowed from the chest without authority to the amount of several thousand pounds. The money was, however, restored. No public care could restrain these funds from their tendency to escape'.

Among the many baffling features of the episode is the record of persistent but vain efforts by Jocelyn and his friends to have the circumstances of his dismissal re-examined judicially, and the confidence with which Jocelyn expected that such an inquiry would 'give me back my reputation', a reputation that had caused Lord Stanhope to declare: 'His character is irreproachable', and others to write in similar vein. There is also reason for conjecture as to the full extent of O'Ferrall's collusion, because of his later fraud in forging deeds to property. All Jocelyn's properties were sold to satisfy private creditors as well as the Crown, and he retired to his son's home, Milford, and later to North Down, which the sons had managed to buy.

Jocelyn's downfall arose from his passion for buying land, and earlier for reclaiming it, a passion probably based on a genuine love of the land. In Ireland he had been 'universally beloved'. Tradition has it that he was a good host and enjoyed company. Henry Savery [q.v.], a contemporary chronicler, portrayed him with 'a hurried quickness in his manner, a sort of absentism . . . a little of the brogue in his style of language'. A granddaughter remembered him walking 'very erect' in the garden at North Down, where he and Charlotte ended their days, he on 7 April 1862, she on 13 November 1873; by then they had more than forty grandchildren.

The two brothers were alike in showing an unwise disregard for risk, one in Wexford Harbour, the other when he walked to his death; both were born and married to wealth, failed to conserve it, and again failed to cope with a strange colonial environment. Bartholomew was imaginative, impulsive and altruistic, and Savery and others indicate that he was generous and likeable in many ways. Physically he was 'uncommonly active'. He was one of those enterprising pioneers whose successors derive the benefit of their labours; his brain-child the Cressy Co. returned good capital gain to its shareholders in the 1850s and the bulk of his North Down property still remains in the hands of Jocelyn's descendants.

HRA (3), 5, 6; J. West, *The history of Tasmania*, 1-2 (Launceston, 1852); R. W. Giblin, *The early history of Tasmania*, 2 (Melb, 1939); H. Savery, *The hermit in Van Diemen's Land*, eds C. Hadgraft and Margriet Roe (Brisb, 1964); *Hobart Town Gazette*, 22 July 1826, 28 June 1828; CSO 1/282 (TA); Arthur papers (ML); Family papers (in author's possession).   H. R. THOMAS

THOMAS, WILLIAM (1793-1867), assistant protector and guardian of Aboriginals, was born in Westminster, England, of Welsh parents. His father and brother were army officers. His education was rounded off by a year on the Continent, mainly in Spain, but details of his upbringing are obscure. He opened a school in the Old Kent Road, London, for teaching potential civil servants. In this capacity, and possibly also because of his Wesleyan beliefs, he met members of the post-Reform Act government.

The humanitarian recommendations of the 1837 select committee on Aboriginals resulted in Glenelg's decision to appoint a chief protector and four assistants for the Aboriginals of the Port Phillip District. He offered an assistantship to Thomas at a salary of £250, with a free passage for his wife Susannah, née Jackson, and family. His acceptance of this task at the age of 44 reflects his dedication and zeal. However, he stipulated that his appointment should rank him as a permanent servant of the British and not of a colonial government.

The family reached Sydney on 3 August 1838 and arrived in Melbourne later that year. The chief protector, G. A. Robinson [q.v.], allocated the Port Phillip, Westernport and Gippsland districts to Thomas, who entered the field during April 1839 and soon established his base at Narre Warren. Years of privation followed during which Thomas moved with Aboriginal groups, rarely seeing his family, whose own housing was also primitive.

His early expectations of a rapid enlightenment of the natives were soon dispelled but, unlike most other protectors, he persisted. When hopes of civilizing the Aboriginals faded, he concentrated on the practical tasks of keeping them alive, shepherding them away from the temptations of city life and maintaining harmony between black and white. His task was hindered by Robinson who failed to support him in many disputes with settlers, bombarded him with excessive paper work, and was dilatory in getting him a field allowance. As he was housed in a tent and moved around with the Aboriginals, it is little wonder that some of his replies to Robinson were terse. Despite difficulties Thomas kept a detailed diary and made various notes for a projected book which never eventuated partly because he lost many of his notes around 1844. He wrote long memoranda on Aboriginal society for Robinson, Lieut-Governor La Trobe and Judge Barry; his data and ethnographic collections were basic sources for R. Brough Smyth's *Aborigines of Victoria*, 1-2 (London, 1878).

The protectorate was terminated in 1849, but La Trobe retained Thomas as guardian in the Counties of Bourke, Mornington and Evelyn from January 1850. His presence ensured some protection during the next decade, although expenditure was minimal. Until his death he was chief government adviser on Aboriginal affairs and was the most influential witness at the 1858-59 select committee of the Legislative Council on Aborigines. His recommendation to establish reserves and supply depots throughout Victoria was accepted in a modified form and in 1860 became the policy implemented by the new Central Board for the Protection of Aborigines. Thomas was designated the official visitor to supervise the work of all stations and depots but after a tour of Gippsland in 1860 his health failed. Later he acted as adviser and as a justice of the peace on suburban benches. Failing eyesight caused his retirement from active duties two months before his death on 1 December 1867 at his home, Merri Ville Lodge, Brunswick. He was survived by three of his nine children.

With no gifts of leadership or strong personality, Thomas was overshadowed by Robinson in the 1840s. His anthropological knowledge was gained through experience, and his understanding of tribal complexity and spiritual bonds was thereby limited. However, he was more successful than any other first generation settler in attempting to comprehend and sustain Aboriginal society. His charges knew him as Marminata (Good Father), and he always administered indirectly through influence on their leaders. He had striking success in settling intertribal disputes and preventing racial strife. His bravery and moral conviction were undoubted, but his advocacy of Aboriginal causes made him unpopular in colonial society. Richard Howitt, who befriended him in 1842, commented upon the 'almost childlike simplicity of manners and . . . his goodness of heart'.

T. F. Bride (ed), *Letters from Victorian pioneers* (Melb, 1898); E. J. B. Foxcroft, *Australian native policy: its history, especially in Victoria* (Melb, 1941); W. Thomas papers (ML and La Trobe Lib, Melb).

D. J. MULVANEY

THOMPSON, ANDREW (1773?-1810), chief constable, farmer and businessman, was baptized on 7 February 1773 at Kirk Yetholm, Scotland, the youngest of six children of John Thompson, weaver, manufacturer and dyer, and his wife Agnes, née Hilson. Educated at the parochial school, he entered his father's business until a breakdown in health forced him to leave and study for the excise. With a friend he became involved in the theft of about £10 worth of cloth from the shop of a local merchant; he pleaded guilty at his trial at Jedburgh in 1790, but was probably the less guilty party. He was sentenced to fourteen years transportation and arrived in Sydney in the *Pitt* in February 1792.

After a year in the men's provision store he joined the police force in 1793 and served with distinction at Toongabbie and other centres. In 1796 Governor Hunter appointed him to the Green Hills (Windsor), the main settlement on the Hawkesbury River, where he remained for the rest of his life. He was pardoned in 1798 and built his home overlooking the river on an acre leased from the government. He rose quickly to the position of chief constable and held that office until 1808, during which time he distinguished himself by investigating crimes, capturing runaway convicts, acting as intermediary between whites and blacks and rescuing settlers from disastrous floods. Hunter appointed him to the responsible position of grain assessor in 1799, and the settlers elected him as trustee of the common lands in the district.

As he carried out his constabulary duties Thompson gradually accumulated land by both purchase and grant. He bought the farms West Hill (the Red House), Glasgow, Wardle Bank and Moxham's Farms, and Governor King granted him Agnes Bank and Killarney, totalling 918 acres altogether. He rented them to suitable tenants. At his home on the river Thompson, with the aid of an English agent, John Braddick, established a general store and later an inn which became the commercial centre of the Hawkesbury. Near by on the South Creek he built the first toll bridge in 1802. King supplied convict labour to help him and then gave him a lease of the tolls until 1820. In 1804 King helped him to set up a salt manufacturing plant in Broken Bay. The first site was Mullet Island but Thompson later moved it to Scotland Island. Because of Thompson's outstanding work in the floods of 1806 King allowed him to establish a brewery on South Creek. In addition Thompson controlled a barge for ferrying passengers and stock across the river, and at the Red House he established a tannery.

Over the same period to 1808, Thompson built four ships: *Nancy, Hope, Hawkesbury* and *Governor Bligh*. He also bought the *Speedwell* from Captain Grono. These ships carried grain, fruit and vegetables to Sydney, transported convicts to the Hunter River and returned with cargoes of cedar and coal; they made sealing voyages to Bass Strait and New Zealand and traded with Tahiti for pork. The *Nancy* placed Thompson's name on the map of the South Island of New Zealand.

When Governor Bligh arrived in 1806 Thompson was the largest grain grower and the wealthiest settler in the colony. As the economy of the colony was based on grain there was great significance in the claim which John Macarthur [q.v.] made on Thompson for £341 10s. based on a note of hand for ninety-nine bushels of wheat and valued before the 1806 floods at £34 10s. Macarthur claimed the grain at the inflated price and lost the case. A later appeal to Bligh was dismissed.

Bligh bought two farms on the Hawkesbury and appointed Thompson to develop them as model farms, to encourage the settlers to follow his example. Bligh supplied convict labour and Thompson appointed the overseer. Thompson forwarded monthly accounts to Bligh and these reports showed that Bligh was using government stock and that Thompson was placing the grain in the stores under his own name. There was a break in their friendship in 1808 when Thompson was fined £100 for misusing a puncheon of rum entrusted by Bligh to his care for distribution to the settlers. Bligh was arrested soon afterwards and the rebels seized Thompson's accounts of the model farm and sent them to London as alleged proof of Bligh's intention to rob the government, but at the court martial of Lieut-Colonel Johnston [q.v.] in London in 1811 the accounts were not produced as evidence against the ex-governor.

Under the rebel régime Thompson continued to prosper. He was dismissed from his position as chief constable and for the next two years devoted himself to his own concerns. Lieut-Governor Foveaux [q.v] gave him a town grant in Macquarie Place where he built a gentleman's town house which was later to be occupied by Ellis Bent [q.v.]. After the devastating floods of 1809 Lieut-Governor Paterson [q.v.] rewarded him with a 1000-acre grant at Minto which he named St Andrew's. Previous leases of land on which he had erected his brewery and salt works were converted into grants. All these grants were later approved by Governor Macquarie.

When Macquarie arrived in 1810 Thompson was in poor health as a result of effects of cold and immersion in the 1809 floods. However, Macquarie restored him to favour and appointed him magistrate at the Green Hills, the first emancipist to be appointed to such a position.

Thompson, Simeon Lord and Samuel Marsden [qq.v.] were then appointed trustees of the new turnpike road between Parramatta and the Hawkesbury, but Marsden refused to act with them on the grounds that they were immoral, thus striking the first blow in the fight against Macquarie's emancipist policy. Thompson's health declined rapidly and he died, still a bachelor, at his home on 22 October 1810, Macquarie's 'worthy and highly esteemed good friend . . . from whose superior local knowledge and good sound sense and the judicious advice', the governor had hoped to 'derive great benefit and advantage'. Thompson left a quarter of his real and personal estate to Macquarie, who estimated that his share would be about £5000. Captain Antill [q.v.] was appointed executor, together with Thomas Moore [q.v.]. Antill selected the site for Thompson's grave and the burial took place according to the Church of England rites.

Thompson's estate was managed by his executors until it became apparent that none of his Scottish legatees intended to claim a share. The buildings at his home on the Hawkesbury River were bought by the government. The granary was bought for £1500, and the brewery, after causing a quarrel with George Palmer [q.v.], was converted into a hospital. Alexander Riley and Richard Jones [qq.v.] gave evidence about the administration of the Thompson estate in London in 1819, and Commissioner Bigge [q.v.] made Thompson and his estate one of the chief subjects of his investigation of Macquarie's administration. Thompson's elevation to the magistracy was a feature of his report, whilst Bigge's conclusions about the administration of the estate were sent to Bathurst in a private letter on 7 February 1823. The executors' accounts have not come to light.

Thompson's life and work in New South Wales and the administration of his estate illuminate many aspects of life in early Australian history. His swift rise to wealth illustrates the government attitude towards emancipists from the beginning; his activities prove the importance of grain as a basis of the economy until it was replaced by wool; his enterprises show him to have been a powerful influence in the development of industry and commerce; his association with Bligh points to the exceptional prosperity of Bligh's farm as one important reason for Bligh's arrest; whilst his appointment to the magistracy became a lever for Macquarie's enemies in their attempts to have the governor removed.

HRNSW, 3-7; HRA (1), 2-7; J. V. Byrnes, 'Andrew Thompson', JRAHS, 48 (1962-63), and for bibliog; J. V. Byrnes, The life and times of Andrew Thompson (M.A. thesis, Univ Syd, 1958).

J. V. BYRNES

THOMPSON, RICHARD (1810-1865), journalist, born in England and baptized William Fane, was sentenced to transportation to New South Wales for fourteen years for the theft of some silver spoons. On arrival in June 1834 he was employed by the government at Port Macquarie; in 1840 he received a ticket-of-leave and two years later a conditional pardon. While at Port Macquarie he published a brief account of the geography and geology of north-eastern Australia and tried unsuccessfully to set up a beef-salting plant. In 1842-43 he worked on newspapers in the Port Phillip district, and in 1843 moved to Sydney where he served on the staff of the *Australian*. In November 1844, when Robert Lowe [q.v.] undertook the publication of the *Atlas* on behalf of the squatters, Thompson was named editor, a title he held until March 1845 when a difference of opinion with the actual editor, Lowe, brought about his resignation. In 1846 Benjamin Boyd and J. P. Robinson [qq.v.] decided that the squatters needed a new medium of propaganda and, with the help of William Bland [q.v.], established another weekly, the *Spectator*, of which Thompson was made editor. At the end of the year, when the squatters' demands had been fulfilled by the British government, publication of the *Spectator* ceased. In 1847 Boyd bought a controlling interest in the *Australian* and installed Thompson as managing editor. With the collapse of Boyd's fortunes in 1848 the *Australian* ceased, and Thompson's career as a journalist seems to have foundered. In 1856 he edited the *Report of the Proceedings at the National Banquet . . . to celebrate the Establishment and Inauguration of Responsible Government in the Colony of New South Wales*.

Thompson dabbled in the theatre in Sydney, furnishing scripts, translating librettos, and acting as critic. The pages of the publications which he edited reveal him as a skilful though unoriginal poet and an able editor. On 5 November 1846 he married Mary Ann, daughter of Charles Righton, an officer of the East India Co.; a son was born of this marriage in 1847. Thompson died in Sydney in 1865.

SMH, 2 June 1842, 18, 20 Apr 1844, 22 Mar 1845, 6 Jan, 27 Feb, 6, 7 Nov 1846, 14, 19 Apr, 4, 25 Sept 1847, 16 Jan, 25 Aug, 19 Oct 1849, 2 Jan 1850; Colonial Observer, 4 Jan 1843; Duncan's Wkly Register, 17 Feb 1844; Commercial J, 5 Apr-2 Aug 1845; Examiner (Syd), 9 Aug-1 Nov 1845; Atlas, 8 Jan 1848.

R. L. KNIGHT

THOMSON, ADAM COMPTON (1800?-1859), Church of England clergyman, studied at the University of Edinburgh in 1825-26. In 1830 he was master of a grammar school at Wooler, Northumberland, when he was accepted by the Society for the Propagation of the Gospel as a missionary in India, subject to ordination. He was ordained deacon in December 1830 at St James's, Westminster, by Bishop Blomfield of London, and priest in January 1835 at Tanjore, South India, by Bishop Wilson of Calcutta. Thomson was stationed at Tanjore (1831-33), Negapatam (1833-35), Vepery (Madras) from 1836, and in 1838 was headmaster of the Vepery seminary for catechists. In 1839 he went to England because of the illness of his wife Adèle Zélée, whom he had married in South India, and who, according to Georgiana McCrae [q.v.], was a niece of Spengler, the curator of the Stockholm museum.

He did not return to India, but instead in March 1840 was appointed to the ecclesiastical establishment of Van Diemen's Land and intended for Launceston. However, Bishop Broughton [q.v.] sent him in September 1840 to Melbourne to relieve Rev. J. Y. Wilson, locum tenens for the chaplain of St James's. In January 1841 he succeeded as locum and later as incumbent, but not until October 1842 was St James's Church opened for worship, replacing the temporary wooden 'Church of the Pioneers'. Wilson had begun a movement for a second church in Melbourne, but depression in the early 1840s stopped progress and it was May 1847 before St Peter's, Eastern Hill, was opened.

Notwithstanding an increasing population, from June 1842 Thomson was the sole Anglican priest for Melbourne and district. He had to conduct services regularly at St James's and Brighton, visit as far as Geelong, Bacchus Marsh and Seymour, and supervise day and Sunday schools; in 1847 he officiated at 583 baptisms, 142 marriages and 171 burials. In 1844, at the request of Superintendent La Trobe, he began the St James's Visiting Society, whose infirmary was a precursor of the Melbourne Hospital, and as E. Finn [q.v.] records was 'foremost in every work of charity or philanthropy'.

The arrival of Bishop Perry with additional clergy in January 1848 meant little lightening of Thomson's responsibilities. Not surprisingly his health broke down, and in June 1850 he resigned from St James's to accept the rural parish of Windermere in northern Tasmania. In 1853 he moved to Evandale, but after the death of his wife in 1855 he obtained leave and went to England. When he had not returned by 1858 his parish was declared vacant. He died suddenly at Norwood Green, London, on 23 September 1859.

Thomson was generally accounted a gifted preacher and an energetic organizer. He was of an amiable disposition and, in contrast to Bishop Perry, maintained friendly relations with his colleagues, the Roman Catholic, P. B. Geoghegan, and the Presbyterian, J. Forbes [q.v.]. He was criticized as being too plausible and familiar, suspected of Tractarian sympathies, while some took offence at his chronic indebtedness. But in general opinion 'Parson' Thomson, as he was universally styled, was a faithful pastor and a good citizen.

Thomson composed occasional hymns but his only published work was a Tamil translation of W. Marsh's *A Short Catechism on the Collects* (Colchester, 1821), printed at Vepery in 1842.

G. Goodman, *The Church in Victoria during the episcopate of . . . Charles Perry* (Melb, 1892); F. Penny, *The Church in Madras*, 2 (Lond, 1904); S. M. Smith, Church of England origins in Victoria to 1848 (Th. Schol. thesis, Mollison Lib, St Paul's Cathedral, Melb, 1961).   JAMES GRANT

THOMSON, ALEXANDER (1800-1866), medical practitioner and pastoralist, was born at Aberdeen, Scotland, the son of Alexander Thomson, shipowner. After medical training at Aberdeen and London he married Barbara Dalrymple in Aberdeen on 24 March 1824. Next year he made the first of his several voyages to Australia as surgeon in a convict transport. Attracted by the colonies, he chartered the *Auriga* in which he arrived at Hobart Town in December 1831 with his wife and three-year-old daughter Jane. They went on to Sydney but returned next February. On an earlier visit he had applied to Lieut-Governor Arthur for a land grant which he received in 1833 in spite of the changed regulations. Half of his capital of £9000 was in the form of two steam-boats which he imported from Britain. After they were assembled he opened a steam ferry service between Hobart and Kangaroo Point in October 1832.

After a year he sold the service to George Watson and moved to Launceston.

In 1835 Thomson became interested in Port Phillip and sent across early consignments of cattle and sheep. He himself followed in the *Caledonia* in 1836 and settled temporarily near the site of the present St Paul's Cathedral. There he held Sunday services. Lonsdale [q.v.] appointed him medical officer to the settlement at a salary of £200. In 1837 he moved to the Geelong district where he chose land at Kardinia 'at the falls on the Barwon', a spot remembered by J. D. Lang [q.v.] as the home of 'people of cultivated minds and refined taste'. Thomson became one of the leaders of early pastoral society. At Kardinia in 1837 he formally welcomed Governor Bourke on his first visit to the Geelong district. He was active in the early exploration and survey of the area west of Geelong, and is said to have driven the first bullock team from Geelong to Melbourne in spite of the hostility of the Aboriginal tribes around Werribee.

As a prominent member of the Geelong community Thomson was active in several fields. First, he was largely responsible for starting Presbyterian services in the district. These were held in his parlour and then in his woolshed; later he headed the subscribers who petitioned for a minister and for a church at Geelong, the foundation stone of which he laid in 1841. In 1845 he chaired the meeting which inaugurated the Geelong branch of the British and Foreign Bible Society. His enthusiastic Presbyterianism kept him in close touch with his friend Lang, whose radical political views he shared in part.

Second, Thomson was interested in the civic development of Geelong, of which city he was sometimes called the founder. He was the town's first mayor in 1851 and served again in 1855-57. He was a director of the Geelong-Melbourne Railway Co., whose line was completed in 1857. Geelong's first bank, a branch of the Union Bank, was opened in 1842 in a house he rented. The welfare of the Aboriginals in the district also interested him; he helped missionaries in their work with the local tribes, particularly in advising Tuckfield [q.v.] on the location and character of his Buntingdale mission.

Third, Thomson was active in more general colonial affairs. In 1843 he was elected one of the Port Phillip members to the New South Wales Legislative Council, but resigned in 1844 in protest against having to attend the sittings in Sydney. Throughout the 1840s he was prominent in the separation movement.

His views on the labour question like Lang's, did not coincide with those of all his fellow squatters, for he opposed Irish immigration and every form of convict labour, including 'exiles' or 'expirees'. He formed a local organization with a fund to resist transportation, and in 1847 quarrelled bitterly with his friend George Russell [q.v.] over the question, using language that was 'more uncompromising than prudent'. Thomson also differed from the squatters when he was elected for Geelong to the Victorian Legislative Council in 1852-54 and to the Legislative Assembly in 1857-59. As an urban liberal, he was appointed to the select committee that in 1853 drafted the Constitution bill. He followed it to Europe and at Vienna won a promise from Lord John Russell that the bill would receive early attention by parliament.

In March 1844 Thomson had found himself in financial difficulties through speculation, but he recovered and increased his holdings to 150,000 acres. Towards the end of his life he was again nearly penniless and had to accept appointment as medical officer at the Sunbury Boys' Home. This setback, according to the *Australian Medical Journal*, was due to his disregard of 'the prevailing rule of looking well to his own interests before endeavouring to promote those of his fellow creatures'.

His popularity still remained; like his old horse, Creamy, he had become an institution in the Geelong district and on the Melbourne road. When he died on New Year's Day 1866 many mourners, representing most public groups, attended his funeral. He was buried in the old Geelong cemetery.

Garryowen (E. Finn), *The chronicles of early Melbourne*, 1-2 (Melb, 1888); T. F. Bride (ed), *Letters from Victorian pioneers* (Melb, 1898); H. G. Turner, *A history of the colony of Victoria*, 1-2 (Lond, 1904); R. H. Croll and R. R. Wettenhall, *Dr. Alexander Thomson: a pioneer of Melbourne and founder of Geelong* (Melb, 1937); A. D. Gilchrist (ed), *John Dunmore Lang*, 1-2 (Melb, 1951); P. L. Brown (ed), *Clyde Company papers*, 2-5, (Lond, 1952-63).

LYNDSAY GARDINER

THOMSON, SIR EDWARD DEAS (1800-1879), public servant and parliamentarian, was born on 1 June 1800 in Edinburgh, the youngest son of Sir John Deas Thomson, sometime accountant-general of the navy, and his wife Rebecca, the daughter of John Freer of South Carolina. He was educated at Edinburgh High School and at Harrow, and for two years at a college at Caen, Normandy, where he gained a facility in French which he kept throughout his life. Thomson returned to London to become a clerk in the firm of Inglis, Forbes & Co. He assisted his father in the Navy Office in a variety of ways, including the introduction of double entry book-keeping. He also attended lectures on political economy by the Scottish writer, J. R. McCulloch, whose ideas on free trade were important in forming Thomson's attitude to the question.

Late in 1826 Thomson went to the United States to attend to business arising out of his mother's death in South Carolina. He travelled widely in the United States and Canada and did not return to England until the autumn of 1827. At his father's request he kept a detailed journal on matters concerning the United States navy and army, as well as on affairs of more general interest. His detailed and perceptive comments were circulated by his father among influential acquaintances in London, including Huskisson, with a view to advancing Thomson's career. An attempt to have him appointed British consul in New York failed, but later he was appointed registrar of the Orphan Chambers in Demerara, West Indies, at a salary of £900. In May 1828 his appointment was altered to clerk of the council in New South Wales, largely through the patronage of Huskisson who thought the condition of New South Wales demanded that the post be filled by someone from England. On 24 January 1829 Thomson took up his appointment in New South Wales as clerk to the Executive and Legislative Councils at £600 a year. Thomson soon won Governor Darling's approval by his competence and industry. He had not expected the dual appointment and, finding the duties arduous, he sought relief through an increased salary which would permit him to employ a clerk. His own work did not flag and it acquainted him with many activities of the colony. He was also a member of several boards concerned with the control of convicts and found particular satisfaction on the Convict Assignment Board, where he suggested the chief regulations introduced in 1835 for the assignment of male convicts.

Thomson established harmonious relations also with Governor Bourke, whom he admired as an administrator and as a man. The link became closer when he married Bourke's second daughter, Anne Maria, on 18 September 1833. Some colonists thought this family association prejudiced Thomson's right to promotion as colonial secretary in place of Alexander

McLeay [q.v.] as Bourke recommended. Although the critics did not attack Thomson's capacity Bourke hesitated before he threw his support behind him officially, as well as unofficially through connexions in England. Despite McLeay's reluctance to vacate his post Thomson was appointed colonial secretary of New South Wales and registrar of the records on 2 January 1837. His new position carried with it membership of the Executive and Legislative Councils. Whatever the propriety of Bourke's relations with McLeay, there can be no doubt that Thomson was the logical choice for the office both for experience and ability. As colonial secretary he became the governor's chief adviser, the second executive officer of the administration, and the channel through which all the governor's correspondence flowed.

Under Governor Gipps Thomson was faced from 1843 with the particularly difficult task of representing an unpopular government in the part-elected Legislative Council. At first he had doubts that he could work happily with Gipps. He was privately critical of the governor's manner and capacity, and uncertain of his role as the chief civil officer of the government if policy and his principles should clash. He accepted Bourke's advice and in 1844 testified to the select committee on general grievances that, although the colonial secretary had a moral responsibility to the legislature, he also had a legal responsibility to the governor whose instructions he was bound to carry out. However, in the Executive Council he did not hesitate to express a contrary opinion whenever the majority view differed from his own. His conservative cast of mind was revealed in other evidence before the same committee when he asserted that responsible government in the colonies was incompatible with the imperial connexion.

Thomson's early doubts about Gipps did not prevent him from serving the governor loyally, and they soon became close friends. Thomson was equally respected by his opponents and supporters in the council, where in stormy debates over land and transportation he ably argued the government's case. He also strove to enforce the highest standards in the public service, giving particular attention to the newly introduced statistical returns. His wife's private letters often mentioned his long hours at his office and in council in these troubled years. By the end of Gipps's term in 1846 Thomson had clearly established himself as an efficient administrator, forceful on the government's behalf and, although conservative, fair-minded in considering all points of view. By this time he had also shown special interest in intercolonial trade, education and steam communication with England.

When Governor FitzRoy arrived he showed himself ready to lean on the advice and experience of his chief civil officer, and soon commended Thomson's zeal. During FitzRoy's governorship Thomson continued to strive for high administrative standards. He had little sympathy for inefficiency and frequently received too little support from other senior public servants such as Riddell and Lithgow [qq.v.]. Further afield he saw the problems of intercolonial relations and recognized the dangers inherent in the nascent protectionist attitudes of some colonies. Thus he was probably responsible for FitzRoy's recommendation in September 1846 that the British government should appoint a 'superior Functionary' in Australia with a right to review and veto colonial legislation. Thomson renewed his support for some central intercolonial authority when in May 1848 he presented to the Legislative Council Earl Grey's proposals for a federal union. Although bound to support Grey's views Thomson himself was clearly convinced that some such body was necessary.

Feeling the strain imposed on his health by his duties and aware that Port Phillip would soon become a separate colony, Thomson asked his father-in-law to pursue the possibility of an appointment there as governor. However, no immediate prospect of the position emerged and with some concern for the future of his growing family, Thomson decided to stay in New South Wales. He thus became closely associated with the two most exciting events of the 1850s: the movement for responsible government and the gold discoveries. At the same time he continued firmly to advocate free trade among the Australian colonies and the establishment of a university in New South Wales. In 1849 he was a member of Wentworth's [q.v.] select committee on Sydney University, and after its report won parliamentary approval he was appointed one of the sixteen original members of the university senate in December 1850, and remained a member until his death.

In December 1851 Thomson introduced a bill which he claimed would be beneficial to New South Wales and yet not inhibit intercolonial trade. The bill was modelled closely on views expressed by Lieut-Governor Denison of Van Diemen's Land, with whom Thomson maintained a close personal correspondence. By proposing reduced duties on some goods, a free list of commodities most commonly exchanged between the colonies, and a 5 per cent *ad valorem* tariff on all other merchandise he claimed to be serving the interests of free trade. The bill was administratively complex and its provisions were attacked in council by John Lamb [q.v.], a Sydney merchant and president of the Chamber of Commerce, who sought even greater freedom of trade. Under this criticism Thomson did not press his bill, but next year he welcomed the advice of the Sydney Chamber of Commerce, which had consulted its Melbourne counterpart, since he was anxious to see as little variation as possible in tariffs between the colonies. His new bill, which proposed the abolition of *ad valorem* tariffs and the retention of duties only on such items as wine, spirits and tobacco, became law in August 1852. It was later known as the Deas Thomson tariff, despite his acknowledgment of help from others.

The gold rush in 1851 strained the capabilities of Thomson and his assistants in the public service. He and the governor were the only civil members at the first five meetings of the Executive Council which discussed the discoveries before regulations to control the diggers were framed in May. He visited the major diggings in August and September. Although ultra-conservatives like James Macarthur [q.v.] wanted to discourage workers from going to the diggings, Thomson advocated no arbitrary official action, such as high licence fees, that might regulate the way in which men chose to work. He was opposed to such tactics on principle and doubted their efficacy in practice. More clearly than others he recognized the immense effect which gold would have on the colony's future. The additional work brought by the discovery of gold and the spread of population impelled him to apply in June 1851 for a salary increase of £500. FitzRoy supported him heartily and the Colonial Office recommended it to the New South Wales Legislative Council. This gave the council an opportunity to record its admiration of Thomson's work by voting the increase and making it retrospective to 1846. Praise for Thomson was unanimous in the council but did not mean that he was without detractors. He was criticized by J. D. Lang [q.v.] and was personally disliked by Sir Thomas Mitchell [q.v.] who resented taking orders from an official sometime his junior.

In a colony moving towards responsible government Thomson's political outlook invited attack whatever the respect for his character. His conservative view was reaffirmed in his bill for the colony's electoral divisions in 1851. He had discussed the general principles of this bill with FitzRoy but the details were his own work. In the Legislative Council Thomson defended the principle that representation should be based not only on population but also on property, supporting his argument by reference to the practice of the imperial parliament and to the fact that two-thirds of the colony's exports came from the pastoral districts. To strengthen his case he published *Corrected Report of the Speeches of the Honourable Edward Deas Thomson . . . in the first session of 1851*. In 1852-53 Thomson played an important part in the two committees on the new Constitution for New South Wales. Although W. C. Wentworth was largely responsible for the final report in 1853, Thomson supported it in the Legislative Council, where he spoke without the governor's control; particularly approving the conservative nature of the upper House but doubting the practicability of the proposed general assembly to settle intercolonial matters. With Wentworth, he was chosen by the Legislative Council to watch over the progress of the Constitution bill in the British parliament. Before his selection for this task he had been granted leave to travel to England to restore his health, which continued to be affected by the heavy strain of his duties. Before his departure a committee under the chairmanship of Sir Charles Nicholson [q.v.] presented him with a testimonial of more than £2000; half of it was invested in a piece of plate and the balance, at Thomson's request, was given to the University of Sydney to found a Deas Thomson scholarship for study in natural sciences.

In England ill health prevented Thomson from taking as active a part as Wentworth in watching over the Constitution bill. He did, however, combine with Wentworth to produce a draft on how the bill should be introduced by Lord John Russell. He deeply regretted that these suggestions were not all adopted and that the British parliament rejected the principle that the right of imperial interference should apply only when imperial interests were involved. At the Colonial Office he discussed many questions with Sir William Molesworth, on whose recommendation he was appointed C.B. in February 1856.

Thomson returned to Sydney in 1856 and reassumed office as colonial secretary on 14 January. A week later Governor Denison asked him to form the first ministry under responsible government. Although Thomson's long association with the colony's government merited that honour, the general opinion seems to have been against him because of his connexion with the old order. This was revealed when he failed to gain sufficient support from those he asked to join him. An attempt by Donaldson to form a ministry failed too, and Denison decided to await the results of the first elections before trying again. Thomson declined an invitation by some electors from West Camden to stand for the Legislative Assembly, and after the elections Denison again asked him to form the first ministry assuming that he would occupy a seat in the Legislative Council. Thomson accepted when he found the results of the elections more conservative than he had expected but again failed to gain sufficient support; of the four men he approached, Plunkett [q.v.], Manning, Donaldson and Parker, only Manning agreed to join him. Hurt by these refusals, he rejected an invitation to a place in Donaldson's ministry, the first under responsible government. In April 1856 he had resigned from the Executive Council, but at the governor's request remained as a caretaker colonial secretary until the new ministry was sworn. In May he accepted nomination to the Legislative Council, but refused to accept nomination as its president since he believed that office was too political. His services as colonial secretary were officially terminated on 6 June 1856, and in accordance with the provisions of the Constitution Act he was granted a pension of £2000. So ended his intimate connexion with the government of New South Wales although he remained a member of the Legislative Council until his death.

Immediately after the introduction of responsible government Thomson and others were asked to make suggestions for the administration of government departments. Thomson's recommendations, although not followed completely, were influential in determining the responsibilities and administrative arrangements of the ministers and their departments; one important suggestion, not accepted, was that there should be a minister of Public Instruction with general responsibility for all educational institutions in the colony, a proposal that revealed Thomson's anxiety for the advancement of education and for the firm control of institutions receiving government finance but administering themselves.

Although briefly entertaining the idea of accepting nomination as a candidate for the city of Sydney to the Legislative Assembly in August 1856, Thomson declined on the grounds of ill health. He did, however, agree to join the Parker ministry in October, and was then appointed vice-president of the Executive Council. As representative of the ministry in the Legislative Council, he called in August 1857 for a select committee to consider the expediency of establishing a federal legislature. A few months earlier he had proposed that seven administrative areas, including tariffs, land and railways, were susceptible to federal control; now he pointed to the United States senate as a possible model. As accepted by the council, the committee's report recommended the establishment of 'a Federal Assembly with the power to discuss and determine on all questions of an intercolonial character arising out of the Australian colonies generally'. When the Parker ministry fell in September 1857 the matter lapsed, but throughout his long membership of the Upper House Thomson never abandoned his advocacy of some federal organization and for the maintenance of free trade.

In the crisis over the Robertson land bills he joined those members of the Legislative Council who resigned rather than remain in a council swamped with Robertson's supporters. Although he strenuously opposed the nomination of members under any precondition, he agreed that the land bills should not be obstructed and accepted nomination to the council for life. However, the swamping tactics and other experiences gradually convinced Thomson that the council would be better constituted by election under a conservative franchise than by nomination.

Freed from public office Thomson was able to pursue his other interests. Foremost among these was the University of Sydney. He was elected vice-chancellor in 1863 and chancellor in 1865, holding office until forced to retire through ill health in 1878. He maintained that university education should be broad in scope, with a foundation of classical knowledge augmented by training in practical scientific subjects. He was always interested in natural science, had become a fellow of the Linnean Society in London in 1828 and sent specimens to England from time to time. As chancellor he probably influenced William John Macleay, who had married his daughter Susan, to give the Macleays' natural history collection to the University of Sydney in December 1873. Particularly in the early years of his chancellorship Thomson faced situations in which the university was poorly financed and often the target of public criticism. At such times his prestige and administrative experience were of great service to the young institution.

The range of Thomson's interests is indicated by the number of institutions of which he was a leading member. At various times he was president of the Sydney Infirmary, the Benevolent Society, the Society for Destitute Children, the Australian Jockey Club, and the Australian Club. In 1866 Thomson was asked by Governor Young and the premier, Henry Parkes, to act as commissioner for the New Zealand government to assist in reorganizing its civil service and to advise on methods of taxation. He declined this request probably because of his health, but accepted the less arduous appointment as a member of the commission that collected and classified specimens for the Paris International Exhibition in 1867. In 1874 his long record of public service was recognized when he was appointed K.C.M.G., an honour which many in the colony felt had been too long delayed. He died in Sydney on 16 July 1879, survived by his widow, two sons and five daughters. He was buried at St Jude's Church of England, Randwick, where he had worshipped for many years. His home, Barham, in Forbes Street, Darlinghurst, in which he lived for most of his colonial life, became part of the Sydney Church of England Girls' Grammar School.

A portrait by Capalti and a marble bust by Fantacchiotti are in the Great Hall of the University of Sydney; another portrait, thought also to be by Capalti, is in the Mitchell Library.

Thomson's career in the public service and in parliament spanned many changes in the colony and his influence was strong through continuity alone. As colonial secretary, particularly under FitzRoy, his detailed knowledge of local conditions and his readiness to assume responsibility gave him great power, although contemporaries may have exaggerated his share in such legislation as the tariff amendments in 1852. Probably his greatest contribution was not in his initiation of particular measures but in his continuing concern for efficient administration. This belief enabled him to face and overcome the difficulties posed by the discovery of gold and by the problems of a developing colony. He was important as one of the early proponents of Australian Federation, although his arguments were prompted more by the fears of an administrator than by any great belief in a national identity. However conservative in his political beliefs, he also had a truly liberal reluctance for unnecessary government interference in an individual's affairs. His great probity and tact carried more than one governor through stormy interludes. In 1851 he summarized his aims in simple words, 'Throughout the long career I have pursued in the public service of this colony it has ever been my study to promote the public welfare; to deal with every public measure without favour or affection to any man; to conduct myself alike to all of whatever party, creed or denomination; to do justice to the poor man as well as to the rich'.

HRA (1), 14-26; SMH, 7 June 1856, 17 July 1879; J. A. La Nauze, 'Merchants in action', Economic Record, 31 (1955); Bourke papers (ML); Deas Thomson papers (ML).

M. E. Osborne

THOMSON, JAMES ALEXANDER (1805-1860), architect, engineer and building contractor, was a native of Haddington, Scotland, and at 20, as 'a wild but clever young man', was transported to Van Diemen's Land for theft. With his brothers William and Joseph he had been discovered in a private house, and the three were tried together for the same offence and sentenced on 18 February 1824. William was considered less culpable and pardoned after imprisonment in Newgate; Joseph and James were transported separately; Joseph, who identified the object of the theft as jewellery to the value of £3000, was drowned after two years in the colony. James, who arrived at Hobart Town in the Medway on 14 December 1825, was assigned to public works and was frequently on loan to the colonial architect, David Lambe, and his successor, John Lee Archer [qq.v.], both of whom professed satisfaction with his work as draughtsman. Archer procured for him a small remuneration and towards the end of his assignment he was superintendent of the church building at Richmond (St Luke's 1834-37). He had also acted from 1830 as overseer of the government plumbers, glaziers and painters; indeed his trade was given in convict records as decorative painter. These records imply that at the date of transportation he had a wife and child living in Park Street, Regent's Park, London. By 3 June 1830, however, he had petitioned the lieutgovernor for permission to marry Eliza Ogilvie, the comfortably endowed widow of a respectable Hobart wine and spirits merchant who had died in 1828 leaving her with three children. A daughter, Alice, appears to have been born on 7 August 1830, although the marriage at Richmond did not take place until 16 October 1832. A son, William, was born on 13 August 1833. By 1859 only one daughter, Fanny, survived, but two sons were living.

Thomson received a conditional pardon on 1 January 1835 and immediately set up a business in Liverpool Street, which lasted for most of his life, not only as architect, engineer and surveyor, but also as valuer, estate agent, map printer and dealer in machinery. His free pardon became effective on 31 July 1839. Despite his several complaints that officers of the Royal Engineers and public servants used their leisure time in architectural activities and caused unfair competition, Thomson seems to have enjoyed reasonably consistent architectural patronage, particularly during the shortage of architects in the 1840s. In 1841 he was a partner of James Blackburn [q.v.] in at least some contracts, though both worked independently as well. Thomson was also one of the first in Hobart to become interested in lithography both in its artistic and in its commercially reproductive applications. In 1850-51 Thomson had been one of the first to seek gold in Tasmania, investigating without success Frenchman's Cap and other areas. On 5 December 1852 his wife Eliza died, aged 51, and on 6 December 1853 Thomson married Catherine, the widow of the Hobart builder, John Jackson. Thomson moved from Liverpool Street to Elboden Street and later to Melrose in Hampden Road. He owned property in Macquarie Street, and worked professionally from the Stone Buildings later, about 1855-56 operating there under the name of Thomson & Cookney.

In 1853 he yielded to the supplications of a large group of supporters to stand as an alderman on the Municipal Council, a position he held until 1857. One of his great concerns was the Hobart water supply. Architecturally the bulk of Thomson's work appears to be in the domestic context: the designing and sometimes building of workmanlike utilitarian structures such as shops, office buildings, terraces and houses and cottages, none being works of paramount importance. One interesting tender let in 1850 was for fifty timber-framed houses for the Californian goldfields. Thomson was also engaged in contracting for jetties, wharves and harbour improvements in Hobart and, with Blackburn, road-making. His spectacular buildings were few. Unquestionably the most interesting and important work is the Hobart Synagogue (1843-45), the most comprehensive example of the Regency Egyptian style in Australia (felt suitable for this religion), surpassing in quality the first synagogues of Launceston, Melbourne and Sydney. Other churches are of plain and rudimentary village Gothicism, such as St Joseph's, Hobart (1841-43, some alterations), St Joseph's, Launceston (1838-42, demolished and replaced), and subsequently St Andrew's, Campbell Town (with Cookney, 1856-58, later spire), little touched by

the more scholarly aspects of Gothic Revivalism. A few other works are attributable. Besides the Bridgewater Bridge (1846-49, with Blackburn) Thomson's best known early work was the pile bridge across the Derwent at New Norfolk (1840-41). An association with the stone bridge at Dunrobin (built 1850-56 under W. P. Kay's [q.v.] supervision) is suggested by an obituary of reserved eulogies, which lists also the bridge at Richmond (presumably reconstruction of earlier fabric), the smelting works at Exmouth Bay, the former Hobart Exchange rooms and attorney-general's offices. Thomson had a long record of devoted service as a Freemason and Lodge treasurer, and committee member of the Hobart Mechanics' Institute. He sailed in the *Isles of the South* on 3 February 1860 for a visit to England, and died of typhoid fever at Helensburgh, near Glasgow, on 15 September 1860, aged 55.

Whatever his merits as architect, and they are relatively minor, Thomson provides a remarkable case of a former convict establishing himself as a successful businessman, despite his small estate, respected in many circles and with a considerable variety of commercial activities and social interests.

Hobart Town Advertiser, 21 Nov 1860; Blackburn papers in author's possession.

HARLEY PRESTON

THRELKELD, LANCELOT EDWARD (1788-1859), missionary and Congregational minister, was born on 20 October 1788 in Southwark, London, the son of Samuel Joseph Threlkeld, a brushmaker, and his wife Mary. After serving a trade apprenticeship Threlkeld became an actor with the Royal Circus and later with the Royalty Theatre. He then engaged in business, and in 1808 at St George's Church, Southwark, he married Martha, née Goss, who bore him five children. Threlkeld moved to Hatherleigh, Devonshire, where he was influenced by the vicar, Cradock Glascott, and became one of his itinerant field preachers, assisting Rev. G. Moase, a Calvinistic Methodist. In 1814 he was accepted as a candidate by the (London) Missionary Society and received brief courses in theology and elementary medicine in London. On 8 November 1815 he was ordained at Mr Leitchfield's Chapel, Kensington, in company with William Ellis, with whom he left for the South Seas in the *Atlas* in January 1816.

His wife lost their first child and became so ill that Threlkeld was detained for a year at Rio de Janeiro, where he ministered to the Protestant community. In January 1817 he joined another company of missionaries in the *Harriet* and went to Sydney, whence they sailed to the Society Islands in the *Active*, arriving at Moorea in November 1817. Threlkeld's independence brought him into conflict with the older missionaries, though he worked amicably with John Williams [q.v.] at Raiatea. When his wife died on 7 March 1824, Rev. Daniel Tyerman and a wealthy layman, George Bennet, were visiting the society's mission fields. Threlkeld accompanied them to Australia, intending to return to England. In Sydney the visitors proposed the establishment of a mission to the Aboriginals. Governor Brisbane was agreeable; in January 1825 a site was fixed at Reid's Mistake (Belmont) on Lake Macquarie, and Threlkeld was appointed missionary.

On 20 October 1824 Threlkeld had married Sarah, daughter of Dr Thomas Arndell [q.v.] of Cattai Creek near Windsor; they had five children. Ten thousand acres were reserved in trust for the mission. Threlkeld settled at Newcastle in May 1825; in 1826 he moved to his station Bahtahbah and began to instruct the Aboriginals in simple agriculture. The apparently excessive expenditure at the mission soon brought him into dispute with Rev. S. Marsden [q.v.], the society's agent, and with the directors in London. The breach over financial matters widened, especially as Threlkeld resented the oversight of Marsden. In April 1828 the directors decided to abandon the mission and dismiss Threlkeld, offering to pay his passage to England.

Threlkeld, however, was able to secure a grant of land from Governor Darling in 1829, and in January 1831 the Executive Council confirmed him as missionary, and voted him a salary of £200 to replace the former stipend. Soon afterwards he moved to Ebenezer (Toronto) on the opposite side of the lake. In the next ten years he consolidated his work; with the assistance of the tribal leader, Biraban [q.v.], he mastered the dialect, acted as interpreter for Aboriginals on trial in Sydney, and printed regular reports. His published language studies are now regarded as landmarks in Aboriginal studies. The station became a show place and was visited by the United States Exploring Expedition and the Quakers, J. Backhouse and G. W. Walker [qq.v.]. Threlkeld also formed an acquaintance with influential persons interested in Aboriginal welfare and later corresponded with Sir George Grey. Despite the support of such men Threlkeld was savagely criticized. In 1836 J. D. Lang [q.v.], who had cast aspersions

on the mission as early as March 1828, reviewed its history in the *Colonist*, 31 March 1836, to Threlkeld's disadvantage. He brought a libel case against Lang, and secured one farthing damages.

Although the mission had some success, Threlkeld regarded it as a failure because he made no apparent converts. By 1840 he reported that very few Aboriginals were left at the station; Governor Gipps terminated government support and refused to sanction his employment at Newcastle. The mission was officially closed on 31 December 1841. Threlkeld continued to sit on committees for the welfare of the Aboriginals and to attend the police courts on behalf of Aboriginal defendants.

As the mission had been costly, Threlkeld had to supplement his personal stipend by grazing stock and, in defiance of the monopoly of the Australian Agricultural Co., by developing the coal seams on his property. In 1840 he opened the first mine in the Lake Macquarie district and held it until January 1845.

In 1841 Threlkeld had moved to Sydney, and in 1842 became minister of the South Head Congregational Church which had been gathered by W. P. Crook [q.v.], and also conducted a day school. He relinquished this pastorate in 1845 when he was appointed chaplain of seamen by the Sydney Bethel Union. A substantial Mariners' Church was built chiefly through his exertions, and he regularly preached on shipboard and in hospitals.

In Sydney he was prominent in the public meetings that protested against the French intervention in the Society Islands, and his declaration, in conjunction with Rev. Robert Bourne, to the colonial secretary was used as evidence in securing the independence of the Leeward Islands. In his later years he contributed numerous articles to the religious press. As a champion of Protestantism, much of his writing was polemical and anti-Catholic. In 1851 he was appointed a member of the Ethnological Society, London, for his Aboriginal studies.

Threlkeld died suddenly on 10 October 1859. His wife had predeceased him on 20 December 1853. Threlkeld had tendencies to be theatrical, improvident and self-righteous, yet he was quick to champion the victims of discrimination, whether Dissenters or Aboriginals. He was convinced that the intellectual capabilities of the Aboriginals were equal to those of Europeans, though his approach to missionary work was coloured by his commitment to the Calvinistic doctrine of natural depravity. Lady Franklin described him in 1839 as a 'dingy elderly plain man'.

Though difficult, he was enterprising and energetic.

Threlkeld's principal publication was *An Australian Grammar . . . of the Language, as Spoken by the Aborigines . . . of Hunter's River*, published at Sydney in 1834 by the Society for Promoting Christian Knowledge in conjunction with the colonial government. Besides his printed annual reports (1836-41) and statements, Threlkeld published in Sydney a number of works including *Aboriginal Mission, New South Wales* (1825); *Specimens of a Dialect, of the Aborigines of New South Wales, being the First Attempt to Form their Speech into a Written Language* (1827); *A Statement chiefly relating to The Formation and Abandonment of a Mission to the Aborigines* (1828); *An Australian Spelling Book, in the Language as Spoken by the Aborigines, in the vicinity of Hunter's River* (1836); and *A Key to the Structure of the Aboriginal Language* (1850). Threlkeld's main linguistic writings were rearranged and edited by Dr John Fraser in 1892. One at least of his polemical works was published in London : *An Appeal to common sense: being a comparison of Mohammed and the Pope with the Messiah: addressed to Christians* (1841).

J. Montgomery (ed), *Journal of voyages and travels by the Rev Daniel Tyerman and George Bennet*, 1-2 (Lond, 1831); S. Humphreys, *The faithful servant, and his reward. A funeral discourse* (Syd, 1859); J. Sibree (ed), *A register of missionaries, deputations . . . from 1796 to 1923, London Missionary Society* (Lond, 1923); L. E. Threlkeld, 'Reminiscences', *Christian Herald* (Syd, 1853-55); B. W. Champion, 'L. E. Threlkeld', *JRAHS*, 25 (1935); *Aust Home Companion and Band of Hope J* (Syd), 4 (1859); LMS archives (Westminster); Threlkeld papers (Camden College, Syd); MS cat under Threlkeld (ML).

NIEL GUNSON

THROSBY, CHARLES (1777-1828), surgeon, settler and explorer, was born at Glenfield, near Leicester, England, the younger son of John Throsby, historian and antiquarian. He joined the navy as a surgeon and served in the armed transports *Coromandel* and *Calcutta* from 1797 until the peace. In June 1802 he arrived in New South Wales as naval surgeon of the *Coromandel* and was complimented by Governor King on the good health of the convicts and settlers under his charge. While in Port Jackson Throsby was engaged by James Thomson to do his duty while he took a year's leave; in October Throsby was appointed medical officer and magistrate at Castle Hill. In January 1804 he was

moved to Sydney; in March he applied for a permanent position in the medical service of the colony, and in August he was sent to Newcastle as assistant surgeon. In March 1805 when Lieutenant Charles Menzies [q.v.], the commandant, resigned, Throsby was appointed superintendent of labour; but next month when Ensign Draffen, who relieved Menzies, became insane, Throsby was given command of the settlement which, according to Governor King, he conducted with 'great Activity and Propriety'. In 1808 he was confirmed as magistrate by the rebel administration, but returned to Sydney in December and next September resigned as surgeon on the grounds of ill health. Lieut-Governor Paterson [q.v.] allowed him to retire 'with the indulgence of a free settler', and to exchange his sheep and cattle at Newcastle for an equivalent number at Sydney. In 1808 Lieut-Governor Foveaux [q.v.] had granted Throsby 500 acres at Cabramatta for his services at Newcastle and in 1809 Paterson made him grants of 500 and 100 acres at Minto. These he had to surrender in 1810, but Governor Macquarie granted him 1500 acres in their place, and confirmed the cattle exchange. He built Glenfield, named after his birthplace, at Upper Minto and for the next few years concentrated there on pastoral activities.

In 1817 Macquarie noted Throsby as one of those colonists who were discontented, but he was later reconciled with the governor, probably as a result of his achievements as an explorer, which Macquarie rated highly. Throsby was one of the first settlers in the Illawarra district, where in November 1816 his stockmen already had a hut, and he was also one of the first to settle in the Moss Vale district. In August 1817 he explored the country west of Sutton Forest with Hamilton Hume [q.v.], a family friend. In March and April 1818 he accompanied Surveyor-General Meehan [q.v.] on a journey from the Cowpastures through Moss Vale to Bundanoon Creek and south-west to Jervis Bay; after the party divided Throsby reached the Shoalhaven River and Jervis Bay. In April 1819 he made a tour from the Cowpastures to Bathurst, opening up fertile country which Macquarie felt would meet the increase of settlers for many years; for this he granted Throsby 1000 acres, and also rewarded his companions and servants. In 1819 Throsby discovered a pass between the Illawarra and Robertson districts and successfully drove a herd of cattle through it. In March 1820 he explored the country around Goulburn and Lake Bathurst and penetrated as far as the Breadalbane Plains. Macquarie gave him superintendence over the building of the road from the Cowpastures to the new country, which was placed under the direction of Throsby's servant Joseph Wild [q.v.]. In 1820 Macquarie visited the work party, which had reached the Cookbundoon Range, and gave Throsby's estate in the new country the name of Throsby Park.

Throsby's return to Macquarie's favour was not easy, for Meehan disagreed with Throsby over the usefulness of the new country and Macquarie was first bound to accept Meehan's judgment; but in time Macquarie came to speak as glowingly of the disputed country as Throsby himself. In a letter to Meehan in 1820 Throsby spoke of his pride in having partly caused the disagreement, for he felt that the dispute would inspire others to inquire into the country's usefulness more fully. By 1820 he felt that his poor health and financial worries would prevent any further explorations; however, in March 1821 he set out again for the new country, going in search of the Murrumbidgee. On this trip he crossed the Molonglo and Queanbeyan Rivers and the country where Canberra now stands. This has been spoken of as Throsby's last journey, but in November he appears to have journeyed again from Sutton Forest to Jervis Bay.

In March 1821 Macquarie made Throsby a magistrate of the territory, with his main jurisdiction over the new County of Argyle created out of part of the land Throsby had explored. He also granted him 700 acres to adjoin Throsby Park or any part of the new country he desired. In 1825 Throsby was appointed to the Legislative Council. However, all this time he was involved in financial troubles brought on by the £5000 surety he had undertaken on behalf of Garnham Blaxcell [q.v.], who in 1817 absconded from the colony and died on board ship, leaving Throsby at the mercy of his creditors. Ten years litigation ended in an adverse verdict for Throsby, who by 1828 was also affected by the drought and by falling prices for wool. Worn down by worry and ill health, he committed suicide on 2 April 1828, aged 51, and was buried in Liverpool cemetery. His wife Jane died on 4 November 1838. He was disappointed that he had no children and had sent for his nephew Charles Throsby junior to become his heir. Charles and his wife Elizabeth, née Broughton, arrived in the *Mangles* in August 1820 and their children carried on the family line.

Irritable and allegedly hampered by a speech defect, Throsby was considerate and evoked strong loyalty from his servants. His attitude to the Aboriginals was enlightened, for he believed that their indiscriminate slaughter would bring only revenge and that it was possible to live in harmony with them

HRNSW, 4-7; HRA (1), 5, 7, 9-11, 14; R. H. Cambage, 'Exploration between the Wingecarribee, Shoalhaven, Macquarie and Murrumbidgee Rivers', *JRAHS*, 7 (1921); H. Norrie, 'Australia's debt to her early medicos', *Univ Syd Medical J*, 27 (1933); H. Throsby, 'Charles Throsby', *Univ Syd Medical J*, 28 (1934); *Sydney Gazette*, 24 Sept 1809, 16 Nov 1816, 17 Mar 1821, 22 Dec 1825, 4 Apr 1828; MS cat under C. Throsby (ML).

VIVIENNE PARSONS

TIMS, MARTIN (1750?-1830?), agriculturist, soldier and public servant, spent part of his early life in North America. There he served Colonel Philip Wharton Skene, from Hallyards, Fife, Scotland, who made his home at Skeneborough on Lake Champlain in northern New York State, became lieut-governor of the forts of Crown Point and Ticonderoga, and held other military, civil and judicial appointments in New York and Quebec. Tims (sometimes spelt Timms) served as bailiff and manager of 'Governor' Skene's extensive estates, where he gained experience in agriculture. These estates were confiscated during the American war of independence, and Skene recommended Tims to Major Grose [q.v.], who was then serving in North America. Enlisting in the army, Tims eventually came to Australia as a private in the New South Wales Corps.

Posted to Norfolk Island, he was appointed a superintendent on 1 July 1792 and resigned from the corps in April 1793. Though almost illiterate he established an impeccable record, managing crop cultivation for some ten years with more than three hundred convicts in his charge and then serving as provost-marshal for another decade. He married on Norfolk Island and had his own small farm. After the closure of the settlement in 1813 he returned to England, petitioning for a pension 'as the means of Comfort and Support in his declining years', taking into account 'his infirmity and age'. Instead he received a fresh appointment as provost-marshal of Van Diemen's Land and arrived there in September 1815.

Lacking in learning and guile and well past the prime of life, he was no match for Hobart Town's complex and corrupting society. Whereas he had been a model of steadfastness on Norfolk Island, his performance in Van Diemen's Land was quite different. There were numerous disputes about his interpretation of the duties of provost-marshal, and Supreme Court verdicts were obtained against him for illegalities in the serving of process. There was never any suspicion of dishonesty on his part, but increasingly he found solace in drink. After various suspensions and admonitions he was dismissed at the end of 1818 following his attempt to have the police magistrate, A. W. H. Humphrey [q.v.], arrested at the gate of Government House, apparently at the suggestion of one of the latter's creditors. According to the land commissioners, 'poor old Timms . . . was turned out of his place, (to make way for the great Mr Beamont,) because he dared to do his duty by arresting some of the would be great Men of the day'.

He held the original grant of a farm in the Green Ponds district, but in impoverished circumstances after his dismissal was compelled to sell this cheaply to Edward Lord [q.v.]. A humble man who achieved much, especially in agriculture, before sinking amid the complexities of the administration of justice in Van Diemen's Land, Tims was last heard of in 1826 'dragging on a miserable existence in Hobart Town, his Wife earning a little pittance by washing Clothes'.

HRA (1), 1, 3, 5, 7-10, (3), 2-4; A. McKay (ed), *Journals of the land commissioners for Van Diemen's Land 1826-28* (Hob, 1962); MS cat under Martin Tims (ML); Correspondence file under Martin Tims (ML).

R. L. WETTENHALL

TOM, WILLIAM (1791-1883), farmer and Methodist leader, was born on 25 May 1791 on a farm at Blisland, Cornwall, England. In December 1817 he married Ann Lane (1796-1870) and in 1823 he and his wife, three children and a nephew, with his brother-in-law William Lane and his wife and two children, sailed in the *Betty Ann* to Sydney where they arrived in the *Jupiter* in November.

After a few months at Parramatta Tom obtained a grant at Tarana, but he found that the trees were hard to burn and moved to Sidmouth Valley and thence to Wallaroi, near Bathurst, where he managed for John Hassall. When the country west of the Macquarie River was opened for settlement he and his two elder sons, now hardy and self-reliant bush boys, went exploring and found good land eleven miles east of Orange. There in 1830 he took up land which he named Springfield, and it was granted to him six years later with additional leasehold. William Lane also took up land not far away at Orton Park, which he named after Rev. Joseph Orton [q.v.].

At Springfield Tom first built a lath and plaster house of four rooms, with a loft for the boys and their tutor, George Hawke. In the early 1830s he was joined by other Wesleyans from Cornwall: two brothers of William Lane, and John Glasson; other Glassons followed later. The district was named the Cornish Settlement. Its religious leader was 'Parson' Tom, as he was known far and wide. Until 1842, when a solid and elaborate little steepled stone church was built by the Cornishmen who were skilled stonemasons, Tom conducted services on Bethel Rock. Orton visited them in 1832 and appointed Tom leader of the first Methodist class west of the mountains. Tom preached as far afield as Molong, at the home of his daughter Mary, who in 1842 had married John Smith (1811-1895), a Cornishman, landowner and later member of the Legislative Council.

During a visit in 1834 Orton discussed with Tom, Lane, Hawke and John Glasson the appointment of a minister and erection of a chapel at Bathurst, and in May 1836 Rev. Frederick Lewis arrived, the first resident Methodist minister west of the mountains; a chapel was opened at Bathurst in 1837.

In the early 1840s the older ones among William Tom's hardy sons, now eight in number, the youngest named Wesley, began droving stock west and south-west. John (1820-1895) and William (1823-1904) drove cattle to Gippsland and took up a run known as Tom's Camp. In 1847 Henry (1827-1896) and Nicholas (1829-1888) bought cattle at Mudgee to drove to Adelaide but met James Tyson, who persuaded them to squat at Booligal, where they remained in occupation with their father as a partner until 1858 when they sold out for £25,000. At various times the brothers also held Tom's Lake, Borambil, Huntawong, Gunningbland, Wilga and Cowl-Cowl.

In November 1847 William Tom laid the foundation stone of a fine two-storied house at Springfield. There in 1851 came E. H. Hargraves who explained to the Toms how to make a cradle; after he left William Tom built a cradle and with his brothers James and Henry worked along the creek, eventually washing sixteen grains of gold in one day. Soon afterwards William Tom and J. H. A. Lister found nuggets totalling four ounces and wrote to Hargraves who hastened back to the field, which was named Ophir. The gold rush followed.

Ann Tom died on 10 October 1870 and William Tom at Springfield on 28 September 1883. In addition to eight sons they left five daughters. Selina (1835-1929) married Edmund Webb (1830-1899) a Cornishman and pioneer merchant of Bathurst, Annie (1840-1872) married Gustavus Glasson.

William Tom lacked the business acumen that enabled other Cornish farmers, including two sons-in-law, to make fortunes in the west in his lifetime. He was a patriarch who won in the new land what he wanted: sturdy children, a house of stone, with his land and flocks around, and a following of devoted Christians. A tablet on Bethel Rock commemorates 'the service rendered to the early Methodist Church by William (Parson) Tom 1830-1883'. Another enduring monument, unveiled at Ophir in 1923, bears an inscription recording the parts played by Hargraves, the Toms and Lister in the discovery of payable gold.

W. H. Webb, The life of the late William Tom (Syd, 1922); W. R. Glasson, Early western glimpses (Molong, 1933); E. G. Clancy, More precious than gold (Orange, 1960); K. R. Cramp, 'Who first discovered payable gold in Australia?' JRAHS, 33 (1947); Tom family Bible (Methodist Church, Orange).

GAVIN LONG

TOMPSON, CHARLES (1807-1883), poet and public servant, was born on 26 June 1807 in Sydney, the eldest child of Charles Tompson (1784?-1871), farmer, and his wife, Elizabeth, née Boggis. His father had been convicted at Warwick, England, in March 1802, arrived in Sydney in the Coromandel in May 1804, and for four years was employed in the office of Commissary Palmer [q.v.]; later he kept a shop at the corner of Pitt and Hunter Streets and about 1819 bought a 700-acre farm, Clydesdale, near Windsor.

In July 1814 Rev. Henry Fulton [q.v.] established a parish school at Castlereagh. Young Tompson was a pupil, and in 1818 wrote an 'Ode to Spring', the forerunner of other youthful works in similar style. He celebrated the thirty-sixth anniversary of the foundation of the colony with 'A Song, for January 26, 1824'; of the eight stanzas, one was

Peace lifts her olive sceptre high,
Brown Industry assumes the plough,
Commerce expands her canvas wings,
Wealth points where honour guides the prow;
These, happy Australasia, these
Proclaim thee "Queen of Southern Seas"!

On 26 February Governor Brisbane promised the young poet 100 acres at Mulwaree Ponds; this grant was gazetted in 1832. Also in 1824 Tompson wrote an elegy on the death of the former governor Macquarie:

Deep in the warm recesses of each heart,
His lib'ral virtues held a grateful part.

Two years later Robert Howe published Wild Notes, from the Lyre of a Native Minstrel. By Charles Tompson, Jun., dedicated to Fulton. Before publication 212 subscriptions had been received.

On 12 April 1830 Tompson married Hannah Morris at St Matthew's, Windsor, and by 1831 was living in Kent Street, Sydney, and had become a clerk in the colonial secretary's office, where he remained until 1836 when he returned to his Doon Moor Cottage, Penrith. In July that year he and Fulton were appointed to the Penrith sub-committee of Bishop Broughton's [q.v.] general committee to resist the introduction of the National school system. In the Sydney Gazette, 17 December 1829, Tompson published Australia. A Translation of the Latin Prize Poem of S. Smith, a student of Hyde Abbey School, Winchester.

By 1855 he was a clerk assistant to the Legislative Council, and in 1856 became a clerk assistant to the new Legislative Assembly, of which he was clerk from 1 January 1860 to his retirement on 31 January 1869. Hannah Tompson died on 12 January 1874. Tompson died on 5 January 1883 at Teddington, Glebe Point, and was buried in the Waverley cemetery. There were no children.

According to H. M. Green, Tompson's 'notes are very far from wild; on the contrary they are so polished and urbane that their appearance in such a place and time is something of a marvel . . . his verses are almost perfect in craftsmanship'. However, anthologists have made little effort to revive Tompson's work.

HRA (1), 18; J. C. L. Fitzpatrick, Those were the days (Syd, 1923); Sydney Gazette, 5 Dec 1832; Aust Almanack, 1831-35; New South Wales Calendar, 1832-37; Records (Soc Aust Gen, Syd).

TOOSEY, JAMES DENTON (1801-1883), pastoralist, was born on 11 March 1801 at King's Lynn, Norfolk, England, the son of James Bramall Toosey and his wife Elisabeth, née Denton. His father served with the British army in Canada and then became a corn merchant and estate manager in Norfolk. His grandfather, Rev. Philip Toosey, was ecclesiastical commissary in Canada in 1784.

After eight years at Walsham School, Norfolk, Toosey learnt farming in 1820 from Charles Champion, a celebrated

Shorthorn and Durham breeder, of Blyth, Nottinghamshire. Next year he worked at Feltwell Place, Norfolk, where his father and his uncle, James Denton, were joint proprietors. When the farm went bankrupt in 1825 he left England with six officers of the Horse Breeding Co. of the New South Wales and Van Diemen's Land Establishment, arriving in Hobart Town in the *Albion* in May 1826. He worked on the Cressy estate of the company, then rented the 5000-acre Trevallyn estate from William Barnes [q.v.] in July 1827. When this venture was not successful, he left for Sydney to manage for twelve months a large agricultural farm at Shoalhaven, belonging to Berry & Wollstonecraft [qq.v.]. He returned to Hobart in 1830, intending to go to India, but was persuaded to rejoin the Cressy establishment. He moved into Cressy House, but the estate was verging on bankruptcy. Toosey appealed to Lieut-Governor Arthur in May 1833 against intended sequestration, and with support from the three directors he became temporary manager in 1833-36. With his understanding and experience he quickly restored its prosperity and improved its stock by imports from England and Dresden.

In April 1836 he visited England, and married Charlotte Septima (1804-1851). They returned to the colony in December 1837. He was gazetted a justice of the peace six years later. After his wife's death on 29 May 1851 Toosey took his only child, James Denton junior, to Hobson's Bay, Victoria, but suffered a severe illness at Ballarat. On recovery he sailed for England in April 1853 to have his son educated at Winchester and at Exeter College, Oxford. While in England he persuaded the proprietors of the Cressy establishment to sell the estate as property prices had risen after the gold discoveries. He returned in 1854 and the estate was sold for £135,000.

Toosey himself bought a part, including Richmond Hill, and in 1858 added McRae's Hills to other land purchases that together involved him in a debt of £35,000, which took him twenty years to clear. His son took up pastoral pursuits at Cressy House, the adjoining property, on his return from England.

A strong Anglican, he acquired two acres for the church and cemetery at Cressy. He held Evangelical views and in 1845 joined the protest against the ritualist innovations of surplice and weekly offertory at Longford. When Christ's College was closed in 1856 Toosey was appointed for his shrewd business ability as one of the trustees, under whose direction the institution was freed from debt in fourteen years. At his death on 4 December 1883 at Cressy he left £400 to enlarge and improve the Cressy Church, and from his Richmond Hill estate endowed both the college and church, the estate later becoming St Wilfred's Theological College. His portrait, painted by Henry Mundy, hangs in the hall of Christ College, Hobart. Kindly and hospitable, he was highly esteemed in the district. The year before his death, he published *Brief Jottings of my Life* (Launceston, 1882). His son survived him, and inherited his public spirit, endowing the Longford Hospital, named in his memory, before he returned to England in 1888.

K. R. von Stieglitz, *Story of Holy Trinity Church, Cressy* (Cressy, 1958); *Examiner* (Launceston), 6 Dec 1883; *Church News* (Hob), Aug 1898.   P. R. HART

TORRENS, ROBERT (1780-1864), officer of marines, political economist and colonization commissioner, was born in Ireland, son of Robert Torrens of Harveyhill, County Londonderry, and his wife Elizabeth, née Bristow, daughter of a clergyman. On 1 February 1796 he joined the marines as a second lieutenant and served in the Channel Fleet and ocean convoys. He was promoted first lieutenant in 1798 and captain in 1806. In August 1810 he was given command of the marine garrison on Anholt Island in the Kattegat; next March he was wounded in 'the romantic defence' of the island and promoted brevet-major. In 1813 he was attached to the Woolwich division, in 1819 promoted brevet-lieut-colonel and in 1823 placed on half-pay. In 1830 he sought appointment as deputy-adjutant-general of marines; although passed over he was restored to full pay, transferred to the Plymouth division and then to Chatham, and in June 1831 promoted substantive major. On 17 October 1834 he announced that as a brevet-lieut-colonel he had retired from the service 'by the sale of an unattached majority'.

Torrens was an inveterate publicist. His active service had seldom interfered with 'those habits of patient investigation' in which he 'delighted to indulge', but it had marked effects on his prolific books and pamphlets. His controversial writings were mostly designed to correct, repeal, reform or change those political and economic policies which he believed were threats to Britain's greatness. In 1818 he contested the seat of Rochester without success but on 17 December 'as a gentleman well informed on, and much interested in, all subjects of natural philosophy' was elected a fellow of the Royal Society. In 1821 he helped to found the Political Economy Club and became a proprietor of the Whig *Traveller*, with which the *Globe* was later combined. In 1826 he was elected for Ipswich but unseated after a protest. In 1831 he was returned for Ashburton and in 1832-35 represented Bolton in the reformed parliament.

Torrens's chief influence on Australia was his promotion of emigration. In 1817 he had sent to the chairman of a select committee a paper on reducing the Irish poor rates by emigration to the colonies. A year earlier he had collected information on Botany Bay, 'having prospects of being sent out as its Governor'. In 1825 he joined a scheme for company colonization at the Bay of Islands and later offered to sell some of its land to the New Zealand Associaiton. In 1828 he applied for land at the Swan River settlement and next year sought a government post there. In 1830 he attacked the National Colonization Society for advocating concentrated settlement in the colonies but was converted when he learnt that concentration meant 'the combination of capital and labour to give maximum production within a given area'. He then became active in seeking from the Colonial Office a charter for the South Australian Land Co. When this attempt failed in 1833 he joined the South Australian Association and, in hope of becoming governor of the proposed colony, reopened negotiations with the Colonial Office. In 1834 he chaired the committee which disgusted E. G. Wakefield [q.v.] by deciding that the minimum price for land should be 12s. an acre. This price was inserted in the South Australian Act, which also provided for a colonization commission to manage land sales and emigration. In May 1835 Torrens was appointed chairman of this commission and in June he published *Colonization of South Australia*, in reply to criticisms in the *Westminster Review*. By December the prescribed guarantee fund had been raised and land orders for 35,000 acres sold; on 19 February 1836 the province of South Australia and its boundaries were established by letters patent.

For the next six years Torrens worked zealously, writing and lecturing to woo capital investment in South Australia and campaigning for emigrant labourers especially from Ireland. Later he claimed that the colonization part of the project was a triumph, but admitted that the financial part had failed. To most colonists, however, his whole administration was a calamity. He did nothing to solve the vexed question of authority divided between commission and Colonial Office, and his inadequate direction and staffing of the survey expedition under Colonel Light [q.v.] caused needless delays in rural production and encouraged reckless land speculation. He also abandoned the Wakefield principle of concentration; instead of limiting landbuyers to the 200 square miles around Adelaide, his promises of free choice soon required the survey of 8000 square miles. Since special surveys of 4000 acres could be selected on the best sites, land sales soared in 1839 and the number of emigrants with free passages nearly doubled. This seeming success disturbed the Colonial Office because the achievement was embittering the neighbouring colonies. Torrens had also fallen out with his unpaid colleagues on the commission in 1837 when he was given, at his own request, a salary of £600. The government's decision to form a general Colonial Land and Emigration Commission in January 1840 was therefore welcomed by Torrens, and as one of its three members his salary increased to £800.

By June the rosy prospects were dimmed. Although emigration was proceeding at a great rate, land sales had collapsed. By that time over £250,000 had been paid into the land fund but less than half of it had been used to provide free passages for 12,000 emigrants, many of whom were outside the prescribed ages of 15 to 30. The balance of the fund had been spent mainly on publicity and costly surveys; without realizing it Torrens had brought the province to bankruptcy. In July the commissioners tried to raise a loan, too late because the newspapers had the story, and in August emigration was stopped. Parliament came to the rescue with a loan, and in April 1841 a select committee on South Australia made Governor Gawler the luckless scapegoat, although none of his bills on London had been dishonoured until October 1840. In 1842 South Australia became a Crown colony and Torrens's 'self-supporting' model of systematic colonization came to an end. Belatedly he was dismissed for violating a rule made by Glenelg in October 1835 that no commissioner was to have a proprietary interest in the colony. Although some of his colleagues had promptly resigned Torrens argued that he had only borrowed £1000 to buy land in South Australia. Since he had repaid the loan by 1838 and then transferred the land titles to his relations his continued appeals for reinstatement were unavailing.

Torrens had continued his study of political economy, for which he won wide repute. In the 1840s he also helped to form companies to mine copper and build railways in South Australia, and in 1855 he advocated nominated upper houses in the new constitutions of responsible government. He died on 27 May 1864 in London. In 1801 at Dublin he had married Charity, daughter of Richard Chute of Roxburgh, County Kerry. Of their children, Robert Richard (1814-1884) became noted for his system of registering land titles. Torrens was also survived by his second wife Esther Sarah, née Serle, whom he had married in September 1820.

F. H. Hitchins, The colonial land and emigration commission (Philadelphia, 1931); D. Pike, Paradise of Dissent (Melb, 1957); L Robbins, Robert Torrens and the evolution of classical economics (Lond, 1958); S. A. Meenai, 'Robert Torrens, 1780-1864', Economica, 23 (1956); F. W. Fetter, 'Robert Torrens: colonel of marines and political economist', Economnomica, 29 (1962); Sel cttee on South Australia, Report, PP (HC), 1841 (394); S. A. Meenai, Robert Torrens (M.Sc.Econ. thesis, Univ Lond, 1948).

TORRES, LUIS VAEZ DE (fl.1605-1607), navigator, was a Spanish subject, but nothing is known of his birth or early life. He must have been an experienced navigator when in 1605 he was given command of the San Pedrico, 40 tons, the second in size of three vessels with which Pedro Fernandez de Quiros [q.v.] set out from Callao, Peru, on 21 December in search of the supposed southern continent. Quiros placed great reliance on Torres, and when they reached an island usually sent him ashore in command of the landing party. Torres protested when, in mid-Pacific, Quiros altered course from WSW., which might have taken them to southeastern Australia, to WNW., which did take them to Espiritu Santo (New Hebrides) on 1 May 1606. Torres took a party ashore, but by his 'indiscreet presumption', got involved in a fracas in which several natives were killed. Appointed camp master he had a stockade built, but before the end of the month Quiros decided to abandon Espiritu Santo and sail onward. In bad weather Quiros was driven out of the bay, and when Torres failed to find him, he opened his sealed orders, which ordained that Quiros's second-in-command, Don Diego de Prado, was to take command, and that he was to

search for land as far as 20°S. but, if none was found, to sail to Manila. Prado seems to have allowed Torres to exert actual command, and Torres wrote that he was determined to carry out the viceroy's orders 'although contrary to the inclinations of many, I may say of the greatest part, but my temper was different from that of Captain Ferdinand de Quiros'. In company with the small Los Tres Reyes Margos, the third vessel, he went south to 21°, found no land (he was then west of New Caledonia and about 300 miles from the coast of Australia) and, failing to reach the east coast of New Guinea, coasted closely along its south side, and sailed through Torres Strait, thus discovering that New Guinea was not the northern peninsula of a southern continent. For more than two months the Spaniards sailed along the coast of New Guinea which they claimed for Philip III, fought with the natives, and captured some. On 22 May 1607 Torres reached Manila, where he disappears from history. The report of his voyage seems to have been filed and forgotten, and knowledge of it was not recovered until the British occupied Manila in 1762.

J. C. Beaglehole, The exploration of the Pacific, 2nd ed (Lond, 1947) and for bibliog; J. W. Forsyth, 'Clio etwas gebuckt', JRAHS, 49 (1964).

TOWNSON, JOHN (1760-1835), army officer and settler, came from Shropshire, England, and was the elder brother of Robert Townson [q.v.]. He was appointed ensign in the 18th Regiment on 13 October 1779 and promoted lieutenant in July 1780. His regiment suppressed a dangerous mutiny at Guernsey and formed part of the Gibraltar garrison after the siege was lifted in 1783. He transferred to the New South Wales Corps in October 1789 and arrived in the colony in the Scarborough in June 1790.

Most of his military service in the colony was spent on Norfolk Island, where he was stationed for some six years between late 1791 and late 1799. He was a member of the court of inquiry in 1794 which investigated Lieut-Governor King's actions during the mutiny on the island the previous year. In May 1795 he was promoted captain and from September 1796 until November 1799 acted as lieutgovernor of Norfolk Island while King was absent in England.

Townson's administration of the island was generally efficient and he appears to have had a steadying influence on its inhabitants. One noteworthy achievement was the building in 1798 of the sloop *Norfolk*, which was used later that year by Matthew Flinders [q.v.] to circumnavigate Van Diemen's Land. Although he enjoyed the esteem of King, Townson and Governor Hunter each lacked confidence in the other, and Townson's complaints to the duke of Portland doubtless played their part in Hunter's recall. Although he stipulated that he would remain until King returned, his leave was approved and he departed early in 1800 for England where through illness, he retired by sale of his commission in July 1803.

He returned to the colony in August 1806 armed with a letter stating the intention of the secretary of state to direct Governor Bligh to grant him 2000 acres. Bligh declined to do this until he received specific instructions, although he said he would allow Townson to select, occupy and make use of the land. This Townson refused as he felt it would leave him at the will and pleasure of Bligh, and he was about to leave the colony when his brother Robert arrived in July 1807. In December the secretary of state directed that the grant be made, along with others which, though promised, Bligh had been unwilling to execute without official authority, but the order had not reached Sydney when the rebellion occurred in January 1808. In July Major Johnston [q.v.] granted Townson 2000 acres in the Bexley and Hurstville districts, and next year he received 250 more from Lieut-Governor Paterson [q.v.]; this was all regranted by Governor Macquarie in 1810 and, because of Townson's severe illness, without the usual restrictions on their alienation. After a brief visit to Van Diemen's Land in the summer of 1811-12, Townson sold his grants and thereafter spent most of his time developing further grants which he had received near Kelso on the River Tamar. He inherited a quarter of his brother Robert's estate in 1827 and died in Sydney on 8 July 1835, leaving an estate sworn at £5000 to his nephew, Captain John Witts, R.M., his nieces and his two sisters.

An efficient, if unspectacular administrator, Townson does not seem to have been engaged in the rum traffic and unlike his younger brother Robert did not take an active part in the 'rum rebellion'. He appears to have been generally well liked by his contemporaries, although his marked deafness and ill health, which no doubt debarred him from taking an active part in public life, earned him in his middle and later years a reputation of being unsettled and querulous.

HRA (1), 1-9, (3), 2-4; P. G. King, Letter-book 1797-1806 (ML); Piper papers (ML).

M. AUSTIN

TOWNSON, ROBERT (1763-1827), scholar, scientist and settler, came from Shropshire, England. There seems no evidence for the widespread belief that he was a Yorkshireman. His zest for natural history dictated his activities for many years. He travelled widely as a gentleman scholar, collaborating with the professors at the universities he visited. In 1791 he was elected a fellow of the Royal Society of Edinburgh. He then visited the Universities of Copenhagen and Uppsala. After contributing a paper to the Linnean Society of London in 1792 on 'The Perceptivity of Plants', he made his headquarters at Göttingen University (D.C.L., 1795). While there he made expeditions into France and Austria, visited the University of Vienna, made an extensive tour of Hungary and he published *Observationes physiologicae de amphibiis* (Göttingen, 1794). A period of authorship followed. In 1797 *Travels in Hungary* was published and appeared in French in Paris in 1798; in that year he published *Philosophy of Mineralogy* and in 1799 *Tracts and Observations in Natural History and Physiology*, which included his Linnean paper and a translation of his Latin work of 1794.

After his plans for the study of mineralogy and geology in India had fallen through, Townson's thoughts turned to Australia. He was often at the home of Sir Joseph Banks [q.v] and had there met William Paterson [q.v.] of the New South Wales Corps. His brother, Captain John Townson[q.v.], also returned to England in 1800, so he had ample opportunities to learn about the new settlement. When John decided to return as a settler, Robert approached the British government. He was warmly received, informed that he was the type most urgently needed in the colony, promised land and indulgences, and allowed £100 to buy books and a laboratory for the colony. Dr Townson arrived in Sydney in the *Young William* on 7 July 1807. Proficient in all branches of natural science and also in Latin, Greek, German, French, he was the most eminent scholar in the young colony.

Much to his surprise Robert found John, who had arrived in August 1806, preparing to leave for England. John had brought a letter stating that the secretary of state intended to direct Governor Bligh to grant him 2000 acres and certain indulgences. Bligh would not 'locate the grant' until he received specific instructions from London, but proposed that meanwhile Townson should select and occupy his land, buy livestock and have the use of four convicts for eighteen months. Robert was armed with a similar letter and received similar treatment.

Townson was further affronted when Bligh displayed neither appreciation nor understanding of his talents, and insisted that he consult the governor over the use of the scientific material he had brought out and that he could not go in the *Porpoise* to the Derwent to settle there but must charter a private ship. Greatly frustrated and deeply chagrined he became an opponent of Bligh, and when rebellion took place some months later he was judged one of the principal six 'who previously concerted together with Major Johnston [q.v.] the arrest and imprisonment of the Governor'. He was present at the dinner at the officers' mess on the eve of the trial of John Macarthur [q.v.] which precipitated the revolt: he signed the requisition to Johnston to depose Bligh on 26 January 1808, though not the declaration of thanks next day, and took part in the formal deposition of Bligh at Government House. He served on the insurrectionary committees set up to obtain evidence against Bligh, but soon fell out with the rebel administration. Johnston refused to give him the land he wanted at Emu Island, near Penrith; though he was given 2000 acres at Botany Bay near the present Blakehurst and twenty-eight government cattle, he claimed that only half the grant was of any use, and his long complaints against Bligh written in 1807 and 1808 were followed by another, equally querulous, in 1809 against his supplanters.

Governor Macquarie had to cancel the grants to Townson, like all others made by the rebels, but in 1811 he regranted him 1680 acres at Botany and added 1000 acres near the present Minto. This became the famous Varro Ville farm, but since these grants were made on the customary condition that the land be cultivated and not sold for five years, Townson again felt aggrieved. He had been living on his capital for nearly four years and was afraid of penury. He sought permission to sell his land and return to England. In the end he remained but developed a psychopathic personality. He subordinated everything to the development of his farms, shut himself off from society, and apparently did no scientific work in New South Wales. He became 'singular' and eccentric, and his rigid economy became a byword. He also nursed undue hostility towards all who had contributed to his critical situation; Macquarie described him as 'discontented' and

one of his leading opponents, though there is no evidence that Townson took part in intrigues against him.

After Macquarie departed Townson began to take his rightful place in the community. In 1822 he became a foundation vice-president of the Agricultural Society and a member of its Horticultural and Stock Fund Committees; Wollstonecraft [q.v.] proposed him for membership of the Philosophical Society of Australasia in the same year, and though the society's records do not disclose whether or not he was elected, it is probable that he was. In 1822 he joined in the protest against the commissariat paying for purchases in dollars, and in 1824 in the memorials against the British duties on wool. In 1826 he was appointed a magistrate. His name appeared regularly on subscription lists, and headed the list of donations towards establishing the Sydney Dispensary to give free medical attention to the poor. His invitations to dinner called for an early arrival so that there could be at least two hours of conversation before the meal. The contents of his library offered for sale after his death reveal his wide interests. Varro Ville became a show place for its beauty, abundance and variety in orchard and garden; his vineyard was second only to that of Gregory Blaxland [q.v.]; his fine-woolled sheep and their clip were in great demand; his cattle were numerous and in the opinion of his contemporaries 'no single man had accomplished more in the rearing of stock'.

Townson died at Varro Ville on 27 June 1827 and was buried at Parramatta. A bachelor, he left his fortune to his brother, Captain John Townson of Van Diemen's Land, to two nieces residing in England and to his nephew, Captain John Witts, R.M.

A portrait, attributed to Augustus Earle [q.v.], was transferred from the Australian Museum to the Mitchell Library in 1961.

HRNSW, 6-7; *Sydney Gazette*, 2 July 1827; MS cat under R. Townson (ML).

V. W. E. GOODIN

TREGURTHA, EDWARD PRIMROSE (1803-1880), sea captain, was born at Newlyn, Cornwall, England, the son of Captain Edward Primrose Tregurtha, R.N., and his wife Mary, née Burgess. Edward was a turbulent youth and after a brief spell in the navy left it for the East India Co.'s maritime service. He sailed the barque *Caroline* from Calcutta to Hobart Town by way of Sydney in 1831 and then took her whaling for two years in the western

Pacific. He returned to England in 1833, when his account of prospects for settlers in Australia encouraged the Dennis and Wettenhall families, with whom he was connected, to emigrate. Alexander Dennis, whose wife Emma was Tregurtha's sister, founded the Tarndwarncoort property in Victoria.

Tregurtha married Elizabeth Bussell in England in 1835 and returned to Van Diemen's Land later that year in the *Derwent* as a prospective colonist, with plans for establishing a fishery. After a fortnight's trawling in D'Entrecasteaux Channel, he gave up the fishing plan and decided to start farming. Instead he went into partnership with Captain Edwin Whiting, who was looking for financial backing to operate the brig *Henry*. This was the beginning of five years' successful operations between northern Tasmania and the new settlements in Port Phillip and South Australia. Their first cargo was 37 cattle for J. H. Wedge [q.v.] of Snake Banks, and in May 1836 the *Henry* transported 750 sheep to Hobson's Bay. A consignment of 380 sheep taken to Adelaide in July 1837 was sold in lots of ten to small farmers at 55s. each. Tregurtha and Whiting doubled their carrying capacity by acquiring the *Charlotte*, and with the two vessels landed 55,000 sheep, hundreds of cattle and horses and about 2000 passengers on the Australian mainland. On one voyage Tregurtha landed a party at Geelong and claimed to have then surveyed the harbour as far as Point Henry, naming the point after the brig. Thereafter most of his operations centred on Geelong.

Tregurtha retired from the sea in 1839 and began business in Launceston as a shipping agent, but in 1850 he became master of the tug *Gipsy* on the Tamar. He was appointed shipping master of the port of Launceston in 1858 and held the position until his death. He was a consistent supporter of St John's Church of England, Launceston. He died in Launceston on 6 August 1880, survived by his wife, four sons and three daughters.

P. L. Brown (ed), *Clyde Company papers*, 2 (Lond, 1952); VHM, 21 (1945-46), 31, 32; *Examiner* (Launceston), 21 Nov 1868, 7 Aug 1880; GO 33/78 (TA).   DECIE DENHOLM

TRIGG, HENRY (1791-1882), superintendent of public works and Congregational lay leader, was born on 30 June 1791 in Gloucester, England. He practised the trade of house carpenter and builder in his home county until in 1829 he decided to emigrate to the new colony of Western Australia.

Arriving in October with some £200 in capital, he applied successfully for a land grant of 2986 acres. His skill as a builder was in great demand. In October 1838 he was appointed superintendent of public works and was responsible for the erection of many of the early government buildings in Perth and the outlying districts.

A deeply religious man of moderately Calvinistic views, he and other Dissenters worshipped with the Methodists, but when a Wesleyan minister arrived in 1840 he became dissatisfied and in 1843 began meetings in his own home that developed into a church based on Congregational principles. The first chapel was designed and built by Trigg in 1846. He was its lay leader for seven years and in April 1851 resigned from his government position to become full-time pastor. He devoted much time to caring for the spiritual and moral welfare of the prisoners in the local roadgangs and gaols. His fervent though unbigoted views on social and moral principles were firmly expressed in pulpit and in print. He died in Perth on 15 February 1882.

In 1813 he had married Amelia Ralph and they had six sons and four daughters. Henry, the eldest son, was his father's partner in the building trade.

S. H. Cox, *Seventy years history of the Trinity Congregational Church, Perth, 1845-1916* (Perth, 1916); H. Trigg, Letters to his wife, 1829-30 (Battye Lib, Perth); P. U. Henn, Genealogical notes (Battye Lib, Perth).
                                        P. J. COLES

TUCKER, JAMES (1808-1888?), convict and supposed author, was born in Bristol, England. Although one theory has him educated as a Catholic at Stonyhurst College, Lancashire, the James Tucker enrolled at that school in 1814-21 is recorded as having been born on 8 August 1803. The first indisputable reference to James Tucker is in 1826, when at 18 he was charged with sending a threatening letter to a cousin, James Stanyford Tucker, of Leytonstone, Essex. Under the name James Rosenberg Tucker, clerk, he was tried at the Essex Assizes on 3 March 1826, found guilty, and sentenced to transportation for life. He arrived at Sydney in the *Midas* in February 1827, and was sent next month to the Emu Plains Agricultural Establishment. By 1831 he was one of the prisoners attached to the Department of Public Works and in 1832-39 was employed in the Colonial Architect's Office. His ticket-of-leave, recommended by the Sydney bench of magistrates in 1833 and issued on 27

June 1835, was suspended in 1839 after he was convicted of drunkenness. However, in recognition of his efforts at a fire at the Royal Hotel in March 1840 he was again recommended for a ticket-of-leave, which was made out on 1 September 1840 for the district of Maitland. He lost it in 1844 when he was convicted of forgery. Sentenced to work in irons for a year, he was transferred to the penal settlement of Port Macquarie, where by September 1846 he was employed as store-keeper to the superintendent.

Tucker is alleged to have written at Port Macquarie three works: 'Jemmy Green in Australia', a comedy in three acts; 'The Grahames' Vengeance', an historical drama in three acts by 'Otto von Rosenberg'; and 'Ralph Rashleigh or the Life of an Exile', by 'Giacomo di Rosenberg', the advertisement of which was dated 31 December 1845. The manuscripts of these works were first noticed publicly in the *Sydney Morning Herald*, 9 April 1892, the author being described as 'a convict, an architect by profession . . . who had been transported for forgery'. They had apparently been bequeathed by the author to Alexander Burnett, who had been overseer in the Road Department and in 1838-41 clerk of works under the colonial architect, and who had them for some thirty years before his death in 1885. First published in 1929, *Ralph Rashleigh* was re-edited in 1952 by Colin Roderick, whose claim for Tucker's authorship has not been conclusively proved. The case for Tucker rests on internal evidence (the manuscripts are in Tucker's hand and the alias of Rosenberg is one he had used in 1826) and on the testimony of a resident of Port Macquarie, Charles Edwin Dick (1875-1953), who had in his youth heard of Tucker's activities from ex-convicts still living there (three other plays were named) and who had in 1889 perused the manuscripts of two other prose works. However, it has also been claimed that Tucker was merely a copyist of works originally composed by another and that the level of education required of the author of *Ralph Rashleigh* is not to be found in other examples of Tucker's hand, such as the blackmailing letter of 1826 and official Port Macquarie papers of 1846. Until further evidence is produced, the question of authorship is likely to remain in dispute.

In 1847 Tucker was granted a ticket-of-leave for the district of Port Macquarie, but in 1849 was arrested for absence from his district and sent to prison at Goulburn. Tickets-of-leave were again issued to him on 18 March 1850 and for Moreton Bay on 30 January 1853. After this date Tucker is not mentioned in convict records and his movements are not easily traced. It has been asserted that he was the James Tucker who died at Liverpool Asylum on 11 June 1866 aged 72; however, this man has been identified as a free assisted immigrant, who arrived in the *Edward Coulson* in November 1833. Another James Tucker, native of Bristol, who died at Prince Alfred Hospital, Sydney, on 20 December 1888, apparently aged 84, had married Louisa Binks at St Laurence Church of England, Sydney, on 19 January 1853 and had at least two children: Valentine Kelso, born at Kelso on 2 November 1858 and Fanny, born at Sydney on 2 August 1864. When registering the birth of his son in 1858 Tucker gave his birthplace as Bristol and age as 49; these details coincide with those of the convict James Tucker.

Though their authorship remains in doubt, the works attributed to Tucker occupy a significant place in the history of Australian literature. In particular *Ralph Rashleigh*, the fruit of a creative talent of high order, is of considerable importance both for its intrinsic literary merit and for its value as a social document.

C. Roderick (ed), *Ralph Rashleigh* (Syd, 1952 and 1962); C. Roderick (ed), *Jemmy Green in Australia* (Syd, 1955); M. H. Ellis, 'Who wrote "Ralph Rashleigh"?', *Bulletin*, 9 Feb 1963.   PETER SCOTT

TUCKFIELD, FRANCIS (1808-1865), missionary, was born on 10 May 1808 in the parish of Germoe, Cornwall, England. In his youth he was a miner and seasonal fisherman; at 18 he was converted to the Wesleyan Methodist faith and became an active local preacher. He was accepted as a candidate for the ministry in 1835 and received two years training at the Theological Institution, Hoxton. Upon representations by Rev. Joseph Orton [q.v.] he was selected, with Rev. Benjamin Hurst, as a missionary to the Aboriginals in the Port Phillip District.

The two young men reached Hobart Town with their families in the *Seppings* in March 1838. Four months later Tuckfield arrived in Melbourne, leaving Hurst to follow. Seeking a suitable mission site, Tuckfield made several journeys around Geelong, often with William Buckley [q.v.] as interpreter, and finally chose an area on the Barwon River, near Birregurra. This was confirmed by Hurst on his arrival as superintendent, by Orton and by Governor Gipps. The station was named Buntingdale, in honour of Rev. Jabez Bunting, an outstanding Wesleyan leader in England. Gipps made a provisional grant of 640 acres with a large encircling reserve to prevent settlers from encroaching too close to the mission station.

While Hurst took charge in Geelong Tuckfield worked at .Buntingdale, where in spite of his devotion and enthusiasm the mission made small progress. The local tribes were nomadic and could not be confined to so small an area. The Colac tribe offered most hope of success and at times Tuckfield travelled and lived with it. Unfortunately, intertribal fights were common and Tuckfield and his family were sometimes in real danger; a fire in 1840 destroyed the mission buildings; Hurst was anxious to be relieved of responsibility for the mission; and Tuckfield found that while he could advance the education of the younger Aboriginals he could make little religious impact upon the tribes.

By 1841 Tuckfield was persuaded that mission work could be satisfactory only among tribes completely divorced from white settlement and in 1842, with Superintendent La Trobe's approval, he travelled to the junction of the Goulburn and Murray Rivers seeking a more suitable place for mission work. However, neither the government nor Tuckfield's committee favoured this idea and it seemed that the whole missionary project was to be unsuccessful. With great courage and determination Tuckfield continued at Buntingdale, keeping a small number of Aboriginals around him, attending to his school and gradually developing the area into an efficient farming property.

The government became convinced that the mission was a failure and informed Tuckfield that the grazing licence, by which he now held the mission station, would be cancelled at the end of 1850. In spite of his dedication to the care of the Aboriginals and his persistence Tuckfield now had no alternative but to abandon the site, an unhappy outcome for both his church's missionary zeal and the government's humanitarian programme. Tuckfield was later appointed in turn to several churches in Victoria, New South Wales and Tasmania. After a break caused by ill health, he took charge of the Portland Church, Victoria, in 1864. Next year he contracted pneumonia after attending a funeral, and died on 21 October 1865. He was buried in the Methodist section of the Portland cemetery.

Tuckfield was twice married: first to Sarah Gilbart of Cornwall; and second to Mary Stevens of Glenorchy, Tasmania. Of his eleven children, three sons became ministers and four daughters married ministers.

Tuckfield was an able and zealous missionary with a gift for native languages; the failure at Buntingdale must fairly be ascribed to causes beyond his control. Later he showed himself to be a greatly loved and self-sacrificing pastor.

J. D. Lang, *Phillipsland* (Edinb, 1847), 123-30; A'sian Wesleyan Methodist Church, *Minutes* (Syd, 1866); W. L. Blamires and J. B. Smith, *The early story of the Wesleyan Methodist Church in Victoria* (Melb, 1886); G. W. Greenwood, 'Rev Francis Tuckfield's magnificent failure at Bunting Dale', *Heritage* (Methodist Hist Soc Vic), no 6 (1956); F. Tuckfield, Journal (La Trobe Lib, Melb).

C. A. McCallum

TURNBULL, ADAM (1803-1891), medical practitioner, public servant and Presbyterian minister, was born on 4 November 1803 at Buccleuch Place, Edinburgh, the eldest son of Dr Adam Turnbull, who served as a surgeon in the 57th Regiment in the American wars and in 1800-10 was medical officer at Edinburgh Castle under the command of his friend, Earl Moira, and his wife Susan(na), née Bayne, who went to New South Wales as a widow in 1819 and to Van Diemen's Land in 1823.

Adam Turnbull junior was educated at Edinburgh High School and obtained the degree of M.D. in that city before he was 21. He married Margaret, daughter of George Young, of Tolcross, Edinburgh. In 1824 the Colonial Office promised him a land grant in Van Diemen's Land, and with his wife and three brothers he arrived at Hobart Town in the *City of Edinburgh* on 13 April 1825. With them were members of his wife's family and mutual friends, the Murrays. They all settled in the Campbell Town district, where Turnbull named his property Winton, after the estate of a relation, Sir James Sandilands, whose bequest had provided the capital which entitled him to a grant.

In 1827 he became a partner of James Reid in a whisky distillery near Campbell Town, but the partnership was dissolved late in 1828 when Turnbull entered the Colonial Medical Service as assistant surgeon in the Richmond district, leaving a younger brother, Francis Moira, in charge of Winton. Late in 1829 Turnbull began private practice in Campbell Street, Hobart. In 1831 when John Montagu [q.v.] returned from England and was moved from post to post by Lieut-Governor Arthur, Turnbull was appointed assistant surgeon, for which he received half-pay while he also acted temporarily as private secretary to Arthur, clerk of the Legislative and Executive Councils and colonial treasurer, sharing the salary of these offices with Montagu. Under Sir John Franklin's administration Turnbull continued to fill vacant positions in the public service, and he was responsible for writing many of the lieut-governor's dispatches. In the events leading to Montagu's dismissal in 1842 Turnbull had the invidious task of mediating between him and Sir John and Lady Franklin, and although unsuccessful he retained the personal confidence of both parties.

Turnbull was recommended to the Colonial Office by Arthur and Franklin for permanent public employment but notions of retrenchment prevailed in the 1840s, although in 1847 he was appointed a member of the Land Commission and chairman of the Caveat Board. He also continued to act from time to time as clerk of the councils and colonial treasurer. Outside his official duties he became a vice-president of the Mechanics' Institute, where he lectured on chemistry and other subjects. On 15 January 1845 he chaired the inaugural meeting of the Hobart Savings Bank and became an original member of the board. In 1847 he was an elder of St Andrew's Presbyterian Church and superintendent of its Sunday school.

In 1851 when the Legislative Council became part-elective Turnbull was appointed an official member and also acted as clerk of the Executive Council. Like many other colonists he was deeply exercised over the need for free immigration, the continued transportation of convicts, and the shortage of labour caused by the Victorian gold discoveries. The activities of the Anti-Transportation League ensured the return of several members to the new Legislative Council, although Lieut-Governor Denison was bitterly opposed to their views. In September 1852 some of the elected members gave notice of motion of an address to the Queen requesting the cessation of convict transportation to the colony. Turnbull informed Denison that he favoured the motion and with another nominee, Henry Samuel Chapman, tendered his resignation from the council. The lieut-governor refused the resignation, and in due course Turnbull voted for the motion, which was carried. Denison angrily maintained that Turnbull as a public servant had no right to vote against the government. In spite of his vigorous defence in memorials, in the Executive Council and at the bar of the Legislative Council, and authorization from London of his appointment as colonial secretary Turnbull was deprived of all his offices and of his right to a pension after twenty years' service.

This was a severe material blow to Turnbull and his family, but less than two years later he was in service again, having been ordained a Presbyterian minister and inducted to the charge of Campbell Town-Tunbridge. Through his energy and help, and with the backing of his congregation, the fine St Andrew's Church was built in Campbell Town. As its minister 'the Doctor' showed the same zeal for truth and courteousness as he had displayed in the public service. He had high moral principles and a sincere Christian faith. After a controversy in the Tasmanian Presbytery in 1863 had been carried to the Supreme Court and a ministerial colleague, Rev. J. Storie, had been dismissed, Turnbull pleaded his case before the presbytery each year until 1870 when Storie was reinstated. The chief justice, Sir Lambert Dobson, feelingly recorded Turnbull's calm, dignified and unruffled bearing throughout the case.

Turnbull resigned from the ministry in 1875 and in his retirement could look back on a full and fruitful life. He was still interested in the land, for as well as owning Winton, he had other Tasmanian properties by grant and lease, and in Victoria he held Dundas, Mount Koroite and Winnimburn stations in the name of Adam Turnbull & Son. In 1884 he and his wife celebrated their diamond wedding. He died in Campbell Town on 17 June 1891.

HRA (3), 4, 5; J. Heyer, The Presbyterian pioneers of Van Diemen's Land (Launceston, 1935); W. A. Townsley, The struggle for self-government in Tasmania 1842-1856 (Hob, 1951); CSO 1 & 5 (TA).   LEX FINLAY

TYERS, CHARLES JAMES (1806-1870), surveyor and public servant, was born in London, the son of John Tyers, a linen merchant in Piccadilly, and his wife Elizabeth, née Theobold. After education at Christ's Hospital he entered the navy in 1828. He served under Admiral Lord Lyons in the Blonde and Captain Bremer [q.v.] in the Alligator. He made a study of marine surveying and computed longitudes in the Channel, Mediterranean, West Indies and South Africa, becoming recognized as an expert, and in 1837 he was commissioned to survey the Port Essington area. He reached the rank of captain, but before he was given a command he left the navy in 1839 to join the colonial service. Later that year he was instructed by Governor Gipps to fix the 141st meridian east longitude, the declared boundary between Port Phillip and South Australia, to ascertain in which colony the mouth of the Glenelg River was situated. Tyers made a triangulation and a chain traverse to Portland from Melbourne, thus fixing the longitude of Portland at 141° 35′ 52″, and made chronometer readings from Sydney and lunar observations. Taking a mean from these three calculations he fixed the meridian, but because of differing opinions on the longitude of Sydney, Captain Lort Stokes [q.v.] placed it 57 chains west and Captain Owen Stanley and Sir Thomas Mitchell [qq.v.] at positions farther west again.Thus Tyers's position was most favourable to South Australia. Governor Gipps wrote to the Colonial Office: 'I have to explain that I have caused Mr Tyers' report to be printed in order that by being circulated amongst the officers of the departments it might stimulate them to exertion, and serve as a model in future operations of this nature'. However, after long disputes the boundary was not finally settled until 1914 when documents had to be sought from Tyers's descendants.

Tyers was appointed surveyor in charge of the Portland district in 1841. His work included the laying out of the town and a marine survey of the bay. He was in close contact with the Aboriginals and compiled a vocabulary of about a hundred of their words. He maintained that if treated as 'gentlemen' they were responsive and friendly. He was gazetted a commissioner of crown lands at Portland Bay in August 1842 and a year later became the first commissioner of crown lands for Gippsland. At La Trobe's request he left Melbourne in September to open a coastal route to Gippsland and then a route over the ranges. However, the task of penetrating the thick bush was aggravated by floods and bad weather and Tyers eventually took the sea route to Port Albert, where he arrived in January 1844. Later a third attempt succeeded despite the difficulty of carrying tents and equipment through the thick scrub. La Trobe was very pleased to have the way mapped and travelled it himself on horseback, surprising Tyers by his unexpected arrival at Alberton.

Tyers was responsible for inaugurating government in Gippsland and virtually became 'King' of the huge isolated area, where lawlessness had been common and the Aboriginals hostile. He made a map showing holdings and their occupants and sent it to La Trobe in July 1844 with a descriptive and statistical report. He regulated the liquor trade and on his recommendations two police stations and a Court of Petty Sessions were established and two justices of the peace appointed. He improved Port Albert to cope with the growing trade with Hobart Town. He made extensive explorations of Gippsland, always making his land valuations after trigonometrical survey and collection of geological specimens. In 1846 he investigated the suitability of Gabo Island for a lighthouse. He was appointed a stipendiary magistrate in 1853 and generally had a staff of two or three constables, bullock drivers and rangers. To this position was added that of warden of the Gippsland goldfields in 1861.

He moved from Old Port to Eagle Point, where in 1849 he married Georgina Caroline, daughter of William Scott, a grazier at Swan Reach. Later he moved to Sale and then built a home, Seabank, at Old Port, where he retired in 1867. He died at Melbourne on 20 September 1870.

Tyers was a man of upright character, with the reputation of showing justice rather than mercy, able to undergo great physical hardship yet setting a standard of civilized life in a remote part of the colony. He was a scholar and aesthete as well as a sailor and administrator and did much for the colony in its early days, as did many other naval men possessing similar qualities.

HRA (1), 22, 23, 25, 26; T. F. Bride (ed), *Letters from Victorian pioneers* (Melb, 1898); A. W. Greig, 'The beginnings of Gippsland', *VHM*, 2 (1912); A. S. Kenyon, 'The South Australian boundary', *VHM*, 11 (1926-27); *Port Phillip Patriot*, 21 Sept, 28 Dec 1843, 24 June 1844; G. Cox, 'Notes on Gippsland history', nos 18, 42, 44, 52, 56, *Gippsland Standard*, 1912-14; MS cat under Tyers (ML).

NOWA TYERS

U

ULLATHORNE, WILLIAM BERNARD (1806-1889), Catholic prelate, was born on 7 May 1806 at Pocklington, Yorkshire, England, the eldest of ten children of William Ullathorn and his wife Hannah, née Longstaff. His family had forfeited its estates in the sequel to the rebellion of 1745. At 12 his schooling was cut short and he entered the family business at Scarborough. Soon afterwards he was apprenticed before the mast and he was at sea for four years. Ashore in Memel however, he experienced a sudden and decisive religious conversion and in February 1823 he entered the English Benedictine school at Downside, where J. B. Polding [q.v.] was then headmaster. Next year, when Ullathorne sought to become a Benedictine, Polding was his novice-master and continued to dominate his spiritual and intellectual formation. Much under the influence of St Bernard of Clairvaux, Ullathorne wished to become a Trappist, but Polding held him to the English Benedictine Congregation, and after his ordination in 1831 turned his thoughts to the Australian mission in which Polding had long been interested, the English Benedictines having had responsibility for it on paper since June 1818. Opportunity for action came with the appointment of the liberal Sir Richard Bourke as governor of New South Wales in 1831 and the consecration in 1832 of W. P. Morris as vicar-apostolic of Mauritius, a mission embracing Australia. On 16 September 1832 Ullathorne sailed for Sydney, empowered to act there as Morris's vicar-general. At 26 he had received under Polding and Browne the best education that the Catholic world could then give, a unique blend of patristic, scholastic and modern learning, which he never ceased to improve on. When equipping himself for Sydney his first concern had been to amass a library of five hundred volumes.

He looked even younger than he was. When he landed in Hobart Town the vicar-general, P. Conolly [q.v.], learnt of his appointment and petitioned the bishop for its revocation. Likewise in Sydney, where he arrived in February 1833, J. J. Therry [q.v.] was at first patronizing. Ullathorne, however, took control without any hesitation, leaning much on the advice of J. McEncroe [q.v.], for Therry commanded a party at odds both with other priests in the colony and with the government. Governor Bourke, McEncroe and the leading Catholic laymen were all relieved to have Ullathorne's clear business head in charge. By July the Legislative Council made grants for the appointment of four new chaplains, the completion of three unfinished churches, and £800 a year for schools and schoolteachers. By Christmas St Mary's was in use and Ullathorne had visited the Hunter River and Bathurst; next year he visited Norfolk Island and the Illawarra district. Meanwhile Bourke had drafted proposals for the complete equality in the colony of the Anglican, Presbyterian and Catholic churches, and had also recommended that Ullathorne's stipend be doubled, enabling the vicar-general to rent a large house near the city.

Encouraged by such progress, Ullathorne followed Commissioner R. Therry [q.v.] and McEncroe in strongly urging the appointment of a bishop resident in Sydney, and in May 1834 Propaganda issued the brief of Polding's appointment as vicar-apostolic for New South Wales. Polding arrived in Sydney in September 1835 with one priest, three ecclesiastical students and a catechist, all paid by the government. Ullathorne, who had suspended the Windsor priest and was serving both Windsor and Parramatta himself from Sydney, now became parish priest of Parramatta, but rode to Sydney twice a week to conduct the bishop's business with the government. Thus he freed Polding for an extraordinarily intense mission among the incoming convicts, which provided a powerful case for further government support of Catholic chaplains to work in the interior and on Norfolk Island. During the controversy over the 1836 Church Act and Bourke's education proposals, Ullathorne found himself with McEncroe in opposition to the governor, Polding and Plunkett [q.v.], who all favoured the introduction of Stanley's Irish school system to the colony. However, Polding expressed his unqualified confidence in Ullathorne and decided to send him to Europe for more priests and schoolteachers and more money. Ullathorne accompanied Polding to Hobart and sailed thence to England, after another visit to Norfolk Island.

He was away for over two years entirely in the service of the Australian mission. In England he could recruit only one priest, C. Lovat, whose arrival in 1837 encouraged Polding to open a seminary. Ullathorne was summoned by Cardinal Weld to Rome, where he arrived in March, just before the cardinal's death. In Rome, without patronage and conspicuously young, he spent his best energies on preparing a report for the Sacred Congregation De Propaganda Fide, which won him the warm approval of Gregory XVI and a doctorate of divinity. He recruited J. A. Goold, O.S.A., later bishop of Melbourne, and in June obtained a rescript authorizing the establishment of an independent Benedictine monastery in New South Wales.

Returning to England, he persuaded the Colonial Office to allow passage money of £40 each for ten schoolteachers, whom he recruited from all parts of the British Isles. He published a substantial pamphlet, *The Catholic Mission in Australasia* (London, 1837), and by preaching throughout Lancashire raised £1500 for the mission. The pamphlet quickly ran into six editions, and 80,000 copies were distributed in French, German, Dutch and Italian. In Liverpool he recruited an Irish priest, F. Murphy [q.v.], later bishop of Adelaide, and with his help proceeded to recruit seven priests, two ecclesiastical students and five Sisters of Charity in Ireland; all except the nuns reached Sydney before Ullathorne. A benefactor in Vienna gave £1250 and the Lyons Society 16,000 francs toward their passages and the government gave £150 each for the priests, though the nuns refused all government assistance. On 8 and 12 February 1838 Ullathorne gave evidence to the Molesworth committee on transportation to the effect that the system had failed altogether as a means of reformation of convicts. The Molesworth evidence was a special ordeal for him, because of his fear of accidentally revealing confessional secrets; he brushed with the chairman in private and spoke to the committee with nervous rapidity; only his concern for the mission carried him through. To convey his convictions about transportation at a popular level he had, while in Ireland for a fortnight during 1837, undertaken to write a pamphlet on *The Horrors of Transportation briefly unfolded to the People*; it was published next year in Dublin and Birmingham. He embarked on 17 August with three priests, four students and five nuns, and the party arrived in Sydney on 31 December 1838. He had now added fifteen clergy to the mission.

Ullathorne resumed his duties in Parramatta, but now he had the nuns to assist him in the Orphan School and the Female Factory, which were the most arduous parts of his work. As before, he became responsible for the bishop's business with government but he had returned from Europe very weary and now had to face abuse from all who favoured the continuance of transportation and those who were alarmed at the sudden emergence of Catholicism as a power in the colony. Even Plunkett, the only Catholic on the Legislative Council, disowned Ullathorne's vehemence on the convict question; his fellow clergy did not defend him for fear of drawing the fire on themselves and some of them, notably F. Murphy, joined Ullathorne's critics. For six months he was subjected almost daily to abuse in the press but was content thus to draw fire from the bishop. The campaign led immediately to the launching of a Catholic newspaper, the *Australasian Chronicle*, in August 1839, under one of Ullathorne's schoolmaster recruits, W. A. Duncan [q.v.].

By this time Ullathorne had determined to leave Australia. His failure to enlist English priests in 1837-38, his success in Ireland, and the warm friendships he then formed with several Irish prelates convinced him that ecclesiastically Australia must become a colony of Ireland, and could never be, as he said, 'Benedictinized'. When he first proposed to leave Polding countered by giving him charge of the infant seminary at Sydney and of the entire administration of the diocese. Nevertheless on 3 December 1839 Ullathorne sent in his formal resignation to Polding and Governor Gipps. Then all parties temporized; 1840 was to be Ullathorne's most active year in Australia, teaching at the seminary, lecturing publicly on the Catholic religion, and administering the diocese while the bishop travelled its length and breadth founding a dozen new churches and schools. In May Ullathorne went to Adelaide, interviewed the governor and assembled the Catholics. On 25 August at the laying of the foundation stone of St Patrick's Church, Sydney, Ullathorne organized a procession, the largest public demonstration the city had witnessed, in order to show the governor the numbers and unity of the Catholic body, and to protest against Gipps's education proposals. But in a long address he had to discourage his flock, which was mainly Irish, from giving the demonstration a nationalistic character. Later that year he published his most substantial and strongly worded colonial publication, *A Reply to Judge Burton, of the Supreme Court of New South Wales, on 'The State of Religion' in the Colony* (Sydney, 1840). In it he denounced the judge's attack on Catholic motives and practices, and gave a fine tribute to C. Lovat, a priest with whom he had had serious personal differences.

Since Polding was sailing for Europe in the mission's interest Ullathorne accompanied him on 15 November 1840 chiefly, he declared, to ensure that further sees were set up in Australia and that he himself should not occupy any of them. The government declined to pay his salary during a second long absence, so in 1841 Polding terminated his appointment to Sydney without giving him any personal explanation. Ullathorne took over the parish of Coventry, and published his colonial sermons. He refused the mitre no less than four times during his connexion with Australia, and a fifth time when the see of Perth was established in 1845; his offers to return and serve in subordinate posts were refused in turn. Nevertheless his combination of energy, close knowledge of canon law and boldness in the face of public opinion made him the key figure behind the establishment of a Catholic hierarchy in Australia by Brief of 5 April 1842.

In Coventry Ullathorne helped to found the English Congregation of St Catherine of Siena. On 27 April 1846 he received notice of his appointment as vicar-apostolic of the west of England. The last and greatest of the English vicars-apostolic, he used his Australian experience in 1848 to pilot the reintroduction of a hierarchy in England in communion with Rome. His later career as bishop and archbishop of Birmingham, where he was outstanding as pastor and theologian, and chief go-between for the Irish, the Anglican converts and the old English Catholics, was likewise built squarely upon his Australian experience. In 1888 Ullathorne retired from his diocese to Oscott College, where he died on 21 March 1889.

Australia had forced him to cultivate an independent judgment in matters of dogmatic, moral and apologetic theology alike, and had given him opportunities to form friendships among the English, Irish and Roman prelates scarcely ever granted so young a priest. At the same time his Australian writings complement his later works; though they display little use of his mysticism and grasp of Catholic philosophy, they show his interest in general social questions and his decisive management of business. He never lost his warm interest in Australia, though after 1845 he never attempted to intervene decisively in Australian church affairs. He wrote his autobiography in 1867, mainly as a memoir of his Australian work. It was published in 1891 in an expurgated form and in 1941 from the original draft. A memorial which Ullathorne signed with three others in 1874 to celebrate the golden jubilee of their monastic profession reveals that his grateful admiration for Polding as a spiritual guide had never diminished.

HRA (1), 16-22; H. N. Birt, *Benedictine pioneers in Australia*, 1-2 (Lond, 1911).

T. L. SUTTOR

UNDERWOOD, JAMES (1776?-1844), shipbuilder, distiller and merchant, is traditionally supposed to have come to New South Wales with the First Fleet but the evidence is confused and it is possible that he was sentenced to seven years transportation at Maidstone in March 1790, and arrived in Sydney in the *Admiral Barrington* in October 1791. He probably learned the trade of boatbuilder under Stephen Todd, formerly a carpenter in the *Barwell* who was engaged to build a 34-ton sloop for the Hawkesbury River trade in 1797; later it became the property of Underwood and his partner Henry Kable [q.v.].

The obscurity veiling Underwood's early career lifts in 1800. In that year he was in partnership with Kable and a mariner, Samuel Rodman Chace, who was master of Kable & Underwood's sloop *Diana* engaged in Bass Strait sealing. The partnership with Kable lasted until 1809. During its course Underwood was primarily concerned with building and maintaining vessels of various sizes employed in sealing, whaling in the Derwent, bringing coal from the Hunter River and an occasional sandalwood venture. In 1805 Simeon Lord [q.v.] joined the partnership. Underwood's boatbuilding activities were the most remarkable of a number of diverse achievements. It is uncertain when he constructed his first, but in June 1801 an official surveying expedition at the mouth of the Hunter River discovered the sole survivor of a crew of three from an Underwood vessel which had been wrecked well to the north. He built a number of craft for others for 'burthen or pleasure', and for his own firm before 1805 he had contructed the sloops *Contest* and *Diana*, the schooner *Endeavour*, a 75-ton brig the *Governor King*, and finally the ship-rigged *King George* of near 200 tons, which played a substantial and varied part in Sydney entrepreneurial activity for many years. These vessels, all launched from his yard at the mouth of the Tank Stream, cost £11,400. From 1805 to 1809 Underwood's yard seems to have been principally engaged in a long succession of refits for the firm's vessels, including the *Sydney Cove*, *Santa Anna* and *Commerce* which they bought with varying degrees of legality, and others like the *Aurora* and *Honduras Packet* which they chartered. In a set of Underwood accounts the volume of work done during these years was valued at almost £26,000, an itemized but possibly inflated figure.

Underwood played a considerable part in the early New South Wales sealing industry. In the 1803-04 season the partners had more than sixty men employed in the trade and gathered not less than 30,000 skins. After 1805 the volume greatly increased as, through Lord, the partners had a secure market in London. Between 1806 and 1809 their London agents sold 127,040 skins, sent in four consignments, for more than £27,000; these were by no means all the skins they exported in this period and they sold a considerable quantity of oil as well. In 1807 Underwood owned a third of the *Sydney Cove* which the partners chartered to the government for a voyage to Sydney with convicts. Underwood sailed for England in her in October, buying out Lord's share on his arrival in London in May 1808. He returned in April 1809 on the ship's second voyage with a very valuable investment, and soon afterwards severed his connexion with Kable. Lawsuits between the partners were not settled until 1819.

Underwood's only connexion with sealing after his return to New South Wales appears to have been as agent for his brother Joseph [q.v.]. In June 1812 James opened the St George Coffee Lounge at which the principle beverages sold seem to have been spirituous, and he certainly held a spirit licence in 1813. In October of that year he took part in the formation of the Commercial Society of Sydney, a currency-issuing venture which the governor quickly dissolved. In June 1819 he ceased to be his brother's agent, as he was about to depart for England in the *Surry*, though it is not certain that he went. In 1821 he was described to Commissioner Bigge [q.v.] as one of the few merchants engaged in importing from Europe and India. In the same year he was appointed a member of the Standing Committee of the Emancipated Colonists of New South Wales.

In 1823 he formed a partnership with Robert Cooper [q.v.] and F. E. Forbes to build and operate the Sydney distillery between Old South Head Road and Rushcutters Bay. He bought Forbes's share in 1824 for £1700 and soon afterwards bought out Cooper, with whom he had quarrelled, for a further £1600. These disputes held up operations, much to the farmers' displeasure, but by July 1824 the works, which included eight vats and a large granary, were ready for business; in October the governor was presented with a sample, and six bay horses drew a 300-gallon cask triumphantly to Under-

wood's house for a celebratory party for his 'mechanics'. The house, built by 1804, was a distinctive three-storey, flat-roofed, brick and stone residence next to the Orphan School, and seems to have been for many years among the three or four finest in Sydney, and much more ambitious than the early Government House.

Underwood's remaining years in New South Wales appear to have been prosperous. Unlike his brother and Simeon Lord he does not appear to have invested widely in farm land and he possessed only 100 acres in 1828; his town property may have been substantial, however, and in April 1826 the Bank of Australia opened for business in part of his George Street premises. Soon after December 1842 he retired to England where he died, aged 67, at his home, Paddington House, Tulse Hill, Brixton, Surrey, on 10 February 1844.

Underwood was married first in January 1793 to Mary Kendall. Between 1802 and 1807 he had three children, Charlotte, Thomas and James, by Phyllis Pounds, and a daughter Sarah by Letitia Reynolds in 1811. He married Mary Ann Powell in 1812 and by her had Joseph, Edward, Mary and Richard. Two other children born in 1822 and 1824 died in infancy and his wife died in February 1825. In November Underwood married Elizabeth Shurwell, but there is no record of any children of this marriage.

HRNSW, 3, 6; HRA (1), 3-14; MS cat under James Underwood (ML); Supreme Court records (NSWA).   D. R. HAINSWORTH

UNDERWOOD, JOSEPH (1779-1833), merchant and sealing master, arrived in New South Wales in the *Sydney Cove* in June 1807. He bore a letter of introduction from the Secretary of State to the governor and was accompanied by his wife and a 'large yet infant family'. In March 1810 he told Governor Macquarie that his knowledge of 'mechanics' had caught the attention of 'prominent Englishmen', that he had invested large sums in various building projects in Sydney, and that he was engaged in mercantile speculations. During the next fifteen years Underwood conducted a series of importing enterprises from India and London; unlike other Sydney merchants, he preferred to supervise the voyages personally. Of one ship in 1821 he was not only owner but master as well. In 1810 he sailed for Calcutta in the *Marian*, chartered her to the Bengal government, and returned to Sydney in the *Campbell Macquarie* in March 1811 with a valuable cargo including spirits. She was probably Underwood's property, but was mortgaged to her nominal owners, Alexander & Co., as part security for her cargo and also to evade the monopoly of the East India Co. This ship brought another Indian cargo for Underwood in January 1812. Underwood then sought to persuade Macquarie that it would be legal to ship New South Wales produce to the Cape of Good Hope in his vessel and exchange it there for Cape wine for the Australian market; when Macquarie disagreed Underwood sent the ship to Macquarie Island on a sealing expedition. There she was wrecked and totally destroyed in June 1812.

Underwood came to the New South Wales sealing industry after its best days were over, but seems to have made a success of sea-elephant hunting in which the object was oil rather than skins. In December 1811 he bought the 186-ton *King George*, built by his brother James [q.v.], and employed her in sealing, whaling and bringing pork from Tahiti in 1815, 1817 and 1819. In addition he bought the locally-built 86-ton schooner *Elizabeth and Mary*, and for fifteen years employed her in sealing and in carrying cedar and coal from the Hunter River. In September 1813 he made another voyage to Asia, sailing to China with his wife in the *Archduke Charles* with a consignment of sealskins, sold them well, probably invested in Chinese merchandise, and sailed for Bengal, where he acquired a new *Campbell Macquarie* and brought her to Sydney with a valuable cargo of teas, china ware, rice and spirits. On the way to Sydney he came across the half-derelict *Seringapatam*, which her skeleton crew claimed to have recaptured from an American cruiser which had taken her; he escorted her to Sydney and acted as the crew's agent in salvage claims. The *Campbell Macquarie* made three round trips to Calcutta and Batavia in 1816-17 and it seems likely that Underwood accompanied her as supercargo. In 1818 he was involved in an abortive Indian speculation with Samuel Terry, Robert Campbell junior, and Thomas Winder [qq.v.], but this did not take him out of the country. He went to England in 1819, arriving back in Sydney early in 1821 in his new ship *Midas*; though she later sailed to Mauritius, Underwood appears to have abandoned overseas voyages after 1821. Before going to England he had bought Ashfield Park from Robert Campbell senior [q.v.]; in August 1821 he was granted 1500 acres and took up land near Newcastle in 1822. In 1828 he was still a merchant operating from George Street, but owned 3758 acres, with

480 cleared, and more than 1000 head of cattle; in 1829 he claimed that during the past eighteen years he had provided employment for an average of between 150 and 200 men annually on various enterprises. He was a subscriber to charities and church building and prominent on committees of various kinds during the 1820s.

Underwood died at Ashfield Park on 30 August 1833, aged 54. His first wife Charlotte had died in February 1818, and he married Mrs Elizabeth Lang, the daughter of Surgeon John Harris [q.v.], at Dover on his arrival there from Australia in the *Surry* in 1819. For some reason they went through a second marriage ceremony at Parramatta in 1829. Underwood had several children by his first wife, including at least two sons, Richard and Thomas, born in England and still living with him in 1828, and at least five others born in the colony, only two of whom seem to have survived infancy. By his second marriage he had three daughters and a son, Frederick, born in 1820 in England, who died at Bathurst in 1904.

HRA (1), 2, 8-10, 13; MS cat under Joseph Underwood (ML); Supreme Court records (NSWA).
D. R. HAINSWORTH

UTHER, REUBEN (1791-1880), merchant and manufacturer, was born in England, the son of William Uther, furrier, of Southwark, London. He was indentured in London on 22 September 1806 to Simeon Lord [q.v.], the emancipist merchant. He arrived in Sydney in the *Sydney Cove* in June 1807 and served Lord as clerk or manager until March 1815, when he established a hat factory in Hunter Street, Sydney; next year he moved it to Pitt Street.

In 1812 Governor Macquarie had granted him 400 acres, later known as the Mount Gilead estate, near the junction of Menangle Creek and the Nepean River which, Uther stated later, was 'a reward for successful enterprise in introducing domestic manufactures'. This land was later sold to Thomas Rose [q.v.].

Like several other Sydney merchants Uther was keenly interested in agriculture. By March 1815 he had a contract to supply meat to the government stores, and Macquarie remarked on the improvements which Uther had made on his farm in the district of Appin. In February 1825 he sailed for England in the *Mangles* and applied to the Colonial Office for a further grant of land. He was given a letter instructing Governor Darling to make this, but Darling refused to grant the 2560 acres which the Land Board recommended, and this led to a further series of unsuccessful petitions by Uther to the Colonial Office.

On 21 November 1812 Uther had married Maria Hacking, by whom he had four daughters and two sons. Maria Uther was found drowned at Hobart in January 1829, and on 9 June he married Ann, eldest daughter of Lancelot Iredale (1785-1844), ironmonger, of Sydney; they had three sons and seven daughters. In October Uther was appointed a member of the missionary committee and in December was elected Worshipful Master of Australian Social Lodge No. 260. In 1833 he took over a retail business in George Street and in 1842-51 acted as agent and attorney for his father-in-law who imported and manufactured iron work. In 1846 he presented a petition to the mayor for a meeting to consider the earlier closing of 'drapery and other business establishments'.

During the later part of his life Uther lived at Surry Hills. He died on 10 July 1880, aged 89, and was buried in the Waverley cemetery. His second wife died on 27 July 1894, aged 83. His estate, including the Imperial Arcade between Pitt and Castlereagh Streets, was valued at £250,000. He was typical of the early merchants in the range of his interests: agriculture, iron and hat manufactures and the general retail trade.

HRA (1), 7, 19; Petitions, correspondence and other land grant papers, 1838 (transcripts, Miss Doris Uther, Homebush, NSW).

DAVID S. MACMILLAN

V

VALE, BENJAMIN (1788-1863), Church of England clergyman, was born in London, the son of Benjamin Vale. At 20 he showed the variety of his interests by publishing in London A *New System of Stenography* and *Rhetoric in Miniature*, both works running to several editions. In June 1811 he was admitted a sizar at Christ's College, Cambridge (LL.B., 1819; LL.D., 1834), and ordained priest by the bishop of London in 1813. Appointed assistant chaplain to the 46th Regiment in New South Wales he sailed with his wife Mary Ann in the *Broxbornebury* and arrived at Sydney in July 1814. Governor Macquarie had not been advised of his appointment and was 'at a Loss in regard to the Conduct I should Strictly pursue toward him', when Vale continually 'expressed much feeling of Disappointment' because promises which he claimed had been made in London could not be fulfilled. Macquarie contemplated sending him to Liverpool as soon as a parsonage was built there, and meanwhile made him assistant to William Cowper [q.v.] at St Philip's Church, Sydney, and 'to render him as Comfortable as his own Temper and my Ability will admit' gave him a convict servant, rations, fuel and lodging money.

In 1815 Vale published A *Pastoral Letter to the Congregation assembling at St Philip's* but his discontent was deepened by association with Jeffery Bent and W. H. Moore [qq.v.]. Aided and abetted by these 'strange characters' while Macquarie was absent on a tour of inspection, Vale seized the American schooner *Traveller* as a lawful prize under the Navigation Act. The governor had permitted this ship to enter Port Jackson on 19 February 1816; he returned a week later, quickly 'removed the Arrest', sent for Vale and rebuked him. Instead of apologizing the chaplain 'Attempted by Argument to Vindicate the Measure', so Macquarie ordered his arrest and trial by court martial. At this trial in March Vale was found guilty of subversive behaviour, insubordination and 'Conduct highly derogatory to his Sacred Character'. Although sentenced to be publicly reprimanded, he was privately admonished by Macquarie at Government House before a few officers.

This episode delayed Vale's return with his sickly wife to England. In June he sailed in the *Alexander* taking with him a 'memorial of settlers in New South Wales respecting the conduct of Governor Macquarie'. On 10 March 1817 this petition was presented to the House of Commons by Henry Grey Bennet, but Castlereagh repudiated its malicious aspersions. At the same time Vale published in London his own account of the trial, claiming that he had acted only on 'patriotic impulse'.

Vale became morning preacher at St Margaret's Chapel, Westminster, afternoon lecturer in 1820 at St Luke's, Old Street, London, curate in 1827-39 of Stoke-upon-Trent and rector in 1839-63 of Longton, Staffordshire. Many of his papers were destroyed in a fire at Longton rectory, but he continued to publish his sermons and devotional books, interspersed with works on geology, ancient history, Druidism, logic, Odd Fellowship, botany, the Zodiac and many other subjects; some were republished in several editions. The restlessness of his mind may have derived from the diseased liver of which he died on 2 March 1863 at Longton. By his own request he was buried 'without pomp or show'. The principal legatee of his £4000 estate was his son Benjamin.

HRA (1), 8, 9; M. H. Ellis, *Lachlan Macquarie* (Syd, 1947); PD (GB), 35 (1817), 920.

VANCOUVER, GEORGE (1757-1798), naval officer and hydrographer, was born on 22 June 1757 at King's Lynn, Norfolk, England, the youngest of five children of John Jasper Vancouver (d. 1773) and his wife Bridget (d. 1768), daughter of William Berners whose forbears included Sir Richard Grenville. At 15 Vancouver joined the navy and spent seven years under Captain James Cook [q.v.] during two voyages to the Pacific. In 1780 he became a lieutenant and in 1781-83 served in the West Indies. Under Sir Alan Gardner at Jamaica in 1784-89 he carried out his first independent surveys. At Gardner's suggestion he was chosen to lead an expedition to the South Seas and in 1790 was promoted commander. Instructed to negotiate with the Spaniards at Nootka Sound and to survey the north-west coast of America and well equipped with 'the latest chronometers and scientific instruments', stores and comforts, he left England in April 1791 in the new sloop *Discovery*, 340 tons, accompanied by the armed tender *Chatham*, 135 tons.

Vancouver had been given permission to examine 'that extent of coast of the south-west side of New Holland, which in the present age appears a real blot in geography'. He planned 'to fall in with the S.W. Cape of New Holland, and should I find the shores capable of being navigated without much hazard to range its coast and determine whether it and Van Diemen's Land are joined, which from all information at present extant appears somewhat doubtful'. On 26 September he sighted land near Cape Leeuwin and, sailing south-east, named Capes Chatham and Howe. Two days later the ships entered a spacious harbour which he named King George the Third's Sound. Vancouver also discovered and named Oyster Bay and other features, claiming them for Great Britain. He reported on the terrain, animal life and the native inhabitants, and planted watercress, vines, almonds, oranges, lemons and pumpkins 'for the benefit of future visitors'. On 11 October the ships journeyed east, surveying some 300 miles of coast, 'in which space we saw no other haven or place of security for shipping than the Sound before mentioned' and, in the westernmost part of the Recherche Archipelago, reached a rocky island which Vancouver called Termination Island.

Adverse winds prevented him from examining the Great Australian Bight, and relinquishing 'with great reluctance' this 'favourite project', he sailed south of Van Diemen's Land. The two ships were separated; off the southern tip of New Zealand Vancouver encountered '7 craggy islands' which he named The Snares, and the *Chatham* discovered and named Chatham Island. Further east in the Pacific he made detailed surveys of the Tahitian and Hawaiian (Sandwich) Islands and the vast and complex north-west coast of America from a point near San Francisco to the Alaskan Peninsula, most of the work being done in open boats. On his voyage Vancouver checked earlier charts, including some by Cook, correcting them with modesty and without disparagement. At Nootka he met the Spanish representative, Don Juan Quadra, but they could not agree in interpreting their separate instructions so decided without acrimony to refer the dispute over territory to their governments.

New South Wales remained Vancouver's only link with British officials during his three years in the Pacific. Orders had been sent to Governor Phillip at Port Jackson to replenish Vancouver with supplies and equipment. The storeship *Daedalus* was sent to him, but her commander and an astronomer were murdered in Hawaii and some of the crew deserted before the ship arrived at Nootka in August 1792. Vancouver provided a new commander and as instructed sent livestock back to Sydney; his friend Don Quadra contributed a few cattle and sheep, and other animals were collected on the way, but most were lost on the voyage. The *Daedalus* also took back dispatches, a report for Governor Phillip of the survey of the south-west coast of New Holland, charts and an appraisal of the King George Sound area which Vancouver thought 'worthy of some further attention'. Phillip had returned to England but Lieut-Governor Grose [q.v.] sent the *Daedalus* back to Vancouver with supplies. By December 1794 Vancouver had completed his surveys and turned homeward by way of Cape Horn and St Helena, where the *Chatham* left his command. He arrived in London in September 1795 to find he had been promoted post captain on 28 August 1794. He retired to Petersham, Surrey, to prepare a full account of his voyage and all his charts for publication, as requested by the Admiralty. His health failing he had to seek help from his brother John, who by March 1797 was doing all the writing. Five volumes were completed and the sixth was in preparation when Vancouver died. It was finished by John with aid from Lieutenant Puget and *A Voyage of discovery to the North Pacific Ocean* . . . was published in London in 1798; a second edition followed in 1801 and a French translation in 1802.

Vancouver was buried at St Peter's, Petersham, on 18 May 1798. His grave, neglected for many years, is now cared for by the people of British Columbia and a tablet was placed in the church by the Hudson Bay Co.

By 1803 Vancouver was almost forgotten by all except those who used his magnificent charts. In some quarters he had been reputed harsh and difficult, yet he was a dedicated naval officer, hard-working though in poor health, strict and demanding. His concern for the welfare of his crew kept the scurvy rate low in his two cramped ships. As a diplomat he was successful with the Spanish and the natives of the Pacific. His competent hydrography deflated the geographic theorists of the late eighteenth century and his astronomical observations greatly advanced the science of navigation. In these ways he fulfilled his ambition 'to deserve the appellation of being zealous in the service of his king and country'.

HRA (1), 1; G. Godwin, *Vancouver, a life, 1757-1798* (Lond, 1930), and for bibliog; G. C. Ingleton, *Charting a continent* (Syd, 1944);

H. M. Cooper, *The unknown coast* (Adel, 1953); T. Dunbabin, 'How British Columbia nearly became a colony of Australia', *British Columbia Hist Q*, Jan-Apr 1951; MS cat under Vancouver (ML); Menzies journal of Vancouver's voyage, microfilm FM4/16 (ML); Adm 55/13-17, 25-33, 42, 51/2251.

NAN PHILLIPS

VAUX, JAMES HARDY (b. 1782), convict and author, was baptized on 20 May 1782 at East Clandon, Surrey, England, the son of Hardy Vaux, butler and house steward to George Holme Sumner, M.P., and his wife Sophia, daughter of James Lowe, an attorney who was clerk of papers and deputy-warden of the Fleet prison. After moving with his parents to London, where Hardy Vaux set up as a hatter in Great Turnstile, Holborn, James Vaux apparently attended a boarding school in Stockwell, but spent most of his childhood with his maternal grandparents in Shifnal, Shropshire. At 14, according to his own account, he persuaded his grandfather to apprentice him to a linen draper in Liverpool and it was here that he began the loose living which led to his downfall. Dismissed by his employer, he induced his grandfather to let him go to London, where he became a copying clerk in a legal firm in Lincoln's Inn but again lost his job owing to dissipation. Other intervals of employment followed including a spell in the navy: he volunteered in December 1798 and served in the frigate *Astraea* in the North Sea, according to the muster as an ordinary seaman, but originally as a midshipman by his own account. He deserted at Yarmouth next August and returned to his old life in London. After working for an attorney in Bury St Edmunds and for a Covent Garden clothing firm he was arrested in April 1800 for pilfering from the latter. He was acquitted but was by this time a professional thief, and in September he was sentenced at the Old Bailey to transportation for seven years for stealing a handkerchief, valued by the jury at elevenpence so that the accused might escape a capital sentence.

Vaux reached Sydney in the *Minorca* in December 1801 and worked as a clerk at the Hawkesbury, in Sydney and in Parramatta. Despite a term in the road-gang after he forged Governor King's initials to commissariat orders he succeeded in ingratiating himself with the Parramatta chaplain and magistrate, Samuel Marsden [q.v.], and with the governor, who agreed to take him home in the *Buffalo* in 1807. Vaux was employed on board in writing King's log and in teaching his and Mars-

den's children, but when his sentence expired he became insubordinate and was compelled to enlist as a seaman. When the ship reached Portsmouth Vaux deserted and resumed his old activities in London. On 21 July at St Paul's, Covent Garden, he married Mary Ann Thomas, a prostitute, in the hope that, if he were again transported, she might be allowed as his wife to join him in New South Wales. In December he narrowly escaped a further conviction, this time for stealing a snuffbox, but in February 1809 he was sentenced to death at the Old Bailey under the alias James Lowe for stealing from a jeweller's shop in Piccadilly. This sentence was commuted to transportation for life and after a period in the hulk *Retribution* he sailed in the *Indian* and reached Sydney in December 1810. Assigned to a Hawkesbury settler and then appointed deputy-overseer of the town gang in Sydney, he was sentenced in 1811 to twelve months hard labour for receiving property stolen from the judge-advocate, Ellis Bent [q.v.], and soon afterwards was sent to the Newcastle penal settlement. In January 1814, after returning to Sydney, he was caught while trying to escape in the *Earl Spencer*, flogged and returned to Newcastle.

During his previous spell there Vaux had compiled a slang dictionary for the use of magistrates, and he was now encouraged to write the famous *Memoirs of the First Thirty-Two Years of The Life of James Hardy Vaux, A Swindler and Pickpocket; Now Transported for the Second Time, and For Life, to New South Wales*. He implied that he wrote at the bidding of Captain Thompson, the commandant, and promised in his dedication that his future conduct would justify this patronage. The manuscript came into the hands of Barron Field [q.v.] who arranged for its publication in London by John Murray, along with the slang dictionary, but Murray's imprint does not appear on most extant copies. Vaux received £33 18s. 8d. in royalties. The *Memoirs* were republished by John Hunt in 1827 and reprinted in 1829 and 1830. As the first full-length autobiography written in Australia the book provides a fascinating picture of criminal life in London and the penal system, while the *Vocabulary of the Flash Language*, probably the first dictionary compiled in Australia, gives a valuable glossary of London slang. In 1827 the *London Magazine* described the work as 'one of the most singular that ever issued from the press'.

On 3 August 1818 at Newcastle, during a visit by Governor Macquarie, Vaux married Frances Sharkey, a former Irish convict. Next month he was allowed to return to Sydney where Field used him as a clerk. In January 1820 he received a conditional pardon and soon became a clerk in the colonial secretary's office. In 1823 Vaux was converted to Roman Catholicism by Father Therry [q.v.], but on 2 April 1827 he was married to his housekeeper, Eleanor Bateman, another Irish convict, by Marsden, although Frances Vaux was still alive. At the end of 1826 Governor Darling dismissed Vaux in accordance with his policy of not employing convicts and ex-convicts as clerks. Vaux was then employed in an ironmonger's store but in April 1829 he absconded and so broke the terms of his conditional pardon. He went to Ireland, where in August 1830 at Dublin he was convicted once more under the alias James Young, this time for passing forged bank-notes. He pleaded guilty and, with the co-operation of the bank concerned, his death sentence was commuted to transportation for seven years. On his arrival at Sydney in the *Waterloo* in May 1831 he was recognized, his previous life sentence was revived and he was sent to Port Macquarie penal settlement. In 1837 he was allowed to return to Sydney and became clerk to a wine merchant. In May 1839 he was charged with criminal assault on a girl aged about 8. He was sentenced to two years imprisonment, and although Governor Gipps decided that his life sentence should be re-applied he was released in 1841 on the recommendation of Chief Justice Dowling [q.v.] and disappeared. No reliable record of his further life and death has been traced. Although he is the only convict known to have been transported three times to New South Wales he was probably not unique in this respect, nor was he an outstanding criminal. What does distinguish him is his *Memoirs*, which were republished (edited and with an introduction and notes by Noel McLachlan) in 1964.

A. F. Fink, 'James Hardy Vaux, convict and fatalist', JRAHS, 48 (1962).

AVERIL F. FINK

VERGE, JOHN (1782-1861), architect, builder and pioneer settler, was born in Hampshire, England, the son of Nicholas Verge, a Christchurch builder who later worked at Bloomsbury in London, and his first wife Mary, née Best. On 5 December 1804 at the Priory Church, Christchurch, John Verge married Catherine Bowles; of their three children, only Philip George

survived. In 1826 Verge had retired through ill health from his successful practice as a London builder to farm his recently acquired country estate, when he was lured by the opportunities of the new colony of New South Wales. He sailed from London in the *Clarkstone* and arrived at Port Jackson on 27 December 1828 with his son, a shepherd, a flock of Hampshire sheep, various supplies and agricultural equipment; with his capital these assets amounted in value to £2738. Upon settling at 70 Pitt Street, Sydney, Verge applied on 12 January 1829 for a land grant, and was allowed the maximum of 2560 acres. After some confusion he finally located his land near Dungog, which he called Lyndhurst Vale. A secondary grant in 1838 added a further 2560 acres on the Macleay River, named Austral Eden, while a further 140 acres, now part of Kempsey, were purchased. Catherine Verge did not emigrate, and after her death, Verge married Mary, aged 50, daughter of John Alford, at Austral Eden on 8 March 1858.

Verge's activities as a farmer seem not to have been spectacularly successful at first, though he had built up a considerable practice as architect and builder; on 24 July 1831 because of the paucity of skilled architects, he was invited by Governor Darling, unavailingly, to tender for government contracts. Verge had bought land on the site of 346 Sussex Street in February 1831 and he built his house there immediately afterwards. Most of his architectural work in Sydney appears to have been done between 1830 and 1837, when he retired to Lyndhurst Vale and later to Austral Eden.

His architectural work after 1837 was more restricted and is difficult to attribute, but in his time of maximum activity, 1830-34, as indeed throughout his whole professional life, Verge was patronized by many prominent colonists, officials and businessmen. Most of his practice was in domestic and professional architecture, in which he was the most prolific figure of his period in Australia. A far from comprehensive list contains more than eighty commissions, some trifling but many of considerable magnitude and local importance, suggesting that Verge was clearly the man the times required. His achievements, which indicate a considerable rise in sophistication when compared with the general run of previous designs, are distinguished by exceptional sureness and competence allied with painstaking craftsmanship. His domestic buildings were the colony's high-water mark of the Regency style, in its austere stucco vernacular, and in this context he was one of the earliest and most important practitioners of the Greek Revival in Australia. Although on superficial examination his design may seem to be conceived within a certain copy-book correctness of taste, this predictability is sometimes varied with personal mannerisms such as the free use of classical members in the groined Doric dining-room of Camden Park. Verge brought a more comprehensive range of Regency 'styles' to Australia than any contemporary architect. Gothic (Tudor) designs were made in 1832 as alternatives to Greek and plain classicist plans for The King's School, Parramatta, and while Verge's ecclesiastical output was small, he is credited with part-authorship of the country churches at Bungonia (Christ Church, 1834-36, abandoned and rebuilt) and Cobbitty (St Paul's, 1840-41, in plain Gothic); the latter is attributed to a partnership with John Bibb [q.v.], with whom Verge was occasionally associated. His simple pre-Gothic Revival gothicism is seen most clearly in the chapel of St Mary the Virgin, at Denham Court, Ingleburn, designed in 1833-35 and built between 1836 and 1838. Other Sydney churches such as the Independent Chapel, 1830-31, and the Baptist Chapel, 1835-36, revealed more felicitous symmetrical classicist elevations. For F. A. Hely [q.v.], superintendent of convicts, and his wife, Verge designed not only the major house Engehurst (1834-35, part remains) but also between 1832 and 1837 a sequence of plans of office and garden buildings: Regency *cottages ornées* with trellising, and picturesque pavilions in playful 'Gothick' and in the Chinese taste (the latter the only known example of this period in Australia) all of high quality; a design also exists for what Verge termed a house in 'the Russian style'. Another curiosity was the wooden Treaty House at Waitangi, New Zealand, designed for James Busby [q.v.] in 1832, on his appointment as British Resident, and shipped over after modification by Ambrose Hallen [q.v.], the next year.

The pre-eminent early nineteenth century country house in Australia, and Verge's masterpiece, is Camden Park, Camden, designed for John Macarthur [q.v.] in 1831-32 and built in 1832-35 under Verge's supervision for his son William (there are some discreet, harmonious additions). A house of paramount importance with exquisite details and in the Greek Revival manner was The Vineyard, Rydalmere (later the Subiaco convent) designed for Hannibal Macarthur [q.v.] in 1833, built about 1835-36 and

demolished in 1961. Another outstanding Regency stucco and stone house is formed by the two-storey additions to Denham Court, 1832-34, built for Richard Brooks [q.v.], in which a finely composed elevation is allied to an impressive stone-flagged central hall. One of the richest and most spatially dramatic interiors in early Australian colonial architecture is seen in the hall at the massive Elizabeth Bay House (exterior somewhat altered) designed in 1833, and built in 1835-37 for Alexander McLeay [q.v.], the colonial secretary, a notable house which, with its former spacious ornamental grounds, was much praised. Other distinguished houses remaining, of the many erected, are Rockwall, Pott's Point, for John Busby [q.v.] and H. C. Semphill, 1830-35 (drastically altered) and near-by Tusculum, 1831-36, surrounded by Ionic colonnades commenced for the merchant Alexander Brodie Spark [q.v.] and completed for Bishop Broughton [q.v.], again considerably altered. Also for Spark was designed in 1834 the small Regency villa, practically a *ferme ornée*, Tempe House, Tempe, built in 1835-36 (now St Magdalene's Retreat, with accretions). Other houses were Toxteth Park, Glebe, for the solicitor George Allen [q.v.], about 1830-31 (now the Convent of the Good Samaritan, much enlarged and modified), Barham, for Edward Deas Thomson [q.v.], 1833 (later part of Sydney C. of E. Girls' Grammar School, built in and mutilated) and Lyndhurst, for James Bowman in 1833-35 (now part-demolished). The important terraces, shops and bazaars designed for such businessmen of Sydney as Samuel Lyons and John Edye Manning [qq.v.], father and son, have all disappeared. The only surviving Verge terrace house is the pair designed and built for the Sydney tradesman Frederick Peterson in 1834-36, 39 and 41 Lower Fort Street, which remains as an example of Verge's many routine commissions for city frontages. Finally several of Verge's skilful and apposite additions to earlier buildings exist, such as the additions of 1833 to Elizabeth Farm, commenced about 1793, and the vestries added in 1832-33 to Greenway's [q.v.] St James's Church, Sydney. A number of works from the late 1830s and early 1840s may be attributed to Verge when he also worked as a surveyor, but they lack the quality of carefully supervised execution, suggesting that designs were perhaps furnished after his retirement from an active architectural career.

Verge died on 9 July 1861, aged 79, at Austral Eden and was buried, as an

Anglican, in the burial ground of St Thomas's, Port Macquarie.

M. Herman, *The early Australian architects and their work* (Syd, 1954); W. G. Verge, *John Verge, early Australian architect; his ledger & his clients* (Syd, 1962); W. G. Verge, 'John Verge', JRAHS, 40 (1954).

HARLEY PRESTON

VICTOR, JAMES CONWAY (1792-1864), soldier and engineer, was born on 17 March 1792 in London. He entered the Royal Military College in 1807, became a second lieutenant in 1810, first lieutenant in 1811, and served in the Peninsular war in 1812-14, seeing action in three major battles. In 1821 he was promoted captain, and on 10 April 1834 married Anne Dashwood, youngest daughter of Alexander Young of Harburn, Midlothian. He had been brigade major for five years when he sailed from London with his wife and daughter in the *Emily*. On arrival in Hobart Town in November 1842 as commander of the Royal Engineers he was immediately appointed to the Board of Public Works and with W. P. Kay and Major Cotton [qq.v.] he reported on the water supplies of Hobart and Launceston. A year later the departments of public works and of roads and bridges were amalgamated and Victor was appointed director, at a salary of £300, in addition to his military duties. After some months Lieut-Governor Eardley-Wilmot reported that the amalgamation was not working well and the two departments were separated. Victor was offered the directorship of public works at £300, but refused because these civil duties interfered with his military service. Soon afterwards he was asked by Lieut-Governor Denison to superintend the building of Franklin's wharf. Again Victor demurred, but Denison insisted and later interfered with professional details of the work. In July 1847 Victor wrote to his superiors in London, claiming that misrepresentations from Hobart had induced the Colonial Office to sanction the building of a wharf which was neither necessary nor likely to pay; most of all he objected to civil authority demanding his obedience. The letter was sent to the Colonial Office where Earl Grey deplored the unpleasant tone of Victor's complaints and his unusual reluctance to co-operate in colonial works. The affair finished amicably, but in December 1848 Victor sold the furniture of his Hampden Road house and left for England in the *Calcutta* with his wife and daughter. In 1854 he was promoted major-general and died at Edinburgh on 4 February 1864. His

wife died on 5 September 1876, survived by her only daughter Sophia.

Victor's best memorial in Hobart was some fine architecture. He designed and built the gaol at the barracks, the convict hospital in Campbell Street, and the outbuildings and cottages at Government House.

GO 1/69/15 (TA).

VIDAL, MARY THERESA (1815-1869), née Johnson, was born on 25 July 1815 at Torrington, Devon, England, the eldest child and only daughter of William Charles Johnson and his wife Mary Theresa, née Furse, whose mother, Elizabeth, was a sister of Sir Joshua Reynolds and also related to Charles Wellington Furse, archdeacon of Westminster, and William, later known as Cory, the classical scholar and author of *Ionica*. At Ideford on 25 April 1835 Mary married Rev. Francis Vidal, curate of Torrington and scion of Jamaican planters. Because of her husband's health Mary and her family sailed for Sydney in the *Earl Grey*. They arrived in February 1840. Francis served as incumbent at Penrith, and in 1845 returned with his family to England, where he succeeded William Cory Furse as a tutor at Eton. Francis and Mary had six sons. Their only daughter, Elizabeth Theresa (Lily), was born in New South Wales in 1841, and in August 1861 married Edward Stone, classics master at Eton and later headmaster of Stonehouse; their seventh child became, through marriage, Faith Compton Mackenzie, whose autobiography *As Much As I Dare* (London, 1938) gives a brief account of the life of her grandmother, Mrs Vidal.

Mrs Vidal's first known fictional work was written in Australia and issued in eight sixpenny parts before being published in book form as *Tales for the Bush* (Sydney, 1845); it ran to at least five editions in London. It is a series of stories in the form of brief novelettes, each carefully constructed and divided into tiny chapters. The tales are homiletic and highly moral and intended to instruct the lower orders of society in such Christian virtues as accepting their station in life, observance of the Sabbath and abhorrence of sin. There is little in the tales to connect them with Australia, and their theme and tone reflect the author's English upbringing rather than any Australian influence.

Mrs Vidal's second Australian work, *The Cabramatta Store*, is set in the Nepean district of New South Wales and was published as part of a volume entitled *Cabramatta, and Woodleigh Farm* (London, 1849), the second part, a short novel *Woodleigh Farm*, being set in England. The profits derived from its sale were offered to the bishop of Sydney for the cathedral fund. *The Cabramatta Store* is sub-titled *A Tale of the Bush* and is less a novel than a series of vignettes reflecting the growth and conditions of that part of Australia in its day. Mostly it deals with the school, domestic and church life of the locality, and introduces rather casually the sensational elements of bushrangers, drought and bush fires, which were later to become a feature of so much early Australian fiction.

Mrs Vidal's third Australian novel, *Bengala: or, Some Time Ago* (London, 1860) was published a year after Henry Kingsley's *The Recollections of Geoffrey Hamlyn* and in her preface the author refers to her 'homelier and greyer tinted sketch' which followed 'the more recent and highly-coloured pictures of the same subject'. *Bengala* is a full length, fully developed novel in two volumes. In the rapid changes of colonial life Mrs Vidal planned 'to seize one of these shifting scenes—a transient period with its own peculiar circumstances, its hopes, fears, evils and enjoyments'. The setting is a fictitious township in New South Wales, just north of Sydney. Into the description of the pastoral society have been introduced many characteristics of the stock in trade of the novel of pioneer settlement, even to the near guiltless victim who turns bushranger. Despite the much stronger Australian emphasis, however, the characters are most marked by the English gentility of their way of life.

Mrs Vidal died in England in 1869. She is important as being the first woman writer of fiction published separately in Australia. She published eight other English works and has been referred to by A E. Shipley as 'a lady of some distinction as a writer'. To the student of Australian literature her works are of interest historically rather than as novels in their own right.

E. Morris Miller, 'First woman novelist', *A'sian Book News and Lib J*, March 1947.

J. C. HORNER

VLAMINGH, WILLEM DE (fl. 1697), a native of Vlieland, Holland, and a skipper of the Dutch East India Co., was sent out with three ships in May 1696 from Holland to look for survivors of a ship which was thought to have been wrecked on the west coast of Australia. They sighted the coast on 24 December and five days later anchored off Rottnest Island at about 31° 47′ S. On 31 December de Vlamingh went ashore and a few days later men were sent to the mainland, where they found traces of Aboriginals. A river with numerous black swans was called Swaanerivier and de Vlamingh rowed some ten miles up it. On 13 January 1697 the vessels weighed anchor and sailed north. As a careful survey was made of the coast, the ships made slow progress and parties were regularly sent ashore.

On 30 January de Vlamingh anchored at 26° 12′ S. near an island where Dirck Hartogsz, a native of Amsterdam and skipper of the Dutch East India Co., had landed when on a voyage to the East Indies in charge of the *Eendracht* in 1616. He had sailed too far east from the Cape of Good Hope and on 25 October anchored off the west Australian coast about 25° S. in a bay called Dirck Hartogsz anchorage, presumably Shark Bay. He and his men went ashore, erected a pole and fastened to it a pewter dish with an inscription commemorating their visit. On 3 February 1697 a party sent ashore from de Vlamingh's ship reported that it had found the dish. De Vlamingh took it away but had another inscribed commemorating the landings of both 1616 and 1697. On 12 February his ships left and sailed up the coast to 21° S. until 21 February when they made for Batavia where they arrived on 20 March.

Hartogsz' dish is now, though highly dilapidated, in the Rijksmuseum, Amsterdam. In 1818 Freycinet [q.v. under Baudin] took de Vlamingh's dish to Paris, where it was rediscovered in 1940. In 1947 it was returned to Australia and is in the Perth Museum. On 30 December 1935 a plaque was unveiled on Rottnest Island, commemorating de Vlamingh's visit there. The date on the plaque should have been 31 December and not 30 December 1696. In 1938 the Australian government had a bronze plaque fitted on the lighthouse of Dirk Hartog Island to commemorate the first recorded landing of Europeans in Australia.

P. A. Leupe, *De reizen der Nederlanders naar het Zuidland of Nieuw-Holland in de 17e en 18e eeuw* (Amsterdam, 1868); F. W. Stapel, *De Oostindische Compagnie en Australië* (Amsterdam, 1937); A. Sharp, *The discovery of Australia* (Oxford, 1963).

J. VAN LOHUIZEN

VON STIEGLITZ, FREDERICK LEWIS (1803-1866), pastoralist, was born on 13 October 1803 in Ireland, the eldest son of Baron Heinrich Ludwig von Stieglitz and

Charlotte, née Atkinson, and grandson of Christian Ludwig von Stieglitz who had been created a baron of the Holy Roman Empire in 1765. In 1802 the family moved from Pilsen, Bavaria, to a property known as Lewis Hill in Ireland and after nine years to Cookstown, County Tyrone. When the baron's death in 1824 left the family of six sons and two daughters poorly provided for, they decided to emigrate to Van Diemen's Land. Frederick Lewis, Francis Walter and Robert William von Stieglitz arrived at Hobart Town in the *Lion* on 7 August 1829.

Frederick, an active and intelligent young man in the lieut-governor's opinion, received 2000 acres, which he took up near Fingal and named Killymoon. In 1830 he married Catherine Christiana McNally, who owned an inn at Kempton. He bought a further 3000 acres near Fingal and in the next decade built Killymoon House in stone in the style of Killymoon Castle, County Tyrone. In 1841 he was appointed a justice of the peace and in 1846 became a nominee in the Legislative Council on the resignation of the Patriotic Six. For some years he was a member of the Avoca Road Trust and in 1851 was elected to represent Fingal in the first elective council. After his wife's death in 1857 he sold Killymoon, returned to Ireland, assumed the title of baron, and became a justice of the peace for the Counties of Armagh and Down. In 1859 he married Hester Anna, the daughter of George Blacker and Anne, née Sloane. He died without issue on 14 May 1866.

The second brother, Henry Lewis von Stieglitz (1808-1890), arrived in Hobart in the *Juno* in November 1830, bringing about £1600, and was granted 1500 acres at Apsley, naming his property Green Lawn. He died at Sunnyside, Nile, Tasmania.

Two other brothers, John Lewis (1809-1868) and Robert William von Stieglitz (1816-1876), received no land in Van Diemen's Land but were among the first settlers at Port Phillip, where they took up sheep runs first in the Geelong district and later at Ballan on the Werribee. John also held Station Peak for eight years. In 1836 he married Emma (1807-1880), the daughter of George Cowie, bookseller and alderman of London. She was a talented artist, producing landscapes and botanical studies. John sold his 16,000 acres at Ballan in 1852 and returned to Ireland, where he became a justice of the peace for County Tyrone. He died there on 22 August 1868 without issue. After acquiring 5000 acres at Ballan and 192,000 acres at Lake Hindmarsh in the Wimmera, Robert also sold out and returned to Ireland, where he died on 18 March 1876.

Francis Walter von Stieglitz (1811-1884), who had studied farming before he emigrated, was given a maximum grant of 2560 acres at Fingal and called it Lewis Hill. In September 1843 he was appointed a justice of the peace for Fingal and in 1864 coroner, officiating both in Fingal and Launceston. In 1840 he married Anne Ransom, by whom he had six sons and two daughters. He retired to Launceston in 1880 where he died in 1889.

The sixth and youngest brother, Charles Augustus (1819-1885), had been left at school when the elder brothers emigrated and he did not arrive until 1839. He joined his brothers in Victoria, acquiring 24,000 acres at Durdidwarrah, Portland. He sold out soon after the death of his mother, the baroness, in November 1852, and returned to Ireland where he bought Knockbarragh Park, County Down, in 1859. He died there in July 1885.

The family is commemorated in Victoria in the old gold-mining town of Steiglitz (so spelt), and in Tasmania in a township reserve at George's Bay.

K. R. von Stieglitz, *The centenary of Christchurch, Cullenswood* (Evandale, 1948); *Colonial Times*, 22 Jan 1830; *Hobart Town Courier*, 6 May 1836; *Examiner* (Launceston), 15 Apr 1889; CSO 1, 5, 8 and 24 (TA).

K. R. VON STIEGLITZ

W

WAINEWRIGHT, THOMAS GRIFFITHS (1794-1847), artist and writer, was born in October 1794 at Richmond near London, the son of Thomas Wainewright and his wife Ann, daughter of the publisher, Ralph Griffiths. His mother died at his birth and his father survived her by only a few years. The boy was brought up by his grandfather, Dr Ralph Griffiths, and after his death by an uncle, George Edward Griffiths. Wainewright was educated at Greenwich Academy where the headmaster, Dr Charles Burney, was another relative. At 19 Wainewright began studying painting under John Linnell and Thomas Phillips. In April 1814 he bought a commission in the 16th Regiment, but resigned after only thirteen months service. About this time he suffered a severe illness accompanied by hypochondria which affected him for the rest of his life

As well as painting he began writing for the London Magazine under the pseudonyms of Janus Weathercock, Egomet Bonmot and Cornelius Van Vinkbooms. His articles soon won him entrée to literary circles where he became friendly with Lamb, Hazlitt, Hood, de Quincey, Dickens and others. At 26 he began exhibiting his paintings at the Royal Academy where he came strongly under the influence of Henry Fuseli. The work Wainewright produced in England was so similar to that of Fuseli that it was sometimes confused with that of the master.

In 1821 he married Eliza Frances Ward, the daughter by a previous marriage of Mrs Abercromby. His grandfather had left him the income from £5250, which amounted to some £200 a year. Wainewright placed the capital sum of his inheritance in trust for his young wife, arranging that the money would go to her at his death. However, he lived above his income and was soon heavily in debt; by forging the signatures of his cousin, Edward Foss, and his father, Edward Smith Foss, a solicitor, to a power of attorney in July 1822 he obtained £2250 of his capital from the Bank of England. Two years later with a second forgery he obtained the remaining £3000.

In 1828 he and his wife went to live with his uncle, George Edward Griffiths, who soon died, leaving him his house and some money. In 1830 'old Mrs Abercromby' died a few days after making her will in favour of Mrs Wainewright. The two other daughters, Helen and Madeleine Abercromby, came to live with the Waine-wrights. Almost immediately Helen, still only 20, took out life policies with various insurance companies for some £16,000. Ten months later Helen Abercromby died after a brief illness. The insurance companies were suspicious and refused to pay. Wainewright, as executor, brought an action for recovery. After long delay the case was heard before Judge Abinger on 29 June 1835, but the jury disagreed. When the case was heard again the verdict was in favour of the defendants on the grounds of 'concealment by Miss Abercromby and an evasion of the statute'. Wainewright had left his wife and son in 1831 and remained out of England for six years. Numerous writers have suggested that Wainewright poisoned his uncle, his mother-in-law and his sister-in-law but, however suspicious the circumstances, there is no known evidence to show that any of the three died from other than natural causes. In the court action between Wainewright and the insurance companies the judge instructed the jury that there was 'no evidence of other crime than fraud'.

During Wainewright's absence in France the Bank of England discovered his forgeries and a warrant was issued for his arrest. He returned to England, was arrested on 9 June 1837 and charged with having attempted to defraud the Bank of England with a forged power of attorney. Although the governor of Newgate gaol on behalf of the Bank of England had persuaded him, with a promise of merely nominal punishment, to plead guilty, he was sentenced to transportation for life. In his own words, he was 'forthwith hurried, stunned with such ruthless perfidy, to the Hulks at Portsmouth, and then, in five days, aboard the Susan, a convict transport bound for Van Diemen's Land'. He arrived at Hobart Town on 21 November.

He worked at first on the roads in a chain-gang and was quartered in the prisoners' barracks in Campbell Street; later he was transferred to the Hobart Hospital as a wardsman. His health started to decline. The doctors were unable to diagnose the complaint, which was probably disseminated sclerosis. He was allowed some freedom and this enabled him to practise his beloved painting. Many of the portraits he produced at this time are among the best of his works and were mostly painted in gratitude for small favours by the subjects. In 1844, helped by the hospital authorities, he petitioned the governor for a ticket-of-leave, but his conditional pardon was not granted until 14 November 1846. He died of apoplexy at St Mary's Hospital on 17 August 1847.

Immediately after his death Wainewright began to appear as a vile monomaniac and poisoner in envenomed 'reminiscences' such as T. N. Talfourd's *Final Memorials of Charles Lamb* (London, 1848) and William Crooke's article in the *Spectator* (Melbourne), 14 July 1866. Highly-coloured fiction based on his alleged misdoings and character, for example, Lord Lytton's *Lucretia, or The Children of Night* (London, 1853) and Charles Dickens's *Hunted Down* (Philadelphia, 1860; London, 1870), added to a legend which was accepted by later biographers, J. T. Fields, A. G. Allen, Jonathan Curling and John Lindsey. Yet to his friends he had been a 'facetious, goodhearted fellow', a Georgian dandy, fond of dress and a collector of engravings and early editions, gems and antiques. He was of good family, accepted socially, well educated, talented and an accomplished artist, but something of an enigma. The portraits he painted during his ten years in Hobart Town show little imitation of Fuseli's extravagance, and some forty of these known to exist are works of art in their own right, full of sensitivity and perception. By leaving him with happiness only when he was painting, the harsh conditions and mental anguish that he suffered may also have stimulated his originality.

Wainewright published 'Some Passages' in the Life, etc. of Egomet Bonmot, Esq. (London, 1825) and his collected *Essays and Criticisms* (London, 1880) were edited by W. Carew Hazlitt.

HRA (1), 16; J. Curling, *Janus Weathercock* (Lond, 1938); R. Crossland, *Wainewright in Tasmania* (Melb, 1954); CSO 5, 8 and 11 (TA); Convict Records (TA); Diary of G. T. W. B. Boyes (Roy Soc Tas, Hob); Humble petition of T. G. Wainewright (ML).

V. W. HODGMAN

WAKEFIELD, EDWARD GIBBON (1796-1862), author and colonial promoter, was born on 20 March 1796 in London, the second of nine children of Edward Wakefield and Susanna, née Crash. Like his younger brothers, Daniel, Arthur and William, he later went to New Zealand, but the youngest, Felix, was the only member of the family to go to Australia. Wakefield was educated at Westminster school and Edinburgh High School. Although admitted to Gray's Inn in October 1813 he became secretary to the British envoy at Turin in 1814. He returned briefly to London and in June 1816 eloped with Eliza Ann Frances Pattle, a ward in Chancery. Through the lord chancellor the marriage was approved by parliament and Wakefield returned with Eliza to another appointment at the Turin legation. Susan Priscilla (Nina) was born on 4 December 1817 and Edward Jerningham ten days before Eliza died on 5 July 1820. From this marriage Wakefield derived a substantial life income. Evidently it was not sufficient to sustain his ambitions, for he abducted a 15-year-old heiress, Ellen Turner, from her school in March 1826. They were married at Gretna Green and fled to Calais, pursued by enraged members and friends of the girl's family. She was induced to return to her parents and Wakefield returned to England for trial. He and his brother William, an accomplice, were convicted of a statutory misdemeanour and on 14 May 1827 were each sentenced to three years imprisonment. The marriage was annulled by parliament in spite of a counter-petition by Wakefield.

Wakefield's imprisonment in Newgate was to transform his whole career. His disgrace led to his critical study of emigration and to his remedy, systematic colonization. Soon after his entry to Newgate, Wakefield occupied himself by inquiring why the prisoners were there, how effective were their punishments and what were their prospects. This and other material he brought before the public, chiefly in *Facts relating to the punishment of death in the metropolis* (1831), but also *Swing unmasked, or the causes of rural incendiarism* (1831), *The hangman and the judge* (1833) and *Popular politics* (1837). His study of emigration aroused his interest in Australasia and his anonymous *Sketch of a Proposal for Colonizing Australasia* was printed in June 1829. It was reprinted with other articles in the *Morning Chronicle* from 21 August to 6 October and in A *Letter from Sydney, the principal town of Australasia*, which was published in December with the name of Robert Gouger [q.v.] as editor. The *Letter* caused some stir in Sydney, for Wakefield claimed that Australian colonies were suffering from chaotic granting of free land, shortage of labour and consequent dependence on convicts. He argued that if settlement were concentrated, waste lands of the crown could be readily sold and the proceeds applied to the emigration of labourers, preferably young married couples, thereby giving maximum population relief in Britain and ensuring a balanced, fruitful colonial society. But

if the price for crown land were made
'sufficient' (high enough to discourage
labourers from immediately acquiring
land they could not use) such tribulations
as those of Thomas Peel [q.v.] at the
Swan River settlement would be avoided.
Sufficiency of labour and a congenial
society would attract capital, encourage
emigration, assure prosperity, and justify
the rights of a colony to elect representatives to its own legislature. British society
and civilization could thus be transplanted
from an old to a new country for their
mutual benefit.

Wakefield advocated his theory of systematic colonization, infallible and self-
regulating, with every available mode of
persuasion. Chief among these was his
personal magnetism; his manner, gesture
and speech, which he projected at meetings, at table, before parliamentary committees, even to passers-by and casual
acquaintances. Although a poor speaker
in public he was most persuasive at his
own fireside and in his writings. He
pressed his cause in a constant spate of
letters, newspapers, pamphlets and books,
in prose as insistent as it was terse. Wakefield was also an inveterate maker of
societies, especially those which, in his
own words, having a public object, 'meet,
appoint a chairman and secretary; pass
resolutions and subscribe money; in
other words they set to work for themselves, instead of seeing what their government may do for them'. What were
the obstacles to his cause? The public
cared nothing for colonies nor did the
government except as a dumping ground
for criminals. Those who saw population
as superabundant argued that there was
no surplus capital for export. Religious
and missionary bodies were jealous of
their native charges and feared the influx
of white colonists. By contrast, those who
saw colonization as a panacea for the
condition of England wanted to propound
their own schemes: Wilmot Horton by
pauper emigration and Robert Torrens
[q.v.] by promising emigrant capitalists
all their needs from a slender land fund.
At the Colonial Office Wakefield faced
the unwillingness of an understaffed instrument of state to add to its administrative and financial burdens, exacerbated
by that natural inertia which welled from
the repeated rejection of unwelcome
petitions. Finally, and increasingly with
time, he faced former disciples disgruntled by his exacting demands and
even the minor details of his views.
Wakefield was a passionate man and
could inspire only allegiance or enmity,
never neutrality.

Wakefield's propaganda recognizably
influenced the issue of several new regulations for the disposal of waste land in
New South Wales and Van Diemen's
Land, especially those that stipulated sale
by auction at a minimum price of 5s. an
acre, with the proceeds devoted to an
immigration fund. Wakefield was unimpressed by such a token salute to his
scheme and began to plan the systematic
colonization of southern Australia.

Wakefield's role in the founding of
South Australia is difficult to estimate.
Torrens later credited him with the major
role and so did Governor Hindmarsh.
Robert Gouger and Anthony Bacon [q.v.]
who submitted the first South Australian
proposals were both associates of Wakefield from his prison days. His biographer,
Richard Garnett, hinted that Wakefield
intended to go to South Australia in 1832,
but that year the first plans for the proposed colony were rejected by the Colonial Office. To explain and elaborate his
theories Wakefield anonymously published England and America. A Comparison of the social and political State
of both Nations, 2 vols (London, 1833;
New York, 1834). Meanwhile another
scheme put forward by the South Australian Land Co. had proved abortive. In
these years Wakefield spent much time
on the Continent. He was absent when
the South Australian Association was
formed late in 1833, but returned next
year to help his brother, Daniel, to draft
the bill to empower His Majesty to erect
South Australia into a British province or
provinces and to provide for the colonization and government thereof. Wakefield
was active in organizing the lobbying
that led to parliament passing the bill.
After it received royal assent on 15
August 1834, he published The New
British Province of South Australia
(London, 1834; Edinburgh, 1835), a
manual of advice and information for intending colonists. Apart from these contributions Wakefield's name appears
rarely in contemporary manuscripts,
though his personal influence must have
been very great. In January 1835 he
took his consumptive daughter to Lisbon,
where she died on 12 February. Grief-
stricken he returned to London to find
that Torrens had been made chairman
of the South Australian Colonization
Commission appointed by the government. Wakefield's interest in the new province was already on the wane, chiefly
because he was disgusted by the low
price of land fixed in his absence and
the misleading 'self-supporting principle'
adopted by Torrens.

In June 1836 Wakefield gave evidence before the select committee on the disposal of land in the British colonies and in December offered himself as a parliamentary candidate for Birmingham but soon withdrew. In 1838 he became a director of the Western Australian Co.; its plans for a settlement, Australind, at Port Leschenault, were not carried out with marked success. Wakefield also spent six months with Lord Durham in Canada and his influence appears markedly in Durham's *Report on the Affairs of British North America*, in its strong recommendation for local self-government in British colonies and in the appendices on public land and emigration. In 1841 Wakefield returned to Canada as agent for his North American Colonial Association, planning to carry out public works with Irish labourers on the security of the colony's land revenues. In December 1842 he was elected to the Canadian General Assembly, and despite an uncertain reception proved a valuable adviser to three successive Canadian governors.

Meanwhile Wakfield's eyes had turned again to the antipodes. In May 1837 the New Zealand Association was formed at his home. A number of intending emigrants were assembled by 1838 but the bill for colonizing the islands was defeated in the House of Commons by missionary interests. Wakefield returned from Canada in 1838 to find that the New Zealand Association had formed the New Zealand Land Co. and that their second bill had been rejected. Undeterred, Wakefield plumped for defiance and in May 1839 dispatched the first shipload of colonists. A British consul had already been appointed and favourable reception at the House of Lords select committee on New Zealand emboldened him to have the company apply for a charter, which was granted in 1841. It was the news of the death of his brother, Arthur (1799-1843), in a conflict with Maoris that brought Wakefield back from Canada in 1844. New Zealand affairs were then in a parlous state. The company was nearly bankrupt and many of its titles were in dispute. In April Wakefield worked zealously to win a favourable report from a House of Commons select committee inquiring into New Zealand affairs. Still ignored by the Colonial Office, he then came to the view that while colonists had no control of their own land policy their titles would remain insecure. This was a decisive step, for previously an essential article of his faith was that disposal of lands and emigration should be an imperial matter and

not subject to local interference. His hopes rose in 1846 when Earl Grey took charge at the Colonial Office. Grey had often shown interest in the Wakefield system but was now violently opposed to Wakefield's espousal of self-government for New Zealand. On 15 August Wakefield, already worn out, suffered a severe stroke from which he never fully recovered. Thenceforth he was obliged to avoid excitement and to retire from London, having only his pen and the penny post to execute his plans unless some man of note could be inveigled to his cottage.

Grey's decision to press for the passing of his Australian colonies government bill in the 1850 session diverted Wakefield from his plans for New Zealand's self-government. Hoping to stir up agitation so that he might match the bill with an opposition measure to include New Zealand with Australia, he organized the Society for the Reform of Colonial Government. Much in the spirit of the 1848 revolutionary upheaval he published *The Southern Colonies: their municipal annexation, or their national independence* (London, 1849), in which he exhorted colonists at the Cape, Australia and New Zealand to act vigorously in favour of the colonial reformers' bill. To introduce it he secured Sir William Molesworth, an associate of long standing. But Molesworth's proposal to grant the colonists power to make their own constitutions proved anathema to the Tory members of the society and it broke up on this issue. Wakefield lost interest in the project.

In February 1849 his *A View of the Art of Colonization* had been published in London, with the object of planting a Church of England colony in New Zealand and thereby disarming missionary opposition. The Association for Founding the Settlement of Canterbury had been formed in March 1848, and in July its surveyor left England with instructions to select and prepare a site for the new colony. The first emigrant ships left England in 1850 for Canterbury. In 1851 Wakefield sent as his agent his youngest brother, Felix (1807-1875), who had been a surveyor in Van Diemen's Land in 1832-47. After a Provincial Council was provided for Canterbury by the New Zealand Constitution Act of 1852 Wakefield himself turned colonist. He arrived at Christchurch in February 1853 and after a short stay moved to Wellington. He was elected to the first New Zealand General Assembly but his influence over the acting governor earned him much unpopularity and led to a fracas which broke Wakefield's health. He lived in retirement at his home in Wellington and his death on 16 May 1862 went almost unnoticed.

Wakefield was an enigma to his contemporaries as he is to posterity. Denied office by his criminal record he devoted his energy to schemes for systematic colonization and responsible government. Not content only to influence men's minds by his pen he sought directly to influence their actions as well. His personal magnetism and imaginative zeal won him many converts but much disappointment when he found that people could not be controlled like puppets. His idealism would not allow him to compromise, and when he ignored the principles of others their reactions were often bitter. In his restless search to achieve his objectives he ranged through the whole spectrum of English politics and society, utilitarian radicals, Whigs, and High Church Tories, and left behind him some claim to success in penal reform, immigration to New South Wales, the Durham report, and the colonization of South Australia and New Zealand. The factious conclusion to his career and his obscure death have given to his life a certain tragic perspective although some writers have credited him with high rank as an architect of the British Commonwealth.

A bust by Joseph Durham, R.A., was placed in the Colonial Office in 1876 and transferred in 1934 to the National Gallery of South Australia; a miniature by an unknown artist is in the National Portrait Gallery, London, and a portrait by E. J. Collins and R. Ansdell in the Provincial Hall, Christchurch, New Zealand.

E. J. Wakefield (ed), *Founders of Canterbury* (Christchurch, 1868); R. Garnett, *Edward Gibbon Wakefield, the colonization of South Australia and New Zealand* (Lond, 1898); A. J. Harrop, *The amazing career of Edward Gibbon Wakefield* (Lond, 1928); Irma O'Connor, *Edward Gibbon Wakefield; the man himself* (Lond, 1928); P. Bloomfield, *Edward Gibbon Wakefield, builder of the British Commonwealth* (Lond, 1961); J. Philipp, 'Wakefieldian influence and New South Wales', *Hist Studies*, no 34, May 1960; D. Pike, 'Wakefield, waste land and empire', *PTHRA*, 12 (1965); G. L. Pretty, 'Edward Gibbon Wakefield and New Zealand, 1846-1852', (B.A. thesis, Univ Syd, 1960).

GRAEME L. PRETTY

WALKER, GEORGE WASHINGTON (1800-1859), Quaker, shopkeeper and humanitarian, was born on 19 March 1800 in London, the twenty-first child of John Walker (1726-1821) by his second wife, Elizabeth, née Ridley. Because of the death of his mother and the absence of his aged father engaged in the saddle trade in Paris, he was brought up by his grandmother in Newcastle. He was educated by a Wesleyan schoolmaster near Barnard Castle, and apprenticed in 1814 to a linen draper. Impressed by the probity and wisdom of his Quaker employers and James Backhouse [q.v.] of York, a leading Quaker minister, he left the Unitarian persuasion of his family in 1827 and became a member of the Society of Friends. The next year he formed the first Temperance Society in Newcastle.

In 1831 he accompanied James Backhouse on a nine-year mission to the Australian and South African colonies. The partnership combined the initiative, imagination and adventurous spirit of James Backhouse and Walker's methodical organizing and secretarial skill. They investigated convict and Aboriginal conditions, returned statistical accounts to Quakers in England, and presented a picture of the emigrant's life and prospects. As they visited from house to house or presented to large gatherings their version of a simple practical Christianity, they encouraged schools for the poor, temperance, cleanliness and care in hospitals, humane treatment of the insane, and generally tried to arouse a social conscience among the inhabitants of every colony.

Walker returned from South Africa to Hobart Town in 1840 to marry Sarah Benson Mather, member of a Wesleyan family turned Quaker. Aware of his reputation for trustworthiness, friendliness and leadership, Walker strove to practise what he advocated and to support the organizations he and Backhouse had promoted. With the help of English Friends he set up a linen draper's shop in 1841 and made half of it available for the distribution of Bibles, religious tracts and temperance literature, with the 'pledge' always ready for signature. In 1845, to encourage thrift among the poor, particularly reformed drunkards, he organized the Hobart Savings Bank and managed it for some months without pay; it grew quickly, and soon required his full-time service. Because he thought that some of his merchandise catered only to luxury and fashion, he sold his linen drapery in 1848 at a loss and restricted his trade to the plainer woollen goods. In 1847 he was publicly thanked by a group of shop assistants for inducing other shopkeepers to adopt 7 o'clock closing, but in 1855 he was publicly threatened with tar and feathering for organizing his Temperance

Committee into vigilante bands to enforce the law of Sunday closing of public houses.

In spite of derision his concern for transported prisoners remained active; he supported Maconochie's [q.v.] penal reforms, and continued to help many individual convicts. His wife was a member of Lady Franklin's committee to visit the female prisoners. In 1843 he was appointed to a board of inquiry into conditions at the Female Factory, built by Lieut-Governor Arthur in 1827 in accord with Elizabeth Fry's recommendations. Worried over the growing number of prostitutes, he formed a committee to 'suppress vice' by finding employment for destitute women. In 1848 Lieut-Governor Denison asked him to share in the task of providing an asylum for these women, and noted in his journal: 'the very personification of a mild, benevolent, and excellent Quaker. Even here, where sectarian and religious party feeling run higher than anywhere I have ever known, men of all denominations unite in speaking well of George Washington Walker'.

He kept in close touch with the Aboriginal mission stations and gave valuable service as a member of the council which built the non-denominational high school on the Domain, of the colonial board of education, and of the council of the Royal Society of Tasmania. His friendship with learned men in every colony enriched his letters and made them invaluable to his scholarly eldest son, James Backhouse Walker.

A respected founder with Backhouse of the Society of Friends in Hobart, Walker was always ready to plead for any convict under punishment by solitary confinement or treadmill for refusing in Quaker custom to remove his hat in respect to authority, to explain to judges the Quaker aversion to oaths, or to reason against state aid to religion. Although unable to repeat his missionary journeys, he managed to visit Friends around the island and encouraged others to travel 'in the ministry' to help new Meetings on the mainland. He also corresponded with Friends in other colonies, supported one lone Quaker in Western Australia in her observance of Quaker testimonies, helped the Australian Meetings to win eventual recognition by the London Yearly Meeting, and assisted the organization of small schools for Friends' children, forerunners of the later Friends' School, North Hobart.

Overconscientious and never robust, he maintained a calm cheerful manner that concealed his anxieties and the overtaxing of his means in support of his ten children

and various charities. He died on 2 February 1859 and was buried in the Friends' burial ground in Providence Valley, West Hobart, mourned by citizens in every colony. Narryna, his home for two years, has become the Van Diemen's Land Folk Museum, and contains mementoes of his famous trip with James Backhouse. Of his benevolent organizations, the Hobart Savings Bank and the Temperance Society remain. His Quaker grey and 'thees and thous' were outward labels of a nineteenth-century puritan, but he contributed to the community the enlightened leaven of a Dissenter, the care for humanity of an Evangelical, and the gentle methodical persuasion of a Quaker resolved to effect a change in a vicious brutal world.

J. Backhouse, A *narrative of a visit to the Australian colonies* (Lond, 1843); J. Backhouse and C. Tylor, *The life and labours of George Washington Walker* (Lond, 1862); W. T. Denison, *Varieties of vice-regal life* (Lond, 1870); G. W. Walker papers (Friends House, Lond); Mthly Meeting minutes (Society of Friends, Hob); Walker papers (Univ Tas).   MARY BARTRAM TROTT

WALKER, JOHN (1799-1874), miller, brewer, merchant and landowner, was born at Ednam, near Kelso on the Scottish border, the son of Robert Thomas Walker, a local flour-miller and farmer. John went to school at Kelso and attended the Presbyterian Kirk of Rev. John Pitcairn. His father failed in the depression after Waterloo, so at 21 John decided to emigrate in order to retrieve the family fortunes. In September 1822 he arrived in Hobart Town in the *Heroine*. By his own account he was 'penniless and unfriended', but among his acquaintances were John Dunn, George Carr Clark and Henry Hopkins [qq.v.]. Within a month he was appointed superintendent of the government flour-mill on the Hobart Town Rivulet. Next year he received a grant of 200 acres and in 1824 built a mill at Richmond. Thanks to convict labour he had five prosperous years, increased his capital to £2000 and received a maximum land grant of 2560 acres. Moving to Launceston in 1830, he built a mill at the foot of Cataract Hill. Back in Hobart he bought the government flour-mill together with its attached residence in Barrack Street and opened a brewery. By adding a steam-engine he greatly increased his milling business and extended his activities to commerce, whaling, shipping and insurance. He became a local director of the Bank of Australasia and of the Bank of

Van Diemen's Land. He also helped to form the Derwent Bank and as managing director had to act as its liquidator in 1850. He was also commissioned to wind up the Tasmanian interests of Lieut-Governor Arthur. As his assets increased Walker acquired the estates of Belmont and Shawfield on the River Ouse and Clarendon on the Derwent where he opened another flour-mill.

Walker served actively as a commissioner for Hobart before the municipal council was formed, and in 1840 he was appointed a justice of the peace. In 1851 he was elected for Brighton to the Legislative Council and after responsible government he represented Hobart in the Upper House. In 1857 he became a member of the ministry under Sir Francis Smith and was admitted to the Executive Council. Private business took him several times to Britain. In these travels he was shipwrecked three times: in the *Schomberg* off Cape Otway, in the *Royal Standard* off Rio de Janeiro and in the *Rangoon* in Galle Harbour. He was a zealous apostle for emigration in Scotland and engaged twenty-nine Welsh miners for the Douglas River Coal Co. of which he was a director. He kept a sharp watch for improvements in agriculture and is credited with introducing steam-engines in Van Diemen's Land. About 1855 he revisited his native village, where he distributed largesse to his kinsfolk, to the poor and to the Kelso Free Church, although in Hobart he was an elder of St Andrew's under the ministry of Rev. John Lillie [q.v.]. He was also secretary and treasurer of the Presbyterian Tract Society, an active member of the Hobart Infant School Society, and energetic in a variety of other causes. He died at his home in Barrack Street on 27 February 1874. Walker was twice married: first in 1827 to Janet Glass; they had several children, all of whom with one exception survived him; and second in 1858 to Julia Speke, née Coverdale, the widow of Charles Bradbury, inspector of schools. At Walker's death she and their only son were in England, and she died there at Cheltenham on 19 December 1891.

P. L. Brown (ed), *Clyde Company papers*, 2 (Lond, 1952); *Mercury*, 23 Mar 1874; *Kelso Chronicle*, 19 June 1874; Correspondence file under John Walker (TA).

WALDEMAR WOLFHAGEN

WALKER, THOMAS (1791-1861), commissary and settler, was born on 3 December 1791 in Yorkshire, England, the third son of John Walker, barrister-at-law, of Headingley near Leeds, and Mary, née Rogerson, whose mother had been Elizabeth Brooke of Rhodes Hall near Leeds. He entered the army before 18 and was attached to Wellington's staff. He served in the commissariat in the Peninsular war, in France, in the Netherlands and at Waterloo. He was appointed assistant deputy-commissary-general in December 1814 and as a passenger in the convict transport *Friendship* arrived at Port Jackson on 13 January 1818. He served in the Sydney stores until October when he was sent to take charge at Port Dalrymple. On taking up his duty he applied successfully for a grant of 800 acres at Port Dalrymple. He also received other 'indulgencies', among them an allotment on which to build a government house at George Town. With the intention of settling permanently he improved his land and stocked it.

During his time in the commissariat at Port Dalrymple he was often at loggerheads with the commandant, Lieut-Colonel Cimitiere [q.v.], whom he accused of trying to make personal profit from supplying the stores. After mutual recrimination he refused to have personal dealings with the commandant and communicated with him through his clerk who sent messages to Cimitiere's clerk. This earned him Lieut-Governor Sorell's severe condemnation, but as Walker was on the point of returning to Sydney nothing was done about it.

He sailed early in October 1819 in the schooner *Sinbad*, and after some time in Sydney was put in charge at Parramatta and Windsor. He built a house on the Parramatta River at Concord which he called Rhodes. On 4 January 1823 at St John's Church, Parramatta, he married Anna Elizabeth, second daughter of John Blaxland [q.v.]. They had four sons and nine daughters.

In 1825 Walker retired on half-pay through ill health which he attributed to his strenuous work in the service. In 1832 he left Sydney, took his family to Van Diemen's Land, and built another Rhodes on his grant at South Esk near Longford. Made a magistrate in October 1837, he lived at Rhodes in Tasmania until he died on 12 April 1861, when his family returned to Rhodes in New South Wales.

Walker was ambitious and had hoped to be made commissary-general; he felt that after eight years service he deserved something better than retirement at the same rank with which he had come to the colony. However, he was more successful as a pioneer, and besides building two fine homes he became the owner, through grants and purchases, of valuable properties in New South Wales, Tasmania and at Port Phillip.

Hobart Town Courier, 20 May 1836; *Cornwall Chronicle*, 29 Sept 1838.

IDA McAULAY

WALKER, THOMAS (1804-1886), merchant, banker and benefactor, was born on 3 May 1804 at Leith, Scotland, the elder son of James Thomas Walker, merchant, and his wife Anne, née Walker, of Perth. Thomas Walker came to Sydney and joined his maternal uncle in the firm of William Walker [q.v.] & Co., general merchants, about 1822. Later, with a cousin, he succeeded to the business. Thomas Walker was a magistrate in 1835.

In 1837 he rode overland with three friends to Melbourne; his journal was published anonymously in London in 1838 as *A Month in the Bush of Australia*. Foreseeing the growth of Melbourne, Walker at once bought four Bourke Street blocks for £135. Other prompt purchases brought his freehold in the Port Phillip District to 12,700 acres, which cost him less than £16,000. Walker's Sydney company also held eight squatting runs and had an interest in at least four others. Prudent sales laid the foundation of a large fortune. In June 1843 he was elected one of Port Phillip's representatives in the first part-elective New South Wales Legislative Council. In 1845 he signed a petition for Port Phillip to be made a separate colony, but soon gave up politics to devote more time to his growing financial interests. He was a director of the Australian Steam Navigation Co. and other companies and a minor shareholder in the Bank of Australia when it crashed; this may explain the ultra-conservative policy he adopted when he was a director in 1859 and president in 1869-86 of the Bank of New South Wales. As president, Walker vigorously opposed showy expenditure. He maintained that some shabby premises the bank occupied, instead of injuring business, won the confidence of thrifty people 'who abhor the display and gilt of modern fashions'. Almost to his death he stubbornly opposed any increase in the bank's capital, which still stood at £1,000,000 though deposits had increased from £5,500,000 to £14,500,000 under his presidency. He argued that increased capital would not necessarily bring a proportionate increase in business.

Walker strongly criticized Robertson's Land Acts of 1861. When they came up for review in 1878 and 1884 Walker wrote several pamphlets condemning the policy of free selection before survey. He claimed that the Acts did irreparable injury to the pastoral industry and the State, created an army of debtors, and disposed of the people's land at less than its true value. Though old he wrote trenchantly, using such terms as fraud, corruption, blackmail, evasion, deceit, perjury and waste, and not hesitating to impute dishonesty to some politicians and Lands Department agents. In place of free selection Walker advocated creation of special agricultural reserves where genuine farmers could obtain land without taking the best from the runs and causing antagonism between squatters and selectors.

Walker was regarded by some as tight-fisted. He was, however, conscientious and benevolent, made many personal benefactions, and for a time employed an agent privately to seek out and relieve people in distress; before visiting Europe in 1882 he left £10,000 to be distributed among Sydney charities. In 1860 he had married Ann, the daughter of Thomas Hart, merchant, of Woolloomooloo. She died in December 1870, leaving one child, Eadith Campbell Walker.

Thomas Walker died on 2 September 1886 at Yaralla, Concord, Sydney. His will set aside £100,000 for the building and support of what is now the Thomas Walker Convalescent Hospital at Concord; in seventy years more than 50,000 patients passed through it. The rest of his fortune he left in trust to his daughter. When she died unmarried in October 1937 the fund, then about £800,000, was divided under Thomas Walker's will into two parts, one to go to next-of-kin, the remainder to charitable trusts. None of Walker's brothers and sisters had left children, and an appeal to next-of-kin brought more than six hundred claimants, from Scotland, England, South Africa, the United States, France, Norway and most Australian States. Finally thirty-three claimants established a fifth-degree blood relationship and each received about £12,000. Of £380,000 which finally went to charity, £100,000 was set aside to found the Dame Eadith Walker Convalescent Hospital for Men at Concord and income from the remainder went to support the Dame Eadith hospital, the Thomas Walker hospital and the Yaralla cottages built by Dame Eadith for elderly people in need. A portrait of Thomas Walker is in the head office of the Bank of New South Wales.

HRA (1), 17, 23, 24; E. J. Brady, *Australia unlimited* (Melb, 1918); *SMH*, 3 Sept 1886, 9, 15, 20 Oct, 26 Nov 1937, 30 Nov 1938; *Australasian*, 8 Dec 1934; *Daily Telegraph* (Syd), 24 June 1939.   W. JOY

WALKER, WILLIAM (1787-1854), merchant, was the second son of Archibald Walker, laird of Edenshead, Fife, Scotland, and his second wife, Isabel, daughter of the laird of Falfield. In 1803 he joined the London branch of a Scottish bank and after a few years joined Fairlie, Ferguson & Co., merchants, whose headquarters were at Calcutta. He was soon sent to Calcutta and in July 1813 went to Sydney in the *Eliza* as agent for his firm, with the immediate task of collecting debts owed to it by Robert Campbell [q.v.]. After his return to Calcutta he resigned from the firm and in March 1820 came back to Sydney in the *Haldane*.

William Walker's eldest brother James, a half-pay naval officer, arrived in Sydney in September 1823. Walker had already formed William Walker & Co., with James and two nephews, Thomas [q.v.] and Archibald Walker, who were in the colony, as shareholders. The firm had a wharf and warehouse at Dawes Point and engaged in coastal shipping and whaling. William received a grant of 1000 acres from Governor Macquarie in 1821 and in 1825 another 1000 from Governor Brisbane at Lue, near Mudgee. James received 2000 acres at Wallerawang and settled there in 1824.

In May 1826 William sailed in the *Mangles* for London. On his return to Australia in the *Numa* in July 1828 he brought 160 Saxon merino ewes from Stettin. While in England he had applied for an increased grant as he now had capital of approximately £25,000 invested in the colony. He was given another 1000 acres and later obtained more land in the central district and at Twofold Bay. In February 1831 both brothers chartered the *Forth* and returned to London to establish the firm of Walker Bros. & Co., which during the late 1830s exported large quantities of wool to London. Their men moved stock to the upper Castlereagh River and squatted on several runs. David, William and Thomas Archer [qq.v.], sons of William Archer and Julia Walker, daughter of William's half-brother Archibald, had arrived at Wallerawang in 1834-38 and David Archer began managing the Walkers' properties. News of losses in the depression and drought brought William Walker to Australia again in 1843, but until he died on 8 July 1854 his permanent residence was in England. On 20 October 1828 in Sydney he had married Elizabeth Kirby; they had nine sons and two daughters

William Walker played an active part in public life during his long residence in New South Wales. He was a director of the Bank of New South Wales in 1820-24, a member of committees appointed to examine the bank's affairs in 1844 and 1845, and was on its first London board in 1853-54. He was president of the Chamber of Commerce and treasurer of the Agricultural Society, a strong supporter of the Scots Church and a subscriber to charitable institutions.

HRA (1), 8, 10, 11, 13, 16, 17; *Sydney Gazette*, 10 July 1813, 1 July 1820, 7 July 1828; *Australian*, 19 Feb 1831; B. H. Crew, The history of the Walker and Archer families (M.A. thesis, ANU, 1963); MS cat under W. Walker (ML). VIVIENNE PARSONS

WALKER, WILLIAM (1800-1855), Methodist minister, was accepted as a candidate for the Wesleyan ministry in England in July 1819. A year later he was preparing for the Gambia Mission, but on 30 August 1820 he was appointed 'to the black natives of New South Wales', since his health would not allow him to go to West Africa. He sailed for Sydney in the *Brixton* with Rev. Samuel Leigh [q.v.] and Rev. and Mrs William Horton. On the voyage Walker's health worried Leigh, but he arrived safely on 16 September 1821.

In October, with Jonathan Hassall, he visited the Aboriginals at Blacktown. 'All they require is a few clothes, agricultural implements and a supply of food until their crops be reaped', he wrote. 'I left them with a consciousness of having never been favoured with a more profitable or serious season during my ministerial career'. However, he later found a different group of them 'idle and vagrant and the colonists too often encourage their vices'. He adopted the son of Bennelong [q.v.] and baptized him on 27 September 1822, but next January the boy died, aged 20. Walker's experience in 1821-23 led the Wesleyan missionaries to support the establishment of a seminary for the maintenance and instruction of a select number of youths. The government approved but the project had little success and in 1824 was abandoned, partly because of conflict between the Wesleyan leaders.

On 14 May 1823 Walker had married Eliza Cordelia, daughter of Rowland Hassall [q.v.], at St John's Church, Parramatta. Walker and Walter Lawry [q.v.] benefited materially from their matrimonial alliances with the Hassalls and both were later accused of having commercial interests outside the scope of their ministerial duties. The Wesleyan Overseas Committee informed the local missionaries 'that if they expect to be acknowledged as Methodist missionaries they will be re-

quired to decline the keeping of all farming and grazing stock and the following
of any worldly business whatever'; and so,
'to break up his connection with temporal
things, Mr. Walker was removed'. This was
suspension rather than expulsion, for on 10
August 1825 the English committee consented to his restoration to office if he
humbled himself before God, delivered up
all the mission property together with £40
for a mare bought for the mission, sold
his farm stock, and engaged 'for the future
to submit yourself to your brethren, both
with respect to the place where you shall
labour and the work you shall perform'.
If he accepted these conditions, Walker
was to go to Van Diemen's Land.

However, the local committee remained
difficult. In May 1825 it 'severely rebuked'
Walker for preaching for Leigh, when the
latter was ill; it also complained that without its consent and contrary to its judgment
he had left the Aboriginal mission to accept appointment as superintendent of the
Female Orphan School. Walker argued
that the mission had proved 'a wasteful
and devouring vortex of public money'
and maintained that he had always acted
with the full knowledge and consent of
Rev. G. Erskine, chairman of the New
South Wales district. At the orphanage
charges were made against Walker's administration, while he accused other Wesleyan missionaries of joining Rev. Samuel
Marsden and Archdeacon Scott [qq.v.] in
opposition to Governor Brisbane.

In November 1825 Scott, who as 'King's
Visitor' had been to the Female Orphan
School in the superintendent's absence,
accused Walker of ill treating the inmates
and made specific charges to the governor
about their health. Though even the benign Anne Hassall criticized Walker, in
due course the Supreme Court decided that
Scott had prematurely assumed his visi-
torial functions. Walker was also criticized
because he attended political meetings,
and in April 1826 he and his wife resigned
from the school.

Walker then took up pastoral pursuits
at Brisbane Grove, O'Connell Plains, and
in 1828 he owned 2000 acres, 230 cattle
and 2300 sheep. Meanwhile in opposition
to public opinion he had been supporting
Governor Darling in anonymous articles
in the press, and later accepted a land
grant from him for his children. Despite a
formal separation from his ministerial
brethren he conducted services in his home
and his popularity with Wesleyan families
and the community generally seems well
established. Rev. Joseph Orton [q.v.],
Erskine's successor, rated him as 'most certainly a clever man . . . injudiciously

managed by those who were placed over
him'. Brisbane declared him the 'best educated man in the colony'. Unfortunately,
when he died on 23 November 1855, leaving two sons and three daughters, he requested that his many manuscripts be destroyed, and only a catalogue of his
library of 1057 books remains as evidence
of this claim; but obituary notices affirmed
the value of his writings.

HRA (1), 10-15); *The fifth report for the
Wesleyan Auxiliary Missionary Society for
New South Wales, for the year 1825* (Syd,
1826); J. Colwell, *The illustrated history of
Methodism, Australia* (Syd, 1904); W. J.
Townsend, H. B. Workman and G. Eayrs,
A new history of Methodism, 1-2 (Lond,
1909); *Aust Mag*, 1-2 (1821-22); *JRAHS*, 35
(1949); *Empire*, 28 Nov 1855; W. Walker,
Letters, 1825-26 (Methodist Missionary Soc,
Lond); MS cat under W. Walker (ML).

S. G. CLAUGHTON

WALLACE, WILLIAM VINCENT (1812-
1865), musician, was born in Waterford,
Ireland, the eldest son of the Irish band-
sergeant of the 29th Regiment. At 8 he
composed marches for his father's band;
at 16 he was first violin in the Theatre
Royal orchestra, Dublin; at 18 he was
organist of the Thurles Roman Catholic
Cathedral and taught piano at the Ursu-
line Convent. He fell in love with a pupil,
Isabella Kelly, whose father consented to
their marriage in 1831 on condition that
Wallace became a Roman Catholic and
took the name of Vincent. He returned to
Dublin as sub-leader of the Theatre Royal
orchestra; after hearing Paganini he practised night and day till he became a
virtuoso.

In November 1835 he emigrated to
Hobart Town with his wife and infant son,
his sister Elisabeth, a soprano, and his
brother Wellington, a flautist. After one
concert the family went to Sydney in
January 1836 and in Bridge Street opened
the first Australian music school. Vincent
also imported pianos for his musical repository in Hunter Street, and during 1837
he gave recitals in Sydney, Parramatta
and Windsor, and was known as 'the
Australian Paganini'. Governor Bourke was
Wallace's constant patron, but the story
that Bourke gave him 100 sheep as a fee
for his first concert is apocryphal. Wallace
was never a farmer; he has almost certainly been confused with William Wallace
of Nithsdale.

In January 1838 at St Mary's Cathedral
he organized the first music festival in Australia; in February he sailed secretly for
Valparaiso, leaving debts of £2000. From
1838 to 1843 he allegedly had wild adven-

tures in three continents although he certainly made a successful tour of the United States and helped to found the New York Philharmonic Society. In 1844 he was in Germany and Holland; in 1845 he gave piano recitals in London and his opera *Maritana* was triumphantly produced at Drury Lane, and later at Vienna and Covent Garden. *Maritana* reached Australia in 1849; there is no real evidence for the tradition that Wallace composed it either in Sydney or Tasmania. His *Lurline* (1860) earned £50,000 for the management of Covent Garden but nothing for Wallace; other operas were *Matilda of Hungary*, *The Amber Witch* and *The Desert Flower*, and the British Museum catalogue of smaller works fills a hundred pages.

Wallace had separated from his wife in Sydney; in 1850 he became an American citizen and went through a form of marriage in New York with Helen Stoepel (d. 1887), a pianist, by whom he had two sons, both of whom committed suicide. He died in 1865 at Château de Haget, near Vieuzos, Hautes-Pyrénées, but was buried in Kensal Green, London. His widow, Isabella, survived till 1900; his son William Vincent died a poor brother of the Charterhouse in 1909.

Wallace's sister, Elisabeth (b. Waterford 1814, d. Sydney 1878) settled in Sydney and married a singer, John Bushelle; she witnessed the Viennese *première* of *Maritana* in 1847 and appeared at Covent Garden in the title role in 1848.

A pen-and-ink sketch of Wallace, aged 42, was reproduced in the *Illustrated London News*, November 1845, and a water-colour portrait by Henshaw, 1853, is in the National Gallery, Dublin.

Wallace was a brilliant musician, but even his famous *Maritana* is now performed only by amateurs. As a man he was charming but unprincipled, and his habitual untruthfulness makes it hard to determine the real facts about him.

H. Berlioz, A *treatise upon modern instrumentation and orchestration*, tr M. Cowden Clarke (Lond, 1856); A. Pougin, *William Vincent Wallace. Etude biographique et critique* (Paris, 1866); W. Spark, *Musical memories*, 2nd ed (Lond, 1888); F. J. Sawyer, *English music 1604-1904* (Lond, 1906); W. H. Grattan Flood, *Wallace. A memoir* (Waterford, 1912); R. Northcott, *Opera Chatter* (Lond, 1921); W. Arundel Orchard, *Music in Australia* (Melb, 1952); 'Anecdotes of Vincent Wallace', *Theatre*, 4 (1884); S. Cole and W. H. Grattan Flood, 'Correspondence on Wallace's marriage', *Musical Times*, Sept 1912; *Hobart Town Courier*, 6, 13 Nov, 4 Dec 1835, 8 Jan 1836.

CATHERINE MACKERRAS

WALLIS, JAMES (1785?-1858), soldier, was the second son of James Wallis, of Cork, Ireland, and his wife Lucinda, née Hewson. He was appointed ensign in the 46th Regiment in December 1803 and lieutenant in April 1804, distinguishing himself in action against the French in Dominica. Appointed captain on 19 December 1811, he arrived in Sydney with his regiment on 7 February 1814 in the transport *General Hewitt*, in which a 'fellow-passenger' was the painter, Joseph Lycett [q.v.]. In April 1816 he commanded a company of grenadiers of the 46th Regiment against hostile Aboriginals near Airds and Appin, and received the thanks of Governor Macquarie for 'zealous exertions and strict attention to the fulfilling of the instructions'. On 1 June 1816 he was appointed to relieve Lieutenant Thompson as commandant at Newcastle at a salary of £136, and on 8 June embarked in the brig *Lady Nelson* with a detachment of his regiment.

He at once introduced new regulations and with severe discipline put an end to the laxity that prevailed. He also began to improve the settlement by constructing new public and government buildings. Assisted by Lycett, whom Wallis persuaded to amend the original plans, he proceeded with the building of Christ Church, the third brick and stone church in Australia. Its foundation stone he laid on 1 January 1817 and it was completed within a year. Wallis read services there for the remainder of his stay, since no clergyman was appointed until 1821, but unfortunately the church's 'elegant Spire' revealed the architectural short-comings of its designers; badly shaken by wind it soon had to be removed. His other buildings included a stone convict hospital, a two-storey brick and stone gaol, a brick subalterns' barracks, a brick barracks for the assistant surgeon, a barracks for convicts, a guard house, a watch house, a boat house, a lumber yard and workshop. A school was set up in 1816. The wreck of the small *Nautilus* on 24 November 1816 at the southern entrance to the harbour prompted Wallis's conception of a breakwater from the mainland to Coal (Nobby) Island. Next year he compiled a comprehensive list of signals to be flown from the flagstaff at Newcastle, and then planned the protection of the harbour and the deepening of its entrance.

When Macquarie visited Newcastle in 1818 he was impressed by Wallis's building activity. On 5 May he laid the foundation stone and first stone of the causeway or pier to be constructed across from the mainland to the island, though it was not completed until 1846. On 31 July he named Wallis Plains, the area now comprising Maitland, and it seems likely that the northern lake in the Myall Lakes was also named after Wallis. In December Wallis was relieved by Captain J. T. Morisset [q.v.] of the 48th Regiment. He reached Sydney on 9 January 1819 and on 3 March sailed in the transport *Tottenham* to join his regiment in India. He proceeded to England and in 1820 at Cork married Anne Mann. On 1 March 1821 he was promoted major and served in India until he retired from the army in 1826. In December 1836 at Clifton, Gloucestershire, England, he married Mary Ann Breach, of Hendon, Middlesex. There seem to have been no children. He lived for a time after his retirement at Douglas, Isle of Man, and thereafter at Prestbury, Gloucestershire, where he died on 12 July 1858.

In his career and in the opinion of his superiors, Wallis appears as a brave, efficient, religious and humane officer whose influence was of profound importance on the developing settlement at Newcastle. Macquarie's high opinion of his 'zeal, ability and judgment' is reflected in the general orders of 24 December 1818, and also in a letter of 15 February 1819 to Bathurst in which Wallis was recommended for 'favour and protection as an officer of high merit, and whose Conduct, as late Commandant of the Settlement of Newcastle . . . has deservedly met with my unqualified approbation and Commendation'. When in England he supervised the publication of *An Historical Account of The Colony of New South Wales and its Dependent Settlements; in illustration of Twelve Views, engraved By W. Preston, a Convict, from drawings taken on the Spot* (London, 1821). Ten of the engravings are in the Mitchell Library. One of the originals survives in the Dixson Library, an oil on wood of a corroboree, which has been described as 'a most exciting and remarkably mature work for an amateur painter'.

HRA (1), 9, 10; Rex and Thea Rienits, *Early artists of Australia* (Syd, 1963); B. W. Champion, 'Captain James Wallis', *JRAHS*, 19 (1933); W. Dixson, Notes on J. Wallis (ML); CO 323/130; WO 31/153, 337.

T. W. BLUNDEN

WALSH, WILLIAM HORATIO (1812-1882), Church of England clergyman, was born on 12 September 1812 in London, the son of Isaac Richard and Sarah Walsh. He was accepted in May 1838 by the Society for the Propagation of the Gospel on the recommendation of the archdeacon of St Alban's, ordained deacon by Bishop Blomfield of London, and appointed a colonial chaplain to Van Diemen's Land. He married Anne Ireland in London and sailed in the *Fairlie*. There was some misunderstanding about his official destination and on his arrival at Sydney on 5 December he was retained as minister to the penal establishments, and in April 1839 licensed to the new parish of St Laurence. He was priested by Bishop Broughton [q.v.] at St James's Church on 22 September.

Services had been held in St Laurence's parish since 1838, in the store-room of a brewery in Elizabeth Street. Walsh immediately began to organize his large and unformed parish, and had rapid and substantial success. Bishop Broughton laid the foundation stone of Christ Church on 1 January 1840 and consecrated it in September 1845. Walsh made it one of the principal churches in the diocese. The large congregation included many of Sydney's poorest inhabitants and some leading citizens. Walsh ministered to the former with the help of the latter. His parochial 'association for the Promotion of Christian Knowledge, more particularly amongst the poor' was one of the largest of its kind; the Christ Church school, founded in 1845 and greatly enlarged in 1861, gained a high standard. T. S. Mort assisted Walsh in these fields and worked under him at the Homoeopathic Dispensary and in promoting the Australian Mutual Provident Society. Walsh gained a reputation for constructive efforts on behalf of the under-privileged and was summoned to give evidence before several parliamentary inquiries into urban poverty. He was intelligent and cultivated, moved easily in what passed for polite society, and never hesitated to use the close friendships that he made among the upper classes to serve the interests of his church.

Walsh was influenced by the Tractarian movement and became its chief practical exponent in the diocese. He lacked scholarship but he sought to make Christ Church a centre of liturgical revival in its services and furnishings. These were modest by later standards but they provoked considerable criticism. When two Sydney clergymen, Sconce and Makinson [qq.v.], were converted to Roman Catholicism Walsh, who had been associated with them, became involved in a bitter pamphlet and press controversy. In all these ecclesiastical developments Walsh was a staunch ally of Bishop Broughton, who thought him 'not to be surpassed . . . in any good and effective quality, so far as his strength, which he taxes to the utmost, will carry him'. Broughton secured a Lambeth M.A. for him and in 1852 made him a canon of St Andrew's Cathedral. Walsh had intended in 1841 to take out a Cambridge divinity degree as a 'ten-year man' but did not persist with this discredited procedure. He visited England in 1850 and on his return was commissioned to act as one of the bishop's commissaries if Archdeacon Cowper [q.v.] could not serve during Broughton's absence in England. The commission remained dormant; Walsh was never anxious to assume high office in the church.

On the arrival in 1855 of Broughton's successor, Frederic Barker, Walsh's influence in diocesan affairs was reduced. He continued his parochial and educational work, he became a fellow of St Paul's College within the University of Sydney, and his social activities remained unabated. But his school of theology was at variance with the strong Evangelical convictions of Barker and he played only a minor part in the debates on the constitution of 'the church. By the early 1860s Walsh's health was failing and a long trip to Tasmania did not effect any improvement. He remained at Christ Church until March 1865, when he took leave to go to England. He had rejected an offer of the precentorship of the cathedral, although he was interested in church music; he declined the incumbency of St Mark's, Darling Point, whither some of his leading parishioners had migrated.

In 1867 he resigned his cure and soon found preferment in the diocese of Lichfield. His close friend G. A. Selwyn, bishop of New Zealand, was translated to the see and promoted Walsh's interests. He held the Staffordshire livings of Alrewas (1869-75) and Penn (1875-82), of which Selwyn was patron; he was given a prebendal stall at Lichfield and an episcopal chaplaincy. He returned to Australia in December 1880 and went to live with the family of T. S. Mort on their Bodalla estate, 'a domestic retreat of unrivalled serenity'. There a fine church was being built in Mort's memory but Walsh's duties were 'in the nature of domestic chaplain . . . rather than a licence to a separate cure of souls'. In 1882 Walsh resigned his English posts and died on 17 December at Bodalla.

R. T. Wyatt, *The history of the diocese of Goulburn* (Syd, 1937); L. M. Allen, *A history of Christ Church S. Laurence, Sydney* (Syd, 1939); MS cat under W. H. Walsh (ML).   K. J. CABLE

WARBY (WALBEY), JOHN (1774?-1851), convict and explorer, was convicted at Hertford, England, on 3 March 1791 and sentenced to transportation for seven years. He reached Sydney in February 1792 in the *Pitt*. At Parramatta on 12 September 1796 he married Sarah Bentley (1780-1869), a convict who had arrived in the *Indispensable* in April 1796; they had nine sons and five daughters.

After his sentence expired Warby acquired fifty acres at Prospect and in 1803 was appointed stockman of the wild cattle at large in the Cowpastures. It was along Warby's track leading from his home through the Cowpastures that James Meehan [q.v.] made a line of road in 1805. In 1806 Warby was a constable of Camden County, and he was one of those who signed a respectful address to Governor Bligh on 1 January 1808. He guided Governor Macquarie and his party from Prospect Hill through the Cowpastures in November 1810 and again in October 1815 on an expedition into the rough country along the Nattai River. He was one of the first to explore the Oaks, the Bargo area and the Burragorang Valley, and continued to be in demand as a guide. Thus in 1814 he was among those rewarded for visiting Aboriginal tribes in the inland area and for arresting Patrick Collins, a bushranger, and in 1816 for guiding soldiers who were pursuing Aboriginal tribes.

In June 1816 he was granted 260 acres at Campbelltown and there built a house where he died on 12 June 1851. His widow died at Campbelltown on 19 October 1869.

HRNSW 6; HRA (1), 10; MS cat under J. Warby (ML).

WARDELL, ROBERT (1793-1834), barrister and newspaper editor, was born in England. He was educated at Trinity College, Cambridge (LL.B., 1817; LL.D., 1823), and had been a barrister of the Middle Temple for two years standing when, on 28 February 1823, he applied without success for the newly-created office of attorney-general in New South Wales. Had he, not Saxe Bannister [q.v.], been appointed to the position, General Darling may have been spared much vexation and resulting proceedings that blemished his administration. In 1824 Wardell sailed with his mother for Sydney. Passengers with them in the *Alfred* included John Mackaness, the newly-appointed sheriff, W. C. Wentworth and Dr and Mrs Redfern [qq.v.]. Wardell sued the owner of the ship for subjecting him to 'a wet and comfortless cabin', and denying him 'sufficient nourishment and refreshments' on the voyage, and was awarded £200 damages and £4 16s. 2d. costs.

On 10 September 1824 Wardell and Wentworth were admitted to practise. Thereupon they at once moved the court for a rule calling upon the local attorneys to show cause why they should not be required, as Wardell said, 'to confine themselves to their own profession'. Having heard argument for and against this proposition, Chief Justice Forbes declined, at this stage in the legal life of the colony, to sanction it. Wardell did not allow the matter to rest, and in September 1829 the Supreme Court made a rule dividing the profession, subject to the proviso that it should not take effect until His Majesty's pleasure anent it was made known. In consequence it did not come into force in the colony until 31 October 1834, by which time Wardell was dead. It is evident, however, that, although they practised in their respective offices as attorneys, both Wardell and Wentworth preferred to give opinions and conduct cases in court.

When he and Wentworth became acquainted in 1819, Wardell was editor of the *Statesman*, a London evening newspaper, and they brought with them materials for the purpose of starting a newspaper in Sydney. On 14 October 1824 their newspaper, meaningfully designated the *Australian*, was put into circulation. It was to be published weekly and its price was 1s. 'These gentlemen', reported Governor Brisbane, 'never solicited my permission to publish their Paper'. They were not bound in law to do so. Their brusque action was a typical Wentworthian gesture of independence.,

'A free press', proclaimed the *Australian* in its first editorial, 'is the most legitimate, and, at the same time, the most powerful weapon that can be employed to annihilate influence, frustrate the designs of tyranny, and restrain the arm of oppression'. Until he voluntarily vacated its editorial chair on 27 June 1828, Wardell was the *Australian*. Through its columns he gained the prominence which secures for him a place in the history of his decade. Read today, his articles repel by their prolixity, undertone of sarcasm, and frequent notes of arrogance and condescension. His favourite medium was satire: sometimes light, often heavy, generally wounding. Yet he could go directly and unerringly to the pith of a matter, and state and elucidate a proposition with concision and precision.

He applauded when the chief justice so construed section 19 of 4 Geo. IV, c. 96

as to make imperative the empanelling of an ordinary jury for the trial of free persons arraigned in Courts of Quarter Sessions. On this decision, handed down on the day that the *Australian* first appeared, the editor wrote, 'We cannot but consider it as a most auspicious coincidence'. The next question related to the composition of such juries. Wardell and Wentworth were of opinion that emancipists, otherwise qualified, should be eligible for the jury box, and they then strove without success to achieve that end.

They were also to the fore as the legal advisers of Captain Mitchell of H.M.S. *Slaney* when, to the consternation of Governor Brisbane, he seized the *Almorah* for allegedly breaching the monopoly of the East India Co. So, too, in September 1825, recrimination reached boiling point when Dr Douglass, William Lawson [qq.v.] and Dr McLeod were presented for indictment at the Court of Quarter Sessions at Parramatta by a Grand Jury, whose foreman was Hannibal Macarthur [q.v.]; the two friends were briefed: Wentworth on behalf of the men presented, Wardell on behalf of Macarthur. The pressure was speedily reduced by a judicious Act of Indemnity, but the editor of the *Australian* snarled very audibly when thus denied his bone.

During the first year of the Darling régime Wardell, cultivated by Henry Dumaresq [q.v.], the governor's brother-in-law, adopted a benevolent attitude towards the administration. Yet, basically, his views on public issues of current moment, such as the institution forthwith of an elected assembly and the abolition of military juries, were irreconcilable with those of Darling. When in 1827 the death of Private Sudds was exploited by Wentworth for political purposes, the *Australian* joined in the hue and cry. Darling's resulting attempts to implement his instructions to control the press evoked articles in the *Australian*, and a letter thereto, transparently written by Wardell but signed Vox Populi, which led to his prosecution by the governor for criminal libel.

'Wardell', wrote Forbes, 'is a very good lawyer, whatever may be his other sins'. Because he was 'a very good lawyer', the barrister was apt to reach the same conclusion as to the illegality of some of the measures of the government as did the chief justice. In this identity of expert professional opinion, Darling unwarrantably detected collusion. Obsessed by what became a fixation, he lent a ready ear to those in his entourage who whispered with intent that the chief justice gave Wardell undue latitude in court and summed up with a bias in his direction.

The upshot of His Excellency's prosecutions of Wardell strengthened his fixation; at the end of each of the two major trials, the jury could not agree on a verdict and, by the consent of the parties, was discharged. The passages cited in the respective informations were undoubtedly libellous, but the Crown law officers, even when assisted by the competent attorney, James Norton [q.v.], were no match for Wardell and Wentworth; and the governor's own maladroitness, as pressed upon the attention of the jury by the defence, helped to tip the scales of some of them in favour of the accused.

In those days another weapon was available to a gentleman who felt that his honour had been aspersed: duelling had not yet been proscribed. Twice Wardell was called out, once by Saxe Bannister, and once by his erstwhile friend, Colonel Dumaresq. On neither occasion was either party injured, but the rencontre with Dumaresq was in itself sufficient to put Wardell beyond the pale of Government House. Yet two years later when the newspaper campaign against the governor again flared up, Darling, bitterly conscious of the professional deficiencies of Attorney-General Baxter [q.v.], approved the engagement of Wardell on behalf of the government. Such are the compulsions of necessity. Wardell accepted the briefs, justified his engagement, and was paid fees which startled the secretary of state by their amount.

By 1834 Wardell was a man of substance. Apart from his lucrative practice, he had speculated to advantage. His holdings included an estate at Petersham of some 2500 acres which was more highly valued, inter alia, for its stands of timber. From 25 cultivated acres of it he garnered 500 bushels of good quality wheat in 1830. Early in the afternoon of Sunday, 7 September 1834, astride his hack, he left his cottage at Petersham to inspect his estate. Near the Cook's River boundary he spotted an unauthorized little humpy, from which on his approach emerged three strangers who, he suspected, correctly as it transpired, were convicts unlawfully at large. After a few inflamed exchanges, John Jenkins, the leader of them, shot him. His body was found next day. The three men were arrested about a week later. The youngest of them turned approver and the other two were executed. An expertly finished marble tablet, on which is moulded, in alto relievo, a side view of the head of Wardell, may be seen on the southern wall of St James's Church, Sydney. It is said to be a good likeness.

Wardell was a bachelor, but he was one of a family of six; through two nephews and a niece, strong ties were established between his kinsfolk and those of two of his close professional friends and a client. One nephew, Thomas John Fisher, married the eldest daughter of W. C. Wentworth; the other, Rev. Charles Frederick Durham Priddle, married a daughter of James Norton. His niece, Margaret Anne Priddle, married George Fairfowl Macarthur who reopened The King's School in 1868. He was a son of Hannibal Macarthur. Wardell's mother, to whom by a will made in 1824 he had left everything of which he died possessed, had died in 1830. Administration with the will annexed was granted to W. C. Wentworth on 16 October 1834.

HRA (1), 11-17; Newspaper indexes under Wardell (ML); W. C. Wentworth, Legal letter-book (ML); Family Bible (1660) annotated by T. D. Mutch (ML); Supreme Court records (NSWA); CO 201/147/540.   C. H. CURREY

WATERFIELD, WILLIAM (1795-1868), Congregational minister, was born on 24 March 1795 at Derby, England. After a youth 'devoted to unprofitable amusements', he became a church member, Sunday school teacher and lay preacher. He was accepted for the ministry and trained at Rotherham College, Yorkshire. In May 1828 he was ordained as a pastor of the Independent Church at Wrexham, north Wales. He remained there for ten years and then offered his services to the Colonial Missionary Society, to which Henry Hopkins [q.v.] of Hobart Town had appealed for a minister for the Port Phillip District. Waterfield was appointed; in December 1837 he sailed from England in the Aberdeenshire, and reached Hobart in the following April and Melbourne in the Adelaide a month later.

Waterfield was cordially welcomed by the small group of Congregationalists in Melbourne as their first minister. On 17 May 1838 he preached to some fifty persons in the little wooden Church of England building in William Street. Later he held services in the home of John Gardiner [q.v.], in a large room fitted as a chapel in J. P. Fawkner's [q.v.] hotel in Market Street, and in a temporary place of worship in Bourke Street. Soon after Waterfield's arrival the Independents applied to the government for a site for a church and school. They were given an acre and three-quarters of section 10 of the Melbourne survey, on the north-eastern corner of Russell and Collins Streets. In December 1839 Henry Hopkins set the foundation stone of a brick church, Melbourne's first permanent place of worship. Waterfield lived in a cottage in the grounds, and until the end of 1839 his stipend was paid privately by Hopkins. The church was opened on 1 January 1841.

The financial crisis of the 1840s seriously obstructed Waterfield's ministry and he met unexpected discouragement from some of his church members. He resigned in March 1843 and in July went with his wife to Van Diemen's Land, where for five years he served as a missionary on the Forth, Don and Leven Rivers. The work proved too heavy for him and in 1848 he accepted the charge of the Congregational Church at Green Ponds. In 1860 he suffered a severe illness which left him with impaired health. He finally retired from active work in 1866 and died of apoplexy on 17 May 1868. He was buried in the Green Ponds cemetery. He was survived by his daughters; his wife Elizabeth, daughter of Liddell Purvis of Berwick upon Tweed, whom he had married in June 1842, had died at Green Ponds in April 1865, aged 48.

Waterfield was a genial and warm-hearted man whose upright life and devotion to his pastoral duties earned him the regard of the members of his own and other denominations. As the first Independent minister in Melbourne he served his church and the community well. He gathered a strong congregation and took a prominent part in religious affairs. He was liberal in his outlook and sought and gained, to an unusual degree, the co-operation of his fellow clergy of the other churches.

J. Burchett, 'History of Victorian Congregationalism', *Jubilee volume of Victorian Congregationalism* (Melb, 1888); *Victorian Congregational year book*, 1870; 'Extracts from the diary of the Rev. W. Waterfield', VHM, 3 (1913-14); *Hobart Town Courier*, 1 Feb 1845; W. Waterfield, Diary 1838-43 (ML).   C. A. McCALLUM

WATERHOUSE, HENRY (1770-1812), naval officer, was the eldest son of William Waterhouse and his wife Susanna, née Brewer. William was a page to the duke of Cumberland who was Henry's godfather. He entered the navy at an early age and saw service in the *Portland, Mediator, Ganges* and *Merlin*. In 1786 he joined the *Sirius* as a midshipman, having been recommended to Governor Phillip by Cumberland House. He was present at the first settlement of New South Wales in 1788 and the settlement of Norfolk Island, and accompanied Phillip on many excursions into the new country, including the landing at Manly where Phillip was speared. In December 1789 Phillip made him acting third lieutenant of the *Sirius* when Lieutenant Maxwell was discharged; the appointment was confirmed in July 1792. His return to England was delayed by the loss of the *Sirius* at Norfolk Island in 1790 and his transfer to the *Supply* in February 1791; he eventually sailed in 1791 with a letter of recommendation from Phillip to Sir Charles Middleton at the Admiralty. In May 1792 Waterhouse was appointed lieutenant in the *Swallow*, was transferred to the *Bellerophon* in March 1793, and was present at Howe's victory on the Glorious First of June 1794.

Meanwhile Captain John Hunter had been appointed governor of New South Wales and had sought the appointment of Waterhouse as second commander of the *Reliance* with the rank of commander and power to act in Hunter's absence. Waterhouse was duly appointed, took charge of the *Reliance* in July 1794, and arrived in Sydney in September 1795. Next year he took her to the Cape of Good Hope to buy stock for the colony. The widow of Colonel Gordon, who had imported Spanish sheep to the Cape, offered her husband's flock for sale; Waterhouse and Lieutenant Kent [q.v.] bought twenty-six after Commissary John Palmer [q.v.] had refused them. The return voyage was very stormy and slow, but more than half of Waterhouse's stock survived to reach Sydney in June 1797. These were the first merino sheep imported into the colony, and Waterhouse supplied lambs to many of the settlers including John Macarthur and Samuel Marsden [qq.v.]; most of the flock was sold to William Cox [q.v.] when Waterhouse left the colony. He was not happy in New South Wales and wrote to Phillip and Lord Sydney seeking their influence to have him sent home. He quarrelled with Hunter at one stage but was later reconciled and supported the governor against the officers of the New South Wales Corps. He was granted 25 acres at Liberty Plains and 4½ acres at Parramatta in 1797, and bought another farm; that year and in 1799 he acquired two leases at Port Jackson, one of which, on Garden Island, he sold to Robert Campbell [q.v.] on his departure. He made several voyages to Norfolk Island but complained bitterly that the *Reliance* was unseaworthy. In March 1800 he achieved his desire to go home when Hunter sent him back to England.

On his arrival in London Waterhouse was promoted first captain of the *Reliance;* he sought leave on account of ill health, but appears to have recovered, for in

October 1800 he began dismantling the *Reliance*, and was appointed captain of the *Raison* the same month. He was one of the witnesses at the marriage of George Bass [q.v.] to his sister, and after 1810 regularly visited Matthew Flinders [q.v.]. Most of his later life was spent at The Hermitage, near Rochester, and his opinions on sheep breeding in New South Wales were sought by John Macarthur and Sir Joseph Banks [q.v.]. He did not marry but had an illegitimate daughter, Maria, by Elizabeth Barnes (Baines), born in Sydney in 1791 and taken to England by the Patersons in 1796. In his last years Waterhouse tried to trace his brother-in-law, Bass, who had disappeared on a voyage to South America. Waterhouse died on 27 July 1812 and was buried at St John's, Westminster.

HRNSW, 2, 3, 4, 6; HRA (1), 1, 2; J. S. Cumpston, *Shipping arrivals and departures Sydney, 1788-1825* (Canberra, 1963); MS cat under Waterhouse (ML); Bass papers and Waterhouse papers (microfilm ML).

VIVIENNE PARSONS

WATLING, THOMAS (b. 1762), convict and artist, was born on 19 September 1762 in Dumfries, Scotland, the son of Ham Watlin, soldier. His parents died during his infancy and he was brought up by a maiden aunt, Marion Kirkpatrick. His education, which was well above average, obviously included a thorough grounding in art and eventually he formed his own 'academy'. In 1788 he was briefly in Glasgow as a coach and chaise painter. Back in Dumfries on 27 November he was charged with having forged guinea notes on the Bank of Scotland. He denied his guilt, but rather than risk conviction and execution he asked to be transported and was sentenced to fourteen years. On his way to join a prison hulk at Plymouth he helped to avert a shipboard mutiny by fellow convicts, but this won him no remission of sentence.

In July 1791 Watling was one of 410 convicts who sailed in the *Pitt* for New South Wales. He escaped at Cape Town, but was soon arrested by the Dutch, imprisoned and taken aboard the *Royal Admiral*, in which he reached Sydney on 7 October 1792. He appears to have been assigned almost immediately to the surgeon-general, John White [q.v.], an ardent naturalist, who made extensive use of his artistic skill.

During his first months in the colony Watling continued a series of letters which he had begun at Cape Town; as *Letters from an exile at Botany-Bay to his Aunt in Dumfries. . .* they were published in Penrith, Scotland, probably in 1794. They frankly and courageously criticized various aspects of life in the colony, particularly the treatment of convicts, and included interesting observations from an artist's viewpoint. When White left the colony in December 1794 it is thought that Watling may have been assigned to the judge-advocate, David Collins. There is positive evidence that at least some of the plates in Collins's *An Account of the English Colony in New South Wales* (London, (1798-1802) were taken from original sketches by Watling.

Watling's prospects improved with the arrival of Governor Hunter, himself an enthusiastic and able artist. Within a year, in September 1796 Watling was given a conditional pardon and on 5 April 1797 it was made absolute. While in the colony Watling had a son, presumably by a convict woman, and when he left Sydney he took the child with him. From 1801 to 1803 he lived in Calcutta, earning a precarious living as a miniature painter. He returned to Scotland and on 10 January 1806 was tried at Edinburgh for a series of forgeries allegedly committed at Dumfries between November 1804 and March 1805. He was discharged on a verdict of 'not proven'. Later he moved with his son to London where, in indigent circumstances and suffering from cancer of the left breast, he applied to Hunter, now an admiral, for help and received some assistance from members of the Royal Academy. Neither the date nor place of his death are known.

Watling wrote and regarded himself as a romantic, but most of his landscapes reveal training in the classical style. The Mitchell and Dixson Libraries, Sydney, have a few examples of his work, but most of that known to have survived is in the so-called Watling Collection in the zoological library of the British Museum (Natural History). This collection, apparently made about Port Jackson between 1788 and 1794, comprises 512 drawings by various artists, of which 123 are signed by Watling and at least another 20 are clearly his work. His contributions include landscapes, studies of Aboriginals and a great number of natural history drawings. Many of these are extensively annotated in John White's hand and there seems little doubt that it was he who gathered the collection and took it to England. Watling's only major work known to have survived is 'Sydney in 1794', a large oil painting, which hangs in the Dixson Gallery, Sydney, and is a composite of several of his sketches. Although impressive it is clumsily painted and lacks the delicacy and deft technique of his landscapes in wash and his bird drawings in water-colour.

H. S. Gladstone, *Thomas Watling, limner of Dumfries* (Dumfries, 1938); Bernard Smith, *Place, taste and tradition* (Syd, 1945); Bernard Smith, *European vision and the south Pacific 1768-1850* (Oxford, 1960); Rex and Thea Rienits, *Early artists of Australia* (Syd, 1963); W. Dixson, 'Notes on Australian artists', *JRAHS*, 5 (1919); G. N. Matthews and T. Iredale, 'Thomas Watling', *Aust Avian Record*, 5 (1922).   REX RIENITS

WATSON, ROBERT (1756-1819), harbourmaster, arrived with the First Fleet as quartermaster of H.M.S. *Sirius*, and was still serving in that capacity when the ship was wrecked at Norfolk Island in 1790. Next year he obtained and cultivated a grant of sixty acres on the island. This farm he sold in 1793 when he became mate of the schooner *Francis*, retaining that post until 1805 when the ship was wrecked off Newcastle. Meanwhile in 1801 Governor King had granted him land at South Head, Sydney, and there he settled, later becoming boatswain of the dockyard. In April 1811 soon after the South Head Road was completed Governor Macquarie visited Watson's Bay, as the site of the grant had come to be called. He followed up the visit by appointing Watson senior pilot and, two years later, harbourmaster. Watson's new stone house with outbuildings and a strong wall was finished about the time of Macquarie's visit and the governor later granted him a free licence to sell spirits there. For his services in piloting the *Kangaroo* in January-March 1814 during the evacuation of Norfolk Island, he was given a gratuity of £20 by order of the governor. Soon afterwards he resigned the post of pilot, but retained the appointments of harbourmaster and boatswain of the dockyard until he was dismissed in November 1816 on a charge of stealing canvas. The offence was not viewed severely for long, for when the South Head lighthouse was finished Watson was installed as its first superintendent in November 1818, on the same salary that he had received as harbourmaster (£50). At the end of October 1819 he requested temporary leave on account of illness, and died at his house on The Rocks, Sydney, on 1 November. He was buried in the Sandhills cemetery, from where his remains were removed in 1901 to La Perouse.

There appears to be no record of the identity of Watson's wife, but two sons and a daughter were with him in Sydney. In 1929 a stone seat bearing the following inaccurate inscription was erected in Robertson Park, Watson's Bay: 'To commemorate Robert Watson after whom this Bay is named Quartermaster of H.M.S. Sirius 1786-1790 Signal-Man South Head 1791-1811 Pilot and Harbour Master 1811-1816 Superintendent of Macquarie Lighthouse 1818 Died 1st November 1819'.

F. J. Bayldon, 'History of the pilotage service of Port Jackson', *JRAHS*, 20 (1934); *Sydney Gazette*, 5 Oct, 2 Nov 1816, 6 Nov 1819; J. Watson to G. Frankland, Feb 1830 (ML); L. Macquarie to D. Wentworth, 4 Nov 1811, 18 Apr 1814 (RAHS Lib, Syd).

E. J. LEA-SCARLETT

WEDGE, JOHN HELDER (1793-1872), surveyor and explorer, was the second son of Charles Wedge of Shudy Camps, Cambridge, England, from whom he learned the rudiments of his profession. Losses during the post-war depression in agriculture induced Wedge and his brother Edward to migrate to Van Diemen's Land, where they arrived in 1824 in the *Heroine*. Before leaving London he had obtained an appointment in the colony as assistant surveyor.

Wedge led many arduous expeditions through heavily timbered mountainous country in the north-east and central highlands. On one journey he found a camp of the bushrangers led by Brady [q.v.] whom he pursued so tenaciously that they wrecked his tent. For his efforts in their capture he was rewarded with a land grant in 1826 and later applied for another grant for the capture of five absconders. He was sent to the far north-west in 1828 to examine the lands of the Van Diemen's Land Co. Wedge reported much rich soil in the heavily timbered area but the company wanted pasture land immediately available and disputed the accuracy of his map. His work included the investigation of grants surveyed earlier by Evans and Scott [qq.v.] who were accused of receiving bribes for measuring more than the authorized acreage to settlers. Wedge proved the accusations well founded.

In February 1835 a large expedition was organized by the surveyor-general, Frankland [q.v.], to explore the country lying between the Derwent, Gordon and Huon Rivers. As leader of one of the parties Wedge proved a resourceful, intelligent bushman, and covered much difficult ground. He won Frankland's praise for his energy in the Survey Department whose staff was overworked, but he was eager for promotion and came to believe that his hopes were being frustrated by nepotism at the Colonial Office. In his survey work Wedge had often visited John Batman [q.v.] at Kingston, and together they planned an expedition across Bass Strait. When Batman returned from his first visit in 1835 Wedge resigned from the Survey Department and crossed to Port Phillip where he explored along the Barwon River and surveyed the 600,000 acres 'acquired' by Batman's Port Phillip Association from the Aboriginals. He opposed the forceful removal of Fawkner's [q.v.] party by its rivals, and played an important part in the founding of Melbourne. He was one of the first to bring over sheep from Tasmania, to his station at Werribee. He also reported to Lieut-Governor Arthur on the wild white man, William Buckley [q.v.], whose pardon he recommended, and on outrages against the Aboriginals, for whose hopeless condition he had much compassion. Earlier he had adopted an Aboriginal boy, May Day, rescued from the surf near Circular Head. His 'Narrative of an excursion amongst the natives of Port Phillip' and 'Description of the country around Port Phillip' were among the expedition papers published by the Van Diemen's Land government in 1835. Next year the *Journal* of the Royal Geographical Society printed his paper 'On the country around Port Phillip, South Australia'. The diaries of his explorations and survey work were sent home to his father; these were published by the Royal Society of Tasmania in 1962.

Wedge visited England in 1838-43. On the death of his father he returned to Tasmania to find his circumstances much reduced by economic depression. In 1843 he married Maria Medland Wills, who had been governess to Bishop Nixon's [q.v.] children, but within a year she died in childbirth. He was then appointed by Nixon to manage (1846-51) the farms which formed the endowment of Christ's College at Bishopsbourne. Elected to the Legislative Council for the district of Morven in 1855, he held office in the short-lived ministry of T. Gregson [q.v.] in 1857 and initiated the inquiry into the convict department under its comptroller, Stephen Hampton [q.v]. An active Anglican, one of his last acts before withdrawing from parliament in 1868 was to support the commutation bill that granted £100,000 to religious denominations in place of annual state aid. He died on 22 November 1872 at Medlands, a home he had built on the River Forth in 1865.

J. Bonwick, *Discovery and settlement of Port Phillip* (Melb, 1856); J. Bonwick, *Port Phillip settlement* (Lond, 1883); W. A. Townsley, *The struggle for self-government in Tasmania 1842-1856* (Hob, 1951); Correspondence file under Wedge (TA).

G. H. STANCOMBE

WELLS, THOMAS (1782-1833), clerk and writer, was convicted, probably of embezzlement, at the London Gaol Delivery on 3 April 1816 and sentenced to transportation for fourteen years. He arrived in Sydney in the *Sir William Bensley* and went on to Hobart Town next year in the *Cochin*, the ship which brought the new lieut-governor, Sorell. He served as Sorell's clerk throughout his governorship, a situation in which he enjoyed such confidence as to have custody of the convict indents and to make out occupation licences, but it was alleged that Wells was improperly favoured in the government meat contracts. He acquired sixty-five acres at New Town immediately on his arrival, and steadily added to it. He received a conditional pardon in 1818 and by 1819 had taken up land beyond New Norfolk and had begun breeding with merinos. At his main property, Allanvale, Macquarie Plains, his wool speculations failed and early in 1824 he was bankrupt. His efforts to recover failed, and in 1828 he was declared insolvent and committed to the debtors' prison. During his five years there he not only assailed the lieut-governor with petitions for relief, but set up as an accountant to such effect that he was said to have achieved considerable comfort for himself and his family, and to have paid off most of his creditors. On his release he briefly continued his business in Hobart until he joined the Cornwall Bank in Launceston as accountant. He died on 10 June 1833, probably from tetanus.

Wells's wife, Charlotte, and family had joined him from England in February 1818 and at the time of his death there were eleven children. The eldest, Samuel Pullen, went to Sydney to be educated under 'his relative', Samuel Marsden [q.v.], but in 1834 was convicted of cattle stealing and transported for life to Port Arthur. Charlotte and a daughter were running a school at New Norfolk in 1842.

Thomas Wells's obituary in the *Colonist*, 18 June 1833, said that though industrious, he was 'luxurious and extravagant; very reserved, and in some measure haughty'. It also referred to his 'many able and beneficial articles' in the colonial press, and said he claimed to be the author of the 'Hermit of Van Diemen's Land' articles, in fact written by Henry Savery [q.v.]. Wells is remembered, however, as the author of the first Tasmanian literary pamphlet, *Michael Howe, the last and worst of the Bush Rangers of Van Diemen's Land*, printed by Andrew Bent [q.v.] in December 1818. This forty page rarity was reprinted in 1819, 1824, 1926, 1945 and in facsimile in 1926 for its curiosity value, but its literary merit is small.

HRA (3), 2-4; Correspondence file under T. Wells (TA).　　　P. R. ELDERSHAW

WELSH, JOHN (d. 1832), master mariner, was baptized John Williams and by royal warrant in 1812 changed his surname 'in grateful regard of James Welsh, late Captain in the Merchant Service'. As an able seaman he visited many countries including Australia, where he took part in coastal surveys and was with Matthew Flinders [q.v.] in August 1803 when the *Porpoise* was wrecked off the Queensland coast. Later as a trading captain he travelled widely, particularly in the East Indies, where he speculated without success in a coffee plantation. In July 1818 he visited Sydney as master of the *Claudine* with a general cargo from England. In 1820 he repeated this voyage and while at Sydney bought from Samuel Marsden [q.v.] a 100-acre farm at Pennant Hills; when a road was cut through this farm he petitioned for a land grant in compensation for damage to his crops and costly double fencing. He was promised 1000 acres but did not locate them.

In April 1822 Welsh arrived at Hobart Town as captain of the *Thalia*. Recommended by the Colonial Office and claiming a capital of £3500 'exclusive of his ship valued at £3000', he was promised a substantial land grant. He located it at Lovely Banks, near Launceston, and later bought more land on Pittwater, near Richmond. He also went into partnership with Henry Heylin, who in May married Welsh's niece Mary Roberts; to his much beloved Mary he gave £3000 as a dower, and 1000 acres to Heylin. Next year Welsh went to Sydney in the *Urania* and returned with horses, and rams from the Macarthurs' [q.v.] flock. When this livestock did not sell profitably Lieut-Governor Arthur had sympathy for the disheartened veteran and in January 1824 appointed him inspector of distilleries. Soon afterwards Heylin left the colony and his 1000 acres had to be surrendered.

In January 1826 Welsh was appointed superintendent of government vessels. With great energy he pursued bushrangers and runaway convicts as far afield as Kangaroo Island, conducted

many boards of inquiry, made surveys of D'Entrecasteaux Channel and harbours on Tasman Peninsula, planned a wharf at Sullivan Cove and examined bridge sites on the Derwent and at Launceston. These strenuous tasks affected his health and in June 1828 he was given leave 'to exercise in the country'. In November he asked for more leave to attend to family affairs at Launceston. In January 1829 Arthur, thinking Welsh quite worn out but a very worthy person, appointed him port officer in Launceston at a salary of £200. He often gave useful help to G. A. Robinson [q.v.] in conciliating the Aboriginals, but had little time to buoy the shifting channel of the Tamar River and several ships went ashore. He had an accident himself in October when his cutter was overturned while towing a brig to its moorings; much government gear was lost and Welsh's own instruments. As usual he claimed and was granted compensation. A year later his wife died, aged 83, and he began to complain that Launceston was a 'horrid swampy place worse than Surinam, Demarara or the city of Batavia'. He asked for transfer to another post, but was given instead a short leave. On his return in ill health to Launceston his sickness was diagnosed as jaundice, and he died on 6 June 1832.

A. McKay (ed), *Journals of the land commissioners for Van Diemen's Land, 1826-28* (Hob, 1962); *Sydney Gazette*, 1 July 1826; *Hobart Town Courier*, 31 Jan, 31 Aug 1829; Col Sec in letters, 4/1744, 4/1832 (NSWA); Piper papers (ML); CSO 1/296/7190, 1/364/8325, 1/427/9610, 1/576/13060 (TA).

WEMYSS, WILLIAM (d. 1862), deputy-commissary-general, was appointed an assistant commissary-general on 7 November 1809. He served with distinction in the Peninsular war. On 25 December 1814 he was appointed deputy-commissary-general and on 31 August 1820, while on half-pay, received instructions to go to New South Wales to replace Frederick Drennan [q.v.] in charge of the commissariat there.

When Wemyss and his wife arrived at the Derwent in the *Medway* on 14 March 1821 he complained about the rations which the master had issued to the convicts on board, a charge which Lieut-Governor Sorell felt was justified. Wemyss then sailed for Sydney and assumed control of the Commissariat Department on 24 May. Between 1822 and 1825 the dollar standard was introduced into the colony, and the immediate institution of a sterling exchange standard and a fixed rate of exchange appears to have been largely the work of Wemyss and the colonial secretary, Frederick Goulburn [q.v.]. The commissariat believed that the Bank of New South Wales was rashly increasing discounts and issuing an excessive number of notes, thus causing a bounty on imports; Wemyss hoped that the new dollar system would remove this bounty and make the bank much more cautious in its actions. The commissariat also announced that it would take dollars only at their bullion value in sterling, which was 4s. 2d.; since the conventional colonial valuation was 5s., by this ruling Wemyss depreciated the currency and reduced government expenditure, but those who sold to the commissariat store received less for their produce and the Bank of New South Wales lost 10d. on each dollar it had in reserve. In November 1822 the commissariat announced that no bills or store receipts in sterling would be recognized and the stabilized exchange rate was abandoned in favour of a rate determined by competitive tender. The change to dollars was also hastened on 5 February 1823 when it was ordered that all public accounts should be expressed in the new currency. The Bank of New South Wales and many merchants and settlers attacked this policy, and John Macarthur [q.v.] accused Wemyss of profiting by improper private contracts; he certainly acquired property quickly, but there is little evidence to evaluate Macarthur's charges and Governor Brisbane praised Wemyss for his 'zealous co-operation' during the change to dollar payments and for his aid in necessary retrenchments.

Wemyss had been appointed a magistrate in December 1821 and a member of the Governor's Court next year. He joined his fellow magistrates in the protest which followed the judgment against W. Howe [q.v.] for issuing a warrant of distress to enforce payment for certain labour, under the Government Order of 21 November 1821, on the ground that such a decision opened the way to fraud and imposition. He was faced with the perennial commissariat problem of attempted bribery, when assistant commissary-general Moodie in Van Diemen's Land accused Edward Lord [q.v.] of attempting by this means to prevent the importation of 6000 bushels of wheat from the Cape of Good Hope. In 1822 he served as a member of the court of inquiry investigating charges of peculation against the colonial engineer, Major Druitt [q.v.].

In 1825 Wemyss and Brisbane clashed bitterly over the case of the *Almorah*, a ship chartered by the government to bring wheat from Batavia, which on its return was seized by Captain Mitchell of H.M.S. *Slaney* for violating the East India Co.'s monopoly by importing tea and dollars for the commissariat on Wemyss's order and without the governor's knowledge. The attorney-general issued a writ against Mitchell for seizing crown property; Mitchell replied with a writ against Wemyss and his deputy for engaging in trade which contravened the East India Co.'s charter. Even Macarthur, who claimed he would rejoice at Wemyss's humiliation, attacked Mitchell for seeking to endanger government property and to impede a public functionary in the course of his duty, but Chief Justice Forbes [q.v.] held that Wemyss had shown a 'great contempt of the government of the colony' in ordering these imports. By this time Brisbane had concluded that Wemyss was 'full of weakness, caprice and malevolence' and, though he believed Wemyss 'an honest Man', asked for his replacement. However, the British Treasury considered that there were no grounds for colonial protest against Wemyss as it was his 'obvious duty . . . to obtain all supplies required for the *Public Service* . . . from the best Market and upon the most favourable terms' and this was all that he had done.

In May 1826 Governor Darling made Wemyss a member of the 'Board for General Purposes' which was created to assist in the administration of the various public establishments, and Wemyss and W. Lithgow [q.v.], the auditor of public accounts, inquired into the state of the colonial Treasury. Earlier Wemyss, Moodie and Lithgow had recommended the separation of the Van Diemen's Land commissariat from that of New South Wales.

Throughout the conflict over commissariat policy Wemyss played an important part in colonial society. In 1823 he was made a vice-president of the Bible Society. He was a regular subscriber to the School of Industry, the Benevolent Society and the Sydney Institution. In 1824 he was elected treasurer of the Reading Society, and in 1825 governor of the proposed public free grammar school. The *Sydney Gazette* credited him with being the moving force in the establishment of Scots Church, though this claim was bitterly opposed by J. D. Lang [q.v.]. Sir George Murray criticized Lang and agreed with Darling's estimate of Wemyss as a highly respectable man, but the government had already notified Wemyss of his impending replacement by James Laidley [q.v.]. In 1827 the deputy-commissary-general offered his furniture for sale by auction at his house on Church Hill, and after a serious illness he sailed for England in the *Caroline* on 4 November 1828. He remained on half-pay until 1862, when he died, probably at his home near Edinburgh.

William Wemyss was one of the most honest and competent commissariat officers to serve in New South Wales. During his administration the tensions caused by the transformation from a gaol to a free economy came to a head, and his activities caused conflict with governors who claimed that he was usurping jurisdiction over matters which rightfully belonged to the duties of their office; but his economic policies reflected the new commercial and financial developments in the colony and his administrative ideas also mark a significant turning point in colonial government.

HRA (1), 10-14; Newspaper indexes under W. Wemyss (ML); MS cat under W. Wemyss (ML); WO 58/116.   GEORGE PARSONS

WENTWORTH, D'ARCY (1762?-1827), medical practitioner and public servant, was born near Portadown, Ireland, the sixth of the eight children of D'Arcy Wentworth and his wife, Martha Dickson, also of County Armagh. The first of the Irish Wentworths to come to Australia could trace his ancestry through twenty generations from Robert of Wentworth Woodhouse in Yorkshire in the thirteenth century. His descendant, D'Arcy Wentworth, went to Ireland as agent in Athlone to Wentworth Dillon, fourth earl of Roscommon, during the reign of Charles II, served in 1689 in the army of William III and established himself as a landowner at Fyanstown Castle in County Meath. Some Irish Wentworths intermarried into the leading Anglo-Irish families, but Robert, the third of the Irish Wentworths of Fyanstown Castle, was an impecunious barrister with political ambitions which he failed to realize even though a distant kinsman of the marquis of Rockingham, and under him the family resources were completely dissipated. His son D'Arcy, the father of the subject of this sketch, was an innkeeper at Portadown; but however far the Irish Wentworths had financially fallen from their high estate, they still claimed relationship with Rockingham, Lord Fitzwilliam and the earl of Strafford. By 1822 William Wentworth, the elder brother of D'Arcy of Parramatta, was probably the senior representative of the male line of the family which had established itself at Wentworth Woodhouse, though he had no hereditary claim to the earldom of Strafford. The continuing friendship shown to the Irish branch of the family by the inheritors of the Yorkshire estate through the female line was entirely due to this acknowledgment of an ancient descent and the recognition of the natural claims of the heirs in name if not in possession. The financially hard-hit Wentworths naturally laid greater stress on this relationship than did the inheritors of Wentworth Woodhouse, the politically important Rockingham and Fitzwilliam, but it is clear from the correspondence of D'Arcy Wentworth and his brother William and from the Fitzwilliam papers that their distinguished relatives accepted a clear and defined responsibility to their kinsfolk, and D'Arcy Wentworth could always rely on the influence with the government and the occasional financial assistance of Fitzwilliam throughout his entire life.

Before embarking on a medical career D'Arcy Wentworth served as an ensign in the First Armagh Company of the Irish Volunteers under Lord Charlemont. The company was trained by the officers of the 36th Regiment then stationed at Armagh, and during and after the war of American independence, threats of French intervention and social and political changes imbued D'Arcy with popular and liberal views towards society and government which remained with him throughout his Australian career. The influence of the Irish volunteers upon contemporary society was very considerable: not merely did they aid the civil power in the execution of the laws but they set an example of equality when tradesmen and merchants, lawyers and physicians, esquires, baronets and noblemen all intermingled.

D'Arcy Wentworth is uniformly described as 'a handsome, tall man with blue eyes who was invariably popular with all classes and both sexes'. While in the volunteers, Wentworth, as was then customary, was also serving his apprenticeship for the medical profession with Dr Alexander Patton of Tanderagee, himself a volunteer officer; on promise of an appointment in the service of the East India Co. he went to London to obtain further evidence of medical proficiency from the hospitals there. He was introduced to the society of the ruling classes by his kinsman Fitzwilliam, and it is claimed, though no valid proofs remain, that he found himself in financial difficulties through living cheerfully beyond his means. At the Old Bailey sessions beginning on 12 December 1787 he was thrice charged with highway robbery: twice he was found not guilty and in the third acquitted for lack of evidence. He again appeared and was again found not guilty at the sessions beginning on 9 December 1789. At the conclusion of the case the prosecutor informed the judge: 'My Lord, Mr. Wentworth, the prisoner at the Bar, has taken a passage to go in a fleet to Botany Bay and has obtained an appointment in it as Assistant Surgeon and desires to be discharged immediately'.

Wentworth arrived at Port Jackson in the transport *Neptune* on 28 June 1790. On 1 August he sailed in the *Surprize* for Norfolk Island where he began his Australian career as an assistant in the hospital. He was appointed superintendent of convicts at Norfolk Island from 10 September 1791. He returned to Sydney in February 1796 and was appointed one of the assistant surgeons of the colony from 7 April. Thereafter Wentworth served in different grades and with differing responsibilities at the three medical centres at Norfolk Island, Sydney and Parramatta, until his appointment as principal surgeon of the Civil Medical Department, first made in February 1809, was approved in July 1811.

Wentworth had relinquished his convict superintendency when leaving Norfolk Island, but during his active career he held many non-medical posts. Appointed a justice of the peace in May 1810, he was selected to sit in the Governor's Court. In December he was put in charge of Governor Macquarie's newly reformed police force, which he was to control very ably for nearly a decade. In this position he became the chief police magistrate in Sydney, and his daily work on its bench was a heavy burden which he willingly and efficiently carried. In 1810 he was appointed with Simeon Lord and Andrew Thompson [qq.v.] one of the first commissioners for the turnpike road to Parramatta when Samuel Marsden [q.v.] refused to associate with these emancipist colleagues. Macquarie's high respect for Wentworth's probity was shown by his appointing him treasurer of the Police Fund, which was devoted to defraying the expenditure on those public works, gaols, police salaries, and grants which were not financed by the British government. Every three months three-quarters (seven-eighths after 1818) of the colonial revenue, received chiefly from import duties and port dues, were paid into the Police Fund, the balance going to the orphan fund. Though unpaid, Wentworth, as treasurer of the former, saw more than £10,000 a year pass through his hands.

In 1816 Wentworth was one of those instrumental in establishing the Bank of New South Wales, and his name appears second among the founders in the charter of 12 February 1817; he was one of the original directors and the second largest original shareholder. He had fewer setbacks than most of the other notable early residents of New South Wales in those days of cantankerousness and duelling, except for his quarrel with Governor Bligh. Early in 1808 Bligh court-martialled Wentworth for allegedly misusing the labour of sick convicts for his private advantage; found guilty, Wentworth was sentenced to be reprimanded, but Bligh was not satisfied and two days later suspended him from his duties until he should hear from the British government. When Bligh refused to state the reason for his action, Wentworth protested to Fitzwilliam and to the Colonial Office, and in due course Castlereagh very properly told Bligh that his attitude was 'highly irregular'. Meanwhile this treatment had made Wentworth sympathetic to the rebels who overthrew the governor in January 1808; a court martial on Bligh's hitherto secret charges, which were discovered in his papers, resulted, as might have been expected, in the surgeon's acquittal. Wentworth was on good but not close terms with Governors Hunter and King, though he ultimately fell out with the latter; he was Governor Macquarie's personal physician as well as being on very friendly terms with him and his successor, Sir Thomas Brisbane. Thirty-seven years continuous residence in the colony made him one of the most significant and influential of the early government officials and free settlers. Politically he was attached to the 'emancipist' party; socially as well as politically he was unacceptable to the party of John Macarthur [q.v.] and his 'exclusive' friends.

Wentworth was of no particular distinction as a medical officer, although the standard of medical science was not high at the beginning of the nineteenth century, but he was conspicuous for his humanity. In 1817 he submitted a valuable report, which was approved and adopted, on improvements in victualling and clothing the patients in the colonial hospitals. Wentworth was also noted for probity in his commercial transactions and for the skill with which he amassed a very considerable fortune, both in land and cash, so that when he died he was probably the wealthiest man in the colony. His salary as a medical officer reached the maximum of £365 when he was principal surgeon, and he also received £200 from the Crown when he was acting as superintendent of police; in 1806 he told Fitzwilliam that his total emoluments from all sources were in the order of £700 to £800 a year. His medical salary was paid directly to his agent in London, an old friend, Charles Cookney, who also acted as agent to Fitzwilliam and to Lord Melbourne; through him Wentworth arranged to import various necessities for his own use and for sale, and in later years Cookney offered a home from home for the successive Wentworth boys who were sent to England for their education. Through Cookney, loans, always repaid, were forthcoming from Fitzwilliam should the junior Wentworths require additional funds at the university, in preparation for the Bar, or to purchase a company in a regiment. A member of the Cookney family later worked in Australia as an architect, encouraged by the younger Wentworths.

In 1810 Wentworth, in conjunction with Alexander Riley and Garnham Blaxcell [qq.v.], contracted to build for Macquarie the so-called 'Rum Hospital', the predecessor of the Sydney Hospital. The direct cost to the government was approximately £4200, representing 80 oxen for slaughter, 20 convicts for three years worth £20 a year each, and 20 draught oxen on loan worth about £5 a year each, but Macquarie agreed to grant these three gentlemen permission to import a total of first 45,000 and then 65,000 gallons of rum, a generic term for all spirits. For four years, while the government and the army might import on their own account, other private importations were restricted. In return Wentworth and his friends contracted to build a hospital of over 3000 square feet to cater for over 200 sick. From the point of view of the governor it was a tremendous bargain; from the point of view of his critics it created an undeserved and undesirable monopoly. As Macquarie pointed out, the contractors were to pay a duty of 3s. a gallon on the spirits they imported; but although the British government did not cancel the contract it strongly criticized it as interfering with the freedom of trade which it desired in order to overcome smuggling, and on the grounds that a higher duty should be levied on imported spirits. Wentworth was far wealthier than either Riley or Blaxcell and without him the scheme would have been impossible. In the upshot the contractors were probably correct in their claim that they lost on the deal, though their enemies asserted that they made at least £10,000 each. This figure is undoubtedly a gross exaggeration.

In 1815 Wentworth had a tremendous row with Judge Bent [q.v.], who refused to pay toll at the gates between Sydney and Parramatta and was accordingly fined 40s. by Wentworth, despite Bent's claim that he was in no way amenable to any criminal jurisdiction in the territory. In 1817 he was again the centre of controversy when Lieut-Colonel Molle [q.v.] demanded his court martial as a result of disputes which arose from W. C. Wentworth [q.v.] writing a scurrilous 'pipe' about Molle's shortcomings. These 'frivolous and ridiculous' charges produced a display of acrimony all too common in New South Wales, including a vicious attack by Molle on Wentworth, but in the end the matter was disposed of by Judge-Advocate Wylde's [q.v.] opportune discovery that Wentworth, as surgeon, was not liable to court martial for the offence alleged; however, Wentworth took care to tell Fitzwilliam of the matter in case another storm would be raised in England when the affair was reported there.

On various occasions Wentworth was appointed either alone or in association with others to undertake special inquiries into such occurrences as the very great mortality of convicts in the transport *General Hewitt* in 1814 and the shooting of prisoners in the *Chapman* in 1817. He also took the lead in supporting trial by jury and in advocating the election of a colonial legislature on the ground of 'no taxation without representation'. He was a member of the deputation which eulogized Governor Brisbane on his departure.

In accordance with normal custom Wentworth's salary as a medical officer was supplemented by land grants which in time, since he was active in land clearance and development, became very extensive. Apart from the land which he might have bought or obtained in payment of debts, Wentworth seems to have obtained his first grant of about 147 acres at Parramatta from Governor Hunter in 1799; by 1821 he had been awarded a total of 17,000 acres while his two sons, William Charles and John, had 3450 more, many of the later grants being in the Illawarra area. By his will Wentworth disposed of at least 22,000 acres of land, much of it purchased. Today the Wentworths are the only family retaining in the male line land grants in Australia originally made by Governor Macquarie.

Despite his general popularity, comparative wealth and powerful connexions at home Wentworth mixed little in non-official social life. Although he held the King's commission and had held it before coming to New South Wales, the liberal views imbibed in the Ireland of his youth, which resulted in more than usual sympathy with the convict population, the background of his trials at the Old Bailey and the circumstances of his personal life in the colony all prevented him from fully sharing in the social round. Although he did not come out as a convict, there were widespread stories of the irregularity of his early days and of his failure to accompany the First Fleet as surgeon in the *Charlotte*. Obviously these could have been lived down and, so far as the later governors of his age were concerned, were lived down, but in addition he proved as popular with the female sex as he was asserted to be with general company. D'Arcy Wentworth acknowledged three sons of his name and descent, William Charles, D'Arcy who died without issue in 1861 aged 65, and John who was drowned as a midshipman in 1820. These three were educated in England and were accepted by Fitzwilliam and by the Irish Wentworths; from William Charles the present Australian Wentworth family is descended. In later years Wentworth supported at least seven other children and there is evidence in contemporary letters of a very happy family environment, even if it did not meet with legal approval. In his will he made ample provision for all his dependants. With his family at home D'Arcy Wentworth retained but a limited correspondence, though a number of his Irish friends and acquaintances, including a niece, Martha Bucknell, and her husband, came to New South Wales and sought his influence. The greater part of his correspondence to Britain was through Cookney, so he maintained his home ties and also his business relationships at the same time. In due course his Irish sisters and brother became proud of his success, admired his sons, especially D'Arcy marching through Portadown as an ensign in the 73rd Regiment, and were thrilled to read *A Statistical, Historical, and Political Description of The Colony of New South Wales . . .* (London, 1819) by William Charles Wentworth.

Wentworth was proud of his family descent and possessed for his own use a Cornelian stone set in gold with the arms of the Elmsal branch of the Wentworth family engraved upon it, as well as a large service of family silver. Annually he gave a dinner to commemorate his arrival in New South Wales, a settlement to which he became increasingly devoted. He was an enthusiastic race-goer, running his own horses and presenting an annual cup together with a liberal subscription to the organization. As early as May 1818 he sought permission to retire on half-pay because of 'my advanced period of life, my daily increasing Infirmities, and the General very precarious State of my Health', yet after his resignation was accepted in 1819 and he was replaced as principal surgeon in October, as superintendent of police in

April 1820 and as treasurer of the Police Fund in June, he was in good enough health to return to duty from 1821 to 1825 as superintendent of police when his successor, W. Minchin [q.v.], died soon after taking office. When Wentworth submitted his resignation in 1818 Macquarie testified to 'the indefatigable zeal, vigilance, activity, honor and integrity, universally manifested by him in the due execution and faithful discharge of his various important Public Duties', and when he died at Homebush on 7 July 1827, the obituary in the *Monitor* was probably truer than most when it stated : 'He was a lover of freedom; a consistent steady friend of the people; a kind and liberal master; a just and humane magistrate; a steady friend and an honest man'. The service at his funeral at Parramatta was conducted by Samuel Marsden; the train of mourners, some 150 of whom had accompanied the body from Homebush, was said to be nearly a mile long.

It is impossible for anyone studying his career to obtain other than a favourable opinion of his character and relationships, whatever the irregularities of his private life. Convicts were ambitious to be in his service and his general outlook was friendly and humane. He made a major contribution to the early development of New South Wales, the more significant because he was so little associated with the belligerence and dissension so conspicuous a part of the local scene. Having regard to the circumstances of his private life the text engraved on his tombstone shows a pleasant sense of humour : 'In my father's house are many mansions'.

HRA (1), 2-13, (4), 1; MS cat under D. Wentworth (ML); Wentworth Woodhouse muniments (Sheffield Public Lib).

J. J. AUCHMUTY

WENTWORTH, WILLIAM CHARLES (1790-1872), explorer, author, barrister, landowner, and statesman, was the son of Catherine Crowley, who was convicted at the Staffordshire Assizes in July 1788 of feloniously stealing 'wearing apparell', was sentenced to transportation for seven years, reached Sydney in the transport *Neptune* in June 1790, and in the *Surprize* arrived at Norfolk Island with the infant William on 7 August. Dr D'Arcy Wentworth [q.v.], who also sailed in the *Neptune* and *Surprize*, acknowledged William as his son. He accompanied his parents to Sydney in 1796 and then to Parramatta, where his mother died in 1800. In 1803 he was sent with his brother D'Arcy to England. Writing home from their first school at Bletchley in 1804, he told of a visit to his father's patron and kinsman: 'We waited, one day, on Lord Fitzwilliam, at his request, he seemed glad to see us, and presented each of us with a guinea . . . We are going on in our Latin studies &c., to the satisfaction of our Master, and hope that we shall continue to do so, well knowing how essentially necessary a good education is to our future welfare in life'. In the holidays they stayed with their father's agent, Charles Cookney. In 1805 Mrs Cookney wrote of William to Dr Wentworth that 'a Surgeon is a very improper profession for Him as from the Cast in the Eye it leads Him differently to the object he intends'. They went on to the Greenwich school of Dr Alexander Crombie, a liberal scholar whose published works ranged over philology, politics, economics, agriculture, science, and theology.

Failing to win a place in the military academy at Woolwich or in the East India Co., Wentworth returned to Sydney in 1810 somewhat at a loose end. He was soon riding Gig, his father's grey gelding, to victory in the Hyde Park races. In October 1811 Macquarie appointed him acting provost-marshal. He was granted 1750 acres on the Nepean, where his estate, Vermont, is still a Wentworth property.

He rapidly became a familiar figure around Sydney, with his tall frame, thick shoulders, Roman head, and auburn hair, his rugged and untidy person. He tended to speak in magniloquent abstractions, his harsh voice resounding with rhetoric and sarcasms and classical allusions; yet he showed a keen eye for detail. He seemed already something of a Gulliver in Lilliput. He knew that his father was slighted by the exclusives, that 'aristocratic body' who, he later wrote, 'would monopolize all situations of power, dignity, and emolument . . . and raise an eternal barrier of separation between their offspring and the offspring of the unfortunate convict': and the knowledge bred in him a determination to destroy their power.

Yet he was no leveller, no democrat. Men must be free, but free to rise—and his own family especially. Like his father he was a monopolist at heart. His adventurous spirit, drought, and the desire to discover new pastures led him in May 1813, in company with William Lawson, Gregory Blaxland [qq.v.], four servants, four horses, and five dogs, to take part in the first great feat of inland exploration, the crossing of the Blue Mountains. At the end of their twenty-one-day passage, as he later wrote,

The boundless champaign burst upon our sight
Till nearer seen the beauteous landscape grew,
Op'ning like Canaan on rapt Israel's view.

Uncertain that they had really crossed the mountains, he wrote in his journal: 'we have at all events proved that they are traversable, and that, too, by cattle'. The discovery gave impetus to great pastoral expansion in which Wentworth amply shared. He was rewarded with another 1000 acres. On the mountain journey, according to his father, he had developed a severe cough; to recover his health and to help his father secure valuable sandalwood from a Pacific island he joined a schooner as supercargo in 1814. He was nearly killed by natives at Raratonga while courageously attempting to save a sailor whom they clubbed to death. The captain died, and Wentworth, with knowledge gained on his earlier voyage from England and no mean mathematical skill, brought the ship safely to Sydney.

The *Sydney Gazette* was then subject to official censorship. The nearest approach to a free press in Governor Macquarie's régime were the anonymous 'pipes', of which the most celebrated was the one directed, in 1816, against Colonel Molle [q.v.], the lieut-governor, for his hypocrisy towards Macquarie. The furore resulting from it lasted for more than a year, till Dr Wentworth revealed that William, on his way to England, had written from Cape Town admitting authorship. Other 'pipes' are in his hand. Their political importance was greater than their literary merit, though it is not fanciful to see Wentworth as a key figure in early Australian literature. The alliance between literature and politics was close, each needing freedom in which to breathe. He helped to keep satire alive in the time of Macquarie and was later to lead it from darkness into light.

In 1816 Wentworth arrived in London and enlisted Fitzwilliam's aid in persuading his father that the army was no longer a feasible career for him now that the Napoleonic wars were over. In February 1817 he entered the Middle Temple to prepare himself to be 'the instrument of procuring a free constitution for my country'. He wrote to Fitzwilliam of 'the more remote objects' of his ambition: 'It is . . . by no means my intention in becoming a member of the Law to abandon the Country that gave me birth . . . In withdrawing myself . . . for a time from that country I am actuated by a desire of better qualifying myself for the performance of those duties, that my Birth has imposed—and, in selecting the profession of the Law, I calculate upon acquainting myself with all the excellence of the British Constitution, and hope at some future period, to advocate successfully the right of my country to a participation in its advantages'.

This remained the master-plan, but for a time he was characteristically restless. He unsuccessfully petitioned the Colonial Office to allow him to explore Australia from east to west. He spent more than a year in Europe, chiefly in Paris, to the benefit of his French but the annoyance of Fitzwilliam. His health improved but he was very short of funds. He saw much of the Macarthurs. In 1819 he published *A Statistical, Historical, and Political Description of the Colony of New South Wales and its dependent Settlements in Van Diemen's Land, With a Particular Enumeration of the Advantages which these Colonies offer for Emigration and their Superiority in many Respects over those possessed by the United States of America.* Young John Macarthur had suggested that he write it, and it owed much to conversations with old John [q.v.], who with little sympathy with Wentworth's constitutional ideas later denounced the book, but whose faith in Australian wool was infectious. Wentworth hoped ardently to marry Elizabeth Macarthur. He envisaged a great Wentworth-Macarthur connexion at the head of the pastoral aristocracy dominating the New South Wales of his dreams, and he seemed about to achieve 'a union' which he described to his father as 'so essential to the happiness of your son and to the accomplishment of those projects for the future respectability and grandeur of our family, with the realisation of which I have no doubt you consider me in a great measure identified'. But his hopes were dashed by a quarrel with her father over a loan of money.

A new blow fell. In 1819 H. G. Bennet declared in his *Letter to Lord Sidmouth* that D'Arcy Wentworth had been sent to Sydney as a convict. Mortified by this slander, William rushed to his father's defence, ready to spill the last drop of his heart's blood in reparation. His own investigations proved disquieting. They revealed that his father was never a convict but had indeed been tried four times in England for highway robbery, though finally acquitted. Wentworth rebuked Bennet and later Commissioner Bigge [q.v.], who repeated the slander in his report, but his pride had suffered a rude shock, though not a shattering one. The greatness of his family and the glory of his country were the two almost synonymous preoccupations of his mind: and the two now became one as Wentworth, wounded in heart and pride, resolutely identified himself with the interests of the Australian-born.

His book did much to stimulate emigration and was reissued in revised and enlarged editions in 1820 and 1824. The various strands in his education are clearly seen in it: the classical, in its rhetorical style and arguments from ancient history; the mathematical, in its calculations about wool as 'the most profitable channel of investment offered in the world'; the scientific, in descriptions of the natural scene; and the legal, in the reforms proposed for New South Wales. After the 'description', he attacks the existing autocracy and presses for a nominated legislative council and an assembly elected on a small property franchise: ex-convicts are not to be denied either membership or the vote. No taxation should be imposed without parliamentary sanction. There should be trial by jury, a proper process of appeal, and free migration. Such reforms will realize the emancipists' dream: to raise Australasia 'from the abject state of poverty, slavery, and degradation, to which she is so fast sinking, and to present her with a constitution, which may gradually conduct her to freedóm, prosperity, and happiness'; its future will then be theirs, and Wentworth's. Yet the book is no tract for democracy. Landed property is 'the only standard' he conceives 'by which the right either of electing, or being elected, can in any country be properly regulated'. The council 'bears many resemblances to the House of Lords': 'It forms that just equipoise between the democratic and supreme powers of the state, which has been found necessary not less to repress the licentiousness of the one, than to curb the tyranny of the other'.

He was called to the Bar in February 1822, and decided then to 'keep a few terms' at Cambridge. Soon after entering Peterhouse, he competed for the chancellor's gold medal for a poem on Australasia. His poem, placed second to W. M. Praed's, was speedily published, with a dedication to Macquarie. Rhetorical and realistic, it ends with a bold prophecy of the day when Britain is vanquished and her spirit rises again in the antipodes:

May all thy glories in another sphere
Relume, and shine more brightly still than here;
May this, thy last born infant, then arise,
To glad thy heart and greet thy parent eyes;
And Australasia float, with flag unfurl'd,
A new Britannia in another world.

He returned to Sydney in 1824, determined 'to hold no situation under government': 'As a mere private person I might lead the colony, but as a servant of the

Governor I could only conform to his whims, which would neither suit my tastes nor principles'. In the third edition of the *Description* he had attacked the report of Commissioner Bigge as 'nauseous trash': it was hostile to Macquarie and it played into the hands of the exclusives. He had some influence on the New South Wales Act of 1823, which instituted a nominated Legislative Council and permitted trial by jury in civil actions only when demanded by both parties. With him came Dr Robert Wardell [q.v.], a lawyer who had edited the *Statesman*. Their plan was that each in his sphere, Wardell in journalism and Wentworth at the Bar, should champion the emancipists and smaller free settlers and campaign for a free press, trial by jury, and self-government.

On 14 October 1824 the first issue of the *Australian*, the plant for which they had brought from London, boldly declared: 'Independent, yet consistent—free, yet not licentious—equally unmoved by favours and by fear—we shall pursue our labours without either a sycophantic approval of, or a systematic opposition to, acts of authority, merely because they emanate from government'. Audacity triumphed. They had not sought permission to publish the paper, but Governor Brisbane thought it 'most expedient to try the experiment of full latitude of freedom of the Press'; despite Colonial Office objections approval continued well into the reign of his successor. The exclusives bitterly prophesied 'a nation of freebooters and pirates', but they could do nothing while the *Australian* retained Government House favour.

Meanwhile Wentworth seized every opportunity to attack the exclusives, and awaited a pretext for attacking autocratic government. In October 1825 he arranged a meeting for free inhabitants to consider a farewell address to Brisbane, acknowledging his emancipist sympathies. He called the first draft a 'milk and water production', and in the revised document the 'two fundamental principles of the British constitution' were demanded: trial by jury and representative government. He spoke passionately against the exclusives, the 'yellow snakes of the Colony'.

The wind turned in November 1826 with the death of Private Sudds in circumstances partly arising from the commutation by Governor Darling of the sentence on him and Private Thompson. Wentworth seized on the alleged illegality of Darling's act and with violent invective demanded his recall. The affair rapidly developed into a bitter feud.

At a crowded meeting on Anniversary Day in 1827, which resulted in a petition calling for an elective assembly of at least a hundred members, Wentworth also called for trial by jury and taxation by consent. The newspapers inflamed public opinion against Darling, whose alleged treatment of Sudds Wentworth described as 'murder, or at least a high misdemeanour'. Convinced that Wentworth, a 'vulgar, ill-bred fellow' and a 'demagogue', was 'anxious to become the man of the people' by insulting the government, and that 'nothing short of positive coercion' would curb the licentiousness of the press, Darling submitted to the Legislative Council two bills, to regulate newspapers and to impose a stamp duty. Chief Justice Forbes [q.v.] refused to certify the licence clauses of one as 'not repugnant to the laws of England'. Wentworth attacked the other because blanks had been left for rates of duty to be inserted later; when they were filled in Forbes would not certify it and the Act though passed by council was suspended and later disallowed. Darling saw no alternative but to prosecute for seditious libel.

The resulting cases occupied the Supreme Court through 1828 and 1829. Wentworth surrendered his shares in the *Australian* and acted as defending counsel. He overwhelmed the lamentably weak Crown prosecutors with torrents of invective and brilliant marshalling of his facts. Darling wrote that he and Wardell kept 'the Court and the Bar by their effrontery and talent equally in subjection'. When Wardell was tried, he challenged the jury as nominees of the governor, who could deprive them of their commissions if they failed to convict. Finally in 1829, as a result of Wentworth's insistent demands, the old system of military juries was abolished. A Privy Council Order of 1830 extended trial by jury to the criminal courts of New South Wales.

A draft of 'impeachment' prepared by Wentworth against Darling did little damage to the governor's reputation at the Colonial Office, but it certainly undermined Wentworth's, so intemperate was its language. Darling served his six-year term, and departed in 1831 to the accompaniment of a riotous celebration at Wentworth's estate overlooking the harbour. The *Australian* reported: 'upward of 4,000 persons assembled at Vaucluse to partake of Mr Wentworth's hospitality and to evince joy at the approaching departure. The scene of the fête was on the lawn in front of Mr Wentworth's villa, which was thrown open for the reception of all respectable visitants, while a marquee filled with piles of loaves and casks of Cooper's gin and Wright's strong beer, was pitched a short way off.

On an immense spit a bullock was roasted entire. Twelve sheep were also roasted in succession; and 4,000 loaves completed the enormous banquet. By 7 p.m. two immense bonfires were lighted on the highest hill . . . Rustic sports, speeches, etc., etc., whiled away the night; and morning dawned before the hospitable mansion was quitted by all its guests'.

By taking up the fight against autocracy and by his imperious courage and oratory in the defence of emancipists at the Bar Wentworth had awakened a political instinct among the smaller people of Sydney and become their hero. He had touched both journalism and the Bar with the fire of his brilliance and given them definition, direction, and the vision of greatness: he may justly be called their prophet in the Australian nation, if not the prophet of that nation itself. The larger fight remained: for the great goal of self-government. But, even as the people of Sydney were flocking out to Vaucluse to join with the popular hero in celebration of the tyrant's departure, changes in Wentworth's own life and activities were beginning to cause disillusion among many who only partially understood his aims. With the swelling tide of immigration into New South Wales, the exclusive-emancipist issue was receding into the background of politics. So fast were events moving that in 1835, when Darling was cleared of Wentworth's charges and knighted, there were few in Sydney who showed concern.

By his father's death in 1827 Wentworth added greatly to his landholdings. In that year he bought Vaucluse, about six miles from Sydney on the south side of the harbour, and later enlarged it to 500 acres. The cottage there was rebuilt into a stately mansion which, in the years after Wentworth's marriage in 1829, provided the setting for both his family life and his activities as statesman. It was adorned with riches from the old world and became a sign of the new time, spacious and leisured, that was coming to the rich in New South Wales. With his large legal earnings, Vaucluse, his father's estate at Homebush, and one sheep station after another (he acknowledged fifteen at one time) Wentworth more and more felt himself the prototype of a new nobility, a governing class which would adapt to Australian conditions the way of life of the Whig aristocracy of eighteenth-century England. His own way of life became spacious even to the point of lapses from his marriage vows.

With Darling's successor, Governor Bourke, a kinsman of Edmund Burke, whose patron Fitzwilliam had been, Wentworth had much in common, though not even Bourke could persuade him to accept nomination to the Legislative Council, in which the governor's own liberal measures were frequently frustrated by the exclusives. In London there was growing support for Wentworth's policies: the Reform Act and events in Canada were fostering a climate of opinion favourable to constitutional change. After the murder of Wardell in 1834, William Bland [q.v.] stepped into his place as Wentworth's chief supporter. At the foundation-day meeting in 1833 another petition for self-government was drafted, which was presented to the Commons by Lytton Bulwer.

In 1835 the Australian Patriotic Association was formed to agitate for an amended constitution. Sir John Jamison [q.v.] was president, Wentworth vice-president, and Charles Buller its agent in London. With Bland's assistance Wentworth drafted two alternative bills for the consideration of the British government: one providing for a nominated council and an elected assembly on the model of Canada; the other for a single house of fifty members, one-fifth nominated and the rest elected on a property franchise similar to that of the 1832 Reform Act in Britain. With support in Sydney from Bourke and his successor, Gipps, and in London from Buller, Wentworth's second bill was adopted, with modifications, in an Act granting a degree of representative government in 1842. In an enlarged Legislative Council the proportion of nominees became one-third, and the property qualification for electors of the remaining twenty-four members was high enough to exclude two-thirds of the adult male population. Though the governor retained control of colonial revenue, he ceased to preside over the Legislative Council and was replaced by an elected Speaker.

In his book Wentworth had commended simultaneously a wide franchise and a property qualification for electors. The 1827 petition had demanded suffrage for 'the entire of the free population'. Now the eighteenth-century Whig in him was running stronger and he was more apt to equate political capacity with property and poverty with ignorance. He had given up his legal practice and was concentrating on his landed interests. Though he was still far less wealthy than James Macarthur [q.v.], who had gone to England on behalf of the exclusives to oppose the demands of the Australian Patriotic Association, Wentworth's riches were increasing rapidly, and the onset of middle age, his experience of the crowd, and the shift in the balance of population caused by assisted migration all tended to strengthen his conservatism. The intention of the British government to abolish convict transportation and to raise the price of crown land drew the exclusives and Wentworth into a common opposition to any change in the conditions allowing them cheap land and labour.

The leading emancipists now found themselves together with the exclusives on the side of the rich. Wentworth now belonged to the pastoral aristocracy he had envisaged in 1819 and it was faced with stern threats. When he expressed approval of the idea of importing coolie labour from Asia, he alienated many former supporters together with the radicals among the recent immigrants. In January 1842 the *Australian* summed up the popular feeling: 'Mr Wentworth . . . was an influential man. His day is gone by. His opinion is worth nothing . . . Certainly he first taught the natives of this colony what liberty was, but he has betrayed them since and they have withdrawn their confidence from him'.

In 1839 Wentworth was recommended for appointment to the Legislative Council by Gipps, but was soon at enmity with the new governor. In 1840, in direct opposition to declared British policy, humanely conceived, Wentworth and some associates bought from seven Maori chieftains, for a song, nearly a third of New Zealand, urging them, moreover, not to acknowledge Queen Victoria without proper safeguards. Gipps, aghast at such a 'job', blocked the scheme in the Legislative Council. But he misunderstood Wentworth. This bid was no jobbery, but Elizabethan in spirit and characteristically splendid and defiant. It would have made him the greatest land-owner on earth; frustrated, he swore 'eternal vengeance'. The enmity between Wentworth and Gipps bedevilled almost every issue until the governor's departure in 1846. It was comparatively easy for Wentworth to lead others against Gipps. As with Darling, he set out to wreck his opponent's policies, but although he was frequently depicted as an unscrupulous politician his powers were bent passionately on ends that seemed to him greater than person or reputation, his own or anybody else's.

Wentworth entered the Legislative Council in 1843 at the head of the poll for Sydney. He wished to be Speaker but was passed over in favour of his enemy, Alexander McLeay [q.v.]. However, with his unrivalled knowledge of parliamentary procedure and colonial affairs, he immediately assumed practical leadership of the council. His achievement was already re-markable. He was an orator of immense power, whether bludgeoning an opponent, or fumbling and growling and calling for his 'extracts', or rising, with harsh and rasping voice, to a broken sublimity of language which moved and enlightened even his enemies. All were affected by the impact of his personality. Robert Lowe [q.v.], mellifluously, dartingly, could mock what he had said, but the twain never really met, for they were of two different orders of being. Though he could marshal arguments brilliantly Wentworth relied little on subtlety or logic. He created a mood and stormed rather than seduced the mind. Careless and even slovenly in manners and dress (he now wore corduroys with his badly-fitting morning-coat), he had, while knowing his power, an unconscious arrogance and was in all things the observed of all observers.

He led the squatters in their demand for new land regulations and, since imperial control over crown land was an obstacle to their interest, for a surrender of that control to the Legislative Council. The squatters wanted security of tenure so that they could improve their runs without fear of displacement. Through a Pastoralists' Association, a select committee of the Legislative Council, a paid agent in the House of Commons, and in other ways they waged unceasing war against Gipps's policies. They won most of their demands in the imperial Act of 1846, which gave them security, for varying periods in the 'settled', 'intermediate', and 'unsettled' districts, unless someone would pay £1 an acre for the land they leased, and this they could thwart by purchasing key-points on their runs, such as around the waterholes. In a sense the squatting age was now over. Henceforward the graziers could build spacious homesteads and develop the way of life of a landed, governing class, whatever political power Wentworth and his followers might win for them.

Because pastoral interests were strong in the part-elective Legislative Council Wentworth was able after 1843 to establish again a leadership of the colony as a whole. He was never again popular as he had been in 1831. At times he was distinctly unpopular but the power of his personality continued to sway even the crowd. In the 1848 election, after a public outcry over the renewal of transportation, he again headed the Sydney poll, though Bland was defeated altogether. In 1851, when his unpopularity stood at its height through his insistence on a preponderance of squatter-controlled rural representation over that of Sydney and his opposition to a wide franchise and to the 'spirit of democracy abroad', he came in third, but was still returned.

Though frequently accused of inconsistency, Wentworth followed unswervingly the same ideals throughout his career. He believed profoundly in intellect, and his fury at unintelligent officialdom, military autocracy, and the social pretensions of the unimaginative exclusives (the imaginative, such as John Macarthur, he admired) sprang from the same source as his distrust of mob rule: a hatred of anything which would prevent the human mind and spirit from developing their latent powers. He at no time denied the right of the intelligent poor to aspire to the seats of government, but they must first become 'men of substance', participating in one of the great interests on which the welfare of the community depended. Preeminent among these was the landed interest which, because of his realistic appraisal of the Australian economy no less than his inherited or acquired Whiggism, he believed was the one to which, as he told them in 1851, the inhabitants of Sydney 'were indebted for all their greatness, all the comforts, all the luxuries, that they possessed'. He told them, too, with no little courage, that he 'agreed with that ancient and venerable constitution that treated those who had no property as infants, or idiots, unfit to have any voice in the management of the State'. The way out of infancy, or idiocy, was through intellect and property: but essential to these, and to the management of the state, was education—and Wentworth's pioneering of both primary and university education in Australia is among the noblest of his achievements.

He played a leading part with Lowe, his erstwhile opponent, in establishing in 1848-49 the first real system of state primary education in New South Wales. Hitherto primary teaching—and most of the children of the colony had none—had been conducted predominantly by the various religious denominations, with much sectarian bitterness. New South Wales was on the brink of gaining responsible government; but this, he argued, would be workable only through national education. Should they fail to give the youth of the colony 'the education which would furnish them with the knowledge of the responsibilities they undertook, the achievement of responsible government will be not to achieve a blessing, but to achieve the greatest curse it is possible to conceive'. He went on in 1849-50 to lead the movement that resulted in the founding of the first full colonial university in the British empire, the University of Sydney. He saw this as serving two ends: 'to enlighten the mind, to refine the understanding, to elevate the soul of our fellow men'; and to train men to fill 'the high offices of state'. He deplored the religious bigotry which had obstructed education: the university should be 'open to all, though influenced by none'. But he denied vigorously that his university would promote infidelity: he believed that 'the best mode of proving the divinity of the great Christian Code was to advance the intellect of those who trusted and relied upon it . . . It was not by stinting the intellect that Christianity was to be promoted'. The university would leave religious education to constituent colleges which he envisaged 'in every part of the colony'. Wentworth also helped to endow the university and was a member of its first senate.

In 1844, after a collision between Gipps and the Legislative Council, Wentworth had advocated 'that control of the Ministers and the Administrators of the Colony . . . which can only exist where the decision of the majority can occasion the choice— as well as the removal—of the functionaries who are entrusted with the chief executive departments'. He lost enthusiasm for this kind of responsible government after Governor FitzRoy eased the friction between executive and legislature, and turned instead to demands for self-government with full control of crown lands and colonial revenue. These demands, expressed in the Remonstrances of 1850 and 1851, remained urgent when gold was discovered, but the pastoral ascendancy seemed likely to be seriously threatened by 'pure democracy'. Although in 1852 the Colonial Office finally agreed that New South Wales should have responsible government, only a limited form of individual responsibility of some members of the executive was provided by the select committee which drafted the constitution in 1853. With Wentworth as chairman it recommended a lower house of fifty members elected on a £10 property franchise, and a nominated upper house consisting of members of an hereditary colonial peerage. The rural bias of the proposed lower house and the idea of a peerage were vociferously opposed in Sydney, by the press and by orators representing nearly every shade of political and social opinion. Wentworth vigorously defended his peerage scheme—which was a logical outgrowth of his basic ideas and assumptions and by no means the ridiculous proposal it has been represented as, then and since—but public opinion was so strongly against it that the bill, as eventually passed, contained in its stead provisions for a legislative council shorn of the hereditary principle altogether. Wentworth, with Edward Deas Thomson [q.v.], colonial secretary for New South Wales, with whom he had been much associated through the lack of interest shown by Governor FitzRoy in colonial politics, sailed for England in 1854. In July 1855 he had the satisfaction of seeing the new Constitution made law, despite the deletion of his favoured safeguard against rash amendments to it, and the early death of the General Association of the Australian Colonies which he conceived as the forerunner of a 'Federal Assembly with power to legislate on all internal subjects'.

His life's work triumphantly achieved, he spent his remaining days in England except for a brief return to Sydney in 1861-62, when he was prevailed on to accept the presidency of the Legislative Council during a crisis, and stood out for the nominative as against the elective principle. He had consolidated his fame more by staying away, and being remembered for his great achievements, than if he had returned and been drawn—as he must have been—into the political fray and tried—as he would have done—to stem the democratic tide. In England he became a member of the Conservative Club, and lived at Merly House, near Wimborne, Dorset. There he died on 20 March 1872, survived by his wife Sarah, second daughter of Francis Cox, an emancipist blacksmith, whom he had married in 1829, and by their seven daughters and two of their three sons. His probate was sworn at £96,000 in Sydney and £70,000 in London. As he had wished, his body was brought to Sydney, and after a state funeral on 6 May 1873 was laid to rest in a vault excavated in a rock on his estate at Vaucluse. A chapel erected over his tomb, portraits by Richard Buckner in the chamber of the Legislative Assembly in Sydney and by James Anderson in the Mitchell Library, and a statue in Carrara marble by Tenerani in the Great Hall of the University of Sydney are his tangible memorials.

His intangible, and truer, memorial is much more than can easily be estimated in present-day Australia. With all his apparent contradictions, more than any other man he secured our fundamental liberties and nationhood. He looked backward in many things to the seventeenth and eighteenth centuries; yet he built, with the strength that his sense of history gave him, for the future. He was a child both of the English past and of his own time. He was an heir to the Whig tradition, with its faith in aristocratic and classical values and in British political institutions

as established, more or less, by the Glorious Revolution and the politicians of the eighteenth century, and at the same time a child of the romantic movement. The chief intellectual influence upon him was Burke's oratory, with all its rhetoric and splendour and its evocation of the greatness of Augustan Rome and England. Emotionally, however, he was more Byronic, a force of nature of the kind which blazed in the sky of his boyhood in the person of Napoleon. He had breathed the air of Liberal Toryism abroad in England in the early 1820s. The subjection of his proud and romantic nature to the classical restraints of law and politics, though sometimes imperfectly achieved, increased rather than diminished his achievement. In his determination to secure in his own country those free institutions which in eighteenth-century England bore an aristocratic form, he may have regretted that their very freedom would allow them to become democratic; but their freedom was more important to him than their form. His love of Australia was, he confessed, the 'master passion' of his life. He felt a natural kinship with the founding fathers of the United States. It is his chief claim to greatness that, more than any other, he secured in Australia, in one lifetime, the fruit of centuries—what he, in common with other men of the eighteenth and nineteenth centuries, revered as the fundamental liberties of the British Constitution.

HRA (1), 7-9, 11-26, (4), 1; A. W. Jose, *Builders and pioneers of Australia* (Lond, 1928); A. C. V. Melbourne, *William Charles Wentworth* (Brisb, 1934); F. L. Wood, 'Some early educational problems, and W. C. Wentworth's work for higher education', JRAHS, 17 (1931); H. M. Green, 'Wentworth as orator', JRAHS, 21 (1935); C. H. Currey, 'The centenary . . . of responsible government', JRAHS, 42 (1956); John V. Byrnes, 'William Charles Wentworth, and the continuity of Australian literature', *Australian Letters* (April 1963); Wentworth papers (ML).

MICHAEL PERSSE

WERE, JONATHAN BINNS (1809-1885), stockbroker, was born on 25 April 1809 at Wellington, Somerset, England, the third son of Nicholas Were and his wife Frances, née Binns. In 1829 he joined the firm of Collins & Co., colonial merchants and bankers, of Plymouth. In 1833 he married Sophia Mullet Dunsford (1811-1881), a Quaker. They had twelve children, three of whom died in infancy. In 1882 he married Elizabeth, daughter of Donald Gordon McArthur of Melbourne.

Were emigrated in 1839 and settled in Melbourne. He brought a prefabricated house and merchandise worth about £1500. He traded at first under his own name, then with his brother George and with other partners until 1861, when the title J. B. Were & Son was adopted. Were's were importers, exporters, and agents for shipping, land, cattle, sheep and wool. In 1851 they became brokers and buyers of gold, and in 1853 began to deal in shares.

Despite his reputation as a financier Were was twice bankrupt and never wealthy. In 1843 he lost heavily as a merchant as well as in a land speculation with Henry Dendy at Brighton, but was re-established from England by his eldest brother, Nicholas. In 1857, after his second bankruptcy, the firm's share dealings rapidly took precedence over its commerce. In 1859 Were was both chairman and secretary of a regular stock exchange and in 1860 began to operate 'solely as Broker and Agent'. He successfully challenged stock jobbing by campaigning for an exchange on which brokers could not be principals and in 1865 was elected first chairman of 'The Stock Exchange of Melbourne'. He was a leading broker until his death, taking into partnership at various times his sons, Jonathan Henry, Francis Wellington and Arthur Bonville, and his son-in-law Sherbourne Sheppard.

In the 1840s Were was prominent in communal and business activities. He was first president of the Chamber of Commerce, one of three on the standing committee for separation, president of the Bible Society, a member of the Melbourne Hospital Committee, the Immigration Board and other institutions, and a director of many companies. He was the first justice of the peace appointed for Port Phillip, was a leading Church of England layman, and helped to run the 1881 Melbourne Exhibition, after which he was appointed C.M.G. In 1856 he was elected for Brighton to the Legislative Assembly, but his second bankruptcy soon caused his retirement. Contemporaries considered him most notable for the extraordinary number of his consular posts. He was knighted by the kings of Sweden and Denmark.

Were was a strange mixture of worldly ambition and idealism, of breadth of vision and rashness. His life seems to divide naturally into two periods at about 1857. Most of his public service took place in the 1840s and it was then that he lived in some style; 'all was English' at Moorabbin House in Brighton. He died on 6 December 1885.

Portraits are in the possession of J. B.

Were & Son, Dr Stuart Were of Balwyn, and the Brighton City Council.

T. W. H. Leavitt and W. D. Lilburn (eds), *The jubilee history of Victoria and Melbourne*, 1 (Melb, 1888); *The house of Were 1839-1854* (Melb, 1954); W. Bate, *A history of Brighton* (Melb, 1962); *Argus*, 7 Dec 1885.

WESTON BATE

WESSELOW;
see SIMPKINSON DE WESSELOW

WEST, JOHN (1809-1873), Congregational minister, author and newspaper editor, was born on 17 January 1809 in England, the son of Rev. William West and his wife Ann, née Ball. He had the advantages of a good home and a literary education. In 1829 he was admitted to the Independent ministry at Thetford, Norfolk, became a home missionary at Great Wakering, Essex, and then had charge of chapels at Southam and Coleshill, Warwickshire. In 1838 he was accepted by the Colonial Missionary Society for service in Van Diemen's Land, sailed from London with his wife Narcissa Sarah, née Lee, and young family in the *Emu*, and arrived at Hobart Town in December. He soon moved to Launceston, where he served as a missionary among the surrounding settlers. In 1842 he accepted the pastorate of the new St John's Square Chapel at Launceston and made his home at Windmill Hill.

At Launceston West's eloquence and sincerity soon gained him an important place, and his affability, honesty and genuine interest in people won him many friends and wide popularity. With James Aikenhead [q.v.] and J. S. Waddell he established the *Examiner* in 1842; he also helped to found the City Mission, public hospital and general cemetery, Mechanics' Institute and the Cornwall Insurance Co. In 1847 he was a founder of the Hobart High School, an undenominational institution to educate boys for careers in the professions, commerce and farming. His greatest contribution, however, was his effective leadership of the movement for abolishing the transportation of convicts to Van Diemen's Land. Convinced that transportation was socially and morally wrong, he attacked it with apostolic zeal from pulpit, platform and press, seeking to awaken the public conscience to its degrading effects. The fervour of his public addresses drew attendances that equalled those of the abolitionist orator, Richard Dry [q.v.].

Three years of campaigning convinced West that local organizations had little influence with the British government; on 9 August 1850 at a large protest meeting in Launceston he won acceptance of his proposal to seek the co-operation of all abolitionists throughout Australia. West drafted the letter which was widely circulated among organizations and influential men known to be opposed to continued transportation to Tasmania. The appeal was successful and led in February 1851 to an abolitionist conference in Melbourne, where steps were taken to form a widely representative organization for protest. West toured and lectured for the cause, and later that year the Australasian League for the Prevention of Transportation was formed. At its conferences West was often the principal speaker; although he was preaching to the converted he stressed that 'Australians are one' and should act together in spite of artificial boundaries. He became such an eminent figure that the league even proposed to send him to plead the cause before the public in England.

Throughout the campaign West was often criticized by a section of the press, but most newspapers were sympathetic and spread his message widely. After the fight was won the Hobart *Advertiser*, always hostile to the cause, made such serious personal attacks on West that he was forced to seek redress. The matter was settled out of court, West receiving apologies and £50, which he gave to the Hobart High School to buy books for its library. His church members showed their confidence by presenting him with a purse of fifty sovereigns and the citizens of Launceston gave him a testimonial. According to the *Examiner*, 25 April 1854, 'His was the inspiring spirit that gave vitality and impetus to every well-concerted and successful movement. He was the guiding hand that chiefly directed the machinery . . . his tongue was ever eloquent, his pen was incessantly occupied. He did all that is permitted to the most gifted to accomplish'.

In 1851-52 he had spent little time with his flock in Launceston. Soon after his return to pastoral duties he found another cause to fight when a bill for providing state aid to churches came before the Legislative Council. West was determined to defeat it, for he was a voluntaryist like most Congregationalists, and in 1849 had written a pamphlet, *The Voluntary support of the Christian Ministry Alone Scriptural and Defensible*. In spite of his efforts the bill became law in 1853.

In the early stages of the abolition

movement in 1847-48 a wealthy Hobart supporter, Henry Hopkins [q.v.], had asked West to write a history of the colony. No doubt the main object was to provide the public with an account of the development of the transportation system but, although the colony was only forty-four years old and many living people remembered its early years, there was wide ignorance of the colony's past. West was particularly well equipped for the task, though he was hampered by the lack of contemporary private papers and having to visit Hobart to read official records; involvement in the abolition campaign also seriously limited his time for research and writing. In spite of these difficulties West's *The History of Tasmania*, 2 vols (Launceston, 1852) was a notable achievement. His even temperament enabled him to write of men and events with fairness and detachment. His own knowledge of the times lent freshness to his work. At its best the style of his first volume is in the highest tradition of early Victorian historiography. The second volume is mainly polemical and concerns the evils of the penal system and the treatment of Tasmanian Aboriginals. Later research has revealed remarkably few inaccuracies, and West is sometimes credited with being one of the founding fathers of Australian historical writing.

Like other prominent abolitionists West was greatly interested in the development of representative and responsible government in the Australian colonies. In common with many educated British-born colonists he regretted the growth of separation movements and strongly advocated some form of constitutional union. Between 30 January and 1 September 1854, as 'John Adams', he contributed to the *Sydney Morning Herald* sixteen articles on the federation of the colonies. These articles were reprinted in 1867 and with support from editorials in the *Sydney Morning Herald* had a wide influence. C. D. Allin has commented that although the articles were 'introductory and educational rather than practical' they were 'the first scientific treatment of the question of federation from the pen of an Australian'.

In 1854 West accepted an invitation to become editor of the *Sydney Morning Herald*. Its owner, John Fairfax, was his friend and a prominent Congregationalist, and as a leading abolitionist had been impressed by his advocacy of the cause. With many regrets West left Launceston and took up his duties in Sydney on 14 November. Although he had no experience as an editor he had been a constant contributor to many journals. His leading articles covered a wide range of current topics and were marked by lucidity and reason. He foresaw the problems facing all the colonies in the post-gold-rush period and was almost alone in his warnings of the growth of foreign interests in the Pacific Islands and New Guinea. His forthright statements won him friends but also attracted criticism, which in Sydney of that period often degenerated into personal vilification and led to much litigation. In his editorials West once denounced the financial aspects of new educational schemes promoted by the fiery Rev. J. D. Lang [q.v.]. Lang retorted in the *Empire* with words so damaging that West took action for libel; he was awarded damages of £100 and characteristically gave the money to charity. Later he lost other suits for libellously condemning what he believed was wickedness in the actions of public men; he also tended towards a more conservative attitude in politics. In spite of the heavy demands in editing a daily newspaper with one of the largest circulations in the British empire West often found time to preach; he also helped to found and govern Camden College, an institution for training young evangelists. He died at his home in Woollahra on 11 December 1873. His widow died on 17 February 1874 aged 72. They were survived by three sons and five daughters.

In his dedication to causes which he believed to be morally right West had little interest in material rewards, yet he was no cold zealot isolated from every day life. Contemporaries recorded his urbanity and friendliness, charity towards the unfortunate, and unusual patience with the misinformed and misguided. His bitterest enemies could not impugn the honesty of his purpose.

C. D. Allin, *The early federation movement in Australia* (Kingston, Ontario, 1907); *A century of journalism. The Sydney Morning Herald, 1831-1931* (Syd, 1931); B. Richmond, 'John West and the anti-transportation movement', PTHRA, 2 (1951-52); E. M. Miller, Biography of J. West (TA).

JOHN REYNOLDS

WESTALL, WILLIAM (1781-1850), landscape artist, was born on 12 October 1781 at Hertford, England, the son of Benjamin Westall (1737-1793) and his second wife, Martha Harbord. He was taught to draw by his elder half-brother Richard (1765-1836), a water-colour painter, Royal Academician, and teacher of painting to Princess Victoria.

In 1799 he was admitted to the Royal Academy School, where he was studying when at 19 he was appointed landscape artist with Matthew Flinders' [q.v.] *Investigator* expedition to Australia, at a salary of 300 guineas. During the voyage he made a large number of pencil and pencil-and-wash landscapes in places visited by the *Investigator* and a series of coast profiles in pencil. When the *Porpoise* ran aground on Wreck Reef his sketches were 'wetted and partly destroyed' and, while Westall travelled in China, the drawings, regarded as part of the official record of the voyage, were taken by Lieutenant Robert Fowler to England. There, at the suggestion of Sir Joseph Banks [q.v.], they were handed to Richard Westall to be 'restored to a proper state'. The library of the Royal Commonwealth Society, London, now holds 139 sheets of these drawings.

After spending some time in China and India Westall returned to London in February 1805, sought access to the sketches to paint a picture for exhibition at the Royal Academy and showed a *View of the Bay of Pines* at the academy later in the year. In the summer of 1805 Westall went to Madeira and twelve months later to Jamaica. After returning to England he painted a series of water-colour views of the places he had visited and these were shown in a Brook Street gallery and at the Associated Artists' exhibition in 1808. Later he received commissions from the Admiralty to paint nine pictures to illustrate Flinders' *A Voyage to Terra Australis . . .* (1814), and was engaged by several London publishers to paint watercolours to be reproduced as aquatints. Plates from his pictures illustrate more than forty-five works; perhaps the best known are those in Ackermann's histories of Oxford, Cambridge and English public schools, but his best plates are probably those in *A Picturesque Tour of the River Thames* (1828).

Though Westall was elected an associate of the Royal Academy in 1812 and showed seventy pictures at its exhibitions between 1801 and 1849, his work, admirably suited to reproduction, was not highly esteemed and he was never elected an academician. On 2 September 1820 he married Ann (1789-1862), youngest daughter of Richard Sedgwick, vicar of Dent, Yorkshire. He died at St John's Wood, London, on 22 January 1850, and was survived by his wife and two sons, Robert and Rev. W. Westall.

M. H. Grant, *A dictionary of British landscape painters* (Leigh-on-Sea, 1952); Bernard Smith, *European vision and the south*

Pacific 1768-1850 (Oxford, 1960); T. M. Perry and D. H. Simpson (eds), *Drawings by William Westall* (Lond, 1962); Rex and Thea Rienits, *Early artists of Australia* (Syd, 1963); *Art J*, 12 (1850), p 95, 105; Westall papers (ML, PRO, BM, Roy Cwlth Soc, Lond).

T. M. PERRY

WESTON, WILLIAM PRITCHARD (1804-1888), pastoralist, was born in Shoreditch, London, the son of John Weston, surgeon. He was educated at Brighton, spent three years in a merchant's counting house and later entered the wool trade. In 1823 he decided to emigrate and sailed for Australia in the *Adrian*; the new lieut-governor of Van Diemen's Land, Colonel George Arthur, was also a passenger. Weston had a letter of recommendation from a friend at the Colonial Office, and his capital was more than £3000. The *Adrian* reached Hobart Town in May 1824, and although Weston was bound for New South Wales, he decided to remain in Van Diemen's Land, for on the voyage he had met Ann Elphinstone, daughter of Peninsular war veteran, Captain William Clark, whose family had embarked at the Cape. They were married in June 1826 at Cluny, a home Clark built at Bothwell, and the lieut-governor lent his carriage to take the clergyman from Hobart for the occasion.

Weston was granted 2000 acres of land which he first considered taking at Great Swan Port and later applied for at Bothwell. There for some time he assisted the settlers, Charles [q.v.] and Horace Rowcroft, and is said to have been the hero of a number of incidents described by Charles Rowcroft in *Tales of the Colonies* (London 1845). Disappointed in his application for land at Bothwell, he took his grant instead at Longford, where by 1826 he had also bought 300 acres. On 8 May 1828 he was appointed catechist and lecturer to the district, but inadequate facilities and lack of co-operation caused misunderstandings between Weston and the local police magistrate; although Weston was cleared of charges of neglect of duty, he preferred to resign. When accepting his resignation, Arthur affirmed his high regard for Weston's character and in 1835 appointed him to the Commission of the Peace. At Longford in 1831 he built Hythe, a fine Regency-style residence, and began the improvement of his flocks and the preparation of wattle bark for export. Eight children were born at Hythe, the eldest dying in infancy.

Weston was a deeply religious man and did much missionary work among the country people of the midlands. He contributed largely to the building of Christ's Church at Longford where he was a churchwarden. In 1840 he visited England with his family. Soon after his return in 1842, he severed his connexion with the Longford church, disapproving Rev. R. R. Davies's [q.v.] introduction of the surplice in the pulpit and the extension of the offertory, which to him were Romish practices. For some years he attended Anglican services at Perth but later left the Church of England and assisted in founding the Congregational Church in Launceston where his friend Rev. John West [q.v.] was minister.

An advocate of individual liberty, he devoted time and money to the establishment of the Anti-Transportation League in Tasmania. He and West were the delegates chosen to represent the colony at the meeting in Melbourne in February 1851 at which the League of Solemn Engagement of the Australian Colonies was adopted, binding the subscribers to reject convict labour arriving after that time and to use their official and legislative power to end transportation. The efforts of the two men contributed largely to the final cessation of transportation.

When responsible government was granted to Tasmania Weston was elected unopposed to the House of Assembly in September 1856 as member for Ringwood. In April 1857, when T. G. Gregson [q.v.] had to resign as premier, Weston was asked to form a ministry. However, rowdy opposition led by Gregson completely demoralized Weston and in May he resigned the premiership in favour of Francis Smith, his attorney-general. Nevertheless the ministry he had chosen remained in office for four years and gave the colony its first stable government since the granting of self-government. In 1857 he became a member of the Legislative Council, and from November 1860 to August 1861 was premier again, after Francis Smith had been raised to the bench. Soon afterwards ill health forced him to retire from politics. His ministry was not marked by any serious issues: the rural municipalities bill and Waste Lands Acts were both aimed at meeting a colonial deficit aggravated by falling population. Much-needed legislation to impose a tax on wool and land and introduce protective tariffs was unthinkable for a House packed with pastoralists and merchants. During the 1860s he moved to Victoria where he had invested in land at Geelong. There his wife died in 1868 and Weston died on 21 February 1888. His eldest son Edward, also a member of the Legislative Council, succeeded to his northern properties, and his second son Maurice inherited Cluny and Mauriceton from his Clark grandfather.

Lieut-Governor Denison, strongly in favour of continuing transportation, referred to Weston as an inveterate agitator; Gregson, radical supporter of the working class, regarded him as a renegade. He was, however, a quiet, determined leader who raised the tone of the new parliament above that of a debating society, and with steady perseverance achieved success in advancing the cause of individual freedom and social reform. A portrait in oils by Robert H. Dowling was presented to him by the Anti-Transportation League and now hangs in the Launceston gallery.

P. L. Brown (ed), *Clyde Company papers*, 1 (Lond, 1941); F. C. Green (ed), *A century of responsible government 1856-1956* (Hob, 1956); *Examiner* (Launceston), 11 Mar 1858, 23 Feb 1888; L. L. Robson, 'Press and politics' (M.A. thesis, Univ Tas, 1954); GO 33/78/179 (TA); CSO 1 (TA); LSD 1 (TA).

J. N. D. HARRISON

WHITE, JOHN (1756?-1832), naval surgeon, entered the navy on 26 June 1778 as third sugeon's mate in H.M.S. *Wasp*. He received his diploma of the Company of Surgeons on 2 August 1781, and in the next five years his naval service took him as far as the West Indies and India. On 26 June 1786 he became surgeon of the *Irresistible*, and four months later, on the recommendation of Captain Sir Andrew Snape Hamond, he was appointed chief surgeon of the expedition to establish a convict settlement at Botany Bay.

Of almost 1500 people in the eleven ships of the First Fleet 778 were convicts, many in poor health from long imprisonment. It is to the credit of White and his assistants that on the voyage of more than eight months there were only thirty-four deaths. Outbreaks of scurvy and dysentery and lack of accommodation for the sick were his first problems in the new colony. Within a year the incidence of sickness was greatly decreased, a hospital was built, and White, a keen amateur naturalist, found time to accompany Governor Phillip on two journeys of exploration. On 12 August 1788 he fought a duel with his third assistant, William Balmain [q.v.], in which, according to one account, both were slightly wounded. Ill feeling between them continued for several years.

On joining the First Fleet White had begun to keep a journal, in which he made many notes of birds examined in the colony. In November 1788 he sent this to a London friend, Thomas Wilson; edited

probably by Wilson it was published in 1790 as *Journal of a Voyage to New South Wales*. Accompanying the text were sixty-five engravings illustrating the natural history and products of the colony, drawn in England from specimens sent by White, with descriptions by English specialists. He also sent drawings and possibly specimens for *The Voyage of Governor Phillip to Botany Bay* (London, 1789). His own book was a big success. A German edition followed, and later there were translations into Swedish and French.

Meanwhile the infant colony had reached the edge of famine. White helped in the erection of a signal station at South Head and was among the officers who volunteered to fish every second night to supplement the rations. The arrival in June 1790 of the Second Fleet tested White and his staff to their utmost. About 500 convicts were landed dying or seriously ill. Despite lack of medicines and hospital accommodation White and his assistants nursed more than half of them back to health. A similar crisis arose with the arrival of the Third Fleet between July and September 1791. At one time about 600 newly-arrived convicts were under medical treatment and incapable of work and in 1792 the appalling total of 436 died.

The strain on White was severe and in December 1792 he applied for leave in England. Nevertheless he pursued his natural history studies and sent many specimens and drawings to England. When Thomas Watling [q.v.], convict and artist, reached the colony in October 1792 he was assigned to White and in the next two years made many drawings for him. It is possible that White himself had some skill as an artist. When Phillip departed in December 1792 control of the colony passed to Major Francis Grose [q.v.], who soon afterwards received permission to make land grants to his officers. White received 100 acres which he named Hamond Hill Farm, afterwards part of the suburb of Leichhardt. Later he was granted a further thirty acres near by, with a frontage to White Bay. He retained these grants until 1822 when they were sold to a settler, Edward Redmond [q.v.]. White's application for leave was eventually granted and when he sailed in the *Daedalus* on 17 December 1794 he had the satisfaction of leaving the colony a far healthier place than it had been for five years. Deaths from all causes in his last year had totalled only 59.

White reached London in July 1795. He was reluctant to return to New South Wales and in August 1796, faced with the alternative of doing so immediately or of resigning his appointment, he chose to resign. He contemplated publishing a second book and sent a rough manuscript and many drawings to A. B. Lambert, a noted botanist, but the project came to nothing. The manuscript appears to have been lost and the drawings are possibly those which form the so-called Watling Collection now preserved in the British Museum (Natural History).

For three years (1796-99) White served in various ships. He was surgeon at Sheerness Navy Yard from December 1799 to September 1803 and at Chatham Yard from September 1803 until he was superannuated in January 1820 at the age of 63. He was granted a half-pay pension of £91 5s. and spent his last years at Brighton. He died at Worthing on 20 February 1832 aged 75 and was buried at St Mary's, Broadwater, where until recent years a small tablet noted this event.

White left an estate valued at £12,000. He had married about 1800 and when he died three children of this union were living : Richard Hamond, a naval lieutenant; Clara Christiana, who became the second wife of Ralph Bernal, M.P.; and Augusta Catherine Anne, who married Lieutenant (later Lieut-General) Henry Sandham, R.E. A fourth child, Andrew Douglass (Douglas), born to White by a convict, Rachel Turner, in Sydney on 23 September 1793 was brought up in England as a member of the household. He joined the Royal Engineers, fought at Waterloo, and in 1823 returned to Sydney to rejoin the mother from whom he had been parted as an infant and who had married Thomas Moore [q.v.], a prominent settler. He lived for some years at Parramatta, married in 1835 and died in 1837.

F. Watson, *History of Sydney Hospital* (Syd, 1911); G. Mackaness, *Admiral Arthur Phillip* (Syd, 1937); H. S. Gladstone, *Thomas Watling* (Dumfries, 1938); J. White, *Journal of a voyage to New South Wales*, ed A. H. Chisholm (Syd, 1962); E. Ford, *Medical practice in early Sydney* (Syd, 1955); Rex and Thea Rienits, *Early artists of Australia* (Syd, 1963); W. B. Alexander, 'White's journal', *Emu*, 23 (1923-24), 24 (1924-25); J. Macpherson, 'Surgeon-General John White', *Univ Syd Medical J*, 21 (1928); D. Anderson, 'John White', *MJA*, 11 Feb 1933; G. P. Whitley, 'Naturalists of the First Fleet', *Aust Museum Mag*, 6 (1936-38).   REX RIENITS

WHITEFOORD, JOHN (1809-1892), magistrate, was born in Ayrshire, Scotland, the son of Caleb Whitefoord (1734-1810), F.R.S., a wit and diplomat, who had been secretary to the commission negotiating a peace with America in 1782. Whitefoord studied for the Bar but was attracted to Van Diemen's Land by letters from his brother-in-law, Malcolm Laing Smith, and sailed before qualifying. He arrived in Hobart Town in the *John Craig* in November 1832, bringing a letter of recommendation from the Colonial Office, where he had been introduced by Lord James Stewart. He was placed on the Commission of the Peace in February 1833 but was not given an expected official appointment until September, when he was sent to Oatlands as police magistrate. He was transferred for a year to Campbell Town in 1834 and then returned to Oatlands, where he later filled the offices of commissioner of the Court of Requests and deputy-chairman of Quarter Sessions and coroner. In 1847 he applied for eighteen months leave in England to cure a pulmonary complaint. His leave was extended for six months, but he returned still weak and had to exchange offices for nine months with John Lee Archer [q.v.], police magistrate of Circular Head, where the climate was less extreme. On his return to Oatlands he was given the additional duties of the Bothwell district; later these were removed but the districts of Green Ponds and Brighton were included in his weekly itinerary.

In October 1857 his long service in the southern midlands was rewarded and he was appointed chairman of Quarter Sessions and commissioner of the Court of Requests in Launceston. Three months later the new office of recorder was created to dispatch court hearings more efficiently and Whitefoord, reputed the only bearer of the title in Tasmania, was empowered to preside at some criminal hearings and hold courts whenever necessary. In 1871 he became also commissioner in bankruptcy and three years later commissioner of circuit Courts of Requests. From 1858 to 1887 he continued to be re-elected annually by the judges as chairman of Quarter Sessions.

After a stroke in May 1886 he retired and parliament voted him a pension equivalent to his full pay. He died in Launceston on 28 September 1892. A special requiem was held in Holy Trinity Church where he had worshipped regularly. His wife Albinia Jane Martyn, daughter of a London actor, R. W. Elliston, and sister of William Gore Elliston [q.v.], had died in 1891. Their two daughters and one of their three sons survived them.

Lieut-Governor Franklin complained that Whitefoord's financial necessities interfered with the proper discharge of his duty as a magistrate, and promotion during his term of office was withheld. He had spent a large sum on improving a rented farm near Oatlands, on which he lost money when he had to sub-let it because Franklin directed him to live in the township. An unreliable innkeeper then financed him and in return had his hotel licence continued, much to the annoyance of other residents. Other governors highly estimated his quiet demeanour and the discretion and efficiency with which he discharged his magisterial duties. He was popular in the Oatlands district and the residents turned out in force to carry him into the town on his return from England in 1850.

His family name is commemorated in the Whitefoord Hills surrounding his brother-in-law's property in northern Tasmania.

Correspondence file under Whitefoord (TA).

G. H. STANCOMBE

WHYTE, THOMAS (1793?-1826), master mariner, a native of Dublin, was tried at the Edinburgh Court of Justiciary on 14 July 1814 and sentenced to transportation for fourteen years. He arrived in New South Wales in September 1815 in the Baring, whose indent states that he was a seaman. He was assigned to the colonial marine, and served in the Lady Nelson, Mary and Elizabeth Henrietta. On 1 January 1817 he was conditionally pardoned and then spent three years in the service of merchants trading between Sydney and East Indian ports. From December 1819 he was master of the Campbell Macquarie for twelve months, when Governor Macquarie granted him 300 acres at Norfolk Plains (Longford) in Van Diemen's Land. After spending about £500 developing this property he had the bad luck in 1821 to lose goods worth an equal amount in the wreck of the schooner Mary on her passage from Sydney. When his creditors obtained a writ against him, his fine farm with its comfortable brick and wood dwelling brought the trifling sum of £85 at auction in 1823. Even the land commissioners commented on the injustice of his case. But he must have continued farming, for two years later he was complaining that his considerable grain crop had been destroyed by fire.

In November 1825 Whyte entered the colonial marine of Van Diemen's Land as master of the Duke of York and was soon sent in pursuit of bushrangers and escaped convicts. On this trip he chased a party of runaways near Swan Port so closely that they had to sink their boat to effect an escape. He then put in to George Town for provisions and took the opportunity to visit Launceston with dispatches. On the way there he was ambushed by Matthew Brady [q.v.] and his associates who robbed him and threatened his life. Thence he went to the Bass Strait islands and at Preservation Island on 7 February 1826 came upon the Caledonia, Captain Smith. Whyte's suspicions were aroused when he found that this ship, which had left Hobart Town in January 1825 as a sloop of seven tons, had been altered to a schooner of almost thirty tons. The registered crew comprised Captain Smith, his son, the nominal owner and master, and two seamen, yet when Whyte arrived the son was absent, the ship was commanded by Smith, and five escaped convicts were aboard, one of whom, J. J. Holland, had been concealed with the son's knowledge when the Caledonia left Hobart. It was commonly rumoured that Smith had intended taking his vessel with its cargo of sealskins to Batavia so that Holland could make his escape. Whyte thereupon seized the Caledonia and sent her to Van Diemen's Land under the care of his mate while Captain Smith and his vagabond crew were taken in the Duke of York. This was well enough but Whyte, who was nearly out of stores, also commandeered his prize's provisions. A committee of inquiry, Colonel W. Balfour, Captain J. Welsh [qq.v.] and Rolla O'Ferrall, was appointed to study Smith's claim for damages and found in May 1826 that Whyte had been justified up to this point, but criticized him for consuming all their tobacco and rum; worse still Smith's whale-boat had been left behind at Preservation. When Whyte returned to Hobart he was not congratulated as he had expected, but suspended. He tried to sustain his deflated spirit by a prolonged bout of drinking and dissipation and, at the end of June when on the way to join his family at Port Dalrymple, shot himself in a miserable hut near Bagdad. The ill-fated expedition to Bass Strait is memorable for the report that Whyte made on the habits of the seals and the state of the trade in general. His seizure of the Caledonia drew attention to the deplorable conditions prevailing in these islands which had long been the refuge of the worst ruffians in the Australian colonies.

On 6 October 1817 at St Philip's Church, Sydney, Thomas Whyte, then master of the colonial brig Elizabeth Henrietta, married Jannette Tinnock, aged 22 and free; they had at least three daughters of whom Jane, the youngest, married Henry Best [q.v.]. Whyte's age is variously stated. The indent of the *Baring* records that he was 22 in 1815, the marriage register of St Philip's Church that he was 28 in 1817, and the burial register of St John's Church, Launceston, that he was 28 when he died in 1826.

Correspondence file under T. Whyte (TA).

G. T. STILWELL

WICKHAM, JOHN CLEMENTS (1798-1864), naval officer and magistrate, was born on 21 December 1798 at Leith, Scotland, the son of Captain Samuel Wickham R.N. He entered the navy as a midshipman in 1812 and from 1827 to 1830 he served as lieutenant under P. P. King [q.v.] in a survey expedition off the coast of South America. From 1831 to 1836 he was second in command of the *Beagle* in the expedition for which Charles Darwin [q.v.] was the naturalist and from 1837 to 1841 he commanded the *Beagle* while charting the north-western coasts of Australia. His health was undermined by long and arduous service and he retired from the navy in 1841. He settled next year in New South Wales, where he married a daughter of Hannibal Macarthur [q.v.].

In January 1843 with a salary of £300 he became police magistrate at Moreton Bay, newly opened to free settlement. Though not in control of other government officers in the district, he was regarded as the senior. He showed much sympathy and understanding, and exercised his authority with judgment and a genuine sense of responsibility; he had the confidence of the settlers and was able to contribute much to the early development of Brisbane. In 1846-47 he added to his duties by carrying out a survey of Moreton Bay, financed by local squatters through a district improvement fund. In 1853 the increasing extent of his duties was recognized by a rise of £200 in salary and in 1857 by his appointment as government resident, a post which necessitated the surrender of his magisterial duties.

To replace the tumbledown commandant's quarters allotted to him, in 1847 he bought from his brother-in-law, Patrick Leslie [q.v.], a property known as Newstead, and it became an unofficial Government House. His first wife died in 1852 leaving him with two sons and a daughter, and in 1857 he married Ellen Deering, of Ipswich, who bore him two sons.

On the eve of the formation of the new colony of Queensland Wickham was offered the post of colonial treasurer in the new administration. Fearing that he could not afford to bear the costs of an election, and that a defeat would leave him with nothing, he refused the offer and sought a pension from the New South Wales government. This was refused on the ground that the responsibility belonged to Queensland. In June 1860 he made a similar request to the secretary of state for the colonies, who passed it on to the Queensland government. Despite strong support by Governor Bowen the request was refused, the chief reasons appearing to be pique that Wickham had refused to stay and help the new colony, and a desire to push the responsibility back on New South Wales, the whole question being complicated by a quarrel between the two colonial governments on adjustment of debts. Offended by what he regarded as ingratitude and forced to live in somewhat straitened circumstances, Wickham retired to the south of France, where he died from a stroke on 6 January 1864, and was buried at Biarritz.

F. W. S. Cumbrae-Stewart, 'Notes on the registers and memorials at St John's Cathedral, Brisbane', *JRHSQ*, 1 (1914-19); C. G. Austin, 'Newstead House and Capt. Wickham, R.N.', *JRHSQ*, 3 (1936-47); G. C. Ingleton, 'A brief history of marine surveying in Australia', *JRAHS*, 30 (1944).

A. A. MORRISON

WILD(E), JOSEPH (1773?-1847), bushman and constable, was sentenced on 21 August 1793 at Chester, England, to transportation for life and arrived in New South Wales in the *Ganges* in June 1797. He is said to have accompanied both Barrallier and Robert Brown [qq.v.] on their explorations into the interior. In August 1810 he received a ticket-of-leave, and in January 1813 was granted a conditional pardon. For a time he superintended George Crossley's [q.v.] farm on the Hawkesbury; in 1814 he was a labourer at Liverpool, but soon afterwards began working for Charles Throsby [q.v.]. He accompanied Throsby on journeys to the country west of Sutton Forest in 1817, to Jervis Bay in 1818, and to Bathurst in 1819; for the last he received a grant of 100 acres, but sold it almost immediately to his companion on the tour, John Wait. When the road to the new country was begun in October 1819 Robert Sills was made superintendent of the road-gang, but Wild replaced him when Sills found that the Aboriginals remembered him for pursuing them in 1816; for supervision of fourteen convicts Wild received £20 a year. Governor Macquarie praised Wild's part in the construction of the road when he visited the final stages across the Cookbundoon Range in October 1820 and named the pass through the mountains Wild's Pass.

In August 1820 Throsby sent Wild with two companions in search of water farther south. He discovered Lake George and in December accompanied Charles Throsby on a search for the Murrumbidgee, but it is not clear whether they reached it. Next March he made his last journey with Throsby, again in search of the Murrumbidgee; during this they crossed the Molonglo and Queanbeyan Rivers. Throsby told Surveyor-General Meehan [q.v.] that Wild was as conversant with the country surrounding the Wollondilly as he was himself and offered him Wild's services as a guide there. In April and May 1823 Wild accompanied Captain Currie and Major Ovens [q.v.] on an expedition south of Bong Bong, which resulted in the discovery of the Monaro Plains.

In December 1815 Macquarie had made Wild a constable for the district of the Five Islands and in March 1821 he became constable for the new County of Argyle. After Throsby's death Wild was head stockman for Charles Throsby junior. When he died on 25 May 1847 he was the first to be buried in Bong Bong cemetery. He was illiterate but played a large part in the colony's expansion into the interior as one of those who came to terms with the bush and without whose assistance the task of the more famous explorers would have been much greater. He and his wife Elizabeth had several children.

HRA (1), 10; J. Gale, Canberra, its history and legends (Queanbeyan, 1927); J. Jervis, 'The Wingecarribee and southern highland district', JRAHS, 23 (1937); J. Jervis, 'The great south road', JRAHS, 25 (1939); Sydney Gazette, 9 Dec 1815, 3 Mar 1821; MS cat under J. Wild (ML).   VIVIENNE PARSONS

WILLIAMS, FRANCIS (1780?-1831), merchant, arrived at Port Jackson in the privateer Lucy in April 1806. He had left England as supercargo of a ship trading with South America which had been lost. He appears to have joined the Lucy on a journey through South American waters attacking Spanish shipping and across the Pacific to Port Jackson for repairs. Soon after his arrival he was employed by the merchant Simeon Lord [q.v.] and in November 1806 married Lord's ward, Joanna Short, who had been born at Sydney in 1792, the orphan daughter of the convicts Joseph Short and Elizabeth Drury.

Williams did not have official permission to enter the colony. As an associate of Lord and a friend of D'Arcy Wentworth [q.v.], in whose quarrels with Governor Bligh he had become involved, he was persona ingrata with the governor, who ordered his deportation and advised the British government that he should not be allowed to return as a settler. He left Sydney in November 1807 as supercargo in Lord's Sydney Cove, carrying commissions from Lord and letters to England for Wentworth, who described him as 'a very respectable young gentleman'. In England Williams executed personal and commercial business for Lord and on his behalf went to America to wind up the matter of the Criterion cargo. In 1809 he applied for permission to settle in New South Wales, returned to Sydney in January 1810 and immediately entered into full partnership with Lord. He acquired farming interests on the Hawkesbury River and Governor Macquarie appointed him a trustee and commissioner of the turnpike between Sydney and the Hawkesbury.

In addition to its wholesale and retail business, the firm of Lord & Williams had interests in manufacturing and the timber trade, and in 1810 it made an unsuccessful attempt to establish a flax industry in New Zealand. In July 1811 Williams sailed for Calcutta in the Aurora, an American brig which the firm had chartered, to expedite contracts on behalf of the government for the shipment of wheat, sugar and rum from Bengal, but it was not till October 1812 that Williams returned in the Hope with the cargo of supplies, which was diverted to the Derwent on Macquarie's orders. He spent several months in Hobart Town and bought stock there to set up as a farmer and grazier. He returned to Sydney in March 1813 and requested Macquarie's permission to exchange the 800-acre grant he had received in 1812 in the Hawkesbury district for a similar grant in Van Diemen's Land. Macquarie agreed and ordered that he receive 'the utmost indulgencies of a free settler'. In July 1813 the partnership with Lord was dissolved and Williams left for Van Diemen's Land. Next year he was appointed a magistrate at Hobart, but his grazing concerns seemed to have little success. In February 1818 he was again in Sydney, obtained the position of accountant with the Bank of New South Wales, and a month later succeeded to the senior position of cashier.

In September 1820 the directors of the bank requested him to resign as he had made unauthorized advances to the extent of £2000 which they were obliged to call in. No doubts of his integrity appear to have been entertained; but a few weeks after his resignation it was discovered that the sealed bags of notes which he left for his successor were £12,000 short. It was then found that he had in effect made unauthorized advances to that extent to oblige various individuals and had concealed his action by entering non-existent deposits in the bank books. In March 1822 he was tried and convicted of embezzlement. He appears to have made little personal profit from these clandestine transactions. The bank recovered £6000 from Williams's sureties and about £4000 from three of the customers to whom he had granted favours, though two of them were still being pressed for a final settlement almost ten years later. Sentenced to transportation for fourteen years, Williams appears to have passed his servitude first as a clerk in the government store and later as clerk to the bench at the Newcastle penal settlement. He was granted a ticket-of-leave in 1828 and set up as an agent at Newcastle. He died at Luskentyre, one of T. W. M. Winder's [q.v.] estates, on 6 October 1831.

His career was an unusual reversal of the Botany Bay success story. After a profitable association with Lord, his decision to abandon trade for the life of a country gentleman was unsuccessful, and his final disgrace seems to have been due to weakness and a desire for prestige and popularity rather than to any premeditated plan for monetary gain.

HRA (1), 6, 8, 10; Supreme Court records (NSWA); MS cat under F. Williams (ML).

R. F. HOLDER

WILLIAMS, JOHN (1796-1839), missionary, was born on 27 June 1796 at Tottenham High Cross, London, the son of John Williams and Hannah (?) Maidment. His ancestors on his father's side had been Baptists for many generations. His mother was influenced by the Calvinistic Methodist movement and brought her son up as a Congregationalist. Williams was taught writing and arithmetic at Lower Edmonton; he was apprenticed to an ironmonger in 1810 and was soon entrusted with the management of the business. In 1814 he underwent an Evangelical conversion and became a member of the Tabernacle Church (Calvinistic Methodist). He was taught grammar and exegesis by Rev. Matthew Wilks and in 1816 volunteered for missionary service with the London Missionary Society.

Williams was accepted and on 3 September 1816 was ordained at Surrey Chapel. On 29 October 1816 he married Mary Chauner, formerly of Denston Hall, near Cheadle, Staffordshire. Williams, Robert Bourne (1794-1871), David Darling (1790-1867), and George Platt (1789-1865) formed the third party of missionaries to arrive in the islands after the nominal conversion of Tahiti in 1815. They sailed in November 1816 and were joined by Rev. L. E. Threlkeld [q.v.] at Rio de Janeiro. They arrived at Hobart Town in March 1817 and held the first Evangelical service conducted in Van Diemen's Land, Williams defying opposition by preaching in the open air. In May the party arrived in Sydney where already an itinerant Evangelical ministry had been established by earlier missionaries. William Ellis (1794-1872), who arrived in July 1816, had visited the 'interior', conducted regular services based on Parramatta, taught reading and writing in a Sunday school at Prospect, and set up the mission press in the home of Rowland Hassall [q.v.]. When Ellis left for Tahiti this work was carried on by John Muggridge Orsmond (1788-1856) and Charles Barff (1792-1866) who had arrived in the Surry in December 1816. Orsmond and Barff had taught many of the young Irish convicts to read and write and Barff continued this work in the country districts after Orsmond went to the islands in February 1817. Orsmond later returned briefly to New South Wales, and on 25 December 1819 married Isabella, daughter of Isaac Nelson, an emancipist farmer and the first schoolteacher at Liverpool. Orsmond was better educated than most visiting missionaries, and studied with the family of Dr William Redfern [q.v.]. He later became principal of the South Sea Academy in Moorea, and as a Polynesian scholar and educationist influenced J. D. Lang [q.v].

All these Dissenting missionaries were received favourably by Governor Macquarie and assisted the evangelistic labours of both Anglicans and Wesleyans. Particular friendships were formed with Edward Eagar and Rev. Samuel Leigh [qq.v.]. Williams, in particular, impressed Samuel Marsden [q.v.] with his ability. The entire mission party left for the islands in September 1817.

Williams was regarded as the most enterprising missionary in the islands. In December 1821 he and his wife paid a three-month visit to Sydney, where he preached and addressed public meetings. On his own initiative he also bought a ship, with Marsden's reluctant approval, to trade between Raiatea and Sydney;

and he engaged Thomas A. Scott [q.v.] to instruct the people of Raiatea in the culture of sugar-cane and tobacco. Governor Brisbane was so impressed by Williams that he supplied stock to the mission and gave him magisterial authority for the islands.

In 1838, when Williams had become a public figure, he returned to Sydney in the mission ship *Camden*, and drew considerable crowds to his meetings. Having recently given evidence before the committee of the House of Commons on Aborigines, he was influential in the establishment of the local Aborigines Protection Society, and was also responsible for founding an Auxiliary Missionary Society in Sydney. News of his violent death at Eromanga in the New Hebrides on 20 November 1839 was received with much public sorrow and a new impetus was given to Australian Congregationalism. His widow died in England in June 1851. Their eldest son, John Chauner Williams (1818-1874), was for a time a produce merchant in Sydney before returning to Samoa where he was appointed British consul in 1858.

Besides the well known Baxter prints of Williams, including those of his landing and death at Eromanga, there is a miniature of Williams in the London Missionary Society archives, Westminster.

Several of Williams's colleagues, besides Threlkeld, returned to Australia. Bourne, who arrived in February 1827, went into partnership with Charles Appleton, merchant, in January 1829 before returning to England where he dissolved connexion with the London Missionary Society. He finally settled in Sydney and assumed full management of the business in May 1831. At the end of 1835 he opened a separate business, resigning his Sydney partnership to David Jones [q.v.], then Appleton's London partner. With W. P. Crook [q.v.] and J. Hayward, he took a prominent part in the formation of the Pitt Street Congregational Church in Sydney and was also a prominent member of various philanthropic organizations. Later he moved to Brisbane where he helped to found the Wharf Street Congregational Church in 1859 and among other duties was secretary of the Board of Public education. He died at Brisbane on 1 June 1871. One of his sons, George Bourne, was Landsborough's colleague when he crossed the continent in 1862. A daughter, Harriet, married the parliamentarian, George Raff. Four of his grandsons held important positions in the Queensland civil service. Both Darling and Barff retired to Sydney and died there. Barff's

grandson, Henry Ebenezer Barff (1857-1925), was registrar of the University of Sydney.

The presence of these missionaries in the colonies aroused public interest in missions and drew attention to trade with the Pacific islands. Williams, who had a dynamic personality, believed that the Christianization of the islands in the Pacific would lead to the greater prosperity of Sydney's business houses. But he also believed Australia had a duty to evangelize and civilize, and wrote to the *Sydney Gazette*, 22 March 1827: 'Prosper, O Australia! in your mercantile pursuits, in the extent of your dominions, in the numbers of your flocks and herds, in the fineness of your fleeces; yet recollect, that in your prosperity you are neglecting the work that God, the author of all your prosperity, has assigned you'.

J. Williams, A *narrative of missionary enterprises in the South Sea islands* (Lond, 1837); E. Prout, *Memoirs of the life of the Rev. John Williams* (Lond, 1843); J. E. Ellis, *Life of William Ellis* (Lond, 1873); J. J. Ellis, *John Williams* (Lond, 1890); J. King, *Ten decades, the Australian centenary story of the London Missionary Society* (Lond, 1895); N. Bartley, *Australian pioneers and reminiscences*, ed J. Knight (Brisb, 1896); Benjamin Williams, *Memorial of the family of Williams* (np, 1904); LMS archives (Westminster).   NIEL GUNSON

WILLIAMS, JOHN (1797?-1872), trader, coal-miner and settler, was born at Wells, Somerset, England, the son of William Williams, plasterer, and his wife Ann, née Edwards. He followed many trades and his later nickname, Butty, was said to derive from his experience as a tributer in a Somerset mine. He was probably the John Williams who in June 1832 arrived at Sydney as a seaman in the convict transport *John*, hard on the heels of his fiancée, Sarah Davis, who at 34 was convicted in London of receiving stolen goods, sentenced to transportation for seven years and reached Sydney in the female transport *Burrill* in May. Next year he twice applied for permission to marry Sarah but was refused because she was said to be already married with three children. By 1837 Sarah was assigned to him as a servant.

In October 1841 Williams's Sydney address was 'Sussex Street, two doors from Moon's Wharf' when he applied for permission to take the cutter *John*, 35 tons, with stores to the penal settlement at Moreton Bay. He was allowed to sail in December and was the first free man to receive a trading licence in Brisbane. At first he squatted on land on the southern bank of the Brisbane River and in the early land sales bought several sections there. In 1842 he was given a three year contract at £45 a year to 'provide a sufficient punt and boat to carry passengers' across the river at Kangaroo Point; his ferry was later known as the Time Killer, perhaps because Williams had too many other interests. His first slab and bark store was soon replaced by a larger building in Russell Street on the main track from Brisbane to Ipswich. This building he called the Captain Piper hotel after he received one of the settlement's first liquor licences; his own house near by was one of the first private residences built in Brisbane.

Williams continued as a trader, sending timber to Sydney, returning with stores and liquor, and carrying passengers each way. He victualled ships, employed timber-getters and built many houses. His *John* was quickly replaced by the schooner *Edward*, 80 tons. After the Hunter River Steam Navigation Co. sent the steamer *Shamrock* from Newcastle to Brisbane in December 1842 Williams began to look for coal. His first shaft at Fairfield was unsuccessful but he soon found a small seam on Oxley Creek. In 1844 on an outcrop at Redbank, sixteen miles from Brisbane, he opened his first mine but after four years the workings became flooded and were abandoned. In 1848 he started a more successful mine at Moggill. By 1850 he had also built several barges and was supplying coal to steamers and town consumers, carrying stores to the head of navigation on the Brisbane River at Limestone (Ipswich) and returning with wool and timber. Later he built the *Gneering*, a stern paddle steamer, for towing his barges, carrying passengers and victualling ships in Moreton Bay. In the mid-1850s he sold the Moggill mine very profitably, but in persistent later searches for coal near Brisbane he lost heavily.

Sarah died on 7 April 1849. On 4 July 1865 Williams married Mary Bailey (1837-1926), a newly-arrived emigrant from Chester, England. When their only son John was born Williams described himself as a plasterer at Fortitude Valley. Soon afterwards he made his home at Bulimba, where he had forty-nine acres and an orchard. There he died, a gentleman, on 18 September 1872 and was buried in the old military cemetery in Brisbane.

J. H. C. McClurg, John Williams: the early Brisbane settler, RHSQ Hist Miscel-

lanea, no 4 (Oxley Lib, Brisb); J. H. Allsopp, The coal industry of Queensland (B.A. Hons thesis, Univ Qld, 1953); Col Sec in letters, 4/3094-3101 (NSWA, microfilm Oxley Lib, Brisb).

WILLIAMS, ZEPHANIAH (1795?-1874), Chartist and mine-owner, was born at Merthyr Tydfil in Glamorganshire, Wales. He married Johan (b. 1801) and they had a son, Llewellyn, and a daughter, Rhoda (b. 1830). The Monmouthshire Chartist, Henry Vincent, described Williams as 'one of the most intelligent men it has ever been my good fortune to meet'. Unlike John Frost [q.v.] he was a free-thinker and by 1831 had won notoriety by his spirited polemics against the local clergy. In 1832 he was charged with assaulting a constable in Monmouthshire but was acquitted. In 1838 he became a Chartist and several Chartist meetings were held at his Royal Oak Inn in Coalbrookvale, Blaina, Monmouthshire, where he combined the occupation of innkeeper with that of a mineral surveyor and coal merchant. With John Frost and William Jones he was one of the leaders of the Newport rising of November 1839, though unlike Jones he appears to have favoured a peaceful demonstration. When the rising failed Williams eluded his pursuers for three weeks but was captured at Cardiff on the point of sailing for Portugal, brought to trial at Monmouth and, together with his two associates, sentenced to be hanged, drawn and quartered for waging war against the Queen. The sentence was commuted to transportation for life; Williams sailed with Frost and Jones in the *Mandarin*, and arrived in Hobart Town on 30 June 1840.

Williams was sent to Port Arthur where he was soon employed as a superintendent in the coal-mines. In November he attempted to escape by canoe and was sentenced to two years hard labour in chains at Impression Bay on Tasman Peninsula. His term of probation ended in November 1843 and he was transferred to the prisoners' barracks at Hobart; from there he went to New Norfolk as a constable at 12s. a week. In August 1846 he left the police force and became a barman in a Launceston hotel. Eighteen months later he made another attempt to escape and received a further sentence of twelve months with hard labour in chains on Tasman Peninsula, three months of which he spent in the coal-mines and the rest at Salt Water River. He was released in November 1848 and entered service first at Providence Valley and later in Hobart. He received his ticket-of-leave on

27 November 1849, a conditional pardon on 27 June 1854, and a free pardon on 24 February 1857.

Williams took no part in public life although he remained in the colony. While in service in 1849 he began mining at Knocklofty without success, but later discovered the coalfield in New Town neglected for twenty years. In partnership with R. J. Collins until 1853 he worked the Triumph mine, producing between thirty and forty tons of coal a day, and helping by this competition to keep the general price low. When coal was found at the Mersey River Williams went to inspect it. Offers from a Launceston syndicate fell through and Williams started his own company. He acquired over 2000 acres, formed a miners' camp and commenced work at Tarleton where the Denison colliery was opened in 1853. He sent to England for miners, built houses for them, a tramway and a deep-water jetty. In 1855 he entered another partnership and until 1859 managed the Denison, Nook and Don mines. Williams left the industry when the mines failed, became a publican at Ballahoo and built a fine house at Tarleton. Meanwhile his family had come out to join him. His son Llewellyn returned to Wales soon afterwards and became a noted harpist, but his daughter Rhoda stayed and married George Atkinson, who became a leading citizen of Latrobe. Johan Williams died in 1863; Zephaniah died at Launceston on 8 May 1874 in his eightieth year. They both lie buried, together with their daughter and son-in-law, at East Devonport.

D. Williams, *John Frost. A study in Chartism* (Cardiff, 1939); *Hobart Town Courier*, 22 Dec 1847, 1 Sept 1855; Correspondence file under Williams (TA).

G. RUDE

WILLIAMSON, JAMES (1758-1826), public servant and landholder, came to New South Wales in September 1795 with Governor Hunter who was impressed by his knowledge of book-keeping and gave him control of the commissariat in August 1796. His conduct when in office was open to serious reproach: smallholders complained that he discriminated against them and Governor King alleged that he was one of the officers who made a fortune from private trade. Certainly he advanced his material interests; by August 1800 he owned 359 acres of land and 419 head of stock including 320 sheep, one of the largest flocks in the settlement. A month later he returned to England

with Hunter. While in London he seized the opportunity to invest £925 in a speculative cargo valued at £10,000 which was dispatched to New South Wales in the brig *Venus*. With Hunter's assistance he secured an appointment as deputy-commissary and much to King's displeasure came back to New South Wales in 1802, commencing duties at Parramatta in October.

Restored to the ranks of officialdom Williamson also resumed control of his farm which he had left in the care of an emancipist, John Brannon. Some of his possessions, however, he had sold and, although he soon acquired more land than he had hitherto owned, he had not by 1806 regained his position as a stock raiser. On the other hand his civic responsibilities broadened and by the time of the Rum Rebellion he was a magistrate and lieut-commandant of the Parramatta Loyal Association.

After the deposition of Governor Bligh Williamson was placed in charge of the commissariat. On 3 September 1808, however, Lieut-Governor Foveaux [q.v.] dismissed him and charged him with fraud. This ended his official career. Early in 1810 he begged Governor Macquarie to restore him to his former post but to no avail. Dispirited, he left for England with Bligh on 12 May and later gave evidence on his behalf at Lieut-Colonel Johnston's [q.v.] court martial. In April 1817 he returned to New South Wales as a free settler, and received an 800-acre grant at Cabramatta. He appears to have remained a farmer until he died on 15 February 1826.

HRNSW, 2-7; *HRA* (1), 1-9; *Proceedings of a general court-martial . . . for the trial of Lieut.-Col. Geo. Johnston* (Lond, 1811); M. H. Ellis, *John Macarthur* (Syd, 1955); MS cat under J. Williamson (ML).

B. H. FLETCHER

WILLIS, JOHN WALPOLE (1793-1877), judge, was born on 4 January 1793, the second son of Captain William Willis (d. 1809) of the 13th Dragoons and his wife Mary (d. 1831), the only daughter and heiress of Robert Hamilton Smith, of Lismore, County Down, Ireland. Statements by McCombie, Garryowen and others that he was the son of Dr Francis Willis (1718-1807), the clergyman-physician who treated George III during his first attack of madness, are mistaken.

Willis attended Rugby and Charterhouse, from which he was expelled in 1809. Admitted to Gray's Inn on 4 November 1811, he was called to the Bar in 1816, and joined the northern circuit in 1817. He was admitted fellow commoner at Trinity Hall, Cambridge, on 28 November 1820. In 1816 he published *Digest of Rules and Practice as to Interrogatories for the Examination of Witnesses*, in 1820 *Pleadings in Equity illustrative of Lord Redesdale's Treatise on the Pleadings in Suits in Chancery by English Bill*, and in 1827 *Duties and Responsibilities of Trustees*.

In 1827 the British government planned to establish a court of equity for Upper Canada. Willis was nominated as the equity judge and in 1827 went with his family to take up his duties. He presented the warrant for his appointment to the lieut-governor, Sir Peregrine Maitland, in September 1827, but he met with opposition from the governor and his advisers and the legal profession, and was soon in conflict with the law officers. The chief justice of Upper Canada was away and Willis declined to sit *in banco*, declaring openly his judicial opinion, which was probably sound, that because of the language of the Act creating it, the court could not sit *in banco* in the absence of the chief justice. Invoking the Act, 22 Geo. III, c.75, the governor, without calling on Willis to show cause, amoved him from office. The House of Assembly of Upper Canada in 1829 voted an address to the King praying for Willis's reinstatement. Willis went to London to seek redress, and the Privy Council, without giving reasons, at first affirmed the amotion, but later reconsidered the matter, and the order amoving him was set aside on the ground that Willis had been entitled to a hearing before the order was made. In 1831 the secretary of state for the colonies declared, in respect of these events, that Willis's 'personal honour and integrity were free from reproach'. In 1831 he was appointed vice-president of the Court of Civil and Criminal Justice of British Guiana. He devoted himself with great energy and success to his duties. Though often at variance with his colleagues, he expected, on the retirement of Chief Justice Wray in November 1835, to be appointed to the vacancy, but was passed over. In February 1836 his health failed and he returned to England on furlough. As he was preparing to leave in 1837 to resume his duties at Demerara, West Indies, he was appointed a judge of the Supreme Court of New South Wales. He arrived in Sydney in February 1838.

His health was still poor, according to medical opinion, because of a 'functional derangement of the liver'. In a long letter to Sir George Gipps on 30 March 1839 he gave his version of his activities in Upper Canada and British Guiana, asserting unfair treatment by the British authorities in the matter of salary, allowances and expenses, and asking for 'fair consideration to a claim to reasonable retirement'. Gipps forwarded the letter to London, stating his fear that Mr Justice Willis's health rendered it improbable that he could long continue to perform efficiently the duties of the bench, but that, in view of the shortness of Willis's services in New South Wales, he would not recommend any portion of his retiring allowance to be charged to the revenue of the colony. Willis quarrelled with the chief justice, Sir James Dowling [q.v.] and, when it was decided to appoint a resident judge for the judicial district of Port Phillip, Gipps selected Willis, the purpose being to get him away from Sydney and thus end the friction with Dowling.

Willis arrived at Melbourne on 10 March 1841. His court-room was a small brick building at the south-west corner of Bourke and King Streets. The Supreme Court opened its sittings on 12 April 1841, and the resident judge was soon in conflict with the Bar and influential citizens. He refused to hear a solicitor who wore a moustache, and he rebuked a barrister who owned a stallion and advertised its services. When he cast doubts on the integrity of the Crown prosecutor because he had given an accommodation bill, the Bar walked out of court. He was in constant conflict with the *Port Phillip Gazette* and the *Herald*, and imposed severe punishment, later remitted, on George Arden [q.v.], the editor of the *Gazette*, for contempt of court. In a dispatch, 13 October 1842, Gipps expressed the opinion that Willis, because of an infirmity of temper, was unfit for 'the calm and dispassionate administration of justice', and stated that the town of Melbourne had been 'kept in a state of continued excitement by the proceedings of Mr Justice Willis and the extraordinary nature of the harangues he is in the habit of delivering from the Bench'. Gipps thought, too, that Willis had discreditably suppressed the truth concerning a loan made by him to John Pascoe Fawkner [q.v.], proprietor of the *Port Phillip Patriot*. In 1843 Willis ordered that a prominent citizen, J. B. Were [q.v.], be imprisoned for prevarication, adding a month at each protest by the witness, until the sentence, which was not served, was six months imprisonment. By this time Willis had incurred the enmity of powerful interests in Melbourne, and it is said that four different memorials, one bearing 523 names and endorsed by the superintendent, C. J. La Trobe, were sent to Gipps praying that Willis should be recalled. Gipps amoved Willis from office by an order dated 17 June 1843. As in Canada, Willis was given no hearing before the order was made. Willis first knew of it when on 24 June he was called from court and handed the order. The executive's action was not universally popular; the *Port Phillip Patriot* demanded that Judge Willis should not 'be sacrificed to gratify the despicable clique from whose tyranny His Honour had rescued the community', and resolutions of protest were adopted at a public meeting. More significantly, the *Gazette*, whose editor Willis had treated harshly, found reason to commend Willis, observing 'that schemes of villainy have been unravelled in his court, that intrigues and even plans of glaring depravity have been exposed by him . . . We like him the better that he has never administered one kind of justice to the rich and another kind to the poor'.

On his return to England Willis presented a petition to the Privy Council, and finally on 8 July 1846 a report was made stating there were sufficient grounds for amoving Willis, but that the governor and council ought to have given him some opportunity of being previously heard, and that the order of 17 June 1843 should be reversed. He was paid arrears of salary and costs amounting to a substantial sum, but he received no further judicial appointment. In 1850 he published *On the Government of British Colonies*, in which he propounded a completely unacceptable scheme of colonial government. He died in England on 10 September 1877.

Willis married twice. The first marriage, on 8 August 1824, to Mary Isabella, elder daughter of Thomas Bowes-Lyon, eleventh earl of Strathmore, was dissolved by Act of parliament in 1833. There was one child, Robert Bruce (1826-1897). On 15 September 1836 he married Ann Susanna Kent (d. 1891), the eldest daughter of Colonel Thomas Henry Bund; they had one son and two daughters.

Willis was an able lawyer, honest and fearless, and alert to prevent fraud and oppression, but he lacked the judicial temperament. Contentious and irascible, he could not work in harmony with the executive or with his colleagues, and once involved in a controversy his methods were often dubious. By the time he reached Australia his unfortunate personal limitations were aggravated by serious and chronic ill health. His temperament and outlook led inevitably to clashes with powerful sections which in his view were intent only on furthering their own interests. While the evidence of his cantanker-ousness and lack of judicial courtesy during his brief period in Melbourne is overwhelming, it must in fairness be said that often his censures were justified, and a contemporary historian, McCombie, took a not unfavourable view of his judicial activities. His notebooks during his Melbourne residence, which are in the possession of the Royal Historical Society of Victoria, reveal him to have been a diligent and competent lawyer.

HRA (1), 19-22; E. F. Moore, *Reports*, 5, 379; T. McCombie, *The history of the colony of Victoria* (Melb, 1858); J. L. Forde, *The story of the Bar of Victoria* (Melb, nd); R. Therry, *Reminiscences of thirty years' residence in New South Wales and Victoria*, 2nd ed (Lond, 1863); Garryowen (E. Finn), *Chronicles of early Melbourne*, 1-2 (Melb, 1888); G. B. Vasey, 'John Walpole Willis', *VHM*, 1 (1911).

JOHN V. BARRY

WILLIS, RICHARD (1777-1855), settler, was the second son of Joseph and Mary Willis of Kirkoswald, Cumberland, England. In 1800 he married Anne, who was born at St Kitts, West Indies, in 1780, the daughter of Thomas Harper of London. Said to have been a shoemaker, Willis lived in London before he migrated with his wife and eleven children. They arrived at Hobart Town in the *Courier* on 2 December 1823. Five children died in childhood (one during the voyage), and ten survived in 1836.

Lieut-Governor Sorell felt that Willis's unusually cordial letter from the Colonial Office, as well as his considerable assets and the size of his family, justified his ordering a reserve of 1000 acres in addition to the maximum grant of 2000 acres. Friends in England took some pains to acquaint the new lieut-governor, Arthur, with Willis's virtues; he had taken to the colony, they said, property worth between £5000 and £7000, and had an independent English income of £300 a year and the promise of a further £10,000 from friends, if needed. His other imports included a hundred pure merinos 'bred from the late King's stock', and stud horses and cattle. His connexions were of the highest respectability, his elder children well educated, he had 'prudence, enterprise, probity and talents', and the friendship of the duke of York.

Willis located his land north of Campbell Town, named it Wanstead after a village in Essex and in 1826 cited extensive improvements and the importation of breeding stock in his application for an extension of his grant. Arthur, taking into consideration also 'his extensive family,

& his conduct respecting Priest the bush-ranger', whom Willis had captured after his horse had been shot under him and his neck wounded by gunshot, gave him another 1000 acres. Two years later Willis applied for more land claiming that he was 'without a competitor in these districts' in improvements, having enclosed more than 1000 acres, put 150 acres into cultivation, just completed 'one of the best houses in the Colony, at an expense of upwards of £1000', and having more than 3000 sheep, 150 cattle and 'one of the most beautiful Stallions ever imported'; he had also purchased another 1800 acres. The Land Board remembered that 5000 acres had already been freely granted to him and considered that he should pay for any more, but they recommended that 1000 acres be given to his second son, Richard, now nearing 18.

In 1832 Willis had the services of thirty-five convicts. Of their uselessness he often complained and at the same time dwelt on his great contribution to the colony; he had been a magistrate since 1825. There is some evidence to suggest that Willis's assumptions of importance did not endear him to his fellow colonists; in 1826 there was a quarrel with Samuel Hill who, Willis asserted, insulted him on the bench. Ten years later, in a long correspondence arising from Frederick Forth's claim that Willis had insulted him as a magistrate, it was revealed that Willis had quarrelled with most of his neighbours. But he remained on excellent terms with Arthur, who appointed him to the Legislative Council, and with Lieut-Governor Franklin, who unsuccessfully recommended him to the Colonial Office for compensation for an alleged loss of land to one of his estranged neighbours, John Leake [q.v.]. Unpopularity may have been a factor in his decision to return to England, though the immediate reason was to present his case personally to the Colonial Office. He and his wife sailed in February 1839, leaving five sons in the colonies; Willis never returned. He died at Southsea on 4 March 1855.

Correspondence file under R. Willis (TA).

P. R. ELDERSHAW

WILLS, HORATIO SPENCER HOWE (1811-1861), pastoralist and politician, was born on 5 October 1811 in Sydney, the sixth child of Edward Spencer Wills and his wife Sarah, née Harding. His father was transported for life for highway robbery and arrived in Sydney in the *Hillsborough* in July 1799 accompanied by his wife and eldest child, Sarah. He appears to have been assigned to his wife and they were soon in business as general merchants and ship-chandlers at 96 George Street North, their premises abutting on Sydney Cove. He also owned several small trading vessels in partnership with Thomas Reibey, merchant. Wills was given an unconditional pardon in 1803 and a full pardon on 30 May 1809. He died on 14 May 1811.

On Horatio Wills's first birthday his mother married George Howe [q.v.], printer-editor of the *Sydney Gazette*, then being published at 96 George Street. Howe's fortunes were greatly changed by the trading and ship-owning business that Sarah Howe continued to conduct after her first husband's death. Social prestige came to her from the marriage of her eldest child Sarah to Dr William Redfern [q.v.], and of Elizabeth, her fourth child, to Major Henry Colden Antill [q.v.].

Wills's youth was spent on Sydney's waterfront. He had little formal education, and at 12 was employed in the *Gazette* office. His mother died on 8 July 1823, two years after George Howe. Soon afterwards young Wills was apprenticed to Robert Howe, who inherited the *Gazette* and the George Street premises from his father. Wills never liked the trade and quarrelled often with his stepbrother-master. A legend has him running away to sea, shipwrecked in the South Seas and rescued dramatically after living with islanders for two years; none of the dates mentioned accord with actual happenings in his early youth, although he did abscond from his apprenticeship at least three times for short periods. Once he shipped in a sealing vessel, the other times he was at the homes of his sisters, Mrs Redfern and Mrs Antill. Brought to court by Howe in 1827, Wills was defended by William Charles Wentworth [q.v.] and agreed to return to his master's service. His apprenticeship ended about the time of Robert Howe's death on 29 January 1829.

Although printer and publisher of the *Gazette* in 1832 Wills also edited, published and printed the *Currency Lad* from 25 August 1832. This four-page weekly journal, whose motto was 'Rise Australia', ceased after eighteen months, by which time Wills's connexion with the *Gazette* had ended.

Wills married Elizabeth McGuire, aged 16, at Parramatta on 2 December 1833. At first they lived at Varroville in the Minto district, then owned by his brother Thomas. From 1834 he held a pastoral lease in the Molonglo district. It was from this holding that Wills overlanded to the

Port Phillip District with 5000 sheep and 500 cattle. The journey began on 29 December 1839 and lasted four months. His wife and first child, Thomas Wentworth Wills, aged 2, were in the party, which included drovers, shepherds and Aboriginal stockmen. Wills's party wintered in 1840 near Mount William in the Grampians district; he noted in his diary some years later that he named a near-by hill, Mount Ararat, 'for here, like the Ark, we rested'. In December 1842 he took over a run of 120,000 acres, which he named Lexington. There he lived for ten years greatly improving the holding, experimenting with wheat, fencing some paddocks with netting that he ordered from England, importing Saxon sheep, and building a fine homestead. He sold Lexington with 28,000 sheep and 3000 cattle for £35,000 in November 1852, and for the next eight years lived on Belle Vue, at Point Henry near Geelong. He made this small property a model farm, and himself something of a country squire, taking active interest in church, agricultural, immigration and charitable movements.

Wills was elected to the Victorian Legislative Council on 10 January 1855, succeeding William Clarke Haines who had become colonial secretary. Next year with Haines he was elected for South Grant to the first Legislative Assembly of Victoria, one of its three native-born members. He made no mark in its deliberations, but actively canvassed land reform, exclusion of Chinese from the goldfields, defence and penal reform. When parliament was dissolved on 24 February 1859 he was in Germany where he placed his three younger sons at school. He did not seek re-election.

In 1860 Wills twice visited central Queensland seeking land. He took over the lease of four blocks, each of twenty-five square miles, from Peter Fitzalan Macdonald on the Nogoa River, 25 miles south-west of the later town of Emerald. The selection was named Cullinlaringo. In January 1861 Wills, his son Thomas, and a party of stockmen, shepherds, other servants and their families left Geelong by ship for Brisbane. The twenty-five men, women and children left Brisbane on 5 February 1861 in bullock wagons and drays with stores for a new station. Some stud rams had been brought from Geelong. Sheep, horses and cattle were bought along the track, mainly in the Darling Downs and Burnett districts. Sixteen weeks later the party reached Rockhampton with 10,500 sheep. Thence they moved slowly along the Dawson track, south of the Fitzroy River, to Cullinlaringo,

250 miles west. The expedition was one of the most lavishly equipped seen along the Dawson, and it attracted much attention from settlers, travellers and Aboriginals who became camp followers. Wills ignored warnings not to encourage them or to display supplies of food, clothing, blankets and other stores.

Cullinlaringo was reached in October 1861, eight months after leaving Brisbane. Immediately the building of stock yards, huts and store-rooms was started. A party of Aboriginals settled into a camp near by. Little attention was paid to them; they were friendly, seemed harmless, and had free run of the station. Wills and his people settled to a regular routine, with a rest after each midday meal. In the early afternoon of 17 October the peace of the station was broken by a woman's scream; Wills, resting in his tent, picked up a pistol and fired at an Aboriginal but was battered down with tomahawk and nulla-nulla. With tragic speed eighteen other people were killed. Only three men on the station escaped death. Thomas Wills and two stockmen were away from the station. It was the worst massacre of white men in the history of Australian pioneer settlement.

Wills's careless, lavish display of food, firearms, blankets and clothing had excited the greed of the Aboriginals. Study of the station habits made the raid an easy matter; it was not resisted because there was no preparation against attack. After the massacre the Aboriginals hastily plundered the stores, wagons, tents and huts, and hurried to the ranges. They were followed by a large party of police and settlers, trapped in a valley, and shot down. Few escaped this act of revenge. Wills and his people were buried in a grave at the scene of the massacre, which is remembered in a headstone.

Ironically, transfer of the Cullinlaringo leases was dated 18 October 1861, the day after the massacre. The leases remained with Wills's sons until 1877. Cedric, the second son, worked the property after his father's death and remained in the Peak Downs district all his life. Descendants are still there. Cullinlaringo was sold for £49,000 to the British Food Corporation in 1949 for grain-sorghum growing. The venture failed; later the property was cut up for closer settlement.

The eldest son, Thomas Wentworth Wills, was a noted cricketer at Rugby School, England, and in intercolonial matches for Victoria in the 1860s. Elizabeth Wills died in 1908. Amongst her memorials to her husband is a cottage in the Old Colonists' Homes, Melbourne.

T. F. Bride (ed), *Letters from Victorian pioneers* (Melb, 1898); J. T. S. Bird, *The early history of Rockhampton* (Rockhampton, 1904); R. V. Billis and A. S. Kenyon, *Pastoral pioneers of Port Phillip* (Melb, 1932); W. R. Brownhill, *History of Geelong and Corio Bay* (Melb, 1955); L. L. Banfield, *Like the ark: the story of Ararat* (Melb, 1955); Wills family papers (in private possession).

C. E. SAYERS

WILLSON, ROBERT WILLIAM (1794-1866), Catholic bishop, was born in Lincoln, England, the third son of William James Willson, builder, and his wife Clarissa, née Tenney. Of this marriage were born one daughter and five other sons, of whom Edward won distinction as an architect (*Gentleman's Magazine*, March 1855). Robert William, after some years at school, was placed at his own wish on a farm in Nottinghamshire, where he acquired habits of industry and a good knowledge of men and their ways. His experiences were of benefit in later pastoral visits to isolated stations in Van Diemen's Land.

In 1816 he went to Oscott College to study for the priesthood. Ordained on 16 December 1824, he went to Nottingham where he was pastor for eighteen years. His stay was marked by the building of two new churches, one, St Barnabas, later becoming the city cathedral, and by his notable work among prisoners and the insane. Not content with leading a movement to provide an asylum for mental patients, he got a licence to take some of them into his own home. Public and private tribute was paid to his work, one typical message recording: 'That the best thanks of the visiting governors of Nottingham Asylum be communicated to the Rev. R. W. Willson for his long continued and zealous services in behalf of this institution and his benevolent attention to its afflicted inmates'.

In 1842 Hobart Town was created a diocese separate from New South Wales. Willson was chosen as its chief pastor and consecrated at Birmingham on 28 October. With four missionaries chosen in England he arrived on 11 May 1844 to find two priests already in the island, churches at Richmond, Hobart and Launceston, and himself the ruler of a kingdom within a kingdom: a penal department and a body of free settlers. For the first ten years he gave his personal services almost exclusively to the penal abodes.

At this time the convict population was growing rapidly in Van Diemen's Land because other Australian colonies were closed to transported offenders. The bishop found as many as thirty-five stations used as temporary prisons for men sentenced to labour on public works. Norfolk Island, then administered from Hobart, and Port Arthur were set aside for those held in closer custody. For this section of his flock the bishop had to provide chaplains until 1853 when transportation ceased. While mindful of his spiritual mission he worked to improve social conditions, always advocating reform as the aim of penal discipline. In May 1846 Bishop Willson saw Norfolk Island for the first time. What he discovered had to be exposed, so he travelled to London at his own expense. Before a committee of the House of Lords he told a tragic story to men who, for the first time, came to realize the enormity of atrocities perpetrated under the British flag. Many of the evils were promptly remedied as a result of the prelate's intervention. To verify the reforms he visited Norfolk Island again in 1849. A marvellous change had taken place, but this time his suggestions for further improvements were ignored by officials, and Norfolk Island soon reached the lowest depths of its unsavoury history. When this news reached the bishop in March 1852 he promptly revisited the island. On his return he wrote to Bishop Davis [q.v.]: 'I am making a vigorous effort by letter of forty-eight pages to induce Her Majesty's Government to abandon Norfolk Island as soon as possible. They cannot resist the facts laid before them. I will not rest until it be done'. Convinced by the bishop's letter, Lieut-Governor Denison joined him in the appeals to the British government that helped to close the island prison in 1855.

In England the Nottingham priest had been a recognized leader in advocating humane treatment for the insane; in Tasmania he was a pioneer. Before his arrival a hospital for the insane had been set up at New Norfolk, its inmates mostly drawn from isolation cells at Port Arthur and Norfolk Island. When responsible government was granted in 1855 Willson joined the board of management. He pleaded, wrote and agitated without respite for a modern hospital in cheerful surroundings. He had chaplains appointed and secured useful reforms, although some of his suggestions had to wait until the training of social workers was recognized. The bishop's influence was soon felt far beyond his own diocese. Asked to inspect the proposed site of an asylum in Melbourne, he condemned it strongly. He urged the government to use extreme care in choosing a proper site, where with adequate comfort and humane treatment even the most desperate case might find relief. In New South Wales the Legislative Council ordered the printing of a long letter from Bishop Willson on conditions at Tarban Creek asylum. His services won attention from the *Journal of Mental Science*, 1863. He even urged Rome to introduce up-to-date methods in their houses of detention.

Bishop Willson's activity was not limited to social reform. As in other pioneer missions, his principal work was the building up of the church in a free community. Progress was impeded for some years by a sordid dispute with Father Therry [q.v.] over debts incurred before his appointment. The bishop was blamed for not settling the matter more speedily but in the end his terms had to be accepted by Therry. One urgent need was a division of his diocese into parishes with pastors in charge. The church had land grants in many centres, but small congregations were depressed by heavy debt. When the time came to say farewell to Tasmania, however, the bishop could rejoice that he was leaving to his successors a splendid cathedral, nineteen priests with their churches, four young men preparing for the ministry, several schools, and about 20,000 Catholics. In ill health the bishop left for England, prepared to resign his office. On board ship an attack of paralysis gave notice that the end was not far off. His last days were spent among friends at Nottingham, where he died on 30 June 1866. His tomb is in the Cathedral of St Barnabas.

Throughout his ministry Bishop Willson was deeply revered. In one of many letters to the Nottingham priest, Daniel O'Connell wrote: 'neither I nor Mrs O'Connell can find words to express our esteem or affectionate admiration of your gentle and most assiduous kindness. God, whose anointed priest you are, formed you with that clearness of intellect unobscured and unsubdued by all the more kindly elements of individual and general charity and practical benevolence which, almost without your knowing it, constitute your moral and social character and compel all (even those who most differ from you on the matters of the most awful importance) to respect and cherish the man'. A verdict on his later life was given by Thomas Arnold [q.v.], who, as inspector of Tasmanian schools, knew him well: 'Bishop Willson . . . was a man whom it was impossible to know and not to love'. With the clergy, the people and the government he always maintained the most cordial relations. He avoided sectional controversies which were a marked feature of his period. A display of temper was so rare as to cause surprise. Dr Ullathorne [q.v.] summed up his character thus: 'He was just in his thoughts, just in his judgements, and just in his actions: to which must be added an unaffected humility united with an elevated sense of what is honourable'.

Correspondence relative to St Joseph's Church, Hobart Town (Hob, 1850); T. Kelsh (comp), *'Personal recollections' of . . .Robert William Willson* (Hob, 1882); W. B. Ullathorne, *Memoir of Bishop Willson* (Lond, 1887); E. M. O'Brien, *Life and letters of Archpriest John Joseph Therry*, 1-2 (Syd, 1922); V & P (LA NSW), 1863-64, 4, p 833, 884; J. H. Cullen, 'Bishop Willson', *A'sian Catholic Record*, 26 (1949), 31 (1954); GO 1 & 33 (TA); CSO 24 (TA).

JOHN H. CULLEN

WILMOT; *see* EARDLEY-WILMOT

WILSHIRE, JAMES (1771-1840), public servant and manufacturer, was the second son and fifth child of William Wilshire, fellmonger, of Aylesbury, Buckinghamshire, England, and his wife Martha, née Thompson. He arrived at Sydney in the *Royal Admiral* in November 1800 recommended by John Palmer [q.v.] and was appointed to the Commissary Department. He served as clerk and store-keeper until March 1804 when he replaced W. N. Chapman [q.v.] as acting deputy-commissary. He held this office until about August 1806; his temporary reinstatement in September 1808 by Lieut-Governor Foveaux [q.v.] was later confirmed by Governor Macquarie at a salary of £91 5s. Posted to Windsor early in 1810, he asked to be appointed as a magistrate in compensation for removal from his 'large concern in the Tanning and soap making line' in Sydney. Macquarie agreed but Wilshire returned to Sydney after three months at Windsor and never sat on the bench. An order from the Commissary Department in England forbidding civil officers to conduct private business compelled him to resign in March 1812.

Soon after his arrival Wilshire acquired land at Lane Cove, which he increased to 245 acres in 1805. He obtained a further grant of 570 acres at Liberty Plains (Strathfield) in November 1808. Through the bankruptcy of his English agent in 1811 Wilshire suffered heavy losses and had to sell some of his land and cattle. In 1821 he petitioned Macquarie for more land to provide support for his young and increasing Family', and in October was given an additional 500 acres 'as a grazing farm'.

On retirement from government service he devoted more attention to his manufacturing interests. In 1803 Wilshire, said to have been 'bred to the business in England', had established a tannery on Brickfield Hill which became the largest in the colony, and its operations continued until 1861. It employed between twenty and thirty hands in the 1820s, and produced all types of leather as well as soap, candles, glue and parchment. In 1815 and 1817 with Simeon Lord [q.v.] Wilshire petitioned the governor in vain for some protection for the leather industry. In 1826 he opened a slaughtering and victualling house at his wharf in Darling Harbour. By 1830 he was treating some 15,000 hides and skins a year at his tannery and was producing enough leather for the colony's needs, with a surplus of green hides for export to England.

Wilshire appears to have been well respected and a supporter of established authority. With many 'free and principal proprietors of landed property' he signed an address in support of Governor Bligh on 1 January 1808, and was named as one of Bligh's original fifteen witnesses for the trial of Colonel Johnston [q.v.] though he did not go to England for the court martial in 1811. He was also a signatory to the address in support of Governor Darling in July 1829.

In February 1805 he married Esther (1775-1836), daughter of Robert Pitt; she had come free to the colony in 1801, and through her mother, Mary Matcham, was a connexion of Lord Nelson. By this marriage there were six sons and five daughters, of whom two died young and the others survived Wilshire. His wife predeceased him in May 1836. On his death in Sydney in September 1840 his manufacturing interests were taken over by his sons James Robert (1809-1860) and Austin Forrest 1811-1889). James Robert Wilshire became the second mayor of Sydney in 1844 and was a member of the New South Wales Legislative Council in 1855-56 and 1858-61 and the Legislative Assembly in 1856-57. The eldest son of James Wilshire, William Pitt (1807-1889), married a sister of Sir John Robertson and achieved some success as an artist.

HRA (1) 4-7, 10, 14, 15; V & P (LA NSW), 1862, 5, p 1158, 1865, 2, p 829; Sydney Gazette, 5 May 1804, 28 Mar 1812, 1 Feb 1826, 10 Sept 1840; Wilshire papers (ML).

G. P. WALSH

WILSON, HENRY CROASDAILE (fl. 1832-1841), barrack master and police magistrate, was a colonel in the army of one of the South American republics before coming to Australia. Through the influence of his relation, Lord Althorp, he was appointed barrack master at Sydney in 1832, but Howick asked Governor Bourke to give him a more lucrative position if a suitable one became available. In 1833 Bourke nominated him first police magistrate in place of Captain F. N. Rossi [q.v.], who had been granted leave and retired in 1834 without resuming his duties. The secretary of state formally appointed Wilson.

It was his duty under the terms of the Act, 4 Wm IV, no 7 NSW, to reorganize the Sydney police on similar lines to the London Metropolitan police. Bourke's intention in introducing this new organization was to separate the judicial and executive functions of the police, thus relieving Wilson of magisterial duties so that he could devote his whole time to the recruitment, training, inspection and executive direction of the police. This plan did not work because of the ever increasing number of cases brought before the Sydney bench, although in other ways, such as the introduction of the beat system, Wilson was able to make the Sydney police organization something like that of London. Governors Bourke and Gipps credited him with reducing the inefficiency of the Sydney police.

Unfortunately Wilson had an irascible temperament and made many enemies in the small colonial society. Gipps twice found it necessary to inquire into violent quarrels between him and other officials. In 1838 Wilson faced charges of misconduct with a female convict, but the Executive Council did not take a very serious view of the matter. In December 1839, however, charges were proved that he had employed policemen to assist in building his home and as liveried domestic servants. Wilson's explanation, that he needed police for his personal protection and that the livery was a disguise, was found unsatisfactory; Wilson was suspended from duty and formally removed from office in July 1840.

In June Wilson, who claimed ownership of some 10,000 acres of land in New Zealand, had been associated with W. C. Wentworth [q.v.] and others in an unsuccessful protest against a bill to empower the governor to appoint commissioners to examine land claims in New Zealand.

On 11 March 1841, at a general meeting of the Australian Club, Wilson was defeated by Major Christie in an election for the office of secretary-treasurer. On 24 March the first of a series of anonymous articles appeared in the Free Press casting aspersions on the committee and secretary for alleged mismanagement of the club's affairs. One article, on 5 May, ended with a Latin tag which Christie interpreted as a reflection on the honour of his wife. Finding that the anonymous author was Wilson, Christie horsewhipped him; a duel threatened, but Wilson could not find a second and Christie was bound over to keep the peace. Wilson, who admitted authorship of the article but denied any intention of referring to Mrs Christie, took action in the Supreme Court against Christie for assault and was awarded £150 damages. On 16 June a general meeting of club members resolved that he be asked to resign.

HRA (1), 17-20; V & P (LC NSW), 1835, 1840; H. King, 'Some aspects of police administration in NSW, 1825-51', JRAHS, 42 (1956-57); Sydney Herald, 18 May, 8 Oct 1835, 26 Mar 1838, 18 June 1841; Free Press, 24, 31 Mar, 3, 14, 24 Apr, 5 May, 16 June 1841; H. King, Police organization and administration . . . NSW 1825-51 (M.A. thesis, Univ Syd, 1956); CO 201/233, 236, 289, 202/27; MS cat under H. C. Wilson (ML).

HAZEL KING

WILSON, JOHN (d. 1800), wild white man and explorer, was convicted in October 1785, at Wigan, Lancashire, England, of having stolen 'nine yards of cotton cloth called velveret, of the value of tenpence', and sentenced to transportation for seven years. He reached Port Jackson in the *Alexander* with the First Fleet in January 1788.

Soon after his term expired Wilson, who had formerly been a mariner, took to the bush and lived with Aboriginals, possibly at intervals, for several years. He may have been, as David Collins said, 'a wild, idle young man who preferred living among the natives to earning the wages of honest industry'; but in so doing he lived 'the hard way', and in his wanderings he acquired an extensive knowledge of much of the country within about 100 miles of Sydney. He established good relations with the Aboriginals, to whom he was 'Bun-bo-e', and so definitely did he become a member of a particular band that his body, clad only in a kangaroo skin, was heavily scarred by tribal markings. In 1795 Wilson accompanied Charles Grimes [q.v.] to Port Stephens, and there he possibly saved his leader's life by wounding a native who was about to hurl a spear. He became a 'vagabond of the woods' again soon afterwards, was declared an outlaw in May 1797, but in November returned to the settlement.

In January 1798 when a number of Irish prisoners were becoming restless in their anxiety to escape and to seek what they believed to be a 'New World' of white people situated about 200 miles south-west of Sydney, Governor Hunter, in order to 'save worthless lives', sent off four of them under an armed guard and with Wilson as guide to see what could be found. The Irishmen soon grew tired of the enterprise and returned with the soldiers to Port Jackson, but Wilson and two companions pushed on into unknown country. Through a misprint in historical records it was long supposed that one of Wilson's two colleagues was named 'Barracks', but he was in fact John Price, aged 19, who had come to Australia as Hunter's servant. Price kept a journal of the expedition, and this record, given by Hunter to Sir Joseph Banks [q.v.] and later acquired by the Mitchell Library, indicates that the three explorers reached the Wingecarribee River, more than 100 miles south-west of Parramatta, endured severe privations and were saved only by Wilson's bushcraft. The diary contains the first record of the shooting of a lyrebird, taken by Price on 26 January 1798, and the first written reference, on the same day, to the existence of the 'cullawine' (koala).

Soon afterwards Hunter sent Wilson and two other men into the same country, and this time the expedition reached Mount Towrang, near the present Goulburn. Those two journeys, which revealed the nature of much of the rich southern tablelands of New South Wales, represented Wilson's last useful service. He reverted to a wild life again in 1799 and next year he was killed by an angry Aboriginal when he attempted to take a young woman of the tribe, against her will, for his 'exclusive accommodation'.

HRNSW, 3; D. Collins, An account of the English colony in New South Wales, 2 (Lond, 1802); A. H. Chisholm, The romance of the lyrebird (Syd, 1960); R. H. Cambage, 'Exploration beyond the upper Nepean in 1798', JRAHS, 6 (1920).

A. H. CHISHOLM

WILSON, JOHN THOMAS (fl. 1834-1840), confidence man, was said to have been born in Birmingham, England, with the name of James Abbot, the son of a journeyman sailmaker. Legend has it that when young he eloped with and married a rich young noblewoman and that when her disgusted family cut her off without a penny Wilson deserted his creditors and his wife, leaving several children to her care, and taking all the money he had earned as an auctioneer in an English country town. He is next supposed to have appeared under the name of John Thomas Soanes as an auctioneer in Boston, America, where he 'succeeded in fleecing the Yankees to a considerable amount'. At the Cape of Good Hope he was recognized and forced to flee to Hobart Town under another name, ostentatiously taking several suitcases which were packed only with stones. According to one account he was a barman in Hobart for several months and then went to Sydney where, as Wilson, he was employed by Lancelot Iredale, ironmonger. However, his behaviour towards one of Iredale's daughters caused his dismissal and he next appeared as a clerk to C. & F. Wilson, merchants of George Street, Sydney, where he reputedly ruined the life and fortune of another rich damsel. He then formed a partnership with John S. Uther and bought a large ironmongery in Sydney but soon dissolved the partnership and took sole possession. Wilson now entered a period of great prosperity: business flourished, he was prominent in many religious, philanthropic and literary organizations in Sydney, and among the managers of joint-stock companies. From February 1834 he owned the steamer *Tamar* which traded on the Hunter River, and another steamer on the run to Parramatta He was also secretary and then treasurer of the Australian Steam Conveyance Co.; in 1835 he was elected treasurer of the Australian Union Benefit Society, and stood as a candidate for the board of the Bank of Australia. In April 1836 he was elected a director of the Australian Gaslight Co., but in August he sold his business to Thomas Burdekin and on 11 November bolted from Sydney in the *Lord Goderich*. His flight was prompted by J. D. Lang's [q.v.] attack in the *Colonist* on him and Mrs Taylor, the actress-wife of a Customs officer. His creditors suffered heavy losses, one alone being reputed to have lost £36,000. Wilson was also said to have talked his way out of paying his fare to England.

On arrival in England Wilson was met by a bailiff and given the choice of gaol or returning to Sydney, and so in January 1838 he sailed in the *Duchess of Kent* for Sydney. There A. Polack, an auctioneer, employed him and went security for him for six months. Under Wilson business began to flourish. In October 1839 he bought the *Nereus* and refitted her on credit, then bolted again leaving pregnant the wife of a convict and debts of over £25,000. His creditors formed a committee which with

remarkable inefficiency brought the matter before the Supreme Court and hired the *Rover's Bride* to search for him. Wilson was never seen again in New South Wales and reports placed him variously in New Zealand, America, Valparaiso and the Solomon Islands. He was also said to have caused the suicide of the captain of the *Nereus* by seducing his wife. In October 1840 it was reported that he was 'cut by all hands' at Manila and had escaped to Singapore in a Hamburg brig.

Wilson's activities aroused wide public interest and long articles appeared in the Sydney press, most of which were in a light vein with no sympathy for Wilson's gullible dupes or for the stupid actions of the self-constituted committee of his creditors who wasted money in useless searches for the swindler.

Newspaper indexes under J. T. Wilson (ML).

A. F. PIKE

WILSON, THOMAS (1787-1863), solicitor and author, was born on 5 September 1787, and was related to the naturalist Alfred Russel Wallace. Educated in Germany, he acquired several modern languages and a knowledge of fine arts and music. Returning to England, he was articled to Bartlett & Beddome. With Wilson & Curtis he was later associated professionally with the building of the Portman market. He bought a country estate in Radnorshire, Wales, and gave evidence before the 1829-32 Royal Commission on the law of real property. He published anonymously A *Descriptive Catalogue of the Prints of Rembrandt* in 1836. Many of his engravings and prints, collected on the Continent, are in the British Museum.

In 1837 Wilson decided to emigrate. With some of his family he sailed in the *Duke of Roxburgh* and arrived in Adelaide in July 1838. He soon built an extensive and highly respectable practice, and for many years was a member of the firm of Smart & Wilson. In 1841 Governor Grey appointed him clerk of the Court of Appeals. He designed the official seal of the Municipal Corporation of Adelaide to which he was elected when it was constituted in 1840; he was elected alderman next year and mayor in 1842.

Wilson soon became equally popular for his literary and artistic attainments, and for his scientific interest in natural history. The *South Australian Magazine* published his lectures on engraving in 1843 and on English painting. He also contributed short translations from Anacreon and other authors to the *South Australian Odd Fellows' Magazine*. He lectured again on engraving to the Mechanics' Institute in 1847, and his lecture to the North Adelaide Institute on eminent female artists was published in 1854. His poems *The Feast of Belshazzar, The Lonely Man of the Ocean*, and *Boyuca; or the Fountain of Youth*, were published in Adelaide in 1856. According to the *South Australian Magazine*, November 1841, 'No man seems to possess more of the attribute of ubiquity than Mr. Wilson. Visit whatever part of Adelaide you may, during the hours of business, there you are sure to meet with him . . . he is blessed with a pair of such singularly active legs, as seemingly to annihilate distance and space, his presence in chambers, in the council room, in his own offices, and at the extremities of the city being apparently coeval in point of time'.

Wilson died on 31 March 1863 at Kensington, South Australia, predeceased by his wife Martha, née Grenell. He was survived by three daughters and five sons, of whom Charles Algernon was an amateur naturalist and became registrar of probates in 1858, and Rev. Theodore Percival was the first headmaster of the Collegiate School of St Peter. A portrait of Thomas Wilson is at the Adelaide Town Hall.

T. Worsnop, *History of the city of Adelaide* (Adel, 1878).

WILSON, THOMAS BRAIDWOOD (1792-1843), medical practitioner and settler, was born on 30 April 1792 at Uphall, West Lothian, Scotland, son of James and Katharine Wilson. He became a surgeon in the navy in 1815 and later served as surgeon-superintendent on several convict transports bound for New South Wales and Van Diemen's Land. He had great success in preserving the lives of convicts under his care by insisting on cleanliness and a daily issue of lime juice and wine. He taught convicts how to read and write, conducted divine service and would not permit 'the slightest slang, flash songs nor swearing', for fear of further personal degradation.

He arrived at Sydney in the *Richmond*, in May 1822, on his first voyage and was aboard when she was later wrecked in Torres Strait. His next voyages were in the *Prince Regent* in 1824 and the *Mangles* in 1826. In that year he married Jane Thompson at Durham; a daughter Mary

was born in 1827. In 1829 he was in the *Governor Ready* on her return voyage when he was again shipwrecked in Torres Strait and with some of the crew rowed 1000 miles to Timor. He left Timor in the *Amity* which then sailed to the Swan River, where he saw Perth as a straggling tented town and observed that Fremantle was so sandy that it could be run through an hour-glass. With Captain Collet Barker [q.v.] he explored inland from King George Sound; Wilson's Inlet is named after him. On another voyage he arrived in Hobart Town in the *John* in 1831, bringing with him many European plants and the first hive of bees to survive in Australia.

In 1822 Wilson had been granted land which he selected on the Macquarie River, Van Diemen's Land, and named Janefield. In 1826 he was allowed to transfer this grant to New South Wales, where he was also given 5000 acres for his explorations in 'the western part of New Holland'. Part of the land chosen by him he called Braidwood, and his original grant was moved a mile to the east when government surveyors decided that his first choice was the best site for a township. Wilson acquired more land by purchase and lease; he also bought stock and left them with a manager. In London in 1835 he published *Narrative of a Voyage round the World*, giving an account of his adventures and commenting on the manners and customs of the Aboriginal tribes with whom he had been on good terms and whose high death rate from European diseases caused him deep concern. In the appendix he commented on the treatment of prisoners in convict transports and praised Australia as a place for intending migrants.

Wilson brought his wife, daughter and son to New South Wales in 1836, his eighth voyage to Australia. They settled at Braidwood, where Wilson won repute for the management of his farm and for his efficiency as a magistrate. He also served on many local committees and took a leading part in the affairs of his district. His wife died on 29 January 1838. In the depression of the early 1840s his health rapidly declined. He became bankrupt in October 1843 and died on 11 November. He was buried on a hill-top overlooking the town of Braidwood.

HRA (1), 17; Agnes Hogg, *Back to Braidwood celebrations* (Syd, 1925); M. Uren, *Land looking west* (Lond, 1948); Newspaper indexes under T. B. Wilson (ML); Mowle papers (ML); Rawson papers (NL).

GWENDOLINE WILSON

WILTON, CHARLES PLEYDELL NEALE

WILTON, CHARLES PLEYDELL NEALE (1795-1859), Church of England chaplain, was born at Stow, Gloucestershire, England, the son of Rev. William Wilton and his wife Charlotte, née Jelf. He was educated at St John's College, Cambridge (B.A., 1817; M.A., 1827), and ordained by the bishop of Gloucester in December 1820. Appointed chaplain for New South Wales in October 1826, he sailed from London with his wife Elizabeth in the *Elizabeth* and arrived in Sydney in April 1827.

Wilton became incumbent of the parish of the Field of Mars and Castle Hill and master of the Female Orphan School at Parramatta, receiving £250 as chaplain, £150 as master, and a house. His wife was the matron and after her health broke down she had to be replaced, but Wilton still claimed her salary. He soon had other quarrels with his superior, Archdeacon Scott [q.v.], over his duties and his connexions with Frederick Wright Unwin, a solicitor and fellow passenger who, as temporary accountant of the trustees of the Church and School Corporation, was thought by Scott to have connived with Wilton in dubious transactions of more than £1000. The charges proved baseless but Wilton resigned his appointments in December 1828 and talked of returning to England. He applied instead for the chaplaincy at Newcastle and was appointed in 1831, the third and last of its chaplains.

At Newcastle Wilton regularly visited the primary school and conducted services at Christ Church, in the gaol and in the general hospital, where he was also a vigorous president of the committee. Although he owned a farm and orchard on Moscheto Island in the Hunter River and personally supervised his assigned convict servants, he was prompt and energetic in his parochial duties. His earliest tour extended as far as Muswellbrook, and he later visited different parts of the Hunter River each month until Rev. G. B. Rusden was appointed at Maitland in 1834 and parishes were formed at Hexham and Raymond Terrace in 1839. Wilton shared actively in forming the Newcastle Church Society in April 1851, and was one of the four senior Hunter River clergymen who helped Bishop Tyrrell in planning a diocesan synod and in drafting a petition to the Queen for an inquiry into the constitution of the Church of England in Australia.

To all his clerical duties Wilton added a lively and versatile concern for the spiritual and intellectual needs of the colonists. He was a fellow of the Cambridge Philosophical Society and of the Ashmolean Society of Oxford, and a corresponding member of the Tasmanian Society. In 1828 he founded and edited the *Australian Quarterly Journal of Theology, Literature and Science*, of which four numbers were published. Through his efforts a Mechanics' Institute was started in June 1835 in a room in King Street, Newcastle; its later home in Watt Street stood for over a century and, when demolished, revealed beneath its foundation stone a copper plate with Wilton's name as president. His lectures and publications ranged from burning mountains to education, from agriculture to sea snakes, from Aboriginals to encrinites, without losing sight of simple eternal verities.

Elizabeth Wilton died at Newcastle on 21 December 1836, aged 39, predeceased by two children. On 14 October 1839 Wilton married Charlotte Albinia, eldest daughter of Benjamin Sullivan, police magistrate at Raymond Terrace. To the end, a conscientious churchman and active in encouraging science, Wilton died on 5 June 1859 at Newcastle. He was survived by his widow, a son and a daughter.

HRA (1), 14-16, 18; R. G. Boodle, *The life and labours of the Right Rev. William Tyrrell* (Lond, 1881); E. C. Rowland, *A century of the English Church in New South Wales* (Syd, 1948); G. H. Nadel, *Australia's colonial culture* (Melb, 1957); A. P. Elkin, 'Some early chaplains and churches in the Hunter River valley', JRAHS, 23 (1937).

HERBERT MARSHALL

WINDER, THOMAS WHITE MELVILLE

WINDER, THOMAS WHITE MELVILLE (1789?-1853), merchant and farmer, was born in London and became a sea captain. He traded for some years in the East and West Indies, but ill health forced him to retire and he decided to settle in New South Wales. He arrived at Port Jackson in 1817 in the *Frederick*. Governor Macquarie granted him permissive occupancy of an allotment in Bligh Street, and there he opened a store. From May 1819 to March 1820 he visited Calcutta and in August, with Samuel Terry [q.v.], established the Lachlan Flour Mills at Kensington. In 1821 he and Terry entered into partnership with William Hutchinson, Daniel Cooper [qq.v.], George Williams and William Laverton and renamed the mill the Lachlan and Waterloo Flour Mills. In October 1821 he told Macquarie that his property amounted to more than £7000 and sought a grant of land. Macquarie granted him 700 acres, which he took up on the Hunter River. In 1823 Winder was exporting cedar from this estate before he withdrew from his commercial partnership. He also claimed to have secured with his Hunter River grant a ten year monopoly of all coal won from the Newcastle penal settlement, apart from that required for government use. In February 1826 Governor Darling complained to the Colonial Office that this agreement was highly inconvenient to the inhabitants of Newcastle, although Winder had received only 600 of the 2000 tons specified in the agreement. The Colonial Office admitted that a lease had been proposed but denied the existence of any formal agreement. Thereupon Darling discontinued Winder's monopoly, for in the meantime a monopoly of coal-mining round Newcastle had been granted to the Australian Agricultural Co. by the British government.

In 1824-25 Winder acquired some 4000 acres near Lochinvar and named his estate Windermere. Like other settlers on the Hunter Winder had trouble with Aboriginals who threatened his crops and livestock, but he still managed to become a substantial pastoralist and wheat-grower. He had foreseen the need of regular shipping between the Hunter and Sydney: in October 1824 with a partner he bought the packet *Lord Liverpool*, and soon acquired the schooner *Jessica* and the hulk *St Michael*. All three were sold in May 1828 when he employed convict labour to build the 90-ton *Currency Lass*.

As one of the largest proprietors on the Hunter Winder held 7400 acres by 1828 and by 1831 had acquired another 2600 acres. In 1836 W. C. Wentworth [q.v.] tried to buy the estate but the sale fell through and Winder leased the land and returned to Sydney. After a trip abroad he returned to Maitland and in the early 1840s, in partnership with Wentworth and Charles Nott, he opened a successful boiling-down establishment at Windermere. In 1851 he sold the estate to Nott and returned to Sydney. Winder died on 30 September 1853. About 1819 he had married Ellen Johnson; they had nine children.

Winder was typical of the enterprising settler who made good in the early years of New South Wales. Like many of his contemporaries he blended his landed interests with varied commercial affairs. Although he shunned activity in politics his signature on many petitions indicated his interest in local movements. He played a major role in the development of the northern shipping trade, which proved extremely beneficial to settlers of the surrounding districts, and was the first to enjoy a monopoly of coal mined in the Newcastle district.

HRA (1), 10-12; J. F. Campbell, 'The genesis of rural settlement in the Hunter', *JRAHS*, 12 (1927); E. S. Lauchland, 'Windermere', *Newcastle and Hunter District Hist Soc, Procs*, 3 (1949); *Sydney Gazette*, 13 Feb 1823, 14 Oct 1824, 16 May, 29 Sept 1828; *Maitland Mercury*, 5 Oct 1853.

ELIZABETH GUILFORD

WINDEYER, ARCHIBALD (1785-1870), landowner and pastoralist, was born on 7 November 1785 in England, the son of Walter Windeyer and younger brother of Charles Windeyer [q.v.]. As a youth he entered the service of the Board of Ordnance and by 1816 he was clerk of works in the Royal Engineers Department of the ordnance depot at Purfleet, where he had a salary of £91 5s., an allowance of a further £92, a house and prospects of advancement. He was later promoted and moved to the depot at Devonport. He retired after thirty years service.

His brother John, a retired purser in the navy, had emigrated to New South Wales in 1835 and died soon after arrival. Windeyer also planned to emigrate, and through his brother Charles bought a property of some 1000 acres on the upper Williams River. With his wife Elizabeth, née Orton, whom he had married in 1819, and eight children he arrived at Sydney in the *James Pattison* in December 1838. He bought Kinross near Raymond Terrace, where in 1840 he made his home and became a successful wine-grower. Some of his sons were active in pioneering enterprises in the 1840s and 1850s. Among their properties were Deepwater in New England, which they took up and named in 1839, and Wantabadgery in the Riverina. One son, Thomas Mark, went further afield and was one of the first settlers on the Dawson River in Queensland.

Windeyer was a God-fearing man of strong character, devoted to his family. He died at Kinross on 19 October 1870, survived by his wife. Several of his children married members of well-known pastoral families, Cadell, Traill, Irby, Macansh. A grandson John Cadell Windeyer (1875-1951) became a professor of obstetrics in the University of Sydney.

E. Irby, *Memoirs of Edward and Leonard Irby* (Syd, 1908); Ordnance records (PRO); A. Windeyer, Journal (in author's possession).

J. B. WINDEYER

WINDEYER, CHARLES (1780-1855), magistrate, was born on 1 July 1780 in Staffordshire, England, the son of Walter

Windeyer (1751-1801) and grandson of John Windeyer (1714-1794) who had left Switzerland, and married and settled in England about 1735. After some training in law he became a journalist and publisher. From 1815 to 1819 he was publisher and proprietor of the weekly *Law Chronicle and Estate Advertiser*, and later a parliamentary reporter for *The Times*. In 1825 he was chosen for the staff of the *Representative*. It soon ceased publication and the outlook became dreary for Windeyer who, by his marriage in London on 8 August 1805 to Ann Mary Rudd of Rochester, now had ten children. His thoughts turned to New South Wales where his friend James Dowling [q.v.] had been appointed a judge, and the opportunity of taking up land was attractive.

Leaving his eldest son Richard [q.v.] in England, Windeyer sailed in the *Sarah* with his wife and other children, arriving at Sydney in July 1828. His capital was sufficient to entitle him to a maximum grant of 2560 acres which he located on the upper Williams River opposite Dowling's grant. This property, Tilligra, was worked by one of his sons. Windeyer himself had to find employment in Sydney to maintain his family. His appointment as chief clerk to the bench of magistrates in September 1828 was grudgingly confirmed by the Colonial Office intent on economy. But Governor Darling was desperately in need of respectable officers, especially those with legal knowledge. Windeyer was soon acting as chief clerk of the police and in October 1830 was promoted assistant superintendent of police. In August 1833 he applied for appointment as principal superintendent of police in place of F. N. Rossi [q.v.] who was about to retire, but Governor Bourke reported, 'I do not think he would succeed in the organization or command of a Police Force, for which his previous habits have in no respect qualified him . . . it will be more for the good of the service to leave Mr Windeyer on the Bench'. He was therefore appointed second police magistrate for the town and port of Sydney at a salary of £400, sitting regularly either in the George Street Police Court or, when dealing with convict offenders, in the Hyde Park Barracks. In 1839 he became officially known as senior police magistrate.

His knowledge of law was competent and he applied it with common sense. Educated, painstaking and kindly, he won general respect. In October 1832 he approved Bourke's policy on the jurisdiction of unpaid magistrates over convict servants, but those who disapproved and thought that discipline could only be maintained by ruthless use of the lash complained of Windeyer's leniency. In March 1834, when he awarded only eighteen lashes to a man who had wilfully destroyed two blankets, the *Monitor* violently criticized him and claimed that fifty lashes were deserved. In these and other disputes Windeyer's refusal to be overborne was resentfully attacked by James Mudie [q.v.] in *The Felonry of New South Wales* (London, 1837). Windeyer bore criticisms and disappointments without bitterness. His only direct incursion into politics was in 1843 when he stood for election to the Legislative Council but was defeated by Alexander McLeay [q.v.].

In addition to his other duties Windeyer was from 1837 a commissioner for examining claims for crown lands, and often served on other official inquiries. In 1842, when Sydney was incorporated as a city, he was appointed its first mayor, filling the office until the first city council was elected. In March 1848 he retired from the bench with a pension of £180. With other members of the family he also had pastoral interests, but these were lost when his son Richard's financial affairs collapsed in 1848. After the gold discoveries, however, he was granted an increase in his pension. He died at Newtown on 30 January 1855, survived by his wife, ten children and numerous grandchildren. Mount Windeyer near Dungog was named after him. A small portrait is in the Mitchell Library and others are in the possession of his descendants.

HRA (1), 14-18; J. Wade, *British history, chronologically arranged* (Lond, 1839); Windeyer family papers (in the possession of Sir Victor Windeyer, Syd).   J. B. WINDEYER

WINDEYER, RICHARD (1806-1847), journalist, barrister, agriculturist and politician, was born on 10 August 1806 in London, the eldest child of Charles Windeyer [q.v.] and his wife Ann Mary, née Rudd. He remained in England when in 1828 his parents with the rest of their family migrated to New South Wales. He was admitted as a student in the Middle Temple in March 1829 and called to the Bar on 23 May 1834. In the meantime, as a journalist and parliamentary reporter, he was connected with the *Morning Chronicle*, the *Sun* and the *Mirror of Parliament*, and in 1834 was London correspondent for the *Australian*, using the initials 'W.R.'. He assisted Dodd in compiling the *Parliamentary Pocket Companion*, and was associated with Colonel Perronet Thompson in the early anti-Corn Law movement. On 26 April 1832 he married Maria, daughter of

William Camfield of Groombridge Place and Burswood, Kent. Their only child, William Charles, was born on 29 September 1834. Although he always intended to follow his parents and their family to Sydney, Windeyer's departure from England was hastened by a letter from his father, saying that Dr Wardell's [q.v.] death and 'Wentworth's [q.v.] expected departure . . . and the division of the Bar . . . makes the moment particularly favourable for your debut'. He set out with his wife and infant son, arriving at Sydney on 28 November 1835.

Windeyer soon gained a considerable practice. Even J. D. Lang [q.v.] described him as 'a barrister of superior abilities'; and of his closing speech in the case of the *Bank of Australasia* v. *Breillat* in 1845, the *Herald* said, 'For learned research, and subtle reasoning, and adroit use of circumstance, and occasional bursts of true eloquence, and powerful appeal to the understandings of the Jury . . . we have no hesitation in believing that at that bar it had never been surpassed'. In July 1846 Windeyer and Robert Lowe [q.v.] appeared for the defendant in *Attorney-General* v. *Brown*, concerning the right of the Crown to grant the Australian Agricultural Co. the sole right to mine coal near Newcastle. The arguments for the defendants failed, but enabled Windeyer to array much legal and historical learning in support of the political view that the lands of the colony should be in the control of the colonists, not in the grant of the crown. However, he spent Christmas 1846 in Darlinghurst gaol, for he and Darvall, the opposing counsel, had almost come to blows during the hearing of a case before the chief justice, Sir Alfred Stephen, who therefore committed them both for contempt of court. The matter rankled with Windeyer until his death.

Windeyer's legal work was only a small part of his activities in the colony. In February 1838 he bought his first land in the Hunter valley, and by 1842 he held about 30,000 acres. Vast sums of money were spent, especially on draining extensive swamp lands in the vicinity of Graham's Town, building a homestead at Tomago and on other improvements, but with little return. He planted thirty acres of vines, imported a German vine-dresser from Adelaide, made his first wine in 1845, and received permission to import seven vine-dressers and one wine-cooper from Europe. He ran cattle, horses and pigs, tried growing sugar-cane and wheat, and in 1846 with Reynolds, president of the local agricultural society, he imported the colony's first reaping machine from South Australia. Despite all his expensive improvements and mechanized farming the one prize he won was for pumpkins. However, after his death wine from Tomago won a certificate of merit at Paris in 1855.

In 1842 Windeyer was present at the meeting at Sydney College at which petitions for representative government in the colony were adopted. In 1843 at the first elections for the Legislative Council he stood for Durham County against Andrew Lang and Ogilvie and polled 122 votes to Ogilvie's 77 and Lang's 55. Windeyer at once took a prominent part in the affairs of the council. In 1843 he introduced his monetary confidence bill. Believing that the current depression was aggravated by a decrease of currency in circulation, and a lack of confidence and credit, he proposed a solution based on the Prussian *Pfand-brief* scheme as outlined by Thomas Holt before a select committee: the government was to give credit in the form of pledge certificates, or *Pfandbriefe*, on the security of land. The bill passed the council, but Governor Gipps withheld his assent. Windeyer's main interest in economic matters was directed at effective supervision and control by the council of revenue and expenditure. He worked so persistently for retrenchment that Lang described him as 'the Joseph Hume of the Council'. As a believer in free trade and the representative of an agricultural county, Windeyer worked to open the Van Diemen's Land market to tobacco from New South Wales and the United Kingdom market to the colony's wheat. In the debate on the tariff bill of 1843, however, he voted for an import duty of 1s. a bushel on foreign wheat but explained that he considered it a revenue not a protective duty.

Always interested in education, Windeyer set up a school on his estate, was on the committees of the Sydney Mechanics' School of Arts and the Australian School Society, and prominent in the education debates. Although a member of the Church of England he favoured a National school system, but in 1844 when its introduction was discussed he proposed an amendment to provide primary education for the poor, 'gratuitously if necessary', and to permit denominational schools to receive government aid in some circumstances.

From his youth Windeyer had been interested in law reform, and in 1844 he introduced a bill to amend the jury laws of New South Wales. Trial by assessors was to be replaced by trial by a jury of four special jurors, with a decision by a majority of three to be acceptable if unanimity were not reached after six hours. His model was an Act that Alfred Stephen had introduced in Van Diemen's Land. The bill was passed, although the clause allowing majority decisions was carried only by the casting vote of the chairman of committees. 'Mr. Windeyer's Libel Act', passed in August 1847, was based on Lord Campbell's Libel Act of 1843, but it went further in adopting almost all of the recommendations of the select committee of the House of Lords. It thus established in New South Wales the principle that in neither a civil action nor in criminal proceedings could a libel be justified by showing that the words published were true; only if its publication were both true and for the public benefit could defamation be justified.

Windeyer was a member of the Aborigines Protection Society. His attention had been attracted to their legal disadvantages in the trial of an Aboriginal, Murrell, and the trials arising out of the Myall Creek 'massacre' in which he had appeared. As the law stood, Aboriginals were not allowed to give evidence in the courts because they could not understand the nature of an oath. Windeyer supported proposals, later in substance adopted, that they should be allowed to make unsworn statements. On his motion a select committee was appointed in 1845 to consider Aboriginal welfare generally, but the committee ceased work with his death. Other ways in which he showed his concern for social welfare were by his membership of the New South Wales Temperance Society, of the committee of the Benevolent Society and as first president of the Debating Society.

In his political activities Windeyer was no friend of Governor Gipps. In 1846 he unsuccessfully challenged the legality of quitrents. But in the disputes arising from Gipps's squatting regulations of 1844 he took a middle line between squatters and the executive. He condemned the squatters as 'cormorants' and 'robbers', but he also opposed the regulations, as he objected to the executive powers on which they were supposedly based. He, with Lang, Lowe and Bland [q.v.], led a 'constitutional' party who sought to secure control of the land revenue for the colonial legislature. It was not as an advocate of squatting interests, but rather because of his insistence on what he asserted was correct constitutional doctrine, that he became a member of the committee of the Pastoral Association. In the Legislative Council he worked hard for what he believed were the interests of the colony and after each session he made a point of touring his electorate to give an account of his stewardship.

Ill from overwork, financial worries and some internal disease, Windeyer died on 2 December 1847 at the home of his wife's brother-in-law William Henty [q.v.], near Launceston. He was described as 'an able, enlightened, honest, and uncompromising public man'. He died when his role was far from completed, as Wentworth and many others recognized. But his private affairs had suffered. His optimism and enterprise had led him to entertain projects that he could not afford and to incur large debts. From this cause and the economic depression of the 1840s, he died impoverished. His widow, a woman of remarkable character and determination, was enabled by money received from her family to retain a part of Tomago, where she lived, devoting herself to the prudent management of the property, the welfare of her infant son and local affairs. The obituary of Windeyer in the *Herald*, written by Lowe, his ally and friend, seems a balanced and fair assessment of his character: vigorous, ambitious, honest, liberal in outlook, but aggressively independent. He was ruthless with opponents, but kind to his family and friends.

A portrait is in the Mitchell Library, Sydney, and others are in private possession.

J. B. Windeyer, Richard Windeyer: aspects of his work in NSW from 1835 to 1847 (B.A. thesis, Univ Syd, 1961); Camfield-Windeyer letters (ML); Windeyer family papers (in possession of Sir Victor Windeyer, Syd).

J. B. WINDEYER

WINSTANLEY; *see* O'FLAHERTY

WISEMAN, SOLOMON (1777-1838), merchant, born on 16 April 1777 in Essex, England, was a journeyman lighterman when convicted at the Old Bailey on 30 October 1805 of stealing from his employers 704 lbs of Brazil wood from a Thames lighter. His death sentence was commuted to transportation for life, and in August 1806 he arrived in New South Wales in the *Alexander* with his wife Jane, née Middleton, and two sons. In June 1810 he received a ticket-of-leave and in February 1812 an absolute pardon. In July 1811 the sloop *Hawkesbury Packet*, built for Wiseman, was launched at Cockle Bay; with it he entered the coastal trade and later added the sloop *Hope*. In December 1815 he was one of the merchants who petitioned Governor Macquarie for permission to visit parts of the coast for cedar and coal to sell in Sydney; their request was refused, but during the next two years he received permission to bring cedar from Port Stephens both on his own behalf and for other merchants. In July 1817 the *Hope* was wrecked at Port Stephens and two of the crew were killed by Aboriginals; two months later the *Hawkesbury Packet* was also wrecked.

In August 1813 Wiseman had received a wine and spirits licence for premises in Bligh Street, Sydney. In 1817 he had agreed to sell them to Samuel Terry [q.v.]; after the wrecks he had to assign his property to Terry. Soon afterwards he was granted 100 acres which he selected on the Hawkesbury River near Wilberforce. He then acquired the *Mary Ann* which the government chartered in 1821 to go to Port Macquarie. In 1823 he received a further grant of 200 acres near Benjamin Singleton's [q.v.] Mill Farm and in 1828 held 1100 acres, acquired by grant and purchase. In 1826 he obtained a licence for his house on the road to Newcastle. Next year he was given a lease of what became known as Wiseman's Ferry on the Hawkesbury River on condition that government horses and property were carried on it free of charge. Richard Jones took this over in 1827. Like many other officials Wiseman was accused of corruption and of contravening port orders, but there is no evidence that these complaints were justified. In his last years he became well known for his hospitality and in May 1833 entertained the governor.

His wife Jane had died on 20 July 1821 after a long illness, leaving him with four sons and two daughters. On 1 November 1826 he married Sophia Warner, the widow of one of his employees at Wilberforce. He died on 28 November 1838, described as a respected colonist and friend of the poor. He was buried with his first wife on his property, reinterred first in the Church of St Mary Magdalene, and after that church was damaged by vandals, in the cemetery at Wiseman's Ferry. Sophia Wiseman returned to England in 1841 and died at Hammersmith in 1870.

C. Swancott, *Wiseman's ferry* (Woy Woy, 1965); F. Walker, 'The great north road', *JRAHS*, 3 (1915-17); J. Jervis, 'Wiseman and his ferry', *JRAHS*, 27 (1941); *Sydney Gazette*, 6 July 1811, 6 Sept 1817, 28 July 1821; *Sydney Herald*, 30 Nov 1838; *Sydney Mail*, 3 Sept 1924; MS cat under S. Wiseman (ML).

VIVIENNE PARSONS

WITTENOOM, JOHN BURDETT (1789-1855), colonial chaplain, was born at Newark, Nottinghamshire, England, the son of Thomas Wittenoom of London. His patronymic came from Dutch grandparents. After education at Winchester and Brasenose College, Oxford (B.A., 1810; M.A., 1813), he became headmaster of Newark Grammar School, where he remained for fifteen years. His first wife was Margaret Mary Teasdale, by whom he had five sons. Soon after her death Wittenoom decided to emigrate. In July 1829 he was appointed chaplain to the civil establishment at Swan River, with a stipend of £250 and the promise of a house, glebe and provisions. He arrived in Fremantle in the *Wanstead* in January 1830 with his mother, sister and four sons, John Burdett, Henry, Frederick Dirck, and Charles.

Wittenoom took up land at Gwambygine, near York, but had to let it until his sons could manage it. Although not the first Anglican clergyman at Swan River, he was the only one for five years after Thomas Hobbes Scott [q.v.] left. Singlehanded until 1836 he conducted service each Sunday at Perth and alternately at Fremantle and Guildford, and on occasion toured the settlements as far afield as Albany. The church sank into apathy, and it was soon obvious that he could not cope alone with the colony's growing needs, but the initiative in asking for new clergymen was left to the Agricultural Society. When relief did come Wittenoom limited his work to the Perth area, where he was also able to further his interest in education; as well as tutoring children of the few well-to-do families in Perth he opened a small grammar school mostly for senior pupils. In 1847 he was appointed to the first education committee and was its chairman for eight years after it became the Board of Education. He also served on charitable committees but showed no interest in politics and made no claim for a seat on the Executive Council. On 3 January 1839 he married Mary Watson Helms, of Perth, by whom he had two daughters and a son who died in infancy. An amateur cellist and a fluent speaker, he encouraged musical evenings and reading parties in his home; but religious enthusiasm was contrary to his High Church views and his colleagues thought him too easygoing and unenterprising as an organizer. With the opening of a convict gaol at Fremantle his duties increased. His health was undermined by domestic worry and too little exercise, and he became a victim of gout. He died in Perth on 23 January 1855. A tablet in his memory was placed in St George's Cathedral, Perth.

After Wittenoom's death his wife and daughter took charge of the government girls' school. Of his sons, Edward died young; John Burdett was in the Swan River mounted police but resigned to prospect for gold in Victoria, where his relatives lost touch with him; Henry was a lifelong invalid but lived to old age at Gwambygine; Frederick Dirck joined the public service of the colony in 1840 and was later appointed guardian of juvenile immigrants, sheriff, and a member of the Executive and Legislative Councils. He was described officially as 'charitable, amiable and of unobtrusive disposition' and he died in 1863.

The fifth son, Charles (1824-1866), whose first wife, Sarah Elizabeth Harding, died in 1861, was responsible for carrying on the Wittenoom line. His children were Edward Horne (1854-1936), Francis Frederick Burdett (1855-1939), Rose Agnes (1857-1902), who became wife of Sir Henry Bruce Lefroy, and James Cornelius, who died in infancy. Charles's second wife was Annie Fletcher Moore, by whom he had one child, Florence Mary Teasdale.

R. E. Cranfield, *Wittenoom family in Western Australia* (Perth, 1962); Research notes 11, 341 (WAA); P. U. Henn, Genealogical notes (Battye Lib, Perth).

R. E. CRANFIELD

WOLLASTON, JOHN RAMSDEN (1791-1856), Anglican archdeacon, was born on 28 March 1791 in London. He was educated at Charterhouse, where his father, Edward Wollaston, was a master and his maternal grandfather headmaster, and at Christ's College, Cambridge (B.A., 1812; M.A., 1815). He took holy orders and in May 1819 married Mary Amelia, youngest daughter of Colonel George Gledstones; they had five sons and two daughters. Finding the income from his cure of West Wickham, Cambridgeshire, insufficient for his growing family, he applied in 1840 for the position of chaplain to the Western Australian Land Co.'s proposed settlement at Australind on Port Leschenault. The company let it be known in its advance publicity that Wollaston's services would be available to the settlement, but gave him no appointment, and it was eventually the British government that assured him of an official stipend if he went to Western Australia.

Wollaston arrived at Fremantle in April 1841, at a time of considerable financial stringency. He bought land at Picton, between Australind and Bunbury, and began to build a chapel on his land. He expected the annual subsidy that Governor Hutt had introduced in an ordinance to encourage the building of churches and the payment of stipends, but he was allowed no government aid until his church was opened for divine service. The small wooden church with a thatched roof (later replaced by shingles), was designed by Wollaston and finished by him and his sons. Consecrated on 18 December 1842, it was still standing in 1966, the oldest church but one in Western Australia.

Such enterprise was remarkable in a newly arrived clergyman, no longer young and not by temperament readily adaptable to the change from English village life to a pioneering society. It contrasted with the apathy and neglect which had tended to characterize the Anglican community under Wittenoom's [q.v.] well-meaning but unenterprising guidance. Stimulated by the activity of Roman Catholics and Nonconformists, Wollaston soon took the initiative in revivifying the organization of the colony's Church of England. In February 1842 he convened a conference of the colony's five clergy at Perth, where the church's problems were assessed and a statement drawn up urging Bishop Broughton [q.v.] to visit Western Australia and set matters in order. The sequel was discouraging; Broughton could not come and Wittenoom failed to respond to Wollaston's suggestion that clergy conferences should become annual. Moreover, Wollaston's congregation was declining after the failure of the Australind scheme. But his continued labours as a parish priest earned him the name of a 'worthy, laborious, energetic, excellent missionary'.

Wollaston's opportunity came in 1848: a new and more sympathetic governor, Fitzgerald, transferred him to the parish of St John's, Albany, and the colony was visited by Bishop Short and Archdeacon Hale of the new diocese of Adelaide. Impressed by Wollaston's qualities, Short appointed him archdeacon of Western Australia early in 1849, an office which he discharged ably and zealously until his death. During these years Wollaston covered many hundreds of miles on horseback in the course of duties which included five visitations throughout the settled areas of the colony. Growth in population and after 1850 the transportation of convicts increased the church's responsibilties, especially as the Anglican clergy had to serve many Nonconformists without ministers of their own. Through his own efficiency and the good relations he developed with the government, Wollaston successfully met this situation. During his time the number of Anglican clergy increased from five to ten, and the regularity of services in the colony's major centres improved greatly.

Although an earlier Aboriginal mission in 1835 had failed, Wollaston established another Anglican mission to Western Australian Aboriginals at Albany in 1851. The temporal affairs of the church were regulated by the passing in 1853 of an Act drafted by Wollaston, providing for the management of each church by trustees elected by the parishioners, and assuring each incumbent a dwelling place, garden and glebe.

Wollaston was not personally ambitious and would willingly have resigned in favour of an archdeacon based on Perth, but his ultimate aim was the establishment of a bishopric in Western Australia. Soon after his arrival in the colony he encouraged a movement among settlers to set aside gifts of land for the endowment of a see. The scheme had little success until it came under his oversight as archdeacon; 1300 acres had been subscribed by 1856. Meanwhile in 1854 arrangements were begun for founding a diocese at Perth with Archdeacon Hale as first bishop. But before the necessary formalities were completed Wollaston died at Albany on 3 May 1856, soon after returning from his fifth pastoral visitation.

Diffident, pessimistic, and often censorious of his colleagues, Wollaston yet proved outstandingly effective in strengthening the framework of the infant church in Western Australia. His journals reveal not merely an observant commentator on colonial manners and character, but a man whose qualities of humility, common sense and devoted perseverance enabled him to give purpose and order to a very isolated branch of the Anglican communion. The Church of England in Western Australia in 1957 commemorated his name in a theological college.

A. Burton, *Church beginnings in the west* (Perth, 1941); A. Burton and P. U. Henn (eds), *Wollaston's Picton journal* (Perth, 1948); C. L. M. Hawtry, *The availing struggle* (Perth, 1949); P. U. Henn (ed), *Wollaston's Albany journals* (Perth, 1954).

G. C. BOLTON

WOLLSTONECRAFT, EDWARD (1783-1832), merchant and landowner, was the son of Edward Wollstonecraft, a London solicitor, who was a brother of Mary Wollstonecraft Godwin. Edward and his sister Elizabeth were therefore cousins of the ill-fated Fanny Imlay and of Mary Godwin who became the second wife of Shelley and was the author of *Frankenstein*. His parents died when relatively young. Wollstonecraft resented the notoriety of his aunt and sought escape and fortune for himself and his sister in travel and trade.

Wollstonecraft had some association with a Spanish merchant, De Zastel, of London, and on a voyage from Lisbon to Cadiz in June 1812 he met Alexander Berry [q.v.]. Berry introduced himself to the 'tall, formal-looking young man, dressed in black', and despite Wollstonecraft's initial reserve they became friends. They shared lodgings in Cadiz during the last stages of Marshal Soult's siege of the city. About this time Wollstonecraft became Berry's 'agent under a power of attorney' and returned to London to investigate matters arising out of Berry's earlier trading ventures. Wollstonecraft, his sister and Berry lived together in London from 1815 to 1819 when Wollstonecraft entered into full partnership with Berry and they both sailed for New South Wales, although in different ships.

Wollstonecraft arrived in Sydney in September 1819 in the *Canada*; Berry soon returned to England. Governor Macquarie promised both men the usual grants of land. In Berry's absence Wollstonecraft was permitted to locate some 500 of his 2000 acres on the north side of Sydney Harbour, and his tenure was made official in June 1825. In spite of ill health he became a magistrate and a central figure in the Sydney commerce of the 1820s. As a director of the Bank of New South Wales and of the Bank of Australia, and as chairman of the Chamber of Commerce, he appears to have been chiefly concerned with maintaining the general financial liquidity of the colony's economy. He argued that the introduction of the Spanish dollar had depreciated colonial values and embarrassed external trade, and he urged the government to make loans to the colonial banks in the financial crises of 1826 and 1828.

A wide variety of merchandise passed through the warehouse of Berry and Wollstonecraft in George Street. In 1820, while Berry was still in London, Wollstonecraft advised him to concentrate on obtaining the solid necessities of a young colony and to beware of fripperies 'and the other female trash by which we are likely to lose so much already'.

Berry returned to Sydney in 1821, chartering the *Royal George* and bringing with him Governor Brisbane and his party as passengers. With Wollstonecraft he successfully applied for a further 10,000 acres on their undertaking to maintain 100 convicts. The grant was taken on the Shoalhaven River on the initiative of Berry, who explored the area, liked it and assured it of safe access from the sea by cutting a canal between the Crookhaven and Shoalhaven Rivers. On this foundation Wollstonecraft's relentless business energy worked, for he believed that the colony's greatest economic need was a reliable export staple. Finding the Shoalhaven region climatically unsuited for sheep, his long term plan at Coolangatta (Cullingatta and Coolungatta), as the property came to be called, was to clear the hillsides and drain the swamps for agriculture. Meanwhile the forests of cedar and blue gum could be put to use. Teams of sawyers, both assigned convicts and freemen, were organized, and by July 1823 thirty-six men were employed in getting and preparing timber for which Wollstonecraft was assiduous in seeking markets. The bulk of it was exported and thus provided a desirable balance to the imports demanded by the diverse trade still carried on by the partners in Sydney. While timber proved an immediate and sure source of wealth, experiments were made at Shoalhaven with other crops of similar economic potential, the chief being tobacco which was normally retailed at enormous profit to the importer. The partners generally arranged that one was at Shoalhaven and the other at the North Shore. The bond between them was strengthened by Berry's marriage in September 1827 to Elizabeth, Wollstonecraft's sister.

Both Wollstonecraft and Berry had the eighteenth-century Englishman's view of the social importance of land, and they saw at Shoalhaven the beginning of a great estate over which eventually they might rule as patriarchs. In pursuit of their object Wollstonecraft was almost morbidly jealous of encroaching settlers. His aim was to exclude them altogether or, failing that, so to encircle their holdings as to make them unworkable. This the partners were increasingly able to do, both by manipulating the location of their own grants before survey, and by buying the promises of grants from other settlers and locating them as strategy required. Wollstonecraft died on 7 December 1832. His life in Australia depended largely on Berry's enterprise, yet Berry could rightly claim that he had 'a naturally defective temper', and that his conduct in his last years was 'such as to render my existence hardly tolerable'. His letters leave an impression of sardonic bitterness which may, however, have been the product of ill health. His business acumen and integrity were beyond question, yet it is doubtful that they would have found any important employment

without the wider vision and more civilized instincts of Berry.

Wollstonecraft never married. A suburb of Sydney was named after him and another after his cottage, Crow's Nest, on the North Shore. In March 1846 his remains were removed from the Sydney burial ground and placed with those of his sister, who died on 11 April 1845, in a magnificent tomb erected by Berry in the cemetery near St Thomas's Church of England, North Sydney.

HRA (1), 10-13; Alexander Berry, *Reminiscences* (Syd, 1912); F. L. Jones (ed), *The letters of Mary W. Shelley*, 1-2 (Norman, Oklahoma, 1944), in which the editorial notes relating to Wollstonecraft are seriously misinformed; Berry papers (ML).

M. D. STEPHEN

WOODRIFF, DANIEL (1756-1842), naval officer, was born on 17 November 1756, the son of John Woodriff, of Deptford, Kent, England, shipwright and carpenter's mate who died probably in 1761. His brother Allen was carpenter in H.M.S. *Centaur*. When 6 he joined H.M.S. *Ludlow Castle* as servant to his uncle George Woodriff, master gunner. In December 1767 he was admitted to the Royal Hospital School at Greenwich, and in 1770 was apprenticed to John White, a captain engaged in the Jamaica trade. In 1778 he was impressed into the navy. After two years service in the North Sea he was transferred to the *Britannia* guardship and in 1782 commissioned lieutenant. He then commanded the *Dependance*, used for evacuating Loyalists from South Carolina and Georgia. After eleven years service on the American Station and in the West Indies, during which he married the daughter of a Loyalist who had been killed in the American war, he returned to England, and in 1792 was sent to Australia in the *Kitty*, primarily to bring out supplies and convicts, but also to make a report on the naval defences of Port Jackson. After his return in 1794 he was promoted commander, served off the coast of Flanders and then acted as resident agent for the Transport Board at Southampton and Lynn. He received the personal thanks of the commander-in-chief for his work in evacuating the British troops from the Low Countries.

After a term as superintendent of prisoners of war, in April 1802 Woodriff was gazetted post captain and next year appointed to command H.M.S. *Calcutta* in Collins's expedition to found a new settlement in Bass Strait. He remained with Collins in Port Phillip Bay until December but, to the annoyance of both Collins and

Governor King, Woodriff then refused to go to the Derwent when Collins decided to move the settlement; because of his instructions to bring to England as quickly as possible the naval stores awaiting him at Port Jackson, he felt he had no alternative but to go at once to Sydney to collect them, for the *Ocean* transport was sufficient for the move to Van Diemen's Land. While in Port Jackson he helped to check the convict insurrection planned to support the one at Castle Hill, and was granted 1000 acres at Penrith. Portion of this grant is still owned by his descendants.

Woodriff sailed in March 1804. Next year, while convoying some 200 merchantmen, he engaged a French fleet of ten sail which included four ships of the line, though his ship, H.M.S. *Calcutta*, was only a converted East Indiaman mounting forty-eight 9-pounders and four 12-pounders. All but one of his convoy escaped, but eventually Woodriff had to surrender and was taken to France as a prisoner of war. In June 1807 he was exchanged on the orders of Napoleon and, after being honourably acquitted for the loss of the *Calcutta*, he was appointed superintendent of prisoners of war at Forton. In 1814 he was appointed resident commissioner at Port Royal, Jamaica, where he instituted important economies. In 1822 he resigned and returned to England, living first at Gosport and later at Greenwich. In 1831 he was created a C.B., and in 1837 was made one of the four resident captains at Greenwich Hospital, preferring that position to rear-admiral's rank.

Woodriff's visits to Australia in 1792 and 1804 had convinced him of the urgent need of a naval squadron based on Port Jackson, and he kept urging this on the Admiralty until his death on 25 February 1842. His portrait and three oils of the celebrated fight are in the National Library, Canberra. His first wife, Asia, died some time after 1823; the date of his second marriage is unknown, but his widow, Sarah, died in January 1860 aged 90. His three sons, Daniel James (1788-1860), John and Robert, all served with their father in the *Calcutta* in 1803-04 and became naval officers. Daniel James, who became a captain, was master's mate in the *Bellerophon* at the battle of Trafalgar, and for a short time took charge of the ship when all her officers were killed or badly wounded. His diary is in the National Library, Canberra.

W. R. O'Byrne, *A naval biographical dictionary* (Lond, 1849); D. C. Tilghman, 'Captain Daniel Woodriff, C.B., R.N.', VHM, 32 (1962).   Douglas Campbell Tilghman

WOODS, ROGER HENRY (fl. 1829-1831), public servant, was a brother of James Dominick Woods, barrister and journalist, one of whose sons, Julian E. Tenison Woods, served as a Roman Catholic priest in Australia in 1856-87. R. H. Woods was appointed principal superintendent of convicts, which had become vacant upon the death of John Lakeland [q.v.] in 1828. Woods claimed to have been an associate of Sir John Hulloch (1767-1829), a judge on the Northern Circuit, and he was recommended by several members of parliament, including Horace Twiss, under-secretary of state for the colonies. Woods arrived in Van Diemen's Land from London in the *Bussorah Merchant* on 18 January 1830. He was accompanied by his wife Ann, five children, his wife's mother, Mrs Margaret Fenton, and brother Richard.

Lieut-Governor Arthur had stressed the need for an officer with a wide knowledge of local affairs, and he must have been distressed to learn from P. A. Mulgrave [q.v.], who had known Woods in England, of the habits of his new appointee. It was clear that Woods was an incorrigible tippler although he claimed that rheumatism in the head sometimes made him appear far from sober. He had imbibed heavily on the ship and continued to do so in the colony. His salary was to be £300 and he had been advanced £310 in London. Arthur offered him a position of assistant police magistrate at the same salary, and when he declined Arthur wrote to London in March officially complaining that Woods did not appear fully qualified for his post, and in a personal letter to Twiss listed his doubts about Woods more candidly. Meanwhile Woods proceeded to carry out his duties in a state of confusion which brought the Convict Department close to chaos. He convicted offenders wrongly, abused a magistrate in open court, left work undone, and employed absconded convicts in his own garden. His aberrations were listed by the colonial secretary, John Burnett [q.v.], in the form of thirteen charges, and in September 1830 he was called before the Executive Council to answer them. He failed to attend and was promptly suspended from duty.

In a long letter Woods attempted to refute the charges, but in November Arthur reported the suspension and requested confirmation by the Colonial Office. Woods loudly protested his innocence and in December was finally permitted to defend himself before the Executive Council. The case dragged on for thirteen days until 4 January, when a letter arrived from the Colonial Office giving Arthur authority to replace him as he thought fit. Woods was then formally dismissed and his salary ceased. Out of sympathy for his family Arthur offered him the post of under-sheriff. Woods refused and his persistent demands for a free passage to London to defend himself at the Colonial Office became so insulting that Arthur declined to correspond with him.

Soon afterwards Woods left the colony, and although only £86 of his salary advance had been repaid Arthur recorded: 'It was utterly impossible for the Government to call upon Mr Woods for the balance before his departure as it was evident that he had no money'. Woods left his family behind, and about a year later his wife went to Sydney, allegedly eloping with an overseer, leaving four children to be brought up in the King's Orphan School.

Woods was undoubtedly one of the worst cases of patronage from Downing Street that Arthur had to contend with. His connexions in England must have been the principal reason for the Executive Council devoting so much time to his case, but changes of control at the Colonial Office seem to have dissipated any interest in his career.

CO 280/31.   J. R. MORRIS

WOOLLEY, THOMAS (1809?-1858), merchant, was born in England, a son of Thomas and Mary Honoria Woolley. He arrived in the *Florentia* at Sydney in January 1834. In partnership with his brother Michael he opened in June an ironmonger's store in the Birmingham and Manchester Warehouse, George Street, and within six months had to enlarge his premises. In May 1835 he bought from Gregory Blaxland [q.v.] an acre, known as Blaxland's salt works, on the coast at Newcastle. Later in the year he appears to have returned to England, where he married Eliza Pilmor; they arrived in the *Tamar* at Sydney in September 1836. When the Australian Gaslight Co. was founded Woolley joined its committee and in 1837 became one of its directors, serving until mid-1840 when he sailed again for England. He returned in March 1842 and in April was appointed treasurer of the Sydney Dispensary. Next year he was a member of the committee that petitioned for the importation of Indian coolies to New South Wales, and in November was elected unopposed for Cook ward to the first Sydney City Council. Meanwhile his business continued to flourish; among many other projects he supplied iron-mongery for the overland expedition to Port Essington and exported whale oil and local produce to pay for his imports. By 1850 he had sold his business to Tomlins & Sloman for £10,000 and returned to London, where that year he published *Reminiscences of the Life of a Bushman: or, how to make happiness, abundance and profit, the results of emigrating to Australia.* On its title page he claimed to have ' "run the gauntlet" through thick and thin, and experienced every state and stage of fortune in several of the Colonies of that vast Continent. "Aide toi, et le Ciel t'aidra".' Woolley retired to Regents Park with his family. Later he moved to the Victoria Hotel, St Leonard's-on-Sea, Sussex, where he died on 18 February 1858, leaving an estate valued at some £20,000 to his wife, his son, two daughters and other relations.

Newspaper indexes under T. Woolley (ML); MS cat under T. Woolley (ML).

WORGAN, GEORGE BOUCHIER (1757-1838), surgeon, was christened on 3 May 1757 at St Andrew's, Holborn, London, the second son and third child of John Worgan (1724-1790), a doctor of music, and his wife Sarah, née Maclean. At 18 he entered the navy, qualified as surgeon's second mate in February 1778 and was gazetted naval surgeon in March 1780. He served for two years in the *Pilote* and in November 1786 joined the *Sirius*, sailing in her next year in the First Fleet to New South Wales and taking with him a piano. In addition to his medical duties he joined several expeditions to such places as Hawkesbury River and Broken Bay. On one excursion from Prospect Hill the upper Nepean was named Worgan River after him. He visited the Cape of Good Hope in the *Sirius* in 1788-89, and then spent a year on Norfolk Island after she was wrecked there, before he returned to England in the *Waaksamheyd* in 1791, leaving his piano with Mrs Macarthur [q.v.]. He continued to serve as surgeon's mate and surgeon until about 1800 when he was judged unfit for service and retired on half-pay. He took up farming with little success, and died of apoplexy at Liskeard on 4 March 1838.

CO 323/132; G. B. Worgan, Journal Jan-July 1788 (ML).   JOHN COBLEY

WORTMAN(N), IGNATZ and ADOLPHUS (fl. 1842-1857), match manufacturers and exporters, came from the northern Hungarian town of Nyitra (now Nitra in

Czechoslovakia), where Adolphus was born in 1825. Ignatz arrived in Sydney in November 1842 and in April 1843 announced in the press that he had 'commenced manufacturing lucifer matches and cigar lights of every description'. The advertisement added 'matches packed with care for any part of the world', a reference to the export activities of the firm which was to be emphasized during fifteen years of business. The first match factory was in Pitt Street South, whence it was moved to King Street and later to York Street. In March 1847 Adolphus arrived from Hungary, bringing from London phosphorus, nitric acid and matchwood. Ignatz handed over the factory to Adolphus, and probably left the colony. Adolphus moved the factory to Campbell Street, where he manufactured matches for ten years and then sold his business to A. Blitz, under whom the establishment prospered for several decades.

The matches made by the Wortmans were advertised as 'lucifers', a name originally denoting a sulphur-type match. Nevertheless the arrival of shipments of phosphorus and nitric acid for their factory proves that their matches were phosphorus matches, a type invented by the Hungarian chemist János Irinyi and concurrently by other Austrian, German and French chemists. Although Irinyi sold his patent in the mid-1830s to the Austrian Römer, he nevertheless operated his own manufactory in Pest between 1840 and 1848. It is almost certain that Ignatz Wortman learnt the phosphoric method, at that time the most advanced in the world, in Irinyi's workshop at Pest, or in one of the other Hungarian match factories using Irinyi's method. The production of this new type of match, named 'Congrave' in England, developed only later in Great Britain and a very large proportion of matches used in the British Isles were of Austro-Hungarian and German manufacture.

The technical skills brought by the two Wortmans from Hungary to Australia enabled them to reverse the trade pattern in their field: they imported matchwood, boxes, and chemicals from Britain, and exported their finished products to New Zealand, the South Sea islands, America and England.

Ignatz invariably spelt his surname with a double 'n'; Adolphus's naturalization certificate shows one 'n', and he used both spellings in his advertisements.

E. F. Kunz, Hungarians in Australia (M.A. thesis, Univ Syd, 1966), and for bibliog.

E. F. Kunz

WRIGHT, EDWARD (1788?-1859), surgeon, claimed a medical training in the University of Edinburgh and, after graduation in 1813, much experience in public hospitals before he became apothecary, house surgeon and superintendent at Bethlem Hospital (Bedlam) in London in 1818. From this position he was dismissed in 1830 for frequent drunkenness, neglect of duties and undue familiarities, even though by this time he had been elected president of the Phrenological Society in London and a member of many other learned societies. He soon contrived to clear his name and then went to Syria. After four years he returned to London but failed to find a suitable practice. He became interested instead in the proposed settlement of South Australia, and in hope of an official appointment joined the managing committee of the South Australian Literary Association, and was employed to sell land and to give public lectures on behalf of the new province. His best service, however, was to help in bringing South Australia to the attention of John Morphett [q.v.] whom he had known first in Beirut and whose acquaintance he renewed in London. In December 1835 the colonization commissioners rejected Wright's application for the position of medical officer in the new province, but he was allowed a free passage and sailed with his wife and four sons in the Cygnet.

Wright arrived at Kangaroo Island in September 1836, and after two busy months was appointed by Colonel Light [q.v.] to the Holdfast Bay station. This appointment terminated after the arrival of Governor Hindmarsh and Wright became dependent on private practice. He bought land in Franklin Street and shared in the social life of the new settlement; his patients included many prominent settlers, among them the Thomas family with whom he was a close friend. He was also caught up in political opposition to the governor's party and played an active part in the public meeting that supported Light's choice of site for Adelaide and in establishing the Southern Australian to compete with the official newspaper.

In January 1845 Wright, seemingly in an intoxicated condition, prescribed heroic doses of morphia for the landlord of a Thebarton hotel imprisoned as a mental case at the Adelaide Jail. Tried for manslaughter in the Supreme Court, Wright claimed in defence that he had 'taken only the quantity becoming a gentleman after dinner'. He was discharged on a technical point, Judge Cooper [q.v.] considering him morally responsible for the man's death. Reading the evidence today it is clear that death was not due to morphia poisoning. Although the trial did not lose him all his friends it did induce him to withdraw from public life. He died at Adelaide on 7 November 1859 in his seventieth year. One son Charles, carried on his practice and the others had a farm at Dry Creek.

Although Wright did not bother to enrol in the medical register of South Australia, commenced in 1844, he appears to have been a good practitioner in the days of cupping, cauterizing and applying leeches. According to Morphett he was very clever; yet for a man of eighteen stone he was unduly reckless and over-indulgent and his continued poverty implies poor management.

Bethlem Hospital, *Minutes of evidence taken by the commission appointed to enquire into the charges against Dr Wright . . . and his answer* (Lond, 1830); Bethlem Hospital, *Various letters addressed to Dr Wright, containing testimonials* (Lond, 1831); J. B. Cleland, *Pioneer medical men in South Australia* (Adel, 1941); E. K. Thomas (ed), *The diary and letters of Mary Thomas* (Adel, 1915); CO 13/3 (SAA).   J. B. CLELAND

WROE, JOHN (1782-1863), evangelist, was born on 19 September 1782 at Bowling, Yorkshire, England, the son of Joseph Roe, a fairly prosperous farmer and businessman. Wroe suffered early ill health and in his thirties began to experience religious trances. In 1819 he associated with Yorkshire followers of Joanna Southcott, led by George Turner; on Turner's death in 1821 Wroe was generally accepted as successor. He quickly replaced Southcott's teaching with his own creed, Christian Israelitism, proclaiming that he was appointed by God to encourage the gathering of the descendants of the 'lost' tribes and to bring about their redemption before personal death and the millennium. But elucidation of these themes became secondary to the statement of prophecies, which Wroe claimed as divinely inspired and had his disciples transcribe and publish. He imposed strict rules of conduct, such as abstinence from shaving, repudiation of conventional medical care, and adherence to a restricted diet.

Inspired to carry his message throughout the world, Wroe conducted an extensive missionary programme. The creed first came to Australia with Charles Robertson. An impressive figure (J. Hood, *Australia and the East*, London, 1843, p. 240) he soon built up a following so enthusiastic that authority considered taking coercive

action. In 1841 *Extracts of Letters* from Australian believers was published. The master himself came to Australia in 1843, receiving his first 'divine communication' there in September. This sojourn lasted until February 1844; he returned in September 1850 and on several later occasions. The first trip covered only Sydney and near-by districts, but later he visited Tasmania and Victoria. Other 'beardies' preached from place to place, especially on the goldfields. These followers included John Cartwright, Thomas Frost, Robert Robertson, and Joseph Donnolan, who in April 1851 sailed with Charles Robertson on an ill-fated mission to China. Permanent groups formed at Sydney, Hobart, Adelaide, Penrith, Geelong, and above all at Melbourne, where the Wroeites developed from the congregation established in Fitzroy by Rev. John Allen. Australian references are scattered throughout Wroe's prophecies, and his faith-healing claimed dramatic miracles in Sydney and Hobart. Although some local followers refused to accept the full discipline, Australia seems to have provided his best audience. In 1966 the Melbourne congregation was the most vigorous of the few which survived, exclusively in Australia and America.

Emotional extremism, with strong sexual undertones, characterized Wroe's preaching. It explained both its appeal, and the ill odour in which critics held it. *The Wroeites* by Allan Stewart (Melbourne, nd), attested the power exercised by the creed and alleged that its rites incorporated sexual play. John Davis, *The Wroeites' Faith* (Sydney, 1850), attacked its theology. Both pamphleteers had British counterparts.

Wroe married Mary Appleby in 1815. Despite various scandals involving him the two remained associated until her death on 16 May 1853. Wroe died in Melbourne on 5 February 1863.

(J. Wroe), *A guide to the people surnamed Israelites* (Boston, Mass, 1847); *Private communications given to J. Wroe from the beginning of 1843 to the end of 1852*, 1-3 (Gravesend, 1853); (J. Wroe), *An abridgement of J.W.'s life and travels, also revelations on the scriptures*, 3rd ed (Boston, Mass, 1849); (J. Wroe), *The life and journal of J.W. with divine communications revealed to him* (Gravesend, 1859).   MICHAEL ROE

WYATT, JOSEPH (1788-1860), theatre lessee and owner, settled in Sydney in the early days and made his money as a haberdasher at 16 Pitt Street. In October 1833 he sold his Cheap Wholesale and Retail Warehouse and invested in property. His first theatrical venture began in

April 1835 when he was one of the six lessees who took over Barnett Levey's [q.v.] Theatre Royal. In May 1836 when Levey resumed nominal ownership Wyatt became the sole lessee, paying him the total amount of £30 a week, which previously had been paid by the group of six lessees. Two months later it became known that Wyatt had begun planning his own larger theatre; he was given the assurance that the governor 'will be very glad to see a more commodious theatre erected in Sydney'. Yet when the Victoria Theatre opened in March 1838 its size, a capacity of 2000, proved rather a disadvantage: Sydney's audience potential was too small to allow the building up of a proper repertoire; there was need for constant change of programme which led to badly rehearsed and shoddily produced performances. When opening the Victoria Theatre Wyatt had purchased the lease of the old Theatre Royal from Levey's widow and in years to come he fought every attempt which threatened his monopoly of the theatre in Sydney.

In March 1841 Wyatt sailed for England to bring out performers for the Victoria Theatre. During his absence the management was in the hands of William Knight, a hotel owner, who might also have been one of the six lessees of the Theatre Royal and who until December 1845 was part-owner of the Victoria. After Knight left Wyatt shared the management with Frederick Gibson, his brother-in-law.

The first group of actors engaged by Wyatt in England came to Sydney in October 1842; the others arrived with him in January 1843. By this time the Sydney actors who had played the decisive part in the young Australian theatre protested against this influx of newcomers and the direct result was the emergence of Joseph Simmons's [q.v.] City Theatre. Of the new engagements the *Sydney Morning Herald*, 25 January 1843, wrote: 'Mr Wyatt certainly made a most unfortunate selection of performers. Of the twelve brought out by him from England there is not one equal in ability to the leading members, male or female, of the old company'.

In 1854 Wyatt sold the Victoria, and in March 1855 opened the Prince of Wales Theatre in Castlereagh Street, Sydney. The building cost was above £30,000 but was sold for £10,000 five years later. Joseph Wyatt died on 20 July 1860, and was buried at St Stephen's cemetery, Newtown. It may be said that his purely commercial approach has left its mark on Australian theatre to this day.

H. L. OPPENHEIM

WYATT, WILLIAM (1804-1886), surgeon, landowner and public servant, was born at Plymouth, Devon, England, the son of Richard Wyatt, gentleman. Apprenticed at 16 to Thomas Stewart, a Plymouth surgeon, he became a licentiate of the Worshipful Company of Apothecaries in London and the surgeon of a large dispensary. In 1828 he was admitted a member of the Royal College of Surgeons and began a private practice at Plymouth, where he was also curator of the museum of the Literary and Scientific Institution, and studied zoology and other sciences allied to medicine. In 1836 he applied without success for a post in South Australia, even though a supporter thought him studious, prudent, moral and much else besides. Wyatt was determined, however, to emigrate with his wife and hoped to practise medicine and be an agricultural proprietor as well. As surgeon in the *John Renwick* he arrived in February 1837 in Adelaide, where at next month's opening land sale he bought six town acres; he later acquired many suburban and rural sections as far afield as Port Lincoln.

Wyatt does not appear to have practised much, although he claimed the first amputation of a leg in the province. He was appointed the third protector of the Aborigines in 1837 when he also became city coroner and colonial magistrate. Next year he was made a justice of the peace, joined the local School Society and helped to found the short-lived South Australian Club. As protector he had an invidious task; with no funds and no proper authority he could do little for the Aboriginals, yet he was blamed for every trouble. He was glad to resign in 1839. Land values were then quickly appreciating and Wyatt sold some of his blocks, making nearly £2000 profit on an investment of £700.

In the 1840s Wyatt bought more land during the depression, became an early member of the Medical Board in 1844 and its secretary until his death; he also helped to free Trinity Church from debt in 1848, served on the Immigrants' Welcome Committee, became a director of the abortive Colonial Railway Co., and was elected one of the first proprietors of the Collegiate School of St Peter, where his name was later given to a house and an annual prize. In the 1850s he took a leading part in the South Australian Institute, Acclimatization Society, Botanic Gardens, Royal Society and Society of Arts. In 1851 he was chosen from a large field as the first inspector of schools. His initial plans were imaginative: a model school, training college, examinations for teachers, and textbook depot. During his long regime none of these was properly implemented. The government pursued a shoe-string policy in education and Wyatt was too dignified to press for funds. He earned his £300 salary by visiting schools, seeking to be loved by children as silver-haired 'Uncle Wyatt', and punishing miscreants by exclusion from singing lessons. After fifteen years the government schools were in a deplorable condition and he could not find a single teacher worthy of a first-class certificate. His resignation in 1874 on the eve of the introduction of compulsory education left the government with a vast and costly programme of belated reform. In retirement Wyatt published a *Monograph on certain Crustacea Entomostraca* (Adelaide, 1883) and 'Some account of the manners and superstitions of the Adelaide and Encounter Bay Aboriginal tribes' appeared in J. D. Woods and others, *Native Tribes of South Australia* (Adelaide, 1879).

Wyatt died in Adelaide on 10 June 1886, leaving an estate of nearly £50,000. His only child to survive infancy had been murdered by a drunken workman. He left his wife well provided for, and various annuities and legacies were specified in his will. The greater part of his city and suburban property, however, was left to the Wyatt Benevolent Institution 'to benefit persons above the labouring class who may be in poor or reduced circumstances'. In 1961 the trustees were helping some 250 persons with monthly gifts to each of £5 10s.

E. L. French (ed), *Melbourne studies in education 1957-58* (Melb, 1958); *Observer* (Adel), 12 June 1886; *Advertiser* (Adel), 30 May 1946; A. A. Lendon, Biographical memoirs (SAA); W. Wyatt, Land cash-book 1837-54 (SAA); CO 13/5.   ALAN RENDELL

WYLDE, SIR JOHN (1781-1859), deputy-judge-advocate, was born on 11 May 1781 at Warwick Square, Newgate Street, London, the eldest son of Thomas Wylde (1758-1821) of London, and his wife Mary Anne, née Knight. He was educated at St Paul's School, London, of which he became captain, and Trinity College, Cambridge (LL.B., 1805). In 1805 he was called to the Bar, and at St Benedict's, Cambridge, married Elizabeth Jane, described in his will as daughter of John and Mary Moore, late of Horningsea, near Cambridge, who bore him nine children. He signed his marriage certificate Wylde and used that spelling thereafter, though some members of the family, including his brother

Thomas, chief justice of the Court of Common Pleas and later lord chancellor as the first Lord Truro, and his nephew John Plaisted, Lord Penzance, baron of the Court of Exchequer, adopted the spelling Wilde.

Wylde was successful at the Bar, and in 1815 accepted the position of deputy-judge-advocate of New South Wales at a salary of £1200. He was also appointed judge in the Vice-Admiralty Court there. On 5 October 1816 he arrived in Sydney in the *Elizabeth*, accompanied by his wife, six children, Joshua John Moore [q.v.], his brother-in-law and clerk, and his father, a man of fashion and amateur naturalist of some distinction, who was estranged from his more noted son, Thomas, and had sold his prosperous practice as a London attorney. Before sailing John Wylde had mentioned Ellis Bent's [q.v.] report of the need for 'a professional person . . . as Clerk of the Peace' to help the judge-advocate and had recommended that his father be appointed to this position. On 1 January 1817 Governor Macquarie made Thomas senior clerk of the peace and crown solicitor. He was the first to hold these offices, which he kept until his death on 4 December 1821, aged 63. John Wylde also recommended to Bathurst the appointment of Barron Field [q.v.] as judge of the Supreme Court. He thought Field would give 'constant and able Co-operation in my judicial functions', but later had cause to regret his choice.

Wylde's judicial duties in New South Wales were onerous and diverse, for as judge-advocate he had to combine the roles of 'committing Magistrate, public prosecutor and Judge'. He discharged these duties faithfully and simplified the rules of procedure and pleading in so far as they related to proceedings before him. Within six weeks of his arrival Wylde expressed his concern about the 'Colonial paper Currency', discussed with the governor the difficulty of recovering debts because of the condition of the notes issued by individuals and the need to ignore the colonial proclamations which declared them void; as he felt that there was no time to refer to London, he drafted the charter of the Bank of New South Wales, assured Macquarie that the power to grant it 'could not but belong' to the governor's Commission and so by 'intelligent and zealous Co-operation' played a prominent part in its foundation in 1817. He refused to allow convict attorneys to practise in his court when the cases they had already begun were disposed of. He raised the question of the domicile of persons sued for debt, soon to become important in the case of G. Blaxcell [q.v.]. He advocated the establishment of a supreme court in Van Diemen's Land. He held that D'Arcy Wentworth [q.v.] as a surgeon was not liable to be tried by court martial, suggested to Macquarie that the judge-advocate's office be used as a register of deeds, successfully opposed the governor's desire to arrest the officers of the convict transport *Chapman* for murder after a shooting affray on board, compiled for the governor a digest of government orders of the colony, revised the port regulations to which Ellis Bent had taken such exception, and took part in inquiries into the administration of Provost-Marshall Gore and Commissary Drennan [qq.v.].

In 1821, after Wylde had conducted a circuit in Van Diemen's Land, Macquarie reported on his 'earnest Zeal for the Public Service'. Later that year the judge-advocate reported at length to Commissioner Bigge [q.v.] on the judicial establishments of the colony, stressing the difficulties incidental to applying the 'laws of England' in New South Wales and recommending a 'modified' jury system and a proper court of appeal to overcome the anomalies of his own position in relation to the governor and the existing military jury. One special grievance was the possible influence of the governor in appointing laymen with no legal knowledge to the Governor's Court, over which the judge-advocate presided. Wylde's report was criticized at length by Bigge in a confidential letter to Bathurst on 9 September 1822. According to Bigge, the judge-advocate 'rendered plain subjects unintelligible' and expressed himself with 'such an habitual and studied obscurity of phrase and meaning that the members of the Criminal Court have been placed in a state of greater embarrassment by written and verbal addresses of the Judge-Advocate than if they had been left to their own unassisted consciences and judgment'; he said that though Macquarie had commented favourably on Wylde's 'friendly and placable disposition' the governor avoided communication with the judge-advocate because of his 'mode of treating and discussing the most trifling subjects of business'. Bigge also criticized the employment of Wylde's connexions in duties which related to his office, stated that he had been informed by several persons who were present that Wylde had shown bias when presiding in the trial of J. T. Campbell [q.v.] for his libel on Samuel Marsden [q.v.], told Bathurst that this trial had had 'powerful effect in producing' a petition for trial by jury, and concluded that the judge-advocate had 'not commanded the respect of the Colony in his judicial capacity'.

This criticism was far too harsh. Wylde,

in his farewell speech on the final sitting of the Governor's Court in May 1824, powerfully and ably defended himself against the charge of bias made by Bigge in his public report, and F. Garling [q.v.], who spoke on behalf of the assembled solicitors, said that 'from his own knowledge of the case' the 'explanations' of Wylde were 'perfectly correct' and assured the judge-advocate that 'he took with him the blessings of the Public'. During Governor Brisbane's administration Wylde was to prove himself a courageous defender of the independence of the judiciary and of the rule of law against the convenience of the executive, but his relations with Brisbane were strained. In August 1822 he joined other magistrates in passing a resolution designed, according to Brisbane, to 'intimidate the measures of my government' in the affair of H. G. Douglass [q.v.]. This followed Wylde's decision three months earlier in *Burn* v. *Howe* that the colonial wage-fixing regulations were illegal, and soon after the case he gave to the justices of the peace his opinion that no civil jurisdiction could be conferred on them by governor's proclamations. Brisbane sharply criticized Wylde's failure to mention this matter earlier, so that it might have been referred to London. Already irritated by Wylde's claim to be a member of the Court of Appeal and not merely an adviser to the governor on it, and by his insistence that few capitally convicted prisoners be reprieved despite the large number of offences then punishable only by death, the governor urged Wylde's recall and said that he hoped he had prevented the recurrence of future mischief by 'the judicious appointment' to the Governor's Court 'of two members on whom he could depend', namely two clerks 'in the employ and pay of the Government'. Bathurst, on the advice of James Stephen junior, upheld Wylde's decision in *Burn* v. *Howe*, and endorsed his objections to what approached an attempt to 'pack' the Governor's Court; though he criticized Wylde's conduct in other respects, he refused to remove him on the ground that the contemplated remodelling of the courts, which was carried out by the New South Wales Act, 1823 (4 Geo. IV, c. 96), would soon make new judicial appointments necessary. When told of the new arrangements Wylde, having regard to the criminal and civil jurisdictions still in his charge, said that he did not feel at liberty to return to England until the new chief justice arrived. Field, less mindful of his obligations, left immediately and, to prevent inconvenience to suitors in the Supreme Court, Wylde offered to add Field's duties to his own.

Brisbane gladly accepted this offer, and Wylde was sworn in as judge of the old Supreme Court on 23 March 1824, and so continued until Francis Forbes [q.v.] opened the new court on 17 May.

Wylde had received several land grants, including 2000 acres at Cabramatta and 50 on Pott's Point, Sydney, where he built a palatial home which he kept for many years. He had founded a famous horse stud, was interested in the formation of the Agricultural Association and became president of the Benevolent Society. Widely read and familiar with the classics as might be expected, he also had a love of music. He imported a piano into New South Wales and among his prize possessions was a choice century-old 'cello and a treasured flute. He sailed for England in February 1825, leaving behind three children with his wife who was about to give birth to her last infant, and having already requested 'a higher official Station' in the colonial department. In 1826 Field told Marsden that there was 'not much chance of [Wylde] getting any appointment anywhere' and asked the chaplain to look after Mrs Wylde; but he gained his LL.D., and in 1827 was knighted and appointed chief justice of the new court of the Cape of Good Hope, which was reconstituted as the Supreme Court in 1834.

Most of his children, to whom he was a very devoted parent, came to live with him, but his wife, whom he divorced in 1836, remained in New South Wales. He never left South Africa, but retired in October 1855 because of ill health and died on 13 December 1859. His portrait, painted in 1827 by Sir Martin Shee, is in Parliament House, Cape Town.

HRA (1), 9-11, 14, 15, (3), 3, 4, (4), 1; A. C. V. Melbourne, *Early constitutional developments in Australia* (Oxford, 1934); M. H. Ellis, *Lachlan Macquarie* (Syd, 1947); S. J. Butlin, *Foundations of the Australian monetary system, 1788-1851* (Melb, 1953); F. St Leger Searle, 'Sir John Wylde', *South African Law J*, 50 (1933); MS cat under Wylde (ML); Bigge Report, Appendix, Bonwick transcripts, Box 28/6710 (ML).   R. J. McKAY

WYLIE, an Aboriginal of the King George Sound tribe, was nearing manhood when taken by ship from Albany to Adelaide by E. J. Eyre [q.v.] in May 1840. He had disappeared in June when Eyre left to explore an overland route to Western Australia, but at Eyre's request was in the *Hero* which arrived at Fowler's Bay with provisions in January 1841. Wylie was older than the two other Aboriginals who, with Eyre and his assistant, Baxter,

made up the party which left Fowler's Bay in February. By April food supplies had dwindled and Wylie, whose good temper largely depended on prodigious meals rich in protein, became sulky and disobedient. On the 22nd he left the camp with one of the native boys, but returned after three days and apologized for his absence. On the night of the 29th he raised the' alarm which roused Eyre, who suspected, despite Wylie's denials, that he had known of the plot to raid the stores and had become horrified when Baxter unexpectedly awoke and was murdered by the other two boys. Eyre also suspected that Wylie was disturbed by the thought of possible consequences on their return to settlement, or that the other boys, who belonged to another tribe, might turn on him. However, he helped Eyre to find the horses and break camp. Together they continued the journey, followed for a time by the deserters who called to Wylie like 'wild dogs'.

In May provisions were very low and both men suffered greatly from exhaustion. At times conditions improved and Wylie went in search of food. Quick, observant and a very good shot, he brought in kangaroos, opossums, ducks and swans. He also found yams and roots, and could eat crabs twice as fast as Eyre. He knew how to take water from certain leaves but his inexperience made him painfully slow. On 22 June they sighted the *Mississippi*. Wylie skipped for joy and bade Eyre go ahead while he attended to the horses. He enjoyed his stay on the French ship and gorged himself on the generous rations. They brought ashore many stores, with pipes and tobacco especially for Wylie who was a great smoker, and cans of treacle which he liked to eat with rice.

Earlier in the expedition they had twice encountered Aboriginals whose language Wylie did not understand, but at Rossiter Bay (near Esperance) they met natives whom Wylie understood completely. Nearer to their destination, Wylie insisted that he knew where to cross the King River; he was not a reliable guide, for they became badly bogged and had to camp overnight instead of reaching the settlement as planned. Next day Wylie met a member of his tribe and learnt that he had been mourned by his people. A sudden shrill cry, picked up by Aboriginals in the area, soon brought an excited crowd to greet the wanderer. He made a statement about Baxter's death to the magistrate at Albany, and was commended to the governor for remaining 'faithful to his white friend when forsaken by his countrymen, although, doubtless, like them he too had his fears whether they would ever survive the hardships and difficulties of this fearful journey'.

Wylie was rewarded with a weekly ration of flour and meat by the government and with £2 and a medal by the Agricultural Society of Perth. For a time he served as a police constable but was soon suspended because his duties were hampered by his tribal connexions and his addiction to drink. In 1848 Eyre heard of his plight and had his small ration increased, but nothing certain is known of his later life.

E. J. Eyre, *Journals of expeditions of discovery into central Australia* . . . 1840-1, 1-2 (Lond, 1845); M. Uren and R. Stephens, *Waterless horizons* (Melb, 1941); M. Uren, *Edward John Eyre* (Melb, 1964); WA *Government Gazette*, 6, 13 Aug 1841; *Perth Gazette*, 7 Aug 1841; Albany Court records, 8 July, 16 Aug 1841 (Battye Lib, Perth); Wollaston's journal B, 1848 (Battye Lib, Perth); CSO files (Battye Lib, Perth).   WENDY BIRMAN

WYNDHAM, GEORGE (1801-1870), farmer, wine-grower and pastoralist, was born at Dinton, Wiltshire, England, the third son of William Wyndham of Dinton House and his wife Letitia, née Popham. He was educated at Harrow and Cambridge with a view to entering the Church of England, but decided to emigrate and in 1824 went to Canada, where he travelled with John Galt, secretary of the Canada Co. and a successful novelist. Returning to Europe, he went to Italy in 1825 and there met Margaret, daughter of John Jay, who kept a school in Brussels; he married her in Brussels in 1827.

Refusing a post under the British government, whose policy he did not approve, he decided to emigrate to Australia as a farmer. Taking with them a number of stock, including Southdown sheep, he and his wife sailed in the *George Horne* in August 1827 and reached Sydney in December. He settled near Branxton in the Hunter River valley, naming his property Dalwood, and began experimental farming. Among crops mentioned in his diary for 1830 were maize, wheat, hemp, mustard, castor oil, tobacco, millet and cape barley. He also planted a vineyard and began wine-making, in which he had long been interested. Both red and white varieties of grape were grown, principally Hermitage, Cabernet and Shiraz; some of these Shiraz vines were still producing in 1966 and were then said to be the oldest wine-producing vines in the world. Dalwood wines later became well known. At one time the vineyard was the second largest in New South Wales. Over the years a number of prizes and trophies were taken, including bronze and silver medals in the Paris International Exhibition of 1867.

Eleven sons and two daughters were born to George Wyndham and his wife. For the first decade his enterprises prospered, but the crisis in labour and prices in the 1840s hit the property hard. After trying various expedients including dairying he decided in 1845 to leave Dalwood under a manager, and with his wife and children he set out with horses, cattle and sheep, a few trusted stockmen and a string of covered bullock-wagons to cross the New England plateau to the Richmond River. After an adventurous journey he took up a property known as Keelgyrah (Kilgra, near Kyogle, named after a Wiltshire village). Stocking the property with cattle and leaving it in charge of a member of the party, they next year recrossed the Dividing Range and took up a property near Inverell, named Bukkulla. By 1847 prices had risen and the party returned to Dalwood. A son had been born during the journey. More prosperous times ensued; Hereford cattle were imported and bred, a vineyard at Bukkulla was worked in conjunction with the Dalwood vineyard, and a racing stud was established. George Wyndham died in Sydney on 24 December 1870, three months after the death of his wife. The properties passed out of Wyndham hands, except for Bukkulla which was later reacquired. The Dalwood vineyard was bought by Penfolds Wines Ltd, in whose hands it has remained.

George Wyndham was an independent man and when young was thought something of a radical by his friends; in England he advocated religious toleration, parliamentary reform and abolition of the Corn Laws and tithes. However, in New South Wales, though he generally kept clear of politics, he took the side of the squatters, supported Governor Darling against W. C. Wentworth [q.v.], and was a signatory to a petition seeking the importation of coolie labour after transportation to the colony had ceased. His published writings include *The Impending Crisis* (Maitland, 1851), and *On the Land Policy of New South Wales* (Maitland, 1866). He was a magistrate in Maitland for some years, but refused a seat in the Legislative Council when it was offered in 1839. He was respected for his leniency to assigned servants in his earlier days, and was himself a hard worker in the field. He overcame the difficulties of the slump with spirit and resource, and directed the work of his widely separated runs with success during his lifetime. His wife Margaret, though wholly untrained in domesticity, reared her large family under most difficult circumstances and appears to have been at least as capable and adaptable as her husband.

H. A. Wyndham, A *family history, 1688-1837, the Wyndhams of Somerset, Sussex and Wiltshire* (Lond, 1950); J. Wright, *Generations of men* (Melb, 1956); (C. M. Wright), Extracts from Dinton-Dalwood letters (ML); MS cat under G. Wyndham (ML); Family papers (in possession of H. S. Wyndham, Syd).

JUDITH WRIGHT MCKINNEY

WYNYARD, EDWARD BUCKLEY (1788-1864), military officer, was born on 23 November 1788 at Kensington Palace, London, the son of Lieut-General William Wynyard, colonel of the 20th Regiment. He entered the army as an ensign in December 1803 and served first in Sicily. In 1807 he went to England to join a regiment in South America but it returned to England before he could leave. In 1808 Wynyard became captain and was appointed to the adjutant-general's staff in the Mediterranean. In 1809 he was present at the capture of Ischia and Procida and served under Lieut-General Sir John Oswald in the Ionian Islands, where he was severely wounded on 22 March 1810 at Santa Maura; he was sent to Malta and returned to London in November. In 1811 he was appointed aide-de-camp to Sir Harry Burrard and then brigade-major under Sir Moore Disney but his wound prevented him from serving with the brigade at Bergen op Zoom. In March 1813 he became brevet major on the recommendation of Oswald and in April 1814 was promoted lieut-colonel in the 58th Regiment. In 1816-20 he served with Sir Hudson Cowe on St Helena, and in July

1830 was appointed aide-de-camp to William IV, and colonel in the Grenadier Guards. In 1837 he was placed on half-pay and in 1838 appointed C.B. In November 1841 he was promoted major-general and in September 1847 succeeded Sir Maurice O'Connell [q.v.] in command of the troops in New South Wales, Van Diemen's Land and New Zealand.

Wynyard arrived at Sydney early in 1848. He was a member of the Legislative Council in 1848-51 and of the Executive Council in 1848-53, but unlike O'Connell he did not insist on being addressed as 'Your Excellency'. He appreciated the climate in Australia, although he thought that conditions there were demoralizing for the troops and encouraged desertion. In constant struggles with the British and colonial governments over military costs he refused to countenance resignations from the army by men who were being urged to become settlers. His general policy was to retain the older men on garrison duties in the colonial capitals and to send less experienced soldiers to New Zealand, where they were more likely to see active service than in Australia. His steady opposition to every proposal for the reduction of troops under his command was justified in 1851 when gold was discovered and each colony began to clamour for protection.

In 1851 Wynyard became lieut-general and two years later left Sydney and returned to London. In January 1860 he was promoted general. He died of bronchitis in London on 24 November 1864. His name is remembered in Wynyard Square, Sydney, and probably in the town Wynyard in northern Tasmania which he visited in 1850-51.

MS cat under E. B. Wynyard (ML); WO 519-25 (PRO).

Y

YAGAN (d. 1833), Aboriginal, was the son of Midgigoroo, chief of the tribe in the district of Beeliar, the native name for the region south of Perth bounded by the Swan and Canning Rivers and the sea. For the first nine months of settlement at Swan River relations between settlers and natives were good. Then, as Aboriginals discovered that they liked the taste of the colonists' provisions and began to thieve and to spear livestock, retaliations were made, for food supplies were scarce. Gradually the settlers became aware that the attacks along the Canning River and the farther banks of the Swan were led by a certain native of striking appearance named Yagan. In May 1832 a labourer, William Gaze, was murdered. Yagan was identified as the killer, and Midgigoroo as participating in other recent attacks. After four months Yagan was captured and sentenced, with two other native culprits, to temporary detention on Carnac Island. Two soldiers were sent as guards, and a settler, Robert Lyon, volunteered to accompany them in order to study Aboriginal ways and language. For six weeks Lyon tried to teach the natives the ways of civilization; then one night Yagan and the others stole a boat and escaped. Boats were unknown to the Aboriginals, and Yagan's courage and skill in managing to propel it eight miles to shore was admired, even if deplored. He returned to his old haunts, and became a conspicuous figure in Perth, boasting of his escape, taking part in spear-throwing contests at which he excelled, and showing himself an admirable dancer at corroborees performed before the governor and people. Lyon praised him as a warrior and a patriot, calling him 'the Wallace of the Age' in articles he wrote for the *Perth Gazette* on his study of the Aboriginals and their language.

Yagan and his tribe were soon in trouble again for several thefts. In April 1833 they were fired upon while stealing flour from a Fremantle store, and Yagan's brother was killed. Yagan, Midgigoroo and others followed some carts taking provisions to settlers on the Canning River, and savagely speared the drivers to death. He, Midgigoroo and another, Munday, were then proclaimed outlaws, with a price of £30 on their heads. Midgigoroo was captured, identified by witnesses to his crime, tried and shot; but Yagan was at large for two months. The colonists feared him while admiring him as a kind of patriot. As a patriot Yagan may have been defending his tribal hunting ground, but such facts as there are indicate that his actions were only directed to providing himself with food, and taking retribution at its denial. While still at large he was finally shot on 11 July 1833 by a young shepherd, William Keates, intent on the government reward. Keates was soon killed in another affray with Aboriginals and, after an official inquiry, his brother received the reward.

R. Dale, *Descriptive account of the panoramic view of King George's Sound and the adjacent country* (Lond, 1834); G. F. Moore, *A descriptive vocabulary of the language in common use amongst the Aborigines of Western Australia* (Lond, 1842); G. F. Moore, *Diary of ten years eventful life of an early settler in Western Australia* (Lond, 1884); *The Western Australian Almanack*, 1842; A. Hasluck, 'Yagan the patriot', JRWAHS, 5 (1955-61); *Perth Gazette*, Mar-July 1833; Swan River papers (Battye Lib, Perth).

ALEXANDRA HASLUCK

YOUL, JOHN (1773-1827), Independent missionary and Anglican clergyman, was born on 30 June 1773 in London, the son of John Youl, whose Scottish ancestors had migrated from Stirling to England. In 1798 he was sent as a layman by the (London) Missionary Society in the *Duff* to Tahiti, but was captured by the French and repatriated. Back in London he engaged in home missions and was one of the founders of the London Itinerant Society. In May 1800 he was ordained at the Congregational chapel, Portsea, and sailed again for Tahiti in the *Royal Admiral* with Rev. James Elder [q.v.] and several other missionaries. Detained at Sydney for three months, he helped Rev. Samuel Marsden [q.v] and preached at Toongabbie, Kissing Point and the Hawkesbury settlement. Impressed with the need for itinerant preachers in New South Wales, he proceeded reluctantly with his companions to Tahiti where he worked until 1807. He then returned to Sydney and accepted a call from the Portland Head Society to the little church of Ebenezer, to be paid in kind. On 31 January 1810 at Parramatta he married Jane, the daughter of 'Sergeant' George Loder, gaoler and pound-keeper of Windsor; they had six sons and three daughters.

Youl returned to England in 1813 for further study and was promised priest's

632

orders by the bishop of London. He received episcopal ordination by the bishop of Chester in 1815. He was later commissioned by Earl Bathurst as the first chaplain to the settlement at Port Dalrymple in northern Van Diemen's Land at a salary of £183. He sailed for Sydney where Governor Macquarie sent him temporarily to Liverpool until a house was ready in Van Diemen's Land for his family. Youl went to Port Dalrymple on 20 December 1818 to inspect his new parish. During this three weeks visit he married forty-one couples, some of whom had anticipated the blessing of the church, and baptized sixty-seven children. After long delay he and his family sailed from Sydney at his own cost in the government brig *Prince Leopold*. He arrived with thirty tons of freight at Launceston in November 1819 and moved into Government Cottage. His first services were held in Cameron Street in what had been a blacksmith's shop, and his parishioners were summoned by an iron drum. In July 1821 he moved to a new parsonage at George Town, where he ministered to the convict establishment and conducted a school, at intervals touring his large parish. On Bathurst's orders his salary was increased to £250 and he received 400 acres of glebe with five assigned servants and government stock. With his own free grant of 700 acres on the South Esk River and rams from Macarthur's flock, he helped his sons to become successful pastoralists.

In December 1824 the foundation stone of St John's Church of England, Launceston, was laid by Lieut-Governor Arthur. To Youl the plan was handsome within, but rather squat outside, since Arthur had thought the plans were too big, and foreshortened the nave with his pen. Youl moved to Launceston but a chest ailment and the prevailing moral laxity drove him to despair. A month after sharing in the consecration of the unfinished church, he died from asthma on 25 March 1827. His widow died at Perth, Tasmania, on 19 July 1877.

L. S. Bethell, *The story of Port Dalrymple* (Hob, 1957); 'The London Itinerant Society', Congregational Hist Soc, *Trans*, 7 (1916-18); Letters of John Youl to Thos Hassall, 1823-24 (ML).
G. H. STANCOMBE

YOUNG, ADOLPHUS WILLIAM (1814-1885), merchant and sheriff, was born at Hare Hatch House, Berkshire, England, the son of John Adolphus Young. He had some legal training before 1837 when he married Anne Eliza Smith and migrated with her to Sydney. In December 1837 he became a provisional director of the Australian Gaslight Co., third police magistrate, and a justice of the peace. In March 1838 he resigned his magistracy because the salary of £300 was inadequate, and joined the legal firm of Carr & Rogers as an attorney. On 22 October 1839 the directors of the Gaslight Co. charged him with corrupt practice for buying land adjoining the works in order to sell it at a profit to the company. Young pleaded that he had not known the exact site of the land when he bought it; he was found guilty 'of indiscretion, but not of any act derogatory to his character as a gentleman'. However, he resigned from the board and in September 1840 sailed with his family in the *Ellen* for England.

In October 1842 Young was appointed sheriff of New South Wales, on the understanding that the duties of that office were to be modified. Soon after his return to Sydney he was sworn in on 2 July 1843. In 1844 he became a director of the Australasian Colonial and General Life Assurance Co., and was elected to represent the Port Phillip District in the Legislative Council at Sydney; a petition filed against his election was dismissed. During his campaign he had pledged himself to oppose the government's policy in the administration of crown lands and in January 1845 he signed a petition to the Queen for the separation of the Port Phillip District from New South Wales. However, he was notified that he could not hold both his seat and his government office, and in July he resigned from the council. Later he found that his office as sheriff was 'everywhere of an invidious and responsible character . . . attended with peculiar and unusual difficulties'. Some of his accounts were questioned by the British Treasury and he resigned in November 1849, receiving from the judges of the Supreme Court very warm commendations for his 'integrity, discretion and ability'.

Young's first wife had died in 1845 and in 1847 he married Jane, daughter of Charles Throsby [q.v.]. With her and his children he returned to England. He lived at Hare Hatch House, which he inherited from his father. He became a justice of the peace, acted as deputy-lieutenant for Berkshire, and in the House of Commons he represented Great Yarmouth in 1857-59, and Helston, Cornwall, in 1868-79. In parliament he showed a keen interest in Australian affairs. In 1873 he helped Sir Charles Cowper in London in his efforts to obtain favourable mail contracts for New South Wales and in 1882 gave much encouragement to Sir Henry Parkes. After his second wife died Young married Mary Clementine. He died at Hare Hatch on 4 November 1885, leaving an estate valued at some £27,000 to his widow and his eight surviving children.

HRA (1), 19, 22-24; Newspaper indexes under A. W. Young (ML); MS cat under A. W. Young (ML); CO 201/425.

A. F. PIKE

YURANIGH (d. 1850), Aboriginal guide, belonged to the Molong district, New South Wales. He was one of three Aboriginals who joined Sir Thomas Mitchell [q.v.] and his twenty-nine men soon after they set out from Boree, near Molong, in December 1845 on the journey of exploration that took them to central Queensland. Yuranigh was first mentioned in Mitchell's journal three weeks after the start of the journey when he tracked and brought back to camp three cattle that had strayed. Thereafter he was frequently and gratefully referred to for finding water, scanning the country from lofty trees, pacifying the Aboriginals who shadowed the expedition, and generally imparting bush lore.

Mitchell wrote of his 'guide, companion, counsellor and friend' that 'his intelligence and his judgment rendered him so necessary to me that he was ever at my elbow . . . Confidence in him was never misplaced. He well knew the character of all the white men in the party. Nothing escaped his penetrating eye and quick ear. Yuranigh was particularly clean in his person, frequently washing, and his glossy shining black hair, always well-combed, gave him an uncommonly clean and decent appearance'.

When the expedition was over Yuranigh and Dicky, another Boree Aboriginal, went with Mitchell to Sydney, where Yuranigh took delight in showing his companion the sights. The governor granted Yuranigh a 'small gratuity' and for a time both blacks were resolved 'to work and live like white men'. However, Yuranigh soon tired of the town and after an 'affecting' leave-taking became a stockman on a northern cattle station. Later he found his way back to his own tribe. He died near Molong probably in April 1850. Mitchell saw to it that Yuranigh's grave was fenced at government expense and later he himself paid for an inscribed headstone. In 1900 the government renovated the headstone, re-erected it on a base of Molong marble and re-fenced the grave. The inscription runs: 'To Native Courage Honesty and Fidelity. Yuranigh who accompanied the expedition of discovery into tropical Australia in 1846 lies buried here according to the rites of his countrymen and this spot was dedicated and enclosed by the Governor General's authority in 1852'. A lagoon, a county in Queensland and a creek near Molong are named Yuranigh.

T. L. Mitchell, Journal of an expedition into the interior of tropical Australia (Lond, 1848); W. R. Glasson, 'Yuranigh', Qld Geog J, 54 (1949-52).